John Lloyd Stephens, Engelbert Kaempfer

Remarkable Voyages and Travels

John Lloyd Stephens, Engelbert Kaempfer

Remarkable Voyages and Travels

ISBN/EAN: 9783337212445

Printed in Europe, USA, Canada, Australia, Japan

Cover: Foto ©Andreas Hilbeck / pixelio.de

More available books at **www.hansebooks.com**

REMARKABLE VOYAGES.

A SPANISH SHIP OF WAR.

REMARKABLE
VOYAGES AND TRAVELS

London:
JAMES BLACKWOOD & CO., LOVELL'S COURT,
PATERNOSTER ROW

BLACKWOOD'S UNIVERSAL LIBRARY OF STANDARD AUTHORS.

REMARKABLE
VOYAGES AND TRAVELS,

CONSISTING OF

ANSON'S VOYAGES ROUND THE WORLD; STEPHENS' INCIDENTS
OF TRAVEL IN GREECE, TURKEY, RUSSIA AND POLAND;
AND KŒMPFER'S ACCOUNT OF JAPAN.

ILLUSTRATED.

LONDON:
JAMES BLACKWOOD & CO., LOVELL'S COURT,
PATERNOSTER ROW.

GLASGOW:
C. L. WRIGHT,
PRINTER.

PART I.

ANSON'S VOYAGES ROUND THE WORLD.

CONTENTS.

BOOK FIRST.

	PAGE
CHAP. I. Of the equipment of the squadron. The incidents relating thereto, from its first appointment to its setting sail from St. Helens	1
II. The passage from St. Helens to the Island of Madeira; with a short account of that Island, and of our stay there	5
III. The history of the squadron commanded by Don Joseph Pizarro	6
IV. From Madeira to St. Catherine's	11
V. Proceedings at St. Catherine's, and a description of the place, with a short account of Brazil . .	13
VI. The run from St. Catherine's to port St. Julian, with some account of that port, and of the country to the southward of the river of Plate	16
VII. Departure from the Bay of St. Julian, and the passage from thence to Straits Le Maire . .	22
VIII. From Straits Le Maire to Cape Noir	24
IX. Observations and directions for facilitating the passage of our future Cruisers round Cape Horn .	26
X. From Cape Noir to the Island of Juan Fernandes	30

BOOK SECOND.

CHAP. I. The arrival of the Centurion at the Island of Juan Fernandes, with a description of that Island .	34
II. The arrival of the Gloucester and the Anna pink at the Island of Juan Fernandes, and the transactions at that place during this interval	39
III. A short narrative of what befel the Anna pink before she joined us, with an account of the loss of the Wager, and of the putting back of the Severn and Pearl, the two remaining ships of the squadron	42
IV. Conclusion of our proceedings at Juan Fernandes, from the arrival of the Anna pink, to our final departure from thence	48
V. Our cruise, from the time of our leaving Juan Fernandes, to the taking the town of Paita . .	53
VI. The taking of Paita, and our proceedings till we left the coast of Peru	58
VII. From our departure from Paita, to our arrival at Quibo	64
VIII. Our proceedings at Quibo, with an account of the place	67

CONTENTS.

	PAGE
CHAP. IX. From Quibo to the Coast of Mexico	69
X. An account of the commerce carried on between the city of Manila on the island of Luconia, and the port of Acapulco on the coast of Mexico	72
XI. Our cruise off the port of Acapulco for the Manila ship	77
XII. Description of the Harbour of Chequetan, and of the adjacent coast and country	80
XIII. Our proceedings at Chequetan and on the adjacent coast, till our setting sail for Asia	83
XIV. A brief account of what might have been expected from our squadron, had it arrived in the South Seas in good time	86

BOOK THIRD.

CHAP. I. The run from the coast of Mexico to the Ladrones or Marian Islands	89
II. Our arrival at Tinian, and an account of the island, and of our proceedings there, till the Centurion drove out to sea.	93
III. Transactions at Tinian after the departure of the Centurion	98
IV. Proceedings on board the Centurion, when driven out to sea	101
V. Employment at Tinian, till the final departure of the Centurion from thence; with a description of the Ladrones	103
VI. From Tinian to Macao	106
VII. Proceedings at Macao	108
VIII. From Macao to Cape Espiritu Santo. The taking of the Manila galleon, and returning back again	113
IX. Transactions in the river of Canton	118
X. Proceedings at the city of Canton, and the return of the Centurion to England	123

ANSON'S VOYAGE ROUND THE WORLD.

BOOK I.

CHAPTER I.

Of the equipment of the Squadron. The incidents relating thereto, from its first appointment to its setting sail from St. Helens.

THE squadron under the command of Mr. Anson (of which I here propose to recite the most material proceedings) having undergone many changes in its destination, its force, and its equipment, in the ten months between its first appointment and its final sailing from St. Helens, I conceive the history of these alterations is a detail necessary to be made public, both for the honour of those who first planned and promoted this enterprise, and for the justification of those who have been entrusted with its execution. Since it will from hence appear, that the accidents the expedition was afterwards exposed to, and which prevented it from producing all the national advantages from the strength of the squadron and the expectation of the public seemed to presage, were principally owing to a series of interruptions, which delayed the commander in the course of his preparations, and which it exceeded his utmost industry either to avoid or get removed.

When in the latter end of the summer of the year 1739, it was foreseen that a war with Spain was inevitable, it was the opinion of several considerable persons then trusted with the administration of affairs, that the most prudent step the nation could take, on the breaking out of the war, was attacking that crown in her distant settlements; for by this means (as at that time there was the greatest probability of success) it was supposed that we should cut off the principal resources of the enemy, and reduce them to the necessity of sincerely desiring a peace, as they would hereby be deprived of the returns of that treasure by which alone they could be enabled to carry on a war.

In pursuance of these sentiments, several projects were examined, and several resolutions taken in council. And in all these deliberations it was from the first determined, that George Anson, Esq., then captain of the Centurion, should be employed as commander-in-chief of an expedition of this kind; and he then being absent on a cruise, a vessel was dispatched to his station so early as the beginning of September, to order him to return with his ship to Portsmouth. And soon after he came there, that is, on the 10th of November following, he received a letter from Sir Charles Wager, ordering him to repair to London, and to attend the board of Admiralty; where, when he arrived, he was informed by Sir Charles that two squadrons would be immediately fitted out for two secret expeditions, which however would have some connection with each other; that he, Mr. Anson, was intended to command one of them, and Mr. Cornwall (who hath since lost his life gloriously in the defence of his country's honour) the other. That the squadron under Mr. Anson was to take on board three independent companies of a hundred men each, and Bland's regiment of foot; that colonel Bland was likewise to embark with his regiment, and to command the land forces; and that, as soon as this squadron could be fitted for the sea, they were to set sail, with express orders to touch at no place till they came to Java-Head, in the East Indies: that there they were only to stop to take in water, and thence to proceed directly to the city of Manila, situated on Luconia, one of the Philippine Islands. That the other squadron was to be of equal force with this commanded by Mr. Anson, and was intended to pass round Cape Horn into the South Seas, and there to range along that coast; and after cruising upon the enemy in those parts, and attempting their settlements, this squadron in its return was to rendezvous at Manila, and there to join the squadron under Mr. Anson, where they were to refresh their men and refit their ships, and perhaps receive further orders.

This scheme was doubtless extremely well projected, and could not but greatly advance the public service, and at the same time the reputation and fortune of those concerned in its execution; for had Mr. Anson proceeded for Manila at the time and in the manner proposed by Sir Charles Wager, he would in all probability have arrived there before they had received any advice of the war between us and Spain, and consequently before they had been in the least prepared for the reception of an enemy, or had any apprehensions of their danger. The city of Manila might be well supposed to have been at that time in the same defenceless condition with all the other Spanish settlements, just at the breaking out of the war: that is to say, their fortifications neglected, and in many places decayed; their cannon dismounted, or useless, by the mouldering of their carriages; their magazines, whether of military stores or provision, all empty; their garrisons unpaid, and consequently thin, ill-affected, and dispirited; and the royal chests in Peru, whence alone all these disorders could receive their redress, drained to the very bottom. This, from the intercepted letters of their viceroys and governors, is well known to have been the defenceless state of Panama, and the other Spanish places on the coast of the South Sea, for near a twelvemonth after our declaration of war. And it cannot be supposed that the city of Manila, removed still farther by almost half the circumference of the globe, should have experienced from the Spanish government a greater share of attention and concern for its security than Panama and the other important ports in Peru and Chili, on which their possession of that immense empire depends. Indeed, it is well known, that Manila was at that time incapable of making any considerable defence, and in all probability would have surrendered only on the appearance of our squadron before it. The consequence of this city, and the island it stands on, may be in some measure estimated, from the healthiness of its air, the excellency of its port and bay, the number and wealth of its inhabitants, and the very extensive and beneficial commerce which it carries on to the principal ports in the East Indies and China, and its exclusive trade to Acapulco, the returns for which, being made in silver, are, upon the lowest valuation, not less than three millions of dollars per annum.

And on this scheme Sir Charles Wager was so intent, that in a few days after this first conference, that is, on November 18, Mr. Anson received an order to take under his command the Argyle, Severn, Pearl, Wager, and Tryal sloop; and other orders were issued to him in the same month, and in the December following, relating to the victualling of this squadron. But Mr. Anson attending the Admiralty the beginning of January, he was informed by Sir Charles Wager, that, for reasons with which he, Sir Charles, was not acquainted, the expedition to Manila was laid aside. It may be conceived that Mr. Anson was extremely chagrined at the losing the command of so infallible, so honourable, and in every respect so desirable an enterprise, especially too as he had already, at a very great expense, made the necessary provision for his own accommodation in this voyage, which he had reason to expect would prove a very long one. However, Sir Charles, to render this disappointment in some degree more tolerable, informed him that the expedition to the South Seas was still intended, and that he, Mr. Anson, and his squadron, as their first destination was now countermanded, should be employed in that service. And on the 10th of January he received his commission, appointing him commander-in-chief of the forementioned squadron, which (the Argyle being in the course of their preparation changed for the Gloucester) was the same he sailed with above eight months after from St. Helens. On this change of destination, the equipment of the squadron was still prosecuted with as much vigour as ever, and the victualling, and whatever depended on the commodore, was so far advanced, that he conceived the ships might be capable of putting to sea the instant he should receive his final orders, of which he was in daily expectation. And at last, on the 28th of June, 1740, the duke of Newcastle, principal secretary of state, delivered to him his majesty's instructions, dated January 31, 1739, with an additional instruction from the lords justices, dated June 19, 1740.[1] On the receipt of these, Mr. Anson immediately repaired to Spithead, with a resolution to sail with the first fair wind, flattering himself that all his delays were now at an end. For though he knew by the musters that his squadron wanted three hundred seamen of their complement (a deficiency which, with all his assiduity, he had not been able to get supplied), yet, as Sir Charles Wager informed him that an order from the board of Admiralty was despatched to Sir John Norris to spare him the numbers which he wanted, he doubted not of his complying therewith. But on his arrival at Portsmouth he found himself greatly mistaken and disappointed in this persuasion; for on his application Sir John Norris told him he could spare him none, for he wanted men for his own fleet. This occasioned an inevitable and a very considerable delay, for it was the end of July before this deficiency was by any means supplied, and all that was then done was extremely short of his necessities and expectation. For Admiral Balchen, who succeeded to the command at Spithead after Sir John Norris had sailed to the westward, instead of three hundred able sailors, which Mr. Anson wanted of his complement, ordered on board the squadron a hundred and seventy men only; of whom thirty-two were from the hospital and sick quarters, thirty-seven from the Salisbury, with three officers of Colonel Lowther's regiment, and ninety-eight marines, and these were all that were ever granted to make up the forementioned deficiency.

But the commodore's mortification did not end here. It has been already observed, that it was at first intended that Colonel Bland's regiment, and three independent companies of a hundred men each, should embark as land-forces on board the squadron. But this disposition was now changed, and all the land-forces that were to be allowed, were five hundred invalids to be collected from the out-pensioners of Chelsea college. As these out-pensioners consist of soldiers who, from their age, wounds, or other infirmities, are incapable of service in marching regiments, Mr. Anson was greatly chagrined at having such a decrepit detachment allotted him; for he was fully persuaded that the greatest part of them would perish long before they arrived at the scene of action, since the delays, he had already encountered, necessarily confined his passage round Cape Horn to the most rigorous season of the year. Sir Charles Wager, too, joined in opinion with the commodore, that invalids were no ways proper for this service, and solicited strenuously to have them exchanged; but he was told that persons, who were supposed to be better judges of soldiers than he or Mr. Anson, thought them the properest men that could be employed on this occasion.[2] And upon this determination they were ordered on board the squadron on the 5th of August; but

[1] See these Instructions in the Introduction.

[2] "The feelings of these excellent judges are not to be envied, when they were afterwards made acquainted with the fact, that not one of these unfortunate individuals who went on the voyage survived to reach their native land—every man had perished."—Sir John Barrow's Life of Lord Anson.

instead of five hundred, there came on board no more than two hundred and fifty-nine; for all those who had limbs and strength to walk out of Portsmouth deserted, leaving behind them only such as were literally invalids, most of them being sixty years of age, and some of them upwards of seventy Indeed it is difficult to conceive a more moving scene than the embarkation of these unhappy veterans: they were themselves extremely averse to the service they were engaged in, and fully apprised of all the disasters they were afterwards exposed to; the apprehensions of which were strongly marked by the concern that appeared in their countenances, which was mixed with no small degree of indignation, to be thus hurried from their repose into a fatiguing employ, to which neither the strength of their bodies, nor the vigour of their minds, were any ways proportioned, and where, without seeing the face of an enemy, or in the least promoting the success of the enterprise they were engaged in, they would in all probability uselessly perish by lingering and painful diseases; and this too, after they had spent the activity and strength of their youth in their country's service.

And I cannot but observe, on this melancholy incident, how extremely unfortunate it was, both to this aged and diseased detachment, and to the expedition they were employed in; that amongst all the out-pensioners of Chelsea Hospital, which were supposed to amount to two thousand men, the most crazy and infirm only should be culled out for so fatiguing and perilous an undertaking. For it was well known, that however unfit invalids in general might be for this service, yet by a prudent choice, there might have been found among them five hundred men, who had some remains of vigour left: and Mr. Anson fully expected, that the best of them would have been allotted him; whereas the whole detachment that was sent to him, seemed to be made up of the most decrepit and miserable objects, that could be collected out of the whole body; and by the desertion above-mentioned, these were a second time cleared of that little health and strength which were to be found amongst them, and he was to take up with such as were much fitter for an infirmary, than for any military duty.

And here it is necessary to mention another material particular in the equipment of this squadron. It was proposed to Mr. Anson, after it was resolved that he should be sent to the South-Seas, to take with him two persons under the denomination of agent-victuallers. Those who were mentioned for this employment had formerly been in the Spanish West-Indies, in the South-Sea Company's service, and it was supposed that by their knowledge and intelligence on that coast, they might often procure provisions for him by compact with the inhabitants, when it was not to be got by force of arms. These agent-victuallers were, for this purpose, to be allowed to carry to the value of 15,000*l.* in merchandise on board the squadron; for they had represented, that it would be much easier for them to procure provisions with goods, than with the value of the same goods in money. Whatever colours were given to this scheme, it was difficult to persuade the generality of mankind, that it was not principally intended for the enrichment of the agents, by the beneficial commerce they proposed to carry on upon that coast. Mr. Anson, from the beginning, objected both to the appointment of agent victuallers, and the allowing them to carry a cargo on board the squadron: for he conceived, that in those few amicable ports where the squadron might touch, he needed not their assistance to contract for any provisions the place afforded; and on the enemy's coast, he did not imagine that they could ever procure him the necessaries he should want, unless (which he was resolved not to comply with) the military operations of his squadron were to be regulated by the ridiculous views of their trading projects. All that he thought the Government ought to have done on this occasion, was to put on board to the value of 2 or 3000*l.* only of such goods, as the Indians, or the Spanish planters in the less cultivated part of the coast, might be tempted with; since it was in such places only that he imagined it would be worth while to truck with the enemy for provisions: and in these places, it was sufficiently evident, a very small cargo would suffice.

But though the commodore objected both to the appointment of these officers, and to their project; yet, as they had insinuated that their scheme, besides victualling the squadron, might contribute to settling a trade upon that coast, which might be afterwards carried on without difficulty, and might thereby prove a very considerable national advantage, they were much listened to by some considerable persons: and of the 15,000*l.* which was to be the amount of their cargo, the Government agreed to advance them 10,000 upon imprest, and the remaining 5000 they raised on bottomry bonds; and the goods purchased with this sum were all that were taken to sea by the squadron, how much soever the amount of them might be afterwards magnified by common report.

This cargo was at first shipped on board the Wager store-ship, and one of the victuallers; no part of it being admitted on board the men-of-war. But when the commodore was at St. Catherine's, he considered, that in case the squadron should be separated, it might be pretended that some of the ships were disappointed of provisions for want of a cargo to truck with, and therefore he distributed some of the least bulky commodities on board the men-of-war, leaving the remainder principally on board the Wager, where it was lost: and more of the goods perishing by various accidents to be recited hereafter, and no part of them being disposed of upon the coast, the few that came home to England, did not produce, when sold, above a fourth part of the original price. So true was the commodore's prediction about the event of this project, which had been by many considered as infallibly productive of immense gains. But to return to the transactions at Portsmouth.

To supply the place of the two hundred and forty invalids who had deserted, as is mentioned above, there were ordered on board two hundred and ten marines detached from different regiments: these were raw and undisciplined men, for they were just raised, and had scarcely any thing more of the soldier than their regimentals, none of them having been so far trained, as to be permitted to fire. The last detachment of these marines came on board the 8th of August, and on the 10th the squadron sailed from Spithead to St. Helens, there to wait for a wind to proceed on the expedition.

But the delays we had already suffered had not yet spent all their influence, for we were now advanced into a season of the year, when the westerly winds are usually very constant, and very violent; and it was thought proper that we should put to sea in company with the fleet commanded by Admiral Balchen, and the expedition under Lord Cathcart. And as we made up in all twenty-one men of war, and a hundred and twenty-four sail of merchantmen and transports, we had no hopes of getting out of the channel with so large a number of ships, without the continuance of a fair wind, for some considerable time. This was what we had every day less and less reason to expect, as the time of the equinox drew near; so that our golden dreams, and our ideal possession of the Peruvian treasures, grew each day more faint, and the difficulties and dangers of the passage round Cape Horn in the winter season filled our imaginations in their room. For it was forty days from our arrival at St. Helens, to our final departure from thence: and even then (having orders to proceed without Lord Cathcart) we tided it down the channel with a contrary wind. But this interval of forty days was not free from the displeasing fatigue of often setting sail, and being as often obliged to return; nor exempt from dangers, greater than have been sometimes experienced in surrounding the globe. For the wind coming fair for the first time, on the 23d of August, we got under sail, and Mr. Balchen showed himself truly solicitous to have proceeded to sea, but the wind soon returning to its old quarter, obliged us to put back to St. Helens, not without considerable hazard, and some damage received by two of the transports, which, in tacking, ran foul of each other: besides this, we made two or three more attempts to sail, but without any better success. And, on the 6th of September, being returned to an anchor at St. Helens, after one of these fruitless efforts, the wind blew so fresh, that the whole fleet struck their yards and topmasts to prevent their driving. And, notwithstanding this precaution, the Centurion drove the next evening, and brought both cables a-head, and we were in no small danger of driving foul of the Prince Frederick, a seventy-gun ship, moored at a small distance under our stern; which she happily escaped, by her driving at the same time, and so preserving her distance: nor did we think ourselves secure, till we at last let go the sheet-anchor, which fortunately brought us up.

However, on the 9th of September, we were in some degree relieved from this lingering vexatious situation, by an order which Mr. Anson received from the lords justices, to put to sea the first opportunity with his own squadron only, if Lord Cathcart should not be ready. Being thus freed from the troublesome company of so large a fleet, our commodore resolved to weigh and tide it down channel as soon as the weather should become sufficiently moderate, and this might easily have been done with our own squadron alone full two months sooner, had the orders of the Admiralty, for supplying us with seamen, been punctually complied with, and had we met with none of those other delays mentioned in this narration. It is true, our hopes of a speedy departure were even now somewhat damped by a subsequent order which Mr. Anson received on the 12th of September; for by that he was required to take under his convoy the St. Albans with the Turkey fleet, and to join the Dragon, and the Winchester, with the Straits' and the American trade at Torbay or Plymouth, and to proceed with them to sea as far as their way and ours lay together: this incumbrance of a convoy gave us some uneasiness, as we feared it might prove the means of lengthening our passage to the Madeiras. However, Mr. Anson, now having the command himself, resolved to adhere to his former determination, and to tide it down the channel with the first moderate weather; and that the junction of his convoy might occasion as little a loss of time as possible, he immediately sent directions to Torbay, that the fleets in wait there to take under his care, might be in a readiness to join him instantly on his approach. And at last, on the 18th of September, he weighed from St. Helens; and though the wind was at first contrary, had the good fortune to get clear of the channel in four days, as will be more particularly related in the ensuing chapter.

Having thus gone through the respective steps taken in the equipment of this squadron, it is sufficiently obvious how different an aspect this expedition bore at its first appointment in the beginning of January, from what it had in the latter end of September, when it left the channel; and how much its numbers, its strength, and the probability of its success were diminished, by the various incidents which took place in that interval. For instead of having all our old and ordinary seamen exchanged for such as were young and able, (which the commodore was at first promised,) and having our numbers completed to their full complement, we were obliged to retain our first crews, which were very indifferent; and a deficiency of three hundred men in our numbers was no otherwise made up to us, than by sending us on board a hundred and seventy men, the greatest part composed of such as were discharged from hospitals, or new-raised marines who had never been at sea before. And in the land-forces allotted us, the change was still more disadvantageous, for there, instead of three independent companies of a hundred men each, and Bland's regiment of foot, which was an old one, we had only four hundred and seventy invalids and marines, one part of them incapable for action by age and infirmities, and the other part useless by their ignorance of their duty. But the diminishing the strength of the squadron was not the greatest inconvenience which attended these alterations; for the contests, representations, and difficulties which they continually produced, (as we have above seen, that in these cases the authority of the Admiralty was not always submitted to,) occasioned a delay and waste of time, which, in its consequences, was the source of all the disasters to which this enterprise was afterwards exposed: for, by this means we were obliged to make our passage round Cape Horn in the most tempestuous season of the year, whence proceeded the separation of our squadron, the loss of numbers of our men, and the imminent hazard of our total destruction: and by this delay too, the enemy had been so well informed of our designs, that a person who had been employed in the South-Sea company's service, and arrived from Panama three or four days before we left Portsmouth, was able to relate to Mr. Anson most of the particulars of the destination and strength of our squadron, from what he had learnt amongst the Spaniards before he left them. And this was afterwards confirmed by a more extraordinary circumstance: for we shall find, that when the Spaniards (fully satisfied that our expedition was intended for the South-Seas) had fitted out a squadron to oppose us, which had so far got the start of us, as to arrive before us off the island of Madeira, the commander of this squadron was so well instructed in the form and make of Mr. Anson's broad pennant, and had imitated it so exactly, that he thereby decoyed the Pearl, one of our squadron, within gun-shot of him, before the captain of the Pearl was able to discover his mistake.

CHAPTER II.

The Passage from St. Helens to the Island of Madeira; with a short account of that Island, and of our stay there.

On the 18th of September, 1740, the squadron, as we have observed in the preceding chapter, weighed from St. Helens with a contrary wind, the commodore proposing to tide it down the channel, as he dreaded less the inconveniences he should thereby have to struggle with, than the risk he should run of ruining the enterprise, by an uncertain, and in all probability, a tedious attendance for a fair wind.

The squadron allotted to this service consisted of five men-of-war, a sloop-of-war, and two victualling ships. They were the Centurion of sixty guns, four hundred men, George Anson, Esq. commander; the Gloucester of fifty guns, three hundred men, Richard Norris, commander; the Severn of fifty guns, three hundred men, the honourable Edward Legg, commander; the Pearl of forty guns, two hundred and fifty men, Matthew Mitchel, commander; the Wager of twenty-eight guns, one hundred and sixty men, Dandy Kidd, commander; and the Tryal sloop of eight guns, one hundred men, the honourable John Murray, commander. The two victuallers were pinks, the largest of about four hundred, and the other of about two hundred tons burthen; these were to attend us, till the provisions we had taken on board were so far consumed as to make room for the additional quantity they carried with them, which, when we had taken into our ships, they were to be discharged. Besides the complement of men borne by the above-mentioned ships as their crews, there were embarked on board the squadron about four hundred and seventy invalids and marines, under the denomination of land-forces, as has been particularly mentioned in the preceding chapter, which were commanded by Lieutenant-Colonel Cracherode. With this squadron, together with the St. Albans and the Lark, and the trade under their convoy, Mr. Anson, after weighing from St. Helens, tided it down the channel for the first forty-eight hours; and, on the 20th, in the morning, we discovered off the Ram-Head the Dragon, Winchester, South-Sea Castle, and Rye, with a number of merchantmen under their convoy; these we joined about noon the same day, our commodore having orders to see them (together with the St. Albans and Lark) as far into the sea as their course and ours lay together. When we came in sight of this last mentioned fleet, Mr. Anson first hoisted his broad pennant, and was saluted by all the men-of-war in company.

When we had joined this last convoy, we made up eleven men-of-war, and about one hundred and fifty sail of merchantmen, consisting of the Turkey, the Straits', and the American trade. Mr. Anson, the same day, made a signal for all the captains of the men-of-war to come on board him, where he delivered them their fighting and sailing instructions, and then, with a fair wind, we all stood towards the south-west; and the next day at noon, being the 21st, we had run forty leagues from the Ram-Head; and being now clear of the land, our commodore, to render our view more extensive, ordered Captain Mitchel, in the Pearl, to make sail two leagues a-head of the fleet every morning, and to repair to his station every evening. Thus we proceeded till the 25th, when the Winchester and the American convoy made the concerted signal for leave to separate, which being answered by the commodore, they left us: as the St. Albans and the Dragon, with the Turkey and Straits' convoy, did on the 29th. After which separation, there remained in company only our own squadron and our two victuallers, with which we kept on our course for the island of Madeira. But the winds were so contrary, that we had the mortification to be forty days in our passage thither from St. Helens, though it is known to be often done in ten or twelve. This delay was a most unpleasing circumstance, productive of much discontent and ill-humour amongst our people, of which those only can have a tolerable idea, who have had the experience of a like situation. And besides the peevishness and despondency which foul and contrary winds, and a lingering voyage, never fail to create on all occasions, we, in particular, had very substantial reasons to be greatly alarmed at this unexpected impediment. For as we had departed from England much later than we ought to have done, we had placed almost all our hopes of success in the chance of retrieving, in some measure at sea, the time we had so unhappily wasted at Spithead and St. Helens. However, at last, on Monday, October the 25th, at five in the morning, we, to our great joy, made the land, and in the afternoon came to an anchor in Madeira Road, in forty fathom water; the Brazenhead bearing from us E. by S., the Loo N.N.W., and the great Church N.N.E. We had hardly let go our anchor, when an English privateer sloop ran under our stern, and saluted the commodore with nine guns, which we returned with five. And, the next day, the consul of the island coming to visit the commodore, we saluted him with nine guns on his coming on board.

This island of Madeira, where we are now arrived, is famous through all our American settlements for its excellent wines, which seem to be designed by Providence for the refreshment of the inhabitants of the torrid zone. It is situated in a fine climate, in the latitude of 32° 27' north; and in the longitude from London of, by our different reckonings, from 18° ½ to 19° ⅙ west, though laid down in the charts in 17°. It is composed of one continued hill, of a considerable height, extending itself from east to west: the declivity of which, on the south-side, is cultivated and interspersed with vineyards; and in the midst of this slope the merchants have fixed their country-seats, which help to form an agreeable prospect. There is but one considerable town in the whole island, it is named Fonchiale, and is seated on the south part of the island, at the bottom of a large bay. This is the only place of trade, and indeed the only one where it is possible for a boat to land. Fonchiale, towards the south, is defended by a high wall, with a battery of cannon, besides a castle on the Loo, which is a rock standing in the water at a small distance from the shore. Even here the beach is covered with large stones, and a violent surf continually beats upon it; so that the commodore did not care to venture the ships' long-boats to fetch the water off, as there was so much danger of their being lost; and therefore ordered the captains of the squadron to employ Portuguese boats on that service.

We continued about a week at this island, watering our ships, and providing the squadron with wine and other refreshments. And, on the 3rd of November, Captain Richard Norris having signified, by a letter to the commodore, his desire to quit his command on board the Gloucester, in order to return to England for the recovery of his health, the commodore complied with his request; and thereupon was pleased to appoint Captain Matthew Mitchel to command the Gloucester in his room, and to remove Captain Kidd from the Wager to the Pearl, and Captain Murray from the Tryal sloop to the Wager, giving the command of the Tryal to Lieutenant Cheap. These promotions being settled, with other changes in the lieutenancies, the commodore, on the following day, gave to the captains their orders, appointing St. Jago, one of the Cape de Verd islands, to be the first place of rendezvous in case of separation; and directing them, if they did not meet the Centurion there, to make the best of their way to the island of St. Catherine's on the coast of Brazil. The water for the squadron being the same day completed, and each ship supplied with as much wine and other refreshments as they could take in, we weighed anchor in the afternoon, and took our leave of the island of Madeira. But before I go on with the narration of our own transactions, I think it necessary to give some account of the proceedings of the enemy, and of the measures they had taken to render all our designs abortive.

When Mr. Anson visited the governor of Madeira, he received information from him, that for three or four days, in the latter end of October, there had appeared, to the westward of that island, seven or eight ships of the line, and a patache, which last was sent every day close in to make the land. The governor assured the commodore, upon his honour, that none upon the island had either given them intelligence, or had in any sort communicated with them, but that he believed them to be either French or Spanish, but was rather inclined to think them Spanish. On this intelligence Mr. Anson sent an officer in a clean sloop, eight leagues to the westward, to reconnoitre them, and, if possible, to discover what they were: but the officer returned without being able to get a sight of them, so that we still remained in uncertainty. However, we could not but conjecture, that this fleet was intended to put a stop to our expedition, which, had they cruised to the eastward of the island instead of the westward, they could not but have executed with great facility. For as, in that case, they must have certainly fallen in with us, we should have been obliged to throw overboard vast quantities of provision to clear our ships for an engagement, and this alone, without any regard to the event of the action, would have effectually prevented our progress. This was so obvious a measure, that we could not help imagining reasons which might have prevented them from pursuing it. And we therefore supposed, that this French or Spanish squadron was sent out, upon advice of our sailing in company with Admiral Balchen and Lord Cathcart's expedition: and thence, from an apprehension of being over-matched, they might not think it advisable to meet with us, till we had parted company, which they might judge would not happen, before our arrival at this island. These were our speculations at that time; and from hence we had reason to suppose, that we might still fall in with them, in our way to the Cape de Verd islands. And afterwards, in the course of our expedition, we were many of us persuaded, that this was the Spanish squadron commanded by Don Joseph Pizarro, which was sent out purposely to traverse the views and enterprises of our squadron, to which, in strength, they were greatly superior. As the Spanish armament then was so nearly connected with our expedition, and as the catastrophe it underwent, though not effected by our force, was yet a considerable advantage to this nation, produced in consequence of our equipment, I have, in the following chapter, given a summary account of their proceedings, from their first setting out from Spain in the year 1740, till the Asia, the only ship which returned to Europe of the whole squadron, arrived at the Groyne in the beginning of the year 1746.

CHAPTER III.
The history of the Squadron commanded by Don Joseph Pizarro.

THE squadron fitted out by the court of Spain to attend our motions, and traverse our projects, we supposed to have been the ships seen off Madeira, as mentioned in the preceding chapter. And as this force was sent out particularly against our expedition, I cannot but imagine that the following history of the casualties it met with, as far as by intercepted letters and other information the same has come to my knowledge, is a very essential part of the present work: for by this it will appear we were the occasion, that a considerable part of the naval power of Spain was diverted from the prosecution of the ambitious views of that court in Europe; and the men and ships, lost by the enemy in this undertaking, were lost in consequence of the precautions they took to secure themselves against our enterprises. This squadron (besides two ships intended for the West Indies, which did not part company till after they had left the Madeiras) was composed of the following men-of-war, commanded by Don Joseph Pizarro:

The Asia of sixty-six guns, and seven hundred men; this was the admiral's ship.
The Guipuscoa of seventy-four guns, and seven hundred men.

The Hermiona of fifty-four guns, and five hundred men.
The Esperanza of fifty guns, and four hundred and fifty men.
The St. Estevan of forty guns, and three hundred and fifty men.
And a patache of twenty guns.

These ships, over and above their complement of sailors and marines, had on board an old Spanish regiment of foot, intended to reinforce the garrisons on the coast of the South Seas. When this fleet had cruised for some days to the leeward of the Madeiras, as is mentioned in the preceding chapter, they left that station in the beginning of November, and steered for the river of Plate, where they arrived the 5th of January, O. S., and coming to an anchor in the bay of Maldonado, at the mouth of that river, their Admiral Pizarro sent immediately to Buenos Ayres for a supply of provisions; for they had departed from Spain with only four months' provisions on board. While they lay here expecting this supply, they received intelligence, by the treachery of the Portuguese governor of St. Catherine's, of Mr. Anson's having arrived at that island on the 21st of December preceding, and of his preparing to put to sea again with the utmost expedition. Pizarro, notwithstanding his superior force, had his reasons (and as some say, his orders likewise) for avoiding our squadron anywhere short of the South Seas. He was besides extremely desirous of getting round Cape Horn before us, as he imagined that step alone would effectually baffle all our designs; and, therefore, on hearing that we were in his neighbourhood, and that we should soon be ready to proceed for Cape Horn, he weighed anchor with the five large ships, (the patache being disabled and condemned, and the men taken out of her) after a stay of seventeen days only, and got under sail without his provisions, which arrived at Maldonado within a day or two after his departure. But notwithstanding the precipitation with which he departed, we put to sea from St. Catherine's four days before him, and in some part of our passage to Cape Horn, the two squadrons were so near together, that the Pearl, one of our ships, being separated from the rest, fell in with the Spanish fleet, and mistaking the Asia for the Centurion, had got within gun-shot of Pizarro, before she discovered her error, and narrowly escaped being taken.

It being the 22d of January when the Spaniards weighed from Maldonado, (as has been already mentioned) they could not expect to get into the latitude of Cape Horn before the equinox; and as they had reason to apprehend very tempestuous weather in doubling it at that season, and as the Spanish sailors, being for the most part accustomed to a fair-weather country, might be expected to be very averse to so dangerous and fatiguing a navigation, the better to encourage them, some part of their pay was advanced to them in European goods, which they were to be permitted to dispose of in the South Seas, that so the hopes of the great profit each man was to make on his small venture might animate him in his duty, and render him less disposed to repine at the labour, the hardships and the perils he would in all probability meet with before his arrival on the coast of Peru.

Pizarro with his squadron having, towards the latter end of February, run the length of Cape Horn, he then stood to the westward in order to double it; but in the night of the last day of February, O. S., while with this view they were turning to windward, the Guipuscoa, the Hermiona, and the Esperanza, were separated from the admiral; and, on the 6th of March following, the Guipuscoa was separated from the other two; and on the 7th (being the day after we had passed Straits le Maire) there came on a most furious storm at N. W., which, in despite of all their efforts, drove the whole squadron to the eastward, and obliged them, after several fruitless attempts, to bear away for the river of Plate, where Pizarro in the Asia arrived about the middle of May, and a few days after him the Esperanza and the Estevan. The Hermiona was supposed to founder at sea, for she was never heard of more; and the Guipuscoa was run ashore, and sunk on the coast of Brazil. The calamities of all kinds, which this squadron underwent in this unsuccessful navigation, can only be paralleled by what we ourselves experienced in the same climate, when buffeted by the same storms. There was indeed some diversity in our distresses, which rendered it difficult to decide whose situation was most worthy of commiseration. For to all the misfortunes we had in common with each other, as shattered rigging, leaky ships, and the fatigues and despondency, which necessarily attend these disasters, there was superadded on board our squadron the ravage of a most destructive and incurable disease, and on board the Spanish squadron the devastation of famine.

For this squadron, either from the hurry of their outset, their presumption of a supply at Buenos Ayres, or from other less obvious motives, departed from Spain, as has been already observed, with no more than four months' provision, and even that, as it is said, at short allowance only; so that, when by the storms they met with off Cape Horn, their continuance at sea was prolonged a month or more beyond their expectation, they were thereby reduced to such infinite distress, that rats, when they could be caught, were sold for four dollars a-piece; and a sailor, who died on board, had his death concealed for some days by his brother, who, during that time lay in the same hammock with the corpse, only to receive the dead man's allowance of provisions. In this dreadful situation they were alarmed (if their horrors were capable of augmentation) by the discovery of a conspiracy among the marines, on board the Asia, the admiral's ship. This had taken its rise chiefly from the miseries they endured: for though no less was proposed by the conspirators than the massacring the officers and the whole crew, yet their motive for this bloody resolution seemed to be no more than their desire of relieving their hunger, by appropriating the whole ship's provisions to themselves. But their designs were prevented, when just upon the point of execution, by means of one of their confessors, and three of their ringleaders were immediately put to death. However, though the conspiracy was suppressed, their other calamities admitted of no alleviation, but grew each day more and more destructive. So that by the complicated distress of fatigue, sickness, and hunger, the three ships which escaped lost the greatest part of their men:

the Asia, their admiral's ship, arrived at Monte Video in the river of Plate, with half her crew only; the St. Estevan had lost in like manner half her hands, when she anchored in the bay of Barragan; the Esperanza, a fifty-gun ship, was still more unfortunate, for of four hundred and fifty hands which she brought from Spain, only fifty-eight remained alive, and the whole regiment of foot perished except sixty men. But to give the reader a more distinct and particular idea of what they underwent upon this occasion, I shall lay before him a short account of the fate of the Guipuscoa, from a letter written by Don Joseph Mendinuetta her captain, to a person of distinction at Lima; a copy of which fell into our hands afterwards in the South Seas.

He mentions, that he separated from the Hermiona and the Esperanza in a fog, on the 6th of March, being then, as I suppose, to the S. E. of Staten-Land, and plying to the westward; that in the night after, it blew a furious storm at N. W., which, at half an hour after ten, split his mainsail, that obliged him to bear away with his foresail; that the ship went ten knots an hour with a prodigious sea, and often ran her gangway under water; that he likewise sprang his main-mast; and the ship made so much water, that with four pumps and baling he could not free her. That on the 19th it was calm, but the sea continued so high, that the ship in rolling opened all her upper works and seams, and started the butt ends of her planking and the greatest part of her top timbers, the bolts being drawn by the violence of her roll. That in this condition, with other additional disasters to the hull and rigging, they continued beating to the westward till the 12th: that they were then in sixty degrees of south latitude, in great want of provisions, numbers every day perishing by the fatigue of pumping, and those who survived being quite dispirited by labour, hunger, and the severity of the weather, they having two spans of snow upon the decks: that then finding the wind fixed in the western quarter, and blowing strong, and consequently their passage to the westward impossible, they resolved to bear away for the river of Plate: that on the 22nd, they were obliged to throw overboard all the upper deck guns, and an anchor, and to take six turns of the cable round the ship to prevent her opening: that on the 4th of April, it being calm but a very high sea, the ship rolled so much that the main-mast came by the board, and in a few hours after she lost, in like manner, her fore-mast and her mizen-mast; and that, to accumulate their misfortunes, they were soon obliged to cut away their bowsprit to diminish, if possible, the leakage at her head: that by this time he had lost two hundred and fifty men by hunger and fatigues: for those who were capable of working at the pumps (at which every officer without exception took his turn) were allowed only an ounce and half of biscuit *per diem*; and those who were so sick or so weak that they could not assist in this necessary labour, had no more than an ounce of wheat; so that it was common for the men to fall down dead at the pumps: that, including the officers, they could only muster from eighty to a hundred persons capable of duty: that the south-west winds blew so fresh after they had lost their masts, that they could not immediately set up jury masts, but were obliged to drive like a wreck between the latitudes of thirty-two and twenty-eight till the 24th of April, when they made the coast of Brazil, at Rio de Patas, ten leagues to the southward of the Island of St. Catherine's; that here they came to an anchor, and that the captain was very desirous of proceeding to St. Catherine's if possible, in order to save the hull of the ship, and the guns and stores on board her; but the crew instantly left off pumping, and being enraged at the hardships they had suffered, and the numbers they had lost, (there being at that time no less that thirty dead bodies lying on the deck,) they all with one voice cried out " on shore, on shore," and obliged the captain to run the ship in directly for the land, where, the 5th day after, she sunk with her stores, and all her furniture on board her, but the remainder of the crew, whom hunger and fatigue had spared to the number of four hundred, got safe on shore.

From this account of the adventures and catastrophe of the Guipuscoa, we may form some conjecture of the manner in which the Hermiona was lost, and of the distresses endured by the three remaining ships of the squadron, which got into the river of Plate. These last being in great want of masts, yards, rigging, and all kind of naval stores, and having no supply at Buenos Ayres, nor in any other of their settlements, Pizarro despatched an advice boat with a letter of credit to Rio Janeiro, to purchase what was wanting from the Portuguese. He at the same time sent an express across the continent to San Jago, in Chili, to be thence forwarded to the viceroy of Peru, informing him of the disasters that had befallen his squadron, and desiring a remittance of 200,000 dollars from the royal chests at Lima, to enable him to victual and refit his remaining ships, that he might be again in a condition to attempt the passage to the South Seas, as soon as the season of the year should be more favourable. It is mentioned by the Spaniards as a most extraordinary circumstance that the Indian charged with this express, (though it was then the depth of winter, when the Cordilleras are esteemed impassable on account of the snow,) was only thirteen days in his journey from Buenos Ayres to St. Jago in Chili; though these places are distant three hundred Spanish leagues, near forty of which are amongst the snows and precipices of the Cordilleras.

The return to this despatch of Pizarro's from the viceroy of Peru, was no ways favourable; instead of 200,000 dollars, the sum demanded, the viceroy remitted him only 100,000, telling him, that it was with great difficulty he was able to procure him even that: though the inhabitants at Lima, who considered the presence of Pizarro as absolutely necessary to their security, were much discontented at this procedure, and did not fail to assert, that it was not the want of money, but the interested views of some of the viceroy's confidants, that prevented Pizarro from having the whole sum he had asked for.

The advice-boat sent to Rio Janeiro also executed her commission but imperfectly; for though she brought back a considerable quantity of pitch, tar, and cordage, yet she could not procure either masts or yards: and, as an additional misfortune, Pizarro was disappointed of some masts he ex pected from Paraguay; for a carpenter, whom he entrusted with a large sum of money, and had sent there to cut masts, instead of prosecuting his business he was employed in, had married in the country, and refused to return. However, by removing the masts of the Esperanza into the Asia, and making use of what spare masts and yards they had on board, they made a shift to refit the Asia and the St. Estevan. And in the October following, Pizarro was preparing to put to sea with these two ships, in order to attempt the passage round Cape Horn a second time; but the St. Estevan, in coming down the river Plate, ran on a shoal, and beat off her rudder, on which, and other damages she received, she was condemned and broke up, and Pizarro in the Asia proceeded to sea without her. Having now the summer before him, and the winds favourable, no doubt was made of his having a fortunate and speedy passage; but being off Cape Horn, and going right before the wind in very moderate weather, though in a swelling sea, by some misconduct of the officer of the watch the ship rolled away her masts, and was a second time obliged to put back to the river of Plate in great distress.

The Asia having considerably suffered in this second unfortunate expedition, the Esperanza, which had been left behind at Monte Video, was ordered to be refitted, the command of her being given to Mindinuetta, who was captain of the Guipuscoa when she was lost. He, in the November of the succeeding year, that is, in November, 1742, sailed from the river of Plate for the South Seas, and arrived safe on the coast of Chili; where his commodore Pizarro passing over land from Buenos Ayres met him. There were great animosities and contests between these two gentlemen at their meeting, occasioned principally by the claim of Pizarro to command the Esperanza, which Mindinuetta had brought round: for Mindinuetta refused to deliver her up to him; insisting, that as he came into the South Seas alone, and under no superior, it was not now in the power of Pizarro to resume that authority which he had once parted with. However, the president of Chili interposing and declaring for Pizarro, Mindinuetta, after a long and obstinate struggle, was obliged to submit.

But Pizarro had not yet completed the series of his adventures; for when he and Mindinuetta came back by land from Chili to Buenos Ayres, in the year 1745, they found at Monte Video the Asia, which near three years before they had left there. This ship they resolved, if possible, to carry to Europe, and with this view they refitted her in the best manner they could: but their great difficulty was to procure a sufficient number of hands to navigate her, for all the remaining sailors of the squadron to be met with in the neighbourhood of Buenos Ayres, did not amount to a hundred men. They endeavoured to supply this defect by pressing many of the inhabitants of Buenos Ayres, and putting on board besides all the English prisoners then in their custody, together with a number of Portuguese smugglers, whom they had taken at different times, and some of the Indians of the country. Among these last there was a chief and ten of his followers, who had been surprised by a party of Spanish soldiers about three months before. The name of this chief was Orellana, he belonged to a very powerful tribe, which had committed great ravages in the neighbourhood of Buenos Ayres. With this motley crew (all of them, except the European Spaniards, extremely averse to the voyage) Pizarro set sail from Monte Video in the river of Plate, about the beginning of November 1745, and the native Spaniards being no strangers to the dissatisfaction of their forced men, treated both those, the English prisoners and the Indians, with great insolence and barbarity; but more particularly the Indians, for it was common for the meanest officers in the ship to beat them most cruelly on the slightest pretences, and oftentimes only to exert their superiority. Orellana and his followers, though in appearance sufficiently patient and submissive, meditated a severe revenge for all these inhumanities. As he conversed very well in Spanish, (these Indians having in time of peace a great intercourse with Buenos Ayres) he affected to talk with such of the English as understood that language, and seemed very desirous of being informed how many Englishmen there were on board, and which they were. As he knew that the English were as much enemies to the Spaniards as himself, he had doubtless an intention of disclosing his purposes to them, and making them partners in the scheme he had projected for revenging his wrongs, and recovering his liberty; but having sounded them at a distance, and not finding them so precipitate and vindictive as he expected, he proceeded no further with them, but resolved to trust alone to the resolution of his ten faithful followers. These, it should seem, readily engaged to observe his directions, and to execute whatever commands he gave them; and having agreed on the measures necessary to be taken, they first furnished themselves with Dutch knives sharp at the point, which being the common knives used in the ship, they found no difficulty in procuring: besides this, they employed their leisure in secretly cutting out thongs from raw hides, of which there were great numbers on board, and in fixing to each end of these thongs the double-headed shot of the small quarter-deck guns; this, when swung round their heads, according to the practice of their country, was a most mischievous weapon, in the use of which the Indians about Buenos Ayres are trained from their infancy, and consequently are extremely expert. These particulars being in good forwardness, the execution of their scheme was perhaps precipitated by a particular outrage committed on Orellana himself. For one of the officers, who was a very brutal fellow, ordered Orellana aloft, which being what he was incapable of performing, the officer, under pretence of his disobedience, beat him with such violence, that he left him bleeding on the deck, and stupified for some time with his bruises and wounds. This usage undoubtedly heightened his thirst for revenge, and made him eager and impatient till the means of executing it were in his power; so that, within a day or two after this incident, he and his followers opened their desperate resolves in the ensuing manner.

It was about nine in the evening, when many of the principal officers were on the quarter-deck, indulging in the freshness of the night air; the waist of the ship was filled with live cattle, and the forecastle was manned with its customary watch.

Orellana and his companions, under cover of the night, having prepared their weapons, and thrown off their trowsers and the more cumbrous part of their dress, came all together on the quarter-deck, and drew towards the door of the great cabin. The boatswain immediately reprimanded them, and ordered them to be gone. On this Orellana spoke to his followers in his native language, when four of them drew off, two towards each gangway, and the chief and the six remaining Indians seemed to be slowly quitting the quarter-deck. When the detached Indians had taken possession of the gangway, Orellana placed his hands hollow to his mouth, and bellowed out the war-cry used by those savages, which is said to be the harshest and most terrifying sound known in nature. This hideous yell was the signal for beginning the massacre: for on this they all drew their knives, and brandished their prepared double-headed shot, and the six with their chief, who remained on the quarter-deck, immediately fell on the Spaniards, who were intermingled with them, and laid near forty of them at their feet, of whom above twenty were killed on the spot, and the rest disabled. Many of the officers, in the beginning of the tumult, pushed into the great cabin, where they put out the lights, and barricadoed the door. And of the others, who had avoided the first fury of the Indians, some endeavoured to escape along the gangways into the forecastle, but the Indians, placed there on purpose, stabbed the greatest part of them, as they attempted to pass by, or forced them off the gangways into the waist. Others threw themselves voluntarily over the barricadoes into the waist, and thought themselves happy to lie concealed amongst the cattle; but the greatest part escaped up the main shrouds, and sheltered themselves either in the tops or rigging. And though the Indians attacked only the quarter-deck, yet the watch in the forecastle finding their communication cut off, and being terrified by the wounds of the few who, not being killed on the spot, had sufficient strength to force their passage along the gangways, and not knowing either who their enemies were, or what were their numbers, they likewise gave all over for lost, and in great confusion ran up into the rigging of the fore-mast and bowsprit.

Thus these eleven Indians, with a resolution perhaps without example, possessed themselves almost in an instant of the quarter-deck of a ship mounting sixty-six guns, with a crew of near five hundred men, and continued in peaceable possession of this post a considerable time. For the officers in the great cabin, (amongst whom were Pizarro and Mindinuetta) the crew between decks, and those who had escaped into the tops and rigging, were only anxious for their own safety, and were for a long time incapable of forming any project for suppressing the insurrection, and recovering the possession of the ship. It is true, the yells of the Indians, the groans of the wounded, and the confused clamours of the crew, all heightened by the obscurity of the night, had at first greatly magnified their danger, and had filled them with the imaginary terrors which darkness, disorder, and an ignorance of the real strength of an enemy, never fail to produce. For as the Spaniards were sensible of the disaffection of their pressed hands, and were also conscious of their barbarity to their prisoners, they imagined the conspiracy was general, and considered their own destruction as infallible; so that, it is said, some of them had once taken the resolution of leaping into the sea, but were prevented by their companions.

However, when the Indians had entirely cleared the quarter-deck, the tumult in a great measure subsided; for those who had escaped were kept silent by their fears, and the Indians were incapable of pursuing them to renew the disorder. Orellana, when he saw himself master of the quarter-deck, broke open the arm-chest, which, on a slight suspicion of mutiny, had been ordered there a few days before, as to a place of the greatest security. Here, he took it for granted, that he should find cutlasses sufficient for himself and his companions, in the use of which weapon they were all extremely skilful, and with these, it was imagined, they proposed to have forced the great cabin: but on opening the chest, there appeared nothing but fire-arms, which to them were of no use. There were indeed cutlasses in the chest, but they were hid by the fire-arms being laid over them. This was a sensible disappointment to them, and by this time Pizarro and his companions in the great cabin were capable of conversing aloud, through the cabin windows and port-holes, with those in the gun-room and between decks, and from hence they learnt, that the English (whom they principally suspected) were all safe below, and had not intermeddled in this mutiny; and by other particulars they at last discovered, that none were concerned in it but Orellana and his people. On this Pizarro and the officers resolved to attack them on the quarter-deck, before any of the discontented on board should so far recover their first surprise, as to reflect on the facility and certainty of seizing the ship by a junction with the Indians in the present emergency. With this view Pizarro got together what arms were in the cabin, and distributed them to those who were with him: but there were no other fire-arms to be met with but pistols, and for these they had neither powder nor ball. However, having now settled a correspondence with the gun-room, they lowered down a bucket out of the cabin-window, into which the gunner, out of one of the gun-room ports, put a quantity of pistol cartridges. When they had thus procured ammunition, and had loaded their pistols, they set the cabin-door partly open, and fired some shot amongst the Indians on the quarter-deck, at first without effect. But at last Mindinuetta, whom we have often mentioned, had the good fortune to shoot Orellana dead on the spot; on which his faithful companions, abandoning all thoughts of farther resistance, instantly leaped into the sea, where they every man perished. Thus was this insurrection quelled, and the possession of the quarter-deck regained, after it had been full two hours in the power of this great and daring chief, and his gallant and unhappy countrymen.

Pizarro, having escaped this imminent peril, steered for Europe, and arrived safe on the coast of Galicia, in the beginning of the year 1746, after having been absent between four and five years, and having, by his attendance on our expedition, diminished the naval power of Spain by above three thousand hands (the flower of their sailors), and by four considerable ships of war and a patache

MADEIRA.

For we have seen, that the Hermiona foundered at sea; the Guipuscoa was stranded, and sunk on the coast of Brazil; the St. Estevan was condemned, and broke up in the river of Plate; and the Esperanza being left in the South Seas, is doubtless by this time incapable of returning to Spain. So that the Asia only, with less than one hundred hands, may be considered as all the remains of that squadron with which Pizarro first put to sea. And whoever attends to the very large proportior which this squadron bore to the whole navy of Spain, will, I believe, confess, that had our undertaking been attended with no other advantages than that of ruining so great a part of the sea-force of so dangerous an enemy, this alone would be a sufficient equivalent for our equipment, and an incontestible proof of the service which the nation has thence received. Having thus concluded this summary of Pizarro's adventures, I shall now return again to the narration of our own transactions.

CHAPTER IV.
From Madeira to St. Catherine's.

I HAVE already mentioned that, on the 3d of November, we weighed from Madeira, after orders had been given to the captains to rendezvous at St. Jago, one of the Cape de Verd Islands, in case the squadron was separated. But the next day, when we got to sea, the commodore considering that the season was far advanced, and that touching at St. Jago would create a new delay, he for this reason thought proper to alter his rendezvous, and to appoint the island of St. Catherine's, on the coast of Brazil, to be the first place to which the ships of the squadron were to repair in case of separation.

In our passage to the island of St. Catherine's, we found the direction of the trade-winds to differ considerably from what we had reason to expect, both from the general histories given of these winds, and the experience of former navigators. For the learned Dr. Halley, in his account of the trade-winds which take place in the Ethiopic and Atlantic Ocean, tells us, that from the latitude of 28° N., to the latitude of 10° N., there is generally a fresh gale of N. E. wind, which towards the African side rarely comes to the eastward of E. N. E., or passes to the northward of N. N. E.: but on the American side, the wind is somewhat more easterly, though most commonly even there it is a point or two to the northward of the east. That from 10° N. to 4° N., the calms and tornadoes take place; and from 4° N. to 30° S., the winds are generally and perpetually between the south and east. This account we expected to have verified by our own experience; but we found considerable variations from it, both in respect to the steadiness of the winds, and the quarter from whence they blew. For though we met with a N. E. wind about the latitude of 28° N., yet from the latitude of 25° to the latitude of 18° N., the wind was never once to the northward of the east, but on the contrary, almost constantly to the southward of it. However, from thence to the latitude of 6° 20' N., we had it usually to the northward of the east, though not entirely, it having for a short time changed to E. S. E. From hence, to about 4° 46' N., the weather was very unsettled; sometimes the wind was N. E. then changed to S. E., and sometimes we had a dead calm attended with small rain and lightning. After this, the wind continued almost invariably between the S. and E., to the latitude of 7° 30' S.; and then again as invariably between the N. and E., to the latitude of 15° 30' S.; then E. and S. E., to 21° 37' S. But after this, even to the latitude of 27° 44' S., the wind was never once between the S. and the E., though we had it at times in all the other quarters of the compass. But this last circumstance may be in some measure accounted for, from our approach to the main continent of the Brazils. I mention not these particulars with a view of cavilling at the received accounts of these trade-winds, which I doubt not are in general sufficiently accurate; but I thought it a matter worthy of public notice, that such deviations from the established rules do sometimes take place. This observation may not only be of service to navigators, by putting them on their guard against these hitherto unexpected irregularities, but may perhaps contribute to the solution of that great question about the causes of trade-winds, and monsoons; a question, which in my opinion, has not been hitherto discussed with that clearness and accuracy, which its importance (whether it be considered as a naval or philosophical inquiry) seems to demand.

On the 16th of November, one of our victuallers made a signal to speak with the commodore, and we shortened sail for her to come up with us. The master came on board, and acquainted Mr. Anson, that he had complied with the terms of his charter-party, and desired to be unloaded and dismissed. Mr. Anson, on consulting the captains of the squadron, found all the ships had still such quantities of provision between their decks, and were withal so deep, that they could not without great difficulty take in their several proportions of brandy from the Industry pink, one of the victuallers only: and, consequently, he was obliged to continue the other of them, the Anna pink, in the service of attending the squadron. And the next day the commodore made a signal for the ships to bring to, and to take on board their shares of the brandy from the Industry pink; and in this, the long-boats of the squadron were employed the three following days; that is, till the 19th in the evening, when the pink being unloaded, she parted company with us, being bound for Barbadoes, there to take in a freight for England. Most of the officers of the squadron took the opportunity of writing to their friends at home by this ship; but she was afterwards, as I have been since informed, unhappily taken by the Spaniards.

On the 20th of November, the captains of the squadron represented to the commodore, that their ships' companies were very sickly, and that it was their own opinion as well as their surgeons', that it would tend to the preservation of the men to let in more air between decks; but that their ships were so deep, they could not possibly open their lower ports. On this representation, the commodore ordered six air-scuttles to be cut in each ship, in such places where they would least weaken it.

And on this occasion I cannot but observe, how much it is the duty of all those who, either by office or authority, have any influence in the direction of our naval affairs, to attend to this important article, the preservation of the lives and health of our seamen. If it could be supposed that the motives of humanity were insufficient for this purpose, yet policy, and a regard to the success of our arms, and the interest and honour of each particular commander, should naturally lead us to a careful and impartial examination of every probable method proposed for maintaining a ship's crew in health and vigour. But hath this been always done? Have the late invented plain and obvious methods of keeping our ships sweet and clean, by a constant supply of fresh air, been considered with that candour and temper, which the great benefits promised hereby ought naturally to have inspired? On the contrary, have not these salutary schemes been often treated with neglect and contempt? And have not some of those who have been entrusted with experimenting their effects, been guilty of the most indefensible partiality, in the accounts they have given of these trials? Indeed, it must be confessed, that many distinguished persons, both in the direction and command of our fleets, have exerted themselves on these occasions with a judicious and dispassionate examination, becoming the interesting nature of the inquiry; but the wonder is, that any could be found irrational enough to act a contrary part, in despite of the strongest dictates of prudence and humanity. I must, however, own, that I do not believe this conduct to have arisen from motives so savage, as the first reflection thereon does naturally suggest: but I rather impute it to an obstinate, and in some small degree superstitious, attachment to such practices as have been long established, and to a settled contempt and hatred of all kinds of innovations, especially such as are projected by landsmen and persons residing on shore. But let us return from this, I hope not, impertinent digression.

We crossed the equinoctial with a fine fresh gale at S. E., on Friday the 28th of November, at four in the morning, being then in the longitude of 27° 59′ W. from London. And on the 2d of December, in the morning, we saw a sail in the N. W. quarter, and the Gloucester's and Tryal's signals to chase; and half an hour after, we let our reefs out and chased with the squadron; and about noon a signal was made for the Wager to take our remaining victualler, the Anna pink, in tow. But at seven in the evening, finding we did not near the chase, and that the Wager was very far a-stern, we shortened sail, and made a signal for the cruisers to join the squadron. The next day but one we again discovered a sail, which, on a nearer approach, we judged to be the same vessel. We chased her the whole day, and though we rather gained upon her, yet night came on before we could overtake her, and obliged us to give over the chase, to collect our scattered squadron. We were much chagrined at the escape of this vessel, as we then apprehended her to be an advice-boat sent from Old Spain to Buenos Ayres, with notice of our expedition. But we have since learned that we were deceived in this conjecture, and that it was our East-India Company's packet, bound to St. Helena.

On the 10th of December, being by our accounts in the latitude of 20° S., and 36° 30′ longitude west from London, the Tryal fired a gun to denote soundings. We immediately sounded, and found sixty fathom water, the bottom coarse ground with broken shells. The Tryal being a-head of us, had at one time thirty-seven fathom, which afterwards increased to 90. And then she found no bottom, which happened to us too at our second trial, though we sounded with a hundred and fifty fathom of line. This is the shoal which is laid down in most charts by the name of the Abrollos; and it appeared we were upon the very edge of it; perhaps farther in it may be extremely dangerous. We were then, by our different accounts, from ninety to sixty leagues east of the coast of Brazil. The next day but one we spoke with a Portuguese brigantine from Rio Janeiro, bound to Bahia del Todos Santos, who informed us that we were thirty-four leagues from Cape St. Thomas, and forty leagues from Cape Frio, which last bore from us W. S. W. By our accounts we were near eighty leagues from Cape Frio; and though, on the information of this brigantine, we altered our course and stood more to the southward, yet by our coming in with the land afterwards, we were fully convinced that our reckoning was much correcter than our Portuguese intelligence. We found a considerable current setting to the southward, after we had passed the latitude of 16° S. And the same took place all along the coast of Brazil, and even to the southward of the river of Plate, it amounting sometimes to thirty miles in twenty-four hours, and once to above forty miles. If this current is occasioned (as it is most probable) by the running off of the water accumulated on the coast of Brazil by the constant sweeping of the eastern trade-wind over the Ethiopic Ocean, then it is most natural to suppose, that its general course is determined by the bearings of the adjacent shore. Perhaps too, in almost every other instance of currents, the same may hold true, as I believe no examples occur of considerable currents being observed at any great distance from land. If this then could be laid down for a general principle, it would be always easy to correct the reckoning by the observed latitude. But it were much to be wished, for the general interests of navigation, that the actual settings of the different currents which are known to take place in various parts of the world, were examined more frequently and accurately than hitherto appears to have been done.

We now began to grow impatient for a sight of land, both for the recovery of our sick, and for the refreshment and security of those who as yet continued healthier. When we departed from St. Helens, we were in so good a condition, that we lost but two men on board the Centurion, in our long passage to Madeira. But in this present run between Madeira and St. Catherine's we have been very sickly, so that many died, and great numbers were confined to their hammocks, both in our own ship and in the rest of the squadron, and several of these past all hopes of recovery. The disorders they in general labour under are such as are common to the hot climates, and what most ships bound to the southward experience in a greater or less degree. These are those kind of fevers which they usually call calentures: a disease, which was not only terrible in its first instance, but even the remains of it often prove fatal to those who considered themselves as recovered from it. For it always left them in a very weak and helpless condition, and usually afflicted with fluxes and tenesmuses. And by our continuance at sea all our complaints were every day increasing, so that it was with great joy that we discovered the coast of Brazil on the 18th of December, at seven in the morning.

The coast of Brazil appeared high and mountainous land, extending from the W. to W.S.W., and when we first saw it, it was about seventeen leagues distant. At noon we perceived a low double land, bearing W.S.W., about ten leagues distant, which we took to be the island of St. Catherine's. That afternoon and the next morning, the wind being N.N.W., we gained very little to windward, and were apprehensive of being driven to the leeward of the island; but a little before noon, the next day, the wind came about to the southward, and enabled us to steer in between the north point of St. Catherine's, and the neighbouring island of Alvoredo. As we stood in for the land, we had regular soundings, gradually decreasing from thirty-six to twelve fathom, all muddy ground. In this last depth of water we let go our anchor at five o'clock in the evening of the 18th, the north-west point of the island of St. Catherine's bearing S.S.W., distant three miles; and the island Alvoredo N.N.E., distant two leagues. Here we found the tide to set S.S.E. and N.N.W., at the rate of two knots, the tide of flood coming from the southward. We could from our ships observe two fortifications at a considerable distance within us, which seemed designed to prevent the passage of an enemy between the island of St. Catherine's and the main. And we could soon perceive that our squadron had alarmed the coast, for we saw the two forts hoist their colours, and fire several guns, which we supposed to be intended for assembling the inhabitants. To prevent any confusion, the commodore immediately sent a boat with an officer on shore, to compliment the governor, and to desire a pilot to carry us into the road. The governor returned a very civil answer, and ordered us a pilot. On the morning of the 20th, we weighed and stood in, and towards noon the pilot came on board of us, who, the same afternoon, brought us to an anchor in five fathom and a half, in a large commodious bay on the continent side, called by the French, Bon Port. In standing from our last anchorage to this place, we everywhere found an oozy bottom, with a depth of water first regularly decreasing to five fathom, and then increasing to seven, after which we had six and five fathom alternately. The next morning we weighed again with the squadron, in order to run above the two fortifications we have mentioned, which are called the castles of Santa Cruiz and St. Juan. And now the soundings between the island and the main were four, five, and six fathom, with muddy ground. As we passed by the castle of Santa Cruiz we saluted it with eleven guns, and were answered by an equal number; and at one in the afternoon, the squadron came to an anchor in five fathom and a half, the Governor's Island bearing N.N.W., St. Juan's Castle N.E. ¼ E., and the island of St. Antonio south. In this position we moored at the island of St. Catherine's, on Sunday the 21st of December, the whole squadron being, as I have already mentioned, sickly, and in great want of refreshments: both which inconveniences we hoped to have soon removed at this settlement, celebrated by former navigators for its healthiness and its provisions, and for the freedom, indulgence, and friendly assistance there given to the ships of all European nations in amity with the crown of Portugal.

CHAPTER V.

Proceedings at St. Catherine's, and a Description of the place, with a short Account of Brazil.

OUR first care, after having moored our ships, was to send our sick men on shore, each ship being ordered by the commodore to erect two tents for that purpose: one of them for the reception of the diseased, and the other for the accommodation of the surgeon and his assistants. We sent about eighty sick from the Centurion, and the other ships sent nearly as many, in proportion to the number of their hands. As soon as we had performed this necessary duty, we scraped our decks, and gave our ship a thorough cleansing; then smoked it between decks, and after all washed every part well with vinegar. These operations were extremely necessary for correcting the noisome stench on board, and destroying the vermin; for from the number of our men, and the heat of the climate, both these nuisances had increased upon us to a very loathsome degree, and besides being most intolerably offensive, they were doubtless in some sort productive of the sickness we had laboured under for a considerable time before our arrival at this island.

Our next employment was wooding and watering our squadron, caulking our ships' sides and decks, overhauling the rigging, and securing our masts against the tempestuous weather we were, in all probability, to meet with in our passage round Cape Horn, in so advanced and inconvenient a season. But before I engage in the particulars of these transactions, it will not be improper to give some account of the present state of the island of St. Catherine's, and of the neighbouring country; both as the circumstances of this place are now greatly changed from what they were in the time of former writers, and as these changes laid us under many more difficulties and perplexities than we had reason to expect, or than other British ships, hereafter bound to the South Seas, may perhaps think it prudent to struggle with.

This island is esteemed by the natives to be nowhere above two leagues in breadth, though about nine in length; it lies in 49° 45′ of west longitude from London, and extends from the south latitude of 27° 35′ to that of 28°. Although it be of a considerable height, yet it is scarcely discernible at the distance of ten leagues, being then obscured under the continent of Brazil, whose mountains are exceedingly high; but on a nearer approach it is easy to be distinguished, and may be readily known by a number of small islands lying at each end, and scattered along the east side of it.

The north entrance of the harbour is in breadth about five miles, and the distance from thence to the island of St. Antonio is eight miles, and the course from the entrance to St. Antonio is S.S.W ¼ W. About the middle of the island, the harbour is contracted by two points of land to a narrow channel, no more than a quarter of a mile broad ; and to defend this passage, a battery was erecting on the point of land on the island side. But this seems to be a very useless work, as the channel has no more than two fathom water, and consequently is navigable only for barks and boats, and therefore seems to be a passage that an enemy could have no inducement to attempt, especially as the common passage at the north end of the island is so broad and safe, that no squadron can be prevented from coming in by any of their fortifications, when the sea-breeze is made. However, the Brigadier Don Jose Sylva de Paz, the governor of this settlement, is esteemed an expert engineer, and he doubtless understands one branch of his business very well, which is the advantages which new works bring to those who are entrusted with the care of erecting them : for besides the battery mentioned above, there are three other forts carrying on for the defence of the harbour, none of which are yet completed. The first of these, called St. Juan, is built on a point of St. Catherine's near Parrot Island ; the second, in the form of a half moon, is on the island of St. Antonio ; and the third, which seems to be the chief, and has some appearance of a regular fortification, is on an island near the continent, where the governor resides.

The soil of the island is truly luxuriant, producing fruits of most kinds spontaneously ; and the ground is covered over with one continued forest of trees of a perpetual verdure, which, from the exuberance of the soil, are so entangled with briars, thorns, and underwood, as to form a thicket absolutely impenetrable, except by some narrow pathways which the inhabitants have made for their own convenience. These, with a few spots cleared for plantations along the shore facing the continent, are the only uncovered parts of the island. The woods are extremely fragrant, from the many aromatic trees and shrubs with which they abound ; and the fruits and vegetables of all climates thrive here, almost without culture, and are to be procured in great plenty ; so that here is no want of pine-apples, peaches, grapes, oranges, lemons, citrons, melons, apricots, nor plantains. There are besides great abundance of two other productions of no small consideration for a sea-store, I mean onions and potatoes. The provisions of other kinds are however inferior to their vegetables : there are small wild cattle to be purchased, somewhat like buffaloes, but these are very indifferent food, their flesh being of a loose contexture, and generally of a disagreeable flavour, which is probably owing to the wild calabash on which they feed. There are likewise great plenty of pheasants, but they are much inferior in taste to those we have in England. The other provisions of the place are monkeys, parrots, and fish of various sorts, which abound in the harbour, and are all exceedingly good, and are easily caught, for there are a great number of small sandy bays very convenient for hauling the seine.

The water both on the island and the opposite continent is excellent, and preserves at sea as well as that of the Thames. For after it has been in the cask a day or two it begins to purge itself, and stinks most intolerably, and is soon covered over with a green scum : but this, in a few days, subsides to the bottom, and leaves the water as clear as crystal, and perfectly sweet. The French (who during their South Sea trade in Queen Anne's reign first brought this place into repute) usually wooded and watered at Bon Port, on the continent side, where they likewise anchored with great safety in six fathom water ; and this is doubtless the most commodious road for such ships as intend to make only a short stay. But we watered on the St. Catherine's side, at a plantation opposite to the island of St. Antonio.

These are the advantages of this island of St. Catherine's ; but there are many inconveniences attending it, partly from its climate, but more from its new regulations, and the late form of government established there. With regard to the climate, it must be remembered that the woods and hills which surround the harbour prevent a free circulation of the air. And the vigorous vegetation which constantly takes place there, furnishes such a prodigious quantity of vapour, that all the night and a great part of the morning a thick fog covers the whole country, and continues till either the sun gathers strength to dissipate it, or it is dispersed by a brisk sea breeze. This renders the place close and humid, and probably occasioned the many fevers and fluxes we were there afflicted with. To these exceptions I must not omit to add, that all the day we were pestered with great numbers of musquitoes, which are not much unlike the gnats in England, but more venomous in their stings. And at sun-set, when the musquitoes retired, they were succeeded by an infinity of sand-flies, which, though scarce discernible to the naked eye, make a mighty buzzing, and wherever they bite raise a small bump in the flesh, which is soon attended with a painful itching, like that arising from the bite of an English harvest-bug.

But as the only light in which this place deserves our consideration, is its favourable situation for supplying and refreshing our cruisers intended for the South Seas, in this view its greatest inconveniences remain still to be related ; and to do this more distinctly, it will not be amiss to consider the changes which it has lately undergone, both in its inhabitants, its police, and its governor.

In the time of Frezier and Shelvocke, this place served only as a retreat to vagabonds and outlaws, who fled thither from all parts of Brazil. They did indeed acknowledge a subjection to the crown of Portugal, and had a person among them whom they called their captain, who was considered in some sort as their governor : but both their allegiance to their king, and their obedience to their captain, seemed to be little more than verbal. For as they had plenty of provisions but no money, they were in a condition to support themselves without the assistance of any neighbouring settlements, and had not amongst them the means of tempting any adjacent governor to busy his authority about them. In this situation they were extremely hospitable and friendly to such foreign ships as came amongst them For these ships wanted only provisions, of which the natives had great store ; and the natives wanting clothes, (for they often despised money, and refused to take it) which the ships furnished them with in exchange for their provisions, both sides found their account in this traffic ; and their captain or governor had neither power nor interest to restrain it or to tax it. But of late (for reasons which shall be hereafter mentioned) these honest vagabonds have been obliged to receive amongst them a new colony, and to submit to new laws and government. Instead of their former ragged bare-legged captain (whom, however, they took care to keep innocent) they have now the honour to be governed by Don Jose Sylva de Paz, a brigadier of the armies of Portugal. This gentleman has with him a garrison of soldiers, and has consequently a more extensive and a better supported power than any of his predecessors; and as he wears better clothes, and lives more splendidly, and has besides a much better knowledge of the importance of money than they could ever pretend to, so he puts in practice certain methods of procuring it with which they were utterly unacquainted. But it may be much doubted, if the inhabitants consider these methods as tending to promote either their interests, or that of their sovereign the king of Portugal. This is certain, that his behaviour cannot but be extremely embarrassing to such British ships as touch there in their way to the South Seas. For one of his practices was placing sentinels at all the avenues, to prevent the people from selling us any refreshments, except at such exorbitant rates as we could not afford to give. His pretence for this extraordinary stretch of power was, that he was obliged to preserve their provisions for upwards of a hundred families, which they daily expected to reinforce their colony. Hence he appears to be no novice in his profession, by his readiness at inventing a plausible pretence for his interested management. However, this, though sufficiently provoking, was far from being the most exceptionable part of his conduct. For by the neighbourhood of the river Plate, a considerable smuggling traffic is carried on between the Portuguese and the Spaniards, especially in the exchanging gold for silver, by which both princes are defrauded of their fifths; and in this prohibited commerce Don Jose was so deeply engaged, that in order to ingratiate himself with his Spanish correspondents (for no other reason can be given for his procedure) he treacherously despatched an express to Buenos Ayres in the river of Plate, where Pizarro then lay, with an account of the arrival, and of the strength of our squadron; particularly the number of ships, guns and men, and every circumstance which he could suppose our enemy desirous of being acquainted with. And the same perfidy every British cruiser may expect, who touches at St. Catherine's, while it is under the government of Don Jose Sylva de Paz.

Thus much, with what we shall be necessitated to relate in the course of our own proceedings may suffice as to the present state of St. Catherine's, and the character of its governor. But as the reader may be desirous of knowing to what causes the late new modelling of this settlement is owing; to satisfy him in this particular, it will be necessary to give a short account of the adjacent continent of Brazil, and of the wonderful discoveries which have been made there within these last forty years, which, from a country of but mean estimation, have rendered it now perhaps the most considerable colony on the face of the globe.

This country was first discovered by Americus Vesputio, a Florentine, who had the good fortune to be honoured with giving his name to the immense continent, some time before found out by Columbus: he being in the service of the Portuguese, it was settled and planted by that nation, and, with the other dominions of Portugal, devolved to the crown of Spain, when that kingdom became subject to it. During the long war between Spain and the States of Holland, the Dutch possessed themselves of the northernmost part of Brazil, and were masters of it for some years. But when the Portuguese revolted from the Spanish government, this country took part in the revolt, and soon repossessed themselves of the places the Dutch had taken; since which time it has continued without interruption under the crown of Portugal, being, till the beginning of the present century, only productive of sugar and tobacco, and a few other commodities of very little account.

But this country, which for many years was only considered for the produce of its plantations, has been lately discovered to abound with the two minerals which mankind hold in the greatest esteem, and which they exert their utmost art and industry in acquiring, I mean, gold and diamonds. Gold was first found in the mountains which lie adjacent to the city of Rio Janeiro. The occasion of its discovery is variously related, but the most common account is, that the Indians, lying on the back of the Portuguese settlements, were observed by the soldiers employed in an expedition against them to make use of this metal for their fish-hooks; and their manner of procuring it being inquired into, it appeared that great quantities of it were annually washed from the hills, and left amongst the sand and gravel, which remained in the valleys after the running off or evaporation of the water. It is now little more than forty years since any quantities of gold worth notice have been imported to Europe from Brazil; but since that time the annual imports from thence have been continually augmented by the discovery of places in other provinces, where it is to be met with as plentifully as at first about Rio Janeiro. And it is now said, that there is a small slender vein of it spread through all the country, at about twenty-four feet from the surface, but that this vein is too thin and poor to answer the expense of digging; however, where the rivers or rains have had any course for a considerable time, there gold is always to be collected, the water having separated the metal from the earth, and deposited it in the sands, thereby saving the expenses of digging: so that it is esteemed an infallible gain to be able to divert a stream from its channel, and to ransack its bed. From this account of gathering this metal, it should follow that there are properly no gold mines in Brazil; and this the governor of Rio Grande (who being at St. Catherine's, frequently visited Mr. Anson) did most confidently affirm, assuring us, that the gold was all collected either from rivers, or from the beds of torrents after floods. It is indeed asserted that, in the mountains, large rocks are found abounding with this metal; and I myself have seen the fragment of one of these rocks with a considerable lump of gold entangled in it; but even in this case, the workmen break off the rocks, and do not properly mine into them; and the great expense in subsisting among these mountains, and afterwards in separating the metal from the stone, makes this method of procuring gold to be but rarely put in practice.

The examining the bottoms of rivers, and the gullies of torrents, and the washing the gold found therein from the sand and dirt, with which it is always mixed, are works performed by slaves, who are principally negroes, kept in great numbers by the Portuguese for these purposes. The regulation of the duty of these slaves is singular: for they are each of them obliged to furnish their master with the eighth part of an ounce of gold *per diem*; and if they are either so fortunate or industrious as to collect a greater quantity, the surplus is considered as their own property, and they have the liberty of disposing of it as they think fit. So that it is said some negroes who have accidentally fallen upon rich washing places have themselves purchased slaves, and have lived afterwards in great splendour, their original master having no other demand on them than the daily supply of the forementioned eighth; which as the Portuguese ounce is somewhat lighter than our troy ounce, may amount to about nine shillings sterling.

The quantity of gold thus collected in the Brazils, and returned annually to Lisbon, may be in some degree estimated from the amount of the king's fifth. This hath of late been esteemed one year with another to be one hundred and fifty arroves of 32*l*. Portuguese weight, each of which, at 4*l*. the troy ounce, makes very near 300,000*l*. sterling; and consequently the capital, of which this is the fifth, is about a million and a half sterling. And the annual return of gold to Lisbon cannot be less than this, though it be difficult to determine how much it exceeds it; perhaps we may not be very much mistaken in our conjecture, if we suppose the gold exchanged for silver with the Spaniards at Buenos Ayres, and what is brought privily to Europe, and escapes the duty, amounts to near half a million more, which will make the whole annual produce of the Brazilian gold near two millions sterling; a prodigious sum to be found in a country which, a few years since, was not known to furnish a single grain.

I have already mentioned, that besides gold this country does likewise produce diamonds. The discovery of these valuable stones is much more recent than that of gold, it being as yet scarce twenty years since the first were brought to Europe. They are found in the same manner as the gold, in the gullies of torrents and beds of rivers, but only in particular places, and not so universally spread through the country. They were often found in washing the gold before they were known to be diamonds, and were consequently thrown away with the sand and gravel separated from it. And it is very well remembered, that numbers of very large stones, which would have made the fortunes of the possessors, have passed unregarded through the hands of those, who now with impatience support the mortifying reflection. However, about twenty years since, a person acquainted with the appearance of rough diamonds, conceived that these pebbles, as they were then esteemed, were of the same kind: but it is said, that there was a considerable interval between the first starting of this opinion, and the confirmation of it by proper trials and examination, it proving difficult to persuade the inhabitants, that what they had been long accustomed to despise, could be of the importance represented by the discovery; and I have been informed, that in this interval, a governor of one of their places procured a good number of these stones, which he pretended to make use of at cards to mark with, instead of counters. But to proceed: it was at last confirmed by skilful jewellers in Europe, consulted on this occasion, that the stones thus found in Brazil were truly diamonds, many of which were not inferior either in lustre, or any other quality, to those of the East-Indies. On this determination the Portuguese, in the neighbourhood of those places where they had first been observed, set themselves to search for them with great assiduity. And they were not without great hopes of discovering considerable masses of them, as they found large rocks of crystal in many of the mountains, from whence the streams came which washed down the diamonds.

But it was soon represented to the king of Portugal, that if such plenty of diamonds should be met with as their sanguine conjectures seemed to indicate, this would so debase their value, and diminish their estimation, that besides ruining all the Europeans who had any quantity of Indian diamonds in their possession, it would render the discovery itself of no importance, and would prevent his Majesty from receiving any advantages from it. And on these considerations his Majesty has thought proper to restrain the general search of diamonds, and has erected a Diamond Company for that purpose, with an exclusive charter. This company, in consideration of a sum paid by them to the king, have the property of all diamonds found in Brazil: but to hinder their collecting too large quantities, and thereby debasing their value, they are prohibited from employing above eight hundred slaves in searching after them. And to prevent any of his other subjects from acting the same part, and likewise to secure the company from being defrauded by the interfering of interlopers in their trade, he has depopulated a large town, and a considerable district round it, and has obliged the inhabitants, who are said to amount to six thousand, to remove to another part of the country; for this town being in the neighbourhood of the diamonds, it was thought impossible to prevent such a number of people, who were on the spot, from frequently smuggling.

In consequence of these important discoveries in Brazil, new laws, new governments, and new regulations have been established in many parts of the country. For not long since, a considerable tract, possessed by a set of inhabitants, who from their principal settlement were called Paulists, almost independent of the crown of Portugal, to which they scarcely acknowledged more than a nominal allegiance.* These are said to be descendants of those Portuguese, who retired from the northern part of Brazil, when it was invaded and possessed by the Dutch. And being for a long time neglected and obliged to provide for their own security and defence, the necessity of their affairs produced a kind of government amongst them, which they found sufficient for the confined manner of life to which they were inured. And therefore rejecting and despising the authority and mandate of the court of Lisbon, they were often engaged in a state of downright rebellion: and the mountains surrounding their country, and the difficulty of clearing the few passages that open into it, generally put it in their power to make their own terms before they submitted. But as gold was found to abound in this country of the Paulists, the present king of Portugal (during whose reign almost the whole discoveries I have mentioned were begun and completed) thought it incumbent on him to reduce this province, which now became of great consequence, to the same dependence and obedience with the rest of the country which, I am told, he has at last, though with great difficulty, happily effected. And the same motives which induced his majesty to undertake the reduction of the Paulists, has also occasioned the changes I have mentioned, to have taken place at the island of St. Catherine's. For the governor of Rio Grande, of whom I have already spoken, assured us, that in the neighbourhood of this island there were considerable rivers which were found to be extremely rich, and that this was the reason that a garrison, a military governor, and a new colony was settled there. And as the harbour at this island is by much the securest and the most capacious of any on the coast, it is not improbable, if the riches of the neighbourhood answer their expectation, but it may become in time the principal settlement in Brazil, and the most considerable port in all South America.

Thus much I have thought necessary to insert, in relation to the present state of Brazil, and of the island of St. Catherine's. For as this last place has been generally recommended as the most eligible port for our cruisers to refresh at, which are bound to the South Seas, I believed it to be my duty to instruct my countrymen, in the hitherto unsuspected inconveniences which attend that place. And as the Brazilian gold and diamonds are subjects about which, from their novelty, very few particulars have been hitherto published, I conceived this account I had collected of them would appear to the reader to be neither a trifling nor a useless digression. These subjects being thus despatched, I shall now return to the series of our own proceedings.

When we first arrived at St. Catherine's we were employed in refreshing our sick on shore, in wooding and watering the squadron, cleansing our ships, and examining and securing our masts and rigging, as I have already observed in the foregoing chapter. At the same time Mr. Anson gave directions, that the ships' companies should be supplied with fresh meat, and that they should be victualled with whole allowance of all the kinds of provision. In consequence of these orders, we had fresh beef sent on board us continually for our daily expense, and what was wanting to make up our allowance we received from our victualler the Anna pink, in order to preserve the provisions on board our squadron entire for our future service. The season of the year growing each day less favourable for our passage round Cape Horn, Mr. Anson was very desirous of leaving this place as soon as possible; and we were at first in hopes that our whole business would be done, and we should be in readiness to sail in about a fortnight from our arrival: but, on examining the Tryal's masts, we, to our no small vexation, found inevitable employment for twice that time. For, on a survey, it was found that the main-mast was sprung at the upper woulding, though it was thought capable of being secured by a couple of fishes; but the fore-mast was reported to be unfit for service, and thereupon the carpenters were sent into the woods, to endeavour to find a stick proper for a fore-mast. But after a search of four days, they returned without having been able to meet with any tree fit for the purpose. This obliged them to come to a second consultation about the old fore-mast, when it was agreed to endeavour to secure it by casing it with three fishes: and in this work the carpenters were employed, till within a day or two of our sailing. In the mean time, the commodore thinking it necessary to have a clean vessel on our arrival in the South Seas, ordered the Tryal to be hove down, as this would not occasion any loss of time, but might be completed while the carpenters were refitting her masts, which was done on shore.

On the 27th of December we discovered a sail in the offing, and not knowing but she might be a Spaniard, the eighteen-oared boat was manned and armed, and sent under the command of our second lieutenant, to examine her before she arrived within the protection of the forts. She proved to be a Portuguese brigantine from Rio Grande. And though our officer, as it appeared on inquiry, had behaved with the utmost civility to the master, and had refused to accept a calf, which the master would have forced on him as a present: yet the governor took great offence at our sending our boat; and talked of it in a high strain, as a violation of the peace subsisting between the crowns of Great Britain and Portugal. We at first imputed this ridiculous blustering to no deeper a cause than Don Jose's insolence; but as we found he proceeded so far as to charge our officer with behaving rudely, and opening letters, and particularly with an attempt to take out of the vessel, by violence, the very calf which we knew he had refused to receive as a present (a circumstance which we were satisfied the governor was well acquainted with,) we had hence reason to suspect that he purposely sought this quarrel, and had more important motives for engaging in it, than the mere captions bias of his temper. What these motives were, it was not so easy for us to determine at that time; but as we afterwards found by letters, which fell into our hands in the South Seas, that he had despatched an express to Buenos Ayres, where Pizarro then lay, with an account of our squadron's arrival at St. Catherine's, together with the most ample and circumstantial intelligence of our force and condition, we thence conjectured that Don Jose had raised this groundless clamour, only to prevent our visiting the brigantine when she should put to sea again, least we might there find proofs of his perfidious behaviour, and perhaps at the same time discover the secret of his smuggling correspondence with his neighbouring governors, and the Spaniards at Buenos Ayres. But to proceed.

It was near a month before the Tryal was refitted; for not only her lower masts were defective, as hath been already mentioned, but her main top-mast and fore-yard were likewise decayed and rotten. While this work was carrying on, the other ships of the squadron fixed new standing rigging, and set up a sufficient number of preventer shrouds to each mast, to secure them in the most effectual manner. And in order to render the ships stiffer, and to enable them to carry more sail abroad, and to prevent their labouring in hard gales of wind, each captain had orders given him to strike down some of their great guns into the hold. These precautions being complied with, and each ship having taken in as much wood and water as there was room for, the Tryal was at last completed, and the whole squadron was ready for the sea: on which the tents on shore were struck, and all the sick were received on board. And here we had a melancholy proof how much the healthiness of this place had been over-rated by former writers, for we found that though the Centurion alone had buried no less than twenty-eight men since our arrival, yet the number of her sick had in the same interval increased from eighty to ninety-six. And now our crews being embarked, and every thing prepared for our departure, the commodore made a signal for all captains, and delivered them their orders, containing the successive places of rendezvous from hence to the coast of China. And then, on the next day, being the 18th of January, the signal was made for weighing, and the squadron put to sea, leaving without regret this island of St Catherine's; where we had been so extremely disappointed in our refreshments, in our accommodations, and in the humane and friendly offices which we had been taught to expect in a place, which hath been so much celebrated for its hospitality, freedom, and convenience.

CHAPTER VI.

The run from St. Catherine's to port St. Julian, with some account of that port, and of the country to the southward of the river of Plate.

In leaving St. Catherine's, we left the last amicable port we proposed to touch at, and were now proceeding to a hostile, or at best, a desert and inhospitable coast. And as we were to expect a more boisterous climate to the southward than any we had yet experienced, not only our danger of separation would by this means be much greater than it had been hitherto, but other accidents of a more pernicious nature were likewise to be apprehended, and as much as possible to be provided against. And therefore Mr. Anson, in appointing the various stations at which the ships of the squadron were to rendezvous, had considered, that it was possible his own ship might be disabled from getting round Cape Horn, or might be lost, and had given proper directions, that even in that case the expedition should not be abandoned. For the orders delivered to the captains, the day before we sailed from St. Catherine's, were, that in case of separation, which they were with the utmost care to endeavour to avoid, the first place of rendezvous should be the bay of port St. Julian; describing the place from Sir John Narborough's account of it. There they were to supply themselves with as much salt as they could take in,

both for their own use, and for the use of the squadron; and if, after a stay there of ten days, they were not joined by the commodore, they were then to proceed through Straits le Maire round Cape Horn, into the South Seas, where the next place of rendezvous was to be the island of Nostra Senora del Socoro, in the latitude of 45° South, and longitude from the Lizard 71° 12′ West. They were to bring this island to bear E.N.E, and to cruise from five to twelve leagues distance from it, as long as their store of wood and water would permit, both which they were to expend with the utmost frugality. And when they were under an absolute necessity to supply a fresh supply, they were to stand in, and endeavour to find out an anchoring-place; and in case they could not, and the weather made it dangerous to supply their ships by standing off and on, they were then to make the best of their way to the island of Juan Fernandes, in the latitude of 33° 37′ South. And as soon as they had there recruited their wood and water, they were to continue cruising off the anchoring-place of that island for fifty-six days; in which time, if they were not joined by the commodore, they might conclude that some accident had befallen him, and they were forthwith to put themselves under the command of the senior officer, who was to use his utmost endeavours to annoy the enemy both by sea and land. That with these views their new commodore was to continue in those seas as long as his provisions lasted, or as long as they were recruited by what he should take from the enemy, reserving only a sufficient quantity to carry him and the ships under his command to Macao, at the entrance of the river Tigris near Canton on the coast of China, where having supplied himself with a new stock of provisions, he was thence, without delay, to make the best of his way to England. And as it was found impossible as yet to unload our victualler the Anna pink, the commodore gave the master of her the same rendezvous, and the same orders to put himself under the command of the remaining senior officer.

Under these orders the squadron sailed from St. Catherine's on Sunday the 18th of January, as hath been already mentioned in the preceding chapter. The next day we had very squally weather, attended with rain, lightning and thunder, but it soon became fair again with light breezes, and continued thus till Wednesday evening, when it blew fresh again; and increasing all night, by eight the next morning it became a most violent storm, and we had with it so thick a fog, that it was impossible to see at the distance of two ships' length, so that the whole squadron disappeared. On this, a signal was made, by firing guns, to bring to with the larboard tacks, the wind being then due east. We ourselves immediately handed the top-sails, bunted the main-sail, and lay to under a reefed mizen till noon, when the fog dispersed, and we soon discovered all the ships of the squadron except the Pearl, which did not join us till near a month afterwards. The Tryal sloop was a great way to leeward, having lost her main-mast in this squall, and having been obliged, for fear of bilging, to cut away the raft. We bore down with the squadron to her relief, and the Gloucester was ordered to take her in tow, for the weather did not entirely abate till the day after, and even then, a great swell continued from the eastward, in consequence of the preceding storm.

After this accident we stood to the southward with little interruption, and here we experienced the same setting of the current, which we had observed before our arrival at St. Catherine's; that is, we generally found ourselves to the southward of our reckoning, by about twenty miles each day. This error continued, with a little variation, till we had passed the latitude of the river of Plate; and even then, we found that the same current, however difficult to be accounted for, did yet undoubtedly take place; for we were not satisfied in deducing it from the error in our reckoning, but we actually tried it more than once, when a calm made it practicable.

When we had passed the latitude of the river of Plate, we had soundings all along the coast of Patagonia. These soundings, when well ascertained, being of great use in determining the position of the ship, and we having tried them more frequently, in greater depths, and with more attention, than I believe had been done before us, I shall recite our observations as succinctly as I can. In the latitude of 36° 52' we had sixty fathom of water, with a bottom of fine black and grey sand; from thence, to 39° 55', we varied our depths from fifty to eighty fathom, though we had constantly the same bottom as before; between the last mentioned latitude, and 43° 16', we had only fine grey sand, with the same variation of depths, except that we once or twice lessened our water to forty fathom. After this, we continued in forty fathom for about half a degree, having a bottom of coarse sand and broken shells, at which time we were in sight of land, and not above seven leagues from it. As we edged from the land, we met with variety of soundings; first black sand, then muddy, and soon after rough ground with stones; but then increasing our water to forty-eight fathom, we had a muddy bottom to the latitude of 46° 10'. We then returned again into thirty-six fathom, and kept shoaling our water, till at length we came into twelve fathom, having constantly small stones and pebbles at the bottom. Part of this time we had a view of Cape Blanco, which lies in about the latitude of 46° 52', and longitude west from London 66° 43'. This is the most remarkable land upon the coast. Steering from hence S. by E. nearly, we, in a run of about thirty leagues, deepened our water to fifty fathom, without once altering the bottom; and then drawing towards the shore with a S.W. course, varying rather to the westward, we had everywhere a sandy bottom, till our coming into thirty fathom, where we had again a sight of land, distant from us about eight leagues, lying in the latitude of 48° 31'. We made this land on the 17th of February, and at five in the afternoon we came to an anchor upon the same bottom, in the latitude of 48° 58', the southermost land then in view bearing S.S.W., the northermost N. ¼ E, a small island N.W., and the westermost hummock W.S.W. In this station we found the tide to set S. by W.; and weighing again at five the next morning, we, an hour afterwards, discovered a sail, upon which the Severn and Gloucester were both directed to give chase; but we soon perceived it to be the Pearl, which separated from us a few days after we left St. Catherine's, and on this we made a signal for the Severn to rejoin the squadron, leaving the Gloucester alone in the pursuit. And now we were surprised to see, that on the Gloucester's approach, the people on board the Pearl increased their sail, and stood from her. However, the Gloucester came up with them, but found them with their hammocks in their nettings, and everything ready for an engagement. At two in the afternoon the Pearl joined us, and running up under our stern, Lieutenant Salt hailed the commodore, and acquainted him that Captain Kidd died on the 31st of January. He likewise informed him, that he had seen five large ships the 10th instant, which he for some time imagined to be our squadron: that he suffered the commanding ship, which wore a red broad pennant, exactly resembling that of the commodore, at the main top-mast head, to come within gun-shot of him before he discovered his mistake; but then finding it not to be the Centurion, he haled close upon the wind, and crowded from them with all his sail, and standing cross a ripling, where they hesitated to follow him, he happily escaped. He made them to be five Spanish men of war, one of them exceedingly like the Gloucester, which was the occasion of his apprehensions when the Gloucester chased him. By their appearance he thought they consisted of two ships of seventy guns, two of fifty, and one of forty guns. The whole squadron continued in chase of him all that day, but at night finding they could not get near him, they gave over the chase, and directed their course to the southward.

And now had it not been for the necessity we were under of refitting the Tryal, this piece of intelligence would have prevented our making any stay at St. Julian's; but as it was impossible for that sloop to proceed round the Cape in her present condition, some stay there was inevitable, and therefore the same evening we came to an anchor again in twenty-five fathom water, the bottom a mixture of mud and sand, and the high hummock bearing S.W. by W. And weighing at nine in the morning, we soon after sent the two cutters belonging to the Centurion and Severn in shore, to discover the harbour of St. Julian, while the ships kept standing along the coast, at about the distance of a league from the land. At six o'clock we anchored in the bay of St. Julian, in nineteen fathom, the bottom muddy ground with sand, the northermost land in sight bearing N. and by E., the southermost S. ½ E., and the high hummock, to which Sir John Narborough formerly gave the name of Wood's Mount, W.S.W. Soon after, the cutter returned on board, having discovered the harbour, which did not appear to us in our situation, the northermost point shutting in upon the southermost, and in appearance closing the entrance.

Being come to an anchor in this bay of St. Julian, principally with a view of refitting the Tryal, the carpenters were immediately employed in that business, and continued so during our whole stay at the place. The Tryal's main-mast having been carried away about twelve feet below the cap, they contrived to make the remaining part of the mast serve again; and the Wager was ordered to supply her with a spare main-top-mast, which the carpenters converted into a new fore-mast. And I cannot help observing, that this accident to the

Tryal's mast, which gave us so much uneasiness at that time, on account of the delay it occasioned, was, in all probability, the means of preserving the sloop, and all her crew. For before this, her masts, how well soever proportioned to a better climate, were much too lofty for these high southern latitudes: so that had they weathered the preceding storm, it would have been impossible for them to have stood against those seas and tempests we afterwards encountered in passing round Cape Horn; and the loss of masts, in that boisterous climate, would scarcely have been attended with less than the loss of the vessel, and of every man on board her; since it would have been impracticable for the other ships to have given them any relief, during the continuance of those impetuous storms.

Whilst we stayed at this place, the commodore appointed the Honourable Captain Murray to succeed to the Pearl, and Captain Cheap to the Wager, and he promoted Mr. Charles Saunders, his first lieutenant, to the command of the Tryal sloop. But Captain Saunders lying dangerously ill of a fever on board the Centurion, and it being the opinion of the surgeons that the removing him on board his own ship, in his present condition, might tend to the hazard of his life; Mr. Anson gave an order to Mr. Saumarez, first lieutenant of the Centurion, to act as master and commander of the Tryal, during the illness of Captain Saunders.

Here the commodore too, in order to ease the expedition of all unnecessary expense, held a farther consultation with his captains about unloading and discharging the Anna pink; but they represented to him that they were so far from being in a condition of taking any part of her loading on board, that they had still great quantities of provisions in the way of their guns between-decks, and that their ships were withal so very deep, that they were not fit for action without being cleared. This put the commodore under a necessity of retaining the pink in the service; and as it was apprehended we should certainly meet with the Spanish squadron in passing the Cape, Mr. Anson thought it advisable to give orders to the captains to put all their provisions, which were in the way of their guns, on board the Anna pink, and to remount such of their guns as had formerly, for the ease of their ships, been ordered into the hold.

This bay of St. Julian, where we were now at anchor, being a convenient rendezvous, in case of separation, for all cruisers bound to the southward, and the whole coast of Patagonia, from the river of Plate to the Straits of Magellan, lying nearly parallel to their usual route, a short account of the singularity of this country, with a particular description of port St. Julian, may perhaps be neither unacceptable to the curious, nor unworthy the attention of future navigators, as some of them, by unforeseen accidents, may be obliged to run in with the land, and to make some stay on this coast, in which case the knowledge of the country, its produce and inhabitants, cannot but be of the utmost consequence to them.

To begin then with the tract of country usually styled Patagonia. This is the name often given to the southernmost part of South America, which is unpossessed by the Spaniards, extending from their settlements to the Straits of Magellan. On the east side, this country is extremely remarkable for a peculiarity not to be paralleled in any other known part of the globe; for though the whole territory to the northward of the river of Plate is full of wood, and stored with immense quantities of large timber trees, yet to the southward of the river no trees of any kind are to be met with, except a few peach-trees, first planted and cultivated by the Spaniards, in the neighbourhood of Buenos Ayres: so that on the whole eastern coast of Patagonia, extending near four hundred leagues in length, and reaching as far back as any discoveries have yet been made, no other wood has been found than a few insignificant shrubs. Sir John Narborough in particular, who was sent out, by King Charles the second, expressly to examine this country, and the Straits of Magellan, and who in pursuance of his orders wintered upon this coast in port St. Julian and port Desire, in the year 1670; Sir John Narborough, I say, tells us, that he never saw a stick of wood in the country large enough to make the handle of a hatchet.

But though this country be so destitute of wood, it abounds with pasture. For the land appears in general to be made up of downs of a light dry gravelly soil, and produces great quantities of long coarse grass, which grows in tufts interspersed with large barren spots of gravel between them. This grass, in many places, feeds immense herds of cattle: for the Spaniards at Buenos Ayres, having brought over a few black cattle from Europe at their first settlement, they have thriven prodigiously by the plenty of herbage which they found here, and are now increased to that degree, and are extended so far into the country, that they are not considered as private property; but many thousands at a time are slaughtered every year by the hunters, only for their hides and tallow. The manner of killing these cattle, being a practice peculiar to that part of the world, merits a more circumstantial description. The hunters employed on this occasion being all of them mounted on horseback (and both the Spaniards and Indians in that part of the world are usually most excellent horsemen), they arm themselves with a kind of spear, which, at its end, instead of a blade fixed in the same line with the wood in the usual manner, has its blade fixed across; with this instrument they ride at a beast, and surround him. The hunter that comes behind him hamstrings him; and as after this operation the beast soon tumbles, without being able to raise himself again, they leave him on the ground, and pursue others, whom they serve in the same manner. Sometimes there is a second party, who attend the hunters, to skin the cattle as they fall: but it is said, that at other times the hunters choose to let them languish in torment till the next day, from an opinion that the anguish, which the animal in the meantime endures, may burst the lymphatics, and thereby facilitate the separation of the skin from the carcase: and though their priests have loudly condemned this most barbarous practice, and have gone so far, if my memory does not fail me, as to excommunicate those who follow it, yet all their efforts to put an entire stop to it have hitherto proved ineffectual.

Besides the numbers of cattle which are every year slaughtered for their hides and tallow, in the manner already described, it is often necessary for the purposes of agriculture, and likewise with other views, to take them alive, and without wounding them. This is performed with a most wonderful and almost incredible dexterity, and principally by the use of a machine which the English who have resided at Buenos Ayres generally denominate a lash. It is made of a thong of several fathoms in length, and very strong, with a running noose at one end of it: this the hunters (who in this case are also mounted on horseback) take in their right hands, it being first properly coiled up, and having its end opposite to the noose fastened to the saddle; and thus prepared, they ride at a herd of cattle. When they arrive within a certain distance of a beast, they throw their thong at him with such exactness, that they never fail of fixing the noose about his horns. The beast, when he finds himself entangled, generally runs, but the horse, being swifter, attends him, and prevents the thong from being too much strained, till a second hunter, who follows the game, throws another noose about one of its hind legs: and this being done, both horses (they being trained for this purpose) instantly turn different ways, in order to strain the two thongs in contrary directions; on which the beast, by their opposite pulls, is presently overthrown, and then the horses stop, keeping the thongs still upon the stretch; being thus on the ground and incapable of resistance, (for he is extended between the two horses) the hunters alight, and secure him in such a manner, that they afterwards easily convey him to whatever place they please. In the same manner they noose horses, and, as it is said, even tigers; and however strange this last circumstance may appear, there are not wanting persons of credit who assert it. Indeed, it must be owned, that the address both of the Spaniards and Indians in that part of the world, in the use of this lash or noose, and the certainty with which they throw it, and fix it on any intended part of the beast at a considerable distance, are matters only to be believed from the repeated and concurrent testimony of all who have frequented that country, and might reasonably be questioned, did it rely on a single report, or had it been ever contradicted or denied by any one who had resided at Buenos Ayres.

The cattle which are killed in the manner I have already observed, are slaughtered only for their hides and tallow, to which sometimes are added their tongues, and the rest of their flesh is left to putrify, or to be devoured by the birds and wild beasts; but the greatest part of this carrion falls to the share of the wild dogs, of which there are immense numbers to be found in that country. They are supposed to have been originally produced by Spanish dogs from Buenos Ayres, who, allured by the great quantity of carrion, and the facility they had by that means of subsisting, left their masters, and ran wild amongst the cattle; for they are plainly of the breed of the European dogs, an animal not originally found in America. But though these dogs are said to be some thousands in a company, they hitherto neither diminish nor prevent the increase of the cattle, not daring to attack them, by reason of the numbers which constantly feed together; but contenting themselves with the carrion left them by the hunters, and perhaps now and then with a few stragglers who, by accidents, are separated from the herd they belong to.

Besides the wild cattle which have spread themselves in such vast herds from Buenos Ayres towards the southward, the same country is in like manner furnished with horses. These too were first brought from Spain, and are also prodigiously increased, and run wild to a much greater distance than the black cattle: and though many of them are excellent, yet their number makes them of very little value; the best of them being often sold, in a country where money is plenty and commodities very dear, for not more than a dollar a-piece. It is not as yet certain how far to the southward these herds of wild cattle and horses have extended themselves; but there is some reason to conjecture, that stragglers of both kinds are to be met with very near the Straits of Magellan; and they will in time doubtless fill the southern part of this continent with their breed, which cannot fail of proving of considerable advantage to such ships as may touch upon the coast; for the horses themselves are said to be very good eating, and as such to be preferred by some of the Indians even before the black cattle. But whatever plenty of this kind may be hereafter found here, there is one material refreshment which this eastern side of Patagonia seems to be very defective in, and that is fresh water; for the land being generally of a nitrous and saline nature, the ponds and streams are frequently brackish. However, as good water has been found there, though in small quantities, it is not improbable but, on a further search, this inconvenience may be removed.

Besides the cattle and horses which I have mentioned, there are in all parts of this country a good number of vicunnas or Peruvian sheep; but these, by reason of their shyness and swiftness, are killed with difficulty. On the eastern coast, too, there abound immense quantities of seals, and a vast variety of sea-fowl, amongst which the most remarkable are the penguins: they are in size and shape like a goose, but instead of wings they have short stumps like fins, which are of no use to them except in the water; their bills are narrow, like that of an albatross, and they stand and walk in an erect posture. From this, and their white bellies, Sir John Narborough has whimsically likened them to little children standing up in white aprons.

The inhabitants of this eastern coast (to which I have all along hitherto confined my relation) appear to be but few, and have rarely been seen more than two or three at a time, by any ships that have touched here. We, during our stay at the port of St. Julian, saw none. However, towards Buenos Ayres they are sufficiently numerous, and oftentimes very troublesome to the Spaniards; but there the greater breadth and variety of the country, and a milder climate, yield them a better protection; for in that place the continent is between three and four hundred leagues in breadth, whereas at port St. Julian it is little more than a hundred: so that I conceive the same Indians, that frequent the western coast of Patagonia and the Straits of Magellan, often ramble to this side. As the Indians near Buenos Ayres exceed these southern Indians in number, so they greatly surpass them in activity and spirit, and seem in their manners to be nearly allied to those gallant Chilian Indians, who have long set the whole Spanish power at defiance, have often ravaged their country, and remain to this hour independent. For the Indians about Buenos Ayres have learnt to be excellent horsemen, and are extremely expert in the management of all cutting weapons, though ignorant of the use of fire-arms, which the Spaniards are very solicitous to keep out of their hands. And of the vigour and resolution of these Indians, the behaviour of Orellana and his followers, whom we have formerly mentioned, is a memorable instance. Indeed, were we disposed to aim at the utter subversion of the Spanish power in America, no means seem more probable to effect it, than due encouragement and assistance given to these Indians and those of Chili.

Thus much may suffice in relation to the eastern coast of Patagonia. The western coast is of less extent; and by reason of the Andes which skirt it, and stretch quite down to the water, is a very rocky and dangerous shore. However, I shall be hereafter necessitated to make further mention of it, and therefore shall not enlarge thereon at this time. But it must be remembered, that the bar at the entrance is often shifting, and has many holes in it. The tide flows here N. and S., and at full and change, rises four fathom.

We, on our first arrival here, sent an officer on shore, in order to procure a quantity of salt for the use of the squadron, Sir John Narborough having observed, when he was here, that the salt produced in that place was very white and good, and that in February there was enough of it to fill a thousand ships; but our officer returned with a sample which was very bad, and he told us, that even of this there was but little to be got: I suppose the weather had been more rainy than ordinary, and had destroyed it.

CHAPTER VII.

Departure from the Bay of St. Julian, and the passage from thence to Straits Le Maire.

THE Tryal being nearly refitted, which was our principal occupation at this bay of St. Julian, and the sole occasion of our stay, the commodore thought it necessary, as we were now directly bound for the South Seas and the enemy's coasts, to regulate the plan of his future operations: and, therefore, on the 24th of February, a signal was made for all captains, and a council of war was held on board the Centurion, at which were present the Honourable Edward Legg, Captain Matthew Mitchel, the Honourable George Murray, Captain David Cheap, together with Colonel Mordaunt Cracherode, commander of the land forces. At this council Mr. Anson proposed, that their first attempt, after their arrival in the South Seas, should be the attack of the town and harbour of Baldivia, the principal frontier of the district of Chili; Mr. Anson informing them, at the same time, that it was an article contained in his Majesty's instructions to him, to endeavour to secure some port in the South Seas, where the ships of the squadron might be careened and refitted. To this proposition made by the commodore, the council unanimously and readily agreed; and in consequence of this resolution, new instructions were given to the captains of the squadron, by which, though they were still directed, in case of separation, to make the best of their way to the island of Nuestra Senora del Socoro, yet (notwithstanding the orders they had formerly given them at St. Catherine's) they were to cruise off that island only ten days; from whence, if not joined by the commodore, they were to proceed, and cruise off the harbour of Baldivia, making the land between the latitudes of 40° and 40° 30′, and taking care to keep to the southward of the port; and, if in fourteen days they were not joined by the rest of the squadron, they were then to quit this station, and to direct their course to the island of Juan Fernandes, after which they were to regulate their further proceedings by their former orders. The same directions were also given to the master of the Anna pink, and he was particularly instructed to be very careful in answering the signals made by any ship of the squadron, and likewise to destroy his papers and orders, if he should be so unfortunate as to fall into the hands of the enemy. And as the separation of the squadron might prove of the utmost prejudice to His Majesty's service, each captain was ordered to give it in charge to the respective officers of the watch, not to keep their ship at a greater distance from the Centurion than two miles, as they would answer it at their peril; and if any captain should find his ship beyond the distance specified, he was to acquaint the commodore with the name of the officer, who had thus neglected his duty.

These necessary regulations being established, and the Tryal sloop completed, the squadron weighed on Friday the 27th of February, at seven in the morning, and stood to the sea; the Gloucester indeed found a difficulty in purchasing her anchor, and was left a considerable way a-stern, so that in the night we fired several guns as a signal to her captain to make sail, but he did not come up to us till the next morning, when we found that they had been obliged to cut their cable, and leave their best bower behind them. At ten in the morning, the day after our departure, Wood's Mount, the highland over St. Julian, bore from us N. by W. distant ten leagues, and we had fifty-two fathom of water. And now standing to the southward, we had great expectation of falling in with Pizarro's squadron; for, during our stay at port St. Julian, there had generally been hard gales between the W. N. W. and S. W., so that we had reason to conclude the Spaniards had gained no ground upon us in that interval. And it was the prospect of meeting with them, that had occasioned our commodore to be so very solicitous to prevent the separation of our ships: for had we been solely intent on getting round Cape Horn in the shortest time, the properest method for this purpose would have been to have ordered each ship to have made the best of her way to the rendezvous, without waiting for the rest.[1]

[1] "The calamities that attended Anson's squadron, after passing through the Straits of Magellan at an improper season of the year, were unquestionably owing, in a great degree, to the delay in leaving England; but many of them would have been avoided, had this passage then been as well understood as now, when the smallest ships of war, merchantmen, and whalers, go round the Cape, or through the Straits, at all seasons of the year. The ships of Anson, were, however, most wretchedly manned; and Sir Charles Wager, an excellent seaman, and a man of good sound sense, could not contend with the Secretaries of State and their excellencies the Lords Justices, who appear to have taken entirely upon themselves the setting forth of this expedition." Anson, when at Spithead, ventured to send on shore two invalid officers, who from age and infirmity

From our departure from St. Julian to the 4th of March, we had little wind, with thick hazy weather, and some rain; and our soundings were generally from forty to fifty fathom, with a bottom of black and grey sand, sometimes intermixed with pebble stones. On the 4th of March we were in sight of Cape Virgin Mary, and not more than six or seven leagues distant from it: this is the northern cape of the Straits of Magellan; it lies in the latitude of 52° 21′ South, and longitude from London 71° 44′ West, and seems to be a low flat land, ending in a point. Off this Cape our depth of water was from thirty-five to forty-eight fathom. The afternoon of this day was very bright and clear, with small breezes of wind, inclinable to a calm; and most of the captains took the opportunity of this favourable weather to pay a visit to the commodore; but while they were in company together, they were all greatly alarmed by a sudden flame, which burst out on board the Gloucester, and which was succeeded by a cloud of smoke. However, they were soon relieved from their apprehensions, by receiving information, that the blast was occasioned by a spark of fire from the forge, lighting on some gunpowder and other combustibles, which an officer on board was preparing for use, in case we should fall in with the Spanish fleet; and that it had been extinguished, without any damage to the ship.

We here found what was constantly verified by all our observations in these high latitudes, that fair weather was always of an exceeding short duration, and that when it was remarkably fine, it was a certain presage of a succeeding storm, for the calm and sunshine of our afternoon ended in a most turbulent night, the wind freshening from the S.W. as the night came on, and increasing its violence continually till nine in the morning the next day, when it blew so hard, that we were obliged to bring-to with the squadron, and to continue under a reefed mizen till eleven at night, having in that time from forty-three to fifty-seven fathom water, with black sand and gravel; and by an observation we had at noon, we concluded a current had set us twelve miles to the southward of our reckoning. Towards midnight, the wind abating, we made sail again; and steering south, we discovered in the morning for the first time the land, called Terra del Fuego, stretching from the S. by W., to the S.E. by E. This indeed afforded us but a very uncomfortable prospect, it appearing of a stupendous height, covered every where with snow. We steered along this shore all day, having soundings from forty to fifty fathom, with stones and gravel. And as we intended to pass through Straits Le Maire next day, we lay-to at night, that we might not overshoot them, and took this opportunity to prepare ourselves for the tempestuous climate we were soon to be engaged in; with which view, we employed ourselves good part of the night in bending an entire new suit of sails to the yards. At four the next morning, being the 7th of March, we made sail, and at eight saw the land; and soon after we began to open the Straits, at which time Cape St. James bore from

us E.S.E., Cape St. Vincent S.E. by E., the middle-most of the Three Brothers S. and by W., Montegorda South, and Cape St. Bartholomew, which is the southernmost point of Statenland, E.S.E. Though Terra del Fuego had an aspect extremely barren and desolate, yet this island of Statenland far surpasses it, in the wildness and horror of its appearance: it seeming to be entirely composed of inaccessible rocks, without the least mixture of earth or mould between them. These rocks terminate in a vast number of ragged points which spire up to a prodigious height, and are all of them covered with everlasting snow; the points themselves are on every side surrounded with frightful precipices, and often overhang in a most astonishing manner; and the hills which bear them are generally separated from each other by narrow clefts, which appeared as if the country had been rent by earthquakes; for these chasms are nearly perpendicular, and extend through the substance of the main rocks, almost to their very bottoms: so that nothing can be imagined more savage and gloomy, than the whole aspect of this coast.

I have above mentioned, that on the 7th of March, in the morning, we opened Straits Le Maire, and soon after, or about ten o'clock, the Pearl and the Tryal being ordered to keep a-head of the squadron, we entered them with fair weather and a brisk gale, and were hurried through by the rapidity of the tide in about two hours, though they are between seven and eight leagues in length. As these Straits are often considered as the boundary between the Atlantic and Pacific Oceans, and as we presumed we had nothing now before us but an open sea, till we should arrive on those opulent coasts where all our hopes and wishes centred, we could not help flattering ourselves that the greatest difficulty of our passage was now at an end, and that our most sanguine dreams were upon the point of being realised; and hence we indulged our imaginations in those romantic schemes, which the fancied possession of the Chilian gold and Peruvian silver might be conceived to inspire. These joyous ideas were heightened by the brightness of the sky, and the serenity of the weather, which was indeed most remarkably pleasing; for though the winter was now advancing apace, yet the morning of this day, in its brilliancy and mildness, gave place to none we had seen since our departure from England. Thus animated by these delusions, we traversed these memorable Straits, ignorant of the dreadful calamities that were then impending, and just ready to break upon us; ignorant that the time drew near, when the squadron would be separated never to unite again, and that this day of our passage was the last cheerful day that the greatest part of us would ever live to enjoy.

1 "On the 7th of March, I entered the Straits Le Maire with a favourable gale and fine weather; but had no sooner got through the Straits than I met very hard gales of wind from the high lands of Terra del Fuego: insomuch that I was obliged to reef my courses, which continued reefed fifty-eight days."—*Anson's official report.*

declared themselves incapable of doing any duty: he immediately received an order, by directions of the Lords Justices, that they should again be received on board, and no man should be dismissed."—*Barrow's Life of Lord Anson.*

CHAPTER VIII.

From Straits Le Maire to Cape Noir.

We had scarcely reached the southern extremity of the Straits of Le Maire, when our flattering hopes were instantly lost in the apprehensions of immediate destruction: for before the sternmost ships of the squadron were clear of the Straits, the serenity of the sky was suddenly changed, and gave us all the presages of an impending storm; and immediately the wind shifted to the southward, and blew in such violent squalls, that we were obliged to hand our top-sails, and reef our main-sail: the tide too, which had hitherto favoured us, now turned against us, and drove us to the eastward with prodigious rapidity, so that we were in great anxiety for the Wager and the Anna pink, the two sternmost vessels, fearing they would be dashed to pieces against the shore of Staten-land; nor were our apprehensions without foundation, for it was with the utmost difficulty they escaped. And now the whole squadron, instead of pursuing their intended course to the S.W. were driven to the eastward, by the united force of the storm and of the currents; so that next day in the morning we found ourselves near seven leagues to the eastward of Staten-land, which then bore from us N.W. The violence of the current which had set us with so much precipitation to the eastward, together with the force and constancy of the westerly winds, soon taught us to consider the doubling of Cape Horn as an enterprise that might prove too mighty for our efforts, though some amongst us had lately treated the difficulties which former voyagers were said to have met with in this undertaking, as little better than chimerical, and had supposed them to arise rather from timidity and unskilfulness, than from the real embarrassments of the winds and seas; but we were severely convinced, that these censures were rash and ill grounded: for the distresses with which we struggled, during the three succeeding months, will not easily be paralleled in the relation of any former naval expedition. This will, I doubt not, be readily allowed by those who shall carefully peruse the ensuing narration.

From the storm which came on before we had well got clear of Straits Le Maire, we had a continual succession of such tempestuous weather, as surprised the oldest and most experienced mariners on board, and obliged them to confess, that what they had hitherto called storms were inconsiderable gales, compared with the violence of these winds, which raised such short, and at the same time such mountainous waves, as greatly surpassed in danger all seas known in any other part of the globe: and it was not without great reason, that this unusual appearance filled us with continual terror; for had any one of these waves broke fairly over us, it must, in all probability, have sent us to the bottom. Nor did we escape with terror only; for the ship rolling incessantly gunwale-to, gave us such quick and violent motions, that the men were in perpetual danger of being dashed to pieces against the decks, or sides of the ship. And though we were extremely careful to secure ourselves from these shocks, by grasping some fixed body, yet many of our people were forced from their hold; some of whom were killed, and others greatly injured; in particular, one of our best seamen was canted overboard and drowned, another dislocated his neck, a third was thrown into the main-hold and broke his thigh, and one of our boatswain's mates broke his collar-bone twice; not to mention many other accidents of the same kind. These tempests, so dreadful in themselves, though unattended by any other unfavourable circumstance, were yet rendered more mischievous to us by their inequality, and the deceitful intervals which they at sometimes afforded; for though we were oftentimes obliged to lie-to for days together under a reefed mizen, and were sometimes reduced to lie at the mercy of the waves under our bare poles, yet now and then we ventured to make sail with our courses double-reefed; and the weather proving more tolerable, would perhaps encourage us to set our top-sails; after which, the wind, without any previous notice, would return upon us with redoubled force, and would in an instant tear our sails from the yards. And that no circumstance might be wanting which could aggrandize our distress, these blasts generally brought with them a great quantity of snow and sleet, which cased our rigging, and froze our sails, thereby rendering them and our cordage brittle, and apt to snap upon the slightest strain; adding great difficulty and labour to the working of the ship, benumbing the limbs of our people, and making them incapable of exerting themselves with their usual activity, and even disabling many of them, by mortifying their toes and fingers. It were indeed endless to enumerate the various disasters of different kinds which befel us; and I shall only mention the most material, which will sufficiently evince the calamitous condition of the whole squadron, during the course of this navigation.

It was on the 7th of March, as has been already observed, that we passed Straits Le Maire, and were immediately afterwards driven to the eastward by a violent storm, and the force of the current which set that way. For the four or five succeeding days we had hard gales of wind from the same quarter, with a most prodigious swell; so that though we stood, during all that time, towards the S.W., yet we had no reason to imagine we had made any way to the westward. In this interval we had frequent squalls of rain and snow, and shipped great quantities of water; after which, for three or four days, though the seas ran mountains high, yet the weather was rather more moderate: but, on the 18th, we had again strong gales of wind with extreme cold, and at midnight the main top-sail split, and one of the straps of the main dead-eyes broke. From hence, to the 23rd, the weather was more favourable, though often intermixed with rain and sleet, and some hard gales; but, as the waves did not subside, the ship, by labouring in this lofty sea, was now grown so loose in her upper works, that she let in the water at every seam, so that every part within board was constantly exposed to the sea-water, and scarcely any of the officers ever lay in dry beds. Indeed it was very rare, that two nights ever passed without many of them being driven from their beds, by the deluge of water that came upon them.

On the 23rd, we had a most violent storm of wind, hail, and rain, with a very great sea; and though we handed the main top-sail before the height of the squall, yet we found the yard sprung; and soon after the foot rope of the main-sail breaking, the main-sail itself split instantly to rags, and, in spite of our endeavours to save it, much the greater part of it was blown overboard. On this the commodore made the signal for the squadron to bring-to ; and the storm at length flattening to a calm, we had an opportunity of getting down our main top-sail yard to put the carpenters at work upon it, and of repairing our rigging ; after which, having bent a new main-sail, we got under sail again with a moderate breeze ; but in less than twenty-four hours we were attacked by another storm still more furious than the former ; for it proved a perfect hurricane, and reduced us to the necessity of lying-to under our bare poles. As our ship kept the wind better than any of the rest, we were obliged in the afternoon to wear ship, in order to join the squadron to the leeward, which otherwise we should have been in danger of losing in the night : and as we dared not venture any sail abroad, we were obliged to make use of an expedient, which answered our purpose ; this was putting the helm a-weather, and manning the fore-shrouds : but though this method proved successful for the end intended, yet in the execution of it one of our ablest seamen was canted overboard ; and notwithstanding the prodigious agitation of the waves, we perceived that he swam very strong, and it was with the utmost concern that we found ourselves incapable of assisting him ; and we were the more grieved at his unhappy fate, since we lost sight of him struggling with the waves, and conceived, from the manner in which he swam, that he might continue sensible, for a considerable time longer, of the horror attending his irretrievable situation.[1]

Before this last mentioned storm was quite abated, we found two of our main-shrouds and one mizen-shroud broke, all which we knotted, and set up immediately ; and from hence we had an interval of three or four days less tempestuous than usual, but accompanied with a thick fog, in which we were obliged to fire guns almost every half hour, to keep our squadron together. On the 31st, we were alarmed by a gun fired from the Gloucester, and a signal made by her to speak with the commodore ; we immediately bore down to her, and were prepared to hear of some terrible disaster ; but we were apprised of it before we joined her, for we saw that her main-yard was broke in the slings. This was a grievous misfortune to us all at this juncture ; as it was obvious it would prove a hindrance to our sailing, and would detain us the longer in these inhospitable latitudes. But our future success and safety was not to be promoted by repining, but by resolution and activity ; and therefore, that this unlucky incident might delay us as little as possible, the commodore ordered several carpenters to be put

[1] It was with reference to this affecting circumstance that Cowper composed his beautiful verses on " The Castaway." One of the stanzas is as follows :—
" He long survives, who lives an hour
    In ocean, self-upheld :
And so long he, with unspent power,
    His destiny repell'd :
And ever, as the minutes flew,
Entreated help, or cried—' Adieu.' "

on board the Gloucester from the other ships of the squadron, in order to repair her damage with the utmost expedition. And the captain of the Tryal complaining at the same time that his pumps were so bad, and the sloop made so great a quantity of water, that he was scarcely able to keep her free, the commodore ordered him a pump ready fitted from his own ship. It was very fortunate for the Gloucester and the Tryal, that the weather proved more favourable this day than for many days, both before and after ; since by this means they were enabled to receive the assistance which seemed essential to their preservation, and which they could scarcely have had at any other time, as it would have been extremely hazardous to have ventured a boat on board[1].

The next day, that is, on the 1st of April, the weather returned again to its customary bias, the sky looked dark and gloomy, and the wind began to freshen and to blow in squalls ; however, it was not yet so boisterous, as to prevent our carrying our top-sail close reefed ; but its appearance was such, as plainly prognosticated that a still severer tempest was at hand : and accordingly, on the 3d of April, there came on a storm, which both in its violence and continuation (for it lasted three days) exceeded all that we had hitherto encountered. In its first onset we received a furious shock from a sea which broke upon our larboard quarter, where it stove in the quarter gallery, and rushed into the ship like a deluge ; our rigging too suffered extremely, for one of the straps of the main dead-eyes was broke, as was also a main-shroud and puttock-shroud, so that to ease the stress upon the masts and shrouds, we lowered both our main and fore-yards, and furled all our sails, and in this posture we lay-to for three days, when the storm somewhat abating, we ventured to make sail under our courses only ; but even this we could not do long, for the next day, which was the 7th, we had another hard gale of wind, with lightning and rain, which obliged us to lie-to again till night. It was wonderful, that notwithstanding the hard weather we had endured, no extraordinary accident had happened to any of the squadron since the breaking of the Gloucester's main-yard : but this wonder soon ceased ; for at three the next morning, several guns were fired to leeward as signals of distress. And the commodore making a signal for the squadron to bring-to, we, at daybreak, saw the Wager a considerable way to leeward of any of the other ships ; and we soon perceived that she had lost her mizen-mast, and main top-sail yard. We immediately bore down to her, and found this disaster had arisen from the badness of her iron-work ; for all the chain-plates to windward had given way, upon the ship's fetching a deep roll. This proved the more unfortunate to the Wager, as her carpenter had been on board the Gloucester ever since the 31st of March, and the weather was now too severe to permit him to return : nor was the Wager the only ship of the squadron that had suffered in the last tempest ; for, the next day, a signal of distress was made by the Anna pink, and, upon speaking with the master, we learnt that they had broken their fore-stay and the gammon of

[1] In Anson's Report of the 31st of March, he makes the first mention of the scurvy, as follows:—" Men falling down every day with scorbutic complaints.'

the bowsprit, and were in no small danger of having all the masts come by the board: so that we were obliged to bear away until they had made all fast, after which we haled upon a wind again.

And now, after all our solicitude, and the numerous ills of every kind, to which we had been incessantly exposed for near forty days, we had great consolation in the flattering hopes we entertained, that our fatigues were drawing to a period, and that we should soon arrive in a more hospitable climate, where we should be amply repaid for all our past sufferings. For, towards the latter end of March, we were advanced, by our reckoning, near 10° to the westward of the westernmost point of Terra del Fuego, and this allowance being double what former navigators have thought necessary to be taken, in order to compensate the drift of the eastern current, we esteemed ourselves to be well advanced within the limits of the southern ocean, and had therefore been ever since standing to the northward, with as much expedition as the turbulence of the weather, and our frequent disasters, permitted. And, on the 13th of April, we were but a degree in latitude to the southward of the west entrance of the Straits of Magellan; so that we fully expected, in a very few days, to have experienced the celebrated tranquillity of the Pacific Ocean.

But these were delusions which only served to render our disappointment more terrible; for the next morning, between one and two, as we were standing to the northward, and the weather, which had till then been hazy, accidentally cleared up, the pink made a signal for seeing land right ahead; and it being but two miles distant, we were all under the most dreadful apprehensions of running on shore; which, had either the wind blown from its usual quarter with its wonted vigour, or had not the moon suddenly shone out, not a ship amongst us could possibly have avoided: but the wind, which some few hours before blew in squalls from the S.W. having fortunately shifted to W.N.W., we were enabled to stand to the southward, and to clear ourselves of this unexpected danger; so that by noon we had gained an offing of near twenty leagues.

By the latitude of this land we fell in with, it was agreed to be a part of Terra del Fuego, near the southern outlet described in Frezier's chart of the Straits of Magellan, and was supposed to be that point called by him Cape Noir. It was indeed most wonderful, that the currents should have driven us to the eastward with such strength; for the whole squadron esteemed themselves upwards of ten degrees more westerly than this land, so that in running down, by our account, about nineteen degrees of longitude, we had not really advanced above half that distance. And now, instead of having our labours and anxieties relieved by approaching a warmer climate and more tranquil seas, we were to steer again to the southward, and were again to combat those western blasts, which had so often terrified us; and this too, when we were weakened by our men falling sick, and dying apace, and when our spirits, dejected by a long continuance at sea, and by our late disappointment, were much less capable of supporting us in the various difficulties, which we could not but expect in this new undertaking. Add to all this too, the discouragement we received by the diminution of the strength of the squadron; for, three days before this, we lost sight of the Severn and the Pearl in the morning; and though we spread our ships, and beat about for some time, yet we never saw them more; whence we had apprehensions that they too might have fallen in with this land in the night, and by being less favoured by the wind and the moon than we were, might have run on shore and have perished. Full of these dejected thoughts and gloomy presages, we stood away to the S.W., prepared by our late disaster to suspect that how large soever an allowance we made in our westing for the drift of the eastern current, we might still, upon a second trial, perhaps find it insufficient.

CHAPTER IX.

Observations and directions for facilitating the passage of our future Cruisers round Cape Horn.

THE improper season of the year in which we attempted to double Cape Horn, and to which is to be imputed the disappointment (recited in the foregoing chapter) in falling in with Terra del Fuego, when we reckoned ourselves at least a hundred leagues to the westward of that whole coast, and consequently well advanced into the Pacific Ocean; this unseasonable navigation, I say, to which we were necessitated by our too late departure from England, was the fatal source of all the misfortunes we afterwards encountered. For from hence proceeded the separation of our ships, the destruction of our people, the ruin of our project on Baldivia, and of all our other views on the Spanish places, and the reduction of our squadron from the formidable condition in which it passed Straits Le Maire, to a couple of shattered half-manned cruisers and a sloop, so far disabled, that in many climates they scarcely durst have put to sea. To prevent therefore, as much as in me lies, all ships hereafter bound to the South-Seas from suffering the same calamities, I think it my duty to insert in this place, such directions and observations, as either my own experience and reflection, or the converse of the most skilful navigators on board the squadron could furnish me with, in relation to the most eligible manner of doubling Cape Horn, whether in regard to the season of the year, the course proper to be steered, or the places of refreshment both on the east and west side of South America.

And first with regard to the proper place for refreshment on the east side of South America. For this purpose the island of St. Catherine's has been usually recommended by former writers, and on their faith we put in there, as has been formerly mentioned: but the treatment we met with, and the small store of refreshments we could procure there, are sufficient reasons to render all ships for the future cautious, how they trust themselves in the government of Don Jose Silva de Paz; for they may certainly depend on having their strength, condition and designs betrayed to the Spaniards, as far as the knowledge, the governor can procure of these particulars, will give leave. And as this treacherous conduct is inspired by the views of private gain, in the illicit commerce carried on to the river of Plate, rather than by any national affection which the Portuguese bear the Spaniards, the same perfidy may perhaps be expected from most of the governors of the Brazil coast; since these smuggling engagements are doubtless very extensive and general. And though the governors should themselves detest so faithless a procedure, yet as ships are perpetually passing from some or other of the Brazil ports to the river of Plate, the Spaniards could scarcely fail of receiving, by this means, casual intelligence of any British ships upon the coast; which, however imperfect such intelligence might be, would prove of dangerous import to the views and interests of those cruisers who were thus discovered.

For the Spanish trade in the South-Seas running all in one track from north to south, with very little deviation to the eastward or westward, it is in the power of two or three cruisers, properly stationed in different parts of this track, to possess themselves of every ship that puts to sea: but this is only so long as they can continue concealed from the neighbouring coast; for, the instant an enemy is known to be in those seas, all navigation is stopped, and consequently all captures are at an end; since the Spaniards, well apprised of these advantages of the enemy, send expresses along the coast, and lay a general embargo on all their trade: a measure which, they prudentially foresee, will not only prevent their vessels being taken, but will soon lay any cruisers, who have not strength sufficient to attempt their places, under a necessity of returning home. Hence then appears the great importance of concealing all expeditions of this kind; and hence too it follows, how extremely prejudicial that intelligence may prove, which is given by the Portuguese governors to the Spaniards, in relation to the designs of ships touching at the ports of Brazil.

However, notwithstanding the inconveniences we have mentioned of touching on the coast of Brazil, it will oftentimes happen that ships bound round Cape Horn will be obliged to call there for a supply of wood and water, and other refreshments. In this case St. Catherine's is the last place I would recommend, both as the proper animals for a live stock at sea, as hogs, sheep, and fowls cannot be procured there, (for want of which we found ourselves greatly distressed, by being reduced to live almost entirely on salt provisions) but also because, from its being nearer the river of Plate than many of their other settlements, the inducements and conveniences of betraying us are much stronger. The place I would recommend is Rio Janeiro, where two of our squadron put in after they were separated from us in passing Cape Horn; for here, as I have been informed by one of the gentlemen on board those ships, any quantity of hogs and poultry may be procured; and this place being more distant from the river of Plate, the difficulty of intelligence is somewhat enhanced, and consequently the chance of continuing there undiscovered, in some degree augmented. Other measures, which may effectually obviate all these embarrassments, will be considered more at large hereafter.

And now I proceed to the consideration of the proper course to be steered for doubling Cape Horn. And here, I think, I am sufficiently authorised by our own fatal experience, and by a careful comparison and examination of the journals of former navigators, to give this piece of advice, which in prudence, I think, ought never to be departed from: that is, that all ships bound to the South Seas, instead of passing through Straits le Maire, should constantly pass to the eastward of Staten-land, and should be invariably bent on running to the southward as far as the latitude of 61 or 62 degrees, before they endeavour to stand to the westward; and that when they are got into that latitude, they should then make sure of sufficient westing, before they once think of steering to the northward.

But as directions diametrically opposite to these have been formerly given by other writers, it is incumbent on me to produce my reasons for each part of this maxim. And first, as to the passing to the eastward of Staten-land. Those who have attended to the risk we ran in passing Straits Le Maire, the danger we were in of being driven upon Staten-land by the current, when, though we happily escaped being put on shore, we were yet carried to the eastward of that island: those who reflect on this, and on the like accidents which have happened to other ships, will surely not esteem it prudent to pass through Straits Le Maire, and run the risk of shipwreck, and after all find themselves no farther to the westward (the only reason hitherto given for this practice) than they might have been in the same time, by a secure navigation in an open sea.

And next, as to the directions I have given for running into the latitude of 61 or 62 south, before any endeavour is made to stand to the westward. The reasons for this precept are, that in all probability the violence of the currents will be hereby avoided, and the weather will prove less tempestuous and uncertain. This last circumstance we ourselves experienced most remarkably; for after we had unexpectedly fallen in with the land, as has been mentioned in the preceding chapter, we stood away to the southward to run clear of it, and were no sooner advanced into sixty degrees or upwards, but we met with much better weather, and smoother water than in any other part of the whole passage: the air indeed was very cold and sharp, and we had strong gales, but they were steady and uniform, and we had at the same time sunshine and a clear sky; whereas in the lower latitudes, the winds every now and then intermitted, as it were, to recover new strength, and then returned suddenly in the most violent gusts, threatening at each blast the loss of our masts, which must have ended in our certain destruction. And that the currents in this high latitude would be of much less efficacy than nearer the land, seems to be evinced from these considerations, that all currents run with greater violence near the shore than at sea, and that at greater distances from shore they are scarcely perceptible: indeed the reason of this seems sufficiently obvious, if we consider, that constant currents are, in all probability, produced by constant winds, the wind driving before it, though with a slow and imperceptible motion, a large body of water, which being accumulated upon any coast that it meets with, this superfluous water must escape along the shore by the endeavours of its surface, to reduce itself to the same level with the rest of the ocean. And it is reasonable to suppose, that those violent gusts of wind which we experienced near the shore, so very different from what we found in the latitude of sixty degrees and upwards, may be owing to a similar cause; for a westerly wind almost perpetually prevails in the southern part of the Pacific Ocean: and this current of air being interrupted by those immense hills called the Andes, and by the mountains on Terra del Fuego, which together bar up the whole country to the southward as far as Cape Horn, a part of it only can escape over the tops of those prodigious precipices, and the rest must naturally follow the direction of the coast, and must range down the land to the southward, and sweep with an impetuous and irregular blast round Cape Horn, and the southernmost part of Terra del Fuego. However, not to rely on these speculations, we may, I believe, establish, as incontestable, these matters of fact, that both the rapidity of the currents, and the violence of the western gales, are less sensible in the latitude of 61 or 62 degrees, than nearer the shore of Terra del Fuego.

But though I am satisfied, both from our own experience and the relations of other navigators, of the importance of the precept I here insist on, that of running into the latitude of 61 or 62 degrees, before any endeavours are made to stand to the westward; yet I would advise no ships hereafter to trust so far to this management, as to neglect another most essential maxim, which is the making this passage in the height of summer, that is, in the months of December and January; and the more distant the time of passing is taken from this season, the more disastrous it may be reasonably expected to prove. Indeed, if the mere violence of the western winds be considered, the time of our passage, which was about the equinox, was perhaps the most unfavourable season; but then it must be considered, that in the depth of winter there are many other inconveniences to be apprehended in this navigation, which are almost insuperable: for the severity of the cold, and the shortness of the days, would render it impracticable at that season to run so far to the southward as is here recommended; and the same reasons would greatly augment the alarms of sailing in the neighbourhood of an unknown shore, dreadful in its appearance in the midst of summer, and would make a winter navigation on this coast to be, of all others, the most dismaying and terrible. As I would, therefore, advise all ships to make their passage in December and January, if possible, so I would warn them never to attempt the seas to the southward of Cape Horn, after the month of March.

And now as to the remaining consideration, that is, the properest port for cruisers to refresh at on their first arrival in the South Seas. On this head there is scarcely any choice, the island of Juan Fernandes being the only place that can be prudently recommended for this purpose. For though there are many ports on the western side of Patagonia, between the Straits of Magellan and the Spanish settlements, where ships might ride in great safety, might recruit their wood and water, and might procure some few refreshments; yet that coast is in itself so terrible, from the rocks and breakers it abounds with, and from the violence of the western winds, which blow constantly full upon it, that it is by no means advisable to fall in with that land, at least till the roads, channels, and anchorage in each part of it are accurately surveyed, and both the dangers and shelter it abounds with are more distinctly known.

Thus having given the best directions in my power for the success of future cruisers bound to the South Seas, it might be expected that I should again resume the thread of my narration. But as both in the preceding and subsequent parts of this work, I have thought it my duty not only to recite all such facts and to inculcate such maxims, as had the least appearance of proving beneficial to future navigators, but also occasionally to recommend such measures to the public, as I conceive are adapted to promote the same laudable purpose, I cannot desist from the present subject without beseeching those to whom the conduct of our naval affairs is committed, to endeavour to remove the many perplexities and embarrassments with which the navigation to the South Seas is, at present, necessarily encumbered. An effort of this kind could not fail of proving highly honourable to themselves, and extremely beneficial to their country. For it is to me sufficiently evident, that whatever advantages navigation shall receive, either by the invention of methods that shall render its practice less hazardous, or by the more accurate delineation of the coasts, roads and ports already known, or by the discovery of new nations, or new species of commerce; it is evident, I say, to me, that by whatever means navigation is promoted, the conveniences hence arising must ultimately redound to the emolument of Great Britain. Since, as our fleets are at present superior to those of the whole world united, it must be a matchless degree of supineness or meanspiritedness, if we permitted any of the advantages which new discoveries, or a more extended navigation may produce to mankind, to be ravished from us.

As therefore it appears that all our future expeditions to the South Seas must run a considerable risk of proving abortive, whilst we are under the necessity of touching at Brazil in our passage thither, an expedient that might relieve us from this difficulty would surely be a subject worthy of the attention of the public; and this seems capable of being effected, by the discovery of some place more to the southward, where ships might refresh and supply themselves with the necessary sea-stock for their voyage round Cape Horn. And we have in reality the imperfect knowledge of two places, which might, perhaps, on examination, prove extremely convenient for this purpose: the first of them is Pepys's Island, in the latitude of 47° south, and laid down, by Dr. Halley, about eighty leagues to the eastward of Cape Blanco, on the coast of Patagonia; the second is Falkland's Isles, in the latitude of 51°½ nearly south of Pepys's Island. The first of these was discovered by Captain Cowley, in his voyage round the world, in the year 1686; who represents it as a commodious place for ships to wood and water at, and says it is provided with a very good and capacious harbour, where a thousand sail of ships might ride at anchor in great safety; that it abounds with fowls, and as the shore is either rocks or sands, it seems to promise great plenty of fish. The second place, or Falkland's Isles, have been seen by many ships, both French and English, being the land laid down by Frezier in his chart of the extremity of South

America, under the title of the New Islands. Woods Rogers, who ran along the N.E. coast of these isles in the year 1708, tells us, that they extended about two degrees in length, and appeared with gentle descents from hill to hill, and seemed to be good ground, with woods and harbours. Either of these places, as they are islands at a considerable distance from the continent, may be supposed, from their latitude, to lie in a climate sufficiently temperate. It is true, they are too little known to be at present recommended for proper places of refreshment for ships bound to the southward: but if the Admiralty should think it advisable to order them to be surveyed, which may be done at a very small expense, by a vessel fitted out on purpose; and if, on this examination, one or both of these places should appear proper for the purpose intended, it is scarcely to be conceived of what prodigious import a convenient station might prove, situated so far to the southward, and so near Cape Horn. The Duke and Duchess of Bristol were but thirty-five days from their losing sight of Falkland's Isles, to their arrival at Juan Fernandes in the South Seas: and as the returning back is much facilitated by the western winds, I doubt not but a voyage might be made from Falkland's Isles to Juan Fernandes, and back again, in little more than two months. This, even in time of peace, might be of great consequence to this nation; and, in time of war, would make us masters of those seas.

And as all discoveries of this kind, though extremely honourable to those who direct and promote them, may yet be carried on at an inconsiderable expense, since small vessels are much the properest to be employed in this service, it were to be wished, that the whole coast of Patagonia, Terra del Fuego, and Staten-land, were carefully surveyed, and the numerous channels, roads, and harbours, with which they abound, accurately examined; this might open to us facilities of passing into the Pacific Ocean, which as yet we may be unacquainted with, and would render all that southern navigation infinitely securer than at present; and particularly, an exact draught of the west coast of Patagonia, from the Straits of Magellan to the Spanish settlements, might perhaps furnish us with better and more convenient ports for refreshment, and better situated for the purposes either of war or commerce, and above a fortnight's sail nearer to Falkland's Islands, than the island of Juan Fernandes. The discovery of this coast hath formerly been thought of such consequence, by reason of its neighbourhood to the Araucos and other Chilian Indians, who are generally at war, or at least on ill terms with their Spanish neighbours, that Sir John Narborough was purposely fitted out in the reign of King Charles II., to survey the Straits of Magellan, the neighbouring coast of Patagonia, and the Spanish ports on that frontier, with directions, if possible, to procure some intercourse with the Chilian Indians, and to establish a commerce and a lasting correspondence with them. His Majesty's views in employing Sir John Narborough in this expedition, were not solely the advantage he might hope to receive from the alliance of those savages, in restraining and intimidating the crown of Spain; but he conceived, that independent of those motives, the immediate traffic with these Indians might prove extremely advantageous to the English nation. For it is well known, that at the first discovery of Chili by the Spaniards, it abounded with vast quantities of gold, much beyond what it has at any time produced since it has been in their possession. And hence it has been generally believed, that the richest mines are prudently concealed by the Indians, as well knowing that the discovery of them to the Spaniards would only excite in them a greater thirst for conquest and tyranny, and render their own independence precarious. But with respect to their commerce with the English, these reasons would no longer influence them; since it would be in our power to furnish them with arms and ammunition of all kinds, of which they are extremely desirous, together with many other conveniences, which their intercourse with the Spaniards has taught them to relish. They would then, in all probability, open their mines, and gladly embrace a traffic of such mutual convenience to both nations; for then their gold, instead of proving the means of enslaving them, would procure them weapons to assert their liberty, to chastise their tyrants, and to secure themselves for ever from the Spanish yoke; whilst with our assistance, and under our protection, they might become a considerable people, and might secure to us that wealth, which formerly by the house of Austria, and lately by the house of Bourbon, has been most mischievously lavished in the pursuit of universal monarchy.

It is true that Sir John Narborough did not succeed in opening this commerce, which in appearance promised so many advantages to this nation. However, his disappointment was merely accidental, and his transactions upon that coast (besides the many valuable improvements he furnished to geography and navigation) are rather an encouragement for future trials of this kind, than any objection against them; his principal misfortune being the losing company of a small barque which attended him, and having some of his people trapanned at Baldivia. However, it appeared, by the precautions and fears of the Spaniards, that they were fully convinced of the practicability of the scheme he was sent to execute, and extremely alarmed with the apprehension of its consequences.

It is said, that his Majesty King Charles the Second was so far prepossessed with the hopes of the advantages redounding from this expedition, and so eager to be informed of the event of it, that having intelligence of Sir John Narborough's passing through the Downs, on his return, he had not patience to attend his arrival at court, but went himself in his barge to Gravesend to meet him.

The two most celebrated charts hitherto published of the southernmost part of South America, are those of Dr. Halley, in his general chart of the magnetic variation, and of Frezier in his voyage to the South Seas. But besides these, there is a chart of the Straits of Magellan, and of some part of the adjacent coast, by Sir John Narborough above-mentioned, which is doubtless infinitely exacter in that part than Frezier, and in some respects superior to Halley, particularly in what relates to the longitudes of the different parts of those Straits. The coast from Cape

Blanco to Terra del Fuego, and thence to Straits Le Maire, we were in some measure capable of correcting by our own observations, as we ranged that shore generally in sight of land. The position of the land, to the northward of the Straits of Magellan, on the west side, is doubtless laid down in our chart but very imperfectly; and yet I believe it to be much nearer the truth than what has hitherto been done: as it is drawn from the information of some of the Wager's crew, who were shipwrecked on that shore, and afterwards coasted it down; and as it agrees pretty nearly with the description of some Spanish manuscripts I have seen.

The channel dividing Terra del Fuego is drawn from Frezier; but in the Spanish manuscripts there are several channels delineated, and I have reason to suppose, that whenever this country is thoroughly examined, this circumstance will prove true, and Terra del Fuego will be found to consist of several islands.

And having mentioned Frezier so often, I must not omit warning all future navigators, against relying on the longitude of Straits Le Maire, or of any part of that coast, laid down in his chart; the whole being being from 8 to 10 degrees too far to the eastward, if any faith can be given to the concurrent evidences of a great number of journals, verified in some particulars by astronomical observation. For instance: Sir John Narborough lays down Cape Virgin Mary in 65° 42' of West longitude from the Lizard, that is, in 71° 20' from London. And the ships of our squadron, who took their departure from St. Catherine's (where the longitude was rectified by an observation of the eclipse of the moon) found Cape Virgin Mary to be from 70° 46', to 71° 30' from London, according to their different reckonings: and there were no circumstances in our run that could render it considerably erroneous, so that it cannot be esteemed in less than 71 degrees of West longitude; whereas Frezier lays it down in less than 66 degrees from Paris, that is, little more than 63 degrees from London, which is doubtless 8 degrees short of its true quantity. Again, our squadron found Cape Virgin Mary and Cape St. Bartholomew, on the eastern side of Straits Le Maire, to be only 2° 8' different in longitude, which in Frezier are distant near 4 degrees; so that not only the longitude of Cape St. Bartholomew is laid down in him near 10 degrees too little, but the whole coast, from the Straits of Magellan to Straits Le Maire, is enlarged to near double its real extent.

But to have done with Frezier, whose errors, the importance of the subject and not a fondness for cavilling, has obliged me to remark (though his treatment of Dr. Halley might, on the present occasion, authorise much severer usage), I must, in the next place, particularise wherein the chart I have here mentioned differs from that of our learned countryman.

It is well known that this gentleman was sent abroad by the public, to make such geographical and astronomical observations as might facilitate the future practice of navigation; and particularly to determine the variation of the compass in such places as he should touch at, and if possible, to ascertain its general laws and affections.

These things Dr. Halley, to his immortal reputation and the honour of our nation, in good measure accomplished, particularly with regard to the variation of the compass; a subject of all others the most interesting to those employed in the art of navigation. He likewise corrected the position of the coast of Brazil, which had been very erroneously laid down by all former hydrographers; and by a judicious comparison of the observations of others, has happily succeeded in settling the geography of many parts of the globe, where he had not himself been. So that the chart he published, with the variation of the needle marked thereon, being the result of his labours on this subject, was allowed by all Europe to be far completer in its geography than any that had then appeared, and at the same time most surprisingly exact in the quantity of variation assigned to the different parts of the globe; a subject so very intricate and perplexing, that all general determinations about it had till then appeared impossible.

But as the only means he had of correcting those coasts where he did not touch himself was the observations of others; where those observations were wanting, or were inaccurate, it was no imputation on his skill that his determinations were defective. And this, upon the best comparison I have been able to make, is the case with regard to that part of his chart which contains the south part of South America. For though the coast of Brazil, and the opposite coast of Peru on the South Seas, are laid down, I presume, with the greatest accuracy, yet from about the river of Plate on the east side, and its opposite point on the west, the coast gradually declines too much to the westward, so as at the Straits of Magellan to be, as I conceive, about fifty leagues removed from its true position: at least, this is the result of the observations of our squadron, which agree extremely well with those of Sir John Narborough. I must add, that Dr. Halley has, in the Philosophical Transactions, given the foundation on which he has proceeded in fixing port St. Julian in 76° ½ of west longitude (which the concurrent journals of our squadron place from 70° ¾ to 71° ½): this, he tells us, was an observation of an eclipse of the moon, made at that place by Mr. Wood, then Sir John Narborough's lieutenant, and which is said to have happened there at eight in the evening, on the 18th of September, 1670. But Capt. Wood's journal of this whole voyage under Sir John Narborough is since published, together with this observation, in which he determines the longitude of port St. Julian to be 73 degrees from London, and the time of the eclipse to have been different from Dr. Halley's account. But the numbers he has given are so faultily printed, that nothing can be determined from them.

CHAPTER X.

From Cape Noir to the Island of Juan Fernandes

AFTER the mortifying disappointment of falling in with the coast of Terra del Fuego, when we esteemed ourselves ten degrees to the westward of it; after this disappointment, I say, recited in the eighth chapter, we stood away to the S.W. till the 22d of April, when we were in upwards of 60° of

South latitude, and by our account near 6° to the westward of Cape Noir; and in this run we had a series of as favourable weather as could well be expected in that part of the world, even in a better season: so that this interval, setting the inquietude of our thoughts aside, was by far the most eligible of any we enjoyed from Straits Le Maire to the West coast of America. This moderate weather continued, with little variation, till the 24th; but on the 24th, in the evening, the wind began to blow fresh, and soon increased to a prodigious storm; and the weather being extremely thick, about midnight we lost sight of the other four ships of the squadron, which, notwithstanding the violence of the preceding storms, had hitherto kept in company with us. Nor was this our sole misfortune; for, the next morning, endeavouring to hand the top-sails, the clew-lines and bunt-lines broke, and the sheets being half flown, every seam in the top-sails was soon split from top to bottom, and the main top-sail shook so strongly in the wind, that it carried away the top-lantern, and endangered the head of the mast; however, at length, some of the most daring of our men ventured upon the yard, and cut the sail away close to the reefs, though with the utmost hazard of their lives. At the same time, the foretop-sail beat about the yard with so much fury, that it was soon blown to pieces; and that we might have full employment, the main-sail blew loose, which obliged us to lower down the yard to secure the sail, and the fore-yard being likewise lowered, we lay-to under a mizen: and besides the loss of our top-sails, we had much of our other rigging broke, and lost a main studding sail-boom out of the chains.

On the 25th, about noon, the weather became more moderate, which enabled us to sway up our yards, and to repair, in the best manner we could, our shattered rigging; but still we had no sight of the rest of our squadron, nor indeed were we joined by any of them again, till after our arrival at Juan Fernandes; nor did any two of them, as we have since learned, continue in company together: and this total separation was the more wonderful, as we had hitherto kept together for seven weeks, through all the reiterated tempests of this turbulent climate. It must indeed be owned, that this separation gave us room to expect, that we might make our passage in a shorter time, than if we had continued together, because we could not make the best of our way without being retarded by the misfortunes of the other ships; but then we had the melancholy reflection, that we ourselves were hereby deprived of the assistance of others, and our safety would depend upon our single ship; so that if a plank started, or any other accident of the same nature should take place, we must all irrecoverably perish; or should we be driven on shore, we had the uncomfortable prospect of ending our days on some desolate coast, without any reasonable hope of ever getting away; whereas with another ship in company, all these calamities are much less formidable, since, in every kind of danger, there would be some probability that one ship at least might escape, and might be capable of preserving or relieving the crew of the other.

The remaining part of this month of April we had generally hard gales, although we had been every day, since the 22d, edging to the northward; however, on the last day of the month, we flattered ourselves with the hopes of soon terminating all our sufferings, for we that day found ourselves in the latitude of 52°, 13', which being northward of the Straits of Magellan, we were assured that we had completed our passage, and had arrived in the confines of the Southern Ocean; and this Ocean being denominated Pacific, from the equability of the seasons which are said to prevail there, and the facility and security with which navigation is there carried on, we doubted not but we should be speedily cheered with the moderate gales, the smooth water, and the temperate air, for which that tract of the globe has been so renowned. And under the influence of these pleasing circumstances, we hoped to experience some kind of compensation for the complicated miseries which had so constantly attended us for the last eight weeks. But here we were again disappointed, for in the succeeding month of May, our sufferings rose to a much higher pitch than they had ever yet done, whether we consider the violence of the storms, the shattering of our sails and rigging, or the diminishing and weakening of our crew by deaths and sickness, and the probable prospect of our total destruction. All this will be sufficiently evident, from the following circumstantial account of our diversified misfortunes.

Soon after our passing Straits Le Maire, the scurvy began to make its appearance amongst us; and our long continuance at sea, the fatigue we underwent, and the various disappointments we met with, had occasioned its spreading to such a degree, that at the latter end of April there were but few on board, who were not in some degree afflicted with it, and in that month no less than forty-three died of it on board the Centurion. But though we thought that the distemper had then risen to an extraordinary height, and were willing to hope that as we advanced to the northward its malignity would abate; yet, we found, on the contrary, that in the month of May, we lost near double that number: and as we did not get to land till the middle of June, the mortality went on increasing, and the disease extended itself so prodigiously, that after the loss of above two hundred men, we could not at last muster more than six fore-mast men in a watch capable of duty.

This disease, so frequently attending all long voyages, and so particularly destructive to us, is surely the most singular and unaccountable of any that affects the human body. For its symptoms are inconstant and innumerable, and its progress and effects extremely irregular: for scarcely any two persons have the same complaints, and where there hath been found some conformity in the symptoms, the order of their appearance has been totally different. However, though it frequently puts on the form of many other diseases, and is therefore not to be described by any exclusive and infallible criterions; yet there are some symptoms which are more general than the rest; and therefore, occurring the oftenest, deserve a more particular enumeration. These common appearances are large discoloured spots dispersed over the whole surface of the body, swelled legs, putrid gums, and, above all, an extraordinary lassitude of the whole body, especially after any exercise, however inconsiderable; and this lassitude at last degenerates into a proneness to swoon on the least exertion of strength, or even on the least motion.

This disease is likewise usually attended with a strange dejection of the spirits, and with shiverings, tremblings, and a disposition to be seized with the most dreadful terrors on the slightest accident. Indeed it was most remarkable, in all our reiterated experience of this malady, that whatever discouraged our people, or at any time damped their hopes, never failed to add new vigour to the distemper; for it usually killed those who were in the last stages of it, and confined those to their hammocks who were before capable of some kind of duty; so that it seemed as if alacrity of mind, and sanguine thoughts, were no contemptible preservatives from its fatal malignity.

But it is not easy to complete the long roll of the various concomitants of this disease; for it often produced putrid fevers, pleurisies, the jaundice, and violent rheumatic pains, and sometimes it occasioned an obstinate costiveness, which was generally attended with a difficulty of breathing; and this was esteemed the most deadly of all the scorbutic symptoms: at other times the whole body, but more especially the legs, were subject to ulcers of the worst kind, attended with rotten bones, and such a luxuriancy of fungous flesh, as yielded to no remedy. But a most extraordinary circumstance, and what would be scarcely credible upon any single evidence, is, that the scars of wounds which had been for many years healed, were forced open again by this virulent distemper: of this, there was a remarkable instance in one of the invalids on board the Centurion, who had been wounded above fifty years before at the battle of the Boyne; for though he was cured soon after, and had continued well for a great number of years past, yet on his being attacked by the scurvy, his wounds, in the progress of his disease, broke out afresh, and appeared as if they had never been healed: nay, what is still more astonishing, the callus of a broken bone, which had been completely formed for a long time, was found to be hereby dissolved, and the fracture seemed as if it had never been consolidated. Indeed, the effects of this disease were in almost every instance wonderful; for many of our people, though confined to their hammocks, appeared to have no inconsiderable share of health, for they ate and drank heartily, were cheerful, and talked with much seeming vigour, and with a loud strong tone of voice; and yet on their being the least moved, though it was only from one part of the ship to the other, and that in their hammocks, they have immediately expired; and others, who have confided in their seeming strength, and have resolved to get out of their hammocks, have died before they could well reach the deck; and it was no uncommon thing for those who were able to walk the deck, and to do some kind of duty, to drop down dead in an instant, on any endeavours to act with their utmost vigour: many of our people having perished in this manner during the course of this voyage.

With this terrible disease we struggled the greatest part of the time of our beating round Cape Horn; and though it did not then rage with its utmost violence, yet we buried no less than forty-three men on board the Centurion, in the month of April, as hath been already observed; but we still entertained hopes, that when we should have once secured our passage round the Cape, we should put a period to this and all the other evils which had so constantly pursued us. But it was our misfortune to find, that the Pacific Ocean was to us less hospitable than the turbulent neighbourhood of Terra del Fuego and Cape Horn: for being arrived, on the 8th of May, off the island of Socoro, which was the first rendezvous appointed for the squadron, and where we hoped to have met with some of our companions, we cruised for them in that station several days. And here we were not only disappointed in our hopes of being joined by our friends, and were thereby induced to favour the gloomy suggestions of their having all perished; but we were likewise perpetually alarmed with the fears of being driven on shore upon this coast, which appeared too craggy and irregular to give us the least hopes that, in such a case, any of us could possibly escape immediate destruction. For the land had indeed a most tremendous aspect: the most distant part of it, and which appeared far within the country, being the mountains usually called the Andes or Cordilleras, was extremely high, and covered with snow; and the coast itself seemed quite rocky and barren; and the water's edge skirted with precipices. In some places indeed there appeared several deep bays running into the land, but the entrance into them was generally blocked up by numbers of little islands; and though it was not improbable but there might be convenient shelter in some of those bays, and proper channels leading thereto; yet as we were utterly ignorant of the coast, had we been driven ashore by the western winds which blew almost constantly there, we did not expect to have avoided the loss of our ships, and of our lives.

And this continued peril, which lasted for above a fortnight, was greatly aggravated by the difficulties we found in working the ship; as the scurvy had by this time destroyed so great a part of our hands, and had in some degree affected almost the whole crew.[1] Nor did we, as we hoped, find the winds less violent, as we advanced to the northward; for we had often prodigious squalls which split our sails, greatly damaged our rigging, and endangered our masts. Indeed, during the greatest part of the time we were upon this coast, the wind blew so hard, that in another situation, where we had sufficient sea-room, we should certainly have lain-to; but in the present exigency we were necessitated to carry both our courses and top-sails, in order to keep clear of this lee-shore. In one of these squalls, which was attended by several violent claps of thunder, a sudden flash of fire darted along our decks, which, dividing, exploded with a report like that of several pistols, and wounded many of our men and officers as it passed, marking them in different parts of the body: this flame was attended with a strong sulphurous stench, and was doubtless of the same nature with the larger and more violent blasts of lightning which then filled the air.

It were endless to recite minutely the various

[1] In Anson's official report, 8th May, he states that "he had not men able to keep the deck sufficient to take in a topsail, all being violently afflicted with the scurvy, and every day lessening our number by six, eight, or ten."

disasters, fatigues and terrors which we encountered on this coast; all these went on increasing till the 22d of May, at which time, the fury of all the storms which we had hitherto encountered seemed to be combined, and to have conspired our destruction. In this hurricane almost all our sails were split, and great part of our standing rigging broken; and, about eight in the evening, a mountainous overgrown sea, took us upon our starboard quarter, and gave us so prodigious a shock, that several of our shrouds broke with the jerk, by which our masts were greatly endangered; our ballast and stores too were so strangely shifted, that the ship heeled afterwards two streaks to port. Indeed it was a most tremendous blow, and we were thrown into the utmost consternation from the apprehension of instantly foundering; and though the wind abated in a few hours, yet, as we had no more sails left in a condition to bend to our yards, the ship laboured very much in a hollow sea, rolling gunwale to, for want of sail to steady her: so that we expected our masts, which were now very slenderly supported, to come by the board every moment. However, we exerted ourselves the best we could to stirrup our shrouds, to reeve new lanyards, and to mend our sails; but while these necessary operations were carrying on, we ran great risk of being driven on shore on the island of Chiloe, which was not far distant from us; but in the midst of our peril the wind happily shifted to the southward, and we steered off the land with the mainsail only, the master and myself undertaking the management of the helm, while every one else on board was busied in securing the masts, and bending the sails as fast as they could be repaired. This was the last effort of that stormy climate; for in a day or two after, we got clear of the land, and found the weather more moderate than we had yet experienced since our passing Straits Le Maire. And now having cruised in vain for more than a fortnight in quest of the other ships of the squadron, it was resolved to take the advantage of the present favourable season and the offing we had made from this terrible coast, and to make the best of our way for the island of Juan Fernandes. For though our next rendezvous was appointed off the harbour of Baldivia, yet as we had hitherto seen none of our companions at this first rendezvous, it was not to be supposed that any of them would be found at the second: indeed we had the greatest reason to suspect, that all but ourselves had perished. Besides, we were by this time reduced to so low a condition, that instead of attempting to attack the places of the enemy, our utmost hopes could only suggest to us the possibility of saving the ship, and some part of the remaining enfeebled crew, by our speedy arrival at Juan Fernandes; for this was the only road in that part of the world where there was any probability of our recovering our sick, or refitting our vessel, and consequently our getting thither was the only chance we had left to avoid perishing at sea.

Our deplorable situation then allowing no room for deliberation, we stood for the island of Juan Fernandes; and to save time, which was now extremely precious (our men dying, four, five and six in a day), and likewise to avoid being engaged again with a lee-shore; we resolved, if possible, to hit the island upon a meridian. And, on the 28th of May, being nearly in the parallel upon which it is laid down, we had great expectations of seeing it: but not finding it in the position in which the charts had taught us to expect it, we began to fear that we had got too far to the westward; and therefore, though the commodore himself was strongly persuaded that he saw it on the morning of the 28th, yet his officers believing it to be only a cloud, to which opinion the haziness of the weather gave some kind of countenance, it was, on a consultation, resolved to stand to the eastward, in the parallel of the island; as it was certain, that by this course we should either fall in with the island, if we were already to the westward of it; or should at least make the main-land of Chili, from whence we might take a new departure, and assure ourselves, by running to the westward afterwards, of not missing the island a second time.

On the 30th of May we had a view of the continent of Chili, distant about twelve or thirteen leagues; the land made exceeding high and uneven, and appeared quite white; what we saw being doubtless a part of the Cordilleras, which are always covered with snow. Though by this view of the land we ascertained our position, yet it gave us great uneasiness to find that we had so needlessly altered our course, when we were, in all probability, just upon the point of making the island; for the mortality amongst us was now increased to a most dreadful degree, and those who remained alive were utterly dispirited by this new disappointment, and the prospect of their longer continuance at sea: our water too began to grow scarce; so that a general dejection prevailed amongst us, which added much to the virulence of the disease, and destroyed numbers of our best men; and to all these calamities there was added this vexatious circumstance, that when, after having got a sight of the main, we tacked and stood to the westward in quest of the island, we were so much delayed by calms and contrary winds, that it cost us nine days to regain the westing, which, when we stood to the eastward, we ran down in two. In this desponding condition, with a crazy ship, a great scarcity of fresh water, and a crew so universally diseased, that there were not above ten fore-mast men in a watch capable of doing duty, and even some of these lame, and unable to go aloft: under these disheartening circumstances, I say, we stood to the westward; and, on the 9th of June, at day-break, we at last discovered the long-wished-for island of Juan Fernandes. And with this discovery I shall close this chapter, and the first book; after observing (which will furnish a very strong image of our unparalleled distresses) that by our suspecting ourselves to be to the westward of the island on the 28th of May, and, in consequence of this, standing in for the main, we lost between seventy and eighty of our men, whom we should doubtless have saved had we made the island that day, which, had we kept on our course for a few hours longer, we could not have failed to have done.

END OF BOOK I.

BOOK II.

CHAPTER I.

The arrival of the Centurion at the Island of Juan Fernandes, with a description of that Island.

On the 9th of June, at day-break, as is mentioned in the preceding chapter, we first descried the island of Juan Fernandes, bearing N. by E. ¼ E., at eleven or twelve leagues' distance. And though, on this first view, it appeared to be a very mountainous place, extremely ragged and irregular; yet as it was land, and the land we sought for, it was to us a most agreeable sight: for at this place only we could hope to put a period to those terrible calamities we had so long struggled with, which had already swept away above half our crew, and which, had we continued a few days longer at sea, would inevitably have completed our destruction. For we were by this time reduced to so helpless a condition, that out of two hundred and odd men which remained alive, we could not, taking all our watches together, muster hands enough to work the ship on an emergency, though we included the officers, their servants, and the boys.

The wind being northerly when we first made the island, we kept plying all that day, and the next night, in order to get in with the land; and wearing the ship in the middle watch, we had a melancholy instance of the almost incredible debility of our people; for the Lieutenant could muster no more than two quarter-masters, and six fore-mast men capable of working; so that without the assistance of the officers, servants and the boys, it might have proved impossible for us to have reached the island, after we had got sight of it; and even with this assistance they were two hours in trimming the sails: to so wretched a condition was a sixty-gun ship reduced, which had passed Straits Le Maire but three months before, with between four and five hundred men, almost all of them in health and vigour.

However, on the 10th, in the afternoon, we got under the lee of the island, and kept ranging along it, at about two miles' distance, in order to look out for the proper anchorage, which was described to be in a bay on the north side. And now being nearer in with the shore, we could discover that the broken craggy precipices, which had appeared so unpromising at a distance, were far from barren, being in most places covered with woods; and that between them there were everywhere interspersed the finest valleys, clothed with a most beautiful verdure, and watered with numerous streams and cascades; no valley, of any extent, being unprovided of its proper rill. The water too, as we afterwards found, was not inferior to any we had ever tasted, and was constantly clear: so that the aspect of this country would, at all times, have been extremely delightful, but in our distressed situation, languishing as we were for the land and its vegetable productions, (an inclination constantly attending every stage of the sea-scurvy) it is scarcely credible with what eagerness and transport we viewed the shore, and with how much impatience we longed for the greens and other refreshments which were then in sight, and particularly for the water, for of this we had been confined to a very sparing allowance for a considerable time, and had then but five tons remaining on board. Those only who have endured a long series of thirst, and who can readily recall the desire and agitation which the ideas alone of springs and brooks have at that time raised in them, can judge of the emotion with which we eyed a large cascade of the most transparent water, which poured itself from a rock near a hundred feet high into the sea, at a small distance from the ship. Even those amongst the diseased, who were not in the very last stages of the distemper, though they had been long confined to their hammocks, exerted the small remains of strength that was left them, and crawled up to the deck to feast themselves with this reviving prospect. Thus we coasted the shore, fully employed in the contemplation of this diversified landscape, which still improved upon us the farther we advanced. But at last the night closed upon us, before we had satisfied ourselves which was the proper bay to anchor in; and therefore we resolved to keep in soundings all night, (we having then from sixty-four to seventy fathom) and to send our boat next morning to discover the road: however, the current shifted in the night, and set us so near the land, that we were obliged to let go the best bower in fifty-six fathom, not half a mile from the shore. At four in the morning, the cutter was despatched with our third lieutenant to find out the bay we were in search of, who returned again at noon with the boat laden with seals and grass; for though the island abounded with better vegetables, yet the boat's-crew, in their short stay, had not met with them; and they well knew that even grass would prove a dainty, and indeed it was all soon and eagerly devoured. The seals too were considered as fresh provision; but as yet were not much admired, though they grew afterwards into more repute: for what rendered them less valuable at this juncture, was the prodigious quantity of excellent fish, which the people on board had taken, during the absence of the boat.

The cutter, in this expedition, had discovered the bay where we intended to anchor, which we found was to the westward of our present station; and, the next morning, the weather proving favourable, we endeavoured to weigh, in order to proceed thither: but though on this occasion, we mustered all the strength we could, obliging even the sick, who were scarce able to keep on their legs, to assist us; yet the capstan was so weakly manned, that it was near four hours before we hove the cable right up and down: after which, with our utmost efforts, and with many surges and some purchases we made use of to increase our power, we found ourselves incapable of starting the anchor from the ground. However, at noon, as a fresh gale blew towards the bay, we were induced to set the sails, which fortunately tripped the anchor; on which we steered along shore, till we came a-breast of the point that forms the eastern part of the bay. On the opening of the bay, the wind, that had befriended us thus far, shifted and blew from thence in squalls; but by means of the head-way we had got, we luffed close in, till the anchor brought us up in fifty-six fathom. Soon after we had thus got to our new berth, we discovered a sail, which we made no doubt was one of our squadron; and on its nearer approach, we found it to be the Tryal sloop. We immediately sent some of our hands on board her, by whose assistance she was brought to an anchor between us and the land. We soon found that the sloop had not been exempted from those calamities which we had so severely felt; for her commander, Captain Saunders, waiting on the commodore, informed him, that out of his small complement, he had buried thirty-four of his men; and those that remained were so universally afflicted with the scurvy, that only himself, his lieutenant, and three of his men, were able to stand by the sails. The Tryal came to an anchor within us, on the 12th, about noon, and we carried our hawsers on board her, in order to moor ourselves nearer in-shore; but the wind coming off the land in violent gusts, prevented our mooring in the birth we intended, especially as our principal attention was now employed on business rather of more importance; for we were now extremely occupied in sending on shore materials to raise tents for the reception of the sick, who died apace on board, and doubtless the distemper was considerably augmented by the stench and filthiness in which they lay; for the number of the diseased was so great, and so few could be spared from the necessary duty of the sails to look after them, that it was impossible to avoid a great relaxation in the article of cleanliness, which had rendered the ship extremely loathsome between decks. But notwithstanding our desire of freeing the sick from their hateful situation, and their own extreme impatience to get on shore, we had not hands enough to prepare the tents for their reception before the 16th; but on that and the two following days we sent them all on shore, amounting to a hundred and sixty-seven persons, besides at least a dozen who died in the boats, on their being exposed to the fresh air. The greatest part of our sick were so infirm, that we were obliged to carry them out of the ship in their hammocks, and to convey them afterwards in the same manner from the water-side to their tents, over a stony beach. This was a work of considerable fatigue to the few who were healthy, and therefore the commodore, with his accustomed humanity, not only assisted herein with his own labour, but obliged his officers, without distinction, to give their helping hand. The extreme weakness of our sick may in some measure be collected from the numbers who died after they had got on shore; for it had generally been found that the land, and the refreshments it produces, very soon recover most stages of the sea-scurvy; and we flattered ourselves, that those who had not perished on this first exposure to the open air, but had lived to be placed in their tents, would have been speedily restored to their health and vigour: but, to our great mortification, it was near twenty days after their landing, before the mortality was tolerably ceased; and for the first ten or twelve days, we buried rarely less than six each day, and many of those, who survived, recovered by very slow and insensible degrees. Indeed, those who were well enough at their first getting on shore, to creep out of their tents, and crawl about, were soon relieved, and recovered their health and strength in a very short time; but in the rest, the disease seemed to have acquired a degree of inveteracy which was altogether without example.

Having proceeded thus far, and got our sick on shore, I think it necessary, before I enter into any longer detail of our transactions, to give a distinct account of this island of Juan Fernandes, its situation, productions, and all its conveniences. These particulars we were well enabled to be minutely instructed in, during our three months' stay there; and as it is the only commodious place in those seas, where British cruisers can refresh and recover their men after their passage round Cape Horn, and where they may remain for some time without alarming the Spanish coast, these its advantages well merit a circumstantial description. And indeed Mr. Anson was particularly industrious in directing the roads and coasts to be surveyed, and other observations to be made, knowing, from his own experience, of how great consequence these materials might prove to any British vessels hereafter employed in those seas. For the uncertainty we were in of its position, and our standing in for the main on the 28th of May, in order to secure a sufficient easting, when we were indeed extremely near it, cost us the lives of between seventy and eighty of our men, by our longer continuance at sea: from which fatal accident we might have been exempted, had we been furnished with such an account of its situation as we could fully have depended on.

The island of Juan Fernandes lies in the latitude of 33° 40′ South, and is a hundred and ten leagues distant from the continent of Chili. It is said to have received its name from a Spaniard, who formerly procured a grant of it, and resided there some time with a view of settling it, but afterwards abandoned it. The island itself is of an irregular figure; its greatest extent being between four and five leagues, and its greatest breadth somewhat short of two leagues. The only safe anchoring at this island is on the North side, where there are three bays, but the middlemost, known by the name of Cumberland Bay, is the widest and deepest, and in all respects much the best; the other two bays, denominated the East and West bays, are scarcely more than good landing-places, where boats may conveniently put their casks on shore. Cumberland Bay is pretty well secured to the southward, lying only exposed from the N. by W. to the E. by S.; and as the northerly winds seldom blow in that climate, and never with any violence, the danger from that quarter is not worth attending to.

As Cumberland Bay is by far the most commodious road in the island, so it is advisable for all ships to anchor on the western side of this bay, within little more than two cables' length of the beach. Here they may ride in forty fathom of water, and be, in a great measure, sheltered from a large heavy sea, which comes rolling in whenever an eastern or a western wind blows. It is however expedient, in this case, to cackle or arm the cables with an iron chain, or good rounding, for five or six fathom from the anchor, to secure them from being rubbed by the foulness of the ground.

I have before observed, that a northerly wind, to which alone this bay is exposed, very rarely blew during our stay here; and as it was then winter, it may be supposed, in other seasons, to be less frequent. Indeed, in those few instances, when it was in that quarter, it did not blow with any great force: but this perhaps might be owing to the highlands on the southward of the bay, which checked its current, and thereby abated its violence; for we had reason to suppose that, a few leagues off, it blew with considerable force, since it sometimes drove before it a prodigious sea, in which we rode fore castle-in. But though the northern winds are never to be apprehended, yet the southern winds, which generally prevail here, frequently blow off the land in violent gusts and squalls, which however rarely last longer than two or three minutes. This seems to be owing to the obstruction of the southern gale by the hills in the neighbourhood of the bay; for the wind being collected by this means, at last forces its passage through the narrow valleys, which, like so many funnels, both facilitate its escape and increase its violence. These frequent and sudden gusts make it difficult for ships to work in with the wind off-shore, or to keep a clear hawse when anchored.

The northern part of this island is composed of high craggy hills, many of them inaccessible, though generally covered with trees. The soil of this part is loose and shallow, so that very large trees on the hills soon perish for want of root, and are easily overturned; which occasioned the unfortunate death of one of our sailors, who being upon the hills in search of goats, caught hold of a tree upon the declivity to assist him in his ascent, and this giving way, he immediately rolled down the hill, and though in his fall he fastened on another tree of considerable bulk, yet that too gave way, and he fell amongst the rocks, and was dashed to pieces. Mr. Brett too met with an accident only by resting his back against a tree, near as large about as himself, which stood on a slope; for the tree giving way, he fell to a considerable distance, though without receiving any harm.

The southern, or rather the S. W. part of the Island, is widely different from the rest, being dry, stony, and destitute of trees, but very flat and low, compared with the hills on the northern part. This part of the island is never frequented by ships, being surrounded by a steep shore, and having little or no fresh water; and besides, it is exposed to the southerly wind, which generally blows here the whole year round, and in the winter solstice very hard. The trees of which the woods on the northern side of the island are composed, are most of them aromatics, and of many different sorts: there are none of them of a size to yield any considerable timber, except the myrtle-trees, which are the largest on the island, and supplied us with all the timber we made use of; but even these would not work to a greater length than forty feet. The top of the myrtle-tree is circular, and appears as uniform and regular, as if it had been clipped by art; it bears on its bark an excrescence like moss, which in taste and smell resembles garlic, and was used by our people instead of it. We found here too the pimento-tree, and likewise the cabbage-tree, though in no great plenty.

Our prisoners observed, that the appearance of the hills in some part of the island resembled that of the mountains in Chili, where the gold is found: so that it is not impossible but mines might be discovered here. We observed, in some places, several hills of a peculiar sort of red earth, exceeding vermilion in colour, which perhaps, on examination, might prove useful for many purposes.

Besides a great number of plants of various kinds which are to be met with upon the island, but which we were not botanists enough either to describe or attend to, we found there almost all the vegetables which are usually esteemed to be particularly adapted to the cure of those scorbutic disorders, which are contracted by salt diet and long voyages. For here we had great quantities of water-cresses and purslain, with excellent wild sorrel, and a vast profusion of turnips and Sicilian radishes: these two last, having some resemblance to each other, were confounded by our people under the general name of turnips. We usually preferred the tops of the turnips to the roots, which were often stringy; though some of them were free from that exception, and remarkably good. These vegetables, with the fish and flesh we found here, and which I shall more particularly describe hereafter, were not only extremely grateful to our palates, after the long course of salt diet which we had been confined to, but were likewise of the most salutary consequence to our sick in recovering and invigorating them, and of no mean service to us who were well, in destroying the lurking seeds of the scurvy, from which perhaps none of us were totally exempt, and in refreshing and restoring us to our wonted strength and activity.

Besides the vegetables I have mentioned, of which we made perpetual use, we found many acres of ground covered with oats and clover. There were also some few cabbage-trees upon the island, as observed before; but as they generally grew on the precipices, and in dangerous situations, and as it was necessary to cut down a large tree for every single cabbage, this was a dainty that we were able but rarely to indulge in.

The excellence of the climate and the looseness of the soil render this place extremely proper for all kinds of vegetation; for if the ground be anywhere accidentally turned up, it is immediately overgrown with turnips and Sicilian radishes; and therefore Mr. Anson having with him garden-seeds of all kinds, and stones of different sorts of fruits, he, for the better accommodation of his countrymen who should hereafter touch here, sowed both lettuces, carrots, and other garden plants, and set in the woods a great variety of plum, apricot, and peach stones: and these last he has been informed have since thriven to a very remarkable degree; for some gentlemen, who in their passage from Lima to Old Spain were taken and brought to England, having procured leave to wait upon Mr. Anson, to thank him for his generosity and humanity to his prisoners, some of whom were their relations, they, in casual discourse with him about his transactions in the South Seas, particularly asked him, if he had not planted a great number of fruit-stones on the island of Juan Fernandes, for they told him, their late navigators had discovered there numbers of peach-trees and apricot-trees, which being fruits before unobserved in that place, they concluded them to be produced from kernels set by him.

And this may in general suffice as to the soil and vegetable productions of this place: but the face of the country, at least of the north part of the island, is so extremely singular, that I cannot avoid giving it a particular consideration. I have already taken notice of the wild, inhospitable air with which it first appeared to us, and the gradual improvement of this uncouth landscape as we drew nearer, till we were at last captivated by the numerous beauties we discovered on the shore. And I must now add, that we found, during the time of our residence there, that the inland parts of the island did no ways fall short of the sanguine prepossessions which we first entertained in their favour.

For the woods which covered most of the steepest hills, were free from all bushes and underwood, and afforded an easy passage through every part of them; and the irregularities of the hills and precipices, in the northern part of the island, necessarily traced out by their various combinations a great number of romantic valleys; most of which had a stream of the clearest water running through them, that tumbled in cascades from rock to rock, as the bottom of the valley, by the course of the neighbouring hills, was at any time broken into a sudden sharp descent: some particular spots occurred in these valleys, where the shade and fragrance of the contiguous woods, the loftiness of the overhanging rocks, and the transparency and frequent falls of the neighbouring streams, presented scenes of such elegance and dignity, as would perhaps with difficulty be rivalled in any other part of the globe. It is in this place, perhaps, that the simple productions of unassisted nature may be said to excel all the fictitious descriptions of the most animated imagination. I shall finish this article with a short account of that spot where the commodore pitched his tent, and which he made choice of for his own residence, though I despair of conveying an adequate idea of its beauty. The piece of ground which he chose was a small lawn, that lay on a little ascent, at the distance of about half a mile from the sea. In the front of his tent there was a large avenue cut through the woods to the sea-side, which sloping to the water, with a gentle descent, opened a prospect of the bay and the ships at anchor. This lawn was screened behind by a tall wood of myrtle sweeping round it, in the form of a theatre, the ground on which the wood stood rising with a much sharper ascent than the lawn itself, though not so much but that the hills and precipices within land towered up considerably above the tops of the trees, and added to the grandeur of the view. There were, besides, two streams of crystal water, which ran on the right and left of the tent, within a hundred yards' distance, and were shaded by the trees which skirted the lawn on either side, and completed the symmetry of the whole.

It remains now only that we speak of the animals and provisions which we met with at this place. Former writers have related, that this island abounded with vast numbers of goats, and their accounts are not to be questioned, this place being the usual haunt of the buccaneers and privateers, who formerly frequented those seas. And there are two instances; one of a Musquito Indian, and the other of Alexander Selkirk, a Scotchman, who were left by their respective ships, and lived alone upon this island for some years, and consequently were no strangers to its produce¹. Selkirk, who was the last, after a stay of between four and five years, was taken off the place by the Duke and Duchess privateers of Bristol, as may be seen at large in the journal of their voyage: his manner of life, during his solitude, was in most particulars very remarkable; but there is one circumstance he relates, which was so strangely verified by our own observation, that I cannot help reciting it. He tells us, among other things, as he often caught more goats than he wanted, he sometimes marked their ears and let them go. This was about thirty-two years before our arrival at the island. Now it happened, that the first goat that was killed by our people at their landing had his ears slit, whence we concluded that he had doubtless been formerly under the power of Selkirk. This was indeed an animal of a most venerable aspect, dignified with an exceeding majestic beard, and with many other symptoms of antiquity. During our stay on the island, we met with others marked in the same manner, all the males being distinguished by an exuberance of beard, and every other characteristic of extreme age.

But the great numbers of goats, which former writers described to have been found upon this island, are at present very much diminished: for the Spaniards being informed of the advantages which the buccaneers and privateers drew from the provisions which goat's-flesh here furnished them with, they have endeavoured to extirpate the breed, thereby to deprive their enemies of this relief. For this purpose, they have put on shore great numbers of large dogs, which have increased apace, and have destroyed all the goats in the accessible part of the country; so that there now remain only a few amongst the crags and precipices, where the dogs cannot follow them. These are divided into separate herds of twenty or thirty each, which inhabit distinct fastnesses, and never mingle with each other: by this means we found it extremely difficult to kill them; and yet we were so desirous of their flesh, which we all agreed much resembled venison, that we got knowledge, I believe, of all their herds, and it was conceived, by comparing their numbers together, that they scarcely exceeded two hundred upon the whole island. I remember we had once an opportunity of observing a remarkable dispute between a herd of these animals and a number of dogs; for going in our boat into the eastern bay, we saw some dogs running very eagerly upon the foot, and being willing to discover what game they were after, we lay upon our oars some time to view them, and at last we saw them take to a hill, and looking a little further, we observed upon the ridge of it a herd of goats, which seemed drawn up for their reception; there was a very narrow path which skirted on each side by precipices, on which the master of the herd posted himself fronting the enemy, th

¹ It was from the circumstance of Alexander Selkirk's sojourn on this beautiful island, that De Foe produced his popular and interesting narrative of Robinson Crusoe

rest of the goats being all behind him, where the ground was more open: as this spot was inaccessible by any other path, excepting where this champion had placed himself, the dogs, though they ran up-hill with great alacrity, yet when they came within about twenty yards of him, durst not encounter him, (for he would infallibly have driven them down the precipice) but gave over the chase, and quietly laid themselves down, panting at a great rate.

The dogs, who, as I have mentioned, are masters of all the accessible parts of the island, are of various kinds, but some of them very large, and are multiplied to a prodigious degree. They sometimes came down to our habitations at night, and stole our provision; and once or twice they set upon single persons, but assistance being at hand, they were driven off without doing any mischief. As at present it is rare for goats to fall in their way, we conceived that they lived principally upon young seals; and indeed some of our people had the curiosity to kill dogs sometimes and dress them, and they seemed to agree that they had a fishy taste.

Goat's-flesh, as I have mentioned, being scarce, we rarely being able to kill above one a day, and our people growing tired of fish, (which, as I shall hereafter observe, abounds at this place) they at last condescended to eat seals, which by degrees they came to relish, and called it lamb. The seal, numbers of which haunt this island, hath been so often described by former writers, that it is unnecessary to say any thing particular about them in this place. But there is another amphibious creature to be met with here, called a sea-lion, that bears some resemblance to a seal, though it is much larger. This too we ate, under the denomination of beef; and as it is so extraordinary an animal, I conceive, it well merits a particular annotation. They are in size, when arrived at their full growth, from twelve to twenty feet in length, and from eight to fifteen in circumference: they are extremely fat, so that after having cut through the skin, which is about an inch in thickness, there is at least a foot of fat before you can come at either lean or bones; and we experienced, more than once, that the fat of some of the largest afforded us a butt of oil. They are likewise very full of blood, for if they are deeply wounded in a dozen places, there will instantly gush out as many fountains of blood, spouting to a considerable distance; and to try what quantity of blood they contained, we shot one first, and then cut its throat, and measuring the blood that came from him, we found, that besides what remained in the vessels, which to be sure was considerable, we got at least two hogsheads. Their skins are covered with short hair of a light dun colour, but their tails, and their fins, which serve them for feet on shore, are almost black; their fins or feet are divided at the ends like fingers, the web which joins them not reaching to the extremities, and each of these extremities is furnished with a nail. They have a distant resemblance to an overgrown seal, though in some particulars there is a manifest difference, especially in the males, who have a large snout or trunk hanging down five or six inches below the end of the upper jaw; this particular the females have not, and this renders the countenance of the male and female easy to be distinguished from each other, and besides, the males are of a much larger size. One of them was the master of the flock, and from his driving off the other males, and keeping a great number of females to himself, he was by the seamen ludicrously styled the Bashaw. These animals divide their time equally between the land and sea, continuing at sea all the summer, and coming on shore at the setting in of the winter, where they reside during that whole season. In this interval they engender and bring forth their young, and have generally two at a birth; these they suckle with their milk, they being at first about the size of a full-grown seal. During the time of these animals' continuance on shore, they feed on the grass and verdure which grows near the bank of the fresh-water streams; and, when not employed in feeding, sleep in herds in the most miry places they can find out. As they seem to be of a very lethargic disposition, and not easily awakened, each herd was observed to place some of their males at a distance in the nature of sentinels, who never failed to alarm them, whenever our men attempted to molest, or even to approach them; and they were very capable of alarming, even at a considerable distance, for the noise they make is very loud and of different kinds, sometimes grunting like hogs, and at other times snorting like horses in full vigour. They often, especially the males, have furious battles with each other, principally about their females; and we were one day extremely surprised by the sight of two animals, which at first appeared different from all we had ever observed; but, on a nearer approach, they proved to be two sea-lions, who had been goring each other with their teeth, and were covered over with blood: and the Bashaw before-mentioned, who generally lay surrounded with a seraglio of females, which no other male dared to approach, had not acquired that envied preeminence without many bloody contests, of which the marks still remained in the numerous scars which were visible in every part of his body. We killed many of them for food, particularly for their hearts and tongues, which we esteemed exceeding good eating, and preferable even to those of bullocks: and in general there was no difficulty in killing them, for they were incapable either of escaping or resisting, their motion being the most unwieldy that can be conceived, their blubber, all the time they are moving, being agitated in large waves under their skins. However, a sailor one day being carelessly employed in skinning a young sea-lion, the female, from whence he had taken it, came upon him unperceived, and getting his head in her mouth, she with her teeth scored his skull in notches in many places, and thereby wounded him so desperately, that though all possible care was taken of him he died in a few days.

These are the principal animals which we found upon the island: for we saw but few birds, and those chiefly hawks, blackbirds, owls, and humming-birds. We saw not the pardela, which burrows in the ground, and which former writers have mentioned to be found here; but as we met with their holes, we supposed that the dogs had destroyed them, as they have almost done the cats, which were very numerous in Selkirk's time, but we saw not above one or two during our whole stay. However, the rats still keep their ground, and continue here in great numbers, and were very troublesome to us, by infesting our tents nightly.

But that which furnished us with the most delicious repasts at this island, remains still to be described. This was the fish, with which the whole bay was most plentifully stored, and with the greatest variety: for we found here cod of a prodigious size; and by the report of some of our crew, who had been formerly employed in the Newfoundland fishery, not in less plenty than is to be met with on the banks of that island. We caught also cavallies, gropers, large breams, maids, silver-fish, congers of a peculiar kind, and above all, a black fish which we most esteemed, called by some a chimney-sweeper, in shape resembling a carp. Indeed the beach is everywhere so full of rocks and loose stones, that there is no possibility of hauling the seine; but with hooks and lines we caught what numbers we pleased, so that a boat with two or three lines would return loaded with fish in about two or three hours' time. The only interruption we ever met with, arose from great quantities of dog-fish and large sharks, which sometimes attended our boats and prevented our sport. Besides the fish we have already mentioned, we found here one delicacy in greater perfection, both as to size, flavour and quantity, than is perhaps to be met with in any other part of the world: this was sea craw-fish; they generally weighed eight or nine pounds apiece, were of a most excellent taste, and lay in such abundance near the water's edge, that the boat-hooks often struck into them, in putting the boat to and from the shore.

These are the most material articles relating to the accommodations, soil, vegetables, animals, and other productions of the island of Juan Fernandes; by which it must appear how properly that place was adapted for recovering us from the deplorable situation to which our tedious and unfortunate navigation round Cape Horn had reduced us. And having thus given the reader some idea of the site and circumstances of this place, which was to be our residence for three months, I shall now proceed, in the next chapter, to relate all that occurred to us in that interval, resuming my narration from the 18th day of June, being the day in which the Tryal sloop, having by a squall been driven out to sea three days before, came again to her moorings, the day in which we finished the sending our sick on shore, and about eight days after our first anchoring at this island.

CHAPTER II.

The arrival of the Gloucester and the Anna pink at the island of Juan Fernandes, and the transactions at that place during this interval.

THE arrival of the Tryal sloop at this island, so soon after we came there ourselves, gave us great hopes of being speedily joined by the rest of the squadron; and we were for some days continually looking out, in expectation of their coming in sight. But near a fortnight being elapsed, without any of them having appeared, we began to despair of ever meeting them again; as we knew that had our ship continued so much longer at sea, we should every man of us have perished, and the vessel, occupied by dead bodies only, would have been left to the caprice of the winds and waves: and this we had great reason to fear was the fate of our consorts, as each hour added to the probability of these desponding suggestions.

But on the 21st of June, some of our people, from an eminence on shore, discerned a ship to leeward, with her courses even with the horizon: and they, at the same time, particularly observed, that she had no sail abroad except her courses and her main-topsail. This circumstance made them conclude that it was one of our squadron, which had probably suffered in her sails and rigging as severely as we had done: but they were prevented from forming more definite conjectures about her; for, after viewing her for a short time, the weather grew thick and hazy, and they lost sight of her. On this report, and no ship appearing for some days, we were all under the greatest concern, suspecting that her people were in the utmost distress for want of water, and so diminished and weakened by sickness, as not to be able to ply up to windward; so that we feared that, after having been in sight of the island, her whole crew would notwithstanding perish at sea. However, on the 26th, towards noon, we discerned a sail in the north-east quarter, which we conceived to be the very same ship that had been seen before, and our conjectures proved true; and about one o'clock she approached so near, that we could distinguish her to be the Gloucester. As we had no doubt of her being in great distress, the commodore immediately ordered his boat to her assistance, laden with fresh water, fish, and vegetables, which was a very seasonable relief to them; for our apprehensions of their calamities appeared to be but too well grounded, as perhaps there never was a crew in a more distressed situation. They had already thrown overboard two thirds of their complement, and of those that remained alive, scarcely any were capable of doing duty, except the officers and their servants. They had been a considerable time at the small allowance of a pint of fresh water to each man for twenty-four hours, and yet they had so little left, that, had it not been for the supply we sent them, they must soon have died of thirst. The ship plied in within three miles of the bay; but, the winds and currents being contrary, she could not reach the road. However, she continued in the offing the next day, but had no chance of coming to an anchor, unless the wind and currents shifted; and therefore the commodore repeated his assistance, sending to her the Tryal's boat manned with the Centurion's people, and a further supply of water and other refreshments. Captain Mitchel, the captain of the Gloucester, was under a necessity of detaining both this boat and that sent the preceding day; for without the help of their crews he had no longer strength enough to navigate the ship. In this tantalising situation the Gloucester continued for near a fortnight, without being able to fetch the road, though frequently attempting it, and at some times bidding very fair for it. On the 9th of July, we observed her stretching away to the eastward at a considerable distance, which we supposed was with a design to get to the southward of the island; but as we soon lost sight of her, and she did not appear for near a week, we were prodigiously concerned, knowing that she must be again in extreme distress for want of water. After great impatience about her, we discovered her again on the 16th, endeavouring to come round the eastern point of the island; but the wind, still blowing directly from the bay, prevented her getting nearer than within four leagues of the land. On this, Captain Mitchel made signals of distress, and our long-boat was sent to him with a store of water, and plenty of fish, and other refreshments. And the long-boat being not to be spared, the coxswain had positive orders from the commodore to return again immediately; but the weather proving stormy the next day, and the boat not appearing, we much feared she was lost, which would have proved an irretrievable misfortune to us all: but, the third day after, we were relieved from this anxiety, by the joyful sight of the long-boat's sails upon the water; and we sent the cutter immediately to her assistance, who towed her alongside in a few hours. The crew of our long-boat had taken in six of the Gloucester's sick men to bring them on shore, two of which had died in the boat. And now we learnt that the Gloucester was in a most dreadful condition, having scarcely a man in health on board, except those they received from us; and, numbers of their sick dying daily, we found that, had it not been for the last supply sent by our long-boat, both the healthy and diseased must have all perished together for want of water. And these calamities were the more terrifying, as they appeared to be without remedy: for the Gloucester had already spent a month in her endeavours to fetch the bay, and she was now no farther advanced than at the first moment she made the island; on the contrary, the people on board her and worn out all their hopes of ever succeeding in it, by the many experiments they had made of its difficulty. Indeed, the same day her situation grew more desperate than ever, for after she had received our last supply of refreshments, we again lost sight of her; so that we in general despaired of her ever coming to an anchor.

Thus was this unhappy vessel bandied about within a few leagues of her intended harbour, whilst the neighbourhood of that place and of those circumstances, which could alone put an end to the calamities they laboured under, served only to aggravate their distress by torturing them with a view of the relief it was not in their power to reach. But she was at last delivered from this dreadful situation, at a time when we least expected it; for after having lost sight of her for several days, we were pleasingly surprised, on the morning of the 23rd of July, to see her open the N. W. point of the bay with a flowing sail; when we immediately despatched what boats we had to her assistance, and in an hour's time from our first perceiving her, she anchored safe within us in the bay. And now we were more particularly convinced of the importance of the assistance and refreshments we so often sent them, and how impossible it would have been for a man of them to have survived, had we given less attention to their wants; for notwithstanding the water, the greens, and fresh provisions which we supplied them with, and the hands we sent them to navigate the ship, by which the fatigue of their own people was diminished, their sick relieved, and the mortality abated; notwithstanding this indulgent care of the commodore, they yet buried three-fourths of their crew, and a very small proportion of the remainder were capable of assisting in the duty of the ship. On their coming to an anchor, our first care was to assist them in mooring, and our next to send the sick on shore: these were now reduced by deaths to less than fourscore, of which we expected to lose the greatest part; but whether it was, that those farthest advanced in the distemper were all dead, or that the greens and fresh provisions we had sent on board had prepared those which remained for a more speedy recovery, it happened, contrary to our expectations, that their sick were in general relieved and restored to their strength, in a much shorter time than our own had been when we first came to the island, and very few of them died on shore.

I have thus given an account of the principal events relating to the arrival of the Gloucester, in one continued narration: I shall only add, that we never were joined by any other of our ships, except our victualler, the Anna pink, who came in about the middle of August, and whose history I shall more particularly relate hereafter. And I shall now return to the account of our own transactions on board and on shore, during the interval of the Gloucester's frequent and ineffectual attempts to reach the island.

Our next employment, after sending our sick on shore from the Centurion, was cleansing our ship and filling our water. The first of these measures was indispensably necessary to our future health, as the numbers of sick, and the unavoidable negligence arising from our deplorable situation at sea, had rendered the decks most intolerably loathsome. And the filling our water was a caution that appeared not less essential to our future security, as we had reason to apprehend that accidents might oblige us to quit the island at a very short warning; for some appearances, which we had discovered on shore upon our first landing, gave us grounds to believe, that there were Spanish cruisers in these seas, which had left the island but a short time before our arrival, and might possibly return there again, either for a recruit of water, or in search of us: for as we could not doubt, but that the sole business they had at sea was to intercept us, so we knew that this island was the likeliest place, in their own opinion, to meet with us. The circumstances, which gave rise to these reflections (in part of which we were not mistaken, as shall be observed more at large hereafter), were our finding on shore several pieces of earthen jars, made use of in those seas for water and other liquids, which appeared to be fresh broken: we saw, too, many heaps of ashes, and near them fish-bones and pieces of fish, besides whole fish scattered here and there, which plainly appeared to have been but a short time out of the water, as they were but just beginning to decay. These appearances were certain indications that there had been ships at this place but a short time before we came there; and as all Spanish merchantmen are instructed to avoid the island, on account of its being the common rendezvous of their enemies, we concluded those who had touched here to be ships of force; and not knowing that Pizarro was returned to Buenos Ayres, and ignorant what strength might have been fitted out at Callao, we were under some

IN A FOREIGN LAND.

p. 40.

concern for our safety, being in so wretched and enfeebled a condition, that notwithstanding the rank of our ship, and the sixty guns she carried on board, which would only have aggravated our dishonour, there was scarcely a privateer sent to sea, that was not an over-match for us. However, our fears on this head proved imaginary, and we were not exposed to the disgrace, which might have been expected to have befallen us, had we been necessitated (as we must have been, had the enemy appeared) to fight our sixty-gun ship with no more than thirty hands.

Whilst the cleaning our ship and the filling our water went on, we set up a large copper-oven on shore near the sick tents, in which we baked bread every day for the ship's company, being extremely desirous of recovering our sick as soon as possible, and conceiving that new bread, added to their greens and fresh fish, might prove a powerful article in their relief. Indeed we had all imaginable reason to endeavour at the augmenting our present strength, as every little accident, which to a full crew would be insignificant, was extremely alarming in our present helpless situation: of this, we had a troublesome instance on the 30th of June; for at five in the morning, we were astonished by a violent gust of wind directly off shore, which instantly parted our small bower cable about ten fathom from the ring of the anchor: the ship at once swung off to the best bower, which happily stood the violence of the jerk, and brought us up with two cables an end in eighty fathom. At this time we had not above a dozen seamen in the ship, and we were apprehensive, if the squall continued, that we should be driven to sea in this wretched condition. However, we sent the boat on shore, to bring off all that were capable of acting; and the wind, soon abating of its fury, gave us an opportunity of receiving the boat back again with a reinforcement. With this additional strength we immediately went to work, to heave in what remained of the cable, which we suspected had received some damage from the foulness of the ground before it parted; and agreeable to our conjecture, we found that seven fathom and a half of the outer end had been rubbed, and rendered unserviceable. In the afternoon, we bent the cable to the spare anchor, and got it over the ship's side; and the next morning, July 1, being favoured with the wind in gentle breezes, we warped the ship in again, and let go the anchor in forty-one fathom; the easternmost point now bearing from us E. ¼ S.; the westernmost N.W. by W.; and the bay as before, S.S.W.; a situation, in which we remained secure for the future. But we were much concerned for the loss of our anchor, and swept frequently for it, in hopes to have recovered it; but the buoy having sunk at the very instant that the cable parted, we were never able to find it.

And now as we advanced in July, some of our men being tolerably recovered, the strongest of them were employed in cutting down trees, and splitting them into billets; while others, who were too weak for this employ, undertook to carry the billets by one at a time to the water-side: this they performed, some of them with the help of crutches, and others supported by a single stick. We next sent the forge on shore, and employed our smiths, who were but just capable of working, in mending our chain-plates, and our other broken and decayed iron-work. We began too the repairs of our rigging; but as we had not a sufficient quantity of junk to make spun-yarn, we deferred the general over-haul, in hopes of the daily arrival of the Gloucester, who we knew had a great quantity of junk on board. However, that we might make as great despatch as possible in our refitting, we set up a large tent on the beach for the sail-makers; and they were immediately employed in repairing our old sails, and making us new ones.

These occupations, with our cleansing and watering the ship (which was by this time pretty well completed), the attendance on our sick, and the frequent relief sent to the Gloucester, were the principal transactions of our infirm crew, till the arrival of the Gloucester at an anchor in the bay. And then Captain Mitchel waiting on the commodore, informed him, that he had been forced by the winds, in his last absence, as far as the small island called Masa-Fuero, lying about twenty-two leagues to the westward of Juan Fernandes; and that he endeavoured to send his boat on shore at this place for water, of which he could observe several streams, but the wind blew so strong upon the shore, and occasioned such a surf, that it was impossible for the boat to land; though the attempt was not altogether useless, as they returned with a boat-load of fish. This island had been represented by former navigators as a barren rock; but Captain Mitchel assured the commodore, that it was almost everywhere covered with trees and verdure, and was near four miles in length; and added, that it appeared to him far from impossible but some small bay might be found on it, which might afford sufficient shelter for any ship desirous of refreshing there.

As four ships of our squadron were missing, this description of the Island of Masa-Fuero gave rise to a conjecture, that some of them might possibly have fallen in with that island, and have mistaken it for the true place of our rendezvous; and this suspicion was the more plausible, as we had no draught of either island that could be relied on. In consequence of this reasoning, Mr. Anson determined to send the Tryal sloop thither, as soon as she could be fitted for the sea, in order to examine all its bays and creeks, that we might be satisfied whether any of our missing ships were there or not. For this purpose, some of our best hands were sent on board the Tryal the next morning, to overhaul and fix her rigging; and our long-boat was employed in completing her water; and whatever stores and necessaries she wanted were immediately supplied, either from the Centurion or the Gloucester. But it was the 4th of August before the Tryal was in readiness to sail, when having weighed, it soon after fell calm, and the tide set her very near the eastern shore: Captain Saunders hung out lights, and fired several guns to acquaint us with his danger: upon which all the boats were sent to his relief, who towed the sloop into the bay; where she anchored until the next morning, and then weighing again, proceeded on her cruise with a fair breeze.

And now, after the Gloucester's arrival, we were employed in earnest in examining and repairing our rigging; but in the stripping our foremast, we were alarmed by discovering it was sprung just above the partners of the upper deck. The spring was two inches in depth, and twelve in circumference; but the carpenters inspecting it, gave it as their opinion, that fishing it with two leaves of an anchor-stock would render it as secure as ever. But our greatest difficulty in refitting was the want of cordage and canvas; for though we had taken to sea much greater quantities of both than had ever been done before, yet the continued bad weather we met with had occasioned such a consumption of these stores, that we were driven to great straits: for after working up all our junk and old shrouds, to make twice-laid cordage, we were at last obliged to unlay a cable to work into running rigging. And with all the canvas and remnants of old sails that could be mustered, we could only make up one complete suit.

Towards the middle of August, our men being indifferently recovered, they were permitted to quit their sick tents, and to build separate huts for themselves, as it was imagined that, by living apart, they would be much cleanlier, and consequently likely to recover their strength the sooner; but at the same time particular orders were given, that on the firing of a gun from the ship, they should instantly repair to the water-side. Their employment on shore was now either the procuring of refreshments, the cutting of wood, or the making of oil from the blubber of the sea-lions. This oil served us for several uses, as burning in lamps, or mixing with pitch to pay the ships' sides, or, when mixed with wood-ashes, to supply the use of tallow, of which we had none left, to give the ship boot-hose tops. Some of the men too were occupied in salting of cod; for there being two Newfoundland fishermen in the Centurion, the commodore made use of them in laying in a considerable quantity of salted cod for a sea-store; but very little of it was made use of, as it was afterwards thought to be as productive of the scurvy as any other kind of salt provisions.

I have before mentioned, that we had a copper-oven on shore to bake bread for the sick; but it happened that the greatest part of the flour, for the use of the squadron, was embarked on board our victualler the Anna pink: and I should have mentioned, that the Tryal sloop, at her arrival, had informed us, that on the 9th of May she had fallen in with our victualler, not far distant from the continent of Chili; and had kept company with her for four days, when they were parted in a hard gale of wind. This gave us some room to hope that she was safe, and that she might soon join us; but all June and July being past without any news of her, we suspected she was lost; and at the end of July the commodore ordered all the ships to a short allowance of bread. And it was not in our bread only, that we feared a deficiency; for since our arrival at this island, we discovered that our former purser had neglected to take on board large quantities of several kinds of provisions, which the commodore had expressly ordered him to receive; so that the supposed loss of our victualler was, on all accounts, a mortifying consideration. However, on Sunday, the 16th of August, about noon, we espied a sail in the northern quarter, and a gun was immediately fired from the Centurion, to call off the people from shore; who readily obeyed the summons, and repaired to the beach, where the boats waited to carry them on board. And now being prepared for the reception of this ship in view, whether friend or enemy, we had various speculations about her; at first, many imagined it to be the Tryal sloop returned from her cruise; but as she drew nearer this opinion was confuted, by observing she was a vessel with three masts; and then other conjectures were eagerly canvassed, some judging it to be the Severn, others the Pearl, and several affirming that it did not belong to our squadron: but about three in the afternoon our disputes were ended, by a unanimous persuasion that it was our victualler the Anna pink. This ship, though, like the Gloucester, she had fallen in to the northward of the island, had yet the good fortune to come to an anchor in the bay, at five in the afternoon. Her arrival gave us all the sincerest joy; for each ship's company was now restored to their full allowance of bread, and we were now freed from the apprehensions of our provisions falling short, before we could reach some amicable port; a calamity, which in these seas is of all others the most irretrievable. This was the last ship that joined us; and the dangers she encountered, and the good fortune which she afterwards met with, being matters worthy of a separate narration, I shall refer them, together with a short account of the other ships of the squadron, to the ensuing chapter.

CHAPTER III.

A short narrative of what befell the Anna pink before she joined us, with an account of the loss of the Wager, and of the putting back of the Severn and Pearl, the two remaining ships of the squadron.

ON the first appearance of the Anna pink, it seemed wonderful to us how the crew of a vessel, which came to this rendezvous two months after us, should be capable of working their ship in the manner they did, with so little appearance of debility and distress: but this difficulty was soon solved when she came to an anchor; for we then found that they had been in harbour since the middle of May, which was near a month before we arrived at Juan Fernandes: so that their sufferings (the risk they had run of shipwreck only excepted) were greatly short of what had been undergone by the rest of the squadron. It seems, on the 16th of May, they fell in with the land, which was then but four leagues distant, in the latitude of 45° 15' south. On the first sight of it, they wore ship and stood to the southward, but their fore-topsail splitting, and the wind being W.S.W., they drove towards the shore; and the captain at last, either unable to clear the land, or as others say, resolved to keep the sea no longer, steered for the coast, with a view of discovering some shelter amongst the many islands which then appeared in sight: and about four hours after the first view of the land, the pink had the fortune to come to an anchor, to the eastward of the island of Inchin; but as they did not run sufficiently near to the east shore of that island, and had not hands to veer away the cable briskly, they were soon driven to the eastward, deepening their water from twenty-five fathom to thirty-five, and still continuing to drive, they, the next day, the 17th of May, let go their sheet-anchor; which though it brought them up for a short time, yet, on the 18th, they drove again, till they came into sixty-five fathom water, and were now within a mile of the land, and expected to be forced on shore every moment, in a place where the coast was very high and steep too, that there was not the least prospect of saving the ship or cargo: and their boats being very leaky, and there being no appearance of a landing-place, the whole crew, consisting of sixteen men and boys, gave themselves over for lost, for they apprehended, that if any of them by some extraordinary chance should get on shore, they would, in all probability, be massacred by the savages on the coast: for those, knowing no other Europeans but Spaniards, it might be expected they would treat all strangers with the same cruelty which they had so often and so signally exerted against their Spanish neighbours. Under these terrifying circumstances, the pink drove nearer and nearer to the rocks which formed the shore: but at last, when the crew expected each instant to strike, they perceived a small opening in the land, which raised their hopes: and immediately cutting away their two anchors, they steered for it, and found it to be a small channel betwixt an island and the main, which led them into a most excellent harbour, which, for its security against all winds and swells, and the smoothness of its waters, may perhaps compare with any in the known world. And this place being scarcely two miles distant from the spot where they deemed their destruction inevitable, the horrors of shipwreck and of immediate death, which had so long and so strongly possessed them, vanished almost instantaneously, and gave place to the more joyous ideas of security, repose, and refreshment.

In this harbour, discovered in this almost miraculous manner, the pink came to an anchor in twenty-five fathom water, with only a hawser, and a small anchor of about three hundred-weight: and here she continued for near two months refreshing her people, who were many of them ill of the scurvy, but were soon restored to perfect health by the fresh provisions, of which they procured good store, and the excellent water with which the adjacent shore abounded. But as this place may prove of the greatest importance to future navigators who may be forced upon this coast by the westerly winds, which are almost perpetual in that part of the world; I shall, before I enter into any farther particulars of the adventures of the pink, give the best account I could collect of this port, its situation, conveniences and productions.

Its latitude, which is indeed an important point, is not well ascertained, the pink having no observation either the day before she came here, or within a day of her leaving it: but it is supposed that it is not very distant from 45° 30′ south, and the large extent of the bay before the harbour renders this uncertainty the less material. The island of Inchin lying before the bay is supposed to be one of the islands of Chonos, which are mentioned in the Spanish accounts, as spreading all along that coast; and are said by them to be inhabited by a barbarous people, famous for their hatred of the Spaniards, and for their cruelties to such of that nation as have fallen into their hands: and it is possible too that the land, near which the harbour itself lies, may be another of those islands, and that the continent may be considerably farther to the eastward. There are two coves where ships may conveniently heave down, the water being constantly smooth: and there are several fine runs of excellent fresh water, which fall into the harbour, and some of them so luckily situated, that the casks may be filled in the long-boat with a hose: the most remarkable of these runs is a fresh-water river, and here the pink's people got some few mullets of an excellent flavour; and they were persuaded that, in a proper season (it being winter when they were there) it abounded with fish. The principal refreshments they met with in this port were greens, as wild celery, nettle-tops, &c. (which after so long a continuance at sea they devoured with great eagerness); shell-fish, as cockles and muscles of an extraordinary size, and extremely delicious; and good store of geese, shags, and penguins. The climate, though it was the depth of winter, was not remarkably rigorous; nor the trees, or the face of the country destitute of verdure; and doubtless in the summer many other species of fresh provision, besides these here enumerated, might be found there. And notwithstanding the tales of the Spanish historians, in relation to the violence and barbarity of the inhabitants, it doth not appear that their numbers are sufficient to give the least jealousy to any ship of ordinary force, or that their disposition is by any means so mischievous or merciless as hath hitherto been represented: and besides all these advantages, it is so far removed from the Spanish frontier, and so little known to the Spaniards themselves, that there is reason to suppose, that with proper precautions a ship might continue here undiscovered for a long time. It is also a place of great defence; for by possessing the island that closes up the harbour, and which is accessible in very few places, a small force might defend this port against all the strength the Spaniards could muster in that part of the world; for this island towards the harbour is steep too, and has six fathom water close to the shore, so that the pink anchored within forty yards of it: whence it is obvious how impossible it would prove, either to board or to cut out any vessel protected by a force posted on shore within pistol-shot, and where those who were thus posted could not themselves be attacked. All these circumstances seem to render this place worthy of a more accurate examination; and it is to be hoped that the important uses which this rude account of it seems to suggest, may hereafter recommend it to the consideration of the public, and to the attention of those who are more immediately entrusted with the conduct of our naval affairs.

After this description of the place where the pink lay for two months, it may be expected that I should relate the discoveries made by the crew on the adjacent coast, and the principal incidents during their stay there: but here I must observe, that, being only a few in number, they did not dare to detach any of their people on distant discoveries; for they were perpetually terrified with the apprehension that they should be attacked either by the Spaniards or the Indians; so that their excursions were generally confined to that tract of land which surrounded the port, and where they were never out of view of the ship. But even had they at first known how little foundation there was for these fears, yet the country in the neighbourhood was so grown up with wood, and traversed with mountains, that it appeared impracticable to penetrate it: so that no account of the inland parts could be expected from them. Indeed they were able to disprove the relations given by Spanish writers, who had represented this coast as inhabited by a fierce and powerful people: for they were certain that no such inhabitants were there to be found, at least during the winter season; since all the time they continued there, they saw no more than one Indian family, which came into the harbour in a periagua, about a month after the arrival of the pink, and consisted of an Indian near forty years old, his wife, and two children, one three years of age, and the other still at the breast. They seemed to have with them all their property, which was a dog and a cat, a fishing-net, a hatchet, a knife, a cradle, some bark of trees intended for the covering of a hut, a reel, some worsted, a flint and steel, and a few roots of a yellow hue and a very disagreeable taste, which served them for bread. The master of the pink, as soon as he perceived them, sent his yawl, who brought them on board; and fearing lest they might discover him if they were permitted to go away, he took, as he conceived, proper precautions for securing them, but without any mixture of ill usage or violence: for in the day-time they were permitted to go where they pleased about the ship, but at night were locked up in the forecastle. As they were fed in the same manner with the rest of the crew, and were often indulged with brandy, which they seemed greatly to relish, it did not at first appear that they were much dissatisfied with their situation, especially as the master took the Indian on shore when he went a shooting (who always seemed extremely delighted when the master killed his game), and as all the crew treated them with great humanity: but it was soon perceived, that though the woman continued easy and cheerful, yet the man grew pensive and restless at his confinement. He seemed to be a person of good natural parts, and though not capable of conversing with the pink's people, otherwise than by signs, was yet very curious and inquisitive, and showed great dexterity in the manner of making himself understood. In particular, seeing so few people on board such a large ship, he let them know that he supposed they were once more numerous: and to represent to them what he imagined was become of their companions, he laid himself down on the deck, closing his eyes, and stretching himself out motionless, to imitate the appearance of a dead body. But the strongest proof of his sagacity was the manner of his getting away; for after being in custody on board the pink eight days, the scuttle of the forecastle, where he and his family were locked up every night, happened to be unnailed, and the following night being extremely dark and stormy, he contrived to convey his wife and children through the unnailed scuttle, and then over the ship's side into the yawl; and to prevent being pursued, he cut away the long-boat, and his own periagua which were towing astern, and immediately rowed ashore. All this he conducted with so much diligence and secrecy, that though there was a watch on the quarter-deck with loaded arms, yet he was not discovered by them till the noise of his oars in the water, after he had put off from the ship, gave them notice of his escape; and then it was too late either to prevent him or to pursue him; for, their boats being all adrift, it was a considerable time before they could contrive the means of getting on shore themselves to search for their boats. The Indian too by this effort, besides the recovery of his liberty, was in some sort revenged on those who had confined him, both by the perplexity they were involved in from the loss of their boats, and by the terror he threw them into at his departure; for on the first alarm of the watch, who cried out "The Indians!" the whole ship was in the utmost confusion, believing themselves to be boarded by a fleet of armed periaguas.

The resolution and sagacity with which the Indian behaved upon this occasion, had it been exerted on a more extensive object than the retrieving the freedom of a single family, might perhaps have immortalised the exploit, and have given him a rank amongst the illustrious names of antiquity. Indeed his late masters did so much justice to his merit, as to own that it was a most gallant enterprise, and that they were grieved they had ever been necessitated, by their attention to their own safety, to abridge the liberty of a person of whose prudence and courage they had now such a distinguished proof. And as it was supposed by some of them that he still continued in the woods in the neighbourhood of the port, where it was feared he might suffer for want of provisions, they easily prevailed upon the master to leave a quantity of such food as they thought would be most agreeable to him, in a particular part where they imagined he would be likely to find it: and there was reason to conjecture that this piece of humanity was not altogether useless to him; for, on visiting the place some time after, it was found that the provision was gone, and in a manner that made them conclude it had fallen into his hands.

But however, though many of them were satisfied that this Indian still continued near them; yet others would needs conclude that he was gone to the island of Chiloe, where they feared he would alarm the Spaniards, and would soon return with a force sufficient to surprise the pink: and on this occasion the master of the pink was prevailed on to omit firing the evening gun; for it must be remembered, (and there is a particular reason hereafter for attending to this circumstance,) that the master, from an ostentatious imitation of the practice of men-of-war, had hitherto fired a gun every evening at the setting of the watch. This he pretended was to awe the enemy, if there was any within hearing, and to convince them that the pink was always on her guard; but it being now represented to him that his great security was his concealment, and that the evening gun might possibly discover him, and serve to guide the enemy to him, he was prevailed on, as has been mentioned, to omit it for the future: and his crew being now well refreshed, and their wood and water sufficiently replenished, he, in a few days after the escape of the Indian, put to sea, and had a fortunate passage to the rendezvous at the island of Juan Fernandes, where he arrived on the 16th of August, as hath been already mentioned in the preceding chapter.

This vessel, the Anna pink, was, as I have observed, the last that joined the commodore at Juan Fernandes. The remaining ships of the squadron were the Severn, the Pearl, and the Wager store-ship: the Severn and Pearl parted company with the squadron off Cape Noir, and, as we afterwards learnt, put back to the Brazils: so that of all the ships which came into the South Seas, the Wager, Captain Cheap, was the only one that was missing. This ship had on board some field-pieces mounted for land service, together with some cohorn mortars, and several kinds of artillery, stores and tools, intended for the operations on shore: and therefore, as the enterprise on Baldivia had been resolved on for the first undertaking of the squadron, Captain Cheap was extremely solicitous that these materials, which were in his custody, might be ready before Baldivia; that if the squadron should possibly rendezvous there (as he knew not the condition they were then reduced to), no delay nor disappointment might be imputed to him.

But whilst the Wager, with these views, was making the best of her way to her first rendezvous off the island of Socoro, whence (as there was little probability of meeting any of the squadron there) she proposed to steer directly for Baldivia, she made the land on the fourteenth of May, about the latitude of 47° South; and, the captain exerting himself on this occasion, in order to get clear of it, he had the misfortune to fall down the after-ladder, and thereby dislocated his shoulder, which rendered him incapable of acting. This accident, together with the crazy condition of the ship, which was little better than a wreck, prevented her from getting off to sea, and entangled her more and more with the land, so that the next morning, at day-break, she struck on a sunken rock, and soon after bilged, and grounded between two small islands, at about a musket-shot from the shore.

In this situation the ship continued entire a long time, so that all the crew had it in their power to get safe on shore; but a general confusion taking place, numbers of them, instead of consulting their safety, or reflecting on their calamitous condition, fell to pillaging the ship, arming themselves with the first weapons that came to hand, and threatening to murder all who should oppose them. This frenzy was greatly heightened by the liquors they found on board, with which they got so extremely drunk, that some of them tumbling down between decks, were drowned, as the water flowed in, being incapable of getting up and retreating to other places where the water had not yet entered: and the captain, having done his utmost to get the whole crew on shore, was at last obliged to leave these mutineers behind him, and to follow his officers, and such as he had been able to prevail on; but he did not fail to send back the boats, to persuade those who remained, to have some regard to their preservation; though all his efforts were for some time without success. However, the weather next day proving stormy, and there being great danger of the ship's parting, they began to be alarmed with the fears of perishing, and were desirous of getting to land; but it seems their madness had not yet left them, for the boat not appearing to fetch them off so soon as they expected, they at last pointed a four-pounder, which was on the quarter-deck, against the hut where they knew the captain resided on shore, and fired two shot, which passed but just over it.

From this specimen of the behaviour of part of the crew, it will not be difficult to frame some conjecture of the disorder and anarchy which took place, when they at last got all on shore. For the men conceived that, by the loss of the ship, the authority of the officers was at an end; and, they being now on a desolate coast, where scarcely any other provisions could be got except what should be saved out of the wreck, this was another insurmountable source of discord: for as the working upon the wreck, and the securing the provisions, so that they might be preserved for future exigencies as much as possible, and the taking care that what was necessary for immediate subsistence might be sparingly and equally distributed, were matters not to be brought about but by discipline and subordination; the mutinous disposition of the people, stimulated by the impulses of immediate hunger, rendered every regulation made for this purpose ineffectual: so that there were continual concealments, frauds and thefts, which animated each man against his fellow, and produced infinite feuds and contests. And hence there was constantly kept on foot a perverse and malevolent turn of temper, which rendered them utterly ungovernable.[1]

But besides these heart-burnings occasioned by petulance and hunger, there was another important point, which set the greatest part of the people at variance with the captain. This was their differing with him in opinion, on the measures to be pursued in the present exigency: for the captain was determined, if possible, to fit up the boats in the best manner he could, and to proceed with them to the northward. For having with him above a hundred men in health, and having gotten some fire-arms and ammunition from the wreck, he did not doubt but they could master any Spanish vessel they should meet with in those seas: and he thought he could not fail of meeting with one in the neighbourhood of Chiloe or Baldivia, in which, when he had taken her, he intended to proceed to the rendezvous at Juan Fernandes; and he farther insisted, that should they meet with no prize by the way, yet the boats alone would easily carry them there. But this was a scheme that, however prudent, was no ways relished by the generality of his people; for, being quite jaded with the distresses and dangers they had already run through, they could not think of prosecuting an enterprise farther, which had hitherto proved so disastrous: and therefore the common resolution was to lengthen the long-boat, and with that and the rest of the boats to steer to the southward, to pass though the Straits of Magellan, and to range along the east side of South America, till they

[1] "It was in consequence of the mutinous and bad conduct of the shipwrecked seamen of the Wager, that Anson, in 1746, when he had the management of the Admiralty in the absence of the Duke of Bedford and Lord Sandwich, got an act passed (21 George 2nd.) for extending the discipline of the navy to the crews of his Majesty's ships, wrecked, lost, or taken, and continuing to them their wages upon certain conditions."—*Barrow's Life of Lord Anson.*

should arrive at Brazil, where they doubted not to be well received, and to procure a passage to Great Britain. This project was at first sight infinitely more hazardous and tedious than what was proposed by the captain; but as it had the air of returning home, and flattered them with the hopes of bringing them once more to their native country, this circumstance alone rendered them inattentive to all its inconveniences, and made them adhere to it with insurmountable obstinacy; so that the captain himself, though he never changed his opinion, was yet obliged to give way to the torrent, and in appearance to acquiesce in this resolution, whilst he endeavoured underhand to give it all the obstruction he could; particularly in the lengthening of the long-boat, which he contrived should be of such a size, that though it might serve to carry them to Juan Fernandes, would yet, he hoped, appear incapable of so long a navigation as that to the coast of Brazil.

But the captain, by his steady opposition at first to this favourite project, had much embittered the people against him; to which likewise the following unhappy accident greatly contributed. There was a midshipman whose name was Cozens, who had appeared the foremost in all the refractory proceedings of the crew. He had involved himself in brawls with most of the officers who had adhered to the captain's authority, and had even treated the captain himself with great abuse and insolence. As his turbulence and brutality grew every day more and more intolerable, it was not in the least doubted, but there were some violent measures in agitation, in which Cozens was engaged as the ringleader: for which reason the captain, and those about him, constantly kept themselves on their guard. But at last the purser, having, by the captain's order, stopped the allowance of a fellow who would not work; Cozens, though the man did not complain to him, intermeddled in the affair with great eagerness; and grossly insulting the purser, who was then delivering out provisions just by the captain's tent, and was himself sufficiently violent, the purser, enraged by his scurrility and perhaps piqued by former quarrels, cried out "a mutiny!" adding, "that the dog had pistols," and then himself fired a pistol at Cozens, which however missed him: but the captain, on this outery and the report of the pistol, rushed out of his tent; and, not doubting but it had been fired by Cozens as the commencement of a mutiny, he immediately shot him in the head without farther deliberation, and though he did not kill him on the spot, yet the wound proved mortal, and he died about fourteen days after.

This incident, however displeasing to the people, did yet, for a considerable time, awe them to their duty, and rendered them more submissive to the captain's authority: but at last, when towards the middle of October the long-boat was nearly completed, and they were preparing to put to sea, the additional provocation he gave them by covertly traversing their project of proceeding through the Straits of Magellan, and their fears that he might at length engage a party sufficient to overturn this favourite measure, made them resolve to make use of the death of Cozens as a reason for depriving him of his command, under pretence of carrying him a prisoner to England, to be tried for murder; and he was accordingly confined under a guard.

But they never intended to carry him with them, as they too well knew what they had to apprehend on their return to England, if their commander should be present to confront them: and therefore, when they were just ready to put to sea, they set him at liberty, leaving him, and the few who chose to take their fortunes with him, no other embarkation but the yawl, to which the barge was afterwards added, by the people on board her being prevailed on to return back.

When the ship was wrecked, there remained alive on board the Wager near a hundred and thirty persons; of these above thirty died during their stay upon the place, and near eighty went off in the long-boat and the cutter to the southward; so that there remained with the captain, after their departure, no more than nineteen persons, which however was as many as the barge and the yawl, the only embarkations left them, could well carry off. It was the 13th of October, five months after the shipwreck, that the long-boat, converted into a schooner, weighed, and stood to the southward, giving the captain, who, with Lieutenant Hamilton of the land forces, and the surgeon, was then on the beach, three cheers at their departure. It was the 29th of January following before they arrived at Rio Grande, on the coast of Brazil: and having, by various accidents, left about twenty of their people on shore at the different places they touched at, and a greater number having perished by hunger during the course of their navigation, there were no more than thirty of them left, when they arrived in that port. Indeed, the undertaking of itself was a most extraordinary one; for, not to mention the length of the run, the vessel was scarcely able to contain the number that first put to sea in her; and their stock of provisions (being only what they had saved out of the ship) was extremely slender, and the cutter, the only boat they had with them, soon broke away from the stern, and was staved to pieces; so that when their provision and their water failed them, they had frequently no means of getting on shore to search for a fresh supply.

When the long-boat and cutter were gone, the captain, and those who were left with him, proposed to pass to the northward in the barge and yawl: but the weather was so bad, and the difficulty of subsisting so great, that it was two months after the departure of the long-boat before he was able to put to sea. It seems the place, where the Wager was cast away, was not a part of the continent, as was first imagined, but an island at some distance from the main, which afforded no other sorts of provision but shell-fish, and a few herbs; and as the greatest part of what they had gotten from the ship was carried off in the long-boat, the captain and his people were often in great necessity, especially as they chose to preserve what little sea-provisions remained, for their store when they should go to the northward. During their residence at this island, which was by the seamen denominated Wager's Island, they had now and then a straggling canoe or two of Indians, which came and bartered their fish and other provisions with our people. This was indeed some little succour, and at another season might perhaps have been greater; for as there were several Indian huts on the shore, it was supposed that in some years, during the height of summer, many of these savages might resort thither to fish: and from what has been related in the account of the Anna pink, it should seem to be the general practice of those Indians to frequent this coast in the summer-time for the benefit of fishing, and to retire in the winter into a better climate, more to the northward.

And, on this mention of the Anna pink, I cannot but observe, how much it is to be lamented that the Wager's people had no knowledge of her being so near them on the coast; for as she was not above thirty leagues distant from them, and came into their neighbourhood about the same time the Wager was lost, and was a fine roomy ship, she could easily have taken them all on board, and have carried them to Juan Fernandes. Indeed, I suspect she was still nearer to them than what is here estimated; for several of the Wager's people, at different times, heard the report of a cannon, which I conceive could be no other than the evening-gun fired from the Anna pink, especially as what was heard at Wager's Island was about the same time of the day. But to return to Captain Cheap.

Upon the 14th of December, the captain and his people embarked in the barge and the yawl, in order to proceed to the northward, taking on board with them all the provisions they could amass from the wreck of the ship; but they had scarcely been an hour at sea, when the wind began to blow hard, and the sea ran so high, that they were obliged to throw the greatest part of their provisions overboard, to avoid immediate destruction. This was a terrible misfortune, in a part of the world where food is so difficult to be got: however, they still persisted in their design, putting on shore as often as they could to seek subsistence. But about a fortnight after, another dreadful accident befell them, for the yawl sunk at an anchor, and one of the men in her was drowned; and as the barge was incapable of carrying the whole company, they were now reduced to the hard necessity of leaving four marines behind them on that desolate shore. But they still kept on their course to the northward, struggling with their disasters, and greatly delayed by the perverseness of the winds, and the frequent interruptions which their search after food occasioned: till at last, about the end of January, having made three unsuccessful attempts to double a headland, which they supposed to be what the Spaniards called Cape Tres Montes, it was unanimously resolved to give over this expedition, the difficulties of which appeared insuperable, and to return again to Wager Island, where they got back about the middle of February, quite disheartened and dejected with their reiterated disappointments, and almost perishing with hunger and fatigue.

However, on their return they had the good luck to meet with several pieces of beef, which had been washed out of the ship, and were swimming in the sea. This was a most seasonable relief to them, after the hardships they had endured; and to complete their good fortune, there came, in a short time, two canoes of Indians, amongst which was a native of Chiloe, who spoke a little Spanish; and the surgeon, who was with Captain Cheap, understanding that language, he made a bargain with the Indian, that if he would carry the captain and his people to Chiloe in the barge, he should have her, and all that belonged to her, for his pains. Accordingly, on the 6th of March, the eleven persons to which the company was now reduced, embarked in the barge on this new expedition; but after having proceeded for a few days, the captain and four of his principal officers being on shore, the six, who together with an Indian remained in the barge, put off with her to sea, and did not return.

By this means there were left on shore, Captain Cheap, Mr. Hamilton lieutenant of marines, the Honourable Mr. Byron, and Mr. Campbel, midshipmen, and Mr. Elliot, the surgeon. One would have thought that their distresses had long before this time been incapable of augmentation; but they found, on reflection, that their present situation was much more dismaying than anything they had yet gone through, being left on a desolate coast, without any provision, or the means of procuring any; for their arms, ammunition, and every convenience they were masters of, except the tattered habits they had on, were all carried away in the barge.

But when they had sufficiently revolved in their own minds the various circumstances of this unexpected calamity, and were persuaded that they had no relief to hope for, they perceived a canoe at a distance, which proved to be that of the Indian, who had undertaken to carry them to Chiloe, he and his family being then on board it. He made no difficulty of coming to them; for it seems he had left Captain Cheap and his people a little before to go a fishing, and had in the mean time committed them to the care of the other Indian, whom the sailors had carried to sea in the barge. But when he came on shore, and found the barge gone and his companion missing, he was extremely concerned, and could with difficulty be persuaded that the other Indian was not murdered; but, being at last satisfied with the account that was given him, he still undertook to carry them to the Spanish settlements, and (as the Indians are well skilled in fishing and fowling) to procure them provisions by the way.

About the middle of March, Captain Cheap and the four who were left with him, set out for Chiloe, the Indian having procured a number of canoes, and gotten many of his neighbours together for that purpose. Soon after they embarked, Mr. Elliot the surgeon died, so that there now remained only four of the whole company. At last, after a very complicated passage by land and water, Captain Cheap, Mr. Byron, and Mr. Campbel, arrived in the beginning of June at the island of Chiloe, where they were received by the Spaniards with great humanity; but, on account of some quarrel among the Indians, Mr. Hamilton did not get thither till two months after. Thus, above a twelvemonth after the loss of the Wager, ended this fatiguing peregrination, which by a variety of misfortunes had diminished the company from twenty to no more than four; and those too brought so low, that had their distresses continued but a few days longer, in all probability none of them would have survived. For the captain himself was with difficulty recovered; and the rest were so reduced by the severity of the weather, their labour, and their want of all kinds of necessaries, that it was wonderful how they supported themselves so long. After some stay at Chiloe, the captain and the three who were with him were sent to Valparaiso, and thence to St. Jago, the capital of Chili, where they continued above a year: but on the advice of a cartel being settled between Great Britain and Spain, Captain Cheap, Mr. Byron, and Mr. Hamilton, were permitted to return to Europe on board a French ship. The other midshipman, Mr. Campbel, having changed his religion, whilst at St. Jago, chose to go back to Buenos Ayres with Pizarro and his officers, with whom he went afterwards to Spain on board the Asia ; and there having failed in his endeavours to procure a commission from the court of Spain, he returned to England, and attempted to get reinstated in the British navy ; and has since published a narration of his adventures, in which he complains of the injustice that had been done him, and strongly disavows his ever being in the Spanish service : but as the change of his religion, and his offering himself to the court of Spain (though not accepted) are matters which, he is conscious, are capable of being incontestably proved ; on these two heads he has been entirely silent. And now, after this account of the accidents which befell the Anna pink, and the catastrophe of the Wager, I shall again resume the thread of our own story.

CHAPTER IV.

Conclusion of our proceedings at Juan Fernandes, from the arrival of the Anna pink, to our final departure from thence.

About a week after the arrival of our victualler, the Tryal sloop, that had been sent to the island of Masa-Fuero, returned to an anchor at Juan Fernandes, after having been round that island, without meeting any part of our squadron. As, upon this occasion, the island of Masa-Fuero was more particularly examined than, I dare say, it had ever been before, or perhaps ever will be again ; and as the knowledge of it may, in certain circumstances, be of great consequence hereafter, I think it incumbent on me to insert the accounts given of this place, by the officers of the Tryal sloop.

The Spaniards have generally mentioned two islands, under the name of Juan Fernandes, styling them the greater and the less : the greater being that island where we anchored, and the less being the island we are now describing, which, because it is more distant from the continent, they have distinguished by the name of Masa-Fuero. The Tryal sloop found that it bore from the greater Juan Fernandes W. by S., and was about twenty-two leagues distant. It is much larger than has been generally reported ; for former writers have represented it as a barren rock, destitute of wood and water, and altogether inaccessible ; whereas our people found it was covered with trees, and that there were several fine falls of water pouring down its sides into the sea : they found too, that there was a place where a ship might come to an anchor on the north side of it, though indeed the anchorage is inconvenient ; for the bank extends but a little way, is steep too, and has very deep water upon it, so that you must come to an anchor very near the shore, and there lie exposed to all the winds but a southerly one : and besides the inconvenience of the anchorage, there is also a reef of rocks running off the eastern point of the island, about two miles in length ; but there is little danger to be feared from them, because they are always to be seen by the seas breaking over them. This place has at present one advantage beyond the island of Juan Fernandes ; for it abounds with goats, who, not being accustomed to be disturbed, were no ways shy or apprehensive of danger, till they had been frequently fired at. These animals reside here in great tranquillity, the Spaniards not having thought the island considerable enough to be frequented by their enemies, and therefore they have not been solicitous in destroying the provisions upon it ; so that no dogs have hitherto been set on shore there. And besides the goats, our people found there vast numbers of seals and sea-lions : and upon the whole, they seemed to imagine, that though it was not the most eligible place for a ship to refresh at, yet in case of necessity it might afford some sort of shelter, and prove of considerable use, especially to a single ship, who might apprehend meeting with a superior force at Fernandes.

The latter part of the month of August was spent in unloading the provisions from the Anna pink ; and here we had the mortification to find that great quantities of our provisions, as bread, rice, groats, &c. were decayed, and unfit for use. This was owing to the water the pink had made by her working and straining, in bad weather ; for hereby several of her casks had rotted, and her bags were soaked through. And now, as we had no farther occasion for her service, the commodore, pursuant to his orders from the board of Admiralty, sent notice to Mr. Gerard her master, that he discharged the Anna pink from the service of attending the squadron ; and gave him, at the same time, a certificate, specifying how long she had been employed. In consequence of this dismission, her master was at liberty, either to return directly to England, or to make the best of his way to any port, where he thought he could take in such a cargo as would answer the interest of his owners. But the master, being sensible of the bad condition of the ship and of her unfitness for any such voyage, wrote the next day an answer to the commodore's message, acquainting Mr. Anson that, from the great quantity of water the pink had made in her passage round Cape Horn, and since that, in the tempestuous weather he had met with on the coast of Chili, he had reason to apprehend that her bottom was very much decayed ; and that besides, her upper-works were rotten abaft ; that she was extremely leaky ; that her fore-beam was broke ; and that, in his opinion, it was impossible to proceed to sea with her, before she had been thoroughly refitted : he therefore requested the commodore, that the carpenters of the squadron might be directed to survey her, that their judgment of her condition might be known. In compliance with this desire, Mr. Anson immediately ordered the carpenters to take a careful and strict survey of the Anna pink, and to give him a faithful report under their hands of the condition in which they found her, directing them at the same time to proceed herein with such circumspection, that, if they should be hereafter called upon, they might be able to make oath of the veracity of their proceedings. Pursuant to these orders, the carpenters immediately set about the examination, and the next day made their report; which was, that the pink had no less than fourteen knees and twelve beams broken and decayed; that one breast-hook was broken, and another rotten; that her water-ways were open and decayed; that two standards were broken, as also several clamps, besides others which were rotten; that all her iron-work was greatly decayed; that her spirkiting and timbers were very rotten; and that, having ripped off part of her sheathing, they found her wales and outside planks extremely defective, and her bows and decks very leaky; and in consequence of these defects and decays, she certified, that in their opinion she could not depart from the island without great hazard, unless she was first of all thoroughly refitted.

The thorough refitting of the Anna pink, proposed by the carpenters, was in our present situation impossible to be complied with, as all the plank and iron in the squadron was insufficient for that purpose. And now the master finding his own sentiments confirmed by the opinion of all the carpenters, he offered a petition to the commodore in behalf of his owners, desiring that, since it appeared he was incapable of leaving the island, Mr. Anson would please to purchase the hull and furniture of the pink for the use of the squadron. Hereupon the commodore ordered an inventory to be taken of every particular belonging to the pink, with its just value: and as by this inventory it appeared that there were many stores which would be useful in refitting the other ships, and which were at present very scarce in the squadron, by reason of the great quantities that had been already expended, he agreed with Mr. Gerard to purchase the whole together for three hundred pounds. The pink being thus broken up, Mr. Gerard, with the hands belonging to the pink, were sent on board the Gloucester; as that ship had buried the greatest number of men in proportion to her complement. But afterwards, one or two of them were received on board the Centurion on their own petition, they being extremely averse to sailing in the same ship with their old master, on account of some particular ill usage they conceived they had suffered from him.

This transaction brought us down to the beginning of September, and our people by this time were so far recovered of the scurvy, that there was little danger of burying any more at present; and therefore I shall now sum up the total of our loss since our departure from England, the better to convey some idea of our past sufferings, and of our present strength. We had buried on board the Centurion, since our leaving St. Helena, two hundred and ninety-two, and had now remaining on board two hundred and fourteen. This will doubtless appear a most extraordinary mortality: but yet on board the Gloucester it had been much greater; for out of a much smaller crew than ours they had buried the same number, and had only eighty-two remaining alive. It might be expected that on board the Tryal, the slaughter would have been the most terrible, as her decks were almost constantly knee-deep in water; but it happened otherwise, for she escaped more favourably than the rest, since she only buried forty-two, and had now thirty-nine remaining alive. The havoc of this disease had fallen still severer on the invalids and marines than on the sailors; for on board the Centurion, out of fifty invalids and seventy-nine marines, there remained only four invalids including officers, and eleven marines; and on board the Gloucester every invalid perished; and out of forty-eight marines, only two escaped. From this account it appears, that the three ships together departed from England with nine hundred and sixty-one men on board, of whom six hundred and twenty-six were dead before this time; so that the whole of our remaining crews, which were now to be distributed amongst three ships, amounted to no more than three hundred and thirty-five men and boys; a number greatly insufficient for the manning the Centurion alone, and barely capable of navigating all the three, with the utmost exertion of their strength and vigour. This prodigious reduction of our men was still the more terrifying, as we were hitherto uncertain of the fate of Pizarro's squadron, and had reason to suppose, that some part of it at least had got round into these seas: indeed, we were satisfied, from our own experience, that they must have suffered greatly in their passage; but then every port in the South Seas was open to them, and the whole power of Chili and Peru would doubtless be united in refreshing and refitting them, and recruiting the numbers they had lost. Besides, we had some obscure knowledge of a force to be refitted out from Callao; and, however contemptible the ships and sailors of this part of the world may have been generally esteemed, it was scarcely possible for any thing, bearing the name of a ship of force, to be feebler or less considerable than ourselves. And had there been nothing to be apprehended from the naval power of the Spaniards in this part of the world, yet our enfeebled condition would nevertheless give us the greatest uneasiness, as we were incapable of attempting any of their considerable places; for the risking of twenty men, weak as we then were, was risking the safety of the whole: so that we conceived we should be necessitated to content ourselves with what few prizes we could pick up at sea, before we were discovered; after which, we should in all probability be obliged to depart with precipitation, and esteem ourselves fortunate to regain our native country, leaving our enemies to triumph in the inconsiderable mischief they had received from a squadron, whose equipment had filled them with such dreadful apprehensions. This was a subject on which we had reason to imagine the Spanish ostentation would remarkably exert itself; though the causes of our disappointment and their security were neither to be sought for in their valour nor our misconduct.

Such were the desponding reflections which at that time arose on the review and comparison of our remaining strength with our original numbers: indeed our fears were far from being groundless, or disproportioned to our feeble and almost desperate situation. It is true, the final event proved more honourable than we had foreboded; but the intermediate calamities did likewise greatly surpass our most gloomy apprehensions, and could they have been predicted to us at this island of Juan Fernandes, they would doubtless have appeared insurmountable. But to return from this digression.

In the beginning of September, as has been already mentioned, our men were tolerably well recovered; and now, the time of navigation in this climate drawing near, we exerted ourselves in getting our ships in readiness for the sea. We converted the fore-mast of the victualler into a main-mast for the Tryal sloop; and still flattering ourselves with the possibility of the arrival of some other ships of our squadron, we intended to leave the main-mast of the victualler, to make a mizen-mast for the Wager. Thus all hands being employed in forwarding our departure, we, on the 8th, about eleven in the morning, espied a sail to the N.E., which continued to approach us, till her courses appeared even with the horizon. In this interval we all had hopes she might prove one of our own squadron; but at length finding she steered away to the eastward, without hauling in for the island, we concluded she must be a Spaniard. And now great disputes were set on foot about the possibility of her having discovered our tents on shore, some of us strongly insisting, that she had doubtless been near enough to have perceived something that had given her a jealousy of an enemy, which had occasioned her standing to the eastward without hauling in; but leaving these contests to be settled afterwards, it was resolved to pursue her, and, the Centurion being in the greatest forwardness, we immediately got all our hands on board, set up our rigging, bent our sails, and by five in the afternoon got under sail. We had at this time very little wind, so that all the boats were employed to tow us out of the bay; and even what wind there was lasted only long enough to give us an offing of two or three leagues, when it flattened to a calm. The night coming on we lost sight of the chase, and were extremely impatient for the return of day-light, in hopes to find that she had been becalmed as well as we; though I must confess, that her greater distance from the land was a reasonable ground for suspecting the contrary, as we indeed found in the morning, to our great mortification; for though the weather continued perfectly clear, we had no sight of the ship from the mast-head. But as we were now satisfied that it was an enemy, and the first we had seen in these seas, we resolved not to give over the search lightly; and, a small breeze springing up from the W.N.W., we got up our top-gallant masts and yards, set all the sails, and steered to the S.E., in hopes of retrieving our chase, which we imagined to be bound to Valparaiso. We continued on this course all that day and the next, and then not getting sight of our chase we gave over the pursuit, conceiving that by that time she must in all probability have reached her port. And now we prepared to return to Juan Fernandes, and hauled up to the S.W. with that view, having but very little wind till the 12th, when, at three in the morning, there sprang up a fresh gale from the W.S.W., and we tacked and stood to the N.W.: and at day-break we were agreeably surprised with the sight of a sail on our weather-bow, between four and five leagues distant. On this we crowded all the sail we could, and stood after her, and soon perceived it not to be the same ship we originally gave chase to. She at first bore down upon us, showing Spanish colours, and making a signal, as to her consort; but observing that we did not answer her signal, she instantly luffed close to the wind, and stood to the southward. Our people were now all in spirits, and put the ship about with great alacrity; and as the chase appeared to be a large ship, and had mistaken us for her consort, we conceived that she was a man of war, and probably one of Pizarro's squadron: this induced the commodore to order all the officers' cabins to be knocked down and thrown overboard, with several casks of water and provisions which stood between the guns; so that we had soon a clear ship ready for an engagement. About nine o'clock we had thick hazy weather and a shower of rain, during which we lost sight of the chase; and we were apprehensive, if the weather should continue, that by going upon the other tack, or by some other artifice, she might escape us; but it clearing up in less than an hour, we found that we had both weathered and fore-reached upon her considerably; and now we were near enough to discover that she was only a merchantman, without so much as a single tier of guns. About half an hour after twelve, being then within a reasonable distance of her, we fired four shot amongst her rigging; on which they lowered their top-sails and bore down to us, but in very great confusion, their top-gallant sails and stay-sails all fluttering in the wind: this was owing to their having let run their sheets and halyards just as we fired at them; after which, not a man amongst them had courage enough to venture aloft (for there the shot had passed but just before) to take them in. As soon as the vessel came within hail of us, the commodore ordered them to bring-to under his lee quarter, and then hoisted out the boat, and sent Mr. Saumarez, his first lieutenant, to take possession of the prize, with directions to send all the prisoners on board the Centurion, but first the officers and passengers. When Mr. Saumarez came on board them, they received him at the side with the strongest tokens of the most abject submission; for they were all of them (especially the passengers, who were twenty-five in number) extremely terrified, and under the greatest apprehensions of meeting with very severe and cruel usage; but the lieutenant endeavoured, with great courtesy, to dissipate their fright, assuring them that their fears were altogether groundless, and that they would find a generous enemy in the commodore, who was not less remarkable for his lenity and humanity, than for his resolution and courage. The prisoners, who were first sent on board the Centurion, informed us, that our prize was called Nuestra Senora del Monte Carmelo, and was commanded by Don Manuel Zamorra. Her cargo consisted chiefly of sugar, and great quantities of blue cloth made in the province of Quito, somewhat resembling our English coarse broad cloths, but inferior to them. They had besides several bales of a coarser sort of cloth, of different colours, somewhat like Colchester bays, called by them *pannio da tierra*, with a few bales of cotton and tobacco; which, though strong, was not ill flavoured. These were the principal goods on board her; but we found besides, what was to us much more valuable than the rest of the cargo this was some trunks of wrought plate, and twenty three serons of dollars, each weighing upwards of 200lbs. avoirdupois. The ship's burthen was about four hundred and fifty tons; she had fifty-three sailors on board, both whites and blacks; she came from Callao, and had been twenty-seven days at sea, before she fell into our hands. She was bound to the port of Valparaiso in the kingdom of Chili, and proposed to have returned from thence loaded with corn and Chili wine, some gold, dried beef, and small cordage, which at Callao they convert into larger rope. Our prize had been built upwards of thirty years; yet as they lie in harbour all the winter months, and the climate is favourable, they esteemed it no very great age. Her rigging was very indifferent, as were likewise her sails, which were made of cotton. She had only three four-pounders, which were altogether unserviceable, their carriages being scarcely able to support them; and there were no small arms on board, except a few pistols, belonging to the passengers. The prisoners informed us that they left Callao in company with two other ships, whom they had parted with some days before, and that at first they conceived us to be one of their company; and by the description we gave them of the ship we had chased from Juan Fernandes, they assured us, she was of their number, but that the coming in sight of that island was directly repugnant to the merchants' instructions, who had expressly forbid it, as knowing that if any English squadron was in those seas, the island of Fernandes was most probably the place of their rendezvous.

And now, after this short account of the ship and her cargo, it is necessary that I should relate the important intelligence which we met with on board her, partly from the information of the prisoners, and partly from the letters and papers which fell into our hands. We here first learnt with certainty the force and destination of that squadron, which cruised off the Madeiras at our arrival there, and afterwards chased the Pearl in our passage to port St. Julian. This we now knew was a squadron composed of five large Spanish ships, commanded by Admiral Pizarro, and purposely fitted out to traverse our designs; as hath been already more amply related in the 3rd chapter of the 1st book. And we had, at the same time, the satisfaction to find, that Pizarro, after his utmost endeavours to gain his passage into these seas, had been forced back again into the river of Plate, with the loss of two of his largest ships: and besides this disappointment of Pizarro, which considering our great debility, was no unacceptable intelligence, we farther learnt that an embargo had been laid upon all shipping in these seas, by the viceroy of Peru, in the month of May preceding, on a supposition that about that time we might arrive upon the coast. But on the account sent over-land by Pizarro of his own distresses, part of which they knew we must have encountered, as we were at sea during the same time, and on their having no news of us in eight months after we were known to set sail from St. Catherine's, they were fully persuaded that we were either shipwrecked, or had perished at sea, or at least had been obliged to put back again; for it was conceived impossible for any ships to continue at sea during so long an interval: and therefore, on the application of the merchants, and the firm persuasion of our having miscarried, the embargo had been lately taken off.

This last article made us flatter ourselves, that, as the enemy was still a stranger to our having got round Cape Horn, and the navigation of these seas was restored, we might meet with some considerable captures, and might thereby indemnify ourselves for the incapacity we were now under of attempting any of their considerable settlements on shore. And thus much we were certain of, from the information of our prisoners, that, whatever our success might be as to the prizes we might light on, we had nothing to fear, weak as we were, from the Spanish force in this part of the world; though we discovered that we had been in most imminent peril from the enemy, when we least apprehended it, and when our other distresses were at the greatest height; for we learnt, from the letters on board, that Pizarro, in the express he despatched to the viceroy of Peru, after his return to the river of Plate, had intimated to him, that it was possible some part, at least, of the English squadron might get round: but that, as he was certain from his own experience, that if they did arrive in those seas, it must be in a very weak and defenceless condition, he advised the viceroy, in order to be secure at all events, to fit out what ships of force he had, and send them to the southward, where, in all probability, they would intercept us singly, and before we had an opportunity of touching anywhere for refreshment; in which case, he doubted not but we should prove an easy conquest. The viceroy of Peru approved of this advice, and immediately fitted out four ships of force from Callao; one of fifty guns, two of forty guns, and one of twenty-four guns: three of them were stationed off the port of Conception, and one of them at the island of Fernandes; and in these stations they continued cruising for us till the 6th of June, when not seeing anything of us, and conceiving it to be impossible that we could have kept the seas so long, they quitted their cruise and returned to Callao, fully satisfied that we had either perished, or at least had been driven back. As the time of their quitting their station was but a few days before our arrival at the island of Fernandes, it is evident, that had we made that island on our first search for it, without hauling in for the main to secure our easting, (a circumstance which at that time we considered as very unfortunate to us, on account of the numbers which we lost by our longer continuance at sea) had we, I say, made the island on the 28th of May, when we first expected to see it, and were in reality very near it, we had doubtless fallen in with some part of the Spanish squadron; and in the distressed condition we were then in, the meeting with a healthy well-provided enemy was an incident that could not but have been perplexing, and might perhaps have proved fatal, not only to us, but to the Tryal, the Gloucester, and the Anna pink, who separately joined us, and who were each of them less capable than we were of making any considerable resistance. I shall only add, that these Spanish ships, sent out to intercept us, had been greatly shattered by a storm during their cruise; and that, after their arrival at Callao, they had been laid up. And our prisoners assured us, that whenever intelligence was received at Lima of our being in these seas, it would be at least two months before this armament could be again fitted out.

The whole of this intelligence was as favourable as we in our reduced circumstances could wish for.

And now we were fully satisfied as to the broken jars, ashes, and fish-bones, which we had observed at our first landing at Juan Fernandes, these things being doubtless the relics of the cruisers stationed off that port. Having thus satisfied ourselves in the material articles, and having gotten on board the Centurion most of the prisoners, and all the silver, we, at eight in the same evening, made sail to the northward, in company with our prize, and at six the next morning discovered the island of Fernandes, where, the next day, both we and our prize came to an anchor.

And here I cannot omit one remarkable incident which occurred, when the prize and her crew came into the bay, where the rest of the squadron lay. The Spaniards in the Carmelo had been sufficiently informed of the distresses we had gone through, and were greatly surprised that we had ever surmounted them: but when they saw the Tryal sloop at anchor, they were still more astonished, that after all our fatigues, we had the industry (besides refitting our other ships) to complete such a vessel in so short a time, they taking it for granted that she had been built upon the spot. And it was with great difficulty they were prevailed on to believe that she came from England with the rest of the squadron; they at first insisting, that it was impossible such a bauble as that could pass round Cape Horn, when the best ships of Spain were obliged to put back.

By the time we arrived at Juan Fernandes, the letters found on board our prize were more minutely examined: and, it appearing from them, and from the accounts of our prisoners, that several other merchantmen were bound from Callao to Valparaiso, Mr. Anson despatched the Tryal sloop the very next morning to cruise off the last-mentioned port, reinforcing him with ten hands from on board his own ship. Mr. Anson likewise resolved, on the intelligence recited above, to separate the ships under his command, and employ them in distinct cruises, as he thought that by this means we should not only increase our chance for prizes, but that we should likewise run a less risk of alarming the coast, and of being discovered. And now the spirits of our people being greatly raised, and their despondency dissipated by this earnest of success, they forgot all their past distresses, and resumed their wonted alacrity, and laboured indefatigably in completing our water, receiving our lumber, and in preparing to take our farewell of the island: but as these occupations took us up four or five days with all our industry, the commodore, in that interval, directed that the guns belonging to the Anna pink, being four six-pounders, four four-pounders, and two swivels, should be mounted on board the Carmelo, our prize: and having sent on board the Gloucester six passengers, and twenty-three seamen to assist in navigating the ship, he directed Captain Mitchel to leave the island as soon as possible, the service requiring the utmost despatch, ordering him to proceed to the latitude of five degrees South, and there to cruise off the highland of Paita, at such a distance from shore as should prevent his being discovered. On this station he was to continue till he should be joined by the commodore, which would be whenever it should be known that the viceroy had fitted out the ships at Callao, or on Mr. Anson's receiving any other intelligence, that should make it necessary to unite our strength These orders being delivered to the captain of the Gloucester, and all our business completed, we, on the Saturday following, being the 19th of September, weighed our anchor, in company with our prize, and got out of the bay, taking our last leave of the island of Juan Fernandes, and steering to the eastward, with an intention of joining the Tryal sloop in her station off Valparaiso.

CHAPTER V.

Our cruise, from the time of our leaving Juan Fernandes, to the taking the town of Paita.

ALTHOUGH the Centurion, with her prize, the Carmelo, weighed from the bay of Juan Fernandes on the 19th of September, leaving the Gloucester at anchor behind her; yet, by the irregularity and fluctuation of the winds in the offing, it was the 22nd of the same month, in the evening, before we lost sight of the island: after which, we continued our course to the eastward, in order to reach our station, and to join the Tryal off Valparaiso. The next night, the weather proved squally, and we split our maintop-sail, which we handed for the present, but got it repaired, and set it again the next morning. And now, on the 24th, a little before sunset, we saw two sail to the eastward; on which, our prize stood directly from us, to avoid giving any suspicion of our being cruisers; whilst we, in the mean time, made ourselves ready for an engagement, and steered towards the two ships we had discovered with all our canvas. We soon perceived that one of these, which had the appearance of being a very stout ship, made directly for us, whilst the other kept at a very great distance. By seven o'clock we were within pistol-shot of the nearest, and had a broadside ready to pour into her, the gunners having their matches in their hands, and only waiting for orders to fire; but as we knew it was now impossible for her to escape us, Mr. Anson, before he permitted them to fire, ordered the master to hail the ship in Spanish; on which the commanding officer on board her, who proved to be Mr. Hughs, lieutenant of the Tryal, answered us in English, and informed us, that she was a prize taken by the Tryal a few days before, and that the other sail at a distance was the Tryal herself, disabled in her masts. We were soon after joined by the Tryal; and Captain Saunders, her commander, came on board the Centurion. He informed the commodore, that he had taken this ship the 18th instant; that she was a prime sailer, and had cost him thirty-six hours' chase, before he could come up with her; that for some time he gained so little upon her, that he began to despair of taking her; and the Spaniards, though alarmed at first with seeing nothing but a cloud of sail in pursuit of them, the Tryal's hull being so low in the water that no part of it appeared, yet knowing the goodness of their ship, and finding how little the Tryal neared them, they at length laid aside their fears, and, recommending themselves to the blessed Virgin for protection, began to think themselves secure. And indeed their success was very near doing honour to their Ave Marias; for, altering their course in the night, and shutting up their windows to prevent any of their lights from being seen, they had some chance of escaping; but a small crevice in one of the shutters rendered all their invocations ineffectual; for through this crevice the people on board the Tryal perceived a light, which they chased, till they arrived within gun-shot; and then Captain Saunders alarmed them unexpectedly with a broadside, when they flattered themselves they were got out of his reach: however, for some time after they still kept the same sail abroad, and it was not observed that this first salute had made any impression on them; but, just as the Tryal was preparing to repeat her broadside, the Spaniards crept from their holes, lowered their sails, and submitted without any opposition. She was one of the largest merchantmen employed in those seas, being about six hundred tons burthen, and was called the Arranzazu. She was bound from Callao to Valparaiso, and had much the same cargo with the Carmelo we had taken before, except that her silver amounted only to about 5000*l*. sterling.

But to balance this success, we had the misfortune to find that the Tryal had sprung her main-mast, and that her maintop-mast had come by the board; and as we were all of us standing to the eastward the next morning, with a fresh gale at South, she had the additional ill-luck to spring her fore-mast: so that now she had not a mast left, on which she could carry sail. These unhappy incidents were still aggravated by the impossibility we were just then under of assisting her; for the wind blew so hard, and raised such a hollow sea, that we could not venture to hoist out our boat, and consequently could have no communication with her; so that we were obliged to lie-to for the greatest part of forty-eight hours to attend her, as we could have no thought of leaving her to herself in her present unhappy situation: and as an accumulation to our misfortunes, we were all the while driving to the leeward of our station, at the very time when, by our intelligence, we had reason to expect several of the enemy's ships would appear upon the coast, who would now gain the port of Valparaiso without obstruction. And I am verily persuaded, that the embarrassment we received from the dismasting of the Tryal, and our absence from our intended station occasioned thereby, deprived us of some very considerable captures.

The weather proving somewhat more moderate on the 27th, we sent our boat for the captain of the Tryal, who, when he came on board us, produced an instrument, signed by himself and all his officers, representing that the sloop, besides being dismasted, was so very leaky in her hull, that even in moderate weather it was necessary to keep the pumps constantly at work, and that they were then scarcely sufficient to keep her free; so that in the late gale, though they had all been engaged at the pumps by turns, yet the water had increased upon them; and, upon the whole, they apprehended her to be at present so very defective, that if they met with much bad weather, they must all inevitably perish; and therefore they petitioned the commodore to take some measures for their future safety. But the refitting of the Tryal, and the repairing of her defects, was an undertaking that in the present conjuncture greatly exceeded his power; for we had no masts to spare her, we had no stores to complete her rigging, nor had we any port where she might be hove down, and her bottom examined: besides had a port and proper requisites for this purpose been in our possession, yet it would have been extreme imprudence, in so critical a conjuncture, to have loitered away so much time as would have been necessary for these operations: The commodore therefore had no choice left him, but that of taking out her people, and destroying her: but, at the same time, as he conceived it necessary for his Majesty's service to keep up the appearance of our force, he appointed the Tryal's prize (which had been often employed by the viceroy of Peru as a man of war) to be a frigate in his Majesty's service, manning her with the Tryal's crew, and giving new commissions to the captain and all the inferior officers accordingly. This new frigate, when in the Spanish service, had mounted thirty-two guns; but she was now to have only twenty, which were the twelve that were on board the Tryal, and eight that had belonged to the Anna pink. When this affair was thus far regulated, Mr. Anson gave orders to Captain Saunders to put it in execution, directing him to take out of the sloop the arms, stores, ammunition, and every thing that could be of any use to the other ships, and then to scuttle her and sink her. And after Captain Saunders had seen her destroyed, he was to proceed with his new frigate (to be called the Tryal's prize) and to cruise off the highland of Valparaiso, keeping it from him N.N.W., at the distance of twelve or fourteen leagues: for as all ships bound from Valparaiso to the northward steer that course, Mr. Anson proposed by this means to stop any intelligence, that might be despatched to Callao, of two of their ships being missing, which might give them apprehensions of the English squadron being in their neighbourhood. The Tryal's prize was to continue on this station twenty-four days, and, if not joined by the commodore at the expiration of that term, she was then to proceed down the coast to Pisco or Nasca, where she would be certain to meet with Mr. Anson. The commodore likewise ordered lieutenant Saumarez, who commanded the Centurion's prize, to keep company with Captain Saunders, both to assist him in unloading the sloop, and also that, by spreading in their cruise, there might be less danger of any of the enemy's ships slipping by unobserved. These orders being despatched, the Centurion parted from them at eleven in the evening, on the 27th of September, directing her course to the southward, with a view of cruising for some days to the windward of Valparaiso.

And now by this disposition of our ships we flattered ourselves, that we had taken all the advantages of the enemy that we possibly could with our small force, since our disposition was doubtless the most prudent that could be projected. For, as we might suppose the Gloucester by this time to be drawing near her station off the highland of Paita, we were enabled, by our separate stations, to intercept all vessels employed either betwixt Peru and Chili to the southward, or betwixt Panama and Peru to the northward: since the principal trade from Peru to Chili being carried on to the port of Valparaiso, the Centurion cruising to the windward of Valparaiso, would, in all probability, meet with them, as it is the constant practice of those ships to fall in with the coast, to the windward of that port: and the Gloucester would, in like manner, be in the way of the trade bound from Panama or the northward, to any part of Peru; since the highland off which she was stationed is constantly made by all ships in that voyage. And whilst the Centurion and Gloucester were thus situated for interrupting the enemy's trade, the Tryal's prize and Centurion's prize were as conveniently stationed for preventing all intelligence, by intercepting all ships bound from Valparaiso to the northward; for it was on board these vessels that it was to be feared some account of us might possibly be sent to Peru.

But the most prudent dispositions carry with them only a probability of success, and can never insure its certainty: since those chances, which it was reasonable to overlook in deliberations, are sometimes of most powerful influence in execution. Thus in the present case, the distress of the Tryal, and the quitting our station to assist her (events which no degree of prudence could either foresee or obviate) gave an opportunity to all the ships, bound to Valparaiso, to reach that port without molestation, during this unlucky interval." So that though, after leaving Captain Saunders, we were very expeditious in regaining our station, where we got the 29th at noon, yet in plying on and off till the 6th of October, we had not the good fortune to discover a sail of any sort: and then, having lost all hopes of making any advantage by a longer stay, we made sail to the leeward of the port, in order to join our prizes; but when we arrived on the station appointed for them, we did not meet with them, though we continued there four or five days. We supposed that some chase had occasioned their leaving their station, and therefore we proceeded down the coast to the highland of Nasca, where Captain Saunders was directed to join us. Here we arrived on the 21st, and were in great expectation of meeting with some of the enemy's ships on the coast, as both the accounts of former voyages, and the information of our prisoners assured us, that all ships bound to Callao constantly make this land to prevent the danger of running to the leeward of the port. But notwithstanding the advantages of this station, we saw no sail till the 2nd of November, when two ships appeared in sight together; we immediately gave them chase, but soon perceived that they were the Tryal's and Centurion's prizes: as they had the wind of us, we brought to and waited their coming up; when Captain Saunders came on board us, and acquainted the commodore, that he had cleared the Tryal pursuant to his orders, and having scuttled her, he remained by her till she sunk, but that it was the 4th of October before this was effected; for there ran so large and hollow a sea, that the sloop, having neither masts nor sails to steady her, rolled and pitched so violently, that it was impossible for a boat to lay alongside of her, for the greatest part of the time; and during this attendance on the sloop, they were all driven so far to the northwest, that they were afterwards obliged to stretch a long way to the westward to regain the ground they had lost; which was the reason that we had not met with them on their station as we expected. We found they had not been more fortunate in their cruise than we were, for they had seen no vessel since they separated from us. The little success we all had, and our certainty, that had any

ships been stirring in these seas for some time past we must have met with them, made us believe, that the enemy at Valparaiso, on the missing of the two ships we had taken, had suspected us to be in the neighbourhood, and had consequently laid an embargo on all the trade in the southern parts. We likewise apprehended, that they might by this time be fitting out the men of war at Callao; for we knew that it was no uncommon thing for an express from Valparaiso to reach Lima in twenty-nine or thirty days, and it was now more than fifty since we had taken our first prize. These apprehensions of an embargo along the coast, and of the equipment of the Spanish squadron at Callao, determined the commodore to hasten down to the leeward of Callao, and to join Captain Mitchel (who was stationed off Paita) as soon as possible, that our strength being united, we might be prepared to give the ships from Callao a warm reception, if they dared to put to sea. With this view we bore away the same afternoon, taking particular care to keep at such a distance from the shore, that there might be no danger of our being discovered from thence; for we knew that all the country ships were commanded, under the severest penalty, not to sail by the port of Callao without stopping; and as this order was constantly complied with, we should undoubtedly be known for enemies, if we were seen to act contrary to it. In this new navigation, not being certain whether we might not meet the Spanish squadron in our route, the commodore took on board the Centurion part of his crew, with which he had formerly manned the Carmelo. And now standing to the northward, we, before night came on, had a view of the small island called St. Gallan, which bore from us N.N.E. ¼ E., about seven leagues distant. This island lies in the latitude of about fourteen degrees South, and about five miles to the northward of a highland, called Morro Veijo, or the old man's head. I mention this island, and the highland near it, more particularly, because between them is the most eligible station on that coast for cruising upon the enemy; as all ships bound to Callao, whether from the northward or the southward, run well in with the land in this part. By the 5th of November, at three in the afternoon, we were advanced within view of the highland of Barranca, lying in the latitude of 10° 36′ South, bearing from us N. E. by E., distant eight or nine leagues: and an hour and a half afterwards we had the satisfaction, we had so long wished for, of seeing a sail. She first appeared to leeward, and we all immediately gave her chase; but the Centurion so much outsailed the two prizes, that we soon ran them out of sight, and gained considerably on the chase: however, night coming on before we came up with her, we, about seven o'clock, lost sight of her, and were in some perplexity what course to steer; but at last Mr. Anson resolved, as we were then before the wind, to keep all his sails set, and not to change his course: for though we had no doubt but the chase would alter her course in the night; yet, as it was uncertain what tack she would go upon, it was thought more prudent to keep on our course, as we must by this means unavoidably near her, than to change it on conjecture; when, if we should mistake, we must infallibly lose her. Thus then we continued the chase about an hour and a half in the dark, some one or other on board us constantly imagining they discerned her sails right a-head of us; but at last Mr. Brett, then our second lieutenant, did really discover her about four points on the larboard-bow, steering off to the seaward: we immediately clapped the helm a-weather, and stood for her; and in less than an hour came up with her, and having fired fourteen shot at her, she struck. Our third lieutenant, Mr. Dennis, was sent in the boat with sixteen men, to take possession of the prize, and to return the prisoners to our ship. This ship was named the Santa Teresa de Jesus, built at Gualaquil, of about three hundred tons burthen, and was commanded by Bartolome Urrunaga, a Biscayer: she was bound from Guaiaquil to Callao; her loading consisted of timber, cocoa, cocoanuts, tobacco, hides, Pito thread (which is very strong, and is made of a species of grass) Quito cloth, wax, &c. The specie on board her was inconsiderable, being principally small silver money, and not amounting to more than 170*l.* sterling. It is true, her cargo was of great value, could we have disposed of it; but, the Spaniards having strict orders never to ransom their ships, all the goods that we took in these seas, except what little we had occasion for ourselves, were of no advantage to us. Indeed, though we could make no profit thereby ourselves, it was some satisfaction to us to consider, that it was so much really lost to the enemy, and that the despoiling them was no contemptible branch of that service, in which we were now employed by our country.

Besides our prize's crew, which amounted to forty-five hands, there were on board her ten passengers, consisting of four men and three women, who were natives of the country, born of Spanish parents, and three black female slaves that attended them. The women were a mother and her two daughters, the eldest about twenty-one, and the youngest about fourteen. It is not to be wondered at, that women of these years should be excessively alarmed at the falling into the hands of an enemy whom, from the former outrages of the buccaneers, and by the artful insinuations of their priests, they had been taught to consider as the most terrible and brutal of all mankind. These apprehensions, too, were in the present instance exaggerated by the singular beauty of the youngest of the women, and the riotous disposition which they might well expect to find in a set of sailors, that had not seen a woman for near a twelvemonth. Full of these terrors, the women all hid themselves when our officer went on board, and when they were found out, it was with great difficulty that he could persuade them to approach the light: however, he soon satisfied them, by the humanity of his conduct and his assurances of their future security and honourable treatment, that they had nothing to fear. And the commodore being informed of the matter, sent directions that they should be continued on board their own ship, with the use of the same apartments, and with all the other conveniences they had enjoyed before, giving strict orders that they should receive no kind of inquietude or molestation whatever: and that they might be the more certain of having these orders complied with, or of complaining if they were not, the commodore permitted the pilot, who in Spanish ships is generally the second person on board, to stay with them, as their guardian and protector. He was particularly chosen for this purpose by Mr. Anson, as he seemed to be extremely interested in all that concerned the women, and had at first declared that he was married to the youngest of them; though it afterwards appeared, both from the information of the rest of the prisoners, and other circumstances, that he had asserted this with a view the better to secure them from the insults they expected on their first falling into our hands. By this compassionate and indulgent behaviour of the commodore, the consternation of our female prisoners entirely subsided, and they continued easy and cheerful during the whole time they were with us, as I shall have occasion to mention more particularly hereafter.

I have before observed, that at the beginning of this chase, the Centurion ran her two consorts out of sight, for which reason we lay by all the night, after we had taken the prize, for Captain Saunders and Lieutenant Saumarez to join us, firing guns, and making false fires every half-hour, to prevent their passing us unobserved; but they were so far a-stern, that they neither heard nor saw any of our signals, and were not able to come up with us till broad day-light. When they had joined us we proceeded together to the northward, being now four sail in company. We here found the sea, for many miles round us, of a beautiful red colour: This, upon examination, we imputed to an immense quantity of spawn spread upon its surface; and taking up some of the water in a wine-glass, it soon changed from a dirty aspect to a clear crystal, with only some red globules of a slimy nature floating on the top. And now having a supply of timber on board our new prize, the commodore ordered our boats to be repaired, and a swivel gun-stock to be fixed in the bow both of the barge and pinnace, in order to increase their force, in case we should be obliged to have recourse to them for boarding ships, or for any attempts on shore.

As we stood from hence to the northward, nothing remarkable occurred for two or three days, though we spread our ships in such a manner, that it was not probable any vessel of the enemy could escape us. In our run along this coast we generally observed, that there was a current which set us to the northward, at the rate of ten or twelve miles each day. And now being in about eight degrees of South latitude, we began to be attended with vast numbers of flying fish and bonitos, which were the first we saw after our departure from the coast of Brazil. But it is remarkable that on the east side of South America they extended to a much higher latitude than they do on the west side; for we did not lose them on the coast of Brazil till we approached the southern tropic. The reason for this diversity is doubtless the different degrees of heat obtaining in the same latitude on different sides of that continent. And on this occasion I must beg leave to make a short digression on the heat and cold of different climates, and on the varieties which occur in the same place in different parts of the year, and in different places lying in the same degree of latitude.

The ancients, as appears in many places, conceived that of the five zones, into which they divided the surface of the globe, two only were habitable, supposing that all between the tropics was too hot, and all within the polar circle too cold, to be supported by mankind. The falsehood of this reasoning has been long evinced; but the particular comparisons of the heat and cold of these various climates, has as yet been very imperfectly considered. However, enough is known safely to determine this position, that all places between the tropics are far from being the hottest on the globe, as many of those within the polar circles are far from enduring that extreme degree of cold, to which their situation should seem to subject them: that is to say, in other words, that the temperature of a place depends much more upon other circumstances, than upon its distance from the pole, or its proximity to the equinoctial.

This proposition relates to the general temperature of places, taking the whole year round; and in this sense it cannot be denied but that the city of London, for instance, enjoys much warmer seasons than the bottom of Hudson's Bay, which is nearly in the same latitude with it; for there the severity of the winter is so great, that it will scarcely permit the hardiest of our garden plants to live. And if the comparison be made between the coast of Brazil and the western shore of South America, as, for example, betwixt Bahia and Lima, the difference will be still more remarkable; for though the coast of Brazil is extremely sultry, yet the coast of the South Seas in the same latitude is perhaps as temperate and tolerable as any part of the globe; since in ranging along it we did not once meet with so warm weather as is frequent in a summer's day in England: and this was the more remarkable, as there never fell any rains to refresh and cool the air.

The causes of this temperature in the South Seas are not difficult to be assigned, and shall be hereafter mentioned. I am now only solicitous to establish the truth of this assertion, that the latitude of a place alone is no rule whereby to judge of the degree of heat and cold which obtains there. Perhaps this position might be more briefly confirmed by observing, that on the tops of the Andes, though under the equinoctial, the snow never melts the whole year round; a criterion of cold, stronger than what is known to take place in many parts far removed within the polar circle.

I have hitherto considered the temperature of the air all the year through, and the gross estimations of heat and cold which every one makes from his own sensation. If this matter be examined by means of thermometers, which in respect to the absolute degree of heat and cold are doubtless the most unerring evidences; if this be done, the result will be indeed most wonderful; for it will appear that the heat in very high latitudes, as at Petersburg for instance, is at particular times much greater than any that has been hitherto observed between the tropics; and that even at London, in the year 1746, there was the part of one day considerably hotter than what was at any time felt by a ship of Mr. Anson's squadron, in running from hence to Cape Horn and back again, and passing twice under the sun; for in the summer of that year, the thermometer in London (being one of those graduated according to the method of Fahrenheit) stood once at 78°; and the greatest height at which a thermometer of the same kind stood in the foregoing ship, I find to be 76°: this was at St. Catherine's, in the latter end of December, when the sun was within about three degrees of the vertex. And as to Petersburg, I find, by the acts of the Academy established there, that in the year 1734, on the 20th and 25th of July, the thermometer rose to 98° in the shade, that is, it was twenty-two divisions higher than it was found to be at St. Catherine's; which is a degree of heat that, were it not authorised by the regularity and circumspection with which the observations seem to have been made, would appear altogether incredible.

If it should be asked, how it comes to pass then, that the heat in many places between the tropics is esteemed so violent and insufferable, when it appears, by these instances, that it is sometimes rivalled or exceeded in very high latitudes not far from the polar circle? I should answer, that the estimation of heat, in any particular place, ought not to be founded upon that degree of heat which may now and then obtain there, but is rather to be deduced from the medium observed in a whole season, or perhaps in a whole year: and in this light it will easily appear, how much more intense the same degree of heat may prove, by being long continued without remarkable variation. For instance, in comparing together St. Catherine's and Petersburg, we will suppose the summer heat at St. Catherine's to be 76°, and the winter heat to be twenty divisions short of it: I do not make use of this last conjecture upon sufficient observation; but I am apt to suspect that the allowance is full large. Upon this supposition then, the medium heat all the year round will be 66°, and this perhaps by night as well as day, with no great variation: now those who have attended to thermometers will readily own that a continuation of this degree of heat for a length of time would by the generality of mankind be styled violent and suffocating. But now at Petersburg, though a few times in the year the heat, by the thermometer, may be considerably greater than at St. Catherine's, yet, as at other times the cold is immensely sharper, the medium for a year, or even for one season only, would be far short of 66°. For I find that the variation of the thermometer at Petersburg is at least five times greater, from its highest to its lowest point, than what I have supposed to take place at St. Catherine's.

But besides this estimation of the heat of a place, by taking the medium for a considerable time together, there is another circumstance which will still augment the apparent heat of the warmer climates, and diminish that of the colder, though I do not remember to have seen it remarked in any author. To explain myself more distinctly upon this head, I must observe, that the measure of absolute heat, marked by the thermometer, is not the certain criterion of the sensation of heat, with which human bodies are affected: for as the presence and perpetual succession of fresh air is necessary to our respiration, so there is a species of tainted or stagnated air, which is often produced by the continuance of great heats, which never fails to excite in us an idea of sultriness and suffocating warmth, much beyond what the mere heat of the air alone, supposing it pure and agitated, would occasion. Hence it follows that the mere inspection of the thermometer will never determine the heat which the human body feels from this cause; and hence it follows too, that the heat in most places between the tropics must be much more troublesome and uneasy, than the same degree of absolute heat in a high latitude: for the equability and duration of the tropical heat contribute to impregnate the air with a multitude of steams and vapours from the soil and water, and these being, many of them, of an impure and noxious kind, and being not easily removed, by reason of the regularity of the winds in those parts, which only shift the exhalations from place to place, without dispersing them, the atmosphere is by this means rendered less proper for respiration, and mankind are consequently affected with what they style a most intense and stifling heat: whereas in the higher latitudes these vapours are probably raised in smaller quantities, and the irregularity and violence of the winds frequently disperse them; so that, the air being in general pure and less stagnant, the same degree of absolute heat is not attended with that uneasy and suffocating sensation. This may suffice in general with respect to the present speculation; but I cannot help wishing, as it is a subject in which mankind, especially travellers of all sorts, are very much interested, that it were more thoroughly and accurately examined, and that all ships bound to the warmer climates would furnish themselves with thermometers of a known fabric, and would observe them daily, and register their observations; for considering the turn to philosophical subjects, which has obtained in Europe for the last fourscore years, it is incredible how very rarely anything of this kind has been attended to. For my own part, I do not recollect that I have ever seen any observations of the heat and cold, either in the East or West Indies, which were made by mariners or officers of vessels, except those made by Mr. Anson's order, on board the Centurion, and by Captain Legge on board the Severn, which was another ship of our squadron.

This digression I have been in some measure drawn into by the consideration of the fine weather we met with on the coast of Peru, even under the equinoctial itself, but the particularities of this weather I have not yet described: I shall now therefore add, that in this climate every circumstance concurred that could render the open air and the daylight desirable. For in other countries the scorching heat of the sun in summer renders the greater part of the day unapt either for labour or amusement; and the frequent rains are not less troublesome in the more temperate parts of the year. But in this happy climate the sun rarely appears: not that the heavens have at any time a dark and gloomy look; but there is constantly a cheerful grey sky, just sufficient to screen the sun, and to mitigate the violence of its perpendicular rays, without obscuring the air, or tinging the daylight with an unpleasant or melancholy hue. By this means all parts of the day are proper for labour or exercise abroad, nor is there wanting that refreshment and pleasing refrigeration of the air, which is sometimes produced in other climates by rains; for here the same effect is brought about by the fresh breezes from the cooler regions to the southward. It is reasonable to suppose that this fortunate complexion of the heavens is principally owing to the neighbourhood of those vast hills, called the Andes, which running nearly parallel to the shore, and at a small distance from it, and extending themselves immensely higher than any other mountains upon the globe, form upon their sides and declivities a prodigious tract of country, where, according to the different approaches to the summit, all kinds of climates may at all seasons of the year be found. These mountains, by intercepting great part of the eastern winds which generally blow over the continent of South America, and by cooling that part of the air which forces its way over their tops, and by keeping besides a prodigious extent of the atmosphere perpetually cool, by its contiguity to the snows with which they are covered; these hills, I say, by thus extending the influence of their frozen crests to the neighbouring coasts and seas of Peru, are doubtless the cause of the temperature and equability which constantly prevail there. For when we were advanced beyond the equinoctial, where these mountains left us, and had nothing to screen us to the eastward, but the high lands on the isthmus of Panama, which are but mole-hills to the Andes, we then soon found that in a short run we had totally changed our climate, passing in two or three days from the temperate air of Peru to the sultry burning atmosphere of the West Indies. But it is time to return to our narration.

On the 10th of November we were three leagues south of the southernmost island of Lobos, lying in the latitude 6° 27' South. There are two islands of this name; this, called Lobos de la Mar, and another, which lies to the northward of it, very much resembling it in shape and appearance, and often mistaken for it, called Lobos de Tierra. We were now drawing near to the station appointed to the Gloucester, for which reason, fearing to miss her, we made an easy sail all night. The next morning, at day-break, we saw a ship in-shore, and to windward, plying up to the coast: she had passed by us with the favour of the night, and we soon perceiving her not to be the Gloucester, got our tacks on board, and gave her chase; but it proving very little wind, so that neither of us could make much way, the commodore ordered the barge, his pinnace, and the Tryal's pinnace, to be manned and armed, and to pursue the chase and board her. Lieutenant Brett, who commanded the barge, came up with her first, about nine o'clock, and running along-side of her, he fired a volley of small shot between the masts, just over the heads of the people on board, and then instantly entered with the greatest part of his men; but the enemy made no resistance, being sufficiently frightened by the dazzling of the cutlasses, and the volley they had just received. Lieutenant Brett ordered the sails to be trimmed, and bore down to the commodore, taking up in his way the two pinnaces. When he was arrived within about four miles of us he put off in the barge, bringing with him a number of the prisoners, who had given him some material intelligence, which he was desirous the commodore should be acquainted with as soon as possible. On his arrival we learnt, that the prize was called Nuestra Senora del Carmin, of about two hundred and seventy tons burthen; she was commanded by Marcos Morena, a native of Venice, and had on board forty-three mariners: she was deep laden with steel, iron, wax, pepper, cedar, plank, snuff, rosarios, European bale goods, powder-blue, cinnamon, Romish indulgences, and other species of merchandize; and though this cargo, in our present circumstances, was but of little value to us, yet with respect to the Spaniards, it was the most considerable capture that fell into our hands in this part of the world; for it amounted to upwards of 400,000 dollars prime cost at Panama. This ship was bound to Callao, and had stopped at Paita in her passage, to take in a recruit of water and provisions, and had not left that place above twenty-four hours, before she fell into our hands.

I have mentioned that Mr. Brett had received some important intelligence from the prisoners, which he endeavoured to acquaint the commodore with immediately. The first person he received it from (though upon further examination it was confirmed by the other prisoners) was one John Williams, an Irishman, whom he found on board the Spanish vessel. Williams was a papist, who worked his passage from Cadiz, and had travelled over all the kingdom of Mexico as a pedlar: he pretended by this business he had got 4 or 5000 dollars · but that he was embarrassed by the papists, who knew he had money, and was at last stripped of all he had. He was indeed at present all in rags, being but just got out of Paita gaol, where he had been confined for some misdemeanor: he expressed great joy upon seeing his countrymen, and immediately informed them, that a few days before, a vessel came into Paita, where the master of her informed the governor, that he had been chased in the offing by a very large ship, which from her size, and the colour of her sails, he was persuaded must be one of the English squadron: this we then conjectured to have been the Gloucester, as we afterwards found it was. The governor, upon examining the master, was fully satisfied of his relation, and immediately sent away an express to Lima to acquaint the viceroy therewith; and the royal officer residing at Paita, being apprehensive of a visit from the English, was busily employed in removing the king's treasure and his own to Piura, a town within land, about fourteen leagues distant. We further learnt from our prisoners, that there was a very considerable sum of money belonging to some merchants at Lima, that was now lodged at the Custom-house at Paita; and that this was intended to be shipped on board a vessel, which was then in the port of Paita; and was preparing to sail with the utmost expedition, being bound for the bay of Sonsonnate, on the coast of Mexico, in order to purchase a part of the cargo of the Manila ship. This vessel at Paita was esteemed a prime sailer, and had just received a new coat of tallow on her bottom; and, in the opinion of the prisoners, she might be able to sail the succeeding morning. The character they gave us of this vessel, in which the money was to be shipped, left us little reason to believe that our ship, which had been in the water near two years, could have any chance of coming up with her, if we once suffered her to escape out of the port. And therefore, as we were now discovered, and the coast would be soon alarmed, and as our cruising in these parts any longer would answer no purpose, the commodore resolved to surprise the place, having first minutely informed himself of its strength and condition, and being fully satisfied, that there was little danger of losing many of our men in the attempt. This surprise of Paita, besides the treasure it promised us, and its being the only enterprise it was in our power to undertake, had these other advantages attending it, that we should in all probability supply ourselves with great quantities of live provision, of which we were at this time in want: and we should likewise have an opportunity of setting our prisoners on shore, who were now very numerous, and made a greater consumption of our food than our stock that remained was capable of furnishing long. In all these lights the attempt was a most eligible one, and what our necessities, our situation, and every prudential consideration, prompted us to. How it succeeded, and how far it answered our expectations, shall be the subject of the following chapter.

CHAPTER VI.

The taking of Paita, and our proceedings till we left the coast of Peru.

THE town of Paita is situated in the latitude of 5° 12′ south, in a most barren soil, composed only of sand and slate: the extent of it is but small, containing in all less than two hundred families. The houses are only ground-floors; the walls built of split cane and mud, and the roofs thatched with leaves: these edifices, though extremely slight, are abundantly sufficient for a climate, where rain is considered as a prodigy, and is not seen in many years: so that it is said, that a small quantity of rain falling in this country in the year 1728, it ruined a great number of buildings, which mouldered away, and as it were melted before it. The inhabitants of Paita are principally Indians and black slaves, or at least a mixed breed, the whites being very few. The port of Paita, though in reality little more than a bay, is esteemed the best on that part of the coast; and is indeed a very secure and commodious anchorage. It is greatly frequented by all vessels, coming from the north; since it is here only that the ships from Acapulco, Sonsonnate, Relaleijo and Panama, can touch and refresh in their passage to Callao: and the length of these voyages (the wind for the greatest part of the year being full against them) renders it impossible to perform them without calling upon the coast for a recruit of fresh water. It is true, Paita is situated on so parched a spot, that it does not itself furnish a drop of fresh water, or any kind of greens or provisions, except fish and a few goats: but there is an Indian town called Colan, about two or three leagues distant to the northward, from whence water, maize, greens, fowls, &c. are brought to Paita on balsas or floats, for the conveniency of the ships that touch here; and cattle are sometimes brought from Piura, a town which lies about fourteen leagues up in the country. The water brought from Colan is whitish, and of a disagreeable appearance, but it is said to be very wholesome; for it is pretended by the inhabitants, that it runs through large woods of sarsaparilla, and that it is sensibly impregnated therewith. This port of Paita, besides furnishing the northern trade bound to Callao with water and necessaries, is the usual place where passengers from Acapulco or Panama, bound to Lima, disembark; for, as it is two hundred leagues from hence to Callao, the port of Lima, and as the wind is generally contrary, the passage by sea is very tedious and fatiguing, but by land there is a tolerably good road parallel to the coast, with many stations and villages for the accommodation of travellers.

The town of Paita is itself an open place; its sole protection and defence being a single fort. It was of consequence to us to be well informed of the fabric and strength of this fort; and by the examination of our prisoners we found, that there were eight pieces of cannon mounted in it, but that it had neither ditch nor outwork, being only surrounded by a plain brick wall; and that the garrison consisted of only one weak company, but the town itself might possibly arm three hundred men more.

Mr. Anson having informed himself of the strength of the place, resolved (as hath been said in the preceding chapter) to attempt it that very night. We were then about twelve leagues distant from the shore, far enough to prevent our being discovered; yet not so far but that, by making all the sail we could, we might arrive in the bay with our ships in the night. However, the commodore prudently considered that this would be an improper method of proceeding, as our ships being such large bodies might be easily discovered at a distance even in the night, and might thereby alarm the inhabitants, and give them an opportunity of removing their valuable effects. He therefore, as the strength of the place did not require our whole force, resolved to attempt it with our boats only, ordering the eighteen-oared barge, and our own and the Tryal's pinnaces, on that service; and having picked out fifty-eight men to man them, well provided with arms and ammunition, he gave the command of the expedition to Lieutenant Brett, and gave him his necessary orders. And the better to prevent the disappointment and confusion which might arise from the darkness of the night, and the ignorance of the streets and passages of the place, two of the Spanish pilots were ordered to attend the lieutenant, and to conduct him to the most convenient landing-place, and were afterwards to be his guides on shore; and that we might have the greater security for their faithful behaviour on this occasion, the commodore took care to assure all our prisoners, that if the pilots acted properly, they should all of them be released, and set on shore at this place; but in case of any misconduct or treachery, he threatened them that the pilots should be instantly shot, and that he would carry all the rest of the Spaniards, who were on board him, prisoners to England. So that the prisoners themselves were interested in our success, and therefore we had no reason to suspect our conductors either of negligence or perfidy.

And on this occasion I cannot but remark a singular circumstance of one of the pilots employed by us in this business. It seems (as we afterwards learnt) he had been taken by Captain Clipperton above twenty years before, and had been forced to lead Clipperton and his people to the surprise of Truxillo, a town within land to the southward of Paita, where, however, he contrived to alarm his countrymen, and to save them, though the place was taken. Now that the only two attempts on shore, which were made at so long an interval from each other, should be guided by the same person, and he too a prisoner both times, and forced upon the employ contrary to his inclination, is an incident so very extraordinary, that I could not help taking notice of it. But to return to the matter in hand.

During our prepara..ons, the ships themselves stood towards the port with all the sail they could make, being secure that we were yet at too great a distance to be seen. But, about ten o'clock at night, the ships being then within five leagues of the place, Lieutenant Brett, with the boats under his command, put off, and arrived at the mouth of the bay without being discovered; but no sooner had he entered it, than some of the people on board a vessel, riding at anchor there, perceived him, who instantly put off in their boat, rowing towards the fort, shouting and crying, "The English dogs," &c. by which the whole town was suddenly alarmed, and our people soon observed several lights hurrying backwards and forwards in the fort, and other marks of the inhabitants being in great motion. Lieutenant Brett, on this, encouraged his men to pull briskly up to the shore, that they might give the enemy as little time as possible to prepare for their defence. However, before our boats could reach the shore, the people in the fort had got ready some of their cannon, and pointed them towards the landing-place; and though in the darkness of the night it might be well supposed that chance had a greater share than skill in their direction, yet the first shot passed extremely near one of the boats, whistling just over the heads of the crew. This made our people redouble their efforts; so that they had reached the shore, and were in part disembarked, by the time the second gun fired. As soon as our men landed, they were conducted by one of the Spanish pilots to the entrance of a narrow street, not above fifty yards distant from the beach, where they were covered from the fire of the fort; and being formed in the best manner the shortness of the time would allow, they immediately marched for the parade, which was a large square at the end of this street, the fort being one side of the square, and the governor's house another. In this march (though performed with tolerable regularity) the shouts and clamours of threescore sailors, who had been confined so long on shipboard, and were now, for the first time, on shore in an enemy's country, joyous as they always are when they land, and animated besides in the present case with the hopes of an immense pillage; the huzzas, I say, of this spirited detachment, joined with the noise of their drums, and favoured by the night, had augmented their numbers, in the opinion of the enemy, to at least three hundred; by which persuasion the inhabitants were so greatly intimidated, that they were much more solicitous about the means of their flight than of their resistance: so that though upon entering the parade, our people received a volley from the merchants who owned the treasure then in the town; and who, with a few others, had ranged themselves in a gallery that ran round the governor's house, yet that post was immediately abandoned upon the first fire made by our people, who were thereby left in quiet possession of the parade.

On this success Lieutenant Brett divided his men into two parties, ordering one of them to surround the governor's house, and if possible to secure the governor, whilst he himself with the other marched to the fort, with an intent to force it. But, contrary to his expectation, he entered it without opposition; for the enemy, on his approach, abandoned it, and made their escape over the walls. By this means the whole place was mastered in less than a quarter of an hour's time from the first landing, with no other loss than that of one man killed on the spot, and two wounded; one of which was the Spanish pilot of the Teresa, who received a slight bruise by a ball which grazed on his wrist: indeed, another of the company, the Honourable Mr. Keppel, son to the Earl of Albemarle, had a very narrow escape; for having on a jockey cap, one side of the peak was shaved off close to his temple by a ball, which however did him no other injury.

And now, Lieutenant Brett, after this success, placed a guard at the fort, and another at the Governor's house, and appointed sentinels at all the avenues of the town, both to prevent any surprise from the enemy, and to secure the effects in the place from being embezzled. And this being done, his next care was to seize on the customhouse where the treasure lay, and to examine if any of the inhabitants remained in the town, that he might know what farther precautions it was necessary to take; but he soon found that the numbers left behind were no ways formidable; for the greatest part of them (being in bed when the place was surprised) had run away with so much precipitation, that they had not given themselves time to put on their clothes. And in this precipitate rout the governor was not the last to secure himself, for he fled betimes half naked, leaving his wife, a young lady of about seventeen years of age, to whom he had been married but three or four days, behind him, though she too was afterwards carried off in her shift by a couple of sentinels, just as the detachment, ordered to invest the house, arrived before it

This escape of the governor was an unpleasing circumstance, as Mr. Anson had particularly recommended it to Lieutenant Brett to secure his person, if possible, in hopes that by that means we might be able to treat for the ransom of the place; but it seems his alertness rendered it impossible to seize him. The few inhabitants who remained were confined in one of the churches under a guard, except some stout negroes which were found in the place; these, instead of being shut up, were employed the remaining part of the night to assist in carrying the treasure from the customhouse and other places to the fort. However, there was care taken that they should be always attended by a file of musketeers.

The transporting the treasure from the customhouse to the fort, was the principal occupation of Mr. Brett's people, after he had got possession of the place. But the sailors, while they were thus employed, could not be prevented from entering the houses which lay near them, in search of private pillage. And the first things which occurred to them, being the clothes which the Spaniards in their flight had left behind them, and which, according to the custom of the country, were most of them either embroidered or laced, our people eagerly seized these glittering habits, and put them on over their own dirty trowsers and jackets; not forgetting, at the same time, the tie or bag-wig and laced hat, which were generally found with the clothes; and when this practice was once begun, there was no preventing the whole detachment from imitating it. And those, who came latest into the fashion, not finding men's clothes sufficient to equip themselves, they were obliged to take up with women's gowns and petticoats, which (provided there was finery enough) they made no scruple of putting on, and blending with their own greasy dress. So that when a party of them thus ridiculously metamorphosed first appeared before Mr. Brett, he was extremely surprised at their appearance, and could not immediately be satisfied they were his own people.

These were the transactions of our detachment on shore at Paita the first night. And now to return to what was done on board the Centurion in that interval. I must observe, that after the boats were gone off, we lay by till one o'clock in the morning, and then supposing our detachment to be near landing, we made an easy sail for the bay. About seven in the morning we began to open the bay, and soon after we had a view of the town; and though we had no reason to doubt of the success of the enterprise, yet it was with great joy that we first discovered an infallible signal of the certainty of our hopes; this was by means of our perspectives, for through them we saw an English flag hoisted on the flag-staff of the fort, which to us was an incontestable proof that our people had got possession of the town. We plied into the bay with as much expedition as the wind, which then blew off shore, would permit us. And at eleven, the Tryal's boat came on board us, loaden with dollars and church-plate; and the officer who commanded her informed us of the preceding night's transactions, such as we have already related them. About two in the afternoon we came to an anchor in ten fathom and a half, at a mile and a half distance from the town, and were consequently near enough to have a more immediate intercourse with those on shore. And now we found that Mr. Brett had hitherto gone on in collecting and removing the treasure without interruption; but that the enemy had rendezvoused from all parts of the country on a hill, at the back of the town, where they made no inconsiderable appearance: for amongst the rest of their force, there were two hundred horse seemingly very well armed and mounted, and, as we conceived, properly trained and regimented, being furnished with trumpets, drums, and standards. These troops paraded about the hill with great ostentation, sounding their military music, and practising every art to intimidate us (as our numbers on shore were by this time not unknown to them), in hopes that we might be induced by our fears to abandon the place before the pillage was completed. But we were not so ignorant as to believe that this body of horse, which seemed to be what the enemy principally depended on, would dare to venture in streets and amongst houses, even had their numbers been three times as great; and therefore, notwithstanding their menaces, we went on, as long as the day-light lasted, calmly, in sending off the treasure, and in employing the boats to carry on board the refreshments, such as hogs, fowls, &c. which we found here in great abundance. But, at night, to prevent any surprise, the commodore sent on shore a reinforcement, who posted themselves in all the streets leading to the parade; and for their greater security, they traversed the streets with barricadoes six feet high. And the enemy continuing quiet all night, we at day-break returned again to our labour of loading the boats and sending them off.

By this time we were convinced of what consequence it would have been to us, had fortune seconded the prudent views of the commodore, by permitting us to have secured the governor. For we found in the place many store-houses full of valuable effects, which were useless to us at present, and such as we could not find room for on board. But had the governor been in our power, he would, in all probability, have treated for a ransom, which would have been extremely advantageous both to him and us: whereas, he being now at liberty, and having collected all the force of the country, for many leagues round, and having even got a body of militia from Piura, which was fourteen leagues distant, he was so elated with his numbers, and so fond of his new military command, that he seemed not to trouble himself about the fate of his government. So that though Mr. Anson sent several messages to him by the inhabitants, who were in our power, desiring him to enter into a treaty for the ransom of the town and goods; giving him, at the same time, an intimation that he should be far from insisting on a rigorous equivalent, but perhaps might be satisfied with some live cattle, and a few necessaries for the use of the squadron, and assuring him too, that if he would not condescend at least to treat, he would set fire to the town and all the warehouses; yet the governor was so imprudent and arrogant, that he despised all these reiterated applications, and did not deign even to return the least answer to them.

On the second day of our being in possession of the place, several negro-slaves deserted from the enemy on the hill, and coming into the town, voluntarily entered into our service: one of these was well known to a gentleman on board, who remembered him formerly at Panama. And the Spaniards without the town being in extreme want of water, many of their slaves crept into the place by stealth, and carried away several jars of water to their masters on the hill; and though some of them were seized by our men in the attempt, yet the thirst among the enemy was so pressing, that they continued this practice till we left the place. And now, on this second day we were assured, both by the deserters and by these prisoners we took, that the Spaniards on the hill, who were by this time increased to a formidable number, had resolved to storm the town and fort the succeeding night; and that one Gordon, a Scotch papist, and captain of a ship in those seas, was to have the command of this enterprise. But we notwithstanding, continued sending off our boats, and prosecuted our work without the least hurry or precipitation till the evening; and then a reinforcement was again sent on shore by the commodore, and Lieutenant Brett doubled his guards at each of the barricadoes; and our posts being connected by the means of sentinels placed within call of each other, and the whole being visited by frequent rounds, attending with a drum, these marks of our vigilance, which the enemy could not be ignorant of, as they could doubtless hear the drum, if not the calls of the sentinels; these marks, I say of our vigilance, and of our readiness to receive them, cooled their resolution, and made them forget the vaunts of the preceding day; so that we passed this second night with as little molestation as we had done the first.

We had finished sending the treasure on board the Centurion the evening before; so that the third morning, being the 15th of November, the boats were employed in carrying off the most valuable part of the effects that remained in the town. And the commodore intending to sail this day, he, about ten o'clock, pursuant to his promise, sent all his prisoners, amounting to eighty-eight, on shore, giving orders to Lieutenant Brett to secure them in one of the churches, under a strict guard, till he was ready to embark his men. Mr. Brett was at the same time ordered to set the whole town on fire, except the two churches (which by good fortune stood at some distance from the other houses), and then he was to abandon the place, and to come on board. These orders were punctually complied with; for Mr. Brett immediately set his men to work, to distribute pitch, tar, and other combustibles (of which great quantities were found here) into houses situated in different streets of the town, so that, the place being fired in many quarters at the same time, the destruction might be more violent and sudden, and the enemy, after our departure, might not be able to extinguish it. These preparations being made, he in the next place ordered the cannon, which he found in the fort, to be nailed up; and then setting fire to those houses which were most windward, he collected his men, and marched towards the beach, where the boats waited to carry them off. And the part of the beach where he intended to embark being an open place without the town, the Spaniards on the hill perceiving he was retreating, resolved to try if they could not precipitate his departure, and thereby lay some foundation for their future boasting. And for this purpose a small squadron of their horse, consisting of about sixty, picked out, as I suppose, for this service, marched down the hill with much seeming resolution; so that, had we not been prepossessed with a juster opinion of their prowess, we might have suspected that, now we were on the open beach with no advantage of situation, they would certainly have charged us: but we presumed (and we were not mistaken) that this was mere ostentation. For, notwithstanding the pomp and parade they advanced with, Mr. Brett had no sooner ordered his men to halt and face about, but the enemy stopped their career, and never dared to advance a step further.

When our people were arrived at their boats, and were ready to go on board, they were for some time delayed, by missing one of their number; but being unable, by their mutual inquiries amongst each other, to inform themselves where he was left, or by what accident he was detained, they, after a considerable delay, resolved to get into their boats, and to put off without him. And the last man was actually embarked, and the boats just putting off, when they heard him calling to them to take him in. The town was by this time so thoroughly on fire, and the smoke covered the beach so effectually, that they could scarcely see him, though they heard his voice. The lieutenant instantly ordered one of the boats to his relief, who found him up to the chin in water, for he had waded as far as he durst, being extremely frightened with the apprehensions of falling into the hands of an enemy, enraged, as they doubtless were, with the pillage and destruction of their town. On inquiring into the cause of his staying behind, it was found that he had taken that morning too large a dose of brandy, which had thrown him into so sound a sleep, that he did not awake till the fire came near enough to scorch him. He was strangely amazed, on first opening his eyes, to see the place all in a blaze on one side, and several Spaniards and Indians not far from him on the other. The greatness and suddenness of his fright instantly reduced him to a state of sobriety, and gave him sufficient presence of mind to push through the thickest of the smoke, as the likeliest means to escape the enemy; and making the best of his way to the beach, he ran as far into the water as he durst, (for he could not swim) before he ventured to look back.

And here I cannot but observe, to the honour of our people, that though there were great quantities of wine and spirituous liquors found in the place, yet this man was the only one who was known to have so far neglected his duty, as to get drunk. Indeed, their whole behaviour, while they were on shore, was much more regular than could well have been expected from sailors, who had been so long confined to a ship: and though part of this prudent demeanour must doubtless be imputed to the diligence of their officers, and to the excellent discipline to which they had been long inured on board the commodore, yet it was doubtless no small reputation to the men, that they should in general refrain from indulging themselves in those intoxicating liquors, which they found ready to their hands in almost every warehouse.

And having mentioned this single instance of drunkenness, I cannot pass by another oversight, which was likewise the only one of its kind, and which was attended with very particular circumstances. There was an Englishman, who had formerly wrought as a ship-carpenter in the yard at Portsmouth, but leaving his country, had afterwards entered into the Spanish service, and was employed by them at the port of Guaiaquil; and it being well known to his friends in England that he was then in that part of the world, they put letters on board the Centurion, directed to him. This man being then by accident amongst the Spaniards, who were retired to the hill at Paita, he was desirous (as it should seem) of acquiring some reputation amongst his new masters. With this view he came down unarmed to a sentinel of ours, who was placed at some distance from the fort towards the enemy, and pretended to be desirous of surrendering himself, and of entering into our service. Our sentinel had a cocked pistol, but being deceived by the other's fair speeches, he was so imprudent as to let him approach much nearer than he ought; so that the shipwright, watching his opportunity, rushed on the sentinel, and seizing his pistol, wrenched it out of his hand, and instantly ran away with it up the hill. By this time, two of our people, who seeing the fellow advance, had suspected his intention, were making towards him, and were thereby prepared to pursue him; but he got to the top of the hill before they could reach him, and then turning about, fired the pistol; at which instant his pursuers fired at him, and though he was at a great distance, and the crest of the hill hid him as soon as they had fired, so that they took it for granted they had missed him, yet we afterwards learnt that he was shot through the body, and had fallen down dead the very next step he took after he was out of sight. The sentinel too, who had been thus grossly imposed upon, did not escape unpunished; for he was ordered to be severely whipt for being thus shamefully surprised upon his post, and for having given an example of carelessness, which, if followed in other instances, might prove fatal to us all. But to return:

By the time our people had taken their comrade out of the water, and were making the best of their way for the squadron, the flames had taken possession of every part of the town, and had got such hold, both by means of combustibles that had been distributed for that purpose, and by the slightness of the materials of which the houses were composed, and their aptitude to take fire, that it was sufficiently apparent no efforts of the enemy (though they flocked down in great numbers) could possibly put a stop to it, or prevent the entire destruction of the place, and all the merchandise contained therein. A whole town on fire at once, especially a place that burnt with such facility and violence, being a very singular and awful spectacle.

Our detachment under Lieutenant Brett having safely joined the squadron, the commodore prepared to leave the place the same evening. He found, when he first came into the bay, six vessels of the enemy at anchor; one of which was the ship, which, according to our intelligence, was to have sailed with the treasure to the coast of Mexico, and which, as we were persuaded she was a good sailer, we resolved to take with us: the others were two snows, a bark, and two row-galleys of thirty-six oars a-piece: these last, as we were afterwards informed, with many others of the same kind built at different ports, were intended to prevent our landing in the neighbourhood of Callao: for the Spaniards, on the first intelligence of our squadron and its force, expected that we would attempt the city of Lima. The commodore, having no occasion for these other vessels, had ordered the masts of all five of them to be cut away on his first arrival; and now, at his leaving the place, they were towed out of the harbour, and scuttled and sunk; and the command of the remaining ship, called the Solidad, being given to Mr. Hughs, the lieutenant of the Tryal, who had with him a crew of ten men to navigate her, the squadron towards midnight, weighed anchor, and sailed out of the bay, being now augmented to six sail, that is the Centurion and the Tryal prize, together with the Carmelo, the Teresa, the Carmin, and our last acquired vessel the Solidad.

And now, before I entirely quit the account of our transactions at this place, it may not perhaps be improper to give a succinct relation of the booty we made here, and of the loss the Spaniards sustained. I have before observed, that there were great quantities of valuable effects in the town; but as the greatest part of them were what we could neither dispose of nor carry away, the total amount of this merchandise can only be rudely guessed at. But the Spaniards, in the representations they made to the court of Madrid (as we were afterwards assured), estimated their whole loss at a million and a half of dollars; and when it is considered, that no small part of the goods we burnt there were of the richest and most expensive species, as broad-cloths, silks, cambrics, velvets, &c., I cannot but think their valuation sufficiently moderate. As to our parts, our acquisition, though inconsiderable in comparison of what we destroyed, was yet in itself far from despicable; for the wrought plate, dollars and other coin, which fell into our hands amounted to upwards of 30,000*l.* sterling, besides several rings, bracelets, and jewels, whose intrinsic value we could not then determine; and over and above all this, the plunder which became the property of the immediate captors, was very great: so that upon the whole it was by much the most important booty we made upon that coast.

There remains, before I take leave of this place, another particularity to be mentioned, which, on account of the great honour which our national character in those parts has thence received, and the reputation which our commodore in particular has thereby acquired, merits a distinct and circumstantial discussion. It has been already related, that all the prisoners taken by us in our preceding prizes were put on shore, and discharged at this place; amongst which there were some persons of considerable distinction, particularly a youth of about seventeen years of age, son of the vice-president of the Council of Chili. As the barbarity of the buccaneers, and the artful use the ecclesiastics had made of it, had filled the natives of those countries with the most terrible ideas of the English cruelty, we always found our prisoners, at their first coming on board us, to be extremely dejected, and under great horror and anxiety. In particular, this youth, whom I last mentioned, having never been from home before, lamented his captivity in the most moving manner, regretting, in very plaintive terms, his parents, his brothers, his sisters, and his native country; of all which he was fully persuaded he had taken his last farewell, believing that he was now devoted, for the remaining part of his life, to an abject and cruel servitude; nor was he singular in his fears, for his companions on board, and indeed all the Spaniards that came into our power, had the same desponding opinion of their situation. Mr. Anson constantly exerted his utmost endeavours to efface these inhuman impressions they had received of us; always taking care, that as many of the principal people among them as there was room for, should dine at his table by turns; and giving the strictest orders too, that they should at all times, and in every circumstance, be treated with the utmost decency and humanity. But notwithstanding this precaution, it was generally observed, that for the first day or two they did not quit their fears, but suspected the gentleness of their usage to be only preparatory to some unthought-of calamity. However, being confirmed by time, they grew perfectly easy in their situation and remarkably cheerful, so that it was often disputable, whether or no they considered their being detained by us as a misfortune. For the youth I have above-mentioned, who was near two months on board us, had at last so far conquered his melancholy surmises, and had taken such an affection to Mr. Anson, and seemed so much pleased with the manner of life, totally different from all he had ever seen before, that it is doubtful to me whether, if his own opinion had been taken, he would not have preferred a voyage to England in the Centurion, to the being set on shore at Paita, where he was at liberty to return to his country and his friends.

This conduct of the commodore to his prisoners, which was continued without interruption or deviation, gave them all the highest idea of his humanity and benevolence, and induced them likewise (as mankind are fond of forming general opinions) to entertain very favourable thoughts of the whole English nation. But whatever they might be disposed to think of Mr. Anson before the taking of the Teresa, their veneration for him was prodigiously increased by his conduct towards those women, whom (as I have already mentioned) he took in that vessel: for the leaving them in the possession of their apartments, the strict orders given to prevent all his people on board from approaching them, and the permitting the pilot to stay with them as their guardian, were measures that seemed so different from what might be expected from an enemy and a heretic, that the Spaniards on board, though they had themselves experienced his beneficence, were surprised at this new instance of it; and the more so, as all this was done without his ever having seen the women, though the two daughters were both esteemed handsome, and the youngest was celebrated for her uncommon beauty.[1] The women themselves, too, were so sensible of the obligations they owed him for the care and attention with which he had protected them, that they absolutely refused to go on shore at Paita, till they had been permitted to wait on him on board the Centurion, to return him thanks in person. Indeed, all the prisoners left us with the strongest assurances of their grateful remembrance of his uncommon treatment. A jesuit in particular, whom the commodore had taken, and who was an ecclesiastic of some distinction, could not help expressing himself with great thankfulness for the civilities he and his countrymen had found on board, declaring that he should consider it as his duty to do Mr. Anson justice

---

[1] "We have heard a great deal of the continence of Scipio Africanus, when that conqueror of Spain refused to see a beautiful princess that had fallen into his power. If Anson, under the circumstances of the times and country, be denied the meed of praise bestowed on the Roman general, as an example of stern Roman virtue, he was amply repaid for his generosity and humanity to his prisoners, by their cordial and grateful remembrance of his treatment, which was applauded and circulated through every corner of Spanish America."—*Barrow's Life of Lord Anson.*

at all times; adding, that his usage of the men-prisoners was such as could never be forgot, and such as he could never fail to acknowledge and recite upon all occasions: but that his behaviour to the women was so extraordinary, and so extremely honourable, that he doubted all the regard due to his own ecclesiastical character, would be scarcely sufficient to render it credible. And indeed we were afterwards informed, that both he and the rest of our prisoners had not been silent on this head, but had, both at Lima and at other places, given the greatest encomiums to our commodore; the jesuit in particular, as we were told, having on his account interpreted in a lax and hypothetical sense that article of his Church, which asserts the impossibility of heretics being saved.

And let it not be imagined, that the impressions which the Spaniards hence received to our advantage, is a matter of small import: for, not to mention several of our countrymen who have already felt the good effects of these prepossessions, the Spaniards are a nation, whose good opinion of us is doubtless of more consequence than that of all the world besides: not only as the commerce we have formerly carried on with them, and perhaps may again hereafter, is so extremely valuable; but also as the transacting it does so immediately depend on the honour and good faith of those who are entrusted with its management. But, however, had no national conveniences attended it, the commodore's equity and good temper would not less have deterred him from all tyranny and cruelty to those whom the fortune of war had put into his hands. I shall only add, that by his constant attachment to these humane and prudent maxims, he has acquired a distinguished reputation amongst the Creolian Spaniards, which is not confined merely to the coast of the South Seas, but is extended through all the Spanish settlements in America; so that his name is frequently to be met with in the mouths of most of the Spanish inhabitants of that prodigious empire.[1]

CHAPTER VII.

From our departure from Paita, to our arrival at Quito.

WHEN we got under sail from the road of Paita (which, as I have already observed, was about midnight, on the 16th of November) we stood to the westward, and in the morning the commodore gave orders that the whole squadron should spread themselves, in order to look out for the Gloucester. For we now drew near to the station where Captain Mitchel had been directed to cruise, and hourly expected to get sight of him; but the whole day passed without seeing him.

And now a jealousy, which had taken its rise at Paita, between those who had been ordered on shore for the attack, and those who had continued on board, grew to such a height that the commodore, being made acquainted with it, thought it necessary to interpose his authority to appease it. The ground of this animosity was the plun-der gotten at Paita, which those who had acted on shore had appropriated to themselves, and considered as a reward for the risks they had run, and the resolution they had shown in that service. But those who had remained on board considered this as a very partial and unjust procedure, urging, that had it been left to their choice, they should have preferred the acting on shore to the continuing on board; that their duty, while their comrades were on shore, was extremely fatiguing; for besides the labour of the day, they were constantly under arms all night to secure the prisoners, whose numbers exceeded their own, and of whom it was then necessary to be extremely watchful, to prevent any attempts they might have formed in that critical conjuncture; that upon the whole it could not be denied, but that the presence of a sufficient force on board was as necessary to the success of the enterprise as the action of the others on shore; and therefore those who had continued on board insisted, that they could not be deprived of their share of the plunder without manifest injustice. These were the contests amongst our men, which were carried on with great heat on both sides: and though the plunder in question was a very trifle, in comparison of the treasure taken in the place (in which there was no doubt but those on board had an equal right), yet as the obstinacy of sailors is not always regulated by the importance of the matter in dispute, the commodore thought it necessary to put a stop to this ferment betimes. And accordingly, the morning after our leaving of Paita, he ordered all hands upon the quarter-deck; where, addressing himself to those who had been detached on shore, he commended their behaviour, and thanked them for their services on that occasion: but then representing to them the reasons urged, by those who had continued on board, for an equal distribution of the plunder, he told them that he thought these reasons very conclusive, and that the expectations of their comrades were justly founded; and therefore he ordered, that not only the men, but all the officers likewise, who had been employed in taking the place, should produce the whole of their plunder immediately upon the quarter-deck; and that it should be impartially divided amongst the whole crew, in proportion to each man's rank and commission: and to prevent those who had been in possession of the plunder from murmuring at this diminution of their share, the commodore added, that as an encouragement to others who might be hereafter employed on like services, he would give his entire share to be distributed amongst those who had been detached for the attack of the place. Thus this troublesome affair, which if permitted to have gone on, might perhaps have been attended with mischievous consequences, was by the commodore's prudence soon appeased, to the general satisfaction of the ship's company: not but there were some few, whose selfish dispositions were uninfluenced by the justice of this procedure, and who were incapable of discerning the force of equity, however glaring, when it tended to deprive them of any part of what they had once got into their hands.

This important business employed the best part of the day, after we came from Paita. And now, at night, having no sight of the Gloucester, the commodore ordered the squadron to bring-to, that

---

[1] "Even to this day the name of Anson is held in the highest respect in the Spanish provinces of America, while the fate of Paita is forgotten, or, if remembered, is so chiefly to reprobate the obstinacy of the governor."—*Barrow's Life of Lord Anson.*

we might not pass her in the dark. The next morning we again looked out for her, and at ten we saw a sail, to which we gave chase ; and at two in the afternoon we came near enough to her to discover her to be the Gloucester, with a small vessel in tow. About an hour after, we were joined by them ; and then we learnt that Captain Mitchel, in the whole time of his cruise, had only taken two prizes ; one of them being a small snow, whose cargo consisted chiefly of wine, brandy, and olives in jars, with about 7000*l.* in specie ; and the other a large boat or launch, which the Gloucester's barge came up with near the shore. The prisoners on board this vessel alleged, that they were very poor, and that their lading consisted only of cotton ; though the circumstances in which the barge surprised them, seemed to insinuate that they were more opulent than they pretended to be ; for the Gloucester's people found them at dinner upon pigeon-pie, served up in silver dishes. However, the officer who commanded the barge having opened several of the jars on board, to satisfy his curiosity, and finding nothing in them but cotton, he was inclined to believe the account the prisoners gave him : but the cargo being taken into the Gloucester, and there examined more strictly, they were agreeably surprised to find, that the whole was a very extraordinary piece of false package ; and that there was concealed amongst the cotton, in every jar, a considerable quantity of double doubloons and dollars, to the amount in the whole of near 12,000*l.* This treasure was going to Paita, and belonged to the same merchants who were the proprietors of the greatest part of the money we had taken there ; so that, had this boat escaped the Gloucester, it is probable her cargo would have fallen into our hands. Besides these two prizes which we have mentioned, the Gloucester's people told us, that they had been in sight of two or three other ships of the enemy which had escaped them ; and one of them we had reason to believe, from some of our intelligence, was of an immense value.

Being now joined by the Gloucester and her prize, it was resolved that we should stand to the northward, and make the best of our way either to Cape St. Lucas on California, or to Cape Corientes on the coast of Mexico. Indeed the commodore, when at Juan Fernandes, had determined with himself to touch in the neighbourhood of Panama, and to endeavour to get some correspondence over-land with the fleet under the command of Admiral Vernon. For when we departed from England, we left a large force at Portsmouth, which was intended to be sent to the West Indies, there to be employed in an expedition against some of the Spanish settlements. And Mr. Anson taking it for granted, that this enterprise had succeeded, and that Porto Bello perhaps might be then garrisoned by British troops, he hoped that on his arrival at the isthmus, he should easily procure an intercourse with our countrymen on the other side, either by the Indians, who were greatly disposed in our favour, or even by the Spaniards themselves, some of whom, for proper rewards, might be induced to carry on this intelligence, which, after it was once begun, might be continued with very little difficulty ; so that Mr. Anson flattered himself, that he might by this means have received a reinforcement of men from the other side, and that by settling a prudent plan of operations with our commanders in the West-Indies, he might have taken even Panama itself; which would have given to the British nation the possession of that isthmus, whereby we should have been in effect masters of all the treasures of Peru, and should have had in our hands an equivalent for any demands, however extraordinary, which we might have been induced to have made on either of the branches of the house of Bourbon.

Such were the projects which the commodore revolved in his thoughts at the island of Juan Fernandes, notwithstanding the feeble condition to which he was then reduced. And indeed, had the success of our force in the West Indies been answerable to the general expectation, it cannot be denied but these views would have been the most prudent that could have been thought of. But in examining the papers which were found on board the Carmelo, the first prize we took, we learnt (though I then omitted to mention it) that our attempt against Carthagena had failed, and that there was no probability that our fleet, in that part of the world, would engage in any new enterprise, that would at all facilitate this plan. And therefore Mr. Anson gave over all hopes of being reinforced across the isthmus, and consequently had no inducement at present to proceed to Panama, as he was incapable of attacking the place ; and there was great reason to believe, that by this time there was a general embargo on all the coast.

The only feasible measure than which was left us, was to get as soon as possible to the southern parts of California, or to the adjacent coast of Mexico, there to cruise for the Manila galleon, which we knew was now at sea, bound to the port of Acapulco. And we doubted not to get on that station, time enough to intercept her ; for this ship does not actually arrive at Acapulco till towards the middle of January, and we were now but in the middle of November, and did not conceive that our passage thither would cost us above a month or five weeks ; so that we imagined, we had near twice as much time as was necessary for our purpose. Indeed there was a business which we foresaw would occasion some delay, but we flattered ourselves that it would be despatched in four or five days, and therefore could not interrupt our project. This was the recruiting of our water ; for the number of prisoners we had entertained on board, since our leaving the island of Fernandes, had so far exhausted our stock, that it was impossible to think of venturing upon this passage to the coast of Mexico, till we had procured a fresh supply ; especially as at Paita, where we had some hopes of getting a quantity, we did not find enough for our consumption during the time we staid there. It was for some time a matter of deliberation, where we should take in this necessary article ; but by consulting the accounts of former navigators, and examining our prisoners, we at last resolved for the island of Quibo, situated at the mouth of the bay of Panama : nor was it but on good grounds that the commodore conceived this to be the properest place for watering the squadron. Indeed, there was a small island called Cocos, which was less out of our way than Quibo, where some of the buccaneers have pretended they found water; but none of our prisoners knew anything of it, and it was thought too hazardous to risk the safety of the squadron, and expose ourselves to the hazard of not meeting with water when we came there, on the mere authority of these legendary writers, of whose misrepresentations and falsities we had almost daily experience. Besides, by going to Quibo we were not without hopes that some of the enemy's ships bound to or from Panama might fall into our hands, particularly such of them as were put to sea before they had any intelligence of our squadron.

Having determined therefore to go to Quibo, we directed our course to the northward, being eight sail in company, and consequently having the appearance of a very formidable fleet; and on the 19th, at day-break, we discovered Cape Blanco, bearing S.S.E.½E. seven miles distant. This cape lies in the latitude of 4° 15′ south, and is always made by ships bound either to windward or to leeward; so that off this cape is a most excellent station to cruise upon the enemy. By this time we found that our last prize, the Solidad, was far from answering the character given her of a good sailer; and she and the Santa Teresa delaying us considerably, the commodore ordered them both to be cleared of everything that might prove useful to the rest of the ships, and then to be burnt; and having given proper instructions, and a rendezvous to the Gloucester and the other prizes, we proceeded in our course for Quibo; and, on the 22d in the morning, saw the island of Plata, bearing east, distant four leagues. Here one of our prizes was ordered to stand close in with it, both to discover if there were any ships between that island and the continent, and likewise to look out for a stream of fresh water, which was reported to be there, and which would have saved us the trouble of going to Quibo; but she returned without having seen any ship, or finding any water. At three in the afternoon Point Manta bore S.E. by E., seven miles distant; and there being a town of the same name in the neighbourhood, Captain Mitchel took this opportunity of sending away several of his prisoners from the Gloucester in the Spanish launch. The boats were now daily employed in distributing provisions on board the Tryal and other prizes, to complete their stock for six months: and that the Centurion might be the better prepared to give the Manila ship (one of which we were told was of an immense size) a warm reception, the carpenters were ordered to fix eight stocks in the main and fore tops, which were properly fitted for the mounting of swivel guns.

On the 25th we had a sight of the island of Gallo, bearing E.S.E.½E., four leagues distant; and from hence we crossed the bay of Panama with a N.W. course, hoping that this would have carried us in a direct line to the island of Quibo. But we afterwards found that we ought to have stood more to the westward; for the winds in a short time began to incline to that quarter, and made it difficult for us to gain the island. And now, after passing the equinoctial, (which we did on the 22d,) and leaving the neighbourhood of the Cordilleras, and standing more and more towards the isthmus, where the communication of the atmosphere to the eastward and the westward was no longer interrupted, we found in very few days an extraordinary alteration in the climate. For instead of that uniform temperature, where neither the excess of heat or cold was to be complained of, we had now for several days together close and sultry weather, resembling what we had before met with on the coast of Brazil, and in other parts between the tropics on the eastern side of America. We had besides frequent calms and heavy rains; which we at first ascribed to the neighbourhood of the Line, where this kind of weather is generally found to prevail at all seasons of the year; but observing that it attended us to the latitude of seven degrees north, we were at length induced to believe that the stormy season, or, as the Spaniards call it, the Vandevals, was not yet over; though many writers, particularly Captain Shelvocke, positively assert, that this season begins in June, and is ended in November; and our prisoners all affirmed the same thing. But perhaps its end may not be always constant, and it might last this year longer than usual.

On the 27th, Captain Mitchel having finished the clearing of his largest prize, she was scuttled, and set on fire; but we still consisted of five ships, and were fortunate enough to find them all good sailers; so that we never occasioned any delay to each other. Being now in a rainy climate, which we had been long disused to, we found it necessary to caulk the decks and sides of the Centurion, to prevent the rain-water from running into her.

On the 3rd of December we had a view of the island of Quibo; the east end of which then bore from us N.N.W., four leagues distant, and the island of Quicara W.N.W., at about the same distance. Here we struck ground with sixty-five fathoms of line, and found the bottom to consist of grey sand, with black specks. When we had thus got sight of the land, we found the wind to hang westerly; and therefore, night coming on, we thought it advisable to stand off till morning, as there are said to be some shoals in the entrance of the channel. At six the next morning Point Mariato bore N.E.½N., three or four leagues distant. In weathering this point, all the squadron, except the Centurion, were very near it; and the Gloucester, being the leewardmost ship, was forced to tack and stand to the southward, so that we lost sight of her. At nine, the island Sebaco bore N.W. by N., four leagues distant; but the wind still proving unfavourable, we were obliged to ply on and off for the succeeding twenty-four hours, and were frequently taken aback. However, at eleven the next morning, the wind happily settled in the S.S.W., and we bore away for the S.S.E. end of the island, and about three in the afternoon entered the Canal Bueno, passing round a shoal which stretches off about two miles from the south point of the island. This Canal Bueno, or Good Channel, is at least six miles in breadth; and as we had the wind large, we kept in a good depth of water, generally from twenty-eight to thirty-three fathoms, and came not within a mile and a half distance of the breakers; though, in all probability, if it had been necessary, we might have ventured much nearer without incurring the least danger. At seven in the evening we came to an anchor in thirty-three fathoms muddy ground; the south point of the island bearing S.E. by S., a remarkable high part of the island W. by N., and the island Sebaco E. by N. Being thus arrived at this island of Quibo, the account of the place, and of our transactions there shall be referred to the ensuing chapter.

CHAPTER VIII.

Our proceedings at Quibo, with an account of the place.

THE next morning, after our coming to an anchor, an officer was despatched on shore to discover the watering-place, who having found it, returned before noon; and then we sent the long-boat for a load of water, and at the same time we weighed and stood farther in with our ships. At two we came again to an anchor in twenty-two fathoms, with a bottom of rough gravel intermixed with broken shells, the watering place now bearing from us N.W.¼N., only three quarters of a mile distant.

This island of Quibo is extremely convenient for wooding and watering; for the trees grow close to the high-water mark, and a large rapid stream of fresh water runs over the sandy beach into the sea: so that we were little more than two days in laying in all the wood and water we wanted. The whole island is of a very moderate height, excepting one part. It consists of a continued wood spread over the whole surface of the country, which preserves its verdure all the year round. Amongst the other wood we found there abundance of cassia and a few lime trees. It appeared singular to us that, considering the climate and the shelter, we should see no other birds there than parrots, parroquets, and macaws; indeed of these last there were prodigious flights. Next to these birds, the animals we found there in most plenty were monkeys and guanos, and these we frequently killed for food; for though we were informed there were many herds of deer upon the place, yet the difficulty of penetrating the woods prevented our coming near them, so that though we saw them often, we killed only two during our stay. Our prisoners assured us that this island abounded with tigers; and we did once discover the print of a tiger's paw upon the beach, but the tigers themselves we never saw. The Spaniards, too, informed us that there was often found in the woods a most mischievous serpent, called the flying snake, which they said darted itself from the boughs of trees on either man or beast that came within its reach; and whose sting they believed to be inevitable death. Besides these mischievous land animals, the sea hereabouts is infested with great numbers of alligators of an extraordinary size; and we often observed a large kind of flat-fish, jumping a considerable height out of the water, which we supposed to be the fish that is said frequently to destroy the pearl divers, by clasping them in its fins as they rise from the bottom; and we were told that the divers, for their security, are now always armed with a sharp knife, which, when they are entangled, they stick into the belly of the fish, and thereby disengage themselves from its embraces.

Whilst the ship continued here at anchor, the commodore, attended by some of his officers, went in a boat to examine a bay which lay to the north-ward; and they afterwards ranged all along the eastern side of the island. And in the places where they put on shore in the course of this expedition, they generally found the soil to be extremely rich, and met with great plenty of excellent water. In particular, near the N.E. point of the island, they discovered a natural cascade, which surpassed, as they conceived, everything of this kind which human art or industry has hitherto produced. It was a river of transparent water, about forty yards wide, which ran down a declivity of near a hundred and fifty yards in length. The channel it ran in was very irregular; for it was entirely formed of rock, both its sides and bottom being made up of large detached blocks; and by these the course of the water was frequently interrupted: for in some places it ran sloping with a rapid but uniform motion, while in other parts it tumbled over the ledges of rocks with a perpendicular descent. All the neighbourhood of this stream was a fine wood; and even the huge masses of rock which overhung the water, and which, by their various projections, formed the inequalities of the channel, were covered with lofty forest trees. Whilst the commodore, and those who were with him, were attentively viewing this place, and were remarking the different blendings of the water, the rocks and the wood, there came in sight (as it were with an intent still to heighten and animate the prospect) a prodigious flight of macaws, which hovering over this spot, and often wheeling and playing on the wing about it, afforded a most brilliant appearance, by the glittering of the sun on their variegated plumage; so that some of the spectators cannot refrain from a kind of transport, when they recount the complicated beauties which occurred in this extraordinary waterfall.

In this expedition, which the boat made along the eastern side of the island, though they met with no inhabitants, yet they saw many huts upon the shore, and great heaps of shells of fine mother-of-pearl scattered up and down in different places: these were the remains left by the pearl-fishers from Panama, who often frequent this place in the summer season; for the pearl oysters, which are to be met with everywhere in the bay of Pa-nama, are so plentiful at Quibo, that by advancing a very little way into the sea, you might stoop down and reach them from the bottom. They are usually very large, and out of curiosity we opened some of them with a view of tasting them, but we found them extremely tough and unpalatable. And having mentioned these oysters and the pearl-fishery, I must beg leave to recite a few particulars relating thereto.

The oysters most productive of pearls are those found in considerable depths; for though what are taken up by wading near shore are of the same species, yet the pearls found in them are very rare and very small. It is said too that the pearl partakes in some degree of the quality of the bottom on which the oyster is found; so that if the bottom be muddy the pearl is dark and ill-coloured.

The taking up oysters from great depths for the sake of the pearls they contain, is a work performed by negro slaves, of which the inhabitants of Panama and the neighbouring coast formerly kept great numbers, which were carefully trained to this business. And these are said not to be esteemed complete divers till they have by degrees been able to protract their stay under water so long, that the blood gushes out from their nose, mouth, and ears. And it is the tradition of the country, that when this accident has once befallen them, they dive for the future with much greater facility than before; and they have no apprehension either that any inconvenience can attend it, the bleeding generally stopping of itself, or that there is any probability of their being ever subject to it a second time. But to return from this digression.

Though the pearl-oyster, as has been said, was incapable of being eaten, yet the sea at this place furnished us with another dainty, in the greatest plenty and perfection: this was the turtle, of which we took here what quantity we pleased. There are generally reckoned four species of turtle; that is, the trunk turtle, the loggerhead, the hawksbill, and the green turtle. The two first are rank and unwholesome; the hawksbill (which furnishes the tortoiseshell) is but indifferent food, though better than the other two; but the green turtle is generally esteemed, by the greatest part of those who are acquainted with its taste, to be the most delicious of all eatables; and that it is a most wholesome food, we are amply convinced by our own experience: for we fed on this last species, or the green turtle, for near four months, and consequently, had it been in any degree noxious, its ill effects could not possibly have escaped us. At this island we took what quantity we pleased with great facility; for as they are an amphibious animal, and get on shore to lay their eggs, which they generally deposit in a large hole in the sand, just above the high-water mark, covering them up, and leaving them to be hatched by the heat of the sun, we usually dispersed several of our men along the beach, whose business it was to turn them on their backs when they came to land; and the turtle being thereby prevented from getting away, we carried them off at our leisure; by this means we not only secured a sufficient stock for the time we staid on the island, but we took a number of them with us to sea, which proved of great service both in lengthening out our store of provision, and in heartening the whole crew with an almost constant supply of fresh and palatable food; for the turtle being large, they generally weighing about 200lbs. weight each, those we took with us lasted us near a month, and by that time we met with a fresh recruit on the coast of Mexico, where we often saw them in the heat of the day floating in great numbers on the surface of the water fast asleep. When we discovered them we usually sent out our boat with a man in the bow, who was a dexterous diver, and when the boat came within a few yards of the turtle, the diver plunged into the water, and took care to rise close upon it; and seizing the shell near the tail, and pressing down the hinder parts, the turtle, when awakened, began to strike with its claws, which motion supported both it and the diver, till the boat came up and took them in. By this management we never wanted turtle for the succeeding four months in which we continued at sea; and though, when at Quibo, we had already been three months on board, without otherwise putting our feet on shore, than in the few days we stayed at this island of Quibo, (except those employed in the attack of Paita,) yet in the whole seven months, from our leaving Juan Fernandes to our anchoring in the harbour of Chequetan, we buried no more in the whole squadron than two men; a most incontestable proof that the turtle, on which we fed for the last four months of this term, was at least innocent, if not something more.

Considering the scarcity of provisions on some part of the coast of these seas, it appears wonderful, that a species of food so very palatable and salubrious as turtle, and so much abounding in those parts, should be proscribed by the Spaniards as unwholesome, and little less than poisonous. Perhaps the strange appearance of this animal may have been the foundation of this ridiculous and superstitious aversion, which is strongly rooted in all the inhabitants of that coast, and of which we had many instances in the course of this navigation. I have already observed, that we put our Spanish prisoners on shore at Paita, and that the Gloucester sent theirs to Manta; but as we had taken in our prizes some Indian and negro slaves, we did not set these on shore with their masters, but continued them on board, as our crews were thin, to assist in navigating our ships. These poor people being possessed with the prejudices of the country they came from, were astonished at our feeding on turtle, and seemed fully persuaded that it would soon destroy us; but finding that none of us died, nor even suffered in our health by a continuation of this diet, they at last got so far the better of their aversion, as to be persuaded to taste it, to which the absence of all other kinds of fresh provisions might not a little contribute. However, it was with great reluctance, and very sparingly, that they first began to eat of it: but the relish improving upon them by degrees, they at last grew extremely fond of it, and preferred it to every other kind of food, and often felicitated each other on the happy experience they had acquired, and the delicious and plentiful repasts it would be always in their power to procure, when they should again return back to their country. Those who are acquainted with the manner of life of these unhappy wretches, need not be told, that next to large draughts of spirituous liquors, plenty of tolerable food is the greatest joy they know, and consequently the discovering a method which would always supply them with what quantity they pleased, of a food more luxurious to the palate than any their haughty lords and masters could indulge in, was doubtless a circumstance which they considered as the most fortunate that could befal them.

After this digression, which the prodigious quantity of turtle on this island of Quibo, and the store of it we thence took to sea, in t une measure led me into, I shall now return to our wn proceedings.

In three days' time we had completed our business at this place, and were extremely impatient to put to sea, that we might arrive time enough on the coast of Mexico to intercept the Manila galleon. But the wind being contrary, detained us a night; and the next day, when we got into the offing, (which we did through the same channel by which we entered,) we were obliged to keep hovering about the island, in hopes of getting sight of the Gloucester; which, as I have in the last chapter mentioned, was separated from us on our first arrival. It was the 9th of December, in the morning, when we put to sea; and continuing to the southward of the island, looking out for the Gloucester, we, on the 10th, at five in the afternoon, discerned a small sail to the northward of us, to which we gave chase, and, coming up with her, took her. She proved to be a barque from Panama, bound to Cheripe, an inconsiderable village on the continent, and was called the Jesu Nazareno. She had nothing on board but some oakum, about a ton of rock-salt, and between 30*l*. and 40*l*. in specie, most of it consisting of small silver money, intended for purchasing a cargo of provisions at Cheripe.

And on occasion of this prize I cannot but observe, for the use of future cruisers, that had we been in want of provisions, we had by this capture an obvious method of supplying ourselves. For at Cheripe, whither she was bound, there is a constant store of provisions prepared for the vessels who go thither every week from Panama, the market of Panama being chiefly supplied from thence: so that by putting a few of our hands on board our prize, we might easily have seized a large store without any hazard, since Cheripe is a place of no strength. And as provisions are the staple commodity of that place and of its neighbourhood, the knowledge of this circumstance may be of great use to such cruisers as find their provisions grow scant, and yet are desirous of continuing on that coast as long as possible. But to return:

On the 12th of December, we were at last relieved from the perplexity we had suffered by the separation of the Gloucester; for on that day she joined us, and informed us that in tacking to the southward, on our first arrival, she had sprung her foretop-mast, which had disabled her from working to windward, and prevented her from joining us sooner. And now we scuttled and sunk the Jesu Nazareno, the prize we took last; and having the greatest impatience to get into a proper station for the galleon, we stood all together to the westward, leaving the island of Quibo (notwithstanding all the impediments we met with) in about nine days after our first coming in sight of it.

CHAPTER IX.

From Quibo to the coast of Mexico.

On the 12th of December we stood from Quibo to the westward, and the same day the commodore delivered fresh instructions to the captains of the men-of-war, and the commanders of our prizes, appointing them the rendezvouses they were to make, and the courses they were to steer, in case of a separation. And first, they were directed to use all possible despatch in getting to the northward of the harbour of Acapulco, where they were to endeavour to fall in with the land, between the latitudes of 18 and 19 degrees; from thence, they were to beat up the coast at eight or ten leagues' distance from the shore, till they came abreast of Cape Corientes, in the latitude of 20° 20′. When they arrived there, they were to continue cruising on that station till the 14th of February; and then they were to proceed to the middle island of the Tres Marias, in the latitude of 21° 25′, bearing from Cape Corientes N.W. by N., twenty-five leagues distant. And if at this island they did not meet the commodore, they were there to recruit their wood and water, and then to make the best of their way to the island of Macao, on the coast of China. These orders being distributed to all the ships, we had little doubt of arriving soon upon our intended station, as we expected, upon the increasing our offing from Quibo, to fall in with the regular trade-wind. But, to our extreme vexation, we were baffled for near a month, either with tempestuous weather from the western quarter, or with dead calms and heavy rains, attended with a sultry air; so that it was the 25th of December before we got a sight of the island of Cocos, which by our reckoning was only a hundred leagues from the continent; and we had the mortification to make so little way, that we did not lose sight of it again in five days. This island we found to be in the latitude of 5° 20′ north. It has a high hummock towards the western part, which descends gradually, and at last terminates in a low point to the eastward. From the island of Cocos we stood W. by N., and were till the 9th of January in running a hundred leagues more. We had at first flattered ourselves, that the uncertain weather and western gales we met with were owing to the neighbourhood of the continent, from which, as we got more distant, we expected every day to be relieved, by falling in with the eastern trade-wind: but as our hopes were so long baffled, and our patience quite exhausted, we began at length to despair of succeeding in the great purpose we had in view, that of intercepting the Manila galleon; and this produced a general dejection amongst us, as we had at first considered this project as almost infallible, and had indulged ourselves in the most boundless hopes of the advantages we should thence receive. However, our despondency was at last somewhat alleviated, by a favourable change of the wind; for on the 9th of January, a gale for the first time sprang up from the N.E., and on this we took the Carmelo in tow, as the Gloucester did the Carmin, making all the sail we could to improve the advantage, for we still suspected that it was only a temporary gale, which would not last long; but the next day we had the satisfaction to find, that the wind did not only continue in the same quarter, but blew with so much briskness and steadiness, that we now no longer doubted of its being the true trade-wind. And as we advanced apace towards our station, our hopes began to revive, and our former despair by degrees gave place to more sanguine prejudices: for though the customary season of the arrival of the galleon at Acapulco was already elapsed, yet we were by this time unreasonable enough to flatter ourselves, that some accidental delay might, for our advantage, lengthen out her passage beyond its usual limits.

When we got into the trade-wind, we found no alteration in it till the 17th of January, when we were advanced to the latitude of 12° 50′, but on that day it shifted to the westward of the north: this change we imputed to our having hauled up too soon, though we then esteemed ourselves full seventy leagues from the coast, which plainly shows that the trade-wind does not take place but at a considerable distance from the continent. After this, the wind was not so favourable to us as it had been: however, we still continued to advance, and, on the 26th of January, being then to the northward of Acapulco, we tacked and stood to the eastward, with a view of making the land.

In the preceding fortnight we caught some turtle on the surface of the water, and several dolphins, bonitos, and albicores. One day, as one of the sail-maker's mates was fishing from the end of the jib-boom, he lost his hold, and dropped into the sea; and the ship, which was then going at the rate of six or seven knots, went directly over him: but as we had the Carmelo in tow, we instantly called out to the people on board her, who threw him over several ends of ropes, one of which he fortunately caught hold of, and twisting it round his arm, they hauled him into the ship, without his having received any other injury than a wrench in his arm, of which he soon recovered.

When, on the 26th of January, we stood to the eastward, we expected, by our reckonings, to have fallen in with the land on the 28th; but though the weather was perfectly clear, we had no sight of it at sunset, and therefore we continued on our course, not doubting but we should see it by the next morning. About ten at night we discovered a light on the larboard-bow, bearing from us N.N.E. The Tryal's prize, too, which was about a mile ahead of us, made a signal at the same time for seeing a sail; and as we had none of us any doubt but what we saw was a ship's light, we were all extremely animated with a firm persuasion that it was the Manila galleon, which had been so long the object of our wishes: and what added to our alacrity, was our expectation of meeting with two of them instead of one, for we took it for granted that the light in view was carried in the top of one ship for a direction to her consort. We immediately cast off the Carmelo and pressed forward with all our canvas, making a signal for the Gloucester to do the same. Thus we chased the light, keeping all our hands to their respective quarters, under an expectation of engaging in the next half hour, as we sometimes conceived the chase to be about a mile distant, and at other times to be within reach of our guns; and some on board us positively averred, that besides the light, they could plainly discern her sails. The commodore himself was so fully persuaded that we should be soon alongside of her, that he sent for his first lieutenant, who commanded between decks, and directed him to see all the great guns loaded with two round-shot for the first broadside, and after that with one round-shot and one grape; strictly charging him, at the same time, not to suffer a gun to be fired, till he, the commodore, should give orders, which he informed the lieutenant would not be till we arrived within pistol-shot of the enemy. In this constant and eager attention we continued all night, always presuming that another quarter of an hour would bring us up with this Manila ship, whose wealth, with that of her supposed consort, we now estimated by round millions. But when the morning broke, and daylight came on, we were most strangely and vexatiously disappointed, by finding that the light which had occasioned all this bustle and expectancy, was only a fire on the shore. Indeed the circumstances of this deception are so extraordinary as to be scarcely credible; for, by our run during the night, and the distance of the land in the morning, there was no doubt to be made but this fire, when we first discovered it, was above twenty-five leagues from us: and yet I believe there was no person on board who doubted of its being a ship's light, or of its being near at hand. It was indeed upon a very high mountain, and continued burning for several days afterwards; it was not a volcano, but rather, as I suppose, stubble or heath set on fire for some purpose of agriculture.

At sun-rising, after this mortifying delusion, we found ourselves about nine leagues off the land, which extended from the N.W. to E.¼N. On this land we observed two remarkable hummocks, such as are usually called paps, which bore north from us: these, a Spanish pilot and two Indians, who were the only persons amongst us that pretended to have traded in this part of the world, affirmed to be over the harbour of Acapulco. Indeed, we very much doubted their knowledge of the coast; for we found these paps to be in the latitude of 17° 56', whereas those over Acapulco are said to be in 17 degrees only; and we afterwards found our suspicions of their skill to be well grounded: however, they were very confident, and assured us, that the height of the mountains was itself an infallible mark of the harbour; the coast, as they pretended (though falsely) being generally low to the eastward and westward of it.

And now being in the track of the Manila galleon, it was a great doubt with us (as it was near the end of January) whether she was or was not arrived: but examining our prisoners about it, they assured us, that she was sometimes known to come in after the middle of February; and they endeavoured to persuade us, that the fire we had seen on shore was a proof that she was as yet at sea, it being customary, as they said, to make use of these fires as signals for her direction, when she continued longer out than ordinary. On this information, strengthened by our propensity to believe them in a matter which so pleasingly flattered our wishes, we resolved to cruise for her for some days; and we accordingly spread our ships at the distance of twelve leagues from the coast, in such a manner, that it was impossible she should pass us unobserved: however, not seeing her soon, we were at intervals inclined to suspect that she had gained her port already; and as we now began to want a harbour to refresh our people, the uncertainty of our present situation gave us great uneasiness, and we were very solicitous to get some positive intelligence, which might either set us at liberty to consult our necessities, if the galleon was arrived, or might animate us to continue on our present cruise with cheerfulness, if she was not. With this view the commodore, after examining our prisoners very particularly, resolved to send a boat, under colour of the night, into the harbour of Acapulco, to see if the Manila ship was there or not, one of the Indians being very positive that this might be done without the boat itself being discovered. To execute this project, the barge was despatched the 5th of February, with a sufficient crew and two officers, who took with them a Spanish pilot, and the Indian who had insisted on the practicability of this measure, and had undertaken to conduct it. Our barge did not return to us again till the eleventh, when the officers acquainted Mr. Anson, that, agreeable to our suspicion, there was nothing like a harbour in the place where the Spanish pilots had at first asserted Acapulco to lie; that when they had satisfied themselves in this particular, they steered to the eastward, in hopes of discovering it, and had coasted alongshore thirty-two leagues; that in this whole range they met chiefly with sandy beaches of a great length, over which the sea broke with so much violence, that it was impossible for a boat to land; that at the end of their run they could just discover two paps at a very great distance to the eastward, which from their appearance and their latitude, they concluded to be those in the neighbourhood of Acapulco; but that not having a sufficient quantity of fresh water and provision for their passage thither and back again, they were obliged to return to the commodore, to acquaint him with their disappointment. On this intelligence we all made sail to the eastward, in order to get into the neighbourhood of that port, the commodore resolving to send the barge a second time upon the same enterprise, when we were arrived within a moderate distance. And the next day, which was the 12th of February, we being by that time considerably advanced, the barge was again dispatched, and particular instructions given to the officers to preserve themselves from being seen from the shore. On the thirteenth we espied a high land to the eastward, which we first imagined to be that over the harbour of Acapulco; but we afterwards found that it was the high land of Seguateneio, where there is a small harbour, of which we shall have occasion to make more ample mention hereafter.

And now, having waited six days without any news of our barge, we began to be uneasy for her safety; but, on the seventh day, that is, on the 19th of February, she returned. The officers informed the commodore, that they had discovered the harbour of Acapulco, which they esteemed to bear from us E.S.E., at least fifty leagues distant: that on the 17th, about two in the morning, they were got within the island that lies at the mouth of the harbour, and yet neither the Spanish pilot, nor the Indian, who were with them, could give them any information where they then were; but that while they were lying upon their oars in suspense what to do, being ignorant that they were then at the very place they sought for, they discerned a small light upon the surface of the water, on which they instantly plied their paddles, and moving as silently as possible towards it, they found it to be in a fishing canoe, which they surprised, with three negroes that belonged to it. It seems the negroes at first attempted to jump overboard; and being so near the land, they would easily have swum on shore; but they were prevented by presenting a piece at them, on which they readily submitted, and were taken into the barge. The officers further added, that they had immediately turned the canoe adrift against the face of a rock, where it would inevitably be dashed to pieces by the fury of the sea.

This they did to deceive those who perhaps might be sent from the town to search after the canoe; for upon seeing several pieces of a wreck, they would immediately conclude that the people on board her had been drowned, and would have no suspicion of their having fallen into our hands. When the crew of the barge had taken this precaution, they exerted their utmost strength in pulling out to sea, and by dawn of day had gained such an offing, as rendered it impossible for them to be seen from the coast.

And now having gotten the three negroes in our possession, who were not ignorant of the transactions at Acapulco, we were soon satisfied about the most material points which had long kept us in suspense: and on examination we found, that we were indeed disappointed in our expectation of intercepting the galleon before her arrival at Acapulco; but we learnt other circumstances which still revived our hopes, and which, we then conceived, would more than balance the opportunity we had already lost; for though our negro prisoners informed us that the galleon arrived at Acapulco on our 9th of January, which was about twenty days before we fell in with this coast, yet they at the same time told us, that the galleon had delivered her cargo, and was taking in water and provisions for her return, and that the viceroy of Mexico had, by proclamation, fixed her departure from Acapulco to the 14th of March, N. S. This last news was most joyfully received by us, as we had no doubt but she must certainly fall into our hands, and as it was much more eligible to seize her on her return, than it would have been to have taken her before her arrival, as the specie for which she had sold her cargo, and which she would now have on board, would be prodigiously more to be esteemed by us than the cargo itself; great part of which would have perished on our hands, and no part of it could have been disposed of by us at so advantageous a mart as Acapulco.

Thus we were a second time engaged in an eager expectation of meeting with this Manila ship, which, by the fame of its wealth, we had been taught to consider as the most desirable prize that was to be met with in any part of the globe. As all our future projects will be in some sort regulated with a view to the possession of this celebrated galleon, and as the commerce which is carried on by means of these vessels between the city of Manila and the port of Acapulco is perhaps the most valuable, in proportion to its quantity, of any in the known world, I shall endeavour, in the ensuing chapter, to give as distinct an account as I can of all the particulars relating thereto, both as it is a matter in which I conceive the public to be in some degree interested, and as I flatter myself, that from the materials which have fallen into my hands, I am enabled to describe it with more distinctness than has hitherto been done, at least in our language.

CHAPTER X.

An account of the commerce carried on between the city of Manila on the island of Luconia, and the port of Acapulco on the coast of Mexico.

ABOUT the end of the 15th century, and the beginning of the 16th, the discovery of new countries and of new branches of commerce was the reigning passion of several of the European princes. But those who engaged most deeply and fortunately in these pursuits were the kings of Spain and Portugal; the first of these having discovered the immense and opulent continent of America and its adjacent islands, whilst the other, by doubling the Cape of Good Hope, had opened to his fleets a passage to the southern coast of Asia, usually called the East Indies, and by his settlements in that part of the globe became possessed of many of the manufactures and natural productions with which it abounded, and which, for some ages, had been the wonder and delight of the more polished and luxurious part of mankind.

In the mean time, these two nations of Spain and Portugal, who were thus prosecuting the same views, though in different quarters of the world, grew extremely jealous of each other, and became apprehensive of mutual encroachments, and therefore, to quiet their jealousies, and to enable them with more tranquillity to pursue the propagation of the catholic faith in these distant countries, (they having both of them given distinguished marks of their zeal for their mother church, by their butchery of innocent pagans,) Pope Alexander VI. granted to the Spanish crown the property and dominion of all places either already discovered, or that should be discovered, a hundred leagues to the westward of the islands of Azores, leaving all the unknown countries to the eastward of this limit, to the industry and future disquisition of the Portuguese: and this boundary being afterwards removed two hundred and fifty leagues more to the westward, by the agreement of both nations, it was imagined that by this regulation all the seeds of future contests were suppressed. For the Spaniards presumed, that the Portuguese would be hereby prevented from meddling with their colonies in America: and the Portuguese supposed that their East Indian settlements, and particularly the Spice Islands, which they had then newly discovered, were secured from any future attempts of the Spanish nation.

But it seems that the infallibility of the holy father had, on this occasion, deserted him, and for want of being more conversant in geography, he had not foreseen that the Spaniards, by pushing their discoveries to the west, and the Portuguese to the east, might at last meet with each other, and be again embroiled; as it actually happened within a few years afterwards. For Frederick Magellan, who was an officer in the king of Portugal's service, having received some disgust from that court, either by the defalcation of his pay, or by having his parts, as he conceived, too cheaply considered, he entered into the service of the king of Spain, and being, as it appears, a man of ability, h was very desirous of signalizing his talents by some enterprise, which might prove extremely vexatious to his former masters, and might teach them to estimate his worth by the greatness of the mischief be brought upon them; this being the most obvious and natural turn of all fugitives, and more especially of those who, being really men of capacity, have quitted their country by reason of the small account that has been made of them. Magellan, in pursuance of these vindictive views, knowing that the Portuguese court considered their possession of the Spice Islands as their most important acquisition in the East Indies, resolved with himself to instigate the court of Spain to an enterprise which, by still pushing their discoveries, would give them a right to interfere both in the property and commerce of those renowned Portuguese settlements; and the king of Spain approving of this project, Magellan, in the year 1519, set sail from the port of Seville, in order to carry this enterprise into execution. He had with him a considerable force, consisting of five ships and two hundred and thirty-four men, with which he stood for the coast of South America, and ranging along the shore, he at last, towards the end of October, 1520, had the good fortune to discover those straits, which have since been denominated from him, and which opened him a passage into the Pacific Ocean. And this first part of his scheme being thus happily accomplished, he, after some stay on the coast of Peru, set sail again to the westward, with a view of falling in with the Spice Islands. In this extensive run he first discovered the Ladrones or Marian Islands; and continuing on his course, he at length reached the Philippine Islands, which are the most eastern part of Asia, where, venturing on shore in a hostile manner, and skirmishing with the Indians, he was slain.

By the death of Magellan, the original project of securing some of the Spice Islands was defeated; for those who were left in command contented themselves with ranging through them, and purchasing some spices from the natives; after which they returned home round the Cape of Good Hope, being the first ships which had ever surrounded this terraqueous globe; and thereby demonstrated, by a palpable experiment obvious to the grossest and most vulgar capacity, the reality of its long disputed spherical figure.

But though Spain did not hereby acquire the property of any of the Spice Islands, yet the discovery made in this expedition of the Philippine Islands was thought too considerable to be neglected; for these were not far distant from those places which produced spices, and were very well situated for the Chinese trade, and for the commerce of other parts of India; and, therefore, a communication was soon established and carefully supported between these islands and the Spanish colonies on the coast of Peru: so that the city of Manila (which was built on the island of Luconia, the chief of the Philippines) soon became the mart for all Indian commodities, which were bought up by the inhabitants, and were annually sent to the South Seas to be there vended on their account; and the returns of this commerce to Manila, being principally made in silver, the place by degrees grew extremely opulent and considerable, and its trade so far increased as to engage the attention of the court of Spain, and to be frequently controlled and regulated by royal edicts.

In the infancy of this trade, it was carried on from the port of Callao to the city of Manila, in which voyage the trade-wind continually favoured them; so that notwithstanding these places were distant between three and four thousand leagues, yet the voyage was often made in little more than two months: but then the return from Manila was extremely troublesome and tedious, and is said to have sometimes taken them up above a twelvemonth, which, if they pretended to ply up within the limits of the trade-wind, is not at all to be wondered at; and it is asserted that, in their first voyages, they were so imprudent and unskilful as to attempt this course. However, that route was soon laid aside, by the advice, as it is said, of a Jesuit, who persuaded them to steer to the northward till they got clear of the trade-winds, and then, by the favour of the westerly winds, which generally prevail in high latitudes, to stretch away for the coast of California. This has been the practice for at least a hundred and sixty years past: for Sir Thomas Cavendish, in the year 1586, engaged, off the south end of California, a vessel bound from Manila to the American coast. And it was in compliance with this new plan of navigation, and to shorten the run both backwards and forwards, that the staple of this commerce to and from Manila was removed from Callao, on the coast of Peru, to the port of Acapulco on the coast of Mexico, where it continues fixed at this time.

Such was the commencement, and such were the early regulations, of this commerce; but its present condition being a much more interesting subject, I must beg leave to dwell longer on this head, and to be indulged in a more particular narration, beginning with a description of the island of Luconia, and of the port and bay of Manila.

The island of Luconia, though situated in the latitude of 15 degrees north, is esteemed to be in general extremely healthy, and the water that is found upon it is said to be the best in the world; it produces all the fruits of the warm climates, and abounds in a most excellent breed of horses, supposed to be carried thither first from Spain: it is very well situated for the Indian and Chinese trade; and the bay and port of Manila, which lies on its western side, is perhaps the most remarkable on the whole globe, the bay being a large circular basin, near ten leagues in diameter, and great part of it entirely land-locked. On the east side of this bay stands the city of Manila, which is very large and populous; and which, at the beginning of this war, was only an open place, its principal defence consisting in a small fort, which was in great measure surrounded on every side by houses; but they have lately made considerable additions to its fortifications, though I have not yet learnt in what manner. The port, peculiar to the city, is called Cabite, and lies near two leagues to the southward; and in this port all the ships employed in the Acapulco trade are usually stationed.

The city of Manila itself is in a very healthy situation, is well watered, and is in the neighbourhood of a very fruitful and plentiful country; but as the principal business of this place is its trade to Acapulco, it lies under some disadvantage from the difficulty there is in getting to sea to the eastward: for the passage is among islands and through channels where the Spaniards, by reason of their unskilfulness in marine affairs, waste much time, and are often in great danger.

The trade carried on from this place to China and different parts of India, is principally for such commodities as are intended to supply the kingdoms of Mexico and Peru. These are spices, all sorts of Chinese silks and manufactures; particularly silk stockings, of which I have heard that no less than fifty thousand pair were the usual number shipped on board the annual ship; vast quantities of Indian stuffs, as calicoes and chintz, which are much worn in America, together with other minuter articles, as goldsmiths' work, &c., which is principally done at the city of Manila itself by the Chinese; for it is said there are at least twenty thousand Chinese who constantly reside there, either as servants, manufacturers, or brokers. All these different commodities are collected at Manila, thence to be transported annually in one or more ships, to the port of Acapulco, in the kingdom of Mexico.

But this trade to Acapulco is not laid open to all the inhabitants of Manila, but is confined by very particular regulations, somewhat analogous to those by which the trade of the register-ships from Cadiz to the West Indies is restrained. The ships employed herein are found by the king of Spain, who pays the officers and crews; and the tonnage is divided into a certain number of bales, all of the same size; these are distributed amongst the convents at Manila, but principally to the Jesuits, as a donation for the support of their mission for the propagation of the catholic faith; and these convents have hereby a right to embark such a quantity of goods on board the Manila ship, as the tonnage of their bales amounts to; or if they choose not to be concerned in trade themselves, they have the power of selling this privilege to others; and as the merchants to whom they grant their shares are often unprovided of a stock, it is usual for the convents to lend them considerable sums of money on bottomry.

The trade is, by the royal edicts, limited to a certain value, which the annual cargo ought not to exceed. Some Spanish manuscripts I have seen, mention this limitation to be 600,000 dollars; but the annual cargo does certainly surpass this sum; and though it may be difficult to fix its exact value, yet, from many comparisons, I conclude, that the return cannot be greatly short of three millions of dollars.

It is sufficiently obvious that the greatest part of the treasure, returned from Acapulco to Manila, does not remain in that place, but is again dispersed into different parts of India. And as all European nations have generally esteemed it good policy to keep their American settlements in an immediate dependence on their mother country, without permitting them to carry on directly any gainful traffic with other powers, these considerations have occasioned many remonstrances to be presented to the court of Spain against the Indian trade, hereby allowed to the kingdom of Peru and Mexico; it having been urged, that the silk manufactures of Valencia and other parts of Spain are hereby greatly prejudiced, and the linens carried from Cadiz are much injured in their sale since the Chinese silks coming almost directly to Acapulco, can be afforded much cheaper there than any European manufactures of equal goodness; and the cottons from the Coromandel coast make the European linens almost useless. So that the Manila trade renders both Mexico and Peru less dependent upon Spain for a supply of their necessities than they ought to be; and exhausts those countries of a considerable quantity of silver, the greatest part of which, were this trade prohibited, would centre in Spain, either in payment for Spanish commodities, or in gains to the Spanish merchant; whereas now the only advantage which arises from it is, the enriching the Jesuits and a few particular persons besides, at the other extremity of the world. These arguments did so far influence Don Joseph Patinho, who was then prime minister, but an enemy to the Jesuits, that about the year 1725, he had resolved to abolish this trade, and to have permitted no Indian commodities to be introduced into any of the Spanish ports in the West Indies, but what were carried there in the register ships from Europe. But the powerful intrigues of the Jesuits prevented this regulation from taking place.

This trade from Manila to Acapulco and back again, is usually carried on in one or at most two annual ships, which set sail from Manila about July, and arrive at Acapulco in December, January, or February following, and having there disposed of their effects, return for Manila sometime in March, where they generally arrive in June; so that the whole voyage takes up very near an entire year; for this reason, though there is often no more than one ship employed at a time, yet there is always one ready for the sea when the other arrives; and, therefore, the commerce at Manila are provided with three or four stout ships, that, in case of any accident, the trade may not be suspended. The largest of these ships, whose name I have not learnt, is described as little less than one of our first-rate men-of-war, and indeed she must be of an enormous size, for it is known that when she was employed with other ships from the same port, to cruise for our China trade, she had no less than twelve hundred men on board. Their other ships, though far inferior in bulk to this, are yet stout large vessels, of the burthen of twelve hundred tons and upwards, and usually carry from three hundred and fifty to six hundred hands, passengers included, with fifty odd guns. As these are all king's ships, commissioned and paid by him, there is usually one of the captains, who is styled the general, and who carries the royal standard of Spain at the main-top gallant mast-head, as we shall more particularly observe hereafter.

And now, having described the port of Manila and the shipping they employ, it is necessary to give a more circumstantial detail of their navigation. The ship having received her cargo on board, and being fitted for the sea, generally weighs from the mole of Cabite about the middle of July, taking the advantage of the westerly monsoon, which then sets in, to carry them to sea. It appears that the getting through the Boccadero to the eastward must be a troublesome navigation, and, in fact, it is sometimes the end of August before they get clear of the land. When they have got through this passage, and are clear of the islands, they stand to the northward of the east, in order to get into the latitude of 30 odd degrees, where they expect to meet with westerly winds, before which they run away for the coast of California. It is most remarkable that, by the concurrent testimony of all the Spanish navigators, there is not one port, nor even a tolerable road, as yet found out betwixt the Philippine Islands and the coast of California and Mexico; so that from the time the Manila ship first loses sight of land, she never lets go her anchor till she arrives on the coast of California, and very often not till she gets to its southernmost extremity; and, therefore, as this voyage is rarely of less than six months' continuance, and the ship is deep laden with merchandise and crowded with people, it may appear wonderful how they can be supplied with a stock of fresh water for so long a time; and indeed their method of procuring it is extremely singular, and deserves a very particular recital.

It is well known to those who are acquainted with the Spanish customs in the South Seas, that their water is preserved on ship-board, not in casks, but in earthen jars, which in some sort resemble the large oil jars we often see in Europe. When the Manila ship first puts to sea, they take on board a much greater quantity of water than can be stowed between decks; and the jars which contain it are hung all about the shrouds and stays, so as to exhibit at a distance a very odd appearance. And though it is one convenience of their jars that they are much more manageable than casks, and are liable to no leakage, unless they are broken, yet it is sufficiently obvious that a six, or even a three months' store of water could never be stowed in a ship so loaded, by any management whatsoever; and therefore without some other supply, this navigation could not be performed. A supply, indeed, they have; but the reliance upon it seems at first sight so extremely precarious, that it is wonderful such numbers should risk the perishing by the most dreadful of all deaths, on the expectation of so casual a circumstance. In short, their only method of recruiting their water is by the rains, which they meet with between the latitudes of 30° and 40° north, and which they are always prepared to catch. For this purpose they take to sea with them a great number of mats, which they place slopingly against the gunwale, whenever the rain descends; these mats extend from one end of the ship to the other; and their lower edges rest on a large split bamboo, so that all the water which falls on the mats drains into the bamboo, and by this, as a trough, is conveyed into a jar; and this method of supplying their water, however accidental and extraordinary it may at first sight appear, has never been known to fail them; so that it is common for them, when their voyage is a little longer than usual, to fill all their water-jars several times over.

However, though their distresses for fresh water are much short of what might be expected in so tedious a navigation, yet there are other inconveniences generally attendant upon a long continuance at sea, from which they are not exempted. The principal of these is the scurvy, which sometimes rages with extreme violence, and destroys great numbers of the people; but at other times their passage to Acapulco (of which alone I would be here understood to speak) is performed with little loss.

The length of time employed in this passage, so much beyond what usually occurs in any other navigation, is perhaps in part to be imputed to the indolence and unskilfulness of the Spanish sailors, and to an unnecessary degree of caution and concern for so rich a vessel; for it is said that they never set their main-sail in the night, and often lie by unnecessarily. And indeed the instructions given to their captains (which I have seen) seem to have been drawn up by such as were more apprehensive of too strong a gale, though favourable, than of the inconveniences and mortality attending a lingering and tedious voyage; for the captain is particularly ordered to make his passage in the latitude of thirty degrees, if possible; and to be extremely careful to stand no farther to the northward than is absolutely necessary for the getting a westerly wind. This, according to our conceptions, appears to be a very absurd restriction; since it can scarcely be doubted, but that in the higher latitudes the westerly winds are much steadier and brisker than in the latitude of thirty degrees; so that the whole conduct of this navigation seems liable to very great censure. For if, instead of steering E.N.E. into the latitude of thirty odd degrees, they at first stood N.E., or even still more northerly, into the latitude of forty or forty-five degrees, in part of which course the trade-winds would greatly assist them, I doubt not but by this management they might considerably contract their voyage, and perhaps perform it in half the time which is now allotted for it; for in the journals I have seen of these voyages, it appears, that they are often a month or six weeks after their laying the land, before they get into the latitude of thirty degrees; whereas, with a more northerly course, it might easily be done in a fourth part of the time; and when they were once well advanced to the northward, the westerly winds would soon blow them over to the coast of California, and they would be thereby freed from the other embarrassments to which they are now subjected, only at the expense of a rough sea and a stiff gale. And this is not merely matter of speculation; for I am credibly informed that, about the year 1721, a French ship, by pursuing this course, ran from the coast of China to the valley of Vanderas, on the coast of Mexico, in less than fifty days. But it was said that this ship, notwithstanding the shortness of her passage, suffered prodigiously by the scurvy, so that she had only four or five of her crew left when she arrived in America.

However, I shall descant no longer on the probability of performing this voyage in a much shorter time, but shall content myself with reciting the actual occurrences of the present navigation. The Manila ship having stood so far to the northward as to meet with a westerly wind, stretches away nearly in the same latitude for the coast of California. And when she has run into the longitude of ninety-six degrees from Cape Espiritu Santo, she generally meets with a plant floating on the sea, which, being called *porra* by the Spaniards, is, I presume, a species of sea-leek. On the sight of this plant they esteem themselves sufficiently near the Californian shore, and immediately stand to the southward; and they rely so much on this circumstance, that on the first discovery of the plant the whole ship's company chant a solemn *Te Deum*, esteeming the difficulties and hazards of their passage to be now at an end; and they constantly correct their longitude thereby, without ever coming within sight of land. After falling in with these signs, as they denominate them, they steer to the southward, without endeavouring to fall in with the coast, till they have run into a lower latitude; for as there are many islands and some shoals adjacent to California, the extreme caution of the Spanish navigators makes them very apprehensive of being engaged with the land; however, when they draw near its southern extremity, they venture to haul in, both for the sake of making Cape St. Lucas to ascertain their reckoning, and also to receive intelligence from the Indian inhabitants, whether or no there are any enemies on the coast; and this last circumstance, which is a particular article in the captain's instructions, makes it necessary to mention the late proceedings of the Jesuits amongst the Californian Indians.

Since the first discovery of California, there have been various wandering missionaries who have visited it at different times, though to little purpose; but of late years the Jesuits, encouraged and supported by a large donation from the Marquis de Valero, a most munificent bigot, have fixed themselves upon the place, and have established a very considerable mission. Their principal settlement lies just within Cape St. Lucas, where they have collected a great number of savages, and have endeavoured to inure them to agriculture and other mechanic arts. And their efforts have not been altogether ineffectual; for they have planted vines at their settlements with very good success, so that they already make a considerable quantity of wine, resembling in flavour the inferior sort of Madeira, which begins to be esteemed in the neighbouring kingdom of Mexico.

The Jesuits, then, being thus firmly rooted on California, they have already extended their jurisdiction quite across the country from sea to sea, and are endeavouring to spread their influence farther to the northward; with which view they have made several expeditions up the gulf between California and Mexico, in order to discover the nature of the adjacent countries, all which they hope hereafter to bring under their power. And being thus occupied in advancing the interests of their society, it is no wonder if some share of attention is engaged about the security of the Manila ship, in which their convents at Manila are so deeply concerned. For this purpose there are refreshments, as fruits, wine, water, &c., constantly kept in readiness for her; and there is besides care taken, at Cape St. Lucas, to look out for any ship of the enemy, which might be cruising there to intercept her; this being a station where she is constantly expected, and where she has been often waited for and fought with, though generally with little success. In consequence then of the measures mutually settled between the Jesuits of Manila and their brethren at California, the captain of the galleon is ordered to fall in with the land to the northward of Cape St. Lucas, where the inhabitants are directed, on sight of the vessel, to make the proper signals with fires; and on discovering these fires, the captain is to send his launch on shore with twenty men, well armed, who are to carry with them the letters from the convents at Manila to the Californian missionaries, and are to bring back the refreshments which will be prepared for them, and likewise intelligence whether or no there are any enemies on the coast. And if the captain finds, from the account which is sent him, that he has nothing to fear, he is directed to proceed for Cape St. Lucas, and thence to Cape Corientes, after which he is to coast it along for the port of Acapulco.

The most usual time of the arrival of the galleon at Acapulco is towards the middle of January; but this navigation is so uncertain, that she sometimes gets in a month sooner, and at other times has been detained at sea above a month longer. The port of Acapulco is by much the securest and finest in all the northern parts of the Pacific Ocean; being, as it were, a basin surrounded by very high mountains. But the town is a most wretched place, and extremely unhealthy, for the air about it is so pent up by the hills, that it has scarcely any circulation. The place is, besides, destitute of fresh water, except what is brought from a considerable distance; and is in all respects so inconvenient, that, except at the time of the mart, whilst the Manila galleon is in the port, it is almost deserted.

When the galleon arrives in this port, she is generally moored on its western side, and her cargo is delivered with all possible expedition. And now the town of Acapulco, from almost a solitude, is immediately thronged with merchants from all parts of the kingdom of Mexico. The cargo being landed and disposed of, the silver and the goods intended for Manila are taken on board, together with provisions and water, and the ship prepares to put to sea with the utmost expedition. There is indeed no time to be lost; for it is an express order to the captain to be out of the port of Acapulco, on his return, before the first day of April, N. S.

And having mentioned the goods intended for Manila, I must observe, that the principal return is always made in silver, and, consequently, the rest of the cargo is but of little account; the other articles, besides the silver, being some cochineal and a few sweetmeats, the produce of the American settlements, together with European millinery ware for the women at Manila, and some Spanish wines, such as tent and sherry, which are intended for the use of their priests in the administration of the sacrament.

And this difference in the cargo of the ship to and from Manila, occasions a very remarkable variety in the manner of equipping the ship for these two different voyages. For the galleon, when she sets sail from Manila, being deep laden with a variety of bulky goods, she has not the convenience of mounting her lower tier of guns, but carries them in her hold till she draws near Cape St. Lucas, and is apprehensive of an enemy. Her hands too are as few as is consistent with the safety of the ship, that she may be less pestered with the stowage of provisions. But on her return from Acapulco, as her cargo lies in less room, her lower tier is (or ought to be) always mounted before she leaves the port, and her crew is augmented with a supply of sailors, and with one or two companies of foot, which are intended to reinforce the garrison at Manila. And there being, besides, many merchants who take their passage to Manila on board the galleon, her whole number of hands on her return is usually little short of six hundred, all which are easily provided for by reason of the small stowage necessary for the silver.

The galleon being thus fitted for her return, the captain, on leaving the port of Acapulco, steers for the latitude of 13° or 14°, and runs on that parallel till he gets sight of the island of Guam, one of the Ladrones. In this run the captain is particularly directed to be careful of the shoals of St. Bartholomew, and of the island of Gasparico. He is also told in his instructions that, to prevent his passing the Ladrones in the dark, there are orders given that, through all the month of June, fires shall be lighted every night on the highest part of Guam and Rota, and kept in till the morning.

At Guam there is a small Spanish garrison, (as will be more particularly mentioned hereafter,) purposely intended to secure that place for the refreshment of the galleon, and to yield her all the assistance in their power. However, the danger of the road at Guam is so great, that though the galleon is ordered to call there, yet she rarely stays above a day or two, but getting her water and refreshments on board as soon as possible, she steers away directly for Cape Espiritu Santo, on the island of Samal. Here the captain is again ordered to look out for signals; and he is told, that sentinels will be posted not only on that cape, but likewise in Catandunnas, Butusan, Birriborongo, and on the island of Batan. These sentinels are instructed to make a fire when they discover the ship, which the captain is carefully to observe: for if, after this first fire is extinguished, he perceives that four or more are lighted up again, he is then to conclude that there are enemies on the coast; and on this he is immediately to endeavour to speak with the sentinel on shore, and to procure from him more particular intelligence of their force, and of the station they cruise in: pursuant to which, he is to regulate his conduct, and to endeavour to gain some secure port amongst those islands, without coming in sight of the enemy; and in case he should be discovered when in port, and should be apprehensive of an attack, he is then to land his treasure, and to take some of his artillery on shore for its defence, not neglecting to send frequent and particular accounts to the city of Manila of all that passes. But if, after the first fire on shore, the captain observes that two others only are made by the sentinels, he is then to conclude, that there is nothing to fear; and he is to pursue his course without interruption, and to make the best of his way to the port of Cabite, which is the port to the city of Manila, and the constant station for all the ships employed in this commerce to Acapulco.

CHAPTER XI.

Our cruise off the port of Acapulco for the Manila ship.

I HAVE already mentioned, in the ninth chapter, that the return of our barge from the port of Acapulco, where she had surprised three negro fishermen, gave us inexpressible satisfaction, as we learnt from our prisoners that the galleon was then preparing to put to sea, and that her departure was fixed, by an edict of the viceroy of Mexico, to the 14th of March, N.S., that is, to the 3d of March according to our reckoning.

What related to this Manila ship being the matter to which we were most attentive, it was necessarily the first article of our examination; but having satisfied ourselves upon this head, we then indulged our curiosity in inquiring after other news; when the prisoners informed us that they had received intelligence at Acapulco of our having plundered and burnt the town of Paita; and that on this occasion the governor of Acapulco had augmented the fortifications of the place, and had taken several precautions to prevent us from forcing our way into the harbour; that, in particular, he had placed a guard on the island which lies at the harbour's mouth, and that this guard had been withdrawn but two nights before the arrival of our barge: so that had the barge succeeded in her first attempt, or had she arrived at the port the second time two days sooner, she could scarcely have avoided being seized on, or if she had escaped, it must have been with the loss of the greatest part of her crew, as she would have been under the fire of the guard before she had known her danger.

The withdrawing of this guard was a circumstance that greatly encouraged us, as it seemed to demonstrate, not only that the enemy had not as yet discovered us, but likewise that they had now no farther apprehensions of our visiting their coast. Indeed the prisoners assured us that they had no knowledge of our being in those seas, and that they had therefore flattered themselves that, in the long interval since our taking of Paita, we had steered another course. But we did not consider the opinion of these negro prisoners as so authentic a proof of our being hitherto concealed, as the withdrawing of the guard from the harbour's mouth; for this, being the action of the governor, was of all arguments the most convincing, as he might be supposed to have intelligence with which the rest of the inhabitants were unacquainted.

Satisfied, therefore, that we were undiscovered, and that the time was fixed for the departure of the galleon from Acapulco, we made all necessary preparations, and waited with the utmost impatience for the important day. As this was the 3d of March, and it was the 16th of February when the barge returned and brought us our intelligence, the commodore resolved to continue the greatest part of the intermediate time on his present station, to the westward of Acapulco, conceiving that in this situation there would be less danger of his being seen from the shore, which was the only circumstance that could deprive us of the immense treasure on which we had at present so eagerly fixed our thoughts. During this interval we were employed in scrubbing and cleansing our ships' bottoms, in bringing them into their most advantageous trim, and in regulating the orders, signals, and stations, to be observed when we should arrive off Acapulco, and the time of the departure of the galleon should draw nigh.

And now, on the first of March, we made the high lands, usually called the paps, over Acapulco, and got with all possible expedition into the situation prescribed by the Commodore's orders. The distribution of our squadron on this occasion, both for the intercepting the galleon and for the avoiding a discovery from the shore, was so very judicious, that it well merits to be distinctly described. The order of it was thus:

The Centurion brought the paps over the harbour to bear N.N.E., at fifteen leagues' distance, which was a sufficient offing to prevent our being seen by the enemy. To the westward of the Centurion there was stationed the Carmelo, and to the eastward were the Tryal prize, the Gloucester, and the Carmin. These were all ranged in a circular line, and each ship was three leagues distant from the next; so that the Carmelo and the Carmin, which were the two extremes, were twelve leagues' distance from each other: and as the galleon could without doubt be discerned at six leagues' distance from either extremity, the whole sweep of our squadron, within which nothing could pass undiscovered, was at least twenty-four leagues in extent; and yet we were so connected by our signals, as to be easily and speedily informed of what was seen in any part of the line: and to render this disposition still more complete, and to prevent even the possibility of the galleon's escaping us in the night, the two cutters belonging to the Centurion and the Gloucester were both manned and sent in shore, and were ordered to lie all day at the distance of four or five leagues from the entrance of the port, where, by reason of their smallness, they could not possibly be discovered; but in the night they were directed to stand nearer to the harbour's mouth, and as the light of the morning came on, they were to return back again to their day-posts. When the cutters should first discover the Manila ship, one of them was ordered to return to the squadron, and to make a signal whether the galleon stood to the eastward or to the westward, whilst the other was to follow the galleon at a distance, and, if it grew dark, was to direct the squadron in their chase by showing false fires.

Besides the care we had taken to prevent the galleon from passing by us unobserved, we had not been inattentive to the means of engaging her to advantage when we came up with her: for, considering the thinness of our hands, and the vaunting accounts given by the Spaniards of her size, her guns, and her strength, this was a consideration not to be neglected. As we supposed that none of our ships but the Centurion and the Gloucester were capable of lying alongside of her, we took on board the Centurion all the hands belonging to the Carmelo and the Carmin, except what were just sufficient to navigate those ships; and Captain Saunders was ordered to send from the Tryal prize ten Englishmen, and as many negroes, to reinforce the crew of the Gloucester: and for the encouragement of our negroes, of which we had a considerable number on board, we promised them that on their good behaviour they should all have their freedom; and as they had been almost every day trained to the management of the great guns for the two preceding months, they were very well qualified to be of service to us; and from their hopes of liberty, and in return for the usage they had met with amongst us, they seemed disposed to exert themselves to the utmost of their power.

And now being thus prepared for the reception of the galleon, we expected with the utmost impatience the so often mentioned 3d of March, the day fixed for her departure. And on that day we were all of us most eagerly engaged in looking out towards Acapulco; and we were so strangely prepossessed with the certainty of our intelligence, and with an assurance of her coming out of port, that some or other on board us were constantly imagining that they discovered one of our cutters returning with a signal. But, to our extreme vexation, both this day and the succeeding night passed over without any news of the galleon. However we did not yet despair, but were all heartily disposed to flatter ourselves that some unforeseen accident had intervened, which might have put off her departure for a few days; and suggestions of this kind occurred in plenty, as we knew that the time fixed by the viceroy for her sailing, was often prolonged on the petition of the merchants of Mexico. Thus we kept up our hopes, and did not abate of our vigilance; and as the 7th of March was Sunday, the beginning of Passion-week, which is observed by the papists with great strictness and a total cessation from all kinds of labour, so that no ship is permitted to stir out of port during the whole week, this quieted our apprehensions for some days, and disposed us not to expect the galleon till the week following. On the Friday in this week our cutters returned to us, and the officers on board them were very confident that the galleon was still in port, for that she could not possibly have come out but they must have seen her. On the Monday morning succeeding Passion-week, that is, on the 15th of March, the cutters were again despatched to their old station, and our hopes were once more indulged in as sanguine prepossessions as before; but in a week's time our eagerness was greatly abated, and a general dejection and despondency took place in its room. It is true there were some few amongst us who still kept up their spirits, and were very ingenious in finding out reasons to satisfy themselves that the disappointment we had hitherto met with had only been occasioned by a casual delay of the galleon, which a few days would remove, and not by a total suspension of her departure for the whole season. But these speculations were not relished by the generality of our people, for they were persuaded that the enemy had by some accident discovered our being upon the coast, and had therefore laid an embargo on the galleon till the next year. And indeed this persuasion was but too well founded, for we afterwards learnt that our barge, when sent on the discovery of the port of Acapulco, had been seen from the shore, and that this circumstance (no embarkations but canoes ever frequenting that coast) was to them a sufficient proof of the neighbourhood of our squadron; on which they stopped the galleon till the succeeding year.

The commodore himself, though he declared not his opinion, was yet in his own thoughts very apprehensive that we were discovered, and that the departure of the galleon was put off; and he had, in consequence of this opinion, formed a plan for possessing himself of Acapulco; for he had no doubt but the treasure as yet remained in the town, even though the orders for the despatching of the galleon were countermanded. Indeed the place was too well defended to be carried by an open attempt; for, besides the garrison and the crew of the galleon, there were in it at least a thousand men, well armed, who had marched thither as guards to the treasure, when it was brought down from the city of Mexico; for the roads thereabouts are so much infested, either by independent Indians or fugitives, that the Spaniards never trust the silver without an armed force to protect it. And besides, the strength of the place been less considerable, and such as might have appeared not superior to the efforts of our squadron, yet a declared attack would have prevented us from receiving any advantages from its success; since, upon the first discovery of our squadron, all the treasure would have been ordered into the country, and in a few hours would have been out of our reach; so that our conquest would have been only a desolate town, where we should have found nothing that could have been of the least consequence to us.

For these reasons, the surprisal of the place was the only method that could at all answer our purpose; and, therefore, the manner in which Mr Anson proposed to conduct this enterprise was, by setting sail with the squadron in the evening, time enough to arrive at the port in the night; and as there is no danger on that coast, he would have stood boldly for the harbour's mouth, where he expected to arrive, and might perhaps have entered it before the Spaniards were acquainted with his designs. As soon as he had run into the harbour, he intended to have pushed two hundred of his men on shore in his boats, who were immediately to attempt the fort; whilst he, the commodore, with his ships, was employed in firing upon the town, and the other batteries. And these different operations, which would have been executed with great regularity, could hardly have failed of succeeding against an enemy, who would have been prevented by the suddenness of the attack, and by the want of daylight, from concerting any measures for their defence; so that it was extremely probable that we should have carried the fort by storm; and then the other batteries, being open behind, must have been soon abandoned; after which, the town, and its inhabitants, and all the treasure, must necessarily have fallen into our hands, for the place is so cooped up with mountains, that it is scarcely possible to escape out of it, but by the great road, which passes under the fort. This was the project which the commodore had settled in general in his thoughts; but when he began to inquire into such circumstances as were necessary to be considered in order to regulate the particulars of its execution, he found there was a difficulty, which, being insuperable, occasioned the enterprise to be laid aside: for on examining the prisoners about the winds which prevail near the shore, he learned (and it was afterwards confirmed by the officers of our cutters) that nearer in-shore there was always a dead calm for the greatest part of the night, and that towards morning, when a gale sprung up, it constantly blew off the land; so that the setting sail from our present station in the evening, and arriving at Acapulco before daylight, was impossible.

This scheme, as has been said, was formed by the commodore upon a supposition that the galleon was detained till the next year; but as this was a matter of opinion only, and not founded on intelligence, and there was a possibility that she might still put to sea in a short time, the commodore thought it prudent to continue his cruise upon this station, as long as the necessary attention to his stores of wood and water, and to the convenient season for his future passage to China, would give him leave; and, therefore, as the cutters had been ordered to remain before Acapulco till the 23d of March, the squadron did not change its position till that day; when the cutters not appearing, we were in some pain for them, apprehending they might have suffered either from the enemy or the weather; but we were relieved from our concern the next morning, when we discovered them, though at a great distance, and to the leeward of the squadron. We bore down to them and took them up, and were informed by them, that, conformable to their orders, they had left their station the day before, without having seen anything of the galleon; and we found that the reason of their being so far to the leeward of us was a strong current, which had driven the whole squadron to windward.

And here it is necessary to mention that, by information which was afterwards received, it appeared that this prolongation of our cruise was a very prudent measure, and afforded us no contemptible chance of seizing the treasure, on which we had so long fixed our thoughts. For it seems, after the embargo was laid on the galleon, as is before mentioned, the persons principally interested in the cargo sent several expresses to Mexico to beg that she might still be permitted to depart. For as they knew, by the accounts sent from Paita, that we had not more than three hundred men in all, they insisted that there was nothing to be feared from us; for that the galleon (carrying above twice as many hands as our whole squadron) would be greatly an overmatch for us. And though the viceroy was inflexible, yet, on the account of their representation, she was kept ready for the sea for near three weeks after the first order came to detain her.

When we had taken up the cutters, all the ships being joined, the commodore made a signal to speak with their commanders; and upon inquiry into the stock of fresh water remaining on board the squadron, it was found to be so very slender, that we were under a necessity of quitting our station to procure a fresh supply; and consulting what place was the most proper for this purpose, it was agreed, that the harbour of Seguataneo or Chequetan, being the nearest to us, was on that account the most eligible; and it was therefore immediately resolved to make the best of our way thither. And that, even while we were recruiting our water, we might not totally abandon our views upon the galleon; which, perhaps upon certain intelligence of our being employed at Chequetan, might venture to slip out to sea. our cutter, under

the command of Mr. Hughes, the lieutenant of the Tryal prize, was ordered to cruise off the port of Acapulco for twenty-four days; that if the galleon should set sail in that interval, we might be speedily informed of it. In pursuance of these resolutions, we endeavoured to ply to the westward to gain our intended port; but were often interrupted in our progress by calms and adverse currents. In these intervals we employed ourselves in taking out the most valuable part of the cargoes of the Carmelo and Carmin prizes, which two ships we intended to destroy as soon as we had tolerably cleared them.

By the first of April we were so far advanced towards Seguataneo, that we thought it expedient to send out two boats, that they might range along the coast and discover the watering-place; they were gone some days, and our water being now very short, it was a particular felicity to us that we met with daily supplies of turtle, for had we been entirely confined to salt provisions, we must have suffered extremely in so warm a climate. Indeed, our present circumstances were sufficiently alarming, and gave the most considerate amongst us as much concern as any of the numerous perils we had hitherto encountered; for our boats, as we conceived by their not returning, had not as yet discovered a place proper to water at, and by the leakage of our casks and other accidents, we had not ten days' water on board the whole squadron: so that, from the known difficulty of procuring water on this coast, and the little reliance we had on the buccaneer writers, (the only guides we had to trust to,) we were apprehensive of being soon exposed to a calamity, the most terrible of any in the long disheartening catalogue of the distresses of a sea-faring life.

But these gloomy suggestions were soon happily ended; for our boats returned on the fifth of April, having discovered a place proper for our purpose, about seven miles to the westward of the rocks of Seguataneo, which, by the description they gave of it, appeared to be the port, called by Dampier the harbour, of Chequetan. The success of our boats was highly agreeable to us, and they were ordered out again the next day, to sound the harbour and its entrance, which they had represented as very narrow. At their return they reported the place to be free from any danger; so that on the seventh we stood in, and that evening came to an anchor in eleven fathoms. The Gloucester came to an anchor at the same time with us; but the Carmelo and the Carmin having fallen to leeward, the Tryal prize was ordered to join them, and to bring them in, which in two or three days she effected.

Thus, after a four months' continuance at sea, from the leaving of Quibo, and having but six days' water on board, we arrived in the harbour of Chequetan, the description of which, and of the adjacent coast, shall be the business of the ensuing chapter.

CHAPTER XII.

Description of the harbour of Chequetan, and of the adjacent coast and country.

THE harbour of Chequetan, which we here propose to describe, lies in the latitude of 17° 36' north, and is about thirty leagues to the westward of Acapulco. It is easy to be discovered by any ship that will keep well in with the land, especially by such as range down coast from Acapulco, and will attend to the following particulars.

There is a beach of sand which extends eighteen leagues from the harbour of Acapulco to the westward, against which the sea breaks with such violence, that it is impossible to land in any part of it; but yet the ground is so clean that ships, in the fair season, may anchor in great safety, at the distance of a mile or two from the shore. The land adjacent to this beach is generally low, full of villages, and planted with a great number of trees; and on the tops of some small eminences there are several look-out towers; so that the face of the country affords a very agreeable prospect. For the cultivated part, which is the part here described, extends some leagues from the shore, and there appears to be bounded by the chain of mountains, which stretch to a considerable distance on either side of Acapulco. It is a most remarkable particularity, that in this whole extent, being, as has been mentioned, eighteen leagues, and containing, in appearance, the most populous and best planted district of the whole coast, there should be neither canoes, boats, nor any other embarkations either for fishing, coasting, or for pleasure.

The beach here described is the surest guide for finding the harbour of Chequetan; for five miles to the westward of the extremity of this beach there appears a hummock, which at first makes like an island, and is in shape not very unlike the hill of Petaplan hereafter mentioned, though much smaller. Three miles to the westward of this hummock is a white rock lying near the shore, which cannot easily be passed by unobserved. It is about two cables' length from the land, and lies in a large bay about nine leagues over. The westward point of this bay is the hill of Petaplan. This hill, too, like the fore-mentioned hummock, may be at first mistaken for an island, though it be in reality a peninsula, which is joined to the continent by a low and narrow isthmus, covered over with shrubs and small trees. The bay of Seguataneo extends from this hill a great way to the westward; at a small distance from the hill, and opposite to the entrance of the bay, there is an assemblage of rocks, which are white from the excrements of boobies and tropical birds. Four of these rocks are high and large, and, together with several smaller ones, are, by the help of a little imagination, pretended to resemble the form of a cross, and are called the "White Friars." These rocks bear W. by N. from Petaplan; and about seven miles to the westward of them lies the harbour of Chequetan, which is still more minutely distinguished by a large and single rock, that rises out of the water a mile and a half distant from its entrance, and bears S. ½ W. from the middle of it.

These are the infallible marks by which the harbour of Chequetan may be known to those who keep well in with the land; and I must add, that the coast is no ways to be dreaded from the middle of October to the beginning of May, nor is there then any danger from the winds; though, in the remaining part of the year, there are frequent and violent tornadoes, heavy rains, and hard gales in all directions of the compass. But, as to those who keep at any considerable distance from the coast, there is no other method to be taken by them for finding this harbour, than that of making it by its latitude: for there are so many ranges of mountains rising one upon the back of another within land, that no drawings of the appearance of the coast can be at all depended on, when off at sea; for every little change of distance or variation of position brings new mountains in view, and produces an infinity of different prospects, which would render all attempts of delineating the aspect of the coast impossible.

This may suffice as to the methods of discovering the harbour of Chequetan. Its entrance is but about half-a-mile broad; the two points which form it, and which are faced with rocks that are almost perpendicular, bear from each other S.E. and N.W. The harbour is environed on all sides, except to the westward, with high mountains overspread with trees. The passage into it is very safe on either side of the rock that lies off the mouth of it, though we, both in coming in and going out, left it to the eastward. The ground without the harbour is gravel mixed with stones, but within it is a soft mud: and it must be remembered that, in coming to an anchor, a good allowance should be made for a large swell, which frequently causes a great send of the sea; as likewise, for the ebbing and flowing of the tide, which we observed to be about five feet, and that it set nearly E. and W.

The watering-place for fresh water has the appearance of a large standing lake, without any visible outlet into the sea, from which it is separated by a part of the strand. The origin of this lake is a spring, that bubbles out of the ground near half-a-mile within the country. We found the water a little brackish, but more considerably so towards the sea-side; for the nearer we advanced towards the spring-head, the softer and fresher it proved: this laid us under a necessity of filling all our casks from the furthest part of the lake, and occasioned us some trouble; and would have proved still more difficult, had it not been for our particular management, which, for the convenience of it, deserves to be recommended to all who shall hereafter water at this place. Our method consisted in making use of canoes which drew but little water; for, loading them with a number of small casks, they easily got up the lake to the spring-head, and the small casks being there filled, were in the same manner transported back again to the beach, where some of our hands always attended to start them into other casks of a larger size.

Though this lake, during our continuance there, appeared to have no outlet into the sea, yet there is reason to suppose that in the wet season it overflows the strand, and communicates with the ocean; for Dampier, who was formerly here speaks of it as a large river. Indeed there must be a very great body of water amassed before the lake can rise high enough to overflow the strand; for the neighbouring country is so low, that great part of it must be covered with water, before it can run out over the beach.

As the country in the neighbourhood, particularly the tract which we have already described, appeared to be well peopled, and cultivated, we hoped thence to have procured fresh provision and other refreshments which we stood in need of. With this view, the morning after we came to an anchor, the commodore ordered a party of forty men, well armed, to march into the country, and to endeavour to discover some town or village, where they were to attempt to set on foot a correspondence with the inhabitants; for we doubted not, if we could have any intercourse with them, but that by presents of some of the coarse merchandise, with which our prizes abounded (which, though of little consequence to us, would to them be extremely valuable) we should allure them to furnish us with whatever fruits or fresh provisions were in their power. Our people were directed on this occasion to proceed with the greatest circumspection, and to make as little ostentation of hostility as possible; for we were sensible, that we could meet with no wealth here worth our notice, and that what necessaries we really wanted, we should in all probability be better supplied with by an open amicable traffic, than by violence and force of arms. But this endeavour of opening an intercourse with the inhabitants proved ineffectual; for towards evening, the party which had been ordered to march into the country, returned greatly fatigued with their unusual exercise, and some of them so far spent as to have fainted by the way, and to be obliged to be brought back upon the shoulders of their companions. They had marched in all, as they conceived, about ten miles, in a beaten road, where they often saw the fresh dung of horses or mules. When they had got about five miles from the harbour, the road divided between the mountains into two branches, one running to the east, and the other to the west: after some deliberation about the course they should take, they agreed to pursue the eastern road, which, when they had followed for some time, led them at once into a large plain or savannah; on one side of which they discovered a sentinel on horseback with a pistol in his hand: it was supposed that when they first saw him he was asleep, but his horse startled at the glittering of their arms, and turning round suddenly rode off with his master, who was very near being unhorsed in the surprise, but he recovered his seat, and escaped with the loss only of his hat and his pistol, which he dropped on the ground. Our people ran after him, in hopes of discovering some village or habitation which he would retreat to, but as he had the advantage of being on horseback, he soon lost sight of them. However, they were unwilling to come back without making some discovery, and therefore still followed the track they were in; but the heat of the day increasing, and finding no water to quench their thirst, they were at first obliged to halt, and then resolved to return; for as they saw no signs of plantations or cultivated land, they had no reason to believe that there was any village or settlement near them; but to leave no means untried of procuring some intercourse with the people, the officers stuck up several poles in the road, to which were affixed declarations, written in Spanish, encouraging the inhabitants to come down to the harbour, and to traffic with us, giving the strongest assurances of a kind reception, and faithful payment for any provisions they should bring us. This was doubtless a very prudent measure, but yet it produced no effect; for we never saw any of them during the whole time of our continuance at this port of Chequetan. But had our men, upon the division of the path, taken the western road instead of the eastern, it would soon have led them to a village or town, which in some Spanish manuscripts is mentioned as being in the neighbourhood of this port, and which we afterwards learned was not above two miles from that turning.

And on this occasion I cannot help mentioning another adventure, which happened to some of our people in the bay of Petaplan, as it may help to give the reader a just idea of the temper of the inhabitants of this part of the world. Some time after our arrival at Chequetan, Lieutenant Brett was sent by the commodore, with two of our boats under his command, to examine the coast to the eastward, particularly to make observations on the bay and watering-place of Petaplan. As Mr. Brett, with one of the boats, was preparing to go on shore towards the hill of Petaplan, he accidentally looking across the bay, perceived, on the opposite strand, three small squadrons of horse parading upon the beach, and seeming to advance towards the place where he proposed to land. On sight of this he immediately put off the boat, though he had but sixteen men with him, and stood over the bay towards them: and he soon came near enough to perceive that they were mounted on very sightly horses, and were armed with carbines and lances. On seeing him make towards them, they formed upon the beach, and seemed resolved to dispute his landing, firing several distant shot at him as he drew near; till at last the boat being arrived within a reasonable distance of the most advanced squadron, Mr. Brett ordered his people to fire, upon which this resolute cavalry instantly ran in great confusion into the wood, through a small opening. In this precipitate flight one of their horses fell down and threw his rider, but, whether he was wounded or not we could not learn, for both man and horse soon got up again, and followed the rest into the wood. In the mean time, the other two squadrons, who were drawn up at a great distance behind, out of the reach of our shot, were calm spectators of the rout of their comrades; for they had halted on our first approach, and never advanced afterwards. It was doubtless fortunate for our people that the enemy acted with so little prudence, and exerted so little spirit; for had they concealed themselves till our men had landed, it is scarcely possible but the whole boat's crew must have fallen into their hands; since the Spaniards were not much short of two hundred, and the whole number, with Mr. Brett, as hath been already mentioned, only amounted to sixteen. However, the discovery of so considerable a force, collected in this bay of Petaplan, obliged us constantly to keep a boat or two before it; for we were apprehensive that the cutter, which we had left to cruise off Acapulco, might, on her return, be surprised by the enemy, if she did not receive timely information of her danger. But now to proceed with the account of the harbour of Chequetan.

After our unsuccessful attempt to engage the people of the country to furnish us with the necessaries we wanted, we desisted from any more endeavours of the same nature, and were obliged to be contented with what we could procure for ourselves in the neighbourhood of the port. We caught fish here in tolerable quantities, especially when the smoothness of the water permitted us to haul the seine. Amongst the rest, we got there cavallies, breams, mullets, soles, fiddle-fish, sea-eggs, and lobsters: and we here, and in no other place, met with that extraordinary fish called the torpedo, or numbing-fish, which is in shape very like the fiddle-fish, and is not to be known from it but by a brown circular spot of about the bigness of a crown-piece near the centre of its back; perhaps its figure will be better understood, when I say it is a flat fish, much resembling the thorn-back. This fish, the torpedo, is indeed of a most singular nature, productive of the strangest effects on the human body: for whoever handles it, or happens even to set his foot upon it, is presently seized with a numbness all over him; but which is more distinguishable in that limb which was in immediate contact with it. The same effect too will be in some degree produced by touching the fish with anything held in the hand; for I myself had a considerable degree of numbness conveyed to my right arm, through a walking cane which I rested on the body of the fish for some time; and I make no doubt but I should have been much more sensibly affected, had not the fish been near expiring when I made the experiment: for it is observable that this influence acts with most vigour when the fish is first taken out of the water, and entirely ceases when it is dead, so that it may be then handled or even eaten without any inconvenience. I shall only add that the numbness of my arm on this occasion did not go off on a sudden, as the accounts of some naturalists gave me reason to expect, but diminished gradually, so that I had some sensation of it remaining till the next day.

To the account given of the fish we met with here, I must add, that though turtle now grew scarce, and we met with none in this harbour of Chequetan, yet our boats, which, as I have mentioned, were stationed off Petaplan, often supplied us therewith; and though this was a food that we had now been so long as it were confined to, (for it was the only fresh provisions which we had tasted for near six months,) yet we were far from being cloyed with it, or from finding that the relish we had of it at all diminished.

The animals we met with on shore were principally guanos, with which the country abounds, and which are by some reckoned delicious food. We saw no beasts of prey here, except we should esteem that amphibious animal, the alligator, as such, several of which our people discovered, but none of them very large. However, we were satisfied that there were great numbers of tigers in the woods, though none of them came in sight; for we every morning found the beach near the watering place imprinted very thick with their footsteps: but we never apprehended any mischief from them;

for they are by no means so fierce as the Asiatic or African tiger, and are rarely, if ever, known to attack mankind. Birds were here in sufficient plenty; for we had abundance of pheasants of different kinds, some of them of an uncommon size, but they were very dry and tasteless food. And besides these we had a variety of smaller birds, particularly parrots, which we often killed for food.

The fruits and vegetable refreshments at this place were neither plentiful, nor of the best kinds: there were, it is true, a few bushes scattered about the woods, which supplied us with limes, but we scarcely could procure enough for our present use; and these, with a small plum of an agreeable acid, called in Jamaica the hog-plum, together with another fruit called the papah, were the only fruits to be found in the woods. Nor is there any other useful vegetable here worth mentioning, except brooklime: this indeed grew in great quantities near the fresh-water banks; and, as it was esteemed an antiscorbutic, we fed upon it frequently, though its extreme bitterness made it very unpalatable.

These are the articles most worthy of notice in this harbour of Chequetan. I shall only mention a particular of the coast lying to the westward of it, that to the eastward having been already described. As Mr. Anson was always attentive to whatever might be of consequence to those who might frequent these seas hereafter; and, as we had observed that there was a double land to the westward of Chequetan, which stretched out to a considerable distance, with a kind of opening, which appeared not unlike the inlet to some harbour, the commodore, soon after we came to an anchor, sent a boat to discover it more accurately, and it was found, on a nearer examination, that the two hills, which formed the double land, were joined together by a valley, and that there was no harbour nor shelter between them.

By all that has been said, it will appear that the conveniences of this port of Chequetan, particularly in the articles of refreshment, are not altogether such as might be desired: but yet, upon the whole, it is a place of considerable consequence, and the knowledge of it may be of great import to future cruisers. For it is the only secure harbour in a vast extent of coast, except Acapulco, which is in the hands of the enemy. It lies at a proper distance from Acapulco for the convenience of such ships as may have any designs on the Manila galleon; and it is a place where wood and water may be taken in with great security, in despite of the efforts of the inhabitants of the adjacent district for there is but one narrow path which leads through the woods into the country, and this is easily to be secured by a very small party, against all the strength the Spaniards in that neighbourhood can muster. After this account of Chequetan, and the coast contiguous to it, we shall return to the recital of our own proceedings.

CHAPTER XIII.

Our proceedings at Chequetan and on the adjacent coast, till our setting sail for Asia.

THE next morning, after our coming to an anchor in the harbour of Chequetan, we sent about ninety of our men well armed on shore, forty of whom were ordered to march into the country, as has been mentioned, and the remaining fifty were employed to cover the watering-place, and to prevent any interruption from the natives.

Here we completed the unloading of the Carmelo and Carmin, which we had begun at sea; at least we took out of them the indigo, cacao, and cochineal, with some iron for ballast, which were all the goods we intended to preserve, though they did not amount to a tenth of their cargoes. Here, too, it was agreed, after a mature consultation, to destroy the Tryal's prize, as well as the Carmelo and Carmin, whose fate had been before resolved on. Indeed the ship was in good repair and fit for the sea; but as the whole numbers on board our squadron did not amount to the complement of a fourth-rate man-of-war, we found it was impossible to divide them into three ships, without rendering them incapable of navigating in safety in the tempestuous weather we had reason to expect on the coast of China, where we supposed we should arrive about the time of the change of the monsoons. These considerations determined the commodore to destroy the Tryal's prize, and to reinforce the Gloucester with the greatest part of her crew. And in consequence of this resolve, all the stores on board the Tryal's prize were removed into the other ships, and the prize herself, with the Carmelo and Carmin, were prepared for scuttling with all the expedition we were masters of; but the greatest difficulties we were under in laying in a store of water (which have been already touched on) together with the necessary repairs of our rigging and other unavoidable occupations, took us up so much time, and found us such unexpected employment, that it was near the end of April before we were in a condition to leave the place.

During our stay here, there happened an incident, which, as it proved the means of convincing our friends in England of our safety, which for some time they had despaired of, and were then in doubt about, I shall beg leave particularly to recite. I have observed, in the preceding chapter, that from this harbour of Chequetan there was but one pathway which led through the woods into the country. This we found much beaten, and were thence convinced that it was well known to the inhabitants. As it passed by the spring-head, and was the only avenue by which the Spaniards could approach us, we, at some distance beyond the spring-head, felled several large trees, and laid them one upon the other across the path; and at this barricado we constantly kept a guard: and we besides ordered our men employed in watering to have their arms ready, and, in case of any alarm, to march instantly to this post. And though our principal intention was to prevent our being disturbed by any sudden attack of the enemy's horse, yet it answered another purpose, which was not in itself less important; this was to hinder our own people from straggling singly into the country, where we had reason to believe they would be surprised by the Spaniards, who would doubtless be extremely solicitous to pick up some of them, in hopes of getting intelligence of our future designs. To avoid this inconvenience, the strictest orders were given to the sentinels to let no person whatever pass beyond their post: but notwithstanding this precaution we missed one Lewis Leger, who was the commodore's cook: and as he was a Frenchman, and suspected to be a papist, it was by some imagined that he had deserted with a view of betraying all that he knew to the enemy; but this appeared, by the event, to be an ill-grounded surmise; for it was afterwards known that he had been taken by some Indians, who carried him prisoner to Acapulco, from whence he was transferred to Mexico, and thence to Vera Cruz, where he was shipped on board a vessel bound to Old Spain: and the vessel being obliged by some accident to put into Lisbon, Leger escaped on shore, and was by the British consul sent from thence to England; where he brought the first authentic account of the safety of the commodore, and of what he had done in the South Seas. The relation he gave of his own seizure was, that he had rambled into the woods at some distance from the barricado, where he had first attempted to pass, but had been stopped and threatened to be punished; that his principal view was to get a quantity of limes for his master's store; and that in this occupation he was surprised unawares by four Indians, who stripped him naked, and carried him in that condition to Acapulco, exposed to the scorching heat of the sun, which at that time of the year shone with its greatest violence: and afterwards at Mexico his treatment in prison was sufficiently severe, and the whole course of his captivity was a continued instance of the hatred which the Spaniards bear to all those who endeavour to disturb them in the peaceable possession of the coasts of the South Seas. Indeed Leger's fortune was, upon the whole, extremely singular; for after the hazards he had run in the commodore's squadron, and the severities he had suffered in his long confinement amongst the enemy, a more fatal disaster attended him on his return to England: for though, when he arrived in London, some of Mr. Anson's friends interested themselves in relieving him from the poverty to which his captivity had reduced him; yet he did not long enjoy the benefit of their humanity, for he was killed in an insignificant night brawl, the cause of which could scarcely be discovered.

And here I must observe that though the enemy never appeared in sight during our stay in this harbour, yet we perceived that there were large parties of them encamped in the woods about us; for we could see their smokes, and could thence determine that they were posted in a circular line surrounding us at a distance; and just before our coming away they seemed, by the increase of their fires, to have received a considerable reinforcement. But to return:

Towards the latter end of April, the unloading of our three prizes, our wooding and watering, and, in short, all our proposed employments at the harbour of Chequetan, were completed: so that, on the 27th of April, the Tryal's prize, the Carmelo and the Carmin, all which we here intended to destroy, were towed on shore and scuttled, and a quantity of combustible materials were distributed in their upper works; and the next morning the Centurion and the Gloucester weighed anchor, but as there was but little wind, and that not in their favour, they were obliged to warp out of the harbour. When they had reached the offing, one of the boats was despatched back again to set fire to our prize, which was accordingly executed. And a canoe was left fixed to a grapnel in the middle of the harbour, with a bottle in it well corked, inclosing a letter to Mr. Hughes, who commanded the cutter, which was ordered to cruise before the port of Acapulco, when we came off that station. And on this occasion I must mention more particularly than I have yet done, the views of the commodore in leaving the cutter before that port.

When we were necessitated to make for Chequetan to take in our water, Mr. Anson considered that our being in that harbour would soon be known at Acapulco; and therefore he hoped that, on the intelligence of our being employed in port, the galleon might put to sea, especially as Chequetan is so very remote from the course generally steered by the galleon: he therefore ordered the cutter to cruise twenty-four days off the port of Acapulco, and her commander was directed, on perceiving the galleon under sail, to make the best of his way to the commodore at Chequetan. As the Centurion was doubtless a much better sailer than the galleon, Mr. Anson, in this case, resolved to have got to sea as soon as possible, and to have pursued the galleon across the Pacific Ocean: and supposing he should not have met with her in his passage, (which, considering that he would have kept nearly the same parallel, was not very improbable,) yet he was certain of arriving off Cape Espiritu Santo, on the island of Samal, before her; and that being the first land she makes on her return to the Philippines, we could not have failed to have fallen in with her, by cruising a few days in that station. But the viceroy of Mexico ruined this project by keeping the galleon in the port of Acapulco all that year.

The letter left in the canoe for Mr. Hughes, the commander of the cutter, (the time of whose return was now considerably elapsed,) directed him to go back immediately to his former station before Acapulco, where he would find Mr. Anson, who resolved to cruise for him there for a certain number of days; after which, it was added, that the commodore would return to the southward to join the rest of the squadron. This last article was inserted to deceive the Spaniards, if they got possession of the canoe, (as we afterwards learnt they did,) but could not impose on Mr. Hughes, who well knew that the commodore had no squadron to join, nor any intention of steering back to Peru.

Being now in the offing of Chequetan, bound across the vast Pacific Ocean in our way to China, we were impatient to run off the coast as soon as possible; for as the stormy season was approaching apace, and as we had no further views in the American seas, we had hoped that nothing would have prevented us from standing to the westward, the moment we got out of the harbour of Chequetan: and it was no small mortification to us, that our necessary employment there had detained us so much longer than we expected; and now we were farther detained by the absence of the cutter, and the standing towards Acapulco in search of her. Indeed, as the time of her cruise had been expired for near a fortnight, we suspected that she had been discovered from the shore; and that the governor of Acapulco had thereupon sent out a force to seize her, which, as she carried but six hands, was no very difficult enterprise. However, this being only conjecture, the commodore, as soon as he was got clear of the harbour of Chequetan, stood along the coast to the eastward in search of her: and to prevent her from passing by us in the dark, we brought-to every night; and the Gloucester, whose station was a league within us towards the shore, carried a light, which the cutter could not but perceive, if she kept along-shore, as we supposed she would do; and as a farther security, the Centurion and the Gloucester alternately showed two false fires every half hour. Indeed, had she escaped us, she would have found orders in the canoe to have returned immediately before Acapulco, where Mr. Anson proposed to cruise for her some days.

By Sunday, the 2d of May, we were advanced within three leagues of Acapulco, and having seen nothing of our boat, we gave her over for lost, which, besides the compassionate concern for our ship-mates, and for what it was apprehended they might have suffered, was in itself a misfortune, which, in our present scarcity of hands, we were all greatly interested in: for the crew of the cutter, consisting of six men and the lieutenant, were the very flower of our people, purposely picked out for this service, and known to be every one of them of tried and approved resolution, and as skilful seamen as ever trod a deck. However, as it was the general belief among us that they were taken and carried into Acapulco, the commodore's prudence suggested a project which we hoped would recover them. This was founded on our having many Spanish and Indian prisoners in our possession, and a number of sick negroes, who could be of no service to us in the navigating of the ship. The commodore therefore wrote a letter the same day to the governor of Acapulco, telling him, that he would release them all, provided the governor returned the cutter's crew; and the letter was despatched the same afternoon by a Spanish officer, of whose honour we had a good opinion, and who was furnished with a launch belonging to one of our prizes, and a crew of six other prisoners who all gave their parole for their return. The officer, too, besides the commodore's letter, carried with him a joint petition signed by all the rest of the prisoners, beseeching his Excellency to acquiesce in the terms proposed for their liberty. From a consideration of the number of our prisoners, and the quality of some of them, we did not doubt but the governor would readily comply with Mr. Anson's proposal, and therefore we kept plying on and off the whole night, intending to keep well in with the land, that we might receive an answer at the limited time, which was the next day, being Monday: but both on the Monday and Tuesday we were driven so far off shore, that we could not hope to receive any answer; and on the Wednesday morning we found ourselves fourteen leagues from the harbour of Acapulco; but as the wind was now favourable, we pressed forwards with all our sail, and did not doubt of getting in with the land in a few hours. Whilst we were thus standing in, the man at the mast-head called out that he saw a boat under sail at a considerable distance to the south-eastward: this we took for granted was the answer of the governor to the commodore's message, and we instantly edged towards it; but when we drew nearer, we found to our unspeakable joy that it was our own cutter. While she was still at a distance, we imagined that she had been discharged out of the port of Acapulco by the governor; but when she drew nearer, the wan and meagre countenances of the crew, the length of their beards, and the feeble and hollow tone of their voices, convinced us that they had suffered much greater hardships than could be expected from even the severities of a Spanish prison. They were obliged to be helped into the ship, and were immediately put to bed, and with rest, and nourishing diet, which they were plentifully supplied with from the commodore's table, they recovered their health and vigour apace: and now we learnt that they had kept the sea the whole time of their absence, which was above six weeks; that when they finished their cruise before Acapulco, and had just begun to ply to the westward in order to join the squadron, a strong adverse current had forced them down the coast to the eastward in spite of all their efforts; that at length their water being all expended, they were obliged to search the coast farther on to the eastward, in quest of some convenient landing-place, where they might get a fresh supply; that in this distress they ran upwards of eighty leagues to leeward, and found everywhere so large a surf, that there was not the least possibility of their landing; that they passed some days in this dreadful situation, without water, and having no other means left them to allay their thirst than sucking the blood of the turtle which they caught; and at last, giving up all hopes of relief, the heat of the climate too augmenting their necessities, and rendering their sufferings insupportable, they abandoned themselves to despair, fully persuaded that they should perish by the most terrible of all deaths; but that they were soon after happily relieved by a most unexpected incident, for there fell so heavy a rain, that by spreading their sails horizontally, and by putting bullets in the centers of them to draw them to a point, they caught as much water as filled all their cask; that immediately upon this fortunate supply they stood to the westward in quest of the commodore; and being now luckily favoured by a strong current, they joined us in less than fifty hours, from the time they stood to the westward, after having been absent from us full forty-three days. Those who have an idea of the inconsiderable size of a cutter belonging to a sixty-gun ship, (being only an open boat about twenty-two feet in length,) and who will attend to the various accidents to which she was exposed during a six weeks' continuance alone, in the open ocean, on so impracticable and dangerous a coast, will readily own, that her return to us at last, after all the difficulties which she actually experienced, and the hazards to which she was each hour exposed, may be considered as little short of miraculous.

I cannot finish the article of this cutter, without remarking how little reliance navigators ought to have on the accounts of the buccaneer writers: for though in this run of hers, eighty leagues to the eastward of Acapulco, she found no place where it was possible for a boat to land, yet those writers have not been ashamed to feign harbours and convenient watering-places within these limits; thereby exposing such as should confide in their relations, to the risk of being destroyed by thirst.

And now having received our cutter, the sole object of our coming a second time before Acapulco, the commodore resolved not to lose a moment's time longer, but to run off the coast with the utmost expedition, both as the stormy season on the coast of Mexico was now approaching apace, and as we were apprehensive of having the westerly monsoon to struggle with when we came upon the coast of China; and therefore he no longer stood towards Acapulco, as he now wanted no answer from the governor; but yet he resolved not to deprive his prisoners of the liberty, which he had promised them; so that they were all immediately embarked in two launches which belonged to our prizes, those from the Centurion in one launch, and those from the Gloucester in the other. The launches were well equipped with masts, sails and oars; and, lest the wind might prove unfavourable, they had a stock of water and provisions put on board them sufficient for fourteen days. There were discharged thirty-nine persons from on board the Centurion, and eighteen from the Gloucester, the greatest part of them Spaniards, the rest Indians and sick negroes: but as our crews were very weak, we kept the mulattoes and some of the stoutest of the negroes, with a few Indians, to assist us; but we dismissed every Spanish prisoner whatever. We have since learnt, that these two launches arrived safe at Acapulco, where the prisoners could not enough extol the humanity with which they had been treated; and that the governor, before their arrival, had returned a very obliging answer to the commodore's letter, and had attended it with a present of two boats laden with the choicest refreshments and provisions which were to be got at Acapulco; but that these boats not having found our ships, were at length obliged to put back again, after having thrown all their provisions overboard in a storm which threatened their destruction.

The sending away our prisoners was our last transaction on the American coast; for no sooner had we parted with them, than we and the Gloucester made sail to the S.W., proposing to get a good offing from the land, where we hoped, in a few days, to meet with the regular tradewind, which the accounts of former navigators had represented as much brisker and steadier in this ocean, than in any other part of the globe: for it has been esteemed no uncommon passage, to run from hence to the easternmost parts of Asia in two months; and we flattered ourselves that we were as capable of making an expeditious passage, as any ships that had ever run this course before us: so that we hoped soon to gain the coast of China, for which we were now bound. And conformable to the general idea of this navigation given by former voyagers, we considered it as free from all kinds of embarrassment of bad weather, fatigue, or sickness; and consequently we undertook it with alacrity, especially as it was no contemptible step towards our arrival at our native country, for which many of us by this time began to have great longings. Thus, on the 6th of May, we, for the last time, lost sight of the mountains of Mexico, persuaded, that in a few weeks we should arrive at the river of Canton in China, where we expected to meet with many English ships, and numbers of our countrymen; and hoped to enjoy the advantages of an amicable, well-frequented port, inhabited by a polished people, and abounding with the conveniences and indulgences of a civilised life; blessings, which now for near twenty months had never been once in our power. But there yet remains (before we take our leave of America) the consideration of a matter well worthy of attention, the discussion of which shall be referred to the ensuing chapter.

CHAPTER XIV.

A brief account of what might have been expected from our squadron, had it arrived in the South Seas in good time.

AFTER the recital of the transactions of the commodore, and the ships under his command, on the coasts of Peru and Mexico, as contained in the preceding part of this book, it will be no useless digression to examine what the whole squadron might have been capable of achieving, had it arrived in those seas in so good a plight, as it would probably have done, had the passage round Cape Horn been attempted in a more seasonable time of the year. This disquisition may be serviceable to those who shall hereafter form projects of the like nature for that part of the world, or may be entrusted with their execution. And therefore I propose, in this chapter, to consider, as succinctly as I can, the numerous advantages which the public might have received from the operations of the squadron, had it set sail from England a few months sooner.

And first, I must suppose, that in the summer-time we might have got round Cape Horn with an inconsiderable loss, and without any damage to our ships or rigging. For the Duke and Duchess of Bristol, who between them had above three hundred men, buried no more than two, from the coast of Brazil to Juan Fernandes; and out of a hundred and eighty-three hands which were on board the Duke, there were only twenty-one sick of the scurvy, when they arrived at that island: whence, as men-of-war are much better provided with all conveniences than privateers, we might, doubtless, have appeared before Baldivia in full strength, and in a condition of entering immediately on action; and therefore, as that place was in a very defenceless state, its cannon incapable of service, and its garrison in great measure unarmed, it was impossible that it could have opposed our force, or that its half-starved inhabitants, most of whom are convicts banished thither from other parts, could have had any other thoughts than that of submitting; and Baldivia, which is a most excellent port, being once taken, we should immediately have been terrible to the whole kingdom of Chili, and should, doubtless, have awed the most distant parts of the Spanish empire. Indeed,

it is far from improbable that, by a prudent use of our advantages, we might have given a violent shock to the authority of Spain on that whole continent; and might have rendered some, at least, of her provinces independent. This would, doubtless, have turned the whole attention of the Spanish ministry to that part of the world, where the danger would have been so pressing. And thence Great Britain and her allies might have been rid of the numerous embarrassments, which the wealth of the Spanish Indies, operating in conjunction with the Gallic intrigues, have constantly thrown in her way.

And that I may not be thought to over-rate the force of this squadron, by ascribing to it a power of overturning the Spanish government in America, it is necessary to premise a few observations on the condition of the provinces bordering on the South Seas, and on the disposition of the inhabitants, both Spaniards and Indians, at that time; by which it will appear, that there was great dissension amongst the governors, and disaffection among the Creolians; that they were in want of arms and stores, and had fallen into a total neglect of all military regulations in their garrisons; and that as to the Indians on their frontier, they were universally discontented, and seemed to be watching with impatience for the favourable moment, when they might take a severe revenge for the barbarities they had groaned under for more than two ages; so that every circumstance concurred to facilitate the enterprises of our squadron. Of all these particulars we were amply informed by the letters we took on board our prizes, none of these vessels, as I remember, having had the precaution to throw her papers overboard.

The ill blood amongst the governors was greatly augmented by their apprehensions of our squadron; for every one being willing to have it believed, that the bad condition of his government was not the effect of negligence, there were continual demands and remonstrances amongst them, in order to throw the blame upon each other. Thus, for instance, the president of St. Jago in Chili, the president of Panama, and many other governors and military officers, were perpetually soliciting the viceroy of Peru to furnish them with the necessary supplies of money for putting their provinces and places in a proper state of defence to oppose our designs. But the customary answer of the viceroy to these representations was the emptiness of the royal chest at Lima, and the difficulties he was under to support the expenses of his own government; and in one of his letters (which we intercepted), he mentioned his apprehensions that he might even be necessitated to stop the pay of the troops, and of the garrison of Callao, the key of the whole kingdom of Peru. Indeed he did at times remit to these governors some part of their demands: but as what he sent them was greatly short of their wants, it rather tended to the raising jealousies and heart-burnings amongst them, than contributed to the purposes for which it was intended.

And besides these mutual janglings amongst the governors, the whole body of the people were extremely dissatisfied; for they were fully persuaded that the affairs of Spain, for many years before, had been managed by the influence of a particular foreign interest, which was altogether detached from the advantages of the Spanish nation. So that the inhabitants of these distant provinces believed themselves to be sacrificed to an ambition, which never considered their convenience or interests, or paid any regard to the reputation of their name, or the honour of their country. That this was the temper of the Creolian Spaniards at that time, might be evinced from a hundred instances; but I shall content myself with one, which is indeed conclusive. This is the testimony of the French mathematicians sent into America, to measure the magnitude of an equatorial degree of latitude. For in the relation of the murder of a surgeon belonging to their company in one of the cities of Peru, and of the popular tumult occasioned thereby, written by one of those astronomers, the author confesses, that the inhabitants, during the uproar, all joined in imprecations on their bad governors, and bestowed the most abusive language upon the French, detesting them, in all probability, more particularly as belonging to a nation, to whose influence in the Spanish councils the Spaniards imputed all their misfortunes.

And whilst the Creolian Spaniards were thus dissatisfied, it appears by the letters we intercepted, that the Indians, on almost every frontier, were ripe for a revolt, and would have taken up arms on the slightest encouragement; in particular, the Indians in the southern parts of Peru; as likewise the Arraucos, and the rest of the Chilian Indians, the most powerful and terrible to the Spanish name of any on that continent. For it seems, that in the disputes between the Spaniards and the Indians, which happened some time before our arrival, the Spaniards had insulted the Indians with an account of the force, which they expected from Old Spain, under the command of Admiral Pizarro, and had vaunted that he was coming thither to complete the great work which had been left unfinished by his ancestors. These threats alarmed the Indians, and made them believe that their extirpation was resolved on. For the Pizarros being the first conquerors of that coast, the Peruvian Indians held the name, and all that bore it, in execration; not having forgot the destruction of their monarchy, the massacre of their beloved Inca, Atupalipa, the extinction of their religion, and the slaughter of their ancestors; all perpetrated by the family of the Pizarros. The Chilian Indians, too, abhorred a chief descended from those, who, by their lieutenants, had first attempted to enslave them, and had necessitated their tribes, for more than a century, to be continually wasting their blood in defence of their independence.

And let it not be supposed, that among those barbarous nations the traditions of such distant transactions could not be continued till the present times; for all who have been acquainted with that part of the world agree, that the Indians, in their public feasts, and annual solemnities, constantly revive the memory of these tragic incidents; and those who have been present at these spectacles have observed, that all the recitals and representations of this kind were received with an enthusiastic rage, and with such vehement emotions, as plainly evinced how strongly the memory of their former wrongs was implanted in them, and how acceptable the means of revenge would at all times prove. To this account I must add,

too, that the Spanish governors themselves were so fully informed of the disposition of the Indians, and were so apprehensive of a general defection among them, that they employed all their industry to reconcile the most dangerous tribes, and to prevent them from immediately taking up arms. Among the rest, the president of Chili in particular made large concessions to the Arraucos, and the other Chilian Indians, by which, and by distributing considerable presents to their leading men, he at last got them to consent to a prolongation of the truce between the two nations. But these negociations were not concluded at the time when we might have been in the South Seas; and had they been completed, yet the hatred of these Indians to the Spaniards was so great, that it would have been impossible for their chiefs to have prevented their joining us.

Thus, then, it appears that on our arrival in the South Sea we might have found the whole coast unprovided with troops, and destitute even of arms; for we well knew, from very particular intelligence, that there were not three hundred fire-arms, of which too the greatest part were matchlocks, in all the province of Chili. At the same time, the Indians would have been ready to revolt, the Spaniards disposed to mutiny, and the governors enraged with each other, and each prepared to rejoice at the disgrace of his antagonist; whilst we, on the other hand, might have consisted of near two thousand men, the greatest part in health and vigour, all well armed and united under a chief, whose enterprising genius (as we have seen) could not be depressed by a continued series of the most sinister events, and whose equable and prudent turn of temper would have remained unvaried, in the midst of the greatest degree of good success; and who besides possessed, in a distinguished manner, the two qualities, the most necessary in these uncommon undertakings; I mean, that of maintaining his authority, and preserving, at the same time, the affections of his people. Our other officers too of every rank, appear, by the experience the public has since had of them, to have been equal to any enterprise they might have been charged with by their commander; and our men (at all times brave if well conducted) in such a cause where treasure was the object, and under such leaders, would doubtless have been prepared to rival the most celebrated achievements hitherto performed by British mariners.

It cannot then be contested, but that Baldivia must have surrendered on the appearance of our squadron; after which it may be presumed that the Arraucos, the Pulches, and Penguinches, inhabiting the banks of the river Imperial, about twenty-five leagues to the northward of this place, would have immediately taken up arms, being disposed, as has been already related, and encouraged by the arrival of so considerable a force in their neighbourhood. As these Indians can bring into the field near thirty thousand men, the greatest part of them horse, their first step would doubtless have been the invading the province of Chili, which they would have found totally unprovided of ammunition and weapons; and as its inhabitants are a luxurious and effeminate race, they would have been incapable, on such an emergency, of giving any opposition to this rugged enemy; so that it is no strained conjecture to imagine, that the Indians would soon have been masters of the whole country. And the other Indians on the frontiers of Peru being equally disposed with the Arraucos to shake off the Spanish yoke, it is highly probable, that they likewise would have embraced the occasion, and that a general insurrection would have taken place through all the Spanish territories in South America; in which case, the only resource left to the Creolians (dissatisfied as they were with the Spanish government) would have been to have made the best terms they could with their Indian neighbours, and to have withdrawn themselves from the obedience of a master, who had shown so little regard to their security. This last supposition may perhaps appear chimerical to those who measure the possibility of all events by the scanty standard of their own experience; but the temper of the times, and the strong dislike of the natives to the measures then pursued by the Spanish court, sufficiently evince at least its possibility. But not to insist on the presumption of a general revolt, it is sufficient for our purpose to conclude that the Arraucos would scarcely have failed of taking arms on our appearance; for this alone would so far have embarrassed the enemy that they would no longer have thought of opposing us, but would have turned all their care to the Indian affairs; as they still remember, with the utmost horror, the sacking of their cities, the rifling of their convents, the captivity of their wives and daughters, and the desolation of their country by these resolute savages, in the last war between the two nations. For it must be remembered, that this tribe of Indians have been frequently successful against the Spaniards, and possess at this time a large tract of country, which was formerly full of Spanish towns and villages, whose inhabitants were all either destroyed or carried into captivity by the Arraucos and the neighbouring Indians, who, in a war against the Spaniards, never fail to join their forces.

But even independent of an Indian revolt, there were but two places on all the coast of the South Sea, which could be supposed capable of resisting our squadron; these were the cities of Panama and Callao: as to the first of these, its fortifications were so decayed, and it was so much in want of powder, that the governor himself, in an intercepted letter, acknowledged it was incapable of being defended; so that I take it for granted it would have given us but little trouble, especially if we had opened a communication across the Isthmus with our fleet on the other side: and for the city and port of Callao, its condition was not much better than that of Panama; for its walls are built upon the plain ground, without either outwork or ditch before them, and consist only of very slender feeble masonry, without any earth behind them; so that a battery of five or six pieces of cannon, raised anywhere within four or five hundred paces of the place, would have had a full view of the whole rampart, and would have opened it in a short time; and the breach hereby formed, as the walls are so extremely thin, could not have been difficult of ascent: for the ruins would have been but little higher than the surface of the ground; and it would have yielded this particular advantage to the assailants, that the bullets, which grazed upon it, would have driven before them such shivers of brick and stone, as would have prevented the garrison from forming behind it, supposing that the troops employed in the defence of the place, should have so far surpassed the usual limits of Creolian bravery, as to resolve to stand a general assault: indeed, such a resolution cannot be imputed to them for the garrison and people were in general dissatisfied with the viceroy's behaviour, and were never expected to act a vigorous part. The viceroy himself greatly apprehended that the commodore would make him a visit at Lima, the capital of the kingdom of Peru; to prevent which, if possible, he had ordered twelve galleys to be built at Guaiaquil and other places, which were intended to oppose the landing of our boats, and to hinder us from pushing our men on shore. But this was an impracticable project, and proceeded on the supposition that our ships, when we should land our men, would keep at such a distance, that these galleys, by drawing little water, would have been out of the reach of their guns; whereas the commodore, before he had made such an attempt, would doubtless have been possessed of several prize ships, which he would not have hesitated to have run on shore for the protection of his boats; and besides there were many places on that coast, and one in particular in the neighbourhood of Callao, where there was good anchoring, though a great depth of water, within a cable's length of the shore; so that the cannon of the men-of-war would have swept all the coast to above a mile's distance from the water's edge, and would have effectually prevented any force from assembling to oppose the landing and forming of our men: and the place had this additional advantage, that it was but two leagues distant from the city of Lima; so that we might have been at that city within four hours after we should have been first discovered from the shore. The place I have here in view is about two leagues south of Callao, and just to the northward of the head-land called, in Frezier's draught of that coast, Morro Solar. Here there is seventy or eighty fathoms of water within two cables' length of the shore; and the Spaniards themselves were so apprehensive of our attempting to land there, that they had projected to build a fort close to the water; but there being no money in the royal chests, they could not go on with that work, and therefore they contented themselves with keeping a guard of a hundred horse there, that they might be sure to receive early notice of our appearance on that coast. Indeed some of them (as we were told) conceiving our management at sea to be as pusillanimous as their own, pretended that the commodore would never dare to bring in his ships there, for fear that in so great a depth of water their anchors could not hold them.

And here let it not be imagined that I am proceeding upon groundless and extravagant presumptions, when I conclude that fifteen hundred or a thousand of our people, well conducted, should have been an over-match for any numbers the Spaniards could muster in South America. For not to mention the experience we had of them at Paita and Petaplan, it must be remembered, that our commodore was extremely solicitous to have all his men trained to the dextrous use of their fire-arms; whereas the Spaniards in this part of the world were in great want of arms, and were very awkward in the management of the few they had; and though, on their repeated representations, the court of Spain had ordered several thousand firelocks to be put on board Pizarro's squadron, yet those, it is evident, could not have been in America time enough to have been employed against us; so that by our arms, and our readiness in the use of them, (not to insist on the timidity and softness of our enemy,) we should in some degree have had the same advantages which the Spaniards themselves had, in the first discovery of this country, against its naked and unarmed inhabitants.

And now let it be considered what were the events which we had to fear, or what were the circumstances which could have prevented us from giving law to all the coast of South America, and thereby cutting off from Spain the resources which she drew from those immense provinces. By sea there was no force capable of opposing us; for how soon soever we had sailed, Pizarro's squadron could not have sailed sooner than it did, and therefore could not have avoided the fate it met with; as we should have been masters of the ports of Chili, we could there have supplied ourselves with the provisions we wanted in the greatest plenty; and from Baldivia to the equinoctial we ran no risk of losing our men by sickness, (that being of all climates the most temperate and healthy,) nor of having our ships disabled by bad weather; and had we wanted hands to assist in the navigating our squadron, whilst a considerable part of our men were employed on shore, we could not have failed of getting whatever numbers we pleased in the ports we should have taken, and the prizes which would have fallen into our hands; and I must observe that the Indians, who are the principal sailors in that part of the world, are extremely docile and dextrous, and though they are not fit to struggle with the inclemencies of a cold climate, yet in temperate seas they are most useful and laborious seamen.

Thus, then, it appears what important revolutions might have been brought about by our squadron, had it departed from England as early as it ought to have done: and from hence it is easy to conclude, what immense advantages might have thence accrued to the public. For, as on our success it would have been impossible for the kingdom of Spain to have received any treasure from the provinces bordering on the South Seas, or even to have had any communication with them, it is certain that the whole attention of that monarchy must have been immediately employed in regaining the possession of these inestimable territories, either by force or compact. By the first of these methods it was scarcely possible they could succeed; for it must have been at least a twelvemonth from our arrival, before any ships from Spain could get into the South Seas, and those perhaps separated, disabled, and sickly; and by that time they would have had no port in their possession, either to rendezvous at or to refit in; whilst we might have been supplied across the Isthmus with whatever necessaries, stores, or even men we wanted, and might thereby have maintained our squadron in as good a plight as when it first set sail from St. Helens. In short, it required but little prudence in the conduct of this business to have rendered all the efforts of Spain, seconded by the power of France, ineffectual, and to have maintained our conquests in defiance of them both: so that they must either have resolved to have left Great Britain masters of the wealth of South America, (the principal support of all their destructive projects,) or they must have submitted to her terms, and have been contented to receive these provinces back again as an equivalent for those restrictions to their future ambition, which her prudence should have dictated to them. Having thus discussed the prodigious weight which the operations of our squadron might have added to the national influence of this kingdom, I shall here end this second book, referring to the next, the passage of the shattered remains of our force across the Pacific Ocean, and all their future transactions till the commodore's arrival in England.

END OF BOOK II.

BOOK III.

CHAPTER I.

The run from the coast of Mexico to the Ladrones or Marian Islands.

WHEN, on the sixth of May, 1742, we left the coast of America, we stood to the S.W. with a view of meeting with the N.E. trade-wind, which the accounts of former writers made us expect at seventy or eighty leagues' distance from the land: we had besides another reason for standing to the southward, which was the getting into the latitude of 13 or 14° north; that being the parallel where the Pacific Ocean is most usually crossed, and consequently where the navigation is esteemed the safest: this last purpose we had soon answered, being in a day or two sufficiently advanced to the south. At the same time we were also farther from the shore than we had presumed was necessary for the falling in with the trade-wind: but in this particular we were most grievously disappointed; for the wind still continued to the westward, or at best variable. As the getting into the N.E. trade, was to us a matter of the last consequence, we stood more to the southward, and made many experiments to meet with it; but all our efforts were for a long time unsuccessful: so that it was seven weeks, from our leaving the coast, before we got into the true trade-wind. This was an interval, in which we believed we should well nigh have reached the easternmost parts of Asia: but we were so baffled with the contrary and variable winds, which for all that time perplexed us, that we were not as yet advanced above a fourth part of the way. The delay alone would have been a sufficient mortification; but there were other circumstances attending it, which rendered this situation not less terrible, and our apprehensions perhaps still greater than in any of our past distresses. For our two ships were by this time extremely crazy; and many days had not passed, before we discovered a spring in the foremast of the Centurion, which rounded about twenty-six inches of its circumference, and which was judged to be at least four inches deep: and no sooner had our carpenters secured this with fishing it, but the Gloucester made a signal of distress; and we learnt that she had a dangerous spring in her main-mast, twelve feet below the trussel-trees; so that she could not carry any sail upon it. Our carpenters, on a strict examination of this mast, found it so very rotten and decayed, that they judged it necessary to cut it down as low as it appeared to have been injured; and by this it was reduced to nothing but a stump, which served only as a step to the topmast. These accidents augmented our delay, and occasioned us great auxiety about our future security: for on our leaving the coast of Mexico, the scurvy had began to make its appearance again amongst our people; though from our departure from Juan Fernandes we had till then enjoyed a most uninterrupted state of health. We too well knew the effects of this disease, from our former fatal experience, to suppose that anything but a speedy passage could secure the greater part of our crew from perishing by it: and as, after being seven weeks at sea, there did not appear any reasons that could persuade us we were nearer the trade-wind than when we first set out, there was no ground for us to suppose but our passage would prove at least three times as long as we at first expected; and consequently we had the melancholy prospect, either of dying by the scurvy, or perishing with the ship for want of hands to navigate her. Indeed, some amongst us were at first willing to believe, that in this warm climate, so different from what we felt in passing round Cape Horn, the violence of this disease, and its fatality, might be in some degree mitigated; as it had not been unusual to suppose that its particular virulence in that passage was in a great measure owing to the severity of the weather: but the havoc of the distemper, in our present circumstances, soon convinced us of the falsity of this speculation; as it likewise exploded some other opinions, which usually pass current about the cause and nature of this disease.

For it has been generally presumed, that plenty of fresh provisions and of water are effectual preventives of this malady; but it happened that in the present instance we had a considerable stock of fresh provisions on board, as hogs and fowls, which were taken at Paita; and we besides almost every day caught great abundance of bonitos, dolphins, and albicores; and the unsettled season, which deprived us of the benefit of the trade-wind, proved extremely rainy; so that we were enabled to fill up our water-casks, almost as fast as they were empty; and each man had five pints of water allowed him every day, during the passage. But notwithstanding this plenty of water, and that the fresh provisions were distributed amongst the sick, and the whole crew often fed upon fish, yet neither were the sick hereby relieved, nor the progress and advancement of the disease retarded: nor was it in these instances only that we found ourselves disappointed; for though it has been usually esteemed a necessary piece of management to keep all ships, where the crews are large, as clean and airy between decks as possible; and it has been believed by many, that this particular, if well attended to, would prevent the appearance of the scurvy, or at least, mitigate its effects; yet we observed, during the latter part of our run, that though we kept all our ports open, and took uncommon pains in cleansing and sweetening the ships, yet neither the progress nor the virulence of the disease were thereby sensibly abated.

However, I would not be understood to assert, that fresh provisions, plenty of water, and a constant fresh supply of sweet air between decks, are matters of no moment: I am, on the contrary, well satisfied, that they are all of them articles of great importance, and are doubtless extremely conducive to the health and vigour of a crew, and may in many cases prevent the fatal malady we are now speaking of from taking place. All I have aimed at, in what I have advanced, is only to show that in some instances, both the cure and the prevention of this disease is impossible to be effected by any management, or by the application of any remedies which can be made use of at sea. Indeed, I am myself fully persuaded, that when it has once got to a certain head, there are no other means in nature for relieving the diseased, but carrying them on shore, or at least bringing them into the neighbourhood of land. Perhaps a distinct and adequate knowledge of the source of this disease may never be discovered; but in general, there is no difficulty in conceiving that as a continued supply of fresh air is necessary to all animal life, and as this air is so particular a fluid, that without losing its elasticity, or any of its obvious properties, it may be rendered unfit for this purpose, by the mixing with it some very subtle and otherwise imperceptible effluvia; it may be conceived, I say, that the steams arising from the ocean may have a tendency to render the air they are spread through less properly adapted to the support of the life of terrestrial animals, unless these steams are corrected by effluvia of another kind, and which perhaps the land alone can supply.

To what hath been already said in relation to this disease, I shall add, that our surgeon (who during our passage round Cape Horn, had ascribed the mortality we suffered to the severity of the climate) exerted himself in the present run to the utmost, and at last declared, that all his measures were totally ineffectual, and did not in the least avail his patients: on which it was resolved by the commodore to try the effects of two medicines, which, just before his departure from England, were the subject of much discourse, I mean the pill and drop of Mr. Ward. For however violent the effects of these medicines are said to have sometimes proved, yet in the present instance, where destruction seemed inevitable without some remedy, the experiment at least was thought advisable: and therefore, one or both of them, at different times, were given to persons in every stage of the distemper. Out of the numbers that took them, one, soon after swallowing the pill, was seized with a violent bleeding at the nose: he was before given over by the surgeon, and lay almost at the point of death; but he immediately found himself much better, and continued to recover, though slowly, till we arrived on shore, which was near a fortnight after.

A few others too were relieved for some days, but the disease returned again with as much violence as ever; though neither did these, nor the rest, who received no benefit, appear to be reduced to a worse condition than they would have been if they had taken nothing. The most remarkable property of these medicines, and what was obvious in almost every one that took them, was, that they operated in proportion to the vigour of the patient; so that those who were within two or three days of dying were scarcely affected; and as the patient was differently advanced in the disease, the operation was either a gentle perspiration, an easy vomit, or a moderate purge: but if they were taken by one in full strength, they then produced all the before-mentioned effects with considerable violence, which sometimes continued for six or eight hours together, with little intermission. But to return to the prosecution of our voyage.

I have already observed, that, a few days after our running off the coast of Mexico, the Gloucester had her main-mast cut down to a stump, and we were obliged to fish our fore-mast; and that these misfortunes were greatly aggravated, by our meeting with contrary and variable winds for near seven weeks. I shall now add, that when we reached the trade-wind, and it settled between the north and the east, yet it seldom blew with so much strength, but the Centurion might have carried all her small sails abroad with the greatest safety; so that now, had we been a single ship, we might have run down our longitude apace, and have reached the Ladrones soon enough to have recovered great numbers of our men, who afterwards perished. But the Gloucester, by the loss of her main-mast, sailed so very heavily, that we had seldom any more than our top-sails set, and yet were frequently obliged to lie-to for her: and, I conceive, that in the whole we lost little less than a month by our attendance upon her, in consequence of the various mischances she encountered. In all this run it was remarkable, that we were rarely many days together, without seeing great numbers of birds; which is a proof that there are many islands, or at least rocks, scattered all along at no very considerable distance from our track. Some indeed there are marked in the Spanish chart, hereafter mentioned; but the frequency of the birds, seem to evince that there are many more than have been hitherto discovered; for the greatest part of the birds we observed were such as are known to roost on shore; and the manner of their appearance sufficiently made out, that they came from some distant haunt every morning, and returned thither again in the evening; for we never saw them early or late; and the hour of their arrival and departure gradually varied, which we supposed was occasioned by our running nearer their haunts or getting further from them.

The trade-wind continued to favour us without any fluctuation, from the end of June till towards the end of July. But on the 26th of July, being then, as we esteemed, about three hundred leagues distant from the Ladrones, we met with a westerly wind, which did not come about again to the eastward in four days' time. This was a most dispiriting incident, as it at once damped all our hopes of speedy relief, especially too as it was attended with a vexatious accident to the Gloucester: for in one part of these four days the wind flattened to a calm, and the ships rolled very deep; by which means the Gloucester's forecap split, and her top-mast came by the board, and broke her fore-yard directly in the slings.* As she was hereby rendered incapable of making any sail for some time, we were obliged, as soon as a gale sprang up, to take her in tow; and near twenty of the healthiest and ablest of our seamen were taken from the business of our own ship, and were employed for eight or ten days together on board the Gloucester in repairing her damages: but these things, mortifying as we thought them, were but the beginning of our disasters; for scarce had our people finished their business in the Gloucester, before we met with a most violent storm in the western board, which obliged us to lie-to. In the beginning of this storm our ship sprang a leak, and let in so much water, that all our people, officers included, were employed continually in working the pumps: and the next day we had the vexation to see the Gloucester, with her top-mast once more by the board; and whilst we were viewing her with great concern for this new distress, we saw her main-top-mast, which had hitherto served as a jury main-mast, share the same fate. This completed our misfortunes, and rendered them without resource; for we knew the Gloucester's crew were so few and feeble, that without our assistance they could not be relieved: and our sick were now so far increased, and those that remained in health so continually fatigued with the additional duty of our pumps, that it was impossible for us to lend them any aid. Indeed we were not as yet fully apprised of the deplorable situation of the Gloucester's crew; for when the storm abated, (which during its continuance prevented all communication with them,) the Gloucester bore up under our stern; and captain Mitchel informed the commodore, that besides the loss of his masts, which was all that had appeared to us, the ship had then no less than seven feet of water in her hold, although his officers and men had been kept constantly at the pumps for the last twenty-four hours.

This last circumstance was indeed a most terrible accumulation to the other extraordinary distresses of the Gloucester, and required, if possible, the most speedy and vigorous assistance; which Captain Mitchel begged the commodore to send him: but the debility of our people, and our own immediate preservation, rendered it impossible for the commodore to comply with his request. All that could be done was to send our boat on board for a more particular condition of the ship; and it was soon suspected that the taking her people on board us, and then destroying her, was the only measure that could be prosecuted in the present emergency, both for the security of their lives and of our own.

Our boat soon returned with a representation of the state of the Gloucester, and of her several defects, signed by Captain Mitchel and all his

---

* "On the 15th of June the Gloucester found her main mast sprung at the head, which, upon examination, was discovered to be entirely rotten. On the 29th of July the Gloucester carried away her foretop-mast and fore-yard. My ship's company are now miserably afflicted with the scurvy, the ship very leaky, the men and officers tho. were well being only able to make one spell at the pump."—*Anson's Official Report.*

"This is all," observes Sir John Barrow, "that Anson says of the second attack of this afflicting malady; but, coming from the commodore, it speaks volumes."

officers; by which it appeared, that she had sprung a leak by the stern-post being loose, and working with every roll of the ship, and by two beams a-midships being broken in the orlop; no part of which the carpenters reported was possible to be repaired at sea: that both officers and men had worked twenty-four hours at the pumps without intermission, and were at length so fatigued, that they could continue their labour no longer, but had been forced to desist, with seven feet of water in the hold, which covered their casks, so that they could neither come at fresh-water, nor provision: that they had no mast standing, except the fore-mast, the mizen-mast, and the mizen topmast, nor had they any spare masts to get up in the room of those they had lost: that the ship was besides extremely decayed in every part, for her knees and clamps were all worked quite loose, and her upper works in general were so loose, that the quarter-deck was ready to drop down: and that her crew was greatly reduced, for there remained alive on board her no more than seventy-seven men, eighteen boys, and two prisoners, officers included; and that of this whole number, only sixteen men and eleven boys were capable of keeping the deck, and several of these very infirm.

The commodore, on the perusal of this melancholy representation, presently ordered them a supply of water and provisions, of which they seemed to be in immediate want, and at the same time sent his own carpenter on board them, to examine into the truth of every particular; and it being found, on the strictest inquiry, that the preceding account was in no instance exaggerated, it plainly appeared, that there was no possibility of preserving the Gloucester any longer, as her leaks were irreparable, and the united hands on board both ships, capable of working, would not be able to free her, even if our own ship should not employ any part of them. What then could be resolved on, when it was the utmost we ourselves could do to manage our own pumps? indeed there was no room for deliberation; the only step to be taken was, the saving the lives of the few that remained on board the Gloucester, and getting out of her as much as possible before she was destroyed. And therefore the commodore immediately sent an order to Captain Mitchel, as the weather was now calm and favourable, to send his people on board the Centurion as expeditiously as he could; and to take out such stores as he could get at, whilst the ship could be kept above water. And as our leak required less attention, whilst the present easy weather continued, we sent our boats with as many men as we could spare, to Captain Mitchel's assistance.

The removing the Gloucester's people on board us, and the getting out such stores as could most easily be come at, gave us full employment for two days. Mr. Anson was extremely desirous to have gotten two of her cables and an anchor, but the ship rolled so much, and the men were so excessively fatigued, that they were incapable of effecting it; nay, it was even with the greatest difficulty that the prize-money, which the Gloucester had taken in the South Seas, was secured, and sent on board the Centurion: however, the prize-goods on board her, which amounted to several thousand pounds in value, and were principally the Centurion's property, were entirely lost; nor could any more provision be got out than five casks of flour, three of which were spoiled by the salt-water. Their sick men, amounting to near seventy, were removed into boats with as much care as the circumstances of that time would permit; but three or four of them expired as they were hoisting them into the Centurion.

It was the 15th of August, in the evening, before the Gloucester was cleared of every thing that was proposed to be removed; and though the hold was now almost full of water, yet as the carpenters were of opinion that she might still swim for some time, if the calm should continue, and the water become smooth, she was set on fire; for we knew not how near we might now be to the island of Guam, which was in the possession of our enemies, and the wreck of such a ship would have been to them no contemptible acquisition. When she was set on fire, Captain Mitchel and his officers left her, and came on board the Centurion: and we immediately stood from the wreck, not without some apprehensions (as we had now only a light breeze) that if she blew up soon, the concussion of the air might damage our rigging; but she fortunately burnt, though very fiercely, the whole night, her guns firing successively, as the flames reached them. And it was six in the morning, when we were about four leagues distant, before she blew up; the report she made upon this occasion was but a small one, but there was an exceeding black pillar of smoke, which shot up into the air to a very considerable height.

Thus perished his Majesty's ship the Gloucester. And now it might have been expected, that being freed from the embarrassments which her frequent disasters had involved us in, we might proceed on our way much brisker than we had hitherto done, especially as we had received some small addition to our strength, by the taking on board the Gloucester's crew; but our anxieties were not yet to be relieved; for, notwithstanding all that we had hitherto suffered, there remained much greater distresses, which we were still to struggle with. For the late storm, which had proved so fatal to the Gloucester, had driven us to the northward of our intended course; and the current setting the same way, after the weather abated, had forced us still a degree or two farther, so that we were now in $17°\frac{1}{2}$ of North latitude, instead of being in $13°\frac{1}{4}$, which was the parallel we proposed to keep, in order to reach the island of Guam: and as it had been a perfect calm for some days since the cessation of the storm, and we were ignorant how near we were to the meridian of the Ladrones, and supposed ourselves not to be far from it, we apprehended that we might be driven to the leeward of them by the current, without discovering them: in this case, the only land we could make would be some of the eastern parts of Asia, where, if we could arrive, we should find the western monsoon in its full force, so that it would be impossible for the stoutest best-manned ship to get in. And this coast being removed between four and five hundred leagues farther, we, in our languishing circumstances, could expect no other than to be destroyed by the scurvy, long before the most favourable gale could carry us to such a distance: for our deaths were now extremely alarming, no day passing in which we did not bury eight or ten, and sometimes twelve, of our men; and those, who had hitherto continued healthy, began to fall down apace. Indeed we made the best use we could of the present calm, by employing our carpenters in searching after the leak, which was now considerable, notwithstanding the little wind we had: the carpenters at length discovered it to be in the gunner's fore-store-room, where the water rushed in under the breast-hook, on each side of the stem; but though they found where it was, they agreed that it was impossible to stop it, till we should get into port, and till they could come at it on the outside; however, they did the best they could within-board, and were fortunate enough to reduce it, which was a considerable relief to us.

We had hitherto considered the calm which succeeded the storm, and which continued for some days, as a very great misfortune; since the currents were driving us to the northward of our parallel, and we thereby risked the missing of the Ladrones, which we now conceived ourselves to be very near. But when a gale sprang up, our condition was still worse; for it blew from the S.W., and consequently was directly opposed to the course we wanted to steer: and though it soon veered to the N.E., yet this served only to tantalise us, for it returned back again in a very short time to its old quarter. However, on the 22d of August we had the satisfaction to find that the current was shifted, and had set us to the southward: and the 23d, at day-break, we were cheered with the discovery of two islands in the western board: this gave us all great joy, and raised our drooping spirits; for before this, a universal dejection had seized us, and we almost despaired of ever seeing land again: the nearest of these islands we afterwards found to be Anatacan; we judged it to be full fifteen leagues from us, and it seemed to be high land, though of an indifferent length: the other was the island of Serigan; and had rather the appearance of a high rock, than a place we could hope to anchor at. We were extremely impatient to get in with the nearest island, where we expected to meet with anchoring-ground, and an opportunity of refreshing our sick: but the wind proved so variable all day, and there was so little of it, that we advanced towards it but slowly; however, by the next morning we were got so far to the westward that we were in view of a third island, which was that of Paxaros, though marked in the chart only as a rock. This was small and very low land, and we had passed within less than a mile of it, in the night, without seeing it: and now at noon, being within four miles of the island of Anatacan, the boat was sent away to examine the anchoring-ground and the produce of the place; and we were not a little solicitous for her return, as we then conceived our fate to depend upon the report we should receive: for the other two islands were obviously enough incapable of furnishing us with any assistance, and we knew not then that there were any others which we could reach. In the evening the boat came back, and the crew informed us that there was no place for a ship to anchor, the bottom being everywhere foul ground, and all, except one small spot, not less than fifty fathoms in depth; that on that spot there was thirty fathoms, though not above half a mile from the shore; and that the bank was steep too, and could not be depended on: they farther told us, that they had landed on the island, but with some difficulty, on account of the greatness of the swell; that they found the ground was everywhere covered with a kind of wild cane, or rush; but that they met with no water, and did not believe the place to be inhabited; though the soil was good, and abounded with groves of cocoa-nut trees.

This account of the impossibility of anchoring at this island occasioned a general melancholy on board; for we considered it as little less than the prelude to our destruction; and our despondency was increased by a disappointment we met with the succeeding night; for, as we were plying under topsails, with an intention of getting nearer to the island, and of sending our boat on shore to load with cocoa-nuts for the refreshment of our sick, the wind proved squally, and blew so strong off shore, that we were driven so far to the southward, that we dared not send off our boat. And now the only possible circumstance, that could secure the few which remained alive from perishing, was the accidental falling in with some other of the Ladrone Islands better prepared for our accommodation; and as our knowledge of these islands was extremely imperfect, we were to trust entirely to chance for our guidance; only as they are all of them usually laid down near the same meridian, and we had conceived those we had already seen to be part of them, we concluded to stand to the southward as the most probable means of falling in with the next. Thus, with the most gloomy persuasion of our approaching destruction, we stood from the island of Anatacan, having all of us the strongest apprehensions (and those not ill founded) either of dying of the scurvy, or of perishing with the ship, which, for want of hands to work her pumps, might in a short time be expected to founder.

CHAPTER II.

Our arrival at Tinian, and an account of the Island, and of our proceedings there, till the Centurion drove out to Sea.

It was on the 26th of August, 1742, in the morning, when we lost sight of Anatacan. The next morning we discovered three other islands to the eastward, which were from ten to fourteen leagues from us. These were, as we afterwards learnt, the islands of Saypan, Tinian, and Aguigan. We immediately steered towards Tinian, which was the middlemost of the three, but had so much of calms and light airs, that though we were helped forwards by the currents, yet next day, at day-break, we were at least five leagues distant from it. However, we kept on our course, and about ten in the morning we perceived a proa under sail to the southward, between Tinian and Aguigan. As we imagined from hence that these islands were inhabited, and knew that the Spaniards had always a force at Guam, we took the necessary precautions for our own security, and for preventing the enemy from taking advantage of our present wretched circumstances, of which they would be sufficiently informed by the manner of our working the ship; we therefore mustered all our hands who were capable of standing to their arms, and loaded our upper and quarter-deck guns with grape-shot; and that we might the more readily procure some intelligence of the state of these islands, we showed Spanish colours, and hoisted a red flag at the fore top-mast-head, to give our ship the appearance of the Manila galleon, hoping thereby to decoy some of the inhabitants on board us. Thus preparing ourselves, and standing towards the land, we were near enough, at three in the afternoon, to send the cutter in shore, to find out a proper berth for the ship; and we soon perceived that a proa came off the shore to meet the cutter, fully persuaded, as we afterwards found, that we were the Manila ship. As we saw the cutter returning back with the proa in tow, we immediately sent the pinnace to receive the proa and the prisoners, and to bring them on board, that the cutter might proceed on her errand. The pinnace came back with a Spaniard and four Indians, which were the people taken in the proa. The Spaniard was immediately examined as to the produce and circumstances of this island of Tinian, and his account of it surpassed even our most sanguine hopes; for he informed us that it was uninhabited, which, in our present defenceless condition, was an advantage not to be despised, especially as it wanted but few of the conveniences that could be expected in the most cultivated country; for he assured us, that there was great plenty of very good water, and that there were an incredible number of cattle, hogs, and poultry running wild on the island, all of them excellent in their kind; that the woods produced sweet and sour oranges, limes, lemons, and cocoa-nuts in great plenty, besides a fruit peculiar to these islands (called by Dampier, bread-fruit); that from the quantity and goodness of the provisions produced here, the Spaniards at Guam made use of it as a store for supplying the garrison; that he himself was a serjeant of that garrison, and was sent there with twenty-two Indians to jerk beef, which he was to load for Guam on board a small bark of about fifteen tons, which lay at anchor near the shore.

This account was received by us with inexpressible joy: part of it we were ourselves able to verify on the spot, as we were by this time near enough to discover several numerous herds of cattle feeding in different places of the island; and we did not any ways doubt the rest of his relation, as the appearance of the shore prejudiced us greatly in its favour, and made us hope, that not only our necessities might be there fully relieved, and our diseased recovered, but that, amidst those pleasing scenes which were then in view, we might procure ourselves some amusement and relaxation, after the numerous fatigues we had undergone: for the prospect of the country did by no means resemble that of an uninhabited and uncultivated place, but had much more the air of a magnificent plantation, where large lawns and stately woods had been laid out together with great skill, and where the whole had been so artfully combined, and so judiciously adapted to the slopes of the hills, and the inequalities of the ground, as to produce a most striking effect, and to do honour to the invention of the contriver. Thus (an event not unlike what we had already seen) we were forced upon the most desirable and salutary measures by accidents, which at first sight we considered as the greatest of misfortunes; for had we not been driven by the contrary winds and currents to the northward of our course, (a circumstance, which at that time gave us the most terrible apprehensions,) we should, in all probability, never have arrived at this delightful island, and consequently, we should have missed of that place, where alone all our wants could be most amply relieved, our sick recovered, and our enfeebled crew once more refreshed, and enabled to put again to sea.

The Spanish serjeant, from whom we received the account of the island, having informed us that there were some Indians on shore under his command, employed in jerking beef, and that there was a barque at anchor to take it on board, we were desirous, if possible, to prevent the Indians from escaping, who doubtless would have given the governor of Guam intelligence of our arrival and we therefore immediately dispatched the pinnace to secure the barque, which the serjeant told us was the only embarkation on the place; and then, about eight in the evening, we let go our anchor in twenty-two fathoms; and though it was almost calm, and whatever vigour and spirit was to be found on board was doubtless exerted to the utmost on this pleasing occasion, when, after having kept the sea for some months, we were going to take possession of this little paradise, yet we were full five hours in furling our sails: it is true, we were somewhat weakened by the crews of the cutter and pinnace, which were sent on shore; but it is not less true, that, including those absent with the boats and some negro and Indian prisoners, all the hands we could muster capable of standing at a gun amounted to no more than seventy-one, most of which number, too, were incapable of duty; but on the greatest emergencies this was all the force we could collect, in our present enfeebled condition, from the united crews of the Centurion, the Gloucester, and the Tryal, which, when we departed from England, consisted altogether of near a thousand hands.

When we had furled our sails, the remaining part of the night was allowed to our people for their repose, to recover them from the fatigue they had undergone; and in the morning a party was sent on shore, well armed, of which I myself was one, to make ourselves masters of the landing-place, as we were not certain what opposition might be made by the Indians on the island: we landed without difficulty, for the Indians having perceived, by our seizure of the barque the night before, that we were enemies, they immediately fled into the woody parts of the island. We found on shore many huts which they had inhabited, and which saved us both the time and trouble of erecting tents; one of these huts which the Indians made use of for a store-house was very large, being twenty yards long and fifteen broad; this we immediately cleared of some bales of jerked beef, which we found in it, and converted it into an hospital for our sick, who, as soon as the place was ready to receive them, were brought on shore, being in all a hundred and twenty-eight: numbers of these were so very helpless, that we were obliged to carry them from the boats to the hospital upon our shoulders, in which humane employment (as before at Juan Fernandes) the commodore himself, and every one of his officers, were engaged without distinction; and, notwithstanding the great debility and the dying aspects of the greatest part of our sick, it is almost incredible how soon they began to feel the salutary influence of the land; for, though we buried twenty-one men on this and the preceding day, yet we did not lose above ten men more during our whole two months' stay here; and in general, our diseased received so much benefit from the fruits of the island, particularly the fruits of the acid kind, that, in a week's time, there were but few who were not so far recovered, as to be able to move about without help.

And now being in some sort established at this place, we were enabled more particularly to examine its qualities and productions; and that the reader may the better judge of our manner of life here, and future navigators be better apprised of the conveniences we met with, I shall, before I proceed any farther in the history of our own adventures, throw together the most interesting particulars that came to our knowledge, in relation to the situation, soil, produce, and conveniences of this island of Tinian.

This island lies in the latitude of 15° 8' north, and longitude from Acapulco 114° 50' west. Its length is about twelve miles, and its breadth about half as much; it extending from the S.S.W. to N.N.E. The soil is everywhere dry and healthy, and somewhat sandy, which being less disposed than other soils to a rank and over luxuriant vegetation, occasions the meadows and the bottoms of the woods to be much neater and smoother than is customary in hot climates. The land rises by easy slope, from the very beach where we watered to the middle of the island; though the general course of its ascent is often interrupted and traversed by gentle descents and valleys; and the inequalities that are formed by the different combinations of these gradual swellings of the ground, are most beautifully diversified with large lawns, which are covered with a very fine trefoil, intermixed with a variety of flowers, and are skirted by woods of tall and well-spread trees, most of them celebrated either for their aspect or their fruit. The turf of the lawns is quite clean and even, and the bottoms of the woods in many places clear of all bushes and underwoods; and the woods themselves usually terminate on the lawns with a regular outline, not broken, nor confused with straggling trees, but appearing as uniform, as if laid out by art. Hence arose a great variety of the most elegant and entertaining prospects, formed by the mixture of these woods and lawns, and their various intersections with each other, as they spread themselves differently through the valleys, and over the slopes and declivities with which the place abounds. The fortunate animals, too, which for the greatest part of the year are the sole lords of this happy soil, partake in some measure of the romantic cast of the island, and are no small addition to its wonderful scenery: for the cattle, of which it is not uncommon to see herds of some thousands feeding together in a large meadow, are certainly the most remarkable in the world; for they are all of them milk-white, except their ears, which are generally black. And though there are no inhabitants here, yet the clamour and frequent parading of domestic poultry, which range the woods in great numbers, perpetually excite the ideas of the neighbourhood of farms and villages, and greatly contribute to the cheerfulness and beauty of the place. The cattle on the island we computed were at least ten thousand; and we had no difficulty in getting near them, as they were not shy of us. Our first method of killing them was shooting them; but at last, when, by accidents to be hereafter recited, we were obliged to husband our ammunition, our men ran them down with ease. Their flesh was extremely well tasted, and was believed by us to be much more easily digested, than any we had ever met with. The fowls too were exceeding good, and were likewise run down with little trouble; for they could scarcely fly further than a hundred yards at a flight, and even that fatigued them so much, that they could not readily rise again; so that, aided by the openness of the woods, we could at all times furnish ourselves with whatever number we wanted. Besides the cattle and the poultry, we found here abundance of wild hogs: these were most excellent food; but as they were a very fierce animal, we were obliged either to shoot them, or to hunt them with large dogs, which we found upon the place at our landing, and which belonged to the detachment which was then upon the island amassing provisions for the garrison of Guam. As these dogs had been purposely trained to the killing of the wild hogs, they followed us very readily, and hunted for us; but though they were a large bold breed, the hogs fought with so much fury, that they frequently destroyed them, so that we by degrees lost the greatest part of them.

But this place was not only extremely grateful to us from the plenty and excellence of its fresh provisions, but was as much perhaps to be admired for its fruits and vegetable productions, which were most fortunately adapted to the cure of the sea scurvy, which had so terribly reduced us. For in the woods there were inconceivable quantities of cocoa-nuts, with the cabbages growing on the same tree: there were besides guavoes, limes, sweet and sour oranges, and a kind of fruit, peculiar to these islands, called by the Indians, rima, but by us the bread-fruit, for it was constantly eaten by us during our stay upon the island instead of bread, and so universally preferred to it, that no ship's bread was expended during that whole interval. It grew upon a tree which is somewhat lofty, and which, towards the top, divides into large and spreading branches. The leaves of this tree are of a remarkable deep green, are notched about the edges, and are generally from a foot to eighteen inches in length. The fruit itself grows indifferently on all parts of the branches; it is in shape rather elliptical than round, is covered with a rough rind, and is usually seven or eight inches long; each of them grows singly and not in clusters. This fruit is fittest to be used when it is full grown, but is still green; in which state its taste has some distant resemblance to that of an artichoke bottom, and its texture is not very different, for it is soft and spongy. As it ripens it grows softer and of a yellow colour, and then contracts a luscious taste, and an agreeable smell, not unlike a ripe peach; but then it is esteemed unwholesome, and is said to produce fluxes. Besides the fruits already enumerated, there were many other vegetables extremely conducive to the cure of the malady we had long laboured under, such as water-melons, dandelion, creeping purslain, mint, scurvy-grass, and sorrel; all which, together with the fresh meats of the place, we devoured with great eagerness, prompted thereto by the strong inclination which nature never fails of exciting in scorbutic disorders for these powerful specifics.

It will easily be conceived from what hath been already said, that our cheer upon this island was in some degree luxurious, but I have not yet recited all the varieties of provision which we here indulged in. Indeed we thought it prudent totally to abstain from fish, the few we caught at our first arrival having surfeited those who ate of them; but considering how much we had been inured to that species of food, we did not regard this circumstance as a disadvantage, especially as the defect was so amply supplied by the beef, pork, and fowls already mentioned, and by great plenty of wild fowl; for I must observe, that near the centre of the island there were two considerable pieces of fresh water, which abounded with duck, teal, and curlew: not to mention the whistling plover, which we found there in prodigious plenty.

And now perhaps it may be wondered at, that an island, so exquisitely furnished with the conveniences of life, and so well adapted, not only to the subsistence, but likewise to the enjoyment of mankind, should be entirely destitute of inhabitants, especially as it is in the neighbourhood of other islands, which in some measure depend upon this for their support. To obviate this difficulty, I must observe, that it is not fifty years since the island was depopulated. The Indians we had in our custody assured us, that formerly the three islands of Tinian, Rota, and Guam, were all full of inhabitants; and that Tinian alone contained thirty thousand souls: but a sickness raging amongst these islands which destroyed multitudes of the people, the Spaniards, to recruit their numbers at Guam, which were greatly diminished by this mortality, ordered all the inhabitants of Tinian thither; where, languishing for their former habitations, and their customary method of life, the greatest part of them in a few years died of grief. Indeed, independent of that attachment which all mankind have ever shown to the places of their birth and bringing up, it should seem, from what has been already said, that there were few countries more worthy to be regretted than this of Tinian.

These poor Indians might reasonably have expected, at the great distance from Spain where they were placed, to have escaped the violence and cruelty of that haughty nation, so fatal to a large proportion of the whole human race: but it seems their remote situation could not protect them from sharing in the common destruction of the western world, all the advantage they received from their distance being only to perish an age or two later. It may perhaps be doubted, if the number of the inhabitants of Tinian, who were banished to Guam, and who died the repining for their native home, was so great as what we have related above; but, not to mention the concurrent assertion of our prisoners and the commodiousness of the island and its great fertility, there are still remains to be met with on the place which evince it to have been once extremely populous, for there are in all parts of the island a great number of ruins of a very particular kind; they usually consist of two rows of square pyramidal pillars, each pillar being about six feet from the next, and the distance between the rows being about twelve feet; the pillars themselves are about five feet square at the base, and about thirteen feet high, and on the top of each of them there is a semi-globe, with the flat part upwards; the whole of the pillars and semi-globe is solid, being composed of sand and stone cemented together and plastered over. If the account our prisoners gave us of these structures was true, the island must indeed have been extremely populous, for they assured us that they were the foundations of particular buildings set apart for those Indians only who had engaged in some religious vow; and monastic institutions are often to be met with in many Pagan nations. However, if these ruins were originally the basis of the common dwelling-houses of the natives, their numbers must have been considerable, for in many parts of the island they are extremely thick planted, and sufficiently evince the great plenty of former inhabitants. But to return to the present state of the island.

Having mentioned the conveniences of this place, the excellence and quantity of its fruits and provisions, the neatness of its lawns, the stateliness, freshness, and fragrance of its woods, the happy inequality of its surface, and the variety and elegance of the views it afforded, I must now observe that all these advantages were greatly enhanced by the healthiness of its climate, by the almost constant breezes which prevail there, and by the frequent showers which fall, and which, though of a very short and almost momentary duration, are extremely grateful and refreshing, and are perhaps one cause of the salubrity of the air, and of the extraordinary influence it was observed to have upon us, in increasing and invigorating our appetites and digestion. This was so remarkable, that those among our officers who were at all other times spare and temperate eaters, who, besides a slight breakfast, made but one moderate repast a day, were here, in appearance, transformed into gluttons; for instead of one reasonable flesh-meal, they were now scarcely satisfied with three, and each of them so prodigious in quantity, as would at another time have produced a fever or a surfeit: and yet our digestion so well corresponded with the keenness of our appetites, that we were neither disordered nor even loaded by this repletion; for after having, according to the custom of the island, made a large beef breakfast, it was not long before we began to consider the approach of dinner as a very desirable though somewhat tardy incident.

And now having been thus large in my encomiums on this island, in which, however, I conceive I have not done it justice, it is necessary I should speak of those circumstances in which it is defective, whether in point of beauty or utility.

And first, with respect to its water. I must own that before I had seen this spot I did not conceive that the absence of running water, of which it is entirely destitute, could have been so well replaced by any other means as it is in this island; for though there are no streams, yet the water of the wells and springs, which are to be met with everywhere near the surface, is extremely good; and in the midst of the island there are two or three considerable pieces of excellent water, whose edges are as neat and even as if they had been basons purposely made for the decoration of the place. It must however be confessed that, with regard to the beauty of the prospects, the want of rills and streams is a very great defect, not to be compensated either by large pieces of standing water, or by the neighbourhood of the sea, though that, by reason of the smallness of the island, generally makes a part of every extensive view.

As to the residence upon the island, the principal inconvenience attending it is the vast numbers of musquitos and various other species of flies, together with an insect called a tick, which, though principally attached to the cattle, would yet frequently fasten upon our limbs and bodies, and if not perceived and removed in time would bury its head under the skin and raise a painful inflammation. We found here too centipedes and scorpions, which we supposed were venomous, but none of us ever received any injury from them.

But the most important and formidable exception to this place remains still to be told. This is the inconvenience of the road, and the little security there is at some seasons for a ship at anchor. The only proper anchoring-place for ships of burthen is at the S.W. end of the island. In this place the Centurion anchored in twenty and twenty-two fathom water, opposite to a sandy bay, and about a mile and a half distant from the shore. The bottom of this road is full of sharp-pointed coral rocks, which, during four months of the year, that is from the middle of June to the middle of October, renders it a very unsafe place to lie at. This is the season of the western monsoons, when near the full and change of the moon, but more particularly at the change, the wind is usually variable all round the compass, and seldom fails to blow with such fury that the stoutest cables are not to be confided in. What adds to the danger at these times is the excessive rapidity of the tide of flood, which sets to the S.E. between this island and that of Aguiguan, a small island near the southern extremity of Tinian. This tide runs at first with a vast head and overfall of water, and occasions such a hollow and overgrown sea as is scarcely to be conceived; so that (as will be hereafter more particularly mentioned) we were under the dreadful apprehension of being pooped by it, though we were in a sixty-gun ship. In the remaining eight months of the year, that is, from the middle of October to the middle of June, there is a constant season of settled weather, when, if the cables are but well armed, there is scarcely any danger of their being so much as rubbed; so that during all that interval it is as secure a road as could be wished for. I shall only add, that the anchoring bank is very shelving, and stretches along the S.W. end of the island, and that it is entirely free from shoals, except a reef of rocks which is visible and lies about half a mile from the shore, and affords a narrow passage into a small sandy bay, which is the only place where boats can possibly land. After this account of the island and its produce, it is necessary to return to our own history.

Our first undertaking after our arrival was the removal of our sick on shore, as hath been mentioned. Whilst we were thus employed, four of the Indians on shore, being part of the Spanish serjeant's detachment, came and surrendered themselves to us, so that with those we took in the proa we had now eight of them in our custody. One of the four who submitted undertook to show us the most convenient place for killing cattle, and two of our men were ordered to attend him on that service; but one of them unwarily trusting the Indian with his firelock and pistol, the Indian escaped with them into the woods: his countrymen who remained behind were apprehensive of suffering for this perfidy of their comrade, and therefore begged leave to send one of their own party into the country, who they engaged should both bring back the arms and persuade the whole detachment from Guam to submit to us. The commodore granted their request, and one of them was despatched on this errand, who returned next day and brought back the firelock and pistol, but assured us he had met with them in a pathway in the wood, and protested that he had not been able to meet with any one of his countrymen. This report had so little the air of truth, that we suspected there was some treachery carrying on, and therefore, to prevent any future communication amongst them, we immediately ordered all the Indians who were in our power on board the ship, and did not permit them to return any more on shore.

When our sick were well settled on the island, we employed all the hands that could be spared from attending them, in arming the cables with a good rounding several fathom from the anchor, to secure them from being rubbed by the coral rocks which here abounded. And this being completed, our next attention was our leak, and in order to raise it out of water, we, on the first of September, began to get the guns aft to bring the ship by the stern; and now the carpenters, being able to come at it on the outside, ripped off the old sheathing that was left, and caulked all the seams on both sides the cut-water and leaded them over, and then new sheathed the bows to the surface of the water. By this means we conceived the defect was sufficiently secured; but upon our beginning to bring the guns into their places, we had the mortification to perceive that the water rushed into the ship in the old place with as much violence as ever. Hereupon we were necessitated to begin again; and that our second attempt might be more effectual we cleared the fore store-room, and sent a hundred and thirty barrels of powder on board the small Spanish bark we had seized here, by which means we raised the ship about three feet out of the water forwards, and the carpenters ripped off the sheathing lower down, and new caulked all the seams, and afterwards laid on new sheathing; and then, supposing the leak to be effectually stopped, we began to move the guns forwards; but, the upper deck guns were scarcely in their places, when, to our amazement, it burst out again; and now, as we durst not cut away the lining within board, lest a but-end or a plank might start, and we might go down immediately we had no other resource left than clinching and caulking within-board; and indeed by this means the leak was stopped for some time; but when our guns were all in their places, and our stores were taken on board, the water again forced its way through a hole in the stem, where one of the bolts was driven in; and on this we desisted from all farther efforts, being now well assured that the defect was in the stem itself, and that it was not to be remedied till we should have an opportunity of heaving down.

Towards the middle of September several of our sick were tolerably recovered by their residence on shore; and on the 12th of September all those who were so far relieved, since their arrival, as to be capable of doing duty were sent on board the ship. And then the commodore, who was himself ill of the scurvy, had a tent erected for him on shore, where he went with the view of staying a few days for the recovery of his health, being convinced, by the general experience of his people, that no other method but living on the land was to be trusted to for the removal of this dreadful malady. The place where his tent was pitched on this occasion was near the well, whence we got all our water, and was indeed a most elegant spot.

As the crew on board were now reinforced by the recovered hands returned from the island, we began to send our casks on shore to be fitted up, which till now could not be done, for the coopers were not well enough to work. We likewise weighed our anchors that we might examine our cables, which we suspected had by this time received considerable damage. And as the new moon was now approaching, when we apprehended violent gales, the commodore, for our greater security, ordered that part of the cables next to the anchors to be armed with the chains of the fire-grapnels; and they were besides cackled twenty fathom from the anchors, and seven fathom from the service, with a good rounding of a 4½ inch hawser; and to all these precautions we added that of lowering the main and fore-yard close down, that in case of blowing weather the wind might have less power upon the ship to make her ride a strain.

Thus effectually prepared, as we conceived, we expected the new moon, which was the 18th of September, and riding safe that and the three succeeding days (though the weather proved very squally and uncertain), we flattered ourselves (for I was then on board) that the prudence of our measures had secured us from all accidents; but on the 22nd the wind blew from the eastward with such fury, that we soon despaired of riding out the storm; and therefore we should have been extremely glad that the commodore and the rest of our people on shore, which were the greatest part of our hands, had been on board with us, since our only hopes of safety seemed to depend on our putting immediately to sea; but all communication with the shore was now effectually cut off, for there was no possibility that a boat could live, so that we were necessitated to ride it out till our cables parted. Indeed it was not long before this happened, for the small bower parted at five in the afternoon, and the ship swung off to the best bower; and as the night came on the violence of the wind still increased; but notwithstanding its inexpressible fury, the tide ran with so much rapidity as to prevail over it; for the tide having set to the northward in the beginning of the storm, turned suddenly to the southward about six in the evening, and forced the ship before it in despite of the storm which blew upon the beam. And now the sea broke most surprisingly all round us, and a large tumbling swell threatened to poop us; the long-boat, which was at this time moored a-stern, was on a sudden canted so high, that it broke the transom of the commodore's gallery, whose cabin was on the quarter-deck, and would doubtless have risen as high as the tafferel, had it not been for this stroke which stove the boat all to pieces; but the poor boat-keeper, though extremely bruised, was saved almost by miracle. About eight the tide slackened, but the wind did not abate; so that at eleven the best bower cable, by which alone we rode, parted. Our sheet anchor, which was the only one we had left, was instantly cut from the bow; but before it could reach the bottom we were driven from twenty-two into thirty-five fathom; and after we had veered away one whole cable, and two thirds of another, we could not find ground with sixty fathom of line. This was a plain indication that the anchor lay near the edge of the bank, and could not hold us long. In this pressing danger, Mr. Saumarez, our first lieutenant, who now commanded on board, ordered several guns to be fired, and lights to be shown, as a signal to the commodore of our distress; and in a short time after, it being then about one o'clock, and the night excessively dark, a strong gust, attended with rain and lightning, drove us off the bank and forced us out to sea, leaving behind us on the island, Mr. Anson, with many more of our officers, and great part of our crew, amounting in the whole to a hundred and thirteen persons. Thus were we all, both at sea and on shore, reduced to the utmost despair by this catastrophe, those on shore conceiving they had no means left them ever to leave the island, and we on board utterly unprepared to struggle with the fury of the seas and winds we were now exposed to, and expecting each moment to be our last.

CHAPTER III.

Transactions at Tinian after the departure of the Centurion.

THE storm which drove the Centurion to sea, blew with too much turbulence to permit either the commodore or any of the people on shore to hear the guns, which she fired as signals of distress; and the frequent glare of the lightning had prevented the explosions from being observed. So that, when at day-break, it was perceived from the shore that the ship was missing, there was the utmost consternation amongst them. For much the greatest part of them immediately concluded that she was lost, and intreated the commodore that the boat might be sent round the island to look for the wreck; and those who believed her safe, had scarcely any expectation that she would ever be able to make the island again. For the wind continued to blow strong at east, and they knew how poorly she was manned and provided for struggling with so tempestuous a gale. And if the Centurion was lost, or should be incapable of returning, there appeared in either case no possibility of their ever getting off the island; for they were at least six hundred leagues from Macao, which was their nearest port; and they were masters of no other vessel than the small Spanish bark of about fifteen tons, which they seized at their first arrival, and which would not even hold a fourth part of their number. And the chance of their being taken off the island by the casual arrival of any other ship was altogether desperate; as perhaps no European ship had ever anchored here before, and it were madness to expect that like incidents should send another here in a hundred ages to come. So that their desponding thoughts could only suggest to them the melancholy prospect of spending the remainder of their days on this island, and bidding adieu for ever to their country, their friends, their families, and all their domestic endearments.

Nor was this the worst they had to fear: for they had reason to expect, that the governor of Guam, when he should be informed of their situation, might send a force sufficient to overpower them, and to remove them to that island; and then, the most favourable treatment they could hope for would be to be detained prisoners for life; since, from the known policy and cruelty of the Spaniards in their distant settlements, it was rather to be expected that the governor, if he once had them in his power, would make their want of commissions (all of them being on board the Centurion) a pretext for treating them as pirates, and for depriving them of their lives with infamy.[*]

In the midst of these gloomy reflections, Mr. Anson had doubtless his share of disquietude; but he always kept up his usual composure and steadiness: and having soon projected a scheme for extricating himself and his men from their present anxious situation, he first communicated it to some of the most intelligent persons about him; and having satisfied himself that it was practicable, he then endeavoured to animate his people to a speedy and vigorous prosecution of it. With this view he represented to them, how little foundation there was for their apprehensions of the Centurion's being lost: that he should have hoped, they had been all of them better acquainted with sea affairs, than to give way to the impression of so chimerical a fright; and that he doubted not, but if they would seriously consider what such a ship was capable of enduring, they would confess that there was not the least probability of her having perished: that he was not without hopes that she might return in a few days; but if she did not, the worst that could be supposed, was, that she was driven so far to the leeward of the island that she could not regain it, and that she would consequently be obliged to bear away for Macao on the coast of China: that as it was necessary to be prepared against all events, he had, in this case, considered of a method of carrying them off the island, and joining their old ship the Centurion again at Macao: that this method was to hale the Spanish bark on shore, to saw her asunder, and to lengthen her twelve feet, which would enlarge her to near forty tons burthen, and would enable her to carry them all to China: that he had consulted the carpenters, and they had agreed that this proposal was very feasible, and that nothing was wanting to execute it but the united resolution and industry of the whole body: he added, that for his own part, he would share the fatigue and labour with them, and would expect no more from any man than what he, the commodore himself, was ready to submit to; and concluded with representing to them the importance of saving time; and that, in order to be the better prepared for all events, it was necessary to set to work immediately, and to take it for granted, that the Centurion would not be able to put back (which was indeed the commodore's secret opinion); since, if she did return, they should only throw away a few days' application; but, if she did not, their situation, and the season of the year, required their utmost despatch.

These remonstrances, though not without effect, did not immediately operate so powerfully as Mr. Anson could have wished: he indeed raised their spirits, by showing them the possibility of their getting away, of which they had before despaired; but then, from their confidence of this resource, they grew less apprehensive of their situation, gave a greater scope to their hopes, and flattered themselves that the Centurion would return and prevent the execution of the commodore's scheme, which they could easily foresee would be a work of considerable labour: by this means it was some days before they were all of them heartily engaged in the project; but at last, being in general convinced of the impossibility of the ship's return, they set themselves zealously to the different tasks allotted them, and were as industrious and as eager as their commander could desire, punctually assembling at daybreak at the rendezvous, whence they were distributed to their different employments, which they followed with unusual vigour till night came on.

And here I must interrupt the course of this transaction for a moment, to relate an incident which for some time gave Mr. Anson more concern than all the preceding disasters. A few days after the ship was driven off, some of the people on shore cried out, "A sail!" This spread a general joy, every one supposing that it was the ship returning; but presently a second sail was descried, which quite destroyed their first conjecture and made it difficult to guess what they were. The commodore eagerly turned his glass towards them, and saw they were two boats; on which it immediately occurred to him that the Centurion was gone to the bottom, and that these were her two boats coming back with the remains of her people; and this sudden and unexpected suggestion wrought on him so powerfully that, to conceal his emotion, he was obliged (without speaking to any one) instantly to retire to his tent, where he passed some bitter moments in the firm belief that the ship was lost, and that now all his views of farther distressing the enemy, and of still signalizing his expedition by some important exploit, were at an end.

But he was soon relieved from these disturbing thoughts by discovering that the two boats in the offing were Indian proas; and, perceiving that they stood towards the shore, he directed every

---

[*] "An enterprising Englishman, John Oxnam by name, having been active in his attacks upon the Spaniards, was at length taken prisoner at the Pearl Islands, by an expedition despatched from Panama, under the command of Juan de Ortega, in 1575. Being carried to that place, and questioned by the governor, as to whether he had the Queen of England's commission, or a licence from any other prince or state? He replied, that he had no commission, but that he acted upon his own authority, and at his own risk. Upon this answer, Oxnam and his men were condemned to death, and the whole, except five boys, were executed."—*Burney's History of Discoveries.*

appearance that could give them any suspicion to be removed, and concealed his people in the adjacent thickets, prepared to secure the Indians when they should land. But after the proas had stood in within a quarter of a mile of the land, they suddenly stopped short, and remaining there motionless for near two hours they then made sail again and stood to the southward. But to return to the projected enlargement of the bark.

If we examine how they were prepared for going through with this undertaking, on which their safety depended, we shall find that, independent of other matters which were of as much importance, the lengthening of the bark alone was attended with great difficulty. Indeed, in a proper place, where all the necessary materials and tools were to be had, the embarrassment would have been much less; but some of these tools were to be made, and many of the materials were wanting, and it required no small degree of invention to supply all these deficiencies. And when the hull of the bark should be completed this was but one article, and there were many others of equal weight which were to be well considered: these were the rigging it, the victualling it, and, lastly, the navigating it for the space of six or seven hundred leagues, through unknown seas, where no one of the company had ever passed before. In some of these particulars such obstacles occurred that, without the intervention of very extraordinary and unexpected accidents, the possibility of the whole enterprise would have fallen to the ground, and their utmost industry and efforts must have been fruitless. Of all these circumstances I shall make a short recital.

It fortunately happened that the carpenters, both of the Gloucester and of the Tryal, with their chests of tools, were on shore when the ship drove out to sea; the smith too was on shore, and had with him his forge and some tools, but unhappily his bellows had not been brought from on board, so that he was incapable of working, and without his assistance they could not hope to proceed with their design. Their first attention therefore was to make him a pair of bellows, but in this they were for some time puzzled by their want of leather; however, as they had hides in sufficient plenty, and they had found a hogshead of lime, which the Indians or Spaniards had prepared for their own use, they tanned some hides with this lime; and though we may suppose the workmanship to be but indifferent, yet the leather they thus made served tolerably well, and the bellows (to which a gun-barrel served for a pipe) had no other inconvenience than that of being somewhat strong scented from the imperfection of the tanner's work.

Whilst the smith was preparing the necessary iron-work, others were employed in cutting down trees and sawing them into planks; and this being the most laborious task, the commodore wrought at it himself for the encouragement of his people. As there were neither blocks nor cordage sufficient for tackles to hale the bark on shore, it was proposed to get her up on rollers, and for these the body of the cocoa-nut tree was extremely useful, for its smoothness and circular turn prevented much labour, and fitted it for the purpose with very little workmanship: a number of these trees were therefore felled and the ends of them properly opened for the reception of handspikes, and in the meantime a dry-dock was dug for the bark, and ways laid from thence quite into the sea, to facilitate the bringing her up. And besides those who were thus occupied in preparing measures for the future enlargement of the bark, a party was constantly ordered for the killing and preparing of provisions for the rest: and though in these various employments, some of which demanded considerable dexterity, it might have been expected there would have been great confusion and delay, yet good order being once established, and all hands engaged, their preparations advanced apace. Indeed the common men, I presume, were not the less tractable for their want of spirituous liquors; for, there being neither wine nor brandy on shore, the juice of the cocoa-nut was their constant drink, and this, though extremely pleasant, was not at all intoxicating, but kept them very cool and orderly.

And now the officers began to consider of all the articles necessary for the fitting out the bark; when it was found, that the tents on shore, and the spare cordage accidentally left there by the Centurion, together with the sails and rigging already belonging to the bark, would serve to rig her indifferently well, when she was lengthened: and as they had tallow in plenty, they proposed to pay her bottom with a mixture of tallow and lime, which it was known was well adapted to that purpose: so that with respect to her equipment, she would not have been very defective. There was, however, one exception, which would have proved extremely inconvenient, and that was her size: for as they could not make her quite forty tons burthen, she would have been incapable of containing half the crew below the deck, and she would have been so top-heavy, that if they were all at the same time ordered upon deck, there would be no small hazard of her oversetting; but this was a difficulty not to be removed, as they could not augment her size beyond the size already proposed. After the manner of rigging and fitting up the bark was considered and regulated, the next essential point to be thought on was, how to procure a sufficient stock of provisions for their voyage; and here they were greatly at a loss what course to take; for they had neither grain nor bread of any kind on shore, their breadfruit, which would not keep at sea, having all along supplied its place: and though they had live cattle enough, yet they had no salt to cure beef for a sea-store, nor would meat take salt in that climate. Indeed, they had preserved a small quantity of jerked beef, which they found upon the place at their landing; but this was greatly disproportioned to the run of near six hundred leagues, which they were to engage in, and to the number of hands they should have on board. It was at last, however, resolved to take on board as many cocoa-nuts as they possibly could; to make the most of their jerked beef, by a very sparing distribution of it; and to endeavour to supply their want of bread by rice; to furnish themselves with which, it was proposed, when the bark was fitted up, to make an expedition to the island of Rota, where they were told that the Spaniards had large plantations of rice under the care of the Indian inhabitants: but as this last measure was to be executed by force, it became necessary to examine what ammunition had been left on shore, and to preserve it carefully; and on this inquiry, they had the mortification to find, that the utmost that could be collected by the strictest search, did not amount to more than ninety charges of powder for their firelocks, which was considerably short of one a-piece for each of the company, and was indeed a very slender stock of ammunition, for such as were to eat no grain or bread for a month, but what they were to procure by force of arms.

But the most alarming circumstance, and what, without the providential interposition of very improbable events, had rendered all their schemes abortive, remains yet to be related. The general idea of the fabric and equipment of the vessel was settled in a few days; and when this was done, it was not difficult to make some estimation of the time necessary to complete her. After this, it was natural to expect that the officers would consider on the course they were to steer, and the land they were to make. These reflections led them to the disheartening discovery, that there was neither compass nor quadrant on the island. Indeed the commodore had brought a pocket-compass on shore for his own use; but Lieutenant Brett had borrowed it to determine the position of the neighbouring islands, and he had been driven to sea in the Centurion, without returning it: and as to a quadrant, that could not be expected to be found on shore, for as it was of no use at land, there could be no reason for bringing it from on board the ship. It was eight days, from the departure of the Centurion, before they were in any degree relieved from this terrible perplexity: at last, in rummaging a chest belonging to the Spanish bark, they found a small compass, which, though little better than the toys usually made for the amusement of school-boys, was to them an invaluable treasure. And a few days after, by a similar piece of good fortune, they found a quadrant on the sea-shore, which had been thrown overboard amongst other lumber belonging to the dead: the quadrant was eagerly seized, but on examination, it unluckily wanted vanes, and therefore in its present state was altogether useless; however, fortune still continuing in a favourable mood, it was not long before a person out of curiosity pulling out the drawer of an old table, which had been driven on shore, found therein some vanes, which fitted the quadrant very well; and it being thus completed, it was examined by the known latitude of the place, and was found to answer to a sufficient degree of exactness.

And now, all these obstacles being in some degree removed, (which were always as much as possible concealed from the vulgar, that they might not grow remiss with the apprehension of labouring to no purpose) the work proceeded very successfully and vigorously: the necessary iron-work was in great forwardness; and the timbers and planks (which, though not the most exquisite performances of the sawyer's art, were yet sufficient for the purpose) were all prepared; so that, on the 6th of October, being the fourteenth day from the departure of the ship, they haled the bark on shore, and, on the two succeeding days she was sawn asunder, (though with great care not to cut her planks) and her two parts were separated the proper distance from each other, and, the materials being all ready before-hand, they, the next day, being the 9th of October, went on with great despatch in their proposed enlargement of her; and by this time they had all their future operations so fairly in view, and were so much masters of them, that they were able to determine when the whole would be finished, and had accordingly fixed the 5th of November for the day of their putting to sea. But their projects and labours were now drawing to a speedier and happier conclusion; for on the 11th of October, in the afternoon, one of the Gloucester's men, being upon a hill in the middle of the island, perceived the Centurion at a distance, and running down with his utmost speed towards the landing-place, he, in the way, saw some of his comrades, to whom he hallooed out with great ecstacy, "The ship, the ship!" This being heard by Mr. Gordon, a lieutenant of marines, who was convinced by the fellow's transport that his report was true, Mr. Gordon ran towards the place where the commodore and his people were at work, and being fresh and in breath, easily outstripped the Gloucester's man, and got before him to the commodore, who, on hearing this happy and unexpected news, threw down his axe with which he was then at work, and by his joy broke through, for the first time, the equable and unvaried character which he had hitherto preserved; the others, who were with him, instantly ran down to the sea-side in a kind of frenzy, eager to feast themselves with a sight they had so ardently wished for, and of which they had now for a considerable time despaired. By five in the evening, the Centurion was visible in the offing to them all; and, a boat being sent off with eighteen men to reinforce her, and with fresh meat and fruits for the refreshment of her crew, she, the next afternoon, happily came to an anchor in the road, where the commodore immediately came on board her, and was received by us with the sincerest and heartiest acclamations: for, from the following short recital of the fears, the dangers and fatigues we in the ship underwent, during our nineteen days' absence from Tinian, it may be easily conceived, that a harbour, refreshments, repose, and the joining of our commander and shipmates, were not less pleasing to us, than our return was to them.

CHAPTER IV.

Proceedings on board the Centurion, when driven out to sea.

The Centurion being now once more safely arrived at Tinian, to the mutual respite of the labours of our divided crew, it is high time that the reader, after the relation already given of the projects and employment of those left on shore, should be apprised of the fatigues and distresses, to which we, who were driven off to sea, were exposed during the long interval of nineteen days that we were absent from the island.

It has been already mentioned, that it was the 22nd of September, about one o'clock, in an extremely dark night, when by the united violence of a prodigious storm, and an exceeding rapid tide, we were driven from our anchors and forced to sea. Our condition then was truly deplorable; we were in a leaky ship, with three cables in our hawses, to one of which hung our only remaining anchor; we had not a gun on board lashed, nor a port barred in; our shrouds were loose, and our top-masts unrigged, and we had struck our fore and main yards close down before the storm came on, so that there were no sails we could set, except our mizen.

In this dreadful extremity we could muster no more strength on board, to navigate the ship, than a hundred and eight hands, several negroes and Indians included: this was scarcely the fourth part of our complement; and of these the greater number were either boys, or such as, being lately recovered from the scurvy, had not yet arrived at half their former vigour. No sooner were we at sea, but by the violence of the storm, and the working of the ship, we made a great quantity of water through our hawse-holes, ports and scuppers, which, added to the constant effect of our leak, rendered our pumps alone a sufficient employment for us all: but though this leakage, by being a short time neglected, would inevitably end in our destruction, yet we had other dangers then impending, which occasioned this to be regarded as a secondary consideration only. For we all imagined, that we were driving directly on the neighbouring island of Aguiguan, which was about two leagues distant; and as we had lowered our main and fore yards close down, we had no sails we could set but the mizen, which was altogether insufficient to carry us clear of this instant peril: we therefore immediately applied ourselves to work, endeavouring, by the utmost of our efforts, to heave up the main and fore yards, in hopes that, if we could but be enabled to make use of our lower canvas, we might possibly weather the island, and thereby save ourselves from this impending shipwreck. But after full three hours' ineffectual labour, the jeers broke, and the men being quite jaded, we were obliged, by mere debility, to desist, and quietly to expect our fate, which we then conceived to be unavoidable: for we imagined ourselves by this time to be driven just upon the shore, and the night was so extremely dark, that we expected to discover the island no otherwise than by striking upon it; so that the belief of our destruction, and the uncertainty of the point of time when it would take place, occasioned us to pass several hours under the most serious apprehensions that each succeeding moment would send us to the bottom. Nor did these continued terrors, of instantly striking and sinking, end but with the daybreak; when we with great transport perceived, that the island, we had thus dreaded, was at a considerable distance, and that a strong northern current had been the cause of our preservation.

The turbulent weather, which forced us from Tinian, did not begin to abate till three days after; and then we swayed up the fore-yard, and began to heave up the main-yard, but the jeers broke and killed one of our men, and prevented us at that time from proceeding. The next day, being the 26th of September, was a day of most severe fatigue to us all; for it must be remembered, that in these exigencies no rank or office exempted any person from the manual application and bodily labour of a common sailor. The business of this day was no less than an attempt to heave up the sheet-anchor, which we had hitherto dragged at our bows with two cables an end[1]. This was a work of great importance to our future preservation. For, not to mention the impediment to our navigation, and the hazard it would be to our ship, if we attempted to make sail with the anchor in its present situation, we had this most interesting consideration to animate us, that it was the only anchor we had left; and, without securing it, we should be under the utmost difficulties and hazards whenever we made the land again; and therefore being all of us fully apprised of the consequence of this enterprise, we laboured at it with the severest application for full twelve hours, when we had indeed made a considerable progress, having brought the anchor in sight; but it then growing dark, and we being excessively fatigued, we were obliged to desist, and to leave our work unfinished till the next morning, when, by the benefit of a night's rest, we completed and hung the anchor at our bow.

It was the 27th of September in the morning, that is, five days after our departure, when we thus secured our anchor; and the same day we got up our main-yard. And having now conquered, in some degree, the distress and disorder which we were necessarily involved in at our first driving out to sea, and being enabled to make use of our canvas, we set our courses, and for the first time stood to the eastward, in hopes of regaining the island of Tinian, and joining our commodore in a few days. For we were then, by our accounts, only forty-seven leagues to the south-west of Tinian; so that on the first day of October, having then run the distance necessary for making the island according to our reckoning, we were in full expectation of seeing it; but we were unhappily disappointed, and were thereby convinced that a current had driven us to the westward. And as we could not judge how much we might hereby have deviated, and, consequently, how long we might still expect to be at sea, we had great apprehensions that our stock of water might prove deficient; for we were doubtful about the quantity we had on board, and found many of our casks so decayed, as to be half-leaked out. However, we were delivered from our uncertainty the next day, by having a sight of the island of Guam, by which we discovered that the currents had driven us forty-four leagues to the westward of our accounts. This sight of land having satisfied us of our situation, we kept plying to the eastward, though with excessive labour, for the wind continuing fixed in the eastern board, we were obliged to tack often, and our crew were so weak, that without the assistance of every man on board, it was not in our power to put the ship about. This severe employment lasted till the 11th of October, being the nineteenth day from our departure; when arriving in the offing of Tinian, we were reinforced from the shore, as hath been already mentioned; and on the evening of the same day, we, to our inexpressible joy, came to an anchor in the road, thereby procuring to our shipmates on shore, as well as to ourselves, a cessation from the fatigues and apprehensions which this disastrous incident had given rise to.

[1] The nautical reader will be surprised at this passage. The first object should have been to heave up the anchor; for how was it possible for the ship to perform, even if they had succeeded in swaying the yards up and making sail, with the sheet anchor at the end of 200 fathoms (400 yards) of cable towing at the bows?

CHAPTER V.

Employment at Tinian, till the final departure of the Centurion from thence; with a description of the Ladrones.

WHEN the commodore came on board the Centurion, on her return to Tinian, as already mentioned, he resolved to stay no longer at the island than was absolutely necessary to complete our stock of water, a work which we immediately set ourselves about. But the loss of our long-boat, which was staved against our poop, when we were driven out to sea, put us to great inconveniences in getting our water on board; for we were obliged to raft off all our casks, and the tide ran so strong, that, besides the frequent delays and difficulties it occasioned, we more than once lost the whole raft. Nor was this our only misfortune; for, on the 14th of October, being but the third day after our arrival, a sudden gust of wind brought home our anchor, forced us off the bank, and drove the ship out to sea a second time. The commodore, it is true, and the principal officers, were now on board; but we had near seventy men on shore, who had been employed in filling our water, and procuring provisions. These had with them our two cutters; but as they were too many for the cutters to bring off at once, we sent the eighteen-oared barge to assist them; and at the same time made a signal for all that could to embark. The two cutters soon came off to us full of men; but forty of the company, who were employed in killing cattle in the wood, and in bringing them down to the landing-place, were left behind; and though the eighteen-oared barge was left for their conveyance, yet, as the ship soon drove to a considerable distance, it was not in their power to join us. However, as the weather was favourable, and our crew was now stronger than when we were first driven out, we, in about five days' time, returned again to an anchor at Tinian, and relieved those we had left behind us from their second fears of being deserted by their ship.

On our arrival, we found that the Spanish bark, the old object of their hopes, had undergone a new metamorphosis. For those we had left on shore began to despair of our return; and conceiving that the lengthening the bark, as formerly proposed, was both a toilsome and unnecessary measure, considering the small number they consisted of, they had resolved to join her again, and to restore her to her first state; and in this scheme they had made some progress; for they had brought the two parts together, and would have soon completed her, had not our coming back put a period to their labours and disquietudes.

These people we had left behind informed us, that just before we were seen in the offing, two proas had stood in very near the shore, and had continued there for some time; but on the appearance of our ship, they crowded away, and were presently out of sight. And, on this occasion I must mention an incident, which, though it happened during the first absence of the ship, was then omitted, to avoid interrupting the course of the narration.

It hath already been observed, that a part of the detachment sent to this island under the command of the Spanish serjeant, lay concealed in the woods; and we were the less solicitous to find them out, as our prisoners all assured us that it was impossible for them to get off, and, consequently, that it was impossible for them to send any intelligence about us to Guam. But when the Centurion drove out to sea, and left the commodore on shore, he one day, attended by some of his officers, endeavoured to make the tour of the island. In this expedition, being on a rising ground, they perceived in the valley beneath them the appearance of a small thicket, which, by observing more nicely, they found had a progressive motion. This at first surprised them; but they soon discovered that it was no more than several large cocoa-bushes, which were dragged along the ground, by persons concealed beneath them. They immediately concluded that these were some of the serjeant's party (which was indeed true); and therefore the commodore and his people made after them, in hopes of finding out their retreat. The Indians soon perceived they were discovered, and hurried away with precipitation; but Mr. Anson was so near them, that he did not lose sight of them till they arrived at their cell, which he and his officers entering found to be abandoned, there being a passage from it down a precipice contrived for the convenience of flight. They found here an old firelock or two, but no other arms. However, there was a great quantity of provisions particularly salted spareribs of pork, which were excellent; and from what our people saw here, they concluded, that the extraordinary appetite which they had found at this island was not confined to themselves alone; for, it being about noon, the Indians had laid out a very plentiful repast, considering their numbers, and had their breadfruit and cocoa-nuts prepared ready for eating, and in a manner which plainly evinced that, with them too, a good meal was neither an uncommon nor an unheeded article. The commodore having in vain endeavoured to discover the path by which the Indians had escaped, he and his officers contented themselves with sitting down to the dinner which was thus luckily fitted to their present appetites; after which they returned back to their old habitation, displeased at missing the Indians, as they hoped to have engaged them in our service, if they could have had any conference with them. But notwithstanding what our prisoners had asserted, we were afterwards assured, that these Indians were carried off to Guam long before we left the place. But to return to our history.

On our coming to an anchor again, after our second driving off to sea, we laboured indefatigably in getting in our water; and having, by the 20th of October, completed itto fifty tons, which we supposed would be sufficient for our passage to Macao, we, on the next day, sent one of each mess on shore, to gather as large a quantity of oranges, lemons, cocoa-nuts, and other fruits of the island, as they possibly could, for the use of themselves and messmates, when at sea. And these purveyors returning on board us in the evening of the same day, we then set fire to the bark and proa, hoisted in our boats, and got under sail, steering away for the south end of the island of Formosa, and taking our leaves, for the third and last time, of the island of Tinian: an island which, whether we consider the excellence of its productions, the beauty of its appearance, the elegance of its woods and lawns, the healthiness of its air, or the adventures it gave rise to, may in all these views be truly styled romantic.

And now, postponing for a short time our run to Formosa, and thence to Canton, I shall interrupt the narration with a description of that range of islands, usually called the Ladrones, or Marian Islands, of which this of Tinian is one.

These islands were discovered by Magellan in the year 1521 ; and by the account given of the two he first fell in with, it should seem that they were the islands of Saypan and Tinian ; for they are described in his expedition as very beautiful islands, and as lying between fifteen and sixteen degrees of north latitude. These characteristics are particularly applicable to the two above-mentioned places; for the pleasing appearance of Tinian hath occasioned the Spaniards to give it the additional name of Buenavista ; and Saypan, which is in the latitude of 15° 22' north, affords no contemptible prospect when seen from the sea.

There are usually reckoned twelve of these islands ; but if the small islets and rocks are counted in, then their whole number will amount to above twenty. They were formerly most of them well inhabited ; and, even not sixty years ago, the three principal islands, Guam, Rota, and Tinian, together, are said to have contained above fifty thousand people : but since that time Tinian has been entirely depopulated ; and only two or three hundred Indians have been left at Rota to cultivate rice for the island of Guam ; so that now no more than Guam can properly be said to be inhabited. This island of Guam is the only settlement of the Spaniards ; here they keep a governor and garrison, and here the Manila ship generally touches for refreshment in her passage from Acapulco to the Philippines. It is esteemed to be about thirty leagues in circumference, and contains, by the Spanish accounts, near four thousand inhabitants, of which a thousand are said to live in the city of San Ignatio de Agand, where the governor generally resides, and where the houses are represented as considerable, being built with stone and timber, and covered with tiles, a very uncommon fabric for these warm climates and savage countries : besides this city there are upon the island thirteen or fourteen villages. As this is a post of some consequence, on account of the refreshment it yields to the Manila ship, there are two castles on the seashore ; one is the castle of St. Angelo, which lies near the road, where the Manila ship usually anchors, and is but an insignificant fortress, mounting only five guns, eight-pounders ; the other is the castle of St. Lewis, which is N.E. from St. Angelo, and four leagues distant, and is intended to protect a road where a small vessel anchors, which arrives here every other year from Manila.' This fort mounts the same number of guns as the former : and besides these forts there is a battery of five pieces of cannon, on an eminence near the seashore. The Spanish troops employed on this island consist of three companies of foot, from forty to fifty men each ; and this is the principal strength the governor has to depend on ; for he cannot rely on any assistance from the Indian inhabitants, being generally upon ill terms with them, and so apprehensive of them, that he has debarred them the use of fire-arms or lances.

The rest of these islands, though not inhabited, do yet abound with many kinds of refreshmen and provision ; but there is no good harbour or road to be met with amongst them all : of that of Tinian we have treated largely already ; nor is the road of Guam much better : for it is not unusual for the Manila ship, though she proposes to stay there but twenty-four hours, to be forced to sea, and to leave her boat behind her. This is an inconvenience so sensibly felt by the commerce at Manila, that it is always recommended to the governor at Guam to use his best endeavours for the discovery of some safe port in this part of the world. How industrious he may be to comply with his instructions I know not ; but this is certain, that, notwithstanding the many islands already found out between the coast of Mexico and the Philippines, there is not yet known any one safe port in that whole tract ; though in other parts of the world it is not uncommon for very small islands to furnish most excellent harbours.

From what has been said it appears that the Spaniards, on the island of Guam, are extremely few compared to the Indian inhabitants ; and formerly the disproportion was still greater, as may be easily conceived from what has been said, in another chapter, of the numbers heretofore on Tinian alone. These Indians are a bold well-limbed people ; and it should seem from some of their practices that they are no ways defective in understanding ; for their flying proas in particular, which have been for ages the only vessels used by them, are so singular and extraordinary an invention, that it would do honour to any nation, however dexterous and acute. For if we consider the aptitude of this proa to the particular navigation of these islands, which, lying all of them nearly under the same meridian, and within the limits of the trade-wind, require the vessels made use of in passing from one to the other to be particularly fitted for sailing with the wind upon the beam ; or, if we examine the uncommon simplicity and ingenuity of its fabric and contrivance, or the extraordinary velocity with which it moves, we shall, in each of these articles, find it worthy of our admiration, and meriting a place amongst the mechanical productions of the most civilised nations, where arts and sciences have most eminently flourished. As former navigators, though they have mentioned these vessels, have yet treated of them imperfectly ; and, as I conceive that, besides their curiosity, they may furnish both the shipwright and seaman with no contemptible observations, I shall here insert a very exact description of the built, rigging, and working of these vessels which I am well enabled to do ; for one of them, as I have mentioned, fell into our hands at our first arrival at Tinian, and Mr. Brett took it to pieces, on purpose to delineate its fabric and dimensions with greater accuracy : so that the following account may be relied on.

The name of flying proa given to these vessels, is owing to the stiffness with which they sail. Of this the Spaniards assert such stories as appear altogether incredible to those who have never seen these vessels move ; nor are the Spaniards the only people who relate these extraordinary tales of their celerity. For those who shall have the curiosity to inquire at the dock at Portsmouth, about a trial made there some years since with a very imperfect one built at that place, will meet with accounts not less wonderful than any the Spaniards have given. However, from some rude estimations made by our people of the velocity with which they crossed the horizon at a distance, while we lay at Tinian, I cannot help believing that, with a brisk trade-wind, they will run near twenty miles an hour: which, though greatly short of what the Spaniards report of them, is yet a prodigious degree of swiftness. But let us give a distinct idea of its figure.

The construction of this proa is a direct contradiction to the practice of all the rest of mankind. For as the rest of the world make the head of their vessels different from the stern, but the two sides alike; the proa, on the contrary, has her head and stern exactly alike, but her two sides very different; the side intended to be always the lee-side being flat, and the windward-side made rounding, in the manner of other vessels; and, to prevent her oversetting, which, from her small breadth, and the straight run of her leeward-side, would, without this precaution, infallibly happen, there is a frame laid out from her to windward, to the end of which is fastened a log fashioned into the shape of a small boat, and made hollow: the weight of the frame is intended to balance the proa, and the small boat is by its buoyancy (as it is always in the water) to prevent her oversetting to windward; and this frame is usually called an outrigger. The body of the proa (at least of that we took) is made of two pieces joined endways, and sewed together with bark, for there is no iron used about her: she is about two inches thick at the bottom, which at the gunwale is reduced to less than one: the mast is supported by a shroud, and by two stays: the sail is made of matting, and the mast, yard, boom, and outriggers, are all made of bamboo: the heel of the yard is always lodged in one of the sockets, according to the tack the proa goes on; and when she alters her tack, they bear away a little to bring her stern up to the wind, then by easing the halyard and raising the yard, and carrying the heel of it along the lee-side of the proa, they fix it in the opposite socket; whilst the boom at the same time, by letting fly one sheet, and haling the other sheet, shifts into a contrary situation to what it had before, and that which was the stern of the proa now becomes the head, and she is trimmed on the other tack. When it is necessary to reef or furl the sail, this is done by rolling it round the boom. The proa generally carries six or seven Indians; two of which are placed in the head and stern, who steer the vessel alternately with a paddle according to the tack she goes on, he in the stern being the steersman; the other Indians are employed either in baling out the water which she accidentally ships, or in setting and trimming the sail. From the description of these vessels it is sufficiently obvious how dexterously they are fitted for ranging this collection of islands called the Ladrones: for as these islands lie nearly N. and S. of each other, and are all within the limits of the trade-wind, the proas, by sailing most excellently on a wind, and with either end foremost, can run from one of these islands to the other and back again, only by shifting the sail, without ever putting about; and, by the flatness of their lee-side, and their small breadth, they are capable of lying much nearer the wind than any other vessel hitherto known, and thereby have an advantage which no vessels that go large can ever pretend to: the advantage I mean is that of running with a velocity nearly as great, and perhaps sometimes greater than that with which the wind blows. This, however paradoxical it may appear, is evident enough in similar instances on shore: for it is well known that the sails of a windmill often move faster than the wind; and one great superiority of common windmills over all others, that ever were, or ever will be contrived to move with a horizontal motion, is analogous to the case we have mentioned of a vessel upon a wind and before the wind: for the sails of a horizontal windmill, the faster they move, the more they detract from the impulse of the wind upon them; whereas the common windmills, by moving perpendicular to the torrent of air, are nearly as forcibly acted on by the wind when they are in motion as when they are at rest.

Thus much may suffice as to the description and nature of these singular embarkations. I must add that vessels bearing some obscure resemblance to these are to be met with in various parts of the East Indies; but none of them, that I can learn, to be compared with those of the Ladrones, either in their construction or celerity; which should induce one to believe that this was originally the invention of some genius of these islands, and was afterwards imperfectly copied by the neighbouring nations: for though the Ladrones have no immediate intercourse with any other people, yet there lie to the S. and S.W. of them a great number of islands, which are supposed to extend to the coast of New Guinea. These islands are so near the Ladrones that canoes from them have sometimes, by distress, been driven to Guam; and the Spaniards did once despatch a bark for their discovery, which left two Jesuits amongst them, who were afterwards murdered: and the inhabitants of the Ladrones with their proas may, by like accident, have been driven amongst these islands. Indeed I should conceive that the same range of islands extends to the S.E. as well as the S.W. and that to a prodigious distance: for Schouten, who traversed the south part of the Pacific Ocean in the year 1615, met with a large double canoe full of people, at above a thousand leagues distance from the Ladrones towards the S.E. If this double canoe was any distant imitation of the flying proa, which is no very improbable conjecture, this can only be accounted for by supposing that there is a range of islands, near enough to each other to be capable of an accidental communication, which is extended from the Ladrones thither. And indeed all those who have crossed from America to the East Indies in a southern latitude, have never failed of meeting with several very small islands scattered over that immense ocean.

And as there may be hence some reason to suppose that the Ladrones are only a part of an extensive chain of islands spreading themselves to the southward towards the unknown boundaries of the Pacific Ocean; so it appears from the Spanish chart, elsewhere spoken of, that the same chain is extended from the northward of the

Ladrones to Japan: so that in this light the Ladrones will be only one small portion of a range of islands, reaching from Japan perhaps to the unknown southern continent. After this short account of these places, I shall now return to the prosecution of our voyage.

CHAPTER VI.

From Tinian to Macao

I HAVE already mentioned, that, on the 21st of October, in the evening, we took our leave of the island of Tinian, steering the proper course for Macao in China. The eastern monsoon was now, we reckoned, fairly settled; and we had a constant gale blowing right upon our stern: so that we generally ran from forty to fifty leagues a-day. But we had a large hollow sea pursuing us, which occasioned the ship to labour much; whence we received great damage in our rigging, which was grown very rotten, and our leak was augmented: but happily for us, our people were now in full health; so that there were no complaints of fatigue, but all went through their attendance on the pumps, and every other duty of the ship, with ease and cheerfulness.

Having now no other but our sheet-anchor left, except our prize-anchors, which were stowed in the hold, and were too light to be depended on, we were under great concern how we should manage on the coast of China, where we were all entire strangers, and where we should doubtless be frequently under the necessity of coming to an anchor. Our sheet-anchor being obviously much too heavy for a coasting anchor, it was at length resolved to fix two of our largest prize-anchors into one stock, and to place between their shanks two guns, four pounders, which was accordingly executed, and it was to serve as a best bower: and a third prize-anchor being in like manner joined with our stream-anchor, with guns between them, we thereby made a small bower; so that, besides our sheet-anchor, we had again two others at our bows, one of which weighed 3900 and the other 2900 pounds.

The 3d of November, about three in the afternoon, we saw an island, which at first we imagined to be the island of Botel Tobago Ximo: but on our nearer approach we found it to be much smaller than that is usually represented; and about an hour after we saw another island, five or six miles farther to the westward. As no chart, nor any journal we had seen, took notice of any other island to the eastward of Formosa, than Botel Tobago Ximo, and as we had no observation of our latitude at noon, we were in some perplexity, being apprehensive that an extraordinary current had driven us into the neighbourhood of the Bashee islands; and therefore, when night came on, we brought to, and continued in this posture till the next morning, which proving dark and cloudy, for some time prolonged our uncertainty; but it cleared up about nine o'clock, when we again discerned the two islands above-mentioned; we then pressed forward to the westward, and by eleven got sight of the southern part of the island of Formosa. This satisfied us that the second island we saw was Botel Tobago Ximo, and the first a small island or rock, lying five or six miles due east from it, which, not being mentioned by any of our books or charts, was the occasion of our fears.

When we got sight of the island of Formosa we steered W. by S. in order to double its extremity, and kept a good look out for the rocks of Vele Rete, which we did not see till two in the afternoon. They then bore from us W.N.W., three miles distant, the south end of Formosa at the same time bearing N. by W. ½ W., about five leagues distant. To give these rocks a good berth, we immediately hauled up S. by W., and so left them between us and the land. Indeed we had reason to be careful of them; for though they appeared as high out of the water as a ship's hull yet they are environed with breakers on all sides, and there is a shoal stretching from them at least a mile and a half to the southward, whence they may be truly called dangerous. The course from Botel Tobago Ximo to these rocks, is S.W. by W and the distance about twelve or thirteen leagues and the south end of Formosa, off which they lie is in the latitude of 21° 50′ north, and in 23° 50 west longitude from Tinian, according to our most approved reckonings, though by some of our accounts above a degree more.

While we were passing by these rocks of Vele Rete, there was an outcry of fire on the forecastle; this occasioned a general alarm, and the whole crew instantly flocked together in the utmost confusion, so that the officers found it difficult for some time to appease the uproar: but having at last reduced the people to order, it was perceived that the fire proceeded from the furnace; and pulling down the brick-work, it was extinguished with great facility, for it had taken its rise from the bricks, which, being over-heated, had begun to communicate the fire to the adjacent wood-work. In the evening we were surprised with a view of what we at first sight conceived to have been breakers, but, on a stricter examination, we found them to be only a great number of fires on the island of Formosa. These, we imagined, were intended by the inhabitants of that island as signals for us to touch there, but that suited not our views, we being impatient to reach the port of Macao as soon as possible. From Formosa we steered W.N.W., and sometimes still more northerly, proposing to fall in with the coast of China, to the eastward of Pedro Blanco; for the rock so called is usually esteemed an excellent direction for ships bound to Macao. We continued this course till the following night, and then frequently brought to, to try if we were in soundings: but it was the 5th of November, at nine in the morning, before we struck ground, and then we had forty-two fathom, and a bottom of grey sand mixed with shells. When we had got about twenty miles farther W.N.W., we had thirty-five fathom, and the same bottom, from whence our soundings gradually decreased from thirty-five to twenty-five fathom; but soon after, to our great surprise, they jumped back again to thirty fathom: this was an alteration we could not very well account for, since all the charts laid down regular soundings everywhere to the northward of Pedro Blanco; and for this reason we kept a very careful look-out, and altered our course to N.N.W., and having run thirty-five miles in this direction, our soundings

tinued the ship under the management of the Chinese who came first on board. By this time we learned that we were not far distant from Macao, and that there were in the river of Canton, at the mouth of which Macao lies, eleven European ships, of which four were English. Our pilot carried us between the islands of Bamboo and Cabouce, but the winds hanging in the northern board, and the tides often setting strongly against us, we were obliged to come frequently to an anchor, so that we did not get through between the two islands till the 12th of November, at two in the morning. In passing through, our depth of water was from twelve to fourteen fathom ; and as we still steered on N. by W. ¼ W., between a number of other islands, our soundings underwent little or no variation till towards the evening, when they increased to seventeen fathom ; in which depth (the wind dying away) we anchored not far from the island of Lantoon, which is the largest of all this range of islands. At seven in the morning we weighed again, and steering W. S. W. and S. W. by W., we at ten o'clock happily anchored in Macao road, in five fathom water, the city of Macao bearing W. by N., three leagues distant ; the peak of Lantoon E. by N., and the grand Ladrone S. by E., each of them about five leagues distant. Thus, after a fatiguing cruise of above two years' continuance, we once more arrived in an amicable port in a civilised country ; where the conveniences of life were in great plenty ; where the naval stores, which we now extremely wanted, could be in some degree procured ; where we expected the inexpressible satisfaction of receiving letters from our relations and friends ; and where our countrymen, who were lately arrived from England, would be capable of answering the numerous inquiries we were prepared to make, both about public and private occurrences, and to relate to us many particulars, which, whether of importance or not, would be listened to by us with the utmost attention, after the long suspension of our correspondence with our country, to which the nature of our undertaking had hitherto subjected us.

CHAPTER VII.

Proceedings at Macao.

THE city of Macao, in the road of which we came to an anchor on the 12th of November, is a Portuguese settlement, situated in an island at the mouth of the river of Canton. It was formerly a very rich and populous city, and capable of defending itself against the power of the adjacent Chinese governors ; but at present it is much fallen from its ancient splendour ; for though it is inhabited by Portuguese, and hath a governor nominated by the king of Portugal, yet it subsists merely by the sufferance of the Chinese, who can starve the place, and dispossess the Portuguese, whenever they please. This obliges the governor of Macao to behave with great circumspection, and carefully to avoid every circumstance that may give offence to the Chinese. The river of Canton, at the mouth of which this city lies, is the only Chinese port frequented by European ships ; and this river is indeed a more commodious harbour, on many accounts, than Macao. But the peculiar customs of the Chinese, only adapted to the entertainment of trading ships, and the apprehensions of the commodore, lest he should embroil the East-India Company with the regency of Canton, if he should insist on being treated upon a different footing than the merchantmen, made him resolve to go first to Macao, before he ventured into the port of Canton. Indeed, had not this reason prevailed with him, he himself had nothing to fear ; for it is certain that he might have entered the port of Canton, and might have continued there as long as he pleased, and afterwards have left it again, although the whole power of the Chinese empire had been brought together to oppose him.

The commodore, not to depart from his usual prudence, no sooner came to an anchor in Macao road, than he despatched an officer with his compliments to the Portuguese governor of Macao, requesting his excellency, by the same officer, to advise him in what manner it would be proper to act to avoid offending the Chinese ; which, as there were then four of our ships in their power at Canton, was a matter worthy of attention. The difficulty which the commodore principally apprehended, related to the duty usually paid by all ships in the river of Canton, according to their tonnage. For as men of war are exempted in every foreign harbour from all manner of port charges, the commodore thought it would be derogatory to the honour of his country, to submit to this duty in China : and therefore he desired the advice of the governor of Macao, who, being a European, could not be ignorant of the privileges claimed by a British man of war, and consequently might be expected to give us the best lights for avoiding this perplexity. Our boat returned in the evening with two officers sent by the governor, who informed the commodore, that it was the governor's opinion, that if the Centurion ventured into the river of Canton, the duty would certainly be demanded ; and, therefore, if the commodore approved of it, he would send him a pilot, who should conduct us into another safe harbour, called the Typa, which was every way commodious for careening the ship (an operation we were resolved to begin upon as soon as possible) and where the above-mentioned duty would in all probability be never asked for.

This proposal the commodore agreed to, and in the morning we weighed anchor, and under the direction of the Portuguese pilot, steered for the intended harbour. As we entered the two islands, which form the eastern passage to it, we found our soundings decreased to three fathom and a half. But the pilot assuring us that this was the least depth we should meet with, we continued our course, till at length the ship stuck fast in the mud, with only eighteen foot water abaft ; and the tide of ebb making, the water sewed to sixteen feet, but the ship remained perfectly upright ; we then sounded all round us, and finding the water deepened to the northward, we carried out our small bower with two hawsers an end, and at the return of the flood, hove the ship afloat ; and a small breeze springing up at the same instant, we set the fore-top sail, and slipping the hawser, ran into the harbour, where we moored in about five fathom water. This harbour of the Typa is formed by a number of islands, and is

again gradually diminished to twenty-two fathom, and we at last, about midnight, got sight of the mainland of China, bearing N. by W., four leagues distant: we then brought the ship to, with her head to the sea, proposing to wait for the morning; and before sunrise we were surprised to find ourselves in the midst of an incredible number of fishing-boats, which seemed to cover the surface of the sea as far as the eye could reach. I may well style their number incredible, since I cannot believe, upon the lowest estimate, that there were so few as six thousand, most of them manned with five hands, and none of those we saw with less than three. Nor was this swarm of fishing vessels peculiar to this spot; for, as we ran on to the westward, we found them as abundant on every part of the coast. We at first doubted not but we should procure a pilot from them to carry us to Macao; but though many of them came close to the ship, and we endeavoured to tempt them by showing them a number of dollars, a most alluring bait for Chinese of all ranks and professions, yet we could not entice them on board us, nor procure any directions from them; though, I presume, the only difficulty was their not comprehending what we wanted them to do, for we could have no communication with them but by signs: indeed we often pronounced the word Macao; but this we had reason to suppose they understood in a different sense; for in return they sometimes held up fish to us, and we afterwards learnt, that the Chinese name for fish is of a somewhat similar sound. But what surprised us most, was the inattention and want of curiosity, which we observed in this herd of fishermen: a ship like ours had doubtless never been in those seas before; perhaps, there might not be one, amongst all the Chinese employed in this fishery, who had ever seen any European vessel; so that we might reasonably have expected to have been considered by them as a very uncommon and extraordinary object; but though many of their vessels came close to the ship, yet they did not appear to be at all interested about us, nor did they deviate in the least from their course to regard us; which insensibility, especially in maritime persons, about a matter in their own profession, is scarcely to be credited, did not the general behaviour of the Chinese, in other instances, furnish us with continual proofs of a similar turn of mind: it may perhaps be doubted, whether this cast of temper be the effect of nature or education; but, in either case, it is an incontestible symptom of a mean and contemptible disposition, and is alone a sufficient confutation of the extravagant panegyrics, which many hypothetical writers have bestowed on the ingenuity and capacity of this nation. But to return:

Not being able to procure any information from the Chinese fishermen about our proper course to Macao, it was necessary for us to rely entirely on our own judgment; and concluding from our latitude, which was 22° 42′ North, and from our soundings, which were only seventeen or eighteen fathoms, that we were yet to the eastward of Pedro Blanco, we stood to the westward: and for the assistance of future navigators, who may hereafter doubt about the parts of the coast they are upon, I must observe, that besides the latitude of Pedro Blanco, which is 22° 18′, and the depth of water, which to the westward of that rock is almost everywhere twenty fathoms, there is another circumstance which will give great assistance in judging of the position of the ship: this is the kind of ground; for, till we came within thirty miles of Pedro Blanco, we had constantly a sandy bottom; but there the bottom changed to soft and muddy, and continued so quite to the island of Macao; only while we were in sight of Pedro Blanco, and very near it, we had for a short space a bottom of greenish mud, intermixed with sand.

It was on the 5th of November, at midnight, when we first made the coast of China; and the next day, about two o'clock, as we were standing to the westward within two leagues of the coast, and still surrounded by fishing vessels in as great numbers as at first, we perceived that a boat a-head of us waved a red flag, and blew a horn: this we considered as a signal made to us, either to warn us of some shoal, or to inform us that they would supply us with a pilot, and in this belief we immediately sent our cutter to the boat, to know their intentions; but we were soon made sensible of our mistake, and found that this boat was the commodore of the whole fishery, and that the signal she had made was to order them all to leave off fishing, and to return in shore, which we saw them instantly obey. On this disappointment we kept on our course, and soon after passed by two very small rocks, which lay four or five miles distant from the shore; but night came on before we got sight of Pedro Blanco, and we therefore brought to till the morning, when we had the satisfaction to discover it. It is a rock of a small circumference, but of a moderate height, and, both in shape and colour, resembles a sugar-loaf, and is about seven or eight miles from the shore. We passed within a mile and a half of it, and left it between us and the land, still keeping on to the westward; and the next day, being the 7th, we were a-breast of a chain of islands, which stretched from east to west. These, as we afterwards found, were called the islands of Lema; they are rocky and barren, and are in all, small and great, fifteen or sixteen; and there are, besides, a great number of other islands between them and the mainland of China. These islands we left on the starboard side, passing within four miles of them, where we had twenty-four fathom water. We were still surrounded by fishing-boats; and we once more sent the cutter on board one of them, to endeavour to procure a pilot, but could not prevail; however one of the Chinese directed us by signs to sail round the westernmost of the island or rocks of Lema, and then to hale up. We followed this direction, and in the evening came to an anchor in eighteen fathom.

After having continued at anchor all night, we on the 9th, at four in the morning, sent our cutter to sound the channel, where we proposed to pass; but before the return of the cutter, a Chinese pilot put on board us, and told us, in broken Portuguese, he would carry us to Macao for thirty dollars. These were immediately paid him, and we then weighed and made sail; and soon after several other pilots came on board us, who, to recommend themselves, produced certificates from the captains of several ships they had piloted in, but we con-

about six miles distant from Macao. Here we saluted the castle of Macao with eleven guns, which were returned by an equal number.

The next day the commodore paid a visit in person to the governor, and was saluted at his landing by eleven guns; which were returned by the Centurion. Mr. Anson's business in this visit, was to solicit the governor to grant us a supply of provisions, and to furnish us with such stores as were necessary to refit the ship. The governor seemed really inclined to do us all the service he could, and assured the commodore, in a friendly manner, that he would privately give us all the assistance in his power; but he, at the same time, frankly owned, that he dared not openly furnish us with anything we demanded, unless we first procured an order for it from the viceroy of Canton; for that he neither received provisions for his garrison, nor any other necessaries, but by permission from the Chinese government; and as they took care only to furnish him from day to day, he was indeed no other than their vassal, whom they could at all times compel to submit to their own terms, only by laying an embargo on his provisions.

On this declaration of the governor, Mr. Anson resolved himself to go to Canton, to procure a license from the viceroy; and he accordingly hired a Chinese boat for himself and his attendants; but just as he was ready to embark, the hoppo, or Chinese custom-house officer at Macao, refused to grant a permit to the boat, and ordered the watermen not to proceed, at their peril. The commodore at first endeavoured to prevail with the hoppo to withdraw his injunction, and to grant a permit; and the governor of Macao employed his interest with the hoppo to the same purpose. Mr. Anson, finding the officer inflexible, told him the next day, that if he longer refused to grant the permit, he would man and arm his own boats to carry him thither; asking the hoppo, at the same time, who he imagined would dare to oppose him. This threat immediately brought about what his intreaties had laboured for in vain. The permit was granted, and Mr. Anson went to Canton. On his arrival there, he consulted with the supercargoes and officers of the English ships, how to procure an order from the viceroy for the necessaries he wanted. But in this he had reason to suppose that the advice they gave him, though doubtless well intended, was yet not the most prudent. For as it is the custom with these gentlemen never to apply to the supreme magistrate himself, whatever difficulties they labour under, but to transact all matters relating to the government by the mediation of the principal Chinese merchants, Mr. Anson was advised to follow the same method upon this occasion, the English promising (in which they were doubtless sincere) to exert all their interest to engage the merchants in his favour. And when the Chinese merchants were applied to, they readily undertook the management of it, and promised to answer for its success; but after near a month's delay, and reiterated excuses, during which interval they pretended to be often upon the point of completing the business, they at last (being pressed, and measures being taken for delivering a letter to the viceroy) threw off the mask, and declared they neither had applied to the viceroy, nor could they; for he was too great a man, they said, for them to approach on any occasion. And, not contented with having themselves thus grossly deceived the commodore, they now used all their persuasion with the English at Canton, to prevent them from intermeddling with anything that regarded him, representing to them, that it would in all probability embroil them with the government, and occasion them a great deal of unnecessary trouble; which groundless insinuations had indeed but too much weight with those they were applied to.

It may be difficult to assign a reason for this perfidious conduct of the Chinese merchants: interest indeed is known to exert a boundless influence over the inhabitants of that empire; but how their interest could be affected in the present case, is not easy to discover; unless they apprehended that the presence of a ship of force might damp their Manila trade, and therefore acted in this manner with a view of forcing the commodore to Batavia; but it might be as natural in this light to suppose, that they would have been eager to have got him despatched. I therefore rather impute their behaviour to the unparalleled pusillanimity of the nation, and to the awe they are under of the government: for as such a ship as the Centurion, fitted for war only, had never been seen in those parts before, she was the horror of these dastards, and the merchants were in some degree terrified even with the idea of her, and could not think of applying to the viceroy (who is doubtless fond of all opportunities of fleecing them) without representing to themselves the pretences which a hungry and tyrannical magistrate might possibly find, for censuring their intermeddling in so unusual a transaction, in which he might pretend the interest of the state was immediately concerned. However, be this as it may, the commodore was satisfied that nothing was to be done by the interposition of the merchants, as it was on his pressing them to deliver a letter to the viceroy, that they had declared they durst not intermeddle, and had confessed, that notwithstanding all their pretences of serving him, they had not yet taken one step towards it. Mr. Anson therefore told them, that he would proceed to Batavia, and refit his ship there; but informed them, at the same time, that this was impossible to be done, unless he was supplied with a stock of provisions sufficient for his passage. The merchants, on this, undertook to procure him provisions, but assured him, that it was what they durst not engage in openly, but proposed to manage it in a clandestine manner, by putting a quantity of bread, flour, and other provisions on board the English ships, which were now ready to sail; and these were to stop at the mouth of the Typa, where the Centurion's boats were to receive it. This article, which the merchants represented as a matter of great favour, being settled, the commodore, on the 16th of December, returned from Canton to the ship, seemingly resolved to proceed to Batavia to refit, as soon as he should get his supplies of provision on board.

But Mr. Anson (who never intended going to Batavia) found, on his return to the Centurion, that her main-mast was sprung in two places, and that the leak was considerably increased; so that, upon the whole, he was fully satisfied, that though he should lay in a sufficient stock of provisions, yet it would be impossible for him to put to sea without refitting: for, if he left the port with his ship in her present condition, she would be in the utmost danger of foundering; and therefore, notwithstanding the difficulties he had met with, he resolved at all events to have her hove down, before he left Macao. He was fully convinced, by what he had observed at Canton, that his great caution not to injure the East-India Company's affairs, and the regard he had shown to the advice of their officers, had occasioned all his embarrassments. For he now saw clearly, that if he had at first carried his ship into the river of Canton, and had immediately applied himself to the mandarins, who are the chief officers of state, instead of employing the merchants to apply for him; he would, in all probability, have had all his requests granted, and would have been soon despatched. He had already lost a month, by the wrong measures he had been put upon, but he resolved to lose as little more time as possible; and therefore, the 17th of December, being the next day after his return from Canton, he wrote a letter to the viceroy of that place, acquainting him, that he was commander-in-chief of a squadron of his Britannic Majesty's ships of war, which had been cruising for two years past in the South Seas against the Spaniards, who were at war with the king his master; that, in his way back to England, he had put into the port of Macao, having a considerable leak in his ship, and being in great want of provisions, so that it was impossible for him to proceed on his voyage, till his ship was repaired, and he was supplied with the necessaries he wanted; that he had been at Canton, in hopes of being admitted to a personal audience of his excellency; but being a stranger to the customs of the country, he had not been able to inform himself what steps were necessary to be taken to procure such an audience, and therefore was obliged to apply to him in this manner, to desire his excellency to give order for his being permitted to employ carpenters and proper workmen to refit his ship, and to furnish himself with provisions and stores, thereby to enable him to pursue his voyage to Great Britain with this monsoon, hoping, at the same time, that these orders would be issued with as little delay as possible, lest it might occasion his loss of the season, and he might be prevented from departing till next winter.

This letter was translated into the Chinese language, and the commodore delivered it himself to the hoppo or chief officer of the emperor's customs at Macao, desiring him to forward it to the viceroy of Canton, with as much expedition as he could. The officer at first seemed unwilling to take charge of it, and raised many objections about it, so that Mr. Anson suspected him of being in league with the merchants of Canton, who had always shown a great apprehension of the commodore's having any immediate intercourse with the viceroy or mandarins; and therefore the commodore, with some resentment, took back his letter from the hoppo, and told him he would immediately send an officer with it to Canton in his own boat, and would give him positive orders not to return without an answer from the viceroy. The hoppo perceiving the commodore to be in earnest, and fearing to be called to an account for his refusal, begged to be entrusted with the letter, and promised to deliver it, and to procure an answer as soon as possible. And now it was soon seen how justly Mr. Anson had at last judged of the proper manner of dealing with the Chinese; for this letter was written but the 17th of December, as hath been already observed; and, on the 19th in the morning a mandarin of the first rank, who was governor of the city of Janson, together with two mandarins of an inferior class, and a great retinue of officers and servants, having with them eighteen half galleys decorated with a greater number of streamers, and furnished with music, and full of men, came to grapnel a-head of the Centurion whence the mandarin sent a message to the commodore, telling him that he (the mandarin) was ordered, by the viceroy of Canton, to examine the condition of the ship, and desiring the ship's boat might be sent to fetch him on board. The Centurion's boat was immediately despatched, and preparations were made for receiving him; for a hundred of the most sightly of the crew were uniformly dressed in the regimentals of the marines, and were drawn up under arms on the main-deck against his arrival. When he entered the ship he was saluted by the drums, and what other military music there was on board; and passing by the new-formed guard, he was met by the commodore on the quarter-deck, who conducted him to the great cabin. Here the mandarin explained his commission, declaring that his business was to examine all the particulars mentioned in the commodore's letter to the viceroy, and to confront them with the representation that had been given of them; that he was particularly instructed to inspect the leak, and had for that purpose brought with him two Chinese carpenters; and that for the greater regularity and despatch of his business, he had every head of enquiry separately written down on a sheet of paper, with a void space opposite to it, where he was to insert such information and remarks thereon, as he could procure by his own observation.

This mandarin appeared to be a person of very considerable parts, and endowed with more frankness and honesty, than is to be found in the generality of the Chinese. After the proper inquiries had been made, particularly about the leak, which the Chinese carpenters reported to be as dangerous as it had been represented, and consequently that it was impossible for the Centurion to proceed to sea without being refitted, the mandarin expressed himself satisfied with the account given in the commodore's letter. And this magistrate, as he was more intelligent than any other person of his nation that came to our knowledge, so likewise was he more curious and inquisitive, viewing each part of the ship with particular attention, and appearing greatly surprised at the largeness of the lower deck guns, and at the weight and size of the shot. The commodore, observing his astonishment, thought this a proper opportunity to convince the Chinese of the prudence of granting him a speedy and ample supply of all he wanted: with this view he told the mandarin, and those who were with him, that, besides the demands he made for a general supply, he had a particular complaint against the proceedings of the custom-house of Macao; that at his first arrival the Chinese boats had brought on board plenty of greens, and variety of fresh provisions for daily use, for which they had always been paid to their full satisfaction, but that the custom-house officers at Macao had soon forbid them, by which means he was deprived of those refreshments which were of the utmost consequence to the health of his men, after their long and sickly voyage; that as they, the mandarins, had informed themselves of his wants, and were eye-witnesses of the force and strength of his ship, they might be satisfied it was not for want of power to supply himself, that he desired the permission of the government to purchase what provisions he stood in need of; that they must be convinced that the Centurion alone was capable of destroying the whole navigation of the port of Canton, or of any other port in China, without running the least risk from all the force the Chinese could collect; that it was true, this was not the manner of proceeding between nations in friendship with each other; but it was likewise true, that it was not customary for any nation to permit the ships of their friends to starve and sink in their ports, when those friends had money to supply their wants, and only desired liberty to lay it out; that they must confess, he and his people had hitherto behaved with great modesty and reserve; but that, as his wants were each day increasing, hunger would at last prove too strong for any restraint, and necessity was acknowledged in all countries to be superior to every other law; and therefore it could not be expected that his crew would long continue to starve in the midst of that plenty to which their eyes were every day witnesses: to this the commodore added, (though perhaps with a less serious air) that if by the delay of supplying him with provisions his men should be reduced to the necessity of turning cannibals, and preying upon their own species, it was easy to be foreseen that, independent of their friendship to their comrades, they would, in point of luxury, prefer the plump well-fed Chinese to their own emaciated shipmates. The first mandarin acquiesced in the justness of this reasoning, and told the commodore, that he should that night proceed for Canton; that on his arrival, a council of mandarins would be summoned, of which he himself was a member; and that by being employed in the present commission, he was of course the commodore's advocate; that, as he was fully convinced of the urgency of Mr. Anson's necessity, he did not doubt but, on his representation, the council would be of the same opinion; and that all that was demanded would be amply and speedily granted: and with regard to the commodore's complaint of the custom-house of Macao, he undertook to rectify that immediately by his own authority; for desiring a list to be given him of the quantity of provisions necessary for the expense of the ship for a day, he wrote a permit under it, and delivered it to one of his attendants, directing him to see that quantity sent on board early every morning; and this order, from that time forwards, was punctually complied with.

When this weighty affair was thus in some degree regulated, the commodore invited him and his two attendant mandarins to dinner, telling them at the same time, that if his provisions, either in kind or quantity, was not what they might expect, they must thank themselves for having confined him to so hard an allowance. One of his dishes was beef, which the Chinese all dislike, though Mr. Anson was not apprised of it; this seems to be derived from the Indian superstition, which for some ages past has made a great progress in China. However, his guests did not entirely fast; for the three mandarins completely finished the white part of four large fowls. But they were extremely embarrassed with their knives and forks, and were quite incapable of making use of them : so that, after some fruitless attempts to help themselves, which were sufficiently awkward, one of the attendants was obliged to cut their meat in small pieces for them. But whatever difficulty they might have in complying with the European manner of eating, they seemed not to be novices in drinking. The commodore excused himself in this part of the entertainment under the pretence of illness, but there being another gentleman present, of a florid and jovial complexion, the chief mandarin clapped him on the shoulder, and told him by the interpreter, that certainly he could not plead sickness, and therefore insisted on his bearing him company; and that gentleman perceiving, that after they had despatched four or five bottles of Frontiniac, the mandarin still continued unruffled, he ordered a bottle of citron-water to be brought up, which the Chinese seemed much to relish; and this being near finished, they arose from table, in appearance cool and uninfluenced by what they had drunk, and the commodore having, according to custom, made the mandarin a present, they all departed in the same vessels that brought them.

After their departure the commodore with great impatience expected the resolution of the council, and the necessary licenses for his refitment. For it must be observed, as has already appeared from the preceding narration, that he could neither purchase stores nor necessaries with his money, nor did any kind of workmen dare to engage themselves to work for him, without the permission of the government first obtained. And in the execution of these particular injunctions the magistrates never fail of exercising great severity; they, notwithstanding the fustian eulogiums bestowed upon them by the catholic missionaries and their European copiers, being composed of the same fragile materials with the rest of mankind, and often making use of the authority of the law, not to suppress crimes, but to enrich themselves by the pillage of those who commit them; for capital punishments are rare in China, the effeminate genius of the nation, and their strong attachment to lucre, disposing them rather to make use of fines; and hence arises no inconsiderable profit to those who compose their tribunals: consequently prohibitions of all kinds, particularly such as the alluring prospect of great profit may often tempt the subject to infringe, cannot but be favourite institutions in such a government. But to return:

Some time before this Captain Saunders took his passage to England on board a Swedish ship, and was charged with despatches from the commodore; and soon after, in the month of December, Captain Mitchel, Colonel Crachcrode, and Mr. Tassel, one of the agent-victuallers, with his nephew Mr. Charles Harriot, embarked on board some of our Company's ships; and I, having obtained the commodore's leave to return home, embarked with them. I must observe too (having omitted it before) that whilst we lay here at Macao, we were informed by some of the officers of our Indiamen, that the Severn and Pearl, the two ships of our squadron which had separated from us off Cape Noir, were safely arrived at Rio Janeiro on the coast of Brazil. I have formerly taken notice that, at the time of their separation, we apprehended them to be lost. And there were many reasons which greatly favoured this suspicion: for we knew that the Severn in particular was extremely sickly; and this was the more obvious to the rest of the ships, as in the preceding part of the voyage her commander Captain Legge had been remarkable for his exemplary punctuality in keeping his station, till, for the last ten days before his separation, his crew was so diminished and enfeebled, that with his utmost efforts it was not possible for him to maintain his proper position with his wonted exactness. The extraordinary sickness on board him was by many imputed to the ship, which was new, and on that account was believed to be the more unhealthy; but whatever was the cause of it, the Severn was by much the most sickly of the squadron: for before her departure from St. Catherine's she buried more men than any of them, insomuch that the commodore was obliged to recruit her with a number of fresh hands; and, the mortality still continuing on board her, she was supplied with men a second time at sea after our setting sail from St. Julians; and, notwithstanding these different reinforcements, she was at last reduced to the distressed condition I have already mentioned: so that the commodore himself was firmly persuaded she was lost; and therefore it was with great joy we received the news of her and the Pearl's safety, after the strong persuasion, which had so long prevailed amongst us, of their having both perished. But to proceed with the transactions between Mr. Anson and the Chinese.

Notwithstanding the favourable disposition of the mandarin governor of Janson at his leaving Mr. Anson, several days were elapsed before he had any advice from him; and Mr. Anson was privately informed there were great debates in council upon his affair: partly perhaps owing to its being so unusual a case, and in part to the influence, as I suppose, of the intrigues of the French at Canton: for they had a countryman and fast friend residing on the spot who spoke the language very well, and was not unacquainted with the venality of the government, nor with the persons of several of the magistrates, and consequently could not be at a loss for means of traversing the assistance desired by Mr. Anson. And this opposition of the French was not merely the effect of national prejudice or contrariety of political interests, but was in a good measure owing to their vanity, a motive of much more weight with the generality of mankind than any attachment to the public service of their community: for, the French pretending their Indiamen to be men-of-war, their officers were apprehensive that any distinction granted to Mr. Anson, on account of his bearing the king's commission, would render them less considerable in the eyes of the Chinese, and would establish a prepossession at Canton in favour of ships of war, by which they, as trading vessels, would suffer in their importance: and I wish the affectation of endeavouring to pass for men-of-war,

and the fear of sinking in the estimation of the Chinese, if the Centurion was treated in a different manner from themselves, had been confined to the officers of the French ships only. However, notwithstanding all these obstacles, it should seem that the representation of the commodore to the mandarins of the facility with which he could right himself, if justice were denied him, had at last its effect: for, on the 6th of January, in the morning, the governor of Janson, the commodore's advocate, sent down the viceroy of Canton's warrant for the refitment of the Centurion, and for supplying her people with all they wanted; and, the next day, a number of Chinese smiths and carpenters went on board, to agree for all the work by the great. They demanded at first to the amount of a thousand pounds sterling for the necessary repairs of the ship, the boats, and the masts: this the commodore seemed to think an unreasonable sum, and endeavoured to persuade them to work by the day; but that proposal they would not hearken to; so it was at last agreed that the carpenters should have to the amount of about six hundred pounds for their work; and that the smiths should be paid for their iron-work by weight, allowing them at the rate of three pounds a hundred nearly for the small work, and forty-six shillings for the large.

This being regulated, the commodore exerted himself to get this most important business completed; I mean the heaving down the Centurion, and examining the state of her bottom: for this purpose the first lieutenant was despatched to Canton to hire two country vessels, called in their language junks, one of them being intended to heave down by, and the other to serve as a magazine for the powder and ammunition: at the same time the ground was smoothed on one of the neighbouring islands, and a large tent was pitched for lodging the lumber and provisions, and near a hundred Chinese caulkers were soon set to work on the decks and sides of the ship. But all these preparations, and the getting ready the careening gear, took up a great deal of time; for the Chinese caulkers, though they worked very well, were far from being expeditious; and it was the 26th of January before the junks arrived; and the necessary materials, which were to be purchased at Canton, came down very slowly; partly from the distance of the place, and partly from the delays and backwardness of the Chinese merchants. And in this interval Mr. Anson had the additional perplexity to discover that his fore-mast was broken asunder above the upper deck partners, and was only kept together by the fishes which had been formerly clapt upon it.

However, the Centurion's people made the most of their time, and exerted themselves the best they could; and as, by clearing the ship, the carpenters were enabled to come at the leak, they took care to secure that effectually whilst the other preparations were going forwards. The leak was found to be below the fifteen foot mark, and was principally occasioned by one of the bolts being worn away and loose in the joining of the stem where it was scarfed.

At last, all things being prepared, they, on the 22nd of February, in the morning, hove out the first course of the Centurion's starboard side, and had the satisfaction to find that her bottom ap peared sound and good; and, the next day, (having by that time completed the new sheathing of the first course) they righted her again to set up anew the careening rigging, which stretched much. Thus they continued heaving down, and often righting the ship from a suspicion of their careening tackle, till the 3rd of March; when, having completed the paying and sheathing the bottom, which proved to be everywhere very sound; they, for the last time, righted the ship, to their great joy; for not only the fatigue of careening had been considerable, but they had been apprehensive of being attacked by the Spaniards, whilst the ship was thus incapacitated for defence. Nor were their fears altogether groundless; for they learnt afterwards, by a Portuguese vessel, that the Spaniards at Manila had been informed that the Centurion was in the Typa, and intended to careen there; and that thereupon the governor had summoned his council, and had proposed to them to endeavour to burn her whilst she was careening, which was an enterprise which, if properly conducted, might have put them in great danger: they were farther told, that this scheme was not only proposed, but resolved on; and that a captain of a vessel had actually undertaken to perform the business for forty thousand dollars, which he was not to receive unless he succeeded; but the governor pretending that there was no treasure in the royal chest, and insisting that the merchants should advance the money, and they refusing to comply with the demand, the affair was dropped: perhaps the merchants suspected that the whole was only a pretext to get forty thousand dollars from them; and indeed this was affirmed by some who bore the governor no good will, but with what truth it is difficult to ascertain.

As soon as the Centurion was righted, they took in her powder, and gunner's stores, and proceeded in getting in their guns as fast as possible, and then used their utmost expedition in repairing the foremast, and in completing the other articles of her refitment. And being thus employed, they were alarmed, on the 10th of March, by a Chinese fisherman, who brought them intelligence that he had been on board a large Spanish ship off the Grand Ladrone, and that there were two more in company with her: he added several particulars to his relation; as that he had brought one of their officers to Macao; and that, on this, boats went off early in the morning from Macao to them: and the better to establish the belief of his veracity, he said he desired no money, if his information should not prove true. This was presently believed to be the forementioned expedition from Manila; and the commodore immediately fitted his cannon and small arms in the best manner he could for defence; and having then his pinnace and cutter in the offing, which had been ordered to examine a Portuguese vessel, which was getting under sail, he sent them the advice he had received, and directed them to look out strictly: but no such ships ever appeared, and they were soon satisfied the whole of the story was a fiction; though it was difficult to conceive what reason could induce the fellow to be at such extraordinary pains to impose on them.

It was the beginning of April before they had new-rigged the ship, stowed their provisions and water on board, and had fitted her for the sea; and before this time the Chinese grew very uneasy, and extremely desirous that she should be gone; either not knowing, or pretending not to believe, that this was a point the commodore was as eagerly set on as they could be. On the 3rd of April, two mandarin boats came on board from Macao to urge his departure; and this having been often done before, though there had been no pretence to suspect Mr. Anson of any affected delays, he at this last message answered them in a determined tone, desiring them to give him no further trouble, for he would go when he thought proper, and not before. On this rebuke the Chinese (though it was not in their power to compel him to be gone) immediately prohibited all provisions from being carried on board him, and took such care that their injunctions should be complied with, that from that time forwards nothing could be purchased at any rate whatever.

On the 6th of April, the Centurion weighed from the Typa, and warped to the southward; and, by the 15th, she was got into Macao road, completing her water as she passed along, so that there remained now very few articles more to attend to; and her whole business being finished by the 19th, she, at three in the afternoon of that day, weighed and made sail, and stood to sea.

CHAPTER VIII.

From Macao to Cape Espiritu Santo: the taking of the Manila galleon, and returning back again.

THE commodore was now got to sea, with his ship very well refitted, his stores replenished, and an additional stock of provisions on board: his crew too was somewhat reinforced; for he had entered twenty-three men during his stay at Macao, the greatest part of which were Lascars or Indian sailors, and some few Dutch.[1] He gave out at Macao, that he was bound to Batavia, and thence to England; and though the westerly monsoon was now set in, when that passage is considered as impracticable, yet, by the confidence he had expressed in the strength of his ship, and the dexterity of his people, he had persuaded not only his own crew, but the people at Macao likewise, that he proposed to try this unusual experiment; so that there were many letters put on board him by the inhabitants of Canton and Macao for their friends at Batavia.

But his real design was of a very different nature: for he knew, that instead of one annual ship from Acapulco to Manila there would be this year, in all probability, two; since, by being before Acapulco, he had prevented one of them from putting to sea the preceding season. He therefore resolved to cruise for these returning vessels off Cape Espiritu Santo, on the island of Samal, which is the first land they always make in the Philippine Islands. And as June is generally the month in which they arrive there, he doubted not but he should get to his intended

---

"[1] The number of men I have now borne is two hundred and one, amongst which are included all the officers and boys which I had out of the Gloucester, Tryal prize, and Anna pink, so that I have not before the mast more than forty-five able seamen."—*Anson's official report.*

station time enough to intercept them. It is true they were said to be stout vessels, mounting forty-four guns a-piece, and carrying above five hundred hands, and might be expected to return in company; and he himself had but two hundred and twenty-seven hands on board, of which near thirty were boys: but this disproportion of strength did not deter him, as he knew his ship to be much better fitted for a sea-engagement than theirs, and as he had reason to expect that his men would exert themselves in the most extraordinary manner, when they had in view the immense wealth of these Manila galeons.

This project the commodore had resolved on in his own thoughts, ever since his leaving the coast of Mexico. And the greatest mortification which he received, from the various delays he had met with in China, was his apprehension, lest he might be thereby so long retarded as to let the galleons escape him. Indeed, at Macao it was incumbent on him to keep these views extremely secret; for there being a great intercourse and a mutual connexion of interests between that port and Manila, he had reason to fear, that if his designs were discovered, intelligence would be immediately sent to Manila, and measures would be taken to prevent the galleons from falling into his hands: but being now at sea, and entirely clear of the coast, he summoned all his people on the quarter-deck, and informed them of his resolution to cruise for the two Manilla ships, of whose wealth they were not ignorant. He told them he should choose a station, where he could not fail of meeting with them; and though they were stout ships, and full manned, yet, if his own people behaved with their accustomed spirit, he was certain he should prove too hard for them both, and that one of them at least could not fail of becoming his prize: he further added, that many ridiculous tales had been propagated about the strength of the sides of these ships, and their being impenetrable to cannon-shot; that these fictions had been principally invented to palliate the cowardice of those who had formerly engaged them; but he hoped there were none of those present weak enough to give credit to so absurd a story: for his own part, he did assure them upon his word, that, whenever he met with them, he would fight them so near that they should find, his bullets, instead of being stopped by one of their sides, should go through them both.

This speech of the commodore's was received by his people with great joy: for no sooner had he ended, than they expressed their approbation, according to naval custom, by three strenuous cheers, and all declared their determination to succeed or perish, whenever the opportunity presented itself. And now their hopes, which since their departure from the coast of Mexico, had entirely subsided, were again revived; and they all persuaded themselves, that, notwithstanding the various casualties and disappointments they had hitherto met with, they should yet be repaid the price of their fatigues, and should at last return home enriched with the spoils of the enemy: for firmly relying on the assurances of the commodore, that they should certainly meet with the vessels, they were all of them too sanguine to doubt a moment of mastering them; so that they considered themselves as having them already in

their possession. And this confidence was so universally spread through the whole ship's company, that, the commodore having taken some Chinese sheep to sea with him for his own provision, and one day inquiring of his butcher, why, for some time past, he had seen no mutton at his table, asking him if all the sheep were killed, the butcher very seriously replied, that there were indeed two sheep left, but that if his honour would give him leave, he proposed to keep those for the entertainment of the general of the galleons.

When the Centurion left the port of Macao, she stood for some days to the westward; and, on the first of May, they saw part of the island of Formosa; and, standing thence to the southward, they, on the 4th of May, were in the latitude of the Bashee islands, as laid down by Dampier; but they suspected his account of inaccuracy, as they found that he had been considerably mistaken in the latitude of the south end of Formosa: for this reason they kept a good look-out, and about seven in the evening discovered from the mast-head five small islands, which were judged to be the Bashees, and they had afterwards a sight of Botel Tobago Ximo. By this means they had an opportunity of correcting the position of the Bashee islands, which had been hitherto laid down twenty-five leagues too far to the westward: for by their observations, they esteemed the middle of these islands to be in 21° 4′ north, and to bear from Botel Tobago Ximo S.S.E. twenty leagues distant, that island itself being in 21° 57′ north.

After getting a sight of the Bashee islands, they stood between the S. and S.W. for Cape Espiritu Santo; and, the 20th of May at noon, they first discovered that cape, which about four o'clock they brought to bear S.S.W., about eleven leagues distant. It appeared to be of a moderate height, with several round hummocks on it. As it was known that there were sentinels placed upon this cape to make signals to the Acapulco ship, when she first falls in with the land, the commodore immediately tacked, and ordered the top-gallant sails to be taken in, to prevent being discovered; and, this being the station in which it was resolved to cruise for the galleons, they kept the cape between the south and the west, and endeavoured to confine themselves between the latitude of 12° 50 and 13° 5′, the cape itself lying, by their observations, in 12° 40′ north and in 4° of east longitude from Botel Tobago Ximo.

It was the last of May, by the foreign style, when they arrived off this cape; and, the month of June, by the same style, being that in which the Manila ships are usually expected, the Centurion's people were now waiting each hour with the utmost impatience for the happy crisis which was to balance the account of all their past calamities. As from this time there was but small employment for the crew, the commodore ordered them almost every day to be exercised in the management of the great guns, and in the use of their small arms. This had been his practice, more or less, at all convenient seasons during the whole course of his voyage; and the advantages which he received from it, in his engagement with the galleon, were an ample recompense for all his care and attention. Indeed, it should seem that there are few particulars of a commander's duty of more importance than this, how much soever it may have been sometimes overlooked or misunderstood: for it will, I suppose, be confessed, that in two ships of war, equal in the number of their men and guns, the disproportion of strength, arising from a greater or less dexterity in the use of their great guns and small arms, is what can scarcely be balanced by any other circumstances whatever. For, as these are the weapons with which they are to engage, what greater inequality can there be betwixt two contending parties, than that one side should perfectly understand the use of their weapons, and should have the skill to employ them in the most effectual manner for the annoyance of their enemy, while the other side should, by their awkward management of them, render them rather terrible to themselves, than mischievous to their antagonists? This seems so plain and natural a conclusion, that a person unacquainted with these affairs would suppose the first care of a commander to be the training his people to the use of their arms.

But human affairs are not always conducted by the plain dictates of common sense. There are many other principles which influence our transactions: and there is one in particular, which though of a very erroneous complexion, is scarcely ever excluded from our most serious deliberations; I mean custom, or the practice of those who have preceded us. This is usually a power too mighty for reason to grapple with; and is the most terrible to those who oppose it, as it has much of superstition in its nature, and pursues all those who question its authority with unrelenting vehemence. However, in these later ages of the world, some lucky encroachments have been made upon its prerogative; and it may reasonably be hoped, that the gentlemen of the navy, whose particular profession hath of late been considerably improved by a number of new inventions, will of all others be the readiest to give up those practices which have nothing to plead but prescription, and will not suppose that every branch of their business hath already received all the perfection of which it is capable. Indeed, it must be owned, that if a dexterity in the use of small arms, for instance, hath been sometimes less attended to on board our ships of war, than might have been wished for, it hath been rather owing to unskilful methods of teaching it, than to negligence: for the common sailors, how strongly soever attached to their own prejudices, are very quick-sighted in finding out the defects of others, and have ever shown a great contempt for the formalities practised in the training of land troops to the use of their arms; but when those who have undertaken to instruct the seamen have contented themselves with inculcating only what was useful, and that in the simplest manner, they have constantly found their people sufficiently docile, and the success hath even exceeded their expectation. Thus on board Mr. Anson's ship, where they were only taught the shortest method of loading with cartridges, and were constantly trained to fire at a mark, which was usually hung at the yard-arm, and where some little reward was given to the most expert, the whole crew, by this management, were rendered extremely skilful, quick in loading, all of them good marksmen, and some of them most extraordinary ones; so that I doubt not but, in the use of small arms, they were more than a match for double their number, who had not been habituated to the same kind of exercise. But to return:

It was the last of May, N.S. as hath been already said, when the Centurion arrived off Cape Espiritu Santo; and consequently the next day began the month in which the galleons were to be expected. The commodore therefore made all necessary preparations for receiving them, having hoisted out his long-boat, and lashed her alongside, that the ship might be ready for engaging, if they fell in with the galleons in the night. All this time too he was very solicitous to keep at such a distance from the cape, as not to be discovered; but it hath been since learnt, that notwithstanding his care, he was seen from the land; and advice of him was sent to Manila, where it was at first disbelieved, but on reiterated intelligence (for it seems he was seen more than once) the merchants were alarmed, and the governor was applied to, who undertook (the commerce supplying the necessary sums) to fit out a force consisting of two ships of thirty-two guns, one of twenty guns and two sloops of ten guns, each, to attack the Centurion on her station: and some of these vessels did actually weigh with this view; but the principal ship not being ready, and the monsoon being against them, the commerce and the governor disagreed, and the enterprise was laid aside. This frequent discovery of the Centurion from the shore was somewhat extraordinary; for the pitch of the cape is not high, and she usually kept from ten to fifteen leagues distant; though once indeed, by an indraught of the tide, as was supposed, they found themselves in the morning within seven leagues of the land.

As the month of June advanced, the expectancy and impatience of the commodore's people each day increased. And I think no better idea can be given of their great eagerness on this occasion, than by copying a few paragraphs from the journal of an officer, who was then on board; as it will, I presume, be a more natural picture of the full attachment of their thoughts to the business of their cruise, than can be given by any other means. The paragraphs I have selected, as they occur in order of time, are as follow:

"May 31, Exercising our men at their quarters, in great expectation of meeting with the galleons very soon; this being the eleventh of June their style."

"June 3, Keeping in our stations, and looking out for the galleons."

"June 5, Begin now to be in great expectation, this being the middle of June their style."

"June 11, Begin to grow impatient at not seeing the galleons."

"June 13, The wind having blown fresh easterly for the forty-eight hours past, gives us great expectations of seeing the galleons soon."

"June 15, Cruising on and off, and looking out strictly."

"June 19, This being the last day of June, N.S. the galleons, if they arrive at all, must appear soon."

From these samples it is sufficiently evident, how completely the treasure of the galleons had engrossed their imagination, and how anxiously they passed the latter part of their cruise, when the certainty of the arrival of these vessels was dwindled down to probability only, and that probability became each hour more and more doubtful. However, on the 20th of June O. S., being just a month from their arrival on their station, they were relieved from this state of uncertainty; when, at sun-rise, they discovered a sail from the mast-head, in the S.E. quarter. On this, a general joy spread through the whole ship; for they had no doubt but this was one of the galleons, and they expected soon to see the other. The commodore instantly stood towards her, and at half an hour after seven they were near enough to see her from the Centurion's deck; at which time the galleon fired a gun, and took in her top-gallant sails, which was supposed to be a signal to her consort, to hasten her up; and therefore the Centurion fired a gun to leeward, to amuse her. The commodore was surprised to find, that in all this time the galleon did not change her course, but continued to bear down upon him; for he hardly believed, what afterwards appeared to be the case, that she knew his ship to be the Centurion, and resolved to fight him.

About noon the commodore was little more than a league distant from the galleon, and could fetch her wake, so that she could not now escape; and, no second ship appearing, it was concluded that she had been separated from her consort. Soon after, the galleon hauled up her fore-sail, and brought-to under top-sails, with her head to the northward, hoisting Spanish colours, and having the standard of Spain flying at the top-gallant mast-head. Mr. Anson, in the mean time, had prepared all things for an engagement on board the Centurion, and had taken all possible care, both for the most effectual exertion of his small strength, and for the avoiding the confusion and tumult, too frequent in actions of this kind. He picked out about thirty of his choicest hands and best marksmen, whom he distributed into his tops, and who fully answered his expectation, by the signal services they performed. As he had not hands enough remaining to quarter a sufficient number to each great gun, in the customary manner, he therefore, on his lower tier, fixed only two men to each gun, who were to be solely employed in loading it, whilst the rest of his people were divided into different gangs of ten and twelve men each, which were constantly moving about the decks, to run out and fire such guns as were loaded. By this management he was enabled to make use of all his guns; and, instead of firing broadsides with intervals between them, he kept up a constant fire without intermission, whence he doubted not to procure very signal advantages; for it is common with the Spaniards to fall down upon the decks when they see a broadside preparing, and to continue in that posture till it is given; after which they rise again, and, presuming the danger to be some time over, work their guns, and fire with great briskness, till another broadside is ready: but the firing gun by gun, in the manner directed by the commodore, rendered this practice of theirs impossible.

The Centurion being thus prepared, and nearing the galleon apace, there happened, a little after noon, several squalls of wind and rain, which often obscured the galleon from their sight; but whenever it cleared up, they observed her resolutely lying-to; and, towards one o'clock, the Centurion hoisted her broad pendant and colours, she being then within gun-shot of the enemy. And the commodore observing the Spaniards to have neglected clearing their ship till that time, as he then saw them throwing overboard cattle and lumber, he gave orders to fire upon them with the chasing, to embarrass them in their work, and prevent them from completing it, though his general directions had been not to engage till they were within pistol-shot. The galleon returned the fire with two of her stern-chasers; and the Centurion getting her sprit-sail-yard fore and aft, that if necessary she might be ready for boarding; the Spaniards in a bravado rigged their sprit-sail-yard fore and aft likewise. Soon after, the Centurion came abreast of the enemy within pistol-shot, keeping to the leeward with a view of preventing them from putting before the wind, and gaining the port of Jalapay, from which they were about seven leagues distant. And now the engagement began in earnest, and, for the first half hour, Mr. Anson over-reached the galleon, and lay on her bow; where, by the great wideness of his ports he could traverse almost all his guns upon the enemy, whilst the galleon could only bring a part of hers to bear. Immediately on the commencement of the action, the mats, with which the galleon had stuffed her netting, took fire, and burnt violently, blazing up half as high as the mizen-top. This accident (supposed to be caused by the Centurion's wads) threw the enemy into great confusion, and at the same time alarmed the commodore, for he feared lest the galleon should be burnt, and lest he himself too might suffer by her driving on board him: but the Spaniards at last freed themselves from the fire, by cutting away the netting, and tumbling the whole mass which was in flames, into the sea. But still the Centurion kept her first advantageous position, firing her cannon with great regularity and briskness, whilst at the same time the galleon's decks lay open to her top-men, who, having at their first volley driven the Spaniards from their tops, made prodigious havoc with their small arms, killing or wounding every officer but one that ever appeared on the quarter-deck, and wounding in particular the general of the galleon himself. And though the Centurion, after the first half hour, lost her original situation, and was close alongside the galleon, and the enemy continued to fire briskly for near an hour longer, yet at last the commodore's grape-shot swept their decks so effectually, and the number of their slain and wounded was so considerable, that they began to fall into great disorder, especially as the general, who was the life of the action, was no longer capable of exerting himself. Their embarrassment was visible from on board the commodore. For the ships were so near, that some of the Spanish officers were seen running about with great assiduity, to prevent the desertion of their men from their quarters: but all their endeavours were in vain; for after having, as a last effort, fired five or six guns with more judgment than usual, they gave up the contest; and, the galleon's colours being singed off the ensign-staff in the beginning of the engagement, she struck the standard at her main-top-gallant mast-head, the person who was employed to do it having been in imminent peril of being killed, had not the commodore, who perceived what he was about, given express orders to his people to desist from firing.

Thus was the Centurion possessed of this rich prize, amounting in value to near a million and a half of dollars. She was called the Nostra Signora de Cabadonga, and was commanded by the general Don Jeronimo de Montero, a Portuguese by birth, and the most approved officer for skill and courage of any employed in that service. The galleon was much larger then the Centurion, had five hundred and fifty men and thirty-six guns mounted for action, besides twenty-eight pidreroes in her gunwale, quarters and tops, each of which carried a four-pound ball. She was very well furnished with small-arms, and was particularly provided against boarding, both by her close quarters, and by a strong net-work of two inch rope, which was laced over her waist, and was defended by half pikes. She had sixty-seven killed in the action, and eighty-four wounded, whilst the Centurion had only two killed, and a lieutenant and sixteen wounded, all of whom, but one, recovered: of so little consequence are the most destructive arms in untutored and unpractised hands!

The treasure thus taken by the Centurion having been for at least eighteen months the great object of their hopes, it is impossible to describe the transport on board, when, after all their reiterated disappointments, they at last saw their wishes accomplished. But their joy was near being suddenly damped by a most tremendous incident: for no sooner had the galleon struck, than one of the lieutenants coming to Mr. Anson to congratulate him on his prize, whispered him at the same time, that the Centurion was dangerously on fire near the powder-room. The commodore received this dreadful news without any apparent emotion, and, taking care not to alarm his people, gave the necessary orders for extinguishing it, which was happily done in a short time, though its appearance at first was extremely terrible. It seems some cartridges had been blown up by accident between decks, whereby a quantity of oakum in the afterhatchway, near the after powder-room, was set on fire; and the great smother and smoke of the oakum occasioned the apprehension of a more extended and mischievous fire. At the same instant, too, the galleon fell on board the Centurion on the starboard quarter, but she was cleared without doing or receiving any considerable damage.

The commodore made his first lieutenant, Mr. Saumarez, captain of this prize, appointing her a post-ship in his Majesty's service. Captain Saumarez, before night, sent on board the Centurion all the Spanish prisoners, but such as were thought the most proper to be retained to assist in navigating the galleon. And now the commodore learnt, from some of these prisoners, that the other ship, which he had kept in the port of Acapulco the preceding year, instead of returning in company with the present prize as was expected, had set sail from Acapulco alone much sooner than usual, and had, in all probability, got into the port of Manila long before the Centurion arrived off Espiritu Santo; so that Mr. Anson, notwithstanding his present success, had great reason to regret his loss of time at Macao, which prevented him from taking two rich prizes instead of one.

The commodore, when the action was ended, resolved to make the best of his way with his prize for the river of Canton, being in the mean time fully employed in securing his prisoners, and in removing the treasure from on board the galleon into the Centurion. The last of these operations was too important to be postponed; for as the navigation to Canton was through seas but little known, and where, from the season of the year, much bad weather might be expected, it was of great consequence that the treasure should be sent on board the Centurion, which ship, by the presence of the commander-in-chief, the greater number of her hands, and her other advantages, was doubtless much safer against all the casualties of winds and seas than the galleon: and the securing the prisoners was a matter of still more consequence, as not only the possession of the treasure, but the lives of the captors, depended thereon. This was indeed an article which gave the commodore much trouble and disquietude; for they were above double the number of his own people; and some of them, when they were brought on board the Centurion, and had observed how slenderly she was manned, and the large proportion which the striplings bore to the rest, could not help expressing themselves with great indignation, to be thus beaten by a handful of boys. The method which was taken to hinder them from rising, was by placing all but the officers and the wounded in the hold, where, to give them as much air as possible, two hatchways were left open; but then (to avoid all danger whilst the Centurion's people should be employed upon the deck) there was a square partition of thick planks, made in the shape of a funnel, which enclosed each hatch-way on the lower deck, and reached to that directly over it on the upper deck; these funnels served to communicate the air to the hold better than could have been done without them; and, at the same time, added greatly to the security of the ship; for they being seven or eight feet high, it would have been extremely difficult for the Spaniards to have clambered up; and still to augment that difficulty, four swivel-guns, loaded with musket-bullets, were planted at the mouth of each funnel, and a sentinel with a lighted match constantly attended, prepared to fire into the hold amongst them, in case of any disturbance. Their officers, who amounted to seventeen or eighteen, were all lodged in the first lieutenant's cabin, under a constant guard of six men; and the general, as he was wounded, lay in the commodore's cabin with a sentinel always with him; and they were all informed, that any violence or disturbance would be punished with instant death. And that the Centurion's people might be at all times prepared, if, notwithstanding these regulations, any tumult should arise, the small arms were constantly kept loaded in a proper place, whilst all the men went armed with cutlasses and pistols; and no officer ever pulled off his clothes, and when he slept had always his arms lying ready by him.

These measures were obviously necessary, considering the hazards to which the commodore and his people would have been exposed, had they been less careful. Indeed, the sufferings of the poor prisoners, though impossible to be alleviated, were much to be commiserated; for the weather was extremely hot, the stench of the hold loathsome, beyond all conception, and their allowance of wate but just sufficient to keep them alive, it not being practicable to spare them more than at the rate of a pint a day for each, the crew themselves having only an allowance of a pint and a half. All this considered, it was wonderful that not a man of them died during their long confinement, except three of the wounded, who died the same night they were taken: though it must be confessed, that the greatest part of them were strangely metamorphosed by the heat of the hold; for when they were first taken, they were sightly, robust fellows; but when, after above a month's imprisonment, they were discharged in the river of Canton, they were reduced to mere skeletons; and their air and looks corresponded much more to the conception formed of ghosts and spectres, than to the figure and appearance of real men.

Thus employed in securing the treasure and the prisoners, the commodore, as hath been said, stood for the river of Canton; and, on the 30th of June, at six in the evening, got sight of Cape Delangano, which then bore west ten leagues distant; and the next day he made the Bashee islands, and the wind being so far to the northward, that it was difficult to weather them, it was resolved to stand through between Grafton and Monmouth islands, where the passage seemed to be clear; but in getting through, the sea had a very dangerous aspect, for it rippled and foamed, as if it had been full of breakers, which was still more terrible, as it was then night. But the ships got through very safe (the prize always keeping a-head), and it was found that the appearance which had alarmed them had been occasioned only by a strong tide. I must here observe, that though the Bashee islands are usually reckoned to be no more than five, yet there are many more lying about them to the westward, which, as the channels amongst them are not at all known, makes it advisable for ships rather to pass to the northward or southward, than through them; and indeed the commodore proposed to have gone to the northward, between them and Formosa, had it been possible for him to have weathered them. From hence the Centurion steering the proper course for the river of Canton, she, on the 8th of July, discovered the island of Supata, the westernmost of the Lema islands, being the double-peaked rock, formerly referred to. This island of Supata they made to be a hundred and thirty-nine leagues distant from Grafton's island, and to bear from it north 82° 37′ west: and, on the 11th, having taken on board two Chinese pilots, one for the Centurion, and the other for the prize, they came to an anchor off the city of Macao.

By this time the particulars of the cargo of the galleon were well ascertained, and it was found that she had on board 1,313,843 pieces of eight, and 35,682 oz. of virgin silver, besides some cochineal, and a few other commodities, which, however, were but of small account, in comparison of the specie. And this being the commodore's last prize, it hence appears, that all the treasure taken by the Centurion was not much short of 400,000*l.* independent of the ships and merchandise, which she either burnt or destroyed, and which, by the most reasonable estimation, could not amount to so little as 600,000*l.* more: so that the whole loss of the enemy, by our squadron, did doubtless exceed a million sterling. To which, if there be added the great expense of the court of Spain, in fitting out Pizarro, and in paying the additional charges in America, incurred on our account, together with the loss of their men-of-war, the total of all these articles will be a most exorbitant sum, and is the strongest conviction of the utility of this expedition, which, with all its numerous disadvantages, did yet prove so extremely prejudicial to the enemy. I shall only add, that there were taken on board the galleon several draughts and journals, from some of which many of the particulars recited in the 10th chapter of the second book are collected. Among the rest there was found a chart of all the ocean, between the Philippines and the coast of Mexico, which was what was made use of by the galleon in her own navigation.

CHAPTER IX.

Transactions in the river of Canton.

THE commodore having taken pilots on board, proceeded with his prize for the river of Canton; and, on the 14th of July, came to an anchor short of the Bocca Tigris, which is a narrow passage forming the mouth of that river: this entrance he proposed to stand through the next day, and to run up as far as Tiger Island, which is a very safe road, secured from all winds. But whilst the Centurion and her prize were thus at anchor, a boat with an officer came off from the mandarin, commanding the forts at Bocca Tigris to examine what the ships were, and whence they came. Mr. Anson informed the officer, that his ship was a ship of war, belonging to the king of Great Britain; and that the other in company with him was a prize he had taken; that he was going into Canton river to shelter himself against the hurricanes which were then coming on; and that as soon as the monsoon shifted, he should proceed for England. The officer then desired an account of what men, guns, and ammunition were on board, a list of all which he said was to be sent to the government of Canton. But when these articles were repeated to him, particularly when he was told that there were in the Centurion four hundred firelocks, and between three and four hundred barrels of powder, he shrugged up his shoulders, and seemed to be terrified with the bare recital, saying, that no ships ever came into Canton river armed in that manner; adding, that he durst not set down the whole of this force, lest it should too much alarm the regency. After he had finished his inquiries, and was preparing to depart, he desired to leave two custom-house officers behind him; on which the commodore told him, that though as a man-of-war he was prohibited from trading, and had nothing to do with customs or duties of any kind, yet, for the satisfaction of the Chinese, he would permit two of their people to be left on board, who might themselves be witnesses how punctually he should comply with his instructions. The officer seemed amazed when Mr. Anson mentioned being exempted from all duties, and told him, that the emperor's duty must be paid by all ships that came into his ports: and it is supposed, that on this occasion, private directions were given by him to the Chinese pilot, not to carry the commodore through the Bocca Tigris; which make-it necessary, more particularly, to describe that entrance.

The Bocca Tigris is a narrow passage, little more than musket-shot over, formed by two points of land, on each of which there is a fort, that on the starboard side being a battery on the water's edge, with eighteen embrasures, but where there were no more than twelve iron cannon mounted, seeming to be four or six pounders; the fort on the larboard side is a large castle, resembling those old buildings which here in England we often find distinguished by that name; it is situated on a high rock, and did not appear to be furnished with more than eight or ten cannon, none of which were supposed to exceed six-pounders. These are the defences which secure the river of Canton; and which the Chinese (extremely defective in all military skill) have imagined were sufficient to prevent any enemy from forcing his way through.

But it is obvious, from the description of these forts, that they could have given no obstruction to Mr. Anson's passage, even if they had been well supplied with gunners and stores; and therefore, though the pilot, after the Chinese officer had been on board, refused at first to take charge of the ship, till he had leave from the forts, yet as it was necessary to get through without any delay, for fear of the bad weather which was hourly expected, the commodore weighed on the 15th, and ordered the pilot to carry him by the forts, threatening him that, if the ship ran aground, he would instantly hang him up at the yard-arm. The pilot, awed by these threats, carried the ship through safely the forts not attempting to dispute the passage. Indeed the poor pilot did not escape the resentment of his countrymen, for when he came on shore, he was seized and sent to prison, and was rigorously disciplined with the bamboo. However, he found means to get at Mr. Anson afterwards, to desire of him some recompense for the chastisement he had undergone, and of which he then carried very significant marks about him; and Mr. Anson, in commiseration of his sufferings, gave him such a sum of money, as would at any time have enticed a Chinese to have undergone a dozen bastinadings.

Nor was the pilot the only person that suffered on this occasion; for the commodore soon after seeing some royal junks pass by him from Bocca Tigris towards Canton, he learnt, on inquiry, that the mandarin commanding the forts was a prisoner on board them; that he was already turned out, and was now carrying to Canton, where it was expected he would be severely punished for having permitted the ships to pass; and the commodore urging the unreasonableness of this procedure, from the inability of the forts to have done otherwise, explaining to the Chinese the great superiority his ships would have had over the forts, by the number and size of their guns, the Chinese seemed to acquiesce in his reasoning, and allowed that their forts could not have stopped him; but they still asserted, that the mandarin would infallibly suffer, for not having done, what all his judges were convinced, was impossible. To such indefensible absurdities are those obliged to submit, who think themselves concerned to support their authority, when the necessary force is wanting. But to return:

On the 16th of July the commodore sent his second lieutenant to Canton, with a letter to the viceroy, informing him of the reason of the Centurion's putting into that port; and that the commodore himself soon proposed to repair to Canton, to pay a visit to the viceroy. The lieutenant was very civilly received, and was promised that an answer should be sent to the commodore the next day. In the mean time Mr. Anson gave leave to several of the officers of the galleon to go to Canton, they engaging their parole to return in two days. When these prisoners got to Canton, the regency sent for them, and examined them, inquiring particularly by what means they had fallen into Mr. Anson's power. And on this occasion the prisoners were honest enough to declare, that as the kings of Great Britain and of Spain were at war, they had proposed to themselves the taking of the Centurion, and had bore down upon her with that view, but that the event had been contrary to their hopes: however, they acknowledged that they had been treated by the commodore, much better than they believed they should have treated him, had he fallen into their hands. This confession from an enemy had great weight with the Chinese, who, till then, though they had revered the commodore's power, had yet suspected his morals, and had considered him rather as a lawless freebooter, than as one commissioned by the state for the revenge of public injuries. But they now changed their opinion, and regarded him as a more important person; to which perhaps the vast treasure of his prize might not a little contribute; the acquisition of wealth being a matter greatly adapted to the estimation and reverence of the Chinese nation.

In this examination of the Spanish prisoners, though the Chinese had no reason in the main to doubt of the account which was given them, yet there were two circumstances which appeared to them so singular, as to deserve a more ample explanation; one of them was the great disproportion of men between the Centurion and the galleon; the other was the humanity, with which the people of the galleon were treated after they were taken. The mandarins therefore asked the Spaniards, how they came to be overpowered by so inferior a force; and how it happened, since the two nations were at war, that they were not put to death when they came into the hands of the English. To the first of these inquiries the Spaniards replied, that though they had more hands than the Centurion, yet she being intended solely for war, she had a great superiority in the size of her guns, and in many other articles, over the galleon, which was a vessel fitted out principally for traffic: and as to the second question, they told the Chinese, that amongst the nations of Europe, it was not customary to put to death those who submitted; though they readily owned, that the commodore, from the natural bias of his temper, had treated both them and their countrymen, who had formerly been in his power, with very unusual courtesy, much beyond what they could have expected, or than was required by the customs established between nations at war with each other. These replies fully satisfied the Chinese, and at the same time wrought very powerfully in the commodore's favour.

On the 20th of July, in the morning, three

mandarins, with a great number of boats, and a vast retinue, came on board the Centurion, and delivered to the commodore the viceroy of Canton's order for a daily supply of provisions, and for pilots to carry the ships up the river as far as the second bar; and at th same time they delivered him a message from t e viceroy, in answer to the letter sen t to Cant. a. The substance of the message was, that the viceroy desired to be excused from receiving the commodore's visit, during the then excessive hot weather; because the assembling the mandarins and soldiers, necessary to that ceremony, would prove extremely inconvenient and fatiguing; but that in September, when the weather would be more temperate, he should be glad to see both the commodore himself, and the English captain of the other ship that was with him. As Mr. Anson knew that an express had been despatched to the court at Pekin, with an account of the Centurion and her prize being arrived in the river of Canton, he had no doubt but the principal motive for putting off this visit was, that the regency at Canton might gain time to receive the emperor's instructions, about their behaviour in this unusual affair.

When the mandarins had delivered their message, they began to talk to the commodore about the duties to be paid by his ships; but he immediately told them, that he would never submit to any demand of that kind; that as he neither brought any merchandise thither, nor intended to carry any away, he could not be reasonably deemed to be within the meaning of the emperor's orders, which were doubtless calculated for trading vessels only; adding, that no duties were ever demanded of men-of-war, by nations accustomed to their reception, and that his master's orders expressly forbade him from paying any acknowledgment for his ships anchoring in any port whatever.

The mandarins being thus cut short on the subject of the duty, they said they had another matter to mention, which was the only remaining one they had in charge; this was a request to the commodore, that he would release the prisoners he had taken on board the galleon; for that the viceroy of Canton apprehended the emperor, his master, might be displeased, if he should be informed, that persons, who were his allies, and carried on a great commerce with his subjects, were under confinement in his dominions. Mr. Anson was himself extremely desirous to get rid of the Spaniards, having, on his first arrival, sent about a hundred of them to Macao, and those who remained, which were near four hundred more, were on many accounts, a great incumbrance to him. However, to inhance the favour, he at first raised some difficulties; but permitting himself to be prevailed on, he at last told the mandarins, that to show his readiness to oblige the viceroy, he would release the prisoners, whenever they, the Chinese, would send boats to fetch them off. This matter being thus adjusted, the mandarins departed; and, on the 28th of July, two Chinese junks were sent from Canton, to take on board the prisoners, and to carry them to Macao. And the commodore, agreeably to his promise, dismissed them all, and ordered his purser to send with them eight days' provision for their subsistence, during their sailing down the river; this being despatched, the Centurion and her prize came to her moorings, about the second bar, where they proposed to continue till the monsoon shifted.

Though the ships, in consequence of the viceroy's permit, found no difficulty in purchasing provisions for their daily consumption, yet it was impossible for the commodore to proceed to England, without laying in a large quantity both of provisions and stores for his use, during the voyage: the procuring this supply was attended with much embarrassment; for there were people at Canton who had undertaken to furnish him with biscuit, and whatever else he wanted; and his linguist, towards the middle of September, had assured him, from day to day, that all was ready, and would be sent on board him immediately. But a fortnight being elapsed, and nothing being brought, the commodore sent to Canton to inquire more particularly into the reasons of this disappointment: and he had soon the vexation to be informed, that the whole was an illusion; that no order had been procured from the viceroy, to furnish him with his sea-stores, as had been pretended; that there was no biscuit baked, nor any one of the articles in readiness, which had been promised him; nor did it appear, that the contractors had taken the least step to comply with their agreement. This was most disagreeable news, and made it suspected, that the furnishing the Centurion for her return to Great Britain might prove a more troublesome matter than had been hitherto imagined; especially, too, as the month of September was nearly elapsed, without Mr. Anson's having received any message from the viceroy of Canton.

And here perhaps it might be expected that some satisfactory account should be given of the motives of the Chinese for this faithless procedure. But as I have already, in a former chapter, made some kind of conjectures about a similar event, I shall not repeat them again in this place, but shall observe, that after all, it may perhaps be impossible for a European, ignorant of the customs and manners of that nation, to be fully apprised of the real incitements to this behaviour. Indeed, thus much may undoubtedly be asserted, that in artifice, falsehood, and an attachment to all kinds of lucre, many of the Chinese are difficult to be paralleled by any other people; but then the combination of these talents, and the manner in which they are applied in particular emergencies, are often beyond the reach of a foreigner's penetration; so that though it may be safely concluded, that the Chinese had some interest in thus amusing the commodore, yet it may not be easy to assign the individual views by which they were influenced. And that I may not be thought too severe in ascribing to this nation a fraudulent and selfish turn of temper, so contradictory to the character given of them in the legendary accounts of the Roman missionaries, I shall here mention an extraordinary transaction or two, which I hope will be some kind of confirmation of what I have advanced.

When the commodore lay first at Macao, one of his officers, who had been extremely ill, desired leave of him to go on shore every day on a neighbouring island, imagining that a walk upon the land would contribute greatly to the restoring of his health: the commodore would have dissuaded him, suspecting the tricks of the Chinese, but the officer continuing importunate, in the end the boat was ordered to carry him. The first day he was put on shore he took his exercise, and returned without receiving any molestation, or even seeing any of the inhabitants; but the second day, he was assaulted, soon after his arrival, by a great number of Chinese who had been hoeing rice in the neighbourhood, and who beat him so violently with the handles of their hoes, that they soon laid him on the ground incapable of resistance; after which they robbed him, taking from him his sword, the hilt of which was silver, his money, his watch, gold-headed cane, snuff-box, sleeve-buttons and hat, with several other trinkets: in the mean time the boat's crew, who were at some little distance, and had no arms of any kind with them, were incapable of giving him any assistance; till at last one of them flew on the fellow who had the sword in his possession, and wresting it out of his hands drew it, and with it was preparing to fall on the Chinese, some of whom he could not have failed of killing; but the officer, perceiving what he was about, immediately ordered him to desist, thinking it more prudent to submit to the present violence, than to embroil his commodore in an inextricable squabble with the Chinese government, by the death of their subjects; which calmness in this gentleman was the more meritorious, as he was known to be a person of an uncommon spirit, and of a somewhat hasty temper: by this means the Chinese recovered the possession of the sword, which they soon perceived was prohibited to be made use of against them, and carried off their whole booty unmolested. No sooner were they gone, than a Chinese on horseback, very well dressed, and who had the air and appearance of a gentleman, came down to the shore, and, as far as could be understood by his signs, seemed to censure the conduct of his countrymen, and to commiserate the officer, being wonderfully officious to assist in getting him on board the boat: but notwithstanding this behaviour, it was shrewdly suspected that he was an accomplice in the theft, and time fully evinced the justice of those suspicions.

When the boat returned on board, and reported what had passed to the commodore, he immediately complained of it to the mandarin, who attended to see his ship supplied; but the mandarin coolly replied, that the boat ought not to have gone on shore, promising, however, that if the thieves could be found out, they should be punished; though it appeared plain enough, by his manner of answering, that he would never give himself any trouble in searching them out. However, a considerable time afterwards, when some Chinese boats were selling provisions to the Centurion, the person who had wrested the sword from the Chinese came with great eagerness to the commodore, to assure him that one of the principal thieves was then in a provision-boat along-side the ship; and the officer, who had been robbed, viewing the fellow on this report, and well remembering his face, orders were immediately given to seize him; and he was accordingly secured on board the ship, where strange discoveries were now made.

This thief, on his being first apprehended, expressed so much fright in his countenance, that it was feared he would have died upon the spot; the mandarin too, who attended the ship, had visibly no small share of concern on the occasion. Indeed he had reason enough to be alarmed, since it was soon evinced that he had been privy to the whole robbery; for the commodore declaring that he would not deliver up the thief, but would himself order him to be shot, the mandarin immediately put off the magisterial air, with which he had at first pretended to demand him, and begged his release in the most abject manner: and the commodore appearing inflexible, there came on board, in less than two hours' time, five or six of the neighbouring mandarins, who all joined in the same intreaty, and, with a view of facilitating their suit, offered a large sum of money for the fellow's liberty. Whilst they were thus soliciting, it was discovered that the mandarin who was the most active amongst them, and who seemed to be most interested in the event, was the very gentleman who came to the officer, just after the robbery, and who pretended to be so much displeased with the villany of his countrymen. And, on further inquiry it was found that he was the mandarin of the island; and that he had, by the authority of his office, ordered the peasants to commit that infamous action. And it seemed, as far as could be collected from the broken hints which were casually thrown out, that he and his brethren, who were all privy to the transaction, were terrified with the fear of being called before the tribunal at Canton, where the first article of their punishment would be the stripping them of all they were worth; though their judges (however fond of inflicting a chastisement so lucrative to themselves) were perhaps of as tainted a complexion as the delinquents. Mr. Anson was not displeased to have caught the Chinese in this dilemma; and he entertained himself for some time with their perplexity, rejecting their money with scorn, appearing inexorable to their prayers, and giving out that the thief should certainly be shot; but as he then foresaw that he should be forced to take shelter in their ports a second time, when the influence he might hereby acquire over the magistrates would be of great service to him, he at length permitted himself to be persuaded, and as a favour released his prisoner, but not till the mandarin had collected and returned all that had been stolen from the officer, even to the minutest trifle.

But notwithstanding this instance of the good intelligence between the magistrates and criminals, the strong addiction of the Chinese to lucre often prompts them to break through this awful confederacy, and puts them on defrauding the authority that protects them of its proper quota of the pillage. For not long after the above-mentioned transaction (the former mandarin, attendant on the ship, being, in the meantime, relieved by another), the commodore lost a topmast from his stern, which, after the most diligent inquiry, could not be traced: and as it was not his own, but had been borrowed at Macao to heave down by, and was not to be replaced in that part of the world, he was extremely desirous to recover it, and published a considerable reward to any who would bring it him again. There were suspicions from the first of its being stolen, which made him conclude a reward was the likeliest method of getting it back: accordingly, soon after, the mandarin told

I

him that some of his, the mandarin's, people had found the topmast, desiring the commodore to send his boats to fetch it, which being done, the mandarin's people received the promised reward; but the commodore told the mandarin that he would make him a present besides for the care he had taken in directing it to be searched for; and accordingly Mr. Anson gave a sum of money to his linguist, to be delivered to the mandarin; but the linguist knowing that the people had been paid, and ignorant that a further present had been promised, kept the money himself: however, the mandarin fully confiding in Mr. Anson's word, and suspecting the linguist, he took occasion, one morning, to admire the size of the Centurion's masts, and thence, on a pretended sudden recollection, he made a digression to the topmast which had been lost, and asked Mr. Anson if he had not got it again. Mr. Anson presently perceived the bent of this conversation, and inquired of him if he had not received the money from the linguist, and finding he had not, he offered to pay it him upon the spot. But this the mandarin refused, having now somewhat more in view than the sum which had been detained: for the next day the linguist was seized, and was doubtless mulcted of all he had gotten in the commodore's service, which was supposed to be little less than two thousand dollars; he was besides so severely bastinadoed with the bamboo, that it was with difficulty he escaped with his life; and when he was upbraided by the commodore (to whom he afterwards came begging) with his folly, in risking all he had suffered for fifty dollars, (the present intended for the mandarin) he had no other excuse to make than the strong bias of his nation to dishonesty; replying, in his broken jargon, "*Chinese man very great rogue truly, but have fashion, no can help.*"

It were endless to recount all the artifices, extortions, and frauds which were practised on the commodore and his people, by this interested race. The method of buying all things in China being by weight, the tricks made use of by the Chinese to increase the weight of the provision they sold to the Centurion, were almost incredible. One time a large quantity of fowls and ducks being bought for the ship's use, the greatest part of them presently died. This alarmed the people on board with the apprehension that they had been killed by poison; but on examination it appeared that it was only owing to their being crammed with stones and gravel to increase their weight, the quantity thus forced into most of the ducks being found to amount to ten ounces in each. The hogs too, which were bought ready killed of the Chinese butchers, had water injected into them for the same purpose; so that a carcass, hung up all night for the water to drain from it, has lost above a stone of its weight; and when, to avoid this cheat, the hogs were bought alive, it was found that the Chinese gave them salt to increase their thirst, and having by this means excited them to drink great quantities of water, they then took measures to prevent them from discharging it again by urine, and sold the tortured animals in this inflated state. When the commodore first put to sea from Macao, they practised an artifice of another kind; for as the Chinese never object to the eating of any food that dies of itself, they took care, by some secret practices, that great part of his live sea-store should die in a short time after it was put on board, hoping to make a second profit of the dead carcases which they expected would be thrown overboard; and two-thirds of the hogs dying before the Centurion was out of sight of land, many of the Chinese boats followed her only to pick up the carrion. These instances may serve as a specimen of the manners of this celebrated nation, which is often recommended to the rest of the world as a pattern of all kinds of laudable qualities. But to return:

The commodore, towards the end of September, having found out (as has been said) that those who had contracted to supply him with sea-provisions and stores had deceived him, and that the viceroy had not sent to him according to his promise, he saw it would be impossible for him to surmount the embarrassment he was under without going himself to Canton, and visiting the viceroy; and therefore, on the 27th of September, he sent a message to the mandarin who attended the Centurion, to inform him that he, the commodore, intended, on the first of October, to proceed in his boat to Canton; adding, that the day after he got there, he should notify his arrival to the viceroy, and should desire him to fix a time for his audience; to which the mandarin returned no other answer, than that he would acquaint the viceroy with the commodore's intentions. In the meantime all things were prepared for this expedition; and the boat's crew in particular, which Mr. Anson proposed to take with him, were clothed in a uniform dress, resembling that of the watermen on the Thames; they were in number eighteen and a coxswain; they had scarlet jackets and blue silk waistcoats, the whole trimmed with silver buttons, and with silver badges on their jackets and caps. As it was apprehended, and even asserted, that the payment of the customary duties for the Centurion and her prize, would be demanded by the regency of Canton, and would be insisted on previous to the granting a permission for victualling the ship for her future voyage; the commodore, who was resolved never to establish so dishonourable a precedent, took all possible precaution to prevent the Chinese from facilitating the success of their unreasonable pretensions by having him in their power at Canton: and therefore, for the security of his ship, and the great treasure on board her, he appointed his first lieutenant, Mr. Brett, to be captain of the Centurion under him, giving him proper instructions for his conduct; directing him, particularly, if he, the commodore, should be detained at Canton on account of the duties in dispute, to take out the men from the Centurion's prize, and to destroy her; and then to proceed down the river through the Bocca Tigris, with the Centurion alone, and to remain without that entrance till he received further orders from Mr. Anson.

These necessary steps being taken, which were not unknown to the Chinese, it should seem as if their deliberations were in some sort embarrassed thereby. It is reasonable to imagine that they were in general very desirous of getting the duties to be paid them; not perhaps solely in consideration of the amount of those dues, but to keep up their reputation for address and subtlety, and to avoid the imputation of receding from claims on which they had already so frequently insisted. However, as they now foresaw that they had no other method of succeeding than by violence, and that even against this the commodore was prepared, they were at last disposed, I conceive, to let the affair drop, rather than entangle themselves in a hostile measure, which they found would only expose them to the risk of having the whole navigation of their port destroyed, without any certain prospect of gaining their favourite point thereby.

However, though there is reason to imagine that these were their thoughts at that time, yet they could not depart at once from the evasive conduct to which they had hitherto adhered. For when the commodore, on the morning of the first of October, was preparing to set out for Canton, his linguist came to him from the mandarin who attended his ship, to tell him that a letter had been received from the viceroy of Canton, desiring the commodore to put off his going thither for two or three days: but in the afternoon of the same day another linguist came on board, who, with much seeming fright, told Mr. Anson that the viceroy had expected him up that day, that the council was assembled, and the troops had been under arms to receive him; and that the viceroy was highly offended at the disappointment, and had sent the commodore's linguist to prison chained, supposing that the whole had been owing to the linguist's negligence. This plausible tale gave the commodore great concern, and made him apprehend that there was some treachery designed him, which he could not yet fathom; and though it afterwards appeared that the whole was a fiction, not one article of it having the least foundation, yet (for reasons best known to themselves) this falsehood was so well supported by the artifices of the Chinese merchants at Canton, that, three days afterwards, the commodore received a letter signed by all the supercargoes of the English ships then at that place, expressing their great uneasiness at what had happened, and intimating their fears that some insult would be offered to his boat if he came thither before the viceroy was fully satisfied about the mistake. To this letter Mr. Anson replied, that he did not believe there had been any mistake; but was persuaded it was a forgery of the Chinese to prevent his visiting the viceroy; that therefore he would certainly come up to Canton on the 13th of October, confident that the Chinese would not dare to offer him an insult, as well knowing it would be properly returned.

On the 13th of October, the commodore continuing firm to his resolution, all the supercargoes of the English, Danish, and Swedish ships came on board the Centurion, to accompany him to Canton, for which place he set out in his barge the same day, attended by his own boats, and by those of the trading ships, which on this occasion came to form his retinue; and he was passed by Wampo, where the European vessels lay, he was saluted by all of them but the French, and in the evening he arrived safely at Canton. His reception at that city, and the most material transactions from henceforward, till his arrival in Great Britain, shall be the subject of the ensuing chapter.

CHAPTER X.

Proceedings at the city of Canton, and the return of the Centurion to England.

WHEN the commodore arrived at Canton he was visited by the principal Chinese merchants, who affected to appear very much pleased that he had met with no obstruction in getting thither, and who thence pretended to conclude, that the viceroy was satisfied about the former mistake, the reality of which they still insisted on; they added, that as soon as the viceroy should be informed that Mr. Anson was at Canton, (which they promised should be done the next morning) they were persuaded a day would be immediately appointed for the visit, which was the principal business that had brought the commodore thither.

The next day the merchants returned to Mr. Anson, and told him, that the viceroy was then so fully employed in preparing his despatches for Pekin, that there was no getting admittance to him for some days; but that they had engaged one of the officers of his court to give them information, as soon as he should be at leisure, when they proposed to notify Mr. Anson's arrival, and to endeavour to fix the day of audience. The commodore by this time too well acquainted with their artifices, not to perceive that this was a falsehood; and had he consulted only his own judgment, he would have applied directly to the viceroy by other hands: but the Chinese merchants had so far prepossessed the supercargoes of our ships with chimerical fears, that they (the supercargoes) were extremely apprehensive of being embroiled with the government, and of suffering in their interest, if those measures were taken, which appeared to Mr. Anson at that time to be the most prudential: and therefore, lest the malice and double-dealing of the Chinese might have given rise to some sinister incident, which would be afterwards laid at his door, he resolved to continue passive, as long as it should appear that he lost no time, by thus suspending his own opinion. With this view, he promised not to take any immediate step himself for getting admittance to the viceroy, provided the Chinese, with whom he contracted for provisions, would let him see that his bread was baked, his meat salted, and his stores prepared with the utmost despatch; but if by the time when all was in readiness to be shipped off, (which it was supposed would be in about forty days) the merchants should not have procured the viceroy's permission, then the commodore proposed to apply for it himself. These were the terms Mr. Anson thought proper to offer, to quiet the uneasiness of the supercargoes; and notwithstanding the apparent equity of the conditions, many difficulties and objections were urged; nor would the Chinese agree to them, till the commodore had consented to pay for every article he bespoke before it was put in hand. However, at last the contract being passed, it was some satisfaction to the commodore to be certain that his preparations were now going on, and being himself on the spot, he took care to hasten them as much as possible.

During this interval, in which the stores and provisions were getting ready, the merchants continually entertained Mr. Anson with accounts of their various endeavours to get a license from the viceroy, and their frequent disappointments; which to him was now a matter of amusement, as he was fully satisfied there was not one word of truth in any thing they said. But when all was completed, and wanted only to be shipped, which was about the 24th of November, at which time too the N.E. monsoon was set in, he then resolved to apply himself to the viceroy to demand an audience, as he was persuaded that, without this ceremony, the procuring a permission to send his stores on board would meet with great difficulty. On the 24th of November, therefore, Mr. Anson sent one of his officers to the mandarin, who commanded the guard of the principal gate of the city of Canton, with a letter directed to the viceroy. When this letter was delivered to the mandarin, he received the officer who brought it very civilly, and took down the contents of it in Chinese, and promised that the viceroy should be immediately acquainted with it; but told the officer, it was not necessary for him to wait for an answer, because a message would be sent to the commodore himself.

On this occasion Mr. Anson had been under great difficulties about a proper interpreter to send with his officer, as he was well aware that none of the Chinese, usually employed as linguists, could be relied on: but he at last prevailed with Mr. Flint, an English gentleman belonging to the factory, who spoke Chinese perfectly well, to accompany his officer. This person, who upon this occasion and many others was of singular service to the commodore, had been left at Canton when a youth, by the late Captain Rigby. The leaving him there to learn the Chinese language was a step taken from his own persuasion of the great advantages which the East India Company might one day receive from an English interpreter; and though the utility of this measure has greatly exceeded all that was expected from it, yet I have not heard that it has been to this day imitated: but we imprudently choose (except in this single instance) to carry on the vast transactions of the port of Canton, either by the ridiculous jargon of broken English which some few of the Chinese have learnt, or by the suspected interpretation of the linguists of other nations.

Two days after the sending the above-mentioned letter, a fire broke out in the suburbs of Canton. On the first alarm, Mr. Anson went thither with his officers, and his boat's crew, to assist the Chinese. When he came there, he found that it had begun in a sailor's shed, and that by the slightness of the buildings, and the awkwardness of the Chinese, it was getting head apace: but he perceived, that by pulling down some of the adjacent sheds it might easily be extinguished; and particularly observing that it was running along a wooden cornice, which would soon communicate it to a great distance, he ordered his people to begin with tearing away that cornice; this was presently attempted, and would have been soon executed; but, in the mean time, he was told, that, as there was no mandarin there to direct what was to be done, the Chinese would make him, the commodore, answerable for whatever should be pulled down by his orders. On this his people desisted; and he sent them to the English factory, to assist in securing the Company's treasure and effects, as it was easy to foresee that no distance was a protection against the rage of such a fire, where so little was done to put a stop to it; for all this time the Chinese contented themselves with viewing it, and now and then holding one of their idols near it, which they seemed to expect should check its progress: however, at last, a mandarin came out of the city, attended by four or five hundred firemen: these made some feeble efforts to pull down the neighbouring houses; but by this time the fire had greatly extended itself, and was got amongst the merchants' warehouses; and the Chinese firemen, wanting both skill and spirit, were incapable of checking its violence; so that its fury increased upon them, and it was feared the whole city would be destroyed. In this general confusion the viceroy himself came thither, and the commodore was sent to, and was entreated to afford his assistance, being told that he might take any measures he should think most prudent in the present emergency. And now he went thither a second time, carrying with him about forty of his people; who, upon this occasion, exerted themselves in such a manner, as in that country was altogether without example: for they were rather animated than deterred by the flames and falling buildings amongst which they wrought; so that it was not uncommon to see the most forward of them tumble to the ground on the roofs, and amidst the ruins of houses, which their own efforts brought down with them. By their boldness and activity the fire was soon extinguished, to the amazement of the Chinese; and the buildings being all on one floor, and the materials slight, the seamen, notwithstanding their daring behaviour, happily escaped with no other injuries than some considerable bruises.

The fire, though at last thus luckily extinguished, did great mischief during the time it continued; for it consumed a hundred shops and eleven streets full of warehouses, so that the damage amounted to an immense sum; and one of the Chinese merchants, well known to the English, whose name was Succoy, was supposed, for his own share, to have lost near two hundred thousand pounds sterling. It raged indeed with unusual violence, for in many of the warehouses there were large quantities of camphor which greatly added to its fury, and produced a column of exceeding white flame, which shot up into the air to such a prodigious height, that the flame itself was plainly seen on board the "enturion, though she was thirty miles distant.

Whilst the commodore and his people were labouring at the fire, and the terror of its becoming general still possessed the whole city, several of the most considerable Chinese merchants came to Mr. Anson, to desire that he would let each of them have one of his soldiers (for such they styled his boat's crew from the uniformity of their dress) to guard their warehouses and dwelling-houses, which, from the known dishonesty of the populace, they feared would be pillaged in the tumult. Mr. Anson granted them this request; and all the men that he thus furnished to the Chinese behaved greatly to the satisfaction of their employers, who afterwards highly applauded their great diligence and fidelity.

By this means, the resolution of the English at

the fire and their trustiness, and punctuality elsewhere, was the general subject of conversation amongst the Chinese: and the next morning, many of the principal inhabitants waited on the commodore to thank him for his assistance; frankly owning to him, that they could never have extinguished the fire themselves, and that he had saved their city from being totally consumed. And soon after a message came to the commodore from the viceroy, appointing the 30th of November for his audience; which sudden resolution of the viceroy, in a matter that had been so long agitated in vain, was also owing to the signal services performed by Mr. Anson and his people at the fire, of which the viceroy himself had been in some measure an eye-witness.

The fixing this business of the audience was, on all accounts, a circumstance which Mr. Anson was much pleased with; as he was satisfied that the Chinese government would not have determined this point, without having agreed among themselves to give up their pretensions to the duties they claimed, and to grant him all he could reasonably ask; for as they well knew the commodore's sentiments, it would have been a piece of imprudence, not consistent with the refined cunning of the Chinese, to have admitted him to an audience, only to have contested with him. And therefore, being himself perfectly easy about the result of his visit, he made all necessary preparations against the day; and engaged Mr. Flint, whom I have mentioned before, to act, as interpreter in the conference; who, in this affair, as in all others, acquitted himself much to the commodore's satisfaction; repeating with great boldness, and doubtless with exactness, all that was given in charge, a part which no Chinese linguist would ever have performed with any tolerable fidelity.

At ten o'clock in the morning, on the day appointed, a mandarin came to the commodore, to let him know that the viceroy was ready to receive him; on which the commodore and his retinue immediately set out: and as soon as he entered the outer gate of the city, he found a guard of two hundred soldiers drawn up ready to attend him; these conducted him to the great parade before the emperor's palace, where the viceroy then resided. In this parade, a body of troops, to the number of ten thousand, were drawn up under arms, and made a very fine appearance, being all of them new clothed for this ceremony: and Mr. Anson and his retinue having passed through the middle of them, he was then conducted to the great hall of audience, where he found the viceroy seated under a rich canopy in the emperor's chair of state, with all his council of mandarins attending: here there was a vacant seat prepared for the commodore, in which he was placed on his arrival: he was ranked the third in order from the viceroy, there being above him only the head of the law, and of the treasury, who in the Chinese government take place of all military officers. When the commodore was seated, he addressed himself to the viceroy by his interpreter, and began with reciting the various methods he had formerly taken to get an audience; adding, that he had imputed the delays he had met with to the insincerity of those he had employed, and that he had therefore no other means left, than to send, as he had done, his own officer with a letter to the gate. On the mention of this the viceroy stopped the interpreter, and bade him assure Mr. Anson, that the first knowledge they had of his being at Canton was from that letter. Mr. Anson then proceeded, and told him, that the subjects of the king of Great Britain trading to China had complained to him, the commodore, of the vexatious impositions both of the merchants and inferior custom-house officers, to which they were frequently necessitated to submit, by reason of the difficulty of getting access to the mandarins, who alone could grant them redress: that it was his (Mr. Anson's) duty, as an officer of the king of Great Britain, to lay before the viceroy these grievances of the British subjects, which he hoped the viceroy would take into consideration, and would give orders, that for the future there should be no just reason for complaint. Here Mr. Anson paused, and waited some time in expectation of an answer; but nothing being said, he asked his interpreter, if he was certain the viceroy understood what he had urged; the interpreter told him he was certain it was understood, but he believed no reply would be made to it. Mr. Anson then represented to the viceroy the case of the ship Hastingfield, which, having been dismasted on the coast of China, had arrived in the river of Canton but a few days before. The people on board this vessel had been great sufferers by the fire; the captain in particular had all his goods burnt, and had lost besides, in the confusion, a chest of treasure of four thousand five hundred tahel, which was supposed to be stolen by the Chinese boat men. Mr. Anson therefore desired that the captain might have the assistance of the government, as it was apprehended the money could never be recovered without the interposition of the mandarins. And to this request the viceroy made answer, that in settling the emperor's customs for that ship, some abatement should be made in consideration of her losses.

And now the commodore having despatched the business with which the officers of the East-India Company had entrusted him, he entered on his own affairs; acquainting the viceroy, that the proper season was now set in for returning to Europe, and that he waited only for a license to ship off his provisions and stores, which were all ready; and that as soon as this should be granted him, and he should have gotten his necessaries on board, he intended to leave the river of Canton, and to make the best of his way for England. The viceroy replied to this that the license should be immediately issued, and that everything should be ordered on board the following day. And finding that Mr. Anson had nothing farther to insist on, the viceroy continued the conversation for some time, acknowledging in very civil terms how much the Chinese were obliged to him for his signal services at the fire, and owning that he had saved the city from being destroyed: and then observing that the Centurion had been a good while on their coast, he closed his discourse, by wishing the commodore a good voyage to Europe. After which, the commodore, thanking him for his civility and assistance, took his leave.[1]

[1] The following is Anson's own account of these proceedings:—" Finding I could not obtain the provisions and stores to enable me to proceed to Europe, I was under the necessity of visiting the Vice King, notwithstanding the

As soon as the commodore was out of the hall of audience, he was much pressed to go into a neighbouring apartment, where there was an entertainment provided; but finding, on inquiry, that the viceroy himself was not to be present, he declined the invitation, and departed, attended in the same manner as at his arrival; only at his leaving the city he was saluted by three guns, which are as many as in that country are ever fired on any ceremony. Thus the commodore, to his great joy, at last finished this troublesome affair, which, for the preceding four months, had given him great disquietude. Indeed he was highly pleased with procuring a license for the shipping of his stores and provisions; for thereby he was enabled to return to Great Britain with the first of the monsoon, and to prevent all intelligence of his being expected: but this, though a very important point, was not the circumstance which gave him the greatest satisfaction; for he was more particularly attentive to the authentic precedent established on this occasion, by which his majesty's ships of war are for the future exempted from all demands of duty in any of the ports of China.

In pursuance of the promises of the viceroy, the provisions were begun to be sent on board the day after the audience; and, four days after, the commodore embarked at Canton for the Centurion; and, on the 7th of December, the Centurion and her prize unmoored, and stood down the river, passing through the Bocca Tigris on the 10th. And on this occasion I must observe, that the Chinese had taken care to man the two forts, on each side of that passage, with as many men as they could well contain, the greatest part of them armed with pikes and match-lock muskets. These garrisons affected to show themselves as much as possible to the ships, and were doubtless intended to induce Mr. Anson to think more reverently than he had hitherto done of the Chinese military power: for this purpose they were equipped with much parade, having a great number of colours exposed to view; and on the castle in particular there were laid considerable heaps of large stones; and a soldier of unusual size, dressed in very sightly armour, stalked about on the parapet with a battle-axe in his hand, endeavouring to put on as important and martial an air as possible, though some of the observers on board the Centurion shrewdly suspected, from the appearance of his armour, that instead of steel, it was composed only of a particular kind of glittering paper.

The Centurion and her prize being now without the river of Canton, and consequently upon the point of leaving the Chinese jurisdiction, I beg leave, before I quit all mention of the Chinese affairs, to subjoin a few remarks on the disposition and genius of that extraordinary people. And though it may be supposed, that observations made at Canton only, a place situated in the corner of the empire, are very imperfect materials on which to found any general conclusions, yet as those who have had opportunities of examining the inner parts of the country, have been evidently influenced by very ridiculous prepossessions, and as the transactions of Mr. Anson with the regency of Canton were of an uncommon nature, in which many circumstances occurred, different perhaps from any which have happened before, I hope the following reflections, many of them drawn from these incidents, will not be altogether unacceptable to the reader.

That the Chinese are a very ingenious and industrious people is sufficiently evinced from the great number of curious manufactures which are established amongst them, and which are eagerly sought for by the most distant nations; but though skill in the handicraft arts seems to be the most important qualification of this people, yet their talents therein are but of a second-rate kind; for they are much outdone by the Japanese in those manufactures which are common to both countries; and they are in numerous instances incapable of rivalling the mechanic dexterity of the Europeans. Indeed, their principal excellence seems to be imitation; and they accordingly labour under that poverty of genius which constantly attends all servile imitators. This is most conspicuous in works which require great truth and accuracy, as in clocks, watches, fire-arms, &c., for in all these, though they can copy the different parts, and can form some resemblance of the whole, yet they never could arrive at such a justness in their fabric as was necessary to produce the desired effect. And if we pass from their manufactures to artists of a superior class, as painters, statuaries, &c., in these matters they seem to be still more defective; their painters, though very numerous and in great esteem, rarely succeeding in the drawing or colouring of human figures, or in the grouping of large compositions; and though in flowers and birds their performances are much more admired, yet even in these some part of the merit is rather to be imputed to the native brightness and excellency of the colours, than to the skill of the painter; since it is very unusual to see the light and shade justly and naturally handled, or to find that ease and grace in the drawing which are to be met with in the works of European artists. In short, there is a stiffness and minuteness in most of the Chinese productions, which are extremely displeasing: and it may perhaps be asserted with great truth, that these defects in their arts are entirely owing to the peculiar turn of the people,

---

Europeans were of opinion that the Emperor's duties would be insisted upon, and that my refusing to pay them would embarrass the trade of the East India Company; not knowing what means they might make use of, when they had me in their power, I gave orders to Captain Brett, whom upon this occasion I had appointed captain under me, that, if he found me detained, he should destroy the galleon (out of which I had removed all the treasure, amounting to one million three hundred and thirteen thousand eight hundred and forty-three pieces of eight, and thirty-five thousand six hundred and eighty-two ounces of virgin silver and plate) and proceed with the Centurion without the river's mouth, out of gun-shot of the two forts.

"Contrary to the general opinion of the Europeans, the Vice-King received me with great civility and politeness, having ten thousand soldiers drawn up, and his council of Mandarins attending the audience, and granted me every thing I desired. I had great reason to be satisfied with the success of my visit, having obtained the principal point I had in view, which was establishing a precedent upon record that the Emperor's duties and measurage had not been demanded from me, by which means His Majesty's ships will be under no difficulties in entering into any of the Emperor of China's ports for the future."—*Anson's official report.*

amongst whom nothing great or spirited is to be met with.

If we next examine the Chinese literature, (taking our accounts from the writers who have endeavoured to represent it in the most favourable light) we shall find that on this head their obstinacy and absurdity are most wonderful: for though, for many ages, they have been surrounded by nations to whom the use of letters was familiar, yet they, the Chinese alone, have hitherto neglected to avail themselves of that almost divine invention, and have continued to adhere to the rude and inartificial method of representing words by arbitrary marks; a method which necessarily renders the number of their characters too great for human memory to manage, makes writing to be an art that requires prodigious application, and in which no man can be otherwise than partially skilled; whilst all reading, and understanding of what is written, is attended with infinite obscurity and confusion; for the connexion between these marks, and the words they represent, cannot be retained in books, but must be delivered down from age to age by oral tradition: and how uncertain this must prove in such a complicated subject, is sufficiently obvious to those who have attended to the variation which all verbal relations undergo when they are transmitted through three or four hands only. Hence it is easy to conclude that the history and inventions of past ages, recorded by these perplexed symbols, must frequently prove unintelligible; and consequently the learning and boasted antiquity of the nation must, in numerous instances, be extremely problematical.

But we are told by some of the missionaries, that though the skill of the Chinese in science is indeed much inferior to that of the Europeans, yet the morality and justice taught and practised by them are most exemplary. And from the description given by some of these good fathers, one should be induced to believe that the whole empire was a well-governed affectionate family, where the only contests were, who should exert the most humanity and beneficence: but our preceding relation of the behaviour of the magistrates, merchants and tradesmen at Canton sufficiently refutes these jesuitical fictions. And as to their theories of morality, if we may judge from the specimens exhibited in the works of the missionaries, we shall find them solely employed in recommending ridiculous attachments to certain immaterial points, instead of discussing the proper criterion of human actions, and regulating the general conduct of mankind to one another on reasonable and equitable principles. Indeed, the only pretension of the Chinese to a more refined morality than their neighbours, is founded, not on their integrity or beneficence, but solely on the affected evenness of their demeanour, and their constant attention to suppress all symptoms of passion and violence. But it must be considered, that hypocrisy and fraud are often not less mischievous to the general interests of mankind than impetuosity and vehemence of temper: since these, though usually liable to the imputation of imprudence, do not exclude sincerity, benevolence, resolution, nor many other laudable qualities. And perhaps, if this matter were examined to the bottom, it would appear that the calm and patient turn of the Chinese, on which they so much value themselves, and which distinguishes the nation from all others, is in reality the source of the most exceptionable part of their character; for it has been often observed, by those who have attended to the nature of mankind, that it is difficult to curb the more robust and violent passions, without augmenting at the same time the force of the selfish ones: so that the timidity, dissimulation, and dishonesty of the Chinese may, in some sort, be owing to the composure, and external decency, so universally prevailing in that empire.

Thus much for the general disposition of the people: but I cannot dismiss this subject without adding a few words about the Chinese government, that too having been the subject of boundless panegyric. And on this head I must observe, that the favourable accounts often given of their prudent regulations for the administration of their domestic affairs, are sufficiently confuted by their transactions with Mr. Anson: for we have seen that their magistrates are corrupt, their people thievish, and their tribunals crafty and venal. Nor is the constitution of the empire, or the general orders of the state, less liable to exception: since that form of government which does not in the first place provide for the security of the public against the enterprises of foreign powers, is certainly a most defective institution: and yet this populous, this rich and extensive country, so pompously celebrated for its refined wisdom and policy, was conquered about an age since by a handful of Tartars; and even now, by the cowardice of the inhabitants, and the want of proper military regulations, it continues exposed not only to the attempts of any potent state, but to the ravages of every petty invader. Nor is the state provided with ships of considerable force to protect them: for at Canton, where doubtless their principal naval power is stationed, we saw no more than four men-of-war junks, of about three hundred tons burthen, and mounted only with eight or ten guns, the largest of which did not exceed a four-pounder. This may suffice to give an idea of the defenceless state of the Chinese empire. But it is time to return to the commodore, whom I left with his two ships without the Bocca Tigris; and who, on the 12th of December, anchored before the town of Macao.

Whilst the ships lay here, the merchants of Macao finished their agreement for the galleon, for which they had offered 6000 dollars; this was much short of her value, but the impatience of the commodore to get to sea, to which the merchants were no strangers, prompted them to insist on so unequal a bargain. Mr. Anson had learnt enough from the English at Canton to conjecture, that the war betwixt Great Britain and Spain was still continued; and that probably the French might engage in the assistance of Spain, before he could arrive in Great Britain; and therefore, knowing that no intelligence could get to Europe of the prize he had taken, and the treasure he had on board, till the return of the merchantmen from Canton, he was resolved to make all possible expedition in getting back, that he might be himself the first messenger of his own good fortune, and might thereby prevent the enemy from forming any projects to intercept him: for these reasons, he, to avoid all delay, accepted of the sum offered for the galleon; and she being delivered to the merchants, the 15th of December 1743, the

Centurion, the same day, got under sail, on her return to England. And, on the 3rd of January, she came to an anchor at Prince's Island in the Straits of Sunda, and continued there wooding and watering till the 8th; when she weighed and stood for the Cape of Good Hope, where, on the 11th of March, she anchored in Table-bay.

The Cape of Good Hope is situated in a temperate climate, where the excesses of heat and cold are rarely known; and the Dutch inhabitants, who are numerous, and who here retain their native industry, have stocked it with prodigious plenty of all sort of fruits and provisions; most of which either from the equality of the seasons, or the peculiarity of the soil, are more delicious in their kind than can be met with elsewhere: so that by these, and by the excellent water which abounds there, this settlement is the best provided of any in the known world, for the refreshment of seamen after long voyages. Here the commodore continued till the beginning of April, highly delighted with the place, which by its extraordinary accommodations, the healthiness of its air, and the picturesque appearance of the country, all enlivened by the addition of a civilised colony, was not disgraced in an imaginary comparison with the valleys of Juan Fernandes, and the lawns of Tinian. During his stay he entered about forty new men; and having, by the 3rd of April 1744, completed his water and provision, he, on that day, weighed and put to sea; and, the 19th of the same month, they saw the island of St. Helena, which however they did not touch at, but stood on their way; and, on the 10th of June, being then in soundings, they spoke with an English ship from Amsterdam bound for Philadelphia, whence they received the first intelligence of a French war; the twelfth, they got sight of the Lizard; and the fifteenth, in the evening, to their infinite joy, they came safe to an anchor at Spithead. But that the signal perils which had so often threatened them, in the preceding part of the enterprise, might pursue them to the very last, Mr. Anson learnt, on his arrival, that there was a French fleet of considerable force cruising in the chops of the Channel; which, by the account of their position, he found the Centurion had run through, and had been all the time concealed by a fog. Thus was this expedition finished, when it had lasted three years and nine months; after having, by its event, strongly evinced this important truth, that though prudence, intrepidity, and perseverance united, are not exempted from the blows of adverse fortune; yet in a long series of transactions, they usually rise superior to its power, and in the end rarely fail of proving successful.[1]

[1] " This remark (observes Sir John Barrow) is certainly just; and no parallel is to be found, in the history of navigation, to the Voyage of Anson, unless it be that of Sir Francis Drake, which comes nearest to it, and in some respects is perhaps still more extraordinary. He left England with five ships, his own, the Hind, of 100 tons, the second 80 the third 30, a fly-boat 50, and a pinnace of 15 tons. He lost, or broke up, or left behind him, all but his own: plundered the Spaniards on the western coast, proceded nearly to 50° N. to look for a north-east passage into the Atlantic, crossed the Pacific, proceeded round the Cape of Good Hope, and after an absence of two years and ten months, reached England with only his own ship and about 50 men out of 160."

One of the survivors of Anson's voyage, a seaman named George Gregory, died so late as 1804, at Kingston, at the great age of 109, having never known a day's illness since he went to sea in 1714.

PART II.

STEPHENS' TRAVELS

IN GREECE, TURKEY, RUSSIA AND POLAND.

CONTENTS.

CHAPTER I.
A Hurricane.—An Adventure.—Missolonghi.—Siege of Missolonghi.—Byron.—Marco Bozzaris.—Visit to the Widow, Daughters, and Brother of Bozzaris 133

CHAPTER II.
Choice of a Servant.—A Turn out.—An Evening Chat.—Scenery of the Road.—Lepanto.—A projected Visit.—Change of Purpose.—Padras.—Vostitza.—Variety and Magnificence of Scenery . . . 137

CHAPTER III.
Quarrel with the Landlord.—Ægina.—Sicyon.—Corinth.—A distinguished Reception.—Desolation of Corinth.—The Acropolis.—View from the Acropolis.—Lechæum and Cenchreæ.—Kaka Scala.—Arrival at Athens 141

CHAPTER IV.
American Missionary School.—Visit to the School.—Mr. Hill and the Male Department.—Mrs. Hill and the Female Department.—Maid of Athens.—Letter from Mr. Hill.—Revival of Athens.—Citizens of the World 145

CHAPTER V.
Ruins of Athens.—Hill of Mars.—Temple of the Winds.—Lantern of Demosthenes.—Arch of Adrian.—Temple of Jupiter Olympus.—Temple of Theseus.—The Acropolis.—The Parthenon.—Pentelican Mountain.—Mount Hymettus.—The Piræus.—Greek Fleas.—Napoli 148

CHAPTER VI.
Argos.—Parting and Farewell.—Tomb of Agamemnon.—Mycenæ.—Gate of the Lions.—A Misfortune.—Meeting in the Mountains.—A Landlord's Troubles.—A Midnight Quarrel.—One good Turn deserves another.—Gratitude of a Greek Family.—Megara.—The Soldier's Revel 155

CHAPTER VII.
A Dreary Funeral.—Marathon.—Mount Pentelicus.—A Mystery.—Woes of a Lover.—Reveries of Glory.—Scio's Rocky Isle.—A blood-stained Page of History.—A Greek Prelate.—Desolation.—The Exile's Return 160

CHAPTER VIII.
A Noble Grecian Lady.—Beauty of Scio.—An Original.—Foggi.—A Turkish Coffee-house.—Mussulman at Prayers.—Easter Sunday.—A Greek Priest.—A Tartar Guide.—Turkish Ladies.—Camel Scenes.—Sight of a Harem.—Disappointed Hopes.—A rare Concert.—Arrival at Smyrna 168

CHAPTER IX.
First Sight of Smyrna.—Unveiled Women.—Ruins of Ephesus.—Ruin, all Ruin.—Temple of Diana.—Encounter with a Wolf.—Love at first Sight.—Gatherings on the Road 175

CHAPTER X.
Position of Smyrna.—Consular Privileges.—The Case of the Lover.—End of the Love Affair.—The Missionary's Wife.—The Casino.—Only a Greek Row.—Rambles in Smyrna.—The Armenians.—Domestic Enjoyments 179

CHAPTER XI.
An American Original.—Moral Changes in Turkey.—Wonders of Steam Navigation.—The March of Mind.—Classic Localities.—Sestos and Abydos.—Seeds of Pestilence 183

CHAPTER XII.
Mr. Churchill.—Commodore Porter.—Castle of the Seven Towers.—The Sultan's Naval Architect.—Launch of the Great Ship.—Sultan Mahmoud.—Jubilate.—A National Grievance.—Visit to a Mosque.—The Burial-grounds 187

CHAPTER XIII.
Visit to the Slave-market.—Horrors of Slavery.—Departure from Stamboul.—The stormy Euxine.—Odessa.—The Lazaretto.—Russian Civility.—Returning Good for Evil 191

CHAPTER XIV.
The Guardiano.—One too many.—An excess of Kindness.—The last Day of Quarantine.—Mr. Baguet.—Rise of Odessa.—City-making.—Count Woronzow.—A Gentleman Farmer.—An American Russian . . 196

CONTENTS.

CHAPTER XV.
Choice of a Conveyance.—Hiring a Servant.—Another American.—Beginning of Troubles.—A Bivouac.—Russian Jews.—The Steppes of Russia.—A *Traveller's* Story.—Approach to Chioff.—How to get rid of a Servant.—History of Chioff 200

CHAPTER XVI.
A lucky encounter.—Church of the Catacombs.—A Visit to the Saints.—A tender Parting.—Pilgrims.—Rough Treatment.—A Scene of Starvation.—Russian Serfs.—Devotion of the Serfs.—Approach to Moscow 206

CHAPTER XVII.
Moscow.—A severe Operation.—An Exile by Accident.—Meeting with an Emigré.—A civil Stranger.—A Spy.—The Kremlin.—Sepulchres of the Czars.—The great Bell.—The great Gun.—Precious Relics . . 210

CHAPTER XVIII.
The Drosky.—Salle des Nobles.—Russian Gaming.—Gastronomy.—Pedroski.—A Sunday in Moscow.—A Gipsy Belle.—Tea-drinking.—The Emperor's Garden.—Retrospective 216

CHAPTER XIX.
Getting a Passport.—Parting with the Marquis.—The Language of Signs.—A loquacious Traveller.—From Moscow to St. Petersburgh.—The Wolga.—Novogorod.—Newski Perspective.—An unfortunate Mistake.—Northern Twilight 220

CHAPTER XX.
Police Requisites.—The Russian Capital.—Equestrian Statue of Peter the Great.—The Alexandrian Column.—Architectural Wonders.—The Summer Islands.—A perilous Achievement.—Origin of St. Petersburgh.—Tombs of dead Monarchs.—Origin of the Russian Navy 224

CHAPTER XXI.
A new Friend.—The Winter Palace.—Importance of a Hat.—An artificial Mine.—Remains of a huge Monster.—Peter the Great's Workshop.—The Greek Religion.—Tomb of a Hero.—A Saint Militant.—Another Love Affair.—The Hermitage.—The Winter and Summer Gardens . . . 229

CHAPTER XXII.
An Imperial Fête.—Nicolas of Russia.—Varied Splendours.—A Soliloquy.—House of Peter the Great.—A Boat Race.—Czarskoselo.—The Amber Chamber.—Catharine II.—The Emperor Alexander . . 235

CHAPTER XXIII.
The Soldier's Reward.—Review of the Russian Army.—American Cannibals.—Palace of Potemkin.—Palace of the Grand-duke Michael.—Equipments for Travelling.—Rough Riding.—Poland.—Vitepsk.—Napoleon in Poland.—The Disastrous Retreat.—Passage of the Berezina . . . 238

CHAPTER XXIV.
Travel by Night.—A Rencounter.—A Traveller's Message.—Lithuania.—Poverty of the Country.—Agricultural Implements.—Minsk.—Polish Jews.—A Coin of Freedom.—Riding in a Basket.—Brezc.—The Bug.—A searching Operation.—Women Labourers.—Warsaw 245

CHAPTER XXV.
Warsaw.—A Polish Doctor.—Battle of Grokow.—The Outbreak.—The fatal Issue.—Present Condition of Poland.—Polish Exiles.—Aspect of Warsaw.—Traits of the Poles . . . 250

CHAPTER XXVI.
Religion of Poland.—Sunday in Warsaw.—Baptized Jews.—Palaces of the Polish Kings.—Sobieski.—Field of Vola.—Wreck of a Warrior.—The Poles in America.—A Polish Lady.—Troubles of a Passport.—Departure from Warsaw.—An official Rachel.—A mysterious Visiter 254

CHAPTER XXVII.
Friendly Solicitude.—Raddom.—Symptoms of a Difficulty.—A Court of Inquisition.—Showing a proper Spirit.—Troubles thickening.—Approaching the Climax.—Woman's Influence.—The Finale.—Utility of the Classics.—Another Latinist.—A lucky Accident.—Arrival at Cracow . . 259

CHAPTER XXVIII.
Cracow.—Casimir the Great.—Kosciusko.—Tombs of the Polish Kings.—A Polish Heroine.—Last Words of a King.—A Hero in Decay.—The Salt-mines of Cracow.—The Descent.—The Mines.—Underground Meditations.—The Farewell 265

INCIDENTS OF TRAVEL

IN

GREECE, TURKEY, RUSSIA, AND POLAND.

CHAPTER I.

A Hurricane.—An Adventure.—Missolonghi.—Siege of Missolonghi. — Byron. — Marco Bozzaris. — Visit to the Widow, Daughters, and Brother of Bozzaris.

On the evening of the — February, 1835, by a bright starlight, after a short ramble among the Ionian Islands, I sailed from Zante, in a beautiful cutter of about forty tons, for Padras. My companions were Doctor W., an old and valued friend from New York, who was going to Greece merely to visit the Episcopal missionary school at Athens, and a young Scotchman, who had travelled with me through Italy, and was going farther, like myself, he knew not exactly why. There was hardly a breath of air when we left the harbour, but a breath was enough to fill our little sail. The wind, though of the gentlest, was fair; and as we crawled from under the lee of the island, in a short time it became a fine sailing breeze. We sat on the deck till a late hour, and turned in with every prospect of being at Padras in the morning. Before daylight, however, the wind chopped about, and set in dead a-head, and when I went on deck in the morning it was blowing a hurricane. We had passed the point of Padras; the wind was driving down the Gulf of Corinth, as if old Æolus had determined on thwarting our purpose; and our little cutter, dancing like a gull upon the angry waters, was driven into the harbour of Missolonghi.

The town was full in sight, but at such a distance, and the waves were running so high, that we could not reach it with our small boat. A long flat extends several miles into the sea, making the harbour completely inaccessible, except to small Greek caiques, built expressly for such navigation. We remained on board all day; and the next morning, the gale still continuing, made signals to a fishing-boat to come off and take us ashore. In a short time she came alongside; we bade farewell to our captain—an Italian, and a noble fellow, cradled and as he said born to die on the Adriatic—and in a few moments struck the soil of fallen but immortal Greece.

Our manner of striking it, however, was not such as to call forth any of the warm emotions struggling in the breast of the scholar, for we were literally stuck in the mud. We were yet four or five miles from the shore, and the water was so low that the fishing-boat, with the additional weight of four men and luggage, could not swim clear. Our boatmen were two long, sinewy Greeks, with the red tarbouch, embroidered jacket, sash, and large trousers, and with their long poles set us through the water with prodigious force; but, as soon as the boat struck, they jumped out, and, putting their brawny shoulders under her sides, heaved her through into better water, and then resumed their poles. In this way they propelled her two or three miles, working alternately with their poles and shoulders, until they got her into a channel, when they hoisted the sail, laid directly for the harbour, and drove upon the beach with canvass all flying.

During the late Greek revolution, Missolonghi was the great debarking-place of European adventurers; and, probably, among all the desperadoes who ever landed there, none were more destitute, and in better condition to "go a-head" than I; for I had all that I was worth on my back. At one of the Ionian Islands I had lost my carpet-bag, containing my note-book, and every article of wearing apparel except the suit in which I stood. Every condition, however, has its advantages; mine put me above porters and custom-house officers; and while my companions were busy with these plagues of travellers, I paced, with great satisfaction, the shore of Greece, though I am obliged to confess that this satisfaction was for reasons utterly disconnected with any recollections of her ancient glories. Business before pleasure: one of our first inquiries was for a breakfast. Perhaps, if we had seen a monument, or solitary column, or ruin of any kind, it would have inspired us to better things; but there was nothing, absolutely nothing, that could recall an image of the past. Besides, we did not expect to land at Missolonghi, and were not bound to be inspired at a place into which we were thrown by accident; and more than all, a drizzling rain was penetrating to our very bones; we were wet and cold, and what can men do in the way of sentiment when their teeth are chattering!

The town stands upon a flat, marshy plain, which extends several miles along the shore. The whole was a mass of new-made ruins —of houses demolished and black with smoke—the tokens of savage and desolating war. In front, and running directly along the shore, was a long street of miserable one-story shantees, run up since the destruction of the old town, and so near the shore that sometimes it is washed by the sea, and at the time of our landing it was wet and muddy from the rain. It was a cheerless place, and reminded me of Communipaw, in bad weather. It had no connexion with the ancient glory of Greece, no name or place on her historic page, and no hotel where we could get a breakfast; but one of the officers of the customs conducted us to a shantee filled with Bavarian soldiers drinking. There was a sort of second story, accessible only by a ladder; and one end of this was partitioned off with boards, but had neither bench, table, nor any other article of housekeeping. We had been on and almost in the water since daylight, exposed to a keen wind and drizzling rain, and now, at eleven o'clock, could probably have eaten several chickens a-piece; but nothing came amiss, and, as we could not get chickens, we took eggs, which for lack of any vessel to boil them in, were roasted. We placed a huge loaf of bread on the middle of the floor, and seated ourselves around it, spreading out so as to keep the eggs from rolling away, and each hewing off bread for himself. Fortunately, the Greeks have learnt from their quondam Turkish masters the art of making coffee, and a cup of this Eastern cordial kept our dry bread from choking us.

When we came out again, the aspect of matters was more cheerful; the long street was swarming with Greeks, many of them armed with pistols and yataghan, but miserably poor in appearance, and in such numbers that not half of them could find the shelter of a roof at night. We were accosted by one dressed in a hat and frock-coat, and, who, in occasional visits to Corfu and Trieste, had picked up some Italian and French, and a suit of European clothes, and was rather looked up to by his untravelled countrymen. As a man of the world who had received civilities abroad, he seemed to consider it incumbent upon him to reciprocate at home, and, with the tacit consent of all around, he undertook to do the honours of Missolonghi.

If, as a Greek, he had any national pride about him, he was imposing upon himself a severe task; for all that he could do was to conduct us among ruins, and as he went along, tell us the story of the bloody siege which had reduced the place to its present woeful state. For more than a year, under unparalleled hardships, its brave garrison resisted the combined strength of the Turkish and Egyptian armies, and when all hope was gone, resolved to cut their way through the enemy or die in the attempt. Many of the aged and sick, the wounded and the women, refused to join in the sortie and preferred to shut themselves up in an old mill, with the desperate purpose of resisting until they should bring around them a large crowd of Turks, when they would blow all up together. An old invalid soldier seated himself in a mine under the Bastion Bozzaris (the ruins of which we saw), the mine being charged with thirty kegs of gunpowder; the last sacrament was administered by the bishop and priests to the whole population, and, at a signal, the besieged made their desperate sortie. One body dashed through the Turkish ranks, and, with many women and children, gained the mountains; but the rest were driven back. Many of the women ran to the sea and plunged in with their children; husbands stabbed their wives with their own hands to save them from the Turks, and the old soldier under the bastion set fire to the train, and the remnant of the heroic garrison buried themselves under the ruins of Missolonghi.

Among them were thirteen foreigners, of whom only one escaped. One of the most distinguished was Meyer, a young Swiss, who entered as a volunteer at the beginning of the revolution, became attached to a beautiful Missolonghiote girl, married her, and, when the final sortie was made, his wife being sick he remained with her, and was blown up with the others. A letter written a few days before his death, and brought away by one who escaped in the sortie, records the condition of the garrison.

"A wound which I have received in my shoulder, while I am in daily expectation of one which will be my passport to eternity, has prevented me till now from bidding you a last adieu. We are reduced to feed upon the most disgusting animals. We are suffering horribly from hunger and thirst. Sickness adds much to the calamities which overwhelm us. Seventeen hundred and forty of our brothers are dead; more than a hundred thousand bombs and balls, thrown by the enemy, have destroyed our bastions and our homes. We have been terribly distressed by the cold, for we have suffered great want of food. Notwithstanding so many privations, it is a great and noble spectacle to behold the ardour and devotedness of the garrison. A few days more, and these brave men will be angelic spirits, who will accuse before God the indifference of Christendom. In the name of all our brave men, among whom are Notho Bozzaris, * * * I announce to you the resolution sworn to, before Heaven, to defend, foot by foot, the land of Missolonghi, and to bury ourselves, without listening to any capitulation, under the ruins of this city. We are drawing near our final hour. History will render us justice. I am proud to think that the blood of a Swiss, of a child of William Tell, is about to mingle with that of the heroes of Greece."

But Missolonghi is a subject of still greater interest than this, for the reader will remember it as the place where Byron died. Almost the first questions I asked were about the poet, and it added to the dreary interest which the place inspired, to listen to the manner in which the Greeks spoke of him. It might be thought that here, on the spot where he breathed his last, malignity would have held her accursed tongue; but it was not so. He had committed the fault, unpardonable in the eyes of political opponents, of attaching himself to one of the great parties that then divided Greece; and though he had given her all that man could give, in his own dying words, "his time, his means, his health, and, lastly, his life," the Greeks spoke of him with all the rancour and bitterness of party spirit. Even death had not won oblivion for his political offences; and I heard those that saw him die in her cause affirm that Byron was no friend to Greece.

His body, the reader will remember, was transported to England and interred in the family sepulchre. The church where it lay in state is a heap of ruins, and there is no stone or monument recording his death; but wishing to see some memorial connected with his residence here, we followed our guide to the house in which he died. It was a large square building of stone; one of the walls still standing, black with smoke, the rest a confused and shapeless mass of ruins. After his death it was converted into a hospital and magazine; and, when the Turks entered the city, they set fire to the powder; the sick and dying were blown into the air, and we saw the ruins lying as they fell after the explosion. It was a melancholy spectacle, but it seemed to have a sort of moral fitness with the life and fortunes of the poet. It was as if the same wild destiny, the same wreck of hopes and fortunes that attended him through life, were hovering over his grave. Living and dead, his actions and his character have been the subject of obloquy and reproach, perhaps justly; but it would have softened the heart of his bitterest enemy to see the place in which he died.

It was in this house that, on his last birthday, he came from his bedroom and produced to his friends the last notes of his dying muse, breathing a spirit of sad foreboding and melancholy recollections; of devotion to the noble cause in which he had embarked, and a prophetic consciousness of his approaching end.

" My days are in the yellow leaf,
 The flowers and fruits of love are gone;
The worm, the canker, and the grief
 Are mine alone.
* * * * * *
" If thou regret'st thy youth, *why live?*
 The land of honourable death
Is here: up to the field, and give
 Away thy breath!
" Seek out—less often sought than found—
 A soldier's grave, for thee the best;
Then look around, and choose thy ground,
 And take thy rest."

Moving on beyond the range of ruined houses, though still within the line of crumbling walls, we came to a spot perhaps as interesting as any that Greece in her best days could show. It was the tomb of Marco Bozzaris! no monumental marble emblazoned his deeds and fame; a few round stones piled over his head, which but for our guide, we should have passed without noticing, were all that marked his grave. I would not disturb a proper reverence for the past: time covers with its dim and twilight glories both distant scenes and the men who acted in them; but, to my mind, Miltiades was not more of a hero at Marathon, or Leonidas at Thermopylæ, than Marco Bozzaris at Missolonghi. When they went out against the hosts of Persia, Athens and Sparta were great and free, and they had the prospect of *glory* and the praise of men, to the Greeks always dearer than life. But when the Suliote chief drew his sword, his country lay bleeding at the feet of a giant, and all Europe condemned the Greek revolution as foolhardy and desperate. For two months, with but a few hundred men, protected only by a ditch and slight parapet of earth, he defended the town where his body now rests against the whole Egyptian army. In stormy weather, living upon bad and unwholesome bread, with no covering but his cloak, he passed his days and nights in constant vigil; in every assault his sword cut down the foremost assailant, and his voice rising above the din of battle, struck terror into the hearts of the enemy. In the struggle which ended with his life, with two thousand men he proposed to attack the whole army of Mustapha Pacha, and called upon all who were willing to die for their country to stand forward. The whole band advanced to a man. Unwilling to sacrifice so many brave men in a death-struggle, he chose three hundred, the sacred number of the Spartan band, his tried and trusty Suliotes. At midnight he placed himself at their head, directing that not a shot should be fired till he sounded his bugle; and his last command was, "If you lose sight of me, seek me in the pacha's tent." In the moment of victory he ordered the pacha to be seized, and received a ball in the loins; his voice still rose above the din of battle, cheering his men until he was struck by another ball in the head, and borne dead from the field of his glory.

Not far from the grave of Bozzaris was a pyramid of sculls, of men who had fallen in the last attack upon the city, piled up near the blackened and battered wall which they had died in defending. In my after wanderings I learned to look more carelessly upon these things; and, perhaps, noticing everywhere the light estimation put upon human life in the East, learned to think more lightly of it myself; but, then, it was melancholy to see bleaching in the sun, under the eyes of their countrymen, the unburied bones of men who, but a little while ago, stood with swords in their hands, and animated by the noble resolution to free their country or die in the attempt. Our guide told us that they had all been collected in that place with a view to sepulture; and that King Otho, as soon as he became of age and took the government in his own hands, intended to erect a monument over them. In the meantime, they are at the mercy of every passing traveller, and the only remark that our guide made was a comment upon the force and unerring precision of the blow of the Turkish sabre, almost every scull being laid open on the side nearly down to the ear.

But the most interesting part of our day at Missolonghi was to come. Returning from a ramble round the walls, we noticed a large square house, which, our guide told us, was the residence of Constantine, the brother of Marco Bozzaris. We were all interested in this intelligence, and our interest was in no small degree increased when he added that the widow and two of the children of the Suliote chief were living with his brother. The house was surrounded by a high stone wall, a large gate stood most invitingly wide open, and we turned toward it in the hope of catching a glimpse of the inhabitants; but, before we reached the gate, our interest had increased to such a point that, after consulting with our guide, we requested him to say that, if it would not be considered an intrusion, three travellers, two of them Americans, would feel honoured in being permitted to pay their respects to the widow and children of Marco Bozzaris.

We were invited in, and shown into a large

room on the right, where three Greeks were sitting cross-legged on a divan, smoking the long Turkish chibouk. Soon after the brother entered, a man about fifty, of middling height, spare-built, and wearing a Bavarian uniform, as holding a colonel's commission in the service of King Otho. In the dress of the dashing Suliote he would have better looked the brother of Marco Bozzaris, and I might then more easily have recognised the daring warrior who, on the field of battle, in a moment of extremity, was deemed, by universal acclamation, worthy of succeeding the fallen hero. Now the straight military frock-coat, buttoned tight across the breast, the stock, tight pantaloons, boots and straps, seemed to repress the free energies of the mountain warrior; and I could not but think how awkward it must be for one who had spent all his life in a dress which hardly touched him, at fifty to put on a stock, and straps to his boots. Our guide introduced us, with an apology for our intrusion. The colonel received us with great kindness, thanked us for the honour done his brother's widow, and requesting us to be seated, ordered coffee and pipes.

And here, on the very first day of our arrival in Greece, and from a source which made us proud, we had the first evidence of what afterward met me at every step, the warm feeling existing in Greece toward America; for almost the first thing that the brother of Marco Bozzaris said was to express his gratitude, as a Greek, for the services rendered his country by our own; and, after referring to the provisions sent out for his famishing countrymen, his eyes sparkled and his cheek flushed as he told us that, when the Greek revolutionary flag first sailed into the port of Napoli di Romania, among hundreds of vessels of all nations, an American captain was the first to recognise and salute it.

In a few moments the widow of Marco Bozzaris entered. I have often been disappointed in my preconceived notions of personal appearance, but it was not so with the lady who now stood before me; she looked the widow of a hero; as one of her Grecian mothers, who gave their hair for bowstrings, their girdle for a sword-belt, and, while their heart-strings were cracking, sent their young lovers from their arms to fight and perish for their country. Perhaps it was she that led Marco Bozzaris into the path of immortality; that roused him from the wild guerilla warfare in which he had passed his early life, and fired him with the high and holy ambition of freeing his country. Of one thing I am certain, no man could look in her face without finding his wavering purposes fixed, without treading more firmly in the path of high and honourable enterprise. She was under forty, tall and stately in person, and habited in deep black, fit emblem of her widowed condition, with a white handkerchief laid flat over her head, giving the Madonna cast to her dark eyes and marble complexion. We all rose as she entered the room: and though living secluded, and seldom seeing the face of a stranger, she received our compliments and returned them with far less embarrassment than we both felt and exhibited.

But our embarrassment, at least I speak for myself, was induced by an unexpected circumstance. Much as I was interested in her appearance, I was not insensible to the fact that she was accompanied by two young and beautiful girls, who were introduced to us as her daughters. This somewhat bewildered me. While waiting for their appearance, and talking with Constantine Bozzaris, I had in some way conceived the idea that the daughters were mere children, and had fully made up my mind to take them both on my knee and kiss them; but the appearance of the stately mother recalled me to the grave of Bozzaris; and the daughters would probably have thought that I was taking liberties upon so short an acquaintance if I had followed up my benevolent purpose in regard to them; so that, with the long pipe in my hand, which, at that time, I did not know how to manage well, I cannot flatter myself that I exhibited any of the benefit of continental travel.

The elder was about sixteen, and even in the opinion of my friend Doctor W., a cool judge in these matters, a beautiful girl, possessing in its fullest extent all the elements of Grecian beauty: a dark, clear complexion, dark hair, set off by a little red cap embroidered with gold thread, and a long blue tassel hanging down behind, and large black eyes, expressing a melancholy quiet, but which might be excited to shoot forth glances of fire more terrible than her father's sword. Happily, too, for us, she talked French, having learned it from a French marquis who had served in Greece and been domesticated with them; but young and modest, and unused to the company of strangers, she felt the embarrassment common to young ladies when attempting to speak a foreign language. And we could not talk to her on common themes. Our lips were sealed, of course, upon the subject which had brought us to her house. We could not sound for her the praises of her gallant father. At parting, however, I told them that the name of Marco Bozzaris was as familiar in America as that of a hero of our own revolution, and that it had been hallowed by the inspiration of an American poet; and I added that, if it would not be unacceptable, on my return to my native country I would send the tribute referred to, as an evidence of the feeling existing in America toward the memory of Marco Bozzaris. My offer was gratefully accepted; and afterward, while in the act of mounting my horse to leave Missolonghi, our guide, who had remained behind, came to me with a message from the widow and daughters reminding me of my promise.

I do not see that there is any objection to my mentioning that I wrote to a friend, requesting him to procure Halleck's "Marco Bozzaris," and send it to my banker at Paris. My friend, thinking to enhance its value, applied to Mr. Halleck for a copy in his own handwriting. Mr. Halleck, with his characteristic modesty, evaded the application; and on my return home I told him the story of my visit, and reiterated the same request. He evaded me as he had done my friend, but promised me a copy of the new edition of his poems, which he afterward gave me, and which, I hope, is now in the hands of the widow and daughters of the Grecian hero.

I make no apology for introducing in a book the widow and daughters of Marco Bozzaris. True, I was received by them in private, without any expectation, either on their part or mine, that all the particulars of the interview would be noted and laid before the eyes of all who choose to read. I hope it will not be considered invading the sanctity of private life; but, at all events, I make no apology; the widow and children of Marco Bozzaris are the property of the world.

CHAPTER II.

Choice of a Servant.—A Turnout—An Evening Chat.— Scenery of the Road.—Lepanto.—A projected Visit.— Change of Purpose. — Padras. — Vostitza.—Variety and Magnificence of Scenery.

BARREN as our prospect was on landing, our first day in Greece had already been full of interest. Supposing that we should not find anything to engage us long, before setting out on our ramble we had directed our servant to procure horses, and when we returned we found all ready for our departure.

One word with regard to this same servant. We had taken him at Corfu, much against my inclination. We had a choice between two, one a full-blooded Greek in fustinellas, who in five minutes established himself in my good graces, so that nothing but the democratic principle of submitting to the will of the majority could make me give him up. He held at that time a very good office in the police at Corfu, but the eagerness which he showed to get out of regular business and go roving, warmed me to him irresistibly. He seemed to be distracted between two opposing feelings: one the strong bent of his natural vagabond disposition to be rambling, and the other a sort of tugging at his heart-strings by wife and children, to keep him in a place where he had a regular assured living, instead of trusting to the precarious business of guiding travellers. He had a boldness and confidence that won me; and when he drew on the sand with his yataghan a map of Greece, and told us the route he would take us, zigzag across the Gulf of Corinth to Delphi and the top of Parnassus, I wondered that my companions could resist him.

Our alternative was an Italian from somewhere on the coast of the Adriatic, whom I looked upon with an unfavourable eye, because he came between me and my Greek; and on the morning of our departure I was earnestly hoping that he had overslept himself, or got into some scrape and been picked up by the guard; but, most provokingly, he came in time, and with more baggage than all of us had together. Indeed, he had so much of his own, that, in obedience to Nature's first law, he could not attend to ours, and in putting ashore some British soldiers at Cephalonia he contrived to let my carpet-bag go with their luggage. This did not increase my amiable feeling toward him, and, perhaps, assisted in making me look upon him throughout with a jaundiced eye; in fact, before we had done with him, I regarded him as a slouch, a knave, and a fool, and had the questionable satisfaction of finding that my companions, though they sustained him as long as they could, had formed very much the same opinion.

It was to him, then, that, on our return from our visit to the widow and daughters of Marco Bozzaris, we were indebted for a turnout that seemed to astonish even the people of Missolonghi. The horses were miserable little animals, hidden under enormous saddles made of great clumps of wood over an old carpet or towcloth, and covering the whole back from the shoulders to the tail the luggage was perched on the tops of these saddles, and with desperate exertions and the help of the citizens of Missolonghi we were perched on the top of the luggage. The little animals had a knowing look as they peered from under the superincumbent mass, and, supported on either side by the by-standers till we got a little steady in our seats, we put forth from Missolonghi. The only gentleman of our party was our servant, who followed on a European saddle which he had brought for his own use, smoking his pipe with great complacency, perfectly satisfied with our appearance and with himself.

It was four o'clock when we crossed the broken walls of Missolonghi. For three hours our road lay over a plain extending to the sea. I have no doubt, if my Greek had been there, he would have given an interest to the road by referring to scenes and incidents connected with the siege of Missolonghi; but Demetrius—as he now chose to call himself—knew nothing of Greece, ancient or modern; he had no sympathy of feeling with the Greeks; had never travelled on this side of the Gulf of Corinth before; and so he lagged behind and smoked his pipe.

It was nearly dark when we reached the miserable little village of Bokara. We had barely light enough to look around for the best khan in which to pass the night. Any of the wretched tenants would have been glad to receive us for the little remuneration we might leave with them in the morning. The khans were all alike, one room, mud floor and walls, and we selected one where the chickens had already gone to roost, and prepared to measure off the dirt floor according to our dimensions. Before we were arranged a Greek of a better class, followed by half a dozen villagers, came over, and, with many regrets for the wretched state of the country, invited us to his house. Though dressed in the Greek costume, it was evident that he had acquired his manners in a school beyond the bounds of his miserable little village, in which his house now rose like the Leaning Tower of Pisa, higher than everything else, but rather rickety. In a few minutes we heard the death-notes of some chickens, and at about nine o'clock sat down to a not unwelcome meal. Several Greeks dropped in during the evening, and one, a particular friend of our host's, supped with us. Both talked French, and had that perfect ease of manner and *savoir faire* which I always remarked with admiration in all Greeks who had travelled. They talked much of their travels; of time spent in Italy and Germany, and particularly of a long residence at Bucharest. They talked, too, of Greece; of her long and bitter servitude, her revolution, and her independence; and from their enthusiasm I could not but think that they had fought and bled in her cause. I certainly was not lying in wait to entrap them, but I afterward gathered from their conversation that they had taken occasion to be on their travels at the time

K

when the bravest of their countrymen were pouring out their blood like water to emancipate their native land. A few years before I might have felt indignation and contempt for men who had left their country in her hour of utmost need, and returned to enjoy the privileges purchased with other men's blood; but I had already learned to take the world as I found it, and listened quietly while our host told us that, confiding in the permanency of the government secured by the three great powers, England, France, and Russia, he had returned to Greece, and taken a lease of a large tract of land for fifty years, paying a thousand drachms,—a drachm being one-sixth of a dollar,—and one-tenth of the annual fruits, at the end of which time one-half of the land under cultivation was to belong to his heirs in fee.

As our host could not conveniently accommodate us all, M. and Demetrius returned to the khan at which we had first stopped, and where, to judge from the early hour at which they came over to us the next morning, they had not spent the night as well as we did. At daylight we took our coffee, and again perched our luggage on the backs of the horses, and ourselves on the top of the luggage. Our host wished us to remain with him, and promised the next day to accompany us to Padras; but this was not a sufficient inducement; and taking leave of him, probably for ever, we started for Lepanto.

We rode about an hour on the plain; the mountains towered on our left, and the rich soil was broken into rough sandy gullies running down to the sea. Our guides had some apprehensions that we should not be able to cross the torrents that were running down from the mountain; and when we came to the first, and had to walk up along the bank, looking out for a place to ford, we fully participated in their apprehensions. Bridges were a species of architecture entirely unknown in that part of modern Greece; indeed, no bridges could have stood against the mountain torrents. There would have been some excitement in encountering these rapid streams if we had been well mounted; but, from the manner in which we were hitched on our horses, we did not feel any great confidence in our seats. Still nothing could be wilder or more picturesque than our process in crossing them, except that it might have added somewhat to the effect to see one of us floating down-stream, clinging to the tail of his horse. But we got over or through them all. A range of mountains then formed on our right, cutting us off from the sea, and we entered a valley lying between the two parallel ranges. At first the road, which was exceedingly difficult for a man or a sure-footed horse, lay along a beautiful stream, and the whole of the valley extending to the Gulf of Lepanto is one of the loveliest regions of country I ever saw. The ground was rich and verdant, and, even at that early season of the year, blooming with wild flowers of every hue, but wholly uncultivated, the olive-trees having all been cut down by the Turks, and without a single habitation on the whole route. My Scotch companion, who had a good eye for the picturesque and beautiful in natural scenery, was in raptures with this valley. I have since travelled in Switzerland, not, however, in all the districts frequented by tourists; but in what I saw, beautiful as it is, I do not know a place where the wildness of mountain scenery is so delightfully contrasted with the softness of a rich valley.

At the end of the valley, directly opposite Padras, and on the borders of the gulf, is a wild road called Scala Cativa, running along the sides of a rocky, mountainous precipice, overlooking the sea. It is a wild and almost fearful road; in some places I thought it like the perpendicular sides of the Palisades;* and when the wind blows in a particular direction it is impossible to make headway against it. Our host told us that we should find difficulty that day; and there was just rudeness enough to make us look well to our movements. Directly at our feet was the gulf of Corinth; opposite a range of mountains; and in the distance the island of Zante. On the other side of the valley is an extraordinary mountain, very high, and wanting a large piece in the middle, as if cut out with a chisel, leaving two strait parallel sides, and called by the unpoetical name of the Armchair. In the wildest part of the Scala, where a very slight struggle would have precipitated us several hundred feet into the sea, an enormous shepherd's dog came bounding and barking towards us; and we were much relieved when his master, who was hanging with his flock of goats on an almost inaccessible height, called him away. At the foot of the mountain we entered a rich plain, where the shepherds were pasturing their flocks down to the shore of the sea, and in about two hours arrived at Lepanto.

After diligent search by Demetrius (the name by which we had taken him, whose true name, however, we found to be Jerolamon), and by all the idlers whom the arrival of strangers attracted, we procured a room near the farthest wall; it was reached by ascending a flight of steps outside, and boasted a floor, walls, and an apology for a roof. We piled up our baggage in one corner, or rather, my companions did theirs, and went prowling about in search of something to eat. Our servant had not fully apprised us of the extreme poverty of the country, the entire absence of all accommodations for travellers, and the absolute necessity of carrying with us everything requisite for comfort. He was a man of few words, and probably thought that, as between servant and master, example was better than precept, and that the abundant provision he had made for himself might serve as a lesson for us; but in our case, the objection to this mode of teaching was, that it came too late to be profitable. At the foot of the hill fronting the sea was an open place, in one side of which was a little cafteria, where all the good-for-nothing loungers of Lepanto were assembled. We bought a loaf of bread and some eggs, and, with a cup of Turkish coffee, made our evening meal

We had an hour before dark, and strolled along the shore. Though in a ruinous condition, Lepanto is in itself interesting, as giving an exact idea of an ancient Greek city, being situated in a commanding position on the side of a mountain running down to the sea, with its citadel on the top, and enclosed by walls and turrets. The port is shut within the walls, which run into the sea, and are erected on the foundations of the ancient Naupactus. At a distance was the promontory of

---

* Rocks so called, rising along the river Hudson, a few miles above New York.—ED.

Actium, where Cleopatra, with her fifty ships, abandoned Antony and left to Augustus the empire of the world; and directly before us, its surface covered with a few straggling Greek caiques, was the scene of a battle which has rung throughout the world, the great battle of the Cross against the Crescent, where the allied forces of Spain, Venice, and the pope, amounting to nearly three hundred sail, under the command of Don John of Austria, humbled for ever the naval pride of the Turks. One hundred and thirty Turkish galleys were taken and fifty-five sunk; thirty thousand Turks were killed, ten thousand taken prisoners, fifteen thousand Christian slaves delivered; and Pope Pius VI., with holy fervour, exclaimed, "There was a man sent from God, and his name was John." Cervantes lost his left hand in this battle; and it is to wounds he received here that he makes a touching allusion when reproached by a rival: "What I cannot help feeling deeply is, that I am stigmatized with being old and maimed, as though it belonged to me to stay the course of time; or as though my wounds had been received in some tavern broil, instead of the most lofty occasion which past ages have yet seen, or which shall ever be seen by those to come. The scars which the soldier wears on his person, instead of badges of infamy, are stars to guide the daring in the path of glory. As for mine, though they may not shine in the eyes of the envious, they are at least esteemed by those who know where they were received; and, even was it not yet too late to choose, I would rather remain as I am, maimed and mutilated, than be now whole of my wounds, without having taken part in so glorious an achievement."

I shall, perhaps, be reproached for mingling with the immortal names of Don John of Austria and Cervantes those of George Wilson, of Providence, Rhode Island, and James Williams, a black of Baltimore, cook on board Lord Cochrane's flagship in the great battle between the Greek and Turkish fleets. George Wilson was a gunner on board one of the Greek ships, and conducted himself with so much gallantry, that Lord Cochrane, at a dinner in commemoration of the event, publicly drank his health. In the same battle James Williams, who had lost a finger in the United States' service under Decatur at Algiers, and had conducted himself with great coolness and intrepidity in several engagements, when no Greek could be found to take the helm, volunteered his services, and was struck down by a splinter, which broke his legs and arms. The historian will probably never mention these gallant fellows in his quarto volumes; but I hope the American traveller, as he stands at sun-set by the shore of the Gulf of Lepanto, and recalls to mind the great achievements of Don John and Cervantes, will not forget *George Wilson* and *James Williams*.

At evening we returned to our room, built a fire in the middle, and, with as much dignity as we could muster, sitting on the floor, received a number of Greek visiters. When they left us we wrapped ourselves in our cloaks and lay down to sleep. Sleep, however, is not always won when wooed. Sometimes it takes the perverse humour of the wild Irish boy: "The more you call me the more I won't come." Our room had no chimney; and though, as I lay all night looking up at the roof, there appeared to be apertures enough to let out the smoke, it seemed to have a loving feeling toward us in our lowly position, and clung to us so closely that we were obliged to let the fire go out, and lie shivering till morning.

Every schoolboy knows how hard it is to write poetry, but few know the physical difficulties of climbing the poetical mountain itself. We had made arrangements to sleep the next night at Castri, by the side of the sacred oracle of Delphi, a mile up Parnassus. Our servant wanted to cross over and go up on the other side of the gulf, and entertained us with several stories of robberies committed on this road, to which we paid no attention. The Greeks who visited us in the evening related, with much detail, a story of a celebrated captain of brigands having lately returned to his haunt on Parnassus, and attacked nine Greek merchants, of whom he killed three; the recital of which interesting incident we ascribed to Demetrius, and disregarded.

Early in the morning we mounted our horses and started for Parnassus. At the gate of the town we were informed that it was necessary, before leaving, to have a passport from the eparchos, and I returned to procure it. The eparchos was a man about forty-five, tall and stout, with a clear olive complexion and a sharp black eye, dressed in a rich Greek costume, and, fortunately, able to speak French. He was sitting cross-legged on a divan, smoking a pipe, and looking out upon the sea; and when I told him my business, he laid down his pipe, repeated the story of the robbery and murder that we had heard the night before, and added that we must abandon the idea of travelling that road. He said, farther, that the country was in a distracted state; that poverty was driving men to desperation; and that, though they had driven out the Turks, the Greeks were not masters of their own country. Hearing that I was an American, and as if in want of a bosom in which to unburden himself, and as one assured of sympathy, he told me the whole story of their long and bloody struggle for independence, and the causes that now made the friends of Greece tremble for her future destiny. I knew that the seat of the muses bore a rather suspicious character, and, in fact, that the rocks and caves about Parnassus were celebrated as the abodes of robbers, but I was unwilling to be driven from our purpose of ascending it. I went to the military commandant, a Bavarian officer, and told him what I had just heard from the eparchos. He said frankly that he did not know much of the state of the country, as he had but lately arrived in it; but, with the true Bavarian spirit, advised me, as a general rule, not to believe anything a Greek should tell me. I returned to the gate, and made my double report to my companions. Dr. W. returned with me to the eparchos, where the latter repeated, with great earnestness, all he had told me; and when I persisted in combating his objections, shrugged his shoulders in a manner that seemed to say, "your blood be on your own heads;" that he had done his duty, and washed his hands of the consequences. As we were going out he called me back, and, recurring to our previous conversation, said that he had spoken to me as an American more freely than he would have done to a stranger, and begged that, as I was going to Athens, I would not repeat his words where they could do him injury. I would not mention the circumstance now, but that the political clouds which then hung over the horizon of Greece have passed away; King Otho has taken his seat on the throne, and my friend has probably long since been driven or retired from public life. I was at that time a stranger to the internal politics of Greece, but I afterward found that the eparchos was one of a then powerful body of Greeks opposed to the Bavarian influence, and interested in representing the state of the country as more unsettled than it really was. I took leave of him, however, as one who had intended me a kindness, and, returning to the gate, found our companion sitting on his horse, waiting the result of our farther inquiries. Both he and my fellow-envoy were comparatively indifferent upon the subject, while I was rather bent on drinking from the Castalian fount, and sleeping on the top of Parnassus. Besides, I was in a beautiful condition to be robbed! I had nothing but what I had on my back, and I felt sure that a Greek mountain robber would scorn my stiff coat and pantaloons and black hat. My companions, however, were not so well situated, particularly M., who had drawn money at Corfu, and had no idea of trusting it to the tender mercies of a Greek bandit. In the teeth of the advice we had received, it would, perhaps, have been foolhardy to proceed; and, to my great subsequent regret, for the first and the last time in my ramblings, I was turned aside from my path by fear of perils on the road. Perhaps, after all, I had a lucky escape; for if the Greek tradition be true, whoever sleeps on the mountain becomes an inspired poet or a madman, either of which, for a professional man, is a catastrophe to be avoided.

Our change of plan suited Demetrius exactly; he had never travelled on this side of the Gulf of Corinth; and besides that, he considered it a great triumph that his stories of robbers were confirmed by others, showing his superior knowledge of the state of the country; he was glad to get on a road which he had travelled before, and on which he had a chance of meeting some of his old travelling acquaintance. In half an hour he had us on board a caique. We put out from the harbour of Lepanto with a strong and favourable wind; our little boat danced lightly over the waters of the Gulf of Corinth; and in three hours, passing between the frowning castles of Romelia and Morea, under the shadow of the walls of which were buried the bodies of the Christians who fell in the great naval battle, we arrived at Padras.

The first thing we recognised was the beautiful little cutter which we had left at Missolonghi, riding gracefully at anchor in the harbour, and the first man we spoke to on landing was our old friend the captain. We exchanged a cordial greeting, and he conducted us to Mr. Robertson, the British vice-consul, who, at the moment of our entering, was in the act of directing a letter to me at Athens. The subject was my interesting carpet-bag. There being no American consul at Padras, I had taken the liberty of writing to Mr. Robertson, requesting him, if my estate should find its way into his hands, to forward it to me at Athens, and the letter was to assure me of his attention to my wishes. It may be considered treason against classical taste, but it consoled me somewhat for the loss of Parnassus, to find a stranger taking so warm an interest in my fugitive habiliments.

There was something, too, in the appearance of Padras, that addressed itself to other feelings than those connected with the indulgence of a classical humour. Our bones were still aching with the last night's rest, or, rather, the want of it, at Lepanto; and when we found ourselves in a neat little locanda, and a complaisant Greek asked us what we would have for dinner, and showed us our beds for the night, we almost agreed that climbing Parnassus and such things were fit only for boys just out of college.

Padras is beautifully situated at the mouth of the Gulf of Corinth, and the windows of our locanda commanded a fine view of the bold mountains on the opposite side of the gulf, and the parallel range forming the valley which leads to Missolonghi. It stands on the site of the ancient Patræ, enumerated by Herodotus among the twelve cities of Achaia. During the intervals of peace in the Peloponnesian war, Alcibiades, about four hundred and fifty years before Christ, persuaded its inhabitants to build long walls down to the sea. Philip of Macedon frequently landed there in his expeditions to Peloponnesus. Augustus Cæsar, after the battle of Actium, made it a Roman colony, and sent thither a large body of his veteran soldiers; and, in the time of Cicero, Roman merchants were settled there just as French and Italians are now. The modern town has grown up since the revolution, or rather since the accession of Otho, and bears no marks of the desolation at Missolonghi and Lepanto. It contains a long street of shops well supplied with European goods; the English steamers from Corfu to Malta touch here; and, besides the little Greek caiques trading in the Gulf of Corinth, vessels from all parts of the Adriatic are constantly in the harbour.

Among others, there was an Austrian man-of-war from Trieste, on her way to Alexandria. By a singular fortune, the commandant had been in one of the Austrian vessels that carried to New York the unfortunate Poles; the only Austrian man-of-war which had ever been to the United States. A day or two after their arrival at New York I had taken a boat at the Battery and gone on board this vessel, and had met the officers at some parties given to them at which he had been present; and though we had no actual acquaintance with each other, these circumstances were enough to form an immediate link between us, particularly as he was enthusiastic in his praises of the hospitality of our citizens and the beauty of our women. Lest, however, any of the latter should be vainglorious at hearing that their praises were sounded so far from home, I consider it my duty to say that the commandant was almost blind, very slovenly, always smoking a pipe, and generally a little tipsy.

Early in the morning we started for Athens. Our turnout was rather better than at Missolonghi, but not much. The day, however, was fine; the cold wind which, for several days, had been blowing down the Gulf of Corinth, had ceased, and the air was warm, and balmy, and invigorating. We had already found that Greece had something to attract the stranger besides the

CORINTH.   p. 141.

recollections of her ancient glories, and often forgot that the ground we were travelling was consecrated by historians and poets, in admiration of its own wild and picturesque beauty. Our road for about three hours lay across a plain, and then close along the gulf, sometimes winding by the foot of a wild precipitous mountain, and then again over a plain, with the mountains rising at some distance on our right. Sometimes we rose and crossed their rugged summits, and again descended to the sea-shore. On our left we had constantly the gulf, bordered on the opposite side by a range of mountains, sometimes receding and then rising almost out of the water, while high above the rest rose the towering summits of Parnassus covered with snow.

It was after dark when we arrived at Vostitza, beautifully situated on the banks of the Gulf of Corinth. This is the representative of the ancient Ægium, one of the most celebrated cities in Greece, mentioned by Homer as having supplied vessels for the Trojan war, and in the second century containing sixteen sacred edifices, a theatre, a portico, and an agora. For many ages it was the seat of the Achaian Congress. Probably the worthy delegates who met here to deliberate upon the affairs of Greece had better accommodations than we obtained, or they would be likely, I should imagine, to hold but short sessions.

We stopped at a vile locanda, the only one in the place, where we found a crowd of men in a small room, gathered around a dirty table, eating, one of whom sprang up and claimed me as an old acquaintance. He had on a Greek capote, and a large foraging cap slouched over his eyes, so that I had some difficulty in recognising him as an Italian who, at Padras, had tried to persuade me to go by water up to the head of the gulf. He had started that morning, about the same time we did, with a crowd of passengers, half of whom were already by the ears. Fortunately, they were obliged to return to their boats, and left all the house to us; which, however, contained little besides a strapping Greek, who called himself its proprietor.

Before daylight we were again in the saddle. During the whole day's ride the scenery was magnificent. Sometimes we were hemmed in as if for ever enclosed in an amphitheatre of wild and gigantic rocks; then from some lofty summit we looked out upon lesser mountains, broken, and torn, and thrown into every wild and picturesque form, as if by an earthquake; and after riding among deep dells and craggy steeps, yawning ravines and cloud-capped precipices, we descended to a quiet valley and the sea-shore.

At about four o'clock we came down, for the last time, to the shore, and before us, at some distance, espied a single khan, standing almost on the edge of the water. It was a beautiful resting-place for a traveller; the afternoon was mild, and we walked on the shore till the sun set. The khan was sixty or seventy feet long, and contained an upper room running the whole length of the building. This room was our bedchamber. We built a fire at one end, made tea, and roasted some eggs, the smoke ascending and curling around the rafters, and finally passing out of the openings in the roof; we stretched ourselves in our cloaks, and, with the murmur of the waves in our ears,

looked through the apertures in the roof upon the stars, and fell asleep.

About the middle of the night the door opened with a rude noise, and a tall Greek, almost filling the doorway, stood on the threshold. After pausing a moment he walked in, followed by half-a-dozen gigantic companions, their tall figures, full dresses, and the shining of their pistols and yataghans, wearing a very ugly look to a man just roused from slumber. But they were merely Greek pedlars or travelling merchants, and, without any more noise, kindled the fire anew, drew their capotes around them, stretched themselves upon the floor, and were soon asleep.

CHAPTER III.

Quarrel with the Landlord.—Ægira.—Sicyon.—Corinth.—A distinguished Reception.—Desolation of Corinth.—The Acropolis.—View from the Acropolis.—Lochæum and Cenchreæ.—Kaka Scala.—Arrival at Athens.

IN the morning Demetrius had a roaring quarrel with the keeper of the locanda, in which he tried to keep back part of the money we gave him to pay for us. He did this, however, on principle, for we had given twice as much as our lodging was worth, and no man ought to have more. His character was at stake in preventing any one from cheating us too much; and, in order to do this, he stopped our funds *in transitu*.

We started early, and for some time our road lay along the shore. It was not necessary, surrounded by such magnificent scenery, to draw upon historical recollections for the sake of giving interest to the road; still it did not diminish that interest to know that, many centuries ago, great cities stood here, whose sites are now desolate, or occupied as the miserable gathering-places of a starving population. Directly opposite Parnassus, and at the foot of a hill crowned with the ruins of an acropolis, in perfect desolation now, stood the ancient Ægira; once numbering a population of ten thousand inhabitants, and in the second century containing three hiera, a temple, and another sacred edifice. Farther on, and toward the head of the Gulf of Corinth, the miserable village of Basilico stands on the site of the ancient Sicyon, boasting as high an antiquity as any city in Greece, and long celebrated as the first of her schools of painting. In five hours we came in sight of the Acropolis of Corinth, and shortly after, of Corinth itself.

The reader need not fear my plunging him deeply into antiquities. Greece has been explored, and examined, and written upon, till the subject is almost threadbare; and I do not flatter myself that I discovered in it anything new. Still no man from such a distant country as mine can find himself crossing the plain of Corinth, and ascending to the ancient city, without a strange and indescribable feeling. We have no old monuments, no classical associations; and our history hardly goes beyond the memory of that venerable personage, "the oldest inhabitant." Corinth is so old that its early records are blended with the history of the heathen gods. The Corinthians say that it was called after the son of Jupiter, and its early sovereigns were heroes of the Grecian mythology. It was the friend of Sparta and the rival of Athens; the first city to build war-galleys, and send forth colonies, which became great empires. It was the assembling-place of their delegates, who elected Philip, and afterward Alexander the Great, to conduct the war against the Persians. In painting, sculpture, and architecture, surpassing all the achievements of Greece or which the genius of man has ever since accomplished. Conquered by the then barbarous Romans, her walls were razed to the ground, her men put to the sword, her women and children sold into captivity; and the historian who records her fall, writes that he saw the finest pictures thrown wantonly on the ground, and Roman soldiers playing on them at draughts and dice. For many years deserted, Corinth was again peopled; rose rapidly from its ruins; and, when St. Paul abode there " a year and six months"—to the Christian the most interesting period in her history—she was again a populous city, and the Corinthians a luxurious people.

Its situation in the early ages of the world could not fail to make it a great commercial emporium. In the inexperienced navigation of early times it was considered difficult and dangerous to go around the point of the Peloponnesus, and there was a proverb, " Before the mariner doubles Cape Malea, he should forget all he holds dearest in the world." Standing on the isthmus commanding the Adriatic and Ægean Seas; receiving in one hand the riches of Asia, and in the other those of Europe; distributing them to every quarter of the then known world, wealth followed commerce, and then came luxury and extravagance to such an extent that it became a proverb, " It is not for every man to go to Corinth."

As travellers having regard to supper and lodging, we should have been glad to see some vestige of its ancient luxury; but times are changed; the ruined city stands where stood Corinth of old, but it has fallen once more; the sailor no longer hugs the well-known coasts, but launches fearlessly into the trackless ocean, and Corinth can never again be what she has been.

Our servant had talked so much of the hotel at Corinth, that perhaps the idea of bed and lodging was rather too prominent in our reveries as we approached the fallen city. He rode on before to announce our coming, and, working our way up the hill through narrow streets, stared at by all the men, followed by a large representation from the juvenile portion of the modern Corinthians, and barked at by the dogs, we turned into a large enclosure, something like a barnyard, on which opened a ruined balcony, forming the entrance to the hotel. Demetrius was standing before it with our host, as unpromising a looking scoundrel as ever took a traveller in. He had been a notorious captain of brigands; and when his lawless band was broken up, and half of its number hanged, he could not overcome his disposition to prey upon travellers, but got a couple of mattresses and bedsteads, and set up a hotel at Corinth. Demetrius had made a bargain for us at a price that made him hang his head when he told it, and we were so indignant at the extortion that we at first refused to dismount. Our host stood aloof, being used to such scenes, and perfectly sure that, after storming a little, we should be glad to take the only beds between Padras and Athens. In the end, however, we got the better both of him and Demetrius; for, as he had fixed separate prices for dinner, beds, and breakfast, we went to a little Greek coffee-house, and raised half Corinth to get us something to eat, and paid him only for our lodging.

We had a fine afternoon before us, and our first movement was to the ruins of a temple, the only monument of antiquity in Corinth. The city has been so often sacked and plundered, that not a column of the Corinthian order exists in the place from which it derives its name. Seven columns of the old temple are still standing, fluted and of the Doric order, though wanting in height the usual proportion to the diameter; built probably before that order had attained its perfection, and long before the Corinthian order was invented; though when it was built, by whom, or to what god it was consecrated, antiquaries cannot agree in deciding. Contrasted with these solitary columns of an unknown antiquity, are ruins of yesterday. Houses fallen, burned, and black with smoke, as if the wretched inmates had fled before the blaze of their dwellings; and high above the ruined city, now as in the days when the Persian and Roman invaded it, still towers the Acropolis, a sharp and naked rock, rising abruptly a thousand feet from the earth, inaccessible and impregnable under the science of ancient war; and in all times of invasion and public distress, from her earliest history down to the bloody days of the late revolution, the refuge of the inhabitants.

It was late in the afternoon when we set out for the Acropolis. About a mile from the city we came to the foot of the hill, and ascended by a steep and difficult path, with many turnings and windings, to the first gate. Having been in the saddle since early in the morning, we stopped several times to rest, and each time lingered and looked out with admiration upon the wild and beautiful scenery around us; and we thought of the frequently recurring times when hostile armies had drawn up before the city at our feet, and the inhabitants, in terror and confusion, had hurried up this path and taken refuge within the gate before us.

Inside the gate were the ruins of a city, and here, too, we saw the tokens of ruthless war: the fire-brand was hardly yet extinguished, and the houses were in ruins. Within a few years it has been the stronghold and refuge of infidels and Christians, taken and retaken, destroyed, rebuilt, and destroyed again, and the ruins of Turkish mosques and Christian churches are mingled together in undistinguishable confusion. This enclosure is abundantly supplied with water issuing from the rock, and is capable of containing several thousand people. The fountain of Pyrene, which supplies the Acropolis, called the most salubrious in Greece, is celebrated as that at which Pegasus was drinking when taken by Bellerophon. Ascending among ruined and deserted habitations, we came to a second gate flanked by towers. A wall about two miles in circumference encloses the whole summit of the rock, including two principal points which still rise above the rest. One is crowned with a tower and the other with a mosque, now in ruins; probably erected where once stood a heathen temple. Some have mistaken it for a Christian church, but all agree that it is a place built and consecrated to divine use, and that, for unknown ages, men have gone up to this cloud-capped point to worship their Creator. It was a sublime idea to erect on this lofty pinnacle an altar to the Almighty. Above us were only the unclouded heavens; the sun was setting with that brilliancy which attends his departing glory nowhere but in the East; and the sky was glowing with a lurid red, as of some great conflagration. The scene around and below was wondrously beautiful. Mountains and rivers, seas and islands, rocks, forests, and plains, thrown together in perfect wantonness, and yet in the most perfect harmony, and every feature in the expanded landscape consecrated by the richest associations. On one side the Saronic Gulf, with its little islands, and Ægina and Salamis, stretching off to " Sunium's marble height," with the ruins of its temple looking out mournfully upon the sea; on the other, the Gulf of Corinth or Lepanto, bounded by the dark and dreary mountains of Cytheron, where Actæon, gazing at the goddess, was changed into a stag, and hunted to death by his own hounds; and where Bacchus, with his train of satyrs and frantic bacchantes, celebrated his orgies. Beyond were Helicon, sacred to Apollo and the Muses, and Parnassus, covered with snow. Behind us towered a range of mountains stretching away to Argos and the ancient Sparta, and in front was the dim outline of the temple of the Acropolis at Athens. The shades of evening gathered thick around us while we remained on the top of the Acropolis, and it was dark long before we reached our locanda.

The next morning we breakfasted at the coffeehouse, and left Corinth wonderfully pleased at having outwitted Demetrius and our brigand host, who gazed after us with a surly scowl as we rode away, and probably longed for the good old days when, at the head of his hanged companions, he could have stopped us at the first mountain-pass and levied contributions at his own rate. I probably condemn myself when I say that we left this ancient city with such a trifle uppermost in our thoughts, but so it was; we bought a loaf of bread as we passed through the market-place, and descended to the plain of Corinth. We had still the same horses which we rode from Padras; they were miserable animals, and I did not mount mine the whole day. Indeed, this is the true way to travel in Greece; the country is mountainous, and the road or narrow horse-path so rough and precipitous that the traveller is often obliged to dismount and walk. The exercise of clambering up the mountains and the purity of the air brace every nerve in the body, and not a single feature of the scenery escapes the eye.

But, as yet, there are other things beside scenery; on each side of the road and within sight of each other are the ruins of the ancient cities of Lechæum and Cenchreæ, the ports of Corinth on the Corinthian and Saronic Gulfs; the former once connected with it by two long walls, and the road to the latter once lined with temples and sepulchres, the ruins of which may still be seen. The isthmus connecting the Peloponnesus with the continent is about six miles wide, and Corinth owed her commercial greatness to the profits of her merchants in transporting merchandise across it. Entire vessels were sometimes carried from one sea and launched into the other. The project of a canal across suggested itself both to the Greeks and Romans, and there yet exist traces of a ditch commenced for that purpose.

On the death of Leonidas, and in apprehension of a Persian invasion, the Peloponnesians built a wall across the isthmus from Lechæum to Cenchreæ. This wall was at one time fortified with a hundred and fifty towers; it was often destroyed and as often rebuilt; and in one place, about three miles from Corinth, vestiges of it may still be seen. Here were celebrated those Isthmian games so familiar to every tyro in Grecian literature and history; toward Mount Oneus stands on an eminence an ancient mound supposed to be the tomb of Melicertes, their founder, and near it is at this day a grove of the sacred pine, with garlands of the leaves of which the victors were crowned.

In about three hours from Corinth we crossed the isthmus, and came to the village of Kalamaki, on the shore of the Saronic Gulf, containing a few miserable buildings, fit only for the miserable people who occupied them. Directly on the shore was a large coffee-house enclosed by mud walls, and having branches of trees for a roof; and in front was a little flotilla of Greek caiques.

Next to the Greek's love for his native mountains is his passion for the waters that roll at their feet; and many of the proprietors of the rakish little boats in the harbour talked to us of the superior advantage of the sea over a mountainous road, and tried to make us abandon our horses and go by water to Athens; but we clung to the land, and have reason to congratulate ourselves upon having done so, for our road was one of the most beautiful it was ever my fortune to travel over. For some distance I walked along the shore, on the edge of a plain running from the foot of Mount Geranion. The plain was intersected by mountain-torrents, the channel-beds of which were at that time dry. We passed the little village of Caridi, supposed to be the Sidus of antiquity, while a ruined church and a few old blocks of marble mark the site of ancient Crommyon, celebrated as the haunt of a wild boar destroyed by Theseus.

At the other end of the plain we came to the foot of Mount Geranion, stretching out boldly to the edge of the gulf, and followed the road along its southern side close to and sometimes overhanging the sea. From time immemorial this has been called the Kaka Scala, or bad way. It is narrow, steep, and rugged, and wild to sublimity Sometimes we were completely hemmed in by impending mountains, and then rose upon a lofty eminence, commanding an almost boundless view On the summit of the range the road runs directly along the mountain's brink, overhanging the sea, and so narrow that two horsemen can scarcely pass abreast, where a stumble would plunge the traveller several hundred yards into the waters beneath. Indeed, the horse of one of my companions stumbled and fell, and put him in such peril that both dismounted and accompanied me on foot. In the olden time this wild and rugged road was famous as the haunt of the robber Sciron, who plundered the luckless travellers, and then threw them from this precipice. The fabulous account is, that Theseus, three thousand years before, on his first visit to Athens, encountered the famous robber, and tossed him from the same precipice whence he had thrown so many better men. According to Ovid, the earth and the sea refused to receive the bones of Sciron, which continued for some time suspended in the open air, until they were changed into large rocks, whose points still appear at the foot of the precipice; and to this day, say the sailors, knock the bottoms out of the Greek vessels. In later days this road was so infested by corsairs and pirates that even the Turks feared to travel on it; at one place, that looks as though it might be intended as a jumping-off point into another world, Ino, with her son Melicertes in her arms (so say the Greek poets), threw herself into the sea to escape the fury of her husband; and we know that in later days St. Paul travelled on this road to preach the gospel to the Corinthians.

But, independently of all associations, and in spite of its difficulties and dangers, if a man were by accident placed on the lofty height without knowing where he was, he would be struck with the view which it commands, as one of the most beautiful that mortal eyes ever beheld. It was my fortune to pass over it a second time on foot, and I often seated myself on some wild point, and waited the coming up of my muleteers, looking out upon the sea, calm and glistening as if plated with silver, and studded with islands in continuous clusters stretching away into the Ægean.

During the greater part of the passage of the Kaka Scala, my companions walked with me; and, as we always kept in advance, when we seated ourselves on some rude rock overhanging the sea to wait for our beasts and attendants, few things could be more picturesque than their approach.

On the summit of the pass we fell into the ancient paved way that leads from Attica into the Peloponnesus, and walked over the same pavement which the Greeks travelled, perhaps, three thousand years ago. A ruined wall and gate mark the ancient boundary; and near this an early traveller observed a large block of white marble projecting over the precipice, and almost ready to fall into the sea, which bore an inscription, now illegible. Here it is supposed stood the Stèle erected by Theseus, bearing on one side the inscription, "Here is Peloponnesus, not Ionia;" and on the other the equally pithy notification, "Here is not Peloponnesus, but Ionia." It would be a pretty place of residence for a man in misfortune: for besides the extraordinary beauty of the scenery, by a single step he might avoid the service of civil process, and set the sheriff of Attica or the Peloponnesus at defiance. Descending, we saw before us a beautiful plain, extending from the foot of the mountain to the sea, and afar off, on an eminence commanding the plain, was the little town of Megara.

It is unfortunate for the reader that every ruined village on the road stands on the site of an ancient city. The ruined town before us was the birth-place of Euclid, and the representative of that Megara which distinguished in history more than two thousand years ago; which sent forth its armies in the Persian and Peloponnesian wars; alternately the ally and enemy of Corinth and Athens; containing numerous temples, and the largest public-houses in Greece; and though exposed, with her other cities, to the violence of a fierce democracy, as is recorded by the historian, "the Megareans retained their independence and lived in peace." As a high compliment, the people offered to Alexander the Great the freedom of their city. When we approached, it its appearance was a speaking comment upon human pride. It had been demolished and burned by Greeks and Turks, and now presented little more than a mass of blackened ruins. A few apartments had been cleared out and patched up, and occasionally I saw a solitary figure stalking amid the desolation.

I had not mounted my horse all day; had kicked out a pair of Greek shoes on my walk, and was almost barefoot when I entered the city. A little below the town was a large building enclosed by a high wall, with a Bavarian soldier lounging at the gate. We entered, and found a good coffee-room below, and a comfortable bed-chamber above, where we found good quilts and mattresses, and slept like princes.

Early in the morning we set out for Athens, our road for some time lying along the sea. About half way to the Piræus, a ruined village, with a starving population, stands on the site of the ancient Eleusis, famed throughout all Greece for the celebration of the mysterious rites of Ceres. The magnificent temple of the goddess has disappeared, and the colossal statue made by the immortal Phidias now adorns the vestibule of the University at Cambridge. We lingered a little while in the village and soon after entered the Via Sacra, by which, centuries ago, the priests and people moved in solemn religious processions from Athens to the great temple of Ceres. At first we passed underneath the cliff along the shore, then rose by a steep ascent among the mountains, barren and stony, and wearing an aspect of desolation equal to that of the Roman Campagna; then we passed through a long defile, upon the side of which, deeply cut in the rock, are seen the marks of chariot-wheels; perhaps of those used in the sacred processions. We passed the ruined monastery of Daphne, in a beautifully picturesque situation, and in a few minutes saw the rich plain of Attica; and our muleteers and Demetrius, with a burst of enthusiasm, perhaps because the journey was ended, clapped their hands and cried out, "Atinæ! Atinæ!!"

The reader, perhaps, trembles at the name of Athens, but let him take courage. I promise to let him off easily. A single remark, however, before reaching it. The plain of Attica lies between two parallel ranges of mountains, and extends from the sea many miles back into the interior. On the border of the sea stands the Piræus, now, as in former times, the harbour of the city; and towards the east, on a little eminence, Athens itself, like the other cities in Greece, presenting a miserable appearance, the effects of protracted and relentless wars. But high above the ruins of the modern city towers the Acropolis, holding up to the skies the ruined temples of other days, and proclaiming what Athens was. We wound around the temple of Theseus, the most beautiful and perfect specimen of architecture that time has spared; and in striking contrast with this monument of the magnificence of past days, here, in the entrance to the city, our horses were struggling and sinking up to their saddle-girths in the mud.

We did in Athens what we should have done in Boston or Philadelphia; rode up to the best hotel, and, not being able to obtain accommodation there, rode to another; where, being again refused admittance, we were obliged to distribute ourselves into three parcels. Dr. Willet went to Mr. Hill's (of whom more anon). M. found entrance at a new hotel in the suburbs, and I betook myself to the *Hotel de France.* The *garçon* was rather bothered when I threw him a pair of old boots which I had hanging at my saddle-bow, and told him to take care of my baggage; he asked me when the rest would come up; and hardly knew what to make of me when I told him that was all I travelled with.

I was still standing in the court of the hotel, almost barefoot, and thinking of the prosperous condition of the owner of a dozen shirts, and other things conforming, when Mr. Hill came over and introduced himself; and telling me that his house was the house of every American, asked me to waive ceremony and bring my luggage over at once. This was again hitting my sore point; everybody seemed to take especial interest in my luggage, and I was obliged to tell my story more than once. I declined Mr. Hill's kind invitation, but called upon him early the next day, dined with him, and during the whole of my stay in Athens, was in the habit, to a great extent, of making his house my home; and this, I believe is the case with all the Americans who go there; besides which, some borrow his money, and others his clothes.

CHAPTER IV.

American Missionary School.—Visit to the School.—Mr. Hill and the Male Department.—Mrs. Hill and the Female Department.—Maid of Athens.—Letter from Mr. Hill.—Revival of Athens.—Citizens of the World.

THE first thing we did in Athens was to visit the American missionary school. Among the extraordinary changes of an ever-changing world, it is not the least that the young America is at this moment paying back the debt which the world owes to the mother of science, and the citizen of a country which the wisest of the Greeks never dreamed of, is teaching the descendants of Plato and Aristotle the elements of their own tongue. I did not expect among the ruins of Athens to find anything that would particularly touch my national feelings, but it was a subject of deep and interesting reflection that, in the city which surpassed all the world in learning, where Socrates, and Plato, and Aristotle taught, and Cicero went to study, the only door of instruction was that opened by the hands of American citizens, and an American missionary was the only schoolmaster; and I am ashamed to say that I was not aware of the existence of such an institution until advised of it by my friend Dr. W.

In eighteen hundred and thirty the Rev. Messrs. Hill and Robinson, with their families, sailed from this city (New York) as the agents of the Episcopal missionary society, to found schools in Greece. They first established themselves in the island of Tenos; but, finding that it was not the right field for their labours, employed themselves in acquiring a knowledge of the language, and of the character and habits of the modern Greeks. Their attention was directed to Athens, and in the spring of eighteen hundred and thirty-one they made a visit to that city, and were so confirmed in their impressions, that they purchased a lot of ground on which to erect edifices for a permanent establishment, and, in the mean time, rented a house for the immediate commencement of a school. They returned to Tenos for their families and effects, and again arrived at Athens about the end of June following. From the deep interest taken in their struggle for liberty, and the timely help furnished them in their hour of need, the Greeks were warmly prepossessed in favour of our countrymen; and the conduct of the missionaries themselves was so judicious, that they were received with the greatest respect and the warmest welcome by the public authorities and the whole population of Athens. Their furniture, printing-presses, and other effects, were admitted free of duties; and it is but justice to them to say that, since that time, they have moved with such discretion among an excitable and suspicious people, that, while they have advanced in the great objects of their mission, they have grown in the esteem and good-will of the best and most influential inhabitants of Greece; and so great was Mr. Hill's confidence in their affections, that, though there was at that time a great political agitation, and it was apprehended that Athens might again become the scene of violence and bloodshed, he told me he had no fears, and felt perfectly sure that, in any out-breaking of popular fury, himself and family, and the property of the mission, would be respected.*

In the middle of the summer of their arrival at Athens, Mrs. Hill opened a school for girls in the magazine or cellar of the house in which they resided; the first day she had twenty pupils, and in two months one hundred and sixty-seven. Of the first ninety-six, not more than six could read at all, and that very imperfectly; and not more than ten or twelve knew a letter. At the time of our visit the school numbered nearly five hundred; and when we entered the large room, all the scholars all rose in a body to greet us as Americans, I felt a deep sense of regret that, personally, I had no hand in such a work, and almost envied the feelings of my companion, one of its patrons and founders. Besides teaching them gratitude to those from whose country they derived the privileges they enjoyed, Mr. Hill had wisely endeavoured to impress upon their minds a respect for the constituted authorities, particularly important in that agitated and unsettled community; and on one end of the wall, directly fronting the seats of the scholars, was printed in large Greek characters, the text of Scripture, "Fear God, honour the king."

It was all-important for the missionaries not to offend the strong prejudices of the Greeks by any attempt to withdraw the children from the reli-

---

* Since my return home I have seen in a newspaper an account of a popular commotion at Syra, in which the printing-presses and books of the missionaries were destroyed, and Mr. Robinson was threatened with personal violence.

gion of their fathers; and the school purports to be, and is intended for, the diffusion of elementary education only; but it is opened in the morning with prayer, concluding with the Lord's Prayer as read in our churches, which is repeated by the whole school aloud; and on Sundays, besides the prayers, the Creed, and sometimes the Ten Commandments, are recited, and a chapter from the Gospels is read aloud by one of the scholars, the missionaries deeming this more expedient than to conduct the exercises themselves. The lesson for the day is always the portion appointed for the gospel of the day in their own church; and they close by singing a hymn. The room is thrown open to the public, and is frequently resorted to by the parents of the children and strangers; some coming, perhaps, says Mr. Hill, to "hear what these babblers will say," and "other some" from a suspicion that "we are setters forth of strange gods."

The boys' school is divided into three departments, the lowest under charge of a Greek qualified on the Lancasterian system. They were of all ages, from three to eighteen; and, as Mr. Hill told me, most of them had been half-clad, dirty, ragged little urchins, who, before they were put to their A, B, C, or rather, their Alpha, Beta, Gamma, Delta, had to be thoroughly washed, rubbed, scrubbed, doctored, and dressed, and, but for the school, would now, perhaps, be prowling vagabonds in the streets of Athens, or training for robbery in the mountains. They were a body of fine-looking boys, possessing, as Mr. Hill told me, in an extraordinary degree, all that liveliness of imagination, that curiosity and eagerness after knowledge, which distinguished the Greeks of old, retaining, under centuries of dreadful oppression, the recollection of the greatness of their fathers, and, what was particularly interesting, many of them bearing the great names so familiar in Grecian history; I shook hands with a little Miltiades, Leonidas, Aristides, &c., in features and apparent intelligence worthy descendants of the immortal men whose names they bear. And there was one who startled me; he was the son of the Maid of Athens! To me the Maid of Athens was almost an imaginary being, something fanciful, a creation of the brain, and not a corporeal substance, to have a little urchin of a boy. But so it was. The Maid of Athens is married. She had a right to marry, no doubt; and it is said that there is poetry in married life, and, doubtless, she is a much more interesting person now than the Maid of Athens at thirty-six could be; but the Maid of Athens is married to a Scotchman! the Maid of Athens is now Mrs. Black! wife of George Black! head of the police! and her son's name is * * * * * Black! and she has other little Blacks! Comment is unnecessary.

But the principal and most interesting part of this missionary school was the female department, under the direction of Mrs. Hill, the first, and, except at Syra, the only school for females in all Greece, and particularly interesting to me from the fact that it owed its existence to the active benevolence of my own countrywoman. At the close of the Greek revolution, female education was a thing entirely unknown in Greece, and the women of all classes were in a most deplorable state of ignorance. When the strong feeling that ran through our country in favour of this struggling people had subsided, and Greece was freed from the yoke of the Mussulman, an association of ladies in the little town of Troy, perhaps instigated somewhat by an inherent love of power and extended rule, and knowing the influence of their sex in a cultivated state of society, formed the project of establishing at Athens a school exclusively for the education of females; and, humble and unpretending as was its commencement, it is becoming a more powerful instrument in the civilization and moral and religious improvement of Greece, than all that European diplomacy has ever done for her. The girls were distributed in different classes, according to their age and advancement; they had clean faces and hands, a rare thing with Greek children, and were neatly dressed, many of them wearing frocks made by ladies at home (probably at some of our sewing societies); and some of them had attained such an age, and had such fine, dark, rolling eyes as to make even a northern temperament feel the powerful influence they would soon exercise over the rising, excitable generation of Greeks, and almost make him bless the hands that were directing that influence aright.

Mr. and Mrs. Hill accompanied us through the whole establishment, and being Americans, we were everywhere looked upon and received by the girls as patrons and fathers of the school, both which characters I waived in favour of my friend; the one because he was really entitled to it, and the other because some of the girls were so well grown that I did not care to be regarded as standing in that venerable relationship. The didaskalissas, or teachers, were of this description, and they spoke English. Occasionally Mr. Hill called a little girl up to us, and told us her history, generally a melancholy one, as, being reduced to the extremity of want by the revolution; or an orphan, whose parents had been murdered by the Turks; and I had a conversation with a little Penelope, who, however, did not look as if she would play the faithful wife of Ulysses, and, if I am a judge of physiognomy, would never endure widowhood twenty years for any man.

Before we went away the whole school rose at once, and gave us a glorious finale with a Greek hymn. In a short time these girls will grow up into women and return to their several families; others will succeed them, and again go out, and every year hundreds will distribute themselves in the cities and among the fastnesses of the mountains, to exercise over their fathers, and brothers, and lovers, the influence of the education acquired here; instructed in all the arts of woman in civilised domestic life, firmly grounded in the principles of morality, and of religion purified from the follies, absurdities, and abominations of the Greek faith. I have seen much of the missionary labours in the East, but I do not know an institution which promises so surely the happiest results. If the women are educated, the men cannot remain ignorant; if the women are enlightened in religion, the men cannot remain debased and degraded Christians.

The ex-secretary Rigos was greatly affected at the appearance of this female school; and, after surveying it attentively for some moments, pointed to the Parthenon on the summit of the Acropolis, and said to Mrs. Hill, with deep emotion, "Lady, you are erecting in Athens a monument more enduring and more noble than yonder temple;" and the king was so deeply impressed with its value, that, a short time before my arrival, he proposed to Mr. Hill to take into his house girls from different districts and educate them as teachers, with the view of sending them back to their districts, there to organise new schools, and carry out the great work of female education. Mr. Hill acceded to the proposal, and the American missionary school now stands as the nucleus of a large and growing system of education in Greece; and, very opportunely for my purpose, within a few days I have received a letter from Mr. Hill, in which, in relation to the school, he says, "Our missionary establishment is much increased since you saw it; our labours are greatly increased, and I think I may say we have now reached the summit of what we had proposed to ourselves. We do not think it possible that it can be extended farther without much larger means and more personal aid. We do not wish or intend to ask for either. We have now nearly forty persons residing with us, of whom thirty-five are Greeks, all of whom are brought within the influence of the gospel; the greater part of them are young girls from different parts of Greece, and even from Egypt and Turkey (Greeks, however), whom we are preparing to become instructresses of youth hereafter in their various districts. We have five hundred, besides, under daily instruction in the different schools under our care, and we employ under us in the schools twelve native teachers, who have themselves been instructed by us. We have provided for three of our dear pupils (all of whom were living with us when you were here), who are honourably and usefully settled in life. One is married to a person every way suited to her, and both husband and wife are in our missionary service. One has charge of the government female school at the Piræus, and supports her father and mother and a large family by her salary; and the third has gone with our missionaries to Crete, to take charge of the female schools there. We have removed into our new house" (of which the foundation was just laid at the time of my visit), "and, large as it is, it is not half large enough. We are trying to raise ways and means to enlarge it considerably, that we may take more boarders under our own roof, which we look up to as the most important means of making sure of our labour; for every one who comes to reside with us is taken away from the corrupt example exhibited at home, and brought within a wholesome influence. Lady Byron has just sent us one hundred pounds towards enlarging our house with this view, and we have commenced the erection of three additional dormitories with the money."

Athens is again the capital of a kingdom. Enthusiasts see in her present condition the promise of a restoration to her ancient greatness; but reason and observation assure us that the world is too much changed for her ever to be what she has been. In one respect, her condition resembles that of her best days; for, as her fame then attracted strangers from every quarter of the world to study in her schools, so now the capital of King Otho has become a great gathering-place of wandering spirits from many near and distant regions. For ages difficult and dangerous of access, the ancient capital of the arts lay shrouded in darkness, and almost cut off from the civilised world. At long intervals, a few solitary travellers only found their way to it; but, since the revolution, it has again become a place of frequent resort and intercourse. It is true that the ancient halls of learning are still solitary and deserted, but strangers from every nation now turn hither; the scholar to roam over her classic soil, the artist to study her ancient monuments, and the adventurer to carve his way to fortune.

The first day I dined at the hotel, I had an opportunity of seeing the variety of material congregated in the reviving city. We had a long table, capable of accommodating about twenty persons. The manner of living was à-la-carte, each guest dining when he pleased, but, by tacit consent, at about six o'clock all assembled at the table. We presented a curious medley. No two were from the same country. Our discourse was in English, French, Italian, German, Greek, Russian, Polish, and I know not what else, as if we were the very people stricken with confusion of tongues at the tower of Babel. Dinner over, all fell into French, and the conversation became general. Every man present was, in the fullest sense of the term, a citizen of the world. It had been the fortune of each, whether good or bad, to break the little circle in which so many are born, revolve, and die; and the habitual mingling with people of various nations had broken down all narrow prejudices, and given to every one freedom of mind and force of character. All had seen much, had much to communicate, and felt that they had much yet to learn. By some accident, moreover, all seemed to have become particularly interested in the East. They travelled over the whole range of Eastern politics, and to a certain extent considered themselves identified with eastern interests. Most of the company were or had been soldiers, and several wore uniforms and stars, or decorations of some description. They spoke of the different campaigns in Greece in which some of them had served; of the science of war; of Marlborough, Eugene, and more modern captains; and I remember that they startled my feelings of classical reverence by talking of Leonidas at Thermopylæ and Miltiades at Marathon, in the same tone as of Napoleon at Leipsic and Wellington at Waterloo. One of them constructed on the table, with the knives and forks and spoons, a map of Marathon, and with a sheathed yataghan pointed out the position of the Greeks and Persians, and showed where Miltiades, as a general, was wrong. They were not blinded by the dust of antiquity. They had been knocked about till all enthusiasm and all reverence for the past were shaken out of them, and they had learned to give things their right names. A French engineer showed us the skeleton of a map of Greece, which was then preparing under the direction of the French Geographical Society, exhibiting an excess of mountains and deficiency of plain which surprised even those who had travelled over every part of the kingdom. One had just come from Constantinople, where he had seen the sultan going to mosque; another had escaped from an attack of the plague in Egypt; a third gave the dimensions of the Temple of the Sun at Baalbeck; and a fourth had been at Babylon, and seen the ruins of the tower of Babel. In short, every man had seen something which the others had not seen, and all their knowledge was thrown into a common stock. I found myself at once among a new class of men; and I turned from him who sneered at Miltiades to him who had seen the sultan, or to him who had been at Bagdad, and listened with interest, somewhat qualified by consciousness of my own inferiority. I was lying in wait, however, and took advantage of an opportunity to throw in something about America; and, at the sound, all turned to me with an eagerness of curiosity that I had not anticipated.

In Europe, and even in England, I had often found extreme ignorance of my own country; but here I was astonished to find, among men so familiar with all parts of the Old World, such total lack of information about the New. A gentleman opposite me, wearing the uniform of the King of Bavaria, asked me if I had ever been in America. I told him that I was born, and, as they say in Kentucky, *raised* there. He begged my pardon, but doubtfully suggested, "You are not black?" and I was obliged to explain to him that in our section of America the Indian had almost entirely disappeared, and that his place was occupied by the descendants of the Gaul and the Briton. I was forthwith received into the fraternity, for my home was farther away than any of them had ever been; my friend opposite considered me a *bijou*, asked me innumerable questions, and seemed to be constantly watching for the breaking out of the cannibal spirit, as if expecting to see me bite my neighbour. At first I had felt myself rather a small affair; but, before separating, *l'Américain*, or *le sauvage*, or, finally, *le cannibal*, found himself something of a lion.

CHAPTER V.

Ruins of Athens.—Hill of Mars.—Temple of the Winds.—Lantern of Demosthenes.—Arch of Adrian.—Temple of Jupiter Olympus.—Temple of Theseus.—The Acropolis.—The Parthenon.—Pentelican Mountain.—Mount Hymettus.—The Piræus.—Greek Fleas.—Napoli.

THE next morning I began my survey of the ruins of Athens. It was my intention to avoid any description of those localities and monuments, because so many have preceded me, stored with all necessary knowledge, ripe in taste and sound in judgment, who have devoted to them all the time and research they so richly merit; but as, in our community, through the hurry and multiplicity of business occupations, few are able to bestow upon these things much time or attention, and, furthermore, as the books which treat of them are not accessible to all, I should be doing injustice to my readers if I were to omit them altogether. Besides, I should be doing violence to my own feelings, and cannot get fairly started in Athens, without recurring to scenes which I regarded at the time with extraordinary interest. I have since visited most of the principal cities in Europe, existing as well as ruined, and I hardly know any to which I recur with more satisfaction than Athens. If the reader tire in the brief reference I shall make, he must not impute it to any want of interest in the subject; and as I am not in the habit of going into heroics, he will believe me when I say that, if he have any reverence for the men or things consecrated by the respect and admiration of ages, he will find it called out at Athens. In the hope that I may be the means of inducing some of my countrymen to visit that famous city, I will add another inducement, by saying that he may have, as I had, Mr. Hill for a cicerone. This gentleman is familiar with every locality, and monument around or in the city, and, which I afterward found to be an unusual thing with those living in places consecrated in the minds of strangers, he retains for them all that freshness of feeling which we possess who only know them from books and pictures.

By an arrangement made the evening before, early in the morning of my second day in Athens, Mr. Hill was at the door of my hotel to attend us. As we descended the steps a Greek stopped him, and, bowing with his hand on his heart, addressed him in a tone of earnestness which we could not understand; but we were struck with the sonorous tones of his voice and the musical cadence of his sentences; and when he had finished, Mr. Hill told us that he had spoken in a strain which, in the original, was poetry itself, beginning, "Americans, I am a Stagyrite. I come from the land of Aristotle, the disciple of Plato," &c. &c.; telling him the whole story of his journey from the ancient Stagyra and his arrival in Athens; and that, having understood that Mr. Hill was distributing books among his countrymen, he begged for one to take home with him. Mr. Hill said that this was an instance of every-day occurrence, showing the spirit of inquiry and thirst for knowledge among the modern Greeks. This little scene with a countryman of Aristotle was a fit prelude to our morning ramble.

The house occupied by the American missionary as a school stands on the site of the ancient Agora, or market-place, where St. Paul "disputed daily with the Athenians." A few columns still remain; and near them is an inscription mentioning the price of oil. The school-house is built partly from the ruins of the Agora; and to us it was an interesting circumstance, that a missionary from a newly-discovered world was teaching to the modern Greeks the same saving religion which, eighteen hundred years ago, St. Paul, on the same spot, preached to their ancestors.

Winding around the foot of the Acropolis, within the ancient and outside the modern wall, we came to the Areopagus, or Hill of Mars, where in the early days of Athens, her judges sat in the open air; and, for many ages, decided with such wisdom and impartiality, that to this day the decisions of the court of Areopagites are regarded as models of judicial purity. We ascended this celebrated hill, and stood on the precise spot where St. Paul, pointing to the temples which rose from every section of the city and towered proudly on the Acropolis, made his celebrated address: "Ye men of Athens, I see that in all things ye are too superstitious." The ruins of the very temples to which he pointed were before our eyes.

Descending, and rising toward the summit of another hill, we came to the Pnyx, where Demosthenes, in the most stirring words that ever fell from human lips, roused his countrymen against the Macedonian invader. Above, on the very summit of the hill, is the old Pnyx, commanding a view of the sea of Salamis, and of the hill where Xerxes sat to behold the great naval battle. During the reign of the thirty tyrants the Pnyx was removed beneath the brow of the hill, excluding the view of the sea, that the orator might not inflame the passions of the people by directing their eyes to Salamis, the scene of their naval glory. But, without this, the orator had material enough; for, when he stood on the platform facing the audience, he had before him the city which the Athenians loved and the temples in which they worshipped, and I could well imagine the irresistible force of an appeal to these objects of their enthusiastic devotion, their firesides and altars. The place is admirably adapted for public speaking. The side of the hill has been worked into a gently inclined plane, semicircular in form, and supported in some places by a wall of immense stones. This plain is bounded above by the brow of the hill, cut down perpendicularly. In the centre the rock projects into a platform about eight or ten feet square, which forms the Pnyx, or pulpit for the orator. The ascent is by three steps cut out of the rock, and in front is a place for the scribe or clerk. We stood on this Pnyx, beyond doubt on the same spot where Demosthenes thundered his Philippics in the ears of the Athenians. On the road leading to the Museum hill we entered a chamber excavated in the rock, which tradition hallows as the prison of Socrates ; and though the authority for this is doubtful, it is not uninteresting to enter the damp and gloomy cavern wherein, according to the belief of the modern Athenians, the wisest of the Greeks drew his last breath. Farther to the south is the hill of Philopappus, so called after a Roman governor of that name. On the very summit, near the extreme angle of the old wall, and one of the most conspicuous objects around Athens, is a monument erected by the Roman governor in honour of the emperor Trajan. The marble is covered with the names of travellers, most of whom, like Philopappus himself, would never have been heard of but for that monument.

Descending toward the Acropolis, and entering the city among streets encumbered with ruined houses, we came to the Temple of the Winds, a marble octagonal tower, built by Andronicus. On each side is a sculptured figure, clothed in drapery adapted to the wind he represents ; and on the top was formerly a Triton with a rod in his hand, pointing to the figure marking the wind. The Triton is gone, and great part of the temple buried under ruins. Part of the interior, however, has been excavated, and probably, before long, the whole will be restored.

East of the foot of the Acropolis, and on the way to Adrian's Gate, we came to the Lantern of Demosthenes (I eschew its new name of the Choragic Monument of Lysichus), where, according to an absurd tradition, the orator shut himself up to study the rhetorical art. It is considered one of the most beautiful monuments of antiquity, and the capitals are most elegant specimens of the Corinthian order refined by Attic taste. It is now in a mutilated condition, and its many repairs make its dilapidation more perceptible. Whether Demosthenes ever lived here or not, it derives an interest from the fact that Lord Byron made it his residence during his visit to Athens. Farther on, and forming part of the modern wall, is the Arch of Adrian, bearing on one side an inscription in Greek, " This is the city of Theseus ; " and on the other, " But this is the city of Adrian." On the arrival of Otho, a placard was erected, on which was inscribed, " These were the cities of Theseus and Adrian, but now of Otho." Many of the most ancient buildings in Athens have totally disappeared. The Turks destroyed many of them to construct the wall around the city, and even the modern Greeks have not scrupled to build their miserable houses with the plunder of the temples in which their ancestors worshipped.

Passing under the Arch of Adrian, outside the gate, on the plain toward the Ilissus, we came to the ruined Temple of Jupiter Olympus, perhaps once the most magnificent in the world. It was built of the purest white marble, having a front of nearly two hundred feet, and more than three hundred and fifty in length, and contained one hundred and twenty columns, sixteen of which are all that now remain ; and these, fluted and having rich Corinthian capitals, tower more than sixty feet above the plain, perfect as when they were reared. I visited these ruins often, particularly in the afternoon: they are at all times mournfully beautiful, but I have seldom known anything more touching than, when the sun was setting, to walk over the marble floor, and look up at the lonely columns of this ruined temple. I cannot imagine anything more imposing than it must have been when, with its lofty roof supported by all its columns, it stood at the gate of the city, its doors wide open, inviting the Greeks to worship. That such an edifice should be erected for the worship of a heathen god! On the architrave connecting three of the columns a hermit built his lonely cell, and passed his life in that elevated solitude, accessible only to the crane and the eagle. The hermit is long since dead, but his little habitation still resists the whistling of the wind, and awakens the curiosity of the wondering traveller.

The Temple of Theseus is the last of the principal monuments, but the first which the traveller sees on entering Athens. It was built after the battle of Marathon, and in commemoration of the victory which drove the Persians from the shores of Greece. It is a small but beautiful specimen of the pure Doric, built of Pentelican marble, centuries of exposure to the open air giving it a yellowish tint, which softens the brilliancy of the white. Three Englishmen have been buried within this temple. The first time I visited it a company of Greek recruits, with some negroes among them, was drawn up in front, going through the manual exercise under the direction of a German corporal ; and, at the same time, workmen were engaged in fitting it up for the coronation of King Otho !

These are the principal monuments around the city, and except the temples at Pæstum, they are more worthy of admiration than all the ruins in Italy ; but towering above them in position, and far exceeding them in interest, are the ruins of the Acropolis. I have since wandered among the ruined monuments of Egypt and the desolate city of Petra, but I look back with unabated reverence to the Athenian Acropolis. Every day I had gazed at it from the balcony of my hotel, and from every part of the city and suburbs. Early on my arrival I had obtained the necessary permit, paid a hurried visit, and resolved not to go again until I had examined all the other interesting objects On the fourth day, with my friend M., I went again. We ascended by a broad road paved with stone. The summit is inclosed by a wall, of which some of the foundation stones, very large, and bearing an appearance of great antiquity, are pointed out as part of the wall built by Themistocles after the battle of Salamis, four hundred and eighty years before Christ. The rest is Venetian and Turkish, falling to decay, and marring the picturesque effect of the ruins from below. The guard examined our permit, and we passed under the gate. A magnificent propylon of the finest white marble, the blocks of the largest size ever laid by human hands, and having a wing of the same material on each side, stands at the entrance. Though broken and ruined, the world contains nothing like it even now. If my first impressions do not deceive me, the proudest portals of Egyptian temples suffer in comparison. Passing this magnificent propylon, and ascending several steps, we reached the Parthenon, or ruined Temple of Minerva; an immense white marble skeleton, the noblest monument of architectural genius which the world ever saw. Standing on the steps of this temple, we had around us all that is interesting in association and all that is beautiful in art. We might well forget the capital of King Otho, and go back in imagination to the golden age of Athens. Pericles, with the illustrious throng of Grecian heroes, orators, and sages, had ascended there to worship, and Cicero and the noblest of the Romans had gone there to admire; and probably, if the fashion of modern tourists had existed in their days, we should see their names inscribed with their own hands on its walls. The great temple stands on the very summit of the Acropolis, elevated far above the Propylæa and the surrounding edifices. Its length is two hundred and eight feet, and breadth one hundred and two. At each end were two rows of eight Doric columns, thirty-four feet high and six feet in diameter, and on each side were thirteen more. The whole temple within and without was adorned with the most splendid works of art, by the first sculptors in Greece, and Phidias himself wrought the statue of the goddess, of ivory and gold, twenty-six cubits high, having on the top of her helmet a sphinx, with griffins on each of the sides; on the breast a head of Medusa wrought in ivory, and a figure of Victory, about four cubits high, holding a spear in her hand and a shield lying at her feet. Until the latter part of the seventeenth century, this magnificent temple, with all its ornaments, existed entire. During the siege of Athens by the Venetians, the central part was used by the Turks as a magazine; and a bomb, aimed with a fatal precision or by a not less fatal chance reached the magazine, and with a tremendous explosion, destroyed a great part of the buildings. Subsequently the Turks used it as a quarry, and antiquaries and travellers, foremost among whom is Lord Elgin, have contributed to destroy "what Goth, and Turk, and Time had spared."

Around the Parthenon, and covering the whole summit of the Acropolis, are strewed columns and blocks of polished white marble, the ruins of ancient temples. The remains of the Temples of Erectheus and Minerva Polias are pre-eminent in beauty; the pillars of the latter are the most perfect specimens of the Ionic in existence, and its light and graceful proportions are in elegant contrast with the severe and simple majesty of the Parthenon. The capitals of the columns are wrought and ornamented with a delicacy surpassing anything of which I could have believed marble susceptible. Once I was tempted to knock off a corner and bring it home, as a specimen of the exquisite skill of the Grecian artist, which it would have illustrated better than a volume of description; but I could not do it; it seemed nothing less than sacrilege.

Afar off, and almost lost in the distance, rises the Pentelican mountain, from the body of which were hewed the rough rude blocks which, wrought and perfected by the sculptor's art, now stand the lofty and stately columns of the ruined temple. What labour was expended upon each single column! how many were employed in hewing it from its rocky bed, in bearing it to the foot of the mountain, transporting it across the plain of Attica, and raising it to the summit of the Acropolis! and then what time, and skill, and labour, in reducing it from a rough block to a polished shaft, in adjusting its proportions, in carving its rich capitals, and rearing it where it now stands, a model of majestic grace and beauty! Once, under the direction of Mr. Hill, I clambered up to the very apex of the pediment, and, lying down at full length, leaned over and saw under the frieze the acanthus leaf delicately and beautifully painted on the marble, and, being protected from exposure, still retaining its freshness of colouring. It was entirely out of sight from below, and had been discovered, almost at the peril of his life, by the enthusiasm of an English artist. The wind was whistling around me as I leaned over to examine it, and, until that moment, I never appreciated fully the immense labour employed and the exquisite-finish displayed in every portion of the temple.

The sentimental traveller must already mourn that Athens has been selected as the capital of Greece. Already have speculators and the whole tribe of "improvers" invaded the glorious city; and while I was lingering on the steps of the Parthenon, a German, who was quietly smoking among the ruins, a sort of superintendant, whom I had met before, came up, and offering me a cigar, and leaning against one of the lofty columns of the temple, opened upon me with "his plans of city improvements; with new streets, and projected railroads, and the rise of lots." At first I almost thought it personal, and that he was making a fling at me in allusion to one of the greatest hobbies of my native city; but I soon found that he was as deeply bitten as if he had been in Chicago or Dunkirk;[*] and the way in which he talked of moneyed facilities, the wants of the community, and a great French bank then

---

[*] Towns lately laid out, in the United States.—ED.

contemplated at the Piræus, would have been no discredit to some of my friends at home. The removal of the court has created a new era in Athens; but, in my mind, it is deeply to be regretted that it has been snatched from the ruin to which it was tending. Even I, deeply imbued with the utilitarian spirit of my country, and myself a quondam speculator in "up-town lots," would fain save Athens from the ruthless hand of renovation; from the building mania of modern speculators. I would have her go on till there was not a habitation among her ruins; till she stood, like Pompeii, alone in the wilderness, a sacred desert, where the traveller might sit down and meditate alone and undisturbed among the relics of the past. But already Athens has become a heterogeneous anomaly; the Greeks in their wild costume are jostled in the streets by Englishmen, Frenchmen, Italians, Dutchmen, Spaniards, and Bavarians, Russians, Danes, and sometimes Americans. European shops invite purchasers by the side of Eastern bazars, coffee-houses, and billiard-rooms, and French and German restaurants are opened all over the city. Sir Pulteney Malcolm has erected a house to hire near the site of Plato's Academy. Lady Franklin has bought land near the foot of Mount Hymettus for a country-seat. Several English gentlemen have done the same. Mr. Richmond, an American clergyman, has purchased a farm in the neighbourhood; and in a few years, if the "march of improvement" continues, the Temple of Theseus will be enclosed in the garden of the palace of Otho; the Temple of the Winds will be concealed by a German opera-house, and the Lantern of Demosthenes by a row of "three-story houses."

I was not a sentimental traveller, but I visited all the localities around Athens, and, therefore, briefly mention that several times I jumped over the poetic and perennial Ilissus, trotted my horse over the ground where Aristotle walked with his Peripatetics, and got muddied up to my knees in the garden of Plato.

One morning my Scotch friend and I set out early to ascend Mount Hymettus. The mountain is neither high nor picturesque, but a long flat ridge of bare rock, the sides cut up into ravines, fissures, and gullies. There is an easy path to the summit, but we had no guide, and about midday, after a wild scramble, were worn out, and descended without reaching the top, which is exceedingly fortunate for the reader, as otherwise he would be obliged to go through a description of the view therefrom.

Returning, we met the king taking his daily walk, attended by two aides, one of whom was young Marco Bozzaris. Otho is tall and thin, and, when I saw him, was dressed in a German military frock-coat and cap, and altogether, for a king, seemed to be an amiable young man enough. All the world speaks well of him, and so do I. We touched our hats to him, and he returned the civility; and what could he do more without inviting us to dinner? In old times there was a divinity about a king; but now, if a king is a gentleman, it is as much as we can expect. He has spent his money like a gentleman, that is, he cannot tell what has become of it. Two of the three-millions loan are gone, and there is no colonisation, no agricultural prosperity, no opening of roads, no security in the mountains; not a town in Greece but is in ruins, and no money to improve them. Athens, however, is to be embellished. With ten thousand pounds in the treasury, he is building a palace of white Pentelican marble, to cost three hundred thousand pounds.

Otho was very popular, because, not being of age, all the errors of his administration were visited upon Count Armansperg and the regency, who, from all accounts, richly deserved it; and it was hoped that, on receiving the crown, he would shake off the Bavarians who were preying upon the vitals of Greece, and gather around him his native-born subjects. In private life he bore a most exemplary character. He had no circle of young companions, and passed much of his time in study, being engaged, among other things, in acquiring the Greek and English languages. His position is interesting, though not enviable; and if, as the first king of emancipated Greece, he entertains recollections of her ancient greatness, and the ambition of restoring her to her position among the nations of the earth, he is doomed to disappointment. Otho is since crowned and married. The pride of the Greeks was considerably humbled by a report that their king's proposals to several daughters of German princes had been rejected; but the king had great reason to congratulate himself upon the spirit which induced the daughter of the Duke of Oldenburgh to accept his hand. From her childhood she had taken an enthusiastic interest in Greek history, and it had been her constant wish to visit Greece; and when she heard that Otho had been called to the throne, she naïvely expressed an ardent wish to share it with him. Several years afterward, by the merest accident, she met Otho at a German watering-place, travelling with his mother, the Queen of Bavaria, as the Count de Missolonghi; and in February last she accompanied him to Athens, to share the throne which had been the object of her youthful wish.

M. dined at my hotel, and, returning to his own, he was picked up and carried to the guard-house. He started for his hotel without a lantern, the requisition to carry one being imperative in all the Greek and Turkish cities; the guard could not understand a word he said until he showed them some money, which made his English perfectly intelligible; and they then carried him to a Bavarian corporal, who, after two hours' detention, escorted him to his hotel. After that we were rather careful about staying out late at night.

"Thursday. I don't know the day of the month." I find this in my notes, the caption of a day of business, and at this distance of time will not undertake to correct the entry. Indeed, I am inclined to think that my notes in those days are rather uncertain and imperfect; certainly not taken with the precision of one who expected to publish them. Nevertheless, the residence of the court, the diplomatic corps, and strangers, form an agreeable society at Athens. I had letters to some of the foreign ministers, but did not present them, as I was hardly presentable myself without my carpet-bag. On "Thursday," however, in company with Dr. W., I called upon Mr. Dawkins, the British minister. Mr. Dawkins went to

Greece on a special mission, which he supposed would detain him six months from home, and had remained there ten years. He is a high tory, but retained under a whig administration, because his services could not well be dispensed with. He gave us much interesting information in regard to the present condition and future prospects of Greece; and, in answer to my suggestion that the United States were not represented at all in Greece, not even by a consul, he said, with emphasis, " You are better represented than any power in Europe. Mr. Hill has more influence here than any minister plenipotentiary among us." A few days after, when confined to my room by indisposition, Mr. Dawkins returned my visit, and again spoke in the same terms of high commendation of Mr. Hill. It was pleasing to me, and I have no doubt it will be so to Mr. Hill's numerous friends in this country, to know that a private American citizen, in a position that keeps him aloof from politics, was spoken of in such terms by the representative of one of the great powers of Europe. I had heard it intimated that there was a prospect of Mr. Dawkins being transferred to this country, and parted with him in the hope at some future day of seeing him the representative of his government here.

I might have been presented to the king, but my carpet-bag—Dr. W. borrowed a hat, and was presented; the doctor had an old white hat, which he had worn all the way from New York. The tide is rolling backward; Athens is borrowing her customs from the barbarous nations of the north; and it is part of the etiquette to enter a drawing-room with a hat (a black one) under the arm. The doctor, in his republican simplicity, thought that a hat, good enough to put on his own head, was good enough to go into the king's presence; but he was advised to the contrary, and took one of Mr. Hill's, not very much too large for him. He was presented by Dr. ——, a German, the king's physician, with whom he had discoursed much of the different medical systems in Germany and America. Dr. W. was much pleased with the king. Did ever a man talk with a king who was not pleased with him? But the doctor was particularly pleased with King Otho, as the latter entered largely into discourse on the doctor's favourite theme, Mr. Hill's school, and the cause of education in Greece. Indeed, it speaks volumes in favour of the young king, that education is one of the things in which he takes the deepest interest. The day the doctor was to be presented we dined at Mr. Hill's, having made arrangements for leaving Athens that night; the doctor and M. to return to Europe. In the afternoon, while the doctor remained to be presented, M. and I walked down to the Piræus, now, as in the days of her glory, the harbour of Athens. The ancient harbour is about five miles from Athens, and was formerly joined to it by *long walls* built of stone of enormous size, sixty feet high, and broad enough on the top for two waggons to pass abreast. These have long since disappeared, and the road is now over a plain shaded a great part of the way by groves of olives. As usual at this time of day, we met many parties on horseback, sometimes with ladies; and I remember particularly the beautiful and accomplished daughters of Count Armansperg,

both of whom are since married and dead.* It is a beautiful ride, in the afternoon particularly, as then the dark outline of the mountains beyond, and the reflections of light and shade, give a peculiarly interesting effect to the ruins of the Acropolis. Toward the other end we paced between the ruins of the old walls, and entered upon a scene which reminded me of home. Eight months before there was only one house at the Piræus; but, as soon as the court removed to Athens, the old harbour revived; and already we saw long ranges of stores and warehouses, and all the hurry and bustle of one of our rising western towns. A railroad was in contemplation, and many other improvements, which have since failed; but an *omnibus!* that most modern and commonplace of inventions, is now running regularly between the Piræus and Athens. A friend who visited Greece six months after me brought home with him an advertisement printed in Greek, English, French, and German, the English being in the words and figures following, to wit:

" ADVERTISEMENT.

" The public are hereby informed, that on the nineteenth instant an omnibus will commence running between Athens and the Piræus, and will continue to do so every day at the undermentioned hours until further notice.

Hours of departure.

From Athens.	From Piræus.
Half past seven o'clock A.M.	Half past eight o'clock A.M.
Ten o'clock A.M.	Eleven o'clock A.M.
Two o'clock P.M.	Three o'clock P.M.
Half past four P.M.	Half past five P.M.

" The price of a seat in the omnibus is one drachme.

" Baggage, if not too bulky and heavy, can be taken on the roof.

" Smoking cannot be allowed in the omnibus, nor can dogs be admitted.

" Small parcels and packages may be sent by this conveyance at a moderate charge, and given to the care of the conducteur.

" The omnibus starts from the corner of the Hermes and Æolus streets at Athens, and from the Bazar at the Piræus, and will wait five minutes at each place, during which period the conducteur will sound his horn.

" Athens, 17th, 29th September, 1836."

Old things are passing away, and all things are becoming new. For a little while yet we may cling to the illusions connected with the past, but the mystery is fast dissolving, the darkness is breaking away, and Greece and Rome, and even Egypt herself, henceforward claim our attention with objects and events of the present hour. Already they have lost much of the deep and absorbing interest with which men turned to them a generation ago. All the hallowed associations of these ancient regions are fading away. We may regret it, we may mourn over it, but we cannot help it. The world is marching onward; I have met parties of my own townsmen while walking in the silent galleries of the Coliseum. I have seen Americans drinking champagne in an excavated dwelling of the ancient Pompeii, and I have

---

* They married two brothers, the young princes Cantacuzenes. Some scruples being raised against this double alliance on the score of consanguinity, the difficulty was removed by each couple going to separate churches with separate priests to pronounce the mystic words at precisely the same moment: so that neither could be said to espouse his sister-in-law.

dined with Englishmen among the ruins of Thebes, but, blessed be my fortune, I never rode in an omnibus from the Piræus to Athens.

We put our baggage on board the caique, and lounged among the little shops till dark, when we betook ourselves to a dirty little coffee-house, filled with Greeks dozing and smoking pipes. We met there a boat's crew of a French man-of-war, waiting for some of the officers, who were dining with the French ambassador at Athens. One of them had been born to a better condition than that of a common sailor. One juvenile indiscretion after another had brought him down, and, without a single vice, he was fairly on the road to ruin. Once he brushed a tear from his eyes as he told us of prospects blighted by his own follies; but, rousing himself, hurried away, and his reckless laugh soon rose above the noise and clamour of his wild companions.

About ten o'clock the doctor came in, drenched with rain and up to his knees in mud. We wanted to embark immediately, but the appearance of the weather was so unfavourable that the captain preferred waiting till after midnight. The Greeks went away from the coffee-house, the proprietor fell asleep in his seat, and we extended ourselves on the tables and chairs; and now the fleas, which had been distributed about among all the loungers, made a combined onset upon us. Life has its cares and troubles, but few know that of being given up to the tender-mercies of Greek fleas. We bore the infliction till human nature could endure no longer; and, at about three in the morning, in the midst of violent wind and rain, broke out of the coffee-house and went in search of our boat. It was very dark, but we found her and got on board. She was a caique, having an open deck with a small covering over the stern. Under this we crept, and with our cloaks and a sailcloth spread over us, our heated blood cooled, and we fell asleep. When we woke we were on the way to Epidaurus. The weather was raw and cold. We passed within a stone's-throw of Salamis and Ægina, and at about three o'clock, turning a point which completely hid it from view, entered a beautiful little bay, on which stands the town of Epidaurus. The old city, the birth-place of Esculapius, stands upon a hill projecting into the bay, and almost forming an island. In the middle of the village is a wooden building containing a large chamber, where the Greek delegates, a band of mountain warriors, with arms in their hands, "in the name of the Greek nation, proclaimed before Gods and men its independence."

At the locanda there was by chance one bed, which not being large enough for three, I slept on the floor. At seven o'clock, after a quarrel with our host, and paying him about half his demand, we set out for Napoli di Romania. For about an hour, we moved in the valley running off from the beautiful shore of Epidaurus; soon the valley deepened into a glen, and in an hour we turned off on a path that led into the mountains, and, riding through wild and rugged ravines, fell into the dry bed of a torrent; following which, we came to the Hieron Elios, or Sacred Grove of Esculapius. This was the great watering-place for the invalids of ancient Greece, the prototype of the Cheltenham and Saratoga of modern days. It is situated in a valley surrounded by high mountains, and was formerly inclosed by walls, within which, that the credit of the god might not be impeached, *no man was allowed to die, and no woman to be delivered.* Within this inclosure were temples, porticoes, and fountains, now lying in ruins hardly distinguishable. The theatre is the most beautiful, and best preserved. It is scooped out of the side of the mountain, rather more than semicircular in form, and containing fifty-four seats. These seats are of pink marble, about fifteen inches high and nearly three feet wide. In the middle of each seat is a groove, in which, probably, woodwork was constructed, to prevent the feet of those above from incommoding them who sat below, and also to support the backs of an invalid audience. The theatre faces the north, and is so arranged that with the mountain towering behind it, the audience was shaded nearly all the day. It speaks volumes in favour of the intellectual character of the Greeks, that it was their favourite recreation to listen to the recitation of their poets and players. And their superiority in refinement over the Romans, is in no way manifested more clearly than by the fact, that in the ruined cities of the former are found the remains of theatres, and in the latter of amphitheatres, showing the barbarous taste of the Romans for combats of gladiators and wild beasts. It was in beautiful keeping with this intellectual taste of the Greeks, that their places of assembling were in the open air, amid scenery calculated to elevate the mind; and, as I sat on the marble steps of the theatre, I could well imagine the high satisfaction with which the Greek, under the shade of the impending mountain, himself all enthusiasm and passion, rapt in the interest of some deep tragedy, would hang upon the strains of Euripides or Sophocles. What deep-drawn exclamations, what shouts of applause had rung through that solitude, what bursts of joy and grief had echoed from those silent benches! And then, too, what flirting and coquetting! the taste of society at the springs in the Grove of Esculapius being probably much the same as at Saratoga in our own days. The whole grove is now a scene of desolation. The lentisculus is growing between the crevices of the broken marble; birds sing undisturbed among the bushes; the timid hare steals among the ruined fragments; and sometimes the snake is seen gliding over the marble steps.

We had expected to increase the interest of our visit by taking our noonday refection on the steps of the theatre, but it was too cold for a picnic *al fresco;* and, mounting our horses, about two o'clock we came in sight of Argos, on the opposite side of the great plain; and in half an hour more, turning the mountain, saw Napoli di Romania beautifully situated on a gentle elevation on the shore of the gulf. The scenery in every direction around Napoli is exceedingly beautiful; and, when we approached it, bore no marks of the sanguinary scenes of the late revolution. The plain was better cultivated than any part of the adjacent country; and the city contained long ranges of houses and streets, with German names, such as Heidecker, Maurer-street, &c., and was seemingly better regulated than any other city in Greece. We drove up to the *Hôtel des Quatre Nations,* the best we had found in Greece; dined at a res-

L

taurant with a crowd of Bavarian officers and adventurers, and passed the evening in the streets and coffee-houses.

The appearance of Otho-street, which is the principal, is very respectable; it runs from what was the palace to the grand square or esplanade, on one side of which are the barracks of the Bavarian soldiers, with a park of artillery posted so as to sweep the square and principal streets; a speaking comment upon the liberty of the Greeks, and the confidence reposed in them by the government!

Every thing in Napoli recalls the memory of the brief and unfortunate career of Capo d'Istria. Its recovery from the horrors of barbarian war, and the thriving appearance of the country around, are ascribed to the impulse given by his administration. A Greek by birth, while his country lay groaning under the Ottoman yoke, he entered the Russian service, distinguished himself in all the diplomatic correspondence during the French invasion, was invested with various high offices and honours, and subscribed the treaty of Paris in 1815 as imperial Russian plenipotentiary. He withdrew from her service because Russia disapproved the efforts of his countrymen to free themselves from the Turkish yoke; and, after passing five years in Germany and Switzerland, chiefly at Geneva, in 1827 he was called to the presidency of Greece. On his arrival at Napoli, amid the miseries of war and anarchy, he was received by the whole people as the only man capable of saving their country. Civil war ceased on the very day of his arrival, and the traitor Grievas placed in his hands the key of the Palimethe. I shall not enter into any speculations upon the character of his administration. The rank he had attained in a foreign service is conclusive evidence of his talents, and his withdrawal from that service for the reason stated is as conclusive of his patriotism; but from the moment he took into his hands the reins of government, he was assailed by every so-called liberal press in Europe with the party cry of Russian influence. The Greeks were induced to believe that he intended to sell them to a stranger; and Capo d'Istria, strong in his own integrity, and confidently relying on the fidelity and gratitude of his countrymen, was assassinated in the streets on his way to mass. Young Mauromichalis, the son of the old Bey of Maina, struck the fatal blow, and fled for refuge to the house of the French ambassador. A gentleman attached to the French legation told me that he himself opened the door when the murderer rushed in with the bloody dagger in his hand, exclaiming, "I have killed the tyrant." He was not more than twenty-one, tall and noble in his appearance, and animated by the enthusiastic belief that he had delivered his country. My informant told me that he barred all the doors and windows, and went up stairs to inform the minister, who had not yet risen. The latter was embarrassed and in doubt what he should do. A large crowd gathered round the house; but, as yet, they were all Mauromichalis' friends. The young enthusiast spoke of what he had done with a high feeling of patriotism and pride; and while the clamour out of doors was becoming outrageous, he ate his breakfast and smoked his pipe with the utmost composure. He remained at the embassy more than two hours, and until the regular troops drew up before the house. The French ambassador, though he at first refused, was obliged to deliver him up; and my informant saw him shot under a tree outside the gate of Napoli, dying gallantly in the firm conviction that he had played the Brutus and freed his country from a Cæsar.

The fate of Capo d'Istria again darkened the prospects of Greece, and the throne went begging for an occupant until it was accepted by the king of Bavaria for his second son Otho. The young monarch arrived at Napoli in February, 1833. The whole population came out to meet him, and the Grecian youth ran breast-deep in the water to touch his barge as it approached the shore. In February, 1834, it was decided to establish Athens as the capital. The propriety of this removal has been seriously questioned, for Napoli possessed advantages in her location, harbour, fortress, and a town already built; but the king of Bavaria, a scholar and an antiquary, was influenced more, perhaps, by classical feeling than by regard for the best interests of Greece. Napoli has received a severe blow from the removal of the seat of government, and the consequent withdrawal of the court, and the manufacturers and mechanics attendant upon it. Still it was by far the most European in its appearance of any city I had seen in Greece. It had several restaurants and coffee-houses, which were thronged all the evening with Bavarian officers and broken-down European adventurers, discussing the internal affairs of that unfortunate country, which men of every nation seemed to think they had a right to assist in governing. Napoli had always been the great gathering-place of the phil-Hellenists, and many appropriating to themselves that sacred name were hanging round it still. All over Europe thousands of men are trained up to be shot at for so much per day; the soldier's is as regular a business as that of the lawyer or merchant, and there is always a large class of turbulent spirits constantly on the look-out for opportunities, and ever ready with their swords to carve their way to fortune. To them the uproar of a rebellion is music, for they know that, in the general turning up of the elements, something may be gained by him who has nothing to lose; and when the Greek revolution broke upon the astonished people of Europe, these soldiers of fortune hastened to take their part in the struggle, and win the profits of success. I believe that there were men who embarked in the cause with as high and noble purposes as ever animated the warrior; but of many of these chivalric patriots there is no lack of charity in saying that, however good they might be as fighters, they were not much as men; and I am sorry to add that, from the accounts I heard in Greece, the American phil-Hellenists were a rather shabby set. Jarvis was about the most active and distinguished, and I never heard in Greece any imputations on his character. Mr. M., then resident in Napoli, was accosted one day in the streets by a young man, who asked him where he could find General Jarvis. "What do you want with him?" said Mr. M. "I hope to obtain a commission in his army." "Do you see that dirty fellow yonder?" said Mr. M., pointing to a ragged patriot passing at the moment: "well, twenty such fellows compose Jarvis's army, and

Jarvis himself is no better off." "Well, then," said the young *American*, "I believe I'll join the Turks!" Allen, another American patriot, was hung at Constantinople. Another behaved gallantly as a soldier, but sullied his laurels by appropriating the money intrusted to him by the Greek committee. One bore the sacred name of Washington; a brave but unprincipled man. Mr. M. had heard him say, that if the devil himself should raise a regiment, and would give him a good commission, he would willingly march under him. He was struck by a shot from the fortress in the harbour of Napoli, while directing a battery against it; was taken on board his Britannic majesty's ship Asia, and breathed his last, uttering curses on his country.

I could have passed a week with great satisfaction in Napoli, if it were only for the luxury of its hotel; but time would not permit, and I went to bed resolving to make up for the last night, and sleep a little in advance for the next.

CHAPTER VI.

Argos.—Parting and Farewell.—Tomb of Agamemnon.—Mycenæ.—Gate of the Lions.—A Misfortune.—Meeting in the Mountains.—A Landlord's Troubles.—A Midnight Quarrel.—One good Turn deserves another.—Gratitude of a Greek Family.—Megara.—The Soldier's Revel.

In the morning, finding a difficulty in procuring horses, some of the loungers about the hotel told us there was a carriage in Napoli, and we ordered it to be brought out, and soon after saw moving majestically down the principal street a bella carozza, imported by its enterprising proprietor from the Strada Toledo at Naples. It was painted a bright flaring yellow, and had a big-breeched Albanian for coachman. While preparing to embark, a Greek came up with two horses, and we discharged the bella carozza. My companion hired the horses for Padras, and I threw my cloak on one of them and followed on foot.

The plain of Argos is one of the most beautiful I ever saw. On every side, except toward the sea, it is bounded by mountains, and the contrast between these mountains, the plain, and the sea is strikingly beautiful. The sun was beating with intense heat; the labourers were almost naked, or in several places lying asleep on the ground, while the tops of the mountains were covered with snow. I walked across the whole plain, being only six miles, to Argos. This ancient city is long since in ruins; her thirty temples, her costly sepulchres, her gymnasium, and her numerous and magnificent monuments and statues, have disappeared, and the only traces of her former greatness are some remains of her Cyclopean walls, and a ruined theatre cut in the rock and of magnificent proportions. Modern Argos is nothing more than a straggling village. Mr. Riggs, an American missionary, was stationed there, but was at that time at Athens with an invalid wife. I was still on foot, and wandered up and down the principal street looking for a horse. Every Greek in Argos soon knew my business, and all kinds of four-legged animals were brought to me at exorbitant prices. When I was poring over the Iliad, I little thought that I should ever visit Argos; still less that I should create a sensation in the ancient city of the Danai; but man little knows for what he is reserved.

Argos has been so often visited, that Homer is out of date. Every middy from a Mediterranean cruiser has danced on the steps of her desolate theatre, and, instead of busying myself with her ancient glories, I roused half the population in hiring a horse. In fact, in this ancient city I soon became the centre of a regular horse-market. Every rascally jockey swore that his horse was the best, and, according to the descendants of the respectable sons of Atreus, blindness, lameness, spavin, and staggers, were a recommendation. A Bavarian officer, whom I had met in the bazars, came to my assistance, and stood by me while I made my bargain. I had more regard to the guide than the horse; and picking out one who had been particularly noisy, hired him to conduct me to Corinth and Athens. He was a lad of about twenty, with a bright sparkling eye, who laughing roguishly at his unsuccessful competitors, wanted to pitch me at once on the horse and be off. I joined my companions, and in a few minutes we left Argos.

The plain of Argos has been immortalised by poetic genius as the great gathering-place of the kings and armies that assembled for the siege of Troy. To the scholar and poet few plains in the world are more interesting. It carries him back to the heroic ages, to the history of times bordering on the fabulous, when fact and fiction are so beautifully blended that we would not separate them if we could. I had but a little while longer to remain with my friends, for we were approaching the point where our roads separated, and about eleven o'clock we halted and exchanged our farewell greetings. We parted in the middle of the plain, they to return to Padras and Europe, and I for the tomb of Agamemnon, and back to Athens, and I hardly know where besides. Dr. W. I did not meet again until my return home. About a year afterward, I arrived in Antwerp in the evening from Rotterdam. The city was filled with strangers, and I was denied admission at a third hotel, when a young man brushed by me in the doorway, and I recognized Maxwell. I hailed him, but in cap and cloak, and with a large red shawl around my neck, he did not know me. I unrolled and discovered myself, and it is needless to say that I did not leave the hotel that night. It was his very last day of two years' travel on the Continent; he had taken his passage in the steamer for London, and one day later I should have missed him altogether. I can give but a faint idea of the pleasure of this meeting. He gave me the first information of the whereabout of Dr. W.; we talked nearly all night, and about noon the next day I again bade him farewell on board the steamer.

I have for some time neglected our servant. When we separated, the question was who should *not* keep him. We were all heartily tired of him, and I would not have had him with me on any account. Still, at the moment of parting in that wild and distant region, never expecting to see him again, I felt some slight leaning toward him. Touching the matter of shirts, it will not be surprising to a man of the world that, at the moment of parting, I had one of M.'s on my back; and, in justice to him, I must say it was a very good one, and lasted a long time. A friend once wrote to me on a like occasion not to wear his out of its turn, but M. laid no such restriction upon me. But this trifling gain did not indemnify me for the loss of my friends. I had broken the only link that connected me with home, and was setting out alone for I knew not where. I felt at once the great loss I had sustained, for my young muleteer could speak only his own language, and, as Queen Elizabeth said to Sir Walter Raleigh of her Hebrew, we had " forgotten our " Greek.

But on that classical soil I ought not to have been lonely. I should have conjured up the ghosts of the departed Atridæ, and held converse on their own ground with Homer's heroes. Nevertheless, I was not in the mood; and, entirely forgetting the glories of the past, I started my horse into a gallop. My companion followed on a full run, close at my heels, belabouring my horse with a stick, which when he broke, he pelted him with stones; indeed, this mode of scampering over the ground seemed to hit his humour, for he shouted, hurraed, and whipped, and sometimes laying hold of the tail of the beast, was dragged along several paces with little effort of his own. I soon tired of this, and made signs to him to stop; but it was his turn now, and I was obliged to lean back till I reached him with my cane before I could make him let go his hold, and then he commenced shouting and pelting again with stones.

In this way we approached the village of Krabata, about a mile below the ruins of Mycenæ, and the most miserable place I had seen in Greece. With the fertile plain of Argos uncultivated before them, the inhabitants exhibited a melancholy picture of the most abject poverty. As I rode through, crowds beset me with outstretched arms imploring charity; and a miserable old woman, darting out of a wretched hovel, laid her gaunt and bony hand upon my leg, and attempted to stop me. I shrank from her grasp, and, under the effect of a sudden impulse, threw myself off on the other side, and left my horse in her hands.

Hurrying through the village, a group of boys ran before me, crying out "Agamemnon," "Agamemnon." I followed, and they conducted me to the tomb of "the king of kings," a gigantic structure, still in good preservation, of a conical form, covered with turf; the stone over the door is twenty-seven feet long and seventeen wide, larger than any hewn stone in the world except Pompey's Pillar. I entered, my young guides going before with torches, and walked within and around this ancient sepulchre. A worthy Dutchman, Herman Van Creutzer, has broached a theory that the Trojan war is a mere allegory, and that no such person as Agamemnon ever existed. Shame upon the cold-blooded heretic! I have my own sins to answer for in that way, for I have laid my destroying hand upon many cherished illusions; but I would not, if I could, destroy the mystery that overhangs the heroic ages. The royal sepulchre was forsaken and empty; the shepherd drives within it his flock for shelter; the traveller sits under its shade to his noonday meal; and, at the moment, a goat was dozing quietly in one corner. He started as I entered, and seemed to regard me as an intruder; and when I flared before him the light of my torch, he rose up to butt me. I turned away and left him in quiet

possession. The boys were waiting outside, and crying "Mycenæ," "Mycenæ," led me away. All was solitude, and I saw no marks of a city until I reached the relics of her Cyclopean walls. I never felt a greater degree of reverence than when I approached the lonely ruins of Mycenæ. At Argos I spent most of my time in the horse-market, and I had galloped over the great plain as carelessly as if it had been the road to Harlem;* but all the associations connected with this most interesting ground here pressed upon me at once. Its extraordinary antiquity, its gigantic remains, and its utter and long-continued desolation, came home to my heart. I moved on to the Gate of the Lions, and stood before it a long time without entering. A broad street led to it between two immense parallel walls; and this street may, perhaps, have been a market-place. Over the gate are two lions rampant, like the supporters of a modern coat-of-arms, rudely carved, and supposed to be the oldest sculptured stone in Greece. Under this very gate Agamemnon led out his forces for the siege of Troy; three thousand years ago he saw them filing before him, glittering in brass, in all the pomp and panoply of war; and I held in my hand a book which told me that this city was so old that, more than seventeen hundred years ago, travellers came as I did to visit its ruins; and that Pausanias had found the Gate of the Lions in the same state in which I beheld it now. A great part is buried by the rubbish of the fallen city. I crawled under, and found myself within the walls, and then mounted to the height on which the city stood. It was covered with a thick soil and a rich carpet of grass. My boys left me, and I was alone. I walked all over it, following the line of the walls. I paused at the great blocks of stone, the remnants of Cyclopic masonry, the work of wandering giants. The heavens were unclouded, and the sun was beaming upon it with genial warmth. Nothing could exceed the quiet beauty of the scene. I became entangled in the long grass, and picked up wild flowers growing over long-buried dwellings. Under it are immense caverns, their uses now unknown; and the earth sounded hollow under my feet, as if I were treading on the sepulchre of a buried city. I looked across the plain to Argos: all was as beautiful as when Homer sang its praises; the plain, and the mountains, and the sea were the same, but the once magnificent city, her numerous statues and gigantic temples, were gone for ever; and but a few remains were left to tell the passing traveller the story of her fallen greatness. I could have remained there for hours; I could have gone again and again, for I had not found a more interesting spot in Greece; but my reveries were disturbed by the appearance of my muleteer and my juvenile escort. They pointed to the sun as an intimation that the day was passing; and, crying "Cavallo," "Cavallo," hurried me away. To them the ruined city was a playground; they followed capering behind; and, in descending, three or four of them rolled down upon me; they hurried me through the Gate of the Lions, and I came out with my pantaloons, my only pantaloons, rent across the knee almost irreparably. In an instant I was another man; I railed at the ruins for their strain upon wearing apparel, and be-

---
* A village so called, near New York.—ED.

moaned my unhappy lot in not having with me a needle and thread. I looked up to the old gate with a sneer. This was the city that Homer had made such a noise about; a man could stand on the citadel and almost throw a stone beyond the boundary-line of Agamemnon's kingdom. In full sight, and just at the other side of the plain, was the kingdom of Argos. The little state of Rhode Island would make a bigger kingdom than both of them together.

But I had no time for deep meditation, having a long journey to Corinth before me. Fortunately, my young Greek had no tire in him; he started me off on a gallop, whipping and pelting my horse with stones, and would have hurried me on, over rough and smooth, till either he, or I, or the horse broke down, if I had not jumped off and walked. As soon as I dismounted he mounted, and then he moved so leisurely that I had to hurry him on in turn. In this way we approached the range of mountains separating the plain of Argos from the Isthmus of Corinth. Entering the pass, we rode along a mountain torrent, of which the channel-bed was then dry, and ascended to the summit of the first range. Looking back, the scene was magnificent. On my right and left were the ruined heights of Argos and Mycenæ; before me, the towering Acropolis of Napoli di Romania; at my feet, the rich plain of Argos, extending to the shore of the sea; and beyond, the island-studded Ægean. I turned away with a feeling of regret that, in all probability, I should never see it more.

I moved on, and in a narrow pass, not wide enough to turn my horse if I had been disposed to take to my heels, three men rose up from behind a rock, armed to the teeth with long guns, pistols, yataghans, and sheep-skin cloaks—the dress of the klept, or mountain robber—and altogether presenting a most diabolically cut-throat appearance. If they had asked me for my purse I should have considered it all regular, and given up the remnant of my stock of borrowed money without a murmur; but I was relieved from immediate apprehension by the cry of Passe porta! King Otho has begun the benefits of civilised government in Greece by introducing passports, and mountain warriors were stationed in the different passes to examine strangers. They acted, however, as if they were more used to demanding purses than passports, for they sprang into the road and rattled the butts of their guns on the rock with a violence that was somewhat startling. Unluckily, my passport had been made out with those of my companions, and was in their possession, and when we parted, neither thought of it; and this demand to me, who had nothing to lose, was worse than that of my purse. A few words of explanation might have relieved me from all difficulty, but my friends could not understand a word I said. I was vexed at the idea of being sent back, and thought I would try the effect of a little impudence; so, crying out "Americanos," I attempted to pass on; but they answered me "Nix," and turned my horse's head towards Argos. The scene, which a few moments before had seemed so beautiful, was now perfectly detestable. Finding that bravado had not the desired effect, I lowered my tone and tried a bribe; this was touching the right chord; half a dollar removed all suspicions from the minds of these trusty guardians of the pass; and, released from their attentions, I hurried on.

The whole road across the mountain is one of the wildest in Greece. It is cut up by numerous ravines, sufficiently deep and dangerous, which at every step threaten destruction to the incautious traveller. During the late revolution, the soil of Greece had been drenched with blood; and my whole journey had been through cities and over battle-fields, memorable for scenes of slaughter unparalleled in the annals of modern war. In the narrowest pass of the mountains, my guide made gestures indicating that it had been the scene of a desperate battle. When the Turks, having penetrated to the plain of Argos, were compelled to fall back again upon Corinth, a small band of Greeks, under Niketas and Demetrius Ypsilanti, waylaid them in this pass. Concealing themselves behind the rock, and waiting till the pass was filled, all at once they opened a tremendous fire upon the solid column below, and the pass was instantly filled with slain. Six thousand were cut down in a few hours. The terrified survivors recoiled for a moment; but, as if impelled by an invisible power, rushed on to meet their fate. "The Mussulman rode into the passes with his sabre in his sheath and his hands before his eyes, the victim of destiny." The Greeks again poured upon them a shower of lead, and several thousand more were cut down before the Moslem army accomplished the passage of this terrible defile.

It was nearly dark when we rose to the summit of the last range of mountains, and saw, under the rich lustre of the setting sun, the Acropolis of Corinth, with its walls and turrets, towering to the sky; the plain forming the Isthmus of Corinth; the dark, quiet waters of the Gulf of Lepanto; and the gloomy mountains of Cithæron, and Helicon, and Parnassus covered with snow. It was after dark when we passed the region of the Nemean Grove, celebrated as the haunt of the lion and the scene of the first of the twelve labours of Hercules. We were yet three hours from Corinth; and, if the old lion had still been prowling in the grove, we could not have made more haste to escape its gloomy solitude. Reaching the plain, we heard behind us the clattering of horses' hoofs, at first sounding in the stillness of evening as if a regiment of cavalry or a troop of banditti was at our heels, but it proved to be only a single traveller, belated like ourselves, and hurrying on to Corinth. I could see through the darkness the shining butts of his pistols and hilt of his yataghan, and took his dimensions with more anxiety, perhaps, than exactitude. He recognised my Frank dress, and accosted me in bad Italian, which he had picked up at Padras (being just the Italian on which I could meet him on equal ground), and told me that he had met a party of Franks on the road to Padras, whom, from his description, I recognised as my friends.

It was nearly midnight when we rattled up to the gate of the old locanda. The yard was thronged with horses and baggage, and Greek and Bavarian soldiers. On the balcony stood my old brigand host, completely crest-fallen, and literally turned out of doors in his own house; a detachment of Bavarian soldiers had arrived that afternoon from Padras, and taken entire possession, giving him and his wife the freedom of the outside. He did not recognise me, and, taking me for an Englishman, began, "Sono Inglesi Signor" (he had lived at Corfu under the British dominion); and, telling me the whole particulars of his unceremonious ouster, claimed, through me, the arm of the British government to resent the injury to a British subject; his wife was walking about in no very gentle mood, but, in truth, very much the contrary. I did not speak to her, and she did not trust herself to speak to me; but, addressing myself to the husband, introduced the subject of my own immediate wants, a supper and night's lodging. The landlord told me, however, that the Bavarians had eaten everything in the house, and he had not a room, bed, blanket, or coverlet to give me; that I might lie down in the hall or the piazza, but there was no other place.

I was outrageous at the hard treatment he had received from the Bavarians. It was too bad to turn an honest innkeeper out of his house, and deny him the pleasure of accommodating a traveller who had toiled hard all day, with the perfect assurance of finding a bed at night. I saw, however, that there was no help for it; and noticing an opening at one end of the hall, went into a sort of store-room filled with all kinds of rubbish, particularly old barrels. An unhinged door was leaning against the wall, and this I laid across two of the barrels, pulled off my coat and waistcoat, and on this extemporaneous couch went to sleep.

I was roused from my first nap by a terrible fall against my door. I sprang up; the moon was shining through the broken casement, and seizing a billet of wood, I waited another attack. In the meantime I heard the noise of a violent scuffling on the floor of the hall, and, high above all, the voices of husband and wife, his evidently coming from the floor in a deprecating tone, and hers in a high towering passion, and enforced with severe blows of a stick. As soon as I was fairly awake I saw through the thing at once. It was only a little matrimonial *tête-à-tête*. The unamiable humour in which I had left them against the Bavarians had ripened into a private quarrel between themselves, and she had got him down, and was pummelling him with a broomstick or something of that kind. It seemed natural and right enough, and was, moreover, no business of mine; and remembering that whoever interferes between man and wife is sure to have both against him, I kept quiet. Others, however, were not so considerate, and the occupants of the different rooms tumbled into the hall in every variety of fancy night-gear, among whom was one whose only clothing was a military coat and cap, with a sword in his hand. When the hubbub was at its highest I looked out, and found, as I expected, the husband and wife standing side by side, she still brandishing the stick, and both apparently outrageous at everything and everybody around them. I congratulated myself upon my superior knowledge of human nature, and went back to my bed on the door.

In the morning I was greatly surprised to find that, instead of whipping her husband, she had been taking his part. Two German soldiers, already half intoxicated, had come into the hall, and insisted upon having more wine; the host refused, and when they moved toward my sleeping-place, where the wine was kept, he interposed, and all came down together with the noise which had woke me. His wife came to his aid, and the blows which, in my simplicity, I had supposed to be falling upon him, were bestowed on the two Bavarians. She told me the story herself; and when she complained to the officers, they had capped the climax of her passion by telling her that her husband deserved more than he got. She was still in a perfect fury; and as she looked at them in the yard arranging for their departure, she added, in broken English, with deep, and, as I thought, ominous passion, "'Twas better to be under the Turks."

I learned all this while I was making my toilet on the piazza, that is, while she was pouring water on my hands for me to wash; and, just as I had finished, my eye fell upon my muleteer assisting in loading their horses. At first I did not notice the subdued expression of his usually bright face, nor that he was loading my horse with some of their camp equipage; but all at once it struck me that they were pressing him into their service. I was already roused by what the woman had told me, and resolving that they should not serve me as they did the Greeks, sprang off the piazza, cleared my way through the crowd, and going up to my horse, already staggering under a burden poised on his back, but not yet fastened, put my hand under one side and tumbled it over with a crash on the other. The soldiers cried out furiously; and, while they were sputtering German at me, I sprang into the saddle. I was in admirable pugilistic condition, with nothing on but pantaloons, boots, and shirt, and just in a humour to get a whipping, if nothing worse; but I detested the manner in which the Bavarians lorded it in Greece; and riding up to a group of officers who were staring at me, told them that I had just tumbled their luggage off my horse, and that they must bear in mind that they could not deal with strangers quite so arbitrarily as they did with the Greeks. The commandant was disposed to be indignant and very magnificent; but some of the others making suggestions to him, he said he understood I had only hired my horse as far as Corinth! but, if I had taken him for Athens, he would not interfere; and, apologising on the ground of the necessities of government, ordered him to be released. I apologised back again, returned the horse to my guide, whose eyes sparkled with pleasure, and went in for my hat and coat.

I dressed myself, and, telling him to be ready when I had finished my breakfast, went out expecting to start forthwith; but, to my surprise, my host told me that the lad refused to go any farther without an increase of pay: and, sure enough, there he stood, making no preparation for moving. The cavalcade of soldiers had gone, and taken with them every horse in Corinth, and the young rascal intended to take advantage of my necessity. I told him that I had hired him to Athens for such a price, and that I had saved him from impressment, and consequent loss of wages, by the soldiers; which he admitted. I added that he was a young rascal; which he neither admitted nor denied, but answered with a roguish laugh. The extra price was no object compared with the vexation of a day's detention; but a traveller is apt to think that all the world is conspiring to impose upon him, and, at times, to be very resolute in resisting. I was peculiarly so then, and, after a few words, set off to complain to the head of the police. Without any ado he trotted along with me, and we proceeded together, followed by a troop of idlers, I in something of a passion, he perfectly cool, good-natured, and considerate, merely keeping out of the way of my stick. Hurrying along near the columns of the old temple, I stumbled, and he sprang forward to assist me, his face expressing great interest, and a fear that I had hurt myself; and when I walked toward a house which I had mistaken for the bureau of the police department, he ran after me to direct me right. All this mollified me considerably; and before we reached the door, the affair began to strike me as rather ludicrous.

I stated my case, however, to the eparchos, a Greek in Frank dress, who spoke French with great facility, and treated me with the greatest consideration. He was so full of professions that I felt quite sure of a decision in my favour; but, assuming my story to be true, and without asking the lad for his excuse, he shrugged his shoulders, and said it would take time to examine the matter, and, if I was in a hurry, I had better submit. To be sure, he said, the fellow was a great rogue, and he gave his countrymen in general a character that would not tell well in print; but, added in their justification, that they were imposed upon and oppressed by everybody, and therefore considered that they had a right to take their advantage whenever an opportunity offered. The young man sat down on the floor, and looked at me with the most frank, honest, and open expression, as if perfectly unconscious that he was doing anything wrong. I could not but acknowledge that some excuse for him was to be drawn from the nature of the school in which he had been brought up, and, after a little parley, agreed to pay him the additional price, if, at the end of the journey, I was satisfied with his conduct. This was enough; his face brightened, he sprang up and took my hand, and we left the house the best friends in the world. He seemed to be hurt as well as surprised at my finding fault with him, for to him all seemed perfectly natural; and, to seal the reconciliation, he hurried on ahead, and had the horse ready when I reached the locanda. I took leave of my host with a better feeling than before, and set out a second time on the road to Athens.

At Kalamaki, while walking along the shore, a Greek who spoke the lingua Franca came from on board one of the little caiques, and when he learned that I was an American, described to me the scene that had taken place on that beach upon the arrival of provisions from America; when thousands of miserable beings who had fled from the blaze of their dwellings, and lived for months upon plants and roots, grayheaded men, mothers with infants at their breasts, emaciated with hunger and almost frantic with despair, came down from their mountain retreats to receive the welcome relief. He might well remember the scene, for he had been one of that starving people; and he took me to his house, and showed me his wife and four children, now nearly all grown, telling me that they had been rescued from death by the generosity of my countrymen. I do not know why, but in those countries it did not seem unmanly for a bearded and whiskered man to weep: I felt anything but contempt for him when, with his heart overflowing and his eyes filled with tears, he told me, when I returned home, to say to my countrymen that I had seen and talked with a recipient of their bounty; and though the Greeks might never repay us, they could never forget what we had done for them. I remembered the excitement in our country in their behalf, in colleges and schools, from the graybearded senator to the prattling school-boy, and reflected that, perhaps, my mite, cast carelessly upon the waters, had saved from the extremity of misery this grateful family. I wish that the cold-blooded prudence which would have checked our honest enthusiasm in favour of a people, under calamities and horrors worse than ever fell to the lot of man struggling to be free, could have listened to the gratitude of this Greek family. With deep interest I bade them farewell, and, telling my guide to follow with my horse, walked over to the foot of the mountain.

Ascending, I saw in one of the openings of the road a packhorse and a soldier in the Bavarian uniform, and, hoping to find some one to talk with, I hailed him. He was on the top of the mountain, so far off that he did not hear me; and when, with the help of my Greek, I had succeeded in gaining his attention, he looked for some time without being able to see me. When he did, however, he waited; but, to my no small disappointment, he answered my first question with the odious "Nix." We tried each other in two or three dialects; but, finding it of no use, I sat down to rest, and he, for courtesy, joined me; my young Greek, in the spirit of good-fellowship, doing the same. He was a tall, noble-looking fellow, and, like myself, a stranger in Greece; and, though we could not say so, it was understood that we were glad to meet and travel together as comrades. The tongue causes more evils than the sword; and, as we were debarred the use of this mischievous member, and walked all day side by side, seldom three paces apart, before night we were sworn friends.

About five o'clock in the afternoon, we arrived at Megara. A group of Bavarian soldiers was lounging round the door of the khan, who welcomed their expected comrade and me as his companion. My friend left me, and soon returned with the compliments of the commandant, and an invitation to visit him in the evening. I had, however, accepted a prior invitation from the soldiers for a rendezvous in the locanda. I wandered till dark among the ruined houses of the town, thought of Euclid and Alexander the Great, and returning, went up to the same room in which I had slept with my friends, pored over an old map of Greece hanging on the wall, made a few notes, and throwing myself back on a sort of divan, while thinking what I should do fell asleep.

About ten o'clock I was roused by the loud roar of a chorus, not like a sudden burst, but a thing that seemed to have swelled up to that point by degrees; and rubbing my eyes, and stumbling down stairs, I entered the banqueting-hall; a long, rough wooden table extended the whole length of the room, supplied with only two articles, wine-flaggons and tobacco-pouches; forty or fifty soldiers were sitting round it, smoking pipes and singing with all their souls, and, at the moment I entered, waving their pipes to the dying cadence of a hunting chorus. Then followed a long thump on the table, and they all rose; my long travelling friend, with a young soldier who spoke a little French, came up, and, escorting me to the head of the table, gave me a seat by the side of the chairman. One of them attempted to administer a cup of wine, and the other thrust at me the end of a pipe, and I should have been obliged to kick and abscond but for the relief afforded me by the entrance of another new-comer. This was no other than the corporal's wife; and if I had been received warmly, she was greeted with enthusiasm. Half the table sprang forward to escort her, two of them collared the president and hauled him off his seat, and the whole company, by acclamation, installed her in his place. She accepted it without any hesitation, while two of them, with clumsy courtesy, took off her bonnet, which I, sitting at her right hand, took charge of. All then resumed their places, and the revel went on more gaily than ever. The lady president was about thirty, plainly but neatly dressed, and, though not handsome, had a frank, amiable, and good-tempered expression, indicating that greatest of woman's attributes, a good heart. In fact, she looked what the young man at my side told me she was, the peace-maker of the regiment; and, he added, that they always tried to have her at their convivial meetings, for when she was among them the brawling spirits were kept down, and every man would be ashamed to quarrel in her presence. There was no chivalry, no heroic devotion about them, but their manner toward her was as speaking a tribute as was ever paid to the influence of woman; and I question whether beauty in her bower, surrounded by belted knights and barons bold, ever exercised in her more exalted sphere a more happy influence. I talked with her, and with the utmost simplicity she told me that the soldiers all loved her; that they were all kind to her, and she looked upon them all as brothers. We broke up at about twelve o'clock with a song, requiring each person to take the hand of his reighbour; one of her hands fell to me, and I took it with a respect seldom surpassed in touching the hand of woman; for I felt that she was cheering the rough path of a soldier's life, and, among scenes calculated to harden the heart, reminding them of mothers, and sisters, and sweet-hearts at home.

CHAPTER VII.

A Dreary Funeral.—Marathon.—Mount Pentelicus.—A Mystery.—Woes of a Lover.—Reveries of Glory.—Scio's Rocky Isle.—A blood-stained Page of History.—A Greek Prelate.—Desolation.—The Exile's Return.

EARLY in the morning I again started. In a little khan at Eleusis I saw three or four Bavarian soldiers drinking, and ridiculing the Greek proprietor, calling him patrioti and capitani. The Greek bore their gibes and sneers without a word; but there was a deadly expression in his look, which seemed to say, "I bide my time;" and I remember then thinking that the Bavarians were running up an account which would one day he settled with blood. In fact, the soldiers went too far; and, as I thought, to show off before me, one of them slapped the Greek on the back, and made him spill a measure of wine which he was carrying to a customer, when the latter turned upon him like lightning, threw him down, and would have strangled him if he had not been pulled off by the by-standers. Indeed, the Greeks had already learned both their intellectual and physical superiority over the Bavarians; and, a short time before, a party of soldiers sent to subdue a band of Maniote insurgents had been captured, and, after a farce of selling them at auction at a dollar a head, were kicked, and whipped, and sent off.

About four o'clock I arrived once more at Athens, dined at my old hotel, and passed the evening at Mr. Hill's.

The next day I lounged about the city. I had been more than a month without my carpet-bag, and the way in which I managed during that time is a thing between my travelling companions and myself. A prudent Scotchman used to boast of a careful nephew, who, in travelling, instead of leaving some of his clothes at every hotel on the road, always brought home *more* than he took away with him. I was a model of this kind of carefulness while my opportunities lasted; but my companions had left me, and this morning I went to the bazars and bought a couple of shirts. Dressed up in one of them, I strolled outside the walls; and while sitting in the shadow of a column of the Temple of Jupiter, I saw coming from the city, through Adrian's Gate, four men, carrying a burden by the corners of a coverlet, followed by another having in his hands a bottle and spade. As they approached I saw they were bearing the dead body of a woman, whom, on joining them, I found to be the wife of the man who followed. He was an Englishman or an American (for he called himself either, as occasion required) whom I had seen at my hotel and at Mr. Hill's; had been a sailor and probably deserted from his ship, and many years a resident of Athens, where he married a Greek woman. He was a thriftless fellow, and, as he told me, had lived principally by the labour of his wife, who washed for European travellers. He had been so long in Greece, and his connexions and associations were so thoroughly Greek, that he had lost that sacredness of feeling so powerful both in Englishmen and Americans of every class in regard to the decent burial of the dead, though he did say that he had expected to procure a coffin, but the police of the city had sent officers to take her away and bury her. There was something so forlorn in the appearance of this rude funeral, that my first impulse was to turn away; but I checked myself and followed. Several times the Greeks laid the corpse on the ground and stopped to rest, chattering indifferently on various subjects. We crossed the Ilissus, and at some distance came to a little Greek chapel excavated in the rock. The door was so low that we were obliged to stoop on entering, and when within we could hardly stand upright. The Greeks laid down the body in front of the altar; the husband went for the priest, the Greeks to select a place for a grave, and I remained alone with the dead. I sat in the door-way, looking inside upon the corpse, and out upon the Greeks digging the grave. In a short time the husband returned with a priest, one of the most miserable of that class of "blind teachers" who swarm in Greece. He immediately commenced the funeral service, which continued nearly an hour, by which time the Greeks returned, and, taking up the body, carried it to the grave-side and laid it within. I knew the hollow sound of the first clod of earth which falls upon the lid of a coffin, and shrunk from its leaden fall upon the uncovered body. I turned away, and, when at some distance, looked back and saw them packing the earth over the grave. I never saw so dreary a burial-scene.

Returning, I passed by the ancient stadium of Herodes Atticus, once capable of containing twenty-five thousand spectators; the whole structure was covered with the purest white marble. All remains of its magnificence are now gone; but I could still trace on the excavated side of the hill its ancient form of a horse-shoe, and walked through the subterraneous passage by which the vanquished in the games retreated from the presence of the spectators.

Returning to the city, I learned that an affray had just taken place between some Greeks and Bavarians, and, hurrying to the place near the bazars, found a crowd gathered round a soldier who had been stabbed by a Greek. According to the Greeks, the affair had been caused by the habitual insults and provocation given by the Bavarians, the soldier having wantonly knocked a drinking-cup out of the Greek's hand while he was drinking. In the crowd I met a lounging Italian (the same who wanted me to come up from Padras by water), a good-natured and good-for-nothing fellow, and skilled in tongues; and going with him into a coffee-house thronged with Bavarians and Europeans of various nations in the service of government, heard another story, by which it appeared that the Greeks, as usual, were in the wrong, and that the poor Bavarian had been stabbed without the slightest provocation, purely from the Greeks' love of stabbing. Tired of this, I left the scene of contention, and a few streets off met an Athenian, a friend of two or three days' standing, and stopping under a window illuminated by a pair of bright eyes from above, happened to express my admiration of the lady who owned them, when he tested the strength of my feelings on the subject by asking me if I would like to marry her. I was not prepared at the moment to give precisely that proof, and he followed up his blow by telling me that, if I wished it, he would engage to secure her for me before the next morning. The Greeks are almost universally poor. With them every traveller is rich, and they are so thoroughly civilised as to think that a rich man is, of course, a good match.

Toward evening I paid my last visit to the Acropolis. Solitude, silence, and sunset are the nursery of sentiment. I sat down on a broken capital of the Parthenon; the owl was already flitting among the ruins. I looked up at the majestic temple and down at the ruined and newly-regenerated city, and said to myself, "Lots must rise in Athens!" I traced the line of the ancient walls, ran a railroad to the Piræus, and calculated the increase on "up-town lots" from building the king's palace near the Garden of Plato. Shall I or shall I not "make an operation" in Athens? The court has removed here, the country is beautiful, climate fine, government fixed, steamboats are running, all the world is coming, and lots must rise. I bought (in imagination) a tract of good tillable land, laid it out in streets, had my Plato, and Homer, and Washington Places, and Jackson Avenue, built a row of houses to improve the neighbourhood where nobody lived, got maps lithographed, and sold off at auction. I was in the right condition to "go in," for I had nothing to lose; but, unfortunately, the Greeks were very far behind the spirit of the age, knew nothing of the beauties of the credit system, and could not be brought to dispose of their consecrated soil "on the usual terms," ten per cent. down, balance on bond and mortgage; so, giving up the idea, at dark I bade farewell to the ruins of the Acropolis, and went to my hotel to dinner.

Early the next morning I started for the field of Marathon. I engaged a servant at the hotel to accompany me, but he disappointed me, and I set out alone with my muleteer. Our road lay along the base of Mount Hymettus, on the borders of the plain of Attica, shaded by thick groves of olives. At noon I was on the summit of a lofty mountain, at the base of which, still and quiet as if it had never resounded with the shock of war, the great battle-ground of the Greeks and Persians extended to the sea. The descent was one of the finest things I met with in Greece; wild, rugged, and, in fact, the most magnificent kind of mountain scenery. At the foot of the mountain we came to a ruined convent, occupied by an old white-bearded monk. I stopped there and lunched, the old man laying before me his simple store of bread and olives, and looking on with pleasure at my voracious appetite.

This over, I hurried to the battle-field. Toward the centre is a large mound of earth, erected over the Athenians who fell in the battle. I made directly for this mound, ascended it, and threw the reins loose over my horse's neck; and, sitting on the top, read the account of the battle in Herodotus.

After all, is not our reverence misplaced, or, rather, does not our respect for deeds hallowed by time render us comparatively unjust? The Greek revolution teems with instances of as desperate courage, as great love of country, as patriotic devotion, as animated the men of Marathon, and yet the actors in these scenes are not known beyond the boundaries of their native land! Thousands whose names were never heard of, and whose bones, perhaps, never received burial, were as worthy of an eternal monument as they upon whose grave I sat. Still that mound is a hallowed sepulchre; and the shepherd who looks at it from his mountain home, the husbandman who drives his plough to its base, and the sailor who hails it as a landmark from the deck of his caique, are all reminded of the glory of their ancestors. But away with the mouldering relics of the past! Give me the green grave of Marco Bozzaris. I put Herodotus in my pocket, gathered a few blades of grass, as a memorial, descended the mound, betook myself to my saddle, and swept the plain on a gallop, from the mountain to the sea.

It is about two miles in width, and bounded by rocky heights inclosing it at either extremity.

Toward the shore the ground is marshy, and at the place where the Persians escaped to their ships are some unknown ruins; in several places the field is cultivated, and toward evening, on my way to the village of Marathon, I saw a Greek ploughing; and when I told him that I was an American, he greeted me as the friend of Greece. It is the last time I shall recur to this feeling; but it was music to my heart to hear a ploughman on immortal Marathon sound in my ears the praises of my country.

I intended to pass the night at the village of Marathon; but every khan was so cluttered up with goats, chickens, and children, that I rode back to the monastery at the foot of the mountain. It was nearly dark when I reached it. The old monk was on a little eminence at the door of his chapel, clapping two boards together to call his flock to vespers. With his long white beard, his black cap and long black gown, his picturesque position and primitive occupation, he seemed a guardian spirit hovering on the borders of Marathon in memory of its ancient glory. He came down to the monastery to receive me, and, giving me a paternal welcome, and spreading a mat on the floor, returned to his chapel. I followed, and saw his little flock assemble. The ploughman came up from the plain, and the shepherd came down from the mountain; the old monk led the way to the altar, and all kneeled down and prostrated themselves on the rocky floor. I looked at them with deep interest. I had seen much of Greek devotion in cities and villages, but it was a spectacle of extraordinary interest to see these wild and lawless men assembled on this lonely mountain to worship in all sincerity, according to the best light they had, the God of their fathers. I could not follow them in their long and repeated kneelings and prostrations; but my young Greek, as if to make amends for me, and, at the same time, to show how they did things in Athens, led the van. The service over, several of them descended with us to the monastery; the old monk spread his mat, and again brought out his frugal store of bread and olives. I contributed what I had brought from Athens, and we made our evening meal. If I had judged from appearances, I should have felt rather uneasy at sleeping among such companions; but the simple fact of having seen them at their devotions gave me confidence. Though I had read and heard that the Italian bandit went to the altar to pray forgiveness for the crimes he intended to commit, and, before washing the stains from his hands, hung up the bloody poniard upon a pillar of the church, and asked pardon for murder, I always felt a certain degree of confidence in him who practised the duties of his religion, whatever that religion might be. I leaned on my elbow, and, by the blaze of the fire, read Herodotus, while my muleteer, as I judged from the frequent repetition of the word Americanos, entertained them with long stories about me. By degrees the blaze of the fire died away, the Greeks stretched themselves out for sleep, the old monk handed me a bunch about four inches high for a pillow, and, wrapping myself in my cloak, in a few moments I was wandering in the land of dreams.

Before daylight my companions were in motion. I intended to return to the marble quarries on the Pentelican Mountain; and crying "Cavallo" in the ear of my still sleeping muleteer, in a few minutes I bade farewell for ever to the good old monk of Marathon. Almost from the door of the monastery we commenced ascending the mountain. It was just peep of day, the weather raw and cold, the top of the mountain covered with clouds, and in an hour I found myself in the midst of them. The road was so steep and dangerous that I could not ride; a false step of my horse might have thrown me over a precipice several hundred feet deep; and the air was so keen and penetrating, that, notwithstanding the violent exercise of walking, I was perfectly chilled. The mist was so dense, too, that, when my guide was a few paces in advance, I could not see him, and I was literally groping my way through the clouds. I had no idea where I was, nor of the scene around me, but I felt that I was in a measure lifted above the earth. The cold blasts drove furiously along the sides of the mountain, whistled against the precipices, and bellowed in the hollows of the rocks, sometimes driving so furiously that my horse staggered and fell back. I was almost bewildered in struggling blindly against them; but, just before reaching the top of the mountain, the thick clouds were lifted as if by an invisible hand, and I saw once more the glorious sun pouring his morning beams upon a rich valley extending a great distance to the foot of the Pentelican Mountain. About half-way down we came to a beautiful stream, on the banks of which we took out our bread and olives. Our appetites were stimulated by the mountain air, and we divided till our last morsel was gone.

At the foot of the mountain, lying between it and Mount Pentelicus, was a large monastery, occupied by a fraternity of monks. We entered and walked through it, but found no one to receive us. In a field near by we saw one of the monks, from whom we obtained a direction to the quarries. Moving on to the foot of the mountain, which rises with a peaked summit into the clouds, we commenced ascending, and soon came upon the strata of beautiful white marble for which Mount Pentelicus has been celebrated thousands of years. Excavations appear to have been made along the whole route, and on the roadside were blocks, and marks caused by the friction of the heavy masses transported to Athens. The great quarries are toward the summit. The surface has been cut perpendicularly smooth, perhaps eighty or a hundred feet high, and one hundred and fifty or two hundred feet in width, and excavations have been made within to an unknown extent. Whole cities might have been built with the materials taken away, and yet, by comparison with what is left, there is nothing gone. In front are entrances to a large chamber, in one corner of which, on the right, is a chapel with the painted figure of the Virgin to receive the Greeks' prayers. Within are vast humid caverns, over which the wide roof awfully extends, adorned with hollow tubes like icicles, while a small transparent petrifying stream trickles down the rock. On one side are small chambers communicating with subterraneous avenues, used, no doubt, as places of refuge during the revolution, or as the haunts of robbers. Bones of animals and stones blackened with smoke showed that but lately some part had been occupied as a habitation. The great excavations around, blocks of marble lying as they fell, perhaps two thousand years ago, and the appearances of having been once a scene of immense industry and labour, stand in striking contrast with the desolation and solitude now existing. Probably the hammer and chisel will never be heard there more, great temples will no more be raised, and modern genius will never, like the Greeks of old, make the rude blocks of marble speak.

At dark I was dining at the *Hôtel de France,* when Mr. Hill came over with the welcome intelligence that my carpet-bag had arrived. On it was pinned a large paper, with the words " Huzzah !" " Huzzah !" " Huzzah !" by my friend Maxwell, who had met it on horseback on the shores of the Gulf of Lepanto, travelling under the charge of a Greek in search of me. I opened it with apprehension, and, to my great satisfaction, found undisturbed the object of my greatest anxiety, the precious note-book from which I now write, saved from the peril of an anonymous publication, or of being used up for gun-waddings.

The next morning, before I was up, I heard a gentle rap at my door, which was followed by the entrance of a German, a missionary, whom I had met several times at Mr. Hill's, and who had dined with me once at my hotel. I apologised for being caught in bed, and told him that he must possess a troubled spirit to send him so early from his pillow. He answered that I was right; that he did indeed possess a troubled spirit; and closing the door carefully, came to my bedside, and said he had conceived a great regard for me, and intended confiding in me an important trust. I had several times held long conversations with him at Mr. Hill's, and very little to my edification, as his English was hardly intelligible; but I felt pleased at having, without particularly striving for it, gained the favourable opinion of one who bore the character of a very learned and a very good man. I requested him to step into the dining-room while I rose and dressed myself; but he put his hand upon my breast to keep me down, and drawing a chair, began, " You are going to Smyrna." He then paused, but, after some moments of hesitation, proceeded to say that the first name I would bear on my arrival there would be his own; that, unfortunately, it was in everybody's mouth. My friend was a short and very ugly middle-aged man, with a very large mouth, speaking English with the most disagreeable German sputter, lame from a fall, and, altogether, of a most uninteresting and unsentimental aspect; and he surprised me much by laying before me a veritable *affaire du cœur.* It was so foreign to my expectations, that I should as soon have expected to be made a confidant in a love affair by the Archbishop of York. After a few preliminaries, he went into particulars: lavished upon the lady the usual quota of charms " in such case made and provided," but was uncertain, rambling, and discursive in regard to the position he held in her regard At first I understood that it was merely the old story, a flirtation and a victim; then that they were very near being married, which I afterward understood to be only so near as this, that he was willing and she not; and, finally, it settled down into the every-day occurrence, the lady smiled, while the parents and a stout two-fisted brother frowned. I could but think, if such a homely expression may be introduced in describing these tender passages, that he had the boot on the wrong leg, and that the parents were much more likely than the daughter to favour such a suitor. However, on this point I held my peace. The precise business he wished to impose on me was, immediately on my arrival in Smyrna to form the acquaintance of the lady and her family, and use all my exertions in his favour. I told him I was an entire stranger in Smyrna, and could not possibly have any influence with the parties; but, being urged, promised him that, if I could interfere without intruding myself improperly, he should have the benefit of my mediation. At first he intended giving me a letter to the lady, but afterward determined to give me one to the Rev. Mr. Brewer, an American missionary, who, he said, was a particular friend of his, and intimate with the beloved and her family, and acquainted with the whole affair. Placing himself at my table, on which were pens, ink, and paper, he proceeded to write his letter, while I lay quietly till he turned over the first side, when, tired of waiting, I rose, dressed myself, packed up, and, before he had finished, stood by the table with my carpet-bag, waiting until he should have done, to throw in my writing materials. He bade me good-by after I had mounted my horse to leave, and, when I turned back to look at him, I could not but feel for the crippled, limping victim of the tender passion, though, in honesty, and with the best wishes for his success, I did not think it would help his suit for the lady to see him.

An account of my journey from Athens to Smyrna, given in a letter to friends at home, was published during my absence and without my knowledge, in successive numbers of the American Monthly Magazine, and perhaps the favourable notice taken of it had some influence in inducing me to write a book. I give the papers as they were then published.

Smyrna, April, 1835.

MY DEAR ******,

I have just arrived at this place, and I live to tell it. I have been three weeks performing a voyage usually made in three days. It has been tedious beyond all things; but, as honest Dogberry would say, if it had been ten times as tedious, I could find it in my heart to bestow it all upon you. To begin at the beginning: on the morning of the second instant, I and my long-lost carpet-bag left the eternal city of Athens, without knowing exactly whither we were going, and sincerely regretted by Miltiades Panajotti, the garçon of the hotel. We wound round the foot of the Acropolis, and, giving a last look to its ruined temples, fell into the road to the Piræus, and in an hour found ourselves at that ancient harbour, almost as celebrated in the history of Greece as Athens itself. Here we took counsel as to farther movements, and concluded to take passage in a caique to sail that evening for Syra, being advised that that island was a great place of rendezvous for vessels, and that from it we could procure a passage to any place we chose. Having disposed of my better half, (I may truly call it so, for what is man without pantaloons, vests, and shirts?) I took a little sail-boat, to float around the ancient harbour and muse upon its departed glories.

The day that I lingered there before bidding farewell, perhaps for ever, to the shores of Greece, is deeply impressed upon my mind. I had hardly begun to feel the magic influence of the land of poets, patriots, and heroes, until the very moment of my departure I had travelled in the most interesting sections of the country, and found all enthusiasm dead within me when I had expected to be carried away by the remembrance of the past; but here, I know not how it was, without any effort, and in the mere act of whiling away my time, all that was great, and noble, and beautiful in her history rushed upon me at once; the sun and the breeze, the land and the sea, contributed to throw a witchery around me; and in a rich and delightful frame of mind, I found myself among the monuments of her better days, gliding by the remains of the immense wall erected to inclose the harbour during the Peloponnesian war, and was soon floating upon the classic waters of Salamis.

If I had got there by accident it would not have occurred to me to dream of battles and all the fierce panoply of war upon that calm and silvery surface. But I knew where I was, and my blood was up. I was among the enduring witnesses of the Athenian glory. Behind me was the ancient city, the Acropolis, with its ruined temples, the tell-tale monuments of by-gone days, towering above the plain; here was the harbour from which the galleys carried to the extreme parts of the then known world the glories of the Athenian name; before me was unconquered Salamis; here the invading fleet of Xerxes; there the little navy, the last hope of the Athenians; here the island of Ægina, from which Aristides, forgetting his quarrel with Themistocles, embarked in a rude boat, during the hottest of the battle, for the ship of the latter; and there the throne of Xerxes, where the proud invader stationed himself as spectator of the battle that was to lay the rich plain of Attica at his feet. There could be no mistake about localities; the details have been handed down from generation to generation, and are as well known to the Greeks of the present day as they were to their fathers. So I went to work systematically, and fought the whole battle through. I gave the Persians ten to one, but I made the Greeks fight like tigers; I pointed them to their city, to their wives and children; I brought on long strings of little innocents, urging them as in the farce, "Sing out, young uns!" I carried old Themistocles among the Persians like a modern Greek fireship among the Turks; I sunk ship after ship, and went on demolishing them at a most furious rate, until I saw old Xerxes scudding from his throne, and the remnant of the Persian fleet scampering away to the tune of "Devil take the hindmost." By this time I had got into the spirit of the thing; and moving rapidly over that water, once red with the blood of thousands from the fields of Asia, I steered for the shore and mounted the vacant throne of Xerxes. This throne is on a hill near the shore, not very high, and as pretty a place as a man could have selected to see his friends whipped and keep out of harm's way himself; for you will recollect that in those days there was no gunpowder nor cannon-balls, and, consequently, no danger from long chance shots. I selected a particular stone, which I thought it probable Xerxes, as a reasonable man, and with an eye to perspective, might have chosen as his seat on the eventful day of the battle; and on that same stone sat down to meditate upon the vanity of all earthly greatness. But, most provokingly, whenever I think of Xerxes, the first thing that presents itself to my mind is the couplet in the Primer,

"Xerxes the Great did die,
And so must you and I."

This is a very sensible stanza, no doubt, and worthy of always being borne in mind; but it was not exactly what I wanted. I tried to drive it away; but the more I tried, the more it stuck to me. It was all in vain. I railed at early education, and resolved that acquired knowledge hurts a man's natural faculties; for if I had not received the first rudiments of education, I should not have been bothered with the vile couplet, and should have been able to do something on my own account. As it was, I lost one of the best opportunities ever a man had for moralising; and you, my dear ——, have lost at least three pages. give you, however, all the materials; put yourself on the throne of Xerxes, and do what you can, and may your early studies be no stumbling-block in your way. As for me, vexed and disgusted with myself, I descended the hill as fast as the great king did of yore, and jumping into my boat, steered for the farthest point of the Piræus; from the throne of Xerxes to the tomb of Themistocles.

I was prepared to do something here. This was not merely a place where he had been; I was to tread upon the earth that covered his bones; here were his ashes; here was all that remained of the best and bravest of the Greeks, save his immortal name. As I approached I saw the large square stones that enclosed his grave, and mused upon his history; the deliverer of his country, banished, dying an exile, his bones begged by his repenting countrymen, and buried with peculiar propriety near the shore of the sea commanding a full view of the scene of his naval glory. For more than two thousand years the waves have almost washed over his grave, the sun has shone and the winds have howled over him; while, perhaps, his spirit has mingled with the sighing of the winds and the murmur of the waters, in moaning over the long captivity of his countrymen; perhaps, too, his spirit has been with them in their late struggle for liberty; has hovered over them in the battle and the breeze, and is now standing sentinel over his beloved and liberated country. I approached as to the grave of one who will never die. His great name, his great deeds, hallowed by the lapse of so many ages; the scene—I looked over the wall with a feeling amounting to reverence, when, directly before me, the first thing I saw, the only thing I could see, so glaring and conspicuous that nothing else could fix my eye, was a tall, stiff, wooden headboard, painted white, with black letters, to the memory of an Englishman with as unclassical a name as that of *John Johnson*. My eyes were blasted with the sight; I was ferocious; I railed at him as if he had buried himself there with his own hands. What had he to do there! I railed at his friends. Did they expect to give him a name by mingling him with the ashes of the immortal dead! Did they expect to steal immortality like fire from the flint! I dashed back to my boat, steered directly for the harbour, gave sentiment to the dogs, and in half-an-hour was eating a most voracious and spiteful dinner.

In the evening I embarked on board my little caique. She was one of the most rakish of that rakish description of vessels. I drew my cloak around me and stretched myself on the deck as we glided quietly out of the harbour; saw the throne of Xerxes, the island of Salamis, and the shores of Greece gradually fade from view; looked at the dusky forms of the Greeks in their capotes lying asleep around me; at the helmsman sitting cross-legged at his post, apparently without life or motion; gave one thought to home, and fell asleep.

In the morning I began to examine my companions. They were, in all, a captain and six sailors, probably all part owners, and two passengers from one of the islands, not one of whom could speak any other language than Greek. My knowledge of that language was confined to a few rolling hexameters, which had stuck by me in some unaccountable way as a sort of memento of college days. These, however, were of no particular use, and, consequently, I was pretty much tongue-tied during the whole voyage. I amused myself by making my observations quietly upon my companions, as they did more openly upon me, for I frequently heard the word "Americanos" pass among them. I had before had occasion to see something of Greek sailors, and to admire their skill and general good conduct, and I was fortified in my previous opinion by what I saw of my present companions. Their temperance in eating and drinking is very remarkable, and all my comparisons between them and European sailors were very much in their favour. Indeed, I could not help thinking, as they sat collectively, Turkish fashion, around their frugal meal of bread, caviari, and black olives, that I had never seen finer men. Their features were regular, in that style which we to this day recognise as Grecian; their figures good, and their faces wore an air of marked character and intelligence; and these advantages of person were set off by the island costume, the fez or red cloth cap, with a long black tassel at the top, a tight vest and jacket, embroidered and without collars, large Turkish trousers coming down a little below the knee, legs bare, sharp-pointed slippers, and a sash round the waist, tied under the left side, with long ends hanging down, and a knife sticking out about six inches. There was something bold and daring in their appearance; indeed, I may say, rakish and piratical; and I could easily imagine that, if the Mediterranean should again become infested with pirates, my friends would cut no contemptible figure among them. But I must not detain you as long on the voyage as I was myself. The sea was calm: we had hardly any wind; our men were at the oars nearly all the time, and passing slowly by Ægina, Cape Sunium, with its magnificent ruins mournfully overlooking the sea, better known in modern times as Colonna's Height, and the scene of Falconer's shipwreck, passing also the island of Zea, the ancient Chios, Thermia, and other islands of lesser note, in the afternoon of the third day we arrived at Syra.

With regard to Syra I shall say but little; I am as loath to linger about it now as I was to stay there then. The fact is, I cannot think of the place with any degree of satisfaction. The evening of my arrival I heard, through a Greek merchant to whom I had a letter from a friend in Athens, of a brig to sail the next day for Smyrna; and I lay down on a miserable bed in a miserable locanda, in the confident expectation of resuming my journey in the morning. Before morning, however, I was roused by "blustering Boreas" rushing through the broken casement of my window; and for more than a week all the winds ever celebrated in the poetical history of Greece were let loose upon the island. We were completely cut off from all communication with the rest of the world. Not a vessel could leave the port, while vessel after vessel put in there for shelter. I do not mean to go into any details; indeed, for my own credit's sake, I dare not; for if I were to draw a true picture of things as I found them; if I were to write home the truth, I should be considered as utterly destitute of taste and sentiment; I should be looked upon as a most unpoetical dog, who ought to have been at home poring over the revised statutes instead of breathing the pure air of poetry and song. And now, if I were writing what might by chance come under the eyes of a sentimental young lady or a young gentleman in his teens, the truth would be the last thing I would think of telling. No, though my teeth chatter, though a cold sweat comes over me when I think of it, I would go through the usual rhapsody, and huzzah for "the land of the East and the clime of the sun." Indeed, I have a scrap in my portfolio, written with my cloak and greatcoat on, and my feet over a brazier, beginning in that way. But to you, my dear ——, who know my touching sensibilities, and who, moreover, have a tender regard for my character and will not publish me, I would as soon tell the truth as not. And I therefore do not hesitate to say, but do not whisper it elsewhere, that in one of the beautiful islands of the Ægean; in the heart of the Cyclades, in the sight of Delos, and Paros, and Antiparos, any one of which is enough to throw one who has never seen them into raptures with their fancied beauties, here, in this paradise of a young man's dreams, in the middle of April, I would have hailed "chill November's surly blast" as a zephyr; I would have exchanged all the beauties of this balmy clime for the sunny side of Kamtschatka; I would have given my room and the whole island of Syra for a third-rate lodging in Communipaw. It was utterly impossible to walk out, and equally impossible to stay in my room; the house, to suit that delightful climate, being built without windows or window-shutters. If I could forget the island, I could remember with pleasure the society I met there. I passed my mornings in the library of Mr. R., one of our worthy American missionaries; and my evenings at the house of Mr. W., the British consul. This gentleman married a Greek lady of Smyrna, and had three beautiful daughters, more than half Greeks in their habits and feelings; one of them is married to an English baronet, another to a Greek merchant of Syra, and the third—

On the ninth day the wind fell, the sun once more shone brightly, and in the evening I embarked on board a rickety brig for Smyrna. At about six o'clock, P. M., thirty or forty vessels were quietly crawling out of the harbour like rats after a storm. It was almost a calm when we started; in about two hours we had a favourable breeze; we turned in, going at the rate of eight miles an hour, and rose with a strong wind dead a-head. We beat about all that day; the wind increased to a gale, and toward evening we took shelter in the harbour of Scio.

The history of this beautiful little island forms one of the bloodiest pages in the history of the world, and one glance told that dreadful history. Once the most beautiful island of the Archipelago, it is now a mass of ruins. Its fields, which once "budded and blossomed as the rose," have become waste places; its villages are deserted, its towns are in ruins, its inhabitants murdered, in captivity, and in exile. Before the Greek revolution the Greeks of Scio were engaged in extensive commerce, and ranked among the largest merchants in the Levant. Though living under hard taskmasters, subject to the exactions of a rapacious pacha, their industry and enterprise, and the extraordinary fertility of their island, enabled them to pay a heavy tribute to the Turks, and to become rich themselves. For many years they had enjoyed the advantages of a college, with professors of high literary and scientific attainments, and their library was celebrated throughout all that country; it was, perhaps, the only spot in Greece where taste and learning still held a seat. But the island was far more famed for its extraordinary natural beauty and fertility. Its bold mountains and its soft valleys, the mildness of its climate and the richness of its productions, bound the Greeks to its soil by a tie even stronger than the chain of their Turkish masters. In the early part of the revolution, the Sciotes took no part with their countrymen in their glorious struggle for liberty. Forty of their principal citizens were given up as hostages, and they were suffered to remain in peace. Wrapped in the rich beauties of their island, they forgot the freedom of their fathers and their own chains; and, under the precarious tenure of a tyrant's will, gave themselves up to the full enjoyment of all that wealth and taste could purchase. We must not be too hard upon human nature; the cause seemed desperate; they had a little paradise at stake; and if there is a spot on earth, the risk of losing which could excuse men in forgetting that they were slaves in a land where their fathers were free, it is the island of Scio. But the sword hung suspended over them by a single hair. In an unexpected hour, without the least note of preparation, they were startled by the thunder of the Turkish cannon; fifty thousand Turks were let loose like blood-hounds upon the devoted island. The affrighted Greeks lay unarmed and helpless at their feet, but they lay at the feet of men who did not know mercy even by name; at the feet of men who hungered and thirsted after blood; of men, in comparison with whom wild beasts are as lambs. The wildest beast of the forest may become gorged with blood; not so with the Turks at Scio. Their appetite "grew with what it fed on," and still longed for blood when there was not a victim left to bleed. Women were ripped open, children dashed against the walls, the heads of whole families stuck on pikes out of the windows of their houses, while their murderers gave themselves up to riot and plunder within. The forty hostages were hung in a row from the walls of the castle; an indiscriminate and universal burning and massacre took place; in a few days the ground was covered with the dead, and one of the loveliest spots on earth was a pile of smoking ruins. Out of a population of one hundred and ten thousand, sixty thousand are supposed to have been murdered, twenty thousand to have escaped, and thirty thousand to have been sold into slavery. Boys and young girls were sold publicly in the streets of Smyrna and Constantinople at a dollar a-head. And all this did not arise from any irritated state of feeling toward them. It originated in the cold-blooded, calculating policy of the sultan, conceived in the same spirit which drenched the streets of Constantinople with the blood of the Janisaries; it was intended to strike terror into the hearts of the Greeks, but the murderer failed in his aim. The groans of the hapless Sciotes reached the ears of their countrymen, and gave a headlong and irresistible impulse to the spirit then struggling to be free. And this bloody tragedy was performed in our own days, and in the face of the civilised world. Surely, if ever Heaven visits in judgment a nation for a nation's crimes, the burning and massacre at Scio will be deeply visited upon the accursed Turks.

It was late in the afternoon when I landed, and my landing was under peculiarly interesting circumstances. One of my fellow-passengers was a native of the island, who had escaped during the massacre, and now revisited it for the first time. He asked me to accompany him ashore, promising to find some friends at whose house we might sleep; but he soon found himself a stranger in his native island: where he had once known everybody he now knew nobody. The town was a complete mass of ruins; the walls of many fine buildings were still standing, crumbling to pieces, and still black with the fire of the incendiary Turks. The town that had grown up upon the ruins consisted of a row of miserable shantees, occupied as shops for the sale of the mere necessaries of life, where the shopman slept on his window-shutter in front. All my companion's efforts to find an acquaintance who would give us a night's lodging were fruitless. We were determined not to go on board the vessel, if possible to avoid it; her last cargo had been oil, the odour of which still remained about her. The weather would not permit us to sleep on deck, and the cabin was intolerably disagreeable. To add to our unpleasant position, and, at the same time, to heighten the cheerlessness of the scene around us, the rain began to fall violently. Under the guidance of a Greek we searched among the ruins for an apartment where we might build a fire and shelter ourselves for the night, but we searched in vain; the work of destruction was too complete.

Cold, and thoroughly drenched with rain, we were retracing our way to our boat, when our guide told my companion that a Greek archbishop had lately taken up his abode among the ruins. We immediately went there, and found him occupying apartments, partially repaired, in what had once been one of the finest houses in Scio. The entrance through a large stone gateway was imposing; the house was cracked from top to bottom by fire, nearly one half had fallen down, and the stones lay scattered as they fell; but enough remained to show that in its better days it had been almost a palace. We ascended a flight of stone steps to a terrace, from which we entered into a large hall, perhaps thirty feet wide and fifty feet long. On one side of this hall the wall had fallen down the whole length, and we looked out upon the mass of ruins beneath. On the other side, in a small room in one corner, we found the archbishop. He was sick, and in bed with all his clothes on, according to the universal custom here, but received us kindly. The furniture consisted of an iron bedstead with a mattress, on which he lay with a quilt spread over him, a wooden sofa, three wooden chairs, about twenty books, and two large leather cases containing clothes, napkins, and, probably, all his worldly goods. The rain came through the ceiling in several places; the bed of the poor archbishop had evidently been moved from time to time to avoid it, and I was obliged to change my position twice. An air of cheerless poverty reigned through the apartment. I could not help comparing his lot with that of more favoured and, perhaps, not more worthy servants of the church. It was a style so different from that of the priests at Rome, the pope and his cardinals, with their gaudy equipages and multitudes of footmen rattling to the Vatican; or from the pomp and state of the haughty English prelates, or even from the comforts of our own missionaries in different parts of this country, that I could not help feeling deeply for the poor priest before me. But he seemed contented and cheerful, and even thankful that, for the moment, there were others worse off than himself, and that he had it in his power to befriend them.

Sweetmeats, coffee, and pipes were served; and in about an hour we were conducted to supper in a large room, also opening from the hall. Our supper would not have tempted an epicure, but suited very well an appetite whetted by exercise and travel. It consisted of a huge lump of bread and a large glass of water for each of us, caviari, black olives, and two kinds of Turkish sweetmeats. We were waited upon by two priests: one of them, a handsome young man, not more than twenty, with long black hair hanging over his shoulders like a girl's, stood by with a napkin on his arm and a pewter vessel, with which he poured water on our hands, receiving it again in a basin. This was done both before and after eating; then came coffee and pipes. During the evening the young priest brought out an edition of Homer, and I surprised *him*, and astounded *myself*, by being able to translate a passage in the Iliad. I translated it in French, and my companion explained it in modern Greek to the young priest. Our beds were cushions laid on a raised platform or divan extending around the walls, with a quilt for each of us. In the morning, after sweetmeats, coffee, and pipes, we paid our respects to the good old archbishop, and took our leave. When we got out of doors, finding that the wind was the same, and that there was no possibility of sailing, my friend proposed a ride into the country. We procured a couple of mules, took a small basket of provisions for a collation, and started.

Our road lay directly along the shore; on one side the sea, and on the other the ruins of houses and gardens, almost washed by the waves. At about three miles' distance we crossed a little stream, by the side of which we saw a sarcophagus, lately disinterred, containing the usual vases of a Grecian tomb, including the piece of money to pay Charon his ferriage over the river Styx, and six pounds of dust; being all that remained of a *man*—perhaps one who had filled a large space in the world; perhaps a hero—buried probably more than two thousand years ago. After a ride of about five miles we came to the ruins of a large village, the style of which would anywhere have fixed the attention, as having been once a favoured abode of wealth and taste. The houses were of brown stone, built together, strictly in the Venetian style, after the models left during the occupation of the island by the Venetians, large and elegant, with gardens of three or four acres, enclosed by high walls of the same kind of stone, and altogether in a style far superior to anything I had seen in Greece. These were the country-houses and gardens of the rich merchants of Scio. The manner of living among the proprietors here was somewhat peculiar, and the ties that bound them to this little village were peculiarly strong. This was the family home; the community was essentially mercantile, and most of their business transactions were carried on elsewhere. When there were three or four brothers in a family, one would be in Constantinople a couple of years, another at Trieste, and so on, while another remained at home; so that those who were away, while toiling amid the perplexities of business, were always looking to the occasional family reunion; and all trusted to spend the evening of their days among the beautiful gardens of Scio. What a scene for the heart to turn to now! The houses and gardens were still there, some standing almost entire, others blank with smoke and crumbling to ruins. But where were they who once occupied them? Where were they who should now be coming out to rejoice in the return of a friend and to welcome a stranger? An awful solitude, a stillness that struck a cold upon the heart, reigned around us. We saw nobody; and our own voices, and the tramping of our horses upon the deserted pavement, sounded hollow and sepulchral in our ears. It was like walking among the ruins of Pompeii; it was another city of the dead; but there was a freshness about the desolation that seemed of to-day; it seemed as though the inhabitants should be sleeping and not dead. Indeed, the high walls of the gardens, and the outside of the houses too, were generally so fresh and in so perfect a state, that it seemed like riding through a handsome village at an early hour before the inhabitants had risen; and I sometimes could not help thinking that in an hour or two the streets would be thronged with a busy population. My friend continued to conduct me through the solitary streets; telling me, as we went along, that this was the house of such a family, this of such a family, with some of whose members I had become acquainted in Greece, until, stopping before a large stone gateway, he dismounted at the gate of his father's house. In that house he was born; there he had spent his youth; he had escaped from it during the dreadful massacre, and this was the first time of his revisiting it. What a tide of recollections must have rushed upon him!

We entered through the large stone gateway into a courtyard beautifully paved in mosaic in the form of a star, with small black and white round stones. On our left was a large stone reservoir, perhaps twenty-five feet square, still so perfect as to hold water, with an arbour over it supported by marble columns; a venerable grapevine completely covered the arbour. The garden covered an extent of about four acres, filled with orange, lemon, almond, and fig-trees; overrun with weeds, roses, and flowers, growing together in wild confusion. On the right was the house, and a melancholy spectacle it was; the wall had fallen down on one side, and the whole was black with smoke. We ascended a flight of stone steps, with marble balustrades, to the terrace, a platform about twenty feet square, overlooking the garden. From the terrace we entered the saloon, a large room with high ceilings and fresco paintings on the walls; the marks of the fire kindled on the stone floor still visible, all the woodwork burned to a cinder, and the whole black with smoke. It was a perfect picture of wanton destruction. The day, too, was in conformity with the scene; the sun was obscured, the wind blew through the ruined building, it rained, was cold and cheerless. What were the feelings of my friend, I cannot imagine; the houses of three of his uncles were immediately adjoining; one of these uncles was one of the forty hostages, and was hanged; the other two were murdered; his father, a venerable-looking old man, who came down to the vessel when we started to see him off, had escaped to the mountains, from thence in a caique to Ipsara, and from thence into Italy. I repeat it, I cannot imagine what were his feelings; he spoke but little; they must have been too deep for utterance. I looked at everything with intense interest; I wanted to ask question after question, but could not, in mercy, probe his bleeding wounds. We left the house and walked out into the garden. It showed that there was no master's eye to watch over it; I plucked an orange which had lost its flavour; the tree was withering from want of care; our feet became entangled among weeds, and roses and rare hothouse plants, growing wildly together. I said that he did not talk much; but the little he did say amounted to volumes. Passing a large vase in which a beautiful plant was running wildly over the sides, he murmured indistinctly "the same vase", (le même vase), and once he stopped opposite a tree, and, turning to me, said, "This is the only tree I do not remember." These, and other little incidental remarks showed how deeply all the particulars were engraved upon his mind, and told me, plainer than words, that the wreck and ruin he saw around him harrowed his very soul. Indeed, how could it be otherwise? This was his father's house, the home of his youth, the scene of his earliest, dearest, and fondest recollections. Busy memory, that source of all our greatest pains as well as greatest pleasures, must have pressed sorely upon him, must have painted the ruined and desolate scene around him in colours even brighter, far brighter, than they ever existed in; it must have called up the faces of well-known and well-loved friends; indeed, he must have asked himself, in bitterness and in anguish of spirit, "The friends of my youth! where are they?" while the fatal answer fell upon his heart, "Gone, murdered, in captivity and in exile."

CHAPTER VIII.

A Noble Grecian Lady.—Beauty of Scio.—An Original.—Fogri.—A Turkish Coffee-house.—Mussulman at Prayers.—Easter Sunday.—A Greek Priest.—A Tartar Guide—Turkish Ladies—Camel Scenes.—Sight of a Harem.—Disappointed Hopes.—A rare Concert.—Arrival at Smyrna.

(Continuation of the Letter.)

WE returned to the house, and seeking out a room less ruined than the rest, partook of a slight collation, and set out on a visit to a relative of my Sciote friend.

On our way my companion pointed out a convent on the side of a hill, where six thousand Greeks, who had been prevailed upon to come down from the mountains to ransom themselves, were treacherously murdered to a man; their unburied bones still whiten the ground within the walls of the convent. Arriving at the house of his relative, we entered through a large gateway into a handsome courtyard, with reservoir, garden, &c., ruinous, though in better condition than those we had seen before. This relative was a widow, of the noble house of Mavrocordato, one of the first families in Greece, and perhaps the most distinguished name in the Greek revolution. She had availed herself of the sultan's amnesty to return; had repaired two or three rooms, and sat down to end her days among the scenes of her childhood, among the ruins of her father's house. She was now not more than thirty; her countenance was remarkably pensive, and she had seen enough to drive a smile for ever from her face. The meeting between her and my friend was exceedingly affecting, particularly on her part. She wept bitterly, though, with the elasticity peculiar to the Greek character, the smile soon chased away the tear. She invited us to spend the night there, pointing to the divan, and promising us cushions and coverlets. We accepted her invitation, and again set forth to ramble among the ruins.

I had heard that an American missionary had lately come into the island, and was living somewhere in the neighbourhood. I found out his abode, and went to see him. He was a young man from Virginia, by name * * * * * *, had married a lady from Connecticut, who was unfortunately sick in bed. He was living in one room in the corner of a ruined building, but was then engaged in repairing a house into which he expected to remove soon. As an American, the first whom they had seen in that distant island, they invited me into the sick-room. In a strange land, and among a people whose language they did not understand, they seemed to be all in all to each other; and I left them, probably for ever, in the earnest hope that the wife might soon be restored to health, that hand-in-hand they might sustain each other in the rough path before them.

Toward evening we returned to the house of my friend's relative. We found there a nephew, a young man about twenty-two, and a cousin, a man about thirty-five, both accidentally on a visit to the island. As I looked at the little party before me, sitting around a brazier of charcoal, and talking earnestly in Greek, I could hardly persuade myself that what I had seen and heard that day was real. All that I had ever read in history of the ferocity of the Turkish character; all the wild stories of corsairs, of murdering, capturing, and carrying into captivity, that I had ever read in romances, crowded upon me, and I saw living witnesses that the bloodiest records of history and the wildest creations of romance were not overcharged. They could all testify in their own persons that these things were true. They had all been stripped of their property, and had their houses burned over their heads; had all narrowly escaped being murdered; and had all suffered in their nearest and dearest connexions. The nephew, then a boy nine years old, had been saved by a maid-servant; his father had been murdered; a brother, a sister, and many of his cousins, were at that moment, and had been for years, in slavery among the Turks; my friend, with his sister, had found refuge in the house of the Austrian consul, and from thence had escaped into Italy; the cousin was the son of one of the forty hostages who were hung, and was the only member of his father's family that escaped death; while our pensive and amiable hostess, a bride of seventeen, had seen her young husband murdered before her eyes; had herself been sold into slavery, and, after two years' servitude, redeemed by her friends.

In the morning I rose early and walked out upon the terrace. Nature had put on a different garb. The wind had fallen, and the sun was shining warmly upon a scene of softness and luxuriance surpassing all that I had ever heard or dreamed of the beauty of the islands of Greece. Away with all that I said about Syra! skip the page. The terrace overlooked the garden filled with orange, lemon, almond, and fig-trees; with plants, roses, and flowers of every description, growing in luxuriant wildness. But the view was not confined to the garden. Looking back to the harbour of Scio, was a bold range of rugged mountains bounding the view on that side; on the right was the sea, then calm as a lake; on both the other sides were ranges of mountains, irregular and picturesque in their appearance, verdant and blooming to their very summits; and for extent of perhaps five miles, were continued gardens like that at my feet, filled with the choicest fruit-trees, with roses, and the greatest variety of rare plants and flowers that ever unfolded their beauties before the eyes of man; above all, the orange-trees, the peculiar favourite of the island, then almost in full bloom, covered with blossoms, from my elevated position on the terrace made the whole valley appear an immense bed of flowers. All, too, felt the freshening influence of the rain; and a gentle breeze brought to me from this wilderness of sweets the most delicious perfume that ever greeted the senses. Do not think me extravagant when I say that, in your wildest dreams, you could never fancy so rich and beautiful a scene. Even among ruins, that almost made the heart break, I could hardly tear my eyes from it. It is one of the loveliest spots on earth. It is emphatically a Paradise lost, for the hand of the Turks is upon it; a hand that withers all that it touches. In vain does the sultan invite the survivors, and the children made orphans by his bloody massacre, to return; in vain do the fruits and the flowers, the sun and the soil, invite them to return; their wounds are still bleeding; they cannot forget that the wild beast's paw might again be upon them, and that their own blood might one day moisten the flowers which grow over the graves of their fathers. But I must leave this place. I could hardly tear myself away then, and I love to linger about it now. While I was enjoying the luxury of the terrace, a messenger came from the captain to call us on board. With a feeling of the deepest interest I bade farewell, probably for ever, to my sorrowing hostess and to the beautiful gardens of Scio.

We mounted our mules, and in an hour were at the port. My feelings were so wrought upon, that I felt my blood boil at the first Turk I met in the streets. I felt that I should like to sacrifice him to the shades of the murdered Greeks. I wondered that the Greeks did not kill every one on the island. I wondered that they could endure the sight of the turban. We found that the captain had hurried us away unnecessarily. We could not get out of the harbour, and were obliged to lounge about the town all day. We again made a circuit among the ruins; examined particularly those of the library, where we found an old woman who had once been an attendant there, living in a little room in the cellar, completely buried under the stones of the fallen building; and returning, sat down with a chibouk before the door of an old Turkish coffee-house fronting the harbour. Here I met an original, in the person of the Dutch consul. He was an old Italian, and had been in America during the revolutionary war as dragoman, as he called it, to the Count de Grasse, though, from his afterward incidentally speaking of the count as "my master," I am inclined to think that the word dragoman, which here means a person of great character and trust, may be interpreted as "valet-de-chambre." The old consul was in Scio during the whole of the massacre, and gave me many interesting particulars respecting it. He hates the Greeks, and spoke with great indignation about the manner in which their dead bodies lay strewed about the streets for months after the massacre. "D—n them," he said, "he could not go anywhere without stumbling over them." As I began to have some apprehensions about being obliged to stay here another night, I thought I could not employ my time better than in trying to work out of the consul an invitation to spend it with him. But the old fellow was too much for me. When I began to talk about the unpleasantness of being obliged to spend the night on board, and the impossibility of spending it on shore, having no acquaintance there, he began to talk poverty in the most up and down terms. I was a little discouraged, but I looked at his military coat, his cocked hat and cane, and, considering his talk merely a sort of apology for the inferior style of housekeeping I should find, was inge-

M

niously working things to a point, when he sent me to the right-about by enumerating the little instances of kindness he had received from strangers who happened to visit the island; among others, from one—he had his name in his pocket-book; he should never forget him; perhaps I had heard of him—who, at parting, shook him affectionately by the hand, and gave him a doubloon and a Spanish dollar. I hauled off from the representative of the majesty of Holland, and perhaps, before this, have been served up to some new visiter as the "mean, stingy American."

In the evening we again got under weigh; before morning the wind was again blowing dead a-head; and about mid-day we put into the harbour of Foggi, a port in Asia Minor, and came to anchor under the walls of the castle, under the blood-red Mussulman flag. We immediately got into the boat to go ashore. This was my first port in Turkey. A huge ugly African, marked with the small-pox, with two pistols and a yataghan in his belt, stood on a little dock, waited till we were in the act of landing, and then rushed forward, ferocious as a tiger from his native sands, throwing up both his hands, and roaring out "Quarantino." This was a new thing in Turkey. Heretofore the Turks, with their fatalist notions, had never taken any precautions against the plague; but they had become frightened by the terrible ravages the disease was then making in Egypt, and imposed a quarantine upon vessels coming from thence. We were, however, suffered to land, and our first movement was to the coffee-house directly in front of the dock. The coffee-house was a low wooden building, covering considerable ground, with a large piazza, or rather projecting roof, all around it. Inside and out there was a raised platform against the wall. This platform was one step from the floor, and on this step every one left his shoes before taking his seat on the matting. There were, perhaps, fifty Turks inside and out; sitting cross-legged, smoking the chibouk, and drinking coffee out of cups not larger than the shell of a Madeira nut.

We kicked our shoes off on the steps, seated ourselves on a mat outside, and took our chibouk and coffee with an air of savoir faire that would not have disgraced the worthiest Moslem of them all. Verily, said I, as I looked at the dozing, smoking, coffee-sipping congregation around me, there are some good points about the Turks, after all. They never think—that hurts digestion; and they love chibouks and coffee—that shows taste and feeling. I fell into their humour, and for a while exchanged nods with my neighbours all around. Suddenly the bitterness of thought came upon me; I found that my pipe was exhausted. I replenished it, and took a sip of coffee. Verily, said I, there are few better things in this world than chibouks and coffee; they even make men forget there is blood upon their hands. The thought started me; I shrank from contact with my neighbours, cut my way through the volumes of smoke, and got into the open air.

My companion joined me. We entered the walls and made a circuit of the town. It was a dirty little place, having one principal street lined with shops or bazars; every third shop, almost, being a cafteria, where a parcel of huge turbaned fellows were at their daily labours of smoking pipes and drinking coffee. The first thing I remarked as being strikingly different from a European city was the total absence of women. The streets were thronged with men, and not a woman was to be seen, except occasionally I caught a glimpse of a white veil or a pair of black eyes sparkling through the latticed bars of a window. Afterward, however, in walking outside the walls into the country, we met a large party of women. When we first saw them they had their faces uncovered; but, as soon as they saw us coming toward them, they stopped and arranged their long white shawls, winding them around their faces so as to leave barely space enough uncovered to allow them to see and breathe, but so that it was utterly impossible for us to distinguish a single one of their features.

Going on in the direction from which they came, and attracted by the mourning cypress, we came to a large burying-ground. It is situated on the side of a hill almost washed by the waves, and shaded by a thick grove of the funereal tree. There is, indeed, something peculiarly touching in the appearance of this tree; it seems to be endowed with feelings, and to mourn over the dead it shades. The monuments were generally a single upright slab of marble, with a turban on the top. There were many, too, in form like one of our oblong tombstones; and, instead of a slab of marble over the top, the interior was filled with earth, and the surface overrun with roses, evergreens and flowers. The burying-grounds in the East are always favourite places for walking in; and it is a favourite occupation of the Turkish women to watch and water the flowers growing over the graves of their friends.

Toward evening we returned to the harbour. I withdrew from my companion, and, leaning against one of the gates of the city, fixed my eyes upon the door of a minaret, watching till the muezzin should appear, and, for the last time before the setting of the sun, call all good Mussulmans to prayer. The door opens towards Mecca, and a little before dark the muezzin came out, and, leaning over the railing with his face toward the tomb of the Prophet, in a voice, every tone of which fell distinctly upon my ear, made that solemn call which, from the time of Mohammed, has been addressed five times a day from the tops of the minarets to the sons of the faithful. "Allah! Allah! God is God, and Mohammed is his prophet. To prayer! to prayer!" Immediately an old Turk by my side fell upon his knees, with his face to the tomb of the Prophet; ten times, in quick succession, he bowed his forehead till it touched the earth; then clasped his hands and prayed. I never saw more rapt devotion than in this pious old Mussulman. I have often marked in Italy the severe observance of religious ceremonies; I have seen, for instance, at Rome, fifty penitents at a time mounting on their knees, and kissing, as they mounted, the steps of the Scala Santa, or holy staircase, by which, as the priests tell them, our Saviour ascended into the presence of Pontius Pilate. I have seen the Greek prostrate himself before a picture until he was physically exhausted; and I have seen the humble and pious Christian at his prayers beneath the simple fanes and before the peaceful altars of my own land; but I never saw that perfect abandonment with which a Turk gives himself up to his God in prayer. He is perfectly abstracted from the things of this world; he does not regard time or place; in his closet or in the street, alone or in a crowd, he sees nothing, he hears nothing; the world is a blank; his God is everything. He is lost in the intensity of his devotion. It is a spectacle almost sublime; and for the moment you forget the polluted fountain of his religion, and the thousand crimes it sanctions, in your admiration of his sincerity and faith.

Not being able to find any place where we could sleep ashore, except on one of the mats of the coffee-house, head and heels with a dozen Turks, we went on board, and toward morning again got under weigh. We beat up to the mouth of the Gulf of Smyrna, but, with the scirocco blowing directly in our teeth, it was impossible to go farther. We made two or three attempts to enter, but in tacking the last time our old brig, which had hardly ballast enough to keep her keel under water, received such a rough shaking that we got her way before the wind, and at three o'clock P.M. were again anchored in the harbour of Foggi. I now began to think that there was a spell upon my movements, and that Smyrna, which was becoming to me a sort of land of promise, would never greet my longing eyes.

I was somewhat comforted, however, by remembering that I had never yet reached any port in the Mediterranean for which I had sailed, without touching at one or two intermediate ports; and that, so far, I had always worked right at last. I was still farther comforted by our having the good fortune to be able to procure lodging ashore, at the house of a Greek, the son of a priest. It was the Saturday before Easter Sunday, and the resurrection of our Saviour was to be celebrated at midnight, or, rather, the beginning of the next day, according to the rites and ceremonies of the Greek church. It was also the last of the forty days' fasting, and the next day commenced feasting. Supper was prepared for us, at which meat was put on the table for me only; my Greek friend being supposed not to eat meat during the days of fasting. He had been, however, two years out of Greece; and though he did not like to offend the prejudices of his countrymen, he did not like fasting. I felt for my fellow-traveller; and, cutting up some meat in small parcels, kept my eye upon the door while he whipped them into his mouth. After supper we lay down upon the divan, with large quilts over us, my friend having promised to rise at twelve o'clock and accompany me to the Greek church.

At midnight we were roused by the chant of the Greeks in the streets, on their way to the church. We turned out, and fell into a procession of five hundred people, making the streets as light as day with their torches. At the door of the church we found our host, sitting at a table with a parcel of wax tapers on one side and a box to receive money on the other. We each bought a taper and went in. After remaining there at least two hours, listening to a monotonous and unintelligible routine of prayers and chants, the priests came out of the holy doors, bearing aloft an image of our Saviour on the cross, ornamented with gold leaf, tassels, and festoons of artificial flowers; passed through the church, and out of the opposite door. The Greeks lighted their tapers and formed into a procession behind them, and we did the same. Immediately outside the door, up the staircase, and on each side of the corridor, allowing merely room enough for the procession to pass, were arranged the women, dressed in white, with long white veils, thrown back from their faces however, laid smooth over the tops of their heads, and hanging down to their feet. Nearly every woman, old or young, had a child in her arms. In fact, there seemed to be as great a mustering of children as of men and women, and, for aught that I could see, as much to the edification of the former as the latter. A continued chant was kept up during the movements of the procession, and perhaps for half an hour after the arrival of the priests at the courtyard, when it rose to a tremendous burst. The torches were waved in the air; a wild, unmeaning, and discordant scream or yell rang through the hollow cloisters, and half a dozen pistols, two or three muskets, and twenty or thirty crackers were fired. This was intended as a feu-de-joie, and was supposed to mark the precise moment of our Saviour's resurrection. In a few moments the frenzy seemed to pass away; the noise fell from a wild clamour to a slow chant, and the procession returned to the church. The scene was striking, particularly the part outside the church; the dead of night; the waving of torches; the women with their long white dresses, and the children in their arms, &c.; but, from beginning to end, there was nothing solemn in it.

Returned to the church, a priest came round with a picture of the Saviour risen; and, as far as I could make it out, holding in his hand the Greek flag, followed by another priest with a plate to receive contributions. He held out the picture to be kissed, then turned his hand to receive the same act of devotion, keeping his eye all the time upon the plate which followed to receive the offerings of the pious, as a sort of payment for the privilege of the kiss. His manner reminded me of the Dutch parson, who, immediately after pronouncing a couple man and wife, touching the bridegroom with his elbow, said, "And now where ish mine dollar?" I kissed the picture, dodged his knuckles, paid my money, and left the church. I had been there four hours, during which time, perhaps, more than a thousand persons had been completely absorbed in their religious ceremonies; and though beginning in the middle of the night, I have seen more yawning at the theatre or at an Italian opera than I saw there. They now began to disperse, though I remember I left a crowd of regular amateurs, at the head of whom were our sailors, still hanging round the desk of an exhorting priest, with an earnestness that showed a still craving appetite.

I do not wonder that the Turks look with contempt upon Christians, for they have constantly under their eyes the disgusting mummeries of the Greek church, and see nothing of the pure and sublime principles our religion inculcates. Still, however, there was something striking and interesting in the manner in which the Greeks in this Turkish town had kept themselves, as it were a peculiar people, and, in spite of the brands of "dog" and "infidel," held fast to the religion they received from their fathers. There was nothing interesting about them as Greeks; they had taken no part with their countrymen in their glorious struggle for liberty; they were engaged in petty business, and bartered the precious chance of freedom once before them for base profits and ignoble ease: and even now were content to live in chains, and kiss the rod that smote them.

We returned to the house where we had slept; and, after coffee, in company with our host and his father, the priest, sat down to a meal, in which, for the first time in forty days, they ate meat. I had often remarked the religious observance of fast-days among the common people in Greece. In travelling there I had more than once offered an egg to my guide on a fast-day, but never could get one to accept anything that came so near to animal food, though, by a strange confusion of the principles of religious obligation, perhaps the same man would not have hesitated to commit murder if he had any inducement to do so. Mrs. Hill, at Athens, told me that, upon one occasion, a little girl in her school refused to eat a piece of cake because it was made with eggs.

At daylight I was lying on the floor looking through a crevice of the window-shutter at the door of the minaret, waiting for the muezzin's morning cry to prayer. At six o'clock I went out, and finding the wind still in the same quarter, without any apparent prospect of change, determined, at all hazards, to leave the vessel and go on by land. My friend and fellow-passenger was also very anxious to get to Smyrna, but would not accompany me, from an indefinite apprehension of plague, robbers, &c. I had heard so many of these rumours, all of which had proved to be unfounded, that I put no faith in any of them. I found a Turk who engaged to take me through in fourteen hours; and at seven o'clock I was in my saddle, charged with a dozen letters from captains, supercargoes, and passengers, whom I left behind waiting for a change of wind.

My Tartar was a big swarthy fellow, with an extent of beard and mustaches unusual even among his bearded countrymen. He was armed with a pair of enormous pistols and a yataghan, and was, altogether, a formidable fellow to look upon. But there was a something about him that I liked. There was a doggedness, a downright stubbornness that seemed honest. I knew nothing about him. I picked him up in the street, and took him in preference to others who offered, because he would not be beaten down in his price. When he saw me seated on my horse he stood by my side a little distance off, and looking at me without opening his lips, drew his belt tight around him, and adjusted his pistols and yataghan. His manner seemed to say that he took charge of me as a bale of goods, to be paid for on safe delivery, and that he would carry me through with fire and sword if necessary. And now, said I, "Let fate do her worst;" I have a good horse under me, and in fourteen hours I shall be in Smyrna. "Blow winds and crack your cheeks;" I defy you.

My Tartar led off at a brisk trot, never opening his lips nor turning his head except occasionally to see how I followed him across a stream. At about ten o'clock he turned off from the horsepath into a piece of fine pasture, and slipping the bridle off his horse, turned him loose to feed. He then did the same with mine, and, spreading my cloak on the ground for me to sit upon, sat down by my side and opened his wallet. His manner seemed to intimate a disposition to throw provisions into a common stock, no doubt expecting the gain to be on his side; but as I could only contribute a couple of rolls of bread which I bought as we rode through the town, I am inclined to think that he considered me rather a sponge.

While we were sitting there a travelling party came up, consisting of five Turks and three women. The women were on horseback, riding crosswise, though there were so many quilts, cushions, &c. piled or the backs of their horses, that they sat rather on seats than on saddles. After a few words of parley with my Tartar, the men lifted the women from the horses, taking them in their arms, and, as it were, hauling them off, not very gracefully, but very kindly; and, spreading their quilts on the ground at a short distance from us, turned their horses loose to feed, and sat down to make their morning meal. An unusual and happy thing for me, the women had their faces uncovered nearly all the time, though they could not well have carried on the process of eating with them muffled up in the usual style. One of the women was old, the other two were exceedingly young; neither of them more than sixteen; each had a child in her arms, and, without any allowance for time and place, both were exceedingly beautiful. I do not say so under the influence of the particular circumstances of our meeting, nor with the view of making an incident of it, but I would have singled them out as such if I had met them in a ball-room at home. I was particularly struck with their delicacy of figure and complexion. Notwithstanding their laughing faces, their mirth, and the kind treatment of the men, I could not divest myself of the idea that they were caged birds longing to be freed. I could not believe that a woman belonging to a Turk could be otherwise than unhappy. Unfortunately, I could not understand a word of their language; and as they looked from their turbaned lords to my stiff hat and frock-coat, they seemed to regard me as something that the Tartar had just caught and was taking up to Constantinople as a present to the sultan. I endeavoured to show, however, that I was not the wild thing they took me to be; that I had an eye to admire their beauty, and a heart to feel for their servitude. I tried to procure from them some signal of distress; I did all that I could to get some sign to come to their rescue, and to make myself generally agreeable. I looked sentimentally. This they did not seem to understand at all. I smiled; this seemed to please them better; and there is no knowing to what a point I might have arrived, but my Tartar hurried me away; and I parted on the wild plains of Turkey with two young and beautiful women, leading almost a savage life, whose personal graces would have made them ornaments in polished and refined society. Verily, said I, the Turks are not so bad after all; they have handsome wives, and a handsome wife comes next after chibouks and coffee.

I was now reminded at every step of my being in an oriental country by the caravans I was constantly meeting. Caravans and camels are more or less associated with all the fairy scenes and glowing pictures of the East. They have always presented themselves to my mind with a sort of poetical imagery, and they certainly have a fine effect in a description or in a picture; but, after all, they are ugly-looking things to meet on the road. I would rather see the two young Turk-esses again, than all the caravans in the East. The caravan is conducted by a guide on a donkey, with a halter attached to the first camel, and so on from camel to camel through the whole caravan. The camel is an exceedingly ugly animal in his proportions, and there is a dead uniformity in his movement; with a dead, vacant expression in his face, that is really distressing. If a man were dying of thirst in the desert, it would be enough to drive him to distraction to look in the cool, unconcerned, and imperturbable face of his camel. But their value is inestimable in a country like this, where there are no carriage roads, and where deserts and drought present themselves in every direction.

One of the camel scenes, the encampment, is very picturesque, the camels arranged around on their knees in a circle, with their heads to the centre, and the camel-drivers with their bales piled up within; and I was struck with another scene; we came to the borders of a stream, which it was necessary to cross in a boat. The boat was then on the other side, and the boatman and camel-driver were trying to get on board some camels. When we came up they had got three on board, down on their knees in the bottom of the boat, and were then in the act of coercing the fourth. The poor brute was frightened terribly; resisted with all his might, and put forth most piteous cries; I do not know a more distressing noise than the cry of a brute suffering from fear; it seems to partake of the feeling that causes it, and carries with it something fearful; but the cries of the poor brute were vain; they got him on board, and in the same way urged on board three others. They then threw in the donkey, and seven camels and the donkey were so stowed in the bottom of the boat, that they did not take up much more room than calves on board of our country-boats.

In the afternoon I met another travelling party of an entirely different description. If before I had occasionally any doubts or misgivings as to the reality of my situation; if sometimes it seemed to be merely a dream, that it could not be that I was so far from home, wandering alone on the plains of Asia, with a guide whom I never saw till that morning, whose language I could not understand, and upon whose faith I could not rely; if the scenes of turbaned Turks, of veiled women, of caravans and camels, of graveyards with their mourning cypress and thousands of tombstones, where every trace of the cities which supplied them with their dead had entirely disappeared; if these and the other strange scenes around me would seem to be the mere creations of a roving imagination, the party which I met now was so marked in its character, so peculiar to an oriental country, and to an oriental country only, that it roused me from my waking dreams, fixed my wandering thoughts, and convinced me, beyond all peradventure, that I was indeed far from home,

among a people "whose thoughts are not as our thoughts, and whose ways are not as our ways;" in short, in a land where ladies are not the omnipotent creatures that they are with us.

This party was no other than the ladies of a harem. They were all dressed in white, with their white shawls wrapped around their faces, so that they effectually concealed every feature, and could bring to bear only the artillery of their eyes. I found this, however, to be very potent, as it left so much room for the imagination; and it was a very easy matter to make a Fatima of every one of them. They were all on horseback, not riding sidewise, but *otherwise*; though I observed, as before, that their saddles were so prepared that their delicate limbs were not subject to that extreme expansion required by the saddle of the rougher sex. They were escorted by a party of armed Turks, and followed by a man in Frank dress, who, as I after understood, was the physician of the harem. They were thirteen in number, just a baker's dozen, and belonged to a pacha who was making his annual tour of the different posts under his government, and had sent them on before to have the household matters all arranged upon his arrival. And no doubt, also, they were to be in readiness to receive him with their smiles; and if they continued in the same humour in which I saw them, he must have been a happy man who could call them all his own. I had not fairly recovered from the cries of the poor camel when I heard their merry voices: verily, thought I, stopping to catch the last musical notes, there are exceedingly good points about the Turks: chibouks, coffee, and as many wives as they please. It made me whistle to think of it. Oh, thought I, that some of our ladies could see these things; that some haughty beauty, at whose feet dozens of worthy and amiable young gentlemen are sighing themselves into premature wrinkles and ugliness, might see these things!

I am no rash innovator. I would not sweep away the established customs of our state of society. I would not lay my meddling fingers upon the admitted prerogatives of our ladies; but I cannot help asking myself, in the rapid changes of this turning world, changes which completely alter rocks and the hardest substances of nature, it may not by possibility happen that the tenour of a lady's humour will change. What a goodly spectacle to see those who are never content without a dozen admirers in their train, following by dozens in the train of one man! But I fear me much that this will never be, at least in our days. Our system of education is radically wrong. The human mind, says some philosopher, and the gentleman is right, is like the sand upon the shore of the sea. You may write upon it what character you please. *We* begin by writing upon their innocent unformed minds, that, "Born for their use, we live but to oblige them." The consequence is, I will not say what; for I hope to return among them and kiss the rod in some fair hand; but this I do know, that here the "twig is so bent" that they become as gentle, as docile, and as tractable as any domestic animal. I say again, there are many exceeding good points about the Turks.

At about six o'clock we came in sight of Smyrna, on the opposite side of the gulf, and still a long way off. At dusk we were directly opposite the city; and although we had yet to make a long circuit round the head of the gulf, I was revelling in the bright prospect before me. Dreams of pulling off my pantaloons; delightful visions of clean sheets and a Christian bed, flitted before my eyes. Yes, said I to my pantaloons and shirt, ye worthy and faithful servants, this night ye shall have rest. While other garments have fallen from me by the way, ye have stuck to me. And thou, my grey pantaloons, little did the neat Parisian tailor who made thee think that the strength of his stitching would ever be tested by three weeks' uninterrupted wear; but tomorrow thou shalt go into the hands of a master, who shall sew on thy buttons and sew up thy rents: and thou, my—I was going on with words of the same affectionate import to my shirt, stockings, and drawers, which, however, did not deserve so well of me, for they had in a measure *dropped off* on the way, when my Tartar came to a dead stop before the door of a cabin, dismounted, and made signs to me to do the same. But I began now to have some notions of my own; heretofore I had been perfectly passive; I had always done as I was told, but in sight of Smyrna I became restive. I talked and shouted to him, pointed to the city, and turned my horse as though I was going on alone. My Tartar, however, paid no attention to me; he very coolly took off my carpet-bag and carried it into the cabin, lighted his pipe, and sat down by the door, looking at me with the most imperturbable gravity. I had hardly had time to admire his impudence, and to calculate the chances of my being able, alone at night, to cross the many streams which emptied into the gulf, when the wind, which had been rising for some time, became very violent, and the rain began to fall in torrents. With a sigh I bade farewell to the bright visions that had deluded me, gave another sigh to the uncertainty of all human calculations, the cup and the lip, &c. and took refuge in the cabin.

What a substitute for the pretty little picture I had drawn! Three Turks were sitting round a brazier of charcoal frying dough-balls. Three rugs were spread in three corners of the cabin, and over each of them were the eternal pistols and yataghan. There was nothing there to defend; their miserable lives were not worth taking; why were these weapons there! The Turks at first took no notice of me, and I had now to make amends for my backwardness in entering. I resolved to go to work boldly, and at once elbowed among them for a seat around the brazier. The one next me on my right seemed a little struck by my easy ways; he put his hand on his ribs to feel how far my elbow had penetrated, and then took his pipe from his mouth and offered it to me. The ice broken, I smoked the pipe to the last whiff, and handed it to him to be refilled; with all the horrors of dyspepsy before my eyes, I scrambled with them for the last doughball, and, when the attention of all of them was particularly directed toward me, took out my watch, held it over the lamp, and wound it up. I addressed myself particularly to the one who had first taken notice of me, and made myself extremely agreeable by always smoking his pipe. After coffee and half a dozen pipes, he gave me to understand that I was to sleep with him upon his mat, at which I slapped him on the back and cried out, "Bono," having heard him use that word, apparently with a knowledge of its meaning.

I was surprised in the course of the evening to see one of them begin to undress, knowing that such was not the custom of the country, but found that it was only a temporary disrobing for sporting purposes, to hunt fleas and bedbugs; by which I had an opportunity of comparing the Turkish with some I had brought with me from Greece; and though the Turk had great reason to be proud of his, I had no reason to be ashamed of mine. I now began to be drowsy, and should soon have fallen asleep; but the youngest of the party, a sickly and sentimental young man, melancholy and musical, and, no doubt, in love, brought out the common Turkish instrument, a sort of guitar, on which he worked with untiring vivacity, keeping time with his head and heels. My friend accompanied him with his voice, and this brought out my Tartar, who joined in with groans and grunts which might have awakened the dead. But my cup was not yet full. During the musical festival my friend and intended bedfellow took down from a shelf above me a large plaster, which he warmed over the brazier. He then unrolled his turban, took off a plaster from the back of his head, and disclosed a wound, raw, gory, and ghastly, that made my heart sink within me: I knew that the plague was about Smyrna; I had heard that it was on this road; I involuntarily recurred to the Italian prayer, "Save me from three miseries of the Levant: plague, fire, and the dragoman." I shut my eyes; I had slept but two hours the night before; had ridden twelve hours that day on horseback; I drew my cloak around me; my head sank upon my carpet-bag, and I fell asleep, leaving the four Turks playing cards on the bottom of a pewter plate. Once during the night I was awakened by my bedfellow's mustaches tickling my lips. I turned my back and slept on.

In the morning my Tartar, with one jerk, stood me upright on the floor, and holding me in that position until I got awake, kicked open the door, and pointed to my horse standing before it ready saddled and bridled. In three hours I was crossing the caravan bridge, a bridge over the beautiful Melissus, on the banks of which Homer was born; and picking my way among caravans, which for ages have continued to cross this bridge laden with all the riches of the East, I entered the long-looked-for city of Smyrna, a city that has braved the reiterated efforts of conflagrations, plagues, and earthquakes; ten times destroyed, and ten times risen from her ruins; the queen of the cities of Anatolia; extolled by the ancients as Smyrna the lovely, the crown of Ionia, the pride of Asia. But old things have passed away, and the ancient city now figures only under the head of arrivals in a newspaper, in the words and figures following, that is to say, "Brig Betsy, Baker master, 57 days from Smyrna, with figs and raisins to order. Mastic dull, opium rising."

In half-an-hour I was in the full enjoyment of a Turkish bath; lolled half an hour on a divan, with chibouk and coffee, and came out fresh as if I had spent the last three weeks training for the ring. Oh, these Turks are luxurious dogs! chibouks, coffee, hot-baths, and as many wives as they please. What a catalogue of human enjoyments! But I intend Smyrna as a place of rest, and, in charity, give you the benefit of it.

* * *

CHAPTER IX.

First Sight of Smyrna.—Unveiled Women.—Ruins of Ephesus.—Ruin, all Ruin.—Temple of Diana.—Encounter with a Wolf.—Love at first Sight.—Gatherings on the Road.

(Another Letter.)

MY DEAR ******,

AFTER my bath I returned to my hotel, breakfasted, and sallied out for a walk. It was now about twelve o'clock, Sunday—the first Sunday after Easter—and all the Frank population was in the streets. My hotel was in an out-of-the-way quarter, and when turning a corner, I suddenly found myself in the main street, I was not prepared for the sight that met my eye. Paris on a fête day does not present so gay and animated a scene. It was gay, animated, striking, and beautiful, and entirely different from anything I had ever seen in any European city. Franks, Jews, Greeks, Turks, and Armenians, in their various and striking costumes, were mingled together in agreeable confusion; and making all due allowance for the circumstance that I had for some time been debarred the sight of an unveiled woman, I certainly never saw so much beauty, and I never saw a costume so admirably calculated to set off beauty. At the same time the costume is exceedingly trying to a lady's pretensions. Being no better than one of the uninitiated, I shall not venture upon such dangerous ground as a lady's toilet. I will merely refer to that part which particularly struck me, and that is the head-dress: no odious broad-brimmed hat; no enormous veils enveloping nose, mouth, and eyes; but simply a large gauze turban, sitting lightly and gracefully on the head, rolled back over the forehead, leaving the whole face completely exposed, and exhibiting clear dark complexions, rosy lips closing over teeth of dazzling whiteness; and then such eyes, large, dark, and rolling. It is matter of history, and it is confirmed by poetry, that

> "The angelic youths of old,
> Burning for maids of mortal mould,
> Bewildered, left the glorious skies,
> And lost their heaven for woman's eyes."

My dear friend, this is the country where such things happened; the throne of the Thunderer, high Olympus, is almost in sight, and these are the daughters of the women who worked such miracles. If the age of passion, like the age of chivalry, were not over and for ever gone, if this were not emphatically a bank-note world, I would say of the Smyrniotes, above all others, that they are that description of women who could

> "Raise a mortal to the skies,
> Or bring an angel down."

And they walk, too, as if conscious of their high pretensions, as if conscious that the reign of beauty is not yet ended; and, under that enchanting turban, charge with the whole artillery of their charms. It is a perfect unmasked battery; nothing can stand before it. I wonder the sultan allows it. The Turks are as touchy as tinder; they take fire as quick as any of the old demi gods, and a pair of black eyes is at any time enough to put mischief in them. But the Turks are a considerate people. They consider that the Franks, or rather the Greeks, to whom I particularly refer, have periodical fits of insanity; that they go mad twice a year, during carnival and after Lent; and if at such a time a follower of the Prophet, accidentally straggling in the Frank quarter, should find the current of his blood disturbed, he would sooner die, nay, he would sooner cut off his beard, than hurt a hair of any one of the light heads that he sees flitting before him. There is something remarkable, by-the-way, in the tenacity with which the Grecian women have sustained the rights and prerogatives of beauty in defiance of Turkish customs and prejudices; while the men have fallen into the habits of their quondam masters, have taken to pipes and coffee, and in many instances to turbans and big trousers, the women have ever gone with their faces uncovered, and to this day one and all eschew the veil of the Turkish women.

Pleased and amused with myself and everything I saw, I moved along unnoticed and unknown, staring, observing, and admiring; among other things, I observed that one of the amiable customs of our own city was in full force here, viz., that of the young gentlemen, with light sticks in their hands, gathering around the door of the fashionable church to stare at the ladies as they came out. I was pleased to find such a mark of civilisation in a land of barbarians, and immediately fell into a thing which seemed so much like home; but, in justice to the Smyrniote ladies, I must say I cannot flatter myself that I stared a single one out of countenance.

But I need not attempt to interest you in Smyrna; it is too every-day a place; every Cape Cod sailor knows it better than I do. I have done all that I could; I have waived the musty reminiscences of its history; I have waived ruin, which are said to exist here, and have endeavoured to give you a faint but true picture of its living and existing beauties, of the bright and beautiful scene that broke upon me the first morning of my arrival; and now, if I have not touched you with the beauty of its women, I should despair of doing so by any description of its beautiful climate, its charming environs, and its hospitable society.

Leave, then, what is, after all, but the city of figs and raisins, and go with me where, by comparison, the foot of civilised man seldom treads; go with me into the desert and solitary places; go with me among the cities of the seven churches of Asia; and, first, to the ruins of Ephesus. I had been several days expecting a companion to make this tour with me, but, being disappointed, was obliged to set out alone. I was not exactly alone, for I had with me a Turk as guide and a Greek as cicerone and interpreter, both well mounted and armed to the teeth. We started at two o'clock in the morning, under the light of thousands of stars; and the day broke upon us in a country wild and desolate, as if it were removed thousands of miles from the habitations of men. There was little variety and little incident in our ride. During the whole day it lay through a country decidedly handsome, the soil rich and fertile, but showing with appalling force the fatal effects of misgovernment, wholly uncultivated, and almost wholly uninhabited. Indeed, the only habitations were the little Turkish coffee-houses and the black tents of the Turcomans. These are a wandering tribe, who come out from the desert, and approach comparatively near the abodes of civilisation. They are a pastoral people; their riches are their flocks and herds; they lead a wandering life, free as the air they breathe; they have no local attachments; to-day they pitch their tents on the hill-side, to-morrow on the plain; and wherever they sit themselves down, all that they have on earth, wife, children and friends, are immediately around them. There is something primitive, almost patriarchal, in their appearance; indeed, it carries one back to a simple and perhaps a purer age, and you could almost realise that state of society when the patriarch sat in the door of his tent and called in and fed the passing traveller.

The general character of the road is such as to prepare one for the scene that awaits him at Ephesus; enormous burying-grounds, with thousands of head-stones shaded by the mourning cypress, in the midst of a desolate country, where not a vestige of a human habitation is to be seen. They stand on the road-side as melancholy telltales that large towns or cities once existed in their immediate neighbourhood, and that the generations who occupied them have passed away, furnishing fearful evidence of the decrease of the Turkish population, and perhaps that the gigantic empire of the Ottoman is tottering to its fall.

For about three hours before reaching Ephesus, the road, crossing a rich and beautiful plain watered by the Cayster, lies between two mountains; that on the right leads to the sea, and on the left are the ruins of Ephesus. Near, and in the immediate vicinity, storks were calmly marching over the plain and building among the ruins; they moved as if seldom disturbed by human footsteps, and seemed to look upon us as intruders upon a spot for a long time abandoned to birds and beasts of prey. About a mile this side are the remains of the Turkish city of Aysalook, or Temple of the Moon, a city of comparatively modern date, reared into a brief magnificence out of the ruins of its fallen neighbour. A sharp hill, almost a mountain, rises abruptly from the plain, on the top of which is a ruined fortress, with many ruins of Turkish magnificence at the base; broken columns, baths overgrown with ivy, and the remains of a grand mosque, the roofs sustained by four granite columns from the Temple of Diana; the minaret fallen, the mosque deserted; the Mussulman no more goes there to pray; bats and owls were building in its lofty roof, and snakes and lizards were crawling over its marble floor.

It was late in the afternoon when I arrived at the little coffee-house at Aysalook; a caravan had already encamped under some fine old sycamores before the door, preparatory to passing the night. I was somewhat fatigued, and my Greek, who had me in charge, was disposed to stop and wait for the morrow; but the fallen city was on the opposite hill at but a short distance, and the shades of evening seemed well calculated to heighten the effect of a ramble among its ruins. In a right line it was not more than half a mile, but we soon found that we could not go directly to it; a piece of low swampy ground lay between, and we had not gone far before our horses sank up to their saddle-girths. We were obliged to retrace our steps, and work our way around by a circuitous route of more than two miles. This, too, added to the effect of our approach. It was a dreary reflection, that a city, whose ports and whose gates had been open to the commerce of the then known world—whose wealth had invited the traveller and sojourner within its walls, should lie a ruin upon a hill-side, with swamps and morasses extending around it, in sight but out of reach, near but unapproachable. A warning voice seemed to issue from the ruins, "*Procul, ó procul este, profani,*" my day is past, my sun is set, I have gone to my grave; pass on, stranger, and disturb not the ashes of the dead.

But my Turk did not understand Latin, and we continued to advance. We moved along in perfect silence, for besides that my Turk never spoke, and my Greek, who was generally loquacious enough, was out of humour at being obliged to go on, we had enough to do in picking our lonely way. But silence best suited the scene; the sound of the human voice seemed almost a mockery of fallen greatness. We entered by a large and ruined gateway into a place distinctly marked as having been a street, and, from the broken columns strewed on each side, probably having been lined with a colonnade. I let my reins fall upon my horse's neck; he moved about in the slow and desultory way that suited my humour; now sinking to his knees in heaps of rubbish, now stumbling over a Corinthian capital, and now gliding over a marble pavement. The whole hill-side is covered with ruins to an extent far greater than I expected to find, and they are all of a kind that tends to give a high idea of the ancient magnificence of the city. To me, these ruins appeared to be a confused and shapeless mass; but they have been examined by antiquaries with great care, and the character of many of them identified with great certainty. I had, however, no time for details; and, indeed, the interest of these ruins in my eyes was not in the details. It mattered little to me that this was the stadium and that a fountain; that this was a gymnasium and that a market-place; it was enough to know that the broken columns, the mouldering walls, the grass-grown streets, and the wide-extended scene of desolation and ruin around me were all that remained of one of the greatest cities of Asia, one of the earliest Christian cities in the world. But what do I say? Who does not remember the tumults and confusion raised by Demetrius the silversmith, "lest the temple of the great goddess Diana should be despised, and her magnificence be destroyed;" and how the people, having caught "Gaius and Aristarchus, Paul's companions in travel," rushed with one accord into the theatre, crying out, "Great is Diana of the Ephesians." My dear friend, I sat among the ruins of that theatre; the stillness of death was around me; far as the eye could reach, not a living soul was to be seen, save my two companions and a group of lazy Turks smoking at the coffee-house in Aysalook. A man of strong imagination might almost go wild with the intensity of his own reflections; and do not let it surprise you, that even one like me, brought up among the technicalities of declarations and replications, rebutters and surrebutters, and in nowise given to the illusions of the senses, should find himself roused, and irresistibly hurried back to the time when the shapeless and confused mass around him formed one of the most magnificent cities in the world; when a large and busy population was hurrying through its streets, intent upon the same pleasures and the same business that engage men now; that he should, in imagination, see before him St. Paul preaching to the Ephesians, shaking their faith in the gods of their fathers, gods made with their own hands; and the noise and confusion, and the people rushing tumultuously up the very steps where he sat; that he should almost hear their cry ringing in his ears, " Great is Diana of the Ephesians;" and then that he should turn from this scene of former glory and eternal ruin to his own far-distant land; a land that the wisest of the Ephesians never dreamed of; where the wild man was striving with the wild beast when the whole world rang with the greatness of the Ephesian name; and which bids fair to be growing greater and greater when the last vestige of Ephesus shall be gone, and its very site unknown.

But where is the temple of the great Diana, the temple two hundred and twenty years in building; the temple of one hundred and twenty-seven columns, each column the gift of a king? Can it be that the temple of the "Great goddess Diana," that the ornament of Asia, the pride of Ephesus, and one of the seven wonders of the world, has gone, disappeared, and left not a trace behind? As a traveller, I would fain be able to say that I have seen the ruins of this temple; but, unfortunately, I am obliged to limit myself by facts. Its site has of course engaged the attention of antiquaries. I am no sceptic in these matters, and am disposed to believe all that my cicerone tells me. You remember the countryman who complained to his minister that he never gave him any Latin in his sermons; and when the minister answered that he would not understand it, the countryman replied that he paid for the best, and ought to have it. I am like that honest countryman; but my cicerone understood himself better than the minister; he knew that I paid him for the best; he knew what was expected from him, and that his reputation was gone for ever if, in such a place as Ephesus, he could not point out the ruins of the great temple of Diana. He accordingly had his temple, which he stuck to with as much pertinacity as if he had built it himself; but I am sorry to be obliged to say, in spite of his authority and my own wish to believe him, that the better opinion is, that now not a single stone is to be seen.

Topographers have fixed the site on the plain, near the gate of the city which opened to the sea. The sea, which once almost washed the walls, has receded or been driven back for several miles. For many years a new soil has been accumulating, and all that stood on the plain, including so much of the remains of the temple as had not been plundered and carried away by different conquerors, is probably now buried many feet under its surface.

It was dark when I returned to Aysalook. I had remarked, in passing, that several caravans had encamped there, and on my return found the camel-drivers assembled in the little coffee-house in which I was to pass the night. I soon saw that there were so many of us that we should make a tight fit in the sleeping part of the khan, and immediately measured off space enough to fit my body, allowing turning and kicking room. I looked with great complacency upon the light slippers of the Turks, which they always throw off, too, when they go to sleep, and made an ostentatious display of a pair of heavy iron-nailed boots, and in lying down, gave one or two preliminary thumps to show them that I was restless in my movements, and, if they came too near me, these iron-nailed boots would be uncomfortable neighbours.

And here I ought to have spent half the night in musing upon the strange concatenation of circumstances which had broken up a quiet practising attorney, and sent him a straggler from a busy, money-getting land, to meditate among the ruins of ancient cities, and sleep pell-mell with turbaned Turks. But I had no time for musing; I was amazingly tired; I looked at the group of Turks in one corner, and regretted that I could not talk with them; thought of the Tower of Babel and the wickedness of man, which brought about a confusion of tongues; of camel drivers, and Arabian Nights' Entertainments; of home, and my own comfortable room in the third story; brought my boot down with a thump that made them all start, and in five minutes was asleep.

In the morning I again went over to the ruins. Daylight, if possible, added to their effect; and a little thing occurred, not much in itself, but which, under the circumstances, fastened itself upon my mind in such a way that I shall never forget it. I had read that here, in the stillness of the night, the jackall's cry was heard; that, if a stone was rolled, a scorpion or lizard slipped from under it; and, while picking our way slowly along the lower part of the city, a wolf of the largest size came out above, as if indignant at being disturbed in his possessions. He moved a few paces towards us with such a resolute air that my companions both drew their pistols; then stopped, and gazed at us deliberately as we were receding from him, until, as if satisfied that we intended to leave his dominions, he turned and disappeared among the ruins. It would have made a fine picture; the Turk first, then the Greek, each with a pistol in his hand, then myself, all on horseback, the wolf above us, the valley, and the ruined city. I feel my inability to give you a true picture of these ruins. Indeed, if I could lay before you every particular, block for block, fragment for fragment, here a column and there a column, I could not convey a full idea of the desolation that marks the scene.

To the Christians, the ruins of Ephesus carry with them a peculiar interest; for here, upon the wreck of heathen temples, was established one of the earliest Christian churches; but the Christian church has followed the heathen temple, and the worshippers of the true God have followed the worshippers of the great goddess Diana; and in the city where Paul preached, and where, in the words of the apostle, "much people were gathered unto the Lord," now not a solitary Christian dwells.

Verily, in the prophetic language of inspiration, "the candlestick is removed from its place;" a curse seems to have fallen upon it, men shun it, not a human being is to be seen among its ruins; and Ephesus, in faded glory and fallen grandeur, is given up to birds and beasts of prey, a monument and a warning to nations.

From Ephesus I went to Scala Nova, handsomely situated on the shore of the sea, and commanding a fine view of the beautiful island of Samos, distant not more than four miles. I had a letter to a Greek merchant there, who received me kindly, and introduced me to the Turkish governor. The governor, as usual, was seated upon a divan, and asked us to take seats beside him. We were served with coffee and pipes by two handsome Greek slaves, boys about fourteen, with long hair hanging down their necks, and handsomely dressed; who, after serving us, descended from the platform, and waited with folded arms until we had finished. Soon after a third guest came, and a third lad, equally handsome and equally well dressed, served him in the same manner. This is the style of the Turkish grandees, a slave to every guest. I do not know to what extent it is carried, but am inclined to think that, in the present instance, if one or two more guests had happened to come in, my friend's retinue of slaves would have fallen short. The governor asked me from what country I came, and who was my king; and when I told him that we had no king, but a president, he said, very graciously, that our president and the grand seignior were very good friends; a compliment which I acknowledged with all becoming humility. Wanting to show off a little, I told him that we were going to fight the French, and he said we should certainly whip them if we could get the grand seignior to help us.

I afterwards called on my own account upon the English consul. The consuls in these little places are originals. They have nothing to do, but they have the government arms blazoned over their doors, and strut about in cocked hats and regimentals, and shake their heads, and look knowing, and talk about their government; they do not know what their government will think, &c., when half the time their government hardly knows of the existence of its worthy representatives. This was an old Maltese, who spoke French and Italian. He received me very kindly, and pressed me to stay all night. I told him that I was not an Englishman, and had no claim upon his hospitality; but he said that made no difference; that he was consul for all civilised nations, among which he did me the honour to include mine.

At three o'clock I took leave of the consul. My Greek friend accompanied me outside the gate, where my horses were waiting for me; and, at parting, begged me to remember that I had a friend, who hardly knew what pleasure was, except in serving me. I told him that the happiness of my life was not complete before I met him; we threw ourselves into each other's arms, and, after a two hours' acquaintance, could hardly tear away from each other's embraces. Such is the force of sympathy between congenial spirits. My friend was a man about fifty, square-built, broad-shouldered, and big-mustached; and the beauty of it was, that neither could understand a word the other said; and all this touching interchange of sentiment had to pass through my mustached, big-whiskered, double-fisted, six-feet interpreter.

At four o'clock, we set out on our return; at seven we stopped in a beautiful valley surrounded by mountains, and on the sides of the mountains were a number of Turcomans' tents. The khan was worse than any I had yet seen. It had no floor and no mat. The proprietor of the khan, if such a thing, consisting merely of four mud walls with a roof of branches, which seemed to have been laid there by the winds, could be said to have a proprietor, was uncommonly sociable; he set before me my supper, consisting of bread and yort—a preparation of milk—and appeared to be much amused at seeing me eat. He asked my guide many questions about me; examined my pistols, took off his turban, and put my hat upon his shaved head, which transformed him from a decidedly bold, slashing-looking fellow, into a decidedly sneaking-looking one. I had certainly got over all fastidiousness in regard to eating, drinking, and sleeping; but I could not stand the vermin at this khan. In the middle of the night I rose and went out of doors; it was a brilliant starlight night, and, as the bare earth was in any case to be my bed, I exchanged the mud floor of my khan for the greensward and the broad canopy of heaven. My Turk was sleeping on the ground, about a hundred yards from the house, with his horse grazing around him. I nestled close to him, and slept perhaps two hours. Toward morning I was awakened by the cold, and, with the selfishness of misery, I began punching my Turk under the ribs to wake him. This was no easy matter; but, after a while, I succeeded, got him to saddle the horses, and in a few minutes we were off, my Greek not at all pleased with having his slumbers so prematurely disturbed.

At about two o'clock, we passed some of the sultan's *volunteers*. These were about fifty men chained together by the wrists and ankles, who had been chased, run down, and caught in some of the villages, and were now on their way to Constantinople, under a guard, to be trained as soldiers. I could but smile as I saw them, not at them, for, in truth, there was nothing in their condition to excite a smile, but at the recollection of an article I had seen a few days before in a European paper, which referred to the new levies making by the sultan, and the spirit with which his subjects entered into the service. They were a speaking comment upon European insight into Turkish politics. But, without more ado, suffice it to say, that at about four o'clock I found myself at the door of my hotel, my outer garments so covered with creeping things that my landlord, a prudent Swiss, with many apologies, begged me to shake myself before going into the house; and my nether garments so stained with blood, that I looked as if a corps of the sultan's regulars had pricked me with their bayonets. My enthusiasm on the subject of the seven churches was in no small degree abated, and just at that moment I was willing to take upon trust the condition of the others, that all that was foretold of them in the Scriptures had come to pass. I again betook me to the bath, and, in thinking of the luxury of my repose, I feel for you, and come to a full stop.

CHAPTER X.

Position of Smyrna.—Consular Privileges.—The Case of the Lover.—End of the Love Affair.—The Missionary's Wife.—The Casino.—Only a Greek Row.—Rambles in Smyrna.—The Armenians.—Domestic Enjoyments.

BUT I must go back a little and make the *amende honorable*, for, in truth, Ghiaour Ismir, or Infidel Smyrna, with its wild admixture of European and Asiatic population, deserves better than the rather cavalier notice contained in my letter.

Before reaching it I had remarked its exceeding beauty of position, chosen as it is with that happy taste which distinguished the Greeks in selecting the sites of their ancient cities, on the declivity of a mountain running down to the shore of the bay, with houses rising in terraces on its sides; its domes and minarets, interspersed with cypresses, rising above the tiers of houses, and the summit of the hill crowned with a large solitary castle. It was the first large Turkish city I had seen, and it differed, too, from all other Turkish cities in the strong foothold obtained there by Europeans. Indeed, remembering it as a place where often, and within a very few years, upon a sudden outbreaking of popular fury, the streets were deluged with Christian blood, I was particularly struck, not only with the air of confidence and security, but, in fact, with the bearing of superiority assumed by the "Christian dog!" among the followers of the Prophet.

Directly on the bay is a row of large houses, running along the whole front of the city, among which are seen emblazoned over the doors the arms of most of the foreign consuls, including the American. By the treaties of the Porte with Christian powers, the Turkish tribunals have no jurisdiction of matters touching the rights of foreign residents; and all disputes between these, and even criminal offences, fall under the cognizance of their respective consuls. This gives the consuls in all the maritime ports of Turkey great power and position; and all over the Levant they are great people; but at Smyrna they are far more important than ambassadors and ministers at the European capitals; and, with their janisaries and their appearance on all public occasions in uniform, are looked up to by the Levantines somewhat like the consuls sent abroad under the Roman Empire, and by the Turks as almost sultans.

The morning after my arrival I delivered letters of introduction to Mr. Offley, the American consul, a native of Philadelphia, thirty years resident in Smyrna, and married to an Armenian lady, Mr. Langdon, a merchant of Boston, and Mr. Styth, of Baltimore, of the firm of Issaverdens, Styth, and Company; one to Mr. Jetter, a German missionary, whose lady told me, while her husband was reading it, that she had met me in the street the day before, and on her return home, told him that an *American* had just arrived. I was curious to know the mark by which she recognised me as an American, being rather dubious whether it was by reason of anything praiseworthy or the reverse; but she could not tell.

I trust the reader has not forgotten the victim of the tender passion who, in the moment of my leaving Athens, had reposed in my sympathising bosom the burden of his hopes and fears. At the very first house in which I was introduced to the female members of the family, I found, making a morning call, the lady who had made such inroads upon his affections. I had already heard her spoken of as being the largest fortune, and, *par conséquent*, the greatest belle in Smyrna, and I hailed it as a favourable omen that I accidentally made her acquaintance so soon after my arrival. I made my observations, and could not help remarking that she was by no means pining away on account of the absence of my friend. I was almost indignant at her heartless happiness, and, taking advantage of an opportunity, introduced his name hoping to see a shade come over her, and, perhaps, to strike her pensive for two or three minutes; but her comment was a death-blow to my friend's prospects, and my mediation : " Poor M. !" and all present repeated " Poor M." with a portentous smile, and the next moment had forgotten his existence. I went away in the full conviction that it was all over with " Poor M. !" and murmuring to myself, Put not your trust in woman, I dined, and in the afternoon called with my letter of introduction upon his friend the Rev. Mr. Brewer, and Mr. Brewer's comment on reading it was about equal to the lady's " Poor M." He asked me in what condition I left our unfortunate friend. I told him his *leg* was pretty bad, though he continued to hobble about; but Mr. Brewer interrupted me; he did not mean his leg, but, he hesitated, and with reluctance, as if he wished to avoid speaking of it outright, added, *his mind*. I did not comprehend him, and, from his hesitation and delicacy, imagined that he was alluding to the lover's heart; but he cleared the matter up, and to my no small surprise, by telling me, that, some time before he left Smyrna, " Poor M." had shown such strong marks of aberration of intellect, that his friends had deemed it advisable to put him under the charge of a brother missionary and send him home, and that they hoped great benefit from travel and change of scene. I was surprised, and by no means elevated in my own conceit, when I found that I had been made the confidant of a crazy man. Mr. Hill, not knowing of any particular intimacy between us, and probably not wishing to publish his misfortune unnecessarily, had not given me the slightest intimation of it, and I had not discovered it. I had considered his communication to me strange, and his general conduct not less so, but I had no idea that it was anything more than the ordinary derangement which every man is said to labour under when in love. I then told Mr. Brewer my story, and the commission with which I was intrusted, which he said was perfectly characteristic, his malady being a sort of monomania on the subject of the tender passion! and every particle of interest which I might nevertheless have taken in the affair, in connecting his derangement in some way with the lady in question, was destroyed by the volatile direction of his passion, sometimes to one object and sometimes with another; and in regard to the lady to whom I was accredited, he had never shown any penchant toward her in particular, and must have given me her name because it happened to be the first that suggested itself at the moment of his unburthening himself to me. Fortunately, I had not exposed myself by any demonstrations in behalf of my friend, so I quietly dropped him. On leaving Mr. Brewer I suggested a doubt whether I could be regarded as an acquaintance upon the introduction of a crazy man; but we had gone so far that it was decided, for that specific purpose, to admit his sanity. I should not mention these particulars if there was any possibility of their ever wounding the feelings of him to whom they refer; but he is now beyond the reach either of calumny or praise, for about a year after I heard, with great regret, that his malady had increased, accompanied with a general derangement of health; and, shortly after his return home, he died.

My intercourse with the Franks was confined principally to my own countrymen, whose houses were open to me at all times; and I cannot help mentioning the name of Mr. Van Lennup, the Dutch consul, the great friend of the missionaries in the Levant, who had been two years resident in the United States, and was intimately acquainted with many of my friends at home. Society in Smyrna is purely mercantile; and having been so long out of the way of it, it was actually grateful to me once more to hear men talking with all their souls about cotton, stocks, exchanges, and other topics of *interest*, in the literal meaning of the word. Sometimes lounging in a merchant's counting-room, I took up an American paper, and heard Boston, and New York, and Baltimore, and cotton, and opium, and freight, and quarter per cent. less bandied about, until I almost fancied myself at home; and when this became too severe I had a resource with the missionaries, gentlemanly and well-educated men, well acquainted with the countries and the places worth visiting, with just the books I wanted, and, I had almost said, the wives; I mean with wives always glad to see a countryman, and to talk about home. There is something exceedingly interesting in a missionary's wife. A soldier's is more so, for she follows him to danger, and, perhaps, to death; but glory waits him if he falls, and while she weeps she is proud. Before I went abroad the only missionary I ever knew I despised, for I believed him to be a canting hypocrite; but I saw much of them abroad, and made many warm friends among them; and, I repeat it, there is something exceedingly interesting in a missionary's wife. She who had been cherished as a plant that the winds must not breathe on too rudely, recovers from the shock of a separation from her friends to find herself in a land of barbarians, where her loud cry of distress can never reach their ears. New ties twine round her heart, and the tender and helpless girl changes her very nature, and becomes the staff and support of the man. In his hours of despondency she raises his drooping spirits; she bathes his aching head; she smooths his pillow of sickness; and, after months of wearisome silence, I have entered her dwelling, and her heart instinctively told her that I was from the same land. I have been welcomed as a brother; answered her hurried, and anxious, and eager questions; and sometimes, when I have known any of her friends at home, I have been for a moment more than recompensed for all the toils and privations of a traveller in the East. I have left her dwelling burdened with remembrances to friends whom she will perhaps never see again. I bore a letter to a father, which was opened by a widowed mother. Where I could, I have discharged every promise to a missionary's wife; but I have some yet undischarged which I rank among the sacred obligations of my life. It is true, the path of the missionary is not strewed with roses; but often, in leaving his house at night, and following my guide with a lantern through the narrow streets of a Turkish city, I have run over the troubles incident to every condition of life, not forgetting those of a traveller, and have taken to whistling, and, as I stumbled into the gate of an old convent, have murmured involuntarily, "After all, these missionaries are happy fellows."

Every stranger, upon his arrival in Smyrna, is introduced at the Casino. I went there the first time to a concert. It is a large building, erected by a club of merchants, with a suite of rooms on the lower floor, billiards, cards, reading and sitting room, and a ball-room above covering the whole. The concert was given in the ball-room, and, from what I had seen in the streets, I expected an extraordinary display of beauty; but I was much disappointed. The company consisted only of the aristocracy or higher mercantile classes, the families of the gentlemen composing the club, and excluded the Greek and Smyrniote women, among whom is found a great portion of the beauty of the place. A patent of nobility in Smyrna, as in our own city, is founded upon the time since the possessor gave up selling goods, or the number of consignments he receives in the course of a year. The Casino, by the way, is a very aristocratic institution, and sometimes knotty questions occur in its management. Captains of merchant-vessels are not admitted. A man came out as owner of a vessel and cargo, and also master: *quere*, could he be admitted? His consignee said Yes; but the majority, not being interested in the sale of his cargo, went for a strict construction, and excluded him.

The population of Smyrna, professing three distinct religions, observe three different Sabbaths; the Mohammedans Friday, the Jews Saturday, and the Christians Sunday, so that there are only four days in the week in which all the shops and bazars are open together, and there are so many fête days that these are much broken in upon. The most perfect toleration prevails, and the religious festivals of the Greeks often terminate in midnight orgies which debase and degrade the Christian in the eyes of the pious Mussulman.

On Saturday morning I was roused from my bed by a loud cry and the tramp of a crowd through the street. I ran to my window, and saw a Greek tearing down the street at full speed, and another after him with a drawn yataghan in his hand; the latter gained ground at every step, and, just as he turned the corner, stabbed the first in the back. He returned with the bloody poniard in his hand, followed by the crowd, and rushed into a little Greek drinking-shop next door to my hotel. There was a loud noise and scuffling inside, and presently I saw him pitched out headlong into the street, and the door closed upon him. In a frenzy of passion he rushed back, and drove his yataghan with all his force into the door, stamped against it with his feet, and battered it with stones; unable to force it open, he sat down on the opposite side of the street, occasionally renewing his attack upon the door, talking violently with those inside, and sometimes the whole crowd laughing loud at the answers from within. Nobody attempted to interfere. Giuseppe, my host, said it was only a row among the Greeks. The Greek kept the street in an uproar for more than an hour, when he was secured and taken into custody.

After dinner, under the escort of a merchant, a Jew from Trieste residing at the same hotel, I visited the Jews' quarter. The Jews of Smyrna are the descendants of that unhappy people who were driven out from Spain by the bloody persecutions of Ferdinand and Isabel; they still talk Spanish in their families; and though comparatively secure, now, as ever, they live the victims of tyranny and oppression, ever toiling and accumulating, and ever fearing to exhibit the fruits of their industry, lest they should excite the cupidity of a rapacious master. Their quarter is by far the most miserable in Smyrna, and within its narrow limits are congregated more than ten thousand of "the accursed people." It was with great difficulty that I avoided wounding the feelings of my companion by remarking its filthy and disgusting appearance; and wishing to remove my unfavourable impression by introducing me to some of the best families first, he was obliged to drag me through the whole range of its narrow and dirty streets. From the external appearance of the tottering houses, I did not expect anything better within; and, out of regard to his feelings, was really sorry that I had accepted his offer to visit his people; but with the first house I entered I was most agreeably disappointed. Ascending outside by a tottering staircase to the second story, within was not only neatness and comfort, but positive luxury. At one end of a spacious room was a raised platform opening upon a large latticed window, covered with rich rugs and divans along the wall. The master of the house was taking his afternoon siesta, and while we were waiting for him I expressed to my gratified companion my surprise and pleasure at the unexpected appearance of the interior. In a few minutes the master entered, and received us with the greatest hospitality and kindness. He was about thirty, with the high square cap of black felt, without any rim or border, long silk gown tied with a sash around the waist, a strongly-marked Jewish face, and amiable expression. In the house of the Israelite the welcome is the same as in that of the Turk; and seating himself, our host clapped his hands together, and a boy entered with coffee and pipes. After a little conversation he clapped his hands again; and hearing a clatter of wooden shoes, I turned my head and saw a little girl coming across the room, mounted on high wooden sabots almost like stilts, who stepped up the platform, and with quite a womanly air took her seat on the divan. I looked at her, and thought her a pert, forward little miss, and was about asking her how old she was, when my companion told me she was our host's wife. I checked myself, but in a moment felt more than ever tempted to ask the same question; and, upon inquiring, learned that she had attained the respectable age of thirteen, and had been then two years a wife. Our host told us that she had cost him a great deal of money, and the expense consisted in the outlay necessary for procuring a divorce from another wife. He did not like the other one at all; his father had married him to her, and he had great difficulty in prevailing on his father to go to the expense of getting him freed. This wife was also provided by his father, and he did not like her much at first; he had never seen her till the day of marriage, but now he began to like her very well, though she cost him a great deal for ornaments. All this time we were looking at her, and she, with a perfectly composed expression, was listening to the conversation as my companion interpreted it, and following with her eyes the different speakers. I was particularly struck with the cool, imperturbable expression of her face, and could not help thinking that, on the subject of likings and dislikings, young as she was, she might have some curious notions of her own: and since we had fallen into this little disquisition on family matters, and thinking that he had gone so far himself that I might waive delicacy, I asked him whether she liked him; he answered in that easy tone of confidence of which no idea can be given in words, "Oh yes;" and when I intimated a doubt, he told me I might ask herself. But I forbore, and did not ask her, and so lost the opportunity of learning from both sides the practical operation of matches made by parents. Our host sustained them; the plan saved a great deal of trouble, and wear and tear of spirit; prudent parents always selected such as were likely to suit each other; and being thrown together very young, they insensibly assimilated in tastes and habits; he admitted that he had missed it the first time, but he had hit it the second, and allowed that the system would work much better if the cost of procuring a divorce was not so great. With the highest respect, and a pressing invitation to come again, seconded by his wife, I took my leave of the self-satisfied Israelite.

From this we went into several other houses, in all of which the interior belied, in the same manner, their external appearance. I do not say that they were gorgeous or magnificent, but they were clean, comfortable, and striking by their Oriental style of architecture and furniture; and being their Sabbath, the women were in their best attire, with their heads, necks, and wrists adorned with a profusion of gold and silver ornaments. Several of the houses had libraries, with old Hebrew books, in which an old rabbi was reading or sometimes instructing children. In the last house a son was going through his days of mourning on the death of his father. He was lying in the middle of the floor, with his black cap on, and covered with a long black cloak. Twenty or thirty friends were sitting on the floor around him, who had come in to condole with him. When we entered, neither he nor any of his friends took any notice of us, except to make room on the floor. We sat down with them. It was growing dark, and the light broke dimly through the latticed windows upon the dusky figures of the mourning Israelites; and there they sat, with stern visages and long beards, the feeble remnant of a fallen people, under scorn, and contumely, and persecution, and oppression, holding on to the traditions received from their fathers, practising in the privacy of their houses the same rites as when the priests bore aloft the ark of the covenant, and out of the very dust in which they lie still looking for the restoration of their temporal kingdom. In a room adjoining sat the widow of the deceased, with a group of women around her, all perfectly silent; and they too took no notice of us either when we entered or when we went away.

The next day the shops were shut, and the streets again thronged as on the day of my arrival. I went to church at the English chapel attached to the residence of the British consul, and heard a sermon from a German missionary. I dined at one o'clock, and, in company with mine host of the Pension Suisse, and a merchant of Smyrna resident there, worked my way up the hill through the heart of the Turks' quarter to the old castle standing alone and in ruins on its summit. We rested a little while at the foot of the castle, and looked over the city and the tops of the minarets upon the beautiful bay, and descending in the rear of the castle, we came to the river Meles winding through a deep valley at the foot of the hill. This stream was celebrated in Grecian poetry three thousand years ago. It was the pride of the ancient Smyrneans, once washed the walls of the ancient city, and tradition says that on its banks the nymph Critheis gave birth to Homer. We followed it in its winding course down the valley, murmuring among evergreens. Over it in two places were the ruins of aqueducts which carried water to the old city, and in one or two places it turns an overshot-mill. On each side, at intervals along its banks, were Oriental summer-houses, with verandahs, and balconies, and latticed windows. Approaching the caravan bridge we met straggling parties, and by degrees fell into a crowd of people, Franks, Europeans of every nation, Greeks, Turks, and Armenians, in all their striking costumes, sitting on benches under the shade of noble old sycamores, or on the grass, or on the river's brink, and moving among them were Turks cleanly dressed, with trays of refreshment, ices, and sherbet. There was an unusual collection of Greek and Smyrniote women, and an extraordinary display of beauty; none of them wore hats, but the Greek women a light gauze turban, and the Smyrniotes a small piece of red cloth worked with gold, secured on the top of the head by the folds of the hair, with a long tassel hanging down from it. Opposite, and in striking contrast, the great Turkish burying-ground, with its thick grove of gloomy cypress, approached the bank of the river. I crossed over and entered the burying-ground, and penetrated the grove of funeral trees; all around were the graves of the dead; thousands and tens of thousands who but yesterday were like the gay crowd I saw flitting through the trees, were sleeping under my feet. Over some of the graves the earth was still fresh, and they who lay in them were already forgotten—but no, they were not forgotten; woman's love still remembered them, for Turkish women, with long white shawls wrapped around their faces, were planting over them myrtle and flowers, believing that they were paying an acceptable tribute to the souls of the dead. I left the burying-ground, and plunged once more among the crowd. It may be that memory paints these scenes brighter than they were; but, if that does not deceive me, I never saw at Paris or Vienna so gay and beautiful a scene, so rich in landscape and scenery, in variety of costume, and in beauty of female form and feature.

We left the caravan bridge early to visit the Armenian quarter, this being the best day for seeing them collectively at home; and I had not passed through the first street of their beautiful quarter before I was forcibly struck with the appearance of a people different from any I had yet seen in the East. The Armenians are one of the oldest nations of the civilised world, and, amid all the revolutions of barbarian war and despotism, have maintained themselves as a cultivated people. From the time when their first chieftain fled from Babylon, his native place, to escape from the tyranny of Belus, king of Assyria, this warlike people, occupying a mountainous country near the sources of the Tigris and Euphrates, battled the Assyrians, Medes, the Persians, Macedonians, and Arabians, until their country was depopulated by the shah of Persia. Less than two millions are all that now remain of that once powerful people. Commerce has scattered them, like the Israelites, among all the principal nations of Europe and Asia, and everywhere they have preserved their stern integrity and uprightness of character. The Armenian merchant is now known in every quarter of the globe, and everywhere distinguished by superior cultivation, honesty, and manners. As early as the fourth century, the Armenians embraced Christianity; they never had any sympathy with, and always disliked and avoided, the Greek Christians, and constantly resisted the endeavours of the popes to bring them within the Catholic pale. Their doctrine differs from that of the orthodox chiefly in their admitting only one nature in Christ, and believing the Holy Spirit to issue from the Father alone. Their first abode, Mount Ararat, is even at the present day the centre of their religious and political union. They are distinguished by a patriarchal simplicity in their domestic manners; and it was the beautiful exhibition of this trait in their character that struck me on entering their quarter at Smyrna. In style and appearance their quarter is superior to any in Smyrna; their streets are broad and clean; their houses large, in good order, and well painted; Oriental in their style of architecture, with large balconies and latticed windows, and spacious halls running through the centre, floored with small black and white stones laid in the form of stars and other fanciful devices, and leading to large gardens in the rear, ornamented with trees, vines, shrubs, and flowers, then in full bloom and beauty. All along the streets the doors of the houses were thrown wide open, and the old Armenian "Knickerbockers" were sitting outside or in the doorway, in their flowing robes, grave and sedate, with long pipes and large amber mouth-pieces, talking with their neighbours; while the younger members were distributed along the hall or strolling through the garden, and children climbing the trees and arbours. It was a fête day for the whole neighbourhood. All was social, and cheerful, and beautiful, without being gay or noisy, and all was open to the observation of every passer-by. My companion, an old resident of Smyrna, stopped with me at the house of a large banker, whose whole family, with several neighbours, young and old, were assembled in the hall.

In the street the Armenian ladies observe the Turkish custom of wearing the shawl tied around the face, so that it is difficult to see their features, though I had often admired the dignity and grace of their walk, and their propriety of manners; but in the house there was a perfect absence of all concealment; and I have seldom seen more interesting persons than the whole group of Armenian ladies, and particularly the young Armenian girls. They were not so dark, and wanted the bold, daring beauty of the Greek, but altogether were far more attractive. The great charm of their appearance was an exceeding modesty, united with affability and elegance of manner: in fact, there was a calm and quiet loveliness about them that would have made any one of them dangerous to be shut up alone with, i. e., if a man could talk with her without an interpreter. This was one of the occasions when I numbered among the pains of life the confusion of tongues. But, notwithstanding this, the whole scene was beautiful; and, with all the simplicity of a Dutchman's fireside, the style of the house, the pebbled hall, the garden, the foliage, and the Oriental costumes, threw a charm around it which now, while I write, comes over me again.

CHAPTER XI.

An American Original—Moral Changes in Turkey.—Wonders of Steam Navigation.—The March of Mind.—Classic Localities.—Sestos and Abydos.—Seeds of Pestilence.

On my return from Ephesus I heard of the arrival in Smyrna of two American travellers, father and son, from Egypt; and the same day, at Mr. Langdon's, I met the father, Dr. N. of Mississippi. The doctor had made a long and interesting tour in Egypt and the Holy Land, interrupted, however, by a severe attack of ophthalmia on the Nile, from which he had not yet recovered, and a narrow escape from the plague at Cairo. He was about fifty-five, of a strong, active, and inquiring mind; and the circumstances which had brought him to that distant country were so peculiar, that I cannot help mentioning them. He had passed all his life on the banks of the Mississippi, and for many years had busied himself with speculations in regard to the creation of the world. Year after year he had watched the deposits and formation of soil on the banks of the Mississippi, had visited every mound and mountain indicating any peculiar geological formation, and, unable to find any data to satisfy him, he started from his plantation directly for the banks of the Nile. He possessed all the warm, high-toned feelings of the Southerner, but a thorough contempt for the usages of society and everything like polish of manners. He came to New York and embarked for Havre. He had never been even to New York before; was utterly ignorant of any language but his own; despised all foreigners, and detested their "jabber." He worked his way to Marseilles with the intention of embarking for Alexandria, but was taken sick, and retraced his steps directly to his plantation on the Mississippi. Recovering, he again set out for the Nile the next year, accompanied by his son, a young man of about twenty-three, acquainted with foreign languages, and competent to profit by foreign travel. This time he was more successful, and, when I saw him, he had rambled over the pyramids and explored the ruined temples of Egypt. The result of his observations had been to fortify his preconceived notions, that the age of this world far exceeds six thousand years. Indeed, he was firmly persuaded that some of the temples of the Nile were built more than six thousand years ago. He had sent on to Smyrna enormous boxes of earth and stones, to be shipped to America, and was particularly curious on the subject of trees, having examined and satisfied himself as to the age of the olive-trees in the Garden of Gethsemane and the cedars of Lebanon. I accompanied him to his hotel, where I was introduced to his son; and I must not forget another member of this party, who is, perhaps, already known to some of my readers by the name of Paolo Nuozzo, or, more familiarly, Paul. This worthy individual had been travelling on the Nile with two Hungarian counts, who discharged him, or whom he discharged (for they differed as to the fact), at Cairo. Dr. N. and his son were in want, and Paul entered their service as dragoman and superintendant of another man, who, they said, was worth a dozen of Paul. I have a very imperfect recollection of my first interview with this original. Indeed, I hardly remember him at all until my arrival at Constantinople, and have only an indistinct impression of a dark, surly-looking, mustached man following at the heels of Dr. N., and giving crusty answers in horrible English.

Before my visit to Ephesus I had talked with a Prussian baron of going up by land to Constantinople, but on my return I found myself attacked with a recurrence of an old malady, and determined to wait for the steam-boat. The day before I left Smyrna, accompanied by Mr. O. Langdon, I went out to Boujac to dine with Mr. Styth. The great beauty of Smyrna is its surrounding country. Within a few miles there are three villages, Bournabat, Boujac, and Sediguey, occupied by Franks, of which Boujac is the favourite. The Franks are always looking to the time of going out to their country houses, and consider their residences in their villages the most agreeable part of their year; and from what I saw of it, nothing can be more agreeable. Not more than half of them had yet moved out, but after dinner we went round and visited all who were there. They are all well acquainted, and, living in a strange and barbarous country, are drawn closer together than they would be in their own. Every evening there is a *reunion* at some of their houses, and there is among them an absence of all unnecessary form and ceremony, without which there can be no perfect enjoyment of the true pleasures of social intercourse. These villages, too, are endeared to them as places of refuge during the repeated and prolonged visitations of the plague, the merchant going into the city every morning and returning at night, and during the whole continuance of the disease avoiding to touch any member of his family. The whole region of country around their villages is beautiful in landscape and scenery, producing the choicest flowers and fruits; the fig-tree, particularly, growing with a luxuriance unknown in any other part of the world. But the whole of this beautiful region lies waste and uncultivated, although, if the government could be relied on, holding out, by reason of its fertility, its climate, and its facility of access, particularly now by means of steam-boats, far greater inducements to European emigration than any portion of our own country. I will not impose upon the reader my speculations on this subject; my notes are burdened with them; but, in my opinion, the Old World is in process of regeneration, and at this moment offers greater opportunities for enterprise than the New.

On Monday, accompanied by Dr. N. and his son and Paolo Nuozzo, I embarked on board the steam-boat Maria Dorothea for Constantinople; and here follows another letter, and the last, dated from the capital of the Eastern empire.

Constantinople, May —, 1835.

MY DEAR * * *

Oh, you who hope one day to roam in Eastern lands, to bend your curious eye upon the people warmed by the rising sun, come quickly, for all things are changing. You who have pored over the story of the Turk, who have dreamed of him as a gloomy enthusiast, hating, spurning, and slaying all who do not believe and call upon the Prophet;

"One of that saintly, murderous brood,
To carnage and the Koran given.
Who think through unbelievers' blood
Lies their directest path to heaven;"

come quickly, for that description of Turk is passing away. The day has gone by when the haughty Mussulman spurned and persecuted the "Christian dog." A few years since, it would have been at peril of a man's life to appear in many parts of Turkey in a European dress; but now the European is looked upon, not only as a creature fit to live, but as a man to be respected. The sultan himself, the great head of the nation and the religion, the vicegerent of God upon earth, has taken off the turban, and all the officers of government have followed his example. The army wears a bastard European uniform, and the great study of the sultan is to introduce European customs. Thanks to the infirmities of human nature, many of these customs have begun to insinuate themselves. The pious follower of the Prophet has dared to raise the wine-cup to his lips; and in many instances, at the peril of losing his paradise of houris, has given himself up to strong drink. Time was, when the word of a Turk was sacred as a precept of the Koran; now he can no more be relied upon than a Jew or a Christian. He has fallen with great facility into lying, cheating, and drinking, and if the earnest efforts to change him are attended with success, perhaps we may soon add stealing and having but one wife. And all this change, this mighty fall, is ascribed by the Europeans here to the destruction of the janisaries, a band of men dangerous to government, brave, turbulent, and bloody, but of indomitable pride; who were above doing little things, and who gave a high tone to the character of the whole people. If I was not bent upon a gallop, and could stop for the jogtrot of an argument, I would say that the destruction of the janisaries is a mere incidental circumstance, and that the true cause is—*steam navigation.* Do not laugh, but listen. The Turks have ever been a proud people, possessing a sort of peacock pride, an extravagantly good opinion of themselves, and a superlative contempt for all the rest of the world. Heretofore they have had comparatively little intercourse with Europeans, consequently but little opportunity of making comparisons, and consequently, again, but little means of discovering their own inferiority. But lately things have changed; the universal peace in Europe and the introduction of steamboats into the Mediterranean, have brought the Europeans and the Turks comparatively close together. It seems to me that the effect of steam-boats here has as yet hardly begun to be felt. There are but few of them, indifferent boats, constantly getting out of order, and running so irregularly that no reliance can be placed upon them. But still their effects are felt, their convenience is acknowledged; and, so far as my knowledge extends, they have never been introduced anywhere yet without multiplying in numbers, and driving all other vessels off the water. Now the Mediterranean is admirably suited to the use of steamboats; indeed, the whole of these inland waters, the Mediterranean, the Adriatic, the Archipelago, the Dardanelles, the Sea of Marmora, the Bosphorus, and the Black Sea, from the Straits of Gibraltar to the Sea of Azoff, offer every facility that can be desired for steam navigation; and when we consider that the most interesting cities in the world are on the shores of these waters, I cannot but believe that in a very few years they will be, to a certain extent, covered with steamboats. At all events, I have no doubt that in two or three years you will be able to go from Paris to Constantinople in fifteen or twenty days; and, when that time comes, it will throw such numbers of Europeans into the East as will have a sensible effect upon the manners and customs of the people. These eastern countries will be invaded by all classes of people, travellers, merchants, and mechanics, gentlemen of elegant leisure, and blacksmiths, shoemakers, tinkers, and tailors, nay, even mantua-makers, milliners, and bandboxes, the last being an incident to civilised life as yet unknown in Turkey. Indeed, wonderful as the effects of steamboats have been under our own eyes, we are yet to see them far more wonderful in bringing into close alliance, commercial and social, people from distant countries, of different languages and habits; in removing national prejudices, and in breaking down the great characteristic distinctions of nations. *Nous verrons,* twenty years hence, what steamboats will have done in this part of the world!

But, in standing up for steam-boats, I must not fail in doing justice to the grand signior. His highness has not always slept upon a bed of roses. He had to thank the petticoats of a female slave for saving his life when a boy, and he had hardly got upon his throne before he found that he should have a hard task to keep it. It lay between him and the janisaries. In spite of them and of the general prejudices of the people, he determined to organise an army according to European tactics. He staked his throne and his head upon the issue; and it was not until he had been pushed to the desperate expedient of unfurling the sacred standard of the Prophet, parading it through the streets of Constantinople, and calling upon all good Mussulmans to rally round it; in short, it was not until the dead bodies of thirty thousand janisaries were floating down the Bosphorus, that he found himself the master in his own dominions. Since that time, either because he is fond of new things, or because he really sees farther than those around him, he is constantly endeavouring to introduce European improvements. For this purpose he invites talent, particularly mechanical and military, from every country, and has now around him Europeans among his most prominent men, and directing nearly all his public works.

The Turks are a sufficiently intelligent people, and cannot help feeling the superiority of strangers. Probably the immediate effect may be to make them prone rather to catch the faults and vices than the virtues of Europeans; but afterward better things will come; they will fall into our better ways; and perhaps, though that is almost more than we dare hope for, they will embrace a better religion.

But, however this may be, or whatever may be the cause, all ye who would see the Turk of Mohammed; the Turk who swept the plains of Asia, who leaned upon his bloody sword before the walls of Vienna, and threatened the destruction of Christendom in Europe; the Turk of the turban, and the pipe, and the seraglio, come quickly, for he is becoming another man. A little longer, and the great characteristic distinctions will be broken down; the long pipe, the handsome pipe-bearer, and the amber mouthpiece, are gone, and oh, death to all that is beautiful in Eastern romance! the walls of the seraglio are prostrated, the doors of the harem thrown open, the black eunuch and the veiled woman are no more seen; while the honest Turk trudges home from a quiet tea-party stripped of his retinue of fair ones, with his one and only wife tucked under his arm, his head drooping between his shoulders, taking a lecture from his better half for an involuntary sigh to the good old days that are gone. And oh you who turn up your aristocratic noses at such parvenus as Mohammed and the Turks; who would go back to those distant ages which time covers with its dim and twilight glories,

"When the world was fresh and young,
And the great deluge still had left it green;"

you who come piping-hot from college, your brains teeming with recollections of the heroic ages; who would climb Mount Ida, to sit in council with the gods, come quickly, also, for all things are changing. A steam-boat—shades of Hector, Ajax, and Agamemnon, forgive the sins of the day!—an Austrian steam-boat is now splashing the island-studded Ægean, and paddling the classic waters of the Hellespont. Oh ye princes and heroes who armed for the Trojan war, and covered these waters with your thousand ships, with what pious horror must you look down from your blessed abodes upon the impious modern monster of the deep, which strips the tall mast of its flowing canvas, renders unnecessary the propitiation of the gods, and flounders on its way in spite of wind and weather!

A new and unaccountable respect for the classics almost made me scorn the new-fangled conveyance, though much to the comfort of wayfaring men; but sundry recollections of Greek caiques, and also an apprehension that there might be those yet living who had heard me in early days speak anything but respectfully of Homer, suggested to me that one man could not stem the current of the times, and that it was better for a humble individual like myself to float with the tide. This idea, too, of currents and tides made me think better of Prince Metternich and his steam-boat; and smothering, as well as I could, my sense of shame, I sneaked on board the Maria Dorothea for a race to Constantinople. Join me, now, in this race; and if your heart does not break at going by at the rate of eight or ten miles an hour, I will whip you over a piece of the most classic ground consecrated in history, mythology, or poetry, and in less time than even the swift-footed Achilles could have travelled it. At eleven o'clock on a bright sunny day the Maria Dorothea turned her back upon the city and the beautiful bay of Smyrna; in about two hours passed the harbour of Vourla, then used as a quarantine station, the yellow plague flag floating in the city and among the shipping; and toward dark, turning the point of the gulf, came upon my old acquaintance Foggi, the little harbour into which I had been twice driven by adverse winds. My Greek friend happened to be on board, and in the honesty of his heart, congratulated me upon being this time independent of the elements, without seeming to care a fig whether he profaned the memory of his ancestors in travelling by so unclassical a conveyance. If he takes it so coolly, thought I, what is it to me! they are his relations, not mine. In the evening we were moving close to the island of Mitylene, the ancient Lesbos, the country of Sappho, Alcæus, and Terpander, famed for the excellence of its wine and the beauty of its women, and pre-eminently distinguished for dissipation and debauchery, the fatal plague flag now floating mournfully over its walls, marking it as the abode of pestilence and death.

Early in the morning I found myself opposite the promontory of Lectum, now Cape Baba, separating the ancient Troas from Æolia; a little to the right, but hardly visible, were the ruins of Assos, where the apostles stopped to take in Paul: a little farther the ruins of Alexandria Troas, one of the many cities founded by Alexander during his conquest in Asia; to the left, at some distance in the sea, is the island of Lemnos, in the songs of the poets overshadowed by the lofty Olympus, the island that received Vulcan after he was kicked out of heaven by Jupiter. A little farther, nearer the land, is the island of Tenedos, the ancient Leucophrys, where Paris first landed after carrying off Helen, and behind which the Greeks withdrew their fleet when they pretended to have abandoned the siege of Troy. Still farther on the mainland, is the promontory of Sigæum, where the Scamander empties into the sea, and near which were fought the principal of Homer's battles. A little farther—but hold, stop the engine! If there be a spot of ground on earth in which the historical, and the poetical, and the fabulous, are so beautifully blended together that we would not separate them even to discover the truth, it is before us now. Extending for a great distance along the shore, and back as far as the eye can reach, under the purest sky that ever overshadowed the earth, lies a rich and beautiful plain, and it is the plain of Troy, the battle-ground of heroes. Oh field of glory and of blood, little does he know, that surly Turk who is now lazily following his plough over thy surface, that every blade of thy grass could tell of heroic deeds, the shock of armies, the meeting of war-chariots, the crushing of armour, the swift flight, the hot pursuit, the shouts of victors, and the groans of the dying. Beyond it, towering to the heavens, is a lofty mountain, and it is Mount Ida, on whose top Paris adjudged the golden apple to the goddess of beauty, and paved the way for those calamities which brought on the ten years' siege, and laid in ruins the ancient city of Priam. Two small streams taking their rise from the mountain of the gods, join each other in the middle of the plain ; Scamander and Simois, whose waters once washed the walls of the ancient city of Dardanus ; and that small, confused, and shapeless mass of ruins, that beautiful sky and the songs of Homer, are all that remain to tell us that "Troy was." Close to the sea, and rising like mountains above the plain, are two immense mounds of earth ; they are the tombs of Ajax and Achilles. Shades of departed heroes, fain would we stop and pay the tribute which we justly owe, but we are hurried past by an engine of a hundred-horse power.

Onward, still onward ! We have reached the ancient Hellespont, the Dardanelles of the Turks, famed as the narrow water that divides Europe from Asia, for the beauties that adorn its banks, and for its great Turkish fortifications. Three miles wide at the mouth, it becomes gradually narrower, until, in the narrowest part, the natives of Europe and Asia can talk together from the opposite sides. For sixty miles (its whole length) it presents a continued succession of new beauties, and in the hands of Europeans, particularly English, improved as country-seats, would make one of the loveliest countries in the world. I had just time to reflect that it was melancholy, and seemed inexplicable, that this and other of the fairest portions of the earth should be in the hands of the Turks, who neither improve it themselves nor allow others to do so. At three o'clock we arrived at the Dardanelles, a little Turkish town in the narrowest and most beautiful part of the straits ; a strong fort with enormous cannon stands frowning on each side. These are the terrible fortifications of Mohammed II., the keys of Constantinople. The guns are enormous ; of one in particular, the muzzle is two feet three inches in diameter ; but, with Turkish ingenuity, they are so placed as to be discharged when a ship is directly opposite. If the ship is not disabled by the first fire, and does not choose to go back and take another, she is safe. At every moment a new picture presents itself ; a new fort, a new villa, or the ruins of an ancient city. A naked point on the European side, so ugly compared with all around it as to attract particular attention, projects into the strait, and here are the ruins of Sestus ; here Xerxes built his bridge of boats to carry over his millions to the conquest of Greece ; and here, when he returned with the wreck of his army, defeated and disgraced, found his bridge destroyed by a tempest, and, in his rage, ordered the chains to be thrown into the sea and the waves to be lashed with rods. From this point, too, Leander swam the Hellespont for love of Hero, and Lord Byron and Mr. Ekenhead for fun. Nearly opposite, close to a Turkish fort, are the ruins of Abydos. Here Xerxes, and Leander, and Lord Byron, and Mr. Ekenhead, landed.

Our voyage is drawing to a close. At Gallipoli, a large Turkish town handsomely situated at the mouth of the Dardanelles, we took on board the Turkish governor, with his pipe-bearer and train of attendants, escorted by thirty or forty boats, containing three or four hundred people, his mightiness taking a deck passage. Toward evening we were entering the Sea of Marmora, the ancient Propontis, like one of our small lakes, and I again went to sleep lulled by the music of a high-pressure engine. At daylight we were approaching Constantinople ; twelve miles this side, on the bank of the Sea of Marmora, is the village of St. Stephano, the residence of Commodore Porter. Here the domes and minarets of the ancient city, with their golden points and glittering crescents, began to appear in sight. High above the rest towered the mosque of Sultan Achmet and the beautiful dome of St. Sophia, the ancient Christian church, but now, for nearly four hundred years, closed against the Christians' feet. We approach the walls and pass a range of gloomy turrets ; there are the Seven Towers, prisons, portals of the grave, whose mysteries few live to publish ; the bowstring and the sea reveal no secrets. That palace, with its blinded windows and its superb garden, surrounded by a triple range of walls, is the far-famed Seraglio ; there beauty lingers in a splendid cage, and, lolling on her rich divan, sighs for the humblest lot and freedom. In front, that narrow water, a thousand caiques shooting through it like arrows, and its beautiful banks covered with high palaces and gardens in the Oriental style, is the Thracian Bosphorus. We float around the walls of the seraglio, enter the Golden Horn, and before us, with its thousand mosques and its myriad of minarets, their golden points glittering in the sun, is the Roman city of Constantinople, the Thracian Byzantium, the Stamboul of the Turks ; the city which, more than all others, excites the imagination and interests the feelings ; once dividing with Rome the empire of the world ; built by a Christian emperor, and consecrated as a Christian city, a "burning and a shining light" in a season of universal darkness, all at once lost to the civilised world ; falling into the hands of a strange and fanatic people, the gloomy followers of a successful soldier ; a city which, for nearly four centuries, has sat with its gates closed in sullen distrust and haughty defiance of strangers ; which once sent forth large and terrible armies, burning, slaying, and destroying, shaking the hearts of princes and people, now lying like a fallen giant, huge, unwieldy, and helpless, ready to fall into the hands of the first invader, and dragging out a precarious and ignoble existence, but by the mercy or policy of the great Christian powers. The morning sun, now striking upon its domes and minarets, covers it, as it were, with burnished gold ; a beautiful verdure surrounds it, and pure waters wash it on every side. Can this beautiful city, rich with the choicest gifts of heaven, be pre-eminently the abode of pestilence and death ? where a man carries about with him the seeds of disease to all whom he holds dear ? if he extend the hand of welcome to a friend, if he embrace his child or rub against a stranger, the friend, and the child, and the stranger, follow him to the grave ? where, year after year, the angel of death stalks through the streets, and thousands and tens of thousands look him calmly in the face, and murmuring " Allah, Allah, God is merciful," with a fatal trust in the Prophet, lie down and die ? We enter the city, and these questions are quickly answered. A lazy, lounging, and filthy population ; beggars basking in the sun, and dogs licking their sores; streets never cleaned but by the winds and rains ; immense burying-grounds all over the city ; tombstones at the corners of the streets ; graves gaping ready to throw out their half-buried dead, the whole approaching to one vast charnel-house, dispel all illusions and remove all doubts, and we are ready to ask ourselves if it be possible that, in such a place, health can ever dwell. We wonder that it should ever, for the briefest moment, be free from that dreadful scourge which comes with every summer's sun and strews its streets with dead.—J. L. S.

CHAPTER XII.

Mr. Churchill.—Commodore Porter.—Castle of the Seven Towers.—The Sultan's Naval Architect.—Launch of the Great Ship.—Sultan Mahmoud.—Jubilate.—A National Grievance.—Visit to a Mosque.—The Burial-grounds.

THERE is a good chance for an enterprising Connecticut man to set up an hotel in Constantinople. The reader will see that I have travelled with my eyes open, and I trust this shrewd observation on entering the city of the Cæsars will be considered characteristic and American. Paul was at home in Pera, and conducted us to the Hôtel d'Italia, which was so full that we could not get admission, and so vile a place that we were not sorry for it. We then went to Madame Josephine's, a sort of private boarding-house, but excellent of its kind. We found there a collection of travellers, English, French, German, and Russian, and the dinner was particularly social ; but Dr. N. was so disgusted with the clatter of foreign tongues, that he left the table with the first course, and swore he would not stay there another day. We tried to persuade him. I reminded him that there was an Englishman among them, but this only made him worse ; he hated an Englishman, and wondered how I, as an American, could talk with one as I had with him. In short, he was resolved, and had Paul running about every street in Pera looking for rooms. Notwithstanding his impracticabilities as a traveller, I liked the doctor and determined to follow him, and before breakfast the next morning we were installed in a suite of rooms in the third story of a house opposite the old palace of the British ambassador.

For two or three days I was hors de combat, and put myself under the hands of Dr. Zohrab, an Armenian, educated at Edinburgh, whom I cordially recommend both for his kindness and medical skill. On going out, one of my first visits was to my banker, Mr. Churchill, a gentleman whose name has since rung throughout Europe, and who at one time seemed likely to be the cause of plunging the whole civilised world into a war. He was then living at Sedikuey, on the site of the ancient Chalcedon, in Asia ; and I have seldom been more shocked than by reading in a newspaper, while in the lazaretto at Malta, that, having accidentally shot a Turkish boy with a fowling-piece, he had been seized by the Turks, and in defiance of treaties, bastinadoed till he was almost dead. I had seen the infliction of that horrible punishment ; and, besides the physical pain, there was a sense of the indignity that roused every feeling. I could well imagine the ferocious spirit with which the Turks would stand around and see a Christian scourged. The civilised world owes a deep debt of gratitude to the English government for the uncompromising stand taken in this matter with the sultan, and the firmness with which it insisted on, and obtained, the most ample redress for Mr. Churchill, and atonement for the insult offered to all Christendom in his person.

My companions and myself had received several invitations from Commodore Porter, and, accompanied by Mr. Dwight, one of our American missionaries, to whom I am under particular obligations for his kindness, early in the morning we took a caique with three athletic Turks, and, after a beautiful row, part of it from the seraglio point to the Seven Towers, a distance of five miles, being close under the walls of the city, in two hours reached the commodore's residence at St. Stephano, twelve miles from Constantinople, on the borders of the Sea of Marmora. The situation is beautiful, abounding in fruit-trees, among which are some fig-trees of the largest size ; and the commodore was then engaged in building a large addition to his house. It will be remembered that Commodore Porter was the first envoy ever sent by the United States' government to the Sublime Porte. He had formerly lived at Buyukdere, on the Bosphorus, with the other members of the diplomatic corps ; but his salary as chargé being inadequate to sustain a becoming style, he had withdrawn to this place. I had never seen Commodore Porter before. I afterward passed a month with him in the lazaretto at Malta, and I trust he will not consider me presuming when I say that our acquaintance ripened into friendship. He is entirely different from the idea I had formed of him ; small, dark, weather-beaten, much broken in health, and remarkably mild and quiet in his manners. His eye is his best feature, though even that does not indicate the desperate hardihood of character which he has exhibited on so many occasions. Perhaps I ought not to say so, but he seemed ill at ease in his position, and I could not but think that he ought still to be standing in the front rank of that service he so highly honoured. He spoke with great bitterness of the Foxardo affair, and gave me an account of an interesting interview between General Jackson and himself on his recall from South America. General Jackson wished him to resume his rank in the navy, but he answered that he would never accept service with men who had suspended him for doing what, they said in their sentence of condemnation, was done "to sustain the honour of the American flag."

At the primitive hour of one we sat down to a regular family dinner. We were all Americans. The commodore's sister, who was living with him, presided, and we looked out on the Sea of Marmora and talked of home. I cannot describe the satisfaction of these meetings of Americans so far from their own country. I have often experienced it most powerfully in the houses of the missionaries in the East. Besides having, in many instances, the same acquaintances, we had all the same habits and ways of thinking; their articles of furniture were familiar to me, and there was scarcely a house in which I did not find an article unknown except among Americans, a Boston rocking-chair.

We talked over the subject of our difficulties with France, then under discussion in the Chamber of Deputies, and I remember that Commodore Porter was strong in the opinion that the bill paying the debt would pass. Before rising from table, the commodore's janisary came down from Constantinople, with papers and letters just arrived by the courier from Paris. He told me that I should have the honour of breaking the seals, and I took out the paper so well known all over Europe, "Galignani's Messenger," and had the satisfaction of reading aloud, in confirmation of the commodore's opinion, that the bill for paying the American claims had passed the Chamber of Deputies by a large majority.

About four o'clock we embarked in our caique, to return to Constantinople. In an hour Mr. D. and I landed at the foot of the Seven Towers, and few things in this ancient city interested me more than my walk around its walls. We followed them the whole extent on the land side, from the Sea of Marmora to the Golden Horn. They consist of a triple range, with five gates, the principal of which is the Cannon Gate, through which Mohammed II. made his triumphal entry into the Christian city. They have not been repaired since the city fell into the hands of the Turks, and are the same walls which procured for it the proud name of the "well-defended city;" to a great extent, they are the same walls which the first Constantine built and the last Constantine died in defending. Time has laid his ruining hand upon them, and they are everywhere weak and decaying, and would fall at once before the thunder of modern war. The moat and fossé have alike lost their warlike character, and bloom and blossom with the vine and fig-tree. Beyond, hardly less interesting than the venerable walls, and extending as far as the eye can reach, is one continued burying-ground, with thousands and tens of thousands of turbaned headstones, shaded by thick groves of the mourning cypress. Opposite the Damascus Gate is an elevated enclosure, disconnected from all around, containing five headstones in a row, over the bodies of Ali Pacha, the rebel chief of Yanina, and his four sons. The fatal mark of death by the bowstring is conspicuous on the tombs, as a warning to rebels that they cannot escape the sure vengeance of the Porte. It was toward the sunset of a beautiful evening, and all Stamboul was out among the tombs. At dark we reached the Golden Horn, crossed over in a caique, and in a few minutes were in Pera.

The next day I took a caique at Tophana, and went up to the ship-yards at the head of the Golden Horn to visit Mr. Rhodes, to whom I had a letter from a friend in Smyrna. Mr. Rhodes is a native of Long Island, but from his boyhood a resident of this city, and I take great pleasure in saying that he is an honour to our state and country. The reader will remember that, some years ago, Mr. Eckford, one of our most prominent citizens, under a pressure of public and domestic calamities, left his native city. He sailed from New York in a beautiful corvette, its destination unknown, and came to anchor under the walls of the seraglio in the harbour of Constantinople. The sultan saw her, admired her, and bought her; and I saw her "riding like a thing of life" on the waters of the Golden Horn, a model of beauty.

The fame of his skill, and the beautiful specimen he carried out with him, recommended Mr. Eckford to the sultan as a fit instrument to build up the character of the Ottoman navy; and afterward, when his full value became known, the sultan remarked of him that America must be a great nation if she could spare from her service such a man. Had he lived, even in the decline of life he would have made for himself a reputation in that distant quarter of the globe equal to that he had left behind him, and doubtless would have reaped the attendant pecuniary reward. Mr. Rhodes went out as Mr. Eckford's foreman, and on his death the task of completing his employer's work devolved on him. It could not have fallen upon a better man. From a journeyman ship-builder, all at once Mr. Rhodes found himself brought into close relations with the seraskier pacha, the reis effendi, the grand vizier, and the sultan himself; but his good sense never deserted him. He was then preparing for the launch of the great ship; the longest, as he said, and he knew the dimensions of every ship that floated, in the world. I accompanied him over the ship and through the yards, and it was with no small degree of interest that I viewed a townsman, an entire stranger in the country, by his skill alone standing at the head of the great naval establishment of the sultan. He was dressed in a blue roundabout jacket, without whiskers or mustache, and, except that he wore the tarbouch, was thorough American in his appearance and manners, while his dragoman was constantly by his side, communicating his orders to hundreds of mustached Turks, and in the same breath he was talking with me of shipbuilders in New York, and people and things most familiar in our native city. Mr. Rhodes knows and cares but little for things that do not immediately concern him; his whole thoughts are of his business, and in that he possesses an ambition and industry worthy of all praise. As an instance of his discretion, particularly proper in the service of that suspicious and despotic government, I may mention that, while standing near the ship and remarking a piece of cloth stretched across her stern, I asked him her name, and he told me he did not know; that it was painted on her stern, and his dragoman knew, but he had never looked under, that he might not be able to answer when asked. I have seldom met a countryman abroad with whom I was more pleased, and at parting he put himself on a pinnacle in my estimation by telling me that, if I came to the yard the next day at one, I would see the sultan! There was no man living whom I had a greater curiosity to see. At twelve o'clock I was at the yard, but the sultan did not come. I went again, and his highness had come two hours before the time; had accompanied Mr. Rhodes over the ship, and left the yard less than five minutes before my arrival; his caique was still lying at the little dock, his attendants were carrying trays of refreshments to a shooting-ground in the rear, and two black eunuchs belonging to the seraglio, handsomely dressed in long black cloaks of fine pelisse cloth, with gold-headed canes and rings on their fingers, were still lingering about the ship, their effeminate faces and musical voices at once betraying their neutral character.

The next was the day of the launch; and early in the morning, in the suite of Commodore Porter, I went on board an old steamer provided by the sultan expressly for the use of Mr. Rhodes's American friends. The waters of the Golden Horn were already covered; thousands of caiques, with their high sharp points, were cutting through it, or resting like gulls upon its surface; and there were ships with the still proud banner of the crescent, and strangers with the flags of every nation in Christendom, and sail-boats, long-boats, and row-boats, ambassadors' barges, and caiques of effendis, beys, and pachas, with red silk flags streaming in the wind, while countless thousands were assembled on the banks to behold the extraordinary spectacle of an American ship, the largest in the world, launched in the harbour of old Stamboul. The sultan was then living at his beautiful palace at Sweet Waters, and was obliged to pass by our boat; he had made a great affair of the launch; had invited all the diplomatic corps, and, through the reis effendi, particularly requested the presence of Commodore Porter; had stationed his harem on the opposite side of the river; and as I saw prepared for himself near the ship a tent of scarlet cloth trimmed with gold, I expected to see him appear in all the pomp and splendour of the greatest potentate on earth. I had already seen enough to convince me that the days of Eastern magnificence had gone by, or that the gorgeous scenes which my imagination had always connected with the East had never existed; but still I could not divest myself of the lingering idea of the power and splendour of the sultan.: His commanding style to his own subjects: " I command you, ———, my slave, that you bring the head of ———, my slave, and lay it at my feet;" and then his lofty tone with foreign powers: " I, who am, by the infinite grace of the great, just, and all-powerful Creator, and the abundance of the miracles of the chief of his prophets, emperor of powerful emperors; refuge of sovereigns; distributor of crowns to the kings of the earth; keeper of the two very holy cities (Mecca and Medina); governor of the holy city of Jerusalem; master of Europe, Asia, and Africa, conquered with our victorious sword and our terrible lance; lord of two seas (Black and White); of Damascus, the odour of Paradise; of Bagdad, the seat of the califs; of the fortresses of Belgrade, Agra, and a multitude of countries, isles, straits, peoples, generations, and of so many victorious armies who repose under the shade of our Sublime Porte; I, in short who am the shadow of God upon earth."

I was rolling these things through my mind when a murmur, "The sultan is coming," turned me to the side of the boat, and one view dispelled all my gorgeous fancies. There was no style, no state; a citizen king, a republican president, or a democratic governor, could not have made a more unpretending appearance than did this "shadow of God upon earth." He was seated in the bottom of a large caique, dressed in the military frock-coat and red tarbouch, with his long black beard, the only mark of a Turk about him, and he moved slowly along the vacant space cleared for his passage, boats with the flags of every nation, and thousands of caiques falling back, and the eyes of the immense multitude earnestly fixed upon him, but without any shouts or acclamations; and when he landed at the little dock, and his great officers bowed to the dust before him, he looked the plainest, mildest, kindest man among them. I had wished to see him as a wholesale murderer, who had more blood upon his hands than any man living; who had slaughtered the janisaries, drenched the plains of Greece, to say nothing of bastinadoes, impalements, cutting off heads, and tying up in sacks, which are taking place every moment; but I will not believe that Sultan Mahmoud finds any pleasure in shedding blood. Dire necessity, or, as he himself would say, fate, has ever been driving him on. I look upon him as one of the most interesting characters upon earth, as the creature of circumstances, made bloody and cruel by the necessities of his position. I look at his past life and at that which is yet in store for him, through all the stormy scenes he is to pass until he completes his unhappy destiny, the last of a powerful and once-dreaded race, bearded by those who once crouched at the footstool of his ancestors, goaded by rebellious vassals, conscious that he is going a downward road, and yet unable to resist the impulse that drives him on. Like the strong man encompassed by a net, he finds no avenue of escape, and cannot break through it.

The seraskier pacha and other principal officers escorted him to his tent, and now all the interest which I had taken in the sultan was transferred to Mr. Rhodes. He had great anxiety about the launch, and many difficulties to contend with; first, in the Turks' jealousy of a stranger, which obliged him to keep constantly on the watch lest some of his ropes should be cut or fastenings knocked away; and he had another Turkish prejudice to struggle against: the day had been fixed twice before, but the astronomers found an unfortunate conjunction of the stars, and it was postponed, and even then the stars were unpropitious; but Mr. Rhodes had insisted that the work had gone so far that it could not be stopped. And, besides these, he had another great difficulty in his ignorance of their language. With more than a thousand men under him, all his orders had to pass through interpreters, and often, too, the most prompt action was necessary, and the least mistake might prove fatal. Fortunately, he was protected from treachery by the kindness of Mr. Churchill and Dr. Zobrab, one of whom stood on the bow and the other in the stern of the ship, and through whom every order was transmitted in Turkish. Probably none there felt the same interest that we did; for the flags of the barbarian and every nation in Christendom were waving around us, and at that distance from home, the enterprise of a single citizen enlisted the warmest feelings of every American. We watched the ship with as keen an interest as if our own honour and success in life depended upon her movements. For a long time she remained perfectly quiet. At length she moved, slowly and almost imperceptibly; and then, as if conscious that the eyes of an immense multitude were on her, and that the honour of a distant nation was in some measure at stake, she marched proudly to the water, plunged in with a force that almost buried her, and, rising like a huge leviathan, parted the foaming waves with her bow, and rode triumphantly upon them. Even Mussulman indifference was disturbed; all petty jealousies were hushed; the whole immense mass was roused into admiration; loud and long-continued shouts of applause rose with one accord from Turks and Christians, and the sultan was so transported that he jumped up and clapped his hands like a school-boy.

Mr. Rhodes's triumph was complete; the sultan called him to his tent, and with his own hands fixed on the lapel of his coat a gold medal set in diamonds, representing the launching of a ship. Mr. Rhodes has attained among strangers the mark of every honourable man's ambition, the head of his profession. He has put upon the water what Commodore Porter calls the finest ship that ever floated, and has a right to be proud of his position and prospects under "the shade of the Sublime Porte." The sultan wishes to confer upon him the title of chief naval constructor, and to furnish him with a house and a caique with four oars. In compliment to his highness, who detests a hat, Mr. Rhodes wears the tarbouch; but he declines all offices and honours, and any thing that may tend to fix him as a Turkish subject, and looks to return and enjoy in his own country and among his own people the fruits of his honourable labours. If the good wishes of a friend can avail him, he will soon return to our city rich with the profits of untiring industry, and an honourable testimony to his countrymen of the success of American skill and enterprise abroad.

To go back a moment. All day the great ship lay in the middle of the Golden Horn, while perhaps more than a hundred thousand Turks shot round her in their little caiques, looking up from the surface of the water to her lofty deck; and in Pera, wherever I went, perhaps because I was an American, the only thing I heard of was the American ship. Proud of the admiration excited so far from home by this noble specimen of the skill of an American citizen, I unburden myself of a long-smothered subject of complaint against my country. I cry out with a loud voice for *reform*, not in the hackneyed sense of petty politicians, but by a liberal and enlarged expenditure of public money; by increasing the outfits and salaries of our foreign ambassadors and ministers. We claim to be rich, free from debt, and abundant in resources, and yet every American abroad is struck with a feeling of mortification at the inability of his representative to take that position in social life to which the character of his country entitles him. We may talk of republican simplicity as we will, but there are certain usages of society and certain appendages of rank which, though they may be unmeaning and worthless, are sanctioned, if not by the wisdom, at least by the practice of all civilised countries. We have committed a fatal error since the time when Franklin appeared at the court of France in a plain citizen's dress; everywhere our representative conforms to the etiquette of the court to which he is accredited, and it is too late to go back and begin anew; and now, unless our representative is rich and willing to expend his own fortune for the honour of the nation, he is obliged to withdraw from the circles and position in which he has a right and ought to move, or to move in them on an inferior footing, under an acknowledgment of inability to appear as an equal.

And again: our whole consular system is radically wrong, disreputable, and injurious to our character and interests. While other nations consider the support of their consuls a part of the expenses of their government, we suffer ourselves to be represented by merchants, whose pecuniary interests are mixed up with all the local and political questions that affect the place, and who are under a strong inducement to make their officesubservient to their commercial relations. I make no imputations against any of them. I could not if I would, for I do not know an American merchant holding the office who is not a respectable man; but the representative of our country ought to be the representative of our country only; removed from any distracting or conflicting interests, standing like a watchman to protect the honour of his nation and the rights of her citizens. And more than this, all over the Mediterranean there are ports where commerce presents no inducements to the American merchant, and there the office falls into the hands of the natives; and at this day the American arms are blazoned on the doors, and the American flag is waving over the houses, of Greeks, Italians, Jews, and Arabs, and all the mongrel population of that inland sea; and in the ports under the dominion of Turkey particularly, the office is coveted as a means of protecting the holder against the liabilities to his own government, and of revenue by selling that protection to others. I will not mention them by name, for I bear them no ill-will personally, and I have received kindness from most of the petty vagabonds who live under the folds of the American flag; but the consuls at Genoa and Algiers are a disgrace to the American name. Congress has lately turned its attention to this subject, and will, before long, I hope, effect a complete change in the character of our consular department, and give it the respectability which it wants; the only remedy is by following the example of other nations, in fixing salaries to the office, and forbidding the holders to engage in trade. Besides the leading inducements to this change, there is a secondary consideration, which, in my eyes, is not without its value, in that it would furnish a valuable school of instruction for our young men. The offices would be sought by such. A thousand or fifteen hundred dollars a year would maintain them respectably in most of the ports of the Mediterranean, and young men resident in those places, living upon salaries, and not obliged to engage in commerce, would employ their leisure hours in acquiring the language of the country, in communicating with the interior, and among them would return upon us an accumulation of knowledge far more than repaying us for all the expense of supporting them abroad.

Doubtless the reader expects other things in Constantinople; but all things are changing. The day has gone by when a Christian could not cross the threshold of a mosque and live. Even the sacred mosque of St. Sophia, the ancient Christian church, so long closed against the Christians' feet, now, upon great occasions, again opens its doors to the descendants of its Christian builders. One of these great occasions happened while I was there. The sultan gave a firman to the French ambassador, under which all the European residents and travellers visited it. Unfortunately, I was unwell, and could not go out that day, and was obliged afterwards to content myself with walking around its walls, with uplifted eyes and a heavy heart, admiring the glittering crescent and thinking of the prostrate cross.

But no traveller can leave Constantinople without having seen the interior of a mosque; and accordingly under the guidance of Mustapha, the janisary of the British consul, I visited the mosque of Sultan Suliman, next in point of beauty to that of St. Sophia, though far inferior in historical interest. At an early hour we crossed the Golden Horn to old Stamboul; threaded our way through its narrow and intricate streets to an eminence near the seraskier pacha's tower; entered by a fine gateway into a large courtyard, more than a thousand feet square, handsomely paved and ornamented with noble trees, and enclosed by a high wall; passed a marble fountain of clear and abundant water, where, one after another, the faithful stopped to make their ablutions; entered a large colonnade, consisting of granite and marble pillars of every form and style, the plunder of ancient temples, worked in without much regard to architectural fitness, yet, on the whole, producing a fine effect; pulled off our shoes at the door, and, with naked feet and noiseless step, crossed the sacred threshold of the mosque. Silently we moved among the kneeling figures of the faithful scattered about in different parts of the mosque and engaged in prayer; paused for a moment under the beautiful dome sustained by four columns from the Temple of Diana at Ephesus; leaned against a marble pillar which may have supported, two thousand years ago, the praying figure of a worshipper of the great goddess; gazed at the thousand small lamps suspended from the lofty ceiling, each by a separate cord, and with a devout feeling left the mosque.

In the rear, almost concealed from view by a thick grove of trees, shrubs, and flowers, is a circular building about forty feet in diameter, containing the tomb of Suliman, the founder of the mosque, his brother, his favourite wife Roxala, and two other wives. The monuments are in the form of sarcophagi, with pyramidal tops, covered with rich Cachmere shawls, having each at the head a large white turban, and enclosed by a railing covered with mother-o'-pearl. The great beauty of the sepulchral chamber is its dome, which is highly ornamented, and sparkles with brilliants. In one corner is a plan of Mecca, the holy temple, and tomb of the Prophet.

In the afternoon I went for the last time to the Armenian burying-ground. In the East the graveyards are the general promenades, the places of rendezvous, and the lounging-places; and in Constantinople the Armenian burying-ground is the most beautiful, and the favourite. Situated in the suburbs of Pera, overlooking the Bosphorus, shaded by noble palm-trees, almost regularly toward evening I found myself sitting upon the same tombstone, looking upon the silvery water at my feet, studded with palaces, flashing and glittering with caiques from the golden palace of the sultan to the seraglio point, and then turned to the animated groups thronging the burying-ground; the Armenian in his flowing robes, the dashing Greek, the stiff and out-of-place-looking Frank; Turks in their gay and bright costume, glittering arms, and solemn beards, enjoying the superlative of existence in dozing over their pipe; and women in long white veils, apart under some delightful shade, in little picnic parties, eating ices and confectionary. Here and there, toward the outskirts, was the araba, the only wheeled carriage known among the Turks, with a long low body, highly carved and gilded, drawn by oxen fancifully trimmed with ribands, and filled with soft cushions, on which the Turkish and Armenian ladies almost buried themselves. Instead of the cypress, the burying-ground is shaded by noble plane-trees; and the tomb-stones, instead of being upright, are all flat, having at the head a couple of little niches scooped out to hold water, with the beautiful idea to induce birds to come there and drink and sing among the trees. Their tombstones, too, have another mark, which, in a country where men are apt to forget who their fathers were, would exclude them even from that place where all mortal distinctions are laid low, viz., a mark indicating the profession or occupation of the deceased; as, a pair of shears to mark the grave of a tailor; a razor that of a barber; and on many of them was another mark indicating the manner of death, the bowstring, or some other mark, showing that the stone covered a victim of Turkish cruelty. But all these things are well known; nothing has escaped the prying eyes of curious travellers; and I merely state, for my own credit's sake, that I followed the steps of those who had gone before me, visited the Sweet Waters, Scutary, and Belgrade, the reservoirs, aqueducts, and ruins of the palace of Constantine, and saw the dancing dervishes; rowed up the Bosphorus to Buyukdere, luncheon under the tree where Godfrey encamped with his gallant crusaders, and looked out upon the Black Sea from the top of the Giant's Mountain.

CHAPTER XIII.

Visit to the Slave-market.—Horrors of Slavery.—Departure from Stamboul.—The stormy Euxine.—Odessa.—The Lazaretto.—Russian Civility.—Returning Good for Evil.

THE day before I left Constantinople I went, in company with Dr. N. and his son, and attended by Paul, to visit the slave-market; crossing over to Stamboul, we picked up a Jew in the bazars, who conducted us through a perfect labyrinth of narrow streets to a quarter of the city from which it would have been utterly impossible for me to extricate myself alone. I only know that it was situated on high ground, and that we passed through a gateway into a hollow square of about a hundred and fifty or two hundred feet on each side. It was with no small degree of emotion that I entered this celebrated place, where so many Christian hearts have trembled; and, before crossing the threshold, I ran over in my mind all the romantic stories and all the horrible realities that I could remember connected with its history: the tears of beauty, the pangs of brave men, and so down to the unsentimental exclamation of Johnson to his new friend Don Juan:

"Yon black eunuch seems to eye us;
I wish to God that somebody would buy us."

The bazar forms a hollow square, with little chambers about fifteen feet each way around it, in which the slaves belonging to the different dealers are kept. A large shed or portico projects in front, under which, and in front of each chamber, is a raised platform, with a low railing around it, where the slave-merchant sits and gossips, and dozes over his coffee and pipes. I had heard so little of this place, and it was so little known among Europeans, taking into consideration, moreover, that in a season of universal peace the market must be without a supply of captives gained in war, that I expected to see but a remnant of the ancient traffic, supposing that I should find but few slaves, and those only black; but, to my surprise, I found there twenty or thirty white women. Bad, horrible as this traffic is under any circumstances, to my habits and feelings it loses a shade of its horrors when confined to blacks; but here whites and blacks were exposed together in the same bazar. The women were from Circassia and the regions of the Caucasus, that country so renowned for beauty; they were dressed in the Turkish costume, with the white shawl wrapped around the mouth and chin, and over the forehead, shading the eyes, so that it was difficult to judge with certainty as to their personal appearance. Europeans are not permitted to purchase, and their visits to this bazar are looked upon with suspicion. If we stopped long opposite a door, it was closed upon us; but I was not easily shaken off, and returned so often at odd times, that I succeeded in seeing pretty distinctly all that was to be seen. In general, the best slaves are not exposed in the bazars, but are kept at the houses of the dealers; but there was one among them not more than seventeen, with a regular Circassian face, a brilliantly fair complexion, a mild and cheerful expression; and in the slave-market, under the partial disguise of the Turkish shawl, it required no great effort of the imagination to make her decidedly beautiful. Paul stopped, and with a burst of enthusiasm, the first I had discovered in him, exclaimed, "Quelle beauté!" She noticed my repeatedly stopping before her bazar; and, when I was myself really disposed to be sentimental, instead of drooping her head with the air of a distressed heroine, to my great surprise she laughed and nodded, and beckoned me to come to her. Paul was very much struck; and repeating his warm expression of admiration at her beauty, told me that she wanted me to buy her. Without waiting for a reply, he went off and inquired the price, which was two hundred and fifty dollars; and added that he could easily get some Turk to let me buy her in his name, and then I could put her on board a vessel, and carry her where I pleased. I told him it was hardly worth while at present; and he, thinking my objection was only to the person, in all honesty and earnestness told me he had been there frequently, and never saw anything half so handsome; adding that, if I let slip this opportunity, I would scarcely have another as good, and wound up very significantly by declaring that, if he was a gentleman, he would not hesitate a moment. A gentleman, in the sense in which Paul understood the word, is apt to fall into irregular ways in the East. Removed from the restraints which operate upon men in civilised countries, if he once breaks through the trammels of education, he goes all lengths; and it is said to be a matter of general remark, that slaves are always worse treated by Europeans than by the Turks. The slave-dealers are principally Jews, who buy children when young, and, if they have beauty, train up the girls in such accomplishments as may fascinate the Turks. Our guide told us that, since the Greek revolution, the slave-market had been comparatively deserted; but during the whole of that dreadful struggle, every day presented new horrors; new captives were brought in, the men raving and struggling, and vainly swearing eternal vengeance against the Turks, and the women shrieking distractedly in the agony of a separation. After the massacre at Scio, in particular, hundreds of young girls, with tears streaming down their cheeks, and bursting hearts, were sold to the unhallowed embraces of the Turks for a few dollars a-head. We saw nothing of the horrors and atrocities of this celebrated slave-market. Indeed, except prisoners of war and persons captured by Turkish corsairs, the condition of those who now fill the slave-market is not the horrible lot that a warm imagination might suppose. They are mostly persons in a semi-barbarous state; blacks from Sennaar and Abyssinia, or whites from the regions of the Caucasus, bought from their parents for a string of beads or a shawl; and, in all probability, the really beautiful girl whom I saw had been sold by parents who could not feed or clothe her, who considered themselves rid of an encumbrance, and whom she left without regret; and she, having left poverty and misery behind her, looked to the slave-market as the sole means of advancing her fortune; and, in becoming the favoured inmate of a harem, expected to attain a degree of happiness she could never have enjoyed at home.

I intended to go from Constantinople to Egypt, but the plague was raging there so violently that it would have been fool-hardy to attempt it; and while making arrangements with a Tartar to return to Europe on horseback across the Balkan, striking the Danube at Semlin and Belgrade, a Russian government steamer was advertised for Odessa; and as this mode of travelling at that moment suited my health better, I altered my whole plan, and determined to leave the ruined countries of the Old World for a land just emerging from a state of barbarism, and growing into gigantic greatness. With great regret I took leave of Dr. N. and his son, who sailed the same day for Smyrna, and I have never seen them since. Paul was the last man to whom I said farewell. At the moment of starting my shirts were brought in dripping wet, and Paul bestowed a malediction upon the Greek while he wrung them out and tumbled them into my carpet-bag. I afterward found him at Malta, whence he accompanied me on my tour in Egypt, Arabia Petræa, and the Holy Land, by which he is, perhaps, already known to some of my readers.

With my carpet-bag on the shoulders of a Turk, I walked for the last time to Tophana. A hundred caiquemen gathered around me, but I pushed them all back, and kept guard over my carpet-bag, looking out for one whom I had been in the habit of employing ever since my arrival in Constantinople. He soon spied me; and when he took my luggage and myself into his caique, manifested that he knew that it was for the last time. Having an hour to spare, I directed him to row once more under the walls of the seraglio; and still loath to leave, I went on shore and walked around the point until I was stopped by a Turkish bayonet. The Turk growled, and his mustache curled fiercely as he pointed it at me. I had been stopped by Frenchmen, Italians, and by a mountain Greek, but found nothing that brings a man to such a dead stand as the Turkish bayonet.

I returned to my caique, and went on board the steamer. She was a Russian government vessel, more classically called a pyroscaphe, a miserable old thing; and yet as much form and circumstance were observed in sending her off as in fitting out an *exploring expedition*. Consuls' and ambassadors' boats were passing and repassing, and after an enormous fuss and preparation, we started under a salute of cannon, which was answered from one of the sultan's frigates. We had the usual scene of parting with friends, waving of handkerchiefs, and so on; and feeling a little lonely at the idea of leaving a city containing a million inhabitants without a single friend to bid me Godspeed, I took my place on the quarter-deck, and waved my handkerchief to my caiqueman, who, I have no doubt, independent of the loss of a few piasters per day, was very sorry to lose me; for we had been so long together, that, in spite of our ignorance of each other's language, we understood each other perfectly.

I found on board two Englishmen whom I had met at Corfu, and a third, who had joined them at Smyrna, going to travel in the Crimea; our other cabin-passengers were, Mr. Luoff, a Russian officer, and aide-de-camp of the emperor, just returned from travels in Egypt and Syria; Mr. Perseani, secretary to the Russian legation in Greece; a Greek merchant, with a Russian protection, on his way to the Sea of Azoff; and a French merchant of Odessa. The tub of a steamboat dashed up the Bosphorus at the rate of three miles an hour; while the classic waters, as if indignant at having such a bellowing, blowing, blustering monster upon their surface, seemed to laugh at her unwieldy and ineffectual efforts. Slowly we mounted the beautiful strait, lined on the European side almost with one continued range of houses, exhibiting in every beautiful nook a palace of the sultan, and at Terapeia and Buyukdere the palaces of the foreign ambassadors; passed the Giant's Mountain, and about an hour before dark were entering a new sea, the dark and stormy Euxine.

Advancing, the hills became more lofty and rugged, terminating on the Thracian side in high rocky precipices. The shores of this extremity of the Bosphorus were once covered with shrines, altars, and temples, monuments of the fears or gratitude of mariners who were about to leave, or who had escaped, the dangers of the inhospitable Euxine; and the remains of these antiquities were so great that a traveller almost in our day describes the coast as "covered by their ruins." The castles on the European and the Asiatic side of the strait are supposed to occupy the sites where stood, in ancient days, the great temples of Jupiter Serapis and Jupiter Urius. The Bosphorus opens abruptly, without any enlargement at its mouth, between two mountains. The parting view of the strait, or, rather, of the coast on each side, was indescribably grand, presenting a stupendous wall opposed to the great bed of the waters, as if torn asunder by an earthquake, leaving a narrow rent for their escape. On each side a miserable lantern on the top of a tower, hardly visible at the distance of a few miles, is the only light to guide the mariner at night; and as there is another opening called the false Bosphorus, the entrance is difficult and dangerous, and many vessels are lost here annually.

As the narrow opening closed before me, I felt myself entering a new world; I was fairly embarked upon the wide expanse of water which once, according to ancient legends, mingled with the Caspian, and covered the great Oriental plain of Tartary, and upon which Jason, with his adventurous Argonauts, having killed the dragon and carried off the golden fleece from Colchis, if those same legends be true (which some doubt), sailed across to the great ocean. I might and should have speculated upon the great changes in the face of nature, and the great deluge recorded by Grecian historians and poets, which burst the narrow passage of the Thracian Bosphorus for the outlet of the mighty waters; but who could philosophise in a steam-boat on the Euxine? Oh, Fulton! much as thou hast done for mechanics and the useful arts, thy hand has fallen rudely upon all cherished associations. We boast of thee: I have myself been proud of thee as an American; but as I sat at evening on the stern of the steamer, and listened to the clatter of the engine, and watched the sparks rushing out of the high pipes, and remembered that this was on the dark and inhospitable Euxine, I wished that thy life had begun after mine was ended. I trust I did his memory no wrong; but if I had borne him malice, I could not have wished him worse than to have all his dreams of the past disturbed by the clatter of one of his own engines.

I turned away from storied associations to a new country grown up in our own day. We escaped, and, I am obliged to say, without noticing them, the Cyaneæ, "the blue Symplegades," or, "wandering islands," which, lying on the European Asiatic side, floated about, or, according to Pliny, "were alive, and moved to and fro more swiftly than the blast," and in passing through which the good ship Argo had a narrow escape, and lost the extremity of her stern. History and poetry have invested this sea with extraordinary and ideal terrors! but my experience both of the Mediterranean and Black Sea was unfortunate for realising historical and poetical accounts. I had known the beautiful Mediterranean a sea of storm and sunshine, in which the storm greatly predominated. I found the stormy Euxine calm as an untroubled lake; in fact, the Black Sea is in reality nothing more than a lake, not as large as many of our own, receiving the waters of the great rivers of the north: the Don, the Cuban, the Phase, the Dnieper, and the Danube, and pouring their collected streams through the narrow passage of the Bosphorus into the Mediterranean. Still, if the number of shipwrecks be any evidence of its character, it is indeed entitled to its ancient reputation of a dangerous sea, though probably these accidents proceed, in a great measure, from the ignorance and unskilfulness of mariners, and the want of proper charts and of suitable lighthouses at the opening of the Bosphorus. At all events, we outblustered the winds and waves with our steam-boat; passed the Serpent isles, the ancient Leuce, with a roaring that must have astonished the departed heroes whose souls, according to the ancient poets, were sent there to enjoy perpetual paradise, and scared the aquatic birds which every morning dipped their wings in the sea, and sprinkled the Temple of Achilles, and swept with their plumage its sacred pavement.

On the third day we made the low coast of Moldavia or Bessarabia, within a short distance of Odessa, the great seaport of Southern Russia. Here, too, there was nothing to realise preconceived notions; for, instead of finding a rugged region of eternal snows, we were suffering under an intensely hot sun when we cast anchor in the harbour of Odessa. The whole line of the coast is low and destitute of trees; but Odessa is situated on a high bank; and, with its beautiful theatre, the exchange, the palace of the governor, &c., did not look like a city which, thirty years ago, consisted only of a few fishermen's huts.

The harbour of Odessa is very much exposed to the north and east winds, which often cause great damage to the shipping. Many hundred anchors cover the bottom, which cut the rope cables; and, the water being shallow, vessels are often injured by striking on them. An Austrian brig going out, having struck one, sunk in ten minutes. There are two moles, the quarantine mole, in which we came to anchor, being the principal. Quarantine flags were flying about the harbour, the yellow indicating those undergoing purification, and the red the fatal presence of the plague. We were prepared to undergo a vexatious process. At Constantinople I had heard wretched accounts of the rude treatment of lazaretto subjects, and the rough, barbarous manners of the Russians to travellers, and we had a foretaste of the light in which we were to be regarded, in the conduct of the health officer who came alongside. He offered to take charge of any letters for the town, purify them that night, and deliver them in the morning; and, according to his directions, we laid them down on the deck, where he took them up with a pair of long iron tongs, and putting them into an iron box, shut it up and rowed off.

In the morning, having received notice that the proper officers were ready to attend us, we went ashore. We landed in separate boats at the end of a long pier, and, forgetting our supposed pestiferous influence, were walking up toward a crowd of men whom we saw there, when their retrograde movements, their gestures, and unintelligible shouts, reminded us of our situation. One of our party, in a sort of ecstacy at being on shore, ran capering up the docks, putting to flight a group of idlers, and, single-handed, might have depopulated the city of Odessa, if an ugly soldier with a bayonet had not met him in full career and put a stop to his gambols. The soldier conducted us to a large building at the upper end of the pier; and carefully opening the door, and falling back so as to avoid even the wind that might blow from us in his direction, told us to go in. At the other end of a large room, divided by two parallel railings, sat officers and clerks to examine our passports and take a general account of us. We were at once struck with the military aspect of things, every person connected with the establishment wearing a military uniform; and now commenced a long process. The first operation was to examine our passports, take down our names, and make a memorandum of the purposes for which we severally entered the dominions of the emperor and autocrat of all the Russias. We were all called up, one after the other, captain, cook, and cabin-boy, cabin and deck passengers; and never, perhaps, did steam-boat put forth a more motley assemblage than we presented. We were Jews, Turks, and Christians; Russians, Poles, and Germans; English, French, and Italians; Austrians, Greeks, and Illyrians; Moldavians, Wallachians, Bulgarians, and Sclavonians; Armenians, Georgians, and Africans; and one American. I had before remarked the happy facility of the Russians in acquiring languages, and I saw a striking instance in the officer who conducted the examination, and who addressed every man in his own language with apparently as much facility as though it had been his native tongue. After the oral commenced a corporeal examination. We were ordered one by one into an adjoining room, where, on the other side of a railing, stood a doctor, who directed us to open our shirt bosoms, and slap our hands smartly under our arms and upon our groins, these being the places where the fatal plague-marks first exhibit themselves.

This over, we were forthwith marched to the lazaretto, escorted by guards and soldiers, who behaved very civilly and kept at a respectful distance from us. Among our deck passengers were forty or fifty Jews, dirty and disgusting objects, just returned from a pilgrimage to Jerusalem. An old man, who seemed to be, in a manner, the head of the party, and exceeded them all in rags and filthiness, but was said to be rich, in going up to the lazaretto amused us and vexed the officers by sitting down on the way, paying no regard to them when they urged him on, being perfectly assured that they would not dare to touch him. Once he resolutely refused to move; they threatened and swore at him, but he kept his place until one got a long pole and punched him on a-head.

In this way we entered the lazaretto; but if it had not been called by that name, and if we had not looked upon it as a place where we were compelled to stay for a certain time, nolens volens, we should have considered it a beautiful spot. It is situated on high ground, within an enclosure of some fifteen or twenty acres, overlooking the

Black Sea, laid out in lawn and gravel walks, and ornamented with rows of acacia-trees. Fronting the sea was a long range of buildings divided into separate apartments, each with a little court-yard in front containing two or three acacias. The director, a fine, military-looking man, with a decoration on his lapel, met us on horseback within the enclosure, and with great suavity of manner said that he could not bid us welcome to a prison, but that we should have the privilege of walking at will over the grounds, and visiting each other, subject only to the attendance of a guardiano; and that all that could contribute to our comfort should be done for us.

We then selected our rooms, and underwent another personal examination. This was the real touchstone; the first was a mere preliminary observation by a medical understrapper; but this was conducted by a more knowing doctor. We were obliged to strip naked; to give up the clothes we pulled off, and put on a flannel gown, drawers, and stockings, and a woollen cap provided by the government, until our own should be smoked and purified. In everything, however, the most scrupulous regard was paid to our wishes, and a disposition was manifested by all to make this rather vexatious proceeding as little annoying as possible. The bodily examination was as delicate as the nature of the case would admit; for the doctor merely opened the door, looked in, and went out without taking his hand from off the knob. It was none of my business, to be sure, and may be thought impertinent, but, as he closed the door, I could not help calling him back to ask him whether he held the same inquisition upon the fair sex; to which he replied, with a melancholy upturning of the eyes, that in the good old days of Russian barbarism this had been part of his duties, but that the march of improvement had invaded his rights, and given this portion of his professional duties to a *sage femme*.

All our effects were then taken to another chamber, and arranged on lines, each person superintending the disposition of his own, so as to prevent all confusion, and left there to be fumigated with sulphuric acid for twenty-four hours. So particular were they in fumigating everything susceptible of infection, that I was obliged to leave there a black riband which I wore round my neck as a guard to my watch. Toward evening the principal director, one of the most gentlemanly men I ever met, came round, and with many apologies and regrets for his inability to receive us better, requested us to call upon him freely for anything we might want. Not knowing any of us personally, he did me the honour to say that he understood there was an American in the party, who had been particularly recommended to him by a Russian officer and fellow-passenger. Afterward came the commissary, or chief of the department, and repeated the same compliments, and left us with an exalted opinion of Russian politeness. I had heard horrible accounts of the rough treatment of travellers in Russia, and I made a note at the time, lest after vexations should make me forget it, that I had received more politeness and civility from these northern barbarians, as they are called by the people of the south of Europe, than I ever found amid their boasted civilisation.

Having still an hour before dark, I strolled out, followed by my guardiano, to take a more particular survey of our prison. In a gravel-walk lined with acacias, immediately before the door of my little court-yard, I came suddenly upon a lady of about eighteen, whose dark hair and eyes I at once recognised as Grecian, leading by the hand a little child. I am sure my face brightened at the first glimpse of this vision which promised to shine upon us in our solitude; and perhaps my satisfaction was made too manifest by my involuntarily moving toward her. But my presumption received a severe and mortifying check; for though at first she merely crossed to the other side of the walk, she soon forgot all ceremony, and, fairly dragging the child after her, ran over the grass to another walk to avoid me; my mortification, however, was but temporary; for though, in the first impulse of delight and admiration, I had forgotten time, place, and circumstance, the repulse I had received made me turn to myself, and I was glad to find an excuse for the lady's flight in the flannel gown and long cap and slippers, which marked me as having just entered upon my season of purification.

I was soon initiated into the routine of lazaretto ceremonies and restrictions. By touching a quarantine patient, both parties are subjected to the longest term of either; so that if a person on the last day of his term should come in contact with another just entered, he would lose all the benefit of his days of purification, and be obliged to wait the full term of the latter. I have seen, in various situations of life, a system of operations called keeping people at a distance, but I never saw it so effectually practised as in quarantine. For this night, at least, I had full range. I walked where I pleased, and was very sure that every one would keep out of my way. During the whole time, however, I could not help treasuring up the precipitate flight of the young lady; and I afterward told her, and, I hope, with the true spirit of one ready to return good for evil, that if she had been in my place, and the days of my purification had been almost ended, in spite of plague and pestilence she might have rushed into my arms without my offering the least impediment.

In making the tour of the grounds, I had already an opportunity of observing the relation in which men stand to each other in Russia. When an officer spoke to a soldier, the latter stood motionless as a statue, with his head uncovered during the whole of the conference; and when a soldier on guard *saw* an officer, no matter at what distance, he presented arms, and remained in that position until the officer was out of sight. Returning, I passed a grating, through which I saw our deck-passengers, forty or fifty in number, including the Jewish pilgrims, miserable, dirty-looking objects, turned in together for fourteen days, to eat, drink, and sleep as best they might, like brutes. With a high idea of the politeness of the Russians toward the rich and great, or those whom they believed to be so, and with a strong impression already received confirming the accounts of the degraded condition of the lower classes, I returned to my room, and, with a Frenchman and a Greek for my room-mates, my window opening upon the Black Sea, I spent my first night in quarantine.

CHAPTER XIV.

The Guardiano.—One too many.—An Excess of Kindness.—The last Day of Quarantine.—Mr. Baguet.—Rise of Odessa.—City-making.—Count Woronzow.—A Gentleman Farmer.—An American Russian.

I SHALL pass over briefly the whole of our *pratique*. The next morning I succeeded in getting a room to myself. A guardiano was assigned to each room, who took his place in the ante-chamber, and was always in attendance. These guardianos are old soldiers, entitled by the rules of the establishment to so much a-day; but, as they always expect a gratuity, their attention and services are regulated by that expectation. I was exceedingly fortunate in mine; he was always in the ante-chamber, cleaning his musket, mending his clothes, or stretched on a mattress looking at the wall; and, whenever I came through with my hat on, without a word he put on his belt and followed me; and very soon, instead of regarding him as an encumbrance, I became accustomed to him, and it was a satisfaction to have him with me. Sometimes, in walking for exercise, I moved so briskly that it tired him to keep up with me; and then I selected a walk where he could sit down and keep his eye upon me, while I walked backward and forward before him. Besides this, he kept my room in order, set my table, carried my notes, brushed my clothes, and took better care of me than any servant I ever had.

Our party consisted of eight, and being subjected to the same quarantine, and supposed to have the same quantum of infection, we were allowed to visit each other; and every afternoon we met in the yard, walked an hour or two, took tea together, and returned to our own rooms, where our guardianos mounted guard in the ante-chamber; our gates were locked up, and a soldier walked outside as sentinel. I was particularly intimate with the Russian officer, whom I found one of the most gentlemanly, best educated, and most amiable men I ever met. He had served and been wounded in the campaign against Poland; had with him two soldiers, his own serfs, who had served under him in that campaign, and had accompanied him in his tour in Egypt and Syria. He gave me his address at St. Petersburgh, and promised me the full benefit of his acquaintance there. I have before spoken of the three Englishmen. Two of them I had met at Corfu; the third joined them at Smyrna, and added another proof to the well-established maxim that three spoil company; for I soon found that they had got together by the ears; and the new-comer having connected himself with one of the others, they were anxious to get rid of the third. Many causes of offence existed between them; and though they continued to room together, they were merely waiting till the end of our pratique for an opportunity to separate. One morning the one who was about being thrown off came to my room, and told me that he did not care about going to the Crimea, and proposed accompanying me. This suited me very well; it was a long and expensive journey, and would cost a mere fraction more for two than for one; and when the breach was widened past all possibility of being healed, the cast-off and myself agreed to travel together. I saw much of the secretary of legation, and also of the Greek and Frenchman, my room-mates for the first night. Indeed, I think I may say that I was an object of special interest to all our party. I was unwell, and my companions overwhelmed me with prescriptions and advice; they brought in their medicine-chests; one assuring me that he had been cured by this, another by that, and each wanted me to swallow his own favourite medicine, interlarding their advice with anecdotes of whole sets of passengers who had been detained, some forty, some fifty, and some sixty days, by the accidental sickness of one. I did all I could for them, always having regard to the circumstance that it was not of such vital importance to me, at least, to hold out fourteen days if I broke down on the fifteenth. In a few days the doctor, in one of his rounds, told me he understood I was unwell, and I confessed to him the reason of my withholding the fact, and took his prescriptions so well, that, at parting, he gave me a letter to a friend in Chioff, and to his brother, a distinguished professor in the university of St. Petersburgh.

We had a restaurant in the lazaretto, with a new bill of fare every day; not first-rate, perhaps, but good enough. I had sent a letter of introduction to Mr. Baguet, the Spanish consul, also to a German, the brother of a missionary at Constantinople, and a note to Mr. Ralli, the American consul, and had frequent visits from them, and long talks at the *parlatoria* through the grating. The German was a knowing one, and came often; he had a smattering of English, and would talk in that language, as I thought, in compliment to me; but the last time he came he thanked me kindly, and told me he had improved more in his English than by a year's study. When I got out he never came near me.

Sunday, June seventh, was our last day in quarantine. We had counted the days anxiously; and though our time had passed as agreeably as, under the circumstances, it could pass, we were in high spirits at the prospect of our liberation. To the last, the attention and civility of the officers of the yard continued unremitted. Every morning regularly the director knocked at each gate to inquire how we had passed the night, and whether he could do anything for us; then the doctor, to inquire into our corporeal condition; and every two or three days, toward evening, the director, with the same decoration on the lapel of his coat, and at the same hour, inquired whether we had any complaints to make of want of attendance or improper treatment.

Our last day in the lazaretto is not to be forgotten. We kept as clear of the rest of the inmates as if they had been pickpockets, though once I was thrown into a cold sweat by an act of forgetfulness. A child fell down before me; I sprang forward to pick him up, and should infallibly have been fixed for ten days longer if my guardiano had not caught me. Lingering for the last time on the walk overlooking the Black Sea, I saw a vessel coming up under full sail, bearing, as I thought, the American flag. My heart almost bounded at seeing the stars and stripes on the Black Sea; but I was deceived, and, almost dejected with the disappointment, called my guardiano, and returned for the last time to my room.

The next morning we waited in our rooms till the doctor paid his final visit, and soon after we all gathered before the door of the directory, ready to sally forth. Every American who has made a European voyage knows the metamorphosis in the appearance of the passengers on the day of landing. It was much the same with us; we had no more slipshod, long-bearded companions, but all were clean-shirted and shaved becomingly, except our old Jew and his party, who probably had not changed a garment or washed their faces since the first day in quarantine, nor perhaps for many years before. They were people from whom, under any circumstances, one would be apt to keep at a respectful distance; and to the last they carried everything before them.

We had still another vexatious process in passing our luggage through the custom-house. We had handed in a list of all our effects the night before, in which I intentionally omitted to mention Byron's poems, these being prohibited in Russia. He had been my companion in Italy and Greece, and I was loath to part with him; so I put the book under my arm, threw my cloak over me, and walked out unmolested. Outside the gate, there was a general shaking of hands; the director, whom we had seen every day at a distance, was the first to greet us, and Mr. Baguet, the brother of the Spanish consul, who was waiting to receive me, welcomed me to Russia. With sincere regret I bade good-bye to my old soldier, mounted a drosky, and in ten minutes was deposited in an hotel, in size and appearance equal to the best in Paris. It was a pleasure once more to get into a wheel-carriage; I had not seen one since I left Italy, except the old hack I mentioned at Argos, and the arabas at Constantinople. It was a pleasure, too, to see hats, coats, and pantaloons. Early associations will cling to a man; and, in spite of a transient admiration for the dashing costume of the Greek and Turk, I warmed to the ungraceful covering of civilised man, even to the long surtout and bell-crowned hat of the Russian marchand; and, more than all, I was attracted by an appearance of life and energy particularly striking after coming from among the dead-and-alive Turks.

While in quarantine I had received an invitation to dine with Mr. Baguet, and had barely time to make one tour of the city in a drosky before it was necessary to dress for dinner. Mr. Baguet was a bachelor of about forty, living in pleasant apartments, in an unpretending and gentlemanly style. As in all the ports of the Levant, except where there are ambassadors, the consuls are the nobility of the place. Several of them were present; and the European consuls in those places are a different class of men from ours, as they are paid by salaries from their respective governments, while ours, who receive no pay, are generally natives of the place, who serve for the honour or some other accidental advantage. We had, therefore, the best society in Odessa at Mr. Baguet's, the American consul not being present, which, by-the-way, I do not mean in a disrespectful sense, as Mr. Ralli seemed every way deserving of all the benefits that the station gives.

In the evening the consul and myself took two or three turns on the boulevards, and at about eleven I returned to my hotel. After what I have said of this establishment, the reader will be surprised to learn that, when I went to my room, I found there a bedstead, but no bed or bedclothes. I supposed it was neglect, and ordered one to be prepared; but, to my surprise, was told that there were no beds in the hotel. It was kept exclusively for the rich seigneurs who always carry their own beds with them. Luckily, the bedstead was not corded, but contained a bottom of plain slabs of wood, about six or eight inches wide, and the same distance apart, laid crosswise, so that lengthwise there was no danger of falling through; and, wrapping myself in my cloak, and putting my carpet-bag under my head, I went to sleep.

Before breakfast the next morning I had learned the topography of Odessa. To an American Russia is an interesting country. True, it is not classic ground; but as for me, who had now travelled over the faded and worn-out kingdoms of the Old World, I was quite ready for something new. Like our own, Russia is a new country, and in many respects resembles ours. It is true that we began life differently. Russia has worked her way to civilisation from a state of absolute barbarism, while we sprang into being with the advantage of all the lights of the Old World. Still there are many subjects of comparison, and even of emulation, between us; and nowhere in all Russia is there a more proper subject to begin with than my first landing-place.

Odessa is situated in a small bay between the mouths of the Dnieper and Dniester. Forty years ago it consisted of a few miserable fishermen's huts on the shores of the Black Sea. In 1796 the Empress Catherine resolved to build a city there; and the Turks being driven from the dominion of the Black Sea, it became a place of resort and speculation for the English, Austrians, Neapolitans, Dutch, Ragusans, and Greeks of the Ionian republic. In eighteen hundred and two, two hundred and eighty vessels arrived from Constantinople and the Mediterranean; and the Duke de Richelieu, being appointed governor-general by Alexander, laid out a city upon a gigantic scale, which, though at first its growth was not commensurate with his expectations, now contains sixty thousand inhabitants, and bids fair to realise the extravagant calculations of its founder. Mr. Baguet and the gentlemen whom I met at his table were of opinion that it is destined to be the greatest commercial city in Russia, as the long winters and the closing of the Baltic with ice must ever be a great disadvantage to St. Petersburgh; and the interior of the country can as well be supplied from Odessa as from the northern capital.

There is no country where cities have sprung up so fast and increased so rapidly as in ours; and, altogether, perhaps nothing in the world can be compared to our Buffalo, Rochester, Cincinnati, &c. But Odessa has grown faster than any of these, and has nothing of the appearance of one of our new cities. We are both young, and both marching with gigantic strides to greatness, but we move by different roads; and the whole face of the country, from the new city on the borders of the Black Sea to the steppes of Siberia, shows a different order of government and a different constitution of society. With us, a few individuals cut down the trees of the forest, or settle themselves by the banks of a stream, where they happen to find some local advantages, and build houses suited to their necessities; others come and join them; and by degrees, the little settlement becomes a large city. But here a gigantic government, endowed almost with creative powers, says, "Let there be a city," and immediately commences the erection of large buildings. The rich seigneurs follow the lead of government, and build hotels to let out in apartments. The theatre, casino, and exchange at Odessa, are perhaps superior to any buildings in the United States. The city is situated on an elevation about a hundred feet above the sea; a promenade three quarters of a mile long, terminated at one end by the exchange, and at the other by the palace of the governor, is laid out in front along the margin of the sea, bounded on one side by an abrupt precipice, and adorned with trees, shrubs, flowers, statues, and busts, like the garden of the Tuileries, the Borghese Villa, or the Villa Recali, at Naples. On the other side is a long range of hotels built of stone, running the whole length of the boulevards, some of them with façades after the best models in Italy. A broad street runs through the centre of the city, terminating with a semicircular enlargement at the boulevards, and in the centre of this stands a large equestrian statue erected to the Duke de Richelieu; and parallel and at right angles are wide streets lined with large buildings, according to the most approved plans of modern architecture. The custom which the people have of taking apartments in hotels causes the erection of large buildings, which add much to the general appearance of the city; while with us the universal disposition of every man to have a house to himself, conduces to the building of small houses, and, consequently, detracts from general effect. The city, as yet, is not generally paved, and is, consequently, so dusty, that every man is obliged to wear a light cloak to save his dress. Paving-stone is brought from Trieste and Malta, and is very expensive.

About two o'clock Mr. Ralli, our consul, called upon me. Mr. Ralli is a Greek of Scio. He left his native island when a boy; has visited every port in Europe as a merchant, and lived for the last eight years in Odessa. He has several brothers in England, Trieste, and some of the Greek islands, and all are connected in business. When Mr. Rhind, who negotiated our treaty with the Porte, left Odessa, he authorised Mr. Ralli to transact whatever consular business might be required, and on his recommendation Mr. Ralli afterward received a regular appointment as consul. Mr. Rhind, by-the-way, expected a great trade from opening the Black Sea to American bottoms; but he was wrong in his anticipations, and there have been but two American vessels there since the treaty. Mr. Ralli is rich and respected, being vice-president of the commercial board, and very proud of the honour of the American consulate, as it gives him a position among the dignitaries of the place, enables him to wear a uniform and sword on public occasions, and yields him other privileges which are gratifying, at least, if not intrinsically valuable.

No traveller can pass through Odessa without having to acknowledge the politeness of Count Woronzow, the governor of the Crimea, one of the richest seigneurs in Russia, and one of the pillars of the throne. At the suggestion of Mr. Ralli, I accompanied him to the palace and was presented. The palace is a magnificent building, and the interior exhibits a combination of wealth and taste. The walls are hung with Italian paintings, and, for interior ornaments and finish, the palace is far superior to those in Italy; the knobs of the doors are of amber, and the doors of the dining-room from the old imperial palace at St. Petersburg. The count is a military-looking man of about fifty, six feet high, with sallow complexion and grey hair. His father married an English lady of the Sydney family, and his sister married the Earl of Pembroke. He is a soldier in bearing and appearance, held a high rank during the French invasion of Russia, and distinguished himself particularly at Borodino; in rank and power he is the fourth military officer in the empire. He possesses immense wealth in all parts of Russia, particularly in the Crimea; and his wife's mother, after Demidoff and Scheremetieff, is the richest subject in the whole empire. He speaks English remarkably well, and, after a few commonplaces, with his characteristic politeness to strangers, invited me to dine at the palace the next day. I was obliged to decline, and he himself suggested the reason, that probably I was engaged with my countryman, Mr. Sontag (of whom more anon), whom the count referred to as his old friend, adding, that he would not interfere with the pleasure of a meeting between two countrymen so far from home, and asked me for the day after, or any other day I pleased. I apologised on the ground of my intended departure, and took my leave.

My proposed travelling companion had committed to me the whole arrangements for our journey, or, more properly, had given me the whole trouble of making them; and, accompanied by one of Mr. Ralli's clerks, I visited all the carriage repositories to purchase a vehicle, after which I accompanied Mr. Ralli to his country-house to dine. He occupied a pretty little place a few versts from Odessa, with a large fruit and ornamental garden. Mr. Ralli's lady is also a native of Greece, with much of the cleverness and *spirituel* character of the educated Greeks. One of her *bons-mots* current in Odessa is, that her husband is consul for the other world. A young Italian, with a very pretty wife, dined with us, and, after dinner and a stroll through the garden, we walked over to Mr. Perseani's, the father of our Russian secretary; another walk in the garden with a party of ladies, tea, and I got back to Odessa in time for a walk on the boulevards and the opera.

Before my attention was turned to Odessa, I should as soon have thought of an opera-house at Chicago as there; but I already found, what impressed itself more forcibly upon me at every step, that Russia is a country of anomalies. The new city on the Black Sea contains many French and Italian residents, who are willing to give all that is not necessary for food and clothing for the opera; the Russians themselves are passionately fond of musical and theatrical entertainments, and government makes up all deficiencies. The interior of the theatre corresponds with the beauty of its exterior. All the decorations are in good tasto, and the Corinthian columns, running from the foot to the top, particularly beautiful. The opera was the Barber of Seville; the company in *full* undress, and so barbarous as to pay attention to the performance. I came out at about ten o'clock, and, after a turn or two on the boulevards, took an ice-cream at the café of the *Hôtel de Petersbourg*. This hotel is beautifully situated at one corner of the main street, fronting the boulevards, and opposite the statue of the Duke de Richelieu; and looking from the window of the café, furnished and fitted up in a style superior to most in Paris, upon the crowd still thronging the boulevards, I could hardly believe that I was really on the borders of the Black Sea.

Having purchased a carriage and made all my arrangements for starting, I expected to pass this day with an unusual degree of satisfaction; and I was not disappointed. I have mentioned incidentally the name of a countryman resident in Odessa; and, being so far from home, I felt a yearning toward an American. In France or Italy I seldom had this feeling, for there Americans congregate in crowds; but in Greece and Turkey I always rejoiced to meet a compatriot; and when, on my arrival at Odessa, being going into the lazaretto, the captain told me that there was an American residing there, high in character and office, who had been twenty years in Russia, I requested him to present my compliments, and say that, if he had not forgotten his father-land, a countryman languishing in the lazaretto would be happy to see him through the gratings of his prison-house. I afterward regretted having sent this message, as I heard from other sources that he was a prominent man, and during the whole term of my quarantine I never heard from him personally. I was most agreeably disappointed, however, when, on the first day of my release, I met him at dinner at the Spanish consul's. He had been to the Crimea with Count Woronzow; had only returned that morning, and had never heard of my being there until invited to meet me at dinner. I had wronged him by my distrust; for, though twenty years an exile, his heart beat as true as when he left our shores. Who can shake off the feeling that binds him to his native land? Not hardships nor disgrace at home; not favour nor success abroad; not even time, can drive from his mind the land of his birth, or the friends of his youthful days.

General Sontag was a native of Philadelphia; had been in our navy, and served as sailing-master on board the Wasp; became dissatisfied from some cause which he did not mention, left our navy, entered the Russian, and came round to the Black Sea as captain of a frigate; was transferred to the land service, and, in the campaign of 1814, entered Paris with the allied armies as colonel of a regiment. In this campaign he formed a friendship with Count Woronzow, which exists in full force at this day. He left the army with the rank of brigadier-general. By the influence of Count Woronzow, he was appointed inspector of the port of Odessa, in which office he stood next in rank to the governor of the Crimea, and, in fact, on one occasion, during the absence of Count Woronzow, lived in the palace and acted as governor for eight months. He married a lady of rank, with an estate and several hundred slaves at Moscow; wears two or three ribands at his button-hole, badges of different orders; has gone through the routine of offices and honours up to the grade of grand-councillor of the empire; and a letter addressed to him under the title of "His Excellency" will come to the right hands. He was then living at his country place, about eight versts from Odessa, and asked me to go out and pass the next day with him. I was strongly tempted, but, in order that I might have the full benefit of it, postponed the pleasure until I had completed my arrangements for travelling. The next day General Sontag called upon me, but I did not see him; and this morning, accompanied by Mr. Baguet the younger, I rode out to his place. The land about Odessa is a dead level, the road was excessively dry, and we were begrimed with dust when we arrived. General Sontag was waiting for us, and, in the true spirit of an American farmer at home, proposed taking us over his grounds. His farm is his hobby: it contains about six hundred acres, and we walked all over it. His crop was wheat, and, although I am no great judge of these matters, I think I never saw finer. He showed me a field of very good wheat which had not been sowed-in three years, but produced by the fallen seed of the previous crops. We compared it with our Genesee wheat, and to me it was an interesting circumstance to find an American cultivating land on the Black Sea, and comparing it with the products of our Genesee flats, with which he was perfectly familiar.

One thing particularly struck me, though, as an American, perhaps I ought not to have been so sensitive. A large number of men were at work in the field, and they were all slaves. Such is the force of education and habit, that I have seen hundreds of black slaves without a sensation; but it struck rudely upon me to see white men slaves to an American, and he one whose father had been a soldier of the Revolution, and had fought to sustain the great principle that "all men are by nature free and equal." Mr. Sontag told me that he valued his farm at about six thousand dollars, on which he could live well, have a bottle of Crimea wine, and another every day for a friend, and lay up one thousand dollars a year: but I afterward heard that he was a complete enthusiast on the subject of his farm; a bad manager, and that he really knew nothing of its expense or profit.

Returning to the house, we found Madame Sontag ready to receive us. She is an authoress of great literary reputation, and of such character that, while the emperor was prosecuting the Turkish war in person, and the empress remained in Odessa, the young archduchesses were placed under her charge. At dinner she talked with much interest of America, and expressed a hope, though not much expectation, of one day visiting it. But General Sontag himself, surrounded as he is by Russian connexions, is all American. Pointing to the riband on his button-hole, he said he was entitled to one order which he should value above all others; that his father had been a soldier of the revolution, and member of the Cincinnati Society, and that in Russia the decoration of that order would be to him the proudest badge of honour that an American could wear. After dining we retired into a little room fitted up as a library, which he calls America, furnished with all the standard American books, Irving, Paulding, Cooper, &c., engravings of distinguished Americans, maps, charts, canal and railroad reports, &c.; and his daughter, a lovely little girl and only child, has been taught to speak her father's tongue and love her father's land. 'n honour of me she played on the piano "Hail, Columbia!" and "Yankee Doodle," and the day wore away too soon. We took tea on the piazza, and at parting I received from him a letter to his agent on his estate near Moscow, and from Madame Sontag one which carried me into the imperial household, being directed to Monsieur l'Intendant du Prince héritier, Petersburgh. A few weeks ago I received from him a letter, in which he says, "the visit of one of my countrymen is so great a treat, that I can assure you you are never forgotten by any one of my little family; and when my daughter wishes to make me smile, she is sure to succeed if she sits down to her piano and plays 'Hail, Columbia,' or 'Yankee Doodle;' this brings to mind Mr. ——, Mr. ——, Mr. ——, and Mr. ——, who have passed through this city; to me alone it brings to mind my country, parents, friends, youth, and a world of things and ideas past, never to return. Should any of our countrymen be coming this way, do not forget to inform them that in Odessa lives one who will be glad to see them." And I say now to any of my countrymen whom chance may throw upon the shores of the Black Sea, that if he would receive so far from home the welcome of a true-hearted American, General Sontag will be glad to render it.

It was still early in the evening when I returned to the city. It was moonlight, and I walked immediately to the boulevards. I have not spoken as I ought to have done of this beautiful promenade, on which I walked every evening under the light of a splendid moon. The boulevards are bounded on one side by the precipitous shore of the sea; are three quarters of a mile in length, with rows of trees on each side, gravel walks and statues, and terminated at one end by the exchange, and at the other by the palace of Count Woronzow. At this season of the year it was the promenade of all the beauty and fashion of Odessa, from an hour or two before dark until midnight. This evening the moon was brighter, and the crowd was greater and gayer than usual. The great number of officers, with their dashing uniforms, the clashing of their swords, and rattling of their spurs, added to the effect; and women never look so interesting as when leaning on the arm of a soldier Even in Italy or Greece I have seldom seen a finer moonlight scene than the columns of the exchange through the vista of trees lining the boulevards. I expected to leave the next day, and I lingered till a late hour. I strolled up and down the promenade, alone among thousands. I sat down upon a bench, and looked for the last time on the Black Sea, the stormy Euxine, quiet in the moonbeams. and glittering like a lake of burnished silver. By degrees the gay throng disappeared; one after another, party after party withdrew; a few straggling couples, seeming all the world to each other, still lingered, like me, unable to tear themselves away. It was the hour and the place for poetry and feeling. A young officer and a lady were the last to leave; they passed by me, but did not notice me; they had lost all outward perceptions; and as, in passing for the last time, she raised her head for a moment, and the moon shone full upon her face, I saw there an expression that spoke of heaven. I followed them as they went out, murmured involuntarily "Happy dog!" whistled "Heigho, says Thimble," and went to my hotel to bed.

CHAPTER XV.

Choice of a conveyance.—Hiring a Servant.—Another American.—Beginning of Troubles.—A Bivouac.—Russian Jews.—The Steppes of Russia.—A Traveller's Story.—Approach to Chioff.—How to get rid of a Servant.—History of Chioff.

I HAD before me a journey of nearly two thousand miles, through a country more than half barbarous, and entirely destitute of all accommodation for travellers. Southern Russia was the Scythia of Darius, "savage from the remotest time." "All the way," says an old traveller, "I never came in a house, but lodged in the wilderness by the river side, and carried provisions by the way, for there be small succour in those parts;" and we were advised that a century had made but little change in the interior of the empire. There were no public conveyances, and we had our choice of three modes of travelling; first, by a Jew's waggon, in which the traveller stretches out his bed, and is trundled along like a bale of goods, always with the same horses, and therefore, of necessity, making slow progress; secondly, the char-de-poste, a mere box of wood on four wheels, with straw in the bottom; very fast, but to be changed always with the post horses; and thirdly, posting with our own carriage. We did not hesitate long in choosing the last, and bought a carriage, fortunately a good one, a large calèche which an Italian nobleman had had made for his own use in travelling on the Continent, and which he not sold, not because he did not want it, but because he wanted money more. Next we procured a podoroshni, under which, "By order of his Majesty Nicholas the First, autocrat of all the Russias, from Odessa to Moscow and Petersburgh, all the post-offices were commanded to give —— and ——, with their servant, four horses with their drivers, at the price fixed by law." Besides this, it was necessary to give security that we left no debts behind us; and if Mr. Ralli undertakes for all Americans the same obligation he did for me, it may happen that his office of consul will be no sinecure. Next, and this was no trifling matter, we got our passports arranged; the Russian ambassador at Constantinople, by-the-way, had given me a new passport in Russian, and my companion, that he might travel with the advantages of rank and title, got himself made "noble" by an extra stroke of his consul's pen.

The last thing was to engage a servant. We had plenty of applications, but, as very few talked any language we understood, we had not much choice; one, a German, a capital fellow, was exactly the man we wanted, only he could not speak a word of Russian, which was the principal qualification we required in a servant. At length came a Frenchman, with an unusual proportion of whiskers and mustaches, and one of the worst of the desperate émigrés whom the French Revolution, or, rather, the Restoration, sent roaming in foreign lands. He had naturally a most unprepossessing physiognomy, and this was heightened by a sabre-cut which had knocked out several of his teeth, and left a huge gash in his cheek and lip, and, moreover, made him speak very unintelligibly. When I asked him if he was a Frenchman, he drew himself up with great dignity, and replied, "*Monsieur, je suis Parisien.*" His appearance was a gross libel upon the Parisians; but, as we could get no one else, we took him, upon little recommendation, the day before our departure, and, during the same day, threatened half-a-dozen times to discharge him. The police regulation, obliging him to pay his debts before leaving Odessa, he seemed to consider peculiarly hard; and, all the time he was with us, kept referring to his having been obliged to fritter away thirty or forty rubles before he could leave. We ought to have furnished ourselves with provisions for the whole road to Moscow, and even cooking utensils; but we neglected it, and carried with us only tea and sugar, a tin teapot, two tin cups, two tin plates, two knives and forks, and some Bologna sausages, trusting, like Napoleon when he invaded Russia, to make up the rest by foraging.

Before beginning our journey we had a foretaste of the difficulty of travelling in Russia. We had ordered post-horses three times, and had sent for them morning and evening, and received for answer that there were none in. At the third disappointment, our own consul being out of town, my friend the Spanish consul went with me to the director of the post, and found that during the time in which they had told us they had no horses, they had sent out more than a hundred. Instead of taxing them with their rascality, he talked the matter over very politely, paid the price of the horses, gave them a bonus of ten rubles, and obtained a promise by all the saints in the Russian calendar for daylight the next morning.

The next morning at eight o'clock the horses came, four shaggy, wild-looking little animals, which no comb or brush had ever touched, harnessed with a collar and rope lines. They were tied in with rope traces, all abreast, two on each side the pole, and a postilion with a low wool cap, sheepskin coat and trowsers, the woolly side next the skin, who would make an English whip stare, mounted the box. Henri followed, and my companion and myself took our seats within. The day before we had a positive quarrel upon a point unnecessary here to mention, in which I thought and still think he acted wrong, and the dispute had run so high that I told him I regretted exceedingly having made arrangements for travelling with him, and proposed even then to part company: he objected, and as we had purchased a carriage jointly, and particularly our passports were prepared, our poduroshni made out, and servant hired in our joint names, I was fain to go on; and in this inauspicious humour toward each other we set out for a journey of nearly two thousand miles, through a wild and desolate country, among a half-civilised people, whose language we could not understand, and with a servant whom we distrusted and disliked.

In spite of all this, however, I felt a high degree of excitement in starting for the capital of Russia; and I will do my companion the justice to say that he had been always ready to receive my advances, and to do more than meet me half way, which I afterward learned was from an apprehension of the taunts of his companions, who, not satisfied with getting rid of him, had constantly told him that it was impossible for an Englishman and an American to travel together, and that we would quarrel and fight the first day. I believe that I am enough of an American in my feelings, but such an idea had never entered my head; I met many Englishmen, and with some formed a friendship which, I trust, will last through life; and among all I met, these two were the only *young* men so far behind the spirit of the age as to harbour such a thought. I did meet one *old* gentleman, who, though showing me personally the greatest kindness, could not forget the old grudge. But men cannot be driving their elbows into each other's ribs, comparing money accounts, and consulting upon the hundred little things that present themselves on such a journey, without getting upon at least sociable terms; and before night of the first day the feelings of my companion and myself had undergone a decided change.

But to go back to Odessa. At the barrier we found a large travelling-carriage stopping the way, in which was my friend Mr. Ralli, with his lady, on his way to Nicolaïf; part of his business there was to erect a monument to the memory of a deceased countryman. Mr. Munroe, son of a former postmaster in Washington, is another instance of the success of American adventurers in Russia. He went out to St. Petersburgh with letters from the Russian ambassador and others, and entered the army, the only road to distinction in Russia. He accompanied the Grand-duke Constantine to Poland, and was made one of his aid-de-camps, and on the death of Constantine was transferred to the staff of the Emperor Nicholas. At the time of the invasion of Turkey by the Egyptians under Ibrahim Pacha, Mr. Munroe held the rank of colonel in the army sent to the aid of the sultan. While the Russians were encamped at the foot of the Giant's Mountain, he visited Constantinople, and became acquainted with the American missionaries, who all spoke of him in the highest terms. He was a tall, well-made man, carried himself with a military air, and looked admirably well in the Russian uniform. On the withdrawal of the Russians from the Black Sea, Mr. Munroe was left in some important charge at Nicolaïf, where he died in the opening of a brilliant career. I heard of him all over Russia, particularly from officers of the army; and being often asked if I knew him, regretted to be obliged to answer, no. But, though personally unacquainted, as an American I was gratified with the name he had left behind him.

To return again to our journey: a few rubles satisfied the officer at the barrier that we were carrying nothing prohibited out of the "free port" of Odessa, and we started on a full run, to the great peril of our necks, and, to use the climax of a Dutch proclamation, "what's more, of breaking our carriage." In less than an hour we brought up before the door of a posthouse. Our wheels were smoking when we stopped. On our hind axle we carried a bucket of grease; half-a-dozen bipeds in sheepskin whipped off the wheels and greased them; four quadrupeds were tied into the carriage, another bête mounted the box, and we were off again at a full run. My companion undertook to keep a memorandum of expenses, and we put a certain sum in a purse and paid out of it till all was gone. This was a glorious beginning for a journey of two thousand miles. The country possessed little interest, being mostly level, and having but few villages. On the way we saw a natural phenomenon that is common enough in Egypt and the East, where the country is level, and known by the name of *mirage*. At a distance it seemed a mere pond or lake, and a drove of cattle passing over it looked as if they were walking in the water. We rolled on rapidly all day, passed through Balgarha, Kodurseve, and Pakra, timing ever post and noting every village with a particularity which it would be tedious here to repeat, and at about eight in the evening dashed into the little town of Vosnezeuski, one hundred and thirty versts from Odessa. Here we came to a dead stand. We had begun to entertain some apprehensions from the conduct of Monsieur Henri, who complained of the hardness of his seat, and asked if we did not intend to stop at night, recommending Vosnezenski as a place where we could sleep in the posthouse; we told him that we had no idea of stopping but to change horses, and should go on immediately.

Vosnezeuski lies on the river Bog, and is the chief town of the Cossacks on the Bog. This river is navigable for large vessels for one hundred and fifty versts; beyond this for three or four hundred versts it is full of cataracts. The Cossacks of the Bog are a warlike tribe, numbering from six to seven thousand, and living under the same military system with the Cossacks of the Don. But we fell into worse hands than the Cossacks. The postmaster was a Jew, and at first told us that he had no horses; then that he had no postilion, but would hire one if we would pay him a certain sum, about four times the amount fixed by law. We had been obliged before to pay a few extra rubles, but this was our first serious difficulty with the postmasters; and, in pursuance of the advice received at Odessa, we talked loud, demanded the book which is nailed to the table in every posthouse for travellers to enter complaints in, and threatened the vengeance of Count Woronzow and every one else, up to the emperor; but the Jew laughed in our faces; looked in our podoroshni, where we were described as simple travellers, without any of the formidable array of titles which procure respect in Russia; told us we were no grand seigneurs, and that we must either pay the price or wait, as our betters had done before us. We found too soon, as we had been advised at Odessa, that these fellows do not know such a character in society as a private gentleman; and if a man is not described in his podoroshni as a count, duke, or lord of some kind, or by some high-sounding military title, they think he is a merchant or manufacturer, or some other common fellow, and pay no regard to him. I relied somewhat upon my companion's having been made "noble," but now found that his consul had been rather chary of his honours, and, by the Russian word used, had not put him up high enough to be of any use. We had a long wrangle with the Jew, the result of which was, that we told him, probably in no very gentle phrase, that we would wait a month rather than submit to his extortion; and, drawing up the window of our carriage, prepared to pass the night at the door of the posthouse.

One of our party was evidently well satisfied with this arrangement, and he was Monsieur Henri. We had hired him by the day to Moscow, and, if we wanted him, to St. Petersburgh, and very soon saw that he was perfectly content with the terms, and in no hurry to bring our journey to a close. From the moment of our arrival we suspected him of encouraging the postmaster in his efforts to detain us, and were so much fortified in this opinion by after circumstances, that, when he was about moving toward the house to pass the night within, we peremptorily ordered him to mount the box and sleep there; he refused, we insisted; and as this was the first day out, and the first moment of actual collision, and it was all-important to decide who should be master, we told him that, if he did not obey, we would discharge him on the spot, at the risk of being obliged to work our way back to Odessa alone. And as he felt that, in that case, his debts would have been paid to no purpose, with a string of suppressed *sacrés* he took his place on the box. Our carriage was very comfortable, well lined and stuffed, furnished with pockets and everything necessary for the road, and we expected to sleep in it; but, to tell the truth, we felt rather cheap as we woke during the night, and looked at the shut door of the posthouse, and thought of the Jew sleeping away in utter contempt of us, and our only satisfaction was in hearing an occasional groan from Henri.

That worthy individual did not oversleep himself, nor did he suffer the Jew to do so either. Early in the morning, without a word on our part, the horses were brought out and harnessed to our vehicle, and the same man whom he professed to have hired expressly for us, and who, no doubt, was the regular postilion, mounted the box. The Jew maintained his impudence to the last, coming round to my window, and then asking a few rubles as a douceur. Good English would have been thrown away upon him, so I resented it by drawing up the window of the carriage and scowling at him through the glass.

Many of the postmasters along this road were Jews; and I am compelled to say that they were always the greatest scoundrels we had to deal with; and this is placing them on very high ground, for their inferiors in rascality would be accounted masters in any other country. No men can bear a worse character than the Russian Jews, and I can truly say that I found them all they were represented to be. They are not allowed to come within the territory of old Russia. Peter the Great refused their application to be permitted to approach nearer, smoothing his refusal by telling them that his Russian subjects were greater Jews than they were themselves. The sagacious old monarch, however, was wrong; for all the money business along the road is in their hands. They keep little taverns, where they sell vodka, a species of brandy, and wring from the peasant all his earnings, lending the money again to the seigneurs at exorbitant interest. Many of them are rich, and though alike despised by rich and poor, by the seigneur and the serf, they are proud of exhibiting their wealth, particularly in the jewels and ornaments of their women. At Savonka, a little village on the confines of old Poland, where we were detained waiting for horses, I saw a young girl about sixteen, a Polonese, sitting on the steps of a miserable little tavern, sewing together some ribands, with a head-dress of brown cloth, ornamented with gold chains and pearls worth six hundred rubles, diamond ear-rings worth a hundred, and a necklace of ducats and other Dutch gold pieces worth four hundred rubles; altogether, in our currency, worth perhaps two hundred and fifty dollars.

Here, too, while sitting with Henri on the steps of the posthouse, I asked him in a friendly way how he could be such a rascal as to league with the postmaster to detain us at Vosnezcuski, whereupon he went at once into French heroics, exclaiming, "*Monsieur, je suis vieux militaire—j'étais chasseur de Napoleon—mon honneur*," &c.; that he had never travelled before except with grand seigneurs, and then in the carriage, more as *compagnon de voyage* than as a servant, and intimated that it was a great condescension to travel with us at all.

We passed through several villages, so much alike and so uninteresting in appearance that I did not note even their names. As night approached we had great apprehensions that Henri would contrive to make us stop again; but the recollection of his bed on the box served as a lesson, and we rolled on without interruption. At daylight we awoke, and found ourselves upon the wild steppes of Russia, forming part of the immense plain which, beginning in northern Germany, extends for hundreds of miles, having its surface occasionally diversified by ancient tumuli, and terminates at the long chain of the Urals, which, rising like a wall, separates them from the equally vast plains of Siberia. The whole of this immense plain was covered with a luxuriant pasture, but bare of trees like our own prairie lands, mostly uncultivated, yet everywhere capable of producing the same wheat which now draws to the Black Sea the vessels of Turkey, Egypt, and Italy, making Russia the granary of the Levant; and which, within the last year, we have seen brought six thousand miles to our own doors. Our road over these steppes was in its natural state; that is to say, a mere track worn by caravans of waggons; there were no fences, and sometimes the route was marked at intervals by heaps of stones, intended as guides when the ground should be covered with snow. I had some anxiety about our carriage; the spokes of the wheels were all strengthened and secured by cords wound tightly around them, and interlaced so as to make a network; but the postilions were so perfectly reckless as to the fate of the carriage, that every crack went through me like a shot. The breaking of a wheel would have left us perfectly helpless in a desolate country, perhaps more than a hundred miles from any place where we could get it repaired. Indeed, on the whole road to Chioff there was not a single place where we could have

any material injury repaired; and the remark of the old traveller is yet emphatically true, that "there be small succour in these parts."

At about nine o'clock we whirled furiously into a little village, and stopped at the door of the posthouse. Our wheels were smoking with the rapidity of their revolutions; Henri dashed a bucket of water over them to keep them from burning, and half a dozen men whipped them off and greased them. Indeed, greasing the wheels is necessary at every post, as otherwise the hubs become dry, so that there is actual danger of their taking fire; and there is a *traveller's* story told (but I do not vouch for its truth) of a postilion, waggon and passengers, being all burned up on the road to Moscow by the ignition of the wheels.

The village, like all the others, was built of wood, plastered and whitewashed, with roofs of thatched straw, and the houses were much cleaner than I expected to find them. We got plenty of fresh milk; the bread, which to the traveller in those countries is emphatically the staff of life, we found good everywhere in Russia, and at Moscow the whitest I ever saw. Henri was an enormous feeder, and, wherever we stopped, he disappeared for a moment, and came out with a loaf of bread in his hand, and his mustache covered with the froth of quass, a Russian small beer. He said he was not always so voracious, but his seat was so hard, and he was so roughly shaken, that eating did him no good.

Resuming our journey, we met no travellers. Occasionally we passed large droves of cattle, but all the way from Odessa the principal objects were long trains of waggons, fifty or sixty together, drawn by oxen, and transporting merchandise toward Moscow or grain to the Black Sea. Their approach was indicated at a great distance by immense clouds of dust, which gave us timely notice to let down our curtains and raise our glasses. The waggoners were short, ugly-looking fellows, with huge sandy mustaches and beards, black woolly caps, and sheepskin jackets, the wool side next the skin; perhaps, in many cases, transferred warm from the back of one animal to that of the other, where they remained till worn out or eaten up by vermin. They had among them blacksmiths and wheelwrights, and spare wheels, and hammer, and tools, and everything necessary for a journey of several hundred miles. Half of them were generally asleep on the top of their loads, and they encamped at night in caravan style, arranging the waggons in a square, building a large fire, and sleeping around it. About midday we saw clouds gathering afar off in the horizon, and soon after the rain began to fall, and we could see it advancing rapidly over the immense level, till it broke over our heads, and in a few moments passed off, leaving the ground smoking with exhalations.

Late in the afternoon we met the travelling equipage of a seigneur returning from Moscow to his estate in the country. It consisted of four carriages, with six or eight horses each. The first was a large, stately, and cumbrous vehicle, padded and cushioned, in which, as we passed rapidly by, we caught a glimpse of a corpulent Russian on the back seat, with his feet on the front, bolstered all around with pillows and cushions, almost burying every part of him but his face, and looking the very personification of luxurious indulgence; and yet, probably, that man had been a soldier, and slept many a night on the bare ground, with no covering but his military cloak. Next came another carriage, fitted out in the same luxurious style, with the seigneur's lady and a little girl; then another with nurses and children; then beds, baggage, cooking utensils, and servants, the latter hanging on everywhere about the vehicle, much in the same way with the pots and kettles. Altogether, it was an equipment in caravan style, somewhat the same as for a journey in the desert, the traveller carrying with him provision and everything necessary for his comfort, as not expecting to procure anything on the road, nor to sleep under a roof during the whole journey. He stops when he pleases, and his servants prepare his meals, sometimes in the open air, but generally at the posthouse. We had constant difficulties with Henri and the postmasters, but, except when detained for an hour or two by these petty tyrants, we rolled on all night, and in the morning again woke upon the same boundless plain.

The posthouse was usually in a village, but sometimes stood alone, the only object to be seen on the great plain. Before it was always a high square post, with black and white stripes, marking the number of versts from station to station; opposite to this Henri dismounted, and presented the podoroshni or imperial order for horses. But the postmasters were high above the laws; every one of them seemed a little autocrat in his own right, holding his appointment rather to prey upon than to serve travellers; and the emperor's government would be but badly administered if his ukases and other high-sounding orders did not carry with them more weight than his podoroshni. The postmasters obeyed it when they pleased, and when they did not, made a new bargain. They always had an excuse; as, for instance, that they had no horses, or were keeping them in reserve for a courier or grand seigneur; but they listened to reason when enforced by rubles, and, as soon as a new bargain was made, half-a-dozen animals in sheepskin went out on the plain and drove up fifteen or twenty horses, small, rugged, and tough, with long and shaggy manes and tails, which no comb or brush had ever touched, and, diving among them promiscuously, caught four, put on rope headstalls, and tied them to our rope traces. The postilion mounted the box, and shouting and whipping his horses, and sometimes shutting his eyes, started from the post on a full gallop, carried us like the wind, *ventre à-terre*, over the immense plain, sometimes without a rut or any visible mark to guide him, and brought us up all standing in front of the next post. A long delay and a short post, and this was the same over and over again during the whole journey. The time actually consumed in making progress was incredibly short, and I do not know a more beautiful way of getting over the ground than posting in Russia with a man of high military rank, who can make the postmasters give him horses immediately on his arrival. As for us, after an infinite deal of vexation and at a ruinous expense, on the morning of the fourth day we were within one post of Chioff. Here we heard with great satisfaction that a diligence was advertised for Moscow, and we determined at once to get rid of carriage, posting, and Henri. We took our seats for the last time in the *calèche*, gave the postilion a double allowance of kopeks, and in half an hour saw at a great distance the venerable city of Chioff, the ancient capital of Russia. It stands at a great height, on the crest of an amphitheatre of hills, which rise abruptly in the middle of an immense plain, apparently thrown up by some wild freak of nature, at once curious, unique, and beautiful. The style of its architecture is admirably calculated to give effect to its peculiar position; and, after a dreary journey over the wild plains of the Ukraine, it breaks upon the traveller with all the glittering and gorgeous splendour of an Asiatic city. For many centuries it has been regarded as the Jerusalem of the North, the sacred and holy city of the Russians; and, long before reaching it, its numerous convents and churches, crowning the summit and hanging on the sides of the hill, with their quadrupled domes, and spires, and chains, and crosses, gilded with ducat gold and glittering in the sun, gave the whole city the appearance of golden splendour. The churches and monasteries have one large dome in the centre, with a spire surmounted by a cross, and several smaller domes around it, also with spires and crosses connected by pendent chains, and gilded so purely that they never tarnish. We drove rapidly to the foot of the hill, and ascended by a long wooden paved road to the heart of the city.

During the whole of our last post our interest had been divided between the venerable city and the rogue Henri. My companion, who, by-the-way, spoke but little French, disliked him from the first. We had long considered him in league with all the Jews and postmasters on the road, and had determined under no circumstances to take him farther than Chioff; but as we had hired him to Moscow, the difficulty was how to get rid of him. He might take it into his head, that, if we did not know when we had a good servant, he knew when he had good masters; but he was constantly grumbling about his seat, and calculated upon three or four days' rest at Chioff. So, as soon as we drove up to the door of the hotel, we told him to order breakfast and post-horses. He turned round as if he had not fully comprehended us. We repeated the order, and for the first time since he had been with us he showed something like agility in dismounting; fairly threw himself from the box, swore he would not ride another verst that day for a thousand rubles, and discharged us on the spot. We afterward paid him to his entire satisfaction, indemnifying him for the money he had squandered in paying his debts at Odessa, and found him more useful at Chioff than he had been at any time on the road. Indeed, we afterward learned, what was rather ludicrous, viz,: that he, our pilot and interpreter through the wilderness of Russia, knew but little more of Russian than we did ourselves. He could ask for post-horses and the ordinary necessaries of life, count money, &c. but could not support a connected conversation, nor speak nor understand a long sentence. This changed our suspicions of his honesty into admiration of his impudence; but, in the mean time, when he discharged us, we should have been rather destitute if it had not been for the servant of a Russian traveller, who spoke French, and, taking our direction from him, we mounted a drosky and rode to the office of the diligence, which was situated in the Podolsk or lower town, and at which we found ourselves particularly well received by the proprietor. He said that the attempt to run a diligence was discouraging; that he had advertised two weeks, and had not booked a single passenger; but, if he could get two, he was determined to try the experiment. We examined the vehicle, which was very large and convenient, and, satisfied that there was no danger of all the places being taken, we left him until we could make an effort to dispose of our carriage. Relieved from all anxiety as to our future movements, we again mounted our drosky. Ascending the hill, we passed the fountain where St. Vladimir baptised the first Russian converts; the spring is held sacred by the Christians now, and a column bearing a cross is erected over it, to commemorate the pious act and the ancient sovereignty of Chioff.

The early history of this city is involved in some obscurity. Its name is supposed to be derived from Kiovi or Kii, a Sarmatian word signifying heights or mountains; and its inhabitants, a Sarmatian tribe, were denominated Kivi, or mountaineers. It is known to have been a place of consequence in the fifth century, when the Suevi, driven from their settlements on the Danube, established themselves here and at Novogorod. In the beginning of the tenth century it was the capital and most celebrated and opulent city in Russia, or in that part of Europe. Boleslaus the Terrible notched upon its "golden gate" his "miraculous sword," called by the monks "The sword of God," and the Poles entered and plundered it of its riches. In the latter part of the same century, the capital of Russia again fell before the conquering arms of the Poles. Kiev was at that time the foster-child of Constantinople and the Eastern empire. The voluptuous Greeks had stored it with all the luxuries of Asia; the noble architecture of Athens was festooned with the gaudy tapestry of Lydia, and the rough metal of Russian swords embossed with the polished gold of Ophir and Persia. Boleslaus II., shut up within the "golden gate" of this city of voluptuousness, quaffed the bowl of pleasure till its intoxicating draught degraded all the nobler energies of his nature. His army of warriors followed his example, and slept away month after month on the soft couches of Kiev; and in the language of the historian, as if they had eaten of the fabled fruit of the lotos-tree, at length forgot that their houses were without masters, their wives without husbands, and their children without parents.

But these tender relations were not in like manner oblivious; and, after seven years of absence, the Poles were roused from their trance of pleasure by the tidings of a revolt among the women at home, who, tired of waiting their return, in revenge gave themselves up to the embraces of their slaves. Burning under the disgrace, the Poles hurried home to wreak their vengeance on wives and paramours; but they met at Warsaw a bloody resistance; the women, maddened by despair, urged on their lovers, many of them fighting in person, and seeking out on the battle-field their faithless husbands; an awful warning to married men!

For a long time Kiev was the prey alternately of the Poles, the Lithuanians, and the Tartars, until in 1686 it was finally ceded by the Poles to Russia. The city is composed of three distinct quarters; the old, with its Polish fortifications, containing the palace of the emperor, and being the court end; the Petcherk fortress, built by Peter the Great, with ditches and high ramparts, and an arsenal capable of containing eighty or a hundred thousand stand of arms; and the Podolsk, or business part, situated at the foot of the hill on the banks of the Dnieper. It contains thirty thousand inhabitants, besides a large military garrison, partly of Cossack troops, and one pretty good hotel; but no beds, and none of those soft couches which made the hardy Poles sleep away their senses; and though a welcome resting-place for a traveller through the wild plains of Russia, it does not now possess any such attraction as to put in peril the faith and duties of husbands. By its position secluded from intercourse with strangers, Kiev is still thoroughly a Russian city, retaining in full force its Asiatic style of architecture; and the old Russian, wedded to the manners and customs of his fathers, clings to it as a place which the hand of improvement has not yet reached; among other relics of the olden time, the long beard still flourishes with the same solemn dignity as in the days of Peter the Great. Lying a hundred miles away from the direct road between Moscow and the Black Sea, few European travellers visit it; and though several of them have done so since, perhaps I was the first American who ever passed through it.

We passed the morning in riding round to the numerous convents and churches, among which is the church of St. Sophia, the oldest in Russia, and, if not an exact model of the great St. Sophia of Constantinople, at least of Byzantine design; and toward evening went to the emperor's garden. This garden is more than a mile in length, bounded on one side by the high precipitous bank of the hill, undulating in its surface, and laid out like an English park with lawn, gravel-walks, and trees; it contains houses of refreshment, arbours, or summer-houses, and a summer theatre. At the foot of the hill flows the Dnieper, the ancient Borysthenes, on which, in former days, the descendants of Odin and Ruric descended to plunder Constantinople. Two or three sloops were lying, as it were, asleep in the lower town, telling of a still interior country, and beyond was a boundless plain covered with a thick forest of trees. The view from this bank was unique and extraordinary, entirely different from anything I ever saw in natural scenery, and resembling more than anything else a boundless marine prospect.

At the entrance of the garden is an open square or table of land overlooking the plain, where, every evening at seven o'clock, the military band plays. The garden is the fashionable promenade, the higher classes resorting to it in carriages and on horseback, and the common people on foot; the display of equipages was not very striking, although there is something stylish in the Russian manner of driving four horses, the leaders with very long traces and a postilion; and soldiers and officers, with their splendid uniforms, caps, and plumes, added a brilliant effect.

Before the music began, all returned from the promenade or drive in the garden, and gathered in the square. It was a beautiful afternoon in June, and the assemblage was unusually large and brilliant; the carriages drew up in a line, the ladies let down the glasses, and the cavaliers dismounted, and talked and flirted with them just as in civilised countries. All Chioff was there, and the peasant in his dirty sheepskin jacket, the shopkeeper with his long surtout and beard, the postilion on his horse, the coachman on his box, the dashing soldier, the haughty noble and supercilious lady, touched by the same chord, forgot their temporal distinctions, and listened to the swelling strains of the music till the last notes died away. The whole mass was then in motion, and in a few moments, except by a few stragglers, of whom I was one, the garden was deserted. At about ten o'clock, I returned to my hotel. We had no beds, and slept in our cloaks on settees stuffed with straw and covered with leather. We had no coverlets; still, after four days and nights in a carriage, it was a luxury to have plenty of kicking room.

CHAPTER XVI.

A lucky Encounter.—Church of the Catacombs.—A Visit to the Saints.—A tender Parting.—Pilgrims.—Rough Treatment.—A Scene of Starvation.—Russian Serfs.—Devotion of the Serfs.—Approach to Moscow.

EARLY in the morning, while I was standing in the yard of the hotel, chaffering with some Jews about the sale of our carriage, an officer in a faded, threadbare uniform, with two or three ribands at his button-hole, and stars sparkling on his breast, came up, and, taking me by the hand, told me, in capital English, that he had just heard of the arrival of two English gentlemen, and had hurried down to see them; that he was a great admirer of the English, and happy to have an opportunity, in the interior of his own country, to show its hospitalities to the natives of the Island Queen. At the risk of losing the benefit of his attentions, I was obliged to disclaim my supposed English character, and to publish, in the heart of a grinding despotism, that I was a citizen of a free republic. Nor did I suffer for my candour; for, by one of those strange vagaries which sometimes happen, we cannot tell how or why, this officer in the service of Russia had long looked to America and her republican government as the perfection of an ideal system. He was in Chioff only by accident. Wounded in the last campaign against the Turks, he had taken up his abode at Ismail, where, upon his pension and a pittance of his own, he was able to live respectably as a poor officer. With no friends or connexions, and no society at Ismail, his head seemed to have run principally upon two things, apparently having no connexion with each other, but intimately connected in his mind, viz., the British possessions in India and the United States of America; and the cord that bound them together was the wide diffusion of the English language by means of these powerful agents. He told me more than I ever knew of the constitution and government of the East India Company, and their plan of operations; and, in regard to our own country, his knowledge was astonishing; he knew the names and character, and talked familiarly of all our principal men, from the time of Washington to the present day; had read all our standard works, and was far more familiar with those of Franklin, Irving, &c., than I was; in short, he told me that he had read every American book, pamphlet, or paper he could lay his hands on; and so intimate was his knowledge of detail, that he mentioned Chestnut-street by name as one of the principal streets in Philadelphia. It may be supposed that I was not sorry to meet such a man in the heart of Russia. He devoted himself to us, and seldom left us, except at night, until we left the city.

After breakfast, accompanied by our new friend with as unpronounceable a name as the best in Russia, we visited the catacombs of the Petcherskoi monastery. I have before remarked that Chioff is the holy city of the Russians, and the crowds of pilgrims we met at every turn in the streets constantly reminded us that this was the great season of the pilgrimage. I was but imperfectly acquainted with the Russian character, but in no one particular had I been so ignorant as in regard to their religious impressions. I had seen Italian, Greek, and Turkish devotees, but the Russian surpassed them all; and, though deriving their religion from strangers, they exceed the punctilious Greeks themselves in the observance of its minutest forms. Censurable, indeed, would he be considered who should pass, in city or in highway, the figure of the cross, the image of the Virgin, or any of the numerous family of saints, without taking off his hat and making on his breast the sacred sign of the cross; and in a city like Chioff, where every turn presents some new object claiming their worship, the eyes of our drosky boy were rapidly turning from one side to the other, and his hand was almost constantly in a quiet mechanical motion.

The Church of the Catacombs, or the Cathedral of the Assumption, attached to the monastery, stands a little out of the city, on the banks of the Dnieper. It was founded in ten hundred and seventy-three, and has seven golden domes with golden spires, and chains connecting them. The dome of the belfry, which rises above the hill to the height of about three hundred feet, and above the Dnieper to that of five hundred and eighty-six, is considered by the Russians a chef-d'œuvre of architecture. It is adorned with Doric and Ionic columns and Corinthian pilasters; the whole interior bears the venerable garb of antiquity, and is richly ornamented with gold, silver, and precious stones and paintings; indeed, it is altogether very far superior to any Greek church I had then seen.

In the immense catacombs under the monastery lie the unburied bodies of the Russian saints, and year after year thousands and tens of thousands come from the wilds of Siberia and the confines of Tartary to kneel at their feet and pray. In one of the porches of the church we bought wax tapers, and, with a long procession of pilgrims, bareheaded and with lighted tapers in our hands, descended a long wooden staircase to the mouth of the catacomb. On each side along the staircase was ranged a line of kneeling devotees, of the same miserable description I had so often seen about the churches in Italy and Greece. Entering the excavated passages of the catacombs, the roof of which was black from the smoke of candles, we saw on each side, in niches in the walls, and in open coffins, enveloped in wrappers of cloth and silk, ornamented with gold and silver, the bodies of the Russian saints. These saints are persons who have led particularly pure and holy lives, and by reason thereof have ascended into heaven, where they are supposed to exercise an influence with the Father and Son; and their bodies are left unburied that their brethren may come to them for intercession, and, seeing their honours after death, study to imitate them in the purity of their lives. The bodies are laid in open coffins, with the stiffened hands so placed as to receive the kisses of pilgrims, and on their breasts are written their names, and sometimes a history of their virtuous actions. But we saw there other and worse things than these, monuments of wild and desperate fanaticism; for besides the bodies of saints who had died at God's appointed time, in one passage is a range of small windows, where men had with their own hands built themselves in with stones against the wall, leaving open only a small hole by which to receive their food; and died with the impious thought that they were doing their Maker good service. These little windows close their dwelling and their tomb; and the devoted Russian, while he kneels before them, believes that their unnatural death has purchased for them everlasting life, and place and power among the spirits of the blessed.

We wandered a long time in this extraordinary burial-place, everywhere strewed with the kneeling figures of praying pilgrims. At every turn we saw hundreds from the farthest parts of the immense empire of Russia; perhaps at that time more than three thousand were wandering in these sepulchral chambers.

The last scene I shall never forget. More than a hundred were assembled in a little chapel, around which were arranged the bodies of men who had died in peculiar sanctity. All were kneeling on the rocky floor, an old priest, with a long white beard streaming down his breast, was in the midst of them, and all there, even to the little children, were listening with rapt attention, as if he were preaching to them matters of eternal moment. There was no hypocrisy or want of faith in that vast sepulchre; surrounded by their sainted dead, they were searching their way to everlasting life, and in all honesty believed that they saw the way before them. We ascended once more to the regions of upper air, and stopped a few moments in the courtyard of the monastery, where the beggar pilgrims were eating the hard bread distributed to them by the monks from the bounty of government. No man seemed more relieved than the major. He was a liberal in religion as well as in politics, but he crossed himself everywhere most devoutly, to avoid, as he said, offending the prejudices of his countrymen, though once he rather scandalised a group of pilgrims by cross-questioning a monk about a new saint, who seemed to be receiving more than a usual share of veneration, and who, he said, had been canonised since he was there last.

But there is a time for all things, and nothing is more absolutely fixed by nature's laws than time for dinner. Almost at the first moment of our acquaintance the major had told me of an engraving representing a scene in New York, which was to be found at a second or third-rate hotel, and I proposed to him, in compliment to the honest publican who had the good taste to have such a picture in his house, to go there and dine. We went, and in a large room, something like a bar-room in our hotels, saw on one of the walls, in a black wooden frame, a gaudy and staring engraving representing the pulling down of the statue of George the Second in the Bowling Green. The Bowling Green was associated with my earliest recollections. It had been my playground when a boy; hundreds of times I had climbed over its fence for my ball, and I was one of a band of boys who held on to it long after the corporation invaded our rights. Captain Cook mentions the effect produced upon his crew by finding at one of the savage islands he visited a silver spoon marked "London;" my feelings were, in a small way, of the same nature. The grouping of the picture was rude and grotesque, the ringleader being a long negro stripped to his trousers, and straining with all his might upon a rope, one end of which was fastened to the head of the statue, and the other tied around his own waist, his white teeth and the whites of his eyes being particularly conspicuous on a heavy ground of black. It was a poor specimen of art, but it was a home scene, we drew up our table opposite the picture, and here, in the very head-quarters of despotism, I found a liberal spirit in an officer wearing the uniform of the autocrat, who pledged me in the toast, "Success to liberty throughout the world."

I had another occupation, which savoured more of home, and served to keep my faculties from rusting; and that was the sale of our carriage. We had made a calculation, and found that it would be cheaper, to say nothing of other advantages, to give it away, and take the diligence to Moscow, than go on posting. We accordingly offered it for sale, and every time we returned to the house found a group of Jews examining it. The poor thing found no favour in their eyes; they told us that we had been riding in it at peril of our lives; that we might be thankful it had not broken down on the road; and, in short, that it was worth nothing except for old iron, and for that it was worth forty-five rubles, or about nine dollars. We could not stand this. It had cost us one hundred and forty less than a week before, was cheap at that, and as good now as when we bought it. On the eve of departure, therefore, we offered it to our landlord for three days' board; but the old Turk (he was a Jew turned Christian, and in his regenerated worse than his natural state) refused our offer, thinking that we would go away and leave it on his hands. But we resolved to burn it first; and while hesitating about offering it to our friend the major, he relieved us from all delicacy by telling us that he did not want it, and had no horses to put to it; to save us from imposition, he would willingly give us the full value, but he was not worth the money. He had, however, a piece of fifty rubles, or about ten dollars, in his pocket, and, if we would take that, he would keep the carriage as a souvenir. We gladly accepted his offer, and had the satisfaction of finding that we had grievously disappointed both the Jews and our landlord.

In the morning the proprietor of the diligence, learning that we had sold our vehicle, raised the price of places fifty rubles a-piece ; the major heard of it, and insisted upon our taking back the carriage, when the proprietor took another tone, talked of the expense of sending his huge vehicle with only two passengers, and we listened and assented. We started to accompany him, and just at the door of the hotel saw two runaway horses coming furiously down the street with a drosky, and an officer entangled and dragging on the ground. We picked him up and carried him into the hotel. He was a noble-looking man, who but a few minutes before had attracted my attention by his proud and manly bearing, now a miserable mangled object, his clothes torn, his plume soiled with mud, and his face covered with dust and blood, and, when we left it was uncertain whether he would live or die.

The major accompanied us to the office of the diligence, and our parting was rather tender ; he rubbed his mustache on both my cheeks, wrote his name in my memorandum-book, and I gave him my address ; he said that our visit had been an interlude relieving the dull monotony of his life ; that we were going to new scenes, and would soon forget him, but he would not forget us. Nor shall I forget him, although it is not probable that he and I will ever meet again.

We took our seats in the diligence for Moscow, and set off with an uncommon degree of satisfaction at having got rid of posting and of Henri, and, with them, of all our troubles. We had nothing to do, no wrangling with postmasters, no cheating to undergo from Jews, and were in that happy state which made the honest Hibernian indifferent to an upset or a breakdown ; that is to say, we were merely passengers. With great pomp and circumstance we drove through the principal streets, to advise the Knickerbockers of Chioff of the actual departure of the long-talked-of diligence, the conducteur sounding his trumpet, and the people stopping in the streets and running to the doors to see the extraordinary spectacle.

We descended the long wooden road to the river, and crossed the Dnieper on a bridge about half a mile long. On the opposite bank I turned for the last time to the sacred city, and I never saw anything more unique and strikingly beautiful than the high, commanding position of " this city on a hill," crowned with its golden cupolas and domes, that reflected the sun with dazzling brightness.

For a short distance the country was rather undulating, but soon settled into the regular steppe. We rolled on all day without anything to annoy us or even to interest us, except processions of pilgrims on their way to Chioff. They travelled on foot in bands of one or two hundred, men, women and children, headed by a white-bearded monk, barefooted, and leaning on a staff. During the night I was roused by a loud chant, and looking out, saw a group of more than a hundred pilgrims gathered round a fire, with an old monk in the midst of them, breaking the stillness of the night with songs of devotion ; and all the night long as we rode swiftly by, I saw by the bright moonlight groups of forty, fifty, or a hundred lying by the roadside asleep under the trees. More than fifty thousand pilgrims that year visited the catacombs of Kiev, coming from every part of the immense empire of Russia, and many from Kamtschatka and the most distant region of Siberia, performing the whole journey on foot, seldom sleeping under a roof, and living upon the precarious charity of the miserable peasants on the road. I have since seen the gathering of pilgrims at Jerusalem, and the whole body moving together from the gates of the city to bathe in the Jordan, and I have seen the great caravan of forty thousand true believers tracking their desolate way through the deserts of Arabia to the tomb of the Prophet at Mecca ; but I remember, as if they were before me now, the groups of Russian pilgrims strewed along the road and sleeping under the pale moonlight, the bare earth their bed, the heavens their only covering.

In the morning we stopped at a little town, where the posthouse had in front four Corinthian columns, supporting a balcony. Inside, mats were placed against the broken windows, the walls were rough logs, the floor of mud, with pigs and children disputing its possession, and the master and mistress stood in special need of the purifying influence of a Russian bath. We brought the tea-urn out on the balcony, and had a cow brought up and milked in our presence. After breakfast we lighted our pipes and strolled up the street. At the upper end, an old man in a civil uniform hailed us from the opposite side, and crossed over to meet us ; supposing him to be some dignitary disposed to show us the civilities of the town, we waited to receive him with all becoming respect ; but, as he approached, were rather startled by the loud tone of his voice and the angry expression of his face, and more so when, as soon as within reach, he gave my pipe-stick a severe rap with his cane, which knocked it out of my mouth, broke the bowl and scattered the contents on the ground. I picked up the stick, and should, perhaps, have laid it over his head but for his grey hairs ; and my companion, seeing him tread out the sparks of fire, recollected that there was a severe penalty in Russia against smoking in the streets. The houses are all of wood ; whole villages and towns are often burned down at once, and probably the old man had begun by a civil intimation to that effect ; but, indignant at my quietly smoking in his face, had used more summary measures. He was in a perfect fury ; and calling at the top of his voice to a man up the street, the latter went off with such a suspicious looking-for-a-police-officer movement, that we hurried back to the diligence, which happened to be ready and waiting for us, and started from the town on a full run.

That night, in a miserable posthouse in a miserable village, we found an old billiard-table. It seemed strangely out of place, and I had a great curiosity to know how it had found its way there ; but it was twelve o'clock, and all were asleep but the postilion. I can give no account of the rest of the night's work, I had a large cushioned seat of the diligence to myself, certainly the softest bed I had yet had in Russia ; and when I put my feet out of the window, it was so comfortable that I felt myself in some danger of falling into luxurious habits.

At daylight we arrived in a large village, the

inhabitants of which were not yet stirring, and the streets were strewed with peasants, grim, yellow-bearded fellows, in sheep-skin dresses and caps, lying on their backs asleep, each of them with a log of wood under his head for a pillow. I descended from the diligence, and found that the whole village consisted of a single street, with log-houses on each side, having their gable ends in front; the doors were all open, and I looked in and saw men and women with all their clothes on, pigs, sheep, and children, strewed about the floor.

In every house was the image of the Panagia, or all-holy Virgin, or the picture of some tutelary saint, the face only visible, the rest covered with a tin frame, with a lamp or taper burning before it; and regularly as the serf rose he prostrated himself, and made his orisons at this domestic shrine.

About noon we passed the chateau and grounds of a seigneur; belonging to the chateau was a large church standing in a conspicuous situation, with a green dome, surmounted by the Greek cross; and round it were the miserable and filthy habitations of his slaves. Entering the village, we saw a spectacle of wretchedness and misery seldom surpassed even on the banks of the Nile. The whole population was gathered in the streets, in a state of absolute starvation. The miserable serfs had not raised enough to supply themselves with food, and men of all ages, half-grown boys, and little children, were prowling the streets or sitting in the door-ways, ravenous with hunger, and waiting for the agent to come down from the chateau and distribute among them bread. I had found in Russia many interesting subjects of comparison between that country and my own, but it was with deep humiliation I felt that the most odious feature in that despotic government found a parallel in ours. At this day, with the exception of Russia, some of the West India Islands, and the republic of the United States, every country in the civilised world can respond to the proud boast of the English common law, that the moment a slave sets foot on her soil he is free. I respect the feelings of others and their vested rights, and would be the last to suffer those feelings or those rights to be wantonly violated; but I do not hesitate to say that, abroad, slavery stands as a dark blot upon our national character. There it will not admit of any palliation; it stands in glaring contrast with the spirit of our free institutions; it belies our words and our hearts; and the American who would be most prompt to repel any calumny upon his country withers under this reproach, and writhes with mortification when the taunt is hurled at the otherwise stainless flag of the free republic. I was forcibly struck with a parallel between the white serfs of the north of Europe and African bondsmen at home. The Russian boor, generally wanting the comforts which are supplied to the negro on our best ordered plantations, appeared to me to be not less degraded in intellect, character, and personal bearing. Indeed the marks of physical and personal degradation were so strong, that I was insensibly compelled to abandon certain theories not uncommon among my countrymen at home, in regard to the intrinsic superiority of the white race over all others. Perhaps, too, this impression was aided by my having previously met with Africans of intelligence and capacity, standing upon a footing of perfect equality as soldiers and officers in the Greek army and the soltan's.

The serfs of Russia differ from slaves with us in the important particular that they belong to the soil, and cannot be sold except with the estate; they may change masters, but cannot be torn from their connexions or their birth-place. One sixth of the whole peasantry of Russia, amounting to six or seven millions, belong to the crown, and inhabit the imperial demesne, and pay an annual tax. In particular districts, many have been enfranchised, and become burghers and merchants; and the liberal and enlightened policy of the present emperor is diffusing a more general system of melioration among these subjects of his vast empire. The rest of the serfs belong to the nobles, and are the absolute property and subject to the absolute control of their masters, as much as the cattle on their estates. Some of the seigneurs possess from seventy to more than a hundred thousand; and their wealth depends upon the skill and management with which the labour of these serfs is employed. Sometimes the seigneur sends the most intelligent to Petersburgh or Moscow to learn some handicraft, and then employs them on his own estates, hires them out, or allows them to exercise their trade on their own account, on payment of an annual sum. And sometimes, too, he gives the serf a passport, under which he is protected all over Russia, settles in a city, and engages in trade, and very often accumulates enough to ransom himself and his family. Indeed, there are many instances of a serf's acquiring a large property, and even rising to eminence. But he is always subject to the control of his master; and I saw at Moscow an old mougik who had acquired a very large fortune, but was still a slave. His master's price for his freedom had advanced with his growing wealth, and the poor serf, unable to bring himself to part with his hard earnings, was then rolling in wealth with a collar round his neck; struggling with the inborn spirit of freedom, and hesitating whether to die a beggar or a slave.

The Russian serf is obliged to work for his master but three days in the week; the other three he may work for himself on a portion of land assigned to him by law on his master's estate. He is never obliged to work on Sunday, and every saint's day or fête day of the church is a holiday. This might be supposed to give him an opportunity of elevating his character and condition; but wanting the spirit of a free agent, and feeling himself the absolute property of another, he labours grudgingly for his master, and for himself barely enough to supply the rudest necessaries of life and pay his tax to the seigneur. A few rise above their condition, but millions labour like beasts of burden, content with bread to put in their mouths, and never even thinking of freedom. A Russian nobleman told me that he believed, if the serfs were all free, he could cultivate his estate to better advantage by hired labour; and I have no doubt a dozen Connecticut men would cultivate more ground than a hundred Russian serfs, allowing their usual non-working days and holidays. They have no interest in the soil, and the desolate and uncultivated wastes of Russia show the truth of the judicious reflection of Catharine II., "that agriculture can never flourish in that nation where the husbandman possesses no property."

It is from this great body of peasantry that Russia recruits her immense standing army, or, in case of invasion, raises in a moment a vast body of soldiers. Every person in Russia entitled to hold land is known to the government, as well as the number of peasants on his estate; and, upon receiving notice of an imperial order to that effect, the numbers required by the levy are marched forthwith from every part of the empire to the places of rendezvous appointed. It might be asked, What have these men to fight for? They have no country, and are brought up on immense levels, wanting the rocks, rivers, and mountains that inspire local attachments. It is a singular fact, that, with the Russian serf, there is always an unbounded love for him who stands at the head of the system of oppression under which they groan, the emperor whom they regard as their protector against the oppression of their immediate masters; but to whatever cause it may be ascribed, whether inability to estimate the value of any change in their condition, or a feeling of actual love for the soil on which they were born, during the invasion of Napoleon the serfs of Russia presented a noble spectacle; and the spirit of devotion which animated the corps of ten thousand in the north extended to the utmost bounds of the empire. They received orders to march from St. Petersburgh to meet the advance of the French army; the emperor reviewed them, and is said to have shed tears at their departure. Arrived at the place appointed, Witgenstein ordered them to fall back to a certain point, but they answered "No; the last promise we made the emperor our father was, that we would never fly before the enemy, and we keep our word." Eight thousand of their number died on the spot; and the spirit which animated them fired the serfs throughout the whole empire. The scholar may sneer, but I defy him to point to a nobler page in Grecian or Roman history.

I shall make amends for this long discussion by hurrying on to Moscow. We rode hundreds of miles without meeting a hill; the country was bare of trees, and almost everywhere presenting the same appearance. We saw the first disk of the sun peeping out of the earth, watched it while soaring on its daily round, and, without a bush to obstruct the view, saw it sink below the horizon; and woke up at all times of night and saw the stars

"Rolling like living cars of light
For gods to journey by."

The principal and only large towns on our road were Orel and Toula, the former containing a population of four or five thousand, and presenting an imposing display of churches and monasteries gaudily painted and with gilded domes; the houses were principally of wood, painted yellow. Toula is the largest manufacturing town, and is called the Sheffield of Russia, being particularly celebrated for its cutlery. Everywhere the diligence created a great sensation; the knowing ones said it would never do; but at Orel one spirited individual said if we would wait three days for him he would go on with us. It can hardly seem credible, in our steam-boat and railroad community, that a public conveyance could roll on for seven days and nights, through many villages and towns, toward the capital of an immense empire, and not take in a single way-passenger; but such was the fact; and on the morning of the seventh day, alone as we started from Chioff, we were approaching the burned and rebuilt capital of the czars, Moscow, with gilded cupolas, the holy Moscow, the sanctified city, the Jerusalem of Russia beloved of God, and dear to men.

CHAPTER XVII.

Moscow.—A severe Operation.—An Exile by Accident.—Meeting with an Emigré.—A civil Stranger.—A Spy.—The Kremlin.—Sepulchres of the Czars.—The great Bell.—The great Gun.—Precious Relics.

At daylight we arrived at the last post; and here, for the first time, we saw evidences of our approach to a great city. Four or five travelling-carriages were waiting for horses, some of which had been waiting all night; but our diligence being a "public accommodation," we were preferred, and had the first that came in. We took our places for the last time in the diligence, and passed two or three fine chateaux, our curiosity and interest increasing as we approached, until, at about five versts from Moscow, as we reached the summit of a gentle eminence, the whole city broke upon us at one view, situated in the midst of a great plain, and covering an extent of more than thirty versts. Moscow is emphatically the city of churches, containing more than six hundred, many of which have five or six domes, with steeples, and spires, and crosses, gilded and connected together with golden chains like those of Chioff. Its convents, too, are almost innumerable, rivalling the churches in size and magnificence, and even to us, coming directly from the capital of the Eastern empire, presenting a most striking and extraordinary appearance. As we passed the barrier, two of the most conspicuous objects on each side were the large Greek convents, enclosed by high walls, with noble trees growing above them; and as we rode through the wide and showy streets, the first thing that struck me as strange, and, in this inhospitable climate (always associated in my mind with rude and wintry scenes), as singularly beautiful, was the profusion of plants and flowers, with the remarkable degree of taste and attention given to their cultivation. In Greece and Turkey I had seen the rarest plants and flowers literally "wasting their sweetness on the desert air;" while here, in the heart of an inhospitable country, every house had a court-yard or garden, and in front a light open portico or veranda, ornamented with plants, and shrubs, and flowers, forced into a glowing though unnatural beauty. The whole appearance of the city is Asiatic; and as the exhibition of flowers in front of the better class of houses was almost universal, Moscow seemed basking in the mild climate of Southern Asia, rioting in its brief period of vernal existence, and forgetting that, in a few weeks, a frost would come and cover their beauty with the dreary drapery of winter.

At the office of the diligence my companion and myself separated. He went to an hotel kept by an English woman, with English company, and I believe, too, with English comfort, and I rode to the *Hôtel Germanico*, an old and favourite stopping-place with the Russian seigneurs when they come up from their estates in the country. Having secured my room, I mounted a drusky and hurried to a bath. Riding out to the suburbs, the drusky boy stopped at a large wooden building, pouring forth steam from every chink and crevice. At the entrance stood several half-naked men, one of whom led me to an apartment to undress, and then conducted me to another, in one end of which were a furnace and apparatus for generating steam. I was then familiar with the Turkish bath, but the worst I had known was like the breath of the gentle south wind compared with the heat of this apartment. The operator stood me in the middle of the floor, opened the upper door of the stove, and dashed into it a bucketful of water, which sent forth volumes of steam like a thick fog into every part of the room, and then laid me down on a platform about three feet high and rubbed my body with a mop dipped in soap and hot water : then he raised me up, and deluged me with hot water, pouring several tubfuls on my head ; then laid me down again, and scrubbed me with soap and water from my head to my heels, long enough, if the thing were possible, to make a blackamoor white ; then gave me another sousing with hot water, and another scrubbing with pure water, and then conducted me up a flight of steps to a high platform, stretched me out on a bench within a few feet of the ceiling, and commenced whipping me with twigs of birch, with the leaves on them, dipped in hot water. It was as hot as an oven where he laid me down on the bench ; the vapour, which almost suffocated me below, ascended to the ceiling, and, finding no avenue of escape, gathered round my devoted body, fairly scalding and blistering me ; and when I removed my hands from my face, I felt as if I had carried away my whole profile. I tried to hold out to the end, but I was burning, scorching, and consuming. In agony I cried out to my tormentor to let me up ; but he did not understand me, or was loath to let me go, and kept thrashing me with the bunch of twigs until, perfectly desperate, I sprang off the bench, tumbled him over, and descended to the floor. Snow, snow, a region of eternal snow seemed paradise ; but my tormentor had not done with me ; and, as I was hurrying to the door, he dashed over me a tub of cold water. I was so hot that it seemed to hiss as it touched me ; he came at me with another, and at that moment I could imagine, what had always seemed a traveller's story, the high satisfaction and perfect safety with which the Russian in mid-winter rushes from his hot-bath and rolls himself in the snow. The grim features of my tormentor relaxed as he saw the change that came over me. I withdrew to my dressing-room, dozed an hour on the settee, and went out a new man. In half an hour I stood in the palace of the czars, within the walls of the Kremlin.

Toward evening I returned to my hotel. In all the large hotels in Russia, it is the custom for every man to dine in his own apartment. Travelling alone, I always avoided this when I could, as, besides my dislike of the thing itself, it prevented my making acquaintances and acquiring such information as I needed in a strange city ; and I was particularly averse to dine alone the first day of my arrival at Moscow ; but it was the etiquette of the house to do so, and as I had a letter of introduction which I intended to deliver, from Count Woronzow to Prince Galitzin, the governor of Moscow, I was bound to make some sacrifice for the credit of my acquaintance. After the table was spread, however, finding it too severe a trial, I went down stairs and invited myself to dine with my landlord. He was a German of about fifty-five or sixty, tall, stout, with grey hair, a frank, manly expression, and great respectability of appearance and manners ; and before the dinner was over I regarded him emphatically as what a Frenchman would call *un brave homme.* He had been in Russia during the whole of the French invasion, and among the other incidents of a stirring life, had been sent in exile to Siberia ; and the curious part of it was, that he was sent there by mistake. Rather an awkward mistake, though, as he said, not so bad as being knouted or hanged by mistake ; and in his case it turned out a rather interesting adventure. He was taken by the French as a Russian spy, and retaken by the Russians as a French spy, when, as he said, he did not care a fig for either of them. He was hurried off to Siberia, but on the journey succeeded in convincing the officer who escorted the prisoners that there was an error in the case, and on his arrival was merely detained in exile, without being put to hard labour, until, through the medium of friends, he had the matter brought before the proper tribunal, and the mistake corrected, when he came back post, in company with a Russian officer, smoking his pipe all the way, at the expense of the government. He gave me many interesting particulars in regard to that celebrated country, its mines, the sufferings of the noble exiles ; and much, also, that was new to me, touching its populousness and wealth, and the comfort and luxury of a residence there. He spoke of Tobolsk as a large, gay, and populous city, containing hotels, theatres, and all kinds of places of amusement. The exiles, being many of them of rank, have introduced there all the luxuries of the capital, and life at Tobolsk is much the same as life at Moscow.

As the rage for travelling is excited by hearing from the lips of a traveller stories of the countries he has visited, before the dinner was over I found myself infected with a strong disposition for a journey to Siberia. Small matters, however, produce great changes in the current of a man's feelings, and in a few moments I had entirely forgotten Siberia, and was carried directly home. While we were smoking our pipes, an old gentleman entered, of singularly aristocratic appearance, whom my host received with the greatest consideration and respect, addressing him as the Marquis de P——. He was a Frenchman, an old *militaire,* and a noble specimen of a race almost extinct ; tall, thin, and grey-headed, wearing a double-breasted blue frockcoat, buttoned up to the throat, with a cane in his hand, and a red riband in his button-hole, the decoration of the Knights of Malta ; and when my host introduced me as an American traveller arrived that day in Moscow, he welcomed me with more than the usual forms of courtesy, and told me that, far off as it was, and little as he knew of it, he almost regarded America as his own country ; that, on the downfall of "the emperor," and in a season of universal scattering, some of his nearest relatives, particularly a sister married to a fellow-soldier and his dearest friend, had taken refuge on the other side of the Atlantic; that, eighteen years before, he had met an American secretary of legation who knew them, but since that time he had not heard from them, and did not know whether they were living or dead. I asked him the name, with very little expectation of being able to give him any information about them; and it was with no small degree of pleasure that I found I was particularly acquainted with the condition of his relatives. His brother-in-law and old comrade was dead, but I brought him a satisfaction to which he had long been a stranger, by telling him that his sister was still living, occupying a large property in a neighbouring state, surrounded by a family of children, in character and standing, ranking among the first in our country. They were intimately connected with the family of one of my most intimate friends, letters to and from different members of which had very often passed through my hands; I knew the names of all his nieces, and personally one of his nephews, a lieutenant, and one of the most promising officers in our navy; and about a year before I had accompanied the friends to whom I refer on a visit to these relatives. At Philadelphia I left them under the charge of the lieutenant; and on my return from Washington, according to agreement, the lieutenant came down to an intersecting point on the rail-road to take me home with him; but circumstances prevented my going, and much as I regretted my disappointment then, I regretted it far more now, as otherwise I might have gladdened the old man's heart by telling him that within a year I had seen his sister. His own history was brief. Born to the possession of rank and fortune, and having won honours and decorations by long service in the field, and risen to the rank of inspector-general in the army of Napoleon, he was taken in the campaign against Russia in 1813, and sent a prisoner of war to Moscow, where he had remained ever since. Immediately on their arrival, his brother-in-law and sister had written to him from America, telling him that, with the wreck of their fortune, they had purchased a large landed estate, and begging him to come over and share their abundance; but, as he told me, he scorned to eat the bread of idleness and dependence; manfully turned to account the advantages of an accomplished education; and now, at the advanced age of seventy-eight, sustained himself by his pencil, an honoured guest at every table, and respected by the most distinguished inhabitants of Moscow. He had accidentally given up his rooms a few days before, and was residing temporarily at the same hotel with myself. He was much agitated by this unexpected intelligence from friends he never expected to hear of more, and left me with a promise to call upon me early in the morning.

Too much interested myself to go back to Siberia with my host, I went to the French theatre. The play was some little every-day thing, and the house but thinly attended. I took my seat in the pit, which was on a dead level, instead of ascending from the stage, containing large cushioned seats, and sprinkled with officers talking with ladies in the boxes above. At the end of the first act, as whole benches were empty above me, I moved up to put myself nearer a pair of bright eyes that were beaming from the box upon a pair of epaulettes below. I was hardly seated before one of the understrappers came up and whispered, or rather muttered, something in my ear. As I did not understand a word he said, and his manner was exceedingly rude and ungracious, I turned my back upon him and looked at the lady with the bright eyes. The fellow continued muttering in my ear, and I began to be seriously annoyed and indignant, when a Frenchman sitting two or three benches behind me came up, and, in an imperious tone, ordered him away. He then cursed the Russians as a set of canaille, from the greatest seigneurs to the lowest serf; remarked that he saw I was a stranger, and, with the easy freedom of a man of the world, took a seat by my side. He was above six feet high, about thirty-three or thirty-four years of age, in robust health, with a large pair of whiskers, rather overdressed, and of manners good, though somewhat imperious and bordering on the swagger. He seemed perfectly at home in the theatre; knew all the actors, and before the evening was over, offered to introduce me to all the actresses. I was under obligations to him, if not for the last offer, at least for relieving me from the impertinent doorkeeper; and, when the curtain fell, accepted his invitation to go to a restaurant and take a petit souper. I accompanied him to the Restaurant au coin du pont des Mareschaux, which I afterward ascertained to be the first in Moscow. He was perfectly at home with the carte, knew exactly what to order, and, in fact, he was a man of great general information, perfectly familiar with all continental Europe, geographically and politically, and particularly at home in Moscow; and he offered his services in showing me all that was curious and interesting. We sat together more than two hours, and in our rambling and discursive conversation I could not help remarking that he seemed particularly fond of railing at the government, its tyranny and despotism, and appealing to me as an American and a liberal, to sustain him. I did not think anything of it then, though in a soldier under Charles the Tenth, driven out, as he said, by the revolution of July, it was rather strange; but, at any rate, either from a spirit of contradiction, or because I had really a good feeling toward everything in Russia, I disagreed with him throughout; he took upon himself the whole honours of the entertainment, scolded the servants, called in the landlord, and, as I observed, after a few words with him, went out without paying. I saw that the landlord knew him, and that there was something constrained and peculiar in his behaviour. I must confess, however, that I did not notice these things at the time so clearly as when I was induced to recur to them by after circumstances, for we went out of the house the best friends in the world; and, as it was then raining, we took a drosky and rode home together, with our arms round each other's neck, and my cloak thrown over us both. About two o'clock, in a heavy rain, I stopped at my hotel, bade him good night, and lent him my cloak to go home with.

The reader, perhaps, smiles at my simplicity, but he is wrong in his conjecture; my cloak came home the next morning, and was my companion and only covering many a night afterward. My friend followed it, sat with me a few minutes, and was taking his departure, having made an appointment to call for me at twelve o'clock, when there was a knock at the door, and my friend the marquis entered. I presented them to each other, and the latter was in the act of bending his body with the formality of a gentleman of the old school, when he caught a full view of my friend of the theatre, and, breaking off his unfinished bow, recovered his erect position, and staring from him to me, and from me to him, seemed to demand an explanation. I had no explanation to give, nor had my friend, who, cocking his hat on one side, and brushing by the marquis with more than his usual swagger, stamped down stairs. The marquis looked after him till he was at the foot of the stairs, and then turning to me, asked how, in the name of wonder, I had already contrived to pick up such an acquaintance. I told him the history of our meeting at the theatre, our supper at the restaurant, and our loving ride home, to which he listened with breathless attention; and after making me tax my memory for the particulars of the conversation at the restaurant, told me that my friend was a disgrace to his country; that he had, no doubt, been obliged to leave France for some rascality, and was now entertained by the emperor of Russia as a *spy*, particularly upon his own countrymen; that he was well fed and clothed, and had the entrée of all the theatres and public houses without paying. With the earnestness of a man long used to a despotic government, and to seeing slight offences visited with terrible punishments, the marquis congratulated me upon not having fallen into what he called the snare laid for me.

It is almost impossible for an American to believe that even in Russia he incurs any risk in speaking what he thinks; he is apt to regard the stories of summary punishment for freedom of speech as bugbears or by-gone things. In my own case, even when men looked cautiously around the room and then spoke in whispers, I could not believe that there was any danger. Still I had become prudent enough not to talk with any unnecessary indiscretion of the constituted authorities, and, even in writing home to my friends, not to say any thing that could prejudice me if the letter should fall into wrong hands; and now, although I did not consider that I had run any great risk, I was rather pleased that I had said nothing exceptionable; and though I had no apprehension, particularly since I had been put on my guard, I determined to drop my new acquaintance, and did not consider myself bound to observe any great courtesy in the mode of doing it. I had had a supper, which it was my original intention to return with a dinner; but I did not consider myself under any obligation to him for civilities shown in the exercise of his despicable calling. The first time I met him I made no apology for having been out when he called according to appointment, and did not ask him to come again. I continued to meet him in the streets and at every public place, but our greetings became colder and colder, and the day before I left Moscow we brushed against each other without speaking at all. So much for acquaintances who, after an intimacy of three or four hours, had ridden home under the same cloak, with their arms around each other's neck.

But to return: as soon as the marquis left me I again went to the Kremlin, to me the great, I had almost said the only, object of interest in Moscow. I always detested a cicerone: his bowing, fawning, and prating annoyed me; and all through Italy, with my map and guide-book under my arm, I was in the habit of rambling about alone. I did the same at Moscow, and again walked to the Kremlin unaccompanied. Unlike many of the places I had visited, all the interest I had felt in looking forward to the Kremlin was increased when I stood within its walls. I had thought of it as the rude and barbarous palace of the Czars; but I found it one of the most extraordinary, beautiful, and magnificent objects I ever beheld. I rambled over it several times with admiration, without attempting to comprehend it at all. Its commanding situation on the banks of the Moskwa river; its high and venerable walls; its numerous battlements, towers, and steeples; its magnificent and gorgeous palaces; its cathedrals, churches, monasteries, and belfries, with their gilded, coppered, and tin-plated domes; its mixture of barbarism and decay, magnificence and ruins; its strong contrast of architecture, including the Tartarian, Hindoo, Chinese, and Gothic; and, rising above all, the lofty tower of Ivan Veliki, with its golden ball reflecting the sun with dazzling brilliancy, altogether exhibited a beauty, grandeur, and magnificence strange and indescribable.

The Kremlin is "the heart" and "sacred place" of Moscow, once the old fortress of the Tartars, and now the centre of the modern city. It is nearly triangular in form, enclosed by a high brick wall painted white, and nearly two miles in extent, and is in itself a city. It has five gates, at four of which there are high watch-towers. The fifth is "our Saviour's," or the Holy Gate, through whose awe-commanding portals no male, not even the emperor and autocrat of all the Russias, can pass except with uncovered head and bended body. Bareheaded, I entered by this gate, and passed on to a noble esplanade, commanding one of the most interesting views of Moscow, and having in front the range of palaces of the Czars. I shall not attempt to describe these palaces. They are a combination of every variety of taste and every order of architecture, Grecian, Gothic, Italian, Tartar, and Hindoo, rude, fanciful, grotesque, gorgeous, magnificent, and beautiful. The churches, monasteries, arsenals, museum, and public buildings are erected with no attempt at regularity of design, and in the same wild confusion of architecture. There are no regular streets, but three open places or squares, and abundance of room for carriages and foot-passengers, with which, in summer afternoons, it is always thronged.

Having strolled for some time about the Kremlin, I entered the Cathedral of the Assumption, the most splendid church in Moscow. It was founded in 1325, and rebuilt in 1472. It is loaded with gorgeous and extravagant ornaments. The iconastos, or screen, which divides the sanctuary from the body of the church, is in many parts covered with plates of solid silver and gold, richly and finely wrought. On the walls are painted the images of more than two thousand three hundred saints, some at full length and some of a colossal size, and the whole interior seems illuminated with gold, of which more than two hundred and ten thousand leaves have been employed in embellishing it. From the centre of the roof is suspended a crown of massive silver, with forty-eight chandeliers, all in a single piece, and weighing nearly three thousand pounds. Besides the portraits of saints and martyrs, there are portraits of the old historians, whose names, to prevent confusion, are attached to their resemblances, as Aristotle, Anacharsis, Thucydides, Plutarch, &c. Some of the paintings on wood could not fail to delight an antiquary, inasmuch as every vestige of paint being obliterated, there is abundance of room for speculation as to their age and character. There is also an image of the Virgin, painted by St. Luke's own hand!!! the face dark, almost black, the head encircled with a glory of precious stones, and the hands and the body gilded. It is reverenced for its miraculous powers, guarded with great care, and enclosed within a large silver covering, which is never removed but on great religious festivals, or on payment of a ruble to the verger. Here, too, is a nail from the cross, a robe of our Saviour's, and part of one of the Virgin's!!! And here, too, are the tombs of the church patriarchs, one of whom, St. Phillippe, honoured by a silver monument, dared to say to John the Terrible, "We respect you as an image of the Divinity, but as a man you partake of the dust of the earth."

The Cathedral of the Assumption is honoured as the place where the sovereigns of Russia are crowned, and there is but a step from their throne to their grave, for near it is the Cathedral of the archangel Michael, the ancient burial-place where, in raised sepulchres, lie the bodies of the Czars, from the time when Moscow became the seat of empire until the close of the seventeenth century. The bodies rest in raised tombs or sepulchres, each covered with a velvet pall, and having on it a silver plate, bearing the name of the occupant and the date of his decease. Close by is an odd-looking church, constantly thronged with devotees; a humble structure, said to be the oldest Christian church in Moscow. It was built in the desert, before Moscow was thought of, and its walls are strong enough to last till the gorgeous city shall become a desert again.

After strolling through the churches I ascended the tower of Ivan Veliki, or John the Great, the first of the Czars. It is about two hundred and seventy feet high, and contains thirty-three bells, the smallest weighing seven thousand, and the largest more than one hundred and twenty-four thousand pounds English. On festivals they are all tolled together, the Muscovites being extremely fond of Ivan Veliki's music. This celebrated tower rises above every other object in the Kremlin, and its large gilded dome and cross are conspicuous from every part of the city. From its top I had the finest view of Moscow and the surrounding country, and, perhaps, the finest panoramic view in the world. Hundreds of churches were in sight, with their almost innumerable domes, and spires, and crosses glittering with gold, Tartaric battlements, terraces, balconies, and ramparts, Gothic steeples, Grecian columns, the star, the crescent, and the cross, palaces, mosques, and Tartar temples, pagodas, pavilions, and verandas, monasteries peeping out over high walls and among noble trees, the stream of the Moskwa winding prettily below, and in the distance the Sparrow Hills, on which the French army first made its appearance on the invasion of Moscow. It may seem strange, but I did not feel myself a stranger on the top of that tower. Thousands of miles away I had read its history. I knew that the magnificent city at my feet had been a sheet of fire, and that, when Napoleon fled by the light of its conflagration, a dreadful explosion shook to their foundation the sacred precincts of the Kremlin, and rent from its base to its top the lofty tower of Ivan.

I descended, and the custode conducted me to another well-known object, the great bell, the largest, and the wonder of the world. It is only a short distance from the foot of the tower, in an excavation under ground, accessible by a trap-door, like the covered mouth of a well. I descended by a broken ladder, and can hardly explain to myself the curiosity and interest with which I examined this monstrous piece of metal. I have no knowledge of or taste for mechanics, and no particular penchant for bells, even when spelled with an additional *e*; but I knew all about this one, and it added wonderfully to the interest with which I strolled through the Kremlin, that, from accidental circumstances, I was familiar with every object within its walls. I impeach, no doubt, my classical taste, but, before seeing either, I had dwelt with more interest upon the Kremlin, and knew more of it, than of the Acropolis at Athens; and I stood at the foot of the great bell almost with a feeling of reverence. Its perpendicular height is twenty-one feet four inches, and the extreme thickness of the metal twenty-three inches; the length of the clapper is fourteen feet, the greatest circumference sixty-seven feet four inches, its weight upward of four hundred thousand pounds English, and its cost has been estimated at more than three hundred and sixty-five thousand pounds sterling. There is some question whether this immense bell was ever hung, but it is supposed that it was suspended by a great number of beams and crossbeams; that it was rung by forty or fifty men, one half on either side, who pulled the clapper by means of ropes, and that the sound amazed and deafened the inhabitants. On one side is a crack large enough to admit the figure of a man. I went inside and called aloud, and received an echo like the reverberations of thunder.

Besides the great bell, there is another noisy musical instrument, namely the great gun, like the bell, the largest in the world, being a four thousand three hundred and twenty pounder. It is sixteen feet long, and the diameter of its calibre nearly three feet. I jumped in and turned round in its mouth, and sat upright, my head not reaching the top. All around were planted cannon taken from the French in their unhappy expedition against the capital of Russia; immense field-pieces, whose throats once poured their iron hail against the walls within which they now repose as trophies. I was attracted by a crowd at the door of one of the principal buildings, which I found to be the treasury, containing what a Russian prizes as his birthright, the repository of sacred heirlooms; the door-keeper demanded a permit, and I answered him with rubles and entered the treasury. On the first floor are the ancient imperial carriages; large, heavy, and extraordinary vehicles, covered with carving and gilding, and having large plate-glass windows; among them was an enormous sleigh, carved and profusely gilded, and containing a long table with cushioned seats on each side; all together, these vehicles were most primitive and Asiatic in appearance, and each one had some long and interesting story connected with it.

I ascended by a noble staircase to the *bel étage*, a gallery composed of five parts, in the first of which are the portraits of all the emperors and czars and their wives, in the exact costume of the times in which they lived; in another is a model of a palace projected by the Empress Catharine to unite the whole Kremlin under one roof, having a circumference of two miles, and make of it one magnificent palace; if it had been completed according to the plan, this palace would probably have surpassed the temple of Solomon or any of the seven wonders of the world. In another is a collection of precious relics, such as the crowns worn by the different emperors and Czars, loaded with precious stones; the dresses worn at their marriages; the canopies under which the emperors are married, surmounted by magnificent plumes; two canopies of red velvet, studded with gold, and a throne with two seats. The crown of Prince Vladimir is surmounted by a golden cross, and ornamented with pearls and precious stones, and, until the time of Peter the Great, was used to crown the Czars; the crown of the conquered kingdom of Cazan was placed there by the victorious hands of John Vassilivitch. Besides these were the crowns of the conquered countries of Astrachan and Siberia. That of John Alexius has eight hundred and eighty-one diamonds, and under the cross which surmounts it is an immense ruby. There were also the crown of Peter the Great, containing eight hundred and forty-seven diamonds; that of Catharine the First, his widow, containing two thousand five hundred and thirty-six fine diamonds, to which the Empress Anne added a ruby of enormous size, bought by the Russian ambassador at Pekin; and, lastly, the crown of unhappy Poland! It is of polished gold, surmounted by a cross, but no other ornament. And there were other emblems of royalty: a throne or Greek fauteuil of ivory, in arabesque, presented to John the Great by the ambassadors who accompanied from Rome to Moscow the Princess Sophia, whom he had demanded in marriage. She was the daughter of Thomas Paleologus Porphyrogenitus, brother of Constantine Paleologus, who died in 1453, after seeing his empire fall into the hands of the Turks. By this marriage John considered himself the heir of Constantine, and took the title of Czar, meaning Cæsar (this is one of the derivations of the name), and thus the emperor and autocrat of all the Russias has the fairest claim to the throne of the Cæsars, and, consequently, has always had an eye upon Constantinople. Then there are the throne of Boris, adorned with two thousand seven hundred and sixty turquoises and other precious stones; that of Michel, containing eight thousand eight hundred and twenty-four precious stones; that of Alexius, containing eight hundred and seventy-six diamonds, one thousand two hundred and twenty-four other jewels, and many pearls, bought of a company of merchants trafficking to Ispahan; the throne of the Czars John and Peter, made of massive silver, separated in the middle, the back a cloth of gold, concealing a hole through which the Czarina used to dictate answers to the foreign ambassadors; and, lastly, the throne of Poland!

In the armoury are specimens of ancient armour, the workmanship of every age and nation; coats of mail, sabres adorned with jewels, swords, batons, crosses in armour, imperial robes, ermines in abundance, and, finally, the clothes in which Peter the Great worked at Saardam, including his old boots, from which it appears that he had a considerable foot. These memorials were all interesting, and I wandered through the apartments till ordered out by the footman, when I returned to my hotel to meet my old friend the marquis, who was engaged to dine with me. At his suggestion we went to a new restaurant, patronised by a different set of people from those who frequented the Restaurant au coin du Pont des Mareschaux, being chiefly Frenchmen, manufacturers, and small merchants of various kinds, who, while they detested the country, found it a profitable business to introduce Parisian luxuries and refinements among the barbarous Russians. A party of about twenty sat at a long table, and relieved the severity of exile by talking of their beautiful and beloved France; many of them were old militaires; and my octogenarian friend, as a soldier distinguished under the empire, and identified with the glory of the French arms, was treated with a consideration and respect honourable to them and flattering to himself. At another table was another circle of strangers, composed almost exclusively of Swiss, forming here, as elsewhere, one of the most valuable parts of a foreign population; keeping alive by intercourse with each other the recollections of home, and looking to the time when, with the profits of successful industry, they might return to their wild and beloved native mountains.

" Dear is that bill to which his soul conforms,
And dear that cliff which lifts him to the storms."

Before we rose from table, my friend of the theatre came in and took his seat at one end; he talked and laughed louder than any one else, and was received generally with an outward appearance of cordiality; but the old marquis could not endure his presence. He said he had become too old to learn, and it was too late in life to temporise with dishonour; that he did not blame his countrymen; fair words cost nothing, and it was not worth their while wilfully to make an enemy who would always be on their haunches; but as to himself, he had but a few years to live, and he would not sully the last moments of his life by tolerating a man whom he regarded as a disgrace to his country. We rose from the table, the old marquis leaning on my arm, and pouring in my ears his honest indignation at the disgraceful character of his countryman, and proceeded to the Kitaigorod, or Chinese Town, the division immediately encircling the Kremlin. It is enclosed by a wall with battlements, towers, and gates; is handsomely and compactly built, with wide, clean, and regular streets, and thronged with every variety of people, Greeks, Turks, Tartars, Cossacks, Chinese, Muscovites, French, Italians, Poles, and Germans, in the costumes of their respective nations. The quarter was entirely Russian, and I did not find in the shops a single person who could speak any language but Russian. In one of them where I was conducted by the marquis, I found the old mongik to whom I before referred, who could not agree with his master for the price of his ransom. The principal shops resemble the bazars in the East, though they are far superior even to those in Constantinople, being built of stone, and generally in the form of arcades. They are well filled with every description of Asiatic goods; and some of them, particularly their tea, and tobacco, and pipe shops, are models of propriety and cleanliness. The façade of the great bazar or market is very imposing, resting the whole length on Corinthian columns. It fronts on a noble square, bounded on the opposite side by the white walls of the Kremlin, and contains six thousand "bargaining shops." The merchants live at a distance, and, on leaving their shops at sundown, each of them winds a piece of cord round the padlock of his door, and seals it with soft wax; a seal being with the Russians more sacred than a lock.

In another section of the Kitaigorod is the finest part of the city, containing the hotels and residences of the nobles, many of which are truly magnificent. The hotel at which I put up would in Italy be called a palace. As we moved slowly along the street by the Pont des Mareschaux, we discoursed of the terrible inroads at this moment making by the French in the capital of the North, almost every shop having an inviting sign of nouveautés from Paris. Foiled in their attempt with the bayonet, they are now advancing with apparently more feeble but far more insidious and fatal weapons; and the rugged Russian, whom French arms could not conquer, bows to the supremacy of the French modistes and artistes, and quietly wears the livery of the great mistress of fashion.

CHAPTER XVIII.

The Drosky.—Salle des Nobles.—Russian Gaming.—Gastronomy.—Pedroski.—A Sunday in Moscow.—A Gipsy Belle.—Tea drinking.—The Emperor's Garden.—Retrospective.

EARLY the next morning I mounted a drosky and rode to a celebrated garden or springs, furnished with every description of mineral water. I have several times spoken of the drosky. This may be called the Russian national vehicle, for it is found all over Russia, and nowhere else that I know of, except at Warsaw, where it was introduced by its Russian conquerors. It is on four wheels, with a long cushioned seat running lengthwise, on which the rider sits astride as on horseback, and so low that he can mount from the street. It is drawn by two horses; one in shafts, with a high arched bow over the neck called the douga, and the other, called "le furieux," in traces alongside, this last being trained to curb his neck and canter while the shaft-horse trots. The seat is long enough for two besides the driver, the riders sitting with their feet on different sides; or sometimes there is a cross-seat behind, on which the riders sit, with their faces to the horses, and the drosky boy, always dressed in a long surtout, with a bell-crowned hat turned up at the sides, sits on the end. But to return to the springs. The waters are prepared under the direction of medical men, who have the chymical analysis of all the principal mineral waters known, and manufacture them to order. As is universally the case in Russia, where there is any attempt at style, the establishment is upon a magnificent scale. The building contains a room perhaps one hundred and fifty feet long, with a clean and highly-polished floor, large looking-glasses, elegant sofas, and mahogany chairs and tables. The windows open upon a balcony extending along the whole front, which is furnished with tables and rustic chairs, and opens upon a large garden ornamented with gravel-walks, trees, and the most rare and valuable plants and flowers, at the time of my visit in full bloom. Every morning, from sunrise till noon crowds of people, and particularly the nobility and higher classes, frequent this establishment, and that morning there was a larger collection than usual. Russian hospitality is conspicuous at a place like this. A stranger, instead of being avoided, is sought out; and after one or two promenades I was accosted by more than one gentleman, ready to show me every civility. In the long room and on the balconies, scattered about at the different tables, I saw the gourmand who had distended his stomach almost to bursting, and near him the gaunt and bilious dyspeptic, drinking their favourite waters; the dashing officer and the blooming girl, the lover and coquette, and, in short, all the style and fashion of Moscow, their eyes occasionally turning to the long mirrors, and then singly, in pairs and in groups, strolling gently through the gardens, enjoying the music that was poured forth from hidden arbours.

Returning through a street not far from my hotel, I saw a line of carriages, and gentlemen and ladies, passing under a light arcade which formed the entrance to a large building. I joined the throng, and was put back by the door-keeper because I was not in a dress-coat. I ran to my hotel and changed my frock-coat, but now I had no biglietto of entrance. A few rubles obviated this difficulty and admitted me to the Salle des Nobles, a magnificent apartment surrounded by a colonnade, capable of containing more than three thousand persons, and said to be the finest ballroom in Europe. It belongs to a club of the nobility, and none are admitted as members but nobles. All games of hazard are forbidden; but, nevertheless, all games of hazard are played. Indeed, among the " on dits" which a traveller picks up, gambling is said to be the great vice of Russia. Young men who have not two rubles to rub together will bet thousands; and, when all other resources fail, the dishonourable will cheat, but the delicate-minded will kill themselves. It is not uncommon for a young man to say at the card-table over night, "I must shoot myself tomorrow;" and he is as good as his word. The Salle was open for a few days, as a sort of fair, for the exhibition of specimens of Russian manufacture; and, besides tables, work-boxes, &c., there were some of the finest living specimens of genuine Russian men and women that I had yet seen though not to be compared, as a Russian officer said, to whom I made the remark, with the exhibition of the same specimens in the waltz and mazourka, when the Salle was lighted up and decorated for a ball.

I returned to my hotel, where I found my old friend the marquis waiting, according to appointment, to dine with me. He would have accompanied me everywhere, but I saw that he suffered from the exertion, and would not allow it. Meeting with me had struck a chord that had not been touched for years, and he was never tired of talking of his friends in America. Every morning he breakfasted in my room, and we dined together every day. We went to the restaurant where I had supped with my friend of the theatre. The saloon was crowded, and at a table next us sat a seigneur, who was dining upon a delicacy that will surprise the reader, viz., one of his own female slaves, a very pretty girl, whom he had hired to the keeper of the restaurant for her maintenance and a dinner à-volonté per annum for himself. This was the second time he had dined on her account, and she was then waiting upon him; a pretty, modest, delicate-looking girl, and the old noble seemed never to know when he had enough of her. We left him gloating over still untasted dishes, and apparently mourning that human ability could hold out no longer. In going out my old friend, in homely but pithy phrase, said the only difference between a Russian seigneur and a Russian serf is, that the one wears his shirt inside his trousers and the other outside; but my friend spoke with the prejudices of a soldier of France aggravated by more than twenty years of exile. So far as my observation extended, the higher classes are rather extraordinary for talent and acquirements. Their government is unfortunate for the development and exercise of abilities. They have none of the learned professions; merchandise is disgraceful, and the army is the only field. With an ardent love of country, and an ambition to distinguish himself, every nobleman becomes a soldier, and there is hardly an old or middle-aged individual of this class who was not in arms to repel the invasion of Napoleon, and hardly a young man who did not serve lately in a less noble cause, the campaign in Poland. The consequence of service in the army seems to have been generally a passion for display and expensive living, which sent them back to their estates, after their terms of service expired, over head and ears in debt. Unable to come often to the cities, and obliged to live at their chateaux, deprived of all society, surrounded only by slaves, and feeling the want of the excitement incident to a military life, many of them become great gourmands, or rather, as my French friend said, gluttons. They do not eat, said he, they swallow; and the manner in which, with the true spirit of a Frenchman who still remembered the cuisine of the Palais Royal, he commented upon their eating entremêts, hors-d'œuvre, rôtis, and desserts all pellmell, would have formed a proper episode to Major Hamilton's chapter upon Americans eating eggs out of wine-glasses. The old marquis, although he retained all his French prejudices against the Russians, and always asserted, as the Russians themselves admit, that, but for the early setting in of winter, Napoleon would have conquered Russia, allowed them the virtue of unbounded hospitality, and enumerated several principal families at whose tables he could at any time take a seat without any express invitation, and with whom he was always sure of being a welcome guest; and he mentioned the case of a compatriot who for years had a place regularly reserved for him at the table of a seigneur, which he took whenever he pleased without any questions being asked, until, having stayed away longer than usual, the seigneur sent to inquire for him, and learned that he was dead.

But to return. Toward evening I parted with the marquis, mounted a drosky, and rode to the country theatre at Pedroski. Pedroski is a place dear to the heart of every Russian, having been the favourite residence of Peter the Great, to whom Russia owes its existence among civilised nations. It is about three versts from the barrier, on the St. Petersburgh road. The St. Petersburgh Gate is a very imposing piece of architecture. Six spirited horses rest lightly upon the top, like the brazen horses at St. Mark's in Venice. A wide road, divided into avenues for carriages and pedestrians, gravelled and lined with trees, leads from the gate. The chateau is an old and singular, but interesting building of red brick, with a green dome and white cornices, and inclosed by a circular wall flanked with turrets. In the plain in front two regiments of Cossack cavalry were going through their exercises. The grounds around the chateau are very extensive, handsomely laid out for carriages and promenades, public and retired, to suit every taste. The principal promenade is about a mile in length, through a forest of majestic old trees. On each side is a handsome footpath of continual shade; and sometimes, almost completely hidden by the luxuriant foliage, are beautiful little summer-houses, abundantly supplied with all kinds of refreshments.

The theatre is at a little distance from the extreme end of the great promenade, a plain and unpretending building; and this and the grand opera-house are the only theatres I have seen built like ours, merely with continued rows of seats, and not partitioned off into private boxes. The opera was some little Russian piece, and was followed by the grand ballet, the Revolt of the Seraglio. He who goes to Russia expecting to see a people just emerging from a state of barbarism, will often be astonished to find himself suddenly in a scene of Parisian elegance and refinement; and in no place will he feel this wonder more than in an opera-house at Moscow. The house was rather full, and contained more of the Russian nobility than I had yet seen at any one time. They were well dressed, adorned with stars and ribands, and, as a class of men, the " biggest in the round " I ever saw. Orders and titles of nobility, by-the-way, are given with a liberality which makes them of no value; and all over Russia princes are as plenty as pickpockets in London.

The seigneurs of Russia have jumped over all intermediate grades of civilisation, and plunged at once into the luxuries of metropolitan life. The ballet was, of course, inferior to that of Paris or London, but it is speaking in no mean praise of it to say, that at this country theatre it might be made a subject of comparison. The dancers were the prettiest, the most interesting, and, what I was particularly struck with, the most modest-looking I ever saw on the stage. It was melancholy to look at those beautiful girls, who, amid the glare and glitter of the stage, and in the

P

graceful movements of the dance, were perfectly captivating and entrancing, and who, in the shades of domestic life, might fill the measure of man's happiness on earth, and know them to be slaves. The whole troop belongs to the emperor. They are selected when young with reference to their beauty and talents, and are brought up with great care and expense for the stage. With light fairy figures, seeming rather spirits than corporeal substances, and trained to inspire admiration and love, they can never give way to these feelings themselves, for their affections and marriages are regulated entirely by the manager's convenience. What though they are taken from the very poorest class of life, leaving their parents, their brothers and sisters, the tenants of miserable cabins, oppressed and vilified, and cold and hungry, while they are rolling in luxuries? A chain does not gall the less because it is gilded. Raised from the lot to which they were born, taught ideas they would never have known, they but feel more sensibly the weight of their bonds; and the veriest sylph, whose graceful movements have brought down the loudest thunders of applause, and whose little heart flutters with the admiration she has excited, would probably give all her short-lived triumph for the privilege of bestowing that little flutterer where it would be loved and cherished. There was one among them whom I long remembered. I followed her with my eyes till the curtain fell and left a blank around me. I saw her go out, and afterward she passed me in one of a long train of dark blue carriages belonging to the direction, in which they are carried about like merchandise from theatre to theatre; but, like many other bright visions that broke upon me for a moment, I never saw her again.

At about eleven I left the steps of the theatre to return home. It was a most magnificent night, or, rather, it is almost profanation to call it by so black a name, for in that bright northern climate the day seemed to linger, unwilling to give place before the shades of night. I strolled on alone, wrapped in lonely but not melancholy meditations; the carriages rolled rapidly by me, and I was almost the last of the throng that entered the gate of Moscow.

A Sunday at Moscow. To one who had for a long time been a stranger to the sound of the "church-going bell," few things could be more interesting than a Sunday at Moscow. Any one who has rambled along the Maritime Alps, and has heard, from some lofty eminence, the convent bell ringing for matins, vespers, and midnight prayers, will long remember the not unpleasing sounds. To me there is always something touching in the sound of the church bell; in itself pleasing by its effect upon the sense, but far more so in its associations. And these feelings were exceedingly fresh when I awoke on Sunday in the holy city of Moscow. In Greece and Turkey there are no bells; in Russia they are almost innumerable, but this was the first time I had happened to pass the Sabbath in the city. I lay and listened, almost fearing to move lest I should lose the sounds; thoughts of home came over me; of the day of rest, of the gathering for church, and the greeting of friends at the church-door. But he who has never heard the ringing of bells at Moscow does not know its music. Imagine a city containing more than six hundred churches and innumerable convents, all with bells, and these all sounding together, from the sharp, quick, hammer-note, to the loudest, deepest peals that ever broke and lingered on the ear, struck at long intervals, and swelling on the air as if unwilling to die away. I arose and threw open my window, dressed myself, and after breakfast, joining the throng called to their respective churches by their well-known bells, I went to what is called the English chapel, where, for the first time in many months, I joined in a regular church service, and listened to an orthodox sermon. I was surprised to see so large a congregation, though I remarked among them many English governesses with children, the English language being at that moment the rage among the Russians, and multitudes of cast-off chambermaids being employed to teach the rising Russian nobility the beauties of the English tongue.

All over the Continent, Sunday is the great day for observing national manners and customs. I dined at an early hour with my friend the marquis, and under his escort, mounting a drosky, rode to a great promenade of the people, called *L'Allée des Peuples*. It lies outside the barrier, and beyond the state prisons, where the exiles for Siberia are confined, on the land of Count Schremetow, the richest nobleman in Russia, having one hundred and thirty thousand slaves on his estate; the chateau is about eight versts from the city, and a noble road through his own land leads from the barrier to his door.

This promenade is the great rendezvous of the people; that is, of the merchants and shopkeepers of Moscow. The promenade is simply a large piece of ground ornamented with noble trees, and provided with everything necessary for the enjoyment of all the national amusements, among which the Russian mountain is the favourite; and refreshments were distributed in great abundance. Soldiers were stationed at different points to preserve order, and the people seemed all cheerful and happy; but the life and soul of the place were the Bohemian or gipsy girls. Wherever they moved, a crowd gathered round them. They were the first I had seen of this extraordinary people, coming no one knows whence, and living no one knows how; wanderers from their birth, and with a history enveloped in doubt. It was impossible to mistake the dark complexion and piercing coal-black eyes of the gipsy women. The men were nowhere to be seen, nor were there any old women with them; and these young girls, well dressed, though, in general, with nothing peculiar in their costume, moved about in parties of five or six, singing, playing, and dancing to admiring crowds. One of them, with a red silk cloak trimmed with gold, and a gold band round her hair, struck me as the very *beau idéal* of a gipsy queen. Recognising me as a stranger, she stopped just in front of me, struck her castanets and danced, at the same time directing the movements of her companions, who formed a circle around me. There was a beauty in her face, combined with intelligence and spirit that riveted my attention, and when she spoke her eyes seemed to read me through. I ought, perhaps, to be ashamed of it, but in all my wanderings I never regretted so much my ignorance of the language as when it denied me the pleasure of conversing with that gipsy girl. I would fain have known whether her soul did not soar above the scene and the employment in which I found her; whether she was not formed for better things than to display her beautiful person before crowds of boors; but I am sorry to add, that the character of my queen was not above reproach; and, as I had nothing but my character to stand upon in Moscow, I was obliged to withdraw from the observation which her attention fixed upon me.

Leaving my swarthy princess with this melancholy reflection, and leaving the scene of humbler enjoyment, I mounted a drosky, and, depositing my old friend in the suburbs of the city, in half an hour was in another world, in the great promenade of Pedroski, the gathering-place of the nobility, where all the rank and fashion of Moscow were vying with each other in style and magnificence. The extensive grounds around the old chateau are handsomely disposed and ornamented with trees, but the great carriage promenade is equal to anything I ever saw. It is a straight road, more than a mile in length, through a thick forest of noble trees. For two hours before dark all the equipages in Moscow paraded up and down this promenade. These equipages were striking and showy without being handsome, and the Russian manner of driving four horses makes a very dashing appearance, the leaders being harnessed with long traces, perhaps twenty feet from the wheel horses, and guided by a lad riding the near leader, the coachman sitting as if nailed to the box, and merely holding the reins. All the rules of good taste, as understood in the capitals of Southern Europe, were set at defiance; and many a seigneur, who thought he was doing the thing in the very best style, had no idea how much his turn-out would have shocked an English whip. But all this extravagance, in my eyes, added much to the effect of the scene; and the star-spangled Muscovite who dashed up and down the promenade on horseback, with two Calmuc Tartars at his heels, attracted more of my attention than the plain gentleman who paced along with his English jockey and quiet elegance of equipment. The stars and decorations of the seigneurs set them off to great advantage; and scores of officers, with their showy uniforms, added brilliancy to the scene, while the footmen made as good an appearance as their masters.

On either side of the grand promenade is a walk for foot passengers, and behind this, almost hidden from view by the thick shade of trees, are little cottages, arbours, and tents, furnished with ices and all kinds of refreshments suited to the season. I should have mentioned long since that tea, the very pabulum of all domestic virtues, is the Russian's favourite beverage. They say that they have better tea than can be obtained in Europe, which they ascribe to the circumstance of its being brought by caravans over-land, and saved the exposure of a sea voyage. Whether this be the cause or not, if I am any judge, they are right as to the superiority of their article; and it was one of the most striking features in the animating scene at Pedroski to see family groups distributed about, all over the grounds, under the shade of noble trees, with their large brass urn hissing before them, and taking their tea under the passing gaze of thousands of people, with as much unconcern as if by their own firesides.

Leaving for a moment the thronged promenade, I turned into a thick forest and entered the old chateau of the great Peter. There all was solitude: the footman and I had the palace to ourselves. I followed him through the whole range of apartments, in which there was an appearance of staid respectability that quite won my heart, neither of them being any better furnished than one of our old-fashioned country-houses. The pomp and show that I saw glittering through the openings in the trees were unknown in the days of the good old Peter; the chateau was silent and deserted; the hand that built it was stiff and cold, and the heart that loved it had ceased to beat; old Peter was in his grave, and his descendants loved better their splendid palaces on the banks of the Neva.

When Moscow was burning, Napoleon fled to this chateau for refuge. I stopped for a moment in the chamber where, by the blaze of the burning city, he dictated his despatches for the capital of France; gave the attendant a ruble, and again mixed with the throng, with whom I rambled up and down the principal promenade, and at eleven o'clock was at my hotel. I ought not to forget the Russian ladies; but, after the gay scene at Pedroski, it is no disparagement to them if I say that, in my quiet walk home the dark-eyed gipsy girl was uppermost in my thoughts.

The reader may perhaps ask if such is indeed what the traveller finds in Russia; "Where are the eternal snows that cover the steppes and the immense wastes of that northern empire, that chill the sources of enjoyment, and congeal the very fountains of life?" I answer, they have but just passed by, and they will soon come again; the present is the season of enjoyment; the Russians know it to be brief and fleeting, and like butterflies, unfold themselves to the sun, and flutter among the flowers.

Like them, I made the most of it at Moscow. Mounted in a drosky, I hurried from church to church, from convent to convent, and from quarter to quarter. But although it is the duty of a traveller to see everything that is to be seen, and although there is a kind of excitement in hurrying from place to place, which he is apt to mistake for pleasure, it is not in this that his real enjoyment is found. His true pleasure is in turning quietly to those things which are interesting to the imagination as well as to the eyes, and so I found myself often turning from the churches and palaces, specimens of architecture and art, to the sainted walls of the Kremlin. Here were the first and last of my visits; and whenever I sauntered forth without any specific object, perhaps to the neglect of many other places I ought to have seen, my footsteps involuntarily turned thitherward.

Outside and beneath the walls of the Kremlin, and running almost the whole extent of its circumference, are boulevards and a public garden, called the Emperor's, made within a few years, and the handsomest thing of the kind in Moscow; I am not sure but that I may add anywhere else. I have compared it in my mind to the gardens of the Luxembourg and Tuileries, and in many respects hold it to be more beautiful. It is more agreeably irregular and undulating in its surface, and has a more rural aspect, and the groves and plants are better arranged, although it has not the statues, lakes, and fountains of the pride of Paris. I loved to stroll through this garden, having on one side of me the magnificent buildings of the great Russian princes, seigneurs, and merchants, among the finest and most conspicuous of which is the former residence of the unhappy Queen of Georgia; and on the other side, visible through the foliage of the trees, the white walls of the Kremlin, and, towering above them, the domes of the palaces and churches within, and the lofty tower of Ivan Veliki Thence I loved to stroll to the Holy Gate of the -Kremlin. It is a vaulted portal, and over the entrance is a picture, with a lamp constantly burning; and a sentinel is always posted at the gate. I loved to stand by it and see the haughty seigneurs and the degraded serf alike humble themselves on crossing the sacred threshold, and then, with my hat in my hand, follow the footsteps of the venerating Russian. Once I attempted to brave the interdict, and go in with my head covered; but the soldier at the gate stopped me, and forbade my violating the sacred prohibition. Within the walls I wandered about, without any definite object, sometimes entering the great church and beholding for a moment the prostrate Russian praying before the image of some saint, or descending to take another look at the great bell, or at other times mounting the tower and gazing at the beautiful panorama of the city.

On the last day of my stay in Moscow, a great crowd drew me to the door of the church, where some fête was in course of celebration, in honour of the birth, marriage, or some other incident in the life of the emperor or empress. The archbishop, a venerable-looking old man, was officiating, and when he came out, a double line of men, women, and children was drawn up from the door of the church to his carriage, all pressing forward and struggling to kiss his hands. The crowd dispersed, and I strolled once more through the repository of heirlooms, and imperial reliques and trophies; but, passing by the crowns loaded with jewels, the canopies and thrones adorned with velvet and gold, I paused before the throne of unhappy Poland! I have seen great cities desolate and in ruins, magnificent temples buried in the sands of the African desert, and places once teeming with fertility now lying waste and silent; but no monument of fallen greatness ever affected me more than this. It was covered with blue velvet and studded with golden stars. It had been the seat of Casimir, and Sobieski, and Stanislaus Augustus. Brave men had gathered round it and sworn to defend it, and died in redeeming their pledge. Their oaths are registered in heaven, their bodies rest in bloody graves; Poland is blotted from the list of nations, and her throne, unspotted with dishonour, brilliant as the stars which glitter on its surface, is exhibited as a Russian trophy, before which the stoutest manhood need not blush to drop a tear.

Toward evening I returned to my favourite place, the porch of the palace of the Czars. I seated myself on the step, took out my tablets, and commenced a letter to my friends at home. What should I write? Above me was the lofty tower of Ivan Veliki; below, a solitary soldier, in his grey overcoat, was retiring to a sentry-box to avoid a drizzling rain. His eyes were fixed upon me, and I closed my book. I am not given to musing, but I could not help it. Here was the theatre of one of the most extraordinary events in the history of the world. After sixty battles and a march of more than two thousand miles, the grand army of Napoleon entered Moscow, and found no smoke issuing from a single chimney, nor a Muscovite even to gaze upon them from the battlements or walls. Moscow was deserted, her magnificent palaces forsaken by their owners, her three hundred thousand inhabitants vanished as if they had never been. Silent and amazed, the grand army filed through its desolate streets. Approaching the Kremlin, a few miserable, ferocious, and intoxicated wretches, left behind as a savage token of the national hatred, poured a volley of musketry from the battlements. At midnight the flames broke out in the city; Napoleon, driven from his quarters in the suburbs, hurried to the Kremlin, ascended the steps, and entered the door at which I sat. For two days the French soldiers laboured to repress the fierce attempts to burn the city. Russian police-officers were seen stirring up the fire with tarred lances; hideous-looking men and women, covered with rags, were wandering like demons amid the flames, armed with torches, and striving to spread the conflagration. At midnight again the whole city was in a blaze; and while the roof of the Kremlin was on fire, and the panes of the window against which he leaned were burning to the touch, Napoleon watched the course of the flames and exclaimed, "What a tremendous spectacle! These are Scythians indeed." Amid volumes of smoke and fire, his eyes blinded by the intense heat, and his hands burned in shielding his face from its fury, and traversing streets arched with fire, he escaped from the burning city.

Russia is not classic ground. It does not stand before us covered with the shadow of great men's deeds. A few centuries ago, it was overrun by wandering tribes of barbarians; but what is there in those lands which stand forth on the pages of history, crowned with the glory of their ancient deeds, that, for extraordinary daring, for terrible sublimity, and undaunted patriotism, exceeds the burning of Moscow? Neither Marathon, nor Thermopylæ, nor the battle of the Horatii, nor the defence of Cocles, nor the devotion of the Decii, can equal it; and when time shall cover with its dim and quiet glories that bold and extraordinary deed, the burning of Moscow will be regarded as outstripping all that we read of Grecian or Roman patriotism, and the name of the Russian governor (Rostopchin), if it be not too tough a name to hand down to posterity, will never be forgotten.

CHAPTER XIX.

Getting a Passport.—Parting with the Marquis.—The Language of Signs.—A Loquacious Traveller—From Moscow to St. Petersburgh.—The Wolga.—Novogorod.—Newski Perspective.—An unfortunate Mistake.—Northern Twilight.

UNABLE to remain longer in Moscow, I prepared for my journey for St. Petersburgh. Several diligences run regularly between these two great cities; one of which, the Vélocifère, is superior to any public conveyance on the continent of Europe. I took my place in that, and two days beforehand sent my passport to be viséd. I sent for it the next day, and it was not ready. I went myself, and could not get it. I knew that nothing could be done at the Russian offices without paying for it, and was ready and willing to do so, and time after time I called the attention of the officer to my passport. He replied coolly, "*Dans un instant*," and, turning to something else, kept me waiting two hours; and when at length he took it up and arranged it, he led me down stairs out of sight to receive the expected *douceur*. He was a well-dressed man, with the large government button on his coat, and rather distingué in his appearance and manners. I took the passport, folded it up, and put it in my pocket with a coolness equal to his own, and with malicious pleasure put into his hand a single ruble, equal to twenty cents of our money; he expected at least twenty-five rubles, or about five dollars, and his look of rage and disappointment amply repaid me for all the vexation he had caused by his delay. I bade him farewell with a smile that almost drove him mad.

Bribery is said to be almost universal among the inferior officers of government, and there is a story of a Frenchman in Russia which illustrates the system. He had an office, of which the salary was so small that he could not live upon it. At first he would not take bribes, but stern necessity drove him to it, and while he was about it he did the thing handsomely. Having overreached the mark, and being guilty of being detected, he was brought before the proper tribunal; and when asked, "Why did you take a bribe?" his answer was original and conclusive, "I take, thou takest, he takes, we take, you take, they take!"

I told the marquis the story of my parting interview at the police-office, which he said was capital, but startled me by suggesting that, if there should happen to be any irregularity, I would have great trouble in getting it rectified; even this, however, did not disturb my immediate satisfaction, and, fortunately, all was right.

The morning of my departure, before I was out of bed, the marquis was in my room. Meeting with me had revived in him feelings long since dead; and at the moment of parting he told me, what his pride had till that moment concealed, that his heart yearned once more to his kindred: and that, if he had the means, old as he was, he would go to America. And yet, though his frame trembled, and his voice was broken, and his lamp was almost burned out, his spirit was as high as when he fought the battles of the empire; and he told me to say to them that he would not come to be a dependant upon their bounty; that he could repay all they should do for him by teaching their children. He gave me his last painting, which he regarded with the pride of an artist, as a souvenir for his sister; but having no means of carrying it safely, I was obliged to return it to him. He remained with me till the moment of my departure, clung to my hand after I had taken my place in the drosky, and when we had started I looked back and saw him still standing in the road. It seemed as if the last link that bound him to earth was broken. He gave me a letter, which I forwarded to his friends at home; his sister was still living, and had not forgotten her long-lost brother; she had not heard from him in twenty years, and had long believed him dead. Pecuniary assistance was immediately sent to him; and, unhappily, since my return home, intelligence has been received that it arrived only at the last moment when human aid could avail him; in time to smooth the pillow of death by the assurance that his friends had not forgotten him. And, perhaps, in his dying moments, he remembered me. At all events, it is some satisfaction, amid the recollections of an unprofitable life, to think that, when his checkered career was drawing to its close, I had been the means of gladdening for a moment the old exile's heart.

I must not forget my host, the quondam exile to Siberia. In his old days his spirit too was chafed at living under despotism, and, like the marquis, he also hoped, before he died, to visit America. I gave him my address, with the hope, but with very little expectation, of seeing him again. A travelling companion once remarked, that if every vagabond to whom I gave my address should find his way to America, I would have a precious set to present to my friends. Be it so; there is not a vagabond among them whom I would not be glad to see.

My English companion and myself had seen but little of each other at Moscow. He intended to remain longer than I did, but changed his mind, and took a place in the same diligence for St. Petersburgh. This diligence was the best I ever rode in; and, for a journey of nearly five hundred miles, we could not have been more comfortably arranged. It started at the hour punctually, as from the Messagerie in Paris. We rolled for the last time through the streets of Moscow, and in a few minutes passed out at the St. Petersburgh Gate. Our companions were, a man about thirty-five, a cattle-driver, with his trousers torn, and his linen hanging out ostentatiously in different places, and an old man about sixty-five, just so far civilised as to have cut off the long beard and put on broadcloth clothes. It was the first time the old man had ever been on a journey from home; everything was new to him, and he seemed puzzled to know what to make of us; he could not comprehend how we could look, and walk, and eat like Russians, and not talk like them. My place was directly opposite his, and, as soon as we were seated, he began to talk to me. I looked at him and made no answer; he began again, and went on in an uninterrupted strain for several minutes, more and more surprised that I did not answer, or answered only in unintelligible sounds. After a while he seemed to come to the conclusion that I was deaf and dumb, and turned to my companion, as to my keeper, for an explanation. Finding he could do nothing there, he appeared alarmed, and it was some time before he could get a clear idea of the matter. When he did, however, he pulled off an amazingly white glove, took my hand and shook it, pointed to his head, shook it, and touched my head, then put his hand to his heart, then to my heart; all which was to say, that though our heads did not understand each other, our hearts did. But though he saw we did not understand him, he did not on that account stop talking; indeed, he talked incessantly, and the only way of stopping him was to look directly in his face and talk back again; and I read him long lectures, particularly upon the snares and temptations of the world into which he was about to plunge, and wound up with stanzas of poetry and scraps of Greek and Latin, all which the old man listened to without ever interrupting me, bending his ear as if he expected every moment to catch something he understood; and when I had finished, after a moment's blank expression he whipped off his white glove, took my hand, and touched significantly his head and heart. Indeed, a dozen times a day he did this; and particularly whenever we got out, on resuming our seats, as a sort of renewal of the compact of good fellowship, the glove invariably came off, and the significant movement between the hand, head, and heart was repeated. The second day a young seigneur named Chickoff, who spoke French, joined the diligence, and through him we had full explanations with the old Russian. He always called me the American graff or noble, and said that, after being presented to the emperor, I should go down with him into the country.

My worthy comrade appeared at first to be not a little bored by the old man's garrulous humour; but at length, seized by a sudden whim, began, as he said, to teach him English. But such English! He taught him, after a fashion peculiarly his own, the manner of addressing a lady and gentleman in English; and very soon, with the remarkable facility of the Russians in acquiring languages, the old man, utterly unconscious of their meaning, repeated the words with extraordinary distinctness; and regularly, when he took his place in the diligence, he accompanied the significant movements of his hand, head, and heart to me with the not very elegant address taught him by my companion. Though compelled to smile inwardly at the absurdity of the thing, I could not but feel the inherent impropriety of the conduct of my eccentric fellow-traveller; and ventured to suggest to him that, though he had an undoubted right to do as he pleased in matters that could not implicate me, yet, independent of the very questionable character of the joke itself (for the words savoured more of Wapping than of St. James's), as we were known to have travelled together, a portion of the credit of having taught the old Russian English might fall upon me—an honour of which I was not covetous, and, therefore, should tell the old man never to repeat the words he had been taught, which I did without assigning any reason for it, and before we arrived at St. Petersburgh he had forgotten them.

The road from Moscow to St. Petersburgh is now one of the best in Europe. It is Macadamized nearly the whole way, and a great part is bordered with trees; the posthouses are generally large and handsome, under the direction of government, where soup, cutlets, &c. are always ready at a moment's notice, at prices regulated by a tariff hanging up in the room, which, however, being written in Russian, was of no particular use to us. The country is comparatively thickly settled, and villages are numerous. Even on this road, however, the villages are forlorn things, being generally the property and occupied by the serfs of the seigneurs, and consisting of a single long street, with houses on both sides built of logs, the better sort squared, with the gable end to the street, the roofs projecting two or three feet from the houses, and sometimes ornamented with rude carving and small holes for windows. We passed several chateaux, large, imposing uildings, with parks and gardens, and a large church, painted white, with a green dome, surmounted by a cross.

In many places on the road are chapels with figures of the Panagia, or all-holy Virgin, or some of the saints; and our old Russian, constantly on the look-out for them, never passed one without taking off his hat and going through the whole formula of crosses; sometimes, on entering a town, they came upon us in such quick succession, first on one side, then on the other, that, if he had not been engaged in, to him, a sacred ceremony, his hurry and perplexity would have been ludicrous. During the night we saw fires ahead, and a little off the road were the bivouacs of teamsters or wayfarers, who could not pay for lodging in a miserable Russian hut. All the way we met the great caravan teams carrying tallow, hides, hemp, and other merchandise to the cities, and bringing back wrought fabrics, groceries, &c., into the interior. They were generally thirty or forty together, one man or woman attending to three or four carts, or, rather, neglecting them, as the driver was generally asleep on the top of his load. The horses, however, seemed to know what they were about; for as the diligence came rolling toward them, before the postilion could reach them with his whip, they intuitively hurried out of the way. The bridges over the streams and rivers are strong, substantial structures, built of heavy hewn granite, with iron balustrades, and ornamented in the centre with the double-headed eagle, the arms of Russia.

At Tver we passed the Wolga on a bridge of boats. This noble river, the longest in Europe, navigable almost from its source for an extent of four thousand versts, dividing, for a great part of its course, Europe and Asia, runs majestically through the city, and rolls on, bathing the walls of the city of Astrachan, till it reaches the distant Caspian; its banks still inhabited by the same tribes of warlike Cossacks who hovered on the skirts of the French army during their invasion of Russia. By its junction with the Tverza, a communication is made between the Wolga and Neva, or, in other words, between the Caspian and Baltic. The impetus of internal improvements has extended even to the north of Europe, and the Emperor Nicolas is now actively engaged in directing surveys of the great rivers of Russia for the purpose of connecting them by canals and railroads, and opening steam communications throughout the whole interior of his empire. A great number of boats of all sizes, for carrying grain to the capital, were lying off the city. These boats are generally provided with one mast, which, in the largest, may equal a frigate's mainmast. "The weight of the matsail," an English officer remarks, "must be prodigious, having no fewer than one hundred breadths in it; yet the facility with which it is managed bears comparison with that of the Yankees with their boom-mainsail in their fore-and-aft clippers." The rudder is a ponderous machine, being a broad piece of timber floating astern twelve or fifteen feet, and fastened to the tiller by a pole, which descends perpendicularly into the water; the tiller is from thirty to forty feet long, and the pilot who turns it stands upon a scaffold at that distance from the stern. Down the stream a group of Cossacks were bathing, and I could not resist the temptation to throw myself for a moment into this king of rivers. The diligence hurried me, and, as it came along, I gathered up my clothes and dressed myself inside.

About eighty versts from St. Petersburgh, we came to the ancient city of Novogorod. In the words of an old traveller, "Next unto Moscow, the city of Novogorod is reputed the chiefest in Russia; for although it be in majestie inferior to it, yet in greatness it goeth beyond it. It is the chiefest and greatest mart-town of all Muscovy; and albeit the emperor's seat is not there, but at Moscow, yet the commodiousness of the river, falling into that gulf which is called Sinus Finnicus, whereby it is well frequented by merchants, makes it more famous than Moscow itself." Few of the ruined cities of the Old World present so striking an appearance of fallen greatness as this comparatively unknown place. There is an ancient saying, "Who can resist the gods and Novogorod the Great!" Three centuries ago it covered an area of sixty-three versts in circumference, and contained a population of more than four hundred thousand inhabitants. Some parts of it are still in good condition, but the larger portion has fallen to decay. Its streets present marks of desolation, mouldering walls, and ruined churches, and its population has dwindled to little more than seven thousand inhabitants. The steeples in this ancient city bear the cross, unaccompanied by the crescent, the proud token showing that the Tartars, in all their invasions, never conquered it, while in the reconquered cities the steeples all exhibit the crescent surmounted by the cross.

Late in the afternoon of the fourth day we were approaching St. Petersburgh. The ground is low and flat, and I was disappointed in the first view of the capital of Russia; but passing the barrier, and riding up the Newski Perspective, the most magnificent street in that magnificent city, I felt the stories of its splendour were not exaggerated, and that this was, indeed, entitled to the proud appellation of the "Palmyra of the North." My English companion again stopped at a house kept by an Englishwoman and frequented by his countrymen, and I took an apartment at an hotel in a broad street with an unpronounceable Russian name, a little off the Newski Perspective. I was worn and fatigued with my journey, but I could not resist the inclination to take a gentle promenade along the Newski Perspective. While in the coffee-room refreshing myself with a cup of the best Russian tea, I heard some one outside the door giving directions to a tailor, and presently a man entered, whom, without looking at him, I told he was just the person I wanted to see, as I had a pair of pantaloons to be mended. He made no answer, and, without being able to see distinctly, I told him to wait till I could go up stairs and change them, and that he must mend them strongly and bring them back in the morning. In all probability, the next moment I should have been sprawling on the floor, but the landlady, a clever Frenchwoman, who saw my error, stepped up, and crying out, "Ah, Monsieur le Colonel, at-

tendez, attendez," explained my mistake as clearly as I could have done myself, and I followed closely with an apology, adding that my remark could not be intended as disrespectful to him, inasmuch as even then, with the windows closed, I could scarcely distinguish his person. He understood the thing at once, accepted my apology with great frankness, and, instead of knocking me down, or challenging me to fight with sabre or some other diabolical thing, finding I was a stranger just arrived from Moscow, sat down at the table, and before we rose offered to accompany me in my walk.

There could be no mistake as to the caste of my new friend. The landlady had called him colonel, and, in repelling the imputation of his being a tailor, had spoken of him as a rich seigneur, who for ten years had occupied the front apartments au premier in her hotel. We walked out into the Newski Perspective, and strolled along that magnificent street down to the Admiralty, and along the noble quays of the Neva. I had reached the terminus of my journey; for many months I had been moving farther and farther away, and the next step I took would carry me toward home. It was the eve of the fourth of July; and as I strolled through the broad streets and looked up at the long ranges of magnificent buildings, I poured into the ear of my companion the recollections connected with this moment at home: in boyhood, crackers and fireworks in readiness for the great jubilee of the morrow; and, latterly, the excursion into the country to avoid the bustle and confusion of "the glorious fourth."*

At Moscow and during the journey I had admired the exceeding beauty of the twilight in these northern latitudes, but this night in St. Petersburgh it was magnificent. I cannot describe the peculiar shades of this northern twilight. It is as if the glare and brilliancy of the sun were softened by the mellowing influence of the moon, and the city, with its superb ranges of palaces, its statues, its bridges, and its clear and rapid river, seemed under the reflection of that northern light, of a brilliant and almost unearthly beauty. I felt as if I should like rambling all night. Even though worn with three days' travel, it was with me as with a young lady at her first ball; the night was too short. I could not bear to throw it away in sleep. My companion was tough, and by no means sentimental, and the scene was familiar to him; but he told me that, even in his eyes, it never lost its interest. Moonlight is something, but this glorious twilight is a thing to enjoy and to remember; and, as the colonel remarked when we sat down in his apartment to a comfortable supper, it always gave him such an appetite! After supper I walked through a long corridor to my apartment, threw myself upon my bed and tried to sleep, but the mellow twilight poured through my window and reproached me with the base attempt. I was not restless, but I could not sleep; lest, however, the reader should find himself of a different humour, I will consider myself asleep the first night in St. Petersburgh.

---

* The anniversary of the American "declaration of independence," July 4th, 1776, held as a holiday in the United States.—ED.

CHAPTER XX.

Police Requisites.—The Russian Capital.—Equestrian Statue of Peter the Great.—The Alexandrine Column.—Architectural Wonders.—The Summer Islands.—A perilous Achievement.—Origin of St. Petersburgh.—Tombs of dead Monarchs.—Origin of the Russian Navy.

JULY FOURTH.—I had intended to pass this day at Moscow, and to commemorate it in Napoleon style by issuing a bulletin from the Kremlin, but it was a long time since I had heard from home. At Constantinople I had written to Paris, directing my letters to be sent to Petersburgh, and, notwithstanding my late hours the night before, I was at the post-office before the doors were open. I had never been so long without hearing from home, and my lips quivered when I asked for letters, my hand shook when I received them, and I hardly drew breath till I had finished the last postscript. My next business was at the bureau of general police for a *carte de séjour*, without which no stranger can remain in St. Petersburgh. As usual, I was questioned as to my reasons for coming into Russia; age, time of sojourn, destination, &c.; and, satisfied that I had no intention of preaching democratic doctrines or subverting the government of the autocrat, I received permission to remain two weeks, which, according to direction, I gave to my landlord to be entered at the police-office of his district. As no stranger can stay in Petersburgh without permission, neither can he leave without it; and, to obtain this, he must advertise three times in the Government Gazette, stating his name, address, and intention of leaving the empire; and as the Gazette is only published twice a week, this formality occupies eight days. One of the objects of this is to apprise his creditors, and give them an opportunity of securing their debts; and few things show the barbarity and imperfect civilization of the Russians more clearly than this; making it utterly impossible for a gentleman to spend a winter in St. Petersburgh and go away without paying his landlord. This must prevent many a soaring spirit from wending its way hither, and keep the residents from being enlivened by the flight of those birds of passage which dazzle the eyes of the denizens of other cities. As there was no other way of getting out of the dominions of the czar, I caused my name and intention to be advertised. It did not create much of a sensation; and though it was proclaimed in three different languages, no one except my landlord seemed to feel any interest in it. After all, to get in debt is the true way to make friends; a man's creditors always feel an interest in him; hope no misfortune may happen to him, and always wish him prosperity and success.

These formalities over, I turned to other things. Different from every other principal city I had visited, St. Petersburgh had no storied associations to interest the traveller. There is no Coloseum, as at Rome; no Acropolis, as at Athens; no Rialto, as at Venice; and no Kremlin, as at Moscow; nothing identified with the men and scenes hallowed in our eyes, and nothing that can touch the heart. It depends entirely upon itself for the interest it creates in the mind of the traveller.

St. Petersburgh is situated at the mouth of the Neva, at the eastern extremity of the Gulf of Finland. It is built partly on islands formed by the Neva, and partly on both sides of that river. But little more than a century ago, the ground now covered with stately palaces consisted of wild morasses and primeval forests, and a few huts tenanted by savage natives, who lived upon the fish of the sea. In seventeen hundred and three, Peter the Great appeared as a captain of grenadiers, under the orders of one of his own generals, on the wild and dreary banks of the Neva, drove the Swedes from their fortress at its mouth, cut down the forests on the rude islands of the river, and laid the foundations of a city which now surpasses in architectural magnificence every other in the world. I do not believe that Rome, when Adrian reared the mighty Colosseum, and the Palace of the Cæsars covered the Capitoline Hill, exhibited such a range of noble structures as now exists in the Admiralty Quarter. The Admiralty itself is the central point, on one side fronting the Neva, and on the other a large open square, and has a façade of marble, with ranges of columns a quarter of a mile in length. A beautiful golden spire shoots up from the centre, towering above every other object, and seen from every part of the city glittering in the sun; and three principal streets, each two miles in length, radiate from this point. In front is a range of boulevards, ornamented with trees, and an open square, at one extremity of which stands the great church of St. Isaac, of marble, jasper, and porphyry, upon a foundation of granite; it has been once destroyed, and reared again with increased splendour, enormous columns of a single block of red granite already lifting their capitals in the air.

On the right of the façade, and near the Isaac Bridge, itself a magnificent structure, a thousand and fifty feet long, and sixty feet wide, with two drawbridges, stands the well-known equestrian statue of Peter the Great. The huge block of granite forming the pedestal is fifteen hundred tons in weight. The height of the figure of the emperor is eleven feet, that of the horse seventeen feet, and the weight of the metal in the group nearly thirty-seven thousand pounds. Both the idea and the execution of this superb monument are regarded as masterpieces of genius. To immortalize the enterprise and personal courage with which that extraordinary man conquered all difficulties and converted a few fishermen's huts into palaces, Peter is represented on a fiery steed, rushing up a steep and precipitous rock to the very brink of a precipice; the horse rears with his forefeet in the air, and seems to be impatient of restraint, while the imperial rider, in an attitude of triumph, extends the hand of protection over his capital rising out of the waters. To aid the inspiration of the artist, a Russian officer, the boldest rider of his time, daily rode the wildest Arabian of Count Orloff's stud to the summit of a steep mound, where he halted him suddenly, with his fore-legs raised pawing the air over the brink of the precipice. The monument is surrounded by an iron railing, and the pedestal bears the simple inscription, PETRO PRIMO CATHARINA SECUNDA, MDCCLXXXII.

On the other side of the square, and in front of the Winter Palace, raised within the last two years, and the most gigantic work of modern

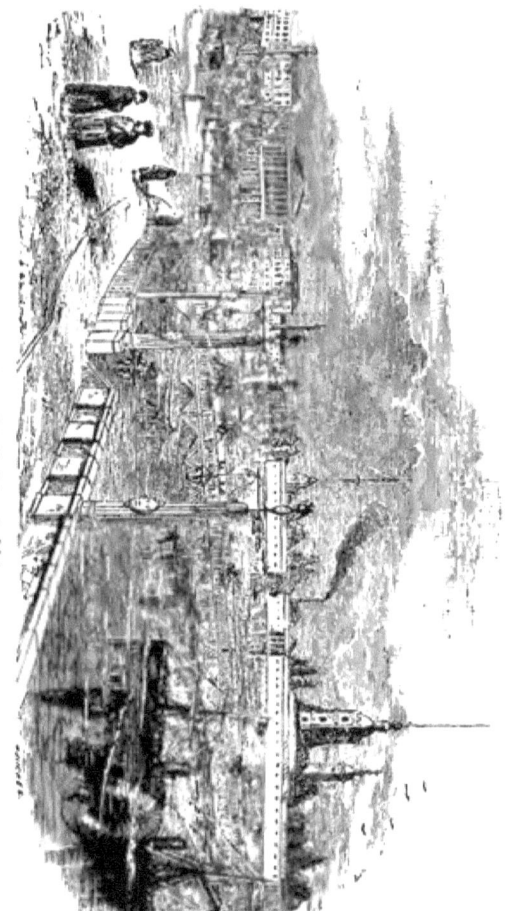

ST. PETERSBURG.—P. 224.

days, rivalling those magnificent monuments in the Old World whose ruins now startle the wondering traveller, and towering to the heavens, as if to proclaim that the days of architectural greatness are not gone by for ever, is the great Alexandrine Column, a single shaft of red granite, exclusive of pedestal and capital, eighty-four feet high. On the summit stands an angel holding a cross with the left hand, and pointing to heaven with the right. The pedestal contains the simple inscription, " To Alexander I. Grateful Russia."

Surrounding this is a crescent of lofty buildings, denominated the Etat-Major, its central portion having before it a majestic colonnade of the Corinthian order, placed on a high rustic basement, with a balustrade of solid bronze, gilt between the columns. In the middle is a triumphal arch, which, with its frieze, reaches nearly to the upper part of the lofty building, having a span of seventy feet, the entablature sculptured with military trophies, allegorical figures, and groups in alto-rilievo. Next, on a line with the Admiralty, and fronting the quay, stands the first of a long range of imperial palaces, extending in the form of a crescent for more than a mile along the Neva. The Winter Palace is a gigantic and princely structure, built of marble, with a façade of seven hundred and forty feet. Next are the two palaces of the Hermitage, connected with it and with each other by covered galleries on bold arches; the beautiful and tasteful fronts of these palaces are strangely in contrast with their simple and unpretending names. Next is the stately Grecian theatre of the Hermitage. Beyond this are the barracks of the guards, then the palace of the French ambassador, then the marble palace built by Catharine II. for her favourite, Prince Orloff, with a basement of granite and superstructure of bluish marble, ornamented with marble columns and pillars. In this palace died Stanislaus Poniatowsky, the last of the Polish sovereigns. This magnificent range, presenting an uninterrupted front of marble palaces upward of a mile in length, unequalled in any city in the world, is terminated by an open square, in which stands a colossal statue of Suwarrow; beyond this, still on the Neva, is the beautiful summer garden fronting the palace of Paul II.; and near it, and at the upper end of the square, is the palace of the Grand-duke Michael.

Opposite is the citadel, with its low bastions of solid granite, washed all round by the Neva; beautiful in its structure, and beautifully decorated by the tall, slender, and richly-gilded spire of its church. On the one side of the Admiralty is the senatorial palace, and beyond opens the English Quay, with a range of buildings that might well be called the residence of " merchant princes ;" while the opposite bank is crowded with public buildings, among which the most conspicuous are the palace of the Academy of the Fine Arts; the Obelisk, rising in the centre of a wide square, recording the glory of some long-named Russian hero; the building of the Naval Cadet Corps, with its handsome front, and the barracks of the Guard of Finland; finally, the great pile of palace-like buildings belonging to the Military Cadet Corps, reaching nearly to the palace of the Academy of Sciences, and terminating with the magnificent Grecian front of the Exchange. I know that a verbal description can give but a faint idea of the character of this scene, nor would it help the understanding of it to say that it exhibits all that wealth and architectural skill can do, for few in our country know what even these powerful engines can effect; as for myself, hardly noting the details, it was my greatest delight to walk daily to the bridge across the Neva, at the Summer Gardens, the view from which more than realised all the crude and imperfect notions of architectural magnificence that had ever floated through my mind; a result that I had never found in any other city I had yet seen, not excepting Venice the rich, or Genoa the proud, although the latter is designated in guide-books as the " city of palaces."

Next to the palaces in solidity and beauty of structure are the bridges crossing the Neva, and the magnificent quays along its course; these last being embankments of solid granite, lining the stream on either side the whole length of its winding course through the city.

I was always at a loss whether to ride or walk in St. Petersburgh; sometimes I mounted a drosky and rode up and down the Newski Perspective, merely for the sake of rolling over the wooden pavement. This street is perhaps more than twice as wide as Broadway; the gutter is in the middle, and on each side are wooden pavements wide enough for vehicles to pass each other freely. The experiment of wooden pavement was first made in this street, and found to answer so well that it has since been introduced into many others; and as the frost is more severe than with us, and it has stood the test of a Russian winter, if rightly constructed it will, no doubt, prove equally successful in our own city. The road is first covered with broken stone, or Macadamised; then logs are laid across it, the interstices being filled up with sand and stone, and upon this are placed hexagonal blocks of pine about eighteen inches long, fitted like joiner's-work, fastened with long pegs, and covered with a preparation of melted lead.

When I left Paris I had no expectation of travelling in Russia, and, consequently, had no letter of introduction to Mr. Wilkins, our minister; but, long before reaching St. Petersburgh, I had made it a rule, immediately on my arrival in a strange place, to call upon our representative, whatever he might be, from a minister plenipotentiary down to a little Greek consul. I did so here, and was probably as well received upon my own introduction as if I had been recommended by letter; for I got from Mr. Wilkins the invitation to dinner usually consequent upon a letter, and besides, much interesting information from home, and, more than all, a budget of New York newspapers. It was a long time since I had seen a New York paper, and I hailed all the well-known names, informed myself of every house to let, every vessel to sail, all the cotton in market, and a new kind of shaving soap for sale at Hart's Bazaar; read with particular interest the sales of real estate by James Bleecker and Sons; wondered at the rapid increase of the city in creating a demand for building lots in one hundred and twenty-seventh street, and reflected that some of my old friends had probably grown so rich that they would not recognise me on my return.

Having made arrangements for the afternoon to

visit the Summer Islands, I dined with my friend the colonel, in company with Prince —— (I have his name in my pocket-book, written by himself, and could give a fac-simile of it, but I could not spell it). The prince was about forty-five, a hightoned gentleman, a nobleman in his feelings, and courtly in his manners, though, for a prince, rather out at elbows in fortune. The colonel and he had been fellow-soldiers, had served in the guards during the whole of the French invasion, and entered Paris with the allied armies as officers in the same regiment. Like most of the Russian seigneurs, they had run through their fortunes in their military career. The colonel, however, had been set up again by an inheritance from a relative, but the prince remained ruined. He was now living upon a fragment saved from the wreck of his estate, a pension for his military services, and the bitter experience acquired by a course of youthful extravagance. Like many of the reduced Russian seigneurs, he was disaffected toward the government, and liberal in politics; he was a warm admirer of liberal institutions, had speculated upon and studied them both in France and America, and analysed understandingly the spirit of liberty as developed by the American and French revolutions; when he talked of Washington, he folded his hands and looked up to heaven, as if utterly unable to express the fulness of his emotions. With us, the story of our revolution is a hackneyed theme, and even the sacred name of Washington has become almost commonplace; but the freshness of feeling with which the prince spoke of him, invested him in my eyes with a new and holy character. After dinner, and while on our way to the Summer Islands, we stopped at his apartments, when he showed me the picture of Washington conspicuous on the wall; under it, by way of contrast, was that of Napoleon; and he summed up the characters of both in few words, by saying, that the one was all for himself, the other all for his country.

The Summer Islands on Sundays and fête-days are the great promenade of the residents of the capital, and the approach to them is either by land or water. We preferred the latter, and at the Admiralty took a boat on the Neva. All along the quay are flights of steps cut in the granite, and descending to a granite platform, where boats are constantly in attendance for passengers. These boats are fantastically painted, and have the stern raised some three or four feet; sometimes they are covered with an awning. The oar is of disproportionate thickness toward the handle, the blade very broad, always feathered in rowing, and the boatman, in his calico or linen shirt and pantaloons, his long yellowish beard and mustaches, looks like any thing but the gondolier of Venice. In passing down the Neva I noticed, about half way between low-water mark and the top of the quay, a ring which serves to fasten vessels, and is the mark to which if the water rises an inundation may be expected. The police are always on the watch, and the fearful moment is announced by the firing of cannon, by the display of white flags from the Admiralty steeple by day, and by lanterns and the tolling of the bells at night. In the last dreadful inundation of 1824, bridges were swept away, boats floated in some parts of the town above the tops of the houses, and many villages were entirely destroyed. At Cronstadt, a vessel of one hundred tons was left in the middle of one of the principal streets; eight thousand dead bodies were found and buried, and probably many thousands more were hurried on to the waters of the Gulf of Finland.

It was a fête-day in honour of some church festival, and a great portion of the population of St. Petersburgh was bending its way toward the Summer Islands. The emperor and empress were expected to honour the promenade with their presence, and all along the quay boats were shooting out loaded with gay parties, and, as they approached the islands, they formed into a fleet, almost covering the surface of the river. We were obliged to wait till perhaps a dozen boats had discharged their passengers, before we could land.

These islands are formed by the branches of the Neva, at about three versts from St. Petersburgh. They are beautifully laid out in grass and gravelwalks, ornamented with trees, lakes, shrubs, and flowers, connected together by light and elegant bridges, and adorned with beautiful little summerhouses. These summer-houses are perfectly captivating; light and airy in their construction, and completely buried among the trees. As we walked along we heard music or gentle voices, and now and then came upon a charming cottage, with a beautiful lawn or garden, just enough exposed to let the passer-by imagine what he pleased; and on the lawn was a light fanciful tent, or an arbour hung with foliage, under which the occupants, with perhaps a party of friends from the city, were taking tea, and groups of rosy children were romping around them, while thousands were passing by and looking on, with as perfect an appearance of domestic *abandon* as if in the privacy of the fireside. I have sometimes reproached myself that my humour changed with every passing scene; but, inasmuch as it generally tended toward at least a momentary satisfaction, I did not seek to check it; and though, from habit and education, I would have shrunk from such a family exhibition, here it was perfectly delightful. It seemed like going back to a simpler and purer age. The gay and smiling faces seemed to indicate happy hearts; and when I saw a mother playing on the green with a little cherub daughter, I felt how I hung upon the community, a loose and disjointed member, and would fain have added myself to some cheerful family group. A little farther on, however, I saw a papa flogging a chubby urchin, who drowned with his bellowing the music from a neighbouring arbour, which somewhat broke the charm of this public exhibition of scenes of domestic life.

Besides these little retiring places or summer residences of citizens, restaurants and houses of refreshment were distributed in great abundance, and numerous groups were sitting under the shade of trees or arbours, taking ices or refreshments; and the grounds for promenade were so large and beautifully disposed, that, although thousands were walking through them, there was no crowd, except before the door of a principal refectory, where a rope-dancer was flourishing in the air among the tops of the trees.

In addition to the many enchanting retreats and summer residences created by the taste, luxury, and wealth of private individuals, there are summer theatres and imperial villas. But the gem of the islands is the little imperial palace at Cammenoi. I have walked through royal palaces, and admired their state and magnificence without one wish to possess them, but I felt a strong yearning toward this imperial villa. It is not so grand and stately as to freeze and chill one, but a thing of extraordinary simplicity and elegance, in a beautifully picturesque situation, heightened by a charming disposition of lawn and trees, so elegant, and, if I may add such an unpoetical word in the description of this imperial residence, so comfortable, that I told the prince if I were a Rasselas escaped from the Happy Valley, I would look no farther for a resting place. The prince replied, that in the good old days of Russian barbarism, when a queen swayed the sceptre, Russia had been a great field for enterprising and adventurous young men, and in more than one instance a palace had been the reward of a favourite. We gave a sigh to the memory of those good old days, and at eleven o'clock returned to the city on the top of an omnibus. The whole road from the Summer Islands and the great street leading to the Admiralty were lighted with little glass lamps, arranged on the side walks about six feet apart, but they almost realised the conceit of illuminating the sun by hanging candles around it, seeming ashamed of their own sickly glare, and struggling vainly with the glorious twilight.

The next morning the valet, who had taken me as his master, and who told others in the house that he could not attend to them, as he was in my service, informed me that a traveller, arrived from Warsaw the night before, had taken apartments in the same hotel, and could give me all necessary information in regard to that route; and, after breakfast, I sent him, with my compliments, to ask the traveller if he would admit me, and shortly after called myself. He was a young man, under thirty, above the middle size, strong and robust of frame, with good features, light complexion, but very much freckled, a head of extraordinarily red hair, and a mustache of the same brilliant colour; and he was dressed in a coloured stuff morning-gown, and smoking a pipe with an air of no small dignity and importance. I explained the purpose of my visit, and he gave me as precise information as could possibly be had; and the most gratifying part of the interview was, that before we separated he told me that he intended returning to Warsaw in about ten days, and would be happy to have me bear him company. I gladly embraced his offer, and left him, better pleased with the result of my interview than I had expected from his rather unprepossessing appearance. He was a Frenchman by descent, born in Belgium, and educated and resident in Poland, and possessed in a striking degree the compounded *amor patriæ* incident to the relationship in which he stood to these three countries. But, as I shall be obliged to speak of him frequently hereafter, I will leave him for the present to his morning-gown and pipe.

Well pleased with having my plans arranged, I went out without any specific object, and found myself on the banks of the Neva. Directly opposite the Winter Palace, and one of the most conspicuous objects on the whole line of the Neva, is the citadel or old fortress, and, in reality, the foundation of the city. I looked long and intently on the golden spire of its church, shooting toward the sky and glittering in the sun. This spire, which rises tapering till it seems almost to fade away into nothing, is surmounted by a large globe, on which stands an angel supporting a cross. This angel, being made of corruptible stuff, once manifested symptoms of decay, and fears were entertained that he would soon be numbered with the fallen. Government became perplexed how to repair it, for to raise a scaffolding to such a height would cost more than the angel was worth. Among the crowd which daily assembled to gaze at it from below was a roofer of houses, who, after a long and silent examination, went to the government and offered to repair it without any scaffolding or assistance of any kind. His offer was accepted; and on the day appointed for the attempt, provided with nothing but a coil of cords, he ascended inside to the highest window, and, looking for a moment at the crowd below and at the spire tapering away above him, stood up on the outer ledge of the window. The spire was covered with sheets of gilded copper, which, to beholders from below, presented only a smooth surface of burnished gold; but the sheets were roughly laid, and fastened by large nails, which projected from the sides of the spire. He cut two pieces of cord, and tied loops at each end of both, fastened the upper loops over two projecting nails, and stood with his feet in the lower; then, clinching the fingers of one hand over the rough edges of the sheets of copper, raised himself till he could hitch one of the loops on a higher nail with the other hand; he did the same for the other loop, and so on he raised one leg after the other, and at length ascended, nail by nail, and stirrup by stirrup, till he clasped his arms around the spire directly under the ball. Here it seemed impossible to go any farther, for the ball was ten or twelve feet in circumference, with a smooth and glittering surface, and no projecting nails, and the angel was above the ball, as completely out of sight as if it were in the habitation of its prototypes. But the daring roofer was not disheartened. Raising himself in his stirrups, he encircled the spire with a cord, which he tied round his waist; and, so supported, leaned gradually back until the soles of his feet were braced against the spire, and his body fixed almost horizontally in the air. In this position he threw a cord over the top of the ball, and threw it so coolly and skilfully that at the first attempt it fell down on the other side, just as he wanted it; then he drew himself up to his original position, and, by means of his cord, climbed over the smooth sides of the globe, and in a few moments, amid thunders of applause from the crowd below, which at that great height sounded only like a faint murmur, he stood by the side of the angel. After attaching a cord to it he descended, and the next day carried up with him a ladder of ropes, and effected the necessary repairs.

But to return. With my eyes fixed upon the spire, I crossed the bridge and entered the gate of the fortress. It is built on a small island, fortified by five bastions, which, on the land side, are mere ramparts, connected with St. Petersburgh quarter by drawbridges, and on the river side it is surrounded by walls cased with granite, in the centre of which is a large gate or sally-port. As a fortress it is now useless; but it is a striking object of embellishment to the river, and an interesting monument in the history of the city. Peter himself selected this spot for his citadel and the foundation of his city. At that time it contained two fishing-huts in ruins, the only original habitations on the island. It was necessary to cut down the trees, and elevate the surface of the island with dirt and stone brought from other places, before he commenced building the fortress; and the labour of the work was immense, no less than forty thousand workmen being employed at one time. Soldiers, Swedish prisoners, Ingrians, Carelians, and Cossacks, Tartars, and Calmues, were brought from their distant solitudes to lay the foundation of the imperial city, labouring entirely destitute of all the comforts of life, sleeping on the damp ground and in the open air, often without being able, in that wilderness, to procure their daily meal; and, moreover, without pickaxes, spades, or other instruments of labour, and using only their bare hands for digging; but, in spite of all this, the work advanced with amazing rapidity, and in four months the fortress was completed. The principal objects of interest it now contains are the Imperial Mint and the Cathedral of St. Peter and St. Paul. Brought up in a community where "making money" is the great business of life, I ought, perhaps, to have entered the former, but I turned away from the ingots of gold and silver, and entered the old church, the burial-place of Peter the Great, and nearly all the czars and czarinas, emperors and empresses, since his time. Around the walls were arranged flags and banners, trophies taken in war, principally from the Turks, waving mournfully over the tombs of the dead. A sombre light broke through the lofty windows, and I moved directly to the tomb of Peter. It is near the great altar, of plain marble, in the shape of a square coffin, without any ornament but a gold plate, on one end of which are engraved his name and title; and at the moment of my entrance an old Russian was dusting it with a brush. It was with a mingled feeling of veneration and awe that I stood by the tomb of Peter. I had always felt a profound admiration for this extraordinary man, one of those prodigies of nature which appear on the earth only once in many centuries; a combination of greatness and cruelty, the sternness of whose temper spared neither age nor sex, nor the dearest ties of kindred; whose single mind changed the face of an immense empire and the character of millions, and yet who often remarked with bitter compunction, "I can reform my people, but I cannot reform myself."

By his side lies the body of his wife, Catharine I., the beautiful Livonian, the daughter of a peasant girl, and the wife of a common soldier, who, by a wonderful train of events, was raised to wield the sceptre of a gigantic empire. Her fascination soothed the savage Peter in his moodiest hours. She was the mediatrix between the stern monarch and his subjects; mercy was ever on her lips, and one who knew her well writes what might be inscribed in letters of gold upon her tomb: "She was a pretty, well-looked woman, but not of that sublimity of wit, or, rather, that quickness of imagnation which some people have supposed. The great reason why the Czar was so fond of her was her exceeding good temper; she never was seen peevish or out of humour; obliging and civil to all, and never forgetful of her former condition, and withal mighty grateful."

Near their imperial parents lie the bodies of their two daughters, Anne of Holstein and the Empress Elizabeth. Peter, on his death-bed, in an interval of delirium, called to him his daughter Anne, as it was supposed with the intention of settling upon her the crown, but suddenly relapsed into insensibility; and Anne, brought up in the expectation of two crowns, died in exile, leaving one son, the unfortunate Peter III.

Elizabeth died on the throne, a motley character of goodness, indolence, and voluptuousness, and extremely admired for her great personal attractions. She was never married, but, as she frequently owned to her confidants, never happy but when in love. She was so tender of heart that she made a vow to inflict no capital punishment during her reign; shed tears upon the news of every victory gained by her troops, from the reflection that it could not have been gained without bloodshed, and would never give her consent for the execution of a felon, however deserving; and yet she condemned two noble ladies, one of them the most beautiful woman in Russia, to receive fifty strokes of the knout in the open square of St. Petersburgh.

I strolled for a few moments among the other imperial sepulchres, and returned to the tombs of Peter's family. Separate monuments are erected over their bodies, all in the shape of large oblong tomb-stones, ornamented with gold, and enclosed by high iron railings. As I leaned against the railing of Peter's tomb, I missed one member of his imperial family. It was an awful chasm. Where was his first-born child and only son? the apparent heir of his throne and empire? Early the object of his unnatural prejudice, excluded from the throne, imprisoned, tortured, tried, condemned, sentenced to death by the stern decree of his offended father.

The ill-starred Alexius lies in the vaults of the church, in the imperial sepulchre, but without any tomb or inscription to perpetuate the recollection of his unhappy existence. And there is something awful in the juxta-position of the dead; he lies by the side of his unhappy consort, the amiable Princess Charlotte, who died the victim of his brutal neglect; so subdued by affliction that, in a most affecting farewell to Peter, unwilling to disturb the tranquillity of her last hour, she never mentioned his name, and welcomed death as a release from her sufferings.

Leaving the church, I went to a detached building within the fortress, where is preserved, in a separate building, a four-oared boat, as a memorial of the origin of the Russian navy. Its history is interesting. About the year 1691 Peter saw this boat at a village near Moscow; and inquiring the cause of its being built differently from those he was in the habit of seeing, learned that it was contrived to go against the wind. Under the direction of Brandt, the Dutch shipwright who built it, he acquired the art of managing it. He afterward had a large pleasure-yatch constructed after the same model, and from this beginning went on till he surprised all Europe by a large fleet on the Baltic and the Black Sea. Twenty years afterward he had it brought up from

Moscow, and gave a grand public entertainment, which he called the consecration of the "Little Grandsire." The fleet, consisting of twenty-seven men-of-war, was arranged at Cronstadt in the shape of a half-moon. Peter embarked in the Little Grandsire, himself steering, and three admirals and Prince Mendzikoff rowing, and made a circuit in the gulf, passing by the fleet, the ships striking their flags and saluting it with their guns, while the Little Grandsire returned each salute by a discharge of three small pieces. It was then towed up to St. Petersburgh, where its arrival was celebrated by a masquerade upon the waters, and, Peter again steering, the boat proceeded to the fortress, and under a discharge of all the artillery it was deposited where it now lies.

Returning, I took a bath in the Neva. In bathing, as in everything else, the Russians profit by the short breath of summer, and large public bathing-houses are stationed at intervals along the quay of the river, besides several smaller ones, tasteful and ornamental in appearance, being the private property of rich seigneurs. I went into one of the former, where a swimming-master was teaching a school of boys the art of swimming. The water of the Neva was the first thing I had found regularly Russian, that is, excessively cold; and though I bathed in it several times afterward, I always found it the same.

At five o'clock I went to dine with Mr. Wilkins. He had broken up his establishment and taken apartments at the house of an English lady, where he lived much in the same style as at home. He had been at St. Petersburgh but a short time, and, I believe, was not particularly well pleased with it, and was then making arrangements to return. I had never met with Mr. Wilkins in our own country, and I consider myself under obligations to him; for, not bringing him any letter, I stood an entire stranger in St. Petersburgh, with nothing but my passport to show that I was an American citizen, and he might have even avoided the dinner, or have given me the dinner, and troubled himself no more about me. But the politeness which he had shown me as a stranger increased to kindness; and I was in the habit of calling upon him at all times, and certainly without any expectation of ever putting him in print. We had at table a parti quarré, consisting of Mr. Wilkins, Mr. Gibson, who has been our consul I believe for twenty years, if, he being still a bachelor, it be not unfriendly to carry him back so far, and Mr. Clay, the secretary of legation, who had been twice left as chargé-d'affaires at the imperial court, and was then lately married to an English lady in St. Petersburgh.(After dinner, three or four American merchants came in; and at eleven o'clock, having made an appointment to go with Mr. Wilkins and see a boat-race on the Neva, Mr. Clay and I walked home along the quay, under that enchanting twilight which I have already so often thrust upon the reader, and which I only regret that I cannot make him realise and enjoy.

CHAPTER XXI.

A new Friend.—The Winter Palace.—Importance of a Hat.—An artificial Mine.—Remains of a huge Monster.—Peter the Great's Workshop.—The Greek Religion.—Tomb of a Hero.—A Saint Militant.—Another Love Affair.—The Hermitage.—The Winter and Summer Gardens.

EARLY in the morning, while at breakfast, I heard a loud knock at my door, which was opened without waiting for an answer, and in stalked a tall, stout, dashing-looking young man, with a blue frock, white pantaloons, and a vest of many colours, a heavy gold chain around his neck, an enormous Indian cane in his hand, and a broad-brimmed hat brought down on one side, over his right eye in particular. He had a terrible scowl on his face, which seemed to be put on to sustain the dignity of his amazing costume, and he bowed on his entrance with as much *hauteur* as if he meant to turn me out of my own room. I stared at him in unfeigned astonishment, when, putting his cane under his arm, and pulling off his hat, his intensely red head broke upon me with a blaze of beauty, and I recognised my friend and intended fellow-traveller, the French Belgian Pole, whom I had seen in an old morning-gown and slippers. I saw through my man at once; and speedily knocking in the head his overwhelming formality, came upon him with the old college salutation, asking him to pull off his clothes and stay a week; and he complied almost literally, for in less than ten minutes he had off his coat and waistcoat, cravat and boots, and was kicking up his heels on my bed. I soon discovered that he was a capital fellow, a great beau in his little town on the frontiers of Poland, and one of a class by no means uncommon, that of the very ugly men who imagine themselves very handsome. While he was kicking his heels over the footboard, he asked me what we thought of red hair in America; and I told him that I could not undertake to speak the public voice, but that, for myself, I did not admire it as much as some people did, though, as to his, there was something striking about it, which was strictly true, for it was such an enormous mop, that, as his head lay on the pillow, it looked like a bust set in a large red frame. All the time he held in his hand a pocket looking-glass and a small brush, with which he kept brushing his mustaches, giving them a peculiar twirl toward the ears. I told him that he was wrong about the mustache; and, taking the brush, brought them out of their twist, and gave them an inclination à la Turque, recommending my own as a model; but he soon got them back to their place, and, rising, shook his gory locks and began to dress himself, or, as he said, to put himself in parchment for a walk.

My new friend was for no small game, and proposed visiting some of the palaces. On the way he confided to me a conquest he had already made since his arrival; a beautiful young lady, of course, the daughter of an Italian music-master, who resided directly opposite our hotel. He said he had applied for an apartment next to mine, which commanded a view of the window at which she sat, and asked me, as a friend, whether it would be interfering with me. Having received my assurance that I had no intentions in that quarter, he said he would order his effects to be removed the same day.

By this time we had arrived at the Winter Palace, presenting, as I have before remarked, a marble front on the Neva of more than seven hundred feet, or as long as the side of Washington Square, and larger and more imposing than that of the Tuileries, or any other royal palace in Europe. We approached the large door of entrance to this stately pile, and, notwithstanding my modest application, backed by my companion's dashing exterior, we were turned away by the imperial footman because we had not on dress-coats. We went home and soon returned equipped as the law of etiquette requires, and were admitted to the imperial residence. We ascended the principal story by the great marble staircase, remarkable for its magnificence and the grandeur of its architecture. There are nearly a hundred principal rooms on the first floor, occupying an area of four hundred thousand square feet, and forming almost a labyrinth of splendour. The great banquetting-hall is one hundred and eighty-nine feet by one hundred and ten, incrusted with the finest marble, with a row of columns at each end, and the side decorated with attached columns, rich gilding, and splendid mirrors. The great Hall of St. George is one of the richest and most superb rooms on the Continent, not excepting the pride of the Tuileries or Versailles. It is a parallelogram of one hundred and forty feet by sixty, decorated with forty fluted Corinthian columns of porphyritic marble, with capitals and bases of bronze richly gilded, and supporting a gallery with a gilded bronze balustrade of exquisite workmanship. At one end, on a platform, is the throne, approached by a flight of eight steps, covered with the richest Genoa velvet, embroidered with gold, with the double-headed eagle expanding his wings above it. The large windows on both sides are hung with the richest drapery, and the room is embellished by magnificent mirrors and colossal candelabra profusely gilded.

We passed on to the *salle blanche*, which is nearly of the same dimensions, and beautifully chaste in design and finish. Its elevation is greater, and the sides are decorated with pilasters, columns, and bas-reliefs of a soft white tint, without the least admixture of gaudy colours. The space between the Hall of St. George and the *salle blanche* is occupied as a gallery of national portraits, where the Russians who distinguished themselves during the French invasion are exhibited in half-length portraits as rewards for their military services. The three field-marshals, Kutuzow, Barclay de Tolly, and the Duke of Wellington, are represented at full length. The symbol which accompanies the hero of Waterloo is that of imperishable celebrity, the British oak, "the triumpher of many storms."

I will not carry the reader through all the magnificent apartments, but I cannot help mentioning the Diamond Room, containing the crowns and jewels of the imperial family. Diamonds, rubies, and emeralds, are arranged round the room in small cases, of such dazzling beauty that it is almost bewildering to look at them. I had already acquired almost a passion for gazing at precious stones. At Constantinople I had wandered through the bazars, under the guidance of a Jew, and seen all the diamonds collected and for sale in the capital of the East, but I was astonished at the brilliancy of this little chamber, and, in my strongly-awakened admiration, looked upon the miser who, before the degrading days of bonds and mortgages, converted his wealth into jewels and precious stones, as a man of elegant and refined taste. The crown of the emperor is adorned with a chaplet of oak-leaves made of diamonds of an extraordinary size, and the imperial sceptre contains one supposed to be the largest in the world, being the celebrated stone purchased by the Empress Catharine II. from a Greek slave for four hundred and fifty thousand rubles and a large pension for life. Eighty thousand persons were employed in the construction of this palace; upwards of two thousand habitually reside in it, and even a larger number when the emperor is in St. Petersburgh. The imperial flag was then floating from the top of the palace, as an indication to his subjects of his majesty's presence in the capital; and about the time that his majesty sat down to his royal dinner, we were working upon a *côtelette de mouton*, and drinking, in *vin ordinaire*, health and long life to Nicolas the First; and afterward, in talking of the splendour of the imperial palace and the courtesy of the imperial footmen, we added health and long life to the Lady Autocrat and all the little autocrats.*

After dinner we took our coffee at the Café Chinois, on the Newski Perspective, equal, if not superior, in style and decoration to anything in Paris. Even the rules of etiquette in France are not orthodox all over the world. In Paris it is not necessary to take off the hat on entering a café or restaurant, and in the south of France a Frenchman will sit down to a dinner next a lady with his head covered; but in Russia, even on entering an apartment where there are only gentlemen, it is necessary to uncover the head. I neglected this rule from ignorance and want of attention, and was treated with rudeness by the proprietor, and afterward learned the cause, with the suggestion that it was fortunate that I had not been insulted. This is a small matter, but a man's character in a strange place is often affected by a trifling circumstance; and Americans, at least I know it to be the case with myself, are, perhaps, too much in the habit of neglecting the minor rules of etiquette.

That night my new friend had his effects removed to a room adjoining mine, and the next morning I found him sitting in his window with a book in his hand, watching the young lady opposite. He was so pleased with his occupation that I could not get him away, and went off without him. Mr. Wilkins having offered to accompany me to some of the public institutions, I called for him; and, finding him disengaged, we took a boat on the Neva, and went first to the Academy of Arts, standing conspicuously on the right bank opposite the English Quay, and, perhaps, the chastest and most classical structure in St. Petersburgh. In the court are two noble Egyptian sphynxes. A magnificent staircase, with a double flight of granite steps, leads to a grand landing-

---

* The Winter Palace has since been destroyed by fire. The author has not seen any account of the particulars, but has heard that the contents of the Diamond Chamber were saved

place with broad galleries around it, supporting, by means of Ionic columns, the cupola, which crowns the whole. The Rotunda is a fine apartment of exquisite proportions, decorated with statues and busts; and at the upper end of the Conference-room stands a large table, at the head of which is a full-length portrait of Nicolas under a rich canopy. In one room are a collection of models from the antique, and another of the paintings of native artists, some of which are considered as indicating extraordinary talent

From hence we went to the *Hotel des Mines*, where the name of the American minister procured us admission without the usual permit. The *Hotel des Mines* was instituted by the great Peter for the purpose of training a mining engineer corps, to explore scientifically the vast mineral resources of the empire, and also engineers for the army. Like all the other public edifices, the building is grand and imposing, and the arrangement of the different rooms and galleries is admirable. In one room is a large collection of medals, and in another of coins. Besides specimens of general mineralogy of extraordinary beauty, there are, native iron from the Lake Olonetz, silver ore from Tobolsk, and gold sand from the Oural Mountains; and in iron-bound cases, beautifully ornamented, there is a rich collection of native gold, found either in the mines belonging to government or in those of individuals, one piece of which was discovered at the depth of three and a half feet in the sand, weighing more than twenty-four pounds. The largest piece of platinum in existence, from the mines of Demidoff, weighing ten pounds, is here also; and, above all, a colossal specimen of amalachite, weighing three thousand four hundred and fifty-six pounds, and, at the common average price of this combination of copper and carbonic acid, worth three thousand seven hundred and fifty pounds sterling.

But the most curious part of this valuable repository is under ground, being the model of a mine in Siberia. Furnished with lighted tapers, we followed our guides through winding passages cut into the bowels of the earth, the sides of which represented, by the aggregation of real specimens, the various stratifications, with all the different ores, and minerals, and different species of earth, as they were found in the natural state; the coal formation, veins of copper, and in one place of gold, being particularly well represented, forming an admirable practical school for the study of geology, though under a chilliness of atmosphere which would be likely very soon to put an end to studies of all kinds.

From here we passed to the imperial Academy of Sciences, by far the most interesting part of our day's visiting. This, too, was founded by the Great Peter. I hardly know why, but I had already acquired a warm admiration for the stout old czar. There was nothing high or chivalric about him, but every step in Russia, from the Black Sea to the Baltic, showed me what he had done to advance the condition of his people. I knew all this as matter of history, but here I felt it as fact. We strolled through the mineralogical and zoological repositories, and stopped before the skeleton of that stupendous inhabitant of a former world, denominated the mammoth, whose fame had been carried over the waste of waters even to our distant country, and beside which even the skeletons of elephants looked insignificant. What was he! where did he live, and is his race extinct? It gave rise to a long train of interesting speculation, to endow him with life, and see him striding with gigantic steps, the living tenant of a former world; and more interesting still to question, as others had done, whether he was not, after all, one of a race of animals not yet extinct, and perhaps wandering even now within a short distance of the Polar Sea.

There is also in this part of the museum a collection of anatomical specimens and of human monsters; an unpleasing exhibition, though, no doubt, useful to medical science; among them was a child with two heads from America. More interesting to me was a large collection of insects, of medals, and particularly of the different objects in gold found in the tumuli of Siberia, consisting of bracelets, vases, crowns, bucklers, rings, sabres with golden hilts, Tartar idols, &c., many of them of great value and of very elegant workmanship, which have given rise to much interesting speculation in regard to the character of the people who formerly inhabited that country. The Asiatic museum contains a library of Chinese, Japanese, Mongolese, and Tibetan books and manuscripts; Mohammedan, Chinese, and Japanese coins; an interesting assemblage of Mongulese idols cut in bronze and gilded, and illustrating the religion of Buddha. There is also an Egyptian museum, containing about a thousand articles. The cabinet of curiosities contains figures of all the different people conquered under the government of Russia, habited in their national costumes; also of Chinese, Persians, Aleutans, Carelians, and the inhabitants of many of the Eastern, Pacific, or Northern islands discovered or visited by Russian travellers and navigators, as well as of the different nations inhabiting Siberia.

But by far the most interesting part of the museum is the cabinet of Peter himself, consisting of a suite of apartments, in which the old czar was in the habit of passing his leisure hours engaged in some mechanical employment. In one room are several brass cylinders turned by his own hands, and covered with battle-scenes of his own engraving. Also an iron bar forged by him; bas-reliefs executed in copper, representing his desperate battles in Livonia; an ivory chandelier of curious and highly-wrought workmanship, and a group in ivory representing Abraham offering up his son Isaac, the ram and the angel Gabriel cut out entire. In another room is his workshop, containing a variety of vessels and models etched in copper, and a copper-plate with an unfinished battle-scene. His tools and implements are strewed about the room precisely in the state in which he left them the last time he was there. In another chamber were the distended skin of his French body-servant, seven feet high; the Arabian horse which he rode at the bloody battle of Pultowa, and the two favourite dogs which always accompanied him; and in another the figure of the old czar himself in wax, as large as life; the features, beyond doubt, bearing the exact resemblance to the original, being taken from a cast applied to his face when dead, and shaded in imitation of his real complexion. The eyebrows and hair are black, the eyes dark, the complexion swarthy, the aspect stern. This figure is surrounded by the portraits of his predecessors, in their barbarian costumes, himself seated in an arm-chair in the same splendid dress which he wore when with his own hands he placed the imperial crown on the head of his beloved Catharine. Here, also, are his uniform of the guards, gorget, scarf, and sword; and hat shot through at the battle of Pultowa; and the last thing which the guide put into my hands was a long stick measuring his exact height, and showing him literally a great man, being six Russian feet. I must not forget a pair of shoes made by his own hands; but the old czar was no shoemaker. Nevertheless, these memorials were all deeply interesting; and though I had seen the fruits of his labours from the Black Sea to the Baltic, I never felt such a strong personal attraction to him as I did here.

I was obliged to decline dining with Mr. Wilkins, in consequence of an engagement with my friend the Pole; and, returning, I found him at the window with a book in his hand, precisely in the same position in which I had left him. After dinner, a servant came in and delivered a message, and he proposed a walk on the Admiralty Boulevards. It was the fashionable hour for promenade, and, after a turn or two, he discovered his fair enslaver, accompanied by her father and several ladies and gentlemen, one of whom seemed particularly devoted to her. She was a pretty little girl, and seemed to me a mere child, certainly not more than fifteen. His admiration had commenced on the Boulevards the first afternoon of his arrival, and had increased violently during the whole day, while he was sitting at the window. He paraded me up and down the walk once or twice, and, when they had seated themselves on a bench, took a seat opposite. He was sure she was pleased with his admiration, but I could not see that her look indicated any very flattering acknowledgment. In fact, I could but remark that the eyes of the gentlemen were turned toward us quite as often as those of the lady, and suggested that, if he persisted, he would involve us in some difficulty with them; but he said there could not be any difficulty about it, for, if he offended them, he would give them satisfaction. As this view of the case did not hit my humour, I told him that, as I had come out with him, I would remain, but if he made any farther demonstrations, I should leave him, and, at all events, after that, he must excuse me from joining his evening promenades. Soon after they left the Boulevards, and we returned to our hotel, where he entertained me with a history of his love adventures at home, and felicitations upon his good fortune in finding himself already engaged in one here.

Sunday. Until the early part of the tenth century the religion of Russia was a gross idolatry. In nine hundred and thirty-five, Olga, the widow of Igor, the son of Runic, sailed down the Dnieper from Kief, was baptized at Constantinople, and introduced Christianity into Russia, though her family and nation adhered for a long time to the idolatry of their fathers. The great schism between the Eastern and Western churches had already taken place, and the Christianity derived from Constantinople was of course of the Greek persuasion. The Greek Church believes in the doctrines of the Trinity, but differs from the Catholic in some refined and subtle distinction in regard to what is called the procession of the Holy Ghost. It enjoins the invocation of saints as mediators, and permits the use of pictures as a means of inspiring and strengthening devotion. The well-informed understand the use for which they are intended, but these form a very small portion of the community, and probably the great bulk of the people worship the pictures themselves. The clergy are, in general, very poor, and very ignorant. The priests are not received at the tables of the upper classes, but they exercise an almost controlling influence over the lower, and they exhibited this influence in rousing the serfs against the French, which may be ascribed partly, perhaps, to feelings of patriotism, and partly to the certainty that Napoleon would strip their churches of their treasures, tear down their monasteries, and turn themselves out of doors. But of the population of fifty-five millions, fifteen are divided into Roman Catholics, Armenians, Protestants, Jews, and Mohammedans, and among the Caucasians, Georgians, Circassians, and Mongol tribes, nearly two millions are pagans or idolaters, Brahmins, Lamists, and worshippers of the sun.

For a people so devout as the Russians, the utmost toleration prevails throughout the whole empire, and particularly in St. Petersburgh. Churches of every denomination stand but a short distance apart on the Newski Perspective. The Russian cathedral is nearly opposite the great Catholic chapel; near them is the Armenian, then the Lutheran, two churches for Dissenters, and a mosque for the Mohammedans! and on Sunday thousands are seen bending their steps to their separate churches, to worship according to the faith handed down to them by their fathers.

Early in the morning, taking with me a valet, and joining the crowd that was already hurrying with devout and serious air along the Newski Perspective, I entered the Cathedral of our Lady of Cazan, a splendid monument of architecture, and more remarkable as the work of a native artist, with a semicircular colonnade in front, consisting of one hundred and thirty-two Corinthian columns thirty-five feet high, somewhat after the style of the great circular colonnade of St. Peter's at Rome, and surmounted by a dome crowned with a cross of exquisite workmanship, supported on a large gilded ball. Within, fifty noble columns, each of one piece of solid granite from Finland, forty-eight feet high and four feet in diameter, surmounted by a rich capital of bronze, and resting on a massive bronze base, support an arched roof richly ornamented with flowers in bas-relief. The jewels and decorations of the altar are rich and splendid, the doors leading to the sanctum sanctorum, with the railing in front, being of silver. As in the Catholic churches, there are no pews, chairs, or benches, and all over the floor were the praying figures of the Russians. Around the walls were arranged military trophies, flags, banners, and the keys of fortresses wrested from the enemies of Russia; but far more interesting than her columns, and colossal statues, and military trophies, is the tomb of the warrior Kutuzow; simple, and remarkable for the appropriate warlike trophy over it, formed of French flags and the eagles of Napoleon. Admiration for heroism owns no geographical or territorial limits, and I pity the man who could stand by the grave of Kutuzow without feeling it a sacred spot. The Emperor Alexander with his own hands took the most precious jewel from his crown and sent it to the warrior, with a letter announcing to him his elevation to the rank of Prince of Smolensko ; but richer than jewels or principalities is the tribute which his countrymen pay at his tomb.

The church of our Lady of Cazan contains another monument of barbarian patriotism. The celebrated leader of the Cossacks, during the period of the French invasion, having intercepted a great part of the booty which the French were carrying from Moscow, sent it to the metropolitan or head of the church, with a characteristic letter, directing it to be "made into an image of the four Evangelists, and adorn the church of the Mother of God of Cazan." The concluding paragraph is, "Hasten to erect in the temple of God this monument of battle and victory ; and while you erect it, say with thankfulness to Providence, the enemies of Russia are no more ; the vengeance of God has overtaken them on the soil of Russia ; and the road they have gone has been strewed with their bones, to the utter confusion of their frantic and proud ambition.

(Signed) "PLATOFF."

From the church of our Lady of Cazan I went to the Protestant church, where I again joined in an orthodox service. The interior of the church is elegant, though externally it can scarcely be distinguished from a private building. The seats are free, the men sitting on one side and the women on the other. Mr. Law, the clergyman, has been there many years, and is respected and loved by his congregation. After church I walked to the convent of Alexander Newski, the burial-place of Prince Alexander, who obtained in the thirteenth century a splendid victory over the allied forces of Sweden, Denmark, and Livonia ; afterwards he became a monk, and for his pure and holy life was canonized, and now ranks among the principal saints in the Russian calendar. The warrior was first buried at Moscow, but Peter the Great had his remains transported with great ceremony to this place, a procession of a thousand priests walking barefoot all the way. The monastery stands at the extreme end of the Newski Perspective, and within its precincts are several churches, and a large cemetery. It is the residence of the distinguished prelates of the Greek Church and a large fraternity of monks. The dress of the monks is a loose black cloak and round black cap, and no one can be admitted a member until the age of thirty. We entered a grand portal, walked up a long avenue, and, crossing a bridge over a stream, worked our way between lines of the carriages of nobles and ladies, and crowds of the people in their best bell-crowned hats ; and, amid a throng of miserable beggars, penetrated to the door of the principal church, a large and beautiful specimen of modern Corinthian architecture. I remarked the great entrance, the lofty dome, the fresco paintings on the ceilings, and the arabesque decorations on the walls ; the altar-piece of white Carrara marble, paintings by Rubens and Vandyck, the holy door in the iconastos, raised on a flight of steps of rich gilded bronze, and surmounted by the representation of a dazzling aureola of different-coloured metals, and in the centre the initials of that awful name which none in Israel save the initiated were permitted to pronounce. I walked around and paused before the tomb of the warrior saint.

A sarcophagus, or coffin of massive silver, standing on an elevated platform, ornamented in bas-relief, representing scenes of battles with the Swedes, contain his relics ; a rich ermine lies upon the coffin, and above is a silver canopy. On each side is a warrior clothed in armour, with his helmet, breastplate, shield and spear, also of massive silver. The altar rises thirty feet in height, of solid silver, with groups of military figures and trophies of warriors, also of silver, as large as life; and over it hangs a golden lamp, with a magnificent candelabrum of silver, together with a vessel of curious workmanship holding the bones of several holy men, the whole of extraordinary magnificence and costliness of material, upward of four thousand pounds' weight of silver having been used in the construction of the chapel and shrine. The dead sleep the same whether in silver coffins or in the bare earth, but the stately character of the church, dimly lighted, and the splendour and richness of the material, gave a peculiar solemnity to the tomb of the warrior saint.

Leaving the churches, I strolled through the cloisters of the monastery and entered the great cemetery. There, as in the great cemetery of Père-la-Chaise, at Paris, all that respect, and love, and affection, can do to honour the memory of the dead, and all that vanity and folly can do to ridicule it, have been accomplished. There are seen epitaphs of affecting brevity, and elaborate amplification ; every design, every device, figure, emblem, and decoration ; every species of material, from native granite to Carrara marble and pure gold. Among the simpler tombs of poets, warriors, and statesmen, a monument of the most gigantic proportions is erected to snatch from oblivion the name of a rich Russian merchant. The base is a solid cubic block of the most superb marble, on which is a solid pedestal of black marble ten feet square, bearing a sarcophagus fourteen feet high, and of most elegant proportions, surmounted by a gold cross twenty feet in height. At each of the four corners is a colossal candelabrum of cast iron, with entwining serpents of bronze gilded. The ground alone cost a thousand pounds, and the whole monument about twenty thousand dollars. Near the centre of this asylum of the dead, a tetrastyle Ionic temple of the purest white marble records the virtues of an interesting lady, the Countess of Potemkin ; and alto-relievos of the most exquisite execution on three sides of the temple tell the melancholy story of a mother snatched from three lovely children. The countess, prophetically conscious of her approaching fate, is looking up calmly and majestically to the figure of religion, and resting with confidence her left hand on the symbol of Christianity. In front are the inscription and arms of the family in solid gold.

But what are the Russian dead to me ? The granite and marble monument of the merchant is a conglomeration of hides, hemp, and tallow ; a man may be excused if he linger a moment at the tomb of an interesting woman, a mother cut off in her prime ; but melancholy is infectious, and induces drowsiness and closing of the book.

Q

In consideration for my valet, at the grand portal I took a drosky, rolled over the wooden pavement of the Newski Perspective, and, with hardly motion enough to disturb my reverie, was set down at the door of my hotel. My Pole was waiting to dine with me, and roused me from my dreams of the dead to recount his dreams of the living. All day he had sat at his window, and a few straggling glances from the lady opposite had abundantly rewarded him, and given him great spirits for his evening's promenade on the Boulevards. I declined accompanying him, and he went alone, and returned in the evening almost in raptures. We strolled an hour by the twilight and retired early.

It will hardly be believed, but early the next morning he came to my room with a letter on fine pink paper addressed to his fair enslaver. The reader may remember that this was not the first time I had been made a confidant in an *affaire du cœur*. To be sure, the missionary at Smyrna turned out to be crazy; and on this point, at least, my Pole was a little touched; nevertheless, I listened to his epistle. It was the regular old-fashioned document, full of hanging, shooting, drowning, and other extravagances. He sealed it with an amatory device, and, calling up a servant in his confidence, told him to carry it over, and then took his place in my window to watch the result. In the meantime, finding it impossible to dislodge him, and that I could not count upon him to accompany me on my visits to the palaces as he had promised, I went to the Hermitage alone. The Great and Little Hermitages are connected with the Winter Palace and with each other by covered galleries, and the theatre is connected with the two Hermitages by means of another great arch thrown over a canal, so that the whole present a continued line of imperial palaces, unequalled in extent in any part of Europe, measuring one thousand five hundred and ninety-six feet, or one-third of an English mile. If I were to select a building designed to realise the most extravagant notions of grandeur and luxury, it would be the gorgeous palace known under the modest name of the Hermitage. I shall not attempt any description of the interior of this splendid edifice, but confine myself to a brief enumeration of its contents. I ascended by a spacious staircase to the ante-room, where I gave, or, rather, where my cane was demanded by the footman, and proceeded through a suite of magnificent rooms, every one surpassing the last, and richer in objects of the fine arts, science, and literature; embellished throughout by a profusion of the most splendid ornaments and furniture, and remarkable for beauty of proportion and variety of design. In rooms and galleries appropriated to the separate schools and masters are upward of thirteen hundred paintings by Raphael, Titian, Guido, Andrea del Sarto, Luca Giordano, the Caracci, Perugino, Coreggio, and Leonardo da Vinci; here is also the best collection in existence of pictures by Wouvermans and Teniers, with some of the masterpieces of Rubens and Vandyck, of the French Claude, Poussin, and Vernet. The celebrated Houghton collection is here, with a gallery of paintings of the Spanish schools, many of them Murillos. In one room is a superb vase of Siberian jasper, of a lilac colour, five feet high, and of exquisite form and polish; in another are two magnificent candelabras, said to be valued at two hundred and twenty thousand rubles, or about fifty thousand dollars; I must mention also the great musical clock, representing an antique Grecian temple, and containing within a combination of instruments, having the power of two orchestras, which accompany each other; two golden tripods, seven feet high, supporting the gold salvers on which salt and bread were exhibited to the Emperor Alexander on his triumphal return from Paris, as emblems of wisdom and plenty; a large musical and magical secretary, which opens spontaneously in a hundred directions at the sound of music, purchased by the late emperor for eight hundred guineas: a room surrounded with books, some of which were originals, placed there by Catharine for the use of the domestics, as she said, to keep the devil out of their heads; a saloon containing the largest collection of engravings and books of engravings in Europe, amounting to upward of thirty thousand; a library of upward of one hundred and ten thousand volumes; an extensive cabinet of medals, and another of gems and pastes; a jewel cabinet containing the rich ornaments which have served for the toilets of succeeding empresses, innumerable precious stones and pearls, many of extraordinary magnitude; a superb collection of antiques and cameos, amounting to upwards of fifteen thousand, the cameos alone affording employment for days. In one room are curious works in ivory and fishbones, by the inhabitants of Archangel, who are skilled in that species of workmanship; and in another is the celebrated clock, known by the name of L'Horloge du Paon. It is enclosed in a large glass case ten feet high, being the trunk of a golden tree, with its branches and leaves all of gold. On the top of the trunk sits a peacock, which, when the chimes begin, expands its brilliant tail, while an owl rolls its eyes with its own peculiar stare, and, instead of a bell striking the hours, a golden cock flaps his wings and crows. The clock is now out of order, and the machinery is so complicated that no artist has hitherto been able to repair it.

But perhaps the most extraordinary and interesting of the wonders of the Hermitage are the Winter and Summer Gardens. As I strolled through the suites of apartments, and looked out through the windows of a long gallery, it was hardly possible to believe that the flourishing trees, shrubs, and flowers stood upon an artificial soil, raised nearly fifty feet above the surface of the earth. The Winter Garden is a large quadrangular conservatory, planted with laurels and orange-trees, in which linnets and Canary birds formerly flew about enjoying the freedom of nature; but the feathered tribe have disappeared. The Summer Garden connected with it is four hundred feet long; and here, suspended as it were in the air, near the top of the palace, I strolled along gravel-walks, and among parterres of shrubs and flowers growing in rich luxuriance, and under a thick foliage inhaled their delightful fragrance. It is idle to attempt a description of the scene.

I returned to my Pole, whom I found at his window with a melancholy and sentimental visage, his beautiful epistle returned upon his hands—

having, in sportsman's phrase, entirely missed fire—and then lying with a most reproving look on his table. My friend had come up to St. Petersburgh in consequence of a lawsuit, and as this occupied but a small portion of his time, he had involved himself in a love-suit, and so far as I could see, with about an equal chance of success in both. *L'amour* was the great business of his life, and he could not be content unless he had what he called *une affaire du cœur*.

CHAPTER XXII.

An Imperial Fête.—Nicolas of Russia.—Varied Splendours.—A Soliloquy.—House of Peter the Great.—A Boat-race.—Czarskoselo.—The Amber Chamber.—Catharine II.—The Emperor Alexander.

The next day was that appointed for the great fête at Peterhoff. In spite of the confining nature of his two suits, my Pole had determined to accompany me thither, being prompted somewhat by the expectation of seeing his damsel; and, no way disheartened by the fate of his first letter, he had manufactured another, by comparison with which the first was an icicle. I admitted it to be a masterpiece, though when he gave it to a servant to carry over, as we were on the point of setting off, suggested that it might be worth while to wait and pick it up when she threw it out of the window. But he had great confidence, and thought much better of her spirit for sending back his first letter.

The whole population of Petersburgh was already in motion and on the way to Peterhoff. It was expected that the fête would be more than usually splendid, on account of the presence of the Queen of Holland, then on a visit to her sister the empress; and at an early hour the splendid equipages of the nobility, carriages, droskys, telegas, and carts, were hurrying along the banks of the Neva, while steam-boats, sail-boats, row-boats, and craft of every description, were gliding on the bosom of the river.

As the last trouble, we chose a steam-boat, and at twelve o'clock embarked at the English Quay. The boat was crowded with passengers, and among them was an old English gentleman, a merchant of thirty years' standing in St. Petersburgh. I soon became acquainted with him, how I do not know, and his lady told me that the first time I passed them she remarked to her husband that I was an American. The reader may remember that a lady made the same remark at Smyrna; without knowing exactly how to understand it, I mentioned it as a fact showing the fine discrimination acquired by persons in the habit of seeing travellers from different countries. Before landing, the old gentleman told me that his boys had gone down in a pleasure-boat, abundantly provided with materials, and asked me to go on board and lunch with them, which, upon the invitation being extended to my friend, I accepted.

Peterhoff is about twenty-two versts from St. Petersburgh, and the whole bank of the Neva on that side is adorned with palaces and beautiful summer residences of the Russian seigneurs. It stands at the mouth of the Neva, on the borders of the Gulf of Finland. Opposite is the city of Cronstadt, the seaport of St. Petersburgh and the anchorage of the Russian fleet. It was then crowded with merchant ships of every nation, with flags of every colour streaming from their spars in honour of the day. On landing, we accompanied our new friends, and found "the boys," three fine young fellows just growing up to manhood, in a handsome little pleasure-boat, with a sail arranged as an awning, waiting for their parents. We were introduced and received with open arms, and sat down to a cold collation in good old English style, at which, for the first time since I left home, I fastened upon an old-fashioned sirloin of roast-beef. It was a delightful meeting for me. The old people talked to me about my travels; and the old lady particularly, with almost a motherly interest in a straggling young man, inquired about my parents, brothers, and sisters, &c.; and I made my way with the frank-hearted "boys" by talking "boat." Altogether, it was a regular home family scene; and, after the lunch, we left the old people under the awning, promising to return at nine o'clock for tea, and with "the boys" set off to view the fête.

From the time when we entered the grounds, until we left at three o'clock the next morning, the whole was a fairy scene. The grounds extended some distance along the shore, and the palace stands on an embankment perhaps a hundred and fifty feet high, commanding a full view of the Neva, Cronstadt with its shipping, and the Gulf of Finland. We followed along the banks of a canal five hundred yards long, bordered by noble trees. On each side of the canal were large wooden frames about sixty feet high, filled with glass lamps for the illumination; and at the foot of each was another high framework with lamps, forming, among other things, the arms of Russia, the double-headed eagle, and under it a gigantic star thirty or forty feet in diameter. At the head of the canal was a large basin of water, and in the centre of the basin stood a colossal group in brass, of a man tearing open the jaws of a rampant lion; and out of the mouth of the lion rushed a *jet-d'eau* perhaps a hundred and fifty feet high. On each side of this basin, at a distance of about three hundred feet, was a smaller basin, with a *jet-d'eau* in each about half its height, and all around were *jets-d'eau* of various kinds, throwing water vertically and horizontally; among them I remember a figure larger than life, leaning forward in the attitude of a man throwing the discus, with a powerful stream of water rushing from his clenched fist. These basins were at the foot of the embankment on which stands the palace. In the centre was a broad flight of steps leading to the palace, and on each side was a continuous range of marble slabs to the top of the hill, over which poured down a sheet of water, the slabs being placed so high and far apart as to allow lamps to be arranged behind the water. All over, along the public walks and in retired alcoves, were frames hung with lamps; and everywhere, under the trees and on the open lawn, were tents of every size and fashion, beautifully decorated; many of them, Oriental in style and elegance, were fitted up as places of refreshment. Thousands of people, dressed in their best attire, were promenading the grounds, but no vehicles were to be seen, until, in turning a point, we espied at some distance up an avenue, and coming quietly toward us, a plain open carriage, with two horses and two English jockey outriders, in which were a gentleman and lady, whom, without the universal taking off of hats around us, I recognised at once as the emperor and empress. I am not apt to be carried away by any profound admiration for royalty, but, without consideration of their rank, I never saw a finer specimen of true gentility; in fact, he looked every inch a king, and she was my beau ideal of a queen in appearance and manners. They bowed as they passed, and, as I thought, being outside of the line of Russians and easily recognised as a stranger, their courtesy was directed particularly to me; but I found that my companion took it very much to himself, and no doubt every long-bearded Russian near us did the same. In justice to myself, however, I may almost say that I had a conversation with the emperor; for although his imperial highness did not speak to me, he spoke in a language which none but I (and the queen and his jockey outriders) understood; for, waving his hand to them, I heard him say in English, "To the right." After this *interview* with his majesty we walked up to the palace. The splendid regiments of cavalier guards were drawn up around it, every private carrying himself like a prince; and I did not admire all his palaces, nor hardly his queen, so much as this splendid body of armed followers. Behind the palace is a large plain cut up into gravel-walks, having in one place a basin of water, with waterworks of various kinds, among which were some of peculiar beauty falling in the form of a semiglobe.

A little before dark we retired to a refectory under a tent until the garden was completely lighted up, that we might have the full effect of the illumination at one *coup-d'œil*, and, when we went out, the dazzling brilliancy of the scene within the semicircular illumination around the waterworks was beyond description. This semicircular framework enclosed in a large sweep the three basins, and terminated at the embankment on which the palace stands, presenting all around an immense fiery scroll in the air, sixty or eighty feet high, and filled with all manner of devices; and for its background a broad sheet of water falling over a range of steps, with lighted lamps behind it, forming an illuminated cascade, while the basins were blazing with the light thrown upon them from myriads of lamps, and the colossal figures of a reddened and unearthly hue were spouting columns of water into the air. More than two hundred thousand people were supposed to be assembled in the garden, in every variety of gay, brilliant, and extraordinary costume. St. Petersburgh was half depopulated, and thousands of peasants were assembled from the neighbouring provinces. I was accidentally separated from all my companions; and, alone among thousands, sat down on the grass, and for an hour watched the throng passing through the illuminated circle, and ascending the broad steps leading toward the palace. Among all this immense crowd there was no rabble; not a dress that could offend the eye; but intermingled with the ordinary costumes of Europeans were, the Russian shopkeeper, with his long surtout, his bell-crowned hat, and solemn beard; Cossacks, and Circassian soldiers, and Calmuc Tartars, and cavalier guards; hussars, with the sleeves of their rich jackets dangling loose over their shoulders, tossing plumes, and helmets glittering with steel, intermingled throughout with the gay dresses of ladies; while near me, and, like me, carelessly stretched on the grass, under the light of thousands of lamps, was a group of peasants from Finland fiddling and dancing; the women with light hair, bands around their heads, and long jackets enwrapping their square forms, and the men with long great-coats, broad-brimmed hats, and a bunch of shells in front.

Leaving this brilliant scene, I joined the throng on the steps, and by the side of a splendid hussar, stooping his manly figure to whisper in the ears of a lovely young girl, I ascended to the palace, and presented my ticket of admission to the *bal masqué*, so called from there being no masks there I had not been presented at court, and, consequently, had only admission to the outer apartments with the people. I had, however, the range of a succession of splendid rooms, richly decorated with vases and tazzas of precious stones, candelabras, couches, ottomans, superb mirrors, and inlaid floors; and the centre room, extending several hundred feet in length, had its lofty walls covered to the very ceilings with portraits of all the female beauties in Russia about eighty years ago. I was about being tired of gazing at these pictures of long-sleeping beauties, when the great doors at one end were thrown open, and the emperor and empress, attended by the whole court, passed through on their way to the banquetting-hall. Although I had been in company with the emperor before in the garden, and though I had taken off my hat to the empress, both passed without recognising me. The court at St. Petersburgh is admitted to be the most brilliant in Europe; the dresses of the members of the diplomatic corps and the uniforms of the general and staff-officers being really magnificent, while those of the ladies sparkled with jewels. Besides the emperor and empress, the only acquaintance I recognised in that constellation of brilliantly-dressed people were Mr. Wilkins and Mr. Clay, who, for republicans, made a very fair blaze. I saw them enter the banquetting-hall, painted in Oriental style to represent a tent, and might have had the pleasure of seeing the emperor and empress and all that brilliant collection eat; but, turning away from a noise that destroyed much of the illusion, viz., the clatter of knives and forks, and a little piqued at the cavalier treatment I had received from the court circles, I went out on the balcony and soliloquised, "Fine feathers make fine birds; but look back a little, ye dashing cavaliers and supercilious ladies. In the latter part of the seventeenth century, a French traveller in Russia wrote that 'most men treat their wives as a necessary evil, regarding them with a proud and stern eye, and even beating them after.' Dr. Collins, physician to the Czar in 1670, as an evidence of the progress of civilisation in Russia, says that the custom of tying up wives by the hair of the head and flogging them 'begins to be left off;' accounting for it, however, by the prudence of parents, who made a stipulative provision in the marriage contract that their daughters were not to be whipped, struck, kicked, &c. But, even in this improved state of society, one man 'put upon his wife a shirt dipped in ardent spirits, and burned her to death,' and was not punished, there being, according to the doctor, ' no punishment in Russia for killing a wife or a slave.' When no provision was made in the marriage contract, he says, they were accustomed to discipline their wives very severely. At the marriage the bridegroom had a whip in one boot and a jewel in the other, and the poor girl tied her fortune by choosing. ' If she happens upon the jewel,' says another traveller, 'she is lucky; but if on the whip, she gets it.' The bridegroom rarely saw his companion's face till after the marriage, when, it is said, ' if she be ugly she pays for it soundly, maybe the first time he sees her.' Ugliness being punished with the whip, the women painted to great excess; and a traveller in sixteen hundred and thirty-six saw the grand duchess and her ladies on horseback, astride, most wickedly bepainted.' The day after a lady had been at an entertainment, the hostess was accustomed to ask how she got home; and the polite answer was, ' Your ladyship's hospitality made me so tipsy that I don't know how I got home ;' and for the climax of their barbarity it can scarcely be believed, but it is recorded as a fact, that the women did not begin to wear stays till the beginning of the present century !"

Soothed by these rather ill-natured reflections, I turned to the illuminated scene and the thronging thousands below, descended once more to the garden, passed down the steps, worked my way through the crowd, and fell into a long avenue, like all the rest of the garden, brilliantly lighted, but entirely deserted. At the end of the avenue I came to an artificial lake, opposite which was a small square two-story cottage, being the old residence of Peter the Great, the founder of all the magnificence of Peterhoff. It was exactly in the style of our ordinary country houses, and the furniture was of a simplicity that contrasted strangely with the surrounding luxury and splendour. The door opened into a little hall, in which were two old-fashioned Dutch mahogany tables, with oval leaves, legs tapering and enlarging at the feet into something like a horse-shoe ; just such a table as every one may remember in his grandfather's house, and recalling to mind the simple style of our own country some thirty or forty years ago. In a room on one side was the old czar's bed, a low, broad wooden bedstead, with a sort of canopy over it, the covering of the canopy and the coverlet being of striped calico ; the whole house, inside and out, was hung with lamps, illumining with a glare that was almost distressing the simplicity of Peter's residence ; and, as if to give greater contrast to this simplicity, while I was standing in the door of the hall, I saw roll by me, in splendid equipages, the emperor and empress, with the whole of the brilliant court which I had left in the banquetting-hall, now making a tour of the gardens. The carriages were all of one pattern, long, hung low, without any tops, and somewhat like our omnibuses, except that, instead of the seats being on one side, there was a partition in the middle not higher than the back of a sofa, with large seats like sofas on each side, on which the company sat in a row, with their backs to each other ; in front was a high and large box for the coachmen, and a footman behind. It was so light that I could distinguish the face of every gentleman and lady as they passed ; and there was something so unique in the exhibition, that, with the splendour of the court dresses, it seemed the climax of the brilliant scenes at Peterhoff. I followed them with my eyes till they were out of sight, gave one more look to the modest pillow on which old Peter reposed his careworn head, and at about one o'clock in the morning left the garden. A frigate brilliantly illuminated was firing a salute, the flash of her guns lighting up the dark surface of the water as I embarked on board the steam-boat. At two o'clock, the morning twilight was like that of day ; at three o'clock I was at my hotel, and, probably, at ten minutes past, asleep.

About eight o'clock the next morning my Pole came into my room. He had returned from Peterhoff before me, and found waiting for him his second epistle, with a note from the mother of the young lady, which he read to me as I lay in bed. Though more than half asleep, I was rather roused by the strange effect this letter had upon him, for he was now encouraged to go on with his suit, since he found that the backwardness of the young lady was to be ascribed to the influence of the mother, and not to any indifference on her part.

In the afternoon I went to a boat-race between English amateurs that had excited some interest among the English residents. The boats were badly matched ; a six-oared boat thirty-two feet long, and weighing two hundred and thirty pounds, being pitted against three pairs of sculls, with a boat twenty-eight feet long and weighing only one hundred and eight pounds. One belonged to the English legation and the other to some English merchants. The race was from the English Quay to the bridge opposite the Suwarrow monument at the foot of the Summer Garden, and back, a little more than two miles each way. The rapidity of the current was between two and three miles an hour, though its full strength was avoided by both boats keeping in the eddies along shore. It was a beautiful place for a boat-race ; the banks of the Neva were lined with spectators, and the six-oared boat beat easily, performing the distance in thirty-one minutes.

The next morning, in company with a Frenchman lately arrived at our hotel, I set out for the imperial palace of Czarskoselo, about seventeen versts from St. Petersburgh. About seven versts from the city we passed the imperial seat of Zechenne, built by the Empress Catharine to commemorate the victory obtained by Orloff over the Turks on the coast of Anatolia. The edifice is in the form of a Turkish pavilion, with a central rotunda containing the full-length portraits of the sovereigns cotemporary with Catharine. Since her death this palace has been deserted. In 1825 Alexander and the empress passed it on their way to the south of Russia, and about eight months after their mortal remains found shelter in it for a night, on their way to the imperial sepulchre. There was no other object of interest on the road until we approached Czarskoselo. Opposite the "Caprice Gate" is a cluster of white houses, in two rows, of different sizes, diminishing as they recede from the road, and converging at the farthest extremity ; altogether a bizarre arrangement, and showing the magnificence of Russian gallantry. The Empress Catharine at the theatre one night happened to express her pleasure at the perspective view of a small town, and the next time she visited Czarskoselo she saw the scene realised in a town erected by Count Orloff at immense expense before the gate of the palace. The façade of the palace is unequalled by any royal residence in the world, being twelve hundred feet in length. Originally, every statue, pedestal, and capital of the numerous columns, the vases, carvings, and other ornaments in front, were covered with gold leaf, the gold used for that purpose amounting to more than a million of ducats. In a few years the gilding wore off, and the contractors engaged in repairing it offered the empress nearly half a million of rubles (silver) for the fragments of gold; but the empress scornfully refused, saying, "*Je ne suis pas dans l'usage de vendre mes vieilles hardes.*" I shall not attempt to carry the reader through the magnificent apartments of this palace. But I must not forget the famed amber chamber, the whole walls and ceilings being of amber, some of the pieces of great size, neatly fitted together, and even the frames of the pictures an elaborate workmanship of the same precious material. But even this did not strike me so forcibly as when, conducted through a magnificent apartment, the walls covered with black paper shining like ebony, and ornamented with gold and immense looking-glasses, the footman opened a window at the other end, and we looked down into the chapel, an Asiatic structure, presenting an *ensemble* of rich gilding of surpassing beauty, every part of it, the groups of columns, the iconastos, and the gallery for the imperial family, resplendent with gold. In one of the state-rooms where the empress's mother resides, the floor consists of a parquet of fine wood inlaid with wreaths of mother-of-pearl, and the panels of the room were incrusted with *lapis lazuli*.

But to me, all these magnificent chambers were as nothing compared with those which were associated with the memory of the late occupant. "Uneasy lies the head that wears a crown;" and perhaps it is for this reason that I like to look upon the pillow of a king, far more on that of a queen. The bedchamber of Catharine II. is adorned with walls of porcelain and pillars of purple glass; the bedclothes are those under which she slept the last time she was at the palace, and in one place was a concealed door, by which, as the unmannerly footman, without any respect to her memory, told us, her imperial highness admitted her six-feet paramours. In the bedchamber of Alexander were his cap, gloves, boots, and other articles of dress, lying precisely as he left them previous to his departure for the southern part of his empire. His bed was of leather, stuffed with straw, and his boots were patched over and over worse than mine, which I had worn all the way from Paris. I tried on his cap and gloves, and moralized over his patched boots. I remembered Alexander as the head of a gigantic empire, the friend and ally, and then the deadly foe, of Napoleon; the companion of kings and princes; the arbiter of thrones and empires, and playing with crowns and sceptres. I sat with the patched boots in my hand. Like old Peter, he had considerable of a foot, and I respected him for it. I saw him, as it were, in an undress, simple and unostentatious in his habits; and there was a domestic air in his whole suite of apartments that interested me more than when I considered him on his throne. His sitting-room showed quiet and gentlemanly as well as domestic habits, for along the wall was a border of earth, with shrubs and flowers growing out of it, a delicate vine trailed around and almost covering a little mahogany railing. The grounds around the palace are eighteen miles in circumference, abounding in picturesque and beautiful scenery, improved by taste and an unbounded expenditure of money, and at this time they were in the fulness of summer beauty. We may talk simplicity and republicanism, but, after all, it must be a pleasant thing to be an emperor. I always felt this, particularly when strolling through imperial parks or pleasure-grounds, and sometimes I almost came to the unsentimental conclusion, that, to be rural, a man must be rich.

We wandered through the grounds without any plan, taking any path that offered, and at every step some new beauty broke upon us: a theatre; Turkish kiosk, or Chinese pagoda; splendid bridges, arches, and columns; and an Egyptian gate; a summer-house in the form of an Ionic colonnade, a masterpiece of taste and elegance, supporting an aerial garden crowded with flowers; and a Gothic building called the Admiralty, on the borders of an extensive lake, on which lay several boats rigged as frigates, elegant barges and pleasure-boats, and beautiful white swans floating majestically upon its surface; on the islands and the shores of the lake were little summer-houses; at the other end was a magnificent stone landing, and in full view a marble bridge, with Corinthian columns of polished marble; an arsenal, with many curious and interesting objects, antique suits of armour, and two splendid sets of horse-trappings, holsters, pistols, and bridles, all studded with diamonds, presented by the sultan on occasion of the peace of Adrianople. Nor must I forget the dairy, and a superb collection of goats and lamas from Siberia. Amid this congregation of beauties, one thing offended me; a Gothic tower, built as a ruin for the sake of the picturesque, which, wanting the associations connected with monuments ruined by time, struck me as a downright mockery. We had intended to visit the palace of Paulowsky, but time slipped away, and it was six o'clock before we started to return to St. Petersburgh.

CHAP. XXIII.

The Soldier's Reward.—Review of the Russian Army.—American Cannibals.—Palace of Potemkin.—Palace of the Grand-duke Michael.—Equipments for Travelling.—Rough Riding.—Poland.—Vitepsk.—Napoleon in Poland.—The Disastrous Retreat.—Passage of the Berezina.

EARLY the next morning I went out about twelve versts from the city to attend a grand military review by the emperor in person. The government of Russia is a military despotism, and her immense army, nominally amounting to a million, even on the peace establishment numbers actually six hundred thousand, of which sixty thousand follow the person of the emperor, and were at that time under arms at St. Petersburgh. When I rode on the parade-ground, the spectacle of this great army, combining the élite of barbaric chivalry with soldiers trained in the best schools of European discipline, drawn up in battle's stern array, and glittering with steel, was brilliant and almost sublime; in numbers and military bearing, in costliness of armour and equipment, far surpassing any martial parade that I had seen, not excepting a grand review of French troops at Paris, or even a *fourth of July parade at home*. I once had the honour to be a paymaster in the valiant one hundred and ninety-seventh regiment of New York State Militia; and I can say—what, perhaps, no other man who ever served in our army can say—that I served out my whole term without being once promoted. Men came in below and went out above me; ensigns became colonels and lieutenants generals, but I remained the same. It was hard work to escape promotion, but I was resolute. Associated with me was a friend as quartermaster, with as little of the spirit of a soldier in him as myself, for which we were rather looked down upon by the warriors of our day; and when, at the end of our term, in company with several other officers, we resigned, the next regimental orders were filled with the military panegyrics, each as, "the colonel has received, with the greatest regret, the resignation of Lieutenant A.;" "the country has reason to deplore the loss of the services of Captain B.," and wound up with, "Quartermaster G. and Paymaster S. have tendered their resignations, *both of which are hereby accepted*." But when strains of martial music burst from a hundred bands, and companies, and regiments, and brigades wheeled and manœuvred before me, and the emperor rode by, escorted by general and field officers, and the most magnificent staff in Europe, and the earth shook under the charge of cavalry, I felt a strong, martial spirit roused within me; perhaps I was excited by the reflection that these soldiers had been in battles, and that the stars and medals glittering on their breasts were not mere holiday ornaments, but the tokens of desperate service on bloody battle-fields.

In a body, the Russian soldiers present an exceedingly fine appearance. When the serf is enrolled, his hair and beard are cut off, except on the upper lip, his uniform is simple and graceful, a belt is worn tightly round the waist, and the breast of the coat is thickly padded, increasing the manliness of the figure, though sometimes at the expense of health. In evolutions they move like a great machine, as if all the arms and legs were governed by a single impulse.

The army under review was composed of representatives from all the nations under the sway of Russia; Cossacks of the Don, and the Wolga, and the Black Sea, in jackets and wide pantaloons of blue cloth, riding on small horses, with high-peaked saddles, and carrying spears eight or ten feet in length. One regiment had the privilege of wearing a ragged flag and caps full of holes, as proofs of their gallant service, being the only regiment that fought at Pultowa. And there were Calmucs in their extraordinary war-dress; a helmet with a golden crest, or a chain-cap with a net-work of iron rings falling over the head and shoulders, and hanging as low as the eyebrows in front; a shirt of mail, composed of steel rings matted together, and yielding to the body, the arms protected by plates, and the back of the hand by steel net-work fastened to the plates on each side; their offensive weapons were bows and arrows, silver-mounted pistols peeping out of their holsters, cartridge-boxes on each side of the breast, and a dagger, sword, and gun.

The Kirguish, a noble-looking race, come from the steppes of Siberia. Their uniform is magnificent, consisting of a blue frock-coat and pantaloons covered with silver lace, a Grecian helmet, and a great variety of splendid arms, the yataghan alone costing a thousand rubles. They are all noble, and have no regular duty, except to attend the imperial family on extraordinary occasions. At home they are always at war among themselves. They are Mohammedans; and one of them said to an American friend who had a long conversation with him, that he had four wives at home; that some had more, but it was not considered becoming to exceed that number. A bearded Russian came up and said that these Kirguish ate dogs and cats, against which the Kirguish protested. The same Russian afterwards observed that the Americans were worse than the Kirguish, for that a patriarch of the church had written, and therefore it must be true, that the number of human beings eaten by Americans could not be counted; adding, with emphasis, "Sir, you were created in the likeness of your Maker, and you should endeavour to keep yourself so." He continued that the Russians were the first Christians, and he felt much disposed to send missionaries among the Americans to meliorate their condition.

The Imperial Guards are the finest-looking set of men I ever saw. The standard is six feet, and none are admitted below that height. Their uniform is a white cloth coat, with buckskin breeches, boots reaching up to the hips, and swords that Wallace himself would not have been ashamed to wield. But perhaps the most striking in that brilliant army was the emperor himself; seeming its natural head, towering even above his gigantic guards, and looking, as Mr. Wilkins once said of him, like one who, among savages, would have been chosen for a chief. In the midst of this martial spectacle, the thought came over me of militia musters at home; and though smiling at the insignificance of our military array as I rode back in my drosky, I could but think of the happiness of our isolated position, which spares us the necessity of keeping a large portion of our countrymen constantly in arms to preserve the rest in the enjoyment of life and fortune.

The next morning my Polish friend, hopeless of success either in his lawsuit or his lovesuit, fixed a day for our departure; and with the suggestion that I am about leaving St. Petersburgh, I turn once more, and for the last time, to the imperial palaces. Not far from the Hermitage is the marble palace; a colossal pile, built by the Empress Catharine for her favourite, Count Orloff, presenting one of its fronts to the Neva. All the decorations are of marble and gilded bronze, and the capitals and bases of the columns and pilasters, and the window-frames and balustrades of the balconies, of cast bronze richly gilded. The effect is heightened by the unusually large dimensions of the squares of fine plate-glass. A traveller in seventeen hundred and fifty-nine says, " that the prodigies of enchantment which we read of in the Tales of the Genii are here called forth into reality; and the temples reared by the luxuriant fancy of our poets may be considered as a picture of the marble palace, which Jupiter, when the burden of cares drives him from heaven, might make his delightful abode." At present, however, there are but few remains of this Olympian magnificence, and I think Jupiter at the same expense would prefer the Winter Palace or the Hermitage.

The Taurida Palace, erected by Catharine II. for her lover, Potemkin, in general effect realises the exaggerated accounts of travellers. The entrance is into a spacious hall, which leads to a circular vestibule of extraordinary magnitude, decorated with busts and statues in marble, with a dome supported by white columns. From thence you pass between the columns into an immense hall or ball-room, two hundred and eighty feet long and eighty wide, with double colonnades of lofty Ionic pillars decorated with gold and silver festoons, thirty-five feet high and ten feet in circumference. From the colonnade, running the whole length of the ball-room, you enter the Winter Garden, which concealed flues and stoves keep always at the temperature of summer; and here, upon great occasions, under the light of magnificent lustres and the reflection of numerous mirrors, during the fierceness of the Russian winter, when the whole earth is covered with snow, and "water tossed in the air drops down in ice," the imperial visiter may stroll through gravel-walks bordered with the choicest plants and flowers, blooming hedges and groves of orange, and inhale the fragrance of an Arabian garden. Paul, in one of his "darkened hours," converted this palace into barracks and a riding-school; but it has since been restored, in some degree, to its ancient splendour.

The palace of Paul in which he was assassinated, has been uninhabited since his death. But the triumph of modern architecture in St. Petersburgh is the palace of the Grand-duke Michael. I shall not attempt any description of this palace; but, to give some notion of its splendours to my calculating countrymen, I shall merely remark that it cost upward of seventeen millions of rubles. But I am weary of palaces; of wandering through magnificent apartments, where scene after scene bursts upon my eyes, and, before I begin to feel at home in them, I find myself ordered out by the footman. Will the reader believe me? On the opposite side of the river is a little wooden house, more interesting in my eyes than all the palaces in St. Petersburgh. It is the humble residence of Peter the Great. I visited it for the last time after rambling through the gorgeous palace of the Grand-duke Michael. It is one story high, low-roofed, with a little piazza around it, and contains a sitting-room, bed-room, and dining-parlours; and Peter himself, with his own axe, assisted in its construction. The rooms are only eight feet in height, the sitting-room is fifteen feet square, the dining-room fifteen feet by twelve, and the bed-chamber ten feet square. In the first there is a chapel and shrine, where the Russian visiter performs his orisons and prays for the soul of Peter. Around the cottage is a neat garden, and a boat made by Peter himself is suspended to one of the walls. I walked around the cottage, inside and out; listened attentively, without understanding a word he said, to the garrulous Russian cicerone, and sat down on the step of the front piazza. Opposite was that long range of imperial palaces extending for more than a mile on the Neva, and surpassing all other royal residences in Europe or the world. When Peter sat in the door of this humble cottage, the ground where they stood was all morass and forest. Where I saw the lofty spires of magnificent churches, he looked out upon fishermen's huts. My eyes fell upon the golden spire of the church of the citadel glittering in the sunbeams, and reminding me that in its dismal charnel-house slept the tenant of the humble cottage, the master-spirit which had almost created out of nothing all this splendour. I saw at the same time the beginning and the end of greatness. The humble dwelling is preserved with religious reverence, and even now is the most interesting monument which the imperial city can show.

And here, at this starting-point in her career, I take my leave of the Palmyra of the North. I am compelled to omit many things which he who speaks of St. Petersburgh at all ought not to omit: her magnificent churches; her gigantic and splendid theatres; her literary, scientific, and eleemosynary institutions, and that which might form the subject of a chapter in her capital, her government and laws. I might have seen something of Russian society, as my friend Luoff had arrived in St. Petersburgh; but, with my limited time, the interchange of these civilities interfered with my seeing the curiosities of the capital.

My intimacy with the colonel had fallen off, though we still were on good terms. The fact is, I believe I fell into rather queer company in St. Petersburgh, and very soon found the colonel to be the most thorough roué I ever met. He seemed to think that travelling meant dissipating; he had never travelled but once, and that was with the army to Paris; and, except when on duty, his whole time had been spent in riot and dissipation; and though sometimes he referred to hard fighting, he talked more of the pleasures of that terrible campaign than of its toils and dangers. In consideration of my being a stranger and a young man, he constituted himself my Mentor, and the advice which, in all soberness, he gave me as the fruits of his experience, was a beautiful guide for the road to ruin. I have no doubt that, if I had given myself up entirely to him, he would have fêted me all the time I was in St. Petersburgh; but this did not suit me, and I afterward fell in with the Pole, who had his own vagaries too, and who, being the proprietor of a cloth manufactory, did not suit the aristocratic notions of the colonel, and so our friendship cooled. My intimacy with his friend the prince, however, increased. I called upon him frequently, and he offered to accompany me everywhere; but as in sight-seeing I love to be alone, I seldom asked him, except for a twilight walk. Old associations were all that now bound together him and the colonel; their feelings, their fortunes, and their habits of life, were entirely different; and the colonel, instead of being displeased with my seeking the prince in preference to himself, was rather gratified. Altogether, the colonel told me, he was much mistaken in me, but he believed I was a good fellow after all; excused my regular habits somewhat on the ground of my health; and the day before that fixed for my departure, asked me to pass the evening with him, and to bring my friend the Pole. In the evening we went to the colonel's apartments. The prince was there, and, after an elegant little supper, happening to speak of a Frenchman and a Prussian living in the hotel, with whom I had become acquainted, he sent down for them to come up and join us. The table was cleared, pipes and tobacco were brought on, and champagne was the only wine. We had a long and interesting conversation on the subject of the road to Warsaw, and particularly in regard to the bloody passage of the Berezina, at which both the colonel and the prince were present. The servant, a favourite serf (who the next day robbed the colonel of every valuable article in his apartment), being clumsy in opening a new bottle of champagne, the colonel said he must return to army practice, and reaching down his sabre, with a scientific blow took off the neck without materially injuring the bottle or disturbing the contents. This military way of decanting champagne aided its circulation, and head after head fell rapidly before the naked sabre. I had for some time avoided emptying my glass, which, in the general hurry of business, was not noticed; but, as soon as the colonel discovered it, he cried out, "Treason, treason against good fellowship, — America is a traitor." I pleaded ill health, but he would not listen to me; upbraided me that the friend and old ally of Russia should fail him; turned up his glass on the table, and swore he would not touch it again unless I did him justice. All followed his example; all decided that America was disturbing the peace of nations; the glasses were turned up all around, and a dead stop was put to the merriment. I appealed, begged, and protested; and the colonel became positive, dogged, and outrageous. The prince came to my aid, and proposed that the difficulty between Russia and America should be submitted to the arbitration of France and Prussia. He had observed these powers rather backing out. The eyes of France were already in a fine frenzy rolling, and Prussia's tongue had long been wandering; and, in apprehension of their own fate, these mighty powers leaned to mercy. It was necessary, however, to propitiate the colonel, and they decided that, to prevent the effusion of blood, I should start once more the flow of wine; that we should begin again with a bumper all around; and, after that, every man should do as he pleased. The colonel was obliged to be content; and swearing that he would drink for us all, started anew.

The Prussian was from Berlin, and this led the colonel to speak of the stirring scenes that had taken place in that capital on the return of the Russian army from Paris; and, after awhile, the Prussian, personally unknown to the colonel, told him that his name was still remembered in Berlin as a leader in Russian riot and dissipation, and particularly as having carried off, in a most daring manner, a lady of distinguished family; and— "go on," said the colonel—"killed her husband." —"He refused my challenge," said the colonel, "but sought my life, and I shot him like a dog." The whole party now became uproarious; the colonel begged me, by all the friendly relations between Russia and America, to hold on till breakfast-time; but, being the coolest man present, and not knowing what farther developments might take place, I broke up the party.

In the morning my passport was not ready. I went off to the police-office for it, and when I returned the horses had not come, and the valet brought me the usual answer, that there were none. My Pole was glad to linger another day for the sake of his flirtation with the little girl opposite, and so we lounged through the day, part of the time in the bazar of a Persian, where I came near ruining myself by an offer I made for a beautiful emerald; and after one more, and the last twilight stroll on the banks of the Neva and up the Newski Perspective, we returned at an early hour, and, for the last time in Russia, slept in a bed.

At nine o'clock the next morning a kibitka drove up to the door of our hotel, demanding an American and a Pole for Warsaw. All the servants of the hotel were gathered around, arranging the luggage, and making a great parade of getting off the distinguished travellers. The travellers themselves seemed equipped for a long journey. One wore a blue roundabout jacket, military cap, and cloak, with whiskers and a mustache tending to red; the other a tall, stout, Herculean fellow, was habited in the most outré costume of a Russian traveller; a cotton dressing-gown of every variety of colours, red and yellow predominating; coarse grey trowsers; boots coming above his knees; a cap tout-à-fait farouche, and there was no mistake about the colour of his hair and mustaches: he was moving slowly around the kibitka in his travelling dress, and looking up to the window opposite, to give his Dulcinea the melancholy intelligence that he was going away, and perhaps to catch one farewell smile at parting. The carriage of these distinguished travellers was the kibitka, one of the national vehicles of Russia, being a long, round-bottomed box or cradle on four wheels, probably the old Scythian waggon, resting, in proud contempt of the effeminacy of springs, on the oaken axles; the hubs of the wheels were two feet long, the linch-pins of wood, the body of the carriage fastened to the wheels by wooden pins, ropes, and sticks; and, except the tires of the wheels, there was not a nail or piece of iron about it. The hinder part was covered with matting, open in front somewhat like an old-fashioned bonnet, and supported by an arched stick, which served as a linch-pin for the hind wheels; a bucket of grease hung under the hind axle, and the bottom of the kibitka was filled with straw; whole cost of outfit, thirteen dollars. Before it were three horses, one in shafts and one on each side, the centre one having a high bow over his neck, painted yellow and red, to which a rein was tied for holding up his head, and also a bell, to a Russian postilion more necessary than harness. The travellers took their places in the bottom of the kibitka, and the postilion, a rough brutal-looking fellow, in grey coat and hat turned up at the sides, mounted in front, catching a seat where he could on the rim of the waggon, about three inches wide; and in this dashing equipage we started for a journey of a thousand miles to the capital of another kingdom. We rolled for the last time through the streets of St. Petersburgh, gazed at the domes, and spires, and magnificent palaces, and in a few moments passed the barrier.

I left St. Petersburgh, as I did every other city, with a certain feeling of regret that, in all probability, I should never see it more; still the cracking of the postilion's whip and the galloping of the horses created in me that high excitement which I always felt in setting out for a new region. Our first stage was to Czarkoselo, our second to Cazena, where there was another palace. It was dark when we reached the third, a small village, of which I did not even note the name. I shall not linger on this road, for it was barren of interest and incident, and through a continued succession of swamps and forests. For two hundred miles it tried the tenure of adhesion between soul and body, being made of the trunks of trees laid transversely, bound down by long poles or beams fastened into the ground with wooden pegs, covered with layers of boughs, and the whole strewed over with sand and earth; the trunks in general were decayed and sunken, and the sand worn or washed away, reminding me of the worst of our western corduroy roads. Our waggon being without springs, and our seats a full-length extension on straw on the bottom, without the bed, pillows, and cushions which the Russians usually have, I found this ride one of the severest trials of physical endurance I ever experienced. My companion groaned and brushed his mustaches, and talked of the little girl at St. Petersburgh. In my previous journey in Russia I had found the refreshment of tea, and on this, often when almost exhausted, I was revived by that precious beverage. I stood it three days and nights, but on the fourth completely broke down. I insensibly slipped down at full length in the bottom of the waggon; the night was cold and rainy; my companion covered me up to the eyes with straw, and I slept from the early part of the evening like a dead man. The horses were changed three times; the waggon was lifted up under me, and the wheels greased; and three times my companion quarrelled with the postmaster over my body without waking me. About six o'clock in the morning he roused me. I could not stir hand or foot; my mouth was full of dust and straw, and I felt a sense of suffocation. In a few moments I crawled out, staggered a few steps, and threw myself down on the floor of a wretched post-house. My companion put my carpet-bag under my head, wrapped cloaks and great-coats around, and prepared me some tea; but I loathed everything. I was in that miserable condition which every traveller has some time experienced; my head ringing, every bone aching, and perfectly reckless as to what became of me. While my companion stood over me I fell asleep, and believe I should have been sleeping there yet if he had not waked me. He said we must go on at all risks until we found a place where we could remain with some degree of comfort. I begged and entreated to be left to myself, but he was inexorable. He lifted me up, hauled me out to the kibitka, which was filled with fresh straw, and seated me within, supporting me on his shoulder.

It was a beautiful day. We moved moderately, and toward evening came to a post-house kept by a Jew, or rather, a Jewess, who was so kind and attentive that we determined to stay there all night. She brought in some clean straw and spread it on the floor, where I slept gloriously. My companion was tougher than I, but he could not stand the fleas and bugs, and about midnight went out and slept in the kibitka. In the morning we found that he had been too late; that the kibitka had been stripped of every article except himself and the straw. Fortunately my carpet-bag had been brought in; but I received a severe blow in the loss of a cane, an old friend and travelling companion, which had been with me in every variety of scene, and which I had intended to carry home with me, and retain as a companion through life. It is almost inconceivable how much this little incident distressed me. It was a hundred times worse than the loss of my carpet-bag. I felt the want of it every moment; I had rattled it on the Boulevards of Paris, in the eternal city, the Coloseum, and the places thereabout; had carried it up the burning mountain, and poked it into the red hot lava; had borne it in the Acropolis, on the field of Marathon, and among the ruins of Ephesus; had flourished it under the beard of the sultan, and the eyes and nose of the emperor and autocrat of all the Russias; in deserts and in cities it had been my companion and friend. Unsparing Nemesis, let loose your vengeance upon the thief who stole it! The rascals had even carried off the rope traces, and every loose article about the kibitka.

Notwithstanding this, however, I ought not to omit remarking the general security of travelling in Russia and Poland. The immense plains; the distance of habitations; the number of forests; the custom of travelling by night as well as by day; the negligence of all measures to ensure the safety of the roads; all contribute to favour robbery and murders; and yet an instance of either is scarcely known in years. It was difficult on those immense levels, which seemed independent of either general or individual proprietors, to recognise even the bounds of empires. The dwina, however, a natural boundary, rolls between Russia and Poland; and at Vitepsk we entered the territories of what was once another kingdom. The surface of Poland forms part of that immense and unvaried plain which constitutes the northern portion of all the central European countries. A great portion of this plain is overspread with a deep layer of sand, alternating, however, with large clayey tracts and extensive marshes; a winter nearly as severe as that of Sweden, and violent winds blowing uninterruptedly over this wide open region, are consequences of its physical structure and position. The Roman arms never penetrated any part of this great level tract, the whole of which was called by them Sarmatia; and Sarmatia and Scythia were in their descriptions always named together as the abode of nomadic and savage tribes. From the earliest era it appears to have been peopled by the Sclavonic tribes; a race widely diffused, and distinguished by a peculiar language, by a strong national feeling, and by a particular train of superstitious ideas. Though shepherds, they did not partake of the migratory character of the Teutonic or Tartar nations; and were long held in the most cruel bondage by the Huns, the Goths, and other nations of Asia, for whom their country was a path to the conquest of the west of Europe.

In the tenth century the Poles were a powerful and warlike nation. In the fourteenth, Lithuania was incorporated with it, and Poland became one of the most powerful monarchies in Europe. For two centuries it was the bulwark of Christendom against the alarming invasions of the Turks; the reigns of Sigismund and Sobieski hold a high place in military history; and, until the beginning of the last century, its martial character gave it a commanding influence in Europe.

It is unnecessary to trace the rapid and irrecoverable fall of Poland. On the second partition, Kosciusko, animated by his recent struggle for liberty in America, roused his countrymen to arms. But the feet of three giants were upon her breast; and Suwarrow, marching upon the capital, storming the fortress of Praga, and butchering in cold blood thirty thousand inhabitants, extinguished, apparently for ever, the rights and the glories of Poland. Living as we do apart from the rest of the world, with no national animosities transmitted by our fathers, it is impossible to realise the feeling of deadly hatred existing between neighbouring nations from the disputes of ancestors centuries ago. The history of Russia and Poland presents a continued series of blood-stained pages. Battle after battle has nourished their mutual hate, and for a long time it had been the settled feeling of both that Russia or Poland must fall. It is perhaps fortunate for the rest of Europe that this feeling has always existed; for, if they were united in heart, the whole south of Europe would lie at the mercy of their invading armies. Napoleon committed a fatal error in tampering with the brave and patriotic Poles; for he might have rallied around him a nation of soldiers who, in gratitude, would have stood by him until they were exterminated.

But to return to Vitepsk. Here, for the first time, we fell into the memorable road traversed by Napoleon on his way to Moscow. The town stands on the banks of the Dwina, built on both sides of the river, and contains a population of about fifteen thousand, a great portion of whom are Jews. In itself, it has but little to engage the attention of the traveller; but I strolled through its streets with extraordinary interest, remembering it as the place where Napoleon decided on his fatal march to Moscow. It was at the same season and on the very same day of the year that the "grand army," having traversed the gloomy forests of Lithuania in pursuit of an invincible and intangible enemy, with the loss of more than a hundred thousand men, emerged from the last range of woods and halted at the presence of the hostile fires that covered the plain before the city. Napoleon slept in his tent on an eminence at the left of the main road, and before sunrise appeared at the advanced posts, and by its first rays saw the Russian army, eighty thousand strong, encamped on a high plain commanding all the avenues of the city. Ten thousand horsemen made a show of defending its passes; and at about ten o'clock, Murat le Beau Sabreur, intoxicated by the admiration his presence excited, at the head of a single regiment of chasseurs charged the whole Russian cavalry. He was repulsed, and driven back to the foot of the hillock on which Napoleon stood. The chasseurs of the French guards formed a circle around him, drove off the assailant lancers, and the emperor ordered the attack to cease; and pointing to the city, his parting words to Murat were, "To-morrow at five o'clock the sun of Austerlitz."

At daylight the camp of Barclay de Tolly was deserted; not a weapon, not a single valuable left behind; and a Russian soldier asleep under a bush was the sole result of the day expected to be so decisive. Vitepsk, except by a few miserable Jews and Jesuits, like the Russian camp, was also abandoned. The emperor mounted his horse and rode through the deserted camp and desolate streets of the city. Chagrined and mortified, he pitched his tents in an open court-yard; but, after a council of war with Murat, Eugene, and others of his principal officers, laid his sword upon the table, and resolved to finish in Vitepsk the campaign of that year. Well had it been for him had he never changed that determination. He traced his line of defence on the map, and explored Vitepsk and its environs as a place where he was likely to make a long residence; formed establishments of all kinds; erected large ovens capable of baking at once thirty thousand loaves of bread; pulled down a range of stone houses which injured the appearance of the square of the palace, and made arrangements for opening the theatre with Parisian actors. But in a few days he was observed to grow restless; the members of his household recollected his expression at the first view of the deserted Vitepsk, "Do you think I have come so far to conquer these miserable huts?" Segur says that he was observed to wander about his apartments as if pursued by some dangerous temptation. Nothing could rivet his attention. Every moment he began, stopped, and resumed his labour. At length, overwhelmed with the importance of the considerations that agitated him, "he threw himself on the floor of his apartment; his frame, exhausted by the heat and the struggles of his mind, could only bear a covering of the slightest texture. He rose from his sleepless pillow possessed once more with the genius of war; his voice deepens, his eyes flash fire, and his countenance darkens. His attendants retreat from his presence, struck with mingled awe and respect. His plan is fixed, his determination taken, his order of march traced out."

The last council occupied eight hours. Berthier, by a melancholy countenance, by lamentations, and even by tears; Lobau by the cold and haughty frankness of a warrior; Caulaincourt, with obstinacy and impetuosity amounting to violence; Duroc, by a chilling silence, and afterward by stern replies; and Daru, straightforward and with firmness immoveable, opposed his going; but, as if driven on by that fate he almost defied, he broke up the council with the fatal determination; "Blood has not been shed, and Russia is too great to yield without fighting. Alexander can only negotiate after a great battle. I will proceed to the holy city in search of that battle, and I will gain it. Peace waits me at the gates of Moscow." From that hour commenced that train of terrible disasters which finally drove him from the throne of France, and sent him to die an exile on a small island in the Indian Ocean. I walked out on the Moscow road, by which the grand army, with pomp and martial music, with Murat, and Ney, and Duroc and Daru, inspired by the great names of Smolensk and Moscow, plunged into a region of almost pathless forests, where most of them were destined to find a grave. I was at first surprised at the utter ignorance of the inhabitants of Vitepsk, in regard to the circumstances attending the occupation of the city by Napoleon. A Jew was my cicerone, who talked of the great scenes of which this little city had in his own day been the theatre, almost as matter of tradition, and without half the interest with which, even now, the Greek points the stranger to the ruins of Argos or the field of Marathon; and this ignorance in regard to the only matters that give an interest to this dreary road I remarked during the whole journey. I was so unsuccessful in my questions, and the answers were so unsatisfactory, that my companion soon became tired of acting as my interpreter. Indeed, as he said, he himself knew more than any one I met, for he had travelled it before in company with an uncle of the Polish legion; but even he was by no means familiar with the ground.

We left Vitepsk with a set of miserable horses, rode all night, and at noon of the next day were approaching the banks of the Berezina, memorable for the dreadful passage which almost annihilated the wretched remnant of Napoleon's army. It was impossible, in passing over the same ground, not to recur to the events of which it had been the scene. The "invincible legions," which left Vitepsk two hundred thousand strong, were now fighting their dreadful retreat from Moscow through regulars and Cossacks, reduced to less than twelve thousand men marching in column, with a train of thirty thousand undisciplined followers, sick, wounded and marauders of every description. The cavalry which crossed the Niemen thirty-seven thousand in number was reduced to one hundred and fifty men on horseback. Napoleon collected all the officers who remained mounted, and formed them into a body, in all about five hundred, which he called his sacred squadron; officers served as privates, and generals of divisions as captains. He ordered the carriages of the officers, many of the waggons, and even the eagles belonging to the different corps, to be burned in his presence; and drawing his sword with the stern remark that he had sufficiently acted the emperor, and must once more play the general, marched on foot at the head of his old guard. He had hardly reorganized before the immense pine forests which border the Berezina echoed with the thunder of the Russian artillery. In a moment all remains of discipline were lost; in the last stage of weakness and confusion they were roused by loud cries before them, and, to their great surprise and joy, recognised the armies of Victor and Oudinot. The latter knew nothing of the terrible disasters of the army of Moscow, and they were thrown into consternation and then melted to tears when they saw behind Napoleon, instead of the invincible legions which had left them in splendid equipments, a train of gaunt and spectral figures, their faces black with dirt, and long bristly beards, covered with rags, female pelisses, pieces of carpet, with bare and bleeding feet, or bundled with rags, and colonels and generals marching pellmell with soldiers, unarmed and shameless, without any order or discipline, kept together and sleeping round the same fires only by the instinct of self-preservation.

About noon we drove into the town of Borizoff. It stands on the banks of the Berezina, and is an old, irregular-looking place, with a heavy wooden church in the centre of an open square. As usual, at the door of the post-house a group of Jews gathered around us. When Napoleon took possession of Borizoff, the Jews were the only inhabitants who remained; and they, a scattered, wandering, and migratory people, without any attachment of soil or country, were ready to serve either the French or Russians, according to the inducements held out to them. A few noble instances are recorded where this persecuted and degraded people exhibited a devotion to the land that sheltered them, honourable to their race and to the character of man; but in general they were false and faithless. Those who gathered round us in Borizoff looked as though they might be the very people who betrayed the Russians. One of them told us that a great battle had been fought there, but we could not find any who had been present at the fatal passage of the river. We dined at the posthouse, probably with less anxiety than was felt by Napoleon or any of the flying Frenchmen; but even we were not permitted to eat in peace; for, before we had finished, our vehicle was ready, with worse horses than usual, and a sorlier postilion. We sent the postilion on a-head, and walked down to the bank of the river. On the night preceding the passage, Napoleon himself had command of Borizoff, with six thousand guards prepared for a desperate contest. He passed the whole night on his feet; and while waiting for the approach of daylight in one of the houses on the border of the river, so impracticable seemed the chance of crossing with the army, that Murat proposed to him to put himself under the escort of some brave and determined Poles, and save himself while there was yet time; but the emperor indignantly rejected the proposition as a cowardly flight. The river is here very broad, and divided into branches. On the opposite side are the remains of an embankment that formed part of the Russian fortifications. When the Russians were driven out of Borizoff by Oudinot, they crossed the river, burned the bridge, and erected these embankments.

Besides the sanguinary contest of the French and Russians, this river is also memorable for a great battle between my companion and our postilion. In the middle of the bridge the postilion stopped and waited till we came up: he grumbled loudly at being detained, to which my companion replied in his usual conciliatory and insinuating manner, by laying his cane over the fellow's shoulders; but on the bridge of Borizoff the blood of the Lithuanian was roused; and, perhaps, urged on by the memory of the deeds done there by his fathers, he sprang out of the waggon, and with a war-cry that would not have disgraced a Cossack of the Don, rushed furiously upon my friend. Oh for a Homer to celebrate that fight on the bridge of Borizoff! The warriors met, not like Grecian heroes with spear and shield, and clad in steel, but with their naked fists, and faces bare to take the blows. My friend was a sublime spectacle. Like a rock, firm and immoveable, he stood and met the charge of the postilion; in short, in the twinkling of an eye he knocked the postilion down. Those who know say that it is more trying to walk over a field of battle after all is over than to be in the fight; and I believe it from my experience in our trying passage of the Berezina; for, when I picked up the discomfited postilion, whose face was covered with blood, I believe that I had the worst of it. All great victories are tested by their results, and nothing could be more decisive than that over the postilion. He arose a wiser and much more tractable man. At first he looked very stupid when he saw me leaning over him, and very startled when he rubbed his hand over his face and saw it stained with blood; but, raising himself, he caught sight of his victor, and without a word got into the waggon, walked the horses over the bridge, and at the other end got out and threw himself on the ground.

It was a beautiful afternoon, and we lingered on the bridge. Crossing it, we walked up the bank on the opposite side toward the place where Napoleon erected his bridges for the passage of his army. All night the French worked at the bridges by the light of the enemy's fires on the opposite side. At daylight the fires were abandoned, and the Russians, supposing the attempt here to be a feint, were soon in full retreat. The emperor, impatient to get possession of the opposite bank, pointed it out to the bravest. A French aide-de-camp and Lithuanian count threw themselves into the river, and, in spite of the ice, which cut their horses' breasts, reached the opposite bank in safety. About one o'clock the bank on which we stood was entirely cleared of Cossacks, and the bridge for the infantry was finished. The first division crossed it rapidly with its cannon, the men shouting "*Vive l'empereur!*" The passage occupied three days. The number of stragglers and the quantity of baggage were immense. On the night of the twenty-seventh the stragglers left the bridge, tore down the whole village, and made fires with the materials, around which they crouched their shivering figures, and from which it was impossible to tear themselves away. At daylight they were roused by the report of Witgenstein's cannon thundering over their heads, and again all rushed tumultuously to the bridges. The Russians, with Platow and his Cossacks, were now in full communication on both sides of the river. On the left bank, Napoleon's own presence of mind and the bravery of his soldiers gave him a decided superiority; but, in the language of Scott, the scene on the right bank had become the wildest and most horrible which war can exhibit.

"Victor, with eight or ten thousand men, covered the retreat over the bridges; while behind his fire thousands of stragglers, old men, women, and children, were wandering by the side of this river, like the fabled spectres which throng the banks of the infernal Styx, seeking in vain for passage. The balls of the Russians began to fall among the disordered mass, and the whole body rushed like distracted beings toward the bridges, every feeling of prudence or humanity swallowed up by the animal instinct of self-preservation. The weak and helpless either shrank from the fray and sat down to wait their fate at a distance, or, mixing in it, were thrust over the bridges, crushed under carriages, cut down with sabres, or trampled to death under the feet of their countrymen. All this while the action continued with fury; and, as if the heavens meant to match their wrath with that of man, a hurricane arose and added terrors to a scene which was already of a character so dreadful. About mid-day the larger bridge, constructed for artillery and heavy carriages, broke down, and multitudes were forced into the water. The scream of the despairing multitude became at this crisis for a moment so universal, that it rose shrilly above the wild whistling of the tempest and the sustained and redoubled hurras of the Cossacks. The dreadful scene continued till dark. As the obscurity came on, Victor abandoned the station he had defended so bravely, and led the remnant of his troops in their turn across. All night the miscellaneous multitude continued to throng across the bridge under the fire of the Russian artillery. At day-break the French engineers finally set fire to the bridge, and all that remained on the other side, including many prisoners, and a great quantity of guns and baggage, became the property of the Russians. The amount of the French loss was never exactly known; but the Russian report concerning the bodies of the invaders, which were collected and burned as soon as the thaw permitted, states that upwards of thirty-six thousand were found in the Berezina."

The whole of this scene was familiar to me as matter of history; the passage of the Berezina had in some way fastened itself upon my mind as one of the most fearful scenes in the annals of war; and, besides this, at St. Petersburgh the colonel and prince had given me a detailed account of the horrors of that dreadful night, for they were both with Witgenstein's army, by the light of the snow, the course of the river, and the noise, directing a murderous fire of artillery against the dark mass moving over the bridge; and nearer still, my companion had visited the place in company with his uncle, of the Polish legion, and repeated to me the circumstances of individual horror which he had heard from his relative, surpassing human belief. The reader will excuse me if I have lingered too long on the banks of that river; and perhaps, too, he will excuse me when I tell him that, before leaving it, I walked down to its brink and bathed my face in its waters. Others have done so at the classic streams of Italy and Greece; but I rolled over the Arno and the Tiber in a vetturino without stopping, and the reader will remember that I jumped over the Ilissus.

CHAPTER XXIV

Travel by Night.—A Rencounter.—A Traveller's Message.—Lithuania.—Poverty of the Country.—Agricultural Implements.—Minsk.—Polish Jews.—A Coin of Freedom.—Riding in a Basket.—Brezc.—The Bug.—A searching Operation.—Women Labourers.—Warsaw.

It was after dark when we returned to our waggon, still standing at the end of the bridge opposite Borizoff. Our postilion, like a sensible man, had lain down to sleep at the head of his horses, so they could not move without treading on him and waking him; and, when we roused him, the pain of his beating was over, and with it all sense of the indignity; and, in fact, we made him very grateful for the flogging by promising him a few additional kopeks.

We hauled up the straw and seated ourselves in the bottom of our kibitka. Night closed upon us amid the gloomy forests bordering the banks of the Berezina. We talked for a little while, and by degrees drawing our cloaks around us, each fell into a reverie. The continued tinkling of the bell, which, on my first entering Russia, grated on my ear, had become agreeable to me, and in a dark night particularly was a pleasing sound. The song of the postilion, too, harmonised with the repose of spirit at that moment most grateful to us; that too died away, the bell almost ceased its tinkling, and in spite of the alarm of war which we had all day been ringing in our own ears, we should probably soon have fallen into a sleep as sound, for a little while at least, as that of them who slept under the waters of the Berezina, but we were suddenly roused by a shock as alarming to quiet travellers as the hurra of the Cossack in the ears of the flying Frenchmen. Our horses sprang out of the road, but not in time to avoid a concussion with another waggon going toward Borizoff. Both postilions were thrown off their seats; and the stranger, picking himself up, came at us with a stream of Lithuanian Russian almost harsh enough to frighten the horses. I will not suggest what its effect was upon us, but only that, as to myself, it seemed at first equal to the voice of at least a dozen freebooters and marauders; and if the English of it had been "stand and deliver," I should probably have given up my carpet-bag without asking to reserve a change of linen. But I was restored by the return fire of our postilion, who drowned completely the attack of his adversary by his outrageous clamour; and when he stopped to take breath my companion followed up the defence, and this brought out a fourth voice from the bottom of the opposite waggon. A truce was called, and waving the question on which side the fault lay, we all got out to ascertain the damage. Our antagonist passenger was a German merchant, used to roughing it twice every year between Berlin, Warsaw, Petersburgh, and Moscow, and took our smashing together at night in this desolate forest as coolly as a rub of the shoulders in the streets; and, when satisfied that his waggon was not injured, kindly asked us if we had any bones broken. We returned his kind inquiries; and, after farther interchanges of politeness, he said that he was happy to make our acquaintance, and invited us to come and see him at Berlin. We wanted him to go back and let us have a look at him by torchlight, but he declined; and, after feeling him stretched out in his bed in the bottom of his waggon, we started him on his way.

We resumed our own places, and without dozing again, arrived at the posthouse, where first of all we made ourselves agreeable to the postmaster by delivering our German friend's message to him, that he ought to be whipped and condemned to live where he was till he was a hundred years old, for putting the neck of a traveller at the mercy of a sleepy postilion; but the postmaster was a Jew, and thought the vile place where he lived equal to any on earth. He was a miserable, squalid-looking object, with a pine torch in his hand lighting up the poverty and filthiness of his wretched habitation, and confessed that he should be too happy to enjoy the fortune which the German would have entailed upon him as a curse. He offered to make us a bed of some dirty straw which had often been slept on before; but we shrunk from it; and, as soon as we could get horses, returned to our kibitka and resumed our journey.

The whole province of Lithuania is much the same in appearance. We lost nothing by travelling through it at night; indeed, every step that we advanced was a decided gain, as it brought us so much nearer its farthermost border. The vast provinces of Lithuania, formerly a part of the kingdom of Poland, and, since the partition of that unhappy country, subject to the throne of Russia, until the fourteenth century were independent of either. The Lithuanians and Samogitians are supposed to be of a different race from the Poles, and spoke a language widely dissimilar to the Polish or Russian. Their religion was a strange idolatry; they worshipped the god of thunder, and paid homage to a god of the harvest; they maintained priests, who were constantly feeding a sacred fire in honour of the god of the seasons; they worshipped trees, fountains, and plants; had sacred serpents, and believed in guardian spirits of trees, cattle, &c. Their government, like that of all other barbarous nations, was despotic, and the nobles were less numerous and more tyrannical than in Poland. In the latter part of the fourteenth century, on the death of Louis, successor to Casimir the Great, Hedwiga was called to the throne of Poland, under a stipulation, however, that she should follow the will of the Poles in the choice of her husband. Many candidates offered themselves for the hand dowered with a kingdom; but the offers of Jagellon, duke of Lithuania, were most tempting; he promised to unite his extensive dominions to the territory of Poland, and pledged himself for the conversion to Christianity of his Lithuanian subjects. But queens are not free from the infirmities of human nature; and Hedwiga had fixed her affections upon her cousin, William of Austria, whom she had invited into Poland; and when Jagellon came to take possession of his wife and crown, she refused to see him. The nobles, however, sent William back to his papa, and locked her up as if she had been a boarding-school miss. And again, queens are not free from the infirmities of human nature: Hedwiga was inconstant; the handsome Lithuanian made her forget her first love, and Poland and Lithuania were united under one crown. Jagellon was baptised, but the inhabitants of Lithuania did not so readily embrace the Christian religion; in one of the provinces they clung for a long time to their own strange and wild superstitions; and even in modern times, it is said, the peasants long obstinately refused to use ploughs or other agricultural instruments furnished with iron, for fear of wounding the bosom of mother Earth.

All the way from Borizoff the road passes through a country but little cultivated, dreary, and covered with forests. When Napoleon entered the province of Lithuania his first bulletins proclaimed, "Here, then, is that Russia so formidable at a distance! It is a desert for which its scattered population is wholly insufficient. They will be vanquished by the very extent of territory which ought to defend them;" and, before I had travelled in it a day, I could appreciate the feeling of the soldier from La Belle France, who hearing his Polish comrades boast of their country, exclaimed, "Et ces gueux là appellent ce pays une patrie!"

The villages are a miserable collection of straggling huts, without plan or arrangement, and separated from each other by large spaces of ground. They are about ten or twelve feet square, made of the misshapen trunks of trees heaped on each other, with the ends projecting over; the roof of large shapeless boards, and the window a small hole in the wall, answering the double purpose of admitting light and letting out smoke. The tenants of these wretched hovels exhibit the same miserable appearance both in person and manners. They are hard-boned, and sallow-complexioned; the men wear coarse white woollen frocks, and a round felt cap lined with wool, and shoes made of the bark of trees, and their uncombed hair hangs low over their heads, generally of a flaxen colour. Their agricultural implements are of the rudest kind. The plough and harrow are made from the branches of the fir-tree, without either iron or ropes; their carts are put together without iron, consisting of four small wheels, each of a single piece of wood; the sides are made of the bark of a tree bent round, and the shafts are a couple of fir branches; their bridles and traces platted from the bark of trees, or composed merely of twisted branches. Their only instrument to construct their huts and make their carts is a hatchet. They were servile and cringing in their expressions of respect, bowing down to the ground and stopping their carts as soon as we came near them, and stood with their caps in their hands till we were out of sight. The whole country, except in some open places around villages, is one immense forest of firs, perhaps sixty feet in height, compact and thick, but very slender. As we approached Minsk the road was sandy, and we entered by a wooden bridge over a small stream and along an avenue of trees.

Minsk is one of the better class of Lithuanian towns, being the chief town of the government of Minsk, but very dirty and irregular. The principal street terminates in a large open square of grass and mean wooden huts. From this another street goes off at right angles, containing large houses, and joining with a second square, where some of the principal buildings are of brick. From this square several streets branch off, and enter a crowd of wooden hovels irregularly huddled together, and covering a large space of ground. The churches are heavily constructed, and in a style peculiar to Lithuania, their gable ends fronting the street, and terminated at each corner by a square spire, with a low dome between them. The population is half Catholic and half Jewish, and the Jews are of the most filthy and abject class.

A few words with regard to the Jews in Poland. From the moment of crossing the borders of Lithuania, I had remarked in every town and village swarms of people differing entirely from the other inhabitants in physical appearance and costume, and in whose sharply-drawn features, long beards, and flowing dresses, with the coal-black eyes and oriental costumes of the women, I at once recognised the dispersed and wandering children of Israel. On the second destruction of Jerusalem, when the Roman general drove a plough over the site of the Temple of Solomon, the political existence of the Jewish nation was annihilated, their land was portioned out among strangers, and the descendants of Abraham were forbidden to pollute with their presence the holy city of their fathers. In the Roman territories, their petition for the reduction of taxation received the stern answer of the Roman, "Ye demand exemption from tribute for your soil; I will lay it on the air you breathe;" and, in the words of the historian, "Dispersed and vagabond, exiled from their native soil and air, they wander over the face of the earth without a king, either human or divine, and even as strangers they are not permitted to salute with their footsteps their native land." History furnishes no precise records of the emigration or of the first settlement of the Israelites in the different countries of Europe; but for centuries they have been found dispersed, as it was foretold they would be, over the whole habitable world, a strange, unsocial, and isolated people, a living and continued miracle. At this day they are found in all the civilised countries of Europe and America, in the wildest regions of Asia and Africa, and even within the walls of China; but, after Palestine, Poland is regarded as their Land of Promise; and there they present a more extraordinary spectacle than in any country where their race is known. Centuries have rolled on, revolutions have convulsed the globe, new and strange opinions have disturbed the human race, but the Polish Jew remains unchanged: the same as the dark superstition of the middle ages made him; the same in his outward appearance and internal dispositions, in his physical and moral condition, as when he fled thither for refuge from the swords of the crusaders.

As early as the fourteenth century, great privileges were secured to the Jews by Casimir the Great, who styled them his "faithful and able subjects," induced, according to the chronicles of the times, like Ahasuerus of old, by the love of a beautiful Esther. While in Germany, Italy Spain, Portugal, and even in England and France, their whole history is that of one continued persecution,—oppressed by the nobles, anathematised by the clergy, despised and abhorred by the populace, flying from city to city, arrested and tortured, and burned alive, and sometimes destroying themselves by thousands to escape horrors worse than death! while all orders were arrayed in fierce and implacable hatred against them, in Poland the race of Israel found rest; and there they remain at this day, after centuries of residence, still a distinct people, strangers and sojourners in the land, mingling with their neighbours in the everyday business of life, but never mingling their blood · the direct descendants of the Israelites who, three thousand years ago, went out from the land of Egypt; speaking the same language, and practising the laws delivered to Moses on the mountain of Sinai; mourning over their fallen temple, and still looking for the Messiah who shall bring together their scattered nation and restore their temporal kingdom.

But notwithstanding the interest of their history and position, the Polish Jews are far from being an interesting people; they swarm about the villages and towns, intent on gain, and monopolising all the petty traffic of the country. Outward degradation has worked inward upon their minds; confined to base and sordid occupations, their thoughts and feelings are contracted to their stations, and the despised have become despicable.

It was principally in his capacity of innkeeper that I became acquainted with the Polish Jew. The inn is generally a miserable hovel communicating with, or a room partitioned off in one corner of, a large shed serving as a stable and yard for vehicles; the entrance is under a low porch of timber; the floor is of dirt; the furniture consists of a long table, or two or three small ones, and in one corner a bunch of straw, or sometimes a few raised boards formed into a platform, with straw spread over it, for beds; at one end a narrow door leads into a sort of hole filled with dirty beds, old women, half-grown boys and girls, and children not overburdened with garments, and so filthy that, however fatigued, I never felt disposed to venture among them for rest. Here the Jew, assisted by a dirty-faced Rachel, with a keen and anxious look, passes his whole day in serving out to the meanest customers, beer, and hay, and corn; wrangling with and extorting money from intoxicated peasants; and, it is said, sometimes, after the day's drudgery is over, retires at night to his miserable hole to pore over the ponderous volumes filled with rabbinical lore; or sometimes his mind takes a higher flight, meditating upon the nature of the human soul; its relation to the Divinity; the connexion between the spirit and the body; and indulging in the visionary hope of gaining, by means of cabalistic form ilm, command over the spirits of the air, the fire, the flood, and the earth.

Though the days of bitter persecution and hatred have gone by, the Jews are still objects of contempt and loathing. Once I remember pointing out to my postilion a beautiful Jewish girl, and, with the fanatic spirit of the middle ages, himself one of the most degraded serfs in Poland, he scorned the idea of marrying the fair daughter of Israel. But this the Jew does not regard; all he asks is to be secured from the active enmity of mankind. "Like the haughty Roman banished from the world, the Israelite throws back the sentence of banishment, and still retreats to the lofty conviction that his race is not excluded as an unworthy, but kept apart as a sacred, people; humiliated, indeed, but still hallowed, and reserved for the sure though tardy fulfilment of the Divine promises."

The Jews in Poland are still excluded from all offices and honours, and from all the privileges and distinctions of social life. Until the accession of Nicolas, they were exempted from military service on payment of a tax; but since his time they have been subject to the regular conscription. They regard this as an alarming act of oppression, for the boys are taken from their families at twelve or thirteen, and sent to the army or the common military school, where they imbibe notions utterly at variance with the principles taught them by their fathers; and, probably, if the system continues, another generation will work a great change in the character of the Jews of Poland.

But to return to the Jews at Minsk. As usual, they gathered around us before we were out of our kibitka, laid hold of our baggage, and in Hebrew, Lithuanian, and Polish, were clamorous in offers of service. They were spare in figure, dressed in high fur caps and long black muslin gowns, shining and glossy from long use, and tied around the waist with a sash; and here I remarked what has often been remarked by other travellers, when the features were at rest, a style of face and expression resembling the pictures of the Saviour in the galleries in Italy. While my companion was arranging for post-horses and dinner, I strolled through the town alone, that is, with a dozen Israelites at my heels; and on my return I found an accession of the stiff-necked and unbelieving race, one of whom arrested my attention by thrusting before me a silver coin. It was not an antique, but it had in my eyes a greater value than if it had been dug from the ruins of a buried city, and bore the image of Julius Cæsar. On the breaking out of the late revolution, one of the first acts of sovereignty exercised by the provincial government was to issue a national coin stamped with the arms of the old kingdom of Poland, the white eagle and the armed cavalier, with an inscription around the rim, "God protect Poland." When the revolution was crushed, with the view of destroying in the minds of the Poles every memento of their brief but glorious moment of liberty, this coin was called in and suppressed, and another substituted in its place, with the Polish eagle, by way of insult, stamped in a small character near the tip end of the wing of the double-headed eagle of Russia. The coin offered me by the Jew was one of the emission of the revolution, and my companion told me it was a rare thing to find one. I bought it at the Jew's price, and put it in my pocket as a memorial of a brave and fallen people.

I will not inflict upon the reader the particulars of our journey through this dreary and uninteresting country. We travelled constantly, except when we were detained for horses. We never stopped at night, for there seldom was any shelter on the road better than the Jews' inns, and even in our kibitka we were better than there. But unluckily, on the seventh day, our kibitka broke down; the off hind-wheel snapped in pieces, and let us down rather suddenly in one of the autocrat's forests. Our first impulse was to congratulate ourselves that this accident happened in day-light; and we had a narrow escape, for the sun had hardly begun to find its way into the dark forest. Fortunately, too, we were but two or three versts from a posthouse. I had met with such accidents at home, and rigged a small tree (there being no such things as rails, property there not being divided by rail fences) under the hind-axle, supporting it on the front. We lighted our pipes and escorted our crippled vehicle to the posthouse, where we bought a wheel off another waggon, much better than the old one, only about two inches lower. This, however, was not so bad as might be supposed, at least for me, who sat on the upper side, and had the stout figure of my companion as a leaning-post.

At Sloghan, about two hundred versts from Breze, the frontier town of Poland, we sold our kibitka for a breakfast, and took the *char-de-poste*, or regular troika. This is the postboy's favourite vehicle; the body being made of twigs interlaced like a long basket, without a particle of iron, and so light that a man can lift up either end with one hand. Our speed was increased wonderfully by the change; the horses fairly played with the little car at their heels; the drivers vied with each other, and several posts in succession we made nearly twenty versts in an hour. It will probably be difficult to throw the charm of romance around the troika driver ; but he comes from the flower of the peasantry ; his life, passed on the wild highways, is not without its vicissitudes, and he is made the hero of the Russian's favourite popular ballads :

> Away, away, along the road
> The gallant troika bounds ;
> While 'neath the douga, sadly sweet,
> Their Valdai bell resounds."*

We passed the house of a very respectable seigneur who had married his own sister. We stopped at his village and talked of him with the postmaster, by whom he was considered a model of the domestic virtues. The same day we passed the chateau of a nobleman who wrote himself cousin to the Emperors of Russia and Austria, confiscated for the part he took in the late Polish revolution : a melancholy-looking object, deserted and falling to ruins, its owner wandering in exile with a price upon his head. It rained hard during the day, for the first time since we left Petersburgh ; at night the rain ceased, but the sky was still overcast. For a long distance, and, in fact, a great part of the way from Petersburgh, the road was bordered with trees. At eleven o'clock we stopped at a wretched posthouse, boiled water, and refreshed ourselves with deep potations of hot tea. We mounted our troika, the postilion shouted, and set off on a run. Heavy clouds were hanging in the sky ; it was so dark that we could not see the horses, and there was some little danger of a break-down ; but there was a high and wild excitement in hurrying swiftly through the darkness on a run, hearing the quick tinkling of a bell and the regular fall of the horses' hoofs, and seeing only the dark outline of the trees. We continued this way all night, and toward morning we were rattling on a full gallop through the streets of Breze. We drove into a large stable-yard filled with kibitkas, troikas, and all kinds of Russian vehicles, at one end of which was a long low building kept by a Jew. We dismounted, and so ended nearly three thousand miles of posting in Russia. The Jew, roused by our noise, was already at the door with a lighted taper in his hand, and gave us a room with a leather-covered sofa and a leather cushion for a pillow, where we slept till eleven o'clock the next day.

We breakfasted, and in the midst of a violent rain crossed the Bug, and entered the territory of Poland Proper. For many centuries, the banks of the Bug have been the battle-ground of the Russians and Poles. In the time of Boleslaus the Terrible, the Russians were defeated there with great slaughter, and the river was so stained with blood that it has retained ever since the name of the *Horrid*. Before crossing we were obliged to exchange our Russian money for Polish rubles and florins, losing, of course, heavily by the operation, besides being subjected to the bore of studying a new currency ; and the moment we planted our feet on the conquered territory, though now nominally under the same government, we were obliged to submit to a most vexatious process. The custom-house stood at the end of the bridge, and, as matter of course our postilion stopped

* The douga is the bow over the neck of the middle horse, to which the bell is attached ; and Valdai the place on the Moscow road where the best bells are made.

there. Our luggage was taken off the waggon, carried inside, every article taken out and laid on the floor, and a Russian soldier stood over, comparing them with a list of prohibited articles as long as my arm. Fortunately for me, the Russian government had not prohibited travellers from wearing pantaloons and shirts in Poland, though it came near faring hard with a morning-gown. My companion, however, suffered terribly ; his wearing apparel was all laid out on one side, while a large collection of curious and pretty nothings, which he had got together with great affection at the capital, as memorials for his friends at home, were laid out separately, boxes opened, papers unrolled, and, with provoking deliberation, examined according to the list of prohibited things. It was a new and despotic regulation unknown to him, and he looked on in agony, every condemned article being just the one above all others which he would have saved ; and when they had finished, a large pile was retained for the examination of another officer, to be sent on to Warsaw in case of their being allowed to pass at all. I had frequently regretted having allowed the trouble and inconvenience to prevent my picking up curiosities ; but when I saw the treasures of my friend taken from him, or, at least, detained for an uncertain time, I congratulated myself upon my good fortune. My friend was a man not easily disheartened ; he had even got over the loss of his love at St. Petersburgh ; but he would rather have been turned adrift in Poland without his pantaloons than be stripped of his precious baubles. I had seen him roused several times on the road, quarrelling with postmasters and thumping postilions, but I had never before seen the full development of that extraordinary head of hair. He ground his teeth and cursed the whole Russian nation, from the Emperor Nicolas down to the soldier at the custom-house. He was ripe for revolution, and, if a new standard of rebellion had been set up in Poland, he would have hurried to range himself under its folds. I soothed him by striking the key-note of his heart. All the way from St. Petersburgh he had sat mechanically, with his pocket-glass and brush, dressing his mustaches ; but his heart was not in the work, until, as we approached the borders of Poland, he began to recover from his Petersburgh affair, and to talk of the beauty of the Polish women. I turned him to this now.

It is a fact that, while for ages a deadly hatred has existed between the Russians and the Poles, and while the Russians are at this day lording it over the Poles with the most arbitrary insolence and tyranny, beauty still asserts its lawful supremacy, and the Polish women bring to their feet the conquerors of their fathers, and husbands, and brothers. The first posthouse at which we stopped confirmed all that my companion had said ; for the postmaster's daughter was brilliantly beautiful, particularly in the melting wildness of a dark eye, indicating an Asiatic or Tartar origin ; and her gentle influence was exerted in soothing the savage humour of my friend, for she sympathised in his misfortunes, and the more sincerely when she heard of the combs, and rings, and slippers, and other pretty little ornaments for sisters and female friends at home ; and my Pole could not resist the sympathy of a pretty woman.

R

We had scarcely left the postmaster's daughter, on the threshold of Poland, almost throwing a romance about the Polish women, before I saw the most degrading spectacle I ever beheld in Europe, or even in the barbarous countries of the East. Forty or fifty women were at work in the fields, and a large, well-dressed man, with a pipe in his mouth and a long stick in his hand, was walking among them as overseer. In our country the most common labouring man would revolt at the idea of his wife or daughter working in the open fields. I had seen it, however, in gallant France and beautiful Italy; but I never saw, even in the barbarous countries of the East, so degrading a spectacle as this; and I could have borne it almost anywhere better than in chivalric Poland.

We were now in the territory called Poland Proper; that is, in that part which, after the other provinces had been wrested away and attached to the dominions of the colossal powers around, until the revolution and conquest of 1830 had retained the cherished name of the kingdom of Poland. The whole road is macadamised, smooth and level as a floor, from the banks of the Bug to Warsaw; the posthouses and postmasters are much better, and posting is better regulated, though more expensive. The road lay through that rich agricultural district which had for ages made Poland celebrated as the granary of Europe; and though the face of the country was perfectly flat, and the scenery tame and uninteresting, the soil was rich, and at that time, in many places, teeming with heavy crops. As yet, it had not recovered from the desolating effects of the war of the revolution. The whole road had been a battle-ground, over which the Poles had chased the Russians to the frontier, and been driven back to Warsaw; time after time it had been drenched with Russian and Polish blood, the houses and villages sacked and burned, and their blackened ruins still cumbered the ground, nursing in the conquered but unsubdued Pole his deep, undying hatred of the Russians.

On this road Diebitsch, the crosser of the Balkan, at the head of eighty thousand men, advanced to Warsaw. His right and left wings manœuvred to join him at Siedler, the principal town, through which we passed. We changed horses three times, and rolled on all night without stopping. In the morning my companion pointed out an old oak, where a distinguished colonel of the revolution, drawing up the fourth Polish regiment against the Imperial Guards, with a feeling of mortal hate commanded them to throw away their primings, and charge with the bayonet, "cœur-à-cœur." In another place, five hundred gentlemen, dressed in black, with pumps, silk stockings, and small swords, in a perfect wantonness of pleasure at fighting with the Russians, and, as they said, in the same spirit with which they would go to a ball, threw themselves upon a body of the guards, and, after the most desperate fighting, were cut to pieces to a man. Farther on, a little off from the road, on the borders of the field of Grokow, was a large mound covered with black crosses, thrown up over the graves of the Poles who had fallen there. About eleven o'clock, we approached the banks of the Vistula. We passed the suburbs of Praga, the last battle-ground of Kosciusko, where the blood-stained Suwarrow butchered in cold blood thirty thousand Poles. Warsaw lay spread out on the opposite bank of the river, the heroic but fallen capital of Poland, the city of brave men and beautiful women; of Stanislaus, and Sobieski, and Poniatowsky, and Kosciusko, and, I will not withhold it, possessing, in my eyes, a romantic interest from its associations with the hero of my schoolboy days, Thaddeus of Warsaw. On the right is the chateau of the old kings of Poland, now occupied by a Russian viceroy, with the banner of Russia waving over its walls. We rode over the bridge and entered the city. Martial music was sounding, and Russian soldiers, Cossacks, and Circassians, were filing through its streets. We held up to let them pass, and they moved like the keepers of a conquered city, with bent brows and stern faces, while the citizens looked at them in gloomy silence. We drove up to the *Hôtel de Leipsic* (which, however, I do not recommend), where I took a bath and a doctor.

CHAPTER XXV.

Warsaw.—A Polish Doctor.—Battle of Grokow.—The Outbreak—The fatal Issue.—Present Condition of Poland. —Polish Exiles.—Aspect of Warsaw.—Traits of the Poles.

A LETTER dated at Warsaw to my friends at home begins thus: "I have reached this place to be put on my back by a Polish doctor. How long he will keep me here I do not know. He promises to set me going again in a week; and, as he has plenty of patients without keeping me down, I have great confidence in him. Besides, having weathered a Greek, an Armenian, and a Russian, I think I shall be too much for a Pole." There was not a servant in the house who understood any language I spoke, and my friend kindly proposed my taking a room with him; and, as he had many acquaintances in Warsaw, who thronged to see him, he had to tell them all the history of the American in the bed in one corner. All the next day I lay in the room alone on a low bedstead, looking up at the ceiling and counting the cracks in the wall. I was saved from a fit of the blues by falling into a passion, and throwing my boots at the servant because he could not understand me. Late in the evening my friend returned from the theatre with three or four companions, and we made a night of it, I taking medicine and they smoking pipes. They were all excellent fellows, and, as soon as they heard me moving, came over to me, and, when I fell back on my pillow, covered me up, and went back, and talked till I wanted them again. Toward daylight I fell asleep, and, when the doctor came in the morning, felt myself a new man. My doctor, by-the-way, was not a Pole, but a German, physician to the court, and the first in Warsaw; he occupied a little country-seat a few miles from Warsaw, belonging to Count Nympsiewitch, the poet and patriot, who accompanied Kosciusko to our country, and married a lady of New Jersey; returned with him to Poland, was with him on his last battle-field, and almost cut to pieces by his side.

In the afternoon, one of my companions of the night before came to see me. He had been in

Warsaw during the revolution, and talked with enthusiasm of their brief but gallant struggle; and, as it was a beautiful afternoon, proposed strolling to a little eminence near at hand, commanding a view of the first battle-ground. I went with him, and he pointed out on the other side of the Vistula the field of Grokow. Below it was the bridge over which General Romarino carried his little army during the night, having covered the bridge, the horses' hoofs, and the wheels of the carriages with straw. This general is now in France under sentence of death, with a price set upon his head.

The battle of Grokow, the greatest in Europe since that of Waterloo, was fought on the twenty-fifth of February 1831, and the place where I stood commanded a view of the whole ground. The Russian army was under the command of Diebitsch, and consisted of one hundred and forty-two thousand infantry, forty thousand cavalry, and three hundred and twelve pieces of cannon. This enormous force was arranged in two lines of combatants, and a third of reserve. Its left wing, between Wavre and the marshes of the Vistula, consisted of four divisions of infantry of forty-seven thousand men, three of cavalry of ten thousand five hundred, and one hundred and eight pieces of cannon; the right consisted of three and a half divisions of infantry of thirty-one thousand men, four divisions of cavalry of fifteen thousand seven hundred and fifty men, and fifty-two pieces of cannon. Upon the borders of the great forest opposite the Forest of Elders, conspicuous from where I stood, was placed the reserve, commanded by the Grand-duke Constantine. Against this immense army the Poles opposed less than fifty thousand men and a hundred pieces of cannon, under the command of General Skrzynecki.

At break of day the whole force of the Russian right wing, with a terrible fire of fifty pieces of artillery and columns of infantry, charged the Polish left with the determination of carrying it by a single and overpowering effort. The Poles, with six thousand five hundred men and twelve pieces of artillery, not yielding a foot of ground, and knowing they could hope for no succour, resisted this attack for several hours, until the Russians slackened their fire. About ten o'clock the plain was suddenly covered with the Russian forces issuing from the cover of the forest, seeming one undivided mass of troops. Two hundred pieces of cannon, posted on a single line, commenced a fire which made the earth tremble, and was more terrible than the oldest officers, many of whom had fought at Marengo and Austerlitz, had ever beheld. The Russians now made an attack upon the right wing; but foiled in this as upon the left, Diebitsch directed the strength of his army against the Forest of Elders, hoping to divide the Poles into two parts. One hundred and twenty pieces of cannon were brought to bear on this one point, and fifty battalions, incessantly pushed to the attack, kept up a scene of massacre unheard of in the annals of war. A Polish officer who was in the battle told me that the small streams which intersected the forest were so choked with dead that the infantry marched directly over their bodies. The heroic Poles, with twelve battalions, for four hours defended the forest against the tremendous attack. Nine times they were driven out, and nine times, by a series of admirably executed manœuvres, they repulsed the Russians with immense loss. Batteries, now concentrated in one point, were in a moment hurried to another, and the artillery advanced to the charge like cavalry, sometimes within a hundred feet of the enemy's columns, and there opened a murderous fire of grape.

At three o'clock the generals, many of whom were wounded, and most of whom had their horses shot under them, and fought on foot at the head of their divisions, resolved upon a retrograde movement, so as to draw the Russians on the open plain. Diebitsch, supposing it to be a flight, looked over to the city and exclaimed, " Well, then, it appears that, after this bloody day, I shall take tea in the Belvidere Palace." The Russian troops debouched from the forest. A cloud of Russian cavalry, with several regiments of heavy cuirassiers at their head, advanced to the attack. Colonel Pientka, who had kept up an unremitting fire from his battery for five hours, seated with perfect sang-froid upon a disabled piece of cannon, remained to give another effective fire, then left at full gallop a post which he had so long occupied under the terrible fire of the enemy's artillery. This rapid movement of his battery animated the Russian forces. The cavalry advanced on a trot upon the line of a battery of rockets. A terrible discharge was poured into their ranks, and the horses, galled to madness by the flakes of fire, became wholly ungovernable, and broke away, spreading disorder in every direction; the whole body swept helplessly along the fire of the Polish infantry, and in a few minutes was so completely annihilated that, of a regiment of cuirassiers who bore inscribed on their helmets the " Invincibles," not a man escaped. The wreck of the routed cavalry, pursued by the lancers, carried along in its flight the columns of infantry; a general retreat commenced, and the cry of " Poland for ever " reached the walls of Warsaw to cheer the hearts of its anxious inhabitants. So terrible was the fire of that day, that in the Polish army there was not a single general or staff officer who had not his horse killed or wounded under him; two-thirds of the officers, and perhaps of the soldiers, had their clothes pierced with balls, and more than a tenth part of the army were wounded. Thirty thousand Russians and ten thousand Poles were left on the field of battle; rank upon rank lay prostrate on the earth, and the Forest of Elders was so strewed with bodies that it received from that day the name of the " Forest of the Dead." The czar heard with dismay, and all Europe with astonishment, that the crosser of the Balkan had been foiled under the walls of Warsaw.

All day, my companion said, the cannonading was terrible. Crowds of citizens, of both sexes and all ages, were assembled on the spot where we stood, earnestly watching the progress of the battle, sharing in all its vicissitudes, in the highest state of excitement as the clearing up of the columns of smoke showed when the Russians or the Poles had fled; and he described the entry of the remnant of the Polish army into Warsaw as sublime and terrible; their hair and faces were begrimed with powder and blood; their armour shattered and broken, and all, even dying men, were singing patriotic songs; and when the fourth regiment, among whom was a brother of my companion, and who had particularly distinguished themselves in the battle, crossed the bridge and filed slowly through the streets, their lances shivered against the cuirasses of the guards, their helmets broken, their faces black and spotted with blood, some erect, some tottering, and some barely able to sustain themselves in the saddle, above the stern chorus of patriotic songs rose the distracted cries of mothers, wives, daughters, and lovers, seeking among this broken band for forms dearer than life, many of whom were then sleeping on the battle-field. My companion told me that he was then a lad of seventeen, and had begged with tears to be allowed to accompany his brother; but his widowed mother extorted from him a promise that he would not attempt it. All day he had stood with his mother on the very spot where we did, his hand in hers, which she grasped convulsively, as every peal of cannon seemed the knell of her son; and when the lancers passed, she sprang from his side as she recognised in the drooping figure of an officer, with his spear broken in his hand, the figure of her gallant boy. He was then reeling in his saddle, his eye was glazed and vacant, and he died that night in their arms.

The tyranny of the Grand-duke Constantine, the imperial viceroy, added to the hatred of the Russians, which is the birthright of every Pole, induced the unhappy revolution of eighteen hundred and thirty. Although, on the death of Alexander, Constantine waived in favour of his brother Nicolas his claim to the throne of Russia, his rule in Poland shows that it was not from any aversion to the exercise of power.

When Constantine was appointed its commander-in-chief, the Polish army ranked with the bravest in Europe. The Polish legions under Dombrowski and Poniatowski had kept alive the recollections of the military glory of their fallen nation. Almost annihilated by the bloody battles in Italy, where they met their old enemies under Suwarrow, the butcher of Praga, the proud remnants reorganised and formed the fifth corps of the "grande armée," distinguished themselves at Smolensk, Borodino, Kalouga, and the passage of the Berezina, took the field with the wreck of the army in Saxony, fought at Dresden and Leipsic, and, when Napoleon told them, brave as they were, that they were free to go home if they pleased, they scorned to desert him in his waning fortunes, and accompanied him to Paris. Alexander promised an amnesty, and they marched with him to Warsaw. Within the first six months many officers of this army had been grossly insulted; an eye-witness told me that he had seen, on the great square of Warsaw, the high-sheriff tear off the epaulettes from the shoulders of an officer, and, in the presence of the whole troops, strike him on the cheek with his hand.

It would, perhaps, be unjust to enumerate, as I heard them, the many causes of oppression that roused to revolt the slumbering spirit of the Poles; in the midst of which the French Revolution threw all Poland into commotion. The three days of July were hailed with rapture by every patriotic heart; the new revolutionary movements in Belgium cheered them on; and eighty young men, torn from the altars while praying for the souls of their murdered countrymen on the anniversary of the butchery at Praga, thrilled every heart and hurried the hour of retribution. The enthusiasm of youth struck the first blow. A band of ardent young men of the first families attended the meetings of secret patriotic associations; and six of them, belonging to the military school, suspecting they were betrayed, early in the evening went to their barracks, and proposed to their comrades a plan for liberating their country. The whole corps, not excepting one sick in bed, amounting in all to about a hundred and fifty, took up arms, and under a lieutenant of nineteen, attacked the palace of Constantine, and almost secured his person. The grand-duke was then asleep on a couch in a room opening upon a corridor of the Belvidere Palace, and, roused by a faithful valet, had barely time to throw a robe over him and fly. The insurgents, with cries of vengeance, rushed into the interior of the palace, driving before them the chief of the city-police and the aide-de-camp of the grand-duke. The latter had the presence of mind to close the door of the grand-duke's apartment, before he was pierced through with a dozen bayonets. The wife of the grand-duke, the beautiful and interesting princess for whom he had sacrificed a crown, hearing the struggle, was found on her knees offering up prayers to Heaven for the safety of her husband. Constantine escaped by a window; and the young soldiers, foiled in their attempt, marched into the city, and, passing the barracks of the Russian guards, daringly fired a volley to give notice of their coming. Entering the city, they broke open the prisons and liberated the state prisoners, burst into the theatres, crying out, "Women, home! men, to arms!" forced the arsenal, and in two hours forty thousand men were under arms. Very soon the fourth Polish regiment joined them; and before midnight, the remainder of the Polish troops in Warsaw, declaring that their children were too deeply implicated to be abandoned, espoused the popular cause. Some excesses were committed; and General Stanislaus Potocki, distinguished in the revolution of Kosciusko, for hesitating was killed, exclaiming with his last breath that it was dreadful to die by the hands of his countrymen.

Chlopicki, the comrade of Kosciusko, was proclaimed dictator by an immense multitude in the Champ de Mars. For some time the inhabitants of Warsaw were in a delirium; the members of the patriotic association, and citizens of all classes, assembled every day, carrying arms, and with glasses in their hands, in the saloon of the theatre and at a celebrated coffee-house, discussing politics and singing patriotic songs. In the theatres the least allusion brought down thunders of applause, and at the end of the piece heralds appeared on the stage waving the banners of the dismembered provinces. In the pit they sang in chorus national hymns; the boxes answered them; and sometimes the spectators finished by scaling the stage and dancing the Mazurka and the Cracoviak.

The fatal issue of this revolution is well known. The Polish nation exerted and exhausted its utmost strength, and the whole force of the colossal empire was brought against it, and, in spite of prodigies of valour, crushed it. The moment, the only moment when gallant, chivalric, and heroic Poland could have been saved and restored to its rank among nations, was suffered to pass by, and no one came to her aid. The minister of France threw out the bold boast that a hundred thousand men stood ready to march to her assistance; but France and all Europe looked on and saw her fall. Her expiring diet ordered a levy in mass, and made a last appeal, "In the name of God; in the name of liberty; of a nation placed between life and death; in the name of kings and heroes who have fought for religion and humanity; in the name of future generations; in the name of justice and the deliverance of Europe;" but her dying appeal was unheard. Her last battle was under the walls of Warsaw; and then she would not have fallen, but even in Poland there were traitors. The governor of Warsaw blasted the laurels won in the early battles of the revolution by the blackest treason. He ordered General Romarino to withdraw eight thousand soldiers and chase the Russians beyond the frontier at Breze. While he was gone, the Russians pressed Warsaw; he could have returned in time to save it, but was stopped with directions not to advance until farther orders. In the mean time Warsaw fell, with the curse of every Pole upon the head of its governor. The traitor now lives ingloriously in Russia, disgraced and despised, while the young lieutenant is an unhappy but not unhonoured exile in Siberia.

So ended the last heroic struggle of Poland. It is dreadful to think so, but it is greatly to be feared that Poland is blotted for ever from the list of nations. Indeed, by a late imperial ukase, Poland is expunged from the map of Europe; her old and noble families are murdered, imprisoned, or in exile; her own language is excluded from the offices of government, and even from the public schools; her national character destroyed; her national dress proscribed; her national colours trampled under foot; her national banner, the white eagle of Poland, is in the dust. Warsaw is abandoned, and become a Russian city; her best citizens are wandering in exile in foreign lands, while Cossack and Circassian soldiers are filing through her streets, and the banner of Russia is waving over her walls.

Perhaps it is not relevant, but I cannot help saying, that there is no exaggeration in the stories which reach us at our own doors of the misfortunes and sufferings of Polish exiles. I have met them wandering in many different countries, and particularly I remember one at Cairo. He had fought during the whole Polish revolution, and made his escape when Warsaw fell. He was a man of about thirty-five years of age, dressed in a worn military frock-coat, and carrying himself with a manly and martial air. He had left a wife and two children at Warsaw. At Constantinople he had written to the emperor requesting permission to return, and even promising never again to take up arms against Russia, but had received for answer that the amnesty was over and the day of grace was past; and the unfortunate Pole was then wandering about the world like a cavalier of fortune or a knight of romance, with nothing to depend upon but his sword. He had offered his services to the sultan and to the pacha of Egypt; he was then poor, and, with the bearing of a gentleman and the pride of a soldier, was literally begging his bread. I could sympathise in the misfortunes of an exiled Pole, and felt that his distress must indeed be great, that he who had perilled life and ties dearer than life in the cause of an oppressed country, should offer his untarnished sword to the greatest despot that ever lived.

The general appearance of Warsaw is imposing. It stands on a hill of considerable elevation on the left bank of the Vistula; the Zamech, or chateau of the kings of Poland, spreads its wings midway between the river and the summit of the hill, and churches and towering spires checker at different heights the distant horizon. Most of the houses are built of stone, or brick stuccoed; they are numbered in one continued series throughout the city, beginning from the royal palace (occupied by Paskiewitch), which is numbered *one*, and rising above number *five thousand*. The churches are numerous and magnificent; the palaces, public buildings, and many of the mansions of noblemen, are on a large scale, very showy, and, in general, striking for their architectural designs. One great street runs irregularly through the whole city, of which Miodowa, or Honey-street, and the Novoy Swiat, or New World, are the principal and most modern portions. As in all aristocratic cities, the streets are badly paved, and have no *trottoirs* for the foot-passengers. The Russian drosky is in common use; the public carriages are like those in Western Europe, though of a low form; the linings generally painted red; the horses large and handsome, with large collars of red or green, covered with small brass rings, which sound like tinkling bells; and the carts are like those in our own city, only longer and lower, and more like our brewers' dray. The hotels are numerous, generally kept in some of the old palaces, and at the entrance of each stands a large porter, with a cocked hat and silver-headed cane, to show travellers to their apartments and receive the names of visiters. There are two principal kukiernia, something like the French cafés, where many of the Varsovians breakfast and lounge in the mornings.

The Poles, in their features, looks, customs, and manners, resemble Asiatics rather than Europeans; and they are, no doubt, descended from Tartar ancestors. Though belonging to the Sclavonic race, which occupies nearly the whole extent of the vast plains of Eastern Europe, they have advanced more than the others from the rude and barbarous state which characterises this race; and this is particularly manifest at Warsaw. An eye-witness, describing the appearance of the Polish deputies at Paris sent to announce the election of Henry of Anjou as successor of Sigismund, says, "It is impossible to describe the general astonishment when we saw these ambassadors in long robes, fur caps, sabres, arrows, and quivers; but our admiration was excessive when we saw the sumptuousness of their equipages; the scabbards of their swords adorned with jewels; their bridles, saddles, and horse-cloths, decked in the same way," &c.

But none of this barbaric display is now seen in the streets of Warsaw. Indeed, immediately on entering it, I was struck with the European aspect of things. It seemed almost, though not quite, like a city of Western Europe, which may, perhaps, be ascribed, in a great measure, to the entire absence of the semi-Asiatic costumes so prevalent in all the cities of Russia, and even at St. Petersburgh; and the only thing I remarked peculiar in the dress of the inhabitants was the remnant of a barbarous taste for show, exhibiting itself in large breast-pins, shirt-buttons, and gold chains over the vest; the mustache is universally worn. During the war of the revolution immediately succeeding our own, Warsaw stood the heaviest brunt; and when Kosciusko fell fighting before it, its population was reduced to seventy five thousand. Since that time it has increased, and is supposed now to be one hundred and forty thousand, thirty thousand of whom are Jews. Calamity after calamity has befallen Warsaw; still its appearance is that of a gay city. Society consists altogether of two distinct and distant orders, the nobles and the peasantry, without any intermediate degrees. I except, of course, the Jews, who form a large item in her population, and whose long beards, thin and anxious faces, and piercing eyes, met me at every corner of Warsaw. The peasants are in the lowest stage of mental degradation. The nobles, who are more numerous than in any other country in Europe, have always, in the eyes of the public, formed the people of Poland. They are brave, prompt, frank, hospitable, and gay, and have long been called the French of the North, being French in their habits, fond of amusements, and living in the open air, like the lounger in the Palais-Royal, the Tuileries, the Boulevards, and Luxembourg, and particularly French in their political feelings, the surges of a revolution in Paris being always felt at Warsaw. They regard the Germans with mingled contempt and aversion, calling them "dumb" in contrast with their own fluency and loquacity; and before their fall were called by their neighbours the "proud Poles." They consider it the deepest disgrace to practise any profession, even law or medicine, and, in case of utmost necessity, prefer the plough. A Sicilian, a fellow-passenger from Palermo to Naples, who one moment was groaning in the agony of sea-sickness and the next playing on his violin, said to me "Canta il, signore?" "Do you sing?" I answered "No;" and he continued, "Suonate?" "Do you play?" I again answered "No;" and he asked me, with great simplicity, "Cosa fatte? Niente!" "What do you do? Nothing?" and I might have addressed the same question to every Pole in Warsaw.

The whole business of the country is in the hands of the Jews, and all the useful and mechanical arts are practised by strangers. I did not find a Pole in a single shop in Warsaw; the proprietors of the hotels and coffee-houses are strangers, principally Germans; my tailor was a German, my shoemaker a Frenchman, and the man who put a new crystal in my watch an Italian from Milan. But though this entire absence of all useful employment, is, on grounds of public policy, a blot on their national character, as a matter of feeling it rather added to the interest with which I regarded the "proud Poles;" and perhaps it was imaginary, but I felt all the time I was in Warsaw that, though the shops and coffee-houses were open, and crowds thronged the streets, a sombre air hung over the whole city; and if for a moment this impression left me, a company of Cossacks, with their wild music, moving to another station, or a single Russian officer riding by in a drosky, wrapped in his military cloak, reminded me that the foot of a conqueror was upon the necks of the inhabitants of Warsaw. This was my feeling after a long summer day's stroll through the streets; and in the evening I went to the theatre, which was a neat building, well filled, and brilliantly lighted; but the idea of a pervading and gloomy spirit so haunted me that in a few moments I left what seemed a heartless mockery of pleasure. I ought to add, that I did not understand a word of the piece; the *triste* air which touched me may have been induced by the misfortunes of the stage here; and, in all probability, I should have astonished a melancholy-looking neighbour if, acting under my interpretation of his visage, I had expressed to him my sympathy in the sufferings of his country.

CHAPTER XXVI.

Religion of Poland.—Sunday in Warsaw.—Baptised Jews.—Palaces of the Polish Kings.—Sobieski.—Field of Vola.—Wreck of a Warrior.—The Poles in America.—A Polish Lady.—Troubles of a Passport.—Departure from Warsaw.—An official Rachel.—A mysterious Visitor.

SUNDAY at Warsaw.—Poland is distinguished above the other nations of Europe as a land of religious toleration. So late as the latter part of the tenth century, the religion of Poland was a gross idolatry; and, mingled with the rites of their own country, they worshipped, under other names, Jupiter, Plato, Mars, Venus, Diana, and other of the pagan deities. During the reign of Mieczylaus I., of the Piast dynasty, the monks introduced Christianity. The prince himself was proof against the monks, but received from woman's lips the principles of the Christian religion. Enamoured of Dombrowska, the daughter of the Duke of Bohemia, a country which had then lately embraced Christianity, who refused to accept his suit unless he was baptised, Mieczylaus sacrificed the superstitions and prejudices of his fathers on the altar of love. But the religion which he embraced for the sake of Dombrowska he afterwards propagated for its own; became an ardent champion of the cross; broke down with his own hands the idols of his country; built Christian churches on the ruins of pagan temples; and, in the ardour of his new faith, issued an edict that, when any portion of the Gospel was read, the hearers should half draw their swords to testify their readiness to defend its truth.

In the reign of the "famous" John Sobieski, the annals of Poland, till that time free from this disgrace, were stained by one of the most atrocious acts of barbarity recorded in the history of religious persecution. A Lithuanian nobleman, a religious and benevolent man, but sufficiently intelligent to ridicule some of the current superstitions, and very rich, on account of a note in a margin of a book written by a stupid German, was tried for atheism by a council of bigoted Catholic bishops, and found guilty, not only of "having denied the existence of a God, but the doctrine of the Trinity and the Divine Maternity of the Virgin Mary." Zuluski, one of the villains concerned in the torment, writes, "The convict was led to the scaffold, where the executioner, with a red-hot iron, tore his tongue and his mouth, *with which he had been cruel toward God;* then they burned his hands, instruments of the abominable production, at a slow fire. The sacrilegious paper was thrown into the flame; himself last; that monster of the age, that deicide, was cast into the flames of expiation, if such a crime could be atoned."

In seventeen hundred and twenty-six the Jesuits, making a public procession with the Host in the streets of Thorn, the young scholars of the order insisted that some Lutheran children should kneel; and on their refusal a scuffle ensued between the Jesuits and townspeople, most of whom were Lutherans, in which the enraged towns-people broke open the Jesuits' college, profaned all the objects of worship, and, among others, an image of the Virgin. The Catholics of Poland, assembled in the diet, almost infuriated with fanatic zeal, condemned to death the magistrates of Thorn for not exercising their authority. Seven of the principal citizens were also condemned to death; many were imprisoned or banished; three persons, accused of throwing the Virgin's image into the fire, lost their right arms, and the whole city was deprived of the freedom of public worship.

This was the last act of religious persecution in Poland; but even yet the spirit of the Reformation has made but little progress, and the great bulk of the people are still groping in the darkness of Catholicism. On every public road and in all the streets of Warsaw stand crosses, sometimes thirty feet high, with a figure of the Saviour large as life, sometimes adorned with flowers and sometimes covered with rags.

As in all Catholic cities, a Sunday in Warsaw is a fête day. I passed the morning in strolling through the churches, which are very numerous, and some of them, particularly the Cathedral Church of St John and that of the Holy Cross, of colossal dimensions. The scene was the same as in the Catholic churches in Italy; at every door crowds were entering and passing out, nobles, peasants, shopmen, drosky boys, and beggars; the highborn lady descended from her carriage, dipped her fingers in the same consecrated water, and kneeled on the same pavement side by side with the beggar; alike equal in God's house, and outside the door again an immeasurable distance between them.

At twelve o'clock, by appointment, I met my travelling companion and another of his friends in the Jardin de Saxe, the principal public garden in Warsaw. It stands in the very heart of the city, in the rear of the Palais de Saxe, built by the Elector of Saxony when called to the throne of Poland. It is inclosed all around by high brick walls, screened by shrubs, and vines, and trees rising above, so as to exclude the view of the houses facing it. It is handsomely laid out with lawns and gravel-walks, and adorned with trees; and as the grounds are exceedingly rural and picturesque, and the high walls and trees completely shut out the view of all surrounding objects, I could hardly realise that I was in the centre of a populous city. It was then the fashionable hour for promenade, and all the élite of Warsaw society was there. I had heard of this Sunday promenade, and, after making one or two turns on the principal walk, I remarked to my companions that I was disappointed in not seeing, as I had expected, a collection of the highborn and aristocratic Poles; but they told me that, changed as Warsaw was in every particular, in nothing was this change more manifest than in the character of this favourite resort. From boyhood, one of them had been in the habit of walking there regularly on the same day and at the same hour; and he told me that, before the revolution, it had always been thronged by a gay and brilliant collection of the nobility of Warsaw; and he enumerated several families whose names were identified with the history of Poland who were in the habit of being there at a certain time, as regularly as the trees which then shaded our walk; but since the revolution these families were broken up and dispersed, and their principal members dead or in exile, or else lived retired too proud in their fallen state to exhibit themselves in public places where they were liable to be insulted by the presence of their Russian conquerors; and I could well appreciate the feeling which kept them away, for Russian officers, with their rattling swords and nodding plumes, and carrying themselves with a proud and lordly air, were the most conspicuous persons present. I had noticed one party, a dark, pale, and interesting-looking man, with an elegant lady and several children and servants, as possessing, altogether, a singularly melancholy and aristocratic appearance; but the interest I was disposed to take in them was speedily dispelled by hearing that he was a baptised Jew, a money broker, who had accumulated a fortune by taking advantage of the necessities of the distressed nobles. Indeed, next to the Russian officers, the baptised Jews were the most prominent persons on the promenade. These persons form a peculiar class in Warsaw, occupying a position between the Israelites and Christians, and amalgamating with neither. Many of them are rich, well educated, and accomplished, and possess great elegance of appearance and manner. They hate most cordially their unregenerated brethren, and it is unnecessary to say that this hate is abundantly reciprocated. It was with a feeling of painful interest that I strolled through this once favourite resort of the nobility of Warsaw; and my companions added to this melancholy feeling by talking in a low tone, almost in whispers, and telling me that now the promenade was always *triste* and dull; and in going out they led me through a private walk, where an old noble, unable to tear himself from a place consecrated by the recollections of his whole life, still continued to take his daily walk apart from the crowd, wearing out the evening of his days in bitter reflections on the fallen condition of his kindred and country.

We dined, as usual, at a restaurant, where at one table was a party of Swiss, here, as at Moscow, exercising that talent, skill, and industry which they exhibit all over the world, and consoling themselves for the privations of exile with the hope of one day being able to return to their native mountains, never to leave them again.

After dinner we took an open carriage, and at the barrier entered one of the numerous avenues of the Ujazdow, leading to Belvidere, the country residence of the late grand-duke Constantine. The avenue is divided by rows of old and stately trees, terminating in a large circular octagon, from which branch off eight other avenues, each at a short distance crossed by others, and forming a sort of labyrinth, said to be one of the finest drives and promenades in Europe, and on Sundays the rendezvous of nearly the entire population of Warsaw. It was a beautiful afternoon, and the throng of carriages, and horsemen, and thousands of pedestrians, and the sun, occasionally obscured and then breaking through the thick foliage, darkening and again lighting up the vista through the trees, gave a beauty to the landscape, and a variety and animation to the scene, that I had not yet found in Warsaw. Passing the Belvidere Palace, my companions described the manner in which the students had made their attack upon it, and pointed out the window by which Constantine escaped. Turning from one of the splendid avenues of the Ujazdow, we crossed a stone bridge, on which stands the equestrian statue of John Sobieski, his horse rearing over the body of a prostrate Turk; it was erected to him as the saviour of Christendom after he had driven the Turks from the walls of Vienna. Beyond this we entered the grounds and park of Lazienki, formerly the country residence of Stanislaus Augustus, situated on a most delightful spot on the banks of the Vistula.

The royal villa stands in the midst of an extensive park of stately old trees, and the walks lead to a succession of delightful and romantic spots, adorned with appropriate and tasteful buildings. Among them, on an island reached by crossing a rustic bridge, are a winter and a summer theatre, the latter constructed so as to resemble, in a great measure, an ancient amphitheatre in ruins; in it performances used formerly to take place in the open air. I am not given to dreaming, and there was enough in the scenes passing under my eyes to employ my thoughts; but, as I wandered through the beautiful walks, and crossed romantic bridges, composed of the trunks and bended branches of trees, I could not help recurring to the hand that had planned these beauties, the good king Stanislaus.

"Dread Pultowa's day,
When fortune left the royal Swede,"

hurled Stanislaus from his throne; and as I stood under the portico of his palace, I could but remember that its royal builder had fled from it in disguise, become a prisoner to the Turks, and died an exile in a foreign land.

From here we rode to the chateau of Villanow, another and one of the most interesting of the residences of the kings of Poland, constructed by John Sobieski, and perhaps the only royal structure in Europe which, like some of the great edifices of Egypt and Rome, was erected by prisoners taken in war, being constructed entirely by the hands of Turkish captives. It was the favourite residence of Sobieski, where he passed most of his time when not in arms, and where he closed his days. Until lately, the chamber and bed on which he died might still be seen. The grounds extend for a great distance along the banks of the Vistula, and many of the noble trees which now shade the walks were planted by Sobieski's own hands. The reign of Sobieski is the most splendid era in the history of Poland. The great statue I had just passed presented him as the conqueror of the Turks, the deliverer of Christendom, the redoubtable warrior, riding over the body of a prostrate Mussulman; and every stone in the palace is a memorial of his warlike triumphs; but if its inner chambers could tell the scenes of which they had been the witness, loud and far as the trumpet of glory has sounded his name, no man would envy John Sobieski. The last time he unsheathed his sword, in bitterness of heart he said "It will be easier to get the better of the enemies I am in quest of than my own sons." He returned broken with vexation and shattered with wounds, more than sixty years old, and two-thirds of his life spent in the tented field; his queen drove his friends from his side, destroyed that domestic peace which he valued above all things, and filled the palace with her plots and intrigues. He had promised to Zaluski an office which the queen wished to give to another. "My friend," said the dying monarch, "you know the rights of marriage, and you know if I can resist the prayers of the queen; it depends, then, on you that I live tranquil or that I be constantly miserable. She has already promised to another this vacant office, and if I do not consent to it I am obliged to fly my house. I know not where I shall go to die in peace. You pity me; you will not expose me to public ridicule." Old and infirm, with grey hairs and withered laurels, a prey to lingering disease, the death-bed of the dying warrior was disturbed by a noise worse than the din of battle; and before the breath had left him, an intriguing wife and unnatural children were wrangling over his body for the possession of his crown. A disgraceful struggle was continued a short time after his death. One by one his children died, and there is not now any living of the name of Sobieski.

The next day I visited the field of Vola, celebrated as the place of election of the kings of Poland. It is about five miles from Warsaw, and was formerly surrounded by a ditch with three gates, one for great Poland, one for little Poland, and one for Lithuania. In the middle were two inclosures, one of an oblong shape, surrounded by a kind of rampart or ditch, in the centre of which was erected, at the time of election, a vast temporary building of wood, covered at the top and open at the sides, which was called the zopa, and occupied by the senate; and the other of a circular shape, called the kola, in which the nuncios assembled in the open air. The nobles, from a hundred and fifty thousand to two hundred thousand in number, encamped on the plain in separate bodies under the banners of their respective palatinates, with their principal officers in front on horseback. The primate having declared the names of the candidates, kneeled down and chanted a hymn; and then, mounting on horseback, went round the plain and collected the votes, the nobles not voting individually, but each palatinate in a body. It was necessary that the election should be unanimous, and a single nobleman peremptorily stopped the election of Ladislaus VII. Being asked what objection he had to him, he answered, "None at all; but I will not suffer him to be king." After being by some means brought over, he gave the king as the reason for his opposition, "I had a mind to see whether our liberty was still in being or not. I am satisfied that it is, and your majesty shall not have a better subject than myself." If the palatinates agreed, the primate asked again, and yet a third time, if all were satisfied; and, after a general approbation, three times proclaimed the king; and the grand marshal of the crown repeated the proclamation three times at the gates of the camp. It was the exercise of this high privilege of electing their own king which created and sustained the lofty bearing of the Polish nobles, inducing the proud boast which, in a moment of extremity, an intrepid band made to their king, "What hast thou to fear with twenty thousand lances? If the sky should fall we would keep it up with their points." But, unhappily, although the exercise of this privilege was confined only to the nobles, the election of a king often exhibited a worse picture than all the evils of universal suffrage with us. The throne was open to the whole world; the nobles were split into contending factions; foreign gold found its way among them, and sometimes they deliberated under the bayonets of foreign troops. Warsaw and its environs were a scene of violence and confusion, and sometimes the field of Vola was stained with blood. Still no man can ride over that plain without recurring to the glorious hour when Sobieski, covered with laurels won in fighting the battles of his country, amid the roar of cannon and the loud acclamations of the senate, the nobles, and the army, was hailed the chosen king of a free people.

I had enough of travelling post, and was looking out for some quiet conveyance to Cracow. A Jew applied to me, and I went with him to look at his carriage, which I found at a sort of "Bull's-head" stopping place, an enormous vehicle without either bottom or top, being a species of framework like our hay-waggons, filled with straw to prevent goods and passengers from spilling out. He showed me a couple of rough-looking fellows, who would be my compagnons de voyage, and who said that we could all three lie very comfortably in the bottom of the vehicle. Their appearance did not add to the recommendation of the waggon; nevertheless, if I had understood the language and been strong enough for the rough work, I should perhaps have taken that conveyance, as, besides the probable incidents of the journey, it would give me more insight into the character of the people than a year's residence in the capital. Returning to my hotel, I found that a Polish officer had left his address, with a request for me to call upon him. I went, and found a man of about forty, middle-sized, pale and emaciated, wounded and an invalid, wearing the Polish revolutionary uniform. It was the only instance in which I had seen this dress. After the revolution it had been absolutely proscribed; but the country being completely subdued, and the government in this particular case not caring to exercise any unnecessary harshness, he was permitted to wear it unmolested. It was, however, almost in mockery that he still wore the garb of a soldier: for if Poland had again burst her chains, and the unsheathed sword were put in his hands, he could not have struck a blow to help her. Unfortunately, he could not speak French, or rather, I may say fortunately, for in consequence of this I saw his lady, a pensive, melancholy, and deeply interesting woman, dressed in black, in mourning for two gallant brothers who died in battle under the walls of Warsaw.

Their business with me was of a most common-place nature. They had lately returned from a visit to some friends at Cracow, in a calèche hired at the frontier; and hearing from the peasant who drove them that a stranger was looking for a conveyance to that place, out of good-will to him desired to recommend him to me. The lady had hardly finished a sort of apologising commencement, before I had resolved to assent to almost anything she proposed; and when she stated the whole case, it was so exactly what I wanted, that I expressed myself under great obligations for the favour done me. I suggested, however, my doubts as to the propriety of undertaking the journey alone, without any interpreter; but, after a few words with the major, she replied that she would give full directions to the peasant as to the route. As the carriage could not go beyond the frontier, her husband would give me a letter to the commissaire at Michoof, who spoke French, and also to the postmaster; and, finally, she would herself make out for me a vocabulary of the words likely to be most necessary, so as to enable me to ask for bread, milk, eggs, &c.; and with this, and the Polish for "how much," I would get along without any difficulty. While she was writing, another officer came in, old and infirm, and also dressed in the Polish uniform. She rose from the table, met him almost at the door, kissed him affectionately, led him to a seat, and barely mentioning him to me as "mon beau-père," resumed her work. While she was writing I watched attentively the whole three, and the expression of face with which the two officers regarded her was unspeakably interesting. They were probably unconscious of it, and perhaps it was only my fancy, but if the transient lighting of their sunken eyes meant anything, it meant that they who sat there in the garb and equipment of soldiers, who had stood in all the pride and vigour of manhood on bloody battle-fields, now looked to a feeble and lovely woman as their only staff and support in life. I would have told them how deeply I sympathised in the misfortunes of their suffering country, but their sadness seemed too deep and sacred. I knew that I could strike a responsive chord by telling them that I was an American, but I would not open their still bleeding wounds; at parting, however, I told them that I should remember in my own country and to their countrymen the kindness shown me here; and as soon as I mentioned that I was an American, the lady asked me the fate of her unhappy countrymen who had landed as exiles on our shores, and I felt proud in telling them that they had found among our citizens that sympathy which brave men in misfortune deserve, and that our government had made a provision in land for the exiled compatriots of Kosciusko. She inquired particularly about the details of their occupation, and expressed the fear that their habits of life, most of them having been brought up as soldiers, unfitted them for usefulness among us. I did not then know how prophetic were her forebodings, and was saved the necessity of telling her, what I afterward read in a newspaper, that an unhappy portion of that band of exiles, discontented with their mode of life, in attempting to cross the Rocky Mountains were cut to pieces by a party of Indians. Under the pressure of their immediate misfortunes they had not heard the fate of the exiles, and a ray of satisfaction played for a moment over their melancholy features on hearing that they had met with friends in America: and they told me to say to the Poles wherever I found them, that they need never again turn their eyes toward home. She added that the time had been when she and her friends would have extended the hand of welcome to a stranger in Poland; that, when a child, she had heard her father and brothers talk of liberty and the pressure of a foreign yoke, but, living in affluence, surrounded by friends and connexions, she could not sympathise with them, and thought it a feeling existing only in men, which women could not know; but actual occurrences had opened her eyes; her family had been crushed to the earth, her friends imprisoned, killed, or driven into exile, and yet, she added, turning to her husband and father, she ought not to mourn, for those dearest to her on earth were spared. But I could read in her face, as she bent her eyes upon their pallid features, that she felt they were spared only for a season.

Reluctantly I bade them farewell. A servant waited to go with me and show me the calèche, but I told him it was not worth while. I was in no humour for examining the spokes of carriage-wheels; and, if I had been obliged to ride on the tongue, I believe I should have taken it. I went to my hotel, and told my friend of my interview with the major and his lady. He knew them by reputation and confirmed and strengthened all the interest I took in them, adding, that both father and son had been among the first to take up arms during the revolution, and at its unhappy termination were so beloved by the people of Warsaw that, in their wounded and crippled state, the Russian government had not proceeded to extremities with them.

I spent my last evening in Warsaw with my Pole and several of his friends at a herbata, that is, a sort of confectioner's shop like a *café* in the south of Europe, where, as in Russia, tea is the popular drink. The next morning, as usual, my passport was not ready. My valet had been for it several times and could not get it. I had been myself to the police-office, and waited until dark, when I was directed to call the next morning. I went at a little after eight, but I will not obtrude upon the reader the details of my vexation, nor the amiable feelings that passed my mind in waiting till twelve o'clock in a large ante-room. In my after wanderings I sometimes sat down upon a stump, or on the sands of the desert, and meditated upon my folly in undergoing all manner of hardships when I might be sitting quietly at home; but when I thought of passports in Russia and Poland, I shook myself with the freedom of a son of the desert, and with the thought that I could turn my dromedary's head which way I pleased, other difficulties seemed light. Ancient philosophers extolled uniformity as a great virtue in a young man's character; and, if so, I was entitled to the highest praise, for in the matter of arranging my passport I was always in a passion. I do not know a single exception to the contrary. And if there was one thing more vexatious than another, it was in the case at Warsaw, where, after having been bandied about from office to office, I received my passport, still requiring the signature of the governor, and walked up to the palace, nursing my indignation, and expecting an accumulation, I was ushered in by guards and soldiers, and at once disarmed of all animosity by the politeness and civility of the principal officers of government. I was almost sorry to be obliged to withhold my intended malediction. I hurried back to my hotel. My friend, with three or four of his Warsaw acquaintances, was waiting to see the last of me; my calèche was at the door, and I was already late for a start. I took my seat and bade them farewell. I promised to write to him on my arrival in Paris, and to continue a correspondence on my return home. Most unfortunately, I lost his address. He lived in some town in Poland, near the frontiers of Prussia, and probably at this moment thinks of me unkindly for my apparent neglect. Possibly we may meet again, though probably never; but if we do, though it do not happen till our heads are grey, we will have a rich fund of satisfaction in the recollections of our long journey to Warsaw.

I was again setting out alone. My guide or *conducteur* was a Polish peasant. Without having seen him I had calculated upon making ordinary human intelligence, to some extent, a medium of communication; but I found that I had been too soaring in my ideas of the divinity of human nature. When I returned to the hotel I found him lying on the sidewalk asleep; a servant kicked him up, and pointed me out as his master for the journey. He ran up and kissed my hands and, before I was aware of his intention, stooped down and repeated the same salutation on my boot. An American, perhaps more than any other, scorns the idea of man's debasing himself to his fellow-man; and so powerful was this feeling in me, that before I went abroad I almost despised a white man whom I saw engaged in a menial office. I had outlived this feeling; but when I saw a tall, strong athletic white man kneel down and kiss my foot, I could have almost spurned him from me. His whole dress was a long shirt coming down to his feet, supported by a broad leathern belt eight inches wide which he used as a pocket, and a low, broad-brimmed hat, turned up all round, particularly at the sides, and not unlike the head-gear of the New Lebanon Shakers.

Before putting myself out of the reach of aid, I held a conversation with him through an interpreter. The lady of the major had made out a chart for me, specifying each day's journey, which he promised to observe, and added that he would be my slave if I would give him plenty to drink. With such a companion, then, I may say most emphatically that I was again setting out alone; but my calèche was even better than the Polish officer represented it, abundantly provided with pockets for provisions, books, &c., and altogether so much more comfortable than anything I was used to, that I threw myself back in it with a feeling of great satisfaction. I rolled for the last time through the streets of Warsaw; looked out upon the busy throng; and though, in the perfectly indifferent air with which they turned to me, I felt how small a space I occupied in the world, I lighted my pipe and smoked in their faces, and, with a perfect feeling of independence toward all the world, at one o'clock I arrived at the barrier.

Here I found, to my great vexation, that I was an object of special consideration to the Emperor of Russia. A soldier came out for my passport, with which he went inside the guardhouse, and in a few minutes returned with the paper in his hands to ask me some question I could not answer him. He talked at me a little while, and again went within doors. After sitting for a few moments, vexed at the detention, but congratulating myself that if there was any irregularity it had been discovered before I had advanced far on my journey, I dismounted and went inside, where, after detaining me long enough to make me feel very uncomfortable, they endorsed the visé and let me go. I again lighted my pipe, and in the mildness and beauty of the day, the comfort of my calèche, and the docility and accommodating spirit of my peasant, forgot my past, and even the chance of future, difficulties. There was nothing particularly attractive in the road; the country was generally fertile, though tame and uninteresting. Late in the afternoon we stopped at a little town, of which I cannot make out the name. Like all the other towns on this side of Warsaw, in the centre was a square, with a range of wooden houses built all around fronting on the square, and the inhabitants were principally Jews. My peasant took off his horses and fed them in the square, and I went into a little kukernia, much cleaner and better than the town promised, where I had a cup of coffee and a roll of bread, and then strolled around the town, which at this moment presented a singular spectacle. The women and children were driving into the square herds of cows from the pasture-grounds in the unenclosed plains around; and, when all were brought in, each proprietor picked out his own cow and drove her home, and in a few moments, opposite almost every house stood the family cow, with a woman or child milking her. After this the cows strolled back into the square to sleep till morning.

A little before dark we started, and, after a fine moonlight ride, at about ten o'clock drove into a sort of caravanserai, being simply a large shed or covered place for waggons and horses, with a room partitioned off in one corner for eating and sleeping. There were, perhaps, fifteen or twenty waggons under the shed, and their waggoners were all assembled in this room, some standing up and eating off a board stretched along the wall, some drinking, some smoking, and some already asleep on the floor. In one corner was a party of Jews, with the contents of a purse emptied before them, which they were dividing into separate parcels. The place was kept by a Jew, who, with his wife, or some woman belonging to the establishment, old and weatherbeaten, was running about serving and apparently quarrelling with all the waggoners. She seemed particularly disposed to quarrel with me, I believe because I could not talk to her, this being, in her eyes, an unpardonable sin. I could understand, however, that she wanted to prepare me a supper; but my appetite was not tempted by what I saw around me, and I lighted my pipe and smoked. I believe she afterward saw something in me which made her like me better; for while the waggoners were strewing themselves about the floor for sleep, she went out, and returning with a tolerably clean sheaf of straw under each arm, called me to her, and shaking them out in the middle of the floor, pointed me to my bed. My pipe was ended, and putting my carpet-bag under my head, I lay down upon the straw; and the old woman climbed up to a sort of platform in one corner, where, a moment after, I saw her sitting up with her arms above her head, with the utmost nonchalance changing her innermost garment.

I was almost asleep, when I noticed a strapping big man, muffled up to the eyes, standing at my feet and looking in my face. I raised my head, and he walked round, keeping his eyes fixed upon me, and went away. Shortly after he returned, and again walking round, stopped and addressed me. "Sprechen sie Deutsch?" I answered by asking him if he could speak French; and not being able, he went away. He returned again, and again walked round as before, looking steadily in my face; I rose on my elbow, and followed him with my eyes till I had turned completely round with him, when he stopped as if satisfied with his observations, and in his broadest vernacular opened bluntly, "Hadn't we better speak English?" I need not say that I entirely agreed with him. I sprang up, and catching his hand, asked him what possessed him to begin upon me in Dutch; he replied by asking why I had answered in French, adding that his stout English figure ought to have made me know better; and after mutual good-natured recriminations, we kicked my straw bed about the floor, and agreed to make a night of it. He was the proprietor of a large iron manufactory, distant about three days' journey, and was then on his way to Warsaw. He went out to his carriage, and one of his servants produced a stock of provisions like the larder of a well-furnished hotel; and as I had gone to bed supperless, he seemed a good, stout, broad-shouldered guardian angel sent to comfort me. We sat on the back seat of the carriage, making a table of the front; and when we had finished, and the fragments were cleared away, we stretched our legs on the table, lighted our pipes, and talked till we fell asleep on each other's shoulder. Notwithstanding our intimacy so far, we should not have known each other by daylight, and at break of day we went outside to examine each other. It was, however, perhaps hardly worth while to retain a recollection of features; for, unless by some such accident as that which brought us together, we never shall meet again. We wrote our names in each other's pocket-book as a memorial of our meeting, and at the same moment started on our opposite roads.

CHAPTER XXVII.

Friendly Solicitude.—Raddom.—Symptoms of a Difficulty.—A Court of Inquisition.—Showing a proper Spirit.—Troubles thickening.—Approaching the Climax.—Woman's Influence.—The Finale.—Utility of the Classic Another Latinist.—A Lucky Accident.—Arrival at Cracow.

AT about eight o'clock we stopped to feed, and at the feeding-place met a German waggoner, who had lived in Hamburgh, and spoke English. He seemed much distressed at my not understanding the language of the country. He was a stout, burly fellow, eating and drinking all the time, and his great anxiety was lest I should starve on the road. He insisted upon my providing against such a fatality, and had a couple of fowls roasted for me, and wrapped in a piece of coarse brown paper; and at parting, backed by a group of friends, to whom he had told my story, he drank schnaps (at my expense) to my safe arrival at Cracow.

At eleven o'clock, we reached Raddom. There was a large swinging gate at the barrier of the town, and the soldier opening it demanded my passport to be viséd by the police; he got into the calèche with me, and we drove into the town, stopped in the public square, and went to the bureau together. He left me in an antechamber, and went within, promising, by his manner, to expedite the business, and intimating an expectation of schnaps on his return. In a few minutes he returned, and barely opening the door for me to enter, hurried off, apparently with some misgivings about his schnaps. I entered, and found three or four men, who took no notice of me. I waited a few moments, and seeing my passport on a table before one of them, went up, and, certainly without intending anything offensive, took up the passport with a view of calling his attention to it; he jerked it out of my hand, and looking at me with an imperious and impertinent air, at the same time saying something I have no doubt in character with the expression of his face, he slapped it down on the table. Two or three officers coming in, looked at it, and laid it down again, until at length one man, the head of that department, I suppose, took it up, wrote a note, and giving the note and passport to a soldier, directed me to follow him. The soldier conducted me to the bureau of the government, the largest building, and occupying a central position in the town, and left me in an antechamber with the usual retinue of soldiers and officers. In about a quarter of an hour he came out without the passport, and pulled me by the sleeve to follow him. I shook my head, asked for the passport, and, in fact, moved toward the door he had left. He seemed a goodhearted fellow, and anxious to save me from any imprudence, pulled me back, held up his fingers, and pointing to the clock, told me to return at one; and touching his hat respectfully, with probably the only French words he knew, "Adieu, seigneur," and a look of real interest, hurried away.

I strolled about the town, dropped in at a kukiernia, went to the square, and saw my peasant friend feeding his horses, apparently in some trouble and perplexity. I went back at one, and was ordered to come again at four. I would have remonstrated, but, besides that I could not make myself understood, when I attempted to speak they turned rudely away from me. I was vexed by the loss of the day, as I had agreed to pay a high price for the sake of going through a day sooner, and this might spoil my plan; and I was particularly vexed by the rough manner in which I was treated. I returned at four, and was conducted into a large chamber, in which were perhaps twenty or thirty clerks and inferior officers in the uniform of the government. As soon as I entered there was a general commotion. They had sent for a young man who spoke a little French to act as interpreter. The passport was put into his hands, and the first question he asked me was how I, an American, happened to be travelling under a Russian passport. I answered that it was not from any wish of mine, but in obedience to their own laws, and added the fact that this passport had been made out by the Russian ambassador at Constantinople; that under it I had been admitted into Russia, and travelled from the Black Sea to St. Petersburgh, and from there down to Warsaw, as he might see from the paper itself, the visés of the proper authorities, down to that of the Governor of Warsaw, being regularly endorsed.

He then asked what my business was in Poland, and what had induced me to come there. I answered, the same that had carried me into Russia, merely the curiosity of a traveller; and he then inquired what in particular I wanted to see in Poland. If I had consulted merely my feelings, I should have told him that, besides being attracted by the interest of her heroic history, I wished to see with my own eyes the pressure of a colossal foot upon the necks of a conquered people: that this very system of inquisition and espionnage was one of the things I expected to see; but I, of course, forbore this, and answered only in general terms, and my answer was not satisfactory. He then began a more particular examination; asked my age, my height, the colour of my eyes, &c. At first I did not see the absurdity of this examination, and answered honestly according to the fact, as I believed it; but all at once, it struck me that, as I did not remember the particulars of the description of my person in the passport, my own impromptu might very easily differ from it, and, catching an insulting expression on his face, I told him that he had the passport in his hands, and might himself compare my person with the description there given of me. He then read aloud the entire description; height, so many feet; eyes, such a colour, &c. &c.; scanned me from head to foot; peered into my eyes, stopping after each article to look at me and compare me with the description. By this time every man in the room had left his business and gathered round looking at me, and, after the reading of each article and the subsequent examination, there was a general shaking of heads and a contemptuous smile.

At the time I remembered, what had before suggested itself to me rather as a good thing, that, before embarking for Europe, I had written on to the department of state for a passport, with a description of my person made out at the moment by a friend, not very flattering, and, perhaps, not very true, but good enough for the Continent, which I expected to be the extent of my tour; and I felt conscious that, on a severe examination, my nose might be longer, or my eyes greyer, or in some other point different from the description. This, added to their close and critical examination, at first embarrassed me considerably, but the supercilious and insulting manner in which the examination was conducted roused my indignation, and restored my self-possession. I saw, from the informal way in which the thing was done, that this was a mere preliminary inquisition, and not the court to sit in judgment; and I had noticed from the beginning that most of these men were Poles, who had sold themselves to Russia for petty place and pay in her offices, traitors in their hearts and lives, apostates from every honourable feeling, and breathing a more infernal spirit against their enslaved country than the Russians themselves; and I told the interpreter, as coolly as the nature of the case would admit, to accept for himself, and to convey to his associates, the assurance that I should remember their little town as long as I lived; that I had then travelled from England through France, Italy, Greece, Turkey, and Russia, and had nowhere met such wanton rudeness and insult as from them; that I did not think it possible that in any European government twenty of its officers would laugh and sneer at the embarrassment of a stranger without a single one stepping forward to assist him; that I deeply regretted the occurrence of such a circumstance in Poland; that I felt convinced that there was not a true-hearted Pole among them, or my character as an American would have saved me from insult.

The interpreter seemed a little abashed, but I could see in the vindictive faces of the rest that they were greatly irritated. The examination was cut short, and I was directed to come again at half-past five, when the commandant, who had been sent for, would be there. By this time there was some excitement in the streets, and, as I afterward learned, it was noised through the little town that an American was detained on suspicion of travelling under a false passport. My calèche had been standing in the public square all day. I had been noticed going to and from the offices with a soldier at my heels, and my poor Pole had been wandering up and down the streets, telling everybody his fears and interest in me, and particularly his anxiety about some ten rubles I had promised him. As I passed along, people turned round and looked at me. I went to a kukiernia, where the dame had been very smiling and attentive, and could not get even a look from her. I went to another; several men were earnestly talking, who became silent the moment I entered. A small matter created an excitement in that little place. It was a rare thing for a traveller to pass through it; the Russian government threw every impediment in the way, and had made the road so vexatious that it was almost broken up. The French, or the citizens of a free country like America, were always suspected of being political emissaries to stir up the Poles to revolution, and it seemed as if, under that despotic government, to be suspected was to be guilty. The Poles were in the habit of seeing slight offences visited with terrible punishments, and probably half the little town looked on me as a doomed man. I went back to the square and took a seat on my calèche; my poor Pole sat on the box looking at me; he had followed me all over, and, like the rest, seemed to regard me as lost. I had probably treated him with more kindness than he was accustomed to receive, though, for every new kindness, he vexed me anew by stooping down and kissing my foot.

At half-past five o'clock, I was again at the door of the palace. On the staircase I met the young man who had acted as interpreter; he would have avoided me, but I stopped him and asked him to return with me. I held on to him, asking him if the commandant spoke French; begged him, as he would hope himself to find kindness in a strange country, to go back and act as a medium of explanation; but he tore rudely away, and hurried down stairs. A soldier opened the door and led me into the same apartment as before. The clerks were all at their desks writing; all looked up as I entered, but not one offered me a seat, nor any the slightest act of civility. I waited a moment, and they seemed studiously to take no notice of me. I felt outrageous at their rudeness. I had no apprehensions of any serious consequences beyond, perhaps, that of a detention until I could write to Mr. Wilkins, our ambassador at St. Petersburgh, and resolved not to be trampled upon by the understrappers. I walked up to the door of the commandant's chamber, when one man, who had been particularly insulting during the reading of the passport, rudely intercepted me, and leaning his back against the door, flourished his hands before him to keep me from entering. Fortunately, I fell back in time to prevent even the tip end of his fingers touching me. My blood flashed through me like lightning and even now I consider myself a miracle of forbearance that I did not strike him.

In a few moments the door opened, and a soldier beckoned me to enter. Directly in front, at the other end of the room, behind a table, sat the commandant, a grim, gaunt-looking figure, about fifty, his military coat buttoned tight up in his throat, his cap and sword on the table by his side, and in his hands my unlucky passport. As I walked toward him he looked from the passport to me, and from me to the passport; and when I stopped at the table he read over again the whole description, at every clause looking at me; shook his head with a grim smile of incredulity, and laid it down, as if perfectly satisfied. I felt that my face was flushed with indignation, and, perhaps, to a certain extent, so distorted with passion that it would have been difficult to recognise me as the person described. I suggested to him that the rude treatment I had met with in the other room had no doubt altered the whole character of my face, but he waved his hand for me to be silent; and, taking up a sheet of paper, wrote a letter or order, or something which I did not understand, and gave it to a soldier, who took it off to one corner and stamped it. The commandant then folded up the passport, enclosed it in the letter, and handed it again to the soldier, who carried it off and affixed to it an enormous wax seal, which looked very ominous and Siberian-like. I was determined not to suffer from the want of any effort on my part, and pulled out my old American passport, under which I had travelled in France and Italy, and also a new one which Commodore Porter had given me in Constantinople. He looked at them without any comment and without understanding them; and, when the soldier returned with the paper and the big seal, he rose, and, without moving a muscle, waved with his hand for me to follow the soldier. I would have resisted if I had dared. I was indignant enough to do some rash thing, but, at every step was a soldier; I saw the folly of it, and, grinding my teeth with vexation and rage, I did as I was ordered.

At the door of the palace we found a large crowd, who, knowing my appointment for this hour, were waiting to hear the result. A line of people was formed along the walk, who, seeing me under the charge of a soldier, turned round and looked at me with ominous silence. We passed under the walls of the prison, and the prisoners thrust their arms through the bars and hailed me, and seemed to claim me as a companion, and to promise me a welcome among them. For a moment I was infected with some apprehensions. In my utter ignorance as to what it all meant, I ran over in my mind the stories I had heard of the exercise of despotic authority, and for one moment thought of my German host at Moscow and a journey to Siberia by mistake. I did not know where the soldier was taking me, but felt relieved when we had got out of the reach of the voices of the prisoners, and more so when we stopped before a large house, which I remarked at once as a private dwelling, though a guard of honour before the door indicated it as the residence of an officer of high rank. We entered, and were ushered into the presence of the governor and commander-in-chief. He was, of course, a Russian, a man about sixty, in the uniform of a general officer, and attended by an aide-de-camp about thirty. I waited till the soldier had delivered his message; and, before the governor had broken the seal, I carried the war into the enemy's country by complaining of the rude treatment I had received, interrupted in my journey under a passport which had carried me all over Russia, and laughed at and insulted by the officers of the government, at the same time congratulating myself that I had at last met those who could at least tell me why I was detained, and would give me an opportunity of explaining anything apparently wrong. I found the governor, as everywhere else in Russia where I could get access to the principal man, a gentleman in his bearing and feelings. He requested me to be seated, while he retired into another apartment to examine the passport. The aide-de-camp remained, and I entertained him with my chapter of grievances; he put the whole burden of the incivility upon the Poles; who, as he said, filled all the inferior offices of government, but told me, too, that the country was in such an unsettled state that it was necessary to be very particular in examining all strangers; and particularly as at that time several French emissaries were suspected to be secretly wandering in Poland, trying to stir up revolution. The governor staid so long that I began to fear there was some technical irregularity which might subject me to detention, and I was in no small degree relieved when he sent for me, and telling me that he regretted the necessity for giving such annoyance and vexation to travellers, handed me back the passport, with a direction to the proper officer to make the necessary visé and let me go. I was so pleased with the result that I did not stop to ask any questions, and to this day I do not know particularly why I was detained.

By this time it was nine o'clock, and when we returned the bureau was closed. The soldier stated the case to the loungers about the door, and now all, including some of the scoundrels who had been so rude to me in the morning, were anxious to serve me. One of them conducted me to an apartment near, where I was ushered into the presence of an elderly lady and her two daughters, both of whom spoke French. I apologized for my intrusion; told them my extreme anxiety to go on that night, and begged them to procure some one to take the governor's order to the commandant; in fact I had become nervous, and did not consider myself safe till out of the place. They called in a younger brother, who started with alacrity on the errand, and I sat down to wait his return. There must be a witchery about Polish ladies. I was almost savage against all mankind; I had been kept up to the extremest point of indignation, without any opportunity of exploding all day, and it would have been a great favour for some one to knock me down; but in a few minutes all my bitterness and malevolence melted away, and before tea was over I forgot that I had been bandied all day from pillar to post, and even forgave the boors who had mocked me, in consideration of their being the countrymen of the ladies who were showing me such kindness. Even with them I began with the chafed spirit that had been goading me on all day; but when I listened to the calm and sad manner in which they replied; that it was annoying, but it was light, very light, compared with the scenes through which they and all their friends had passed, I was ashamed of my petulance. A few words convinced me that they were the Poles of my imagination and heart. A widowed mother and orphan children, their staff and protector had died in battle and a gallant brother was then wandering an exile in France. I believe it is my recollection of Polish ladies that gives me a leaning towards rebels. I never met a Polish lady who was not a rebel, and I could but think, as long as the startling notes of revolution continue to fall like music from their pretty lips, so long the Russian will sleep on an unquiet pillow in Poland.

It was more than an hour before the brother returned, and I was sorry when he came; for, after my professions of haste, I had no excuse for remaining longer. I was the first American they had ever seen; and if they do not remember me for anything else, I am happy to have disabused them of one prejudice against my country, for they believed the Americans were all black. At parting, and at my request, the elder daughter wrote her name in my memorandum-book, and I bade them farewell.

It was eleven o'clock when I left the house, and at the first transition from their presence the night seemed of pitchy darkness. I groped my way into the square and found my caleche gone. I stood for a moment on the spot where I had left it, ruminating what I should do. Perhaps my poor Pole had given me up as lost, and taken out letters of administration upon my carpet-bag. Directly before me, intersecting the range of houses on the opposite side of the square, was a street leading out of the town. I knew that he was a man to go straight a-head, turning neither to the right hand nor the left. I walked on to the opening, followed it a little way, and saw on the right a gate opening to a shed for stabling. I went in, and found him with his horses unharnessed, feeding them, whipping them, and talking at them in furious Polish. As soon as he saw me he left them and came at me in the same tone, throwing up both his hands, and almost flourishing them in my face; then went back to his horses, began pitching on the harness, and, snatching up the meal-bag, came back again toward me. All the time talking and gesticulating like a bedlamite. I was almost in despair. What have I done now? Even my poor peasant turns against me; this morning he kissed my foot; now he is ready to brain me with a meal-bag. Roused by the uproar, the old woman, proprietor of the shed, came out, accompanied by her daughter, a pretty little girl about twelve years old, carrying a lantern. I looked at them without expecting any help. My peasant moved between them and me and the horses, flourishing his meal-bag, and seeming every moment to become more and more enraged with me. I looked on in dismay, when the little girl came up, and dropping a courtesy before me, in the prettiest French I ever heard, asked me, "Que voulez-vous, monsieur?" I could have taken her up in my arms and kissed her. I have had a fair share of the perplexity which befalls every man from the sex, but I hold many old accounts cancelled by the relief twice afforded me this day. Before coming to a parley with my Pole, I took her by the hand, and, sitting down on the tongue of a waggon, learned from her that she had been taken into the house of a rich seigneur to be educated as a companion for his daughter, and was then at home on a visit to her mother; after which she explained the meaning of my postilion's outcry. Besides his apprehensions for me personally, he had been tormented with the no less powerful one of losing the promised ten rubles upon his arrival at a fixed time at Michoof, and all his earnestness was to hurry me off at once, in order to give me a chance of still arriving within the time. This was exactly the humour in which I wanted to find him, for I had expected great difficulty in making him go on that night; so I told him to hitch on his horses, and at parting did give the little girl a kiss, and the only other thing I could give her without impoverishing myself was a silk purse as a memento. I lighted my pipe, and worn out with the perplexities of the day, in a short time forgot police and passports, rude Russians and dastardly Poles, and even the Polish ladies and the little girl.

I woke the next morning under a shed, horses harnessed, postilion on the box whipping, and a Jew at their head holding them, and the two bipeds quarrelling furiously about the stabling. I threw the Jew a florin, and he let go his hold, though my peasant shook his whip, and roared back at him long after we were out of sight and hearing. At a few miles' distance we came to a stopping-place where we found a large calèche with four handsome horses, and the postilion in the costume of a peasant of Cracow, a little square red cap with a red feather, a long white frock somewhat like a shooting-jacket, bordered with red, a belt covered with pieces of brass like scales lapping over each other, and a horn slung over his right shoulder. It belonged to a Polish seigneur, who, though disaffected toward government, had succeeded in retaining his property, and was the proprietor of many villages. He was accompanied by a young man about thirty, who spoke a very little French; less than any man whom I ever heard attempt to speak it at all. They had with them their own servants and cooking apparatus and abundance of provisions. The seigneur superintended the cooking, and I did them the honour to breakfast with them. While we were breakfasting, a troop of waggoners or vaga-

bonds were under the shed dancing the mazurka. The better class of Poles are noble, high-spirited men, warm and social in their feelings, and to them, living on their estates in the interior of their almost untrodden country, a stranger is a curiosity and a treasure. The old seigneur was exceedingly kind and hospitable, and the young man and I soon became on excellent terms. I was anxious to have a friend in case of a new passport difficulty, and at starting gladly embraced his offer to ride with me. As soon as we took our seats in the calèche we lighted our pipes, and shook hands as a bargain of good-fellowship. Our perfect flow of confidence, however, was much broken by the up-hill work of making ourselves understood. I was no great scholar myself, but his French was execrable; he had studied it when a boy, but for more than ten years had not spoken a word. At one time, finding it impossible to express himself, he said, "Parlatis Latinum?" "Can you speak Latin?" I at first thought it was some dialect of the country, and could not believe that he meant the veritable stuff that had been whipped into me at school, and which, to me, was most emphatically a dead language; but necessity develops all that a man has, and for three hours we kept up an uninterrupted stream of talk in bad Latin and worse French.

Like every Pole whom I met, except the employés in the public offices, from the bottom of his heart he detested a Russian. He had been a soldier during the revolution, and lay on his back crippled with wounds when it was crushed by the capture of Warsaw. I showed him the coin which had accidentally come into my hands, and when we came to the point where our roads separated, he said that he was ashamed to do so, but could not help begging from me that coin; to me it was merely a curiosity, to him it was a trophy of the brilliant but short-lived independence of his country. I was loath to part with it, and would rather have given him every button on my coat; but I appreciated his patriotic feeling, and could not refuse. I got out, and he threw his arms around me, kissed me on both cheeks, called me his friend and brother, and mounted the kibitka with the old seigneur. The latter invited me to go with him to his château, about a day's journey distant, and if I had expected to write a book I should certainly have done so.

I went on again alone. At about twelve o'clock we arrived at the town of Kielse. I felt nervous as we approached the barrier. I threw myself back in the calèche, and drew my cap over my eyes in grand seigneur style, the soldier touched his hat as he opened the gate, and we drove into the public square unmolested. I breathed more freely, but almost hesitated to leave the calèche while the horses fed. I smiled, however, at thinking that any effort to avoid observation was the very way to attract it, and went to a kukernia, where I drank coffee, ate bread encrusted with sugar, and smoked a pipe until my Pole came in and kissed my foot as an intimation that the horses were ready.

No questions were asked at the carrier; and we rode on quietly till nine o'clock, when we drove under the shed of a caravanserai. Fifteen or twenty waggoners were eating off a bench, and, as they finished, stretched themselves on the floor for sleep. It was a beautiful moonlight night, and I strolled out for a walk. The whole country was an immense plain. I could see for a great distance, and the old shed was the only roof in sight. It was the last night of a long journey through wild and unsettled countries. I went back to the time when, on a night like that, I had embarked on the Adriatic for Greece; thought of the many scenes I had passed through since, and bidding farewell to the plains of Poland, returned to my calèche, drew my cloak around me, and was soon asleep.

At nine o'clock we stopped at a feeding-place, where a horde of dirty Jews were at a long table eating. I brushed off one corner, and sat down to some bread and milk. Opposite me was a beggar woman dividing with a child, about ten years old, a small piece of dry black bread. I gave them some bread and a jar of milk, and I thought, from the lighting up of the boy's face, that it was long since he had had such a meal.

At twelve o'clock we reached Michoof, the end of my journey with the calèche. I considered my difficulties all ended, and showed at the posthouse my letter from the Polish captain to the commissario. To my great annoyance, he was not in the place. I had to procure a conveyance to Cracow; and having parted with my poor Pole overwhelmed with gratitude for my treatment on the road and my trifling gratuity at parting, I stood at the door of the posthouse with my carpet-bag in my hand, utterly at a loss what to do. A crowd of people gathered round, all willing to assist me, but I could not tell them what I wanted. One young man in particular seemed bent upon serving me; he accosted me in Russian, Polish, and German. I answered him in English, French, and Italian, and then both stopped. As a desperate resource, and almost trembling at my own temerity, I asked him the question I had learned from my yesterday's companion, "Parlatis Latinum ?" and he answered me with a fluency and volubility that again threw me into another perplexity, caught my hand, congratulated me upon having found a language both understood, praised the good old classic tongues, offered his services to procure anything I wanted, &c., and all with such rapidity of utterance that I was obliged to cry out with something like the sailor's "'vast heaving," and tell him that, if he went on at that rate, it was all Russian to me. He stopped, and went on more moderately, and with great help from him I gave him to understand that I wanted to hire a waggon to take me to Cracow. "Venite cum me," said my friend, and conducted me round the town until we found one. I then told him I wanted my passport viséd for passing the frontier. "Venite cum me," again said my friend, and took me with him and procured the visé; then that I wanted a dinner; still he answered "Venite cum me," and took me to a trattoria, and dined with me. At dinner my classical friend did a rather unclassical thing. An enormous cucumber was swimming in a tureen of vinegar. He asked me whether I did not want it; and, taking it up in his fingers, ate it as a dessert, and drinking the vinegar out of the tureen, smacked his lips, wiped his mustaches with the table-cloth, and pronounced it "optimum."

For three hours we talked constantly, and talked nothing but Latin. It was easy enough for him, for, as he told me, at school it had been the language of conversation. To me it was like breaking myself into the treadmill; but, once fairly started, my early preceptors would have been proud of my talk. At parting he kissed me on both cheeks, rubbed me affectionately with his mustaches, and, after I had taken my seat, his last words were, "Semper me servate in vestra memoria."

We had four and a half German, or about eighteen English, miles to Cracow. We had a pair of miserable, ragged little horses, but I promised my postilion two florins extra if he took me there in three hours, and he started off so furiously that in less than an hour the horses broke down, and we had to get out and walk. After breathing them a little they began to recover, and we arrived on a gentle trot at the frontier town, about half way to Cracow. My passport was all right, but here I had a new difficulty in that I had no passport for my postilion. I had not thought of this, and my classical friend had not suggested it. It was exceedingly provoking, as to return would prevent my reaching Cracow that night. After a parley with the commanding officer, a gentlemanly man, who spoke French very well, he finally said that my postilion might go on under charge of a soldier to the next posthouse, about a mile beyond, where I could get another conveyance and send him back. Just as I had thanked him for his courtesy, a young gentleman from Cracow, in a barouche with four horses, drove up, and, hearing my difficulty, politely offered to take me in with him. I gladly accepted his offer, and arrived at Cracow at about dark, where, upon his recommendation, I went to the *Hôtel de la Rose Blanche* and cannot well describe the satisfaction with which I once more found myself on the borders of civilized Europe, within reach of the ordinary public conveyances, and among people whose language I could understand. "Shall I not take mine ease in mine own inn ?" Often, after a hard day's journey, I have asked myself this question, but seldom with the same self-complacency and the same determination to have mine ease as at Cracow. I inquired about the means of getting to Vienna, which, at that moment, I thought no more of than a journey to Boston. Though there was no particular need of it, I had a fire built in my room, for the associations connected with a cheerful blaze. I put on my morning-gown and slippers, and hauling up before the fire an old chintz-covered sofa, sent for my landlord to come up and talk with me. My host was an Italian, and an excellent fellow. Attached to his hotel was a large restaurant, frequented by the first people at Cracow. During the evening an old countess came there to sup; he mentioned to her the arrival of an American, and I supped with her and her niece; neither of them, however, so interesting as to have any effect upon my slumber.

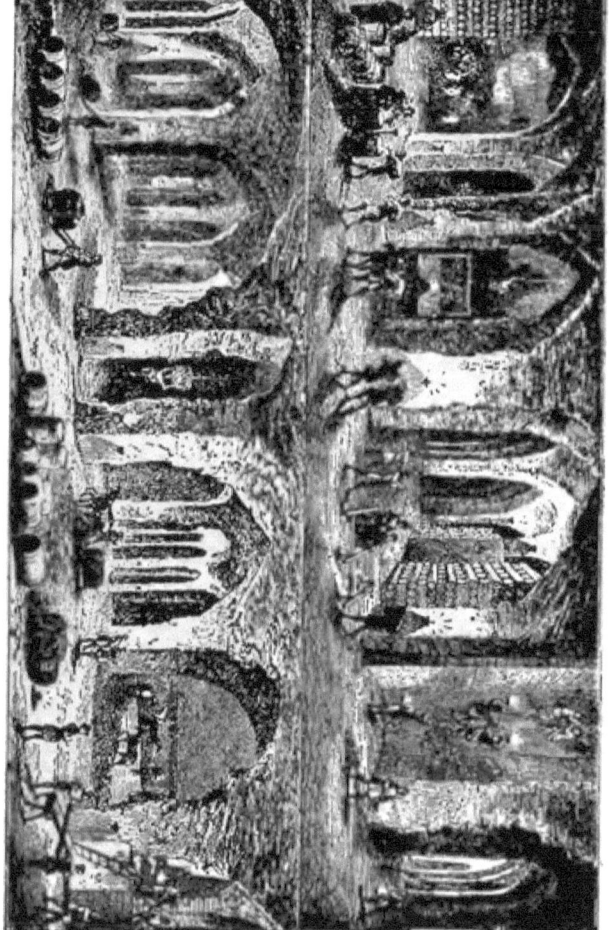

SALT MINES OF CRACOW.

p. 265.

CHAPTER XXVIII.

Cracow.—Casimir the Great.—Kosciusko.—Tombs of the Polish Kings.—A Polish Heroine.—Last Words of a King.—A Hero in Decay.—The Salt-mines of Cracow.—The Descent.—The Mines.—Underground Meditations.—The Farewell.

CRACOW is an old, curious, and interesting city, situated in a valley on the banks of the Vistula; and approaching it as I did, toward the sunset of a summer's day, the old churches and towers, the lofty castles and the large houses spread out on the immense plains, gave it an appearance of actual splendour. This faded away as I entered, but still the city inspired a feeling of respect, for it bore the impress of better days. It contains numerous churches, some of them very large, and remarkable for their style and architecture, and more than a hundred monasteries and convents. In the centre is a large square, on which stands the church of Notre Dame, an immense Gothic structure, and also the old palace of Sobieski, now cut down into shops, and many large private residences, uninhabited and falling to ruins. The principal streets terminate in this square. Almost every building bears striking marks of ruined grandeur. On the last partition of Poland, in eighteen hundred and fifteen, by the Holy Alliance, Cracow, with a territory of five hundred square miles and a population of a hundred and eight thousand, including about thirty thousand Jews, was erected into a republic; and at this day it exists nominally as a *free city*, under the protection of the three great powers; emphatically, such protection as vultures give to lambs; three masters instead of one, Russia, Prussia, and Austria, all claiming the right to interfere in its government.

But even in its fallen state Cracow is dear to the Pole's heart, for it was the capital of his country when Poland ranked high among nations, and, down to him who last sat upon her throne, was the place of coronation and of burial for her kings. It is the residence of many of the old Polish nobility, who, with reduced fortunes, prefer this little foothold in their country, where liberty nominally lingers, to exile in foreign lands. It now contains a population of about thirty thousand, including Jews. Occasionally the seigneur is still seen, in his short cassock of blue cloth, with a red sash and a white square-topped cap; a costume admirably adapted to the tall and noble figure of the proud Pole, and the costume of the peasant of Cracow is still a striking feature in her streets.

After a stroll through the churches, I walked on the old ramparts of Cracow. The city was formerly surrounded with regular fortifications, but, as in almost all the cities of Europe, her ancient walls have been transformed into boulevards; and now handsome avenues of trees encircle it, destroying altogether its gothic military aspect, and on Sundays and fête days the whole population gathers in gay dresses, seeking pleasure where their fathers stood clad in armour and arrayed for battle.

The boulevards command an extensive view of all the surrounding country. "All the sites of my country," says a national poet, "are dear to me; but, above all, I love the environs of Cracow; there at every step I meet the recollections of our ancient glory and our once imposing grandeur."

On the opposite bank of the river is a large tumulus of earth, marking the grave of Cracus, the founder of the city. A little higher up is another mound, reverenced as the sepulchre of his daughter Wenda, who was so enamoured of war that she promised to give her hand only to the lover who should conquer her in battle. Beyond this is the field of Zechino, where the brave Kosciusko, after his return from America, with a band of peasants, again struck the first blow of revolution, and, by a victory over the Russians, roused all Poland to arms.

About a mile from Cracow are the ruins of the palace of Lobzow, built by Casimir the Great, for a long time the favourite royal residence, and identified with a crowd of national recollections; and, until lately, a large mound of earth in the garden was reverenced as the grave of Esther, the beautiful Jewess, the idol of Casimir the Great. Poetry has embellished the tradition, and the national muse has hallowed the palace of Lobzow and the grave of Esther.

"Passer-by, if you are a stranger, tremble in thinking of human destruction; but if you are a Pole, shed bitter tears; heroes have inhabited this palace..... Who can equal them?....

* * * *

" Casimir erected this palace: centuries have hailed him with the name of the great...

* * * *

" Near his Esther, in the delightful groves of Lobzow, he thought himself happy in ceasing to be a king to become a lover.

* * * *

" But fate is unpitiable for kings as for us, and even beauty is subject to the common law. Esther died, and Casimir erected a tomb in the place she had loved.

" Oh! if you are sensible to the grief caused by love, drop a tear at this tomb and adorn it with a crown. If Casimir was tied to humanity by some weaknesses, they are the appendage of heroes! In presence of this chateau, in find ng again noble remains, sing the glory of Casimir the Great."

I was not a sentimental traveller, nor sensible to the grief that is caused by love, and I could neither drop a tear at the tomb of Esther, nor sing the glory of Casimir the Great; but my heart beat high as I turned to another monument in the environs of Cracow; an immense mound of earth, standing on an eminence visible from every quarter, towering almost into a mountain, and sacred to the memory of Kosciusko! I saw it from the palace of the kings and from the ramparts of the fallen city, and with my eyes constantly fixed upon it, descended to the Vistula, followed its bank to a large convent, and then turned to the right, direct for the mound. I walked to the foot of the hill, and ascended to a broad table of land. From this table the mound rises to a conical form, from a base three hundred feet in diameter, to the height of one hundred and seventy-five feet At the four corners formerly stood small houses, which were occupied by revolutionary soldiers who had served under Kosciusko. On the farther side, enclosed by a railing, was a small chapel, and within it a marble tomb covering Kosciusko's heart! A circular path winds round the mound; I ascended by this path to the top. It is built of earth sodded, and was then covered with a thick carpet of grass, and reminded me of the tumuli of the Grecian heroes on the plains of Troy; and perhaps, when thousands of years shall have rolled by, and all connected with our age be forgotten, and time and exposure to the elements shall have changed its form, another stranger will stand where I did, and wonder why and for what it was raised. It was erected in 1819 by the voluntary labour of the Polish people; and so great was the enthusiasm, that, as an eye-witness told me, wounded soldiers brought earth in their helmets, and women in their slippers; and I remembered with a swelling heart, that on this consecrated spot a nation of brave men had turned to my country as the star of liberty, and that here a banner had been unfurled and hailed with acclamations by assembled thousands, bearing aloft the sacred inscription, "Kosciusko, the friend of Washington!"

The morning was cold and dreary, the sky was overcast with clouds, and the sun, occasionally breaking through, lighted up for a moment with dazzling brilliancy the domes and steeples of Cracow, and the palace and burial-place of her kings, emblematic of the fitful gleams of her liberty flashing and dazzling, and then dying away. I drew my cloak around me, and remained there till I was almost drenched with rain. The wind blew violently, and I descended and sheltered myself at the foot of the mound, by the grave of Kosciusko's heart!

I returned to the city and entered the Cathedral Church. It stands by the side of the old palace, on the summit of the rock of Wauvel, in the centre of and commanding the city, enclosed with walls and towers, and allied in its history with the most memorable annals of Poland; the witness of the ancient glory of her kings, and their sepulchre. The rain was pattering against the windows of the old church as I strolled through the silent cloisters and among the tombs of the kings. A verger in a large cocked hat, and a group of peasants, moved like myself, with noiseless steps, as if afraid to disturb the repose of the royal dead. Many of the kings of Poland fill but a corner of the page of history. Some of their names I had forgotten, or, perhaps, never knew until I saw them inscribed on their tombs; but every monument covered a head that had worn a crown, and some whose bones were mouldering under my feet will live till the last records of heroism perish.

The oldest monument is that of Wladislaus le Bref, built of stone, without any inscription, but adorned with figures in bas-relief, which are very much injured. He died in thirteen hundred and thirty-three, and chose himself the place of his eternal rest. Charles the Twelfth of Sweden, on his invasion of Poland, visited the Cathedral Church, and stopped before this tomb. A distinguished canon who attended him, in allusion to the position of John Casimir, who was then at war with the king of Sweden, remarked, "And that king was also driven from his throne, but he returned and reigned until his death." The Swede answered with bitterness, "But your John Casimir will never return." The canon replied respectfully. "God is great and fortune is fickle:" and the canon was right, for John Casimir regained his throne.

I approached with a feeling of veneration the tomb of Casimir the Great. It is of red marble; four columns support a canopy, and the figure of the king, with a crown on his head, rests on a coffin of stone. An iron railing encloses the monument. It is nearly five hundred years since the palatines and nobles of Poland, with all the insignia of barbaric magnificence, laid him in the place where his ashes now repose. The historian writes, "Poland is indebted to Casimir for the greatest part of her churches, palaces, fortresses, and towns," adding that "he found Poland of wood and left her of marble." He patronised letters, and founded the University of Cracow; promoted industry and encouraged trade; digested the unwritten laws and usages into a regular code; established courts of justice; repressed the tyranny of the nobles, and died with the honourable title of King of the Peasants; and I did not forget, while standing over his grave, that beneath me slept the spirit that loved the groves of Lobzow and the heart that beat for Esther the Jewess.

The tomb of Sigismund I. is of red marble, with a figure as large as life reclining upon it. It is adorned with bas-reliefs, and the arms of his republic, the white eagle and the armed cavalier of Lithuania. He died in fifteen hundred and forty-one, and his monument bears the following inscription in Latin: "Sigismund Jagellon, King of Poland, Grand-duke of Lithuania, Conqueror of the Tartars, of the Wallachians, of the Russians and Prussians, reposes under this stone, which he prepared for himself." Forty years ago Thaddeus Czacki, the Polish historian, opened the tombs of the kings and found the head of Sigismund resting upon a plate of silver bearing a long Latin inscription; the body measured six feet and two inches in height, and was covered with three rich ermines; on the feet were golden spurs, a chain of gold around the neck, and a gold ring on one finger of the left hand. At his feet was a small pewter coffin enclosing the body of his son by Bona Sforza.

By his side lies the body of his son Sigismund II., the last of the Jagellons, at whose death began the cabals and convulsions of an elective monarchy, by which Poland lost her influence among foreign powers. His memory is rendered interesting by his romantic love for Barbe Radzewill. She appeared at his father's court, the daughter of a private citizen, celebrated in Polish history and romance as uniting to all a woman's beauty a mingled force and tenderness, energy and goodness. The prince had outlived all the ardour of youth; disappointed and listless amid pleasures, his energy of mind destroyed by his excesses, inconstant in his love, and at the summit of human prosperity, living without a wish or a hope; but he saw Barbe, and his heart beat anew with the pulsations of life. In the language of his biographer, he proved, in all its fulness, that sentiment which draws to earth by its sorrows and raises to heaven by its delights. He married her privately, and on his father's death proclaimed her queen. The whole body of nobles refused to acknowledge the marriage; and one of the nuncios, in the name of the representatives of the nation, supplicated him for himself, his country, his blood, and his children, to extinguish his passion; but the king swore on his sword that neither the diet, nor the nation, nor the whole universe, should make him break his vows to Barbe; that he would a thousand times rather live with her out of the kingdom, than keep a throne which she could not share; and was on the point of abdicating, when his opponents offered to do homage to the queen. When Czacki opened the coffin of this prince, he found the body perfectly preserved, and the head, as before, resting on a silver plate containing a long Latin inscription.

At the foot of his coffin is that of his sister and successor, Anne; and in a separate chapel is the tomb of Stephen Battory, one of the greatest of the kings of Poland, raised to the throne by his marriage with Anne.

I became more and more interested in this asylum of royal dead. I read there almost the entire history of the Polish republic, and again I felt that it was but a step from the throne to the grave, for near me was the great chair in which the kings of Poland were crowned. I paused before the tomb of John Casimir: and there was something strangely interesting in the juxtaposition of these royal dead. John Casimir lies by the side of the brother whom he endeavoured to supplant in his election to the throne. His reign was a continued succession of troubles and misfortunes. Once he was obliged to fly from Poland. He predicted what has since been so fearfully verified, that his country, enfeebled by the anarchy of its government and the licentiousness of the nobles, would be dismembered among the neighbouring powers; and, worn out with the cares of royalty, abdicated the throne, and died in a convent in France. I read at his tomb his pathetic farewell to his people.

"People of Poland,

"It is now two hundred and eighty years that you have been governed by my family. The reign of my ancestors is past, and mine is going to expire. Fatigued by the labours of war, the cares of the cabinet, and the weight of age; oppressed with the burdens and vicissitudes of a reign of more than twenty-one years, I, your king and father, return into your hands what the world esteems above all things, a crown, and choose for my throne six feet of earth, where I shall sleep with my fathers. When you show my tomb to your children, tell them that I was the foremost in battle and the last in retreat; that I renounced regal grandeur for the good of my country, and restored my sceptre to those who gave it me."

By his side, and under a monument of black marble, lies the body of his successor, Michel Wisniowecki, an obscure and unambitious citizen, who was literally dragged to the throne, and wept when the crown was placed upon his head, and of whom Casimir remarked, when informed of his late subjects' choice, "What, have they put the crown on the head of that poor fellow?" And again I was almost startled by the strange and unnatural mingling of human ashes. By the side of that "poor fellow" lies the "famous" John Sobieski, the greatest of the long line of kings of a noble and valorous nation;

"One of the few, the immortal names,
That were not born to die."

On the lower floor of the church, by the side of Poniatowski, the Polish Bayard, is the tomb of one nobler in my eyes than all the kings of Poland or of the world. It is of red marble ornamented with the cap and plume of the peasant of Cracow, and bears the simple inscription " T. Kosciusko." All over the church I had read elaborate panegyrics upon the tenants of the royal sepulchres, and I was struck with this simple inscription, and remembered that the white marble column reared amid the magnificent scenery of the Hudson, which I had often gazed at from the deck of a steam-boat, and at whose base I had often stood, bore also in majestic simplicity the name of "Kosciusko." It was late in the afternoon, and the group of peasants, two Poles from the interior, and a party of the citizens of Cracow, among whom were several ladies, joined me at the tomb. We could not speak each other's language; we were born and lived thousands of miles apart, and we were strangers in our thoughts and feelings, in all our hopes and prospects, but we had a bond of sympathy at the grave of Kosciusko. One of the ladies spoke French, and I told them that, in my far distant country, the name of their nation's idol was hallowed; that schoolboys had erected a monument to his memory. They knew that he had fought by the side of Washington, but they did not know that the recollection of his services was still so dearly cherished in America; and we all agreed that it was the proudest tribute that could be paid to his memory, to write merely his name on the monument. It meant that it was needless to add an epitaph, for no man would ask, Who was Kosciusko?

It was nearly dark when I returned to my hotel. In the restaurant, at a small table directly opposite me, sat the celebrated Chlopicki, to whom, on the breaking out of the last revolution, Poland turned as to another Kosciusko, and who, until he faltered during the trying scenes of that revolution, would have been deemed worthy to lie by Kosciusko's side. Born of a noble family, a soldier from his birth, he served in the memorable campaigns of the great patriot, distinguished himself in the Polish legions in Italy under Dombrowski, and, as colonel of a regiment of the army of the Vistula, behaved gloriously in Prussia. In Spain he fought at Saragossa and Sagunta, and was called by Suchet *le brave des braves*; as general of brigade in the army of Russia, he was wounded at Valentina, near Smolensk, and was general of a division, in eighteen hundred and fourteen, when Poland fell under the dominion of the autocrat. The grand-duke Constantine censured him on parade, saying that his division was not in order; and Chlopicki, with the proud boast, "I did not gain my rank on the parade-ground, nor did I win my decorations there," asked his discharge the next day, and could never after be induced to return to the service. The day after the revolutionary blow was struck, all Poland turned to Chlopicki as the only man capable of standing at the head of the nation. The command of the army, with absolute powers, was conferred upon him by acclamation, and one of the patriot leaders concluded his address to him with these words: "Brother, take the sword of your ancestors and predecessors, Czarnecki, Dombrowski, and Kosciusko. Guide the nation that has placed its trust in you in the path of honour. Save this unhappy country." Chlopicki, with his silver head grown white in the service of Poland, was hailed by a hundred thousand people on the Champ de Mars with shouts of "Our country and its brave defender, Chlopicki, for ever!" He promised never to abuse their confidence, and swore that he would defend the liberty of Poland to the last moment. The whole nation was enthusiastic in his favour; but in less than three months, at a stormy session of the diet, he threw up his high office of dictator, and refused peremptorily to accept command of the army. This brave army, enthusiastically attached to him, was struck with profound grief at his estrangement; but, with all the faults imputed to him, it never was charged that he attempted to take advantage of his great popularity for any ambitious purposes of his own.

At the battle of Grokow he fought nominally as a private soldier, though Skryznecki and Radziwill being both deficient in military experience, the whole army looked to him for guidance. Once, when the battle was setting strong against the Poles, in a moment of desperation he put himself at the head of some disposable battalions, and turning away from an aide-de-camp who came to him for orders, said "Go and ask Radziwill; for me I seek only death." Grievously wounded, his wounds were dressed in presence of the enemy; but at two o'clock he was borne off the field, the hopes of the soldiers died, and the army remained without any actual head. Throughout the revolution his conduct, was cold, indifferent, and inexplicable; private letters from the Emperor of Russia were talked of, and even *treason* was whispered in connexion with his name. The Poles speak of him more in sorrow than in anger; they say that it was not enough that he exposed his person on the field of battle; that he should have given them the whole weight of his great military talents, and the influence of his powerful name; that, standing alone, without children or relations to be compromised by his acts, he should have consummated the glory of his life by giving its few remaining years for the liberty of his country. He appeared about sixty-five, with hair perfectly white, a high florid complexion, a firm and determined expression, and in still unbroken health, carrying himself with the proud bearing of a distinguished veteran soldier. I could not believe that he had bartered the precious satisfaction of a long and glorious career for a few years of ignoble existence; and, though a stranger, could but regret that, in the wane of life, circumstances, whether justly or not, had sullied an honoured name. It spoke loudly against him that I saw him sitting in a public restaurant at Cracow, unmolested by the Russian government.

The next day I visited the celebrated salt-mines at Wielitska. They lie about twelve miles from Cracow, in the province of Galicia, a part of the kingdom of Poland, which, on the unrighteous partition of that country, fell to the share of Austria. Although at so short a distance, it was necessary to go through all the passport formalities requisite on a departure for a foreign country. I took a fiacre and rode to the different bureaus of the city police, and, having procured the permission of the municipal authorities to leave the little territory of Cracow, rode next to the Austrian consul, who thereupon, and in consideration of one dollar to him in hand paid, was graciously pleased to permit me to enter the dominions of his master, the Emperor of Austria. It was also necessary to have an order from the director of the mines to the superintendant; and furnished with this, I again mounted my fiacre, rattled through the principal street, and in a few minutes crossed the Vistula. At the end of the bridge an Austrian soldier stopped me for my passport, a *douanier* examined my carriage for articles subject to duty, and, these functionaries being satisfied, in about two hours from the time at which I began my preparations I was fairly on my way.

Leaving the Vistula, I entered a pretty, undulating, and well-cultivated country, and saw at a distance a high dark line, marking the range of the Carpathian mountains. It was a long time since I had seen anything that looked like a mountain. From the Black Sea the whole of my journey had been over an immense plain, and I hailed the wild range of the Carpathian as I would the spire of a church, as an evidence of the approach to regions of civilization.

In an hour and a half I arrived at the town of Wielitska, containing about three thousand inhabitants, and standing, as it were on the roof of the immense subterraneous excavations. The houses are built of wood, and the first thing that struck me was the almost entire absence of men in the streets, the whole male population being employed in the mines, and then at work below. I rode to the office of the superintendant, and presented my letter, and was received with great civility of manner, but his *Polish* was perfectly unintelligible. A smutty-faced operative, just out of the mines, accosted me in Latin, and I exchanged a few shots with him, but hauled off on the appearance of a man whom the superintendant had sent for to act as my guide; an old soldier who had served in the campaigns of Napoleon, and, as he said, become an amateur and proficient in fighting and French. He was dressed in miner's costume, fanciful and embroidered with gold, holding in his hand a steel axe; and, having arrayed me in a long white frock, conducted me to a wooden building covering the shaft which forms the principal entrance to the mine. This shaft is ten feet square, and descends perpendicularly more than two hundred feet into the bowels of the earth. We arranged ourselves in canvas seats, and several of the miners who were waiting to descend, attached themselves to seats at the end of the ropes, with lamps in their hands, about eight or ten feet below us.

When my feet left the brink of the shaft I felt, for a moment, as if suspended over the portal of a bottomless pit; and as my head descended below the surface, the rope, winding and tapering to a thread, seemed letting me down to the realms of Pluto. But in a few moments we touched the bottom. From within a short distance of the surface, the shaft is cut through a solid rock of salt, and from the bottom passages almost innumerable are cut in every direction through the same bed. We were furnished with guides, who went before us bearing torches, and I followed through the whole labyrinth of passages, forming the largest excavations in Europe, peopled with upward of two thousand souls, and giving a complete idea of a subterraneous world. These mines are known to have been worked upward of six hundred years, being mentioned in the Polish annals as early as twelve hundred and thirty-seven, under Boleslaus the Chaste, and then not as a new discovery, but how much earlier they had existed cannot now be ascertained. The tradition is, that a sister of St. Casimir, having lost a gold ring, prayed to St. Anthony, the patron saint of Cracow, and was advised in a dream that, by digging in such a place, she would find a treasure far greater than that she had lost, and within the place indicated these mines were discovered.

There are four different stories or ranges of apartments; the whole length of the excavations is more than six thousand feet, or three quarters of an hour's walk, and the greatest breadth more than two thousand feet; and there are so many turnings and windings that my guide told me, though I hardly think it possible, that the whole length of all the passages cut through this bed of salt amounts to more than three hundred miles. Many of the chambers are of immense size. Some are supported by timber, others by vast pillars of salt; several are without any support in the middle, and of vast dimensions, perhaps eighty feet high, and so long and broad as almost to appear a boundless subterraneous cavern. In one of the largest is a lake covering nearly the whole area. When the King of Saxony visited this place in eighteen hundred and ten, after taking possession of his moiety of the mines as Duke of Warsaw, this portion of them was brilliantly illuminated, and a band of music, floating on the lake, made the roof echo with patriotic airs. We crossed the lake in a flatboat by a rope, the dim light of torches, and the hollow sound of our voices, giving a lively idea of a passage across the Styx; and we had a scene which might have entitled us to a welcome from the prince of the infernals, for our torch-bearers quarrelled, and in a scuffle that came near carrying us all with them, one was tumbled into the lake. Our Charon caught him, and, without stopping to take him in, hurried across, and as soon as we landed beat them both unmercifully.

From this we entered an immense cavern, in which several hundred men were working with pickaxes and hatchets, cutting out large blocks of salt, and trimming them to suit the size of barrels. With their black faces begrimed with dust and smoke, they looked by the light of the scattered torches like the journeymen of Beelzebub, the prince of darkness, preparing for some great blow-up, or like the spirits of the damned condemned to toil without end. My guide called up a party, who disengaged with their pick-axes a large block of salt from its native bed, and in a few minutes cut and trimmed it to fit the barrels in which they are packed. All doubts as to their being creatures of our upper world were removed by the eagerness with which they accepted the money I gave them; and it will be satisfactory to the advocates of that currency to know that paper money passes readily in these lower regions.

There are more than a thousand chambers or halls, most of which have been abandoned and shut up. In one is a collection of fanciful things, such as rings, books, crosses, &c., cut in the rock-salt. Most of the principal chambers had some name printed over them, as the "Archduke," "Caroline," &c. Whenever it was necessary, my guides went a-head, and stationed themselves in some conspicuous place, lighting up the dark caverns with the blaze of their torches, and, after allowing me a sufficient time, struck their flambeaux against the wall, and millions of sparks flashed and floated around and filled the chamber. In one place, at the end of a long, dark passage, a door was thrown open, and I was ushered suddenly into a spacious ball-room lighted with torches; and directly in front, at the head of the room, was a transparency with coloured lights, in the centre of which were the words "Excelso hospiti," "To the Illustrious guest," which I took to myself, though I believe the greeting was intended for the same royal person for whom the lake chamber was illuminated. Lights were ingeniously arranged around the room, and at the foot, about twenty feet above my head, was a large orchestra. On the occasion referred to a splendid ball was given in this room; the roof echoed with the sound of music; and nobles and princely ladies flirted and coquetted the same as above ground; and it is said that the splendid dresses of a numerous company, and the blaze of light from the chandeliers reflected upon the surface of the rock-salt, produced an effect of inconceivable brilliancy. My chandeliers were worse than Allan M'Aulay's strapping Highlanders, with their pine torches, being dirty, ragged, smutty-faced rascals, who threw the light in streaks across the hall. I am always willing to believe fanciful stories; and if my guide had thrown in a handsome young princess as part of the welcome to the "Excelso hospiti," I would have subscribed to anything he said; but, in the absence of a consideration, I refused to tax my imagination up to the point he wished. Perhaps the most interesting chamber of all is the chapel dedicated to that Saint Anthony who brought about the discovery of these mines. It is supposed to be more than four hundred years old. The columns, with their ornamented capitals, the arches, the images of the Saviour, the Virgin and saints, the altar and the pulpit, with all their decorations, and the figures of two priests represented at prayers before the shrine of the patron saint, are all carved out of the rock-salt, and to this day grand mass is regularly celebrated in the chapel once every year.

Following my guide through all the different passages and chambers, and constantly meeting miners and seeing squads of men at work, I descended by regular stairs cut in the salt, but in some places worn away and replaced by wood or stone, to the lowest gallery, which is nearly a thousand feet below the surface of the earth. I was then a rather veteran traveller, but up to this time it had been my business to move quietly on the surface of the earth, or, when infected with the soaring spirit of other travellers, to climb to the top of some lofty tower or loftier cathedral; and I had fulfilled one of the duties of a visiter to the Eternal City by perching myself within the great ball of St. Peter's; but here I was far deeper under the earth than I had ever been above it; and at the greatest depth from which the human voice ever rose, I sat down on a lump of salt and soliloquised,

"Through what varieties of untried being,
Through what new scenes and changes must we pass!"

I have since stood upon the top of the Pyramids

and admired the daring genius and the industry of man, and at the same time smiled at his feebleness when, from the mighty pile, I saw in the dark ranges of mountains, the sandy desert, the rich valley of the Nile and the river of Egypt, the hand of the world's great Architect; but I never felt man's feebleness more than here; for all these immense excavations, the work of more than six hundred years, were but as the work of ants by the roadside. The whole of the immense mass above me, and around and below, to an unknown extent, was of salt; a wonderful phenomenon in the natural history of the globe. All the different strata have been carefully examined by scientific men. The uppermost bed at the surface is sand; the second clay, occasionally mixed with sand and gravel, and containing petrifactions of marine bodies; the third is calcareous stone; and from these circumstances it has been conjectured that this spot was formerly covered by the sea, and that the salt is a gradual deposit formed by the evaporation of its waters. I was disappointed in some of the particulars which had fastened themselves upon my imagination. I had heard and read glowing accounts of the brilliancy and luminous splendour of the passages and chambers, compared by some to the lustre of precious stones; but the salt is a dark grey colour, almost black, and although sometimes glittering when the light was thrown upon it, I do not believe it could ever be lighted up to shine with any extraordinary or dazzling brightness. Early travellers, too, had reported that these mines contained several villages, inhabited by colonies of miners, who lived constantly below; and that many were born and died there, who never saw the light of day; but all this is entirely untrue. The miners descend every morning and return every night, and live in the village above. None of them ever sleep below. There are, however, two horses which were foaled in the mines, and have never been on the surface of the earth. I looked at these horses with great interest. They were growing old before their time; other horses had perhaps gone down and told them stories of a world above which they would never know.

It was late in the afternoon when I was hoisted up the shaft. These mines do not need the embellishment of fiction. They are, indeed, a wonderful spectacle, and I am satisfied that no traveller ever visited them without recurring to it as a day of extraordinary interest. I wrote my name in the book of visiters, where I saw those of two American friends who had preceded me about a month, mounted my barouche, and about an hour after dark reached the bank of the Vistula. My passport was again examined by a soldier and my carriage searched by a custom-house officer; I crossed the bridge, dined with my worthy host of the *Hôtel de la Rose Blanche*, and, while listening to a touching story of the Polish revolution, fell asleep in my chair.

And here, on the banks of the Vistula, I take my leave of the reader. I have carried him over seas and rivers, mountains and plains, through royal palaces and peasants' huts, and in return for his kindness in accompanying me to the end, I promise that I will not again burden him with my Incidents of Travel.

PART III.

KŒMPFER'S ACCOUNT OF JAPAN.

INTRODUCTION.

The earliest known accounts brought to Europe of the islands forming the empire of Japan, are contained in the narrative of the travels of Marco Polo. This celebrated Venetian, born in 1250, undertook, when only twenty-one years old, a journey to the furthest parts of Asia. The passage to India, by way of the Cape of Good Hope, was then unknown, so that the journey was entirely overland. He was absent twenty-four years, and during that time, he travelled through the greater part of Eastern Asia, and had peculiar sources of information. After his return, he was captured by a Genoese vessel, and thrown into prison at Genoa, where, with the assistance of a fellow captive, a Frenchman, he drew up a narrative of his travels. For some time his accounts were regarded as extravagant, if not fabulous; but as information has accumulated, his general accuracy has become more and more established. He resided for some time in Pekin, which he calls Kambalu; and it was there most probably that he obtained the following information about Japan.

"Zipangu (*i. e.*, Japan) is an island on the east, one thousand five hundred miles distant from the shores of Mangi, very great; the people, of white complexion, of gentle behaviour, in religion idolaters, and have a king of their own. They have gold in great plenty, for few merchants come thither, and the king permits no exportation of it; and they which have carried on commerce there speak of the king's house covered with gold, as churches here with lead,—gilded windows,—floors of gold. There are also many pearls. Once the fame of these riches made Cublai-Khan to send, to conquer it, two of his barons, with a great fleet of ships, one named Abbaca, and the other Venfanjin, who, going from Zaitung and Quinsay, arrived there; but, falling out between themselves, could take but one city, and there beheaded all they took except eight persons, which, by an enchanted precious stone, enclosed in the right arm between the skin and flesh, could not be wounded with iron; whereupon, with wooden clubs, at the command of the two barons, they were slain. It happened one day, that a northern wind blew hard, which was dangerous to the ships riding there; so that some were lost, some put out farther to sea, and others, with the two leaders and a few principal persons, returned home. Out of many broken ships, some escaped, by boards and swimming, to an island, not inhabited, four miles off Zipangu, and were about thirty thousand, without provisions or arms, against whom the Zipanguaners, after the tempest was calmed, sent out a fleet of ships and an army. These coming on land, to seek the wrecked Tartars, without order, gave occasion to the Tartars to wheel about the island, being high in the midst, and to get unseen to their ships, which were left unmanned, with the streamers displayed; and in them they sailed to the chief city of Zipangu, where they were admitted without suspicion, and found few others but women.

"The king of Zipangu besieged them six months, and they, having no relief, yielded themselves, and their lives were saved. This happened, A.D. 1264.

"The Khan, for the ill conduct of his two commanders, cut off the head of one, and sent the other to a desert island called Zerga, where he caused offenders to die, by sewing them, their hands bound, in a new-slayed hide of a buffalo, which, drying, shrinketh so as it puts them to vast tortures, which lead to a miserable death. The idols in this and the adjoining islands are made with heads of kine, swine, dogs; and in other fashions more monstrous, as, with faces on their shoulders, with four, ten, or even a hundred hands; and to these they ascribe most power, and do most reverence, and say that so they learned of their progenitors. They sometimes eat their enemies, which they take with great joy and for great dainties; at least, so it is reported of them. The sea in which this island lies, is called the Sea of Cin or Chin, that is, the sea against Mangi; and in the language of that island, Mangi is called Chin, or Chint; which sea is so large, that the mariners and expert pilots, who frequent it, say that there are seven thousand four hundred and forty islands therein, the most part of them inhabited; that there grows no tree which yields not a good smell; and that there grow many spices of divers kinds, especially lignum aloes, and pepper, black and white. The ships of Zaitum are a year in their voyage; for they go in winter and return in summer, having winds of two sorts, which keep their seasons, and this country is far from India: but I will leave them, for I never was there—nor are they subjects to the Khan: and return to Zaitum, from hence sailing south-westward one thousand five hundred miles, passing a gulf called Cheinan, which continues two months' sailing to the northward, still confining on the south-east of Mangi, and elsewhere, with Ania and Toloman, and other provinces before-named. Within it are infinite islands, all in a manner inhabited; in them is found abundance of gold; and they trade one with another."

The first visit of Europeans to Japan was purely accidental. A Portuguese vessel in the year 1548, on its voyage from Siam to China, was forced out of its course, and driven upon the coast of Japan. The chief men on board were named Antonio da Matta, Francisco Zamioto and Antonio Paixola. They were well received by the Japanese, among whom they resided for some time, and no feeling of jealousy or mistrust was manifested by the inhabitants, who, on the contrary, desired to establish a friendly intercourse with the strangers. On their return, the report of the Portuguese was so favourable, that a trade with Japan was immediately opened.

At that time the Dutch and the Portuguese were the most important European powers in the East. England was scarcely known either as a commercial nation or a maritime power. The Eastern trade was the most lucrative of the time, and it may be naturally supposed that rivalry and jealousy often resulting in actual warfare were created. Another element of opposition existed; the Reformation had divided Christians into the two great sections of Protestants and Catholics, and perhaps there could not be found in all Christendom a nation more Protestant than the Dutch, or more Catholic than the Portuguese. The knowledge of Japan, and of the lucrative trade with it, soon spread among the Dutch, who were eager to establish a traffic with the country. Their first intercourse arose from a very singular circumstance. A Kentish man, William Adams by name, one of the genuine old English seamen of the school of Cavendish and Drake, after serving in the navy of his own country, and roaming over the seas under the flags of other nations, engaged himself as pilot on board one of a fleet of five ships fitted out by the Dutch India Company. The object of the expedition does not appear at all distinct on the face of the records. but like similar expeditions in those days, it is highly probable that it was partly piratical, partly commercial. They sailed from Holland in 1598, and cruised for about a year off the coast of South America. Much of their cargo consisted of woollen cloth. and finding it either unprofitable or dangerous to remain much longer at their cruising ground, they set sail for Japan, hoping that the Japanese would readily purchase their Dutch manufactured broad cloth. But before they arrived at that country, they were so buffeted about by winds and waves, and so roughly used by their enemies, that four ships were lost; and in the fifth, of which Adams was pilot, there were only seven men who were not rendered incapable of duty by sickness. Fortunately our countryman, Adams, was fit for his work, and to him the rest looked up for assistance and direction. It was with great difficulty they cast anchor, and having done so, they were immediately surrounded by a fleet of Japanese boats, whose crews came on board, and though they did not attempt to injure any of the men, yet they made as free with the goods on board as though they had been their own property. This continued, however only for one day, as the Japanese authorities took the vessel and cargo into their own custody. The sailors were well treated, but the dastardly Dutchmen leagued with the Portuguese to libel the character of the English, and to bring Adams and another Englishman on board into disgrace. Both the Portuguese and these veracious Hollanders, represented the English as a race of pirates and sea-rovers, and not merchants at all, and that to give them any encouragement would produce not benefits through commerce, but serious evils through war. However, the Emperor ordered Adams to appear at court, and through interpreters, underwent a long examination by the Emperor, which he appears to have sustained with great calmness, and to have given answers with much prudence and discretion. Of this interview, Adams himself gives the following clear and straightforward account:—

"The king demanded of what land I was, and what moved us to come to his land, being so far off. I showed unto him the name of our country, and that our land had long sought out the East Indies, and desired friendship with all the kings and potentates in way of merchandise, having in our land divers commodities which these lands had not; and also, to buy such merchandises in this land as our country had not. Then the great king asked whether our country had wars? I answered him, yea, with the Spaniards and Portugals, being in peace with all other nations. Further, he asked me in what I did believe? I said, in God that made heaven and earth. He asked me divers other questions of things of religion, and many other things, as what way we came to his country. Having a chart of the whole world with me, I showed him through the Straits of Magelhaens; at which he wondered, and thought me to lie. Thus, from one thing to another, I abode with him till midnight. And having asked me what merchandise we had in our ship, I showed him samples of all. In the end, he being ready to depart, I desired that we might have trade of merchandise, as the Portugals had. To which he made me an answer, but what it was I did not understand. So he commanded me to be carried to prison. But two days after he sent for me again, and inquired of the qualities and conditions of our countries, of wars and peace, of beasts and cattle of all sorts, of heaven and the stars. It seemed that he was well content with all mine answers. Nevertheless, I was commanded to prison again; but my lodging was bettered in another place."

In the meantime the Jesuits and Portuguese left no means untried to prejudice Adams and his companions in the eyes of the Emperor, but without success. Adams became a favourite at court, and pleased the Emperor much by his practical English skill. By the Emperor's orders he built a trading vessel, which made several voyages, some of them as far even as Acapulco; and through his influence both the Dutch and English obtained a commercial footing in Japan. Adams often sought permission to return to England, where he had left a wife and children; but the Emperor refused, and he died at Firando, in the year 1620.

The first attempt of the English to have commercial intercourse with Japan, was made during the reign of James I. by Captain Saris. He was invited to court, where he was accompanied by Adams, and after delivering his presents, credentials, &c., the Emperor granted the following privileges:—

"Privileges granted by OGOSHOSAMA, Emperor of Japan, unto the Right Worshipful Sir THOMAS SMITH, Knight, Governor, and others the Honourable and Worshipful Adventurers to the East Indies.

I. *Imprimis*, We give free licence to the subjects of the King of Great Britain, viz, Sir Thomas Smith, Governor, and Company of the East India merchants and adventurers, for ever safely to come into any of our ports of our empire of Japan, with their shippes and merchandizes, without any hindrance to them or their goods. And to abide, buy, sell, and barter, according to their owne manner, with all nations; to tarry here as long as they think good, and to depart at their pleasures.

II. *Item*, We grant unto them freedom of custom, for all such merchandizes as either now they have brought, or hereafter shall bring into our kingdom, or shall from hence transport to any foreign part. And doe authorize those shippes that hereafter shall arrive, and come from England, to proceed to present sale of their commodities, *without further coming or sending up to our court.*

III. *Item*, If any of their shippes shall happen to lie in danger of shipwrecke, we will our subjects not only to assist them, but that such part of shippes and goods as shall be saved, be returned to their captains or Cape merchants or their assignes. And that they shall, or may build one house or more for themselves in any part of our empire, where they shall thinke fittest, and at their departure to make sale thereof at their pleasure.

IV. *Item*, If any of the English merchants, or other, shall depart this life, within our dominions, the goods of the deceased, shall remaine at the disposal of the Cape merchant. And that all offences committed by them shall be punished by the said Cape merchant, according to his discretion: and our laws to take no hold of their persons or goods.

V. *Item*, We will that ye, our subjects, trading with them for any of their commodities, pay them for the same, according to agreement, without delay, or returne of their wares again unto them.

VI. *Item*, For such commodities as they have now brought, or shall hereafter bring, fitting for our service and proper use; We will, that no arrest be made thereof, but that the price be made with the Cape merchant, according as they may sell to others, and present payment upon the delivery of the goods.

VII. *Item*, If in discovery of other countries for trade, and return of their shippes, they shall neede men or victuals, We will, that ye our subjects, furnish them for their money, as their needs shall require.

VIII. *Item*, And that without other passeport, they shall, and may set out upon the discovery of Yeadzo, or any other part in or about our empire.

From our castle in Surunga, the first day of ninth month, and in the eighteenth year of our Dary, according to our computation. Sealed with our broad Seale.

(*Underwritten.*)   MINNA MOTTONO, *Yei. Ye. Yeas.*"

A factory was established by the East India Company on the strength of these privileges, but the Dutch made numerous attempts to undermine the English. The civil wars that broke out in England about this time also operated very prejudicially, and the marriage of Charles II. to Catherine of Portugal was used by the Dutch to show that the English were in alliance with the Portuguese, who were then hated in Japan. The factory was ultimately broken up, and subsequent attempts to re-establish it have been unsuccessful.

We have already in the preface spoken of the injudicious conduct of the Jesuit missionaries, and the consequent persecution that resulted in the expulsion of the Portuguese and the virtual closing of Japan to foreign nations. The Russians have made several attempts to open up commercial relations with the country, but in vain. The positive laws of Japan have defeated every attempt. There is now, however, some probability that the barriers separating Japan from the rest of the world will, to some extent, be thrown down. Many vessels belonging to the United States of America frequent for fishing purposes the seas in the neighbourhood of Japan, and several have been wrecked on the Japanese coasts, which are proverbially stormy and dangerous. By the cruel laws of Japan, the crews have been either killed or otherwise maltreated, and all demands for redress have been treated with contempt. To such treatment a powerful energetic nation like the Americans will not submit, and an armed expedition is now preparing against Japan. What the result of that expedition will be it is extremely difficult even to conjecture. The Japanese are preparing to repel force by force, but their knowledge of the art of war is too old by many centuries. It is greatly to be hoped that no blood will be shed, but that the result may be the establishment of friendly intercourse between the youngest nation of the new world, and one of the oldest of the old. All who have visited the country represent the natives as very anxious for the removal of the present oppressive restrictions, and if the present Emperor be as enlightened as some of his predecessors, he will doubtless relax these laws, the cause of which has long ceased to exist. But let him act as he may, the spirit of the present age is entirely opposed to allowing any people to place themselves out of the pale of society and to break with impunity the universally respected law of nations.

PREFACE.

THE empire of Japan has for the last two centuries been an unknown land to the nations of Europe. The little information that was collected regarding both the country and the people excited a curiosity which hitherto it has been impossible to gratify, and a desire for familiar and beneficial intercourse, which has been firmly and invariably repulsed. The floating idea in the public mind about Japan has been that of a rich country, an active industrious people, with a peculiar but advanced civilisation, a despotic government, an immense population, and a deep-rooted jealousy and distrust of every other people. With only two nations, the Chinese and the Dutch, will the people of Japan allow any intercourse, and that is fenced round with so many restrictions that it can scarcely be regarded as intercourse at all. It is confined to two ports, to a limited number of ships every year; and the Dutch, so far from being allowed to mingle freely with the inhabitants, are virtually prisoners during the period of their stay, and if found straying beyond the precincts of their own fort, they are liable to be illtreated, if not actually murdered. Again, if any inhabitants of Japan leave their own country, prompted either by desire to see the world or of commercial gain, they are not permitted to return to their native land, and any unfortunate seamen who may be cast away on the Japanese shores are either put to death or carefully precluded from the slightest intercourse with the natives. Isolated thus by arbitrary laws from the rest of mankind, morally and intellectually, they are no less separated geographically, for the insular position of Japan, its wild, rock-bound shores, and stormy seas, make its coasts the terror of the mariners of the Northern Pacific Ocean.

But the laws and the feelings of the people of Japan were not always of this jealous and exclusive kind. When they first became acquainted with Europeans they had a strong desire to cultivate friendly intercourse, and to all foreign traders they for many years gave a hearty welcome and great encouragement. Nay, so strong was this feeling, that in 1619 the Japanese emperor sent an embassy to the Pope at Rome, in order to cultivate the friendship of the great head of the Roman Catholic Church. Had the Europeans acted with prudence or justice, such feelings would still have existed, and most probably Japan would have become by this time one of the greatest eastern marts for European commerce. So long as the visitors confined themselves to trade, so long did they prosper, and so long did the Japanese regard them as friends; but when they aimed at power and influence in the country, the Japanese became animated with the opposite feelings, and adopted the most effectual measures to close their country against strangers. It is to the Jesuits that society owes all these jealousies and restrictions. That powerful, ambitious, and doubly dangerous set of ecclesiastics soon acquired a footing in Japan, and were held in high estimation at first, more perhaps on account of their scientific knowledge than on account of their superior moral and religious character. They soon made many converts to Christianity, and their labours were in no degree interfered with by the emperor, in whose dominions all sects of religion were at that time on an almost equal footing. But that spiritual pride, that lust of power, and that insatiable desire to be supreme in temporal as well as spiritual affairs, which the Jesuits have ever displayed, were very soon manifested, and their conduct at last became so haughty as to excite the jealousy of the Japanese court. Rumours also were spread, which would appear to have been not without foundation, that the aim of the Jesuits was not only to convert, but to conquer, the empire, and that they were to be assisted in this by an insurrection in Japan, and a fleet and army from Europe. The emperor took the alarm; the Jesuits were expelled, the Christian converts were massacred, the Dutch with great difficulty retained even a slight footing in the country, and the arbitrary restrictive laws were passed which are now in force. The history of Siam and other eastern states presents about the same time exactly the same picture: of proud Jesuits trying to subdue the nation, of their failure, of their expulsion, and of the terrible and lasting Asiatic revenge.

Having thus been cut off from almost all intercourse with foreign nations for such a long period, it is not to be expected that, considering that circumstance and the stationary character of eastern civilisation, the manners, habits, customs, &c., of the Japanese should have materially altered during that time. From the stray leaves of information that have come to us recently, it would appear that the accounts given by the early writers are just as descriptive of Japan in the nineteenth, as of Japan in the seventeenth century. It is, therefore, chiefly from these old authors that information regarding Japan is to be obtained.

PREFACE.

The first European traveller by whom the country is mentioned is Marco Polo, whose account we shall give, but he was never in Japan, and his information was obtained in China. The first important work published in Europe was a collection of letters written by the Jesuits in Japan "to those of the same company; in which a notice is given of the various customs and idolatries of those Pagans, and a notice of the beginning, success, and goodness of the Christians in those parts." This work was written in Spanish, and published in 1575, at Alcala, the seat of the famous university founded by Cardinal Ximenes. Many other similar works of the Jesuits were published soon after: one at Naples in 1580, another at Cologne in 1586, and a great many compilations from these works also appeared. Accounts of Japan also appear in many voyages and travels of the period, and several works were published, chiefly in Dutch, giving an account of events in Japan during certain periods. The Dutch accounts of the country, which are numerous, but many of them very heavy reading, are, however, regarded as the best and most authentic. Among these, the work of Engelburtus Kœmpfer is regarded as holding the highest place. Kœmpfer was in Japan as medical officer of the Dutch factory for several years during the end of the seventeenth century. He had many opportunities of observation and collecting knowledge, which he turned to good account. His work was translated into English in 1728, and has been selected for the UNIVERSAL LIBRARY as the most trustworthy account of a strange country to which the attention of the world is now directed by the American Expedition. The work has in many places been considerably abridged, wherever the author was prolix, or repeated himself, or entered into uninteresting details, or into statements applicable only to the time at which he wrote. Prefixed to the work is an introduction, which gives a brief sketch of European intercourse with Japan, which, it is hoped, will add to the completeness of the work.

T

CONTENTS.

	PAGE
INTRODUCTION	278

CHAPTER I.
OF THE EMPIRE OF JAPAN IN GENERAL, AS TO ITS SITUATION, AND THE LARGENESS OF ITS SEVERAL ISLANDS 287

CHAPTER II.
THE DIVISION AND SUB-DIVISION OF THE EMPIRE OF JAPAN INTO ITS SEVERAL PROVINCES; AS ALSO OF ITS REVENUE AND GOVERNMENT 292

CHAPTER III.
THE AUTHOR'S OPINION OF THE TRUE ORIGIN AND DESCENT OF THE JAPANESE . 297

CHAPTER IV.
OF THE ORIGIN OF THE JAPANESE, ACCORDING TO THEIR OWN FABULOUS OPINION 304

CHAPTER V.
OF THE CLIMATE OF JAPAN, AND ITS PRODUCE AS TO MINERALS 307

CHAPTER VI.
OF THE FERTILITY OF THE COUNTRY, AS TO PLANTS 312

CHAPTER VII.
OF THE PLENTY OF THE COUNTRY AS TO BEASTS, BIRDS, REPTILES, AND INSECTS . 316

CHAPTER VIII.
OF FISH AND SHELLS 320

CHAPTER IX.

NAMES OF THE GODS, DEMI-GODS, AND EMPERORS, WHO ARE MENTIONED IN THE JAPANESE HISTORIES, AS THE FIRST MONARCHS AND GOVERNORS OF THAT EMPIRE 324

CHAPTER X.

OF THE ECCLESIASTICAL HEREDITARY EMPERORS OF JAPAN IN GENERAL; OF THEIR SUCCESSION, RESIDENCE, AND COURT; AS ALSO OF THE CHRONOLOGY OF THE JAPANESE 326

CHAPTER XI.

OF THE RELIGIONS OF THIS EMPIRE IN GENERAL, AND OF THE SINTOS RELIGION IN PARTICULAR 331

CHAPTER XII.

OF THE SINTOS TEMPLES, BELIEF, AND WORSHIP 333

CHAPTER XIII.

OF THE SINTOS REBI, THAT IS, THEIR FORTUNATE DAYS AND HOLIDAYS; AND THE CELEBRATION THEREOF 336

CHAPTER XIV.

OF THE SANGA, OR PILGRIMAGE TO ISJE 340

CHAPTER XV.

OF THE JAMMABOS, OR MOUNTAIN-PRIESTS, AND OTHER RELIGIOUS ORDERS . . 343

CHAPTER XVI.

OF THE BUDSDO, OR, FOREIGN PAGAN WORSHIP, AND ITS FOUNDER . . . 348

CHAPTER XVII.

OF THE SIUTO, THAT IS, THE DOCTRINE AND WAY OF LIFE OF THEIR MORALISTS AND PHILOSOPHERS 351

CHAPTER XVIII.

PREPARATIONS FOR OUR JOURNEY TO THE EMPEROR'S COURT AT JEDO OR YEDO, WITH A DESCRIPTION OF THE MANNER OF TRAVELLING IN THIS COUNTRY . 352

CHAPTER XIX.

A GENERAL DESCRIPTION OF THE WAY BY WATER AND LAND, FROM NAGASAKI TO JEDO, THE EMPEROR'S RESIDENCE 357

CHAPTER XX.

A GENERAL DESCRIPTION OF THE SEVERAL EDIFICES AND BUILDINGS, PUBLIC AND PRIVATE, WE MET WITH ALONG THE ROAD. 359

CHAPTER XXI.

OF THE POST-HOUSES, INNS, EATING-HOUSES, AND TEA-BOOTHS . . . 364

CHAPTER XXII.

OF THE GREAT NUMBERS OF PEOPLE WHO DAILY TRAVEL ON THE ROADS . . . 368

CHAPTER XXIII.

OF OUR JOURNEY TO THE EMPEROR'S COURT IN GENERAL; AND HOW WE WERE ACCOMMODATED ON THE ROAD 373

CHAPTER XXIV.

DESCRIPTION OT THE CITY OF JEDO, OR YEDO; ITS CASTLE AND PALACE, WITH AN ACCOUNT OF WHAT HAPPENED DURING OUR STAY THERE; OUR AUDIENCE AND DEPARTURE 377

CHAPTER XXV.

THE AUDIENCE AT COURT, ON THE SECOND JOURNEY 386

KŒMPFER'S
ACCOUNT OF JAPAN.

CHAPTER I.

OF THE EMPIRE OF JAPAN IN GENERAL, AS TO ITS SITUATION, AND THE LARGENESS OF ITS SEVERAL ISLANDS.

THIS empire is by the Europeans called Japan. The natives give it several names and characters. The most common, and most frequently used in their writings and conversation, is Nipon, which is sometimes in a more elegant manner, and particular to this nation, pronounced Nifon, and by the inhabitants of Nankin, and the southern parts of China, Sippon. It signifies "the foundation of the sun;" being derived from *ni*, "fire," and in a more sublime sense, "the sun," and *pon*, the "ground, or foundation of a thing."

There are still some other names and epithets, which are seldom mentioned in conversation, but occur more frequently in their writings. Such are for instance; 1. Tenka, that is, "the subcelestial empire;" as if it were the only one existing under heaven. Hence the Emperor is called Tenkasama, "the subcelestial Monarch." In former times, this name was peculiar to the empire of Japan alone; but since commerce hath made known to them several other countries, they now condescend to honour them also with the same epithet, particularly such whose inhabitants are admitted and tolerated among them. Thus they call the empire of China, To Sin Tenka; the United Provinces of the Netherlands, known to them by the name of Holland, Hollanda Tenka. 2. Fino Motto, is much the same with Nipon, and signifies, properly speaking, "the root of the sun," *fi*, being the sun, and *motto*, a root; *no*, is only a particle, by which these two words are combined together. 3. Awadsissima, is the original name of this country, and is as much as to say, a "terrestrial scum Island;" *awa*, signifying scum, *dsi*, the earth, and *sima*, an island. This name is grounded upon the following fabulous tradition, recorded in their histories, of the origin and first creation of the several islands, which compose this mighty empire; which in former times, for want of communication with other countries, was looked upon by the natives as the only inhabited part of the globe. In the beginning of the creation, the supreme of the seven first celestial spirits (of which more in the seventh chapter of this book), stirred the then chaos, or confused mass of the earth with a staff, which, as he took out, there dropped from it a muddy scum, which running together, formed the Japanese islands; one of which, of the fourth magnitude, still retains this name, being particularly called Awadsissima. 4. D Sin Kokf, or Camino Kuni, "the Country or Habitation of the Gods." For by *Sin* and *Cami* are denoted the gods which were particularly and originally worshipped in Japan; and both *kokf* and *kuni* signify a country. 5. Akitsima, or according to the common pronunciation, Akitsussima, is another name given to this country of old, and frequently to be met with in their chronicles and legends. 6. Tontsio, "the true morning." 7. Sio, all, viz. all the several islands subject to the Emperor of Japan. 8. Jamatto, which name is also given to one of its provinces. Several others, as Asijwara, Asijwara Kokf, Qua, or Wa, and some more I forbear mentioning, to avoid being too tedious on so trifling a subject.

The empire of Japan lies between 31° and 42° of northern latitude. The Jesuits, in a late map of China, made and corrected by their astronomical observations, place it between 157° and 175° 30' of longitude.* It extends to north-east and east-north-east, being irregularly broad, though in the main pretty narrow in comparison to its length, which from one end of the province Fisen, to the extremity of the province Osiu, is supposed to be two hundred German miles [a German mile is equal to nearly six English], in a straight line, all the further distant coasts and islands, though subject to the Japanese Emperor, not reckoned.

It may, in different respects, be compared to the kingdoms of Great Britain and Ireland; being much after the same manner, though in a more eminent degree, divided and broke through by corners and forelands, arms of the sea, great bays and inlets, running deep into the country, and forming several islands, peninsulas, gulfs, and harbours. Besides, as the King of Great Britain is sovereign of three kingdoms, England, Scotland, and Ireland, so likewise the Japanese Emperor hath the supreme jurisdiction of three separate large islands. The first and largest is called Nipon, from the name of the whole empire. It runs lengthways, from east to west in the form of a jaw-bone, whose crooked part is turned to the north. A narrow channel, or

---

* The correct longitude, calculating from the meridian of Greenwich, is between 130° and 150° East. On the old maps the longitude was usually calculated from Ferro in the Canary Isles.—Ed.

strait, full of rocks and islands, some inhabited, some uninhabited, parts it from the second, which is next to it in largeness, and which, from its situation, lying to the south-west of Nipon, is called Saikokf, that is, "the Western Country." It is also called Kiusiu, or, "the Country of Nine;" being divided into nine large provinces. It hath one hundred and forty-eight German miles in circumference; and, according to the Japanese, it hath one hundred and forty of their own miles in length, and between forty and fifty in breadth. The third island lies between the first and second. It is almost square; and being divided into four provinces, the Japanese call it Sikokf, that is, "the Country of Four," viz. provinces. These three large islands are encompassed with an almost inconceivable number of others, some of which are small, rocky, and barren, others large, rich, and fruitful enough to be governed by petty princes, as will appear more fully in the course of this work.

All these several islands and dominions, composing the mighty empire of Japan, were, by the ecclesiastical hereditary monarch Siusiun, divided into Gokisitzido, as they are called by the Japanese, or seven large tracts of land, in the year of Christ 590. Many years after, in the year of Christ 681, Ten Mu divided the seven chief tracts into sixty-six provinces, appointing so many lords of his court to command and govern them, as princes, or his lieutenants. Two more islands, Iki and Tsussima, formerly belonging to the kingdom of Corea, having been conquered in the last (that is the sixteenth) century, and added to the empire of Japan, there are now in all sixty-eight provinces. Both these divisions of the Japanese empire, though they subsist till now, yet through the misery of time its sixty-eight provinces have been since their first constitution torn into six hundred and four lesser districts. In the first and happiest ages of the Japanese monarchy, every prince enjoyed the government of the province, which he was entrusted with by the Emperor, in peace and tranquillity. The miseries of ensuing times, the frequent quarrels and contentions, which arose among the chief branches of the imperial family about the succession to the throne, by degrees involved the whole empire in blood and confusion. Its princes espoused different parties, and no sooner were arms introduced among them, as the surest and most powerful means to make up their dissensions, but every one endeavoured thereby to maintain himself in the possession of those lands, whose government he was owing entirely to the imperial bounty: such as had not been provided for by the Emperor took care to provide for themselves. The princes divided their hereditary dominions among their sons, who, though possessed of but one portion of their father's estate, would not be behind them in grandeur and magnificence. What wonder then, if the number of princedoms and dominions went on perpetually increasing? The emperors of the now reigning family, usurpers themselves of the throne of which they are possessed, think this great division of the provinces of the empire no ways detrimental to their government, but rather conducive to make them the better acquainted with the true state of their riches and revenues; therefore, far from reducing them to their former standard, they still tear and divide them more and more, as they please, or as their interest requires, of which there are some late instances. The province of Tsikusen was not long ago divided into two governments, Janagawa and Kurume, and the Prince of Tsikungo had orders from court to surrender part of his dominions to the prince of the two islands abovementioned, Iki and Tsussima, who till then had nothing in possession upon the continent of Japan.

The borders of this empire are its rocky, mountainous coasts, washed by a tempestuous sea, which by reason of its shallowness admits none but small vessels to approach the shore, and even those not without imminent danger: the depth of most of its gulphs and harbours is not yet known, and others, which the pilots of the country are better acquainted with, are unfit for harbouring ships of any considerable bulk. Indeed, it seems Nature purposely designed these islands to be a sort of a little world, separate and independent of the rest, by making them of so difficult an access, and by endowing them plentifully, with whatever is requisite to make the lives of their inhabitants both delightful and pleasant, and to enable them to subsist without a commerce with foreign nations.

Besides the several islands and provinces already mentioned, there are some further distant countries, which do not, properly speaking, belong to the empire of Japan; but either acknowledge the supremacy of the Emperor, or live under his protection. Of these I think it necessary to give some preliminary account before I proceed to a more particular description of the Japanese empire itself. They are, 1. The islands of Riuku, or Liquejo, the inhabitants of which style themselves subjects, not of the Emperor of Japan, but of the Prince of Satsuma, by whom they were subdued and conquered. 2. Tsiosin, is the third and lowest part of the peninsula of Corea, which is governed, in the name of his Imperial Majesty, by the Prince of Iki and Tsussima. 3. The island Jeso, which is governed for the Emperor by the Prince of Matsumai, whose own dominions make part of the great province Osju.

I. The Liquejo Islands,* as they are set down in our maps, or the islands of Riuku, as they are called by the inhabitants, must not be confounded with the *Insulæ Leuconiæ*, or the Philippine Islands. They lie to the south-west of the province Satzuma, which is situate upon the continent of Saikokf, and the neighbouring island Tana, or Tanagasima, and according to our maps, reach down almost to the 26° of northern latitude. If we believe the Japanese, they are so fruitful as to yield the rice-harvest twice a year. The inhabitants, which are for the most part either husbandmen or fishermen, are a goodnatured, merry sort of people, leading an agreeable contented life, diverting themselves after their work is done with a glass of rice-beer, and playing upon their musical instruments,

---

* These are the islands now known by the name of Loo Choo, and so well described in Captain Basil Hall's well-known voyages. They are now subject to the Chinese.—ED.

which they for this purpose carry out with them into the fields. They appear, by their language, to be of Chinese extraction. In the late great revolution in China, when the Tartars invaded and possessed themselves of that mighty empire, the natives retired in great numbers, and were dispersed all over the East Indies. Not a few fled to these islands, where they applied themselves chiefly to trade, being well skilled in navigation, and well acquainted with those seas. Accordingly, they still carry on a commerce with Satzuma, and go there once a year. Some centuries ago, these islands were invaded and conquered by the Prince of Satzuma, whose successors still keep them in awe by their bugios, or lieutenants, and strong garrisons, though otherwise, by reason of their remoteness from Satzuma, the inhabitants are treated with much regard and kindness; for they are obliged to give their sovereign only one-fifth part of the produce of their country, whilst his own natural subjects, the Satzumese, are taxed at two-thirds. But besides what they pay to the Prince of Satzuma, they raise a contribution among themselves, to be sent by way of a present, once a year, to the Tartarian Monarch of China, in token of loyalty and submission. They have, like the Tonquinese and Japanese, a Dairi of their own, or an ecclesiastical hereditary monarch, to whom they pay great respect, supposing him to be lineally descended from the gods of their country. He resides at Jajama, one of the chief of these islands, situate not far from the island Osima, which is of the second magnitude.

II. Corea, or Coræa, is a peninsula, which stands out from Tartary, running towards Japan, opposite to the coasts of China. It hath been, as the Japanese relate, divided of old into three provinces. That which is lowest, and nearest to Japan, is by the Japanese called Tsiosijn; the second, which makes up the middle part of the whole peninsula, Corea; and the third and uppermost, which confines upon Tartary, Fakkusuai. Sometimes the name of either of these provinces is given to the whole peninsula. The natives, according to the account of the Japanese, are of Chinese extraction. They served often and under different masters. Their neighbours, the Tartars, sometimes entered into alliances with them; at other times, they invaded and subdued them. Mikaddo Tuiuu Ai, Emperor of Japan, persecuted them with war; but he dying before he could put an end to this enterprise, Daïn Gu, his relict, a princess of great parts and personal bravery, pursued it with the utmost vigour, wearing the arms of the deceased emperor, her husband, till at last she made them tributary to Japan, about the year of Christ 201. Some time after, they entered into fresh alliances with their neighbours, the Tartars, and so continued unmolested by the Japanese, till Taiko possessed himself of the secular throne of Japan. This valiant prince, reading the histories of his empire, found it recorded that the Coreans had been subdued by one of his predecessors, and made tributary to Japan: as in the mean time he was but lately come to the throne, he doubted not but that he should get time fully to settle and to secure himself in the possession thereof, if he could send some of the most powerful princes of the empire abroad upon some such military expedition, and by this means remove them from court and country. He therefore gladly seized this opportunity, and resolved to renew and support his pretensions to the kingdom of Corea, and through this kingdom, as he gave out his main design was, to open to himself a way to the conquest of the great empire of China itself. Accordingly he sent over some ambassadors to Corea, to desire the natives to acknowledge the supremacy of the Japanese emperor, and to give tokens of their loyalty and submission. But the Coreans, instead of an answer, killing the emperor's ambassador, by this hostile act, gave him just reason to prosecute them with war. Accordingly, a numerous army was sent over without further delay, under the command of such of the princes of the empire whose presence he had the most reason to be apprehensive of. This war lasted seven years, during which time his generals, with much ado, broke at last through the strong opposition made by the natives and their allies, the Tartars, and, after a brave defence, made the country again tributary to Japan. Taiko dying about that time, and the army returning, Ijejas, his successor, ordered that they should, once in three years, send an embassy to court, to acknowledge his sovereignty. Since that time, they relapsed by degrees, under the domination of the Tartars, and drove the garrisons left by the Japanese down to the very coasts of the province Tsiosijn, the only thing they have now remaining of all their conquests in Corea. As things now stand, the Emperor of Japan seems to be satisfied, for the security of his own dominions, to be master of the coasts, the care and government whereof he committed to the prince of the islands Iki and Tsussima, who keeps there a garrison only of fifty men, under the command of a captain, or bugio, as they are here called. And the inhabitants are ordered to send an embassy to court, and to take the oath of allegiance and supremacy only once at the beginning of every new emperor's reign.* The coasts of Corea are about forty-eight Japanese water leagues, or about ninety English miles, distant from the island of Tsussima, and this as much from the continent of Japan. Numbers of rocks and small islands lie between them, which though they be for the most part uninhabited, yet the Japanese keep strong garrisons in some of the chief, to watch what ships sail by, and to oblige them to show what commodities they have on board, as claiming the sovereignty of those seas. The commodities brought from Tsiosijn are the best cod, and other fish, pickled; walnuts, scarce medicinal plants, flowers and roots, particularly the ninseng, so famous for its excellent virtues, which grows in great plenty in the provinces of Corea and Fakusai, as also in Siamsai, a province of the neighbouring Tartary; this plant, though it be found elsewhere, yet the kind growing in the provinces abovesaid, is believed far to excel others in goodness and virtues. The natives have also a few manufactures. Among the rest, a certain sort of earthen pots, made in Japij and Niuke, two Tartarian provinces, were brought over from thence by the Coreans, which were much esteemed by the Japanese, and bought

---
* Corea is now entirely subject to the Chinese.—ED.

very dear. But of late, it was ordered by the emperor, that there should be no more imported for the future. The boats made use of by the Tsioneese are very bad indifferent structures, in which one scarce would venture further than Tsussima.

III. Jeso, or Jesogasima, that is, "the Island of Jeso," is the most northern island the Japanese have in possession out of their own empire. It was invaded and conquered, as I was informed in Japan, by Joritomo, the first Cubo, or secular monarch, who left it to the Prince of Matsumai, (a neighbouring island belonging to the great province of Osiu,) to be by him governed and taken care of. Some time after, the inhabitants, weary of a foreign government, fell upon the garrison the Prince of Matsumai left there, and killed them all to a man. This act of hostility no sooner reached the prince's ears, than he sent over a good army, with three hundred horse, to demand, and in case of refusal to take, ample satisfaction, and to chastise the rebels. But the Prince of Jeso, to prevent further mischievous consequences, sent over an embassy to Matsumai; and, to take off all suspicion of his having had any intelligence or hand in the affair, he delivered up twenty of the ringleaders, who were executed, and their heads impaled upon the coasts of Jeso. This act of submission entirely reconciled him to his superiors; but the natives being ever since looked upon as a stubborn and tumultuous people, strong garrisons are constantly kept upon the southern coasts of this island, to put it out of their power ever to attempt the like; and the prince is obliged to send, once a year, an embassy to Matsumai, with presents to the value of one mangokf.* This island lies in 42° of northern latitude, to the north-north-east, right opposite to the great province Oosiu, where its two promontories Sugaar and Tsajasaki, running out very far into the sea, form a large gulf, which directly faces it. The passage over to this island is said to be of one day, and it is not to be made at all times, by reason of the currents, which run strongly, sometimes to the east and sometimes to the west; though otherwise it be but forty Japanese water leagues, and in some places not above twenty five or thirty English miles distant from the coast of Japan. It is said to be as large as the island of Kiusiu, but so thoroughly full of woods and forests, that it produces nothing which might be of use to the Japanese, besides some pelts and furs, which even the inhabitants of the southern parts of Japan have no occasion for. Nor do the Jesoans bring over anything else but that and the famous fish karasaki, which is caught in great plenty about the island, and which the Japanese reckon a great dainty, boiling and eating it like cod. As to its figure, I could not gather anything positive, neither from the accounts I had from the Japanese, nor from the maps I met with in the country, they differing much from each other. Some represent it very near round, others make it of a very irregular figure, with large promontories, gulfs, and bays; the sea running in several places so far up into the country, that one might be easily induced to believe it composed of several different islands. I am apt to believe that the country discovered by De Vries, to the north of Japan, was part of this island. I took notice, that in some of the Japanese maps, the south-west and larger part is called Matsuki: but it was, generally speaking, so indifferently drawn, that I should be at a loss to determine whether it be an island by itself or joined to the rest. According to the account the Japanese give of the inhabitants, they are a strong but savage people, wearing long hair and beards, well skilled in the management of bows and arrows, as also in fishing; the greatest part living almost wholly on fish. They describe them further, as very dirty and nasty; but the truth of this accusation is not so strictly to be relied on, since they, the Japanese themselves, are so extremely nice and superstitious in frequently washing and cleaning their bodies, as to have found the very same fault with the Dutch. The language of Jeso is said to have something of that which is spoke in Corea.

Behind this island, to the north, lies the continent of Okujeso, as it is called by the Japanese, that is, Upper or High Jeso. That there is such a country is not in the least questioned among geographers; but they have not as yet been able to determine whether it confines on Tartary or America, consequently where they are to place the Strait of Anain, or the so long wished-for passage out of the North Sea into the great Indian Ocean, supposing that there be such a one, or whether it is closely joined either to Tartary or America, without any intermediate strait or passage at all. I made it my business, both in my travels through Muscovy and Persia, and during my stay in Japan, to inquire, with all the diligence I was capable of, into the true state of those northern countries, though, in the main, to very little purpose, having hardly met with anything worth the notice of the public. At Moscow,* and at Astrakan, I spoke to several people, who either in their travels through Siberia and Kataya into China, or during their stay in Siberia, whither they had been banished by the Czar, and lived many years, picked up what little and uncertain information they could, but could learn nothing farther than that Great Tartary is an isthmus, or neck of land, joined to a neighbouring continent, which they supposed to be America; and from thence concluded that, in all probability, there is no such thing as a communication between the Icy Sea and the Indian Ocean. In a map of Siberia, which was made and cut upon wood, by one who was banished thither, and the names of the places marked in Sclavonian characters, there were several considerable promontories, which from the eastern coasts stood out into the sea, one of which, too great to be brought upon the table, was cut off at the edge. He that showed me this map, told me at the same time that according to the accounts which could be procured from the Tartars living in those parts,

---

* This appears to be a compound measure; the *gokf* (or kolf, as some authors write it) containing three thousand sacks or bales of rice, each sack containing sufficient to support one man for a hundred days. The *man* prefixed stands for ten thousand, so that mangokf is actually thirty millions of sacks of rice.—ED.

* It must be borne in mind that this was written in 1692, and it was not till 1696 that Peter the Great ascended the throne of Russia.—ED.

this very promontory is nothing but an isthmus, which runs towards a neighbouring large continent, on which it confines, but that it is composed of high, rough, and almost inaccessible mountains, and that in his opinion, if ever there hath been a passage there, for the first inhabitants of the world to get over into America, and to people that continent, such another undertaking would be at present utterly impossible. This map of Siberia, such as it was, is extremely ill done, and without any scale of distances, or degrees of longitude or latitude, was yet the first which could give the Czar of Muscovy some, though very imperfect, notions of the great extent of his Tartarian dominions to the north. And it is from the same my particular friend, the ingenious Mr. Winius, who was by the Czar appointed inspector-general over the apothecaries and druggists' shops in Muscovy, made the first rude sketch of his map of Russia and Tartary, which he afterwards considerably corrected and augmented by several accounts procured from different parts, and withal reduced to the necessary degrees of longitude and latitude. He was not a little assisted in this undertaking by Mr. Spitshary, Greek and Latin interpreter at the court at Muscovy. This learned and industrious man was, by the then reigning monarch of Russia, sent as his ambassador to the Emperor of China, with secret orders and instructions to spare neither trouble nor expenses to get himself acquainted with the true state, situation, and extent of the Czar's dominions. Accordingly he went to Pekin through the northern parts of Russia and Tartary, and having dispatched his business at the court of China, returned through the southern provinces, and came back to Moscow about the year 1680. During my stay at the court of Moscow it so happened that he was to be our interpreter, which brought me much acquainted with him, and fed me with no small hopes of learning somewhat new and more particular, than was hitherto known, about the state of those countries; but I found him too distrustful and secret, and very unwilling to communicate what observations he had made upon his journey. The late illustrious N. olaus Witsen, LL.D., and Burghermaster at Amsterdam, a person to whom the public is greatly indebted, met with much better success in his own inquiries, for in his last embassy to the court of Muscovy he did, by his extraordinary good conduct, great learning and affability, insinuate himself so far into the favour of the Czar, and the grandees of his court, that whatever accounts they had procured from all parts of Russia, were without reserve communicated to him, which enabled him to compose that excellent and accurate map of all the Russian empire, and the Great Tartary, with its mountains, rivers, lakes, cities and provinces, for the most part till then unknown—a work which by reason of its great usefulness could not but highly oblige the curious. But however accurate this map of Dr. Witsen's was, which afterwards proved very useful to Mr. Isbrand Ides, in his journey by land to China, where he went ambassador, yet the full extent of the eastern coasts of Siberia, and the Great Tartary, remains as yet undetermined, and we are still in the dark as to what relation they bear to the neighbouring continent, which is probably that of Oku Jeso.

The Japanese on their side are so little acquainted with the state and extent of that country, which lies behind the island of Jeso Gasima, and which is by them called Oku Jeso, that they say it is only 300 Japanese miles long; but what authority they have to support this assertion I cannot tell. A ship having some years ago been accidentally cast upon the coasts of that continent, they met among the rude and savage inhabitants, some persons clad in fine Chinese silk, by which may be very probably conjectured some communication the natives have with the neighbouring Dnats, or Tartary; at least that these countries are not very remote from each other. A jonk, which was sent thither for purposes of discovery, about the year 1684, returned after having been three months upon her voyage, and brought the very same account. An experienced Japanese pilot, who was well acquainted with the seas about Japan, as having been everywhere round this empire, upon my inquiry could give me no other satisfactory answer, but that between Japan and Jesogasima the currents run alternately, sometimes east, sometimes west, and that behind Jesogasima there is only one, which runs constantly, and directly north, whence he concluded that near Dnats, so they call Tartary, there must be some communication with another sea to the north. A few years ago another imperial jonk was sent out in quest of those countries. They sailed from the eastern coasts of Japan, and after many troubles and incommodities endured between forty and fifty degrees of northern latitude, they discovered a very large continent, supposed to be America, where, having met with a good harbour, they stayed there during the winter, and so returned the next year, without any the least account of that country or its inhabitants, excepting only that it run further to the north-west. Since that time it was resolved at the court of Japan to be at no further pain or expense about the discovery of those countries. I was but little the better for consulting the Japanese maps of those seas, though I saw several of them in different places, as at Jedo, in the palace of Tsussimano Cami, governor of Nagaski, in the temple of Symmios, near Osacca, and in several other temples. They all represent a large continent, which stands out from the Great Tartary, and extends itself behind the island Jesogasima, reaching about fifteen degrees of longitude further east than the eastern coasts of Japan. A large space is left empty between it and the neighbouring America. The country itself is divided into the following provinces, marked with their common writing characters, Kabersari, Orankai, Sitsij, Fcrosan; and Amarisi. Between the two last provinces is marked a considerable river, which loses itself into the sea behind the island Jeso, to the south-east. But as all their maps are very indifferently done, without any scale of distances or degrees, and as besides the names of the provinces above-mentioned are only in their canna, or common writing and not, as other more authentic records, in their sini, or significant characters, I shall leave to the reader's own judgment to determine how much there is to be depended upon them. And this is all I could learn in Japan about the state of those countries which lie to the north of this empire.*

Before I leave off this general geographical description of the Japanese empire, I must not forget to mention two other islands, which lie further off to the east or east-north-east, of the coasts of Osiu, at least at one hundred and fifty miles' distance, but as the Japanese pretend, belong to their empire. They have given them very high-sounding names, the smaller, more northern, and more remote from Japan, being called Ginsima, the Silver Island; the larger and nearer, Kinsima, the Gold Island. They keep their state and situation very secret from all foreigners, chiefly the Europeans, forasmuch as their rich names have already tempted them to go in quest thereof. The King of Spain having been informed that they lie westward of America, in that part of the world, which by the Pope's division was assigned to him, as all those lands, which should be discovered from the east, were to the King of Portugal, sent out a very expert pilot to look for them about the year 1620. But this voyage proved unsuccessful. The Dutch attempted the same at different times with no better success. They fitted out one ship for that purpose at Batavia in 1639, and two others in 1643, which had orders to go further, and to attempt the discovery of the coasts of Tartary and America. The voyage of these two ships, one of which was called Bresken, the other the Castrecoom, proved very unfortunate. For besides that they suffered much by storms, the captain of the Bresken having hazarded himself on shore, with some of his ship's company, in a port of Japan lying under the 40 of northern latitude, they were all seized upon, put in irons, carried prisoners to Jedo, and as barbarously treated as if their intention had been to betray or to invade the empire.

About the year 1675, the Japanese accidentally discovered a very large island, one of their barks having been forced there in a storm from the island Fatsisio, from which they computed it to be three hundred miles distant towards the east. They met with no inhabitants, but found it to be a very pleasant and fruitful country, well supplied with fresh water, and furnished with plenty of plants and trees, particularly the arrack-tree, which however might give room to conjecture, that the island lay rather to the south of Japan, than to the east, these trees growing only in hot countries. They called it Bunesima, or the island Bune, and because they found no inhabitants upon it, they marked it with the character of an uninhabited island. On the shores they found an incredible quantity of fish and crabs, some of which were from four to six feet long.

Fatsisio, I just now had occasion to mention, or Fatsisio Gasima, which is as much as to say, the Eighty Fathom Island, is the most remote island the Japanese have in possession southward. It lies under the same meridian with Jedo, and is reckoned to be about eighty Japanese water leagues distant from the continent of Japan, being the furthermost of a long row of small islands, almost contiguous to each other. It is the chief island where the great men of the Emperor's court, when out of favour, are usually confined. pursuant to a very ancient custom, and kept prisoners on a rocky coast, from the extraordinary height of which the whole island hath borrowed its name. As long as they continue on this island, they must work for their livelihood. Their chief occupation is weaving, and some of the silk stuffs wrought by them, as they are generally men of ingenuity and good understanding, are so inimitably fine, that the Emperor hath forbid, under severe penalties, to export or to sell them to foreigners. This island, besides being washed by a rough tempestuous sea, is so well guarded by nature itself, that when there is some provision of the common necessaries of life, or some new prisoners to be brought in, or the guard to be relieved, the whole boat, with all the lading, must be drawn up, and again let down by a crane, the coasts being so steep and rocky as to admit of no other access.

CHAPTER II.

THE DIVISION AND SUB-DIVISION OF THE EMPIRE OF JAPAN INTO ITS SEVERAL PROVINCES; AS ALSO OF ITS REVENUE AND GOVERNMENT.

In the general geographical description of Japan, which I have laid down in the preceding chapter, I took notice that this empire hath been divided into seven great tracts of land, which were again sub-divided into sixty-eight considerable provinces, and these into 604 smaller districts, or counties, as one might call them. I proceed now more particularly to consider the largeness, extent, fertility, produce and revenues of each province, as I found them in a Japanese description of this empire, published in Japan, by the title of Sitzi Jossu.

But before I proceed to a particular consideration of the seven large tracts of land, which the empire of Japan hath been divided into, and of their several provinces, I shall take notice of the Gokinai, or Gokinai goka Kokf, that is the five provinces of the imperial revenues, so called, because all the revenue of these five provinces is particularly appropriated for the support and maintenance of the imperial court. They amount to 148 mans, and 1200 kokfs of rice. The reader is desired to observe in general, that all the revenues in this country are reduced to these two measures in rice. A man contains 10,000 kokf, and a kokf 3000 bales or bags of rice. These five imperial provinces are, 1. Jamasijro, otherwise Sansju: it is a large and fruitful country. Its length from south to north is a hundred Japanese miles; and there are several good towns and other places of note within its compass. It is divided into eight districts—Otokuni, Kadono, Okongi, Kij, Udsi, Kusse, Sakanaka, and Tsukugi. 2. Jamatto, or Wosju, is likewise a very good country, and much of the same length with the former, going from south to north. It had formerly several places of note within its compass, which are at present

---

* All this laboured description and conjecture evidently refer, not to the coast of North America, but to the peninsula of Kamkschatka.—ED.

reduced to a very small number. It is divided into fifteen districts, Soono Cami, Scouosimo, Feguri, Firole, Katzu-Dsiau, Katsunge, Okuno Umi, Utz, Josino, Uda, Sikino Simo, Sikino Cami, Takaiidz, Tooidz, and Jammanobe. 3. Kawutzij, or Kisiu, a tolerably good country, about two days' journey in length, and divided into fifteen districts,—Nistori, Isikawa, Fukaitz, Jaskabe, Ooknke, Tukajatz, Kawatz, Sarara, Umbarada, Katanno, Wakaje, Sibukaja, Sick, Tanbokf, and Tannan. 4. Idsumi, or Seusju, is a very large country, but indifferently fruitful. Its length is a hundred Japanese miles from south to west. It is bordered on one side by the sea, on the other by a ridge of high mountains. It is plentifully supplied with fish by the neighbouring sea: it produces also some buck-wheat, rice, peas and beaus, though but few, and not of the best sort. It hath but three smaller districts, Ootori, Idsume, and Fine. 5. Sitzu, otherwise Tsinokumi, and Sisju. It hath two days' journey and a half in circumference. It is the furthermost country westwards on a large gulph. The southern parts of it are very warm, but the northern colder, and abound more in what they call gokokf, which are the five chief sorts of peas eaten in this country. It affords also some fish, and salt, and is in the main a very good country. It is divided into thirteen districts, Sij Jos, or Symmious, Ratatz, Fingassinai, Nisijuari, Jatsan, Simasimo, Simakami, Tesijma, Kawanobe, Muko, Awara, Arima, and Nosje.

I proceed now to the seven large tracts of land, which the Japanese empire hath been divided into by the Emperor Siusiun.

1. The first is Tookaido, that is, the south-eastern tract. I have observed above, that the said seven large tracts have been by the Emperor Tenmu further divided into sixty-eight provinces, the five provinces above mentioned included, to which some hundred years after two more were added. The Tookaido consists of fifteen of these sixty-eight provinces, which are:—1. Iga, otherwise Isju, which is limited on the south and east by the sea. To the north it is separated from the neighbouring provinces by a ridge of high mountains. It is a hot country, but indifferently fruitful, producing some plants, trees, and bamboos. It is divided into four districts, Aije, Namanda, Iga, and Nabari. 2. Isie, otherwise Sesju, is three days' journey long, going from south to north. It is almost wholly encompassed by the sea, but extremely fruitful, with an agreeable variety of hills and plains. It is divided into fifteen districts, Quana, Asaki, Susuka, Itaisi, Aanki, Taato, Nisikissima, Gosasuma, Inabe, Mije, Ano, Itaka, Watakei, Ino, and Taki. 3. Ssima, or Sisio, is but a small province, which one may travel across in half a day's time. It is a very barren country, but the neighbouring sea supplies it plentifully with fish, oysters, shells, and the like. It hath but three districts, Toosij, Ako, and Kamesima. 4. Owari, otherwise Bisiu, is an inland country, entirely separate from the sea, but one of the most fruitful provinces of the whole empire, and richly stocked with inhabitants. It is three days' journey long, going from south to north, and divided into nine districts, Amabe, Nakassima, Kaquuri Nirva, Kassuogale, Jamada, Aitsi, Tsitta, and Tocsijnossima. 5. Mikawa, otherwise Misiu, is a very barren and poor country, with too many shallow rivers, and ponds, which are very prejudicial to the growth of the gokokf. It is one day's journey and a half long, going from east to west, and divided into eight districts, Awoumi, Kamo, Nukada, Batz, Fori, Jana, Tsitarra, and Akumi. 6. Tootomi, otherwise Jensju, a very good and fruitful country, and one of the pleasantest provinces for a curious variety of hills, rivers, fertile plains, towns and villages. Its length is supposed to be two days' journey and a half, going from east to west, and it is divided into fourteen districts, Fammano, Futz, Fuusa, Aratuma, Nangukami, Nagnasimo, Sutz, Janmmana, Kikoo, Faifara, Tojota, Jamaka, Sanno, and Jwatn. 7. Surunga, or Siusju, deserves likewise to be commended for the variety of its towns, villages, hills, and fruitful plains. It is of the same length with Tootomi, going from east to west, and divided into seven districts, Tsta, Masiasu, Udo, Itabo, Rofarn, Fusij, and Suringa. 8. Kai, otherwise Kaisiu, and Kajoohu, is a flat country, and abounds in rice, fields and pasturage, plants and trees. It breeds also some cattle, chiefly horses. It is two days' journey long from south to north, and divided into four districts, Jamanassiro, Jaatzsiro, Coma, and Tsur. 9. Idsu, or Toosju, a long peninsula, being almost surrounded by the sea. It affords a large quantity of salt, and all sorts of fish, and is reckoned in the main a tolerable good country. It is pretty mountainous, with some flat ground, and some few rice-fields. It hath but three districts upon the continent of Nipon, Takato, Naka, and Camo, whereto are added two neighbouring islands, Oosima, and Firkasima. 10. Sangami or Soosiu, is three days' journey long; a flat and barren country, which affords hardly any thing for the sustenance of human life, but tortoises, fish and crabs from the sea, besides a good quantity of timber out of its large woods. It is divided into eight districts, Asikaranno Cami, Asikaranno Simu, Oosimi, Juringi, Ajikoo Tukangi, Camakura, Mijura, and Jesima. 11. Musasi, or Busiu, a very large province, having five days' journey and a half in circumference. It is a flat country, without woods and mountains, but very fruitful, abounding in rice, gokokf, garden-fruits, and plants. It is divided into twenty-one districts, which are Kuraggi, Tsukuki, Tama, Tatsinbana, Kaikura, Iruma, Tosma, Fijki, Jokomi, Saitama, Kedama, Tsibu Sima, Fabara, Fasisawa, Naka, Kami, Adats, Tsitsubu, Jebara, Totoosima, and Oosato. 12. Awa, otherwise Foosiu, a middling good country, with mountains, hills, rivers, and plains, affording both rice and corn; it is tolerably well inhabited and plentifully supplied by the neighbouring sea with fish and oysters, whose shells the inhabitants make use of to manure their ground. It is one day's journey and a half long from south to north, and divided into four districts, Fekuri, Awa, Asaima, and Nakaha. 13. Kadsusa, otherwise Kocaju, is three days' journey long, going from south to north, a tolerable good country, though not without high rough mountains; great numbers of the inhabitants get their livelihood by weaving of cannib, or hemp-stuffs, which they understand very well. It is divided into eleven

districts, Ssuesu, Amafa, Itsuwara, Umingami, Foiko, Mooki, Issimi, Farinib, Nagawa, Jammanobe, and Mussa. 14. Simoosa, otherwise Soosju, is said to be three days' journey long, going from south to north, a mountainous country, indifferently fruitful, but abounding in fowls and cattle. It is divided into twelve districts, Kaddosika, Tsibba, Imba, Sooma, Sasjuma, Iuuki, Tooda, Koosa, Unagami, Katori, Fannibu, and Okanda. 15. Fitats, or Sjoo, a very large province; my author makes it almost square, and says that it is three days' journey long on each side. It is but a middling country, as to its fruitfulness, but produces a great quantity of silk-worms and silk, of which there are several manufactures established there, as there are also some other things, the inhabitants being a very industrious people. They likewise carry on a trade in cattle. It hath eleven districts, Nijbari, Makaije, Tsukkumba, Kawaata, Saida, Umbaraki, Naminguta, Naka, Kussi, Taka, and Ienguko. Ienguko signifies a distant country, by which is probably meant some neighbouring island. The revenues of these fifteen provinces of the first large tract called Tookaido, amount in all to 494 mankokf.

11. Toosando, that is, the eastern mountainous tract, hath eight large provinces within its compass, which are:—1. Oomi, an extraordinary good and fruitful country, with variety of mountains, hills, rivers, and fruitful fields, producing both rice and corn, and affording to the labourer a thousandfold reward (according to my Japanese author's way of expressing the fruitfulness of this country). It hath three days' journey and a half in circumference, and is divided into thirteen districts: Singa, Karimotto, Ius, Cammoo, Kansaki, Inuugami, Sakatta, Jetz, the upper and lower Assai, Imito, Takassima, Kooka, and Joositzoomi. 2. Mino, or Diosiu, is not inferior to the former, neither in an agreeable variety of hills and plains, nor in fertility, producing plenty of rice, corn, and gokokf, and other necessaries of life. It is three days' journey long from south to north, and divided into eighteen districts: Isijntsu, Fufa, Awadsi, Ikenda, Oono, Mottos, Mussijroda, Katakata, Atsumi, Kakumi, Iamangata, Muggi, Guundsjo, Camo, Cako, Tokki, Jenna, and Taki. 3. Fida, otherwise Fisju, falls far short of the two former, both in largeness and fertility. Its utmost extent from south to north doth not exceed two days' travelling. It abounds in woods and forests, and yields a great quantity of fire-wood, and timber for buildings. It hath but four districts, Ofarra, Masijuda, Ammano, and Araki. 4. Sinano, otherwise Sinsju, a very cold country. Salt and fish are very scarce here, because of its great remoteness from the sea; and it is not well provided with cattle, by reason of its few pastures. It is otherwise tolerably fruitful, and produces a good quantity of mulberry trees, silk, and cannib, of which there are several good manufactures established there. It is said to be five days' journey long from south to north, and is divided into eleven districts: Midsutz, Takaij, Fannissina, Teisagatta, Sacku, Ina, Sauwa, Taikumma, Atsumi, Sara, and Sijna. 5. Koodsuke, otherwise Dsiosju, is four days' journey long, going from east to west, a warm and tolerable good country, producing plenty of mulberry trees, though the silk they yield is not of the best sort, and the stuffs brought from thence but coarse. It is divided into fourteen districts: Ussui, Aassa, Ssikanne, Ssetta, Sai, Nitta, Kattaoka, Soora, Gumma, Kanva, Tago, Midorino, Naba, and Jammada. 6. Simcodsuke, or Jasju, is three days' journey and a half long, going from east to west, a tolerable good country, not very mountainous, but rather flat, with abundance of pasture-ground and rice-fields, which plentifully supply it with grass, rice, corn, and the gokokf. It hath nine districts, Askara, Jamada, Aso, Tsuga, Taka, Sawingawa, Suwooja, Nasu, and Mukabo. 7. Mutsu, or Oosju, is by much the largest province in Japan, being full sixteen days' journey long, from south to north. It is an extraordinary good and fruitful country, and wants nothing for the support of human life. This whole province was formerly subject to one prince, together with the neighbouring province Dewa, of which more hereafter. It is divided into fifty-four (and according to others fifty-five) districts, Sijrakawa, Kurokawa, Juwasi, Mijaki, Aitz, Nama, Oda, Asaka, Adatz, Sibutto, Karida, Tooda, Natori, Sinnobu, Kikkunda, Sibanne, Assonusa, Naminguta, Iwadewaga, Kawatz, Fitzungi, Takano, Wattari, Tamadsukuri, Oonato, Kami, Saida, Kursiwara, Jesan, Jeki, Misawa, Nagaooka, Tojone, Munowara, Oosika, Gunki, Kaddono, Fasikami, Tsuugaru, Uda, Iku, Motnjes, Isbara, Taidsi, Sikamma, Inaga, Siwa, Iwasaki, Kimbara, Kadsinda, Datte, Socka, Fei, and Kisen. 8. Dewa, otherwise, Usju, is five days' journey long, a very good country, abounding in good pasture-ground, plants, and trees. It is said to have the spring fifteen days earlier than other provinces. It belonged formerly to Osju, but is now a separate province, divided into twelve districts, Akumi, Kawanobe, Murajama, Ojtama, Ookatz, Firaka, Tangaira, Diwa, Akindaturi, Senboku, Mogumi, and Jamamottu. All the revenues of these eight provinces amount to 563 mangokf, according to the old rentals, but at present they are considerably improved.

III. Foku Rokkudo, that is, the northern tract, hath seven provinces within its compass:—1. Wackasa, otherwise Siakusju, is one day's journey and a half long, going from south to north. It is limited to the north by the sea, which plentifully supplies it with fish, crabs, tortoises, and the like. It hath some iron-mines, and is divided into three districts, Oonibu, Ooi, and Micatta. 2. Jetsissen, otherwise Jeetsju. Its length, from south to north, is of three days' travelling. It is very mountainous towards the south, but more flat and fruitful to the north, with abundance of good pasture-ground, where the inhabitants breed plenty of cattle. It produces also cannib, mulberry trees, and silk, and the gokokf very plentifully. It is divided into twelve districts: Tauraga, Nibu, Imadats, Asijba, Oono, Sakai, Kuroda, Ikiogomi, Takakida, Joosdsida, Sakagita, and Naand-jo. 3. Kaga, otherwise Kasju, is two days' journey and a half long, going from east to west, a tolerable good country, yielding as much of the gokokf as is necessary for the sustenance of the inhabitants. Some silk manufactures are carried on here; and it affords the best vinegar, sacki, and soja, which are exported into other provinces. It hath four districts, Jenne, Nomi, Isikawa, and Kanga, to which some add Kaboku.

4. Noto, otherwise Seoaju, is a sort of a peninsula, almost wholly encompassed by the sea, and on this account plentifully supplied with fish and crabs. It hath several iron-mines, but not much good ground, and the gokokf ripen considerably later than in other provinces. It is two days' journey and a half long, going from east to west, and is divided into four districts: Bagui, Noto, Fukesaund, and Saus. 5. Jeetaju, otherwise Jaeesju, hath three days' journey in circumference, a tolerable good country, pretty well supplied with gokokf. A particular sort of earthen pots is made here. It affords also some wood, which is made use of particularly for bridges. It is divided into four districts, Tonami, Imidsu, Mebu, and Nijkawa. 6. Jetsingo, otherwise Jeesju, a large province, having six days' journey in circumference. It is very mountainous to the south, otherwise tolerably fruitful, producing silk, cannib, and the gokokf, though not of the best sort. It is divided into seven districts: Kabiki, Kof, Misaima, Iwoodai, Camhara, Nutari, and Iwafuue. 7. Sado, or Sasju, a pretty large island, of three days' journey and a half in circumference, situate to the north of Japan, just over against the two provinces Jeetaju and Jetsingo. It is a very fruitful island, plentifully supplied with corn, rice, and gokokf. It hath also some woods and good pasture-ground. The sea affords fish and crabs. It is divided into three districts, Umo, Soota, and Camo. The yearly revenue of these seven provinces amounts to 243 mangokf.

IV. Sanindo, that is, the "Northern Mountainous, or Cold Tract," consists of eight provinces: 1. Tanba, otherwise Tansju, is two days' journey long, a middling good country, producing plenty of rice, besides several sorts of pease and pulse. It affords also some fire-wood, and is divided into six districts: Kuwada, Funaji, Taki, Amada, Fingumi, and Ikarunga. 2. Tango, otherwise Tansju, is one day's journey and a half broad, going from south to north, likewise a middling good country, where silk and cannib may be had at a very easy rate. It is plentifully supplied by the sea with fish, crabs, and the like. It is divided into five districts: Kaki, Joki, Tango, Katano, and Kumano. 3. Tasima, otherwise Tansju, is two days' journey long, going from east to west, a middling good country, much like the two former, and divided into eight districts: Asami, Jahu, Idsu, Ketta, Kinnosaki, Flangako, Sitzumi, and Mikummi. 4. Imaba, otherwise Insju, is much of the same length and degree of fruitfulness with Tasima. It is limited to the north by the sea, and on the south by a ridge of mountains. It hath several manufactures of coarse silk stuffs, and is divided into seven provinces: Togomi, Jagami, Tsidsu, Oomi, Takaguso, Ketta, and Konno. 5. Fouki, otherwise Fakusju, is two days' journey and a half long, going from south to north, a middling good country, producing plenty of gokokf, cannib, and silk, of which last there are several good manufactures carried on here. It is divided into six districts: Kawamura, Kume, Jawata, Aneeri, Oomi, and Fino. 6. Idsumo, otherwise Unsju, is two days' journey and a half broad, going from east to west, almost wholly encompassed by the Corean sea, after the manner of a peninsula. It is a very fruitful country, producing variety of trees, grass, and plants. It hath also some manufactures of coarse silk stuffs. It is divided into ten districts: Iju, Nomi, Semane, Akisika, Tattenui, Judsumo, Kanto, Ijis, Ninda, and Oofara. 7. Iwami, otherwise Sekisju, is two days' journey long, going from south to north, a middling good country, producing plenty of cannib, and affording some salt. The inhabitants give twice as much a year to their prince as they do in other provinces. It is divided into five districts: Tsikama, Naka, Oota, Mino, and Canoah. 8. Oki, otherwise Inaju, an island erected into a province, and situate in the Corean sea, opposite to the coasts of that peninsula. It is a very barren country, producing a few gokokf. It hath two days' journey in circumference, and is divided into five districts. All the yearly revenues of these eight provinces amount to 123 mangokf.

V. Sanjodo, that is, the "Southern Mountainous, or Warm Tract," is composed of eight provinces, which are, 1. Farima, otherwise Bansju, hath three days' journey and a half in circumference, a very fruitful country, producing in plenty all manner of necessaries. It hath several manufactures of silk-stuffs, paper, and cloth. It is divided into fourteen districts, Akas, Kata, Kamo, Inami, Sikama, Iwo, Akato, Saijo, Sitz, Kansaki, Taka, Mitzubo, Issai, and Itto. 2. Mimasaka, otherwise Sakusju, is three days' journey long, going from east to west, a middling good country, affording as much fruits, plants, victuals, and cloth, as is necessary for the support of its inhabitants. It is observed as somewhat remarkable, that this province is less subject to winds than any other in the empire. It is divided into seven districts, Aida, Katzunda, Tomanisi, Tomafigasi, Khume, Ooha, and Masuma. 3. Bidsen, or Bisju, hath three days' journey in circumference, a middling good country, producing plenty of silk. Its soil is pretty warm, and the produce of the fields and gardens are observed to ripen earlier than in other provinces. It is divided into eleven districts, Kosuma, Waki, Iwanasi, Ooku, Akosaka, Kandatz, Minne, Oona, Tsitaka, Tsingosima, and Kamosima. 4. Bitsju, otherwise Fisin, is one day's journey and a half long, going from east to west, a very good country, plentifully supplied with all the necessaries of life. The gokokf and cannib in particular are extremely cheap here. It is divided into nine districts, Utz, Kaboja, Kaija, Simomitz, As-anguts, Oda, Sitzuki, Teta, and Fanga, to which are added two inlands, Saburosima, and Jorisima. 5. Bingo, otherwise Fisju, is somewhat more than two days' journey long, going from south to north, a middling good country, plentifully supplied with rice and gokokf, which are likewise observed to ripen here much earlier than they do elsewhere. It is divided into fourteen districts, Abe Futsitz. Kamijai, Asuka, Numasimi, Bonitz, Asijda, Kooni, Mikami, Camidami, Mitsuki, Jesso, Sirra, and Mijwara. 6. Aki, otherwise Geaju, is two days' journey and a half long, going from south to north, a mountainous and barren country. Upon the coasts they make salt. Corn, rice, and gokokf will hardly grow here, but it abounds with woods and forests, which afford plenty of mushrooms. It is divided into eight districts, Numada, Takatta, Tojoda, Seda, Cammo, Sahaku, Aki, Takamija, and Iku Kussima; which last is the name of a place particularly famous in this province. 7. Suwo, or Seosju, is three days' journey long, going from east to west, a middling good country, abounding chiefly in plants and good pasture-ground. The coasts afford as much fish, crabs, shells, and other submarine substances as any other province whatever. It is divided into six districts, Oosima, Kuka, Kumade, Taino, Sawa, and Jooski. 8. Nagata, otherwise Tsiosju, is two days' journey and a half long, from east to west, a middling good country, limited to the south and west by the sea, to the north by a ridge of mountains. It produces gokokf, fish, crabs, and other necessaries, twice as much as there is requisite for the maintenance of the inhabitants. It is divided into six districts, Atsa, Trojoro, Miue, Ootz, Amu, and Misijma. The whole yearly revenue of these eight provinces amounts to 270 mangokf.

All the several tracts of land, provinces and districts, hitherto mentioned, belong to the great island Nipon. I proceed now to the second island, which is next to Nipon in largeness, and which is by the Japanese called Kiusju, the Western Country, and Saikokf, the Country of Nine. This offers to our view the

VI. Great tract of land, called Saikaido, that is, the "Western Coast Tract." It is composed of nine large provinces: 1. Tsikudsen, otherwise Tsikusiu, is from south to north four days' journey long, a middling good country, producing both corn and rice. It hath several Chinaware manufactures, and is divided into twenty-four districts, Sima, Kama, Jassijka, Nosima, Mikasa, Monagatta, Onka, Musiroda, Fouami, Sara, Naka, Cassija, Siaka, Musima, Ito, Musijro, Vutz, Kurande, Nokosima, Sinotz, Kasakura, Kamitakasakura, Kokuf, and Tassai. 2. Tsikuugo, otherwise Tsikusju, is, from south to south, five days' journey long, a tolerable good country, producing corn, rice, and peas in great plenty: the coasts afford fish, crabs, and shells. A great deal of sweetmeat is made here, and exported into other provinces. It is divided into ten districts, Mijwara, Mij, Ikwa, Mi, Mike, Kandsima, Simodsima, Jammacando, Jammaseta, and Takeno. 3. Budsen, or Foosju, is four days' journey long from south to north, a tolerable good country, particularly famous for producing extraordinary good medicinal plants. Great numbers of silk manufactures are carried on in this province, some of which the Prince takes in part of payment for his revenue. It is divided into eight districts, Tangawa, Sakku, Mijako, Nakatz, Tsuiki, Kamitzki, Simotzki, and Usa. 4. Bungo, otherwise Foosju, is three days' journey long, middling fruitful. It affords silk from its mulberry-trees, cloth, hemp, gokokf, and some scarce medicinal plants. It is divided into eight districts, Fita, Kees, Nawori, Oono, Amabe, Ookata, Faijami, and Kunisaki. 5. Fidsen, otherwise Fisju, is, from south to north, full five days' journey long, a good and middling fruitful country, besides the produce of corn and rice, plentifully stored with fish and fowls. It hath also some cloth manufactures, and is divided into eleven districts, Kickij, Jabu. Mine, Ooki, Kansoki, Saaga, Maatsura, Kissima, Fusitz, Kadsuraki, and Takaku. 6. Figo, otherwise Fisju, hath about five days' journey in circumference, a middling fruitful country, affording plenty of firewood, and wood for building, also corn, peas, fish, crabs, and other necessaries, as much as will supply the want of the inhabitants. It is divided into fourteen districts, Tamana, Jamaga, Jamamatto, Kikuta, Aso, Takuma, Kuma. Aida, Masika, Udo, Jaadsiro, Koos, Amakusa, and Askita. 7. Fiugo, otherwise Nisju, is about three days' journey long, a poor country, mountainous, and producing hardly what corn, rice, and fruits are necessary for the sustenance of its inhabitants; some few mulberry-trees grow there. It is divided into five districts, Uski, Koiju, Naka, Mijasaka, and Morokata. 8. Oosumi, otherwise Gusju, is, from east to west, two days' journey long, a small but fruitful province, plentifully supplied with all the necessaries of life, particularly such as the sea affords. There is a great quantity of paper made here, and some few silk stuffs. It is divided into eight districts, Oosumi, Fisingari, Kuwabara, Soo, Sijra, Kimodsuki, Komadsij, and Kumagge, to which is added the neighbouring island Tanegasima. 9. Satzuma, or Satzju, is much of the same length with the former, middling fruitful, producing chiefly mulberry-trees and hemp. It hath a few cloth manufactures, but the cloth is very good. It can furnish other provinces with hemp. It is divided into fourteen districts, Idsumi, Takaki, Satzuma, Feki, Isa, Ala, Kawanobe, Jene, Juumaki, Fire, Fuai, Jamma, Okinokosima, and Kosakisiua. The yearly revenue of these nine provinces amounts to 344 mangokf.

An island of the third magnitude, which lies between the two former, and is by the Japanese called Sikokf, that is, the Country of Four, viz., provinces, together with the neighbouring island Awadsi, situate to the north-east of Sikokf, and the great province Kijnokuni, which stands out from the continent of Nipon, make up the seventh large tract of land, which is by the Japanese called

VII. Nankaido, that is, the "Tract of the Southern Coasts." It is composed of the six following provinces: 1. Kijnokuni, otherwise Kisju, is four days' journey and a half long, going from south to north, a flat and barren country, washed by the sea on three sides, and producing neither corn and rice, nor peas and pulse. It is divided into seven districts, Ito, Naka, Nagusa, Amabe, Arida, Fitaka, and Muro. 2. Awadsi, an island of about a day's journey in length, in the main very barren, affording, however, cloth, fish, and salt, as much as there is necessary for the maintenance of the inhabitants. It hath but two districts, Tsina and Mijwara, to which are added two of the chief neighbouring islands, Mussima and Jesima. 3. Awa, otherwise Aaju, is two days' journey long, a middling good country, somewhat mountainous, and plentifully stored with cattle, fowl, fish, crabs, and shells. It is divided into nine districts, Miosi, Ojen, Nasingasi, Nanisi, Katsura, Naka, Itano, Awa, and Mima. 4. Sanuki, otherwise Sansju, is three days' journey long, going from east to west, a middling good and fruitful country, with variety of rivers, mountains, and fields, producing rice, corn, peas, and pulse. The sea affords plenty of fish and crabs. This province is famous for having given birth to several great and eminent men. It is divided into eleven districts, Owutsi, Samingawa, Miki, Mino, Jamada, Kanda, Ano, Utari, Naka, Tado, and Kako. 5. Ijo, otherwise Josju, is two days' journey long, a middling good country, mountainous in some parts, flat in others, some of the fields being sandy, others producing rice, hemp, mulberry-trees, grass, and plants. Some salt is made upon the coasts. It is divided into fourteen districts, Nij, Sucki, Kuwamira, Ootz, Kasafaja, Nooma, Tsike, Otsumi, Kume, Fuke, Jio, Kits, Uwa, and Uma. 6. Tosa, otherwise Tosju, is two days' journey long, going from east to west, a middling good country, supplied with plenty of peas and pulse, wood, fruits, and several other necessaries of life. It is divided into seven provinces, Tosa, Agawa, Taka, Oka, Fata, Namaoka, Katasima, and Kami. The yearly revenue of these six provinces amounts to 140 mangokf.

There remain still two other islands not hitherto mentioned, which were conquered, and annexed to the empire of Japan, in the late war with the inhabitants of Corea. They are called Iki Tsussima, both their names being put together, and have now a prince of their own, having been formerly subject to the Prince, or petty King of Satzuma. The first of these two islands is Iki, otherwise Iaju; it is a day's journey long, and hath two districts, Iki and Isijda. The second island is Tsussima, otherwise Tuisju; this is somewhat larger than the former, and likewise divided into two districts, Akato, and Simoakata, that is, Upper and Lower Akata. The fruitfulness of these islands is said not to be very considerable, but they say that some foreign curiosities are to be seen there, and the number of idols worshipped by the inhabitants is much talked of. The yearly revenue of these two islands amounts to three man, and 5000 kokf.

The whole revenue of all the islands and provinces belonging to the great empire of Japan makes up in all a yearly sum of 2328 man, and 6200 kokf, according to the account above given. My Japanese author, however, puts it only at 2257 mangokf.

Though it be not a proper place here to enter into particulars concerning the government of the Japanese empire, its provinces and districts, yet, for the better understanding of my history, it seems necessary that, before I proceed any further, somewhat should be said on this head. The whole empire, in general, is governed by the emperor, with an absolute and monarchical power; and so is every province in particular, by the prince who, under the emperor, enjoys the government thereof. The present kubo, or secular monarch, is Tsinajos, fourth successor, and great grandson of Jejassuma, first emperor of the now reigning family, who usurped the throne upon the lawful heir, and reigned about the beginning of the sixteenth century. Tsinajos hath the character of a severe, but just and prudent monarch. He inherited from his ancestors, along with the crown, an absolute and unlimited power over all his subjects, from the meanest extraction up to the highest rank. Even the greatest princes and lords of the empire are so far his vassals that he can disgrace, exile, and deprive them of their lives and dominions as he pleases, or as he thinks the peace and welfare of the empire requires, or their crimes deserve.

Particular provinces are governed by hereditary princes, called daimio, which signifies "high-named:" that is, princes and lords of the highest rank. Some of these have found means, by force of arms, to enlarge their dominions. Thus, the Prince of Satzuma made himself master of the two neighbouring provinces, Ooeumi and Fiugo, and the Prince of Canga of the neighbouring province, Noto; on which account these two princes are said to be the most powerful in the empire.

The lords of smaller districts are called Siomio, "well-named," lords of an inferior rank. Their dominions, whether they be islands, as Goto, Firando, Amakusa, Matsaki, and several others, or situate upon the continent of the three chief islands composing the empire of Japan, are mentioned in the list of the sixty-six great provinces, each under that province whereto they belong, or in which they lie. All the siomio are so far subject to the emperor that they are allowed but six months' stay in their hereditary dominions; the other half year they must spend in the imperial capital, Jedo, where their wives and families are kept all the year round as hostages of their fidelity.

Some of these smaller districts are imperial demesne, or crown lands, either because they have been appropriated of old for the support of the crown, or because in course of time, as occasion offered, they were taken from their hereditary possessors by way of punishment, and annexed thereunto, it having been always one of the chief political maxims followed by the Emperors of Japan to maintain themselves in peaceable possession of the throne by splitting large dominions into several small ones, and by endeavouring, by all possible means, to weaken the power and authority of the Princes of the empire. The largest of these crown lands are governed by what they call bugios, acting in the nature of lieutenants; the smaller ones by daiquans, as they are called, or stewards. All the revenues must be brought into the Emperor's exchequer.

CHAPTER III.

THE AUTHOR'S OPINION OF THE TRUE ORIGIN AND DESCENT OF THE JAPANESE.

It hath been the constant opinion of most European geographers, that the Japanese are originally of Chinese extraction, descended from the inhabitants of that mighty empire. This opinion is grounded upon the following two stories, which were brought out of the East by European travellers. The first is: It once happened in China that several families conspired against the Emperor. Upon discovery of the plot, it was ordered, that all those who had any hand in it, should be put to death without mercy. But the number of accomplices was so great, that at last the executioners themselves grow weary of shedding so much blood; the affair was again laid before the Emperor, who thereupon resolved, that their sentence of death should be converted into transportation and banishment into the neighbouring, then rude and uninhabited, islands of Japan, which they peopled, and thereby became the progenitors of that numerous and powerful nation they are now inhabited by. The second story hath been reported as follows: One of the Emperors of China, unwilling to part with his empire, and all that grandeur and power he was possessed of, within the short term human life is limited to, endeavoured to find out, if possible, some universal medicine, which could make him immortal; on this account, he sent expert and able men into all parts of the world. Among the rest, one of his chief physicians persuaded him, that the proper ingredients for such a medicine were, to his knowledge, to be met with in the neighbouring islands of Japan; but that they were of so tender and singular a structure, that they would wither, and lose their virtues, if touched by any other but chaste and pure hands. And, the better to execute this design, he proposed that three hundred young men, and so many young women, all of a strong and healthful constitution, should be carried over thither, which accordingly he did himself, though far from having any real intention to satisfy his Sovereign, but rather out of a desire to escape his tyranny, to settle in happier climes, and to people these then uninhabited islands. As to the first of these two stories, Linschoot is the author of it; but he not acquainting his reader what authority he had for it, or how he came by it, and there being not the least mention made, neither in Chinese nor Japanese histories, of any such conspiracy, it deserves no credit, but ought to be entirely rejected as forged and fabulous. But as to the second, the coming over of a Chinese physician, with so many young men and young women, the same is not at all denied by the Japanese; nay, far from it, they still show a place upon Khumano (so they call the southern coasts of the provinces), Kijnokuni, and some neighbouring provinces, where he landed and afterwards settled with his gallant colony; and the remains of a temple, which was there erected to his memory, for having brought over to them from China good manners, and useful arts and sciences. As to the occasion of his coming over, it is recorded in Japanese histories, that there was great search made after an universal medicine, during the reign of the Emperor Si, or Sikwo, or, as the vulgar pronounce it, Sino Sikwo. This Emperor was one of the three Chinese Neros, Sinosko, Ketzuwo, and Thuwo, whose memory will be for ever abhorred. He not only governed his empire with unparalleled tyranny, but lived with the greatest pride, and mos, profuse magnificence imaginable, of which there are several remarkable instances mentioned in the history of his life. He caused once a large spot of ground to be dug up for a lake, and having ordered it to be filled with Chinese beer, he sailed over it in stately barges. He caused a stately palace, named Kojaku, to be built for his residence, the floors whereof were paved with gold and silver, and the whole building of such an extent, that the Emperor Kooll, who afterwards usurped the throne, having sat it on fire, it burnt in the ashes for the space of three months; which memorable event gave birth to a proverb, whereby the Japanese express the sudden changes, and short duration, human grandeur and happiness are liable to. It was this Emperor who, out of a strong desire for ever to enjoy the empire, ordered that great search should be made after a medicine, which could render him immortal. If it be therefore under his reign, the above said physician went over into Japan with his colony, it must be granted to the Japanese, that they came by much too late to be the progenitors of their nation, which was then already governed by Koken, their eighth monarch; for the arrival of the Chinese was in the seventh year of the reign of Koken, 453 years after Synmu, first Emperor of Japan, and 209 before the birth of our Saviour, the very same year in which Sinosikwo died in the fiftieth year of his age. Since therefore these two stories are by no means a sufficient proof that the Japanese nation is descended from the Chinese, it will not be amiss to inquire whether it be not possible to assign it another more probable origin.

It is unquestionably true that languages, and their laws, are as sure and certain marks, as perhaps it is possible to produce, whereby to discern, and trace out, not only the true origin of a nation, but likewise to find out how in process of time it increased, by being, as it were, incorporated with other nations. Of this most European nations afford us evident proofs. Thus, for instance, we may easily find by the language alone, that the Polanders, Bohemians, and Muscovites, are of Sclavonian extraction; that the Italians, French, and Spaniards descend from the Romans; that the Germans, Low Dutch, Danes, and Swedes, are the offspring of the ancient Goths. Nay, we may go still further, and assert, that the languages alone of several nations, and proper considerations thereupon, will qualify and enable us to form probable conjectures what revolutions happened among them, whether and what neighbouring nations they were conquered by, as also, whether and how from time to time they increased by fresh supplies and colonies from foreign parts: for it may be laid down as a constant rule, that in proportion to the number of strangers who come to settle and live in a country, words of the tongue spoke by them will be brought into the language of that country, and by degrees, as it were, naturalized, and become so familiar to the natives, as if they had been of their own growth. The number of Saxon, Danish, and Norman-French words, in the English language, doth it not prove, that England was successively conquered by the Saxons, Danes, and Normans? Not even the Latin tongue was able to preserve its purity, but Greek words were freely, and in great number, adopted into it, after the Romans became master of that country, then the seat of learning and politeness. The language now spoken in Transylvania has a considerable mixture both of the Latin and neighbouring Hungarian. The language of the inhabitants of Semigallia (a small country near Russia), is composed of the Lettish, Sclavonian, and Latin. The same observation holds true in other parts of the world, as well as in Europe. John de Barros in his Decades, and Flacourt in his history of Madagascar, assure us that the language spoken by the inhabitants of that large African island is full of Javan and Malayan words, as remaining proofs of the trade and commerce which these two nations, about two thousand years ago, the richest and most powerful of Asia, had carried on with Madagascar, where they settled in great numbers. The language spoken in the peninsula Crimea, or Taurica Chersonesus, in Asia (Europe?), still retains many German words, brought thither, as is supposed, by a colony of Goths, who went to settle there about eight hundred and fifty years after the deluge. The late Mr. Busbeq, who had been Imperial Ambassador at the Ottoman Porte, collected and published a great number of these words in his fourth letter; and in my own travels through that country I took notice of many more. If we were better acquainted with the languages of the Javans, Ceylonese, Malabarians, Siamites, and other Indian nations, they would doubtless enable us to trace out their origin, mixture with their neighbours, and the revolutions that happened among them. But to apply what hath been said nearer to our purpose, I may venture to affirm, that if the Japanese language was to be thoroughly and most rigorously examined into, we would find it entirely pure, and free from all mixture with the languages of their neighbours, at least to such a degree, as would give room to conjecture an original descent from them. By their neighbours I mean chiefly the Chinese, who inhabit the eastern maritime provinces of that empire, and carry on a commerce with Japan. They speak three different languages, according to the three chief provinces they belong to, which are Nanking, Tsiakteju, and Foktsju. Now a native of Japan doth not understand one word of either of these languages, excepting the names of a few things which were brought by the Chinese into Japan along with the things themselves, and which conclude no more for an original descent of the Japanese from China, than some few Portuguese words, as pan, palma, bolan, cappa, frasco, bidou, tante, and a few more, still left there, would be allowed a sufficient proof of the Japanese being originally descended from the Portuguese. Nor was the number of Chinese, who came from time to time to settle in Japan ever considerable enough to occasion any remarkable alteration in the mother-tongue of the Japanese, though they could and actually did communicate and introduce among them the arts and sciences, which had long before flourished in China, nay even the knowledge of the learned and significant character-language of that country, which is likewise received in Corea, Tonquin, and other neighbouring kingdoms, much alter the same manner as the Latin is in most European countries. But besides, there are two other essential proprieties of a language, I mean the construction and pronunciation, in the Japanese language so entirely different from that of the Chinese, that there is no room left to think that these two nations gave birth to each other. And first as to the construction and way of writing, the Chinese set their characters one below another in a row, without any intermediate particles to connect them: the Japanese indeed do the same; but the genius of their language requires besides, that the words and characters should be sometimes transposed, sometimes joined together by other words and particles, particularly invented for this purpose, and which are so absolutely necessary, that even in reprinting the books of the Chinese, they must be added, to enable their people to read and to understand them. And as to the pronunciation, that also is vastly different in both languages, whether we consider it in general, or with regard to particular letters, and this difference is so remarkable, that it seems the very instruments of voice are differently formed in the Japanese than they are in the Chinese. The pronunciation of the Japanese language, in general, is pure, articulate, and distinct, there being seldom more than two or three letters (according to our alphabet) combined together in one syllable; that of the Chinese, on the contrary. is nothing but a confused noise of many consonants pronounced with a sort of a singing accent, very disagreeable to the ear. The same difference appears with regard to particular letters. Thus, the Chinese pronounce our letter H very distinctly, but the Japanese can give it no other sound but that of an F. Again, the Japanese pronounce the letters R and D very distinctly, of which the Chinese, particularly those of Nanking, always make an L, even such as are otherwise well skilled in the European languages. I could give several other instances of this kind, and further show, that what hath been observed of the difference between the Chinese and Japanese languages, holds equally true with regard to the languages spoken in Corea and Jeso, compared with that of the natives of Japan; but it is needless to give the reader, and myself, so much trouble, the rather, since nobody ever pretended to draw the original descent of the Japanese from either of these two nations.

Another argument against the descent of the Japanese from the Chinese, I could draw from the difference of the religion of both nations. If the Japanese were a colony of the Chinese, they would have doubtless brought over from thence, into the uninhabited islands of Japan, the religion and worship of their ancestors, and propagated the same upon their posterity. But this appears quite otherwise. The old, and probably original, religion of the Japanese, which is by them called Sintos, and the gods and idols, worshipped by its adherents, Sin and Came, is peculiar only to this empire, nor hath it ever been admitted, nor their gods acknowledged and worshipped, nor the religious way of life of the Japanese followed by the Chinese, or indeed any other heathen nation. It was besides the only one established in Japan during a succession of many ages. For the foreign pagan doctrine of Siaka, which the Japanese now call Bupo, or Budedo, and the gods which it commands to worship, Buds and Fotoge, though ever since its early beginnings it met with uncommon success, and speedily spread over the best part of Asia, yet it was not introduced into Japan till sixty-six years after our Saviour's nativity, under the reign of the Emperor Synnin, when it was brought over from Corea. And although afterwards, through the connivance of the Japanese monarchs, it was successfully propagated by several missionaries, who came over from China, and the neighbouring kingdoms and speedily spread all over the empire, yet it never could prevail so far as to banish the respect and veneration for the old religion of their ancestors out of the minds of a constant and stedfast nation. On the contrary, the more the Bupo doctrine got ground, the more pains were taken for the preservation of the Sintos worship, by embellishing the same with new gods, temples, festivals and fables.

What hath been inferred from the difference of religion against the original descent of the Japanese from China, could be further supported by the wide difference there is between the characters anciently used by both nations; I mean the gross and rude common characters, as they call them, of the Japanese, and the simple and plain images of the Chinese. But this being an argument of less moment, I will not insist upon it, and only mention in a few words two other remarkable differences.

And first I could plainly show that the Japanese greatly differ from the Chinese in their civil customs and way of life, as to eating, drinking, sleeping, dressing, shaving of the head, saluting, sitting, and many more. Secondly, the very inclinations of the mind are remarkably different in both nations. The Chinese are peaceable, modest, great lovers of a sedate, speculative, and philosophical way of life, but withal very much given to fraud and usury. The Japanese, on the contrary, are warlike, inclined to rebellions and a dissolute life, mistrustful, ambitious, and always bent on high designs.

By what hath been hitherto observed, it appears plainly, that the Japanese are an original nation, at least that they are not descended from the Chinese. The difficulty now remaining to be cleared up, is, how, and from what parts of the world, to trace out their true original descent. In order to this we must go up higher, and perhaps it is not inconsistent with reason and the nature of things to assert, that they are descended of the first inhabitants of Babylon, and that the Japanese language is one of those, which sacred writs mention, that the all-wise Providence thought fit, by way of punishment and confusion, to infuse into the minds of the vain builders of the Babylonian tower. This at least seems to be the most probable conjecture, whatever way they went into Japan, or whatever time they spent upon this their first peregrination. Nay, considering the purity of the Japanese language, I may pursue my conjectures, and further affirm, that they cannot have spent much time on their first journey to Japan, forasmuch as we cannot suppose that they made any considerable stay in any one country, or with any one people then existing, without granting at the same time, that in all probability they would have adopted some words of the language of that nation into their own, of which yet it would be found upon examination to be entirely free, contrary to what we find in all European and most Eastern languages known to us, which seem to have been from their very beginning so thoroughly mixed and confounded, that there is scarce any but what hath some words of another though never so remote. If then our Japanese colony did reach that part of the world, which divine Providence assigned for their future abode, as soon as the Chinese, Tonquinese, and other neighbouring nations did theirs, it must be supposed that they fortunately fell in with such a road as could with safety and speed bring them to the eastern extremities of Asia, from whence there is but a short passage over to Japan. In order therefore to trace out what road it is probable they took, we must consider the first Babylonians in the condition they were in, after that dreadful confusion of languages, wholly disappointed from going on with their vain design, and brought to the fatal necessity to part with each other, and to be dispersed all over the world. And in order to this let us suppose, first: That among the different parties there arose in all likelihood a strong emulation to choose for their future abode such countries as were not only fruitful and delightful, but thought to be less exposed to the invasion of other parties, either because of their commodious situation towards the sea, or between large rivers, and high mountains, or by reason of their great distance. And in this regard it is highly probable that such countries, as were very remote, but situate under a temperate climate, became not the last inhabited. This seems to be the case of the empire of Japan, whose remoteness, as well as its fruitfulness, and pleasant situation, between $34°$ and $40°$ of northern latitude, could fully answer all the expectations of a first colony. But, secondly, let us suppose, that the chief care of these first colonies, in their search for a country fit for their habitation, must needs have been to follow such roads and tracts of land, where, in the mean time, they could be provided with the necessaries of life. This intention could scarce be answered more effectually than by travelling, either along the sea-coasts, or, and with more probability, along great rivers and lakes, where they could be supplied with fish for their own nourishment, with sweet water to quench their thirst, and where they were like to meet with good pasture-ground for their cattle, till at last they alighted at a country, where they thought they could settle with safety and convenience.

If, therefore, the dreadful confusion of tongues at Babylon brought its inhabitants, as indeed it must have done, to an indispensable necessity to part with one another, and to be dispersed all over the world, such parties as spoke the same language keeping together, and settling in what country they best liked, we may take it for granted that not a few went towards the neighbouring Black and Caspian seas, and that by this means the country of Hircania, which is situate between the Caucasus and Caspian shores, as the best and most delightful spot of Persia, became first inhabited, as did soon after the neighbouring fruitful countries, situate between the Black and Caspian Seas. Such as intended, or thought it expedient, to pursue their journey further, met here with two different ways, one up the rivers Tanais and Wolga to the north, the other along the eastern shores of the Caspian Sea into Asia. It is foreign to my present purpose to show what became of the former. And as to those that went along the eastern Caspian coasts, they must have at least reached to the mouth of the great river Oxus, or Daiehuun, where it discharges itself into the Caspian Sea, and if we suppose that they followed that river up to its source, it was then no very difficult matter for them to penetrate into the very midst of India, where they must have soon met with the source of the rivers Indus and Ganges, and, going down the different branches of it, got into Indostan, Bengala, Pegu, Siam, and other neighbouring kingdoms, much easier and safer than if they had been obliged to travel over the barren and still uninhabited Mahurounian mountains, or to cross the large deserts of Siftuun and Snablestuun. Even to this day, travellers going from Ispahan to Candahar choose rather to go through Mesihed, a journey of 375 miles, than to take the shortest road, which is but 250 miles, across these wild and dangerous deserts. But to return to the Caspian Sea, before I carry off our Japanese colony from thence on their journey to Japan, I must beg leave to make a short digression in favour of a famous and valiant nation of the Turks, or Turcomans and Usbecks, as they are now called, which settled upon its eastern and north-eastern coasts. Turk signifies a shepherd, and Turkestaan, a shepherd's country. Jusbeek is as much as to say, hundred lords, which seems to imply that the country of Usbeck was once governed by so many princes. Both nations have the same language, the same religion, the same manners and customs, and must therefore be looked upon as originally one, on which we may deservedly bestow the glorious epithets of being a mother of many nations, a nurse of illustrious heroes, and a stem of mighty monarchs. They spread from the north-eastern coasts of the Caspian Sea, between forty and fifty degrees of northern latitude, as far as the borders of Kitaija. Their way of life answered to their name; for during many centuries they lived together in hordes and small commonwealths, wandering from place to place with their cattle, wherein their chief riches consisted. Of these Turks, or Turcomans, are descended the Dagestaan and Nagajan Tartars, the Tartarian inhabitants of the kingdom of Casau, the Boscarian Tartars, the inhabitants of the province of Mogestan in Persia, and some other Tartars, which dwell in that kingdom under tents. The Kisilbacs, or noblemen and great families in Persia, value themselves mightily upon their being of Turcoman extraction. There are likewise descended of them the Crim Tartars, which live between the Dnieper and Danube, upon the coasts of the Black Sea, as also those Tartars whom the great conqueror Sinchischam (a prince who well deserved a Plutarch or Quintus Curtius to write the history of his life, conquests, and heroic actions) sent out upon an expedition into Poland, and who, not meeting with all the expected success, chose rather to stay and to people the then as yet uninhabited Poutus, than to return without honour and victory. I must silently pass over many other branches of the same race, which fell by degrees under the dominion of some neighbouring, chiefly northern, nations, with whom they were in course of time so thoroughly mixed and incorporated, that even the very footsteps of their original descent would have been lost, were it not for some few remains of their former language. I will only add, that the famous Tamerlane was an Usbeckian Scythe,

and that the Ottoman Emperor, the great Mogul and the King of Sopra, are all of Turcoman extraction. Thus much of the Turks and Usbecks. In order now to come nearer to our purpose I will avoid speaking of those companies which went along the river Inike, or from the source of the river Obij down the same towards the Tartarian Ocean, and became the first progenitors of the Tartarian nations living in those parts. Nor will I pretend at present to determine what way the Chinese colony took in their journey to China. It is only six months travelling from the coasts of the Caspian Sea to the borders of China. Jagen Audasen, in his voyage to China in 1647, did not stay longer. Two Tartarian merchants, whom I conversed with at Astracan, and who had been several times in China, gave me the following account of their journey thither. They went from Astracan over the Caspian Sea (which they took to be 200 miles long and 150 broad), to Scrataijk in fifteen days; from thence by land to Ugentz the residence of an Usbeckian prince, in five days; from thence to Bochau in fifteen days, travelling through a wild large desert: from Bochau there are two different ways, whereof travellers may choose which they please. The one going over Chasger was then infested with rovers: so they took to the other, which, across a well-inhabited country, brought them to Tasakond in fourteen days; thence to Oxiend in seven days; thence to Knasker, the capital of Turkistano, and the chief town between Buchara and Kattai, in [this number was omitted in the original] days; thence to Tsutsijk, the first frontier town of Kattai, in thirty days; thence to Hamtsijk in five days; thence to the great wall of Kattai, Chatai, or China, in sixty days, travelling through a well inhabited country; and lastly, from the great wall to Cambalu, or Peking, the capital of China, and residence of the Chinese emperor, in ten days, completing the whole journey within six months' time. A Calmuckian merchant of the retinue of a Calmuckian prince's ambassador to the King of Persia, whom I knew at Ispahan, where he offered me for sale the root taichuun, that is "great yellow root," or rhubarb, which he had brought himself out of China, gave me the journal of his voyage from Mienkisilaag to the great wall of China, thus. He went from Mienkisilaag to Daiem in twenty days; from thence to Gilgaas, where they cross a large river, in fifteen days; from thence to Torkai in a few days, thence to Milantsij in ten days, thence to Toktan in ten days, thence to Tsienrohfu in five days; thence to Isijel in ten days, thence to Kalah in four days, thence to Balane in six days, thence to Karbokatai in ten days, thence to the great wall of China in nine days, travelling through a desert and uninhabited country, where he met only a few Tartarian shepherds dwelling under black tents. Mienkisilaag signifies, in the country language, hundred winter-quarters, or resting places. It is an island situated on the eastern coasts of the Caspian Sea, near forty-five degrees of northern latitude, and the residence of Ajukeh, the Prince of the Calmuckian Tartars living in those parts, who expelled the Turks, or Turcomans, out of their country, and forced them to depart even from the Caspian shores. After all I think it no ways probable that the first Chinese went into China through such desert and barren countries, where travellers are oftentimes necessitated to carry the necessary provisions of water and victuals along with them. I am more inclined to believe that their journey was more to the south, and perhaps along the north side of the Imaasian mountains, where the country is very fruitful with rich pastures and plenty of sweet water, and fish, and other necessaries of life, and where they were like to meet either the source, or else some of the branches, of the large river Croceus, which could conveniently and safely bring them into the very heart of China.

But now, at last, it is high time to make a step backwards, and to fetch the first Japanese colony from the Caspian shores, where we left them above, on their journey to Japan. If we suppose, that for some time they travelled along the east, and north-eastern coasts of the Caspian Sea, till they came to the island Mienkisilag, and that thence they followed up some of the rivers, which there discharge themselves into the said sea, we will find, that by this means they got into a large and fruitful country, extending itself far eastwards, and very proper, by reason of its happy situation and great fertility, for the leisurely and easily pursuing of their journey. Considering this, it will not appear improbable further to suppose, that having once met with so good and pleasant a country, where there was no want of provision for them and their cattle, they resolved to keep to it, avoiding to enter the hot, desert, and barren provinces, now inhabited by the Turkestanus, on one, or on the other side to go down the rivers Istisi, Jenesi, Silinga, and others, which arise thereabouts, and would have brought them to the less agreeable and cold northern countries. Thus, moving on insensibly eastward, they perhaps discovered in time the lake of Arguun, whence arises a large river of that name, and continuing their journey along the said river, for very near an hundred German miles, they must have necessarily met there another much more considerable river, called Amuur, which runs E. S. E., and could, in a journey of about 200 German miles, bring them to the eastern coasts of Asia into the then uninhabited peninsula Corea, where the said river loses itself to the eastern ocean. Perhaps, also, if our travellers went down the river Jenisi for about 780 English miles, to fifty-five degrees of northern latitude, they might have there discovered a much more commodious and pleasant way to the river Amuur, which hath of late been very advantageously followed by the Muscovites in their journeys to China. But as to the whole plan of this journey, I must refer the reader to the accurate and excellent map of Russia, and the great Tartary, which the late illustrious Nicholaus Witzen, LL.D., Burghermaster at Amsterdam, and sometime the States Ambassador to the Russian court, published in 1687, and thereby so highly obliged the curious, that he justly deserves the honours due to discoverers of unknown worlds. This map was afterwards corrected in some places, and abridged by Mr. Isbrand Ydes, who prefixed it to the account he imparted to the world of his journey through Tartary into China.

Having once brought our Japanese colony as far as the peninsula Corea, it will be no difficult matter, considering the nearness of Nagatto, the furthermost province, lying westwards on the continent of the great island Nipon, to bring them over thither, and this the rather, because of the several islands which lie between Corea and Nagatto, in an almost continued row, particularly the two larger ones, Iki and Tsussima: for it is but reasonable to suppose that a colony which had courage enough to venture so far upon their first peregrination, and which had been often necessitated, not only to have recourse to lakes and rivers, but frequently to cross the same, had natural curiosity enough left, in still and fair weather, to go out in canoes or boats, such as then probably they made use of, upon discovery of the state and extent of the Corean Sea, and the neighbouring islands; and that having by this means discovered the continent of Nipon, they resolved to go over thither, which they might easily do, even in ordinary fishing boats, and to choose that country for their future abode. Now, if anybody knows how to bring them hither through the Eastern Tartary and the country of Jeso (which way perhaps the American colonies went), safer and speedier, I am very willing to submit. Meanwhile I do not think it probable that our Japanese colony made any considerable stay upon these western coasts of Nipon. Their innate curiosity and travelling humour, and perhaps also the fear of being followed and disturbed by other parties, must needs have prompted them to travel up the country till they came to its southern extremities, and particularly into the province Isje, which by reason of its fruitfulness, good air, and remoteness from the western coasts, fully answered all the expectations of a secure and pleasant abode. I am the more inclined to believe that they first settled in this province since their posterity still look upon it as the place where their ancestors dwelled, and as such honour it with frequent pilgrimages and other acts of devotion. Thus far my conjectures, for as such only I deliver them, concerning the true original descent of the Japanese nation.

Before I put an end to this chapter, it will not be amiss to say something of the increase of this first Japanese colony, after they had once taken the resolution to stay, and to people the country, where doubtless for several ages before any considerable improvements were made in agriculture and other arts and sciences, they led a simple and indigent life, living on their cattle, on what the earth produced of plants, roots, and fruits, and the sea afforded of fish and crabs. It was unquestionably and chiefly owing to themselves, that in process of time they became so numerous and powerful a nation, and the present inhabitants of Japan must be looked upon in general as descendants of those, who, after the confusion of languages at Babel, came over and settled in these islands. But, on the other hand, it cannot be denied, but that from time to time new colonies were sent over thither, chiefly from China and Corea, and perhaps also from some other neighbouring countries. The Japanese themselves make frequent mention in their histories of learned Chinese, who brought over into Japan their books, and the knowledge of useful arts and sciences, though not till the latter ages, when the Japanese monarchy was already become a powerful empire. And indeed since so few foreign words have been brought into the Japanese language that it is hardly visible that there hath been any alteration at all made in it, and since the religion and old customs subsist till now, it appears plainly that whatever foreign colonies did from time to time voluntarily, or by chance, come over into Japan, their number must have been very inconsiderable with regard to the bulk of the Japanese nation.

Considering further, that the islands of Japan are encompassed with a dangerous and stormy sea, it is highly probable that from time to time ships coming from foreign countries stranded upon the Japanese coasts, and that if any of the ship's company were fortunate enough to save their lives, they chose rather to stay in Japan, and to settle among the natives, than to trust themselves again to the mercy of the sea, and to run the hazard of a perilous return into their own country. Though navigation by this time be highly improved, yet the like accidents still happen very frequently, and there is hardly a year but some ships are forced upon the coasts of Japan, coming sometimes from countries either so remote, or so entirely unknown, that scarce any conjectures can be made about them, neither by the shape nor the language and customs of the ship's company. Several remarkable instances of such accidents are recorded in Japanese histories. The Japanese having some centuries ago accidentally discovered the island Genkaisima, situate to the north of Japan, found it inhabited, as their histories relate, by Oni, that is, black devils, which they prosecuted with war, and having purged the island from this vermin, as they call it, they peopled it with a colony of their own. It is highly probable that these blacks had been forced upon the coasts of this (then uninhabited) island in a storm. It is further observed in the history of this war, that they wore long hairs spread over their shoulders, and that they had a strange sort of household goods, as among the rest high European hats. As to the Japanese calling them devils, we need not in the least wonder at it, considering either their black colour, or the natural pride of the Japanese nation, which so far despises all other countries as to call them Umakokf, that is, the countries of devils. Otherwise, what countrymen these blacks had been, is not very difficult to conjecture by their wearing long hair, by their furniture, and some other circumstances; and I don't believe to impose upon anybody, if I assert that they have been Malayans. It is well known that the Malayans to this day are extremely fond of their own hair, and delighted with wearing it of a considerable length beyond any other of the black nations of Asia. Besides, they had in former times by much the greatest trade in the Indies, and frequented with their merchant ships, not only all the coasts of Asia, but ventured over even to the coasts of Africa, particularly to the great island of Madagascar. The title which the King of the Malayans assumed to himself of Lord of the winds and seas to the east and to the west, is an evident proof of this, but much more the Malayan language, which spread most all over the east, much after the same manner as formerly the Latin, and of late the French, did all over Europe. The high hats, which were found among the household goods of these blacks, must have been brought out of Europe, they having never been fabricated any where else. It was an ancient custom of most eastern princes (which subsists till now in the kingdoms of Cambodia, Siam, Pegu, and some others) to present their prime ministers of state and chief favourites with such hats, as tokens of their particular favour, and they alone had the privilege of wearing them, as singular badges of honour. They were formerly brought out of Europe by land to Ormus,* and from thence exported all over the east by the Malayans, Armenians, and other trading nations; but after the Portuguese had discovered a new way to the Indies, round the Cape of Good Hope, they exported them from Europe (where they are now out of fashion) directly by sea. Now whether there was not among these black inhabitants of Genkaisima some great man who received these hats from his prince, or whether they fell by some other accident into their hands, is not material to inquire. There is also mention made in Japanese histories of black inhabitants, who were found in some of the islands lying to the south of Japan, and who in all probability must have been either Malayan merchants, or else inhabitants of some of the Molucca islands, who having been forced thither in a storm, and finding them uninhabited, resolved to stay and to people them. Not long before my arrival, and during my stay in Japan, several ships stranded upon the coasts coming from remote and unknown countries. In this case all the ship's company, as well those that remain alive as the bodies of such as are drowned, when thrown on shore, and all the ship's tackle, and the boat, if any, must be brought up to Nagasaki,† as the place appointed for a general inquiry into maritime affairs. The governors of this place examine into all the most minute circumstances of the unhappy accident with that care and jealous circumspection which is peculiar only to this nation, and in order to discover if possible what country the ship came from, and what language those that saved their lives speak, this examination is sometimes made in presence of the Dutch resident, who did me the favour upon these occasions to carry me along with him. It is a duty incumbent on every Prince of the empire to take care, in case any ships strand upon the coasts of his province, that they be sent up, as aforesaid, to Nagasaki, which is commonly, out of respect for the Emperor, done with great expense. Not long ago a jonk coming from Manilla, on board which were some Topassians, a sort of black Christians, was wrecked upon the coasts of Satzuma. Most of the ship's company were

---

* Ormuz, an island in the Persian Gulf, was for centuries a great emporium of trade. Goods were brought to it overland from Europe and Asia Minor, and then distributed to India and the East. It is now almost a mass of ruins.—ED.

† The modern spelling of this name is Nangasaki; we have, however, allowed it to stand all through as the worthy Dutchman wrote it.—ED.

drowned, some died on shore, and only three were brought up alive to Nagasaki, the last of whom died there in prison, after having taken some physic ordered him by a Japanese physician. Of another ship which stranded upon the same coasts, only three black sailors were saved, which could not pronounce one distinct word besides that of tobacco; after having lain for some time in prison, they were delivered to us, to be transported on board our ships. Another ship was brought to Nagasaki, which had been forced upon the northern coasts of Japan without anybody on board. The odd, uncommon structure of this vessel, and the remains of three Chinese characters upon the stern, made the Japanese conjecture that it came from the extremities of Jeso. Not long ago another ship perished upon the coasts of the island Riuku, and only two of the company were saved, which were brought first to Satzuma, and from thence to Nagasaki, with a convoy of eight barges, which must have put the prince of Satzuma at the expense of some thousand rixdollars. They were well shaped comely persons, and had their heads shaved much after the manner of the Polanders, no beards, and three holes in each ear. They shewed by their decent and civil behaviour, and free but modest appearance, a tolerable education, and a good clear understanding, by endeavouring to give the Japanese some notions of the number, situation, and largeness of the islands from whence they came, which they did by putting stones of different sizes upon a table, calling each by its name; among the rest, that island where they lived themselves was by them called Patan. We had reason to apprehend that the good understanding and quick apprehension they showed when under examination, would be the occasion of their imprisonment for life at Nagasaki. If we believe the Japanese, there is another unknown nation, and very different from theirs as to their customs, shape, and language, which inhabits the island Kubitesima, one of the most northern islands belonging to Japan. They describe them as Pygmies, and from thence call the whole island the Pygmy Island. What extraction they be of, and how they came to inhabit this island, I will leave to themselves to determine. I will only add on this head, that the first European ship which came into Japan was a Portuguese merchant-ship, forced thither accidentally in a storm.

Upon the whole, the wide difference which is still observed between the Japanese inhabitants of several provinces, as to their shape, seems to argue strongly that, from time to time, different and new branches were grafted into the original tree of this nation. For although the Japanese in the main, particularly the common people of Nipon, be of very ugly appearance, short-sized, strong, thick-legged, tawny, with flattish noses, and thick eye-lids, (though the eyes stand not so deep in the forehead as in the Chinese,) yet the descendants of the eldest and noblest families, of the princes and lords of the empire, have somewhat more majestic in their shape and countenance, being more like the Europeans. The inhabitants of the provinces Satzuma, Oosijmi, and Fiuga, are of middle size, strong, courageous, and manly, otherwise civil and polite. The same is observed of the inhabitants of some of the northern provinces in the great island Nipon, excepting those of the great province Oaju, who are said to be beyond others cruel and unmerciful. The inhabitants of some provinces of Saikokf, particularly Fisen, are short, slender, but well shaped, of a good handsome appearance, and extremely polite. The inhabitants of the great island Nipon, particularly of its eastern provinces, are known from others by their big heads, flat noses, and musculous fleshy complexion.

Now, to close this chapter, and to sum up in a few words what hath been therein largely dwelt on; it appears that in the first ages of the world, not long after the deluge, when the confusion of languages at Babel obliged the Babylonians to drop their design of building a tower of uncommon height, and occasioned their being dispensed all over the world, when the Greeks, Goths, and Sclavonians departed for Europe, others for Asia and Africa, others for America, that then the Japanese also set out on their journey: that in all probability, after many years travelling, and many incommodities endured, they alighted at this remote part of the world; that, being well pleased with its situation and fruitfulness, they resolved to choose it for the place of their abode; that in all likelihood they spent many centuries in a polyarchical way of life, such as is led to this day by the Tartars, living in hordes, and wandering with their cattle and families up and down the country; that being insensibly, and by degrees, grown to be a numerous and powerful nation, they thought it expedient, for the good of the country, and for their own safety, to deliver up the government into the hands of one prince, and choose for their first monarch the valiant Dain Mu Ten Oo; that consequently they are an original nation, no ways indebted to the Chinese for their descent and existence, and that, though they received from them several useful arts and sciences, as the Latins did from the Greeks, yet they were never made subject, and conquered, neither by them nor by any other neighbouring nation.

CHAPTER IV.

OF THE ORIGIN OF THE JAPANESE, ACCORDING TO THEIR OWN FABULOUS OPINION.

THE Japanese fancy themselves highly affronted by the endeavours of some who busy themselves to draw the original descent of their nation from the Chinese or others of their neighbours. They pretend that they arose within the compass of their own empire, though not out of the earth, like mice and worms, as the proud Athenians, for that same reason, were upbraided with, by that cynic Diogenes. They claim a birth much higher and nobler, and esteem themselves no less than offsprings of their very deities, whom otherwise they do not look upon as eternal, but suppose that in the first motion of the chaos, out of which all things were formed, their gods also were brought forth by its invisible power. They have two differing genealogies of their deities. The first is a succession of celestial spirits, of beings absolutely free from all manner of mixture with corporeal substances, who ruled the Japanese world during an undetermined and incomprehensible series of centuries. The second is a race of terrestrial spirits, or god-men, who were not possessed of that pure being peculiar only to their predecessors. They governed the Japanese empire by a lineal succession, each a long but limited number of years, till at last they begot that third race of men which Japan is now inhabited by, and who have nothing left of the purity and perfections of their divine progenitors. It will not be amiss, as a further proof of what I advance, here to insert the names of these two successions of deities, taken out of their own writings. The names of the first succession are purely metaphorical, and the only thing mentioned of it in their historical books, for there is no account given neither of their lives and actions, nor of their government. They succeeded each other in the following order.

Ten d Sin Sitzi Dai, that is, the succession of the seven great spiritual gods.
1. Kuni toko dat sij no Mikotto.
2. Kuni Satfu Tsi no Mikotto.
3. Tojo Kun Nan no Mikotto.

These three gods had no wives; but the four following of the same succession were married, and begot each his successor by his wife, though in a manner far beyond the reach of human understanding. These were—
4. Utsij Nino Mikotto, and his wife Sufitsi Nino Mikotto.
5. Oo Tono Tsino Mikotto, and his wife Oo Toma fe no Mikotto.
6. Oo mo Tarno Mikotto, and his wife Oo si Wote no Mikotto.
7. Isanagi no Mikotto, and his wife Isanami no Mikotto.

These seven gods are by them represented as beings purely spiritual, and the histories of their lives and governments as dreams. The real existence of such a time, when such spiritual beings governed the Japanese world, is what they religiously believe, though, at the same time they own that it is far above their understanding to conceive how it happened, and entirely out of their power to determine how long their government lasted.

The last of the first succession, Isanagi Mikotto, and his wife Isanami Mikotto, are held in peculiar veneration by the Japanese, as being the progenitors of the second succession of god-men, of whom issued the third race of the now existing inhabitants of Nipon. (Mikotto is an epithet peculiar only to the first succession of spiritual gods, and signifies the incomprehensible bliss and happiness of these first monarchs of Japan: sometimes, however, they will bestow it on such of the inferior gods, for whom they have a peculiar veneration.) Those of the Japanese who turned Christians called them their Adam and Eve. They are said to have lived in the province Isje, though it is not known in what particular part of that province they were born, lived, or died. They observe only, that this preadamitical Adam (if I may have the leave thus to call him) was the first who taught, by the example of the bird sekire, or according to the vulgar, Isitataki, lay with his wife in a carnal manner and begot by her sons and daughters of a nature excellent indeed, and far superior to ours, but greatly below that of the divine beings, of which they sprung. Isanami's first-born son, and the first of the second succession of god-men, is supposed by the very law of primogeniture to have been entitled to a superiority over his brothers and sisters, upon which, and a lineal descent from him, is grounded the right the Dairis, or ecclesiastical hereditary Emperor's eldest son's claim to the crown of Japan, upon their father's demise. The second succession is called Dai Sin Go Dai; that is, the "succession of five terrestrial gods or god-men;" who are—

1. Tensio Dai Dsin, in the language of the learned, and Ama Teru Oon Gami, in that of the vulgar. The characters whereby this name is expressed signify, "a great spirit streaming out celestial rays." He is the first-born son of Isanagi, and the only one that left children behind him. For it was his posterity, creatures not of a mean extraction, but of an excellent and almost divine nature, who inhabited the country for many millions of years, till they begot the third race of its present short-living inhabitants. All the Japanese, without exception, look upon themselves as immediate descendants of Tensio Dai Dsin; because they say that all his younger brothers left the world without issue. But particularly the ecclesiastical hereditary Emperor grounds his right to the empire (which is of late gone over into secular hands, he himself having preserved nothing but his title, and a shadow of his former power and grandeur) upon a lineal descent from Tensio Dai Dsin's first-born son, and so down. Tensio Dai Dsin committed not only during his reign many noble and heroic actions, but even after he left this world, as is recorded in Japanese histories, he sufficiently proved by many miracles, and manifested himself to be the most powerful of all the gods of the country, the very life, soul, light, and supreme monarch of nature. For this reason he is devoutly worshipped by all the faithful adherents of the old Japanese religion, as it was of old established in Japan. And the adherents of all other sects, even their greatest philosophers and atheists, show a particular regard and veneration for his name and memory, as that of their first parent. Devout pilgrimages are made yearly by the Japanese of all ranks and qualities to the province where he lived, and where there is a temple erected to his memory. Nor is there any province or town throughout the empire but what has at least one temple where Tensio Dai Dsin is worshipped; and, in hopes of obtaining by his power and assistance great temporal blessings, worshipped with much more assiduity and devotion than any other of their gods. There is otherwise no mention made in Japanese histories of his wife, nor of the wives of his successors, and their names are entirely lost to posterity. After some hundred thousands of years Tensio Dai Dsin was succeeded by his eldest son.

2. Oosiwo ni no Mikotto, or with his full title, Massni Ja su Katz Katz fsi ja fi Amani Oosi woni no Mikotto. His successor was

3. Ninikino Mikotto, or with his full title,

Amatsu fiko fiko Fono ni Niniki no Mikotto. He was succeeded by

4. Do mi no Mikotto, or with his full title, Fikofoo foo Do mi no Mikotto. He was succeeded by

5. Awase Dsu no Mikotto, or with his full title, Tuki Magisa Take Ugei Jakussa fuki awadsi Dsuno Mikotto. With him ends this second, or silver age, as one might call it, of the Japanese world. Something more shall be said on this head in the first chapter of the second book. The names of the five terrestrial gods of this second succession are expressed in Tab. xvi.

These are the two successions of divine and half divine beings, from whence the Japanese draw the original descent of their nation. The account they give how these gods were created, and how they begot each other, is no less chimerical and fabulous. The first of the seven great celestial spirits, they say, was the very first thing that arose out of the chaos, being its purest and invisible part and power. His son and heir went out of him in a manner beyond the reach of human understanding, or as some pretend to explain it and to make it intelligible, by the motion and active power of the heavens and subcelestial elements. Thus were begot the seven great celestial spirits of the first succession. It was the last of them who, knowing his wife in a carnal manner, begot the second succession of god-men, or beings half divine and half human. These, though they fell far short of the perfection of their progenitors, yet by virtue of those divine qualities they had still left them they preserved their lives and continued the succession of their government unto their posterity, which they begot in a more comprehensible manner, for an immemorial time, far exceeding the term human life is now limited to. At last all expired in the person of Awase Dsuno, the last of this second race, who himself became the first parent of the third, the now living inhabitants of Japan. To those of this third race, who descend lineally from the first-born son of Awase Dsuno Mikotto, from his first-born, and so down, or their issue wanting to their next heirs, is by the Japanese attributed to a supernatural, almost divine power, and an unlimited authority over their fellow-creatures. This is in some measure expressed by the great titles and high-sounded epithets they give to this whole family, but particularly to its head and prince. Such are Ooda, the great generation: Mikaddo, Emperor, (Mikotto being peculiar only to the first and second succession of gods and god-men.) Tenoo, Heavenly Prince; Tensi, Son of Heaven; Tee, Prince; and Dairi; by which last name is frequently denoted the whole court of the ecclesiastical hereditary Emperor.

Thus far the common tradition of the Japanese about the original descent of their nation, which is esteemed as sacred among them as the authority of holy scriptures is among Christians. It were needless to refute it, it being of itself of so weak a nature that it will not bear the inquiry of even the most common understanding. Some people, perhaps will think it not unlikely that, under these two successions of gods and god-men, is allegorically couched an obscure account of the Gold and Silver age of Greek writers, or of the first ages of the world before and after the deluge. But then how will they reconcile that infinite time during which the Japanese pretend that these two successions of spiritual beings governed the world, to that short number of years which passed since the creation, according to the divine account delivered to us in holy writ. The Japanese, it seems, would not be behind hand with the Egyptians, Chaldeans, Bramines, and others of their neighbours in the East; who all, pursuant to that pride and vanity which is natural to eastern nations, dated their origin as high as they could, and esteemed it glorious to show a long series of monarchs that ruled over them. But what they seem to have more particularly aimed at is to outdo their neighbours the Chinese; for they make Tensio Dai Dsin, the first progenitor of the Japanese nation, in their historical writings, many thousand years anterior to the first and fictitious, as they call him, founder of the Chinese nation, Sinkwosi, or, according to the Chinese pronunciation, Tien Hoamtsij. And lest even this should not be sufficient to clear them of all suspicion of being any ways descended from the Chinese, they prefix the succession of the first great celestial spirits, which they derive from the very beginning of the creation. They are, however, at a loss what to answer when asked how it came about that Awase Dsuno, the last of their terrestrial gods, a being endowed with so many excellent and supernatural qualities, as they ascribe to him, begot so poor and miserable a race as that of the present inhabitants of Japan. They have as little to say concerning the state of their country, and the history of their ancestors before the time of Sinmu, their first monarch. For this reason several of their own writers have ventured to call Japan, Atarasikokf, and Sinkokf, that is, New Country; as if it had been newly found out and peopled under the reign of their first emperor. Thus much is true, that the genuine Japanese history begins but with the reign of this first monarch, who lived about 660 years before Christ. And herein the Chinese are gone far beyond them, for they begun to write the history of their country at least 2000 years before; and they can show what I believe no other nation can boast of, a succession of monarchs, with an account of their lives, government, and remarkable actions, down to this time, for now upwards of 4000 years. It must be owned, however, that the Japanese nation must needs have existed, and lived in the country, a considerable time before their first Odai, Mikaddo, or Emperor; since, when he was raised to the throne, they were then already grown very numerous, and since, not long after, as is recorded in their histories, great wars arose among them, and many thousands perished by plague and famine; unless one would bring them over at once from another country, or out of the earth like mushrooms, which is either impertinent or improbable. I am more inclined to believe that, from the time of their ancestors coming into the country, they led for many ages a wandering life, erring from place to place, with their families and cattle, which the very disposition of the country, divided by mountains, seas, and rivers, seems to have required; till the happy Ninus Dsin Mu Ten Oo civilized and brought them into better order, and became himself, whether by force or choice, their first monarch. Since that time they have been accurate and faithful in writing the history of their country, and the lives and reigns of their monarchs. To conclude, as Dsitsijno Mikotto is by them believed to have been the greatest of the first succession of celestial spirits, and Tensio Dai Dsin, that of the second of god-men, so they look upon Sin Mu Ten Oo as the greatest of the third race of the now living inhabitants; in whose family the hereditary right to the crown, with a more than human authority, was continued down to Kinsen Kiwotei, the present one hundred and fourteenth Mikaddo, that is 2360 years, computing to the year of Christ 1700. I say, the hereditary right to the crown; for the government of the empire itself is of late gone over into secular hands, as will be shown more particularly in another place.

CHAPTER V.

OF THE CLIMATE OF JAPAN, AND ITS PRODUCE AS TO MINERALS.

Japan boasts of a happy and healthful climate. The air is very inconstant and subject to frequent changes, in the winter loaded with snow, and liable to sharp frosts, in the summer on the contrary, particularly during the dog-days, intolerably hot. It rains frequently throughout the whole year; but with the greatest profusion in the months of June and July, which are for this reason called Satsuki, that is Water-months. However, the rainy season in Japan is far from coming up to that regularity which is observed in other and hotter parts of the East Indies. Thunder and lightning happen very frequently.

The sea, which encompasses the islands of Japan, is very rough and stormy; which, with the many rocks, cliffs, and shoals, above and under water, make its navigation very dangerous. It hath two remarkable and dangerous whirlpools. The one is called Faisaki, and lies near Simabara, below Amakusa. It is dangerous, chiefly when the tide turns; for in high water it becomes even with the surface of the sea, but as soon as the tide begins to go out, it also, after some violent turnings, falls in of a sudden, as I was informed, to the depth of fifteen fathom, swallowing up with great force what ships, boats, and other things happen at that fatal juncture to come within its reach, which are dashed to pieces against the rocks at the bottom. The shattered pieces sometimes remain under water, sometimes they are thrown out again at some German miles' distance. The other whirlpool lies near the coasts of the province Kijnokuni. It is called Narrotto; and from the neighbourhood of the province of Awa, Awano Narrotto, which signifies, "the rushing of Awa," because it rushes with a great boisterous noise about a small rocky island, which is by the violence of the motion kept in perpetual trembling. This, though of a formidable aspect, is yet esteemed less dangerous than the other, because its noise being heard at a considerable distance, it may be easily avoided. Japanese authors, especially poets, frequently allude in their writings to the wonderful nature and motion of this Narrotto, as do also the priests in the pulpit.

Water-spouts also are frequently observed to rise in the Japanese seas, and to turn towards the coasts. The Japanese fancy, that they are a kind of water dragons, with a long watery tail, flying up into the air with a swift and violent motion, for which reason they are by them called Tatsmaki, that is, "spouting dragons."

The soil of Japan in itself is, for the major part, mountainous, rocky, and barren, but through the indefatigable care and industry of the natives, it hath been made fruitful enough to supply them with all manner of necessaries, besides what the neighbouring sea affords of fish, crabs, and shells. Even the most rocky and uncultivated places yield their plants, fruits, and roots for the sustenance of the inhabitants, which their indigent ancestors by experience learned to dress and to prepare, so as not only to make them fit for food, but likewise pleasing and agreeable to the taste. Considering this, and the frugal way of living of the Japanese in general, we need not wonder, that this vast and populous empire is so abundantly provided with all the necessaries of human life, that as a particular world, which Nature seems purposely to have separated from the rest of the globe, by encompassing it with a rocky and tempestuous sea, it easily can subsist of itself without any assistance from foreign countries, as long as arts and agriculture are followed and improved by the natives.

The country besides is plentifully supplied with fresh water, there being very many fountains, lakes, and rivers up and down the empire. Some of the rivers in particular, are so large and rapid, by reason either of the steep high mountains and rocks, where they arise, or because of the profuse showers of rain, which fall frequently, that they are not to be passed over without danger, the rather, since some are so impetuous as to bear no bridges. Some of the most famous rivers are, 1. Ujingava, that is, the River Ujio. It is about a quarter of a German mile (or an English mile and a half) broad, and there being no bridge laid over it, it must be forded through. The force and rapidity with which this river falls down from the mountains is such, that even when the water is low, and scarce knee-deep, five strong men, well acquainted with the bed of it, must be employed to ford a horse through; which with the many large stones lying at the bottom, makes the passage equally difficult and dangerous. The people, whose business it is to ford passengers through this and other such-like rivers, lest they should not take due care, are, by the laws of the country, made answerable for their lives. This is the reason why so few accidents happen. 2. The river Oomi is famous for its surprising beginning; for it is recorded in Japanese histories, that it sprung up of a sudden in one night in the year before Christ 285. It borrowed its name from the province where it arises. 3. The river Askagava is remarkable, for that the depth of its bed alters perpetually, on which account it is frequently alluded to by Japanese authors, chiefly poets.

Japan is very much subject to earthquakes, which happen so frequently, that the natives dread them no more than we Europeans do an ordinary storm of thunder and lightning. They are of opinion, that the cause of earthquakes is a huge large whale's creeping under ground, and that they signify nothing. Sometimes, however, the shakes are so violent, and last so long, that whole cities are thereby destroyed, and many thousands of the inhabitants buried under the ruins. Such a dreadful accident happened, as Father Lewis de Froes relateth (*in Opere de Rebus Japonicis collecto à Joh. Hayo*), in the year 1586, he himself being then in Japan.* The like accidents happened frequently since that time. In 1704, I had a letter from Batavia, from a friend of mine, then lately arrived from Japan, wherein among other things, he gave me an account of such a violent shock, which happened there in 1703, whereby, and by a great fire which broke out at the same time, almost the whole city of Jedo, and the imperial palace itself, were destroyed and laid in ashes, and upwards of 200,000 inhabitants buried under the ruins. It is remarkable, that some particular places in Japan are observed to be free from all manner of successions. The Japanese reason variously upon this phenomenon. Some attribute it to the holiness and sanctity of the place, and to the powerful protection of its genius, or tutelar god. Others are of opinion, that these places are not shook, because they immediately repose upon the unmoved centre of the earth. The fact itself is not called in question; and there are noted for having this singular privilege, the islands of Gotho; the small island Siknbusima, on which stands a most stately temple of Bonzes, being one of the first that was built in the country; the large mountain Kojasan near Miaco, famous for the number of its convents, monasteries, and monks, besides some few others.

* The effects of this earthquake were so stupendous and dreadful, that I could not forbear, with the reader's leave, to insert at length, the account which F. Lewis de Froes gives of it, in a letter dated at Simonofeki, in the province Nagutto, October 15, 1586. His words are: "In the year of Christ 1586, Japan was shook by such dreadful earthquakes, that the like was never known before. From the province Sacajo, as far as Miaco, the earth trembled for forty days successively. In the town of Sacaja sixty houses were thrown down. At Nagafuma, a small town of about a thousand houses, in the kingdom Oomi, the earth gaped and swallowed up one half of that place; the other half was destroyed by a fire. Another place in the province Facata, much frequented by merchants, and likewise called Nagafama by the natives, after it had been violently shook for some days, was at last swallowed up by the sea; the waters rising so high that they overflowed the coasts, washed away the houses, and whatever they met with; drowned the inhabitants, and left no footstep of that once rich and populous town, but the place on which the castle stood, and even that under water. A strong castle in the kingdom of Mino, built at the top of a high hill, after several violent shocks, sunk down and disappeared on a sudden, the earth gaping, that not the least footstep remained, a lake quickly filling the place where the foundations of the castle had been. Another accident of this kind happened in the province Ikoja. Many more gaps and openings were observed up and down the empire, some of which were so wide and deep, that guns being fired into them, the balls could not be heard to reach the other end, and such a stench and smoke issued out of them, that people would not venture to travel that way. Quabacundono (who was afterwards called Taicosama) resided at Sacomot, in the castle Achec, when these earthquakes begun, but they growing too thick and violent, he retired hastily to Osacca. His palaces were violently shaken, but not thrown down."

The greatest riches of the Japanese soil, and those wherein this empire exceeds most known countries, consist in all sorts of minerals and metals, particularly in gold, silver, and copper. The many hot wells in several parts of the empire, and the several smoking and burning mountains, show what a stock of sulphur, which is the mother and main ingredient of mineral and metallic bodies, is hid in the bowels of the earth, besides the vast quantities of this substance dug up in several places. Not far from Firando, where we had our factories and warehouses before we removed to Nagasaki, lies a small rocky island (one of those which, by reason of their great number, are called by the Japanese Kiukin Sima, that is, the ninety-nine islands), which though never so small, and encompassed by the sea, hath been burning and trembling for many centuries. Another small island opposite to Satzuma, which is by the Japanese called Fuogo, which name they borrowed from the Portuguese, and retained ever since; and which is marked in our maps by the name of Vulcanus, hath an ignivomous mountain, which hath been likewise burning, at different intervals, for many ages. At the top of a mountain in the province Figo is to be seen a large cavern, formerly the mouth of a volcano, but the flame ceased of late, probably for want of combustible matter. In the same province there is another place called Aso; famous for a temple called Asa no Gongen, or the "Temple of the jealous God of Aso," not far from which there is an almost perpetual flame issuing out of the top of a mountain, and more visible in the night than it is in the day time. Another burning mountain lies in the province Tsikunsen, not far from a place called Kujanosse. It was formerly a coal-mine, which through the carelessness of the miners accidentally took fire, and continued burning ever since. Sometimes a black stench and smoke is observed to issue out of the top of the famous mountain Fesi, in the province Suruga, which in height is surpassed only by the Pic of Teneriffe, but in shape and beauty hath, I think, not its equal; the top of it is covered with everlasting snow, which being, as it frequently is, blown up into flocks by the violence of the wind, and dispersed about, represents, as it were, a smoking hat. The Japanese histories mention that formerly the top of it burnt, but that upon a new opening which was made by the violence of the fire at the side of the mountain, the flame ceased soon after. Unseen is a deformed, large, but not very high mountain, near Simabara. At all times the top of it is bare, whitish from the colour of the sulphur, and withal resembling a *caput mortuum*, or burnt out massa. It smokes little; however, I could discern the smoke arising from it at three miles distance. Its soil is burning hot in several places, and besides so loose and spongious, that a few spots of ground excepted, on which stand some trees, one cannot walk over it without continual fear, for the crackling, hollow noise perceived under foot. Its sulphurous smell is so strong that for many miles round there is not a bird to be seen; when it rains, the water bubbles up, and the whole mountain seems then as it were boiling. Many cold springs and hot baths arise on and about it. Among others, there is a famous hot bath which they believe to be an infallible cure for the venereal disease, if the patient for several days together goes in but for a few moments a day and washes himself in it. He must begin the cure with another hot bath, not quite so strong, called Obamma, situate a few leagues off; and all the while he uses the waters, he must keep to a hot, warming diet, and, as soon as he comes out of the bath, go to bed, and, covering himself very well, endeavour to sweat. Not far from this hot bath is a monastery of the sect of Tendai. The monks of this place have given peculiar names to each of the hot springs arising in the neighbourhood, borrowed from their quality, from the nature of the froth a-top, or the sediment at bottom, and from the noise they make as they come out of the ground; and they have assigned them as purgatories for several sorts of tradesmen and handicraftsmen, whose professions seem to bear some relation to any of the qualities above mentioned. Thus, for instance, they lodge the deceitful beer and sackibrewers at the bottom of a deep muddy spring; the cooks and pastrycooks in another, which is remarkable for its white froth; wranglers and quarrelsome people in another, which rushes out of the ground with a frightful murmuring noise, and so on. After this manner imposing upon the blind and superstitious vulgar, they squeeze large sums of money out of them, making them believe that by their prayers and intercession they may be delivered from these places of torment after death. In that dreadful persecution which was raised in Japan against the Christian religion, and which hath not its equal in history, amongst innumerable other torments inflicted on the new converts to make them abandon their newly embraced faith and return to the Paganism of their fathers, they were brought hither and tortured with the hot waters of this place. Of other hot baths in Japan, that called Obamma is one of the most eminent, and most efficacious. It lies to the west of the mountain Usen, about three miles off, and is said to have extraordinary virtues in curing several external and internal distempers. The province Figo hath several hot springs, about which grow, as I was informed, camphire trees of an uncommon size, hollow and full of water. The chief and most eminent for its virtues is a hot bath not far from the above-mentioned temple Asano Gongen. There are also several hot springs in the province Fisen, one for instance in the village Takijo, another in the village Urisino. Both would prove very beneficial in curing several distempers, if the natives did but know how to use them. I observed it in all Asiatic countries which I passed through in my travels, that the natives use the hot baths seldom more than three or at furthest eight days, by which, probably enough, they will find some benefit and relief, which they are too apt to mistake for an actual cure, and in case of a relapse to lay all the fault on the waters.

The greatest quantity of sulphur is brought from the province Satzuma. It is dug up in a small neighbouring island, which from the great plenty it affords of this substance, is called Iwogasima, or the Sulphur Island. It is not above a hundred years since they first ventured thither. It was thought before that time to be wholly inaccessible, and by reason of the thick smoke which was observed continually to arise from it, and of the several spectres and other frightful uncommon apparitions people fancied to see there chiefly in the night, it was believed to be a dwelling-place of devils, till at last a resolute and courageous man offered himself, and obtained leave accordingly, to go and to examine the state and situation of it. He chose fifty resolute fellows for this expedition, who upon going on shore found neither hell nor devils, but a large flat spot of ground at the top, which was so thoroughly covered with sulphur that wherever they walked a thick smoke issued from under their feet. Ever since that time this island brings in to the Prince of Satzuma about twenty chests of silver per annum, arising only from the sulphur dug up there, besides what he gets by the trees and timber growing along the shore. The country of Simabara, particularly about the hot baths above mentioned, affords also a fine pure native sulphur, which, however, the inhabitants dare not venture to dig up, for fear of offending the tutelar genius of the place, they having found upon trial that he was not willing to spare it. I pass over in silence several other places, for want of a thorough information.

Gold, the richest of all metals, is dug up in several provinces of the Japanese empire. The greatest quantity of it is melted out of its own ore. Some they wash out of gold sand. Some small quantity also is contained in the copper. The emperor claims the supreme jurisdiction of all the gold mines, and indeed all other mines in the empire, none of which may be opened and worked without his express leave and consent. Of the produce of all the mines which are worked, he claims two-thirds, and one-third is left to the Lord of the Province in which the mine lies; the latter, however, as they reside upon the spot, know how to improve their third parts so as to share pretty equally with the emperor. The richest gold ore, and which yields the finest gold, is dug up in Sado, one of the northern provinces in the great island Nipon. Some of the veins there were formerly so rich, that one catti of the ore yielded one, and sometimes two thails of gold. But of late, as I was informed, the veins there and in most other mines, not only run scarcer, but yield not nearly the quantity of gold they did formerly, which, we were told, was the occasion, amongst other reasons, of the late strict orders relating to the trade and commerce with us, and the Chinese. There is also a very rich gold sand in the same province, which the Prince causes to be washed for his own benefit, without so much as giving notice of it, much less part of the profit, to the court at Jedo. After the gold mines of Sado, those of Surunga were always esteemed the richest, for besides that this province yielded at all times a great quantity of gold ore, there is some gold contained even in the copper dug up there. Among the gold mines of the province Satzuma there was one so rich that a catti of the ore was found upon trial to yield from four to six thails of gold, for which reason the emperor hath given strict orders not to work it, for fear so great a treasure should be exhausted too soon. A mountain on the Gulf Ookus, in the district of

Omura, which had leaned on one side for a considerable time, happened some years ago to fall over into the sea, and there was found at the bottom of the place where it stood so rich a gold sand that, as I was credibly informed, it yielded one half of pure gold. It lay somewhat deep, and was to be fetched up by divers. But this rich harvest lasted not long, for a few years after, in a great storm and extraordinary high tide, the sea overflowed all that spot of ground, and covered at once those inestimable riches with mud and clay to the depth of some fathoms. The poor people in the neighbourhood still busy themselves washing the sand about this mountain, which contains some gold, but in so inconsiderable a quantity, that they can hardly get a livelihood by it. There is another gold mine in the province Tsikungo, not far from a village called Tossino, but so full of water that they cannot go on with working it. However, the situation of the mine is such that by cutting the rock, and making an opening beneath the mouth of the mine, the water might be easily drawn off. This was attempted accordingly; but as they went to work there arose of a sudden such a violent storm of thunder and lightning, that the workmen were obliged to desist and to fly for shelter, which made the superstitious vulgar believe that the tutelar god and protector of the place, unwilling to have the bowels of the earth committed to his trust thus rifled, raised this storm purposely to make them sensible how much he was displeased at this undertaking. Nor was there any further attempt made since, for fear of provoking his anger and wrath still more. Such another accident, and which had the same effect, happened at the opening of a gold mine in the island Amakusa, for it was so suddenly filled with water, which broke out of the mountain and destroyed all the works, that the miners had scarce time to escape and to save their lives.

There are some silver mines in the province Bingo. Others, and these much richer, at a place called Kattami, in one of the northern provinces; others in other places, which I forbear mentioning for want of sufficient information. The two islands Ginsima and Kinsima, that is, gold and silver islands, which lie to the east of Japan, and which I had occasion to speak of in the fourth chapter of this book, deserve a place here, if it be true what the Japanese boast, and what their very names and characters seem to imply, of their wealth and riches.

Copper is the most common of all metals dug up in Japan, and the produce of copper mines enriches several provinces of this empire. It is at present dug up chiefly in the provinces of Surugu, Atsingo, and Kijnokuni. That of Kijnokuni is the finest, most malleable, and fittest for work of any in the world. That of Atsingo is coarse, and seventy cattis of it must be mixed with thirty cattis of the Kijnese to make it malleable and fit for use. That of Suruga is only exceedingly fine and without faults, but charged with a considerable quantity of gold, which the Japanese at present separate and refine much better than they did formerly, which occasions great complaints among the refiners and Brahmines upon the coasts of Cormandel. There are also some copper mines in the province of Satzuma, which the emperor very lately gave leave to work. All the copper is brought to Saccai, one of the five imperial towns, where it is refined and cast into small cylinders, about a span and a half long and a finger thick. As many of these cylinders as amount to one pickel, or 125lb. weight, are packed up into square wooden boxes, and sold to the Dutch from twelve to thirteen mass the pickel. It is one of the cheapest commodities the Dutch buy in Japan, and they carry on a great trade with it. There is besides a sort of coarser copper, which is cast into large, flat, roundish lumps, or cakes, and is bought a great deal cheaper than the other, as it is also much inferior in goodness and beauty. Brass is very scarce in Japan, and much dearer than copper, the calamine-stone being imported from Tunquin in flat cakes, and sold at a very good price.

The province of Bungo affords a small quantity of tin, which is so exceedingly fine and white, that it almost comes up to silver. There is but little use made of this metal in the country.

Iron is dug up only upon the confines of three provinces, Mimasaca, Bitsju, and Bisen; but it is found there in very large quantities. It is refined upon the spot, and cast into staffs, or cylinders, two spans long. Japanese merchants buy it at the place, and export it all over the empire. It is much of a price with copper, iron tools being full as dear or rather dearer than those of copper and brass. Such household goods, hooks, cramp-irons in buildings and ships, and other instruments, as are in other countries made of iron, are made in Japan, of copper or brass. They do not dress their victuals in brass pans, but have a particular sort of kettles or pans which are made of a composition of iron, and are pretty thin. The old ones of this sort are very much esteemed, and bought at a great rate, they having somewhat particular in their shape and make, which at present they have lost the art to imitate.

They have no want of coals in Japan, they being dug up in great quantity in the province Tsikusen about Kujanisse, and in most northern provinces.

Salt is made of sea-water in several maritime provinces. They make it thus. They close in a spot of ground, and fill it with fine loose sand; then they pour the sea-water upon it, and let it dry. This they repeat several times, till they think the sand is sufficiently saturated with salt. Then they take it out and put it into a large trough, with holes at the bottom, and putting fresh sea-water upon it, let it filtrate through the sand. The lye is boiled to a good consistence, and the salt thus obtained is calcined in earthen pots, till it becomes white, and fit for use and sale.

Agates, of several sorts, some extraordinary fine, of a bluish colour not unlike sapphires, as also some cornelians and jaspers, are brought from the mountain Tsugaar, upon the northern extremities of the great province Osju, opposite to the country of Jedo.

Pearls, by the Japanese called kainetamma, which is as much as to say, shell-jewels, or jewels taken out of shells, are found almost everywhere about Saikokf in oysters, and several other seashells. Everybody is at liberty to fish them. Formerly the natives had little or no value for them, till they were apprised of it by the Chinese, who would pay good prices for them, the Chinese women being very proud of wearing necklaces, and other ornaments of pearls. The largest and finest pearls are found in a small sort of oyster, called akoja, which is not unlike the Persian pearl-shell, much of the same shape, both valves shutting close, about a hand broad, exceeding thin and brittle, black, smooth, and shining on the outside, within pretty rough and unequal, of a whitish colour, and glittering like mother of pearl. These pearl-shells are found only in the seas about Satzuma, and in the gulf of Omura. Some of the pearls weigh from four to five condonins, and these are sold for a hundred cohns a-piece. The inhabitants of the Riuku islands buy most of those which are found about Satzuma, they trading to that province. Those on the contrary which are found in the gulf of Omura, are sold chiefly to the Chinese and Tunquinese, and it is computed that they buy for about 3000 thails a year. This great profit occasioned the strict orders which were made not long ago by the Princes both of Satzuma and Omura, importing, that for the future there should be no more of these oysters sold in the market with other oysters, as had been done formerly. I procured some in private from Omura, not without great difficulty. I was told a very extraordinary thing of this sort of pearls, and strongly assured of the truth of the fact, which is, that they have somewhat of a prolific quality, by virtue of which, when some of the largest are put into a box full of a peculiar Japanese cheek varnish, made of another shell called Takaragai (which I shall describe in another place); one or two young pearls will grow on the sides, and when come to maturity, which they do in about three years time, drop off. These pearls, by reason of their scarcity, are kept in private families, and the possessors seldom part with them, unless upon urgent necessity. All this, however, I deliver only upon hearsay, having myself seen none of this sort of pearl. There is another shell which sometimes yields pearls, found plentifully upon all the Japanese coasts, and called by the natives awabi. It is an univalve, in shape almost oval, pretty deep, open on one side, where it sticks to the rocks and to the bottom of the sea, with a row of holes, which grow bigger the nearer they come to the circumference of the shell; rough and limy on its outward surface, frequently with corals, sea-plants, and other shells sticking to it; on the inside of an exquisite mother of pearl's glimmering, sometimes raised into whitish pearly excrescences, which are likewise observed in the common Persian pearl-shell. A great lump of flesh fills the cavity of this shell, for which sole reason they are looked for by fishermen, being a very good commodity for the market. They have an instrument made on purpose to pull them off from the sides of the rocks, to which they stick close. Another shell, the name of which I could not learn, yields a very large pearl, which sometimes weighs from five to six condonins, but they are of a dirty yellow colour, ill-shaped, and worth but little. A pretty good sort of pearl is sometimes observed to grow in the very flesh of a shell, which is called by the natives tairuggi, and is found in the gulf of Arima, between Janagava and Isafaje. It is a flat sort of a shell, oblong, almost triangular, a little crooked on each side, about a span and a half long, and a span broad; where broadest, thin, transparent, smooth, and polished like horn, but very brittle.

Naphtha, of a reddish colour, by the Japanese called tsutsono abra, which signifies red earth, is found in a river of the province Jetsingo. It is taken up in such places where the water hath little or no run, and the natives burn it in lamps, instead of oil.

Some ambergris is found upon the coasts of Satzuma, and of the Riuku islands. A much greater quantity comes from the coasts of Khumano, as they call them, whereby must be understood the southern coasts of Kijnokuni, Isje, and some neighbouring provinces. It is found chiefly in the intestines of a whale, which is caught frequently upon the Japanese coasts, and is by the natives called fiakfiro, that is, the hundred-fathom fish, because of the length of its intestines, which is supposed to equal that number of fathoms. It is found, as I observed, in the intestines of this whale, mixed with chalky limy excrements, almost as hard as stone, and it is from the hardness of these excrements, they conjecture, upon dissecting, whether or no they are like to meet with ambergris. The natives have given a very despicable name to this precious commodity. The ambergris, as it is torn off by the waves from the bottom of the sea, and thrown upon the coasts, before it is swallowed by the whales, is a deformed, flat, slimy substance, and withal of a very disagreeable ungrateful smell. People that find it thus floating on the surface of the water, or lying upon the coasts, take several small pieces, squeeze and press them close together, into the form of a round ball, which as it grows dry, becomes also more solid and weighty. Others mix and knead it with meal, or flower of rice-husks, by which means they not only increase the quantity, but heighten and better the colour. However, the ambergris thus adulterated is easily known; for if you take any quantity and burn it, there will remain a coal, proportionable to the quantity of the stuff mixed with it. It is observed, besides, that the worms get quickly into this spurious sort of ambergris. Others adulterate it by mixing it with a certain powdered rosin of a very agreeable scent, but this cheat also is easily discovered, for upon burning a piece of it, the mixture of rosin will evidently appear by the very colour, smell, and quality of the smoke. The Chinese have another way of trying whether it be genuine; they scrape some of it very fine upon hot boiling tea-water; if genuine, it will dissolve and diffuse equally, which the adulterated sort doth not. The natives use it no otherwise but as an ingredient of other well-scented species, in order, as they say, to fix their volatile smell. In the main they value it but little, and it is owing entirely to the Dutch and Chinese, who would buy it up at any rate, that they have now learnt to prize it. And yet everybody is at liberty to take it up, where he finds it, and to sell it as his own property. During my stay in Japan, there was a piece to be sold of 140 cattis weight, and of a greyish colour. It was too large for any single person to purchase, for which reason they sold it by retail, from sixty to seventy thails a catti. I bought myself for about thirty thails of that which was blackest.

All sorts of submarine plants, shrubs, corals, stones, mushrooms, sea-fans, corallines, fuci, algæ, and the like, as also shells of all kinds, are found plentifully in the Japanese seas, no ways inferior in beauty to those found about Amboina, and the spice islands. But the natives value them so little, that they won't be at the trouble of looking for them, and if by chance they happen to fish them up amongst other things, their way is to carry them to the next temple, or chapel of Jebus, who is the Neptune of the country, thinking that it is not an unpleasing offering to this god, whom they look upon, and worship, as the protector of sea-faring people.

It remains to say something of the minerals and mineral substances, which have not as yet been found in Japan, and are imported from beyond sea. Antimony and sal-ammoniac are absolutely wanted, nor are their qualities and uses in the least known to the natives. Quicksilver and borax are imported by the Chinese. I met, however, with two sorts of borax, growing naturally in Japan, but they are so thoroughly mixed with heterogeneous substances, that the inhabitants don't think it worth their while to pick them up. Sublimate mercury is very much asked for by some private people, who will give an extravagant price for it. They use it as the chief ingredient of a mercurial water, which is in great vogue among them for the cure of ulcers, cancers, and other cutaneous diseases. Native cinnabar is by them given inwardly, in several distempers. The artificial cinnabar they make use of for a colour. Both are imported from China. The buying and selling of this commodity is in the hands of private merchants, who monopolise it by virtue of letters patent from the Emperor. The native cinnabar in general is of a beautiful red colour, but some of it is so exquisitely fine, that it is sold for more than its weight in silver.

CHAPTER VI.

OF THE FERTILITY OF THE COUNTRY, AS TO PLANTS.

It is not in the least surprising, considering either the peculiar happiness of the Japanese climate, or the industry of its laborious inhabitants, that the country affords so large a stock, and such an infinite variety of plants and fruits, both wild and cultivated, as it may deservedly boast of. Most of these their forefathers, indigent and frugal as they were, used for their food and sustenance. In succeeding ages, as wealth and riches increased, the taste also became more refined, and their tables more sumptuous and magnificent. In this present chapter I will take notice only of such plants as are of a more extensive use, and as to the rest refer the more curious reader to my Amœnitates Exoticæ, wherein I have given a catalogue, and begun a more accurate and botanical description of them.

Among the trees the mulberry-tree deservedly claims the first place; for although its fruits, both black and white, be altogether insipid, and not fit for eating, yet this defect is sufficiently made good by the extensive usefulness of its leaves, which are the common food of silkworms. It grows in most parts of Japan, but in great plenty in the northern provinces, where many cities and villages subsist almost wholly upon the silk manufactures, though the silk wove there be not of the finest. The best and most curious stuffs are made by the banished grandees in the island Fatsinsio, weaving being their chief amusement; but they make them of fine foreign silk. The kadsi, or paper-tree, is of the mulberry kind: though it grows wild in the country, yet they transplant and cultivate it in several places, by reason of its great usefulness. It is observed to grow with surprising quickness, and to spread its branches very far. It affords a great quantity of bark, out of which they make paper, as also ropes, matches, stuffs, cloth, and several other things.

The urusi or varnish-tree, is another of the noblest and most useful trees of this country. It affords a milky juice, which the Japanese make use of to varnish, and as we call it, to japan all their household-goods, dishes, and plates of wood, and this from the Emperor down to the meanest peasant. For even at court, and at the imperial table, services of lackered ware are preferred to those of gold and silver. Another kind of varnish-tree, with narrow leaves, is called faasi: it grows wild on hills and mountains. It affords a small quantity of milk, and that too of a very bad sort, and therefore the natives think it hardly worth their while to gather it. The true urusi is of a kind peculiar to this country. It grows in the provinces Figo and Tsikoku; but that which grows in Jamatto is reckoned the fittest for use, and to yield a better sort of varnish than it doth anywhere else out of this province. The Indian varnish-tree, which I take to be the true anacardinus, is a tree quite different from the urusi of the Japanese. At Siam it is called rack-tree. It grows and bears fruits in most eastern countries, but is observed to afford none of its milky juice to the west of the river Ganges, whether because of the barrenness of the soil, or through the carelessness and ignorance of the natives, who do not know how to manage its culture. The greatest quantity of the milk of this Indian varnish-tree is brought from the kingdoms of Siam and Cambodia, and sold very cheap all over the East Indies. It is imported even into Japan, where the natives use it to lacker things of little value, and also as an ingredient of their scarcer and better sort of varnish.

Lauri, or bay-trees, of several kinds grow in Japan. That which bears red berries is a cannelifera spuria, or rather, by reason of its viscosity, a cassia lignea. It resembles exactly the cinnamon-tree, both in its shape, and in the figure and substance of its leaves. But the bark falls far short of that agreeable sweetness which is peculiar only to the bark of the true cinnamon, and it hath more of the aromatic sharpness of a costus. The imperfection I take to be owing entirely to the quality of the soil wherein it grows; for I observed also, that the bark of the

Malabarian, Sumatran, and Javan cinnamon-trees (which latterly is wholly neglected), bath not near that eminent degree of sharpness and agreeableness to the taste, which the true Ceylonese cinnamon is so much and so deservedly esteemed for; that besides it is apt either to lose its aromatic quality in a short time, or that its sharp pungent particles are so wrapt up in a viscous substance, as to make it altogether unworthy of bearing the very name of cinnamon, a substance which is supposed to yield a fine, pleasant, fragrant oil, which no cassia ligoea ever will.

The kua, or camphire-tree, is also of the laurel-kind. It bears black and purple berries. The camphire is prepared by the country-people in the province Satzuma, and the islands Gotho, by a simple decoction of the roots and wood cut into small pieces. It is extremely cheap, and 50 to 100 cattis of the Japanese boiled camphire may be had for one single catti of the true Bornean camphire, which is said to be a natural substance gathered on the stumps of old camphire-trees in the island of Borneo, upon incisions made between the bark and wood.

Tsiauoki, that is the tea shrub, is one of the most useful plants growing in Japan, and yet it is allowed no other room but round the borders of rice and corn fields, and in other barren places, unfit for culture of other things. The common drink of the Japanese is brewed of the larger leaves of this shrub; but the young and tender leaves dried, powdered, and mixed in a cup of hot water into a sort of soup, are drank in houses of people of quality before and after their meals; and it is the custom of the country to present friends that come to visit them, with one or more dishes of tea, both when they come and go.

Sansio is a middle-sized tree, with prickles. They make use of its bark and husks instead of pepper or ginger, and they eat the leaves by reason of their pleasant aromatic taste, as they do also the riches, which grow in the country.

There are three different sorts of fig-trees growing in Japan. One is called kaki, if otherwise it may be called a fig-tree, it differing from it in several particulars. It grows very plentifully in all parts of the empire. It is a very ugly deformed sort of a tree to look at, much like a short old apple-tree. It hath long oval leaves, without notches. The fruit resembles a reddish apple, both in shape and colour, and its fleshy part hath the taste of a delicate fig. The seed is of a hard and almost stony substance, and not unlike gourd-seeds. It is no less commendable for its great fruitfulness, than it is for its extensive use, for the fruits of it dried afford a pleasant and agreeable food for rich and poor. The Chinese preserve them with sugar. The second sort of figs is not unlike that which grows with us in Europe, only it grows on a tree, with broad, oblong, rough leaves, without notches. Our European fig-tree makes up the third sort. It was brought into the country, and planted there by the Portuguese. It bears a very large fruit, bigger than ours, and I think better tasted. But it is very scarce. I need not mention here anything of the sycomorus, or wild fig-tree, because its fruits are not eat in the country, though it grows there very plentifully.

Chesnut-trees grow in great plenty in Japan, particularly in the province Tsikusen, and they bear chesnuts much larger and better than ours. Apple-trees, such as we have them in Europe, they know nothing of. Nor have they more than one sort of pears, of that kind, which we call winter pears. They grow in great plenty, and come to an extraordinary bigness, the least weighing seldom less than a pound: but they are not fit to be eaten raw.

Walnut-trees grow chiefly in the northern provinces. In the same provinces grows a certain tall kind of tarus, called by the Japanese kaja, with oblong nuts, inclosed in a fleshy pulp, and not unlike, in bigness and shape, to the arrack-nut. These nuts are not very agreeable to the taste when fresh, though taken out of the pulp, for they have something astringent in them: they taste better when dried. They have a gentle purging quality, which is owing to their sweet oil, and are, for their many medicinal virtues, served at table along with the dessert. The oils expressed out of these nuts is very sweet and agreeable, and tastes not unlike the oil of sweet almonds. It is much commended for its medicinal virtues, and also made use of to dress victuals. The smoke of the kernels of these nuts is the chief ingredient of the best and dearest Japanese ink.

Another sort of nuts, called Ginau, as big as large pistaches, grow very plentifully almost everywhere in Japan, on a fine tall tree, the leaves of which are not unlike the large leaves of an adianthum. The Japanese call it Itsionoki. The nuts afford plenty of oil, which is also much commended for several uses. As to a more accurate description of this tree, I refer the reader to the Amœuitates Exoticæ, p. 812. There are two sorts of oaks grow in the country, both different from ours. The acorns of the larger sort are boiled and eat by the common people. The fruit of the naatsme, or paliurus of Prosp. alpinus, as it grows in the country, is extraordinary good, and I think much larger than I saw it anywhere else. Pome-citron trees are to be seen only in the gardens of the curious. Oranges and lemons grow very plentifully, and of different sorts. That sort of lemons which is reckoned the best is called micau. It resembles a peach, both in shape and bigness, and hath an excellent aromatic flavour, but tastes somewhat sour. Another sort they call kinkan. It is much scarcer, in shape and bigness not unlike a nutmeg, and exceedingly sour. It grows on a shrub, rather than a tree, and is much used in dressing their victuals, and in what they call atsiaer.

They plant but few vines, because they observe that the grapes would not easily ripen. Brambleberries and raspberries, are not very agreeable to the taste. Strawberries are entirely insipid and not eat. With peaches, apricots, and plums, they are plentifully supplied. Of plums, particularly, they have two sorts, both different from ours, one white, the other purple, both granulated like mulberries, and ingredients of what they call atsiaer. Cherry-trees, and the like, are kept only for the sake of the flowers, as are also by some the apricot and plum-trees, which they improve much by culture, so that the flowers become as big as roses, and in the spring, when they are in full blossom, afford a most delightful sight about their temples, in their gardens and walks, the trees being thick covered with the flowers, as with snow.

Firs and cypress-trees are the most common trees in their woods and forests. There are several different sorts of both. Houses and ships are built of the wood, of which are made also all sorts of household-goods, as cabinets, trunks, boxes, tubs and the like. The branches, and what falls down, serve for fuel and fire-wood. The common people burn also the nuts and leaves, which fall down from the trees, and gathering the same daily they keep the ground and roads neat and clean. For ornament-sake, they are planted in rows along the roads, and over the ridges of hills and mountains, which makes travelling very pleasant. The natives, as they improve every inch of ground, take care to plant them in sandy and barren places, which are good for nothing else. No firs nor cypress-trees may be cut down, without leave from the magistrate of the place; and lest the felling of them should in time too much prejudice their growth they must always plant young ones instead of those they cut down.

Bamboos are very common, and of great use here, as everywhere in the Indies. Several sorts of household goods, baskets, matches, and other things are made of them, as are also gutters and spouts, and the walls of houses. A particular sort of bamboo grows in the province Oomi, which the Dutch export by the name of rottang, and sell for walking canes. Both firs and bamboos are in great esteem among the Japanese, for their constant verdure; and the superstitious believe that they have no small influence over the happy occurrences of human life. The temple-walks, and other holy places, are adorned with them, chiefly upon their festivals and other solemn days; and they make frequent allusions to them in their emblematical and poetical writings, particularly in congratulatory poems: for they are of opinion, that they will subsist a long while, that common bamboos will stand several hundred years, and that the common fir, which they call matznoki, will come to the age of a thousand, that then it will bend down its branches towards the ground, as not being able to support itself any longer. And lest the truth of this assertion should be called in question, they show up and down the country some firs and bamboos of an uncommon size indeed, and pretended long standing. I have seen some extraordinary large ones myself.

Finoki and suggi are two sorts of cypress trees, yielding a beautiful light whitish wood, but nevertheless of a good substance, and remarkable for this singular quality, that it sucks in no water, and might well pass for cedar-wood. The emperor has sometimes forbidden the felling of these trees for any use whatsoever. But little regard is had to orders of this kind, particularly in those provinces which are remote from court, unless there be a very severe punishment put upon transgression thereof. Ksamaki, that is, a stinking maki-tree; asinoki, a sort of oak; and jusmoki, that is, iron-tree, so called from the uncommon hardness of its wood, are all very common trees. Most houses are built of the wood of them. Fatzmoki, a tree growing about the city of Jeseri, and the root of the camphire-tree, afford the best and scarcest wood for cabinets, chests of drawers, and such sort of work, by reason of the curious running of its grain.

Japan, I think, may vie with most, if not all, known countries, for a great variety of beautiful plants and flowers, wherewith kind Nature has most liberally and curiously adorned its fields, hills, woods and forests. Some of these they transplanted into gardens, and improved by assiduity and culture to the utmost, and indeed to a surprising degree of perfection. It is foreign to my present purpose to enumerate and to describe all those I met withal during my stay in the country. I reserve this for another work, and will here confine myself barely to mention some of the chief. Tsubacki is a pretty large shrub, bearing flowers not unlike roses. It grows in woods and hedges, it hath many beautiful varieties, of which, in the Japanese language, copious as it is, there are 900 names, if it be true what the natives report. Satsuki is another shrub, with lily-flowers. Of this, the natives say, there are upwards of an hundred varieties to be met with in gardens. The two kinds, which grow wild, one with purple, the other with incarnate flowers, are a great ornament to hills and fields in the proper season, affording a sight pleasing beyond expression. Sakanandsio is another shrub with lily-flowers, but much larger than the former. It is also much scarcer, and there are three varieties of it.

Momidsi is a kind of maple. It is so called from the purple colour of its leaves. There are two varieties of it, which differ one from another only in this particular, that the leaves of one turn purple in the spring, and of the other in autumn. Both afford to the eye a very curious sight. The fasi-tree is also said to change the colour of its leaves into a fine purple in autumn.

There are two varieties of feverfews (matricariæ) and lilies growing in this country. The first—the flowers of which art and culture hath improved to the bigness of roses—are the chief ornament of houses and gardens, the others of desert and uncultivated places. Nor hath Nature been less kind with regard to the narcissus, flower-de-lys, clove gilliflowers, and the like. But one thing I cannot help observing, which is, that these several flowers fall as short of others of their kind growing in other countries, in strength and agreeableness of smell, as they exceed them in the exquisite beauty of their colours. The same holds true with regard to most fruits growing in Japan, which are far from coming up to the pleasant aromatic taste of those which grow in China, and other eastern countries.

They cultivate as much hemp and cotton as they can spare ground in their fields. Sijro, or the wild hemp-nettle, grows plentifully in most uncultivated places. This plant makes good in some measure what want there is of hemp and cotton; for several sorts of stuffs, fine and coarse, are fabricated of it.

The seeds of the following plants afford their oil for several uses, both physical and domestic. Kiri is a very large but scarce tree. It hath leaves like burdock, flowers like the digitalis, set to a long stalk, and seeds resembling marshmallow seeds. The mikaddo, or ecclesiastical hereditary emperor, bears the leaf of this tree, with three flowering stalks, in his coat of arms. Abrasin is a middle-sized tree, with the leaves of a platanus. Its flowers resemble roses in shape and bigness, and the seeds are like the seeds of the ricinus, which made me call it ricinus arboreus folio alceæ. The assdiracht avicennæ, the teu-backi, above-mentioned, as also the urusi, faasi, and kainoki trees. The cotton shrub and plant. Sesami of two kinds, with white and black seeds. Of all the oils expressed out of the seeds of these several plants, only that of the sesamum and kai are made use of in the kitchen, and even these but sparingly, victuals being commonly dressed in this country without either butter or oil.

The Japanese are as good husbandmen as perhaps any people in the world. Nor indeed is it very surprising that they have made great improvements in agriculture, considering not only the extreme populousness of the country, but chiefly that the natives are denied all commerce and communication with foreigners, and must necessarily support themselves by their own labour and industry. Hence the laws on this head are very particular and severe. Not only the fields and flat country, which are seldom or never turned into meadows and pasture-ground, but likewise the hills and mountains, afford corn, rice, peas, pulse, and numberless edible plants. Every inch of ground is improved to the best advantage; and it was not without great admiration we beheld, in our journeys to and from court, hills and mountains, many inaccessible to cattle, which would lie wholly neglected in other countries, cultivated up to their tops. They are very dexterous and skilful in manuring their ground, which they do in various ways, and with many different substances, as I shall have occasion to show in several places of this history. Flat, low grounds are ploughed with oxen, steep and high ones by men: and both manured with human dung. As to rice in particular, which is the main food of the natives, what ground they can conveniently spare, and will admit of its culture, is turned into rice-fields, particularly low, flat land, which they can cut through by canals, and where they have a command of water, which surprisingly quickens the growth of this plant, it loving a wet, muddy soil. The Japanese rice accordingly is esteemed the best of all Asia, particularly what grows in the northern provinces, which will keep many years, and which for this reason they choose to fill their store-houses withal, having first washed it in muddy water and then dried it. All lands must be surveyed every year, before they are sown, by Kemme, as they call them, being sworn surveyors, who are very big of their skill in geometry, and have the privilege of wearing two swords, which is otherwise allowed to none but to the nobility and soldiers. When the harvest draws near they are surveyed once more, at which time it is computed what the whole crop is likely to amount to, which they do generally indeed by guess, but yet with a surprising accuracy, and thereby prevent the tenants cheating their landlords. If the harvest is like to prove extraordinary good, they cause a square piece of ground to be cut and threshed, and thence infer as to the whole. The landlords claim rokubu, six parts in ten, of all the produce of their land, whether rice, corn, wheat, peas, pulse, or other, and the tenant for his trouble and maintenance keeps sijbu, or four parts in ten. Such as hold lands of the crown give but four parts in ten to the emperor's stewards; the remainder is for themselves. For encouragement's sake, such as cultivate untilled ground, have the whole crop left them for the first two or three years. The ground in general is divided into three sorts:—1. Sso, the best; 2. Tsju, middling; and 3. Ge, poor ground. But they admit likewise of Dso no sio, next to the best; Dso no Isju, next to the middling; and Dso no Ge, next to the bad. Some regard is had as to the scot, the good or the bad quality of the soil; and it varies also considerably in different provinces, but in the main it amounts to six parts in ten. Among many excellent laws which relate to agriculture, they have one, by virtue o. which, whoever doth not cultivate his ground for the term of one year, forfeits his title and possession.

The chief produce of the fields which contributes most to the sustenance of life, is by the Japanese comprehended under the name of gokokf, that is, "the five fruits of the fields." It is by their good or bad growth they estimate the value of the ground; the fruitfulness of the year, and the wealth of the possessor. They make up the chief dishes at their meals, and make good the want there is of flesh-meat, which custom and religion forbid them to eat. The gokokf are, 1. Kome, or rice. There are several varieties of rice grow in the country. The best sort hath not its equal in the Indies. It is perfectly white, like snow, and so nourishing and substantial, that foreigners who are not used to it, can eat but little of it at a time. Boiled to a good consistence, they eat it at their meals instead of bread. Out of what remains from their yearly provision they brew a sort of strong fat beer, called sacki, but no more than they think their families shall have occasion for. Foreigners can export no more rice, or beer than what the magistrate will allow them. 2. Oomuggi, which is as much as to say, "great corn," is what we call barley. They feed their cattle and horses with it: some dress their victuals with the flour, and make cakes of it. There is a sort of barley grows in Japan, with purple-coloured ears, which, when ripe, are a curious ornament to the fields. 3. Koomuggi, that is, "small corn," is what we call wheat. It is extremely cheap, and I know of nothing they make of it, but a particular sort of cakes made of the flour. 4. Daidsu, that is, daidbeans, is a certain sort of beans about the bigness of Turkish peas, growing after the manner of lupins. They are next to the rice in use and esteem. Of the meal of these beans is made what they call midsu; a mealy pap, which they dress their victuals withal, as we do with butter. What they call soeju, is also made of it, which is a sort of an embamma, as they call it, which they eat at meals to get a good stomach. This soeju is exported by the Dutch, and brought even into Holland. I have described their way of making 't in my Amœnitates Exoticœ, p. 839, where the ·lant itself, bearing these beans, is figured and described. 5. Adsuki, or sodsu, that is, sobeans. They grow likewise after the manner of lupins, and are black, not unlike lentils, or the Indian cajan. The flour is baked with sugar into mansjo and other cakes. Besides the several sorts of gokokf just mentioned, the following plants are comprehended under the same name: awa, Indian corn (*panicum Indicum Tabern.*): kibi, or *milium vulgare nostras*, millet: fije, or *panicum vulgare juba minore semine nigricante:* and in general, all sorts of corn, and mami, that is peas and pulse.

Turnips grow very plentifully in the country, and exceeding large ones. Of all the produce of the fields they perhaps contribute most to the sustenance of the natives. But the fields being manured with human dung, they smell so strong that foreigners, chiefly Europeans, cannot bear them. The natives eat them raw, boiled, or pickled. Horse-radishes, carrots, gourds, melons, cucumbers, mala insana, fennel, and some sorts of lettuce, which with us are cultivated in gardens, grow wild in Japan. The *pastinaca hortensis*, or garden parsnip, is not to be met with. But wild parsnip grows plentifully everywhere. Parsley, cummin, succory, and our common European lettuce, are cultivated by the Dutch, as they were formerly by the Portuguese, and thrive extraordinary well.

Besides the plants I have hitherto mentioned, there are numberless others that grow in the fields, upon hills and mountains, in woods and forests, in morassy grounds, in barren and uncultivated places, along the sea-coasts, and, in short, everywhere. Of all these, there are very few but what afford their roots, leaves, flowers, and fruits, not only for the sustenance of the common people, but even for the delicious tables of people of quality. There is a great variety of mushrooms, most of which are eat. Some, indeed, are poisonous, and unlucky accidents happen frequently. The use of some other plants is often attended with the like dangerous consequences, the venomous being sometimes mistook for the wholesome by ignorant people. Some, indeed, they know how to deprive of their hurtful and venomous qualities. Thus, out of the konjakf, which is a poisonous sort of a dracunculus, they prepare a sweet mealy pap. In the like manner, by expressing the juice, by macerating and boiling the roots of the *warabi* or fern, of the ren, or *faba Ægyptica*, called by some tarrate flour, as also of what they call kasne, they make a fine sort of flour; which is of great use in dressing their victuals, and which they eat besides by itself, dissolved in water. Of all the soft submarine plants there is hardly one but what the natives eat. Fishermen's wives wash, sort, and sell them; and they are likewise very dexterous in diving them up from the bottom of the sea in twenty to forty fathoms deep.

CHAPTER VII.

OF THE PLENTY OF THE COUNTRY AS TO BEASTS, BIRDS, REPTILES, AND INSECTS.

OF the animals of this country some are merely chimerical, not existing in nature, nor invented by the Japanese themselves, but borrowed from their neighbours the Chinese. Of these it will not be improper to give some account, before I proceed to describe those which really exist.

Kirin, according to the description and figure which the Japanese give of it, is a winged quadruped, of incredible swiftness, with two soft horns standing before the breast, and bent backwards with the body of a horse, and claws of a deer, and a head which comes nearest to that of a dragon. The good-nature and holiness of this animal are so great that they say it takes special care, even in walking, not to trample over any the least plant, nor to injure any the most inconsiderable worm or insect that might by chance come under its feet. Its conception and birth require a particular constellation in heaven, and the birth of a sesin upon earth. Sesin is a man endowed by nature with an incomparable understanding, and a more than human penetration, a man capable to dive into the mysteries of divine and supernatural things, and withal so full of love towards mankind as to reveal his discoveries for their common benefit. There are famous, as such, the two Chinese emperors, Gio and Sium; the memory of whose excellent government, and the great discoveries they made in the knowledge and virtues of plants, will be always dear in that empire: Koosi and Moosi, two Chinese philosophers: Siaka, an Indian philosopher, and great discoverer of supernatural truths: Darma in China, and Sotoktais in Japan, both founders of particular sects, and persons of an unspotted holy life.

Besides the kirin, there are two other chimeras of the quadruped kind: one is called fuugu. It is not unlike a leopard as to its shape, but hath two soft horns before the breast, bent backwards. The other is called kaitsu, or kuisai. This hath something of the fox in its shape, two horns before the breast, another horn in the forehead, and a row of prickles, like the crocodile, along the back.

After the four-footed chimeras, the tats, dria, or daja, as it is called by the Japanese, that is the dragon, must be mentioned. The chronicles and histories of their gods and heroes are full of fabulous stories of this animal. They believe that it dwells at the bottom of the sea, as in its proper element. They represent it in their books as a huge, long, four-footed snake, scaly all over the body, like the crocodile, with sharp prickles along the back, but the head is beyond the rest monstrous and terrible. The tail of the Japanese dragon ends as it were into a two-edged sword. Some of the Japanese Emperor's cloth, his arms, scimeters, knives, and the like, as also the furniture and haugings of the imperial palace, are adorned with figures of this dragon, holding a round jewel, or pearl, in the right fore-claw. The Japanese dragon hath but three claws on each foot, whereby it is distinguished from the Chinese imperial dragon, which is represented with five. Tatsmaki is another dragon with a long watery tail. It is believed that this also lives at the bottom of the sea, and, by flying up thence into the air, occasions by its violent turnings what we call a water-spout; which phenomenon is very common on the Japanese seas.

and observed frequently to break towards the coasts.

Foo is a chimerical but beautiful large bird of paradise, of a near kin to the phœnix of the ancients. It dwells in the high regions of the air, and it hath this, common with the kirin, that it never comes down from thence, as the Japanese religiously believe, to honour the earth with its blessed presence but upon the birth of a sesin, or that of a great emperor, or upon some such other extraordinary occasion. Thus far the chimerical animals. I proceed now to give an account of such as do really exist.

Considering the largeness and extent of the Japanese empire, it is but sparingly supplied with four-footed beasts, wild or tame. The former find but few desert places, where they could increase and multiply, and follow their usual shy way of life. The latter are bred up only for carriage and agriculture. Pythagoras's doctrine of the transmigration of the soul being received almost universally, the natives eat no flesh meat, and living, as they do, chiefly upon vegetables, they know how to improve the ground to much better advantage than by turning it into meadows and pastures for breeding of cattle. To begin with the tame beasts. There are horses in the country : they are indeed little in the main, but some of them not inferior in shape, swiftness, and dexterity to the Persian breed. They serve for state, for riding, for carriage and ploughing. The best horses come from the provinces Satzuma and Osju ; and a certain breed of little horses from Kai, is very much esteemed. Oxen and cows serve only for ploughing and carriage. Of milk and butter they know nothing. They have a sort of large buffles, of a monstrous size, with bunches on the back, like camels, which serve for carriage and transport of goods only, in large cities. They know nothing of asses, mules, camels, and elephants. Sheep and goats were kept formerly by the Dutch and Portuguese at Firando, where the kind still subsists. They might be bred in the country to great advantage, if the natives were permitted to eat the flesh, or knew how to manage and manufacture the wool. They have but few swine, which were brought over from China, and are bred by the country people in Fisen, not indeed for their own use, which would be contrary to their superstitious notions, but to sell them to the Chinese, who come over for trade every year, and are great admirers of pork, though otherwise the doctrine of Pythagoras, about the transmigration of souls, hath found place likewise in China. Since the now reigning emperor came to the throne, there are more dogs bred in Japan than perhaps in any one country whatever, and than there were before even in this empire. They have their masters, indeed, but lie about the streets, and are very troublesome to passengers and travellers. Every street must, by special command of the emperor, keep a certain number of these animals, and provide them with victuals. There are huts built in every street where they are taken care of when they fall sick. Those that die must be carried up to the tops of mountains and hills, as the usual burying places, and very decently interred. Nobody may, under severe penalties, insult or abuse them, and to kill them is a capital crime, whatever mischief they do. In this case, notice of their misdemeanours must be given to their keepers, who are alone empowered to chastise and to punish them. This extraordinary care for the preservation of the dog kind is the effect of a superstitious fancy of the now [1690] reigning Emperor, who was born in the sign of the Dog. [The reader is desired to take notice that the Dog is one of the twelve celestial signs of the Japanese,] and hath for this reason so great an esteem for this animal, as the great Roman emperor, Augustus Cæsar, is reported in histories to have had for rams. The natives tell a pleasant tale on this head :—A Japanese, as he was carrying up the dead carcase of a dog to the top of a mountain, in order to its burial, grew impatient, grumbled, and cursed the Emperor's birth-day and whimsical commands. His companion, though sensible of the justice of his complaints, bid him hold his tongue and be quiet, and, instead of swearing and cursing, return thanks to the gods that the emperor was not born in the sign of the horse, because, in that case, the load would have been much heavier. Greyhounds and spaniels are wanting. They hunt but little, and only with common dogs; this kind of diversion being not very proper for so populous a country, and where there is so little game. They have a particular kind of cats, which is a domestic animal with them as with us. They are of a whitish colour, with large yellow and black spots, and a very short tail, as if it had been purposely cut off. They do not care for mousing, but love mightily to be carried about, and caressed, chiefly by women.

Of four-footed wild beasts the country produces deer, hares, and boars ; all which the adherents of some sects are permitted to eat at certain times of the year. The island Mijosima, or Akino Mijosima, so called from the neighbourhood of the province Aki, is famous for a particular breed of deer which, they say, are very tame and familiar with the inhabitants. It is contrary to the laws of the country to chase and to kill them. The country people take care to remove their dead carcases from their houses and fields, forasmuch as the governor of the island is empowered, by virtue of another law, to sentence those before whose doors, or upon whose ground such carcases are found, to some days' work, either at the temples or for the public. They have some few monkeys, of a docile kind, with short tails, of a brownish dark colour, with naked red faces and backs. A mountebank showed one about the country which he pretended was one hundred and six years old, and which played several artful tricks with great dexterity. They have some few bears in the northern provinces, but of a small kind. Tanuki is a very singular kind of an animal, of a brownish dark colour, with a snout not unlike a fox's snout, and pretty small : it seems otherwise to be of the wolf's kind. They have likewise a sort of wild dogs with large gaping snouts. Itutz is a small animal of a reddish colour. Another large sort of it is called tin : they both live in houses and lodge themselves under the roofs ; they are so tame that they might be ranked among the domestic animals. They are very dexterous at catching of fowl, chiefly chickens, and fish. The whole country swarms with rats and mice. The rats are tamed by the natives and taught to perform several tricks. Rats thus taught are the common diversion of some poor people. The best of the kind, and which play with most dexterity, are to be seen at Osacca, as the place which mountebanks, jugglers, and raree-show people resort to from all parts of the empire. Foxes also are very common. The natives believe that they are animated by the devil; and their historical and sacred writings are full of strange accounts of several odd accidents which happened with, and with regard to foxes. The fox-hunters, however, are very expert in conjuring and stripping this animated devil; the hair and wool being very much coveted for their writing and painting-pencils. They make the same distinction between the kis, or fox, and oni, or devil, as they do in Sweden between faan and diehlen. Of tigers, panthers, lions, and such other voracious animals Japan is entirely free.

Thus much of the four-footed wild and tame beasts which are to be met with in Japan. The insects of the reptile kind are next to be taken into consideration. Among these a mischievous small creature, known all over the East Indies by the name of white ant, claims the first place. It is a small slender worm, perfectly white, like snow. They live together in commonalty, as our European ants do, from whom they do not much differ in shape and bigness. Their head and breast are of a brownish dark colour, and hard to the touch. The Japanese call them Doo-toos, which is as much as to say "piercers," an epithet which they well deserve, for they pierce and perforate whatever they meet with, stones only and ores excepted; and when once they get into a merchant's warehouse, they are able within a very short compass of time to ruin and destroy his best goods. Nothing hath been as yet found out that will keep them off but salt laid under the goods and spread about them. Our common European ants are their mortal enemies, and whatever place the one sort takes possession of, the others must necessarily quit it. They are no more able than moles to support the open air, and whenever they go out upon an expedition they defend themselves by building arches or trenches all along their march, which they know how to tie fast to the ground. These arches are much of the same substance with that of wasps' nests. I was told surprising and melancholy stories of their quick and mischievous marches and expeditions; but I will only relate what I was an eye-witness of myself. During my stay at Coylang, a Dutch fort upon the coasts of Malabar, I had an apartment assigned me in the governor's own house. One night I did not go to bed till about midnight, having been very busy. The next morning when I rose, I took notice of the marks of such arches upon my table, which were about the bigness of my little finger, and upon a more accurate inspection, I found that these animals had pierced a passage of that thickness up one foot of the table, then across the table (though as good luck would have it, without any damage done to the papers and things I had left there), and so down again through the middle of the foot into the floor. All this was performed within a few hours' time.

Mukadde, according to the common Japanese dialect, and goko, in their significant or character-language, are not what we call aselli, or wood-lice, but the Indian millepedes, palmer-worms, or forty-legs; a worm of about two or three inches in length, slender, of a brown colour, having a great number of legs on both sides, from whence it hath borrowed its name. The Indian forty-legs are very venomous, and their bites are reckoned more dangerous and painful than those of the scorpion. There are but few in Japan, and those not very mischievous. The part which is stung or bit is dressed with spittle, and the bite seldom observed to be attended with ill consequences.

The lizards of this country do not differ from our common European lizards.

There are but few snakes in the country. One of the most famous is called fitakutz, and fibakari. It is of a green colour, with a flat head and sharp teeth. It hath borrowed its name from the length of the day, or the time the sun stays upon the horizon; because people bit by it are said to die before sunset. Soldiers are very fond of its flesh, which they eat, firmly believing that it hath the virtue of making them bold and courageous. This snake calcined in an earthen pot, hermetically sealed, gives that powder which they call gawatsio, and which is very famous for its virtues in curing several internal distempers. This same powder put under the gutters of a house is said in a short time to produce young snakes of the same kind. I met with this sort of snake nowhere else but upon the coasts of Malabar, where I was shown some by the Bramines. Another sort of snakes of a monstrous size, called jamakagata, or, according to the common dialect, uwabami, and sometimes dsja, that is, "dragon," is found in waters and upon mountains. It is very scarce, and when taken shown about for money. From the reptiles I proceed to the birds.

Of tame fowl they keep chickens, and sometimes ducks; but being, as I took notice above, imbued with the superstitious notions of Pythagoras, the generality will not eat them, and they are killed and sold to such as do venture to eat them, only by persons of a mean extraction. When a man lies at the point of death, as also upon those days which are sacred to the memory of deceased persons, none of their relations and friends may kill any bird or beast whatever. In the mourning years for the death of an emperor, and at any other time when the emperor thinks fit to order it, no living creature whatever may be killed or brought to market in any part of his dominions. The cocks oftener find pardon than hens, and are kept alive with great care, because they are held in great esteem, chiefly among the religious orders, by reason of their measuring the time, and foretelling future changes of the weather. Wild fowl, though naturally shy, are in this populous country grown so familiar that many kinds of them might be ranked among the tame. The tsuri, or crane, is the chief of the wild birds of the country, and hath this particular imperial privilege, that nobody may shoot him without an express order from the emperor, and only for the emperor's own pleasure or use. In

Saikokf, however, and in other provinces remote from court, a less strict regard is had to the like imperial commands. The cranes and tortoises are reckoned very happy animals in themselves, and thought to portend good luck to others, and this by reason of their pretended long and fabulous life, of which there are several remarkable instances recorded in their historical writings. For this reason the imperial apartments, walls of temples, and other happy places, are commonly adorned with figures of them, as also with figures of firs and bamboos, for the like reason. I never heard country people and carriers call this bird otherwise than O Tsurisama, that is, "My great Lord Crane." There are two different kinds of them; one white as snow, the other grey or ash-coloured. There are several kinds of saggi, or herons, which differ in colour and size. The chief are sijro saggi, the white heron; goi saggi, the grey heron, both very common; and awoi saggi, a heron of a bluish colour, and almost as big as a crane. There are two different sorts of wild geese, which couple each with their kind. One sort is as white as snow, only the extremities of the wings are black; the other is grey or ash-coloured. Both are very common in this country, particularly the grey ones, and so familiar that they might be taken for tame; for they will not fly up, nor get out of the way at anybody's approach. They do a great deal of mischief in the fields, and yet nobody may disturb or kill them under pain of death, except those who have bought the privilege to shoot them in some tracts of ground. The country people, to keep them off, surround their fields with nets, though to very little purpose, for they will fly over the nets, as I have seen myself, to get at their food.

Of ducks also there are several different kinds, and as tame as the geese. One kind particularly I cannot forbear mentioning, because of the surprising beauty of its male, called kinmodsui, which is so great, that, being shown its picture in colours, I could hardly believe my own eyes, till I saw the bird itself, it being a very common one. Its feathers are wonderfully diversified with the finest colours imaginable; about the neck and breast chiefly they are red. The head is crowned with a most magnificent topping. The tail rising obliquely, and the wings standing up over the back in a very singular manner, afford to the eye a sight as curious as it is uncommon. There are also pheasants of uncommon beauty. One kind particularly is remarkable for the various colours and lustre of its feathers, and for the beauty of its tail, which equals half a man's length, and in a curious variety and mixture of the finest colours, chiefly blue and gold, is no ways inferior to that of a peacock. Woodcocks are a very common bird; they are eat by the adherents of some sects, as are also the pheasants, geese, and ducks. There is a sort of wild pigeons with black and blue feathers, though otherwise they are no great beauties. The natives will not suffer them to nest in their houses; because they found by experience, that their dung upon removal is very apt to take fire, and they say that many an unlucky accident happened thereby.

Storks stay in the country all the year round.

The best falcons are caught in the northern provinces, and are kept more for state than sport.

Hawks are common here as they are everywhere in the East Indies, and a very proud bird; as is also a kind of ravens, of a middling size, which was first brought over from China, as a present to the Emperor.

Another scarce bird was sent over from Corea, by way of present to the Emperor; and is thence called Coreigaras, that is, a "Corean raven."

Our common European crows, as also parrots, and some other Indian birds, are not to be met with in Japan.

Foken, or, according to the common dialect, fototenis, is a scarce night-bird, of an excellent and delicious taste, and a dish only for the tables of people of quality upon extraordinary occasions. The ashes of this bird calcined, and put into old sour sacki, are said to restore it to its former taste and goodness.

Misago, or bisago, is a voracious sea-bird, of the hawk kind. It preys chiefly upon fish. It makes a hole in some rock upon the coasts, where it lays up its prey and provision, which is observed to keep as well as pickled fish, or atsinar, and is thence called, bisagonosusi, or the "bisago's atsinar." It tastes very salt, and is sold dear. Whoever knows such a cave can make a good deal of money of it, provided he do not take out too much at a time.

Mews, sea-ravens, snipes, sea-pies, sparrows, swallows, and some other small birds, are as common here as in Europe.

Larks sing much better here than they do in Europe.

The nightingales, if they have a good voice, are sold sometimes to curious people for twenty copangs a-piece. Thus far, what I had to observe concerning the birds of this country.

Of flying insects, the country hath bees, consequently some honey and wax, though but in a small quantity. Humble-bees, wasps, common flies, gnats, fire-flies, several sorts of beetles and bugs, as also locusts, and a great variety of other insects of this tribe, it hath common with Europe, besides some other particular and remarkable sorts; the chief of which I will here give a short account of.

Among the butterflies there is one very large sort, called jamma tsio, or the mountain-butterfly. It is either entirely black, or party-coloured, and curiously diversified with white, black, and other spots, chiefly upon its forked wings. Komuri is a large, spotted, party-coloured, hairy, beautiful night-fly. The same name is given also to bats. Of beetles, they have several scarce and beautiful kinds. One, in particular, is very large, in shape not unlike the dung-fly, shining black, with two crooked and branched horns, one larger, standing over the nose, after the manner of a rhinoceros's horn, the other smaller, standing out on one side from the shoulder. This animal cannot walk easily. It lives chiefly under ground. It is scarce, and the natives have as yet given it no name.

A certain kind of brown beetle, called sebi, and sometimes semi, affords several curious and remarkable things to the attentive eye of an inquisitive naturalist. They are of three different kinds. The largest is called kuma sebi,

It resembles in shape and higness that sort of flies which with us in Europe are generally observed to fly about in the evening, but it hath no wings. In the spring they creep out of the ground (where they have lain in winter-quarters) in the night-time, and fasten themselves with their hoary legs to trees, their branches, or leaves, or whatever in their march they can lay hold of. A little while after they burst, and split their back lengthways, to give room to another fly, not unlike a beetle, which was enclosed within it, though much bigger than the prison to which it was confined. Some hours after, this second fly flies away with a hurrying noise. This curious little animal hath been described by Gessner by the name of *Cicada*. Bursting open the shell in which it lay, and, at the same time, spreading out its four wings, it makes a sharp and loud noise, which, they say, may be heard (a thing almost incredible) very indistinctly at full an English mile's distance. Woods and mountains are full of the noise these little creatures make. They disappear gradually in the dog-days; and it is said, that they creep into the ground again, in order to undergo a new metamorphosis or change, and to re-appear in the same state the next year. How far this agrees with truth, I am not able to determine, for want of proper observations. The name semi, or sebi, which they bear, is borrowed from their music, which begins slowly and upon a low tune, then increases gradually in swiftness and loudness, and again ends pretty low. This music, I thought, was not unlike the noise a button-maker's spindle makes in turning. They begin to sing with the rising sun, and end about noon. The *exuviæ*, called semi or mukigara, are preserved for physical uses, and sold publicly in shops both in Japan and China. Another smaller kind is from its smallness called kosebi, or the small sebi. They appear later in the year, much about the time when the others disappear. They sing from noon to sunset, and live till late in autumn. Their music is not so loud as that of the first kind, and is by the common people called tsuku tsukuboo. The third kind differs from the second neither in shape nor higness, only they sing from morning to night. The females of all the three kinds are mute, and have their breast shut: in all other respects they are like the males.

The cantharides, or Spanish flies, are of the same colour with our Spanish flies, but somewhat bigger and rounder, and very near as big as our common European beetles. Their use is entirely unknown in Japan. Another particular sort of Spanish flies is called fanmio. They are extremely caustic, and ranked among the poisons. They are found upon rice-ears, and are long, slender, and smaller than the Spanish flies, blue or gold-coloured, with scarlet or crimson spots and lines, which makes them look very beautiful. But the finest of all the flying tribe of insects, and which, by reason of its incomparable beauty, is kept by the ladies among their curiosities, is a peculiar and scarce night-fly, about a finger long, slender, round-bodied, with four wings, two of which are transparent and laid under a pair of others, which are shining, as it were polished, and most curiously adorned with blue and golden lines and spots.

The following fable owes its origin to the unparalleled beauty of this little creature: They say that all other night-flies fall in love with it, and to get rid of their importunities it maliciously bids them (for a trial of their constancy) to go and to fetch fire. The blind lovers scruple not to obey commands, and, flying to the next fire or candle, they never fail to burn themselves to death. The female is not near so beautiful as the male, but grey, or ash-coloured and spotted.

CHAPTER VIII.

OF FISH AND SHELLS.

THE sea, and its productions, contribute full as much towards the sustenance of the natives as the growth of the country, rice only excepted. The sea all about Japan is plentifully stored with all sorts of submarine plants, fish, crabs, and shells; of all which there are very few, but what were eaten by their indigent ancestors, and are so to this day. There are even many which, in these wealthy and refined ages, appear upon the sumptuous tables of people of the highest quality. Both fish, crabs, and shells, are comprehended under one general name, kiokai, or iwokai. In this present chapter, which may be looked upon as an introduction to one of the following, wherein I intend to treat of their tables and kitchen, I will set down as many of them as came to my knowledge, along with their true Japanese names; though it must be observed in general, that several of them are found likewise in our European and other seas.

Of all the animal productions of the Japanese seas, I know of none of so extensive an use, for rich and poor, as the kudsuri, or whale. It is caught frequently about Japan, but particularly in the sea Khumano, which washes the southern coasts of the great island Nipon, as also about the islands Tsussima and Goto, and upon the coasts of Omura and Nomo. The common way of catching them is with darts, or harping-irons, as they do in the Greenland fishery, but the Japanese boats seem to be fitter for this purpose than ours, being small, narrow, tapering into a sharp point at one end, with five oars, or ten men each, who row them with incredible swiftness. About 1680, a rich fisherman in the province Omura, whose name was Gitaijo, found out a new way of catching whales with nets made of strong ropes about two inches thick. This method was afterwards followed with good success by a countryman in the islands of Gotho, whose name was Iwonomo. They say, that as soon as the whale finds his head entangled in a net, he cannot, without great difficulty, swim further, and may be very easily killed with harpoon-irons after the common manner. The reason why this new method, which seemed to bid very fair for success, hath not been universally received is, because it requires a greater and much more expensive set of proper tackle, than common fishermen can afford. For whereas the expense of whale-fishing after the common manner, seldom exceeds twenty chests of silver, this cannot be so much as attempted with a less sum.

There are several sorts of whales, which differ

in their names, shape, and bigness. 1. Sebio is the chief, and indeed the largest fish of the whale-kind. It affords most train oil, and its flesh is very good and wholesome, so far that fishermen and the common people attribute their good state of health, amidst all the injuries of cold and weather, which they are continually exposed to, chiefly to their eating this flesh. 2. Awo fangi, commonly kokadsura, that is a small whale, is grey or ash-coloured, smaller than the sebio, from which it also differs something in shape. 3. Nagass, is commonly twenty to thirty fathoms long, and hath this particular, that he can stay under water for two or three hours, during which time he can travel a vast way, whereas other whales must continually come up to the surface of the water for fresh supplies of air. 4. Sotookadsura, that is, the whale of blind people, so called from the figure of a bijwu, or a sort of a lute, which blind people in this country use to play upon, which is said to be naturally represented on its back. It is not a very large sort, and seldom exceeds ten fathoms in length. It is caught frequently about Japan, but the flesh is reckoned unwholesome food, being as they say, too hot, and occasioning coughs, fevers, eruptions on the skin, and sometimes the small-pox. It is brought to market with other fish, and sold for the flesh of the sebio, but those who know it will never buy it. 5. Mako never exceeds three or four fathoms in length. This same name is given to the young ones of the other kinds. That which I here speak of is caught frequently upon the eastern coasts of Japan, as also upon the coasts of Kijuokuni and Satzuma. Ambergris is found in the intestines of this whale. The head yields a small quantity of train-oil. 6. Iwasikura, that is, sardin's-eater, hath a tail and fins like common fish. We saw this sort when we went up to court, between Caminoseki and Simonoseki; and I took it to be that fish which the Dutch call noord caper. Of all these several kinds of whales nothing is thrown away as useless, excepting only the large shoulder-bone. The skin, which is black in most kinds; the flesh which is red and looks like beef; the intestines, which, from their remarkable length, are called fiakfiro, that is, "an hundred fathoms long," and all the inward parts, are eaten, pickled, boiled, roasted, or fried. The fat, or blubber, is boiled into train-oil, and even the sediments of the second boiling are eaten. The bones, such as are of a cartilaginous substance, are boiled when fresh, and eaten, or scraped, cleaned and dried for the use of the kitchen. Out of the nervous and tendinous parts, both white and yellow, they make cords and ropes, chiefly for their cotton manufactures, as also for their musical instruments. Not even the garbage is thrown away, but kept for some use in the kitchen. Several little things are made of the jaw-bones, fins, and other bones, which are of a more solid substance; particularly their fine steelyards for weighing gold and silver are made of them, and have borrowed their name from thence.

Sateifoko is a fish two, three, and sometimes five or six fathoms long, with two long teeth or tusks, standing out of the mouth upwards, which are sometimes, by way of ornament, put at the top of castles, temples, and public buildings. I was informed by fishermen, that this fish is a cunning and mortal enemy of whales, and that he kills them by creeping into the mouth, and devouring their tongues. He hath a way, as he creeps in, to put his head and teeth into such a posture, that they are no hindrance to him.

Iruku is a known fish, called tenije in the Indies: furube is another fish, not very large: the Dutch call him blazer, which signifies blower, because he can blow and swell himself up into the form of a round ball. He is ranked among the poisonous fish, and if eat whole, is said unavoidably to occasion death. There are three different sorts of it found in the Japanese seas, all in great plenty. The first sort called susume-buka is small, and seldom eat. The second is called mabuku, that is the true buku. This the Japanese reckon a very delicate fish, and they are very fond of it. But the head, guts, bones, and all the garbage must be thrown away, and the flesh carefully washed and cleaned before it is fit to eat. And yet many people die of it, for want, as they say, of thoroughly washing and cleaning it. People that by some long and tedious sickness are grown weary of their lives, or are otherwise under miserable circumstances, frequently choose this poisonous fish, instead of a knife or halter, to make away with themselves. A few years ago five persons of Nagasaki having eaten of this fish, fainted soon after dinner, grew convulsive and delirious, and fell into such a violent spitting of blood, as made an end of their lives in a few days. And yet the Japanese would not deprive themselves of a dish so delicate in their opinion, for all they have so many instances of how fatal and dangerous are the consequences of eating it. Soldiers only and military men, are by special command of the Emperor forbidden to buy and to eat this fish. If any one dies of it, his son forfeits the succession to his father's post, which otherwise he would have been entitled to. It is sold much dearer than common fish, and not eaten, but when fresh. The third sort is called kitamakura, which signifies north cushion. I could not learn the reason of this appellation. The same name is given to a person that sleeps with his head turned to the north. The poison of this sort is absolutely mortal; no washing nor cleaning will take it off. It is therefore never asked for, but by those who intend to make away with themselves.

The sea-horse, or sea-dog, and as the Germans call him, wasserbauch, is a very singular fish, much about the length of a boy of ten years of age, without either scales or fins, with a large head, mouth and breast, a large thin belly like a bag, which will hold a large quantity of water. He hath thin sharp teeth in the chops much like a snake. The inner parts are so minute that they are scarce visible. He hath two flat cartilaginous feet with fingers, not unlike the hands of a child, under the belly, by means of which, he creeps, in all likelihood, or walks at the bottom of the sea. All his parts are eaten, none excepted. He is caught frequently in the gulf of Jedo, between Kamakura and that capital, where I saw him brought to market.

Tai is what the Dutch in the Indies call steenbrassem. This is very much esteemed by the Japanese as the king of fish, and a peculiar emblem of happiness, partly because he is sacred to their Jebis, or Neptune, partly by reason of a beautiful variety of shining colours, which appear on him when under water. It is a very scarce fish, not unlike a carp, and finely variegated with red and white. The female hath some red spots. It is so scarce, that upon some great entertainment at court, or other extraordinary occasions, it is not to be had under a thousand copangs. Another sort of this fish is called kharo tai, or black steenbrassem, from the colour. This is not near so much esteemed, and is caught frequently about Saikokf.

Susuki is what the Germans call kahlkopf, that is, baldhead. Funa is a fish not unlike a carp, and much commended for its medicinal virtues, chiefly against worms. A larger kind of the same is called najos. Mebaar is a red-coloured fish, in bigness and shape not unlike a carp, or steenbrassem, with the eyes standing out of the head like two balls. It is caught everywhere in great plenty, and is the common food of poor people. Koi is another sort of it, which also resembles a carp, and is sometimes one sakf and a half long. This sort is caught in rivers, chiefly about water-falls, against which they endeavour to swim. They are so strong that two men can hardly hold them. They are exported all over the empire, fresh and pickled. They take some in the lake of Saifa, or Tensiu, which are four sakf long. Maar, the salmon, is taken in rivers and fresh water lakes. Itojori is a salmonat, or small salmon. Makuts, is what the Dutch call harder. Sawara, a king's fish. Fiuwo is what the Dutch call draatvish. Ara is what the Dutch in the Indies call Jacob's ewertz. Kusuna, a short nose. Kamas, a pike. Susuki is the schaarvish of the Dutch, only a longer and narrower sort. Adsi is the maasbancker of the Dutch. Of this there are several different kinds, the chief and largest whereof is called ooadsi. Taka is what the Dutch call a kaye. Kame, and takasame, are rays, of the hard skins of which they make cases and other curious things in Japan. The skin of this fish is imported also from Siam, where it is found much finer. Jeje is a broad flat fish, with a long tail. There is one sort of it, which hath a small horny or bony sting at the end of the tail, which the Dutch in the Indies call pijlstaart. The Japanese believe, that this sting taken from a live fish is an infallible remedy against the bite of snakes, rubbing the bitten part with it. For this reason they carry it along with them among other house medicines. Come, or jei, are soles, and karei, bots or bruts. Bora is a fish much like a pike, with a white and delicious flesh. Some call him songaats fish, because he is taken in the Songaats, or first month of the Japanese year. They pickle and smoke them, as they do pikes at Bremen. These and all pickled fish in general, are called karasumi. They export them from Nagasaki and Nomo, where they are frequently caught, and carry them to Jedo, and into several other parts of the empire, tied to straw-ropes, ten to a piece. They are exported by the Dutch and Chinese. Other fish made into karasumi are valued but little by the natives. The best sort of the katsumo fish is caught about Gotho. They cut this fish into four pieces, which they dry by degrees over the damp of hot boiling water, and bring it upon the table along with the liquors. The Dutch export it by the name of comblomaas, which, however, is not the true name. Managatsuwo is a flat fish, not unlike a but, with one eye on each side. Sake, perhaps a sort of cablian, is a pickled fish not unlike cod. It is imported from the country of Jeso, and hath borrowed its name from its smell, which is not unlike the smell of their sake beer. Tara is a sort of cod, imported from the northern provinces; the best of the kind comes from Tsiosija, whence it is called tsiosijn tara. Sajori, is what the inhabitants of Nagasaki call susumoiwo, and the Dutch naadelvish, which signifies needle-fish. It is a small fish, not above a span long, thin, with a row of sharp long prickles along the back. Tobiwo is what the Dutch call a springer, (flying-fish) because it leaps out of the water. The Japanese one seldom exceeds a foot in length, and is very delicious, but rarely taken. Iwas is the sardin; kissugo, the smelt, or sand-smelt. Jeso, by the Dutch called sandkruper, is a middling fish, between a smelt and an eel. Saba are mackerels. Ai, or ai-no-iwo, by the Dutch called modevish, is a fresh-water fish, not above a span long, swimming with surprising swiftness. Sijroiwo, is what the Dutch call kleiner stind : they also call him weissvish, that is white fish. He is caught in the spring about the mouths of rivers. Konosijro, called by the Dutch sassap, is a sort of herring, not unlike the Swedish strohmlings. Kingjo, the gold-fish, is a small fish, seldom exceeding a finger in length, red, with a beautiful shining, yellow or gold-coloured tail, which in the young ones is rather black. In China and Japan, and almost all over the Indies, this fish is kept in ponds, and fed with flies before their wings come out. Another kind hath a silver-coloured tail. Unagi is the common eel. Oounagi is another sort of eel much larger than the common. Jaatzme unagi, that is, an eel with eight eyes, is what is called in Germany neunaug, that is, nine-eye, or an eel with nine eyes. Doodsio is by the Dutch called puyt aal. It is a fish about a finger long, with a very large head in proportion to the body, found frequently in watery rice-fields and muddy ponds. They are of two different kinds, the one with, the other without a beard. They have a notion, that they may be brought forth artificially out of straw, cut, and mixed with mud and dirt, and exposed to the heat of the sun early in the morning. Fammo, by the Dutch called conger aal, is larger than a common eel, which it resembles, when under water, but slenderer.

Ika is common sea-qualm. Both the Chinese and Japanese esteem it a scarce and delicate bit. Fish also are easier caught with the flesh of this qualm than with any other bait. Jako, or sepia, is another sea-qualm, with long tails or feet, at the end whereof are, as it were, small hooks, wherewith the creature fastens itself to rocks, or the bottom of the sea; it is a common soccano or side-dish, and eat either fresh, boiled, or pickled. There are two sorts of kurrugge, which is also of the sea-qualm kind. One is called midsukurage, that is, the white qualm. This is common in all seas, whitish, transparent, watery, and not fit to eat. The other is scarcer, fleshy, and eatable after it has been prepared and deprived of its sharpness. It is prepared after the following manner. They first macerate them in a dissolution of alum for three days together; then they rub, wash, and clean it, till it grows transparent; which done, it is pickled and preserved for use. Before the infusion, the skin is taken off, washed, pickled, and kept by itself. Some of these seaqualms are so large, that two men can scarce lift them up. Pickled, as they are brought upon the table, they are of the same substance, colour, and taste with the edible birds'-nests, (Nidi alcyonum) brought from China; and I have been credibly informed by Chinese fishermen, that these birds'-nests are made of the very flesh of this animal.

Namako, by the Dutch at Batavia called kafferkull, is edible. Imori is a small venomous waterlizard, black, with a red belly. Takanomakura, which is as much as to say, the pillow of the seaqualm tako, is the common sea-star, and is not eaten.

Of all the footed animal-produce of the water, the ki, or came, tortoises, are most esteemed by the Japanese, being looked upon as peculiar emblems of happiness, by reason of the long life which is ascribed to them. That kind particularly which hath a broad tail, much like a large, round beard, and which in their learned language is called mooke, and by the common people minogame, for all it doth not exist in nature, is yet frequently to be seen among other emblematical figures, wherewith they adorn the walls of their temples, the sides of their altars, and the apartments of the emperor and princes. The most common tortoises are, isicame, or sanki, that is, the stone, or mountain-tortoise, which is so called because found in these places, and is nothing else but the common land-tortoise. Io game, or doo game, that is, fishy, or water-tortoise, because of its living in the water. They say, that upon the southern and eastern coasts of Japan there are found tortoises large enough to cover a man from head to toe.

All sorts of crabs and shrimps both of fresh and salt water, are called in general jebi. The following particular kinds have come to my knowledge. Jebisako is the common small crab, which is found in great plenty upon the coasts of the Baltic. Sako signifies all sorts of small fish in general. Si jebi differ but little from the common crabs, no more than what they call dakma jebi, excepting only that the latter are caught in fresh water, and will within a year turn black. Kuruma jebi is as much as to say wheel-crabs; they are so called from the figure of their tail. Umi jebi, that is, great crabs, or lobsters, are commonly a foot long. They are boiled, then cut into small pieces, and brought upon the table, as a soccana or side-dish. Care must be taken not to eat their black tail, because it hath been observed, that it gives people the belly-ache, or throws them into a cholera morbus. Siakwa is a crab with a broad tail, which is caught frequently with other small fish. It hath but little flesh, and almost none at the time of the full moon. All the testaceous and crustaceous animals, which are found in these seas, and indeed everywhere in the Indian ocean beyond the eastern shores of the Ganges, are observed to be fleshier and fuller at the time of the new moon, contrary to what happens in our European seas.

Gamina, otherwise koona, is a crab, which lives in a beautiful shell, diversified with various colours; (this is what the English call soldiers' crab, fresh water soldier, hermit crab, because they live in other people's quarters); kani, which signifies pocket crab, is our common European fresh-water crab. It bears the name of the whole tribe of the fresh-water crabs. Kabutogani, or unkiu, is a crab of a singular structure, with a sharp, long, serrated prickle or sword, standing out from the head, and a roundish, smooth back. Gadsame is no bigger than the common crab, with the upper shell tapering into a point on both sides. It hath four claws, two large ones before, and two behind, which are smaller. Simagani, that is, a striated pocket-crab. It might be called wart-crab, from the great number of warts and prickles which cover the shell all over, the hind claws only excepted, which are smooth and almost cylindrical. They are caught frequently upon the eastern coasts, as also in the gulf of Suruga. Some of this sort are incredibly large. I bought one of the hind claws at Suruga in a cook-shop, which was as long, and full as big, as a man's shin-bone.

All sorts of oysters, muscles, and shells, of which there is a great plenty and surprising variety in the Japanese seas, are eaten, none excepted, raw, pickled, salted, boiled, or fried. They are daily gathered on the coasts in low water. Divers dive for them to a considerable depth; others fish them with nets. The following sorts are the most common and best known; awabi, which I have already mentioned, when I spoke of the pearls of this country, is an open univalve, as big as a middle-sized Persian pearl-shell, but deeper. They lie deep under water, sticking fast to rocks, or to the bottom of the sea, from whence they are taken up by fishermen's wives, they being the best divers of the country. They go down armed with darts or long knives, to defend themselves against kayes and porpoises, and when they see an awabi, they pull it off suddenly before the animal is aware, because otherwise it would fasten itself to the rocks, or to the bottom of the sea, so strongly, that no force will be strong enough to tear it off. This shell is filled with a large piece of flesh of a yellowish or whitish colour, and a very tough substance, though without fibres. They say it was the common food of their necessitous ancestors, in memory whereof, when they entertain company at dinner, they always provide a dish of it. It is also become a custom with them, as well among the vulgar as among people of quality, that when they send one another presents of money, cloth, stuffs, fruits, or anything else, a string, or at least a small bit, of the dried flesh of this shell is sent along with them, as a good omen, and in order to put them in mind of the indigency of their forefathers. The flesh is cut into thin slices or strings, which are extended on a board, and dried. A large pearl is found sometimes in this shell, but of an ugly yellowish colour, a deformed shape, and of no value. Tairagi is a flat, long, thin, and very large bivalve, almost transparent, near of a triangular figure, running from a large base tapering into a point. The animal is tied fast to both sides of the shell with a strong tendon. The best of the kind are found in the gulf of Arima, where it sometimes yields pearls. Akoja is a flat bivalve, about a hand broad, scaly on its outward surface, and of a very ugly appearance; within of an exquisite mother of pearl glimmering. The best of the kind, and which yield the finest pearls, are found in the gulf of Omura. Mirakai is the common black fresh water mussel, which is found also in our rivers and lakes in Germany. Famaguri are bivalves much of the same shape and bigness, but thicker, smooth and white within; without of a brown or chesnut colour. Divers curious figures are painted on the inside, and they serve as an amusement to the court of the Dairi, or Ecclesiastical Hereditary Emperor, where they are played with after the following manner. Large heaps are thrown on the ground, and every one of the company having taken his portion, he wins that can show the most pairs. Every pair hath proper hooks, by the means of which they are easily known, and brought together, though never so much mixed. The best are gathered and in greatest plenty upon the coasts of Quano. Sidsimi is a small bivalve not unlike the famaguri, but thinner, and is found sticking in mud. Katsi or utsikaki, are oysters. The oysters found about Japan are deformed, rough, stony, growing together, and to rocks. There are chiefly two sorts, one remarkably large, the other smaller. The best and largest are found in great plenty in the gulf of Kamakura. Kisa, or akagai, is also a bivalve, white without, with deep furrows, running as it were parallel to each other, within of a reddish colour. They fix a handle to this shell, and use it in the kitchen instead of a spoon, or pail. Nakatagai is a large, ugly, roundish, striated and black shell. Asari is a small thin shell, gray or ash-coloured. Te or matee, is an oblong thin bivalve, gaping at both ends. The animal that lives within it is reckoned very delicious. Umi fake is another bivalve, much of the same kind, about a span long, and so big, that one can scarce grasp it between the thumb and fore-finger. Its flesh is pickled and kept for use. This shell is found only upon the coasts of Tsikungo, where, by express order of the prince of that country, it is forbid to fish them, till a sufficient quantity hath been provided for the Emperor's own table. Takaragai, called in the Indies cowries, are brought from the Maldive and other islands, and imported into Bengal, Pegu, and Siam, where they go for current money. Those found about Japan are of different sorts. The best are brought from the Riuku Islands, and are the chief ingredient of their white cheek varnish. Sasai is a large, thick, odoriferous, turbinated univalve, white and prickled. Its mouth is shut close, with a flat, thick covering, of operculum, a stony substance, rough, on the outside not unlike the lapis judaicus, only sharper and smooth. Nisi is an univalve much of the same shape, but larger, and hath not near so good a flesh. Both can fasten themselves very close to rocks, and the bottom of the sea, like the awabi. Common people make use of the shell instead of pots to spit in. Tannisi are the common black land snails, gathered for food in muddy rice fields. They have their mouth shut, with an oblong, almost stony operculum. Bai is a snail in a common oblong, turbinated, white shell. Ras or mina is another of the same kind, but black and smaller. Both are gathered on the shore in low water. Kabuto is a small, oval, not turbinated univalve. Another small turbinated univalve is called sugai.

CHAPTER IX.

NAMES OF THE GODS, DEMI-GODS AND EMPERORS, WHO ARE MENTIONED IN THE JAPANESE HISTORIES, AS THE FIRST MONARCHS AND GOVERNORS OF THAT EMPIRE.

THE better to understand the opinion of the Japanese about the original state of their country (which formerly they looked upon as the only inhabited part of the earth), and the succession of their emperors and monarchs down to this present time, I have thought fit to divide the history and chronology of this empire into three eras, a fabulous, a doubtful, and a certain.

The first and fabulous epocha of the Japanese government reaches far beyond the time of the creation, as fixed in sacred writs. Japan, they say, was during that period of time, governed by a succession (or rather evolution) of seven celestial spirits or gods, which are by them called Ten Dsin Sitzi Dai, that is, "the seven great celestial spirits," each of which reigned an immense, but undetermined number of years. The history of the Japanese gods is full of strange wonderful adventures, and great bloody wars, which are said to have happened in this first age of the Japanese world. The two chronological authors, whom I have followed in writing this history, barely mention their names, as also that the three first were not married, but that their four successors had each his wife, as a companion of his government, whose names are likewise set down. Of this first succession of gods, I have had already occasion to speak more amply in a previous part of this work, where I treated of the origin of the Japanese nation according to the opinion of the natives. I must therefore refer the reader to that chapter, and beg leave here to repeat, that the last of this first succession, Isanagi Mikotto, having carnally known his wife and goddess Isanami Mikotto, begot a second race of demi-gods or god-men, who succeeded the first in the government of Japan, and being five in number are thence called, Dsi Sin Go Dai, that is, "the five great terrestrial gods," or monarchs. They reigned in the following order:—

1. Ten Se O Dai Sin, eldest son and heir of Isanagi Mikotto, for whose memory, and that of his brethren and posterity, the Japanese still possess a most profound respect and veneration. He is said to have reigned 250,000 years. China, they say, was during his reign governed by Ten Kwo Si, to whom they also attribute a long and fabulous government, and further mention, that three descendants of his family successively ruled the empire of China.

2. Osiwo Ni no Mikotto lived and reigned in all 300,000 years. During his reign, and during the reign of his successor, to the beginning of that of the fourth Japanese Dsi Sin, Sat Teiki governed the empire of China.

3. Ni ni ki no Mikotto reigned 318,533 years. During his whole reign Saitei Ki was Emperor of China.

4. Fiko Oo Demi no Mikotto reigned 637,892 years. China was then governed by the Emperor Katsura Kaki, who was succeeded by five princes of his family.

5. The fifth and last of these demi-gods was Fuki Awa se dsu no Mikotto. He reigned 836,042 years, so that the whole space of time, during which this race of god-men governed Japan, takes in 2,342,467 years. This is all the Japanese know of the ancient state and government of their empire—a tradition which some of the wiser people, even among them, are very sensible is liable to great doubts and uncertainties, if not entirely fabulous and chimerical. However all, without exception, profess a peculiar veneration for Isanagi and his consort Isanami, as being the progenitors of their nation, and, if I may be allowed thus to express myself, their Adam and Eve. The right which the family of the Ecclesiastical Hereditary Emperors claims to the crown and government of Japan, and which they have enjoyed free and undisturbed during a succession of many ages, is grounded upon a lineal descent from Ten Seo Dai Sin, Isanagi's first-born son and heir, from his eldest son, and so down. There is hardly a town, or village, throughout the empire but what hath one or more temples erected to his memory, and the place of his residence, which is said to have been in the province Isje, is held so sacred, that, at certain times of the year, people of all ranks and qualities resort thither in pilgrimage. Thus much of this first and fabulous epocha of the Japanese government, of which I have treated more at large in the above-mentioned seventh chapter of the first book.

I proceed now to the second and doubtful era. It is little known what was the state of these countries, and the way of life of the inhabitants, from the beginning of the creation (when, according to the description of that great lawgiver, Moses, the Supreme Being called this globe of our earth out of nothing, and formed it by his infinite power into a state altogether becoming his divine goodness and wisdom), to the time of their first monarch, Sin Mu Ten Oo, whose reign comes down pretty low, and within 660 years of our Saviour's nativity. It is highly probable that in those early times they lived up and down the country dispersed in hordes (as to this day the Scythian inhabitants of the Great Tartary), separate from the rest of the world by a rocky tempestuous sea, which encompasses their islands, being as yet in a state of nature and freedom, without a settled form of government, and destitute of arts and sciences. The neighbouring empire of China was already grown very powerful; arts and sciences flourished there, and were by the Chinese brought over likewise into Japan. It was owing to this that the Japanese became in time polite and civilised; and it is not unlikely that, in imitation of their neighbours, by whom they were imbued with notions of a monarchical government, they submitted with more cheerfulness when Sin Mu Ten Oo began to reign over them; the rather as this prince was descended of a family so much beloved, and esteemed so sacred among them. In the meantime, that so considerable a period of time should not remain empty in their chronological books, they have filled up the vacancy with the names of the most eminent monarchs who, after the demise of Katsurakuki, and the five descendants of his family, sat on the throne of China.

The first Chinese emperor mentioned in this second era is Fuki, and with his full title Tai Ko Fuki (the Chinese pronounce it Fohi). This prince had, according to some, the body, and according to others, the head, of a serpent with a most sublime understanding. He discovered the motions of the heavens, and the twelve celestial signs, and divided the time into years and months. He invented, besides, many other useful arts and sciences, and communicated them to the world for the common benefit of mankind. The Chinese made him their first emperor, and the founder of their monarchy; and many among them pretend that from his reign down to this present age, they can show an accurate history of their empire, and a true chronological succession of their emperors, which before his time had been very doubtful and fabulous. But if, according to one of my Japanese historians, he began to reign 20,446 years before Synmu, or 21,106 before Christ, that is, many thousand years before the creation, he cannot be allowed a place in this second era, but ought to be rejected into the first and fabulous one. My other chronological author, with more probability, puts the beginning of his reign in the year before Synmu, 2928, which is the year before Christ 3588, or according to Petavius, 396 years after the creation. He reigned, according to one author, 110, and according to the other 115 years. I think it necessary here to acquaint the reader that having found the latter author in many instances more accurate, I chose to follow him preferably to the first. The Rev. Father Couplet, in the Preface to his Chronological Tables, puts the beginning of the reign of Fohi in the year before Christ 2953, which comes 520 nearer our Saviour's nativity; being just that space of time during which Xinum, and the seven descendants of his family, whom he omits, sat on the throne of China.

The second Chinese emperor was Sin Noo (the Chinese pronounce it Xin Num, or Sijannu), and with his full title, Jen Tei Sin Noo Si. Some authors begin the chronology of the Chinese empire with the reign of this emperor. He came to the throne in the year before Synmu, 2549, which is the year before Christ 3209, or, according to Petavius's chronology, 775 years after the creation. This illustrious prince, like another Egyptian Serapis, taught mankind agriculture, and those arts which relate to the support of our life. For this reason he is by some represented with the head of an ox; by others, only with two horns on his forehead. He also discovered the virtues of several plants, and communicated them to the world in a treatise he wrote on this subject, which was doubtless the first herbal that ever was written. His picture is held in high esteem among the Chinese. The physicians particularly have it hung up in one of the best apartments of their houses, with a plant or leaf in his mouth, which he is smelling. He reigned

140 years, and was succeeded by seven descendants of his family, who reigned 380 years; so that the empire continued in this family 520 years.

After the demise of the last emperor of the family of Xin Num, Kwo Tei (or according to the Chinese, Hoam Ti), and with his full title Hon Tei Juu Hin Si, came to the crown. The Chinese historians unanimously agree that this prince reigned in China. Those who call the existence of the preceding reigns in question, begin the history and chronology of the Chinese empire with the reign of Hoam Ti. He began to reign in the year before Synmu 2029, before Christ 2689, or according to Father Couplet, whom Dr. Mentzelius accurately follows, 2697. He was but eleven years old when he came to the crown. During his minority the empire was governed by wise and prudent councillors, who took great care to give the young monarch an education becoming so great a prince, and to instruct him in all the useful arts and sciences then known. The Chinese stand indebted to this emperor for the art of feeling the pulse, which he learnt himself from his tutors, and afterwards commanded that it should be published to the world. He reigned 100 years and lived 111 years. He was succeeded by five descendants of his family, in which the empire continued 313 years.

Of the five princes, Hoam Ti's successors, Tei Gio, or according to the Chinese pronunciation, Ti Jao, was the most illustrious. He was a great sezin—that is, a man incomparably well versed in occult arts and sciences. He was also a very virtuous prince, and a true father of his country. His death was universally lamented by all his subjects, who went into mourning for three years. He came to the crown in the year before Synmu 1697, before Christ 2357. He reigned seventy-two years, and died under the reign of his successor, in the 118th year of his age. Though he had twelve children, ten sons and two daughters, yet he delivered the crown and government of the empire to an honest and wise husbandman, to whom he married his two daughters.

Tei Sijun, otherwise Gu, and according to the Chinese, Ju Ti Sijun, or Ju Ti Xun, was Ti Jao's son-in-law and successor. He reigned eight-and-twenty years with Ti Jao, and thirty-three alone, in all sixty-one. My author puts the beginning of his reign in the year before Synmu, 1634, which is the year before Christ 2294. During his reign a great deluge happened in China, which overflowed many provinces, and drowned great numbers of the inhabitants. The country continued under water in some parts for several years after.

Uu, and with his full title, Katewu, that is Emperor Uu, of the family Ka, or as the Chinese pronounce it, Ju of the family Hia, reigned seventeen years with the Emperor Tei Sjun, and ten years after his death, in all twenty-seven years. He was crowned in the year before Synmu 1573, before Christ 2233. This emperor caused canals and sluices to be cut, to convey the waters, which overflowed great part of China under the reign of his predecessor, down to the sea. By this means deep rivers arose, and the country was freed from the floods. He lived an hundred years, and was succeeded by eleven descendants of his family, who reigned 431 years, so that the crown remained in this family 458 years. The last of this family was famous for his uncommon strength; but he very much tyrannised his subjects, and lived with such a profuseness, that he caused a lake to be dug by two thousand men, and to be filled with Chinese beer. He is said also to have built a tower of gold and precious stones for one of his mistresses. He was deposed and banished in the fifty-second year of his age.

Sioo Sei Too, that is, King Too of the family of Sjoo, (or, as the Chinese pronounce it, King Tam of the family of Kajam), came to the crown in the year before Synmu 1106, before Christ 1766, being then eighty-seven years old. He reigned thirteen years, and died in the hundredth year of his age. During his reign there was a great famine in China, which lasted seven years, like that famous Egyptian famine mentioned in holy writ. He was succeeded by twenty-seven princes of his family, who reigned in all 631 years, so that the empire remained in this family for 644 years. The last emperor of this family was a great tyrant, for which reason the princes his subjects raised war and rebellion against him; and having reduced him to great straits, he set fire to his palace, and burnt himself with his family and domestics, leaving the empire to the conqueror.

Siu no Bu O, that is, Emperor Bu of the family of Siu, (or according to the Chinese, Uu Vam of the family Sjeu,) who came to the crown 462 years before Synmu, and 1122 before Christ. He reigned seven years, and was succeeded by thirty-seven descendants of his family, in which the empire continued, according to the Japanese histories, 868 years, that is, to the year before Christ 255, and 206 years after Synmu. Under Soowoo, and according to the Chinese pronunciation Sjoovam, the fourth emperor of this family, in the twenty-second year of his reign, which was the year before Synmu 367, before Christ 1027, upon the eighth day of the fourth month, was born in India the great heathen prophet Siaka; who for his incomparable qualities was afterwards called Fo, or Fotoge, that is, "the God," and by the Chinese, Sitajun, that is, "the great and perfect." His doctrine was soon spread by his disciples into several parts of the East Indies. He died seventy-nine years old, in the year before Synmu 289, before Christ 949. Thus far what I had to observe concerning the second, and doubtful era, of the Japanese.

CHAPTER X.

OF THE ECCLESIASTICAL HEREDITARY EMPERORS OF JAPAN IN GENERAL; OF THEIR SUCCESSION, RESIDENCE, AND COURT; AS ALSO OF THE CHRONOLOGY OF THE JAPANESE.

The third and last epocha of the Japanese monarchy, which is that of their Oo Dai Sin Oo, or Ecclesiastical Hereditary Emperors, begins with the year before Christ 660; being the seventeenth year of the reign of the Chinese Emperor Kaiwo, or, as the Chinese pronounce it, Huivam, (who was the seventeenth emperor of the family of Sjeu). From that time to the year of Christ 1693, one hundred and fourteen Emperors, all of the same family, sat successively on the throne of Japan. They value themselves extremely upon being the eldest branch of the family of Tensio Dai Sin, that most sacred founder of the Japanese nation, and the lineal issue of his first-born son, and so down. Uncommon respect, and more than human veneration, is, on that account, paid them by their subjects and countrymen. But before I proceed to the history of their succession, lives, and actions, it will not be amiss to give some preliminary account of their sacred persons, and court; as also of the chronology of the empire, whereby the succession of the emperors must be calculated.

And here it must be observed, in the first place, that the ecclesiastical hereditary monarchs, though they are heirs of the throne and government of their divine predecessors, yet they have not inherited the title of Mikotto; a title which is sacred only to the divine and half divine beings of the first and second succession. They are called Mikaddo (which is a diminutive of Mikotto), as also Dai, and Oo, and Kwo and Tai, all which signify an emperor, a prince, and great lord. They are likewise called Tensin, that is, "Sons of Heaven;" and many more titles of the like nature have been given them. In common conversation they are frequently called Dairi, which name properly denotes their whole court; on which account also he is sometimes called Kintsiusama, that is, the head, or Lord of the Ecclesiastical Court. When he speaks of himself he assumes the title of Tsin, and when he signs, that of Maro.

But to come nearer to our purpose. It was about the time mentioned above, that the Japanese, who had been till then without any settled form of government, either monarchical or other, following a course of life not unlike that of the patriarchs, where the several families lived under the command and authority of their fathers, or else obeyed to the most prudent among themselves; it was, I say, about that time, they agreed to submit to the government of one prince. It is not improbable, but that the Chinese, who came over from time to time into Japan, as they were bred up themselves under a monarchical government, had no small share in persuading the Japanese to prefer the same. In this posture of affairs, surely nobody had a better claim to the supreme power and authority, than a prince lineally descended of the first-born issue of the family of Tensio Dai Sin, who, by the very law of primogeniture, seemed to be naturally entitled to the sovereignty ascribed to that founder of their nation, whose holiness and virtues he inherited besides.

Even to this day the princes descended of this family, more particularly those who sit on the throne, are looked upon as persons most holy in themselves, and as Popes by birth. And, in order to preserve these advantageous notions in the minds of their subjects, they are obliged to take an uncommon care of their sacred persons, and to do such things, which, examined according to the customs of other nations, would be thought ridiculous and impertinent. It will not be improper to give a few instances of it. He thinks that it would be very prejudicial to his dignity and holiness to touch the ground with his feet; for this reason, when he intends to go anywhere, he must be carried thither on men's shoulders. Much less will they suffer, that he should expose his sacred person to the open air, and the sun is not thought worthy to shine on his head. There is such a holiness ascribed to all the parts of his body, that he does not dare to cut off his hair, or his beard, or his nails. However, lest he should grow too dirty, they may clean him in the night when he is asleep; because, they say, that what is taken from his body at that time, hath been stolen from him, and that such a theft doth not prejudice his holiness or dignity. In ancient times, he was obliged to sit on the throne for some hours every morning, with the imperial crown on his head, but to sit altogether like a statue, without stirring either hands or feet, head or eyes, nor indeed any part of his body, because, by this means, it was thought that he could preserve peace and tranquillity in his empire: for if, unfortunately, he turned himself on one side or the other, or if he looked a good while towards any part of his dominions, it was apprehended that war, famine, fire, or some other great misfortune was near at hand to desolate the country. But it having been afterwards discovered, that the imperial crown was the palladium, which by its mobility could preserve peace in the empire, it was thought expedient to deliver his imperial person, consecrated only to idleness and pleasures, from this burthensome duty, and therefore the crown is at present placed on the throne for some hours every morning. His victuals must be dressed every time in new pots, and served at table in new dishes: both are very clean and neat, but made only of common clay; that without any considerable expense they may be laid aside, or broken, after they have served once. They are generally broken, for fear they should come into the hands of laymen, for they believe religiously, that if any layman should presume to eat his food out of these sacred dishes, it would swell and inflame his mouth and throat. The like ill effect is dreaded from the Dairi's sacred clothes; for they believe that if a layman should wear them, without the emperor's express leave or command, they would occasion swellings and pains in all parts of his body.

As soon as by the demise of a Mikaddo the throne becomes vacant, he is by the ministry of this ecclesiastical court put into the deceased's place, whom they think the nearest heir, without regard had to age or sex. Hence it is, that often Princes under age, or young unmarried Princesses ascend the throne, and there are also instances, that the deceased Emperor's relict succeeded her husband. If there be several pretenders to the crown, and it doth not appear plainly who it is that hath the nearest title, the difference is adjusted in an amicable way, according to equity, and the supreme power delivered successively to each of them for some years, in proportion to the degree of kindred they bore to the deceased Mikaddo. Sometimes the father resigns the crown successively to one or more of his children, that he, and their mothers, whilst yet alive, may have the pleasure to see them upon the throne, of which perhaps after their demise, they would stand excluded. All this is done at court with as little trouble as possible; and a Mikaddo may die, or resign, and another be put in his place, and no persons but those around the court know of it, till the affair is over. However it happened sometimes, that those of the imperial family who thought themselves entitled to the succession, but were excluded, maintained their right by force of arms, endeavouring to turn out the Dairi, whom they thought unlawfully possessed of the throne. Hence arose wars and dissensions very prejudicial to the empire. The Princes of the empire espoused different interests, and these quarrels seldom ended but with the entire destruction of one of the contending parties, followed by a cruel extirpation of whole families.

The Dairi's whole court is of the family of Tensio Dai Dsin, and it is on account of a birth so eminent and noble, that they esteem themselves entitled to a far greater degree of respect and deference, than laymen could pretend to. Though they are all descended of one family, yet by degrees they spread out into different branches, and are at present many thousands in number. A few are provided with abbeys, and priories of rich monasteries, founded up and down the empire. But the greatest part of them remain at court, religiously attached to the Dairi's most holy person, on whom they must entirely depend as to their support and maintenance, each according to the office or dignity he is invested with.

At present the Secular Emperor grants the necessary subsidies for the maintenance of the Dairi, and his ecclesiastical court. He hath for this purpose assigned him the whole revenue of the city of Miaco, and all its appurtenances; but because they fell far short of balancing his expenses, it hath been agreed, that the deficiencies should be made up out of the Secular Emperor's exchequer: but those allowances are so small, and besides so indifferently paid, that the court can hardly subsist by it; at least, that they cannot make that figure which they did formerly, when the Dairi was himself master of the empire, and had all the revenues at his own disposal. However, they still keep up their former grandeur and magnificence; and it can most truly be said of this court, that it is remarkable for a splendid poverty. The great ones run themselves in debt, and the inferior officers and servants, whose allowances are far from being sufficient to maintain them, must work for their livelihood. Accordingly they make and sell straw baskets, tables, shoes for men and horses, and other mean things of this nature. The Mikaddo, indeed, though his revenues are but small, in comparison of what they were in former times, yet as he still hath them in his own management, he is sure, in the first place, to take care of himself, and to provide what is requisite to keep up his former splendour, and to satisfy his luxury and profuseness. He is the better able to do this, as one very considerable prerogative of the crown and supreme authority he once enjoyed, hath been still left him by the Secular Monarch, which is the granting of titles of honour to the great men of the empire, their children and relations, which brings in vast treasures into his exchequer. He follows the custom of his predecessors, keeping twelve wives, one of whom being the mother of the hereditary Prince or Princess, hath the title of Empress. It would be too tedious to relate all the splendid and pompous ceremonies which are observed upon his marriage; upon the lying-in of the Empress; upon the choosing of a nurse for the heir of the crown, and his education. It is enough to say, that they are great and magnificent beyond expression, and that if all the happiness and welfare of the empire entirely depended upon the birth of this hereditary Prince, they could not be greater.

There are several eminent dignities that belong to this ecclesiastical court, and its nobility is composed of persons of different ranks and quality. The Mikaddo himself is the fountain of honour. There are, indeed, certain employments annexed to certain titles; but other honours are merely titular, and these are frequently conferred by the Mikaddo on secular persons, on the Princes of the empire, and men of note. This is done either at the recommendation of the Secular Monarch, or at their own desire, upon condition of paying a large sum of money. All the honours and titles are divided into six I's, as they call them, that is ranks, or classes. The title of the first class is Dai Seo Dai Sin. The person who is honoured with this title is esteemed so great and sacred, that they believe that his soul becomes a Cami, or god, the moment of her departure from the body. For this reason the Mikaddo keeps it for himself, and seldom bestows it on anybody. The dignity of Quanbuku belongs likewise to this first class. Quanbuku is the second person of the ecclesiastical court, and the Dairi's vicegerent and prime minister in all affairs relating to the empire. (This title is assumed by the Secular Monarch, or given to the presumptive heir of the crown, and is the same with that of Quabacondono, of which there is so frequent mention made in the letters of the Jesuits.) The following three titles belong to the second I, or rank, Sa Dai Sin, U Dai Sin, and Nai Dai Sin. They are never conferred on more than three persons at court. The Dai Nagon and Tsu Nagon make up the third rank. These two titles are always annexed to certain employments. The titles which belong to the fourth and fifth I, rank or class, are Seonagon, Tsiunagon, Tsiuseo, Seosjo, and Sidsiu. Both these classes are very numerous, and again subdivided into several differing ranks. The persons of this class are likewise called Tensio hito, that is, "a heavenly people;" and the whole ecclesiastical court in general assumes the title of Kuge, which signifies as much as Ecclesiastical Lords; and this they do by way of distinction from the Gege, under which name they comprehend all the laity and inferior sort of people, who are not of so holy and so honourable a descent. The titles of the sixth and last class are Tai U, Goi, and many more of less note. All titles and degrees of honour whatsoever are conferred, as I have already observed, by the Mikaddo, and by him alone. When the Secular Monarchs took the government of the empire into their hands, the

Dairi reserved to himself, along with the supreme authority, this considerable branch of the imperial prerogatives. Hence, whatever titles the Secular Emperors intend to bestow on their favourites and prime ministers, must be obtained of the Mikaddo. There are chiefly two titles which the Secular Emperor, with the consent of the Dairi, can confer on his prime ministers, and the Princes of the empire, which are Maquaudairo and Cami. The first was formerly hereditary, and signifies as much as a Duke or Earl; the second denotes a Knight. It must be observed in this place, that the character which denotes a deified soul, is likewise pronounced Cami, but then it is of a nature quite different from that which expresses the title and honour of knighthood. All the gods and idols of this country in general have the name and character of Kami.

The persons of this ecclesiastical court, among other marks of distinction, are clad after a particular fashion, peculiar to themselves, and widely differing from the habits of secular persons, whom they scorn and despise, as being of a mean, unholy extraction. There is so much difference even among themselves, as to their habits, that thereby alone it is easily known what rank they are of, or what employment they have at court. They wear long wide breeches and a large gown over them, which is very wide and made after a singular fashion, chiefly about the shoulders, and hath a long train, which they trail after them on the ground. They cover their heads with a black lackered cap, by the different shape and figure of which it is known, among other marks of distinction, what quality they are of, or what places they have at court. Some have a broad band of black crape or silk stitched to their caps, which is either tied up, or hangs down behind their shoulders. Others have a sort of a lap, made after the fashion of a fan, standing out before their eyes. Some wear a sort of scarf, or a broad band, which hangs down forwards from their shoulders. The length of this scarf is again different, according to every one's quality or dignity; for it is the custom of this court, that nobody bows down lower, but to reach the floor with the end of his scarf. The women's dress at the court of the Dairi is also very particular and different from that of secular women. But chiefly the Dairi's twelve wives are dressed in as many sumptuous gowns, not lined, interwoven with flowers of gold and silver, and withal so large and wide that it is a matter of great difficulty for them to walk when thus completely dressed.

Studies and learning are the chief amusement of this ecclesiastical court. Not only the Kuge, or courtiers, but even many of the fair sex, have acquired great reputation by their poetical, historical, and other writings. All the almanacks were formerly made at court: but now it is a learned citizen at Miaco that makes them. However, they must be examined and approved of at court by persons commissioned for it, who take care that they be sent to Isje, as to a holy place, to be there printed. They are great lovers of music, the women particularly play with great dexterity upon all sorts of musical instruments. Young noblemen divert themselves with riding, running races, fighting, playing at tennis, and such other exercises becoming their quality. I did not inquire whether they act comedies and tragedies at court. But as the Japanese in general are very fond of plays, and will spend a great deal of money upon them, I am inclined to believe that these ecclesiastical persons, notwithstanding their gravity and holiness, would not willingly want so agreeable and entertaining, and withal so innocent a diversion.

In former times, when the Dairi was sole master of the country, he resided, with his court, wherever he pleased, honouring with his sacred presence now this, then another town, or province of his empire, and it seldom happened that two succeeding emperors chose the same place to live at. Of late their residence hath been in a manner fixed to Miaco. They are possessed of the north-east part of this large capital, which well deserves the name of a separate town, not only by reason of its great extent, and the number of streets, palaces, and houses built within its compass, but also because it is actually separated from Miaco, and defended against the sudden approach of an unexpected enemy, by ditches, walls, ramparts, and gates. The Mikaddo himself lives about the middle of it, in a large and spacious palace, known from others by the height and magnificence of its tower. His imperial consort lives with him in the same palace, and the palaces of his other wives stand next to his. A little way further are the houses of the lords of the Dairi's bed-chamber, and of such other persons whose offices require a constant and more immediate attendance on his sacred person. If a Mikaddo resigns, a separate palace is assigned to him, to his family and court, as is also another to the hereditary Prince, and to his court. The rest of the streets and houses are divided among the officers of this court, according to their rank and dignity. The Secular Monarch constantly keeps a strong guard of bugios and soldiers at the Dairi's court, as it were, out of tenderness and care for the preservation and safety of his sacred person and family, but in fact to put it out of his power ever to attempt the recovery of the throne and the supreme authority which he took from him.

Thus much of the Dairi, his court and government in general. It now remains, before I proceed to the history and succession of the Ecclesiastical Emperors, to lay down some general observations tending to explain the chronology made use of in the same.

The Japanese have two principal eras, or epochs. The first, and also the more common, begins with the reign of their first Emperor Synmu in the year before Christ 660. Consequently the year of Christ, 1693, which was the sixth year of Nengo Genrokf, was the 2353 from Synmu. This epoch is by them called Nin O, which, properly speaking, signifies "a very great and powerful lord or monarch," and in a more sublime sense, "the very first."

The second epoch made use of in Japan is called Nengo. It was invented by the Chinese for a greater certainty in chronology than they thought their common epochs would admit of, and it was not introduced into Japan till the reign of the thirty-sixth emperor. It takes in a period only of a few years, commonly less than twenty, seldom beyond this number. The beginning, as also the proper figure to express it, are determined by the emperor, which is done commonly in memory of some remarkable accident, or of some considerable alteration in church or state. As the emperor hath the sole power of instituting them, so he can continue them as long as he pleases. The Japanese character expressing the Nengo, then current, when I was in Japan, the sixth year of which falls in with the year of Christ 1693, was pronounced Genrokf, which signifies the "Happiness of Nature and Art," whereby the then reigning Mikaddo alluded to the desirable happiness and tranquillity of a private life, which the late emperor, his father, resolved to lead after his resignation of the crown. This epoch is made use of in their almanacks, orders, proclamations, journals, letters, and writings. In their printed books, chiefly such as relate to history and chronology, the current year of the epoch Nin O is added to it. It must be observed that a new Nengo begins always with a new year, though it was ordered and instituted several months before. Sometimes also it happens that although a new Nengo hath been already begun, yet the years of the preceding Nengo are continued in the title-pages of their books, their letters, journals, and so on. This I take to be owing either to the people's not liking the character expressing the new Nengo, or to its not being as yet known, which is not impossible in an empire of so great an extent. Thus, for instance, the almanacks of the first and second year of the Nengo Genrokf were printed with the fifth and the sixth year of the preceding Nengo, Dsiokio, though it was then already expired. In this case, however, care is taken that no error or confusion should be occasioned in their chronology by such an inadvertency. And for this reason it was that the next almanack, which was that of the year of Christ 1690, the third year of the Nengo Genrokf then current, was set down accordingly without any mention made of the two first. The character of a Nengo is composed of two, seldom of more figures, which are, and must be taken out of a particular table composed for this purpose.

There remains still a third epoch, which is likewise made use of in the chronology of the Japanese. This consists of cycli or periods of sixty years, and the Japanese stand indebted for it to the Chinese, as they are also for their Nengos. These sixty years arise from a combination of the Jetta, which are the names of the twelve celestial signs, with the ten names of their elements. The characters of the celestial signs being combined with those of the ten elements five different times, or these six times with the former, there arise sixty compound figures or characters, each of which is taken for a year. When the sixty years are expired a new cyclus is begun, which runs again through all these several combinations. The Japanese use this period of sixty years, the better to ascertain the most remarkable occurrences in church and state, which are recorded in their histories, and are referred under the current year of the cyclus, as well as that of the two other epochs Nin O and Nengo, by which means also they obtain a perpetual harmony between their own history and chronology and that of the Chinese; with this difference however, that whereas the Chinese in their historical writings mention not only the year, but likewise the number of the cyclus wherein such or such things happened, the Japanese on the contrary set down only the year. The cycli of the Japanese are not numbered at all, the reason of which will appear plainly, if we consider the natural pride of this nation, and how far short they would fall, in this particular, of their neighbours the Chinese, who can show a succession of cycli for many centuries before the very foundation of the Japanese monarchy. In the following history which I propose to give of the succession of the Japanese monarchs, I shall avoid troubling the reader with all these different epochs, though I thought it requisite to give some preliminary account of them.

The Jetta, or twelve Celestial Signs of the Japanese, are

1. *Ne*, the Mouse.	8. *Tsitsuse*, the Sheep.
2. *Us*, the Ox or Cow.	9. *Sar*, the Monkey.
3. *Torra*, the Tiger.	10. *Torri*, the Cock, or Hen.
4. *Ow*, the Hare.	
5. *Tats*, the Dragon.	11. *In*, the Dog.
6. *Mi*, the Serpent.	12. *I*, the Boar.
7. *Uma*, the Horse.	

The same names are given, and in the same order, to the twelve hours of the natural day, and to the twelve parts, which every hour is by them divided into, by which means they are able to mention in their histories, with great accuracy, not only what day the most remarkable occurrences happened, but also what hour, and what part of the hour. It must be observed, however, that what they call day, is that interval of time between sunrise and sunset, and that the same is divided into six equal parts or hours, as is also the night, from sunset to sunrise into six others. Hence it is, that their hours differ in length every day, that in the summer the hours of the day are much longer than those of the night, and shorter on the contrary in the winter.

As to their elements, there are properly speaking but five, and it is only by giving two different names and characters to each of them, that they have raised the number to ten, which was absolutely necessary, because by their combination with the twelve celestial signs, repeated five times, they were to obtain the cyclus of sixty years. The names of their ten elements are,

1. *Kino Je*,	Wood.	2. *Kino To*,	Wood.
3. *Fino Je*,	Fire.	4. *Fino To*,	Fire.
5. *Tsutsno Je*,	Earth.	6. *Tsutsno To*,	Earth.
7. *Kanno Je*,	Air.	8. *Kanno To*.	Air.
9. *Midsno Je*,	Water.	10. *Midsno To*,	Water.

The beginning of the Japanese year falls in between the winter solstice and spring equinox, about the fifth of February. But as the Japanese are extremely superstitious in celebrating the day of the new moon, they commonly begin it with the new moon, which immediately precedes or follows the fifth of February. Thus the first year of the Nengo Genrokf, which in the cyclus is called Tsutsno Je Tats, being the year of Christ 1688, began on the second of February, the second of Genrokf, in the cyclus Tsutsnoto Mi, (of Christ 1689) on the twenty-first of January; the third of Genrokf in the cyclus Kano Je Uma, (of Christ 1690) on the ninth of February; the fourth of Genrokf, in the cyclus Kanoto Fitsuse (of Christ 1691) on the twenty-first of January; the fifth of Genrokf, in the cyclus Midsno Je Sar, (of Christ 1692) on the seventeenth of February; and the sixth of Genrokf, (of Christ 1693) on the 6th of February. The Japanese have a leap-year every other or third year, or seven leap-years in nineteen common years.

CHAPTER XI.

OF THE RELIGIONS OF THIS EMPIRE IN GENERAL, AND OF THE SINTOS RELIGION IN PARTICULAR.

LIBERTY of conscience, so far as it doth not interfere with the interest of the secular government, or affect the peace and tranquillity of the empire, hath been at all times allowed in Japan, as it is in most other countries of Asia. Hence it is that foreign religions were introduced with ease, and propagated with success, to the great prejudice of that which was established in the country from remotest antiquity.* In this last hundred years, there were chiefly four religions, considerable for the number of their adherents, to wit:—

1. Sinto, the old religion, or idol-worship of the Japanese.
2. Budsdo, the worship of foreign idols, which were brought over into Japan from the kingdom of Siam, and the empire of China.
3. Siuto, the doctrine of their moralists and philosophers.
4. Deivus, or Kiristando, is as much as to say, the way of God and Christ, whereby must be understood the Christian religion.

It was owing to the commendable zeal, and the indefatigable care of the Spanish and Portuguese missionaries, particularly the Jesuits, that the Christian religion was first introduced into Japan, and propagated with a success infinitely beyond their expectation; insomuch, that from the first arrival of the fathers of the society in the province Bongo, which was about the year of Christ 1549, (or six years after the first discovery of Japan,) to the year 1625, or very near 1630, it spread through most provinces of the empire, many of the princes and lords openly embracing the same. Considering what a vast progress it had made till then, even amidst the many storms and difficulties it had been exposed to, there was very good reason to hope, that within a short compass of time the whole empire would have been converted to the faith of our Saviour, had not the ambitious views, and impatient endeavours of these fathers to reap the temporal as well as the spiritual fruits of their care and labour so provoked the supreme majesty of the empire, as to raise against themselves and their converts a persecution which hath not its parallel in history, whereby the religion they preached, and all those that professed it, were in a few years' time entirely exterminated.

Of the three chief religions which now flourish and are tolerated in Japan, the *Sintos* must be considered in the first place, more for its antiquity and long standing, than for the number of its adherents.

Sinto, which is also called Sinsju, and Kamimitsi, is the idol-worship, as of old established in the country. Sin and Kami denote the idols, which are the object of this worship. Jo and Mitsi is as much as to say, the way or method of worshipping these idols. Sin signifies faith, or religion. Sinsja, and in the plural number Sinsju, are the persons who adhere to this religion.

The more immediate end which the followers of this religion propose to themselves is a state of happiness in this world. They have indeed some, though but obscure and imperfect, notions of the immortality of our souls and a future state of bliss or misery. And yet, as little mindful as they are of what will become of them in that future state, so great is their care and attention to worship those gods whom they believe to have a peculiar share in the government and management of this world, with a more immediate influence, each according to his functions, over the occurrences and necessities of human life. And although indeed they acknowledge a Supreme Being, which, as they believe, dwells in the highest of heaven, and though they likewise admit of some inferior gods, whom they place among the stars, yet they do not worship and adore them, nor have they any festival days sacred to them, thinking, *quæ supra nos nihil ad nos*; that beings, which are so much above us, will little concern themselves about our affairs. However, they swear by these superior gods, whose names are constantly inserted in the form of their oath: but they worship and invoke those gods, whom they believe to have the sovereign command of their country, and the supreme direction of its produce, of its elements, water, animals, and other things, and who, by virtue of this power, can more immediately affect their present condition, and make them either happy or miserable in this life. They are the more attentive in paying a due worship to these divinities, as they seem to be persuaded that this alone is sufficient to cleanse and to purify their hearts, and that doubtless by their assistance and intercession they will obtain in the future life rewards proportionable to their behaviour in this. This religion seems to be nearly as ancient as the nation itself. If it is any ways probable that the first Japanese are descended of the Babylonians, and that, whilst at Babel, they acquired some notions of the true religion, of the creation of the world, and its state before that time, as they are delivered to us in sacred writ, we may upon as good grounds suppose, that by the alteration of their language, and by the troubles and fatigues of so long and tedious a journey, the same were almost surely worn out of their minds; that upon their arrival in this extremity of the east, they deservedly bore a most profound respect to their leader, who had happily conducted them through so many dangers and difficulties; that after his

---

* It is related as an instance of the toleration enjoyed by all religious sects in Japan, that shortly after the introduction of Christianity, one of the native priests wished the emperor to expel the Christians. The emperor inquired how many religious sects already existed in his empire, and on the number, which was considerable, being named, he said if he could tolerate all those, he could surely tolerate one other additional sect.—ED.

death they deified him; that in succeeding ages other great men, who had well deserved of their country, either by their prudence and wisdom, or by their courage and heroic actions, were likewise related among their Kami, that is among the immortal spirits worthy to have divine honours paid them, and that to perpetuate their memory, mias, or temples, were in time erected to them. (Mia, properly speaking, signifies the house or dwelling-place of a living soul). The respect due to these great men became in process of time so universal, that ever since it is thought to be a duty incumbent on every sincere lover of his country, whatever sect otherwise he adheres to, to give public proofs of his veneration and grateful remembrance of their virtues and signal services, by visiting their temples, and bowing to their images, either on such days as are more particularly consecrated to their memory, or on any other proper occasion; provided they be not in a state of impurity, and unfit to approach these holy places. Thus, what was at first intended as a simple act of respect and gratitude, turned by degrees into adoration and worship: superstition at last was carried so far, that the Mikaddos, or ecclesiastical hereditary emperors, being lineal descendants of these great heroes, and supposed heirs of their excellent qualities, are looked upon, as soon as they have taken possession of the throne, as true and living images of their Kamis or gods; as Kamis themselves, possessed of such an eminent degree of purity and holiness, that no Gege (Gege is a vile name, which the Kuge, that is, the members of the emperor's ecclesiastical court, give to their countrymen who are not of the same noble and divine extraction) dare presume to appear in their presence; nay, what is still more, that all the other Kamis or gods of the country are under an obligation to visit him once a year, and to wait upon his sacred person, though in an invisible manner, during the tenth month. They are so far persuaded of the truth of this, that during the said month, which is by them called Kaminatsuki, that is, the month without gods, no festival days are celebrated, because the gods are supposed not to be at home in their temples, but at court waiting upon their Dairi. This Japanese pope assumes also to himself the sole power and authority of deifying and canonising others, if it appears to him that they deserve it, either by the apparitions of their souls after their death, or by some miracles wrought by them. In this case the emperor confers an eminent title upon the new god, or saint, and orders a mia, or temple, to be built to his memory, which is done either at his own expense or by the charitable contributions of pious, well-disposed persons. If afterwards it so happens that those who worship in this temple, and more particularly devote themselves to the new god, prosper in their undertakings, but much more if some extraordinary miracle hath been wrought seemingly by his power and assistance, it will encourage other people to implore his protection, and by this means the number of his temples and worshippers will quickly increase. Thus the number of divinities is augmented every age. But besides all the illustrious men who from time to time, for their heroic actions or singular piety, have been by the spiritual emperors related among the divinities of the country, they have another series of gods of a more ancient date. Of these two successions are mentioned. The first is the succession of the Tensin Sitzi Dai, or seven great celestial spirits, who are said to have existed in the most ancient times of the sun, long before the existence of men and heaven, and to have inhabited the Japanese world (the only country, in their opinion, then existing) many millions of years. The seventh and last of these great celestial spirits, whose name was Isanagi, having carnally known his divine consort Isanami, in imitation of what he had observed of the bird Isitadakki, begot a second succession of divinities, inferior, indeed, to the first, but still superior to all those who existed since their time. This second succession is from the number of its chief heads, called Dsi Sin Go Dai, or the succession of the five terrestrial divinities, who lived and governed the country of Japan a long but limited time. It is needless here to enlarge any further on this head; a full account of the ridiculous and fabulous notions of the Japanese with regard to these two successions of divinities, having been already given. I will only add that the history of the second succession is full of strange and uncommon adventures, knight-errantries, defeats of giants, dragons, and other monsters, which then desolated the country, to the great terror of its semi-divine inhabitants. Many cities and villages in the empire have borrowed their names from some such memorable action which happened in the neighbourhood. They still preserve in some of their temples swords, arms, and other warlike instruments, which they look upon as remains of that ancient time, and believe to be the very same which in the hands of these semi-divine heroes proved so destructive and fatal to the disturbers of the peace and tranquillity of the country. Uncommon respect is paid by the adherents of the Sintos religion to these sacred relics, which are by some still believed to be animated by the souls of their former possessors. In short, the whole system of the Sintos divinity is such a lame, ridiculous contexture of monstrous, inconceivable fables, that even those who have made it their business to study it are ashamed to own and to reveal all those impertinences to their own adherents, much less to the Budsdoists and the adherents of other religions. And perhaps it would not have stood its ground so long, had it not been for its close connection with the civil customs, in the observation of which this nation is exceedingly nice and scrupulous. The temples of the Sintoists are not attended by priests and ecclesiastical persons, but by laymen, who are generally speaking entirely ignorant of the grounds and reasons of the religion they profess, and wholly unacquainted with the history of the gods whom they worship. Some few, however, there are among the Sintosju, or adherents of the Sintos religion, chiefly of the order of the Canusis, who will now and then make a sermon to the people, and be at some pains in instructing young children. During my stay in Japan one of these Canusis came from Miaco to preach at the temple of Tensi, and afterwards at that of Suwa. He made a sermon every day, in order to explain the law or commandment Nacottominotarrai, or Nacottamibarrai; but his sermons at best were ill-disposed, confused compositions of romantic and ridiculous stories of their gods and spirits. They will teach their system of divinity to others for a proper consideration, and under an obligation of secrecy; particularly when they come to the last article, which relates to the beginning of all things, they take special care not to reveal the same to their disciples till he hath obliged himself with an oath signed with his hand and seal not to profane such sacred and sublime mysteries by discovering them to the ignorant and incredulous laity. The original text of this mysterious doctrine is contained in the following words taken out of a book which they call Odaiki: "Kai fakuno fasime Dsjusio Fuso Tatojaba Jujono sui soni ukunga Gotosi Tentaijuo utsijni Itai butsu wo sconu Katata Igeno gotosi fenquas ste sin to uar kuni toko datsuo Mikotto to goos;" that is: "In the beginning of the opening of all things, a chaos floated, as fishes swim in the water for pleasure. Out of this chaos arose a thing like a prickle, moveable and transformable; this thing became a soul or spirit, and this spirit is called Kunitokodatano Mikotto."

CHAPTER XII.

OF THE SINTOS TEMPLES, BELIEF AND WORSHIP.

The Sinsju, that is, the adherents of the Sintos religion, call their temples or churches mia, which word, as I have observed, signifies dwelling-places of immortal souls. They come nearest to the fana of the ancient Romans, as they are, generally speaking, so many lasting monuments erected to the memory of great men. They call them also jasijro, and sia, or sinsja, which last takes in the whole court of the mia, with all other buildings and dependencies belonging to the same. The gods who are the subject of their worship they call Sin and Kami, which signifies souls or spirits. Sometimes also they honour them with the epithet of Miosin, sublime, illustrious, holy; and Gongen, just, severe, jealous. The adherents of other religions call the convents of their religious men, and the places of their worship, sisia tira, that is, temples, and the gods themselves which they adore, Fotoge. All other foreign idols, the worship of whom was brought into Japan from beyond sea, are comprehended under one general name of Bosatz, or Budz. The mias, as indeed all convents and religious houses in general, as well of this as of their other sects, are seated in the pleasantest parts of the country, on the best spots of ground, and commonly within or near great cities, towns, villages, and other inhabited places. I will confine myself in this chapter only to the mias of the Sintoists. A broad and spacious walk, planted with rows of fine cypress trees, which grow in the country, and are a tall, fine tree, leads straight to the mia, or else to the temple-court, on which there are sometimes several mias standing together, and in this case the walk aforesaid leads directly to that which is reckoned the chief. The mias are, generally speaking, seated in a pleasant wood, or in the ascent of a fine green hill, and have neat stone staircases leading up to them. Next to the highway, at the entry of the walk which leads to the temple, stands, for distinction's sake from common roads, a particular fashioned gate, called torij, and built either of stone or wood. The structure of these gates is but very mean and simple, they consisting of two perpendicular posts or pillars, with two beams laid across, the uppermost of which is, for ornament's sake, depressed in the middle, the two extremities standing upwards. Between the two cross-beams is placed a square table, commonly of stone, whereon is engraved the name of the god to whom the mia is consecrated, in golden characters. Sometimes such another gate stands before the mia itself, or before the temple-court, if there be several mias built together in one court. Not far from the mia is a bason, commonly of stone, and full of water for those who go to worship to wash themselves. Close to the mia stands a great wooden alms-chest. The mia itself is neither a splendid nor a magnificent building, but very mean and simple, commonly quadrangular, and built of wood, the beams being strong and neat. It seldom exceeds twice or thrice a man's height, and two or three fathoms in breadth. It is raised about a yard or upwards, from the ground, being supported by short wooden posts. There is a small walk, or gallery, to go round it, and a few steps lead up to this walk. The frontispiece of the mia is as simple as the rest, consisting only of one or two grated windows, for those that come to worship to look through, and to bow towards the chief place within. It is shut at all times, and often without anybody to take care of it. Other mias are somewhat larger, sometimes with an antechamber, and two side-rooms, wherein the keepers of the mia sit, in honour of the Kami, richly clad in their fine ecclesiastical gowns. All these several rooms have grated windows and doors, and the floor is covered with curious mats. Generally speaking, three sides of the temple are shut with deal-boards, there being no opening left but in the front. The roof is covered with tiles of stone, or shavings of wood, and jets out on all sides to a considerable distance, to cover the walk, which goes round the temple. It differs from other buildings by its being curiously bent, and composed of several layers of fine wooden beams, which jetting out underneath make it look very singular. At the top of the roof there is sometimes a strong wooden beam, bigger than the rest, laid lengthways, at the extremities of which two other beams stand up, crossing each other; sometimes a third one is laid athwart behind them. This structure is in imitation as well as in memory of the first Isje temple, which though simple, was yet very ingeniously and almost inimitably contrived, so that the weight and connection of these several beams was to keep the whole building standing. Over the temple-door hangs sometimes a wide flat bell, and a strong, long, knotted rope, wherewith those that come to worship, strike the bell, as it were, to give notice to the gods of their presence. This custom, however, is not very ancient, nor did it originally belong to the Sintos religion, for it was borrowed from the Budsdo or foreign idol-worship. Within the temple is hung up white paper, cut into small bits, the intent of which is to make people sensible of the purity of the place. Sometimes a large looking-glass is placed in the middle, for the worshippers to behold themselves, and withal to consider, that as distinctly as the spots of their face appear in the looking-glass, so conspicuous are the secret spots and frauds of their hearts in the eyes of the immortal gods. These temples are very often without any idols, or images of the Kami to whom they are consecrated. Nor indeed do they keep any images at all in their temples, unless they deserve it on a particular account, either for the reputation and holiness of the carver, or because of some extraordinary miracles wrought by them. In this case a particular box is contrived at the chief and upper end of the temple, opposite to its grated front, and it is called fongu, which is as much as to say, the real, true temple. In this box, which the worshippers bow to, the idol is locked up, and never taken out, but upon the great festival day of the Kami whom it represents, which is celebrated but once in a hundred years. In the same shrine are likewise locked up what relics they have of the bones, habits, swords, or handyworks of the same god. The chief mia of every place hath one or more mikosi, as they call them, belonging to it, being square, or six, or eight cornered sacella, or smaller temples, curiously lacquered, adorned without with gilt cornices, within with looking-glasses, cut white paper, and other ornaments, and hanging on two poles in order to be carried about upon proper occasions, which is done with great pomp and solemnity, when upon the Jennitz, that is, the chief festival day of the god, to whom the mia itself is consecrated, the Canusi, or officers of the temple, celebrate the Matsuri, of which more in another place. Sometimes the idol of the Kami, to whom the mia is dedicated, or such of his relics as are there kept, are carried about in these mikosis upon the same solemn occasion. The chief of the Canusis takes them out of the shrine of the temple, where they are kept in curious white boxes, carries them upon his back to the mikosi, and places them backwards into the same, the people in the meantime retiring out of the way, as being too impure and unworthy a race to behold these sacred things. The outside of the mia, or the ante-chamber, and other rooms built close to it, are commonly hung with divers ornaments, scimiters curiously carved, models of ships, images of different sorts, or other uncommon curiosities, affording an agreeable amusement for the idle spectators, who come to view and to worship in these temples upon their holidays. These several ornaments are called jemma, and are generally speaking free gifts to the temple, given by the adherents of this religion, pursuant to vows, which they made, either for themselves, or for their relations and friends, when taken ill of some violent sickness, or labouring under some other misfortunes, and which they afterwards very scrupulously put in execution, both to show the power of the gods, whose assistance they implored, and their own deep sense of gratitude for the blessings received from them. The same custom is likewise observed by the adherents of the Bosatz, or Budsdo religion. These mias, or Sintos temples are not attended by spiritual persons, but by secular married men, who are called Negi, and Canusi, and Siannin, and are maintained, either by the legacies left by the founder of the mia, or by the subsidies granted them by the Mikaddo, or by the charitable contributions of pious well-disposed persons, who come to worship there. Mikaddo, according to the literal sense of the word, signifies the Sublime Porte, Mi being the same with on, goo, oo, gio, high, mighty, illustrious, supreme, sublime, and kado, signifying a port, gate, or door. These Canusis, or secular priests, when they go abroad, are for distinction's sake, clad in large gowns, commonly white, sometimes yellow, sometimes of other colours, made much after the fashion of the Mikaddo's court. However, they wear their common secular dress under these gowns. They shave their beards, but let their hair grow. They wear a stiff, oblong, lackered cap, in shape not unlike a ship, standing out over their forehead, and tied under their chins with twisted silk strings, from which hang down fringed knots, which are longer or shorter, according to the office or quality of the person that wears them, who is not obliged to bow down lower to persons of a superior rank, but to make the ends of these knots touch the floor. Their superiors have their hair twisted up under a black gauze, or crape, in a very particular manner, and they have their ears covered by a particular sort of a lap, about a span and a half long, and two or three inches broad, standing out by their cheeks, or hanging down, more or less according to the dignities or honourable titles conferred upon them by the Mikaddo. In spiritual affairs, they are under the absolute jurisdiction of the Mikaddo; but in temporalities, they, and all other ecclesiastical persons in the empire, stand under the command of two Dsi Sin Bugios, as they call them, or imperial temple-judges, appointed by the Secular Monarch. They are haughty and proud beyond expression, fancying themselves to be of a far better make and nobler extraction than other people. When they appear in a secular dress, they wear two scimiters, after the fashion of the noblemen. Though secular persons themselves, yet they think it their duty, and becoming their station, to abstain religiously from all communication and intimacy with the common people. Nay, some carry their scrupulous conceits about their own purity and holiness so far, that they avoid conversing, for fear of injuring the same, even with other religious persons, who are not of the same sect. As to this conduct, however, I must own, that something may be said on their behalf, for as much as this their uncommon carriage, and religious abstinence from all sort of communication with other people, seems to be the best means to conceal their gross ignorance, and the enormity and inconsistency of their system of divinity, which could not but be very much ridiculed, if in conversation the discourse should happen to fall upon religious affairs. For the whole Sintos religion is so mean and simple, that besides a heap of fabulous and romantic stories of their gods, demi-gods and heroes, inconsistent with reason and common-sense, their divines have nothing, neither in their sacred books, nor by tradition, wherewithal to satisfy the inquiries of curious persons, about the nature and essence of their gods, about their power and government, about the future state of our soul, and such other essential points, whereof other heathen systems of divinity are not altogether silent. For this reason it was, that when the foreign pagan Budsdo religion came to be introduced in Japan, it spread not only quickly, and with surprising success, but soon occasioned a difference and schism even between those, who remained constant and faithful to the religion of their ancestors, by giving birth to two sects, into which the Sintoists are now divided. The first of these sects is called Juits. The orthodox adherents of this, continued so firm and constant in the religion and customs of their ancestors, that they would not yield in any the least point, how insignificant soever; but they are so very inconsiderable in number, that the Canusis, or priests, themselves make up the best part. The other sect is that of the Riobus; these are a sort of syncretists, who for their own satisfaction, and for the sake of a more extensive knowledge in religious matters, particularly with regard to the future state of our souls, endeavoured to reconcile, if possible, the foreign pagan religion, with that of their ancestors. In order to this they suppose, that the soul of Amida, whom the Budsdoists adore as their Saviour, dwelt by transmigration in the greatest of their gods Ten Sio Dai Sin, the essence, as they call him of light and sun. Most Sintoists confess themselves to this sect. Even the Dairi, or the Ecclesiastical Hereditary Emperor's whole court, perhaps sensible enough of the falsity and inconsistency of the religion which they profess, and convinced how poor and weak their arguments are, whereby they endeavour to support the almost divine majesty and holiness which their master arrogates to himself, seem to incline to this syncretism. Nay they have shown not long ago, that they are no great enemies even to the foreign pagan worship, for they conferred the arch-bishopric and the two bishoprics, of the Ikosiu, the richest and most numerous sect of the Budsdoists, upon Princes of the imperial blood. The Secular Monarch professes the religion of his forefathers, and pays his respect and duty once a-year to the Mikaddo, though at present not in person, as was done formerly, but by a solemn embassy and rich presents. He visits in person the tombs of his imperial predecessors, and frequents also the chief temples, and religious houses, where they are worshipped. When I was in Japan, two stately temples were built by order of the Secular Monarch in honour of the Chinese philosopher Kooajuu, or as we call him Confutius, whose philosophy they believe, was communicated to him immediately from Heaven, which same opinion the Greeks formerly had of the philosophy of Socrates. One thing remains worthy of observation, which is, that many and perhaps the greatest part of those, who in their life-time constantly professed the Sintos religion, and even some of the Siutosju, or moralists, recommend their souls on their death-bed to the care of the Budsdo clergy, desiring that the namanda might be sung for them, and their bodies burned and buried after the manner of the Budsdoists. The adherents of the Sintos religion do not believe the Pythagorean doctrine of the transmigration of souls, although almost universally received by the eastern nations. However, they abstain from killing and eating of those beasts which are serviceable to mankind, thinking it an act of cruelty and ungratefulness. They believe that the souls, after their departure from the bodies, transmigrate to a place of happiness, seated just beneath the thirty-three heavens, and dwelling-places of their gods, which, on this account, they call Takamanofarra, which signifies, "high and subcelestial fields;" that the souls of those who have led a good life in this world are admitted without delay, but that the souls of the bad and impious are denied entrance and condemned to err, without a time sufficient to expiate their crimes. This is all they know of a future state of bliss. But besides these Elysian fields, these stations of happiness, they admit no hell, no places of torment, no Cimmerian darkness, no unfortunate state attending our souls in a world to come. Nor do they know of any other devil, but that which they suppose to animate the fox; a very mischievous animal in this country, and so much dreaded, that some are of opinion that the impious after their death are transformed into foxes; which their priests call Ma, that is, evil spirits.

The chief points of the Sintos religion (and those, the observation whereof its adherents believe, makes them agreeable to the gods, and worthy to obtain from their divine mercy an immediate admission into the stations of happiness after their death, or, what is more commonly aimed at, a train of temporal blessings in this life,) are,—1. The inward purity of the heart. 2. A religious abstinence from whatever makes a man impure. 3. A diligent observation of the solemn festival and holy days. 4. Pilgrimages to the holy places at Isje. Of these, to which by some very religious people is added 5. Chastising and mortifying their bodies; I proceed now to treat severally.

To begin, therefore, with the inward purity of the heart, the same consists in doing, or omitting, those things which are ordered to do, or to avoid; either by the law of nature, and the dictates of reason, or the more immediate and special command of civil magistrates. The law of external purity, of which more hereafter, is the only one, the observation of which is more strictly recommended to the followers of this religion. They have no other laws given them, either by divine or ecclesiastical authority, to direct and to regulate them in their outward behaviour. Hence, it would be but natural to think, that they should abandon themselves to all manner of voluptuousness and sinful pleasures, and allow themselves without restraint, whatever can gratify their wishes and desires, as being free from fear of acting contrary to the will of the gods, and little apprehensive of the effects of their anger and displeasure. And this, perhaps, would be the miserable case of a nation in this condition, were it not for a more powerful ruler within their hearts, natural reason, which here exerts itself with full force, and is of itself capable enough to restrain from indulging their vices, and to win over to the dominion of virtue, all those that will but hearken to its dictates. But besides, the civil magistrates have taken sufficient care to supply what is wanting on this head; for, by their authority, there are very severe laws now in force against all sorts of crimes and misdemeanors. And certainly the Japanese nation, considered in the main, makes it evident, that the dictates of natural reason, and the laws of civil magistrates, are sure guides enough to all those that will lead a good and virtuous life, and preserve their hearts in a state of purity.

But as to the external purity, the observance whereof, though less material in itself, hath yet been more strictly commanded, it consists in abstaining from blood; from eating of flesh, and from dead bodies. Those who have rendered themselves impure by any of these things, are thereby disabled from going to the temples; from visiting holy places, and in general from appearing in presence of the gods. Whoever is stained with his own, or other blood, is fusio for seven days, that is, impure and unfit to approach holy places. If, in building a mia or temple, one of the workmen should happen to be hurt, so as to bleed in any part of his body, it is reckoned a very great misfortune, and such a one as makes him altogether incapable to work for the future on that sacred building. If the same accident should happen in building or repairing any of the temples of Tensio Dai Sin at Isje, the misfortune doth not affect the workman alone, but the temple itself must be pulled down and rebuilt anew. No woman may come to the temple whilst she hath her monthly terms. It is commonly believed that, in their holy pilgrimages to Isje, the monthly terms do for that time entirely cease, which, if true, must be owing either to the fatigues of a long and tedious journey, or to their taking great pains to conceal it, for fear their labour and expenses should thereby become useless. Whoever eats the flesh of any fourfooted beast, deer only excepted, is fusio for thirty days. On the contrary, whoever eats a fowl, wild or tame, water-fowls, pheasants, and cranes excepted, is fusio but a Japanese hour, which is equal to two of ours. Whoever kills a beast, or is present at an execution, or attends a dying person, or comes into a house where a dead body lies, is fusio that day. But of all the things which make them impure, none is reckoned so very contagious as the death of parents and near relations. The nearer they are related to the dead person, so much the greater the impurity is. All ceremonies which are to be observed on this occasion, the time of mourning, and the like, are determined by this rule. By not observing these precepts, people make themselves guilty of external impurity, which is detested by the gods, and become unfit to approach their temples. Overscrupulous people, who would be looked upon as great saints, strain things still further, and fancy that even the imparities of others will affect them in three different ways, viz., by the eyes, which see impure things; by the mouth, which speaks of them; and by the ears, which hear them. These three ways to sin and impurity are represented by the emblem of three monkeys sitting at the feet of Daijso, and shutting, with their fore feet, one both his eyes, the other his mouth, the third his ears. This emblem is to be seen in most temples of the Budsdoists, of whom it hath been borrowed. We found it also in several places upon the highway. An acquaintance of mine at Nagasaki was so exceedingly nice and scrupulous on this head that, when he received but a visit of one whom he had reason to suspect of being a fusio, he caused his house to be washed and cleaned with water and salt from top to bottom, and yet, all this superstitious care notwithstanding, the wiser of his countrymen looked upon him as a downright hypocrite.

CHAPTER XIII.

OF THE SINTOS REBI, THAT IS, THEIR FORTUNATE DAYS AND HOLIDAYS; AND THE CELEBRATION THEREOF.

THE celebration of solemn festivals and holidays, which is the third essential point of the Sintos religion, consists in what they call Majiru; that is, in going to the mias and temples of the gods and deceased great men. This may be done at any time, but ought not to be neglected on those days which are particularly consecrated to their worship, unless the faithful be in a state of impurity, and not duly qualified to appear in the presence of the immortal gods, who detest all uncleanness. Scrupulous adorers carry things still further, and think it unbecoming to appear in the presence of the gods even when the thoughts or memory of their misfortunes possess their mind. For, as these immortal beings dwell in an uninterrupted state of bliss and happiness, such objects, it is thought, would be offensive and unpleasing to them, as the addresses and supplications of people whose hearts, the very inmost of which is laid open to their penetrating sight, labour under deep sorrow and affliction. They perform their devotions at the temples in the following manner: the worshippers having first washed and cleaned themselves, put on the very best clothes they have, with a kamisijno, as they call it, or a garment of ceremony, every one according to his ability. Thus clad, they walk with a composed and grave countenance to the temple court, and, in the first place, to the basin of water, there to wash their hands, if needful, for which purpose a pail is hung by the side of it; then, casting down their eyes, they move on, with great reverence and submission, towards the mia itself; and having got up the few steps which lead to the walk round the temple, and are placed opposite to the grated windows of the mia, and the looking-glass within, they fall down upon their knees, bow their head quite to the ground, slowly and with great humility; then lift it up again, still kneeling and turning their eyes towards the looking-glass, make a short prayer, wherein they expose to the gods their desires and necessities, or say a takamano farokami jodomari, and then throw some putjes, or small pieces of money, by way of an offering to the gods and charity to the priests, either through the grates upon the floor of the mia, or into the

A STREET IN A JAPANESE CITY.—P. 377.

alms-box which stands close by: all this being done, they strike the bell thrice, which is hung up over the door of the mia, for the diversion of the gods, whom they believe to be highly delighted with the sound of musical instruments; and so retire to divert themselves the remaining part of the day with walking, exercises, eating or drinking, and treating one another in the very best manner they can. This plain and simple act of devotion, which may be repeated at any time, even when they are not clad in their best clothes, is on the solemn festivals performed by all the Sintos worshippers, at the temples of one or more gods, whom they more peculiarly confide in, either for being the patrons of the profession they follow, or because otherwise they have it in their power to assist and to forward them in their private undertakings. They have no settled rites and church ceremonies; no beads, nor any stated forms of prayers. Every one is at liberty to set forth his necessities to the gods in what words, and after what manner he pleases. Nay, there are among them who think it needless to do it in any at all, upon a supposition that the very inmost of their hearts, all their thoughts, wishes, and desires, are as fully known to the immortal gods, as their faces are distinctly seen in the looking-glass. Nor is it in the least requisite that, by any particular mortification of their bodies, or other act of devotion, they should prepare themselves worthily to celebrate their festival days, ordinary or extraordinary, or the days of commemoration of their deceased parents, or nearest relations. Even on those days which are more particularly consecrated to commemorate the death of their parents, and which they observe very religiously, they may eat or drink anything they please, provided it be not otherwise contrary to the customs of the country. It is observable in general that their festivals and holidays are days sacred rather to mutual compliments and civilities, than to acts of holiness and devotion; for which reason also they call them rebis, which implies as much as visiting days. It is true, indeed, that they think it a duty incumbent on them, on those days, to go to the temple of Tensio Dai Sin, the first and principal object of their worship, and the temples of their other gods and deceased great men. And, although they are scrupulous enough in the observance of this duty, yet the best part of their time is spent with visiting and complimenting their superiors, friends, and relations. Their feasts, weddings, audiences, great entertainments, and in general all manner of public and private rejoicings, are made on these days preferably to others; not only because they are then more at leisure, but chiefly because they fancy that their gods themselves are very much delighted when men allow themselves reasonable pleasures and diversions. All their rebis, or holidays in general, are unmoveable and fixed to certain days. Some are monthly, others yearly; both which I proceed now more particularly to enumerate.

The monthly holidays are three in number. The first is called Tsitatz, and is the first day of each month. It ought rather to be called a day of compliments and mutual civilities, than a religious day or Sunday. The Japanese on it rise early in the morning, and pass their time going from house to house to see their superiors, friends, and relations; to pay their respects and compliments to them; and to wish them medito, or joy on the happy return of the new moon. The remainder of the day is spent about the temples, and in other pleasant places where there is agreeable walking. Some divert themselves with drinking of soccana, a sort of liquor peculiar to this country. Others pass the afternoon in company with women. In short, every one follows that day what pleasures and diversion he likes best. And this custom is grown so universal, that not only the Sintoists, but the Japanese in general, of all ranks and religions, observe it as a custom derived down to them from their ancestors, and worthy, were it but on this sole account, that some regard should be paid to it.

The second monthly holiday is the fifteenth of each month, being the day of the full moon. The gods of the country have a greater share in the visits the Japanese make on this day, than their friends and relations.

Their third monthly holiday is the twenty-eighth of each month, being the day before the new moon, or the last day of the decreasing moon. Not near so much regard is paid to this, than to either of the former two; and the Sintos temples are very little crowded on it. There is a greater concourse of people on this day at the Budsdo's temples, it being one of the monthly holidays sacred to Amida.

They have five great yearly rebi, or sekf, that is, festivals or holidays; which, from their number, are called gosekf, that is, the five solemn festivals. They are purposely laid upon those days which, by reason of their imparity, are judged to be the most unfortunate; and they have also borrowed their names from thence. They are:—1. Songuatz, or the new-year's day. 2. Sanguatz sannitz, the third day of the third month. 3. Goguatz gonitz, the fifth day of the fifth month. 4. Sitsiguatz fanuka, the seventh day of the seventh month; and 5. Kuguatz kunitz, the ninth day of the ninth month.

These five great yearly festivals are again little else but festa politica, days of universal rejoicings. It hath been already observed, that they were by their ancestors purposely and prudently appointed to be celebrated on those days, which were judged by their imparity to be the most unfortunate; and this, in order to divert those Kamis, or gods, by their universal mirth, and by their wishing of joy and happiness to each other to decline and to avoid all unhappy accidents that might otherwise befal them: on this account also, and because of their being days sacred not so much to the worship of their gods as to joy and pleasure, they are celebrated indifferently, not only by the Sintoists, but by the generality of the Japanese, whatever sect or religion they otherwise adhere to.

But to take them into a more particular consideration, I will begin with the Songuatz, or new year's-day, which is celebrated in Japan with the utmost solemnity, preferably to all other holidays. The main business of the day consists in visiting and complimenting each other on the happy beginning of the new year; in eating and drinking; and going to the temples, which some do to worship, but far the greater part for pleasure and diversion. Whoever is able to stir, gets up betimes in the morning, put on his best clothes, and repairs to the houses of his patrons, friends, and relations, to whom he makes, with a low bow, his medito, as they call it, or compliment suitable to the occasion, and at the same time presents them with a box, wherein are contained two or three fans, with a piece of the dried flesh of the awabi, or auris marina, tied to them, and his name written upon the box, for the information of the person to whom the present is made, in case he should not be at home, or not at leisure to receive company. The piece of the awabi flesh in particular, is intended to remind them of the frugality, as well as the poverty of their ancestors, who lived chiefly upon this shell-fish, and to make them sensible of their present happiness and plenty. In houses of people of quality, where a number of visitors on such days must needs be very considerable, they keep a man on purpose, waiting at the entry of the house, or in one of the lowermost apartments, to receive both the compliments and presents that are made that day; and to set down in writing the names of the persons who came to wait upon his master, and what presents they brought along with them. The forenoon being thus spent, and by repeated draughts of strong liquors, which they are presented with in several places, a good foundation laid for the ensuing frolic, they crown the solemnity of the day with a plentiful dinner, which is commonly provided by the head or chief of the family. This visiting and rambling about from place to place, lasts three days, but the eating and drinking, and treating one another, is not discontinued for the whole month. The first three or four days everything is provided for in plenty, and every one clad as elegantly and handsomely as his abilities will allow. Even poor labouring people, on this occasion, wear a camisijno, as they call it, or a garment of ceremony with a scimiter stuck in their girdle. If they have none of their own, they borrow them of other people, for fear of being excluded from honest companies, and deprived of their share in the universal mirth and pleasure. A few go to perform their devotions at the temples, particularly that of Tensio Dai Sin.

The second sekf, or great yearly festival, is called Sanguatz Sannitz, because of its being celebrated on the third day of the third month. On this also, after the usual compliments and visits, which friends and relations pay one to another, and inferiors to their superiors, every one diverts himself in the best manner he can. The season of the year; the beginning of the spring; the trees, chiefly plum, cherry, and apricot trees, which are then in full blossom, and loaded with numberless white and incarnate flowers, single and double, and no less remarkable for their largeness and plenty than for their singular beauty, invite everybody to take the diversion of the country, and to behold Nature in her new and inimitable dress. But this same festival is besides a day of pleasure and diversion for young girls, for whose sake a great entertainment is commonly prepared by their parents, whereto they invite their nearest relations and friends. A large and spacious apartment is curiously adorned with puppets of a considerable value, which are to represent the court of the Dairi, or Ecclesiastical Hereditary Emperor, with the person of Finakuge. A table with Japanese victuals is placed before each puppet, and among other things, cakes made of rice and the leaves of young mugwort. These victuals, and a dish of saki, the guests are presented with by the girls, for whose diversion the entertainment is intended, or, if they be too young, by their parents. The following story gave birth to this custom: A rich man, who lived near Riusagava, which is as much as to say the Bird-River, had a daughter called Bunajo, who was married to one Symmios Dai Miosin. Not having any children by her husband for many years, she very earnestly addressed herself in her prayers to the Kamis or gods of the country, and this with so much success, that soon after she found herself big, and was brought to bed of five hundred eggs. The poor woman extremely surprised at this extraordinary accident and full of fear, that the eggs, if hatched, would produce monstrous animals, packed them all up into a box, and threw them into the river Riusagava, with this precaution however, that she wrote the word, fosjoroo, upon the box. Sometime after an old fisherman, who lived a good way down the river, found this box floating, took it up, and having found it full of eggs, he carried them home to present them to his wife, who was of opinion that there could not be anything extraordinary in them, and that certainly they had been thrown into the water for some good reason, and therefore she advised him to carry them back, where he found them. But the old man replied thus: "We are both old, my dear, and just on the brink of the grave, it will be a matter of very little consequence to us whatever comes out of the eggs, and therefore I have a mind to hatch them, and to see what they will produce." Accordingly he hatched them in an oven, in hot sand, and between cushions, as the way is in the Indies; and having afterwards opened them, they found in every one a child. To keep such a number of children proved a very heavy burthen for this old couple. However they made a shift, and bred them up with mugwort-leaves minced, and boiled rice. But in time they grew so big, that the old man and his wife could not maintain them any longer, so that they were necessitated to shift for themselves, as well as they could, and took to robbing on the highway. Among other projects, it was proposed to them to go up the river to the house of a rich man, who was very famous for his great wealth in that part of the country. As good luck would have it, this house proved to be that of their mother. Upon application made at the door, one of the servants asked what their names were; to which they answered, that they had no names; that they were a brood of five hundred eggs; that mere want and necessity had obliged them to call; and that they would go about their business, if they would be so charitable as to give them some victuals. The servant having brought the message in to his lady, she sent him back to enquire, whether there had not been something writ upon the box in which the eggs had been found; and being answered, that the word fosjoroo was found writ upon it, she could then no longer doubt, but that they all were her children; and accordingly acknowledged and received them as such, and made a great entertainment, whereat everyone of the guests was presented with a dish of sokana, cakes of mugwort and rice, and a branch of the apricot-tree. This is the reason they give, why, on this festival, branches of apricot-trees are laid over the kettle, and cakes made of mugwort and rice, which they call futsumotzi, that is, mugwort-cakes, and prepared after the following manner: the mugwort-leaves are soaked in water over night, then pressed, dried and reduced to powder, afterwards mixed with rice, which hath been boiled in water, then again reduced to powder and mixed with boiled rice and adsuki, or red beans grossly powdered, and so baked into cakes. The mother of these children was afterwards placed amo g the goddesses of the country, by the name of Bensaiten. They believe that she is waited upon in the happy regions of the gods by her five hundred sons; and they worship her as the goddess of riches.

The third seku, or yearly festival, is Goguatz-Gonitz, or the fifth day of the fifth month. It is also called Tangono Seku, and is much of the same natu re with the last; with this difference only, that it is intended chiefly for the diversion of young boys, who in this, as well as in other countries, neglect no opportunity to make a holiday, and to play about. The inhabitants of Nagasaki divert themselves on the water on this and some following days, rowing up and down in their boats, which are for this purpose curiously adorned; and crying, according to the custom of the Chinese, Peiruun, Peiruun. Mugwort-leaves are put upon the roofs and over the doors of their houses. It is commonly believed, that the mug-wort gathered about this time of the year, and particularly on these holidays, makes the best and strongest moxa, when three or four years old. This festival owes its origin to the history of Peiruun, a King of the island Manrigasima. It began to be celebrated at Nagasaki, by the Foktsui peop'e, who introduced it at first among the young boys, and kept it for some time, before elderly and grave people would conform themselves to the custom. It is said, that at the place where the island stood, some remains of it do still appear in low-water. The very best earth for porcelain-ware is found at the same place, and sometimes entire vessels of a fine, thin, greenish, old China are taken up by the divers, which the Japanese have a very great value for, both for their antiquity and for the good quality, which it is said they have, not only to preserve tea a long while, but even to restore old tea which begins to decay, to its former strength and goodness.

The fourth great yearly festival is called Sissiguatz Nanuka, because of its being celebrated on the seventh day of the seventh month. They give it also the name of Sisseki Tanabatta, which implies as much, and Tanomunoseku, which is as much as to say an auxiliary festival. The usual pleasures and diversions consisting in visiting one another, in eating and drinking, are followed on this day with the same freedom as on other solemn days. The school-boys in particular, among various sorts of plays, erect poles or posts of bamboos, and tie verses of their own making to them, to show their application and progress at school.

The fifth and last of the great yearly festivals is Kunitz, or Kugnatz Kokonok, so called because of its being celebrated on the ninth day of the ninth month. Drinking is the favourite diversion on this festival, though without prejudice to their other usual rejoicings. No expenses are spared to provide victuals and good liquors in plenty, every one according to his ability. The joy and mirth is universal. Neighbours treat one another by turns for that and some following days. Not even strangers and unknown persons are suffered to pass by without being invited to make merry with the company. In short, one would imagine that the Bacchanals of the Romans had been brought over into Japan, and established there. At Nagasaki the solemnity is so much the greater, as the festival of Suwa, formerly a renowned hunter, and now god and protector of hunting, luckily happens to fall upon this same day. All sorts of diversions and public shows, dancing, plays, processions, and the like, (which they call matsuri, or an offering and matsurn, that is, making an offering,) so greatly divert and amuse the people, that many choose rather to lose their dinner than to give over sauntering and staring about the streets till late at night.

But besides these five great yearly festivals, their are many more holidays observed in Japan, of less note indeed, and sacred to particular gods and idols, in whose honour they are celebrated, either universally and throughout the empire, or only in such particular places, which in a more peculiar manner acknowledge their favour and protection. It would be needless, and almost endless to mention them all: however, to give some satisfaction to my reader, I will confine myself to some of the most eminent. But before I proceed, I must beg leave to observe, that, for the major part, they are not of so great antiquity and long standing as the great yearly festivals mentioned above, but of a later date, and instituted at different times in honour and memory of some of their emperors, and other great men, who had either in their lifetime done signal services to their country, or by their apparitions after their death, by extraordinary miracles wrought by them, and by their powerful assistance in private undertakings convinced their countrymen, that having been transported into the regions of immortal spirits, they had no small share in the government of this world, and were worthy on this account, to have divine worship paid them.

Tensio Dai Sin is the supreme of all the gods of the Japanese, and acknowledged as patron and protector of the whole empire. His annual festival falls upon the sixteenth day of the ninth month, and is celebrated in all cities and villages throughout the empire, among other things, with solemn matsuris, as they call them, or processions and public shows, in honour, and often in presence, of his idol and priests. It is a custom which obtains in all cities and villages, to have two such matsuris celebrated every year with great pomp and solemnity in honour of that god, to whose more particular care and protection they have devoted themselves. As to Tensio Dai Sin, besides his great yearly festival, which is on the sixteenth day of the ninth month, the sixteenth, twenty-first, and twenty-sixth days of every month are likewise sacred to him, but not celebrated with any great solemnity.

The ninth—common people: dd the nineteenth and twenty-ninth—of every month are sacred to Suwa. All lovers of hunting, and such persons as recommend themselves to Suwa's more immediate protection, never fail on these days to pay their duty and worship to him at his temples. His annual festival is celebrated with more than ordinary pomp and solemnity on the ninth day of the sixth month. The Canusis on this day make all those who come to worship at Suwa's temples creep through a circle or hoop, made of bamboos, and wound about with linen, in memory of a certain accident, which is said to have happened to the saint in his life-time. But the greatest of his yearly festivals is celebrated at Nagasaki, on the ninth day of the ninth month. This city hath a particular veneration for Suwa; and the matsuris, and other public and private rejoicings made on this occasion, last three days successively.

Tensin hath two yearly festivals, one on the twenty-fifth day of the second month, the other on the twenty-fifth day of the eighth month, which last is celebrated with much greater solemnity than the first. His chief temple is at Saif, the place of his banishment. He hath another at Miaco, where he manifested himself by many miracles. His adorers resort in pilgrimage to these two places from all parts of the empire, chiefly on the twenty-fifth day of the eighth month. He hath also a private monthly holiday, every twenty-fifth day of the month.

The festival of Fatzman, a brother of Tensio Dai Sin, is likewise celebrated on the twenty-fifth day of the eighth month. He was in his life-time called Oosin, and was the sixteenth emperor of Japan.

The festival of Mori Saki Dai Gongen is on the eleventh day of the third month. Simios Dai Miosin. Siteuno.

Gotsutenuo, or Giwon, hath his festival at Nagasaki, on the fifteenth day of the sixth month. His monthly holiday is the same with Fatzman's, but little regarded.

Inari Dai Miosin, is the great god of the foxes. His yearly festival is on the eighth day of the eleventh month, and his monthly holiday every eighth day of the month.

Idsumo no O Jasijro, that is, O Jasijro of the province Idsumo, is another god, for whom they have a great respect. Amongst several glorious exploits, he killed a mischievous, terrible dragon. He is called also Osjuwo ni no Mikotto.

Kassino Dai Miosin. She was Empress of Japan, and in her life-time called Singukoga.

Ben Saiten. Her festival is on the seventh day of the eighth month. The history of this goddess is amply described at the beginning of this chapter.

Kumano Gongen. Naniwa Takakuno Mai Kokfirano Dai Miosin was the seventeenth emperor of Japan, and in his life-time called Nintoku.

Askano Dai Miosin was the twenty-seventh emperor of Japan, and when alive called Kei Tei.

Kimbo Senno Gogin was in his life-time called Ankan, and was the twenty-eighth emperor of Japan.

The merchants worship and devote themselves in a more peculiar manner to the four following gods, as gods of fortune and prosperity. 1. Jebisu was Tensio Dai Sin's brother, but by him disgraced and banished into an uninhabited island. It is said of him, that he could live two or three days under water. He is, as it were, the Neptune of the country, and the protector of fishermen and sea-faring people. They represent him sitting on a rock, with an angling-rod in one hand, or the celebrated fish tai, or steenbrassem in the other. 2. Daikoku is said to have the power, that wherever he knocks with his hammer, he can fetch out from thence anything he wants, as for instance, rice, victuals, cloth, money, &c. He is commonly represented sitting on a bale of rice, with his fortunate hammer in his right hand, and a bag laid by him, to put up what he knocks out. 3. Toosi toku, and by some called Kurokusi. The Japanese worship him at the beginning of the new year, in order to obtain from his assistance success and prosperity in their undertakings. He is represented standing, clad in a large gown with long sleeves, with a long beard, a huge, monstrous forehead, and large ears, and a fan in his right hand. 4. Fottei, by some called Miroku, is represented with a great, huge belly. His worshippers expect from his benevolent assistance, among other good things, health, riches, and children.

These are the greatest of their gods, and the festival-days sacred to them. There are many more saints and great men, whose memory is celebrated on particular days, because of their noble actions and great services done to their country. But as they are confined to particular places, being called the saints of such or such a place, and besides, as they were never canonised by the mikaddo, who alone can make saints, nor honoured with an okurina as they call it, or illustrious title, which is usually given to new gods and saints, I did not think it worth while to make any inquiries about them.

Thus far, what an attentive traveller can learn in the country, concerning the Sintos religion, and the gods, who are the objects of its worship. A more extensive and accurate account of both is contained in two Japanese books, one of which is called Nippon Odaiki, being an historical and chronological account of their kinteju, or great men, and their memorable actions; the other, Sin Dai Ki, that is, the history and actions of their great gods.

CHAPTER XIV.

OF THE SANGA, OR PILGRIMAGE TO ISJE.

THE Japanese are very much addicted to pilgrimages. They make several, and to different places. The first and chief goes to Isje, the second to the thirty-three chief Quanwon temples of the empire, the third to some of the most eminent Sin, or Kami, and Fotoje or Buds temples, famous for the great miracles wrought there, and the help and benefit pilgrims found by going to worship there: such are, for instance, Nikotira, that is, the Temple of the Splendour of the Sun, in the province Oaju; some temples of Fatzman-, .ome temples of the great teacher Jakuai; and some more, whereof every one is at liberty to choose which he likes best, or which it best suits his convenience to resort to. A true orthodox Sintoist visits no other temples in pilgrimage but those of his own gods, and the temple Saif, in Tsikusen, where Tensin died. It may not be amiss to observe in general, that of the three several sorts of pilgrimages mentioned above, the last are made indifferently, by the Sintoists, as well as the Budsdoists, with this difference, however, that everyone goes only to those temples, and worships only those gods, whom his religion commands him to worship. The second, which is the pilgrimage to the thirty-three Quanwon temples, is peculiar to neither of these two religions, but made indifferently by the adherents of both, and looked upon by the generality of the Japanese as a sure means to obtain happiness in this world, and bliss in that to come. But the first of all, which is made to Isje, I propose to take into a more particular consideration in this chapter.

Sanga, in the literal sense of the word, is as much as to say, the Ascent, or going up the temple, and must be understood only of this most eminent temple of Tensio Dai Sin, or Tensio ko Dai Sin, that is, according to the literal signification of these words, the great Hereditary Imperial God of the Celestial Generation. This Tensio Dai Sin is the greatest of all the gods of the Japanese, and the first and chief object of the Sintos worship, on which account also his temple is called Dai Singu, that is, the Temple of the Great God, for Dai signifies great Sin, and Kami a god, a spirit, or immortal soul, and Gu, in conjunction with these words, a mia, that is, a temple, or holy building erected in honour and memory of a god, or immortal spirit. The common people call it Isje Mia, or the temple of Isje, from a province of that name, wherein it stands. A particular and extraordinary holiness is ascribed to this province, because Tensio Dai Sin was born, lived, and died there, whence also they derive the name Isje.

This temple, according to the account of those that have been to see it, is situated in a large plain, and is a sorry, low building of wood, covered with a low, flattish, thatched roof. Particular care is taken to preserve it as it was built originally, that it should be a standing monument of the extreme poverty and indigence of their ancestors and founders of the temple, or the first men, as they call them. In the middle of the temple is nothing else but a looking-glass, cast of metal, and polished, according to the fashion of the country, and some cut paper is hung round the walls; the looking-glass is placed there as an emblem of the all-seeing eye of this great god, and the knowledge he hath of what passes in the inmost heart of his worshippers; the white cut paper is to represent the purity of the place, and to put his adorers in mind that they ought not to appear before him but with a pure unspotted heart and clean body. This principal temple is surrounded with nearly a hundred small chapels, built in honour of other inferior gods, which have little else of a temple but the mere shape, being for the greatest part so low and small that a man can scarce stand upright in them. Each of these chapels is attended by a Canusi, or secular priest of the Sintos religion. Next to the temples and chapels live multitudes of Nege, Lords or officers of the Temple, and Taije, as they also style themselves, that is, Evangelists or Messengers of the Gods, who keep houses and lodgings to accommodate travellers and pilgrims. Not far off lies a town, or rather a large borough, which bears the same name with the temple, and is inhabited by inn-keepers, printers, paper-makers, book-binders, cabinet-makers, joiners, and such other workmen whose business and profession are any ways related to the holy trade carried on at this place.

Orthodox Sintoists go in pilgrimage to Isje once a year, or at least once in their life. Nay, it is thought a duty incumbent on every true patriot, whatever sect or religion he otherwise adheres to, and a public mark of respect and gratitude which every one ought to pay to Tensio Dai Sin, if not as to the god and protector of the nation, at least as to its founder and first parent. But besides that they look upon it as a duty, there are many considerable advantages which, as they believe, accrue to those that visit in pilgrimage these holy places; such as, for instance, absolution and delivery from sin, assurances of a happy state in the world to come, health, riches, dignities, children, and other temporal blessings in this life. To keep up the superstitious vulgar in these advantageous notions, every pilgrim is presented by the Canusis, for a small consideration, with an ofarrai, as they call it, that is, a great purification, being, as it were, a public and undoubted instrument of the absolution and remission of their sins insured to themselves by this holy act. But as many people are not able to fetch them at Isje in person, by reason either of sickness and old age, or because of their employments, attendance upon their prince, or for some such other weighty cause, care is taken not to let them want so great and singular a benefit, but to provide them at home. Many of the Budsdoists resort in pilgrimage to this place at least once, if not oftener in their life, were it but in order to get the reputation of a true patriot amongst their countrymen. But still there are very many who stay at home, and think it sufficient for the ease and quietness of their conscience, besides the yearly indulgences of their own priests, to purchase the ofarrais from Isje, great quantities whereof are sent yearly to all parts of the empire.

This pilgrimage is made at all times of the year; but the greatest concourse of people is in the three first months (March, April, and May), when the season of the year, and the good weather, make the journey very agreeable and pleasant. Persons of all ranks and qualities, rich and poor, old and young, men and women, resort thither, the lords only of the highest quality, and the most potent princes of the empire, excepted, who seldom appear there in person. An embassy from the emperor is sent there once every year, in the first month, at which time also another with rich presents goes to Miaco, to the Ecclesiastical Hereditary Monarch. Most of the princes of the empire follow the emperor's example. As to the pilgrims, who go there in person, every one is at liberty to make the journey in what manner he pleases. Able people do it at their own expense in litters, or on horseback, with a retinue suitable to their quality. Poor people go on foot, living upon charity which they beg along the road. They carry their bed along with them upon their back, being a straw mat rolled up, and have a pilgrim's staff in their hands, and a pail hung by their girdle, out of which they drink, and wherein they receive people's charity, pulling off their hats much after the European manner. Their hats are very large, twisted of split reeds. Generally speaking their names, birth, and the place from whence they come, are written upon their hats and pails, that in case of sudden death, or if any other accident should befal them upon the road, it might be known who they are, and to whom they belong; those that can afford it wear a short white coat, without sleeves, over their usual dress, with their names stitched upon it before the breast and on the back. Multitudes of these pilgrims are seen daily on the road. It is scarcely credible what numbers set out only from the capital city of Jedo, and from the large province Osju. It is no uncommon thing at Jedo for children to run away from their parents in order to go in pilgrimage to Isje. The like attempt would be more difficult in other places, where a traveller that is not provided with the necessary passports would expose himself to no small trouble. As to those that return from Isje, they have the privilege that the ofarrai which they bring from thence is allowed everywhere as a good passport.

After the pilgrim is set out on his journey to Isje, a rope with a bit of white paper twisted round it is hung up over the door of his house, as a mark for all such as labour under an ima, as they call it, that is, under a considerable degree of impurity, occasioned chiefly by the death of their parents or near relations, to avoid entering the same, it having been observed that when by chance, or through inadvertency, such an impure person came into a pilgrim's house, the pilgrim at the same time found himself very much troubled with strange uneasy dreams, or exposed to some misfortunes. The like marks of purity are also hung up over the walks which lead to the mias, or temples.

But it is required besides that the pilgrim himself when he is about, or hath already undertaken, this holy journey should abstain religiously from all things that make a man impure, or are likely to divert his mind at the solemn season. Should a fusio, a person that labours under any degree of impurity, presume to undertake this holy journey, before he hath sufficiently purified himself, he would undoubtedly draw upon him and his family the sinbats, that is, the displeasure and vengeance of the just and pure gods. The Siukkie, or priests of the Budsdo religion, stand excluded for ever from these holy places, because they follow an impure profession, and are obliged to attend sick people, and to bury the dead.

When the pilgrim is come to Isje, the desired end of his journey, which is done daily by great numbers, and upon some particular days by several thousands, he repairs forthwith to one of the Canusis, with whom he is acquainted, or hath been addressed to, or by whom he hath been before furnished with ofarrais, and accosts him in a civil and humble manner, bowing his forehead quite down to the ground, according to the country fashion. The Canusi upon this, either conducts himself, with other pilgrims that applied to him for the same purpose, or commands his servant to go along with them, to show them the several temples, and to tell them the names of the gods to whom they were built, which being done, he himself carries them before the chief temple of Tensio Dai Sin, where, with great humility, they prostrate themselves flat on the ground, and in this abject posture address their supplications to this powerful god, setting forth their wants and necessities, and praying for happiness, riches, health, long life, and the like. After this manner it is that they discharge their duty towards Tensio Dai Sin, and complete the end of their pilgrimage. They are entertained afterwards, as long as they stay at Isje, by the Canusi, who lodges them at his own house, if they are not able to bear the expense of a lodging at a public inn. The pilgrims, however, are generally so grateful as to make the Canusi a handsome return for his civility, should it be even out of what they get by begging, and he hath complaisance enough not to refuse it.

Having performed all the acts of devotion this pilgrimage requires, the pilgrim is by the Canusi presented with an ofarrai, or indulgence. This ofarrai is a small oblong square box, about a span and a half long, two inches broad, an inch and a half thick, made of small thin boards, and full of thin small sticks, some of which are wrapt up in bits of white paper, in order to remind the pilgrim to be pure and humble, these two virtues being the most pleasing to the gods. The name of the temple, Dai Singu, that is, the temple of the great god, printed in large characters, is pasted to the front of the box, and the name of the Canusi who gave the box (for there are great numbers that carry on this trade) on the opposite side, in a smaller character, with the noble title of Taiju, which is as much as to say, Messengers of the gods, a title which all the officers of the Mias assume to themselves.

This ofarrai the pilgrims receive with great tokens of respect and humility, and immediately tie it under their hats, in order to keep it from the rain. They wear it just under their forehead, and balance it with another box, or a bundle of straw, much of the same weight, which they fasten to the opposite side of the hat. Those that travel on horseback have better conveniences to keep and hide it. When the pilgrims are got safe home, they take especial care for the preservation of this oarrai, as being a relic of very great moment and consequence to them. And although the effects and virtues of it be limited only to a year, yet, after this term is expired, they allow it a very honourable place in one of the chief apartments of their houses, on a shelf made for this purpose, and raised above a man's height. In some places the custom is to keep the old ofarrais over the doors of their houses, underneath a small roof. Poor people, for want of a better place, keep them in hollow trees behind their houses. In like manner the ofarrais of deceased people, and those that are dropped upon the road, when found, are put up carefully in the next hollow tree.

Large quantities of these ofarrais are sent by the Canusis every year into all parts of the empire, to supply those who cannot conveniently, or are not willing to come and fetch them at Isje. These ofarrai merchants make it their business to resort to the principal and most populous towns towards the Sanguatz, as they call it, or New-year's day, this being one of their most solemn festivals, and a day of great purification, and certainly the time when they are most likely to dispose of their merchandise quickly, and to advantage. They sell at the same time new almanacks, which are made by the command of the Mikaddo, or Ecclesiastical Hereditary Emperor, and cannot be printed anywhere else but at Isje. One may buy an ofarrai and an almanack together for a maas, or an itzebo. Able people will give more by way of charity. Those that buy them once are sure to be called upon the next year, and to be presented with three things, to wit, a receipt from the Canusi, or rather a compliment of thanks to the buyer, a new ofarrai, and a new almanack. Such as pay handsomely, and more than is due, which common people seldom do, receive moreover a sakkant, or a varnished wooden cup, as a small return for their generosity.

The following account of the present state and situation of the temples at Isje is taken out of Itznobe, a Japanese author. There are two temples at Isje, about the length of twelve streets distant from each other, both indifferent low structures. The ground whereon they stand hath not above six mats in compass, including the place where the Canusis sit in honour of Tensio Dai Sin. They are both covered with a thatched roof, and both built, which is very remarkable, without any one of the workmen receiving the least hurt in any part of his body. Behind these two temples, on a small eminence, stands the small, but true temple of Tensio Dai Sin, which is called Fongu, that is, the true Temple, and which hath been purposely built higher than the others, in like manner as the temple of Suwa is at Nagasaki: within this temple there is nothing to be seen but a looking-glass and bits of white paper.

The first of the temples mentioned above is called Geku ; it hath several Canusis to attend it, and about fourscore massia, or smaller temples, around it, built in honour of inferior gods, each about four mats large, and guarded by a Canusi sitting within to receive people's charity, that being his perquisite for his attendance.

The second mia is called Naiku, and stands about the length of twelve streets further off. It hath likewise great numbers of Canusis, and forty massia, or smaller temples round it, each with a Canusi as above. The Canusis of these smaller temples have a very singular title, being called Mia Dsusume, which signifies temple-sparrows.

Those who have a mind to see these temples, and what is remarkable in and about them, without being conducted by a Canusi, or his servants, must observe the following rules. They go, in the first place, to the river Mijangawa, which runs by the village Isje, opposite to the temples, there to wash and to clean themselves. Thence walking towards the houses of the Canusis, and other merchants, which are about the length of three or four streets distant from the banks of the river, and passing the said houses, they come to a broad gravelly walk, which leads them straight to the Geku Mia. Here they worship in the first place, and then go round to view the inferior temples, beginning on the right hand, and so going on till they come again to the said temple, from whence they proceed straight forward to the second, called Naiku, where they worship as before, and see the massias round it. From this second temple they proceed further up a neighbouring hill, situate not far from the coasts, and having walked the length of about fifteen streets, they come to a small cavern, called Awano Matta, that is, the coast of heaven, which is not above twenty ikins distant from the sea. It was in this cavern the great Tensio Dai Sin hid himself, and thereby depriving the world, sun and stars, of their light, showed that he alone is the lord and fountain of light, and the supreme of all the gods. This cavern is about a mat and a half large, with a small temple or chapel, wherein they keep a cami or idol sitting on a cow, and called Dainitz no rai, that is the great representation of the sun. Hard by live some Canusis in two houses built upon the coasts, which are hereabouts very steep and rocky. The pilgrim performs his devotions also at this cavern and temple, and then presents the Canusis with a few putjes, desiring them withal to plant a sugi-plant in memory of his having been there. From the top of this hill, a large island is seen at a distance, lying about a mile and a half off the coasts, which they say arose out of the ocean in the times of Tensio Dai Sin. These are the most remarkable things to be seen at Isje. Curious pilgrims before they return to Isje, go a couple of miles further to see a stately Budado temple, called Asamadaki, where they worship a Quau-won, called Kokusobosatz.

CHAPTER XV.

OF THE JAMMABOS, OR MOUNTAIN-PRIESTS, AND OTHER RELIGIOUS ORDERS.

THE superstitious Japanese are no less inclined to make religious vows, than they are to visit in pilgrimage holy places. Many among them, and those in particular who aim at a quick unhindered passage into their Elysian Fields, or a more eminent place in these stations of happiness, devote themselves to enter into a certain religious order of hermits, called jammabos in the country-language. Others, who labour under some temporal misfortune, or are upon the point to go about some affair of consequence, frequently make a vow, that in case of delivery from present danger, or good success in their undertakings, they will, out of respect and gratitude to the gods, go to worship at certain temples, or keep to a rigorous abstinence on certain days, or build temples, or make valuable presents to the priests and extensive charities to the poor, and the like.

Jammabos signifies, properly speaking, a mountain soldier. The character indeed, whereby this word is expressed, doth not altogether answer to this signification, which depends more upon the rules of their order, and their original establishment, whereby all the individual members of this society are obliged, in case of need, to fight for the gods and the religion of the country. They are a sort of hermits, who pretend to abandon the temporal for the sake of the spiritual and eternal; to exchange an easy and commodious way of life for an austere and rigorous one; pleasures for mortifications; spending most of their time in going up and down holy mountains, and frequently washing themselves in cold water, even in the midst of the winter. The richer among them, who are more at their ease, live in their own houses. The poorer go strolling and begging about the country, particularly in the province Syriga, in the neighbourhood of the high mountain Fusi Jamma; to the top whereof they are by the rules of their order obliged to climb every year, in the sixth month. A few have miss, or temples, but, generally speaking, so ill provided for, that they can scarce get a livelihood by them.

The founder of this order was one Gienno Giossa, who lived about 1100 years ago. They can give no manner of account of his birth, parents, and relations. Nor had he any issue. He was the first that chose this solitary way of life for the mortification of his body. He spent all this time erring and wandering through desert, wild, and uninhabited places, which in the end proved no inconsiderable service to his country, insomuch as thereby he discovered the situation and nature of such places, which nobody before him ventured to view, or to pass through, because of their roughness and wild aspect, and by this means found out new, easier, and shorter roads from places to places, to the great advantage of travellers. His followers, in succession of time, split in two differing orders. One is called Tosanna. Those who embrace this, must once a year climb up to the top of Fikoosan, a very high mountain in the province Busen, upon the confines of Tsikusen, a journey of no small difficulty and danger, by reason of the height and steepness of this mountain, and the many precipices all round it, but much more, because, as they pretend, it hath this singular quality, that all those who presume to ascend it, when fusios, that is, labouring under any degree of impurity, are by way of punishment for their impious rashness possessed with the fox (others would say, the devil) and turn stark mad. The second order is called Fonsanfa. Those who enter into this, must visit in pilgrimage, once a year, the grave of their founder at the top of a high mountain in the province Jostaijno, which by reason of its height is called Omine, that is, the top of the high mountain. It is said to be excessively cold on the top of this mountain, the steepness and precipices whereof make its ascent no less dangerous than that of the other mentioned above. Should any one presume to undertake this journey, without having first duly purified and prepared himself for it, he would run the hazard of being thrown down the horrid precipices, and dashed to pieces, or at least by a lingering sickness, or some other considerable misfortune, pay for his folly, and his contempt of the just anger of the gods. And yet, all these dangers and difficulties notwithstanding, all persons, who enter into any of these two orders, must undertake this journey once a year. In order to this they qualify themselves by a previous mortification, by virtue whereof they must for some time abstain from lying with their wives from impure food, and other things, by the use of which they might contract any degree of impurity, though never so small, not forgetting frequently to bathe and to wash themselves in cold water. As long as they are upon the journey, they must live only upon what roots and plants they find on the mountain.

If they return safe home from this hazardous pilgrimage, they repair forthwith, each to the general of his order, who resides at Miaco, make him a small present in money, which if poor, they must get by begging, and receive from him a more honourable title and higher dignity, which occasions some alteration in their dress, and increases the respect that must be shown them by their brethren of the same order. So far is ambition from being banished out of these religious societies. For thus they rise by degrees, much after the same manner and in the same order as they do in the society of the blind, of which I shall have occasion to speak in the latter part of this chapter.

The religious of this order wear the common habit of secular persons, with some additional ornaments, directed by the statutes of the order, each of which hath a peculiar name and meaning: they are—

Wakisasi, a scimeter of Fudo, which they wear stuck in their girdle on the left side. It is somewhat shorter than a katanna, and kept in a flat sheath.

Sakkudsio, a small staff of the god Daiso, with a copper head, to which are fastened four rings, likewise of copper. They rattle this staff in their prayers upon uttering certain words.

Foranokai, a large shell, which will hold about a pint of water, and is wound like a buccinum, or trumpet, smooth, white, with beautiful red spots and lines. It is found chiefly about Array, in low water. It hangs down from their girdle, and serves them in the nature of a trumpet; having for this purpose a tube fastened to the end, through which they blow upon approach of travellers, to beg their charity. It sounds not unlike a cowherd's horn.

Dsusukake, a twisted band or scarf, with fringes at the end. They wear it about their neck. By the length of this scarf, as also by the shape and size of the fringes, it is known what titles and dignities they have been raised to by their superiors.

Foki, a cap or head-dress, which they wear on their forehead. It is peculiar only to some few among them.

Oji, a bag wherein they keep a book, some money, and cloth. They carry it upon their back.

Jatzuwono warandzie are their shoes or sandals, which are twisted of straw, and the stalks of the tarate flower; which plant is in a peculiar repute of holiness among them. They wear them chiefly in their penitential pilgrimages to the tops of the two holy mountains above-mentioned.

Izu Taka no Dsiusu is their rosary, or string of beads, by which they say their prayers. It is made of rough balls. The invention and use of it are of a later date than the institution of the order; accordingly there is no mention made of it in the statutes of the same. Kongo Dauje, a thick strong staff, a very useful instrument for their journey to the top of the mountains aforesaid.

The most eminent among them have the hair cut off short behind their heads. Others let it grow, and tie it together. Many shave themselves close, as do in particular the novices upon their entering the order, in imitation of the Budsdo priests, of whom they have borrowed this custom.

These Sintos hermits are now very much degenerated from the austerity of their predecessors; who, in imitation of their founder's example, and pursuant to the rules laid down by him, lived, from their first entering the order, upon nothing else but plants and roots, and exposed themselves to perpetual and very rude trials and mortifications, fasting, washing themselves in cold water, wandering through woods and forests, desert and uninhabited places, and the like. In like manner they deviated very much from the simplicity of the religion they formerly professed, admitting the worship of such foreign idols as are thought by them to have the greatest power and influence over the occurrences of human life. They enlarged their system of divinity, and increased the number of superstitious ceremonies. Among other things, they betook themselves to a sort of trade, which proves very beneficial to them; and to impose upon the vulgar, they give out that they are peculiarly versed in magical arts and sciences, pretending by virtue of certain ceremonies, and mystical obscure words and charms, to command all the gods worshipped in the country, as well of the Sintoists as those of the Budsdoists, the worship of whom was brought over from beyond sea; to conjure and drive out evil spirits; to do many things beyond the power of nature; to dive into secrets and mysteries; to recover stolen goods, and to discover the thieves; to foretel future events; to explain dreams; to cure desperate distempers; to find out the guilt or innocence of persons accused of crimes and misdemeanors, and the like.

I flatter myself the reader will not be displeased to receive some farther information about their way of proceeding in several of these particulars. To begin with the cure of distempers. The patient is to give the jammabos as good an account as possibly he can of his distemper, and the condition he is in. The jammabos, after a full hearing, writes some characters on a bit of paper, which characters, as he pretends, have a particular relation to the constitution of the patient, and the nature of his distemper. This done, he places the paper on an altar before his idols, performing many superstitious ceremonies, in order, as he gives out, to communicate a healing faculty to it, after which he makes it up into pills, whereof the patient is to take one every morning, drinking a large draught of water upon it, which again must be drawn up from the spring or river, not without some mystery, and towards such a corner of the world as the jammabos directs. These character-pills are called goof. It must be observed, however, that the jammabos seldom administer and the patients still seldomer resolve to undergo this mysterious cure, till they are almost past all hopes of recovery. In less desperate cases recourse is had to more natural remedies.

The trials of the guilt or innocence of persons accused of crimes and misdemeanors are made in the presence of an idol called Fudo, sitting amidst fire and flames, not indeed in a judicial and public way, after the manner of the Brahmins, Siamites, and other heathens, nor by giving the question, as is often done in Europe, chiefly in cases of witchcraft, but privately in the house where the act was committed, and in presence of the domestics, either by a simple conjuring and uttering certain words, or by fire, or by a draught of khumano goo. If the first, a simple conjuration, proves ineffectual, recourse is had to the second, a trial by fire; to be performed by making the suspected persons walk thrice over a coal-fire, about a fathom long, which if they can do without being burnt on the soles of their feet, they are acquitted. Some are brought to confession by a draught of khumano goo. Goo is a paper filled with characters and pictures of black birds, as ravens and others, and sealed with the seals of the jammabos. It is pasted to the doors of houses to keep off evil spirits, and serves for several other superstitious purposes. It is made indifferently by all jammabos, but the best come from Khumano, whence the name. A little bit torn off this paper must be swallowed by the accused person in a draught of water; and it is said, that if he be guilty, it will work and trouble him most cruelly till he confesses. They talk very big of the surprising and wonderful virtues of their charms and conjurations, whereby they pretend to be able to manage and handle burning coals and red-hot iron, without receiving any the least hurt; suddenly to extinguish fires; to make cold water boiling hot and hot water ice-cold, in an instant; to keep people's swords and scimiters so fast in the sheath that no force is able to draw them out; to keep themselves from being hurt by these or other weapons; and to perform many more such uncommon and surprising things, which, if more nicely examined, would be found perhaps to be little else than jugglers' tricks, and effects of natural causes. They call it jamassu, which signifies conjuring strokes. These mighty strokes are nothing else but certain motions of their hands and fingers, whereby they pretend to represent crocodiles, tigers, and other monstrous animals, at the same time uttering certain obscure sounds. By this, and by frequently altering these positions and representations, as also by lifting up and letting fall their voice, they endeavour, they say, as with so many cross-strokes, to come within reach of the object to be charmed, till at last, having removed and cut through all obstacles and hindrances, they obtain their desired end.

One of their chief and most mysterious sin, as

they call them, or charms, is, when holding up both hands, and twisting the fingers, as it were, one within another, they represent the Si Tensi O, that is, the four most powerful gods of the thirty-third and last heaven. The position which they put their fingers in is thus: they hold up the two middle fingers, one against another almost perpendicular, and make the two next fingers, on each side, cross one another in such a manner, that they point towards four different corners of the world, in representation of these four gods, whom they call Tammonden, Tsigokten, Sosioten, and Kamokten. The two middle fingers held up, as I observed, almost perpendicularly, serve them, as they pretend, in the nature of a spy-glass, whereby to spy out the spirits and distempers, to see the kitz or fox, and the ma, or evil spirit, lodged in people's bodies, and to find out precisely what sort they be of, in order afterwards to square their charms and ceremonious superstitions to the more effectual driving of them out. But this same position of the middle fingers with regard to the rest is to represent besides Fudo mio wo, that is, the holy great Fudo, formerly a giosia, a mighty devotee of their order, who, among other extraordinary mortifications, sat down daily in the midst of a large fire, though without receiving any hurt; and by whose powerful assistance they believe, on this account, to be able, not only to destroy the burning quality of fire when they please, but also to make it serve at command to what purposes they think fit. A lamp filled with an oil made of a certain black venomous water lizard, called iuari, is kept continually burning before the idol of Fudo.

The jammabos make a mighty secret of these charms and mysterious arts. However, for a handsome reward, they will communicate and teach them to other people, though under condition of secrecy. The account I have given in this chapter of this singular order, I had chiefly from a young Japanese, well versed in the affairs of his country, whom during my stay in Japan I taught physic and surgery, and who had been one of their scholars himself. He further told me, that before they would let him into the secret, they made him undergo a very rude noviciate. And, in the first place, he was to abstain from everything that had life in it, and to subsist only upon rice and herbs for six days together. In the next place, they commanded him to wash himself seven times a day in cold water, and kneeling down on the ground, with his buttocks to his heels, and clapping his hands over his head, to lift himself up seven hundred and fourscore times every day. This last part of his trial he found also the rudest; for by getting up and down two or three hundred times, he brought himself all into a sweat, and grew so tired and weary, that he was often upon the point to run away from his masters; but being a young lusty fellow, shame rather than curiosity prevailed upon him to hold out to the last.

Thus much of the jammabos. There are still many more religious orders and societies established in this country, a particular account of which would swell this chapter to an unbecoming length. From the superstitious veneration of the vulgar for their ecclesiastics and the ease and pleasures of a religious life, it is no wonder that the number of costly temples, rich monasteries and convents, where, under the cloak of retirement and divine worship, the monks give themselves up to an uninterrupted pursuit of wantonness and luxury, is grown to an excess scarce credible. But there are also some particular societies not purely ecclesiastical, nor confined to the clergy alone, but rather of a mixed nature, with an alloy of secularity. Out of many, that of the blind is not unworthy of consideration; a singular, but very ancient and numerous body, composed of persons of all ranks and professions. Originally they made up but one society, but in process of time they split into two separate bodies; one of which is called Feekisado, or the Blind Feekis, the other Bussetz Sato, or the Blind Bussetz. It will not be amiss to inquire into the origin and constitutions of both. The Bussetz Sato must be considered first, as being of a more ancient standing. At present this society is composed only of ecclesiastical persons, whose rules and customs are not very different from those of the jammahos. Their founder was Senmimar, the Emperor Jengino Mikaddo, his third (and according to some authors, his fourth) son, and the occasion of their institution is recorded in Japanese histories to have been as follows: Senmimar was a youth of incomparable beauty, and exceedingly beloved by all that came near him. It happened that a princess of the imperial blood fell desperately in love with him: her beauty and virtues proved charms as irresistible to the young prince as his graceful person and princely qualities had been to her. For some time the happy lovers enjoyed all the satisfaction and mutual returns of passion and friendship, when the death of the princess intervening, Senmimar took it so much to heart, that not long after, through grief and sorrow, he lost his sight. Upon this, to perpetuate the memory of his dearly beloved, and to make known to posterity what an unfortunate effect his unfeigned concern and sorrow for her loss had had upon himself, he resolved, with his father's leave, and under his imperial charter, to erect a society, whereinto none should be admitted but such as had the misfortune to be blind by birth or accident. His design was put in execution accordingly. The new erected society prospered exceedingly, and flourished, and got into great repute at court, and in the empire. For some centuries they continued united in one body, till a new society of the Feki Blind, as they are now called, sprung up, which in a short time got so far the better of the former, many great men in the empire, who were blind, voluntarily entering into it, that by degrees they lost much of their reputation, and were reduced very low in number, none being left at last but ecclesiastical persons, to whom it remains now confined. Ever since their first institution, the Feki Blind continued in uninterrupted possession of all the esteem and authority the Bussetz had once enjoyed. Nay, being still more numerous, they are also much more considered in proportion. They owe their origin to the civil wars between the Fekis and Gendzis, both contending for the empire. Whole volumes have been written of the long and bloody dissensions between these two once considerable and powerful parties, and the manifold calamities which thence befel the empire. The cause of Feki and his adherents appearing more just to the then reigning Dairi than that of Gendzi, he thought himself bound in conscience to support; which he did so effectually, that Gendzi and his party were defeated and almost totally destroyed. The victorious Feki, as success is often followed by pride and ambition, soon forgot the obligations he lay under to the Dairi, and behaved himself with so much insolence and ungratefulness towards him, that he resolved to espouse the interest, though almost totally sunk, of Gendzi and his adherents; promising all manner of encouragement and assistance, if they would once more gather all their strength together, and take up arms against Feki and his party. Affairs upon this soon took another turn; victory in a decisive battle favoured the Gendzis; Feki himself was slain near Simonoseki, and his whole army defeated, but few escaping. Amongst those who escaped with their lives, was Kakekigo, a general very much renowned for his valour and supernatural strength, which, it was believed, he obtained from Quanwon, as a reward for his constant devotion to that god. This general fled in a small boat. Joritomo, general of the Gendzis, and himself a very resolute soldier, knew of what consequence it was to secure the person of Kakekigo; and till then thinking his victory incomplete, he caused him to be pursued and taken. However, when he was brought before him, he treated him kindly, and with all the respect due to a person of his rank and character, withal confining him so little, that Kakekigo found means several times to make his escape, but was as often retaken. The generous Joritomo had no thoughts of putting him to death, though his enemy and his prisoner. Nay, far from it, he put such a value upon the friendship and affection of a person of his note, as to think it worth his while to purchase it at any price. One day, when he was pressing him very closely to enter into his service, upon whatever terms he pleased, the captive general returned him the following resolute answer: "I was once, (said he,) a faithful servant to a kind master. Now he is dead, no other small boast of my faith and friendship. I own that you have laid me under great obligations. I owe even my life to your clemency. And yet such is my misfortune, that I cannot set my eyes on you, but with a design, in revenge of him and me, to cut off your head. These, therefore, these designing instruments of mischief I will offer to you, as the only acknowledgment for your generous behaviour towards me, my unhappy condition will allow me to give you." This said, he plucks out both his eyes, and on a plate, presents them to Joritomo, undaunted like that bold Roman, who, in sight of Porsenna, burnt his right hand on the altar. Joritomo, astonished at so much magnanimity and resolution, forthwith set the captive general at liberty, who thereupon retired into the province Fiuga, where he learnt to play upon the bywa, a particular musical instrument used in Japan, and gave birth to this society of the Feki Blind, of which he himself was the first Kengio or head. This is the account Japanese histories give of the original institution of this society, which is since grown very numerous, being composed of persons of all ranks and professions. They shave their heads, as do also the Bussets sato, or ecclesiastical blind. Otherwise, being secular persons, they wear also a secular habit, different however from the common dress of the Japanese, and different among themselves according to their rank and dignities. They do not live upon charity, but make a shift, in their several capacities, to get a livelihood for themselves, and to provide for the maintenance of their commonwealth, following divers professions, not altogether inconsistent with their unhappy condition. Many of them apply themselves to music, in which capacity they are employed at the courts of princes and great men, as also upon public solemnities, festivals, processions, weddings, and the like. Whoever is once admitted a member of this society must remain such for life. They are dispersed up and down the empire, but their general resides at Miaco, where the cash of the company is kept. He is called Oniokf, and has 4300 thails a year allowed him for his maintenance by the Dairi. He governs the commonwealth, being assisted by ten counsellors called Siu Ro, which signifies elder-men, alder-men, of which he, the general, himself is the eldest. They reside at Miaco, and have, jointly with the general, power of life and death, with this restriction however, that no person can be executed, unless the sentence be approved of, and the death-warrant signed by the Lord Chief Justice of Miaco. The council of ten appoint their inferior officers, who reside in the several provinces: some of these are called kengio, as it were father provincials; being each in his province what the general is with regard to the whole society. The founder himself took only the title of Ken Gio. But the society having in process of time grown very numerous, it was thought necessary to alter the government, and to appoint a court superior to the kengios. Every kengio has his kotos, as they are called, to assist and advise him. The kotos sometimes govern particular districts by themselves. At Nagasaki there is a kengio and two kotos, under whose command stand all the blind of that town and adjacent country. The kengios and kotos have many other inferior officers subordinate to them, who are called sijbun, and are again subordinate to one another. They differ from the common body of the blind by wearing long breeches. As they have different ranks and titles among themselves, so they are obliged every five years to purchase a new quan, that is, a new and higher title from their kengio, for 20 to 50 thails. If they neglect, or are not able to do it, they are removed to a lower rank. The main body of the blind are comprehended under one general name of Mukwan. These wear no breeches, and are divided into four quans, ranks, or classes. Those of the fourth and last class are capable of being made sijbuns, from which office they gradually rise to the dignity of kota, kengio, and so on. Sometimes, through money or favour, they rise very suddenly.

CHAPTER XVI.

OF THE BUDSDO, OR, FOREIGN PAGAN WORSHIP, AND ITS FOUNDER.

FOREIGN idols, for distinction's sake from the Kami, or Sin, which were worshipped in the country in the most ancient times, are called Budsd and Fotoke. The characters also, whereby these two words are expressed, differ from those of Sin and Kami. Budsdo, in the literal sense, signifies the way of foreign idols, that is, the way of worshipping foreign idols. The origin of this religion, which quickly spread through most Asiatic countries to the very extremities of the East (not unlike the Indian fig-tree, which propagates itself, and spreads far round, by sending down new roots from the extremities of its branches), must be looked for among the Brahmins. I have strong reasons to believe, both from the affinity of the name, and the very nature of this religion, that its author and founder is the very same person, whom the Brahmins called Budha, and believe to be an essential part of Wisthnu, or their Deity, who made its ninth appearance in the world under this name, and in the shape of this man. The Chinese and Japanese call him Buds and Siaka. These two names indeed became in course of time a common epithet of all gods and idols in general, the worship of whom was brought over from other countries: sometimes also they were given to the saints and great men who preached these new doctrines. The common people in Siam call him Prah Pudi Dsau, that is, the Holy Lord, and the learned among them, in their pali, or holy language, Sammona Khodum. The Peguans call him Samman a Khutama.

His native country, according to the Japanese (with regard to whom he is chiefly considered in this place), is Magattakokf, or the province Magatta in the country Tensik. Teusik, in the literal sense, signifies a heavenly country, a country of heavens. The Japanese comprehend under this name the island of Ceylon, the coasts of Malabar and Coromandel, and in general all the countries of South Asia, the continent as well as the neighbouring islands, which are inhabited by Blacks, such as the peninsula of Malacca, the islands of Sumatra, Java, the kingdoms of Siam, Pegu, &c.

He was born in the twenty-sixth year of the reign of the Chinese Emperor Soowo, who was fourth successor of the famous Suno Buo, on the eighth day of the fourth month. This was according to some the year before our Saviour's nativity, 1029, and according to others, 1027, when I was in Siam, in 1690, the Siamites then told 2232 years from their Budha, who, if he be the same with the Siaka of the Japanese, his birth comes up no higher than 542 years before Christ. His father was king of Magattakokf, a powerful kingdom in the country Tensikf. I conjecture this to be the island of Ceylon. The kingdom of Siam indeed is so called to this day by the common people in Japan.

Siaka, when he came to be nineteen years of age, quitted his palace, leaving his wife and an only son behind him, and voluntarily, of his own choice, became a disciple of Arara Seunin, then a hermit of great repute, who lived at the top of a mountain called Dandokf. Under the inspection of this holy man, he betook himself to a very austere life, wholly taken up with an almost uninterrupted contemplation of heavenly and divine things, in a posture very singular in itself, but reckoned very proper for this sublime way of thinking, to wit, sitting cross-legged, with his hands in the bosom placed so that the extremities of both thumbs touched one another; a posture which is thought to engage one's mind into so profound a meditation, and to wrap it up so entirely within itself, that the body lies for a while as it were senseless, unattentive, and unmoved by any external objects whatsoever. This profound enthusiasm is by them called safen, and the divine truths revealed to such persons, satori. As to Siaka himself, the force of his enthusiasm was so great, that by its means he penetrated into the most secret and important points of religion, discovering the existence and state of heaven and hell, as places of reward and punishment, the state of our souls in a life to come, the transmigration thereof, the way to eternal happiness, the divine power of the gods in the government of this world, and many more things beyond the reach of human understanding, which he afterwards freely communicated to the numerous crowds of his disciples, who, for the sake of his doctrine and instructions, followed him in flocks, embracing the same austere way of life which he led himself.

He lived seventy-nine years, and died on the fifteenth day of the second month, in the year before Christ 950.

The most essential points of his doctrine are as follows:—

The souls of men and animals are immortal: both are of the same substance, and differ only according to the different objects they are placed in, whether human or animal.

The souls of men, after their departure from their bodies, are rewarded in a place of happiness or misery, according to their behaviour in this life.

The place of happiness is called Gokurakf, that is, a place of eternal pleasures. As the gods differ in their nature, and the souls of men in the merit of their past actions, so do likewise the degrees of pleasure and happiness in their Elysian fields, that every one may be rewarded as he deserves. However the whole place is so thoroughly filled with bliss and pleasure, that each happy inhabitant thinks his portion the best, and far from envying the happier state of others, wishes only for ever to enjoy his own. Amida is the sovereign commander of these heavenly stations (for all his doctrine hath not been introduced by the Brahmins, till after our Saviour's glorious resurrection). He is looked upon as the general patron and protector of human souls, but more particularly as the god and father of those who happily transmigrate into these places of bliss. Through his and his sole mediation, men are to obtain absolution from their sins, and a portion of happiness in the future life.

Leading a virtuous life, and doing nothing that is contrary to the commandments of the law of

Siaka, is the only way to become agreeable unto Amida, and worthy of eternal happiness.

The five commandments of the doctrine Siaka, which are the standing rule of the life and behaviour of all his faithful adherents, are called Gokai, which implies as much as the five cautions, or warnings: they are—

Se Seo, the law not to kill any thing that hath life in it.

Tsu To, the law not to steal.

Sijain, the law not to commit impurity.

Mago, the law not to lie.

Onsiu, the law not to drink strong liquors; a law which Siaka most earnestly recommended to his disciples, to be by them strictly observed.

Next to these five chief and general commandments, which contain in substance the whole law of Siaka, follow ten Sikkai, as they call them, that is, counsels or admonitions, being nothing else but the five first laws branched out, and applied to more particular actions, and tending to a stricter observance of virtue. For the sake of the learned, and such as aim at a more than ordinary state of virtue and perfection, even in this world, a still further subdivision has been contrived into Gosiakkai, that is, five hundred counsels and admonitions, wherein are specified, and determined with the utmost exactness and particularity, whatever actions have, according to their notions, the least tendency to virtue and vice, and ought on this account to be done or omitted.

The number of these Gosiakkai being so very extensive, it is no wonder that those, who will oblige themselves to a strict observance thereof, are so few in proportion; the rather, since they tend to such a thorough mortification of their bodies, as to measure and prescribe the very minutest parts of their diet, allowing scarce so much as is necessary to keep them from starving. Nothing but the ambition of acquiring a great repute of perfection and sanctity in this world, and the desire of being raised to a more eminent station of happiness in the next, can prompt any body to undergo such a rude and severe discipline as is prescribed by the Gosiakkai, and few there are, even among the best part of their clergy, who, for the sake of a greater portion of happiness in a future world, would willingly renounce the very least pleasures of this.

All persons, secular or ecclesiastical, who by their sinful life and vicious actions, have rendered themselves unworthy of the pleasures prepared for the virtuous, are sent after their death to a place of misery, called Dsigokf, there to be confined and tormented, not indeed for ever, but only during a certain undetermined time. As the pleasures of the Elysian fields differ in degrees, so do likewise the torments in these infernal places. Justice requires that every one should be punished, according to the nature and number of his crimes, the number of years he lived in the world, the station he lived in, and the opportunities he had to be virtuous and good. Jemma, or with a more majestic character, Jemma O (by which same name he is known also to the Brahmins, Siamites, and Chinese), is the severe judge and sovereign commander of this place of darkness and misery. All the vicious actions of mankind appear to him in all their horror and heinousness, by the means of a large looking-glass, placed before him, and called ssofarino kagami, or the looking-glass of knowledge. The miseries of the poor unhappy souls confined to these prisons of darkness are not so considerable and lasting but that great relief may be expected from the virtuous life and good actions of their family, friends, and relations, whom they left behind. But nothing is so conducive to this desirable end, as the prayers and offerings of the priests to the great and good Amida, who by his powerful intercession can prevail so far upon the almost inexorable judge of this infernal place, as to oblige him to remit from the severity of his sentence, to treat the unhappy imprisoned souls with kindness, at least so far as is not inconsistent with his justice, and the punishment their crimes deserve, and last of all, to send them abroad into the world again as soon as possible.

When the miserable souls have been confined in these prisons of darkness a time sufficient to expiate their crimes, they are, by virtue of the sentence of Jemma O, sent back into the world, to animate, not indeed the bodies of men, but of such vile creatures whose natures and properties are nearly related to their former sinful inclinations, such as, for instance, serpents, toads, insects, birds, fishes, quadrupeds, and the like. From the vilest of these, transmigrating by degrees into others, and nobler, they at last are suffered again to enter human bodies, by which means it is put in their power, either by a good and virtuous life to render themselves worthy of a future uninterrupted state of happiness, or by a new course of vices to expose themselves once more to undergo all the miseries of confinement in a place of torment, succeeded by a new unhappy transmigration.

Thus far the most essential points of the doctrine of Siaka.

Among the disciples of Siaka arose several eminent men, who contributed greatly to the propagation of his doctrine, and were succeeded by others equally learned and zealous, insomuch that we need not wonder that his religion, within a very short compass of time, spread to the very extremities of the East, even all the difficulties they had to struggle with notwithstanding.

The most eminent of his disciples were Annan and Kasia, or with their full titles, Annan Sonaja, and Kasus Sonaja. They collected his wise sentences, and what was found after his death, written with his own hands on the leaves of trees, into a book, which, for its peculiar excellency, is called Fokekio, that is, the book of fine flowers (in comparison with the holy tarate-flower), and sometimes also, by way of pre-eminence, Kio, the book, as being the most perfect performance in its kind, and the bible of all eastern nations beyond the Ganges, who embraced Siaka's doctrine. The two compilers of it, for their care and pains, were related among the saints, and are now worshipped jointly with Siaka, in whose temples, and upon whose altars, they are placed, one to his right, the other to his left hand.

Before the doctrine of Siaka was brought over into China, and from thence through Corea into Japan, the old Sintos or Cami worship, mean and simple as it was, was yet the only one flourishing in this empire. They had but few temples, and few holidays, and the yearly pilgrimage to the temple of Tensio Dai Sin at Iaje, was thought the best and surest way to happiness. 'Tis true, in course of time, the number of gods and saints increased, their system of divinity was embellished with new fables, arts also and sciences were improved, chiefly since the time of Synmu Ten O, their first monarch. But still a certain simplicity prevailed, and people following the dictates of reason, aimed at nothing so much as to live morally well. The Chinese also, before that time, followed the illustrious examples and moral precepts of their two great emperors Tee Gio, that is the Emperor Gio, who, according to their chronological computation, lived 2359 years before Christ, and his successor Tee Siun, or the Emperor Siun, who though a peasant, was yet for his prudence and honesty, made by Gio, first his co-partner in the government, and afterwards his successor, though in prejudice to his, Gio's twelve children, viz., ten sons and two daughters. These two illustrious princes were the two first Sesins. Sesin is a philosopher, able to find out truth and wisdom, merely by the force of his own understanding and without being taught by others. By mistake, this same name hath been sometimes given to some of their most eminent divines. Some hundred years after the reign of these princes, the Pagan doctrine of Roos arose in China. This man was born in Sokokf. that is, the province So, on the fourth day of the ninth month, 346 years after the death of Siaka, or 604 before our Saviour's nativity. They say, that his mother had been big with child eighty-one years, for which reason, when she was brought to bed, they called him Roos, which implies as much as old son, or old child. They further add, that the soul of Kassobosatz, or the holy Kasso, the eldest disciple of Siaka, by transmigration dwelt in him, which made it easy to him to attain to such a high pitch of knowledge about the nature of gods and spirits, the immortality of our souls, a future state, and such other important points as are highly conducive to the instruction of such as are desirous of learning, and fill the credulous vulgar with admiration. He lived eighty-four years.

Meanwhile the doctrine and philosophy of Roos got ground in China, another incomparable sesin appeared on the philosophical stage of that empire. This was Koosi, or as we Europeans call him, Confutius, born in the province Kok, on the fourth day of the eleventh month, 399 years after the death of Siaka, and fifty-three after the birth of Roosi, who was then still alive. His birth was in a manner miraculous, attended with no obscure signs of a future sesin. He had some natural marks on his head, like those of the Emperor Gio, and his forehead was of the same shape with that of the Emperor Siun. At the time of his birth music was heard in heaven, and two dragons were observed to attend when the child was washed. His stature, when grown up, was very noble and majestic, of nine saku and nine suns, proportionable to the greatness of his genius. Passing over in silence what is fabulous and romantic, in the history of his life, it cannot be denied but that he had an incomparable understanding, and excellent sense, and was perhaps the greatest philosopher the East ever produced. His writings and philosophy have maintained a constant uninterrupted reputation for upwards of two thousand years, and are thought in China to have been brought down from heaven, as was formerly supposed of the philosophy of Socrates. A profound respect is shown to his memory both in China and Japan, by public as well as private persons. Very lately the Emperor of Japan caused two temples to be built to him, in his capital Jedo, whither he repaired in person as soon as they were finished, and on this occasion set forth, in a handsome speech to his courtiers, the merits of this great man, and the peculiar excellency of the maxims of government laid down by him. His picture is allowed the most honourable place in the houses of philosophers, and all persons who apply themselves to studies and learning, never mention his name without particular tokens of respect. It is no wonder then, that the chimerical, and in several particulars, incomprehensible doctrine of Roosi was not able to stand its ground against the reasonable and pleasing moral of Confutius, but was, as it were, smothered in its infancy, and sensibly decreased, in proportion as the adherents of Confutius increased, of whom there was a concourse from all parts of the empire, almost beyond imagination. He died in the seventy-third year of his age, leaving behind him many able men, who propagated his doctrine and philosophy, not only by teaching it to others, but by gathering all his wise sentences and moral maxims, which he communicated to them in his lifetime, into a book, which is called Siudo, that is, the philosophical way of life, or the way of life agreeable to philosophy, which ever since, for now upwards of two thousand years, hath been looked upon as a performance incomparable in its kind, and an excellent pattern of a good and virtuous life; a book extolled not only by the admirers of Confutius, but admired for its morals and political maxims, even by the adherents of the Budsdo and other religions, in the very same manner as the writings of the ancient Greek and Roman philosophers, which have escaped the common shipwreck of time, deservedly stand the admiration of all Europe, and a lasting monument of the excellent genius of their great authors.

While thus the doctrine and pleasing philosophy of Confutius began to flourish in China, and to spread to the neighbouring empire of Japan, the doctrine and religion of Siaka, which had then already penetrated to the kingdoms of Siam and Laos, was not likely to meet with a favourable reception in this furthermost part of the East. If we believe the Japanese historians, the first that taught this religion in China, came over thither about the year of Christ 63, and obtained leave to build a temple, which is still called Fakubasi, that is, the temple of the white horse, because the kio, or holy book of Siaka, was brought over on a white horse. The greatest difficulty the preachers of this new doctrine had to struggle with, was the philosophy of Confutius, then shining in its full lustre, and universally approved. And indeed it appears that for several hundred years the religion of Siaka made a very slow and insignificant progress, till about the year of Christ 518, one Darma, a great saint, and thirty-third successor on the holy see of Siaka, came over into China from Seitensiku, as the Japanese writers explain it (that is from that part of the world which lies westward with regard to Japan), and laid, properly speaking, the first sure foundations of Budsdoism in that mighty empire. The fame of his dignity and holiness, the austerity of his life, his ardent uninterrupted devotion, which was so strong, that he did not scruple, in the height of his zeal, to cut off his own eyelids, because they had once drawn him out of his enthusiastic meditations into a sleep, soon brought a crowd of admirers about him. But the most effectual and most persuasive arguments he made use of to induce people to the worship of the gods, were, the doctrine of the immortality of our souls, and the promises of a reward in a future life, which they should not fail to obtain, if they would but worship them, as his doctrine, religion, and example should direct. This new worship having once got ground in China, soon spread into Fakkusai (which was then the name given to the peninsula of Corea, and is now that of one of its three provinces), where the first Budz, or idol of Siaka, was erected and worshipped in the year of Christ 543. Japan, whose inhabitants were then divided between the old religion of the country, and the philosophical doctrines communicated to them from China, could now hold out no longer, but soon admitted the religion of Siaka, following in that, as they had done in many other things, the example of the neighbouring countries. The first Bukkio was brought over into Japan, about the year of Christ 550. About eighteen years after, according to Japanese writers, a curious carved idol of Amida, which had been some years before brought over from Tensiku into Fakusai, appeared in a miraculous manner in the province Tsino Cami, all surrounded with sparkling rays, upon which a temple was built in Sinano, in memory of this remarkable event, which was called Sanquosi, and is still the chief and largest temple of that province. About that time Kimmei ruled over Japan, who was no enemy to this religion, and connived at its introduction and spreading. This was the same emperor who divided the time into Neugos, in imitation of the Chinese. The nengo then subsisting, when this temple was built, was called Cengo.

CHAPTER XVII.

OF THE SIUTO, THAT IS, THE DOCTRINE AND WAY OF LIFE OF THEIR MORALISTS AND PHILOSOPHERS.

SIUTO, in the literal sense, signifies the way or method of the Philosophers. Siudosja, or, in the plural number, Siudosju, are the philosophers, who follow this method. These people have, properly speaking, no religion at all, that is, they conform themselves to none of those forms of worshipping the gods, which are established in the country. They say that the greatest perfection and the supreme good, men are able to acquire, consist in that pleasure and delight which our minds find in a good and virtuous life. They admit of none but temporal rewards or punishments, and only such as are the necessary consequences of the practice of virtue or vice. They say, that we are obliged to be virtuous, because nature hath endowed us with reason, on purpose, that living according to the dictates of reason, we should show our difference and superiority over irrational brutes. Koosi, or Confutius, born in China 2243 years ago, computing from the fifth year of Genrokf (of Christ 1692), was the first who taught that the supreme good consists in the practice of virtue, and must consequently be looked upon as the founder of this philosophical sect. It hath been observed above, how prejudicial the Sioogakf, or the book wherein are contained his precepts and morals, proved to the then flourishing doctrine of Roosi. Moosi, one of Confutius's disciples, was very instrumental in establishing and propagating this philosophy, which he published in Sisio, or four Books, which are still held in great esteem, and read in all countries, where the learned language, wherein they were written, is understood.

This philosophy, so far as it relates to the practice of virtue and good morals, may be reduced to the following five points, which they call Dsin, Gi, Re, Tsi, and Sin. Dsin, teaches them to live virtuously: hence Dsinsja, a virtuous man ; Gi, to do right and justice to everybody ; Re, to be civil and polite ; Tsi sets forth the maxims of a good and prudent government ; and Sin treats of a free conscience and uprightness of heart. They admit no transmigration of souls, but believe an *anima mundi*, an universal soul spirit or power, diffused throughout the whole world, which animates all things, which re-assumes the departing souls (as the sea doth all rivers and waters that flow into it from all parts of the globe), as into a common receptacle, and lets them, as it were, flow out again indifferently to animate other creatures. This universal spirit they confound with the Supreme Being, attributing to one the same divine qualities which only belong to the other. They often make use of the word Ten, heaven or nature, in things which more immediately concern our life and actions. Thus, they thank heaven and nature for their victuals and the necessaries of life. Some among them, with whom I conversed, admitted an intellectual or incorporeal being, but only as governor and director, not as the author of nature ; nay, they pretended, that it is an effect of nature produced by In and Jo, heaven and earth, one active, the other passive ; one the principle of generation, the other of corruption: after the same manner also they explained some other active powers of nature to be spiritual beings. They make the world eternal, and suppose men and animals to have been produced by In Jo, the heaven and five terrestrial elements. Admitting no gods, they have no temples, no forms of worship. Thus far, however, they conform themselves to the general custom of the country, in that they celebrate the memory of their deceased parents and relations, which is done by putting all sorts of victuals, raw and dressed, on a Biosiu, as they call it, or table purposely made with this view, by burning candles before them, by bowing down to the ground as if they were yet alive, by monthly or anniversary dinners, whereto are invited the family and friends of the deceased, who appear all in the best cloth, and wash and clean themselves by way of preparation for three days before, during which time they abstain from lying with their wives, and from all impure things, and by many other tokens of respect and gratitude. As to the burial of their dead, they do not burn them, but keep the corpse three days, and then lay it on the back into a coffin, after the European manner, with the head raised. Sometimes the coffin is filled with spices and sweet-scented herbs, to preserve the body from corruption, and when everything is ready, they accompany it to the grave, and bury it without any further ceremony.

These philosophers do not only admit of self-murder, but look upon it as a heroic and highly commendable action, and the only honourable means to avoid a shameful death, or to prevent falling into the hands of a victorious enemy.

They celebrate no festivals, nor will they pay any respect to the gods of the country, any more than common civility and good manners require. The practice of virtue, free conscience, and a good and honest life, is all that they aim at. They were even suspected of secretly favouring the Christian religion; for which reason, after the said religion had been entirely abolished by cross and fire, and proper means taken to prevent its ever reviving again, they also were commanded to have each the idol, or, at least, the name of one of the gods worshipped in the country, put up in their houses, in a conspicuous and honourable place, with a flower-pot, and incensory before them. They commonly choose Quanwon or Amida, whose idols they place behind the hearth, according to the country fashion. Some have besides, of their own free choice, the Biosiu in their houses, or else the name of some learned man. In their public schools is hung up the picture of Koosi or Confutius. Formerly this sect was very numerous. Arts and sciences were cultivated and improved among them, and the best part of the nation professed it. But that unparalleled persecution of the Christian religion weakened it very much, and it lost ground ever since; the extreme rigour of the imperial edicts made people cautious even as to reading their books, which formerly have been the delight and admiration of the nation, held in as great an esteem as the writings of Plato, Socrates, and other heathen philosophers are in Europe.

About thirty years ago, the Prince of Sisen and Inaba, a great Siudosja and patron of learned men, endeavoured to revive his philosophy, then almost extinct, in his dominions. In order to this, he founded an university, endowed it with great privileges, and settled handsome pensions upon able learned men, whom he sent for from all parts of the empire. The design of this undertaking was to open the eyes of his subjects, and to teach them, if possible, to make use of their reason, which they no sooner did, but they began to see through the impertinent and ridiculous fables of their priests, and discovering their cheats refused to grant them any further subsistence, whereby this numerous crew, which till then lived only upon the charity of credulous people, was reduced to a starving condition. Of so dangerous an innovation heavy complaints were made to both emperors, and the unhappy Prince was like to fall a sacrifice to his good intentions, had he not, by a voluntary resignation of his dominions to his son, prevented the fatal blow of the imperial disgrace ready to fall upon him and his family. His son was of a more prudent and reserved behaviour, yet his life and conduct leave no room to doubt, but that his principles were nearly the same with those of his father—an instance whereof, though foreign to my present purpose, will not be improper to close this chapter.

On the Songuats, or New-year's-day, one of their greatest festivals, there was a numerous appearance at court of gentlemen and ladies, who came thither in their richest apparel, to compliment the Prince on the occasion of the day, and were by him entertained at dinner. Amongst other presents made to him that day, there happened to be a peacock and hen. Every one was delighted, and struck with admiration, by the uncommon beauty of these scarce foreign birds, whence the Prince took occasion to ask their opinion, which of the two they thought was the cock, and which the hen. The gentlemen, out of civility to the ladies, unanimously pitched upon the most beautiful to be the hen; the ladies, on the contrary, very modestly apprehended that the finest of the two was the cock. "You are in the right," answered thereupon the Prince, "nature itself will have the man best clad; and, it seems to me incomprehensible, that the wife should have more pride, and go richer dressed than her husband, who must be at the expense of maintaining her." An excellent New-year's sermon from a heathen Prince.

CHAPTER XVIII.

PREPARATIONS FOR OUR JOURNEY TO THE EMPEROR'S COURT AT JEDO OR YEDO, WITH A DESCRIPTION OF THE MANNER OF TRAVELLING IN THIS COUNTRY.

EVER since the time of Joritomo, the first secular monarch of Japan, who laid the foundation of the present form of government, it hath been a custom observed, not only by the governors of the imperial cities, and lords lieutenants of the provinces, lands, and demesnes, belonging to the crown, but likewise by all other Daimio, and Siomjo, as they are here called, (that is, the lords of all ranks and qualities throughout this vast empire,) to go to court once a year, and to pay their duties, the lords of a higher rank, who, for the extent of their power and dominions, could well be styled Kings, or Princes, to the Emperor himself, the rest only to his prime ministers assembled in council. Both accompany their reverences with presents proportionable to their quality and riches, in token of their acknowledging the supremacy of the Emperor. The Dutch, when they came to settle in Japan, conformed themselves to this ancient custom, as did also in their time the Portuguese. The resident of our East India Company, and chief director of our trade for the time being, makes this journey, with a physician, or surgeon, and one or two secretaries, and attended with numerous flocks of Japanese of different ranks and qualities, whom the governors of Nagasaki, as our magistrates in this country, whose instructions and orders we are to follow, appoint, as it were to honour and convoy us, as persons that are going to see the supreme Majesty of the empire, but in fact and chiefly, to guard and watch us, to keep a good eye over our conduct, to prevent us from having any suspicious and unlawful conversation and communication with the natives, from conveying secretly to them crosses, images, relics, or any other things, which bear any relation to the Christian religion, from presenting them with other European rarities, or from selling the same to them in private, and more particularly to take care, that none of us should escape into the country, there either to attempt the reviving and propagating of the Christian faith, or otherwise to occasion tumults and disturbances, in prejudice of the tranquillity now established in the empire. So important a trust being laid upon the Japanese companions of our journey, the reader may easily imagine, that none are chosen but persons of known candour and fidelity, and who are otherwise employed in affairs relating to the inspection and regulation of our trade, besides some of the governor's own domestics. Nay, far from relying merely on their faithfulness and sincerity, though perhaps never so often approved of, all those that are to go with us, from the leader down to the meanest servant, (those only excepted, who must look after the horses, and are frequently changed,) must, before they set out on this journey, oblige themselves by a solemn and dreadful oath, signed as usual with their blood, to give notice to the government at Nagasaki, of whatever they observe to be done, either by the Dutch, or by their own countrymen, contrary to the standing laws of the country, and the many particular instructions which are given them.

I went to the Emperor's court twice myself, to my very great satisfaction: the first time, in the year 1691, with Henry von Butenheim, a gentleman of great candour, affability, and generosity, and well versed in the customs and language of the Japanese, who, by his good conduct, knew how to keep up the reputation of his masters without prejudice to their interest; the second time, in 1692, with Cornelius van Oouthoorn, brother to the Governor-general at Batavia, a gentleman of great learning, excellent sense, and well skilled in several languages, who, by his innate affability, found means particularly to ingratiate himself into the affection of this proud and jealous nation, and promoting the interests of his masters so much as lay in his power, discharged all the duties of his office to the entire satisfaction both of those who sent him, and of those to whom he was sent. I will here give a particular account, by way of a journal, of what occurred to me remarkable in the journey to court, having first premised some general observations, which seemed to me to be necessary to facilitate the understanding of what I shall lay down in the journals themselves, with all the sincerity I am capable of.

The preparations for our journey consist in the following particulars: The very first thing to be done, is to look out proper presents for his Imperial Majesty, for his privy councillors, and some other great officers at Jedo, Miako, and Osacca, the whole amounting as near as possible, to a certain sum, to sort them, and particularly to assign to whom they are to be delivered. Afterwards they must be put up into leather bags, which are carefully wrapt up in mats, in order to preserve them from all accidents in so long a journey, and for a further security several seals are affixed unto them. It is the business of the governors of Nagasaki to judge and determine what might prove acceptable to the court. They take out of the goods laid up in our warehouses what they think proper, and give instructions to the departing director, about such things as should be sent over from Batavia the next year. Sometimes some of their own goods they have been presented with by the Chinese, are put in among these presents; because, by this means, they can dispose of them to the best advantage, either by obliging us to buy them at an excessive and their own price, or by exchanging them for other goods. Now and then some uncommon curiosities, either of nature or art, are brought over from Europe, and other parts of the world, on purpose to be presented to the Emperor. But it often happens that they are not approved of by these rigid censors. Thus, for instance, there were brought over in my time, two brass fire-engines of the newest invention, but the governors did not think it proper that they should be presented to the Emperor, and so returned them to us, after they had first seen them tried and taken a pattern of them: another time the bird Casuar was sent over from Batavia, but likewise disliked and denied the honour of appearing before the Emperor; because they heard he was good for nothing but to devour a large quantity of victuals. After some time spent in choosing and getting ready these presents, they are brought on board a barge with necessary provisions, three or four weeks before our departure, and sent by water to Simonoseki, a small town, situate upon the extremity of the great island Nipon, where they wait our arrival by land. Formerly our ambassador, with his whole retinue, embarked at the same time, to go thither by water, whereby we saved a great deal of trouble and expense we must now be at in travelling by land, but a violent storm having once put the whole company into imminent danger, and the voyage having been often, by reason of the contrary winds, too long and too tedious, the Emperor had ordered, that for the future we should go thither by land. The barge, on board which the imperial presents are carried to Simonoseki, is kept in the harbour of Nagasaki, at the expense of the company, for this sole purpose, and cannot be made use of for any other whatsoever. The presents for the imperial court, and other heavy baggage, being sent before us, the rest of the time till our departure is spent upon such vast preparations for our journey, as if we designed some great expedition into a remote part of the world.

The first, and indeed the most essential part of these preparations, consists in nominating, and giving proper instructions, to the several officers, and the whole retinue that is to go with us to court. The governors appoint one of their Jorikis, or military officers of the first rank, to be Bugio, that is, head and commander in chief.

He is to represent the authority of his masters, as a badge whereof he hath a pike carried after him. A Dosin or inferior military officer, is ordered to assist him in quality of his deputy. Both the joriki and dosin are taken from among the domestics of one of the governors, who stays that year at Nagasaki. To these are added two beadles, by the name and in quality of Tsioosin, or town-messengers. Both the tsioosin and the dosin carry by virtue of their office a halter about them, to arrest and secure, at command or wink from the joriki, any person guilty, or only suspected to be guilty of any misdemeanor. All these persons besides the officers attending the bugio, are looked upon as military men, and as such have the privilege of wearing two swords. It is from thence they are called Samurai, which signifies persons who wear two swords, or soldiers, all persons that are not either noblemen by birth, or in some military employment, being by a late imperial edict denied this privilege.

I have observed in the preceding book, that our interpreters are divided into two companies, the upper or superior, consisting of the eight chief interpreters, and the inferior including all the rest. The Ninban, or president for the time being, of each of these companies, is appointed of course to attend us in this journey. To these is now added a third, as an apprentice, whom they take along with them to qualify him for the succession, and to show him betimes, and by proper experience, how for the future he must behave himself on the like occasion. All the chief officers, and all other persons that are able to do it, take some servants along with them, partly to wait upon them, partly for state. The bugio, or commander in chief, and the principal interpreter take as many as they please; the other officers, each two or three, as they are able, or as their office requires. The Dutch captain, or ambassador may take three, and every Dutchman of his retinue is allowed one. The interpreters commonly recommend their favourites to us; the more ignorant they are of the Dutch language, the better it answers their intention; not to mention some other persons, who by order, or special leave of the governors and interpreters, make the journey in company with us, and indeed at our expense too, though otherwise they have no manner of business upon our account. All these future companions of our voyage, whom I have hitherto mentioned, have leave to make us some friendly visits at Desima, some time before our departure, in order to get beforehand a little acquainted with us. There are many among them who would willingly be more free and open with us, were it not for the solemn oath they must all take before their departure, but much more for the fear of being betrayed by others, since by virtue of the same oath, they are obliged, all and every one of them, to have a strict and watchful eye, not only over the Dutch, but also over the conduct of each other, particularly with regard to the Dutch.

Another essential branch of the necessary preparations for our journey is the hiring of horses and porters, for us and our baggage. This is the chief interpreter's business, as keeper of our purse, who is also appointed to take care, that whatever is wanted during the whole journey,

be provided for. It is he likewise that gives orders to keep everything in readiness to march, the minute the bugio, as commander in chief, is pleased to set out.

Two days before our departure from Nagasaki, every one must deliver his cloak-bag and portmanteau to proper people, to be bound up, so that in an instant they may be tied to the horses, and again untied. This is not done after our European manner, but after a particular one of their own, which deserves to be here described.

A plain wooden saddle, not unlike the pack-saddles of the Swedish post-horses, is girded on the horse with a poitral, or breast-leather, and crupper. Two latchets are laid upon the saddle, which hang down on both sides of the horse, in order to their being conveniently tied about two portmanteaus, which are put on each side, in that situation which is thought the most proper to keep them in a due balance. For when once tied together, they are barely laid on the horse's back, without any other thong or latchet to tie them faster, either to the saddle or to the horse. However, to fasten them in some measure, a small long box, or trunk, called by the Japanese adofski, is laid over both portmanteaus upon the horse's back, and tied fast to the saddle with thongs; over the whole is spread the traveller's covering and bedding, which are tied fast to the adofski and side-trunks, with broad lined sashes, the middle cavity between the two trunks filled up with some soft stuff, is the traveller's seat, where he sits, as it were, upon a flat table, otherwise commodiously enough, and either cross-legged or with his legs extended hanging down by the horse's neck, as he pleases, or finds it most convenient. Particular care must be taken to sit right in the middle, and not to lean too much on either side, which would either make the horse fall or else the side-trunks and rider. In going up and down hills the footmen and stable grooms hold the two side trunks fast, for fear of such an accident. The traveller mounts the horse, and alights again, not one side as we Europeans do, but by the horse's breast, which is very troublesome for stiff legs. The horses are unsaddled and unladen in an instant; for having taken the bed-clothes away, which they do first of all, they need but untie a latchet or two, which they are very dexterous at, and the whole baggage falls down at once. The latchets, thongs, and girths, made use of for these several purposes, are broad and strong, made of cotton, and withal very neatly worked, with small oblong, cylindrical pieces of wood at both ends, which are of great use to strain the latchets, and to tie things hard.

The saddle is made of wood, very plain, with a cushion underneath, and a caparison behind, lying upon the horse's back, with the traveller's mark, or arms, stitched upon it. Another piece of cloth hangs down on each side, as a safeguard to the horse, to keep it from being daubed with dirt. These two pieces are tied together loosely under the horse's belly. The head is covered with a net-work of small but strong strings, to defend it, and particularly the eyes from flies, which are very troublesome to them. The neck, breast, and other parts, are hung with small bells.

The side-trunks or portmanteaus, which are

filled only with light stuff, and sometimes only with straw, are a sort of a square trunk, made of stiff horse-leather, about five spans long, three broad, and three deep. The cover is made likewise of leather, somewhat larger, and so deep as to cover the lower part down to the bottom. Though they hold out rain very well, yet for a greater security they are wrapt up in mats, with strong ropes tied about them, for which reason, and because it requires some time to pack them up, they are seldom unpacked till you are come to the journey's end, and the things which are most wanted upon the road are kept in the adofaki.

The adofaki is a small thin trunk or case, about six spans in length, one broad, and one deep. It contains one single drawer, much of the same length, breadth, and depth. It hath a little door, or opening on one side, which can be locked up, and by which you can come conveniently at the drawer, without untying the adofaki. What things are daily wanted upon the road must be kept in this trunk. It serves likewise to fasten the two portmanteaus, or side-trunks, which would otherwise require a stick. It is made of thick, strong grey paper, and further, to secure it against all accidents of a long voyage, blue strings are tied about it in form of a net very neatly.

To complete our traveller's equipage, some other things are requisite, which are commonly tied to the portmanteaus. Such are:

A string with senni, or puties, a brass money with a hole in the middle; they being more proper to buy what necessaries are wanted on the road than silver money, which must be weighed. People that travel on horseback tie this string behind them to one of the sashes of their seats. Foot-travellers carry it in a basket upon their back.

A lanthorn of varnished and folded paper, with the possessor's arms painted upon its middle. This is carried before travellers by their footmen upon their shoulder in travelling by night. It is tied behind one of the portmanteaus, put up in a net or bag, which again hath the possessor's arms or marks printed upon it, as have in general the clothes and all other moveables travellers of all ranks and qualities carry along with them upon their journeys.

A brush made of horse's hairs, or black cock feathers, to dust your seat and clothes. It is put behind your seat on one side, more for show than use.

A water-pail, which is put on the other side of the seat opposite to the brush, or anywhere else.

Shoes or slippers for horses and footmen. These are twisted of straw, with ropes likewise of straw hanging down from them, whereby they are tied about the horse's feet, instead of our European iron horse-shoes, which are not used in this country. They are soon worn out in stony slippery roads, and must be often changed for new ones. For this purpose, the men that look after the horses always carry a competent stock along with them, tied to the portmanteaus, though they are to be met with in every village, and are even offered for sale by poor children begging along the road. Hence it may be said that this country hath more farriers than perhaps any other, though in fact it hath none at all.

I must beg leave to observe, that besides the several things hitherto mentioned which travellers usually carry along with them in their journeys, I had for my own private use a very large Japan box, which I had brought with me from Batavia. In this box I privately kept a large mariner's compass, in order to measure the directions of the roads, mountains, and coasts; but openly, and exposed to everybody's view, was an inkhorn, and I usually filled it with plants, flowers, and branches of trees, which I figured and described (nay, under this pretext, whatever occurred to me remarkable): doing this, as I did it free and unhindered, to everybody's knowledge, I should be wrongly accused to have done anything which might have proved disadvantageous to the Company's trade in this country, or to have thereby thrown any ill suspicion upon our conduct from so jealous and circumspect a nation. Nay, far from it, I must own that from the very first day of our setting out till our return to Nagasaki, all the Japanese companions of our voyage, and particularly the bugio, or commander-in-chief, were extremely forward to communicate to me what uncommon plants they met with, together with their true names, characters, and uses, which they diligently inquired into among the natives. The Japanese, a very reasonable and sensible people, and themselves great lovers of plants, look upon botany as a study both useful and innocent, which pursuant to the very dictates of reason and the law of nature, ought to be encouraged by everybody. Thus much I know by my own experience, that of all the nations I saw and conversed with in my long and tedious travels, those the least favoured botanical learning who ought to have encouraged it most. Upon my return to Nagasaki, Tounemon, secretary and chief counsellor to the governors, being once at Desima, sent for me, and made me, by the chief interpreter, Siukobé, the following compliment: that he had heard with great pleasure from Asagina Sindsamosin, our late bugio, how agreeably I had spent my time, and what diversion I had taken upon our journey in that excellent and most commendable study of botany, whereof he, Tonnemon himself, was a great lover and encourager. But I must confess likewise that at the beginning of our journey I took what pains, and tried what means I could to procure the friendship and assistance of my fellow travellers, obliging some with a submissive humble conduct, and ready assistance as to physic and physical advice, others with secret rewards for the very meanest services and favours I received from them.

A traveller must not forget to provide himself with a large cloak against rainy weather. This is made of double varnished oil paper, and withal so very large and wide, that it covers and shelters at once man, horse, and baggage. It seems the Japanese have learnt the use of it, together with the name kappa, from the Portuguese. Foot travellers wear it in rainy weather, instead of cloaks or coats of the same stuff.

To keep off the heat of the sun, travellers must be provided with a large hat, which is made of split bamboos, or straw, very neatly and artfully twisted, in form of an extended sombreiro, or umbrella. It is tied under the chin with broad silk bands, lined with cotton. It is transparent and exceedingly light, and yet, if once wet, will let no rain come through. Not only the men wear such hats upon their journeys, but also the women in cities and villages, at all times, and in all weather, and it gives them no disagreeable look.

The Japanese upon their journeys wear very wide breeches, tapering towards the end, to cover the legs, and slit on both sides to put in the ends of their large long gowns, which would otherwise be troublesome to them in walking or riding. Some wear a short coat or cloak over the breeches. Some, instead of stockings, tie a broad ribbon about their legs. Ordinary servants, chiefly Norimon men and pikebearers, wear no breeches at all, and for expedition sake tack their gowns quite up to their belt, exposing their backs, naked to everybody's view, which they say they have no reason at all to be ashamed of.

The Japanese of both sexes never go abroad without fans, as we Europeans seldom do without gloves. Upon their journeys they make use of a fan, which hath the roads printed upon it, and tells them how many miles they are to travel, what inns they are to go to, and what price victuals are at. Some, instead of such a fan, make use of a road-book, which is offered them for sale by numbers of poor children begging along the road. The Dutch are not permitted, at least publicly, to buy any of these fans or road-books.

After this manner travellers equip themselves for their journeys in this country. A Japanese on horse-back, tucked up after this fashion, makes a very odd comical figure at a distance. For besides that they are generally short-sized and thick, their large hat, wide breeches, and cloaks, together with their sitting cross-legged, make them appear broader than long. Upon the road they ride one by one. Merchants have their horses, with the heavy baggage, packed up in two or three trunks or bales, led before them. They follow sitting on horseback, after the manner above described. As to the bridle, the traveller has nothing to do with that, the horse being led by it by one of his footmen, who walks at the horse's right side next by the head, and together with his companions, sings some merry song or other, to divert themselves, and to animate their horses.

The Japanese look upon our European way of sitting on horseback, and holding the bridle one's self, as warlike, and properly becoming a soldier. For this very reason they seldom or never use it in their journeys. It is more frequent among people of quality in cities, when they go a visiting one another. But even then the rider (who makes but a sorry appearance, when sitting after our manner,) holds the bridle merely for form, the horse being nevertheless led by one, and sometimes two footmen, who walk on each side of the head, holding it by the bit. The saddling of the horses differs but little from ours. Their saddles come nearer our German saddles, than those of any Asiatic nation. The stirrup-leathers or gambados are very short. A broad round leather hangs down on both sides, after the fashion of the Tartars, to defend the legs. The stirrup is made of iron, or sowaas, and withal very thick and heavy, not unlike the sole of a foot, and open on one side, for the rider to get his foot loose with ease in case of a fall. The stirrups are commonly of an exceeding neat workmanship, and inlaid with silver. The reins are not of leather, as ours, but of silk, and fastened to the bit.

Besides going on horseback, there is another more stately and expensive way of travelling in this country, and that is, to be carried in norimons and cangos, or particular sorts of chairs, or litters. The same is usual likewise in cities. People of quality are carried about after this manner for state, others for ease and convenience. There is a wide difference between the litters men of quality go in and those of ordinary people: the former are sumptuous and magnificent, according to every one's rank and riches; the latter are plain and simple. The former are commonly called norimons, the latter cangos. The vulgar (in all nations master of the language) have called them by two different names, though in fact they are but one thing. Norimon signifies, properly speaking, a thing to sit in; cango, a basket or dosser. Both sorts rise through such a variety of degrees, from the lowest to the highest, from the plainest to the most curious, that a fine cangos is scarce to be distinguished from a plain and simple norimon, but by its pole. The pole of a cango is plain, massy, all of one piece, and smaller than that of a norimon, which is large, curiously adorned, and hollow. The pole of a norimon is made up of four thin boards, neatly joined together in form of a wide arch, and much lighter than it appears to be. The bigness and length of these poles hath been determined by the political laws of the empire, proportionable to every one's quality. Princes and great lords show their rank and nobility, amongst other things particularly, by the length and largeness of the poles of their norimons. People, who fancy themselves to be of greater quality than they really are, are apt now and then to get the poles of their norimons or cangos made larger than they ought to have them. But then also they are liable to be obliged by the magistrates, if they come to know of it, to reduce them to the former size, with a severe reprimand, if not a considerable fine into the bargain. This regulation, however, doth not concern the women; for they may, if they please, make use of larger poles than otherwise their own and their husband's quality would entitle them to. The norimon itself is a small room, of an oblong square figure, big enough for one person conveniently to sit or lie in, curiously twisted of fine thin split bamboos, sometimes japanned and finely painted, with a small folding door on each side, sometimes a small window before and behind. Sometimes it is fitted up for the conveniency of sleeping. It ends in a small roof, which in rainy weather is covered with a covering of varnished paper. It is carried by two, four, eight, or more men, according to the quality of the person in it, who, if he be a prince, or lord of a province, they carry the pole on the palms of their hands, otherwise they lay it upon their shoulders. All these norimon-men are clad in the same livery, with the coat of arms, or mark of their masters. They are every now and then relieved by others, who in the mean time walk by the norimon's side. But of this more in another place. The cangos are not near so fine, nor so well attended. They are much of the same figure, but smaller, with a square, solid, sometimes with a round pole, which is either fastened to the upper part of the roof, or put through it underneath. The cangos commonly made use of for travelling, chiefly for carrying people over mountains, are very poor and plain, and withal so small, that one cannot sit in them without very great inconvenience, bowing his head downward, and laying the legs across; for they are not unlike a basket with a round bottom and flat roof, which one reaches with his head. In such cangos we are carried over the rocks and mountains, which are not easily to be passed on horseback. Three men are appointed for every cango, who indeed, for the heaviness of their burden, have enough to do.

CHAPTER XIX.

A GENERAL DESCRIPTION OF THE WAY BY WATER AND LAND, FROM NAGASAKI TO JEDO, THE EMPEROR'S RESIDENCE.

MANY centuries ago the empire of Japan was divided into seven great tracts of land, as I have already shown. To make travelling easy and convenient, every one of these tracts is bounded by a highway, and because in course of time they have been again subdivided into several provinces, so there are particular ways leading to and from every one of these provinces, and all ending in the great highway, as small rivers lose themselves into great ones. They borrowed their name from that tract, or province, to which they lead. But of this more in another place.

These highways are so broad and large, that two companies, though never so great, can conveniently and without hindrance pass by one another. In this case that company, which according to their way of speaking, goes up, that is, to Miaco, takes the left side of the way, and that which comes from Miaco, the right. All the highways are divided, for the instruction and satisfaction of travellers, into measured miles, which are all marked, and begin from the great bridge at Jedo, as the common centre of all highways. This bridge is by way of pre-eminence called Nipon-bas, that is, the bridge of Japan. By this means a traveller, in whatever part of the empire he may be, knows at any time, how many Japanese miles it is from thence to Jedo, the imperial residence. The miles are marked by two small hills, thrown up one on each side of the way, opposite one to another, and planted at the top with one or more trees.

At the end of every tract, province, or smaller district, a wooden, or stone post, or pillar, is set up in the highway, with characters upon it, showing what provinces, or lands they are, which there bound one upon another, and to whom they belong.

The like posts, or pillars, are erected at the entry of sideways, which turn off from the great highway, likewise with characters upon them, showing what province, or dominion they lead to, and how many leagues the next remarkable place is from thence.

In our journey to court we pass through two of these chief highways, and go by water from one to the other, so that our whole journey is divided into three parts. In the first place we set out from Nagasaki, to go by land across the island Kiusju, to the town of Kokura, where we arrive in five days' time. From Kokura we pass the straits in small boats going over to Simonoseki, which is about two leagues off, where we find our above-mentioned barge, riding at anchor and waiting our arrival, this harbour being very convenient and secure. The way from Nagasaki to Kokura, is called by the Japanese Saikaido, which is as much as to say, the western grounds way. At Simonoseki, we go on board our barge to proceed from thence to Osacca, where we arrive in eight days, more or less, according as the wind proves favourable or contrary; sometimes we go no farther with our barge, than Fiogo, because of the shallowness and unsafe riding at anchor in the harbour of Osacca. Osacca is a city very famous for the extent of its commerce, and the wealth of its inhabitants. It lies about thirteen Japanese water leagues from Fiogo, which we make in small boats, leaving our large barge at that place to wait our return. From Osacca we go again by land, over the continent of the great island Nipon, as far as Jedo, the Emperor's residence, where we arrive in about fourteen days or more. The way from Osacca to Jedo is by the Japanese called Tookaido, that is, the sea or coastway. We stay at Jedo about twenty days, or upwards, and having had our audience of his Imperial Majesty, and paid our respects to some of his chief ministers and great favourites, we return to Nagasaki the same way, completing our whole journey in about three months' time.

Our journey from Nagasaki to Jedo is at least of three hundred and twenty-three Japanese leagues of different length. From Nagasaki to Kokura they compute fifty-three leagues and a half; from Kokura to Osacca, a hundred thirty-six at least, and a hundred forty-six at farthest; and from Osacca to Jedo a hundred thirty-three leagues and thirteen tajo; so that the whole comes to three hundred and twenty-three at least, and at farthest three hundred and thirty-three Japanese leagues, which may be computed equal to about 1150 English miles.

The Japanese leagues, or miles, are not equally long. The land leagues upon the island Kiusiu, and in the province Isje, are of fifty tajo each, the other common leagues only of thirty-six. Tajo is the measure of the length of a street. Upon good roads I found the former long leagues to be of a good hour's riding, the latter and shorter only of three quarters of an hour. The tajo contains sixty kin, or mats, according to their way of measuring, or about as many European fathoms, so that the great leagues contain three thousand, and the small ones two thousand one hundred and sixty kins or fathoms each. As to their water leagues, each is a little more than two English miles, without their country, but within it, as they express themselves, that is, between and about their islands, they measure them according to the course of the coasts, without any certainty at all, so that I am not well able to determine what proportion they bear to the land leagues; only I found in general, that they are shorter than the land leagues.

In most parts of Saikaido, and everywhere upon Tookaido, between the towns and villages, there is a straight row of firs planted on each side of the road, which by their agreeable shade make the journey both pleasant and convenient. The ground is kept clean and neat; convenient ditches and outlets are contrived to carry the rain water off towards low fields, and strong dikes are cast up to keep off that which comes down from higher places. This makes the road at all times good and pleasant, unless it be just rainy weather and the ground slimy. The neighbouring villages must jointly keep them in repair, and take care that they be swept and cleaned every day. People of great quality, in their journeys, cause the road to be swept with brooms, just before they pass it; and there lie heaps of sand in readiness at due distances (which are brought thither some days before) to be spread over the road in order to dry it in case it should rain upon their arrival. The lords of the several provinces, and the Princes of the imperial blood in their journeys, find at every two or three leagues' distance, huts of green-leaved branches erected for them, with a private apartment, where they may step in for their pleasures or necessities. The inspectors for repairing the highway, are at no great trouble to get people to clean them; for whatever makes the roads dirty and nasty, is of some use to the neighbouring country people, so that they rather strive who should first carry it away. The pine-nuts, branches, and leaves, which fall down daily from the firs, are gathered for fuel, and to supply the want of wood, which is very scarce in some places. Nor doth horses' dung lie long upon the ground, but it is soon taken up by poor country children and serves to manure the fields. For the same reason care is taken, that the refuse of travellers be not lost, and there are in several places, near country people's houses, or in their fields, necessary conveniencies. Old shoes of horses and men, which are thrown away as useless, are gathered in the same houses, and burnt to ashes along with the filth, for common dung, which they manure all their fields withal. Provisions of this nasty composition are kept in large tubs, or tuns, which are buried even with the ground, in their villages and fields, and being not covered, afford full as ungrateful and putrid a smell of radishes (which is the common food of country people) to tender noses, as the neatness and beauty of the road is agreeable to the eyes.

In several parts of the country the roads go over hills and mountains, which are sometimes so steep and high, that travellers are necessitated to get themselves carried over them in cangos, such as I have described in the preceding chapter, because they cannot without great difficulty and danger pass them on horseback. But even this part of the road, which may be called bad in comparison to others, is green and pleasant, for the abundance of springs of clear water and verdant bushes, and this all the year round, but particularly in the spring, when the flower-bearing trees and shrubs, as the fusi, tsubacki, satsuki, utsugi, temariqua, being then in their full blossom, prove such an additional beauty, affording to the eye so curious a view, and filling the nose with so agreeable a scent, as one should scarce meet with anywhere else.

Several of the rivers we are to cross over, chiefly upon Tookaido, run with so impetuous a rapidity towards the sea, that they will bear no bridge nor boat, and this by reason, partly of the neighbouring snow-mountains, where they rise, partly of the frequent great rains, which swell them to such a degree, as to make them overflow their banks. These must be forded through in shallow places. Men, horses, and baggage, are delivered up to the care of certain people, bred up to this business, who are well acquainted with the bed of the river, and the places which bear the most proper for fording. These people, as they are made answerable for their passengers' lives, and all accidents that might befal them in the passage, exert all their strength, care and dexterity to support them with their arms, against the impetuosity of the river, and the stones rolling down from the mountains, where the rivers arise. Norimons are carried over by the same people upon their arms.

The chief of these rivers is the formidable Ojingawa, which separates the two provinces Tootomi and Surunga. The passage of this river is what all travellers are apprehensive of, not only for its uncommon rapidity and swiftness but because sometimes, chiefly after rains, it swells so high, that they are necessitated to stay several days on either bank, till the fall of the water makes it passable, or till they will venture the passage, and desire to be set over at their own peril. The rivers Fusi, Jodagawa, and Abikawa, in the last mentioned province, are of the like nature, but not so much dreaded.

There are many other shallow and rapid rivers; but because they are not so broad as those above-mentioned, nor altogether so impetuous, passengers are ferried over them in boats, which are built after a particular fashion proper for such a passage, with flat thin bottoms, which will give way, so that if they run aground, or upon some great stone, they may easily rub over it without any danger slide over it and get off again. The chief of these are, the river Tenriu in the province Tootomi; Fudsikawa, in the province Suruga; Benrju, in the province Musasi, and the river Askagawa, which is particularly remarkable, for that its bed continually alters, for which reason inconstant people are compared to it in proverb.

Strong broad bridges are laid over all other rivers, which do not run with so much rapidity, nor alter their beds. These bridges are built of cedar-wood, and very curiously kept in constant repair, so that they look at all times as if they had been but lately finished. They are railed on both sides. The perpendicular rails stand at about a fathom's distance from each other, and there are two upon every arch, if they be not of a larger size, for the commodious passage of boats and ships under the bridge. As one may travel all over Japan without paying any taxes or customs, so likewise they know nothing of any money to be paid by way of a toll for the repair of highways and bridges. Only in some places the custom is, in winter-time, to give the bridge keeper, who is to look after the bridge, a senni, or farthing, for his trouble.

The most famous bridges in Japan, and the most remarkable for their structure and magnitude are, 1. Setanofus, the bridge over the river Jedogawa, where it comes out of a large freshwater lake, in the province Oomi. This bridge is supported, in the middle, by a small island, and consequently consists of two parts, the first whereof hath thirty-six kins, or fathoms,* in length, and the second ninety-six. This river, which runs through Osacca, and then loses itself in the sea, hath several other bridges laid over it, some of which are still larger. There is one for instance, near the small town of Udsi, two near Fusimi, two near Jodo and seven in the city of Osacca, not to mention some smaller ones, which are laid over its arms. This river is also navigable for small boats, but they do not come up higher than Udsi. 2. Jafugibas, near the city Okasacki, in the province Mikawa, is 208 fathoms long. This river is also navigable for small boats, which from the sea-side come up as far as this bridge. 3. Josidanobas, near the city Josida, in the same province, is 120 kins, or fathoms, long. In high water even large barges can come up this river as far as this city. 4. Rokugonofus, in the province Musasi, was 109 kins long. This bridge was, by the impetuosity of the river, swelled by great rains, washed away in 1687, and in all likelihood will never be rebuilt, because the river being very near the residence of the Emperor, its security seems to require that there be no bridge over it. 5. Niponbas, that is, the bridge of Japan, so called by way of pre-eminence. It lies just opposite to the imperial palace, in the middle of the capital city of Jedo, and is particularly famous, because the leagues, which all the highways in Japan are divided into, begin to be computed from thence, and are continued to the very extremities of this mighty and powerful empire. All the bridges are laid over the banks of the river at least two fathoms on each side, and open with their rails like two wings. For this reason four kins, or fathoms, must be added to the length above-mentioned.

That part of our journey to court which we are to make by water, is made along the coasts of the great island Nipon, which we have on our left, steering our course so as to continue always in sight of land, not above one or two leagues off at farthest, that in case of a storm arising, it should not be out of our power forthwith to put into some harbour or other. Coming out of the straits of Simonoseki, we continue for some time in sight of the south-eastern coasts of the island Kiusju, which we went over by land, going from Nagasaki to Kokura. Having left the coasts of Kiusju, we come in sight of those of the island Tsiokoku, we then made the island Awadsi, and steering between this island on our right, and the main continent of the province Idsumi, on our left, we at last put into the harbour of Osacca, and so end that part of our journey to court which must be made by sea. All these coasts are very much frequented, not only by the princes and lords of the empire, with their retinues, travelling to and from court, but like-

* A fathom contains six feet.

wise by the merchants of the country going from one province to another to traffic, to dispose of their goods and to buy others, so that one may chance, on some days, to see upwards of an hundred ships under sail. The coasts hereabouts are rocky and mountainous, and many of the mountains cultivated up to their very tops; otherwise they are well inhabited, and stocked with villages, castles, and small towns. There are very good harbours in several places, where ships put in at night to lie at anchor, commonly upon good clean ground in four to eight fathoms.

In this voyage we pass by innumerable small islands, the straits, particularly between Tsikoko and Nipon, are full of them. They are all mountainous, and are for the most part barren and uncultivated rocks. A few have a tolerably good soil and sweet water. These are inhabited, and the mountains, though very steep, are cultivated up to their tops. The mountains of such islands as are inhabited (as also of the main continent of Nipon), have several rows of fire planted for ornament's sake along their ridge at top, which makes them look at a distance as if they were fringed, and withal affords a very curious prospect. There is hardly an island of the inhabited ones but what hath a convenient harbour, with good anchoring-ground where ships may lie safe. All Japanese pilots know this very well, and will sometimes come to an anchor upon very slight pretences. Nor indeed are they much to be blamed for an over carefulness, or too great a circumspection, which some would be apt to call fear and cowardice. For it must be considered, that by the laws of the empire, their ships must not be built strong enough to bear the shocks and tossing of huge raging waves; the cabin itself, and the goods on board, are scarce secure from rain and sea-water before they drop anchor and take down the mast. The deck is built so loose that it will let the water run through, before the mast hath been taken down, and the ship covered, partly with mats, partly with the sails. The stern is laid quite open, and if the sea runs high, the waves will beat in on all sides. In short, the whole structure is so weak and thin, that a storm approaching, unless anchor be forthwith cast, the sails taken in, and the mast let down, it is in danger every moment to be shattered to pieces and sunk.

CHAPTER XX.

A GENERAL DESCRIPTION OF THE SEVERAL EDIFICES AND BUILDINGS, PUBLIC AND PRIVATE, WE MET WITH ALONG THE ROAD.

IN our journey to court we met with the following structures and buildings: all sorts of ships and barges in our voyage by sea; and in our journey by land, many sacred and civil, public and private buildings; as for instance, castles, cities, boroughs, villages, hamlets, post-houses, inns, eating-houses, public places for proclamations and orders from the government, places of execution, temples, convents, idols, and relics; of all which I propose to give a general description in this and the following chapter.

All the ships and boats we met with in our

voyage by sea, were built of fir or cedar-wood, both which grow in great plenty in the country. They are of a different structure, according to the purposes and the waters they are built for. The pleasure-boats, which make up one sort, and are made use of only for going up and falling down rivers or to cross small bays, are again widely different in their structure, according to the possessor's fancy. Commonly they are built for rowing. The first and lowermost deck is flat and low. Another more lofty, with open windows, stands upon it; and this may be by folding screens divided as they please into several partitions. The roof, and several parts of the ship, are curiously adorned with a variety of flags and other ornaments.

The merchant ships which venture out at sea, though not very far from the coasts, and serve for the transport of men and goods from one island or province to another, are the largest naval structures of this country. They deserve a more accurate description, as by their means trade and commerce is carried on with all parts of the empire. They are commonly fourteen fathoms long, and four fathoms broad, built for sailing as well as rowing; they run tapering from the middle towards the stem; both ends of the keel stand out of the water considerably. The body of the ship is not built roundish as our European ones, but that part which stands below the surface of the water runs almost in a straight line towards the keel. The stern is broad and flat, with a wide opening in the middle, which reaches down almost to the bottom of the ship, and lays open all the inside to the eye. This opening was originally contrived for the easier management of the rudder, but since the emperor hath taken the resolution to shut up his dominions to all foreigners, orders were issued at the same time, that no ship should be built without such an opening; and this in order to prevent his subjects from attempting to venture out to the main sea, on any voyage whatever. The deck is somewhat raised towards the stern. It is broader on the sides where it is flat and straight. It consists only of deal boards laid loose, without anything to fasten them together. It rises but little above the surface of the water, when the ship hath its full lading. It is almost covered with a sort of a cabin, full a man's height, only a small part of it towards the stem being left empty, to lay up the anchor and other tackle. This cabin juts out of the ship about two feet on each side, and there are folding windows round it, which may be opened or shut, as pleasure or occasion require. In the furthermost part are the cabins, or rooms for passengers, separate from each other by folding screens and doors, with the floors covered with fine neat mats. The furthermost cabin is always reckoned the best, and for this reason assigned to the chief passenger. The roof, or upper deck, is flattish, and made of neat boards curiously joined together. In rainy weather the mast is let down upon the upper deck, and the sail extended over it for sailors, and the people employed in the ship's service to take shelter under it, and to sleep at night. Sometimes, and the better to defend the upper deck, it is covered with common straw mats, which for this purpose lie there at hand. The ship hath but one sail, made of hemp, and withal very large. She hath also but one mast, standing up about a fathom behind her middle towards the stern. This mast, which is of the same length with the ship, is wound up by pulleys, and again let down upon the deck, when the ship comes to an anchor. The anchors are of iron, and the cables of twisted straw, and stronger than one would imagine. Ships of this burden have commonly thirty or forty hands a-piece to row them, if the wind fails. The watermen's benches are towards the stern. They row according to the air of a song, or the tune of some words, or other noise, which serves at the same time to direct and regulate their work, and to encourage one another. They do not row after our European manner, extending their oars straight forwards, and cutting just the surface of the water, but let them fall down in the water almost perpendicularly, and then lift them up again. This way of rowing not only answers all the ends of the other, but is done with less trouble, and seems to be much more advantageous, considering either the narrowness of the passage ships chance sometimes to have when they pass either through straits, or by one another, or that the benches of the rowers are raised considerably above the surface of the water. Their oars are besides made in a particular manner, calculated for this way of rowing, being not all straight, like our European oars, but somewhat bent, with a moveable joint in the middle, which, yielding to the violent pressure of the water, facilitates the taking of them up. The timber-pieces and boards are fastened together in their joints and extremities with hooks and bands of copper. The stem is adorned with a knot of fringes, made of thin long black strings. Men of quality, in their voyages, have their cabin hung all about with cloth, whereupon are stitched their coats of arms. Their pike of state, as the badge of their authority, is put up upon the stern on one side of the rudder. On the other side there is a weather-flag for the use of the pilot. In small ships, as soon as they come to an anchor, the rudder is wound up and put ashore; so that one may pass through the opening of the stern, as through a back door, and walking over the rudder as over a bridge, get ashore. Thus much of the ships. I proceed now to the structures and buildings travellers meet with in their journeys by land.

It may be observed in general, that all the buildings of this country, whether ecclesiastical or civil, public or private, are by no means to be compared to ours in Europe, neither in largeness nor magnificence, they being commonly low and built with wood. By virtue of the laws of the empire, the houses of private persons are not to exceed six kins, or fathoms, in height. Nay, it is but seldom they build their houses so high, unless they design them for warehouses. Even the palaces of the Dairi, or Ecclesiastical Hereditary Emperor, those of the Secular Monarch, and of all the princes and lords of the empire, are not above one story high. And although there are many common houses, chiefly in towns, of two stories, yet the upper story, if otherwise it deserves that name, is generally very low, unfit to be inhabited, and good for little else, but to lay up some of the least necessary household goods.

It being often without a ceiling, or any other cover but the bare roof. The reason of their building their houses so very low, is the frequency of the earthquakes to which this country is subject, and which prove much more fatal to lofty and massy buildings of stone than to low and small houses of wood. If the houses of the Japanese be not so large, lofty, or so substantially built as ours, they are, on the other hand, greatly to be admired for their uncommon neatness and cleanliness, and curious furniture. I could not help taking notice, that their furniture and the several ornaments of their apartments, make a far more graceful and handsome appearance in rooms of a small compass, than they would do in large lofty halls. They have none, or but few partition walls, to divide their rooms from each other; but, instead of them make use of folding screens made of coloured or gilt paper, and laid into wooden frames, which they can put on or remove, whenever they please, and by this means enlarge their rooms, or make them narrower, as it best suits their fancy or convenience. The floors are somewhat raised above the level of the street, and are all made of boards, neatly covered with well stuffed, fine mats, the borders of which are curiously fringed, embroidered, or otherwise neatly adorned. Another law of the country directs, that all mats should be of the same size in all parts of the empire, to wit, a kin or fathom long, and half a kin broad. All the lower part of the house, the staircase leading up to the second story, if there be any, the doors, windows, posts and passages are curiously painted and varnished. The ceilings are neatly covered with gilt or silver-coloured paper, embellished with flowers, and the screens in several rooms curiously painted. In short, there is not one corner in the whole house but what looks handsome and pretty, and this the rather, since all their furniture being the produce of the country, may be bought at an easy rate. I must not forget to mention, that it is very healthful to live in these houses, and that in this particular they are far beyond ours in Europe, because of their being built all of cedar-wood, or firs, whereof there is a great plenty in the country; and because of the windows being generally contrived so, that upon opening them, and upon removing the screens which separate the rooms, a free passage is left for the air to strike through the whole house. I took notice, that the roof, which is covered with planks, or shingles of wood, rests upon thick, strong, heavy beams, as large as they can get them, and that the second story is generally built stronger and more substantial than the first. This they do by reason of the frequent earthquakes, which happen in this country, because they observe, that in case of a violent shock, the pressure of the upper part of the house upon the lower, which is built much lighter, keeps the whole from being overthrown.

The castles of the Japanese nobility are built, either on great rivers, or upon hills and rising grounds. They take in a vast deal of room, and consist commonly of three different fortresses, or enclosures, which either cover and defend, of if possible, encompass one another. Every enclosure is surrounded and defended by a clean deep ditch, and a thick strong wall built of stone or earth, with strong gates. Guns they have none. The principal and innermost castle, or inclosure, is called fon mas, that is, the true, or chief castle. It is the residence of the prince or lord who is in possession of it, and as such it is distinguished from others by a square, large, white tower, three or four stories high, with a small roof encompassing each story, like a crown or garland. In the second, called ninmas, that is, the second castle, are lodged the gentlemen of the prince's bed-chamber, his stewards, secretaries, and other chief officers, who are to give a more constant attendance about his person. The empty spaces are cultivated, and turned either into gardens or sown with rice. The third and outwardmost is called sotogamei, that is, the outwardmost defence, as also ninmomas, that is, the third castle. It is the abode of a numerous train of soldiers, courtiers, domestics, and other people, everybody being permitted to come into it. The white walls, bastions, gates, each of which has two or more stories built over it, and above all the beautiful tower of the innermost castle, are extremely pleasant to behold at a distance. There is commonly a place without the castle called oo-te-guts, that is, the great frontier mouth, designed for a rendezvous and review of troops. Hence it appears, that considering war and sieges are carried on in this country without the use of great guns, these castles are well enough defended, and of sufficient strength to hold out against a long siege. The proprietors are bound besides to take particular care, that they be kept in constant repair. However, if there be any part thereof going to ruin, the same cannot be rebuilt, without the knowledge and express leave of the emperor. Much less doth the emperor suffer new ones to be built in any part of his dominions. The castles where the princes or lords reside are commonly seated at the extremity of some large town, which encompasses them in the form of a half moon.

Most of the towns are very populous and well built. The streets are, generally speaking, regular, running straight forward, and crossing each other at right angles, as if they had been laid out at one time, and according to one general ground plan. The towns are not surrounded with walls and ditches. The two chief gates, where people go in and out, are no better than the ordinary gates which stand at the end of every street, and are shut at night. Sometimes there is part of a wall built contiguous to them on each side, merely for ornament's sake. In larger towns, where some prince or other resides, these two gates are a little handsomer, and kept in better repair, and there is commonly a strong guard mounted there, all out of respect for the residing prince. The rest of the town generally lies open to the fields, and is but seldom inclosed even with a common hedge or ditch. The frontier towns of the imperial demesnes, or crown lands, although they be not fortified with any great art, yet in those narrow passages which lead to them, and which cannot be well avoided, they are defended with strong gates, where a good imperial inquisition guard is constantly mounted. In our journey to court I counted thirty-three towns and residences of princes of the empire, some whereof we passed through, but saw others only at a distance. Common towns and large villages

2 A

or boroughs, I computed from seventy-five to eighty or upwards: not to mention some large palaces, inhabited only by sheriffs of counties, or surveyors of some tracts of land; as also some others built to lodge men of great quality in their journeys to and from court. I could not help admiring the great number of shops we met with in all the cities, towns and villages, whole large streets being scarce anything else but continued rows of shops on both sides; and I own, for my part, that I could not well conceive how the whole country is able to furnish customers enough only to make the proprietors get a livelihood, much less to enrich them.

The villages along the highways in the great island Nipon are but thinly inhabited by country people and labourers, the far greater part of the inhabitants being made up by other people, who resort there to get their livelihood, either by selling some odd things to travellers, or by servile daily labour. Hence it is that most villages consist only of one long street, bordering on each side of the highway, which is sometimes extended to such a length as to reach the next village within a quarter of a mile more or less. Hence, likewise, it is, that some villages have two names; for having been originally two villages, which by the gradual increase of the inhabitants and houses came to be joined together, each part retained its former name, though by people not apprised of this distinction the name of either part is sometimes by mistake given to the whole village. I must here desire the reader to observe that the names and words are not always written and pronounced after the same manner, it being not inconsistent with the beauty of the Japanese language to abbreviate some words, to alter some letters in others, just as it pleases every one's fancy, or to add to some syllables the letter n, which they do frequently for the sake of an easier and more agreeable pronunciation. Thus sometimes they write Fonda for Fon Tomida; Mattira for Matzidira; Tagawa for Takawa; Firangawa for Firakawa; Nangasaki for Nagasaki, and so on. I thought it necessary once for all to make this observation, and to entreat the reader not to take it amiss if he meets with the same names differently written in different places.

The houses of country-people and husbandmen are so small and poor that a few lines will serve to give the reader a full idea of them. They consist of four low walls, covered with a thatched or shingled roof. In the back part of the house the floor is somewhat raised above the level of the street, and there it is they place the hearth; the rest is covered with neat mats. Behind the street door hangs a row of coarse ropes made of straw, not to hinder people from coming in or going out, but to serve instead of a lattice-window, to prevent such as are without from looking in and observing what passes within doors. As to household goods they have but few. Many children and great poverty generally make up all their possessions, and yet with some small provision of rice, plants, and roots, they live content and happy.

Passing through cities and villages, and other inhabited places, we always found upon one of the chief public streets a fudanotsiusi, as they call it, being a small place encompassed with gratings, for the *supreme will*, as the usual way of speaking is in this country, that is, for the imperial orders and proclamations. It is the lord, or governor, of every province that publishes them in his own name for the instruction of passengers. They are written, article by article, in large fair characters, upon a square table of a foot or two in length, standing upon a post at least two fathoms high. We saw several of these tables as we travelled along, of different dates and upon different subjects. The chief, largest, and oldest contains the edict against the Roman Catholic religion, setting forth also proper orders relating to the inquisition, specifying what reward is to be given to any person or persons that discover a Christian or a priest. The lords or governors of provinces put up their own orders and edicts in the same place. This is the reason why there are sometimes so many standing behind or near one another, that it is scarce possible to see and to read them all. Sometimes also there are pieces of money, in gold and silver, struck or nailed to some, which are to be given as a reward to any person or persons that will discover any fact, person, or criminal therein mentioned. These grated proclamation-cases are commonly placed in great cities just at the entry, in villages and hamlets in the middle of the chief streets, where there is the greatest passage through, or in any other place where they are the most likely to be taken notice of. Going along the road in such places as are not inhabited, there are some other orders and instructions for passengers put up in the like manner, but upon lower posts. These come from the sheriffs, surveyors of the roads, and other inferior officers, and although the things therein ordered or intimated be generally very trifling, yet they may involve a transgressor or negligent observer in great troubles and expense.

Another remarkable thing we met with as we travelled along were the places of public execution. These are easily known by crosses, posts, and other remains of former executions. They usually lie without the cities or villages, on the west side. It is the common opinion, supposed to hold true in all countries,—the more laws the more offenders. As to the magistrates of this, it is no inconsiderable proof of their wisdom and circumspection, as well as the tenderness and love for their people, that they made it their endeavour to put a stop even to all imaginable opportunities which might tempt and induce people to commit crimes, by express and severe laws, which are so far from being not or but slightly observed, that none but corporal punishments, or an unavoidable death, are known to attend the least transgression thereof. Hence it is, that in this heathen country fewer capital crimes are tried before the courts of justice, and less criminal blood shed by the hands of public executioners, than perhaps in any part of Christianity. So powerfully works the fear of an inevitable shameful death upon the minds of a nation otherwise so stubborn as the Japanese, and so regardless of their lives, that nothing else but such an unbounded strictness would be able to keep them within due bounds of continence and virtue. It is true indeed, Nagasaki cannot boast of that scarcity of executions. For besides that this place hath been in a manner consecrated to cruelty and blood, by being made the place of common butchery of many thousand Japanese Christians, who in the last persecution sealed up their faith with their blood, there have not been since wanting criminals and frequent executions, particularly of those people who, contrary to the severe imperial edicts, cannot leave off carrying on a smuggling trade with foreigners, and who alone perhaps of the whole nation seem to be more pleased with this unlawful gain than frightened by the shameful punishment which they must inevitably suffer if caught in the fact or betrayed to the governors. But it is time to turn our eyes from these unpleasing objects, and to proceed to consider others more agreeable.

Of all the religious buildings to be seen in this country, the tira, that is, the Bud's temples, or temples built to foreign idols, with the adjoining convents, are doubtless the most remarkable, as being far superior to all others, by their stately height, curious roofs, and numberless other beautiful ornaments, which agreeably surprise and amaze the beholder. Such as are built within cities or villages, stand commonly on rising grounds, and in the most conspicuous places. Others, which are without, are built in the ascent of hills and mountains. All are most sweetly seated; a curious view of the adjacent country, a spring or rivulet of clear water, and the neighbourhood of a wood, with pleasant walks, being necessary qualifications of those spots of ground these holy structures are to be built upon. For they say, that the gods are extremely delighted with such high and pleasant places, and I make no doubt but that their priests readily condescend to be of the same opinion, they being the most proper for their own pleasures and diversion. All these temples are built of the best cedars and firs, and adorned within with many carved images. In the middle of the temple stands a fine altar, with one or more gilt idols upon it, and a beautiful candlestick, with sweet scented candles burning before it. The whole temple is so neatly and curiously adorned, that one would fancy himself transported into a Roman Catholic church, did not the monstrous shape of the idols which are therein worshipped evince the contrary. They are not unlike the pagodas of the Siamites and Chinese, both in structure and ornaments, which it is not here the proper place to give a more accurate description of. The whole empire is full of these temples, and their priests are without number. In and about Miaco alone, they count 3893 temples, and 37,093 sinkku, or priests, to attend them.

The sanctity of the mija, or temples sacred to the idols, as of old worshipped in the country, requires also that they should be built in some eminent place, or at least at some distance from unclean common grounds. I have elsewhere observed, that they are attended only by secular persons. A neat broad walk turns in from the highway towards these temples. At the beginning of the walk is a stately and magnificent gate, built either of stone or of wood, with a square table about a foot and a half high, on which the name of the god, to whom the temple is consecrated, is written or engraved in golden characters. Of this magnificent entry may justly say *parturiunt montes:* for if you come to the end of the walk, which is sometimes several hundred paces long, instead of a pompous magnificent building, you find nothing but a low mean structure of wood, often all hid amidst trees and bushes, with one single grated window to look into it, and within either all empty, or adorned only with a looking-glass of metal, placed in the middle, and hung about with some bundles of straw, or cut white paper, tied to a long string in form of fringes, as a mark of the purity and sanctity of the place. The same white paper is also hung round the tooris, and galleries adjoining to most of them. The most magnificent gates stand before the temples of Tensio Dai Sin, Fstzman, and that Cami, or god, whom particular places choose to worship as their tutelar god, and him who takes a more particular care to protect and defend them. I need not enlarge upon this subject, having already and amply considered it.

Other religious objects travellers meet with along the roads, are the fotoge, or foreign idols of stone, chiefly those of Amida and Daisoo, as also other monstrous images and idols, which we found upon the highways in several places, at the turning-in of side-ways, near bridges, convents, temples, and other buildings. They are set up partly as an ornament to the place, partly to remind travellers of the devotion and worship due to the gods, and the paths of virtue and piety which they ought to tread in. For this same purpose draughts of these idols, printed upon entire or half sheets of paper, are pasted upon the gates of cities and villages, upon wooden posts, near bridges, upon the proclamation-cases above described, and in several other places upon the highway, which stand the most exposed to the traveller's view. Travellers, however, are not obliged to fall down before them, or to pay them any other mark of worship and respect than they are otherwise willing to do.

On the doors and houses of ordinary people (for men of quality seldom suffer theirs to be thus disfigured) there is commonly pasted a sorry picture of one of their lares, or house-gods, printed upon one half-sheet of paper. The most common is the black-horned Giwon, otherwise called Godsu Ten Oo, that is, according to the literal signification of the characters this word is expressed by, the ox-headed prince of heaven, whom they believe to have the power of keeping the family from distempers, and other unlucky accidents, particularly from the sekbio, or small-pox, which proves fatal to great numbers of their children. Others fancy they thrive extremely well, and live happy, under the protection of a countryman of Jæso, whose monstrous frightful picture they paste upon their doors, being hairy all over his body, and carrying a large sword with both hands, which they believe he makes use of to keep off and, as it were, to parry all sorts of distempers and misfortunes, endeavouring to get into the house. On the fronts of new and pretty houses, I have sometimes seen dragons' or devils' heads painted with a wide open mouth, large teeth and fiery eyes. The Chinese and other Indian nations, nay, even the Mahometans in Arabia and Persia, have the same placed over the doors of their houses, by the frightful aspect of this monstrous figure, to keep off, as the latter say, the envious from disturbing the peace in families. Often also they put a branch of the fanna skimmi tree over their doors, which is in like manner believed to bring good luck into their houses; or else liverwort, which they fancy hath the particular virtue to keep off evil spirits; or some other plants or branches of trees. In villages they often place their indulgence-boxes, which they bring back from their pilgrimage to Isje, over their doors, thinking also, by this means, to bring happiness and prosperity upon their houses. Others paste long pieces of paper to their doors, which the adherents of the several religious sects and converts are presented with by their clergy for some small gratuity. There are odd unknown characters, and divers forms of prayers, writ upon these papers, which the superstitious firmly believe to have the infallible virtue of conjuring and keeping off all manner of misfortunes. Nay, they hang up these very papers within doors, in several apartments of their houses. Many more amulets of the like nature are pasted to their doors, such as are particularly directed against the plague, distempers, and particular misfortunes. There is also one directed against poverty. Houses with this last mark must needs be very safe from thieves and house-breakers.

CHAPTER XXI.

OF THE POST-HOUSES, INNS, EATING-HOUSES, AND TEA-BOOTHS.

To accommodate travellers, there is in all the chief villages and hamlets a post-house belonging to the lord of the place, where at all times they may find a competent number of horses, porters, footmen, and what else they might be wanting to continue the journey in readiness, at certain settled prices. Horses, or men, which are either much fatigued by their journey, or were hired no further, may be exchanged at these places. Travellers of all ranks and qualities, with their retinues, resort to these post-houses, which are by the Japanese called siuku, because of that conveniency of finding everything ready they may have occasion for. They lie at from eight to twenty-one English miles distance from each other, but are generally speaking not so good, nor so well furnished upon Kiusju, in the way from Nagasaki to Kokura, as we found them upon the great island Nipon, where we came to fifty-six, going from Osacca to Jedo. The post-houses, properly speaking, are not built for innkeeping, but only for convenient stabling of horses, for which reason and in order to prevent the exchanging horses and men from being troublesome to the public streets, a spacious court belongs to each. Clerks and book-keepers there are enough, who keep accounts, in their master's name, of all the daily occurrences. The price of all such things, as are to be hired at these post-houses, is settled in all parts of the empire, not only according to the distance of places from each other, but with due regard had to the goodness or badness of the roads, to the price of victuals or forage, and the like. One way with another, a norikaki, that is, a horse to ride on, with two portmanteaus and an adofski, or trunk, may be had for thirty-three senni a mile. A karassiri, that is, a horse which is only saddled, and hath neither men nor baggage to carry, will cost twenty-five senni; porters, and cangos men, nineteen senni, and so on. Messengers are waiting day and night at all these post-houses, in order to carry the letters, edicts, proclamations, &c., of the emperor, and princes of the empire, which they take up the moment they are delivered at the post-house, and carry them to the next with all speed. They are kept in a small black varnished box, bearing the coat of arms of the emperor, or prince who sent them, and the messenger carries them upon his shoulder tied to a small staff. There are always two of these messengers sent together, that in case any accident should befal either of them upon the road, the other may take his place and deliver the box at the next siuku. All travellers whatsoever, even the princes of the empire, and their retinues, must retire out of the way, and give a free passage to these messengers, who carry letters or orders from the emperor, which they take care to signify at a due distance, by ringing a small bell, which for this particular purpose they always carry about them.

There are inns enough, and tolerably good ones, all along the road. The best are in those villages where there are post-houses. At these even princes and princely retinues may be conveniently lodged, treated suitably to their rank, and provided with all necessaries. They are, like other well-built houses, only one story high, or if there be two stories, the second is low, and good for little else but stowage. The inns are not broader in front than other houses, but considerably deep, sometimes forty fathoms, with a tsuboo, that is, a small pleasure-garden behind, enclosed with a neat, white wall. The front hath only lattice windows, which are kept open all day long, as are also the folding-screens, and moveable partitions, which divide the several apartments, unless there be some man of quality with his retinue at that time lodged there. This lays open to travellers, as they go along, a very agreeable perspective view across the whole house into the garden behind. The floor is raised about half a fathom above the level of the street, and jutting out to some distance both towards the street and garden, forms a sort of a small bench, or gallery, which is covered with a roof, where travellers pass their time, diverting themselves with sitting or walking. From thence also they mount their horses, for fear of dirtying their feet by mounting in the street. In some great inns there is a passage contrived for the ease and conveniency of people of quality, that coming out of their norimons, they may walk directly to their apartments, without being obliged to pass through the fore-part of the house, which is commonly not over clean, and besides very obscure, making but an indifferent figure. It is covered with poor sorry mats, and the rooms divided only by common lattice windows. The kitchen also is in this fore-part of the house, and often fills it with smoke, they having no chimneys, but only a hole in the roof to let the smoke pass through. Here foot travellers and ordinary people live among the servants. People of fashion are accommodated in the back part of the house, which is kept clean and neat to admiration. Not the least spot is to be seen upon the walls, floors, carpets, posts, windows, screens, in short nowhere in the room, which looks at all times as if it were quite new, and but newly furnished. There are otherwise no tables, chairs, benches, or other household goods to be found in these rooms. They are only adorned with some miseratsies, as they call them, which are commonly things of value, artfully made and held in great esteem by this nation. They are put into or hung up in the rooms, for travellers to spend some of their leisure moments to consider and to examine them, which indeed some of them very well deserve. The tsuboo, or garden behind the house, is also very curiously kept for travellers to divert themselves with walking therein, and beholding the fine beautiful flowers it is commonly adorned with. A more accurate description, both of the miseratsse and tsuboo, will I hope not be thought improper, but I shall first take a short and general survey of the rooms themselves.

The rooms in Japanese houses have seldom more than one solid wall, which is pargetted and cast over with clay of Osacca, it being a good fine sort, and so left bare without any other ornament. It is besides made so thin, that the least kick would break it to pieces. On all other sides the room is enclosed, either with windows or folding screens and doors, which move in double joints both above and below, on purpose that they might be easily put on, or removed, as occasion requires. The lower joints are cut in a sill, which runs even with the carpets covering the floor, and the upper joints run in a beam, which comes down about two or three feet lower than the ceiling. The paper windows, which let the light come into the room, have wooden shutters on both sides, which are hid in the daytime, but put on at night, lest anybody should get into the house out of the court, or from the gallery, which runs along the outside of the house. The beams, in which the joints are, are in like manner cast over with clay of Osacca, as is also the place from thence up to the ceiling. The ceiling is sometimes neither planed nor smoothed, by reason of the scarcity and curious running of the veins and grain of the wood, in which case it is only covered with a thin slight coat of a transparent varnish, to preserve it from decaying. Sometimes they paste it over with the same sort of variously coloured and flowered paper, which their screens are made of.

In the solid wall of the room there is always a tokko, as they call it, or a sort of a cupboard, raised about a foot or more above the floor, and very near two feet deep. It commonly stands in that part of the wall which is just opposite to the door, it being reckoned the most honourable, as in Russian houses that corner where they hang up their bog, or saint. Just below this tokko, or cupboard, two extraordinary fine carpets are laid one upon the other, and both upon the ordinary mats or carpets, which cover the floor. These are for people of the first quality to sit upon, for upon the arrival of travellers of less note, they are removed out of the way. At the side of the tokko is a tokkiwari, as they call it, or sidecupboard, with some few boards in the middle, standing over one another in a very particular manner, the view whereof affords some amusement to a curious traveller. The boards themselves are called Tsigaidanna, and serve for the landlord or travellers, if they please, to lay their most esteemed book upon, they holding it, as the Mahometans do their Alcoran, too sacred to be laid on the ground. Upon the arrival of the Dutch, this sacred book of the landlord is put out of the way. Above the tsigui is a particular drawer, where they put up the iukhorn, paper, writings, books, and other things of this kind. Here also travellers find sometimes the wooden trunk, which the natives use at night instead of pillows. It is almost cubical, hollow, and made of six thin boards joined together, curiously varnished, smoothed, and very neat without, about a span long, but not quite so broad, that travellers, by turning it as they please, may lay their head in that posture which they find the most easy. Travellers have no other night clothes or bedding to expect from the landlord, and must carry their own along with them, or else lie on the carpet, which covers the floor, covering themselves with their own clothes, and laying their heads on this piece of wood, as on a pillow. In that side of the room which is next to the tokko, is usually a very fine balcony, of an uncommon but very beautiful structure, serving for the person who is lodged in this, as in the chief room of the house, to look out into the neighbouring garden, or fields, or upon the next water, without stirring from the carpets placed below the tokko.

Beneath the floor, which is covered with fine well-stuffed mats and carpets, is a square walled hole, which in the winter season, after having first removed the carpets, they fill with ashes, and lay coals upon them to keep the room warm. The landladies in their room, put a low table upon this fire hole, and spread a large carpet or tablecloth over it, for people to sit underneath, and to defend themselves against the cold, much in the same manner as they do in Persia under a kurtaij. In rooms where there are no fireholes, they make use in the winter of brass or earthen pots, very artfully made, and filled with ashes, with two iron sticks, which serve them instead of firetongs, much after the same manner as they use two other small sticks at table, instead of forks.

I come now to the above-mentioned miseratsies, as they call them, being curious and amusing ornaments of their rooms. In our journey to court, I took notice of the following, though not altogether in one room, but in the several inns we came to, as we went along: 1. a paper neatly bordered with a rich piece of embroidery, instead of a frame, either with the picture of a saint, done with a coarse pencil to all appearance, and in a few, perhaps three or four strokes, wherein however the proportions and resemblance have been so far observed, that scarce anybody can miss finding out whom it was designed to represent, nor help admiring the ingenuity and skill of the master; or else a judicious moral sentence of some noted philosopher, or poet, written with his own hand; or the hand of some noted writing-master in that city or province, who had a mind to show his skill by a few hasty strokes or characters, indifferent enough at first view, but nevertheless very ingeniously drawn, and such as will afford sufficient matter of amusement and speculation to a curious and attentive spectator. And lest anybody should call their being genuine into question, they are commonly signed, not only by the writing-masters themselves, but have the hands and seals of some other witnesses put to them. They are hung up nowhere else but in the tokko, as the most honourable place of the room, and this because the Japanese set a very great value upon them. 2. The pictures of old Chinese, as also of birds, trees, landscapes and other things, upon white screens, done by some eminent master, or rather scratched with a few hasty, affected strokes, after such a manner, that unless seen at a proper distance, they scarcely appear natural. 3. A flower-pot standing under the tsigaidanoa, which they take particular care to keep constantly in good order, filled with all sorts of curious flowers, and green branches of trees, such as the season affords, and curiously ranged according to the rules of art, it being as much an art in this country to range a flower-pot in proper order, as it is in Europe to carve, or to lay the table-cloth and napkins. Sometimes, there is instead of a flower-pot, a perfuming-pan of excellent good workmanship, cast in brass or copper, resembling a crane, lion, dragon, or other strange animal. I took notice once, that there was an earthen pot of Cologne, such as they use to keep Spa-water in, with all the cracks and fissures carefully mended, put in lieu of a flower-pot, it being esteemed a very great rarity, because of the distant place it came from, of the clay it was made of, and of its uncommon shape. 4. Some strange, uncommon pieces of wood, wherein the colours and grain either naturally run after a curious and unusual manner, or have been brought by art to represent something extraordinary. Sometimes, the tsigaidanna itself is made of such a scarce sort of wood, and sometimes the frame and case of the balcony, or the tokko, or the tokowara, or the door which leads into the room, or that which opens into the gallery towards the garden, sometimes also, the pillars and posts which are in the room, chiefly that which supports the tokko. Whatever things they be that are made of such uncommon pieces of wood, they very often, for fear of lessening the natural beauties, keep them rough and unpolished, with the bark on in several places, and only to preserve them, as well as for neatness sake, they cover them with a thin, slight, transparent varnish. 5. Some neat and beautiful net-work, or branched work, adorning either the balcony and windows towards the garden, or the tops of the doors, screens and partitions of the chief apartments. 6. Some other scarce and uncommon piece of wood, or a branch of a tree, or a piece of a rotten root of an old stump, remarkable for their monstrous deformed shape, which are either hung up in some corner of the room, or lie in the tokowara.

After this manner the chief and back apartments are furnished in great inns, and houses of substantial people. The other rooms gradually decrease from that cleanliness, neatness, and delicacy of furniture, because the screens, windows, mats, carpets, and other ornaments and household goods, after they have for some time adorned the chief apartments, and begin to be spotted, and to grow old, are removed by degrees into the other rooms, there to be quite worn. The chief and largest of the other rooms is that where they keep their plate, China ware, and other household goods, ranged upon the floor in a curious and very particular order, according to their size, shape, and use. Most of these goods are made of wood, thin, but strongly varnished, the greatest part upon a dark red ground. They are washed with warm water every time they are used, and wiped clean with a cloth, and so laid by against the next time. By this means, if they be lackered, and the varnish good, they will, though constantly used, keep clean and neat, and in their full lustre for several years.

The bagnio, or bathing-place, is commonly built at the back of the garden. They build it of cypress wood. It contains either a froo, as they call it, a hot-house to sweat in, or a cisfroo, that is a warm bath, and sometimes both together. It is made warm and got ready every evening, because the Japanese usually bathe or sweat after their day's journey is over, thinking by this means to refresh themselves and to sweat off their weariness. Besides, as they can undress themselves in an instant, so they are ready at a minute's warning to go into the bagnio; for they need but untie their sash, and all their clothes fall down at once, leaving them quite naked, excepting a small band which they wear close to the body about the waist. For the satisfaction of the curious I will here insert a more particular description of their froo, or hot-house, which they go into only to sweat. It is an almost cubical trunk or stove, raised about three or four feet above the ground, and built close to the wall of the bathing-place, on the outside. It is not quite a fathom high, but one fathom and a half long, and of the same breadth. The floor is laid with small planed laths or planks, which are a few inches distant from each other, both for the easy passage of the rising vapours, and the convenient outlet of the water people wash themselves with. You are to go or rather to creep in through a small door or shutter. There are two other shutters, one on each side, to let out the superfluous damp. The empty space beneath this stove, down to the ground, is inclosed with a wall to prevent the damps from getting out on the sides. Towards the yard is a furnace just beneath the hot-house. The fire-hole is shut up towards the bathing stove, to prevent the smoke getting in there. Part of the furnace stands out towards the yard, where they put in the necessary water and plants. This part is shut with a clap-board when the fire is burning, to make all the damp and vapours ascend through the inner and open part into the hot-house. There are always two tubs, one of warm, the other of cold water, put into these hot houses, for such as have a mind to wash themselves, either for their diversion, or out of necessity.

The garden is the only place we Dutchmen, being treated in all respects little better than prisoners, have liberty to walk into. It takes in all the room behind the house. It is commonly square with a back door, and walled in very neatly, like a cistern or pond, for which reason it is called tsubo, which, in the Japanese language, signifies a large water-trough or cistern. There are few good houses and inns but what have their tsubo. If there be not room enough for a garden, they have at least an old ingrafted plum, cherry, or apricot tree. The older, the more crooked and monstrous this tree is, the greater value they put upon it. Sometimes they let the branches grow into the rooms. In order to make it bear larger flowers, and in greater quantity, they commonly cut it to a few, perhaps two or three branches. It cannot be denied but that the great number of beautiful, incarnate, and double flowers which they bear in the proper season, are a surprisingly curious ornament to this back part of the house, but they have this disadvantage, that they bear no fruit. In some small houses and inns of less note, where there is not room enough either for a garden or trees, they have at least an opening or window to let the light fall into the back rooms, before which, for the amusement and diversion of travellers, is put a small tub, full of water, wherein they commonly keep some gold or silver fish, as they call them, being fish, with gold or silver-coloured tails, alive. For a farther ornament of the same place, there is generally a flower-pot or two standing there. Sometimes they plant some dwarf trees, which will grow easily upon pumice or other porous stone, without any ground at all, provided the root be put into the water, from whence it will suck up sufficient nourishment. Ordinary people often plant the same kind of trees before the street-doors, for their diversion, as well as for an ornament to their houses. But to return to the tsubo, or garden; if it be a good one, it must have at least thirty feet square, and consist of the following essential parts:—1. The ground is covered partly with roundish stones of different colours, gathered in rivers or upon the sea-shore, well washed and cleaned, and those of the same kind laid together in form of beds, partly with gravel, which is swept every day, and kept clean and neat to admiration, the large stones being laid in the middle, as a path to walk upon without injuring the gravel, the whole in a seeming but ingenious confusion. 2. A few flower-bearing plants planted confusedly, though not without some certain rules. Amidst the plants stands sometimes a saguer, as they call it, or scarce outlandish tree, sometimes a dwarf-tree or two. 3. A small rock or hill in the corner of the garden, made in imitation of nature, curiously adorned with birds and insects, cast in brass, and placed between the stones; sometimes the model of a temple stands upon it, built, as for the sake of the prospect they generally are, on a remarkable eminence, or the borders of a precipice. Often a small rivulet rushes down the stones with an agreeable noise, the whole in due proportions, and as near as possible resembling nature. 4. A small bush, or wood, on the side of the hill, for which the gardeners choose such trees as will grow close to one another, and plant and cut them according to their largeness, nature, and the colour of their flowers and leaves, so as to make the whole very accurately imitate a natural wood or forest. 5. A cistern, or pond, as mentioned above, with live fish kept in it, and surrounded with proper plants, that is such as love a watery soil, and would lose their beauty and greenness if planted in a dry ground. It is a particular profession to lay out these gardens, and to keep them so curiously and nicely as they ought to be, as I shall have an opportunity to show more at large in the sequel of this history. Nor doth it require less skill and ingenuity to contrive and fit out the rocks and hills above-mentioned, according to the rules of art. What I have hitherto observed will be sufficient to give the reader a general idea of the inns in Japan. The accommodation travellers meet with in the same, I intend to treat of in a chapter by itself.

There are innumerable smaller inns, cook-shops, sacki or ale-houses, pastry-cooks, and confectioners' shops, all along the road, even in the midst of woods and forests, and at the tops of mountains, where a weary foot traveller and the meaner sort of people, find at all times, for a few farthings, something warm to eat, or hot tea-water or sacki, or somewhat else of this kind, wherewith to refresh themselves. It is true, these cookshops are but poor sorry houses, if compared to larger inns, being inhabited only by poor people, who have enough to do to get a livelihood by this trade; and yet even in these there is always something or other to amuse passengers, and to draw them in; sometimes a garden and orchard behind the house, which is seen from the street looking through the passage, and which by its beautiful flowers, or the agreeable sight of a stream of clear water falling down from a neighbouring natural, or artificial hill, or by some other curious ornament of this kind, tempts people to come in and to repose themselves in the shadow; at other times a large flower-pot stands in the window, filled with flowering branches of trees (for the flowers of the plants, though ever so beautiful, are too common to deserve a place in such a pot), disposed in a very curious and singular manner; sometimes a handsome well-looking house-maid, or a couple of young girls well dressed, stand under the door, and with great civility invite people to come in and to buy something. The eatables, such as cakes, or whatever they be, are kept before the fire, in an open room, sticking to skewers of bamboos, to the end that passengers, as they go along, may take them, and pursue their journey without stopping. The landladies, cooks, and maids, as soon as they see anybody coming at a distance, blow up the fire, to make it look as if the victuals had been just got ready. Some busy themselves with making the tea, others prepare the soup in a cup; others fill cups with sacki or other liquors, to present them to passengers, all the while talking and chattering and commending their merchandise with voices loud enough to be heard by their next neighbours of the same profession.

The eatables sold at these cook-shops besides tea, and sometimes sacki, are mauaje, a sort of round cakes, which they learnt to make from the Portuguese; they are as big as common hen's eggs, and sometimes filled within with black bean flour and sugar; cakes of the jelly of the kaad's root, which root is found upon mountains, and cut into round slices, like carrots, and roasted snails, oysters, shell-fish, and other small fish, roasted, boiled, or pickled; Chinese laxa is a thin sort of a pap or paste, made of fine wheat flour, cut into small, thin, long slices, and baked; all sorts of plants, roots, and sprigs, which the season affords, washed and cleaned, then boiled in water with salt; innumerable other dishes peculiar to this country, made of seeds of plants, powdered roots, and vegetable substances, boiled or baked, dressed in many different ways, of various shapes and colours; a still subsisting proof of the indigent and necessitous way of life of their ancestors, and the original barrenness of the country, before it was cultivated and improved to what it now is. The common sauce for these and other dishes is a little soje, as they call it, mixed with sakki or the beer of the country. Sansjo leaves are laid upon the dish for ornament's sake, and sometimes thin slices of fine ginger and lemon peel. Sometimes they put powdered ginger, sansjo, or the powder of some root growing in the country, into the soup. They are also provided with sweatmeats of several different colours and sorts, which generally speaking are far more agreeable to the eye than pleasing to the taste, being but indifferently sweetened with sugar, and withal so tough that one must have good teeth to chew them. Foot-travellers find it set down in their printed road-books, which they always carry about them, where and at what price the best victuals of the kind are to be got.

It now remains to add a few words concerning the tea, the rather since most travellers drink scarcely anything else upon the road. It is sold at all the inns and cook-shops along the road, besides many tea-booths set up only for this trade, in the midst of fields and woods, and at the tops of mountains. The tea sold at all these places is but a coarse sort, being only the largest leaves which remain upon the shrub after the youngest and tenderest have been plucked off at two different times for the use of people of fashion, who constantly drink it before or after their meals. These larger leaves are not rolled up and curled as the better sort of tea is, but simply roasted in a pan, and continually stirred whilst they are roasting, lest they should get a burned taste. When they are done enough, they put them by in straw baskets under the roof of the house, near the place where the smoke comes out. They are not a bit nicer in preparing it for drinking, for they commonly take a good handful of the tea-leaves and boil them in a large iron kettle full of water. The leaves are sometimes wrapt up in a small bag, but if not, they have a little basket swimming in the kettle, which they make use of to keep the leaves down. when they have a mind to take out some of the clear decoction. Half a cup of this decoction is mixed with cold water, when travellers ask for it. Tea thus prepared smells and tastes like lye, the leaves it is made of, besides that they are of a very bad sort, being seldom less than a year old; and yet the Japanese esteem it much more healthful for daily use, than the young tender leaves prepared after the Chinese manner, which they say affect the head too strongly, though even

these lose a great part of their narcotic quality when boiled.

I omit taking notice in this place of the shops and warehouses, which are without number within and without cities, in villages and hamlets, by reason of their being not very different from ours in Germany, and because I have elsewhere mentioned the goods and manufactures of the country, which are therein exposed to sale.

CHAPTER XXII.

OF THE GREAT NUMBERS OF PEOPLE WHO DAILY TRAVEL ON THE ROADS.

It is scarce credible what numbers of people daily travel on the roads in this country, and I can assure the reader, from my own experience, having passed it four times, that Tokaido, which is one of the chief and indeed the most frequented of the seven great roads in Japan, is upon some days more crowded than the public streets in any of the most populous towns in Europe. This is owing partly to the country being extremely populous, partly to the frequent journeys which the natives undertake, oftener than perhaps any other nation, either willingly and out of their own free choice, or because they are necessitated to it. For the reader's satisfaction, I will here insert a short preliminary account of the most remarkable persons, companies, and trains, travellers daily meet upon the road.

The princes and lords of the empire, with their numerous retinues, as also the governors of the imperial cities and crown-lands, deserve to be mentioned in the first place. It is their duty to go to court once a year, and to pay their homage and respect to the secular monarch, at certain times determined by the supreme power. Hence, they must frequent these roads twice every year, going up to court and returning from thence. They are attended in this journey by their whole court, and commonly make it with that pomp and magnificence which is thought becoming their own quality and riches, as well as the majesty of the powerful monarch whom they are going to see. The train of some of the most eminent among the princes of the empire fills up the road for some days. Accordingly, though we travelled pretty fast ourselves, yet we often met the baggage and fore-troops, consisting of the servants and inferior officers, for two days together, dispersed in several troops, and the prince himself followed but the third day, attended with his numerous court, all marching in admirable order. The retinue of one of the chief Daimios, as they are called, is computed to amount to about 20,000 men, more or less; that of a Sjomio, to about 10,000; that of a governor of the imperial cities and crown-lands, to one, or several hundreds, according to his revenues.

If two or more of these princes and lords, with their numerous retinues, should chance to travel the same road at the same time, they would prove a great hindrance to one another, particularly if they should happen at once to come to the same siuku or village, forasmuch as often whole great villages are scarce large enough to lodge the retinue of one single Daimio. To prevent these inconveniences, it is usual for great princes and lords to bespeak the several siukus they are to pass through, with all the inns, sometime before; as for instance, some of the first quality, a month, others a week or two before their arrival. Moreover the time of their future arrival is notified in all the cities, villages, and hamlets they are to pass through, by putting up small boards on high poles of bamboos, at the entry and end of every village, signifying in a few characters what day of the month such or such a lord is to pass through that village, to dine or to lie there.

To satisfy the reader's curiosity, it will not be amiss to describe one of these princely trains, omitting the fore-runners, baggage, led-horses, cangos, and palanquins, which are sent a day or two before. But the account, which I propose to give, must not be understood of the retinue of the most powerful princes and petty kings, such as the lords of Satzuma, Cango, Owari, Kijnokuni, and Mito, but only of those of some other Daimios, several of which we met in our journey to court, the rather as they differ but little, excepting only the coats of arms, and particular pikes, some arbitrary order in the march, and the number of led-horses, fassanbacks, norimons, cangos, and their attendants.

1. Numerous troops of fore-runners, harbingers, clerks, cooks, and other inferior officers, begin the march, they being to provide lodgings, victuals, and other necessary things for the entertainment of their prince and master and his court. They are followed by

2. The prince's heavy baggage, packed up either in small trunks, such as I have above described, and carried upon horses, each with a banner, bearing the coat of arms and the name of the possessor, or else in large chests covered with red lackered leather, again with the possessor's coat of arms, and carried upon men's shoulders, with multitudes of inspectors to look after them.

3. Great numbers of smaller retinues, belonging to the chief officers and noblemen attending the prince, with pikes, scimeters, bows and arrows, umbrellas, palanquins, led-horses, and other marks of their grandeur, suitable to their birth, quality, and office. Some of these are carried in norimons, others in cangos, others go on horseback.

4. The prince's own numerous train, marching in an admirable and curious order, and divided into several troops, each headed by a proper commanding officer: as—1. Five, more or less, fine led-horses, led each by two grooms, one on each side, two footmen walking behind. 2. Five or six, and sometimes more porters, richly clad, walking one by one, and carrying fassanbacks, or lackered chests, and japanned neat trunks and baskets upon their shoulders, wherein are kept the gowns, clothes, wearing-apparel, and other necessaries for the daily use of the prince; each porter is attended by two footmen, who take up his charge by turns. 3. Ten, or more fellows, walking again one by one, and carrying rich scimeters, pikes of state, fire arms, and other weapons in lackered wooden cases, as also quivers with bows and arrows. Sometimes for magnificence-sake, there are more fassanback bearers, and other led-horses follow this troop. 4. Two, three, or more men, who carry the pikes of state, as the badges of the prince's power and authority, adorned at the upper end with bunches of cock-feathers, or certain rough hides, or other particular ornaments, peculiar to such or such a prince. They walk one by one, and are attended each by two footmen. 5. A gentleman carrying the prince's hat, which he wears to shelter himself from the heat of the sun, and which is covered with black velvet. He is attended likewise by two footmen. 6. A gentleman carrying the prince's somberiro or umbrella, which is covered in like manner with black velvet, attended by two footmen. 7. Some more fassanbacks and varnished trunks, covered with varnished leather, with the prince's coat of arms upon them, each with two men to take care of it. 8. Sixteen, more or less, of the prince's pages, and gentlemen of his bed-chamber, richly clad, walking two and two before his norimon. They are taken out from among the first quality of his court. 9. The prince himself sitting in a stately norimon or palanquin, carried by six or eight men, clad in rich liveries, with several others walking at the norimon's sides, to take it up by turns. Two or three gentlemen of the prince's bed-chamber walk at the norimon's side, to give him what he wants and asks for, and to assist and support him in going in or out of the norimon. 10. Two or three horses of state, the saddles covered with black. One of these horses carries a large elbow-chair, which is sometimes covered with black velvet, and placed on a norikako of the same stuff. These horses are attended each by several grooms and footmen in liveries, and some are led by the prince's own pages. 11. Two pike-bearers. 12. Ten or more people carrying each two baskets of a monstrous large size, fixed to the ends of a pole, which they lay on their shoulders in such a manner, that one basket hangs down before, another behind them. These baskets are more for state than for any use. Sometimes some fassanback bearers walk among them, to increase the troop. In this order marches the prince's own train, which is followed by

5. Six or twelve led-horses, with their leaders, grooms, and footmen, all in liveries.

6. A multitude of the prince's domestics, and other officers of his court, with their own very numerous trains and attendants, pike-bearers, fassanback-bearers, and footmen in liveries. Some of these are carried in cangos, and the whole troop is headed by the prince's high-steward, carried in a norimon.

If one of the prince's sons accompanies his father in this journey to court, he follows with his own train immediately after his father's norimon.

It is a sight exceedingly curious and worthy of admiration, to see all the persons who compose the numerous train of a great prince, the pike-bearers only, the norimon-men and liverymen excepted, clad in black silk, marching in an elegant order, with a decent becoming gravity, and keeping so profound a silence, that not the least noise is to be heard, save what must necessarily arise from the motion and rustling of their habits, and the trampling of the horses and men.

KŒMPFER'S ACCOUNT OF JAPAN.

On the other hand it appears ridiculous to a European, to see all the pike-bearers and norimon-men, with their habits tucked up above the waist, exposing their naked backs to the spectators' view. What appears still more odd and whimsical, is to see the pages, pike-bearers, umbrella and hat-bearers, fassanbock or chest-bearers, and all the footmen in liveries, affect a strange mimic march or dance, when they pass through some remarkable town or borough, or by the train of another prince or lord. Every step they make, they draw up one foot quite to their back, in the meantime stretching out the arm on the opposite side as far as they can, and putting themselves in such a posture, as if they had a mind to swim through the air. Meanwhile the pikes, hats, umbrellas, fassanbacks, boxes, baskets, and whatever else they carry, are danced and tossed about in a very singular manner, answering the motion of their bodies. The norimon-men have their sleeves tied with a string as near the shoulders as possible, and leave their arms naked. They carry the pole of the norimon either upon their shoulders, or else upon the palm of the hand, holding it up above their heads. Whilst they hold it up with one arm, they stretch out the other, putting the hand into a horizontal posture, whereby, and by their short deliberate steps and stiff knees, they affect a ridiculous fear and circumspection. If the prince steps out of his norimon into one of the green huts which are purposely built for him, at convenient distances on the road, or if he goes into a private house, either to drink a dish of tea, or for any other purpose, he always leaves a cobang with the landlord as a reward for his trouble. At dinner and supper the expense is much greater.

All the pilgrims who go to Isje, whatever province of the empire they come from, must travel over part of this great road. This pilgrimage is made at all times of the year, but particularly in the spring; and it is about that time vast multitudes of these people are seen upon the roads. The Japanese of both sexes, young and old, rich and poor, generally speaking, undertake this meritorious journey, on foot, in order to obtain at this holy place indulgences and remission of their sins. Some of these pilgrims are so poor, that they must live wholly upon what they get by begging along the road. It is particularly on this account, and by reason of their great number, that they are exceedingly troublesome to the princes and lords, who, at that time of the year, go to court, or come from thence, though otherwise they address themselves in a very civil manner, bare-headed, and with a low submissive voice, saying, "Great lord, be pleased to give the pilgrim a farthing towards the expense of his journey to Isje," or words to this effect. Of all the Japanese, the inhabitants of Jedo and the province Osju are the most inclined to this holy pilgrimage, and frequently resort to Isje, often without the knowledge of their parents and relations, or leave from their magistrates, which they are otherwise obliged to take in that and other provinces. Nay children, if apprehensive of a severe punishment for their misdemeanors, will run away from their parents and go to Isje, there to fetch an ofarrai, or indulgence, which, upon their return, is deemed a sufficient expiation of their crimes, and a sure means to reconcile them to their parents. Multitudes of these pilgrims are obliged to pass whole nights, lying in the open fields, exposed to all the injuries of wind and weather, some for want of room in inns, all the inns and houses of great villages being at some times of the year not sufficient to harbour them; others out of poverty: and of these last many are found dead upon the road, in which case their ofarrai, if they have any about them, is carefully taken up, and hid in the next tree or bush. Sometimes idle and lazy fellows, under pretence of this pilgrimage, go begging all the year round, or so long as they can get enough wherewithal to subsist and to carry on this idle way of life. Others make this pilgrimage in a comical and merry way, drawing people's eyes upon them, as well as getting their money. Some of these form themselves into a society, which is generally composed of four persons, clad in white linen, after the fashion of the kuge, or persons of the holy ecclesiastical court of the Dairi, or ecclesiastical hereditary emperor. Two of them walking a grave, slow, deliberate pace, and standing often still, carry a large barrow adorned and hung about with fir branches, and cut white paper, on which they place a large bell made of light substance, or a kettle, or something else taken out and alluding to some old romantic history of their gods and ancestors; whilst a third, with a commander's staff in his hand, adorned out of respect to his office, with a bunch of white paper, walks or rather dances before the barrow, singing with a dull heavy voice a song relating to the subject they are about to represent. Meanwhile the fourth goes before the houses, or addresses himself to charitable travellers, and receives and keeps the money which is given them out of charity. Their day's journeys are so short, that they can easily spend a whole summer upon such an expedition.

The Siunre are another remarkable sight travellers meet with upon the roads. Siunre are people who go to visit in pilgrimage the thirty-three chief Quanwon temples, which lie dispersed in several provinces of the empire. They commonly travel two or three together, singing a miserable Quanwon song from house to house, and sometimes playing upon a fiddle, or upon a guitar, as vagabond beggars do in Germany: however they do not importune travellers for their charity. They have the names of such Quanwon temples as they have not yet visited, written upon a small board hanging about their neck in proper order. They are clad in white, after a very singular fashion, peculiar only to this sect. Some people like so well to ramble about the country after this manner, that they will apply themselves to no other trade and profession to get a livelihood by, but choose to end their days in this perpetual pilgrimage. Sometimes one meets with very odd strange sights; as for instance, people running stark naked about the streets in the hardest frosts, wearing only a little straw about their waist to cover their privities. These people, generally undertake so extraordinary and troublesome a journey, to visit certain temples, pursuant to religious vows, which they promised to fulfil in case they should obtain from the bounty of their gods deliverance from some fatal distemper they themselves, their parents or relations laboured under, or from some other great misfortunes they were threatened with. They live very poorly and miserably upon the road, receive no charity, and proceed on their journey by themselves, almost perpetually running.

Multitudes of beggars crowd the roads in all parts of the empire, but particularly on the so much frequented Tokaido. Among them there are many lusty young fellows, who shave their heads. This custom of shaving the head was originally introduced by Sotoktais, a zealous propagator of the Fotoge, or doctrine of the foreign pagan worship, and has been kept up ever since. For being vigorously opposed in the propagation of his doctrine by one Moria, he commanded all that had embraced his worship, to shave part of their heads, and to be thereby distinguished from the adherents of Moria, and likewise ordered, that their male children should have their whole head shaved, after the manner of their priests, and by virtue of this solely enjoy the privilege of begging.

To this shaved begging tribe belongs a certain remarkable religious order of young girls called Bikuni, which is as much as to say nuns. They live under the protection of the nunneries at Kamakura and Miaco, to whom they pay a certain sum a year, of what they get by begging, as an acknowledgment of their authority. Some pay besides a sort of tribute or contribution to the Khumano temples at Iaje. Their chief abode is in the neighbourhood of Khumano, from whence they are called Khumano No Bikuni, or the nuns of Khumano, for distinction sake from other religious nuns. They are, in my opinion, by much the handsomest girls we saw in Japan. The daughters of poor parents, if they be handsome and agreeable, apply for and easily obtain this privilege of begging in the habit of nuns, knowing that beauty is one of the most persuasive inducements for travellers to let them feel the effects of their generosity. The jammabos, or begging mountain-priests (of whom more hereafter) frequently incorporate their own daughters into this religious order, and take their wives from among these bikunis. Some of them have been bred up in houses of ill fame, and having served their time there, buy the privilege of entering into this religious order, therein to spend the remainder of their youth and beauty. They live two or three together, and make an excursion every day a few miles from their dwelling houses. They particularly watch people of fashion who travel in norimons, or in cangos, or on horseback. As soon as they perceive somebody coming, they draw near and address themselves, though not altogether, but singly, every one accosting a gentleman by herself, singing a rural song: if he proves very liberal and charitable, she will keep him company and divert him for some hours. As on the one hand very little religious blood seems to circulate in their veins, so on the other it doth not appear that they labour under any considerable degree of poverty. It is true, indeed, they conform themselves to the rules of their order by shaving their heads, but they take care to cover and to wrap them up in caps or hoods made of black silk. They go decently and neatly dressed after the fashion of ordinary people, and wear gloves without fingers on their arms. They wear also a large hat to cover their faces, which are often painted, and to shelter themselves from the heat of the sun. They commonly have a shepherd's rod or hook in their hands. Their voice, gestures, and apparent behaviour, are neither too bold and daring, nor too much dejected and affected, but free, comely, and seemingly modest. However, not to extol their modesty beyond what it deserves, it must be observed, that they make nothing of laying their bosoms quite bare to the view of charitable travellers, all the while they keep them company under pretence of its being customary in the country, and that for aught I know, they may be, though never so religiously shaved, full as impudent and lascivious as any prostitute.

Having thus given an account of these Bikunis, it will not be improper to add a few words of another religious begging order of the Jammabos, as they are commonly called, that is mountain-priests, or rather Jammabus, that is mountain-soldiers, because at all times they go armed with swords and scimitars. They do not shave their heads, and follow the rules of the first founder of this order, who mortified his body by climbing up steep high mountains, at least they conform themselves thereunto in their dress, apparent behaviour, and some outward ceremonies, for they are fallen far short of his rigorous way of life. They have their head, or general of their order, residing at Miaco, to whom they are obliged to bring up a certain sum of money every year, and in return obtain from him a higher dignity, with some additional ornament whereby they are known among themselves. They commonly live in the neighbourhood of some famous Cami temple, and accost travellers in the name of that Cami which is worshipped there, making a short discourse of his holiness and miracles, with a loud coarse voice, meanwhile, to make the noise still louder, they rattle their long staffs loaded at the upper end with iron rings to take up the charity-money which is given them; and last of all they blow a trumpet made of a large shell. They carry their children along with them upon the same begging errand, clad like their fathers, but with their heads shaved. These little bastards are exceedingly troublesome and importunate with travellers, and commonly take care to meet them, as they are going up some hill or mountain, where, because of the difficult ascent, they cannot well escape, nor indeed otherwise get rid of them without giving them something. In some places they and their fathers accost travellers in company with a troop of Bikunis, and with their rattling, singing, trumpeting, chattering, and crying, make such a horrid frightful noise, as would make one mad or deaf. These mountain-priests are frequently addressed by superstitious people, for conjuring, fortune-telling, foretelling future events, recovering lost goods, and the like purposes. They profess themselves to be of the Cami religion, as established of old, and yet they are never suffered to attend or to take care of any of the Cami temples.

There are many more beggars travellers meet

with along the roads. Some of these are old, and to all appearance honest men, who, the better to prevail upon people to part with their charity, are shaved and clad after the fashion of the Siuko or Budsdo priests. Sometimes there are two of them standing together, each with a small oblong book before him, folded much after the same manner as public instruments are in the chancery of Siam. This book contains part of their Fokekio, or Bible, printed in the significant or learned language. However, I would not have the reader think, as if they themselves had any understanding in that language, or knew how to read the book placed before them. They only learn some part of it by heart, and speak it aloud, looking towards the book, as if they did actually read in it, and expecting something from their hearers as a reward for their trouble. Others are found sitting near some river, or running water, making a siegaki, a certain ceremony for the relief of departed souls. This siegaki is made after the following manner: They take a green branch of the fanna skimmi tree, and murmuring certain words with a low voice, wash and scour with it some shavings of wood, whereon they had written the names of some deceased persons. This they believe to contribute greatly to relieve and refresh their departed souls confined in purgatory, and, for ought I know, it may answer the purpose full as well as any number of masses, as they are celebrated to the same end in Roman Catholic countries. Any person that hath a mind to purchase the benefit of this washing for himself or his relations and friends, throws a senni upon the mat, which is spread out near the beggar, who doth not so much as offer to return him any manner of thanks for it, thinking his art and devotion deserve still better, besides, that it is not customary amongst beggars of note to thank people for their charity. Any one who hath learned the proper ceremonies necessary to make the siegaki, is at liberty to do it. Others of this tribe, who make up far the greater part, sit upon the road all day long upon a small coarse mat. They have a flat bell, like a broad mortar, lying before them, and do nothing else but repeat with a lamentable singing tune the word Namanda, which is contracted from Namu Amida Budsu, a short form of prayers wherewith they address the god Amida, as the patron and advocate of departed souls. Meanwhile they beat almost continually with a small wooden hammer upon the aforesaid bell, and this they say, in order to be the sooner heard by Amida, and I am apt to think, not without an intent to be the better taken notice of by passengers too.

Since I have hitherto entertained the reader with an account of the beggars, and numerous begging companies of this country, I must beg leave, before I quit this subject, to mention two or three more. Another sort we met with as we went along were differently clad, some in an ecclesiastical, others in a secular habit. These stood in the fields next to the road, and commonly had a sort of an altar standing before them, upon which they placed the idol of their Briareus, or Quanwon, as they call him, carved in wood and gilt; or the pictures of some other idols scurvily done; as for instance, the picture of Amida, the supreme judge of departed souls; of Jemau O, or the head keeper of the prison whereunto the condemned souls are confined; of Dsisco, or the supreme commander in the purgatory of children, and some others; wherewith, and by some representations of the flames and torments prepared for the wicked in a future world, they endeavour to stir up in passengers compassion and charity.

Other beggars, and these to all appearance honest enough, are met sitting along the road, clad much after the same manner with the Quanwon beggars, with a Dsisco staff in their hand. These have made a vow not to speak during a certain time, and express their want and desire only by a sad dejected, woeful countenance.

Not to mention numberless other common beggars, some sick, some stout and lusty enough, who get people's charity by praying, singing, playing upon fiddles, guitars, and other musical instruments, or performing some juggler's tricks, I will close the account of this vermin with an odd remarkable sort of a beggar's music, or rather chime of bells, we sometimes, but rarely, meet with in our journey to court, and which is from the number of bells called fatsio canne, the chime or music of eight. A young boy with a sort of a wooden roof or machine pendant from his neck, and a rope with eight strings about it, from which hung down eight bells of different sounds, turns round in a circle, with a swiftness scarce credible, in such a manner, that both the machine which rests upon his shoulders, and the bells turn round with him horizontally, the boy in the meanwhile, with great dexterity and quickness, beating them with two hammers, makes a strange odd sort of a melody. To increase the noise, two people sitting near him beat, one upon a large, the other upon a smaller drum. Those who are pleased with their performance throw them some sennis, or farthings, upon the ground.

The crowd and throng upon the roads in this country is not a little increased by numberless small retail merchants and children of country people, who run about from morning to night, following travellers, and offering for sale their poor, for the most part eatable, merchandise; such as for instance several cakes and sweetmeats, wherein the quantity of sugar is so inconsiderable, that it is scarce perceptible; other cakes of different sorts, made of flour, succani, or else all sorts of roots boiled in water and salt, road books, straw-shoes for horses and men, ropes, strings, tooth-pickers, and a multitude of other trifles made of wood, straw, reed and bamboos, such as the situation of every place affords.

In some places, both within and without cities and villages, one meets sometimes empty cangos and palanquins, or empty and saddled, though otherwise but mean-looking horses, with the men to attend them, who offer themselves and their horses to carry weary foot-travellers to the next post-house, or where they please, for a small sum. Commonly they have been already employed, and would be obliged to return empty to the place from whence they set out if they did not pick up somebody by the way that will, or hath occasion to make use of them.

To complete the account I proposed to give, of what multitudes of people travellers daily meet with along the road, I must not forget to take particular notice of numberless wenches, the great and small inns, tea-booths and cook-shops, chiefly in villages and hamlets, in the great island Nipon, are abundantly and at all times furnished with. About noon, when they have done dressing and painting themselves, they make their appearance, standing under the door of the house, or sitting upon the small gallery or bench which is before the house, from whence, with a smiling countenance and good words, they invite the several travelling troops that pass by, to call in at their inn preferably to others. In some places, where there are several inns standing near one another, chiefly in the siuku, or such villages as have post-houses, they make with their chattering and rattling no inconsiderable noise, and prove not a little troublesome.

CHAPTER XXIII.

OF OUR JOURNEY TO THE EMPEROR'S COURT IN GENERAL; AND HOW WE WERE ACCOMMODATED ON THE ROAD.

ALL the princes, lords and vassals of the Japanese empire, being obliged to make their appearance at court once a year, it hath been determined by the emperor, what time and what day they are to set out on their journey. The same was observed with regard to the Dutch, and the 15th or 16th day of the first Japanese month, which commonly falls in with the middle of our February, hath been fixed for our constant departure for times to come. It is towards that time we get everything ready to set out, having first sent the presents we are to make at Osacca, Miaco, and at the emperor's court, (sorted and carefully packed,) together with the victuals and kitchen-furniture for our future voyage by sea, and other heavy baggage, to the city of Simonoseki, on board a barge built for this sole purpose. Every other year this barge must be provided with new tackle, and the cabin hung with new furniture, according to the custom of the country, and it is with no little expense that it is kept in constant good repair. If she grows out of use, a new one must be bought or built for a considerable sum. All the presents and other goods being put on board, she sets sail for Simonoseki, some time before our own departure, because as we make that part of our journey by land, and in less time, she must wait our arrival there, in order to take us and our retinue on board, and to carry us to Osacca. Formerly we went on board ourselves in the harbour of Nagasaki, and made the whole voyage from thence to Osacca by sea, but a very sudden and violent storm having once occurred and put us into imminent danger, the emperor, out of a tender regard for the security of our persons, hath since ordered, that we should make this first part of our journey by land. Three or four weeks after this barge hath set sail to Simonoseki, and a few days before our departure, our resident attended with his usual train, goes to visit the two governors of Nagasaki, at their palaces, in order to take his leave of them, and to recommend the Dutch, who remain in our factory, to their favour and protection. The next day, all the goods and other things which must be carried along with us, either by horses or men are marked, every bale or trunk with a small board, whereon is written the possessor's name, and the things it contains.

The very day of our departure all the officers of our island, and all persons who are any ways concerned with our affairs, particularly the future companions of our voyage, come over to Desima early in the morning. They are followed soon after by both governors, attended with their whole numerous court, or else by their deputies, who come to visit us, and to wish us a good journey, as persons that are now going to have the singular honour of being admitted into the presence of the supreme majesty of the empire. The governors, or their deputies, having been entertained as usual upon this occasion, and taken their leave, are by us accompanied out of our island, which is done commonly about nine in the morning, at which time also we set out on our journey. The bugio, or commander-in-chief of our train, and the Dutch resident enter their norimons. The chief interpreter, if he be old, is carried in an ordinary cango; others mount on horseback, and the servants go a-foot. All the Japanese officers of our island, and several friends and acquaintances of the Japanese companions of our voyage, keep us company out of the town so far as the next inn.

Our train is not the same in the three several parts of our journey to court. In that part which we make by land from Nagasaki to Kokura, travelling over the island Kiusju, it may amount with all the servants and footmen, as also the gentlemen, whom the lords of the several provinces we pass through send to compliment us, and to keep us company during our stay in their dominions, to about an hundred persons. In our voyage by sea it is not much less, all the sailors and watermen taken in. But in the last part of our journey, when passing over the great island Nipon, as we go from Osacca to Jedo, it is considerably greater, and consists of no less than one hundred and fifty people, and this by reason of the presents and other goods which came from Nagasaki as far as Osacca by sea, but must now be taken out and carried by land to Jedo by horses and men. All our heavy baggage is commonly sent away some hours before we set out ourselves, lest it should be a hindrance to us, as also to give timely notice to our landlords of our arrival.

Our days' journeys are very long and considerable; for we set out early in the morning, and save only one hour we rest at dinner, travel till evening, and sometimes till late at night, making from ten to thirteen Japanese miles a day. In our voyage by sea, we put into some harbour and come to an anchor every night, advancing forty Japanese water-leagues a day at farthest.

We are better treated, and more honourably received, everywhere in our journey over Kiusju, than we are upon the great island Nipon, and, in general, we have much more civility shown us by strangers, I mean by the natives of Japan, than by the Nagasakian companions of our voyage, and our own servants, who eat our bread and travel at our expense. In our journey across the island Kiusju, we have nearly the same honours and civility done us by the lords of the several provinces we pass through, which they show only to travelling princes and their retinues. The roads are swept and cleaned before us, and in cities and villages they are watered to lay the dust. The common people, labourers, and idle spectators,(who are so very troublesome to travellers upon the great island Nipon, are kept out of the way, and the inhabitants of the houses, on either side of the roads and streets, see us go by, either sitting in the back part of their houses, or kneeling in the fore part behind the skreens, with great respect and in a profound silence.

All the princes and lords of the island Kiusju, whose dominions we are to pass through, send one of their noblemen to compliment us, as soon as we enter upon their territories; but as he is not suffered to address us in person, he makes his compliment in his master's name to the bugio, or commander-in-chief of our train, and to the chief interpreter, offering at the same time, what horses and men we want for us and our baggage. He likewise orders four footmen to walk by every Dutchman's side, and two gentlemen of some note at his court, who are clad in black silk, with staves in their hands to precede the whole train. After this manner they lead us through their master's territories, and when we come to the limits thereof, the Japanese companions of our voyage are by them treated with sacki and sokana, and so they take their leave. For our passage over the harbours of Omura and Simabara, the lords of these two places lend us their own pleasure barges, and their own watermen, besides that they furnish us with abundance of provisions, without expecting even so much as a small present in return for their civil and courteous behaviour; and yet our thievish interpreters never miss to lay hold of this advantage, putting this article upon our account, as if we had actually been at the expense, and they commonly put the money in their pocket. In our whole journey over Saikokf, from Nagasaki to Kokura, everybody we meet with shows us and our train that deference and respect which is due only to the princes and lords of the country. Private travellers, whether they travel on foot or on horseback, must retire out of the way, and bare-headed humbly bowing wait in the next field, till our whole retinue is gone by. Those who will not pay us this respect willingly, and of their own free choice, are compelled to do it by the officers aforesaid, who precede our train. Peasants and common foot-travellers, generally speaking, are so civil as to retire out of the way into the next field, before they are compelled to it, and there they wait bare-headed and prostrate almost flat to the ground, till we are gone by. I took notice of some country people, who do not only retire out of the way, but turn us their back, as not worthy to behold us; which same respect is paid in Siam to the women of the king's seraglio, and indeed almost all over the East Indies to persons of a superior rank. In Japan it is the greatest mark of civility a native can possibly show us, whether it be out of respect for the supreme majesty of the empire, into whose presence we are going to be admitted, or, as our interpreters would fain persuade us, out of deference to the bugio, as representing the authority of the imperial governors of Nagasaki. Howbeit, thus much is certain, that none, or but few of these public marks of honour and respect, are shown us in our journey over the great island Nipon.

Farther, as to what concerns our accommodation on the road, the same is for our money as good as we could possibly desire, with regard to the carriage of us and of our baggage, the number of horses and men provided for the same, the inns, lodgings, eating, and attendance. But on the other hand, if we consider the narrow compass of liberty allowed us, we have too much reason to complain. For we are treated in a manner like prisoners, deprived of all liberty excepting that of looking about the country from our horses, or out of our cangos, which indeed it is impossible for them to deny us. As soon as a Dutchman alights from his horse (which is taken very ill, unless urgent necessity obliges him to do it), he that rides before our train, and the whole train after him, must stop suddenly; and the dozen and two bailys must come down from their horses to take immediate care of him: nay, they watch us to that degree, that they will not leave us alone, not even when nature obliges us to retire. The bugio, or commander-in-chief of our train, studies day and night not only the contents of his instructions, but the journals of two or three preceding voyages, that none of his care and application should be wanting, exactly and step by step to follow the actions and behaviour of his predecessors. It is looked upon as the most convincing proof of his faithfulness and good conduct still to exceed them. Nay, some of these blockheads are so capricious, that no accident whatsoever can oblige them to go to any other inns but those we had been at the year before, should we upon this account be forced in the worst weather, with the greatest inconveniency, and at the very peril of our lives to travel till late at night.

We go to the same inns which the princes and lords of the country resort to, in their own journeys to the imperial court, that is, to the very best of every place. The apartments are at that time hung with the colour and arms of the Dutch East India Company, and this in order to notify to the neighbourhood by the livery who they are that lodge there, as is customary in the country. We always go to the same inns, with this difference only, that upon our return from Jedo, we lie at the place we dined at in going up; by this means equally to divide the trouble the inn-keepers must be at upon our account, which is much greater at night than at dinner. We always take up our lodging in the back apartment of the house, which is by much the pleasantest, because of the view into a curious garden. It is also otherwise reckoned the chief, by reason of its being the remotest from the noise and tumult of the street and forepart of the house.

The landlord observes the same customs upon our arrival, which he doth upon the arrival of the princes and lords of the empire. He comes out of the town or village into the fields to meet us and our train, being clad in a camisimo or garment of ceremony, and wearing a short scimiter stuck in the girdle. In this attire he addresses every one of us, making his compliments with a low bow, which before the norimons of the bugjo, and our resident, is so low, that he touches the ground with his hands, and almost with his forehead. This done, he hastens back to his house, and receives us at the entry of the same a second time, in the same manner, and with the same compliments.

As soon as we are come to the inn, our guardians and keepers carry us forthwith across the house to our apartments. Nor indeed are we so much displeased at this, since the number of spectators, and the petulant scoffing of the children, but above all the troubles of a fatiguing journey, make us desirous to take our rest, the sooner the better. We are otherwise, as it were, confined to our apartment, having no other liberty allowed us, but to walk out into the small but curious garden, which is behind the house. All other avenues, all the doors, windows, and holes, which open any prospect towards the streets or country, are carefully shut and nailed up, in order, as they would fain persuade us, to defend us and our goods from robbers, but in fact to watch and guard us as thieves and deserters. It must be owned, however, that this superabundant care and watchfulness is considerably lessened upon our return, when we have found means to insinuate ourselves into their favour, and by presents and otherwise to procure their connivance. The bugjo takes possession of the best apartment after ours, in whatever part of the house it be. The several other rooms, which are next to our own, are taken up by the dozen interpreters and other chief officers of our retinue, in order to be always near at hand to watch our conduct, and to take care that none of our landlord's domestics, nor any other person, presume to come into our apartment, unless it be by their leave, and in their presence. In their absence they commit this care to some of their own or our servants, though all the companions of our voyage in general are strictly charged to have a watchful eye over us. Those who exceed their fellow servants in vigilance and good conduct, are by way of encouragement permitted to make the voyage again the next year: otherwise they stand excluded for two years.

As soon as we have taken possession of our apartment, the landlord comes in with some of his chief male domestics, each with a dish of tea in his hand, which they present to every one of us with a low bow, according to his rank and dignity, and repeating with a submissive deep-fetched voice the word, ah, ah, ah! They are all clad in their compliment gowns, or garments of ceremony, which they wear only upon great occasions, and have each a short scimiter stuck in their girdle, which they never quit so long as the company stays in the house. This done, the necessary apparatus for smoking is brought in, consisting of a board of wood or brass, though not always of the same structure, upon which are placed a small fire-pan with coals, a pot to spit in, a small box filled with tobacco cut small, and some long pipes with small brass heads; as also another japanned board or dish, with socano, that is, something to eat, as, for instance, several sorts of fruits, figs, nuts, several sorts of cakes, chiefly mausie, and rice cakes hot, several sorts of roots boiled in water, sweet-meats, and other trumperies of this kind. All these several things are brought in, first into the bugjo's room, then into ours. As to other necessaries travellers may have occasion for, they are generally served by the house-maids, if they be natives of Japan. These wenches also lay the cloth and wait at table, taking this opportunity to engage their guests to further favours. But it is quite otherwise with us. For the landlords themselves, and their male domestics, after they have presented us with a dish of tea as aforesaid, are not suffered, upon any account whatever, to approach or enter our apartments; but whatever we want, it is the sole business of our own servants to provide us with the same.

There are no other spitting pots brought into the room but those which come along with the tobacco. If there be occasion for more, they make use of small pieces of bamboos, a hand broad and high being sawed from between the joints, and hollowed. The candles brought in at night are hollow in the middle; the wick, which is of paper, being wound about a wooden stick before the tallow is laid on. For this reason also the candlesticks have a punch or bodkin at top, which the candles are fixed upon. They burn very quick, and make a great deal of smoke and stink, because the oil or tallow is made out of the berries of bay-trees, camphire trees, and some others of this kind. It is somewhat odd and ridiculous to see the whirling motion of the ascending smoke followed by the flame, when the candle is taken off from the punch at the top of the candlestick. Instead of lamps, they make use of small flat earthen vessels, filled with train oil made of the fat of whales, or with oil made of cotton seed. The match is made of rush, and the above-said earthen vessel stands in another filled with water, or in a square lanthorn, that in case the oil should by chance take fire, no damage might therefrom come to the house. What obliges them to be very careful, is the great havoc fires make in this country, where the houses are all built of wood.

The Japanese in their journeys sit down to table thrice a day, besides what they eat between meals. They begin early in the morning and before break of day, at least before they set out, with a good substantial breakfast; then follows the dinner at noon, and the day is concluded with a plentiful supper at night. Their table is spread, and their victuals dressed after the fashion of the country, which I have described elsewhere. It being forbid to play at cards, they sit after meals drinking and singing some songs to make one another merry, or else they propose some riddles round, or play at some other game, and he that cannot explain the riddle, or loses the game, is obliged to drink a glass. It is again quite otherwise with us in this respect, for we sit at table and eat our victuals very quietly. Our cloth is laid, and the dishes dressed after the European manner, but by Japanese cooks. We are presented besides by the landlord each with a Japanese dish. We drink European wines, and the rice-beer of the country hot. All our diversion is confined in the day-time to the small garden, which is behind the house, at night to the bagnio, in case we please to make use of it. No other pleasure is allowed us, no manner of conversation with the domestics, male or female, excepting what, through the connivance of our inspectors, some of us find means to procure at night in private and in their own rooms.

When everything is ready for us to set out again, the landlord is called, and our resident, in presence of the two interpreters, pays him the reckoning in gold, laid upon a small board. He draws near in a creeping posture, kneeling, holding his hands down to the floor, and when he takes the table which the money is laid upon, he bows down his forehead almost quite to the ground, in token of submission and gratitude, uttering with a deep voice the word, ah, ah, ah! whereby in this country inferiors show their deference and respect to their superiors. He then prepares to make the same compliment to the other Dutchmen, but our interpreters generally excuse him this trouble, and make him return in the same crawling posture. Every landlord hath two cobangs paid him for dinner, and three for supper and lodgings at night. For this money he is to provide victuals enough for our whole train, the horses, the men that look after them, and the porters only excepted. The same sum is paid to the landlords in the cities, where we stay some days, as at Osacca, Miaco, and Jedo, viz., five cobangs a day, without any further recompense—a small matter indeed, considering that we must pay double for everything else we want. The reason of our being kept so cheap as to victuals and lodging is, because this sum was agreed on with our landlords a long while ago, when our train was not so bulky as it now is. The landlords upon Saikaido, in our journey from Nagasaki to Kokura, receive only a small matter by way of reward for the trouble we give them, for our own cooks take care to provide themselves what is requisite for our table. It is a custom in this country, which we likewise observe, that guests before they quit the inn order their servants to sweep the room they lodged in, not to leave any dirt or ungrateful dust behind them.

From this reasonable behaviour of the landlords, on our behalf, the reader may judge of the civility of the whole nation in general, always excepting our own officers and servants, and the companions of our voyage. I must own, that in the visits we made or received in our journey, we found the same to be greater than could be possibly expected from the most civilised nation. The behaviour of the Japanese, from the meanest countryman up to the greatest prince or lord, is such, that the whole empire might be called a school of civility and good manners. They have so much sense and innate curiosity, that if they were not absolutely denied a free and open conversation and correspondence with foreigners, they would receive them with the utmost kindness and pleasure. In some towns and villages only we took notice that the young boys, who are childish all over the world, would run after us, call us names, and crack some malicious jests or other, levelled at the Chinese, whom they take us to be. One of the most common, and not much different from a like sort of a compliment which is commonly made to Jews in Germany, is, *Toosin, bay bay*, which in broken Chinese signifies, Chinese, have ye nothing to truck?

To give the reader an idea of the expenses of our journey to court, I will here set down the chief articles expressed in round sums and rix dollars (about 5 rix dollars being equal to 1*l*.)

	Rix dol.
For victuals and lodging at 50 rix dollars a day, in our journey by land, makes in two months' time	3000
For 40 horses, and so many men, to carry our baggage from Osacca to Jedo, which number is greater in going up to court and less upon our return, at 15 thails a horse, and 6 thails a man, as hath been agreed on of old (half of which money the interpreters put in their pockets), amounts to	3000
A sum of money divided among our retinue, to bear some extraordinary expenses of the journey, of which every Dutchman receives 54 thails, and the others more or less, according to their office and quality, amounts to about .	1000
For hiring a barge (or if she be ours, for building her) 420 thails, to the sailors 50 thails: for the cabin-furniture and tackle 90 thails; for maintaining and repairing the said barge 40 thails; amounts in all to 600 thails, or .	1000
For victuals, drink, tea, tobacco, and other necessary provisions for our voyage by sea	1000
For the usual presents in money; as for instance, to the bugjo or commander-in-chief of our train, 300 thails (or 500 rix dollars), and much the same to the innkeepers, their sons and domestics, at Osacca, Miaco, and Jedo, in all .	1000
Hire for the norimon-men, as also for the cangos we make use of instead of horses, in order to be carried over mountains and bad roads, as also to visit certain temples and pleasure-houses; for passage-money to be ferried over rivers and harbours; for some extraordinary expenses and presents, whether necessary, or for our diversion, may amount in all to	2000
Presents to be made to his Imperial Majesty, of little value indeed for so powerful a monarch, but what, if sold, would bring in a sum of at least .	2500
Presents to be made to fourteen of the prime ministers, and chief officers of the imperial court at Jedo; to the two governors of that city, to the chief judge at Miaco, as also to the two governors of that city, and of the city of Osacca. These presents consist in some foreign commodities, and are but a trifle to every one of them, but bring us to an expense of at least . .	3000
Presents to the two governors of Nagasaki, which they receive before our departure in raw silk and stuffs, which they sell again to very good advantage, make to us a sum of	2500
Sum total of all the expenses of our journey (or about 4000*l*. sterling) .	20,000

Before I proceed to the journal of our journey to the imperial court, it may not be amiss to observe, that it is not an indifferent matter to travellers in this country, what day they set out on their journey. For they must choose for their departure a fortunate day, for which purpose they make use of a particular table, which they say hath been observed to hold true by a continued experience of many ages, and wherein are set down all the unfortunate days of every month, upon which, if travellers were to set out on any journey, they would not only expose themselves to some considerable misfortune, but likewise be liable to lose all their expenses and labour, and to be disappointed in the chief intent of their journey. However, the most sensible of the Japanese have but little regard for this superstitious table, which is more credited by the common people, the mountain-priests, and monks. A copy of this table is printed in all their road and house-books, and is as follows:

A TABLE, showing what days of the month are unfortunate and improper to begin a journey, invented by the wise and experienced astrologer Abino Seimei.

Month.	Unfortunate days.			
1	7	3	11	19	27
2	8	2	10	18	26
3	9	1	9	17	25
4	10	4	12	20	28
5	11	5	13	21	29
6	12	6	14	22	30

To give the more weight and authority to this table, they say, that it was invented by the aforesaid astrologer Seimei, a man of great quality and very eminent in his art. He was born a prince. King Abino Jassima was his father, and a fox his mother. Abino Jassima was married to this fox upon the following occasion: he once happened with a servant of his to be in the temple of Inari, who is the god and protector of the foxes; meanwhile some courtiers were hunting the fox without doors, in order to make use of the lungs for the preparation of a certain medicine. It happened upon this that a young fox, pursued by the hunters, fled into the temple, which stood open, and took shelter in the very bosom of Jassima. The king unwilling to deliver up the poor creature to the unmerciful hunters, was forced to defend himself and his fox, and to repel force, wherein he behaved himself with so much bravery and success, that having defeated the hunters, he could set the fox at liberty. The hunters ashamed, and highly offended at the courageous behaviour of the king, seized in the height of their resentment an opportunity which offered, to kill his royal father. Jassima mustered up all his courage and prudence to revenge his father's death, and with so much success, that he killed the traitors with his own hands. The fox, to return his gratitude to his deliverer, appeared to him after the victory, which he obtained over the murderers of his father, in the shape of a lady of incomparable beauty, and so fired his breast with love, that he took her to his wife. It was by her he had this son, who was endowed with divine wisdom, and the precious gift of prognosticating, and foretelling things to come. Nor did he know, that his wife had been that very fox, whose life he saved with so much courage in the temple of Inari, till soon after her tail and other parts beginning to grow, she resumed by degrees her former shape.

This is not one of the least considerable of the histories of their gods. And I must take this opportunity, once for all, to beg the reader's pardon, if in the account of our journey to court I shall trouble him, as occasion shall require, with other stories of the same kind, there being scarce anything else worth observing, that relates to the antiquities of this country. Seimei not only calculated the above-mentioned table, by the knowledge he acquired of the motions and influence of the stars, but as he was at the same time a perfect master of the cabalistic sciences, he found out certain words, which he brought together into an uta or verse, the sound and pronunciation whereof is believed to have the infallible virtue of keeping off all those misfortunes, which upon the days determined in the said table to be unfortunate, would otherwise befal travellers. This was done for the use and satisfaction of poor ordinary servants, who have not leisure to accommodate themselves to this table, but must go when and wherever they are sent by their masters. The verse itself is as follows:—

Sada Mejesi Tabisatz Fidori Josi Asijwa, Omojitatz Figo Kitz Nito Sen.*

CHAPTER XXIV.

DESCRIPTION OF THE CITY OF JEDO, OR YEDO; ITS CASTLE AND PALACE, WITH AN ACCOUNT OF WHAT HAPPENED DURING OUR STAY THERE; OUR AUDIENCE AND DEPARTURE.

OF the five great trading towns, which belong to the imperial demesnes, or crown lands, Jedo is the first and chief, the residence of the emperor, the capital, and by much the largest city of the empire, by reason of the many princes and lords, who with their families and numerous trains swell up the imperial court, and the inhabitants of the city, to an incredible number. It is seated in the province Musasi in 35°, 32″ of northern latitude, according to my own observations, on a large plain at the end of a gulf, which is plentifully stored with fish, crabs, and shells, and hath Kamakura and the province Idsu on the right, sailing down from Jedo, and the two provinces Awa and Kudsu on the left, but is so shallow, with a muddy clay at the bottom, that no ships of any considerable bulk can come up to the city, but must be unladen a league or two below it. Towards the sea the city hath the figure of a half moon, and the Japanese will have it to be seven miles long, five broad, and twenty in circumference. It is not enclosed with a wall, no more than other towns in Japan, but cut through by many broad ditches and canals, with high ramparts raised on both sides, at the top whereof are planted rows of trees, but

* The details of the author's journey along the coast being of little moment, are omitted. It is to be regretted that no traveller has penetrated through the centre of this interesting country.

this has been done, not so much for the defence of the city, as to prevent the fires, which happen here frequently, from making too great a havoc. I took notice, however, that towards the tile, these ramparts are shut up by strong gates, probably because they serve there for defence too. A large river rising westwards of the city runs through it, and loses itself in the harbour. It sends off a considerable arm, which encompasses the castle, and thence falls down into the said harbour in five different streams, every one of which has its particular name, and a stately bridge laid over it. The chief and most famous of these bridges, by reason of its bigness and stateliness, is called Nipombas, or the bridge of Japan, described in a preceding chapter. Another is called Jedo Baschi, that is, the bridge of Jedo. This city is extremely populous,* and the number of natives, foreigners and ecclesiastics, almost incredible, and indeed it cannot be otherwise, considering the multitude of officers of all ranks, posts, and quality, who compose the imperial court, but more particularly the families of all the princes of the empire, which stay all the year round, with numerous retinues suitable to their quality, whilst the princes themselves are allowed but six months' absence from court, during which they take care of the government of the hereditary dominions, and then return to Jedo.

Jedo is not built with that regularity which is observable in most other cities in Japan, (particularly Miaco,) and this because it swelled by degrees to its present bulk. However, in some parts of the town the streets run regularly enough, cutting each other at right angles. This regularity is entirely owing to accidents of fire, whereby some hundred houses being laid in ashes at once, as indeed very frequently happens, the new streets may be laid out, upon what plan the builders please. Many of these places, which have been thus destroyed by fire, still lie waste, the houses being not built here with that despatch as they are at Moscow, where they sell them ready made, so that there needs nothing but to remove and set them up where they are wanted, without lime, clay, or nails, any time after the fire. The houses in Jedo are small and low, as indeed they are in all other parts of the empire, built of fir-wood, with thin clayed walls, adorned within, and divided into rooms by paper screens, and lattice windows. The floors are covered with fine mats, the roofs with shavings of woods. In short, the whole edifice is a composition of so much combustible matter, that we need not wonder at the great havoc fires make in this country. Almost every house has a place under the roof or upon it, where they constantly keep a tub full of water, with a couple of mops which may be easily come at, even without the house, by the help of ladders. By this precaution, indeed, they often quench a fire in particular houses, but it is far from being sufficient to stop the fury of a raging flame, which has got ground already, and laid several houses in ashes, against which they know no better remedy at present but to pull down some of the neighbouring houses, which have not yet been reached, for which purpose whole companies of firemen patrol about the streets day and night. The city is well stocked with monks, temples, monasteries, and other religious buildings, which are seated in the best and pleasantest places, as they are also in Europe, and I believe, all other countries. The dwelling houses of private monks are no ways different from those of the laity, excepting only that they are seated in some eminent conspicuous place, with some steps leading up to them, and a small temple, or chapel hard by, or if there be none, at least a hall or large room, adorned with a few altars, on which stand several of their idols. There are, besides, many stately temples built to Amida, Siaka, Quanwon, and several other of their gods, of all sects and religions established in Japan: but they do not differ much either in form or structure from other temples erected to the same gods at Miaco.

There are many stately palaces in this city, as may be easily conjectured by its being the residence of a powerful emperor, and the abode of all the noble and princely families of this mighty empire. They are separated and distinguished from other houses by large courtyards and stately gates; fine varnished stair-cases, of a few steps, lead up to the door of the house, which is divided into several magnificent apartments, all of a floor, they being not above one story, nor adorned with towers, as the castles and palaces are, where the princes and lords of the empire reside in their hereditary dominions. The city of Jedo is a nursery of artists, handicraftsmen, merchants, and tradesmen, and yet everything is sold dearer than anywhere else in the empire, by reason of the great concourse of people, and the number of idle monks and courtiers, as also the difficult importing of provisions and other commodities. The political government of this city is much the same as at Nagasaki and Osacca, whereto I refer the reader as to a more ample description. Two governors have the command of the town by turns, each for the space of one year. The chief subaltern officers are the burgher-masters, as the Dutch call them, or mayors, who have the command of particular quarters, and the ottonas, who have the inspection and subordinate command of single streets.

The castle and residence of the emperor is seated about the middle of the city. It is of an irregular figure, inclining to the round, and is five Japanese miles in circumference. It consists of two enclosures, or fore-castles, as one may call them, the innermost and third castle, which is properly the residence of the emperor, two other strong, well fortified, but smaller castles at the sides, and some large gardens behind the imperial palace. I call all these several divisions castles, because they are separately and every one by itself, enclosed with walls and ditches. The first and outermost castle takes in a large spot of ground, which encompasses the second, and half the imperial residence, and is enclosed itself with walls and ditches, and strong, well-guarded gates. In this outermost castle reside the princes of the empire, with their families, living in commodious and stately palaces, built in streets, with spacious courts shut up by strong, heavy gates.

---

* Authorities differ greatly about the population of Jedo, but it seems to range about a million.—ED

The second castle takes in a much smaller spot of ground; it fronts the third, and residence of the emperor, and is enclosed by the first, but separated from both by walls, ditches, drawbridges, and strong gates: the guard of this second castle is much more numerous than that of the first. In it are the stately palaces of some of the most powerful princes of the empire, the counsellors of state, the prime ministers, chief officers of the crown, and such other persons, who must give a more immediate attendance upon the emperor's person. The castle itself, where the emperor resides, is seated somewhat higher than the others, on the top of a hill, which has been purposely flattened for the imperial palace to be built upon it. It is enclosed with a thick, strong wall of freestone, with bastions standing out much after the manner of the European fortifications. A rampart of earth is raised against the inside of this wall, and at the top of it stand, for ornament and defence, several long buildings and square guardhouses built in form of towers several stories high. The structures particularly on that side where the imperial residence is, are of an uncommon strength, all of freestone of an extraordinary size, which are barely laid upon each other, without being fastened, either with mortar or braces of iron, which was done, they say, that in case of earthquakes, which frequently happen in this country, the stones yielding to the shock, the wall itself should receive no damage. Within the palace a square white tower rises aloft above all other buildings. It is many stories high, adorned with roofs, and other curious ornaments, which make the whole castle look at a distance magnificent beyond expression, amazing the beholders, as do also the many other beautiful bended roofs, with gilt dragons at the top and corners, which cover the rest of the buildings within the castle. The second castle is very small, and more like a citadel, without any outward ornament at all. It has but one door, and there is but one passage to it, out of the emperor's own residence, over a high, long bridge. The third castle lies on the side of this second, and is much of the same structure. Both are enclosed with strong, high walls, which for a still better defence are encompassed with broad, deep ditches filled by the great river. In these two castles are bred up the imperial princes and princesses, if there be any. Behind the imperial residence there is still a rising ground, beautified according to the country fashion, with curious and magnificent gardens and orchards, which are terminated by a pleasant wood at the top of a hill, planted with two particular differing and curious kinds of plane-trees, whose starry leaves variegated with green, yellow, and red, are very pleasing to the eye. It is remarkable, what they affirm of these trees, that one kind is in full beauty in the spring, the other towards the autumn. The palace itself has but one story, which however is of a fine height. It takes in a large spot of ground, and has several long galleries and spacious rooms, which upon putting on or removing of screens, may be enlarged or brought into a narrower compass, as occasion requires, and are contrived so as to receive at all times a convenient and sufficient light. The chief apartments have each its particular name. Such are, for instance, the waiting-room, where all persons, that are to be admitted to an audience, either of the emperor or of his prime ministers of state, wait till they are introduced; the council-chamber, where the ministers of state and privy counsellors meet upon business; the hall of thousand mats, where the emperor receives the homage and usual presents of the princes of the empire, and ambassadors of foreign powers; several halls of audience; the apartments for the emperor's household, and others. The structure of all these several apartments is exquisitely fine, according to the architecture of the country. The ceilings, beams, and pillars are of cedar, or camphire, or jeseriwood, the grain whereof naturally runs into flowers and other curious figures, and is therefore in some apartments covered only with a thin transparent layer of varnish, in others japanned, or curiously carved with birds and branched work neatly gilt. The floor is covered with the finest white mats, bordered with gold fringes or bands; and this is all the furniture to be seen in the palaces of the emperor and princes of the empire. I was told that there is a particular private apartment under ground, which instead of the ceiling has a large reservoir of water, and that the emperor repairs thither, when it lightens, because they believe that the force of lightning is broken in the water. But this I deliver only upon hearsay. There are also two strong rooms wherein are kept the imperial treasures, and these are secured from fire and thieves by strong iron doors and roofs of copper. In this castle resided the successors of the emperor Jejas, the first of this family who governed the empire of Japan in the following order:—1. Jejas, after his death called Gongin; 2. Teitokwin, his son; 3. Daijojin, a son of Teitokwin; 4. Genjojin, a son of Daijojin; and, 5. Tsinajos, the now reigning monarch, Genjojin's brother's son. Thus much of the castle and residence of the secular emperor of Japan. I proceed now to resume the thread of my journal.

As soon as we came to our inn, we sent our second interpreter, the first and chief not being able to go out by reason of his indisposition, to notify our arrival to the imperial commissioners appointed for inspecting and regulating foreign affairs, and to that of the governor of Nagasaki, who was then at Jedo, being Genseimon, who for his great care in regulating the affairs of foreign trade, in the year 1685, to the advantage of his country, and the entire satisfaction of the emperor, was by him honoured with the title and character of Sino Cami. He forthwith gave orders to our bugio to keep us close to our apartments, and to suffer nobody to come up to us, besides our own servants, which orders they never fail strictly to comply with, though otherwise one would have thought our apartments sufficiently remote from the street, being the upper story of a back house, to which there was no entry, but through a narrow passage, which could be locked up, if needful. For a further security there were two doors, one at the upper, and another at the lower end of the staircase, and the rooms were shut up on three sides. My room had one single narrow window, through which I could, with much ado, observe the meridian height of the sun. We were told, that four days before our arrival forty streets and upwards of 4000 houses had been burnt down. This very evening a fire broke out about two leagues from our inn to the east, but was soon extinguished, having laid only a few houses in ashes.

On the 14th of March, the imperial commissioners, and Sino Cami, sent to congratulate us upon our happy arrival, and to acquaint us in the mean time, that they had notified the same to the counsellors of state. The same day we opened, in the presence of our bugjo, and another officer sent by Sino Cami, the presents which were to be made to the emperor and the great men at court, and bespoke the necessary boxes for calamback and camphire of Borneo.

On the 15th of March, two tailors came to cut the European stuffs for the emperor, as usual. The same day we bespoke bottles and other vessels for the tent and Spanish wines, and wooden tables to lay the presents upon. Our bugjo went to pay a visit to Sino Cami, by whom he was strictly forbidden to give anybody leave to see us, before we had been admitted to an audience of the emperor, unless he received express orders from him, Sino Cami, for so doing. This evening another fire broke out about two leagues from our ion, but did no great damage.

On the 17th of March, we were acquainted by our bugjo with news from Nagasaki, importing, that within a fortnight after our departure from thence, twenty Chinese jonks were got safe into that harbour. He desired us at the same time not to throw any papers, with European characters upon them, out of our windows among the dust. This morning we again perceive fire not far from us.

On the 18th of March, we were busy about drawing the tent and Spanish wines into long bottles and flasks, and putting the calamback and camphire into boxes, and regulating all things as they were to be presented to the emperor at the next audience. This evening a violent fire broke out near a mile and a half from our inn westwards, and a northerly wind blowing pretty strong at the same time, it burnt with such violence, that it laid twenty-five streets, though they were broad there, and about 600 houses in ashes, within four hours time, before it could be put out. It was said to have been caused by incendiaries, two of whom were seized.

On the 20th of March, we were told that Matzandairo Inaba Cami, who was to go to Miaco in quality of chief justice of that place, set out from Jedo accordingly on his way thither, attended by another lord, who was to present him to the people, and at the same time to bring presents from the emperor to Dairi. Sino Cami sent this day one of his officers to acquaint us, that he hoped we should have our audience from the emperor on the 28th of this month, and withal to command us to preserve our health, and to keep everything in readiness towards that time.

On the 21st of March, our chief interpreter went to pay a visit to the imperial commissioners, and to desire leave to be carried to court on the day of our audience in a cango, which was granted to him, after he had first made affidavit upon oath, signed with his blood, that by reason of his sickness he was not able to go otherwise.

Goto Taiosimoo, burgher-master of Nagasaki, set out to day for that place, having had his audience of the counsellors of state on the 15th of the second Japanese month, and his audience of leave on the 21st.

On the 23rd of March, we sent by our second interpreter Trojemon, a present of a bottle of aqua vitæ to the young lord of Firando, who was then at Jedo, as a small token of our grateful remembrance of the kind protection his father had given us, when we had our factory upon the island Firando. This day, about an hour before noon, the weather being calm, there was felt of a sudden a violent earthquake, which shook our house with great noise. It lasted so long, that one could have told fifty. This sudden accident convinced me of the reasonableness and necessity of that law, whereby it is forbidden throughout the empire to build high houses, and that it is no less requisite to build them as they do in this country, all of slight stuff and wood, and to lay a strong heavy beam under the roof, by its weight and pressure upon the walls of the house, to keep them together in case of such a shock.

On the 24th of March, being Saturday, the weather was very cold, with snow and rain, though it had been excessively hot just the night before. This day Makino Bengo, counsellor of state and the emperor's chief favourite, sent a compliment to our director, and desired some Dutch cheese; we presented him with a whole cheese of Eidam, and half a saffron cheese taken from our own provision.

On the 25th of March, we were busy with putting the presents, which were to be made to his Imperial Majesty, and to some of the great men at court, in proper order, in hopes that we should be admitted to an audience on the 28th of this month, being a holiday: we also sent to desire Sino Cami and the imperial commissioners to use their good endeavours to forward the same. The ministers of state, and other great men at court, some of whom we were only to visit, and to make presents to others, were the five chief imperial counsellors of state, called Goradzi, or the five elderly men, who were:—1. Makino Bingono Cami. 2. Okubo Canga No Cami. 3. Abi Bungono Cami. 4. Toda Jamajiro Cami. 5. Tsutsia Sagami Cami: four imperial under or deputy counsellors of state, called Waka Goridzi, who were:—1. Akimotto Tadsijma Cami. 2. Katta Saddono Cami. 3. Naito Tambaro Cami. And 4. Inagi Sawa Dewano Cami. The Dsiaju, as they are called, that is, lords of the temple, being three: 1. Toda No Tono Cami. 2. Fondakino Cami. And, 3. Ongasawara Saddono Cami. Matzaro Ikno Cami, lord of Firando, of the family of Fisen. The imperial commissioners, as we commonly call them, who are, as it were the emperor's attorney-generals for the city of Jedo, Todo Ijono Cami, and Obutto Sabboro Saijemon Sama: the two governors of Jedo, Fodso, Awana Cami and Nosij Ismono Cami: last of all the governor of Nagasaki, who is at Jedo, being then Kawagatz Gensaimon, or according to his new title, Kawagatz Taino Cami, the two others, Jama Okkasiubioje and Mijaki Tono Mo, being upon their government.

On the 26th of March, Sino Cami sent to acquaint us, that our audience was deferred a day longer, to wit, to the 29th of March, because of the death of Makino Bingo his brother, which would not permit that favourite of the emperor, and first counsellor of state, to appear in public before that day.

On the 27th of March, after dinner, Firanno Sofata, one of the emperor's physicians, an elderly fat man, came to pay me a visit, and to ask my advice about the cure of some distempers.

On the 28th of March, the two imperial commissioners and Sino Cami, sent their secretaries to acquaint us, that we should have our audience from the emperor the next morning, that therefore we should repair to court betimes, and stay there in the great imperial guard-room, till we could be introduced.

The 29th of March, being the last of the second Japanese month, is one of the usual court days, on which the emperor gives audience. And yet we could hardly have flattered ourselves of so quick a dispatch, had not Makino Bengo purposely appointed it for the day of our audience, in order to get rid of us, because on the fifth of the ensuing third Japanese month, he was to have the honour to treat the emperor at dinner, a favour which requires a good deal of time and vast preparations. This Bengo, or Bingo, was formerly tutor to the now reigning monarch, before he came to the crown, but is now his chief favourite, and the only person whom he absolutely confides in. At our audience, it is he that hath the honour to receive the emperor's words and commands from his own mouth, and to address the same to us. He is near seventy years of age, a tall but lean man, with a long face, a manly and German-like countenance, slow in his actions, otherwise very civil in his whole behaviour. He has the character of a just and prudent man, no ways given to ambition, nor inclined to revenge, nor bent upon heaping up immoderate riches, in short, of being altogether worthy of the great confidence and trust the emperor puts in him. About three years ago, he had the honour to treat the emperor at dinner, and was then by him presented with a scimeter, esteemed worth 15,000 thails, which the emperor took from his own side, with 3000 cobangs in gold, 300 shuits of silver, several damask and fine Chinese silk stuffs, and an addition of 300,000 bags of rice to his yearly revenues, which were then already of 400,000, so that now he has in all 700,000. It is reckoned an inestimable honour to treat the emperor, but such a one as may undo and ruin the person upon whom this particular favour is bestowed, because, whatever is scarce and uncommon must be provided, and everything paid at an excessive rate. As an instance of this, it will suffice to mention what Bengo did a few days ago. There being then a ball at court, he sent a socanno, as the Japanese call it (being a small treat of a few things laid on a wooden machine, made in form of a table, which the Japanese send to each other in token of friendship), to the emperor, consisting of two tah, or steenbrassems, as we call them, which he bought for 150 cobangs, and a couple of shell-fish, which cost him 90 cobangs. A cobang is worth about five ducats, so that the whole treat amounted to 1200 ducats, or to about 550*l.* sterling. These two sorts of fish are the scarcest and dearest in Japan, particularly the steenbrassems, which, when in season, are never sold under two cobangs a piece, but in winter-time and for great feasts any price is given for them. In this case it is not only very profitable to the fishmonger, but the buyer esteems it a peculiar happiness to have met with a scarce and dear dish for such a guest as he hath an uncommon value for. But there is something peculiar and superstitious hid in the very name of this fish, it being the last syllable of the word meditah, which the Japanese make use of when they wish one another joy.

On the 29th of March therefore, being Thursday, and the day appointed for our audience, the presents designed for his Imperial Majesty were sent to court, attended by the deputies of Sino Cami, and of the commissioners for inspecting foreign affairs, to be there laid in due order on wooden tables, in the hall of a hundred mats, as they call it, where the emperor was to view them. We followed soon after with a very inconsiderable equipage, clad in black silk cloaks, as garments of ceremony according to the fashion of Europe. We were attended by three stewards of the governors of Nagasaki, our doseon or deputy bugio, two town-messengers of Nagasaki, and an interpreter's son, all walking on foot. We three Dutchmen and our second interpreter rode on horseback, behind each other. Our horses were led by grooms, who took them by the bridle, one groom for each horse, walking at his right side, on which side also it is the fashion of this country to mount and to alight. Formerly we used to have two grooms to each horse, but of late this custom was left off, as putting us only to an unnecessary expense. Our resident or captain, as the Japanese call him, came after us, carried in a norimon, and was followed by our old chief interpreter, carried in a cango. The procession was closed by the rest of our servants and retinue, walking on foot at proper distances, so far as they were permitted to follow us. In this order we moved on towards the castle, and after about half an hour's riding, we came to the first enclosure, which we found well fortified with walls and ramparts. This we entered over a large bridge, with balusters adorned at the upper end with brass balls, laid over a broad river which seemed to run northwards about the castle, and on which we then saw great numbers of boats and vessels. The entry is through two strong gates, with a small guard between them. As soon as we passed through the second gate, we came to a large place where we found another and more numerous guard to our right, which however seemed to be intended more for state than defence. The guard-room was hung about with cloth; pikes were planted in the ground near the entry, and within it was curiously adorned with gilt arms, lackered guns, pikes, shields, bows, arrows, and quivers. The soldiers sat down on the ground cross-legged, in good order, clad in black silk, each with two scimeters stuck in his girdle. Having passed across this first enclosure, riding between the houses and palaces of the princes and lords of the empire, built within its compass, we came to the second, which we found fortified much after the same manner as the first. The bridge only and gates, and inner guard and palaces were much more stately and magnificent. We left our norimon and cango here, as also our horses and servants, and were conducted across this second enclosure to the Foumatz, or imperial residence, which we entered over a long stone bridge, and having passed through a double bastion, and as many strong gates, and thence about twenty paces further, through an irregular street, built as the situation of the ground would allow it, with walls of an uncommon height on both sides, we came to the fiakninban, that is guard of a hundred men, or the great guard of the castle, which was on our left, at the upper end of the above-said street, hard by the last door leading to the emperor's palace. We were commanded to wait in this guard-room till we could be introduced to an audience, which we were told should be done as soon as the great council of state was met in the palace. We were civilly received by the two captains of the guard, who treated us with tea and tobacco. Soon after Sino Cami and the two commissioners came to compliment us, along with some gentlemen of the emperor's court who were strangers to us. Having waited about an hour, during which time most of the imperial counsellors of state, old and young, went into the palace, some walking on foot, others being carried in norimons; we were conducted through two stately gates over a large square place to the palace, to which there is an ascent of a few steps leading from the second gate. The place between the second gate and the front of the palace is but a few paces broad, and was then excessively crowded with throngs of courtiers and troops of guards. From thence we were conducted up two other staircases to the palace itself, and first into a spacious room, next to the entry on the right, being the place where all persons that are to be admitted to an audience, either of the emperor himself or of the counsellors of state, wait till they are called in. It is a large and lofty room, but when all the screens are put on, pretty dark, receiving but a sparing light from the upper windows of an adjoining room, wherein is kept some furniture for the imperial apartments. It is otherwise richly furnished, according to the country fashion, and its gilt posts, walls, and screens are very pleasing to behold. Having waited here upwards of an hour, and the emperor having in the meanwhile seated himself in the hall of audience, Sino Cami and the two commissioners came in and conducted our resident into the emperor's presence, leaving us behind. As soon as he came thither they cried out aloud 'Hollanda Captain,' which was the signal for him to draw near and make his obeisances. Accordingly he crawled on his hands and knees to a place shown him, between the presents ranged in due order on one side, and the place where the emperor sat on the other, and then kneeling he bowed his forehead quite down to the ground, and so crawled backwards like a crab, without uttering one single word. So mean and short a thing is the audience we have of this mighty monarch. Nor are there any more ceremonies observed in the audience he gives even to the greatest and most powerful princes of the empire. For having been called into the hall, their names are cried out aloud, then they move on their hands and feet humbly and silently towards the emperor's seat, and having shown their submission by bowing their foreheads down to the ground, they creep back again in the same submissive posture.

The hall of audience, otherwise the hall of hundred mats, is not in the least like that which has been described and figured by Montanus, in his memorable embassies of the Dutch to the Emperors of Japan. The elevated throne, the steps leading up to it, the carpets pending from it, the stately columns supporting the building which contains the throne, the columns between which the princes of the empire are said to prostrate themselves before the emperor, and the like, have all no manner of foundation but in that author's fancy. For in our second voyage to court, the audience being over, the governor of Nagasaki was pleased to show us the hall, which gave me an opportunity of taking a sketch of it, which in the end was no very difficult matter, considering that it required nothing but to tell over the number of mats, posts, screens, and windows. The floor is covered with a hundred mats, all of the same size. Hence it is called Sen sio siki, that is, the hall of a hundred mats. It opens on one side towards a small court which lets in the light; on the opposite side it joins to two other apartments, which are on this occasion laid open towards the same court, one of which is considerably larger than the other, and serves for the counsellors of state when they give audience by themselves. The other is narrower, deeper, and one step higher than the hall itself. In this the emperor sits when he gives audience, cross-legged, raised only on a few carpets. Nor is it an easy matter to see him, the light reaching not quite so far as the place where he sits, besides that the audience is too short, and the person admitted to it in so humble and submissive a posture, that he cannot well have an opportunity to hold up his head, and to view him. This audience is otherwise very awful and majestic, by reason chiefly of the silent presence of all the counsellors of state, as also of many princes and lords of the empire, the gentlemen of his majesty's bed-chamber, and other chief officers of his court, who line the hall of audience and all its avenues, sitting in good order, and clad in their garments of ceremony.

Formerly all we had to do at the emperor's court was completed by the captain's paying him the usual homage, after the manner above related. A few days after some laws concerning our trade and behaviour were read to him, which, in the name of the Dutch, he promised to keep, and so was dispatched back to Nagasaki. But for about these twenty years last past, he and the rest of the Dutchmen that came up with the embassy to Jedo, were conducted deeper into the palace to give the empress and the ladies of her court, and the princesses of the blood, the diversion of seeing us. In this second audience the emperor and the ladies invited to it, attend behind screens and lattices, but the counsellors of state, and other officers of the court, sit in the open rooms in their usual and elegant order. As soon as the captain had paid his homage, the emperor retired into his apartment, and not long after we three Dutchmen were likewise called up, and conducted, together with the captain, through several apartments into a gallery curiously carved and gilt, where we waited about a quarter of an hour, and were then, through several other walks and galleries, carried further into a large room, where they desired us to sit down, and where several shaved courtiers, being the emperor's physicians, the officers of his kitchen, and some of the clergy, came to ask after our names, age, and the like; but gilt screens were quickly drawn before us, to deliver us from their throng and troublesome importunity. We staid here about half an hour; meanwhile the court met in the imperial apartments, where we were to have our second audience, and whither we were conducted through several dark galleries. Along all these several galleries there was one continued row of lifeguard-men, and nearer to the imperial apartments followed in the same row some great officers of the crown, who lined the front of the hall of audience, clad in their garments of ceremony, bowing their heads and sitting on their heels. The hall of audience consisted of several rooms, looking towards a middle place, some of which were laid open towards the same, others covered by screens and lattices. Some were of fifteen mats, others of eighteen, and they were a mat higher or lower, according to the quality of the persons seated in the same. The middle place had no mats at all, they having been taken away, and was consequently the lowest, on which floor, covered with neat varnished boards, we were commanded to sit down. The emperor and his imperial consort sat behind the lattices on our right. As I was dancing at the emperor's command, I had an opportunity twice of seeing the empress through the slits of the lattices, and took notice that she was of a brown and beautiful complexion, with black European eyes, full of fire, and from the proportion of her head, which was pretty large, I judged her to be a tall woman, and about 36 years of age. By lattices I mean hangings made of reed, split exceeding thin and fine, and covered on the back with a fine transparent silk, with openings about a span broad for the persons behind to look through. For ornament's sake, and the better to hide the persons standing behind, they are painted with divers figures, though otherwise it would be impossible to see them at a distance, chiefly when the light is taken off behind. The emperor himself was in such an obscure place, that we should scarce have known him to be present had not his voice discovered him, which yet was so low as if he purposely intended to be there incognito. Just before us, behind other lattices, were the princes of the blood, and the ladies of the empress's court. I took notice that pieces of paper were put between the reeds in some parts of the lattices, to make the openings wide, in order to obtain a better sight. I counted about thirty such papers, which made me conclude that there was about that number of persons sitting behind. Bengo sat on a raised mat in an open room by himself just before us, towards our right on that side, on which I took notice above, that the emperor sat behind the lattices. On our left, in another room, were the counsellors of state of the first and second rank, sitting in a double row in good and becoming order. The gallery behind us was filled with the chief officers of the emperor's court, and the gentlemen of his bedchamber. The gallery which led into the room where the emperor was, was filled with the sons of some princes of the empire then at court, the emperor's pages and some priests lurking. After this manner it was, that they ordered the stage on which we were now to act. The commissioners for foreign affairs having conducted us into the gallery before the hall of audience, one of the counsellors of state of the second rank came to receive us there, and to conduct us to the above described middle place, on which we were commanded to sit down, having first made our obeisances after the Japanese manner, creeping and bowing our heads to the ground, towards that part of the lattices behind which the emperor was. The chief interpreter sat himself a little forward, to hear more distinctly, and we took our places on his left hand all in a row. After the usual obeisances made, Bengo bid us welcome in the Emperor's name. The chief interpreter received the compliment from Bengo's mouth and repeated it to us. Upon this the ambassador made his compliment in the name of his masters, withal returning their most humble thanks to the emperor, for having graciously granted the Dutch liberty of commerce. This the chief interpreter repeated in Japanese, having prostrated himself quite to the ground, and speaking loud enough to be heard by the emperor. The emperor's answer was again received by Bengo, who delivered it to the chief interpreter, and he to us. He might have indeed received them himself from the emperor's own mouth, and saved Bengo this unnecessary trouble; but I fancy that the words, as they flow out of the emperor's mouth, are esteemed too precious and sacred for an immediate transit into the mouth of persons of a low rank. The mutual compliments being over, the succeeding part of this solemnity turned to a perfect farce. We were asked a thousand ridiculous and impertinent questions. Thus for instance, they desired to know, in the first place, how old each of us was, and what was his name, which we were commanded to write upon a bit of paper, having for these purposes taken an European ink-horn along with us. This paper, together with the ink-horn itself, we were commanded to give to Bengo, who delivered them both into the emperor's hands, reaching them over below the lattice. The captain, or ambassador, was asked concerning the distance of Holland from Batavia, and of Batavia from Nagasaki? Which of the two was the most powerful, the Director-general of the Dutch East India Company at Batavia, or the Prince of Holland? As for my own particular, the following questions were put to me: What external and internal distempers I thought the most dangerous, and most difficult to cure? How I proceeded in the cure of cancerous humours and imposthumations of the inner parts? Whether our European physicians did not search after some medicine to render people immortal, as the Chinese physicians had done for many hundred years? Whether we had made any considerable progress in this search, and which was the last remedy conducive to long life, that had been found out in Europe? To which I returned in answer, that very many European physicians had long laboured to find out some medicine, which should have the virtue of prolonging human life, and preserving people in health to a great age; and having thereupon been asked, which I thought the best? I answered, that I always took that to be the best which was found out last, till experience taught us a better: and being further asked, which was the last? I answered, a certain spirituous liquor, which could keep the humours of our body fluid, and comfort the spirits. This general answer proved not altogether satisfactory, but I was quickly desired to let them know the name of this excellent medicine, upon which, knowing that whatever was esteemed by the Japanese, had long and high-sounding names, I returned in answer, it was the Sal volatile Oleosum Sylvij. This name was minuted down behind the lattices, for which purpose I was commanded to repeat it several times. The next question was, who it was that found it out, and where it was found out? I answered, Professor Sylvius in Holland. Then they asked, whether I could make it up? upon this our resident whispered me to say, No; but I answered, Yes, I could make it up, but not here. Then it was asked, whether it could be had at Batavia? and having returned in answer, that it was to be had there, the emperor desired that it should be sent over by the next ships. The emperor, who hitherto sat among the ladies, almost opposite to us, at a considerable distance, did now draw nearer, and sate himself down on our right behind the lattices, as near us as possibly he could. Then he ordered us to take off our cappa, or cloak, being our garment of ceremony, then to stand upright, that he might have a full view of us; again to walk, to stand still, to compliment each other, to dance, to jump, to play the drunkard, to speak broken Japanese, to read Dutch, to paint, to sing, to put our cloaks on and off. Meanwhile we obeyed the emperor's commands in the best manner we could; I joined to my dance a love-song in High German. In this manner, and with innumerable such other apish tricks, we must suffer ourselves to contribute to the Emperor's and the court's diversion. The ambassador, however, is free from these and the like commands, for as he represents the authority of his masters, some care is taken that nothing should be done to injure or prejudice the same. Besides that he showed so much gravity in his countenance and whole behaviour, as was sufficient to convince the Japanese that he was not at all a fit person to have such ridiculous and comical commands laid upon him. Having been thus exercised for a matter of two hours, though with great apparent civility, some servants shaved came in, and put before each of us a small table with Japanese victuals, and a couple of ivory sticks, instead of knives and forks. We took and ate some little things, and our old chief interpreter, though scarce able to walk, was commanded to carry away the remainder for himself. We were then ordered to put on our cloaks again and to take our leave, which we gladly, and without delay, complied with, putting thereby an end to this second audience. We were then conducted back by the two commissioners to the waiting-room, where we took our leave of them also.

It was now already three o'clock in the afternoon, and we had still several visits to make to the counsellors of state, of the first and second rank, as I have set them down above under the 25th of March. Accordingly we left the Fonmar forthwith, saluted as we went by the officers of the great imperial guard, and made our round afoot. The presents had been carried before-hand to every one's house by our clerks, and because we did not see them in our audiences, I conjectured that they had been actually presented to the persons to whom they belonged. They consisted in some Chinese, Bengalese, and other silk stuffs, some linen, black serge, some yards of black cloth, gingangs, pelangs, and a flask of tent wine. We were everywhere received by the stewards and secretaries with extraordinary civility, and treated with tea, tobacco and sweetmeats, as handsomely as the little time we had to spare would allow. The rooms, where we were admitted to audience, were filled behind the screens and lattices with crowds of spectators, who would fain have obliged us to show them some of our European customs and ceremonies, but could obtain nothing excepting only a short dance at Bengo's house (who came home himself a back way), and a song from each of us, at the youngest counsellors of state, who lived in the northern part of the castle. We then returned again to our cangos and horses, and having got out of the castle through the northern gate, we went back to our inn another way, on the left of which we took notice that there were strong walls and ditches in several places. It was just six in the evening when we got home, heartily tired.

On Friday the 30th of March, we rode out again betimes in the morning, to make some of our remaining visits. The presents, as above described, were sent before us by our Japanese clerks, who took care to lay them on boards, and to range them in good order, according to the country fashion. We were received at the entry of the house by one or two of the principal domestics, and conducted to the apartment where we were to have our audience. The rooms round the hall of audience were everywhere crowded with spectators. As soon as we had seated ourselves, we were treated with tea and tobacco. Then the steward of the household came in, or else the secretary, either alone or with another gentleman, to compliment us, and to receive our compliments in his master's name. The rooms were everywhere so disposed as to make us turn our faces towards the ladies, by whom we were very generously and civilly treated with cakes and several sorts of sweetmeats. We visited and made our presents, this day, to the two governors of Jedo, to the three ecclesiastical judges, and to the two commissioners for foreign affairs, who lived near a mile from each other, one in the south-west, the other in the north-east part of the castle. They both profess themselves to be particular patrons of the Dutch, and received us accordingly with great pomp and magnificence. The street was lined with twenty men armed, who, with their long staffs, which they held on one side, made a very good figure, besides that they helped to keep off the throng of the people from being too troublesome. We were received upon our entering the house, and introduced to audience, much after the same manner as we had been in other places, only we were carried deeper into their palaces, and into the innermost apartment, on purpose that we should not be troubled with numbers of foreign spectators, and be at more liberty, ourselves as well as the ladies, who were invited to the ceremony. Opposite to us in the hall of audience, there were grated lattices, instead of screens, for the length of two mats and upwards, behind which sat such numbers of women of the commissioner's own family, and their relations and friends, that there was no room left. We had scarce seated ourselves, when seven servants, well clad, came in, all in a row, and brought us pipes and tobacco, with the usual apparatus for smoking. Soon after, they brought in something baked, laid on japanned boards; then some fish fried, all after the same manner, by the same number of servants, and always but one piece in a small dish; then a couple of eggs—one baked, the other boiled and shelled,—and a glass of old strong sacki standing between them. After this manner we were entertained for about an hour and a half, when they desired us to sing a song, and to dance: the first we refused to comply with, but satisfied them as to the last. In the house of the first commissioner, a soup made of sweet plums was offered us instead of brandy. In the second commissioner's house we were presented first of all with Mange bread, in a brown liquor, cold, with some mustard-seed and radishes laid about the dish, and at last with some orange-peels with sugar, which is a dish given only upon extraordinary occasions, in token of fortune and goodwill. We then drank some tea, and having taken our leave, went back to our inn, where we arrived at five in the evening.

On the 31st of March, we rode out again at ten in the morning, and went to the houses of the three governors of Nagasaki, two of whom were then absent and upon their government. We presented them on this occasion only with a flask of tent each, they having already received their other presents at Nagasaki. We were met by Sino Cami just by the door of his house. He was attended with a numerous retinue, and having called both our interpreters to him, he commanded them to tell us, that his desire was that we should make ourselves merry in his house: accordingly we were received extraordinary well, and desired to walk about and to divert ourselves in his garden, as being now in the house of a friend at Jedo, and not in the palace of our governor and magistrate at Nagasaki. We were treated with warm victuals and tea, much after the same manner as we had been by the commissioners, and all the while civilly entertained by his own brother and several persons of quality of his friends and relations. Having staid about two hours, we went to Tonosama's house, where we were conducted into the innermost and chief apartment, and desired twice to come nearer the lattices on both sides of the room. There were more ladies behind the screens here than I think we had as yet met with in any other place. They desired us very civilly to show them our clothes, the captain's arms, rings, tobacco-pipes, and the like, some of which were reached them between or under the lattices. The person that treated us in the absent governor's name, and the other gentlemen who were then present in the room, entertained us likewise very civilly, and we could not but take notice that everything was so cordial, that we made no manner of scruple of making ourselves merry, and diverting the company each with a song. The magnificence of this family appeared fully by the richness and exquisiteness of this entertainment, which was equal to that of the first commissioner's, but far beyond it in courteous civility, and a free open carriage. After an hour and a half we took our leave. Tonosama's house is the furthermost to the north or north-west we were to go to, a mile and a half from our inn, but seated in certainly the pleasantest part of the town, where there is an agreeable variety of hills and bushes. Zubosama's family lives in a small sorry house near the ditch which encompasses the castle. We met here but a few women behind a screen, who took up with peeping at us through a few holes, which they made as they sat down. The strong liquors, which we had been this day obliged to drink in larger quantities than usual, being by this time got pretty much into our heads, we made haste to return home, and took our leave as soon as we had been treated, after the usual manner, with tea and tobacco. We were the more impatient to be gone, because we were apprehensive lest our interpreters, who had been pretty much exercised all day, should grow too weary, and unwilling hereafter to attend us so long on the like occasions. The gentleman also, who was to entertain us in the governor's name, although he affected a great civility, had something so froward and disagreeable in his countenance, as hastened very much our departure: for we looked upon ourselves, on this occasion, not as merchants sent there to trade, but as ambassadors to a potent monarch, who ought to be treated with some regard and honour.

On the first of April, in the afternoon, we were promised by Josamma, that the next day we should have our audience of leave.

On the 2nd of April, in the morning, we went to court on horseback in the same order, and the same way, as on the day of our audience. We staid about an hour and a half in the guard-room before the castle, where we received a visit from the two commissioners and Sino Cami. We staid much about the same time in the great waiting-room of the castle, which is taken in with gilt screens, and the floor covered with six and thirty mats. We were again saluted here by the two commissioners and Sino Cami, who called our old chief interpreter out, in order to show him the room, where the ambassador should be admitted to audience, as also to acquaint him what ceremonies should be observed on that occasion. Soon after, the ambassador was called out himself, and was conducted from the waiting-room to a great hall to the left, where with the usual obeisances he took his audience of leave, and had the commands of the emperor read to him, consisting in five articles, relating among other things chiefly to the Portuguese trade. This being over, he was by Sino Cami conducted back to the waiting-room, where we staid for him, and where this governor took his leave of him with great apparent civility, withal telling him, he hoped he should see him at Nagasaki. And so we went away from court, without paying our respects to the two commissioners, and came home about one o'clock in the afternoon. Meanwhile we staid in the waiting-room; several officers at court and the sons of some princes of the empire came to see us. Among the rest was the Prince of Facatta's grandson, who, although he was blind of one eye, had nevertheless orders from the emperor to stay at court, among other young gentlemen of his quality, for no other reason but to serve as a hostage of his grandfather's fidelity. Some of these people asked after the captain's name, and there was one among the rest, who had already taken it down in writing, but this was so quickly betrayed, that minute orders were sent by Sino Cami, that our names should be told to nobody. Our departure from court was preceded by thirty gowns, laid on three tables, as a present from the emperor. In the afternoon, some of the gentlemen, whom we had visited and made presents to, sent us also their gowns, to wit: 1. Noji Jsemono, governor of Jedo, two black gowns; 2. Todotamasijro, one of the counsellors of state, ten gowns; 3. Tsutsia Sagamisama, likewise ten; 4. Fodioawanasama, the other governor of Jedo, two; 5. Kaganni K. S.; and 6. Bongosama, each ten.

On the 3rd of April, we were presented with some more gowns, to wit, with three by each of the two commissioners, and with six by each of the extraordinary counsellors of state. All our business at Jedo was completed this day by one o'clock.

On the 4th of April, the emperor dined at Bengo's, for which reason the gates of the castle were shut, which is a custom the now reigning monarch observes upon these occasions, many people wondering why.

CHAPTER XXV.

THE AUDIENCE AT COURT, ON THE SECOND JOURNEY.

On the 20th of April, the following year, though it continued to rain pretty hard, as it had done for two days before, yet we were obliged at eight o'clock that morning to repair to the castle, which we did on horseback, attended by the bugjos of the three governors of Nagasaki. Passing through the second castle we came to the third, and found Siubosama waiting for us in the great guard-room. We staid there ourselves till half an hour after ten; meanwhile the members of the council of state met in the castle, and we changed our wet stockings and shoes for clean ones. From thence we were conducted into the palace, where we staid till noon. Our captain, as they call him, went first alone to make his submission to the emperor, according to the fashion of the country, and in the company's name to offer the presents. He returned soon after to us in the waiting-room, and that moment we were by Siubosama conducted to audience, and first going round the hall, where the emperor had given orders to our ambassador, and received the presents, which still stood there; thence passing through several long galleries, all gilt and curiously adorned; we came into a long room, where they desired us to stay till we could be admitted into the emperor's presence, which they said should be done immediately. We found the imperial commissioners and other great men walking there, and ten or twelve young noblemen of great quality, sitting. But lest the sitting down so long and so often should tire us at last, we were conducted back into an adjoining gallery, where we could have the liberty to walk about, for which purpose also the shutters of some windows were laid open for us, to have a view into the garden. While we staid in this gallery, several young gentlemen of great quality came to see and salute us, and the commissioners showed us a gold ring, wherein was set a loadstone, with the names of the Jetta, or twelve celestial signs, engraved round it. They showed us likewise an European coat of arms, and some other things. But just as we were examining them, and were going to explain them according to their desire, the emperor sent for us in. So we were conducted through a gallery to our left where we found eighteen gentlemen of the emperor's bedchamber sitting, clad in their garments of ceremony, under which they wore their ordinary gowns; then passing by twenty other gentlemen, sitting in one continued row, we entered the hall of audience, where we found the six counsellors of state sitting on our left as we came in, and on our right some more gentlemen of the emperor's bedchamber of a higher rank, sitting in a gallery. The emperor and two ladies sat behind the grated screens on our right, and Bingosama, president of the council of state, opposite to us, in a room by himself. Soon after we came in, and had after the usual obeisances seated ourselves on the place assigned us, Bingosama welcomed us in the emperor's name, and then desired us to sit upright, to take off our cloaks, to tell him our names and age, to stand up, to walk, to turn about, to dance, to sing songs, to compliment one another, to be angry, to invite one another to dinner, to converse one with another, to discourse in a familiar way like father and son, to show how two friends, or man and wife, compliment or take leave of one another, to play with children, to carry them about upon our arms, and to do many more things of the like nature. Moreover, we were asked many more questions, serious and comical; as for instance, what profession I was of, whether I ever cured any considerable distempers? to which I answered, Yes, I had, but not at Nagasaki, where we were kept no better than prisoners. What houses we had; whether our customs were different from theirs; how we buried our people, and when? to which was answered that we buried our dead in the daytime. How our prince did; what sort of a man he was; whether the governor-general at Batavia was superior to him, or whether he was under his command; whether we had prayers and images like the Portuguese? which was answered in the negative. Whether Holland, and other countries abroad, were subject to earthquakes and storms of thunder and lightning as well as Japan? Whether there be houses set on fire, and people killed by lightning in European countries? Then again we were commanded to read, and to dance separately and jointly, and I to tell them the names of some European plaisters, upon which I mentioned some of the hardest I could remember. The ambassador was asked concerning his children, how many he had, what their names were, as also how far distant Holland was from Nagasaki? In the meanwhile some shutters were opened on the left hand, by order of the emperor, probably to cool the room. We were then further commanded to put on our hats, to walk about the room discoursing with one another, to take off our perukes. I had several opportunities of seeing the empress, and heard the emperor say in Japanese, how sharp we looked at the room where he was, and that we surely could not but know, or at least suspect him to be there, upon which he removed and went to the ladies which sat just before us. Then I was desired once more to come nearer the screen, and to take off my peruke. Then they made us jump, dance, play gambols, and walk together, and upon that they asked the ambassador and me how old we guessed Bengo to be, he answered 50, and I 45, which made them laugh. Then they made us kiss one another, like man and wife, which the ladies particularly showed by their laughter to be well pleased with. They desired us further to show them what sort of compliments it was customary in Europe to make to inferiors, to ladies, to superiors, to princes, to kings. After this they begged another song of me, and were satisfied with two, which the company seemed to like very well. After this farce was over, we were ordered to take off our cloaks, to come near the screen one by one, and to take our leave in the very same manner we would take it of a prince, or king in Europe, which being done seemingly to their satisfaction, we went away. It was already four in the afternoon, when we left the hall of audience, after having been exercised in this manner for two hours and a half. We had been introduced, and were conducted back by the two imperial commissioners and Siube, and immediately repaired to Bengo's house, who received us with uncommon civility. At last in the evening we got home.

On the 22nd of April, we went to make a visit to the new lord of the temple, as they call him, who was a son of the Prince of Firando. His house was full of spectators. But his steward who received us, was one of the greatest coxcombs we had as yet met with in the country, a man entirely unacquainted with compliments, and an utter stranger even to common civility. His ill manners and unpoliteness were made good in some measure by the complaisant carriage of the ladies, who treated us with sweetmeats. He examined with some attention our hats and swords, and then said, let them sing once, which he did to please his master. However, we did not all think fit to comply with commands made with such an ill grace. From thence we repaired to the castle to salute the two governors. Upon the great place before the castle, we took notice that there was a secretary's office, wherein besides the several boxes and cabinets filled with papers, were hung up all sorts of arms. At the first governor's we were only presented with tea, nor were there any ladies present at the audience we had of him. We then made two more visits, and last of all we went to the two imperial commissioners, who received us both with great civility, and treated us very splendidly, so that we did not at all scruple at their desire to entertain the company with a song. At the first commissioner's the treat consisted of the following things:—1. Tea. 2. Tobacco, with the whole set of instruments for smoking. 3. Philosophical, or white syrup. 4. A piece of Steenbrassen, a very scarce fish, boiled in a brown sauce. 5. Another dish of fish, dressed with bean-flower and spices. 6. Cakes of eggs rolled together. 7. Fried fish, which were presented us on green skewers of bamboos. 8. Lemon peels with sugar. After every one of these dishes, they made us drink a dish of sacki, as good as ever I tasted. We were likewise presented twice, in dram cups, with wine made of plums, a very pleasant and agreeable liquor. In short, the whole treat was equally various and good. Only we had nothing made of rice. Last of all we were presented with a dish of tea, and so we took our leave, having staid an hour and a half.

At the second commissioner's we were treated, after tea and tobacco, with the following things:— 1. Two long slices of mange, dipt into a brown sup or sauce, with some ginger. 2. Hard eggs. 3. Four common fish, fried and brought on skewers of bamboos. 4. The stomachs of carps salt, in a brown sauce. 5. Two small slices of a goose roasted, and warm, presented in unglazed earthen dishes. Good liquor was drank about plentifully all the while, and the commissioner's surgeon, who was to treat us, did not miss to take his full dose. Just before us behind a screen, at about two mats distance and a half, sat a gentleman unknown to us, sometimes also ladies appeared on that side. But the greatest throng of women was on the left, in a gallery. The audience being over, we went straight home about an hour and a half before it was dark.

On the 23rd of April, we received the compliments of thanks from the gentlemen we had been to visit the day before, and in the afternoon we had orders given us to prepare ourselves for audience of leave against the next day. We did not go this day to salute the governors according to custom, by reason of its being one of the mourning days for the death of Jejas, the now reigning emperor's father, on which days it would be thought a want of respect for the emperor to treat anybody. He lies buried in Gosio, a temple behind Atogo, about two miles from our inn. The burial-place of the emperors, his predecessors, is at Nikko, three days' journey from Jedo. My servant, a very intelligent young man in the affairs of his country, told me, that the temple where Jejas is buried, is covered with golden obanis instead of tiles, and that his tomb is enclosed with black posts. He was to see me this day, because he was sent to us by a man of quality, our servants being forbidden to see us all the while we stay at Jedo.

On the 24th of April, we went to court on horseback, at seven o'clock in the morning.

attended as before by three Jorikis of the governors of Nagasaki.

We staid in the Fiakninban, or guard of hundred men, till we were conducted into the palace upon orders given by the governors and commissioners. Having staid about half an hour in the waiting-room, the captain was called in before the counsellors of state, who ordered one of the commissioners to read the usual orders to him, which they do by turns; the orders were among the rest, and chiefly to the following effect, that we should not molest any ships, or boats of the Chinese or Liqueans, nor bring any Portuguese or priests into the country on board our ships, and that upon these conditions we should be allowed a free commerce. The orders being read, the ambassador was presented with thirty gowns laid on three present boards, each of which was somewhat longer than two mats, and a letter of fortune, as they call it, as a mark of the emperor's favour, upon which he crept on all-fours to receive the same, and in token of respect, held a piece of the gowns over his head, and so returned to us; but the gowns along with the boards were carried out of the castle to the Fiakninban, where they were packed up in bundles. After the captain came back, we were desired by the governor to stay at dinner, which should be provided for us by order from the emperor. Having therefore waited about half an hour, we were conducted into another room, where two fellows with their heads shaved close, and clad in the garments of ceremony, received us. We guessed them to be some of the chief officers of the emperor's kitchen.

He that hath the direction of the kitchen is called Osobaboos; he sits next to the emperor when he dines, and tastes all the dishes that come upon the table. The interpreters, and Japanese that attend us, were carried into another room to dine by themselves. We had scarce seated ourselves when several young noblemen came into the room to see us, and to discourse with us. A small table made of shavings of matzwood, put together with wooden nails, was set before each of us, on which lay five fresh hot white cakes called amakas, as tough as glue, and two hollow breads of two spans in circumference, made of flour and sugar, with the seeds of the sesamum album spread about them. A small porcelain cup stood by the bread, with some small bits of pickled salmon in a brown sauce, which was not quite so strong, but somewhat sweeter than what they call soje. By the cup were laid two wooden chopsticks, according to the fashion of the Chinese and Japanese. We tasted a little of these dishes only for civility's sake, for we had taken care to provide ourselves with a good substantial breakfast before we went out in the morning, and besides had been treated in the guard-room with fresh manges, and sweet brown cakes of sugar and bean-flour. They desired us very civilly to eat more, and asked us whether we would drink any tea, and being told that we would, the above-mentioned kitchen officer sent for it up. But upon trial we found it to be little better than mere warm water, besides that, the brown varnished dishes, wherein it was presented to us, and which they call miseruaties, looked very poor and sorry. While we were eating our dinner the spectators busied themselves viewing and examining our hats, swords, dress, and what we had about us. After dinner, which was so far from answering the majesty and magnificence of so powerful a monarch as the emperor of Japan is, that we could not have had a worse at any private man's house, we were conducted back to the waiting-room, and having waited there for about an hour, or upwards, we were by the governor conducted through several passages and galleries, which we could not remember to have seen before, towards the hall of audience, and desired to sit down in the same room where we had been before our last audience, or to walk about in the gallery next to it. Some shutters being now opened, which had been shut in our last audience, and some other apartments being laid open, the disposition of the court and hall of audience was thereby so altered, that it looked quite different to what it was before. We took notice that there was scarce a room without some gentleman or other sitting in it. In a large room, and two galleries leading to it, were hung up several imperial orders, on large boards, consisting each of five rows of characters, only with seven characters in each row. These we had not seen in our first audience, perhaps because they were not yet hung up, or because they had now carried us another way. While we were waiting in this room till we should be called in, which might be about half an hour, a priest of about thirty years of age, clad in white and blue silk, with a bag of the same colour, came into the room, and with great affectation of shame and modesty enquired after our names and age, which had been done before by most of the spectators then present. We saw likewise another priest clad in orange-coloured silk, but he staid in the gallery and did not come into the room. As we were waiting, three washing basons, in appearance of silver, were carried into the inner imperial apartments. Soon after the same basons, and a black japanned covered table, on which stood several dishes and plates, were brought out again, whence we concluded that they had been at dinner there. Upon this we were forthwith conducted into a side gallery next to the imperial apartments, and having staid there but a little while, one of the extraordinary counsellors of state, and the two commissioners, came to introduce us, and made us sit down near the grated screen, on the very same place we had been at in our former audiences. The two commissioners did not enter the hall of audience. The emperor sat behind the middle screen on a place which was somewhat raised above the level of the room. Bengo sat in the middle against a paper screen, and the three ordinary and four extraordinary counsellors of state took their usual places. Behind the grated screen, on our right, we could discern only a priest lurking. The place where in our first audience the gobohasi sat, was now left empty, but there were a few in the gallery. Five-and-twenty sat behind us in one row, and eighteen more in the same row, who were out of sight of the emperor, though waiting for his commands. The other side of the hall was lined with the same number of people, and in the same order. After the audience began, more came in, so that all the avenues were pretty much crowded. We made our obeisance first according to the fashion of the Japanese, but were soon commanded to come nearer the screens, and to do it after the European manner. The obeisances made, I was ordered to sing a song; I chose one, which I had formerly composed for a lady, for whom I had a peculiar esteem, and as at the latter end I extolled her beauty and other excellent qualities, in a poetical style, above the value of hundreds, thousands, and millions of pieces of money, I was asked, by order of the emperor, what the meaning of it was: upon which I returned in answer, it was nothing but a sincere wish of mine, that heaven might bestow millions of portions of health, fortune, and prosperity upon the emperor, his family, and court. We were then commanded, as we had been in former audiences, to take off our cloaks, to walk about the room, which the ambassador likewise did, then to show how upon occasion we complimented, or took leave of our friends, parents, or a mistress; how we scolded at one another, how we made up our differences and got friends again. Upon this a priest was commanded to come in, who had a fresh ulcer upon one of his shins of no consequence, only with a little trifling inflammation about it; he had laid on a plaister spread thick upon European cloth. I was ordered to feel his pulse, and to give my opinion about his case, both which I did accordingly, and judged him to be a healthy strong fellow, and his case such as was not like to have any dangerous consequences, and would easily heal by keeping only the plaister on. I advised him, however, not to be too familiar with sacki beer, pretending to guess by his wound, what I did upon much better ground by his red face and nose, that he was pretty much given to drinking, which made the emperor and whole court laugh. Then two of the emperor's surgeons were sent for in, whom Bengo called himself, they being in one of the inner imperial apartments. They appeared forthwith coming down the screen; they were both shaved and clad like priests; one of them was quite blind of one eye, the other looked but little better; otherwise they seemed to be in pretty good health. Hearing that they were the emperor's surgeons, I gave them the precedency, and let them feel my pulse first, then I felt theirs, and judged them both to be in good health, the first rather of a cold constitution and wanting sometimes a dram of brandy to raise his spirits and to quicken the motion of his blood; the second of a hotter temper, and much troubled with headache, which I could very easily perceive by his countenance. Upon this they entered into a discourse with me upon physical matters, and the first asked me whether or no imposthumes were dangerous, at what time and in what distempers we ordered people to be let blood. He also affected to have some knowledge of our European plaisters, and mentioning the names of some, which however he could not well pronounce, I set him right in broken Japanese. This our jargon being half Latin and half Japanese, sounded so oddly, that the emperor asked what language it was the Dutchman spoke in, upon which he was answered, it was a broken Japanese. This farce being also over, a table was brought in with chopsticks of wood for each of us, and placed just before the third mat. On each table were brought in the following victuals, dressed after the Japanese manner.

1. Two small hollow loaves with sesamum seed thrown upon them.
2. A piece of white refined sugar, as it were striped.
3. Five candied kainokis, or kernels of the kai-tree, which are not unlike our almonds.
4. A square flat slice of a cake.
5. Two cakes made of flour and honey, shaped like a tunnel, brown and thick, but somewhat tough. They have on one side the impression of a sun, or rose, and on the other that of the Dairi Tsiap, that is, the Dairi's coat of arms, being the leaf and flower of a large tree called kiri. The leaf is not unlike that of the bardana, and the flower comes nearest to that of the digitalis, several being set to a stalk.
6. Two square slices of a cake made of bean-flour and sugar. They were of a dark reddish colour and brittle.
7. Two other slices of a rice-flour cake, yellow and tough.
8. Two slices of another cake, which was quite of another substance within than the crust seemed to be.
9. A large mange, boiled and filled with brown bean-sugar, like treacle.
10. Two small manges of the common bigness, dressed after the same manner.

We tasted a little of these things, and the chief interpreter was commanded to take up the rest, for which purpose boards and white paper were brought in. The interpreter having taken up his load, we were ordered to put on our cloaks again, to come nearer the screen, and to take our leave one after another. This being done, two gentlemen, one of whom was the youngest extraordinary counsellor of state, conducted us out of the hall of audience, to the end of the gallery, where the gentlemen of the fourth and fifth rank sat, eighteen of each class. They left us here with the two commissioners and the governor, who went with us as far as the waiting-room, where we took our leave of them, amidst the compliments and loud acclamations of the courtiers, so favourable a reception as we had met with from his imperial majesty being much beyond whatever they remembered anybody could boast of. Our interpreter was so loaded with the quantity of victuals, that he was scarce able to follow us. We made no further stay in the waiting-room, but went away immediately, saluting the imperial guard as we went by, and being come into the third castle, we there mounted our horses again. The governor Siube, or as he is now called Tsusimano Cami, happened just then to be carried by in his norimon, which he opened to speak a few words with the joriki. His retinue consisted of eight footmen, walking before his norimon, four pages walking by the norimon's side, a pike-bearer, a white led horse, and three porters carrying bundles on their backs. We repaired instantly to his house, where he caused the shutters of his room to be laid open, and sat himself down before us, with a young gentleman, and the secretary of the younger commissioner. He received us himself, complimented us on the good reception we had met with from the emperor, and desired us to be merry at dinner, which was brought in after a dish of tea, and consisted of the following dishes:—boiled fish in a very good sauce, oysters boiled and brought in the shells, with vinegar, which it was intimated, that he had ordered on purpose to be provided for us, knowing it was a favourite dish with the Dutch; several small slices of a roasted goose; fried fish, and boiled eggs. The liquor drunk between the dishes was also extraordinarily good. After dinner they desired to see our hats, swords, tobacco-pipes, and watches, which were carried out of the room, for there were no ladies present at this audience, and consequently no uta, or dance. Then two maps were brought in, one of which was without the names of the countries and places, otherwise well enough made, and in all likelihood copied from an European map. The other was a map of the whole world, of their own making, in an oval form, and marked with the Japanese Kattakanna characters. I took this opportunity to observe, after what manner they had represented the countries to the north of Japan, which I found to be as follows: beyond Japan, opposite to the two great northern promontories of the province Osju, was the island Jesogasima, and beyond that island a country twice as big in proportion as China, divided into several provinces, reaching about one-third of its bigness beyond the arctic circle towards the pole, and running a good deal farther east than the eastern coasts of Japan: it had a large gulf on the eastern shore opposite to America, and was very nearly of a square figure. There was but one passage between this country and the continent of America, in which lay a small island, and beyond that, further north, another long island, nearly reaching with its two extremities the two continents; to wit, that of Jeso to the west, and that of America to the east, and after this manner, shutting as it were the passage to the north. Much after the same manner all the unknown countries about the antarctic pole were represented as islands. From Tsusimano Cami's we went to Gensejmon Sino Cami, where we were likewise civilly treated in presence of several strangers who, though unknown to us, yet affected a great familiarity. Among the rest were Siube's and Gensejmon's brothers, one of whom had a son with sore legs, and the other a brother with pimples in his face, for both which distempers they asked my advice. The ladies were crowded up behind screens in a light room, for whose diversion we sung and danced. At Tonnemon's, whom we visited last, everything was done as the preceding year, with the utmost splendour and magnificence; so that we did not in the least scruple, in return for so much civility, to entertain the company with singing and dancing to the best of our abilities. Thus at last we got home a little after sun-set, as glad of having got over that day's work, as we were pleased with the favourable reception we had met with everywhere.

This afternoon, before we got home, several of the ordinary counsellors of state and one of the governors sent their gowns, some of which were left with our joriki, but others would stay till our return, to deliver them to our ambassador in person. Several also brought a present for our chief interpreter and the landlord's son, by whom they were introduced to us. The reception of these gowns, when made by our ambassador in person, is done with the following ceremonies: Some kulis march before, carrying the gowns in boxes, one carries the board or table on which the gowns are to be laid, with a letter of fortune, as they call it, being some flat strings twisted together at one end, and wound up in a paper, which is tied about with an unequal number of pairs of silk or paper strings, as for instance, three, five, seven, eleven, &c., of different colours, sometimes gilt or silver coloured. Then the person who is to present the gowns, being commonly the gentleman's steward that sends them, is by our joriki introduced into the ambassador's apartment, in presence of his own retinue, our landlords and interpreters, and seating himself over against the ambassador, at a proper distance, makes the following compliment: "N. N., my master, sends me to congratulate you on your having had your audience, and your audience of leave, and good weather, which is *medithe* (good luck): your presents were very acceptable to him, and he desires you would accept in return of these few gowns." At the same time he delivers to the interpreter, who gives it to the ambassador, a large sheet of paper, on which is written, in large characters, the number of gowns sent, and sometimes also what colours they are of. The captain, in token of respect, holds the sheet of paper over his head, the persons then present in the room all in a profound silence, some sitting, some kneeling, and so returns him with a bow the following compliment: "I give N. N., your master, my most humble thanks for his assistance in procuring us a quick and favourable audience, and intreat him farther to continue his favours to the Dutch: I thank him also for his valuable present, and will not fail to acquaint my masters of Batavia therewith." The mutual compliments being over, tobacco, and the whole set of instruments for smoking, and a dish of tea, are brought in; after that distilled liquors, with a table, on which are laid five silver plates, with sweetmeats. This table is placed before the person that brought the present, and he is civilly desired to taste of the Dutch liquors distilled at Batavia, and to regard not the meanness of the things offered him, but the sincerity and goodwill with which they were offered. Then a small dram-glass is filled with tent wine, which the Japanese call sinti, which, according to the fashion of the Japanese, he takes with both hands, holds it up to his mouth, and, with seeming eagerness, drinks it out to the last drop at two or three gulps, then holding the glass over the tobacco, or the empty space between the mats, to let it drop out clean, and wiping the bottom on the outside with his thumb or a bit of paper, he returns it to the ambassador, who pledges him in the same liquor, and after the same manner. He pledges the ambassador again, and with the same ceremonies returns it to the joriki, who drinks to another, and so it goes round. After this manner several sorts of liquors are drunk about, till every one has tasted of them, and commended them as miseraties. Last of all the glass is returned again to the ambassador, who drinks only a little, and then orders the liquors to be carried away. The landlord in the meantime puts up the sweetmeats in a paper parcel, ties it about with silk strings, and gives it to one of his servants. Then the gentleman takes his leave, thanking for the civility showed him, and particularly for the excellent miserantie liquors. The ambassador once more desires him to assure his master of his sincere respects, and unfeigned thanks for his favour and assistance. The joriki also makes a compliment for himself much to the same effect. Them the gentleman is conducted out of the room, where, with mutual compliments and bowing, he takes his leave a second time.

On the 25th of April, we had ten fine gowns sent us by Bengo, five as good as any wove with flowers, by the young Prince of Firando, who was lately made one of the lords of the Temple, in the room of him who is now lord chief justice of Miaco, and a couple of sorry ones by the second governor of Jedo, who has the inspection of all criminal affairs and executions in this capital. The other governor had sent us the same number, and full as bad the day before. The number of gowns we received was thirty from the emperor, ten from Bengo, and as many from each of the four ordinary counsellors of state, six from each of the four extraordinary counsellors of state, five from each of the three lords of the temples, two from each of the two governors of Jedo,—in all 123; thirty of which being those given by the emperor, belong to the company, and all the rest to the ambassador. All this business was over by two in the afternoon.

On the 26th of April, we were busy with packing up our baggage, hiring a sufficient number of kulis or porters, and fifteen horses for our journey. This morning we felt an earthquake; the shocks were violent but slow, that one might tell forty between each; after midnight it returned with more violence.

www.ingramcontent.com/pod-product-compliance
Lightning Source LLC
Chambersburg PA
CBHW050845300426
44111CB00010B/1139